The **Summary of Learning Objectives** at the end of each chapter again emphasizes each Learning Objective's goal.

summary of learning objectives

Firms increasingly compete in a global market characterized by high uncertainty, many players, and great complexity. This chapter's discussion will help you in your future career as a manager, as a member of a work team, or as an individual to succeed in this new global environment. The material presented to meet each of the chapter's learning objectives stated at the outset of the chapter is summarized below.

1 Describe the changing pattern of international business.

- *Changing world output and world trade picture.* The United States no longer dominates the world economy. Large U.S. multinationals no longer dominate international business. Centrally planned economies are opening to Western businesses, and national barriers to labor markets are folding (particularly in knowledge intensive industries).
- *Changing demographics.* The population in industrialized countries is getting older, and immigration is growing worldwide.
- *Lower trade barriers.* While some protectionism is still present and perhaps receiving growing political support in some areas, lower trade restrictions are now the norm.
- *Greater market integration.* Economic integration between groups of countries is growing, and today there are 34 such agreements, compared to 11 in the 1980s. Of these, the greatest level of integration has been achieved by the European Union composed of 25 countries.
- *Converging global consumer preferences.* Consumer tastes and preferences are becoming more similar around the world.
- *More globalization of production.* A growing number of firms spread their production around the world in order to realize savings, particularly in labor costs.
- *Rapid technological innovations.* Advances in communications, information processing, and transportation are making it much easier to conduct business across geographical boundaries.
- *Greater cultural diversity.* To be effective, firms need to learn to adapt to an increasingly diverse set of customers, employees, and ways of doing business.

2 Identify major factors affecting international business.

- *General business environment.* You must consider of all factors that might influence the costs, benefits, and risks of operating in particular world areas or countries.
- *Legal systems.* The firm must be able to comply with vastly different rules and regula-

Finally, the **Testbank** questions are tagged according to AACSB guidelines, Bloom's taxonomy, and by feature (i.e., Opening Vignette, Management Close-Up, etc.). Ask your local McGraw-Hill sales representative for more information on the Testbank.

IMPORTANT

HERE IS YOUR REGISTRATION CODE TO ACCESS MCGRAW-HILL PREMIUM CONTENT AND MCGRAW-HILL ONLINE RESOURCES

For key premium online resources you need THIS CODE to gain access. Once the code is entered, you will be able to use the web resources for the length of your course.

Access is provided only if you have purchased a new book.

If the registration code is missing from this book, the registration screen on our website, and within your WebCT or Blackboard course will tell you how to obtain your new code. Your registration code can be used only once to establish access. It is not transferable.

To gain access to these online resources

1. USE your web browser to go to: www.mhhe.com/gomez3e

2. CLICK on "First Time User"

3. ENTER the Registration Code printed on the tear-off bookmark on the right

4. After you have entered your registration code, click on "Register"

5. FOLLOW the instructions to setup your personal UserID and Password

6. WRITE your UserID and Password down for future reference. Keep it in a safe place.

If your course is using WebCT or Blackboard, you'll be able to use this code to access the McGraw-Hill content within your instructor's online course.

To gain access to the McGraw-Hill content in your instructor's WebCT or Blackboard course simply log into the course with the user ID and Password provided by your instructor. Enter the registration code exactly as it appears to the right when prompted by the system. You will only need to use this code the first time you click on McGraw-Hill content.

These instructions are specifically for student access. Instructors are not required to register via the above instructions.

The McGraw-Hill Companies

Mc Graw Hill **Higher Education**

GOMEZ: MANAGEMENT 3/E
ISBN: 978-0-07-302748-7
MHID: 0-07-302748-0

Thank you, and welcome to your McGraw-Hill Online Resources.

third edition

management

people · performance · change

Luis R. Gomez-Mejia
Arizona State University

David B. Balkin
University of Colorado

Robert L. Cardy
The University of Texas at San Antonio

Boston   Burr Ridge, IL   Dubuque, IA   New York   San Francisco   St. Louis
Bangkok   Bogotá   Caracas   Kuala Lumpur   Lisbon   London   Madrid   Mexico City
Milan   Montreal   New Delhi   Santiago   Seoul   Singapore   Sydney   Taipei   Toronto

McGraw-Hill
Irwin

MANAGEMENT: PEOPLE, PERFORMANCE, CHANGE
Published by McGraw-Hill/Irwin, a business unit of The McGraw-Hill Companies, Inc., 1221 Avenue of the Americas, New York, NY, 10020.

This book is printed on acid-free paper.

Printed in China

2 3 4 5 6 7 8 9 0 SDB/SDB 0 9 8 7

ISBN 978-0-07-302743-2
MHID 0-07-302743-X

Editorial director: *John E. Biernat*
Senior sponsoring editor: *Kelly H. Lowery*
Senior developmental editor: *Christine Scheid*
Marketing manager: *Anke Braun*
Senior project manager: *Susanne Riedell*
Production supervisor: *Debra R. Sylvester*
Senior designer: *Adam Rooke*
Senior photo research coordinator: *Jeremy Cheshareck*
Photo researcher: *Jennifer Blankenship*
Lead media project manager: *Becky Szura*
Interior design: *Kaye Farmer*
Typeface: *10.5/13 Palatino*
Compositor: *Carlisle Publishing Services*
Printer: *Shenzhen Donnelley Printing Co., Ltd.*

Library of Congress Cataloging-in-Publication Data

Gomez-Mejia, Luis R.
   Management : people, performance, change / Luis R. Gomez-Mejia, David B. Balkin, Robert L. Cardy. -- 3rd ed.
     p. cm.
   Includes index.
   ISBN-13: 978-0-07-302743-2 (alk. paper)
   ISBN-10: 0-07-302743-X (alk. paper)
   1. Management. I. Balkin, David B., 1948- II. Cardy, Robert L., 1955- III. Title.
HD31.G58955 2008
658--dc22
                            2006027131

www.mhhe.com

dedicated

to my sons, Vince and Alex, my daughter
Dulce Maria, and my wife Ana—LG-M

to my parents, Daniel and Jeanne—DBB

to my wife and daughters,
Laurel, Lara, and Emery—RLC

about the authors

Luis R. Gomez-Mejia is a full professor of management in the College of Business at Arizona State University. Before joining ASU, he taught at the University of Colorado and the University of Florida. He has also been on the faculty at Universidad Carlos III de Madrid and Instituto de Empresas and has offered seminars in both Spanish and English in many countries and universities around the world.

He received his Ph.D. and M.A. in industrial relations from the College of Business at the University of Minnesota and a B.A. (summa cum laude) in economics from the University of Minnesota. Prior to entering academia, Professor Gomez-Mejia worked in human resources for the City of Minneapolis and Control Data Corporation and served as consultant to numerous organizations.

He has served two terms on the editorial board of the *Academy of Management Journal* and is editor and co-founder of two journals: *Journal of High Technology Management Research* and *Management Research.* Dr. Gomez-Mejia has published more than 100 articles in the most prestigious management journals including the *Academy of Management Journal, Academy of Management Review, Administrative Science Quarterly, Strategic Management Journal, Industrial Relations,* and *Personnel Psychology.* He has also written and edited a dozen management books.

Dr. Gomez-Mejia has received numerous awards including "best article" in the *Academy of Management Journal* and the Outstanding Alumni Award at University of Minnesota. He has been named a Dean's Council of 100 Distinguished Scholar at Arizona State University every year since 1994, holds the Horace Steel Chair at Arizona State University, is a member of the *Academy of Management Journal's* Hall of Fame, and is a Fellow of the Academy of Management.

He is also president of the Iberoamerican Academy of Management (an affiliate of the Academy of Management), which covers Spain and Portugal, all of Latin America, and Hispanic faculty in U.S. universities.

David B. Balkin is the chair of the Management Division and is a full professor in the College of Business and Administration at the University of Colorado. Previously he was an associate professor at the university. Before joining the University of Colorado in 1988, he taught at Louisiana State University and Northeastern University. He served as a visiting professor for the University of Toulouse in France and the University of Montreal in Quebec, Canada, and has also taught courses in Norway, Spain, Israel, and Santo Domingo, Dominican Republic.

He received his Ph.D. in industrial relations from the University of Minnesota Graduate School of Business, where he specialized in human resources management. He earned a master's degree in industrial relations at the University of Minnesota Graduate School of Business and a bachelor's degree in political science at the University of California at Los Angeles. Dr. Balkin has been a management consultant for Control Data Corporation, a personnel analyst for Honeywell Corporation, and a marketing research associate for National Broadcasting Company. He also serves as an expert witness in cases involving pay and employment discrimination.

Professor Balkin has served as associate editor for *Human Resource Management Review* since 1997 and as a member of the editorial review board for the *Journal of High Technology Management Research* since 1990. He has also been a member of the editorial review board for the *Academy of Management Journal* and serves as a reviewer for several publications. He is widely published in the professional literature, most recently in the *Academy of Management Journal, Journal of Business and Psychology, Group and Organization Management, Human Resource Management Review, Journal of Compensation and Benefits, Journal of Occupational and Organizational Psychology*, and *HR Magazine*.

He is the author and editor of several books on human resources, the management of innovation, compensation, and other topics. He has received the North American Case Research Association's Curtis E. Tate Jr. Outstanding Case Writer award, the National Academy of Management's Best Article of the Year award, and the Western Academy of Management's Outstanding Paper award.

Robert L. Cardy is chair of the Department of Management at the University of Texas at San Antonio. Before joining UT–San Antonio, he taught at Arizona State University and the State University of New York at Buffalo.

He received his Ph.D. in industrial/organizational psychology from Virginia Tech. His masters and undergraduate degrees are from Central Michigan University. Dr. Cardy has consulted with a variety of organizations, particularly in the areas of performance appraisal and competency model development and implementation.

Professor Cardy has served multiple terms as a member of the executive committee of the Human Resource Management Division of the Academy of Management. He has regularly written columns for the *HR Division Newsletter* on new and innovative issues since 1991. Dr. Cardy was the co-founder and editor of the former *Journal of Quality Management.* He has been a member of the editorial review boards for the *Journal of Applied Psychology* and the *Journal of Organizational Behavior* and serves as a reviewer for several publications. He has published articles in a variety of journals including *Journal of Applied Psychology, Organizational Behavior and Human Decision Processes, Journal of Management, Management Communication Quarterly*, and *HR Magazine.*

Dr. Cardy has authored or edited several books on human resource management and performance management. He has twice received a "best paper" award from the Human Resource Management Division of the Academy of Management. He has received a "University Mentor Award" for his work with doctoral students at Arizona State University. He is also an honors Fellow of the W. P. Carey School of Business for which he is a faculty mentor to teams of honors students working on community development projects.

brief contents

Gomez-Mejia | Balkin | Cardy:

Ask your incoming students what "management" is, and they'll talk about the kind of management they know from their own (limited) work experience. Managers assign people their hours, give raises or promotions, tell people what job to do—the manager, in other words, is "the boss."

In most other work settings, however, management means something far more important and complex. In addition to people, managers also manage performance, processes, relationships, and more increasingly in today's world, deal with the pressure and flux of constant change. This, coupled with the fact that workplaces have steadily become less hierarchical and more team- and group-driven, means the traditional responsibilities of the manager have gradually been dispersed throughout the organization. Students preparing to work in today's business environment may not start in a corner office with an assistant, but they still need to *think like* managers and understand the strategic goals of the organization.

Management prepares your students to join a new kind of workplace, one where management is *everyone's* business.

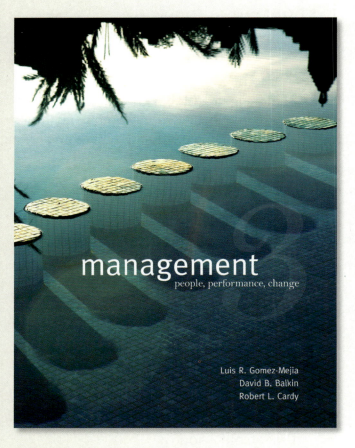

management
people, performance, change

Luis R. Gomez-Mejia
David B. Balkin
Robert L. Cardy

In order to prepare your students for a rapidly changing workplace, *Management* seeks to go beyond the scope of other management textbooks in our approach and our content. It does this in three key aspects:

Management Is Everyone's Business

Beyond the ordinary.

Your students start the course thinking of managers as little more than traditional "bosses." *Management* helps your students to move beyond this perception by offering coverage and exercises that emphasize the multifaceted nature of modern management. In particular, the "Management Close-Up" boxed feature offers unique perspectives. Each close-up has a theme of either Ethics, Customer Focus, and/or Dealing With Change to illustrate contemporary issues that managers and organizations confront that go beyond merely "being the boss."

Beyond theory.

Nothing as complex as management can be understood merely by reading the theory. While *Management* is careful to ground students in the relevant theories, it gives your students numerous opportunities to apply their learning to real-world management situations. Strategically placed throughout the chapter, the Learning Objective Check-Ins or LOC-Ins help students apply information that they've just read by asking scenario-based multiple choice questions based on a Learning Objective at the beginning of the chapter. Answers for the LOC-Ins can be found in the Instructor's Manual online within the Instructor Resources at www.mhhe.com/gomez3e. More than 40 interactive exercises can be found online highlighted with a Web site icon throughout the book—put your students in the manager's chair to deal with important and complex issues. Sixteen The Entrepreneurial Manager videos give your students insight into such entrepreneurs as Todd McFarlane, famed for his comic books, Major League Baseball figurines, and movies such as *Spawn*; or Jim McCann of 1800 Flowers.com and his path to success; or how companies like Joe to Go, New Belgium Brewery, and Cirque Du Soleil began, and reached their current success. Additionally, the end-of-chapter material provides a variety of exercises, including mini-cases, collaborative learning exercises, Internet exercises, and skill-building exercises.

Beyond your expectations.

We've worked hard to make the *Management* textbook package more comprehensive, more useful, and more flexible than any other on the market. Our ancillaries will open whole new avenues of teaching for you - from our impressive range of video cases and our "Manager's Hot Seat" videos which put real managers in the hot seat of a sticky management issue to a Test Bank that incorporates AACSB guidelines with questions tagged to corresponding goals.

Management

is full of innovative chapter features to make studying productive and hassle-free. The following pages show the kind of engaging, helpful pedagogical features that make up Management's powerful approach.

NEW! Learning Objective Check-Ins or LOC-Ins

In response to the need for better assessment of learning objective goals, these scenario-based multiple choice questions occur within each chapter and directly correspond to a Learning Objective specified at the beginning of the chapter. Each question is designed to assess the application of the Learning Objective, with answers found in the Instructor's Manual. Professors can choose to share the answers with their students by either posting to an online course-delivery site, or by printing and distributing.

LOC-In

1 Learning Objective Check-In

Gen-Art is a custom framing and art service boutique that is considering expansion into the surrounding regional market. The 20-person company has highly decentralized job authority and decision making. Instead of strict functional areas, the firm uses a team-based approach to satisfying client needs. Gen-Art avoids many levels of management in favor of a barebones approach to structure, with executives, project managers, and teams of technical staff. Ginny and Mercedes are two managers at Gen-Art.

1. *Ginny is the Vice President of Operations at Gen-Art. She helps make decisions regarding growth, goals, and longer-term issues. Ginny is a _____.*
   a. *strategic manager*
   b. *operational manager*
   c. *front-line manager*
   d. *tactical manager*

2. *As one of the project managers for Gen-Art, Mercedes operates at the _____ level. She is the direct link between the executive level of the firm and the technical staff she oversees.*
   a. *strategic*
   b. *controlling management*
   c. *tactical*
   d. *bureaucratic management*

The next sections of the ... scribe the critical aspects of mo... ment jobs. Figure 1.1 above s... these aspects, namely, the ability... basic managerial functions (pla... strategizing, organizing, leading... trolling) and the ability to perf... managerial roles (interpersona... tional, and decisional). While the... portance of each aspect may... instance, strategic managers may... volved in planning and strategizi... operational managers), those cap... ing well on each of these job aspec... likely to have a successful manag... and be promoted to more respor... tions over time.

The Four Management Fun...
More than once the question has b... "What do managers do?" Or pe... precisely, "What *should* they do?"

video: THE ENTREPRENEURIAL MANAGER

The McFarlane Companies

Summary

What do comics, sports, monsters, toys, and rock'n roll have in common? They all have benefited from the creative artistry of Todd McFarlane. He is responsible for the most successful comic books in history. He has produced a hit movie, directed music videos for Korn and Pearl Jam, won Grammys and Emmys, and runs one of the most successful toy companies in the world. He has licenses ranging from Shrek, Austin Powers, and The Beatles to Major League Baseball, the National Football League, and the NBA. McFarlane also owns part of the Edmonton Oilers hockey team.

McFarlane grew up playing baseball, and wanted to become a major league center fielder. He knew that was a long-shot, and that dream did not materialize for him. He developed an interest in comics late in high school. He wondered if he could make money drawing superheroes. He was self-taught through high school and college, and decided to send off samples to people in the business. He faced 300 rejection letters before finally getting a freelance job with Marvel Comics. They happened to be the biggest name in the industry. McFarlane worked his way up through the ranks, doing increasingly challenging characters with great success. By 1990, he was the highest paid comic book artist in the industry. McFarlane's success came with a downside, however. He was unsatisfied because he lacked ownership of the characters he was producing. He was also frustrated over creative differences. So he quit, started his own company, and took six other artists with him.

NEW! Video: The Entrepreneurial Manager

Many students upon graduation will begin their career with smaller businesses, or perhaps even starting a business of their own. These boxes consist of a summary and discussion questions for videos found on the Online Learning Center (**www.mhhe.com/gomez3e**) that pertain to an entrepreneur or a successful small business and management concepts that relate to the chapter.

Manager's Notebook

These features supplement chapter content with a practicing manager's perspective. Manager's Notebooks provide valuable insider tips to dealing with common situations and are an ideal jumping-off point for classroom discussion.

3.2 manager's notebook

EIGHT STEPS TO SOUND ETHICAL DECISION MAKING IN BUSINESS

1. *Gather the facts.* Avoid jumping to conclusions without having the facts available to you. Consider the following questions: How did the situation occur? Are there historical facts I should know? Are there facts concerning the current situation I should know?

2. *Define the ethical issues.* Identify the ethical values at stake in this problem. Sometimes two important values are in conflict. For example, the right to privacy may conflict with the right to expect a safe workplace. Is there a code of ethics that suggests which values have the highest priority?

3. *Identify the affected parties.* Start with the parties directly affected by the outcome of the decision. Next, think broadly and include other parties who may also be affected, such as employees in other units, people in the community, or customers. How would your decision affect all these parties?

4. *Identify the consequences.* Think about the consequences for all the parties that you have identified. What is the probability of each different consequence for each party? Do you see any highly negative consequences that must be avoided? What are the short-term and long-term consequences of the decision?

5. *Identify your obligations.* Identify the obligations you feel and the reasons for each. For example, did you make a promise to another employee that you could be in jeopardy of breaking? Is your duty at odds with keeping your word to this person? Can you justify making an exception for this decision? Since we each enact numerous roles (as employee, leader, parent, spouse, volunteer, etc.), we are bound to have role conflicts that force us to favor one role over another for a given situation. It is important to be aware of all our obligations when considering a decision.

6. *Consider your character and integrity.* How would others judge your character and integrity if they knew all the facts about the decision that you were about to make? Would you feel good about disclosing your decision to a newspaper that would be read by the members of your community? If you would be ashamed of disclosing your decision to others, perhaps you should rethink your decision so that you feel more comfortable with it when scrutinized by others.

Pedagogy

Management Close-Ups

2.1 MANAGEMENT CLOSE-UP

Global Is Local in a New World Order of Business

THEME: DEALING WITH CHANGE A group of IBM computer programmers at Tsinghua University in Beijing writes software using Java technology. At the end of each day, the work is sent via the Internet to an IBM facility in Seattle, where programmers build on it during their workday. Then, the Seattle programmers send the working files another 5,222 miles to the Institute of Computer Science in Belarus and Software House Group in Latvia, which work on it and send it east to India's Tata Group. The Tata Group sends the software back to Tsinghua by morning in Beijing. The cycle continues until the project is done. "We call it Java Around the Clock," says John Patrick, vice president of Internet technology for IBM. "It's like we've created a 48-hour day through the Internet."

Communications technology has transformed the world into a single work place. As in the IBM programming cycle, workers collaborate in different locations using a computer network in ways they never could before. Caterpillar's global engineers in different countries simultaneously collaborate on tractor designs with a 3-D model over a computer network. ParaGraph International, a software company started by a Russian, Stepan Pachikov, links product development in

The Internet creates possibilities far beyond the phone or private data networks that used to be the backbone of international business. The Web is inexpensive and open to customers and suppliers worldwide, not just to the company's workers. Says Irving Wladawsky-Berger, head of IBM's Internet division, "The difference between Peoria and Romania on the Web is not very large."

In 2006, MCI was the world's largest provider of conferencing services, according to Telespan publishing. Its products include audio, video and Web conferencing, and related services, which help organizations worldwide to meet more productively without the time and costs associated with business travel. This enables companies such as Boeing, which has a multiyear agreement with MCI, "to create an efficient virtual collaboration environment."

The cost of doing business globally has also diminished thanks to technology. Eastman Chemical found the cost of three or four managers in the United States is the same as the cost of stationing one U.S. manager abroad; its U.S.-based managers can now use communication technology to manage by long distances. Of the company's 1,500 employees who work outside the United States, only 130 are Americans.

1.1 MANAGEMENT CLOSE-UP

How Outsourcing Is Transforming Whole Industries and Changing the Way We Work

THEME: CUSTOMER FOCUS In theory, it is becoming increasingly possible to buy, off the shelf, practically any function you need to run a company. Want to start a budget airline but don't want to invest in a huge back office? Accenture's Navitaire unit can manage reservations, plan routes, assign crew, and calculate optimal prices for each seat. Have a cool new telecom or medical device but lack market researchers? For about $5,000, analytics outfits such as New Delhi–based Evalueserve Inc. will, within a day, assemble a team of Indian patent attorneys, engineers, and business analysts, start mining global databases, and call dozens of U.S. experts and wholesalers to provide an independent appraisal.

Want to quickly market a new mutual fund or insurance policy? IT services providers such as India's Tata Consultancy Services Ltd. are building software platforms that furnish every business process needed and secure all regulatory approvals. A sister company, Tata Technologies, boasts 2,000 Indian engineers and recently bought 700-employee Incat International PLC, a Novi, Michigan, auto- and aerospace-engineering firm. Tata Technologies can now handle everything from turning a conceptual design into detailed specs for interiors, chassis,

from IT infrastructure and human resources to management of its offices from Cincinnati to Moscow.

Cost savings aside, many companies believe that outsourcing improves customer service. Five years ago, Penske Truck Leasing, a joint venture between GE and Penske Corp., paid $768 million for trucker Rollins Thick Leasing Corp. just in time for the recession. Customer service, spread among four U.S. call centers, was inconsistent. "I realized our business needed a transformation," says CFO Frank Cocuzza. He began by shifting a few dozen data-processing jobs to GE's huge Mexican and Indian call centers, now called Genpact. He then hired Genpact to help restructure most of his back office. That relationship now spans 30 processes involved in leasing 216,000 trucks and providing logistical services for customers.

Now, if a Penske truck is held up at a weigh station because it lacks a certain permit, for example, the driver calls an 800 number. Genpact staff in India obtains the document over the Web. The weigh station is notified electronically, and the truck is back on the road within 30 minutes. Before, Penske thought it did well if it accomplished that in two hours. And when a driver finishes his job, his entire log, in-

1.2 MANAGEMENT CLOSE-UP

The New Ethics Enforcers

THEME: ETHICS With rock music pounding and lasers painting a brilliant light show on giant screens behind him, Patrick J. Gnazzo restlessly paced the broad stage at the Venetian's convention center in Las Vegas. Because he is the new chief compliance officer at Computer Associates International Inc. (CA), Gnazzo's presentation was one of the main events just before CA World, the company's annual sales extravaganza. Striding before 1,200 CA staffers, the blustery 59-year-old former chief trial attorney for the U.S. Navy took a page from tent revivalists, leading a call-and-response chant: "What happens at CA World," Gnazzo shouted, as the crowd echoed his words, "can make us great." Winding up his talk, he exhorted: "Don't lie, don't cheat, don't steal!"

CA staffers can thank the Justice Department for Pat Gnazzo. To avoid a criminal trial over alleged accounting fraud, CA accepted a deferred prosecution agreement in late 2004 that required it to set aside $225 million for shareholders and impose a variety of reforms, including hiring an internal cop to prevent future chicanery.

The job went to Jesuit-trained Gnazzo, who once considered the priesthood but instead opted for the law. At the $3.5-

Patrick J. Gnazzo is the first compliance officer at Computer Associates International Inc., charged with preventing fraud at the firm. He

---

To help students look up-close at the issues real managers deal with, *Management* includes "Management Close-Up" boxes. Ethics, Customer Focus, or Dealing With Change subtitle these boxes and highlight aspects of management particularly important today.

Dealing With Change

New technology or new CEOs, globalization and the information economy, regulatory changes: all of these factors constantly conspire to reshape the contemporary business workplace or a particular organization. The successful manager needs to be able to anticipate and adapt to change, and these boxes illustrate how a particular change can impact the successful functioning of a firm.

Customer Focus

In today's hyper-competitive world, relationships and trust are increasingly important. For the manager, everyone is a customer, whether they are *internal* or *external*. Within their organizations, managers rely on maintaining good relationships with managers and employees in other departments to get things done. Just as important are relationships with external customers, potential partnerships, and alliances. The Customer Focus boxes offer real-world examples of how relationships play crucial roles in the success of organizations.

Ethics

Ethical conduct in business has become an increasingly public issue. Whether the issue is recognizing the importance of stakeholders, a regulatory issue, or issues with employees, ethical behavior and policies cut across all management issues. Nearly every chapter of *Management* includes these special illustrations of how ethics and trust play an important role in all aspects of business.

End-of-chapter exercises and applications

Focusing on the Future

NEW!

Falling at the end of the chapter but before the Summary, "Focusing on the Future" boxes give students a glimpse of how they will use the skills they are acquiring from the text in their future careers. A "day in the life" snapshots from five types of managers - accounting/finance, operations/general, human resources, marketing/communications, and entrepreneurs - show students how working managers use the theories discussed in the text to solve real-world problems. The author of the feature, Carol Moore, California State University – Hayward, interviewed real-life managers, including: Roxana Carbajal - HR Director, Embassy Suites; Mary Molacavage - Lab Associate, Biotech organization; "Barbara DeLong" - HR Director, telecommunications industry; Mary Kelley - CEO, Sleep Garden; Mark Hasting - Group Vice President, Target Corporation; Brendan Geary - Director of Human Resources, Panalpinia Corporation; David Moore - Pastor, New Summit Presbyterian Church.

Skill Building Exercises

Most chapters now include skill-building exercises that summarize management skills crucial to workplace effectiveness. "Manager's Check-Up" exercises provide students a fun and interesting way to practice and refine those skills, and are found with the End-of-Chapter material.

Individual/Collaborative Learning Case/Exercises

Each chapter includes an in-class exercise designed to be completed in teams. Teams read the case and then recommend a course of action for the issue or problem presented in the exercise.

Management Mini-Cases

These popular exercises have been completely revamped for the 3rd edition. At least half of the cases have been replaced by newer ones, and many have been expanded to provide a more comprehensive approach to the issue. Each chapter has two Management Mini-Cases.

Focusing on the Future: Using Management Theory in Daily Life

Managing in a Global Environment

Bruce Humphrys serves in a general manager capacity for a nonprofit technical organization. As the Executive Director of Compatible Technology International (CTI), he must encourage his employees—a group of volunteer engineers, food scientists, and technicians—to create food processing tools that can be used in underdeveloped nations all over the world. To create products that will be used, rather than abandoned, Bruce has to take into consideration the general business environment, legal systems, the country's economic environment, and cultural environments. Take the case of the breadfruit dryer, for instance.

One of Bruce's senior food scientists, George Ewing, saw a need to give people in Haiti a way to dry breadfruit. Fresh, breadfruit is a vegetable similar to squash. It has a very short shelf-life; fruit lasts only a day or so after being harvested. But when breadfruit is dried, it can be turned into a flour which keeps well and enriches both the islanders' diet and their economy. Fortunately, Ewing met Camille George, a professor at the University of St. Thomas in St. Paul, Minnesota, at a political lunch. She had the expertise in heat transfer technology to help him create a simple breadfruit drying machine.

manager's checkup 3.1

What Are Your Ethical Beliefs?

Instructions: Answer the following questions as honestly as you can. Circle the number between 1 and 5 that best represents your own beliefs about business.

	Strongly Disagree				Strongly Agree
1. Financial gain is all that counts in business.	1	2	3	4	5
2. Ethical standards must sometimes be compromised in business practice.	1	2	3	4	5
3. The more financially successful the businessperson, the more unethical the behavior.	1	2	3	4	5
4. Moral values are irrelevant in business.	1	2	3	4	5
5. The business world has its own rules.	1	2	3	4	5
6. Businesspersons care only about making profits.	1	2	3	4	5
7. Business is like a game—one plays to win.	1	2	3	4	5
8. In business, people will do anything to further their own interest.	1	2	3	4	5
9. Competition forces business managers to resort to shady practices.	1	2	3	4	5
10. The profit motive pressures managers to	1	2	3	4	5

individual/ collaborative learning case 4.1

Enterprise Resource Planning: An Example of Organizational Change

Being the champion of a change, or a change agent, isn't always easy. Enterprise Resource Planning (ERP), software that integrates information from accounting, manufacturing, distribution, and human resource departments, can give management a unified view of these processes in an organization. Unfortunately, the ERP software began gaining a reputation for being difficult to implement and often failing. The majority of these failures were attributed to software performance problems, but the reality was that in most of these situations the failure was due to inadequate attention to change. In other words, technology was not usually the problem; rather it was a lack of management recognition of ERP as an organizational change. An ERP system can add administrative tasks that may not seem needed, but without an understanding of the system, workers may not complete these tasks. Further, an ERP implementation may require a change in roles and increased technical expertise. The implementation of an ERP system at SI Corporation, a small manufacturer of industrial textiles, is an example of an ERP success story. SI expected the implementation of ERP to have a serious impact on its organizational culture.

After deciding to implement an ERP system, SI management created the position of "change management leader" with the responsibility of managing the human element of the implementation. The person hired for this new job, Patrick Keebler, started by assessing the environment for potential problem areas. He considered the levels of workers' computer skills and whether there were areas with a history of resistance to change. Keebler developed a change management strategy that focused on communication and training. As Keebler stated, if you unilaterally "announce that you've launched a new system, you'll get a lot of push back, but if you share your strategy and why it's important early on, people will embrace it."

management minicase 3.1

Starbucks Gambles that Encouraging Its Coffee Suppliers to Act Socially Responsible Is Good for Business

Starbucks, the fast growing coffee retailer with over $4 billion in annual sales, places a high priority on corporate social responsibility. It gives all its employees who work over 20 hours per week health insurance benefits and stock options. It strives to give back to the communities that it does business in by supporting local schools, literacy programs, and environmental activities. One of its newest social responsibility initiatives is to cultivate and reward environmentally and socially responsible coffee suppliers, a practice it calls sustainable sourcing. Company executives reason that such sourcing an important cornerstone of its global growth strategy will help build the Starbucks brand. The impetus for Starbucks to start a program of social responsibility with coffee growers originally had been a way to respond to critics from the "fair trade" movement—which advocates fair payments to farmers in developing nations—that had accused Starbucks of underpaying coffee growers, a claim Starbucks denied after it opened its books to them to prove that was not the case.

There were sound economic reasons for the initiative as well. With an annual growth rate of 20 percent Starbucks executives wanted to make sure that the future supply of coffee would be predictable and reliable for its customers. If the supply of the specialty coffee beans that Starbucks uses were disrupted, its growth plans and quality of its coffee would be at risk. To protect its coffee supply, Starbucks realized it had to identify and nurture partners that could meet its quality standards and keep up with increasing demand. At the same time, to protect its brand, the company needed to be certain that its suppliers shared its commitment to corporate citizenship. Therefore in 2001 the company launched its preferred supplier program to attract and reward farmers committed to socially and environmentally responsible farming. The com-

Video Cases

A Unique Use of Video

video: THE ENTREPRENEURIAL MANAGER

Cirque du Soleil

Summary

Guy Laliberte started as a street performer, with the dream to take his group of jugglers, fire-eaters, stilt-walkers, and clowns on a world tour to have fun and entertain people. He had no idea that he was embarking on a journey that would revive the traditional circus and reinvent live entertainment, making him one of the most successful people in international business. Today, Cirque du Soleil has numerous shows playing worldwide. The troupe who originally formed Cirque in 1984 had to locate in a warmer climate, because performing under a tent in Canada year-round was not an option. So, they decided to go to Los Angeles in 1987, and were given the opportunity to do the opening show at the Los Angeles Arts Festival.

Guy hit the road around the same time that businesses around the world began moving toward globalization, taking regional businesses into the international markets. With the Cold War over, and trade barriers all over the world dropping for the first time in history, companies like Cirque found it much easier to penetrate new markets. The show was fortunately a press and public success immediately.

Cirque is not without significant challenges, however, that relate directly to globalization. First, Cirque must search the globe for specific talents in its shows. Cirque also looks to the Olympics to find talent. They do not approach an athlete until they are sure it is the athlete's last Olympics, which is something the same symbol don't expect to see the athlete use after their...

China Brands

video summary

Summary

Today, Japan leads the electronics market, with Korea a safe second. But the world's most populous country, China, is showing significant potential to explode in the electronics market. China is also making headway by marketing TsingTao beer as a global brand. China's brands are currently becoming successful by marketing to their billion and a half population at home. Xerox and Sony are already manufacturing within China, but it's the nation's own brands that are showing the potential to become global giants in the years ahead. One day China could have some of the world's most popular brands.

There has been a total quality management "revolution" in China, and Haier, a refrigerator manufacturer, is leading the way. The Chinese are placing an emphasis on the quality of their products; the next step, according to Berntt Schmidt of Columbia Business School, is to focus on building brands. Lenovo is the number one selling PC in China, is well known throughout Asia, and plans to launch internationally during its sponsorship of the 2008 Olympics in Beijing. In addition to these, SVA is a popular Chinese television manufacturer that has shelf space in Wal-Mart, Target, Sears, and other retail stores in the United States.

Discussion Questions

1. A company cannot succeed without applying as part of its strategy the technologies that have evolved (and continue to evolve). How has China used technology to improve its position for success in the global economy?

2. New entrants into an industry compete with established companies that control the current market share. What are some barriers to entry for Chinese companies looking to expand in the electronics industry? The beverage industry? How might these firms overcome such barriers?

3. Customers purchase products and services and thus give brands legitimacy. Customers can influence pricing, quality, and service they demand from a company. How does China have an edge concerning its current customer base in China?

The Entrepreneurial Manager

Nearly every chapter contains 2 possible video teaching opportunities. The first, "The Entrepreneurial Manager" feature is located *within* the chapter. This feature contains a summary and discussion questions that pertain to an entrepreneur or a successful small business and relevant management concepts. These videos can be found on the Online Learning Center (OLC) for student viewing outside the class, or on the Instructor DVD for viewing inside the classroom.

End of Chapter Video

The second opportunity offers a stimulating mix of topical reinforcement and real-world insight to help students master the most challenging management topics, with segments such as the "Government vs. Google," "Privacy in the Workplace," and "Economic Rebuilding in New Orleans." The videos can be found on the Instructor DVD-Rom, with summaries and discussion questions for the students found at the end of each chapter.

Finally, **Manager's Hot Seat Videos** are video-based cases used to present stimulating, real-world management situations in the classroom. Focusing on tough issues and sensitive topics, the scenarios include:

- **Negotiation amidst cultural differences**

- **Group dynamics**

- **Conflict management**

- **Personal disclosure**

- **Working in teams**

- **HR issues**

The Manager's Hot Seat collection can now be found online at **http://www.mhhe.com/MHS**. You can also access it though the text's Online Learning Center (**www.mhhe.com/gomez3e**). Please check with your Sales Representative on how your students can receive access to this resource.

What's NEW! in

Chapter 1

- New discussion of how environmental changes are likely to influence future careers.
- New discussion of how internal/external customers are affected by globalization.
- New discussion of how globalization complicates ethical decision making, bringing in recent examples of Yahoo, Google, Microsoft and Cisco in China.
- New discussion of how organizations are appointing ethics officers which are given a lot of power and who report directly to CEO.
- New discussion on what successful managers at any level have in common.
- New discussion on important role emerging technologies exert on control systems.
- New tie-ins of managerial roles to subsequent chapters (before we only had it for management functions).
- Added discussion of why classical management insights are still valuable today and are not a thing of the past.
- Brand new section on emergent cutting-edge perspectives and issues to the study of management for 2000-2020. These include the "Modular Organization" and the "Intangible Organization."
- Brand new and extensive response to "critical thinking questions" posed for new vignette.
- Brand new introductory vignette on the management problems

suffered by Ford and General Motors, brand new critical thinking questions, and brand new answers to critical thinking questions posed earlier.
- All of the Management Close Ups were replaced with brand new ones. These include a "customer driven" close up on global outsourcing, an "ethics" close up concerning ethics enforcers, and an "emergent trends" close up concerning the use of new technologies in organizational control systems.
- Brand new skill building exercise on what college students expect organizations to offer them in the future and how this affects their career/employer choice.
- Three brand new figures have been added to clarify materials and break up text:
  - Figure 1.1 on key aspects of managerial success.
  - Figure 1.2 on origins of key management perspectives overtime.
  - Figure 1.3 on the Modular Organization.
- All of the management MiniCases and Collaborative Learning Exercises have been replaced with new ones. These include one on ethics, one on effective use of organizational culture to achieve success, and one on the 2006 National Academy report concerning the global brain race.
- One brand new section of chapter has been written on emergent organizational forms.

Chapter 2

- Brand new examples of effects of global shift including Delphi Automobile, graduates of China, and illustrations of how several countries are attracting executive talent from Microsoft, etc. Relatedly, discussion of the globalization of labor markets by providing brand new examples of international hires by Japanese and Chinese firms (such as Sony, Nissan, etc.).
- Recent trends in economic unions around the world, including challenges to European Union (due to failure to ratify constitution in 2005 as per Insert 60-1), updates on NAFTA; and brand new economic union agreement (similar to NAFTA) between US and five Central American/Caribbean countries.
- New example of successful joint venture between MCI and Boeing for virtual collaboration on global scale.
- New example of cultural problems when Arab Satellite TV decided to introduce "The Simpsons" to Arab viewers.
- New example of political intervention using the case of Chirac and other French officials to prevent Hewlett Packard from laying off workers in France.
- Several new examples of how practices that are perfectly legal in USA (such as sales volume linked rebates) may be illegal overseas.

- New example of how political events affect stability of currency such as the Paris riots resulting in a 10% drop in value of euro overnight.
- Updates on recent upturn of Japanese economy and how it affects foreign firms, providing new example of Wal-Mart.
- Update on the situation of Mexican economy and how it affects American firms doing business there.
- Update on the situation of China's economy and how it affects American firms doing business there. See also new example of Motorola's investments in China.
- Updates on the situation of India's economy, particularly the enormous growth of software industry and its effect on American firms.
- New examples of global strategic alliances between GM-Daewoo and Texas Instrument-Compel Communication.
- Discussion of new trends in expatriate assignments using survey data.
- Update on cost of living overseas for cities like London, Paris or Tokyo.
- Discussion of new initiative on global social responsibility and ethics called Joint Initiative on Corporate Accountability and Worker Rights by Nike, GAP, Adidas, etc., to monitor foreign suppliers for abuses.
- Two new Management Close Ups. These include IKEA (customer focus) and use of hotlines in Europe.
- Three new mini-cases and collaborative learning cases.

the 3rd edition

Chapter 3

- New table (table 3.1) which provides categories of "selected ethical issues in business" developed from an idea by one of the reviewers.
- New graphic figure 3.1 which compares ethics approaches and a new section in the text which explains how these approaches to ethics compare across some criteria.
- Explantion of the whistleblower provision of the recently enacted Sarbanes-Oxley law that protects individuals who inform on executives who are suspected of performing financial malfeasance.
- A new example of social responsibility problems – this example describes the difficulties Merck the pharmaceutical firm faces when its drug Vioxx was recalled from the market in 2004.
- New examples of firms acting socially responsible to the community – Home Depot example of building playgrounds in communities; Nike example of raising funds for cancer research; Starbucks example of sponsoring literacy programs and giving to seriously ill children.
- New example of a social activist group – Rainforest Action Network (RAN) put economic pressure on Citibank to stop lending money to logging, mining and oil-drilling projects that destroy rain forests.
- New Management Minicase 3.1 "Starbucks Gambles that Encouraging its Coffee Suppliers to Act Socially Responsible is Good for Business." Case about Starbucks

giving preferential business to farmers in third world countries who use sustainable environmental farming practices, which protect the scarce land that can grow coffee beans.

Chapter 4

- New Manager's Checkup (The checkup makes change real by asking the student to consider proactively addressing change at a personal and workgroup level.)
- New figures added (figs. 4.2, 4.3, 4.7) that summarize the text and should help guide the student's reading comprehension.
- Update of opening vignette about SAS.
- New research cited demonstrating the importance of congruence in values for post-merger financial performance.
- Limitation to Lewin's three-step model noted. This addition was suggested by a reviewer. (Lewin's model does not apply when change is dynamic and ongoing.)

Chapter 5

- Brand new example of successful long range planning by GE in China.
- Brand new update on the situation of Kodak and how its past planning efforts have largely failed.
- Brand new example of Genentech as an excellent planner of innovation activities.
- Brand new examples of unanticipated results after careful planning: a) Blockbuster's bad plan to drop the "never late fee"

in 2005; and b) General Motor's discounts which resulted in multibillion dollar losses yet failed to increase GM's market share.
- Brand new example of Katrina and how unforeseen events affect planning.
- Brand new example of excellent long-term product planning by Apple with ideas conceived as far back as 1987.
- Brand new discussion of ethical lapses in planning with several company examples.
- Two brand new Management Close Ups have been added. One on "planning for what if" and one on "bottoms up planning" at several organizations.
- Two Management Mini-Cases are brand new. One brand new Ethical Checklist has been added.

Chapter 6

- Information providing background on the meaning of risk is expanded.
- New example concerning decision making in "crisis situations" is provided from Wal-Mart's use of its Emergency Operations Center in the wake of 2005 Hurricane Katrina to distribute bottled water and food to the stricken area along the Gulf Coast that arrived days ahead of the federal government relief efforts.
- Figure 6.3 is new and provides a decision tree analysis which illustrates how managers can systematically evaluate alternatives in the decision making process. The idea for this figure came from a

suggestion by one of the reviewers of this chapter.
- Description of decision tree analysis which is used for analyzing alternatives to decisions is provided in the text.
- Two new sections in the text that describe the use of "intuition" in decision making and the "escalation of commitment" concept are provided in the section of the chapter that describes the Limits to Rational Decision Making. The idea for this addition came from suggestions by reviewers of this chapter.
- A new section is added to the text: "Personal Decision Making Styles" which describes four different decision making styles: directive, analytical, conceptual and behavioral. The text describes the context that is best suited to use each of these styles. The idea for this addition came from a suggestion from one of the reviewers of this chapter.
- New Management Minicase 6.2. "Merck's Decision to Withdraw its Vioxx Drug from the Market." This case discusses the concept of bounded awareness in decision making, where cognitive blinders may prevent a decision maker from sensing or using important information in the decision making process. In the case of Merck, this error in ignoring critical information had tragic consequences both for the company and the customers who were mislead in using a pain relieving drug that could increase the likelihood of heart attacks and strokes to users. Sadly,

continued

What's (NEW!) in

evidence of these medical risks were available in research that Merck had undertaken four years before it decided to withdraw the drug from the market.

Chapter 7

- Updated situation of what is happening to Ford's new strategy for 2006-2010, and how it has evolved from prior unsuccessful strategies.
- Updated situation of American Express portfolio of products targeted to specific customer groups.
- Updated situation to what is happening to GM and problems with recent GM strategies.
- Brand new example of strategic imitation referring to introduction of organic products by supermarket chains (such as Fry's and Safeway) putting a dent on the market niche of Whole Foods.
- Updated situation with Total, top selling toothpaste in US.
- Brand new discussion of how several emerging countries are becoming "first world" in their innovation capabilities.
- Brand new example of competitive pressures, using as an illustration how Wal-Mart is putting a big dent on earnings of Best Buy and Circuit City by offering half price warranties (which represent half of Best Buy and Circuit City earnings).
- Brand new example of how even Wal-Mart is vulnerable to attack, in this case by Google.

- Update on situation of Boeing's capacity to absorb and capitalize on new technologies by referring to commercial satellite consumers.
- Brand new examples of the impact of demographic changes on business, including Cochlear Ltd. and condo developers.
- Brand new discussion of the impact of politics on firms' discretion, including example of Maryland Legislature's decision to require companies such as Wal-Mart to provide health insurance to employees.
- Update of situation of Microsoft concerning antitrust cases against it.
- Brand new discussion of McDonald's attempt to change its image of "junk food" in France as well as U.S.A.
- Brand new story of how a reborn AT&T plans to move aggressively into TV, web, and wireless services. This is a great recent example of adaptation.
- Brand new story of pressures that relative newcomer Google is putting on Yahoo, surpassing it on advertising sales.
- Brand new examples of strategic alliances and their reasons, including Sony and Korea's Samsung.
- Update of the situation of Kodak as it tried to move from film to digital. Also, brand new example of the impact of technology by discussing how musical downloads has greatly depressed CD sales.
- Brand new example of risk of price wars, describing what

happened to Independence Air as it tried to compete against established airlines.
- Brand new report of firms that create the most patents around the world including specific examples.
- Brand new example of how Volkswagen has successfully used benchmark analysis.
- Brand new example of highly successful single product firm, RIM and the Blackberry.
- Brand new examples of risk faced by single product firms.
- Brand new example of product differentiation, referring to United Airline's conscious decision not to compete on price for passengers but on amenities.
- Brand new example of intense competition between Blockbuster Inc. and Netflix, Inc.
- Updated information on the aftermath of Sarbanes-Oxley, and how it has affected corporations.
- New discussion on how what may be good for some stakeholders may be damaging to other stakeholders, including brand new example of hospitals.
- Five brand new figures were added as a map to guide students through what is a difficult and comprehensive chapter.
- All Management Close Ups boxes were replaced with new examples.
- All Management Mini-Cases and Collaborative Learning Case are brand new, replacing prior ones.
- Brand new SWOT analysis Skill Building Box created, replacing old SWOT analysis Skill Building Exercise.

Chapter 8

- New figures added (figs. 8.1 & 8.2) that graphically summarize the text.
- New Manager's Checkup. (Checkup asks student to take the perspective of the customer as a means to drive innovation.)
- New Management Minicase on outsourcing innovation.
- New management minicase on high tech fabrics. (The case asks students to consider entrepreneurial opportunities in this developing area and to consider whether the blendings of technology and fabric are inventions or innovations.)
- Example added of entrepreneur who is now president of a virtual reality company.
- Updated revenue and employment level reported in Management Close-Up of Dell Computer.
- Management Close-Up of E-ink updated to include receipt of "Best of Small Tech" award.
- Updates on statistics including number of new businesses, number of jobs created by new start-ups, and business ownership levels for minorities and females.
- The concepts of innovation and invention are now differentiated (with the Segway people mover being more of an invention while the simple disposable diaper is more of an innovation).
- Increasing importance of innovation is discussed. The inclusion of imagination to measure leaders at GE is cited and the customer-driven innovation process at Procter &

the 3rd edition

Gamble is discussed.
- Google's formula for managing to maintain an innovative culture is cited.

Chapter 9

- A paragraph description of the "conglomerate" form of product based divisional structure is added to the text.
- A new figure (figure 9.6) that provides a schematic of the conglomerate based organization structure.
- A new section in the text about the strategic factor of technology and how it influences organization design. A typology of different technologies that affect organization design is given. The idea for this new section was provided by one of the reviewers of an earlier edition of the text.
- A new figure that illustrates the strategic factors that influence organization design. The idea for this new figure came from a reviewer.
- A new figure that shows how organization structures can vary from mechanistic to organic on a continuum. The idea for this new figure came from a reviewer.
- A new example of acquisitions made by Oracle that spent over $15 billion to buy PeopleSoft and Siebel Systems software companies.
- An update of the Sara Lee Management close up that indicates how Sara Lee continues to re-organize its structure.
- A new Management Mini-case 9.1 that examines how Microsoft

decided to re-organize itself in order to increase its ability to make entrepreneurial decisions and respond to competitors' moves.

Chapter 10

- New example of effective use of orientation and training at Baptist HealthCare.
- New discussion of how incentives can help strategic objectives but often raise potential ethical issues, including examples.
- ALL Management Close Ups were replaced with new stories and new firms.
- ALL Management Mini-Cases and Individual/Collaborative Learning Cases were replaced with new stories.

Chapter 11

- Discussion of why occupational segregation is still important for women.
- Discussion of new research appearing in Academy of Management Journal showing that power distance affects the benefits of team heterogeneity internationally.
- Discussion of why CEOs believe diversity is important, including quotation by CEO of PriceWaterhouse Coopers, LLP.
- Update of why many blacks believe there is still racial discrimination in the corporate world and a more recent phenomena of African-Americans feeling displaced in unskilled/semiskilled jobs by Hispanics.

- Discussion of recent survey revealing that Asian Americans still feel like "forever foreigners."
- New figures on income of Asian American households being much higher than that of whites.
- Recognition that some organizations are starting to provide assistance for parents of children with disabilities.
- New data on international migrants coming to USA as well as Western Europe.
- New discussion of how Hispanics are not staying in segregated areas by dispersing throughout the country.
- New discussion on health care debate, as it pertains to older employees.
- Updated discussion of religious tolerance and conflict, referring to Paris riots and widespread protests by Muslim believers in response to what they see as insensitivity to their faith.
- Totally brand new section on undocumented workers (with many brand new references).
- Brand new discussion of women entering occupations previously reserved for men.
- Updated data on professional women who drop from labor force.
- Brand new discussion of issues that should be considered in diversity training.
- Tie back to the IBM's opening vignette in the conclusions.
- All of the Management Close Ups were replaced with brand new ones. These include banks targeting Hispanics, saving labor

costs by penalizing older workers, and how women are making inroads in what used to be all male occupations, in this case firefighters.
- All of the Management Mini-Cases and Collaborative Learning Exercises have been replaced with new ones. The skill building exercise on how to deal with stereotypes has been completely replaced.
- Two brand new figures have been added to summarize material and break text, Figure 11.2 and Figure 11.3.
- One brand new section of chapter has been written for undocumented workers.
- One brand new figure (Figure 11.6) has been added containing recommendations by the Society for Human Resource Management on diversity training.

Chapter 12

- Figure added (per reviewer comment) that graphically depicts goal setting process.
- Figure added that portrays cascading goals.
- New management minicase on the motivational impact of recognition.
- New Manager's Checkup - applies expectancy model to assessing student's motivation to manage.
- New internet exercise focused on goal setting.
- Recent survey finding regarding importance of intrinsic factors to career satisfaction and retention.

continued

What's NEW!

- Applied implications of equity theory for managing workers are now discussed (per reviewer suggestion).

Chapter 13

- New Manager's Notebook added on practical leadership skills.
- Opening vignette revised and updated. (It now focuses on Nissan and the leadership of Carlos Ghosn.)

Chapter 14

- There is a new opening vignette on rapid-response teams that save lives at Tenet Healthcare Corporation. New critical thinking questions and new Concluding Thoughts that answer the critical thinking questions at the end of the chapter have been provided.
- A new figure (Figure 14.2) has been added that provides diagrams that illustrate the three major types of interdependence: pooled, sequential, and reciprocal interdependence.
- New content has been added that enriches the section on conflict management. The difference between task conflict and relationship conflict is explained that contributes to the understanding of functional and dysfunctional conflict. The idea for this new content was provided by reviewers of the text.
- A new Management Minicase 14.1 has been added. This minicase looks at different approaches that companies use to encourage teamwork and collaborative behavior among the employees. One approach focuses on changing the reward

environment, while another approach focuses on building the "soft skills" of employees.
- A new Internet exercise has been added (Internet exercise 14.1). The exercise asks the students to visit the Taco Bell website and view how teamwork skills are deeply embedded in the career path of all the positions at Taco Bell. As one advances along the career path one can observe that different team behaviors become more prominent in performing the expected role related to the job.

Chapter 15

- A new opening vignette: "Call center jobs are outsourced to the home thanks to broadband communications technology." New critical thinking questions for the vignette and new Concluding Thoughts are written to correspond to the new opening vignette feature for chap. 15.
- A new figure 15.2 is provided that visually shows organizational communication patterns including downward, upward and horizontal communication.
- New text content concerning electronic communication as pertains to e-mail is provided that discusses the use of smilies or emoticons that are symbols that represent different emotions and used at the end of text sentences to clarify the emotional content of a message.
- A new figure 15.4 that provides illustrations of smilies that are used as symbols for emotions in email messages.
- New content about informal communication is added to the

text that describes the formation of cliques which are informal social groups which can disrupt the flow of communication unless this problem is recognized as a communication barrier and positive steps taken by managers to deal with this situation.
- A new Minicase 15.1 is provided that explains the trend of the use of employee blogs as unofficial communication channels where employees can share their candid feelings and attitudes about the company without worrying about management retribution for expressing their true feelings. The case explores both opportunities and threats that should be of concern to managers concerning the use of employee blogs.

Chapter 17

- Management Close-Up of a shortage for a new drug was updated with new info.
- Discussion of Kanban system expanded and updated.

Chapter 18

- New content on "Knowledge Management Systems" (KMS) used for storing and retrieving organizational knowledge.
- New content on "Customer Relationship Management" (CRM) systems that maintain data about customers and all their interactions with an organization.
- A new Figure 18.2 that provides a diagram of a Customer Relationship Management system (CRM).
- Additional examples of business

to consumer e-commerce strategies used at big box stores such as Target, Lowe's and Wal-Mart.
- New Management Minicase 18.1 that examines "Online Knowledge Sharing at Xerox" - an extended illustration of a knowledge sharing system and how it provides better service to customers.
- New Management Minicase 18.2 that examines "Dun and Bradstreet Use E-Commerce to Sell Financial Services" and how the use of e-commerce provides valuable marketing information that can be used to improve current products and services and suggest ideas for new ones.
- New Manager's Checkup 18.1 - examines the ethical use of the corporate computer. Individuals who score high on this self-assessment are likely to have developed good ethical judgment within the context of using the corporate computer.

Supplements

Instructor Supplements

Instructor's Resource CD-ROM

ISBN 0073027472

Allowing instructors to create a customized multimedia presentation, this all-in-one resource incorporates the Computerized Test Bank, PowerPoint® Slides, Instructor's Resource Guide, downloaded figures from the text, and links to the Online Learning Center.

Instructor's Resource Guide and Video Manual

To help with organizing your classroom presentation, this supplement contains extensive chapter-by-chapter lecture outline notes, chapter overviews, tips for teaching difficult topics, and highlighted key terms. It also includes embedded powerpoint slide notations, alternative examples for difficult topics, answers to the box questions and end-of-chapter material, and a guide to using the videos.

Group and Video Resource Manual: An Instructor's Guide to an Active Classroom

(in print 0073044342 or online at www.mhhe.com/mobmanual)

This manual created for instructors contains everything needed to successfully integrate activities into the classroom. It includes a menu of items to use as teaching tools in class. All of our self-assessment exercises, Test Your Knowledge quizzes, group exercises, and Manager's Hot Seat exercises are located in this one manual along with teaching notes and PowerPoint slides to use in class. Group exercises include everything you would need to use the exercise in class – handouts, figures, etc.

This manual is organized into 25 topics like ethics, decision-making, change and leadership for easy inclusion in your lecture. A matrix is included at the front of the manual that references each resource by topic. Students access all of the exercises and self-assessments on their textbook's website. The Manager's Hot Seat exercises are located online at **www.mhhe.com/MHS**

Test Bank

We've aligned our Testbank with Bloom's Taxonomy and new AACSB guidelines, tagging each question according to the applicable knowledge and skills areas. AACSB categories include Global, Ethics and Social Responsibility, Legal and other External Environment, Communication, Diversity, Group Dynamics, Individual Dynamics, Production, and IT. Previous designations aligning questions with Learning Objectives, boxes and features still exist as well.

PowerPoint slides

Organized in an outline format, and containing additional material, the powerpoint presentation slides number 20-25 per chapter. All of the above can also be found in the Instructor Resources section of the OLC.

DVD format Videos

ISBN 0073027502

Three sets of video are available with this text. One DVD package provides you with two set of video (1) End of Chapter video: Each chapter has a corresponding video that ties in with chapter topics, supplemented with notes and information in the Instructor's Resource Guide. (2) The Entrepreneurial Manager video: In text video cases are supported with video to connect chapter concepts to how they've been applied successfully in entrepreneurial ventures and small businesses. Students are able to access the videos on the Online Learning Center.

The third set, the Manager's Hot Seat collection of video materials are linked to from within this text's Online Learning Center **www.mhhe.com/gomez3e** and available at **http://www.mhhe.com/MHS**.

Student Supplements

Online Learning Center (OLC)

More and more students are studying online. That's why we offer an Online Learning Center (OLC) that follows Management chapter by chapter. It doesn't require any building or maintenance on your part. It's ready to go the moment you and your students type in the URL.

As your students study, they can refer to the OLC Website for such benefits as:

- **Internet-based activities**
- **Self-grading quizzes**
- **Learning objectives**
- **Videos and video quizzes**

Reviewers

We are very grateful to Kelly Lowery, Sponsoring Editor, and John Biernat, Editorial Director, at McGraw-Hill/Irwin for their continuing commitment to our book and making it a reality. We also appreciate the efforts of Christine Scheid, Senior Developmental Editor; Susanne Riedell, Senior Project Manager; Debra Sylvester, Production Supervisor; Adam Rooke, Senior Designer; Jeremy Chesharek, photo research coordinator.

1st Edition Reviewers

Charles Beavin, Miami-Dade Community College

Gunther S. Boroschek, University of Massachusetts—Boston

Ken Dunegan, Cleveland State University

Janice M. Feldbauer, Austin Community College

William Jedlicka, Harper College

Jon Kalinowski, Mankato State University

Joan Keeley, Washington State University

Stephen T. Margulis, Grand Valley State University

J. L. Morrow, Jr., Mississippi State University

Nga T. Nguyen, Temple University

Carl L. Swanson, University of North Texas

James R. Terborg, University of Oregon

Kenneth R. Thompson, DePaul University

Walter Wheatley, University of West Florida

2nd Edition Reviewers

Dave Adams, Manhattanville College

Cheryl Adkins, Longwood University

Baltasar Allende, Sul Ross State University—Alpine

Joseph Anderson, Northern Arizona University

Allen Amason, University of Georgia

M Ruhul Amin, Bloomsburg University of Pennsylvania

Michael Avery, Northwestern College

Barry Axe, Florida Atlantic University—Boca Raton

Harold Babson, Columbus State Community College

Richard Bacha, Pennsylvania State University—York

Kristin Backhaus, State University College—New Paltz

Mark Bagshaw, Marietta College

Kevin Baker, Roanoke College

Mark Baker, Illinois State University

John Bedient, Albion College

James Bell, Southwest Texas State University

Toni Bell, Williston State College

Richard Benedetto, Merrimack College

Ellen Benowitz, Mercer Community College

Dan Benson, Kutztown University of Pennsylvania

Bill Bergman, California State University—Chico

Sharon Berner, Manhattan Christian College

Danielle Beu, Louisiana Tech University

Wesley Bitters, Utah Valley State College—Orem

Don Boyer, Jefferson College

Bill Brown, Montana State University—Bozeman

James Browne, University of Southern Colorado

Rochelle Brunson, Alvin Community College

Diane Caggiano, Fitchburg State College

Elizabeth Cameron, Alma College

Anthony Cantarella, Murray State University

James Carlson, Manatee Community College—Bradenton

Nancy Carr, Community College of Philadelphia

Lesley Casula, Lord Fairfax Community College

Denise Chachere, St. Louis University

Aruna Chandra, Indiana State University—Terre Haute

Bruce Charnov, Hofstra University

Walter Childs, Pennsylvania State University—Abington

Jack Chirch, Hampton University

Janet Ciccarelli, Herkimer County Community College—Herkimer

Tony Cioffi, Lorain County Community College

Alfred Colonies, Community College of Rhode Island—Flanagan

Dennis Conley, University of Nebraska—Lincoln

Suzanne Crampton, Grand Valley State University

Barbara Dalby, University of Mary Hardin Baylor

David Danforth, Bethel College

Ajay Das, Bernard M. Baruch College

Miles Davis, Shenandoah University

Dave Day, Columbia College—Columbia

Gita De Souza, Pennsylvania State University—Delaware Campus

Tom Deckelman, Owens Community College

Paul Dellinger, Western Piedmont Community College

Kate Demarest, Carroll Community College

Mike Drafke, College of Dupage

Sally Dresdow, University of Wisconsin—Green Bay

Linda Duncan, Arkansas State University—Newport

Wendy Eager, Eastern Washington University

Ellen Fagenson Eland, George Mason University

Ray Eldridge, Freed—Hardeman University

Elizabeth Evans, Concordia University

Steve Farner, Bellevue University

Judson Faurer, Metro State College of Denver

Lou Firenze, Northwood University

Paul Fisher, Rogue Community College

David Foote, Middle Tennessee State University

Monique Forte, Stetson University

Mark Fox, Indiana University—South Bend

William Fox, Brenau University

Jennifer Frazier, James Madison University

Pat Fuller, Brevard Community College—Titusville

Richard Gayer, Antelope Valley College

Peter Georgelas, Bridgewater State College

Carmine Gibaldi, St. John's University—Jamaica

Carol Gilmore, University of Maine

Catherine Giunta, Seton Hill College

Norma Givens, Fort Valley State University

Connie Golden, Lakeland Community College

Luis Gonzalez, Bloomfield College

Hugh Graham, Loras College

Wesley Green, Lindsey Wilson College

Mark Grimes, Georgia Southwestern State University

Allison Grindle, Messiah College

Douglas Guthe, University of North Carolina—Chapel Hill

Dave Hall, Saginaw Valley State University

Robert Hanna, California State University—Northridge

Roberta Hanson, Metro State College of Denver

James Harbin, Texas A & M University—Texarkana

Bob Hatfield, Morehead State University

Carolyn Hatton, Cincinnati State Tech & Community College

Ellis Hayes, Wingate University

Brad Hays, North Central State College Ot112

Samuel Hazen, Tarleton State University

Jeff Hefel, St. Mary's University

Gary Hensel, Mc Henry County College

James Herbert, Kennesaw State University

Ronald Herrick, Mesa Community College

David Herzog, St. Louis Community College—Flors Valley

James Hess, Ivy Tech State College—Fort Wayne

Dorothy Hetmer-Hinds, Trinity Valley Community College

Bob Hoerber, Westminster College

David Holloman, Victor Valley College

John Howery, Lindsey Wilson College

Fred Hughes, Faulkner University

Alvin Hwang, Pace University

Lynn Isvik, Upper Iowa Unive—Fayette

Joe Izzo, Alderson—Broaddus College

Elizabeth Jackson, Keystone College

Donna Jarrell, West Virginia State College

Tom Jay, Flathead Valley Community College—Kalispell

Velma Jesser, Lane Community College

Jack Johnson, Cosumnes River College

Sharon Johnson, Cedarville University

Jordan Kaplan, Long Island University—Brooklyn

Joseph Kavanaugh, Sam Houston State University

George Kelley, Erie Community College City Campus—Buffalo

Claire Kent, Mary Baldwin College

Sara Kiser, Alabama State University

Judith Kizzie, Clinton Community College

Tom Knapke, Wright State University—Celina

Margareta Knopik, College of St. Mary

Dennis Kovach, Community College Allegheny City N—Pittsburgh

Kenneth Kovach, University of Maryland—College Park

Subodh Kulkarni, Howard University

Doug Laher, Whitworth College

Lowell Lamberton, Central Oregon Community College

Patrick Langan, Wartburg College

John Leblanc, Cedarville University

Martin Lecker, Rockland Community College

Reviewers

Robert Leonard, Lebanon Valley College

Andrea Licari, St. John's University—Jamaica

Benyamin Lichtenstein, University of Hartford

Meilee Lin, State University College—Potsdam

Tom List, Finlandia University

Paul Lister, Eureka College

Woody Liswood, Sierra Nevada College

Thomas Lloyd, Westmoreland Community College—Youngwood

Bruce Locker, Southwestern Oregon Community College

Victor Lopez, SUNY—Delhi

Tom Loughman, Columbus State University

Richard Lowery, Bowie State University

Barbara Luck, Jackson Community College

William Lyke, Webster University—375 Mssq/Mse

Cheryl Macon, Butler County Community College

Zam Malik, Governors State University

Joseph Manno, Montgomery College—Rockville

Santo Marabella, Moravian College

Michel Marette, Northern Virginia Community College—Loudon Campus

Jackie Mayfield, Texas A & M University International

Martha Mc Creery, Rend Lake College

Loretta McAdam, Seminole Community College—Sanford

Tom McFarland, Mt. San Antonio College

Michael Messina, Gannon University—Erie

Stuart Milne, Georgia Institute of Technology

Barbara Minsky, Troy State University—Dothan

Carol Moore, California State University – Hayward

Mark Moore, St. Cloud State University

Bill Morgan, Felician College

Jaideep Motwani, Grand Valley State University

Peter Moutsatson, Montcalm Community College

Carolyn Mueller, Stetson University

David Murphy, Madisonville Community College

Tom Murphy, Ozarks Technical Community College

Brian Murray, University of Dallas

Robert Nale, Coastal Carolina University

Maria Nathan, Lynchburg College

Chris Neck, Virginia Polytechnic Institute

Albert Novak, St. Vincent College

John O'Brian, Adams State College

Ronald O'Neal, Camden County College

David Olson, California State University—Bakersfield

Floyd Ormsbee, State University College—Potsdam

Pam Pack, Pikeville College

Ranjna Patel, Bethune Cookman College

John Paxton, Wayne State College

Michael Pepper, Transylvania University

Nicholas Peppes, St. Louis Community College—Forest Park

Donna Perkins, University of Wisconsin—Platteville

Sheila Petcavage, Cuyahoga Community College Western—Parma

Barbara Petzall, Maryville University

Jim Pfister, St. Petersburg College—Clearwater

Eustace Phillip, Emmanuel College

Jeff Phillips, Thomas College

Allayne Pizzolato, Nicholls State University

Carl Poch, Northern Illinois University

Brian Porter, Hope College

Larry Potter, University of Maine—Presque Isle

Paula Potter, Western Kentucky University

James Powell, Chaffey College

Michael Provitera, St. Peters College

Richard Raspen, Wilkes University

Nancy Ray-Mitchell, McLennan Community College

Doug Reed, University of Pittsburgh—Johnstown

Bob Reese, Illinois Valley Community College

Erella Regev, Montclair State University

Clint Relyea, Arkansas State University—State University

Danny Rhodes, Anderson College

Shelton Rhodes, Bowie State University

Rick Ringer, Illinois State University

Orlando Roybal, Northern New Mexico Community College—Español

Terry Rumker, Ashland University

Cyndy Ruszkowski, Illinois State University

Tracey Ryan, Longwood University

James Salvucci, Curry College

Hindy Schachter, New Jersey Institute of Technology

Rebecca Schaupp, Fairmont State College

Gerald Schoenfeld, Florida Gulf Coast University

Shirley Schooley, Birmingham Southern College

Greg Schultz, Carroll College

Marian Schultz, The University of West Florida

Michael Schultz, Menlo College

Connie Schwass, West Shore Community College

Mark Seabright, Western Oregon University

Pat Setlik, William Rainey Harper College

Richard Shapiro, Cuyahoga Community College—Metro—Cleveland

Paul Shibelski, Trinity College

Ted Shore, Kennesaw State University

Marion Sillah, South Carolina State University

Cynthia Simerly, Lakeland Community College

Roy Simerly, East Carolina University

Richard Slovacek, North Central College

James Smith, Rocky Mountain College

Nellie Smith, Rust College

Paul Smith, Mars Hill College

Andrea Smith-Hunter, Siena College

R. Spear, University of Idaho

Vernon Stauble, California State Polytechnic University—Pomona

Jeff Strom, Va Western Community College

Mary Kay Sullivan, Maryville College

Harry Sweet, University of Mary Hardin Baylor

James Swenson, Minnesota State University Moorhead

Sarina Swindell, Tarleton State University

Patricia Tadlock, Horry Georgetown Tech Col

Robert Tansky, St. Clair County Community College

Virginia Taylor, William Paterson University

Ira Teich, Yeshiva University

Frank Titlow, St. Petersburg College

Ricardo Trujillo, Red Rocks Community College

Richard Tyler, Anne Arundel Community College—Arnold

Anthony Urbaniak, Northern State University

Matthew Valle, Elon University

Barry Vanhook, Arizona State University—Tempe

Gina Vega, Merrimack College

Roger Volkema, American University

Cheryl Waddington, Wayne State College

Betty Wanielista, Valencia Community College—East Campus

Gary Ward, Reedley Community College

William Ward, Susquehanna University

John Washbush, University of Wisconsin—Whitewater

Harry Waters, California State University—Hayward

William Waxman, Edison Community College

Mark Weber, University of Minn/3—150 Carsmgmt

Steve Welch, West Chester University of Pennsylvania

Richard Wertz, Concordia University

Kenneth Wheeler, University of Texas – Arlinton

David White, Southwest Missouri State University—West Plains

Kathleen White, Macmurray College

Sam White, University of Colorado—Colorado Springs

Ellen Whitener, University of Virginia—Charlottesville

Timothy Wiedman, Thomas Nelson Community College

Dave Wilderman, Wabash Valley College

Ethlyn Williams, University of South Florida

Kathy Wilson, North Carolina Wesleyan College

Laura Wolfe, Louisiana State University—Baton Rouge

Colette Wolfson, Ivy Tech State College—South Bend

Michael Yahr, Robert Morris College

Ray Zagorski, Kenai Peninsula Community College

Austin Zekeri, Lane College

Jason Zimmerman, South Dakota State University

3rd Edition Reviewers

Randall G. Sleeth, Virginia Commonwealth University

Peggy Brewer, Eastern Kentucky University

Michael Buckley, University of Oklahoma

Kevin Carlson, Virginia Tech University

Bruce Charnov, Hofstra University

Shirley Fedorovich, Embry-Riddle University

Peter Hulten, Texas Weslyan University

Edward Johnson, University of North Florida

Jeffrey Podoshen, Franklin and Marshall College

Roy Iraggi, New York City College of Technology

Kelly Ottman, University of Wisconsin-Milwaukee

Sheila Petcavage, Cuyahoga Community College

Xiang Yi, Western Illinois University

Chad Higgins, University of Washington

Dennis Brode, Sinclair Community College

Geoffrey Love, University of Illinois

table of contents

6 Decision Making 224

7 Strategic Management 262

8 Entrepreneurship and Innovation 308

PART FOUR: Organization Management   346

9   Managing the Structure and Design of Organizations   348

11 Managing Employee Diversity 428

14 Managing Teams 534

15 Managing Communication 574

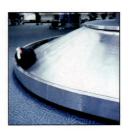

17 Operations Management 644

18 Managing Information Systems 676

management

people • performance • change

part one

Overview

Welcome to the exciting world of management! A rapidly accelerating trend in recent years has seen management become a significant part of everyone's job duties, from front-line employees serving customers to the executives who are at the top of the organization hierarchy. The increasing competitive pressures on companies to make decisions rapidly and to delegate more responsibilities to employees closest to customers, along with wide accessibility of massive amounts of information provided by the Internet, have given rise to a need for everyone to develop management skills—individuals and teams as well as managers. At minimum, employees now have responsibilities for managing information in addition to managing their relationships with customers both internal and external to the organization and with organizational peers, subordinates, and managers. How well employees can manage these relationships and the information for which they are responsible will have a critical impact on their success or failure.

In Part One we provide an overview of the four functions of management: planning and strategizing, organizing, leading, and controlling. These functions are what the work of management is about. Then we explore the evolution of management ideas from their earliest origins to the most recent thinking that influences managers in the 21st century.

1

chapter 1

Management and Its Evolution

Learning Objectives

1. Understand the challenges organizations face in the new millennium.

2. Specify the functions and roles of successful managers.

3. Explain the origins of management as an academic discipline.

4. Describe the bureaucratic and administrative approaches to the study of management.

5. Explain the behavioral perspective in analyzing management issues.

6. Interpret recent approaches to the study of management.

Why GM and Ford Lost while Toyota Won

The bad news from GM and Ford keeps on mounting: 60,000 U.S. and Canadian jobs will go in the next few years, 24 giant factories will close, North American losses in the billions will continue, retirement obligations will be curtailed, and on and on. Clearly, MoTown needs a new approach, and it is natural in the car industry to think the secret must be a killer model—a Toyota Prius hybrid or some other concept—to replace the big pickups and SUVs that floated the American firms for 15 years.

Toyota is leading the charge against Detroit—largely from inside the United States—with a fundamentally different management approach. Compared against Toyota practices, GM's and Ford's approach has five fatal weaknesses:

- *GM and Ford can't design vehicles that Americans want to pay "Toyota money" for.* This is not a matter of bad bets on product concepts or bad engineers. It's a matter of Toyota's better use of its engineers and greater efficiency in its operations. The Prius is not the result of a hunch or luck but rather of a development system that tries out many approaches to every problem, then gets the winning concept to the customer very quickly with low engineering cost, low manufacturing cost, and near perfect quality.

- *GM and Ford do not seem to work well with their suppliers.* Sometimes they seem to try to crush their suppliers' bones—which works only when the suppliers have any profits to squeeze, and few currently do. Then they embrace an ill-defined cooperation with suppliers that briefly makes everyone feel better but fails to produce lower costs, higher quality, or new and better technology. Toyota, by contrast, is getting brilliant results and lower prices from American suppliers while also giving suppliers adequate profit margins. How? By creating mutual trust while at the same time relentlessly analyzing every step in their shared design and production process to take out the waste and put in the quality.

- *At GM and Ford employees depend on orders coming from superiors and individual initiative is discouraged.* These management practices turn competent people into Dilberts. By contrast, Toyota does a brilliant job of making one person responsible for every key business process, like the chief engineer overseeing each new model. And Toyota teaches managers how to ask the right questions (rather than give the usual big-boss answers) in order to engage everyone involved in every process to go faster and do a better job with fewer resources.

- *GM and Ford find it difficult to respond to environmental changes and often become committed to a failing corporate strategy.* This is illustrated by their clinging to a wide range of brands: Chevy, Pontiac, Buick, Cadillac, Saab, GMC, and Hummer at GM; Ford, Mercury, Lincoln, Mazda, Jaguar, Volvo, Aston Martin, and Range Rover at Ford. And they still talk about brand revitalization as the way ahead. Yet the most successful car companies in the world—Toyota and BMW—have only two or three brands. A plethora of brands that can't pull their weight drains management energy and company coffers, yet GM and Ford seem unable to change their course.

- *GM and Ford still treat customers as strangers engaged in one-time transactions.* Toyota's Lexus, by contrast, has created a new and better customer experience. Customers cheerfully pay more for the car and the service and then come back for more cars because they love the treatment. As Toyota applies its fabled process management to retailing to take out costs, which it is now starting to do at Lexus, customer touch becomes the final weapon in the Toyota arsenal.

But note that we haven't mentioned the creaky factories, vast pension obligations, and cranky unions that commentators on the current situation seem obsessed with. In fact, Ford's and GM's factories are now good enough to compete in terms of labor productivity and quality. They just can't support employees with no work in "job banks" and unsustainable pension and health care benefits for retirees as the companies continue to shrink. Union and management both know this, yet no accommodation has been reached on these issues because their conversation has broken down. In the meantime, Toyota seems to be able to work effectively with unions. Toyota has good relations with United Auto Workers, which represents workers at United Motor Manufacturing Inc. in Fremont, California, and the Teamsters at TABC Inc., a Toyota subsidiary in Long Beach, California, that performs various manufacturing functions in North America.

Source: Adapted with permission from J. P. Womack, "Why Toyota Won," *The Wall Street Journal*, February 13, 2006, p. C-3. See also L. Chappell, "Toyota to Spurn Michigan," www.autoweek.com, February 7, 2006. For related stories see J. McCracken, "Detroit's Symbol of Dysfunction: Paying Employees Not to Work.," *The Wall Street Journal*, March 1, 2006, p. A-1, and J.W. Peters, "Both Ford and GM Scale Back," *The New York Times*, March 1, 2006, p. C-1.

CRITICAL THINKING QUESTIONS

1. *Why have Ford and General Motors allowed their financial situation to deteriorate while Toyota is prospering?*

2. *What seems to separate Toyota's management style from that of Ford and General Motors?*

3. *Why has Toyota (a foreign company) been so successful in entering the American market, beating the largest domestic automobile manufacturers on their own turf?*

We'll revisit these questions again in our Concluding Thoughts on page 36, after you have had the opportunity to read the discussion in this chapter.

This chapter provides the "big picture," or an overview, of the field of management. First, we explain what management is. We discuss the different types of managers, the functions that managers perform, and the skills needed to successfully carry out managerial activities. Next, we describe the history and evolution of the field, along with ideas that have affected the practice of management. Some ideas, such as bureaucratic management, were in vogue and then fell out of favor, while other ideas have withstood the test of time and continue to be used by managers today.

Management in the New Millennium

Organizational performance depends, to a large extent, on how resources are allocated and management's ability to adapt to changing conditions. In successful organizations, people are managed wisely and resources are used efficiently and effectively. This helps managers reach key organizational goals, such as keeping the company functioning in a changing external environment in which technology, governmental activities, and competition create constant challenges.

To be successful, a company must be both efficient and effective. A firm is *efficient* when it makes the best possible use of people, money, the physical plant, and technology. It is *effective* when goals are met which sustain a company's competitive advantage. A firm with excellent goals could still fail miserably by being *inefficient*, meaning that the company hired the wrong people, lost key contributors, relied on outdated technology, and made poor investment decisions. A firm is *ineffective* when it fails to reach goals that sustain a company's competitive advantage. High quality companies do things right (they are efficient) and do the right things (they are effective).

The 21st century world of business is strongly influenced by three issues. The first is the *management of change.* Organizational leaders must cope with and adapt to rapid change on a daily basis. Change creates uncertainty and risk. The number of competitors and product offerings are greater than ever before. Globalization means that most firms are exposed to competitive challenges both domestically and internationally. Many products (such as software) become obsolete in a matter of a few years or even months, forcing the firm to continuously innovate or die. Today's managers must effectively deal with a host of technological, legal, cultural, and organizational changes, such as downsizing, restructuring, and mergers.

Skills for Managing 1.1 on page 9 provides an exercise to help you and your classmates think about your future career in light of these changes.

The second major new issue is an increasing emphasis on *customer service.* The company must satisfy the needs of customers in ways that contribute to long-term loyalty. The term *customer* is now used in a broader sense. It refers to anyone who receives a service from an employee. Customers are both external (current or prospective consumers of the firm's products or service) and internal (other managers or employees who depend on the manager's performance or inputs in some capacity). For most successful operations, the customer represents the starting point and an ending point for almost every activity.

Globalization is playing an increasingly important role in the process of serving both internal and external customers as many companies are outsourcing entire functions overseas (see Management Close-Up 1.1, "How Outsourcing Is Transforming Whole Industries and Changing the Way We Work" on page 10).

The third critical issue affecting the management profession in the 21st century is the need for higher *business ethics.* Ethics are the standards and values which are considered necessary for the collective interests of employees, shareholders, and society. Recently, several well-publicized examples of cheating,

Among the many cultural changes facing business managers today is the rising number of Hispanic consumers in the United States, which advertisers see as akin to the baby boom, and the increasing assimilation of Latino culture into the mainstream. Companies' desire to reach this fast-growing market (as in this TV ad for the "Got Milk" campaign) with its divergent tastes and preferences is spurring a creative revolution in Spanish-language television advertising.

dishonesty, and use of the firm's resources for personal gain have emerged in firms such as WorldCom, Tyco, General Dynamics, Enron, Arthur Andersen, and Radio Shack. In the long run, these violations will have a negative impact on those who are influenced by such managers' bad decisions, including employees, other managers, and customers.

Globalization also complicates ethical decision making as companies may feel that they have to compromise ethical standards to do business in certain countries. For instance, during 2006–2007 Yahoo!, Google, Microsoft, and Cisco have come under criticism after revelations that they have cooperated with the Chinese government to censor online searches and even to turn in dissidents to the government.[1]

Many organizations are appointing ethics officers to advise top executives, enforce ethical standards, and monitor potential misconduct at any level within the firm (see Management Close-Up 1.2, "The New Ethics Enforcers" on page 12).

In this book, we will deal with managing change and improving customer service, along with various ethical concerns as various topics are discussed. We will provide examples of what we consider to be both good and bad management practices.

Traditionally, the term *manager* referred only to individuals responsible for making resource allocation decisions and with the formal authority to direct others. There are three levels of management: **strategic managers**, the senior executives with overall responsibility for the firm; **tactical managers** responsible for implementing the directives of strategic managers; and **operational managers** responsible for day-to-day supervision.

In varying degrees successful managers at any level have certain things in common. Each chapter of this book has a feature called "Management Is Everyone's Business" that summarizes how successful *managers* apply sound principles derived from that particular chapter. A broad set of managerial implications of the

strategic managers

The firm's senior executives who are responsible for overall management.

tactical managers

The firm's management staff who are responsible for translating the general goals and plan developed by strategic managers into specific objectives and activities.

operational managers

The firm's lower-level managers who supervise the operations of the organization.

WHAT THE FUTURE WILL BRING

You might think college students aren't looking much farther into the future than next week's exam or Friday's beer bash. As the first decade of the 2000s draws to a close, college students are contemplating something quite different, say campus recruiters and researchers: their future security.

As companies begin their next round of campus visits to recruit the undergraduate class, recruiters say it's clear that the bad news of the past few years—from September 11 and the tech crash to Enron, layoffs, and worries about Social Security's demise—has shaken this new crop of grads. More than any recruits in memory, they're asking employers for assurances of security, so they don't wind up at the next Enron.

Asked in a recent survey what they expect in their compensation packages, recent grads at 123 universities came up with the most detailed list of long-term benefits in the 11-year history of the poll, from retirement plans to health insurance for dependents, even though most undergrads don't even have dependents. Caludia Tattanelli, CEO of Universum, the research and consulting firm that conducted the survey of 29,046 undergrads in all fields of study, says: "This generation is really trying to take their future in their own hands, and do something about it." Asked what elements of compensation they valued most, college seniors gave health insurance and retirement plans higher priority than vacations, bonuses, and stock options.

Although grads are benefiting from the best job market in four years, they learned from watching the tech crash that corporate fortunes can turn—and campus job offers can be rescinded—on a dime. Grads are showing a preference for stable, diversified companies, helping propel such giants as Lockheed Martin and Johnson & Johnson sharply higher in Universum's ratings of grads' "ideal employers" among big corporations in all fields, from consulting and finance to manufacturing and retailing. Martin Slevin, manager, retail recruitment, for Walgreen Co., says today's campus recruits are far more interested in his company's 105-year history and 31 straight years of record profits than grads have been in the past.

"In light of all the corporate scandals like Enron and Worldcom, where people lost all their savings, I wanted to seek out companies that are stable and will live up to benefits promises," says Tiffany Samuels, a recruit from Xavier University, Cincinnati, who turned down two other offers to sign on with Staples.

Skill Building Exercise

Make a list of five things that are highest in priority for you when considering alternative employment opportunities. Submit your list to your instructor, who will merge the lists provided by you and the rest of your class members and distribute it to the entire class (with names removed). As a class, discuss what it is that new employees expect from their organizations, whether or not those expectations are realistic, and what factors are likely to impinge upon companies' success or failure in meeting those expectations.

Source: Adapted from S. Shellenbarger, "Avoiding the Next Enron: Today's Crop of Soon to Be Grads Seeks Job Security," *The Wall Street Journal*, February 16, 2006, P. D-1.

---

contents discussed in this introductory chapter, several of which will be explored in greater detail in subsequent chapters, appears in Management Is Everyone's Business 1.1 on page 13.

Managers still have authority over people and financial resources, but today's organizations are more decentralized than ever before, and employees have more autonomy to define their jobs, prioritize tasks, allocate time, monitor their own work, and set their own objectives. By being *empowered* to make these important choices, employees are less dependent on superiors to tell them what to do and are encouraged to use their own expertise and ideas. In a very real sense, employees are increasingly being asked to manage themselves.

Each chapter of this book has a "Management Is Everyone's Business" feature that emphasizes working as an individual and that summarizes the practical implications of the material being discussed for your *individual* success in

How Outsourcing Is Transforming Whole Industries and Changing the Way We Work

THEME: CUSTOMER FOCUS

In theory, it is becoming possible to buy, off the shelf, practically any function you need to run a company. Want to start a budget airline but don't want to invest in a huge back office? Accenture's Navitaire unit can manage reservations, plan routes, assign crew, and calculate optimal prices for each seat. Have a cool new telecom or medical device but lack market researchers? For about $5,000, analytics outfits such as New Delhi–based Evalueserve Inc. will, within a day, assemble a team of Indian patent attorneys, engineers, and business analysts, start mining global databases, and call dozens of U.S. experts and wholesalers to provide an independent appraisal.

Want to quickly market a new mutual fund or insurance policy? IT services providers such as India's Tata Consultancy Services Ltd. are building software platforms that furnish every business process needed and secure all regulatory approvals. A sister company, Tata Technologies, boasts 2,000 Indian engineers and recently bought 700-employee Incat International PLC, a Novi, Michigan, auto- and aerospace-engineering firm. Tata Technologies can now handle everything from turning a conceptual design into detailed specs for interiors, chassis, and electrical systems to designing the tooling and factory floor layout. "If you map out the entire vehicle development process, we have the capability to supply every piece of it," says Chief Operating Officer Jeffrey D. Sage, an IBM and General Motors veteran. Tata is designing all doors for a future truck, for example, and the power train for a U.S. sedan. The company is hiring 100 experienced U.S. engineers at salaries of $100,000 and up.

Many American companies are quickly taking advantage of these opportunities. Take Procter and Gamble, for instance. Over the past three years the $57 billion consumer-products company has outsourced everything from IT infrastructure and human resources to management of its offices from Cincinnati to Moscow.

Cost savings aside, many companies believe that outsourcing improves customer service. Five years ago, Penske Truck Leasing, a joint venture between GE and Penske Corp., paid $768 million for trucker Rollins Thick Leasing Corp. just in time for the recession. Customer service, spread among four U.S. call centers, was inconsistent. "I realized our business needed a transformation," says CFO Frank Cocuzza. He began by shifting a few dozen data-processing jobs to GE's huge Mexican and Indian call centers, now called Genpact. He then hired Genpact to help restructure most of his back office. That relationship now spans 30 processes involved in leasing 216,000 trucks and providing logistical services for customers.

Now, if a Penske truck is held up at a weigh station because it lacks a certain permit, for example, the driver calls an 800 number. Genpact staff in India obtains the document over the Web. The weigh station is notified electronically, and the truck is back on the road within 30 minutes. Before, Penske thought it did well if it accomplished that in two hours. And when a driver finishes his job, his entire log, including records of mileage, tolls, and fuel purchases, is shipped to Mexico, punched into computers, and processed in Hyderabad. In all, 60 percent of the 1,000 workers handling Penske back office processes are in India or Mexico, and Penske is still ramping up. Under a new program, when a manufacturer asks Penske to arrange for a delivery to a buyer, Indian staff helps with the scheduling, billing, and invoices. The $15 million in direct labor-cost savings are small compared with the gains in efficiency and customer service, Cocuzza says.

Big Pharma is pursuing huge boosts in efficiency as well. Eli Lilly & Co.'s labs are more productive than most, having released

organizations, whether or not you have or will have supervisory responsibilities. The first such Management Is Everyone's Business feature reflects much of what we discuss in this introductory chapter, although these issues will be revisited in greater depth in future chapters. See Management Is Everyone's Business 1.2 on page 13.

Barriers between departments are also breaking down. Functional areas, rivalries, and divisions cause people to develop narrow, parochial views of their jobs and this discourages innovation. Departmentalization prevents employees from understanding corporatewide objectives and promotes interunit conflict rather than cooperation, so the organization loses flexibility and is unable to respond to competitive challenges in a more integrated, cohesive fashion. For this

Penske Truck Leasing and India's Genpact collaborate closly on the documentation required when Penske buys a truck and leases it to a U.S. customer (left). Genpact's Indian staff works remotely to secure titles, registrations, and permits online. When the truck comes back, the driver's log and other documentation for fuel and taxes are forwarded to Genpact's Mexican office (center) for entry to Penske's computer system. Genpact in Hyderabad, India (right), processes the data for tax filings and accounting.

eight major drugs in the past five years. But for each new drug, Lilly estimates it invests a hefty $1.1 billion. That could reach $1.5 billion in four years. "Those kinds of costs are fundamentally unsustainable," says Steven M. Paul, Lilly's science and tech executive vice president. Outsourcing figures heavily in Lilly's strategy to lower that cost to $800 million. The drugmaker maker now does 20 percent of its chemistry work in China for one-quarter the U.S. cost and helped fund a start-up lab, Shanghai's Chem-Explorer Co., with 230 chemists. Lilly now is trying to slash the costs of clinical trials on human patients, which range from $50 million to $300 million per drug, and is expanding such efforts in Brazil, Russia, China, and India.

Other manufacturers and tech companies are learning to capitalize on global talent pools to rush products to market sooner at lower costs. OnStor Inc., a Los Gatos, California, developer of storage systems, says its tie-up with the Bangalore engineering-services outfit HCL Technologies Ltd. enables it to get customized products to clients twice as fast as its major rivals. "If we want to recruit a great engineer in Silicon Valley, our lead time is three months," says CEO Bob Miller. "With HCL, pick up the phone and get somebody in two or three days."

Source: Adapted from P. Engardio, "The Future of Outsourcing," *Business-Week*, January 30, 2006, pp. 50–56.

reason, firms are increasingly relying on employee *teams* that form to work on common projects. When these teams are composed of individuals from different parts of the organization, they are referred to as *cross-functional teams;* when team members have diverse backgrounds, the teams are *cross-disciplinary.* Teams are asked to perform many of the managerial roles of traditional managers. That is, rather than relying on a superior for direction, a team often defines the problem, sets objectives, establishes priorities, proposes new ways of doing things, and assigns members to different tasks. Teams fulfill important managerial roles by linking various parts of the organization to focus on common problems, issues, and complex tasks that require integration and concerted actions by dissimilar individuals.

The New Ethics Enforcers

With rock music pounding and lasers painting a brilliant light show on giant screens behind him, Patrick J. Gnazzo restlessly paced the broad stage at the Venetian's convention center in Las Vegas. Because he is the new chief compliance officer at Computer Associates International Inc. (CA), Gnazzo's presentation was one of the main events just before CA World, the company's annual sales extravaganza. Striding before 1,200 CA staffers, the blustery 59-year-old former chief trial attorney for the U.S. Navy took a page from tent revivalists, leading a call-and-response chant: "What happens at CA World," Gnazzo shouted, as the crowd echoed his words, "can make us great." Winding up his talk, he exhorted: "Don't lie, don't cheat, don't steal!"

CA staffers can thank the Justice Department for Pat Gnazzo. To avoid a criminal trial over alleged accounting fraud, CA accepted a deferred prosecution agreement in late 2004 that required it to set aside $225 million for shareholders and impose a variety of reforms, including hiring an internal cop to prevent future chicanery.

The job went to Jesuit-trained Gnazzo, who once considered the priesthood but instead opted for the law. At the $3.5-billion-a-year Islandia, New York, management-software provider, he reports directly to the board's audit committee, as well as to the general counsel, and can buttonhole any manager from chief executive officer on down. "I have unfettered access," says Gnazzo, who earned total compensation in excess of $675,000 last year.

Gnazzo is among the more visible examples of a new species of executive: high-profile former government lawyers and judges who have been tapped, usually by scandal-tainted companies, to police employees. Others in this group include former Securities and Exchange Commission Chairman Richard C. Breeden, who was named outside monitor of KPMG in 2006 and is now taking a similar role at Hollinger International Inc. Eric R. Dinallo and Beth L. Golden, alumni of New York Attorney General Eliot Spitzer's office, have taken jobs at Morgan Stanley and Bear, Steams & Co., respectively.

Patrick J. Gnazzo is the first compliance officer at Computer Associates International Inc., charged with preventing fraud at the firm. He says, "I've never been in a situation where I had to do anything more than to say to a CEO, 'You know you did something I don't think is right.'"

Old-style ethics officers reported to managers far down the ladder. But now they can report directly to the Board, bypassing even the CEO. For instance, Gnazzo has the power to go right to independent directors with problems. Whenever needed, he can quiz CEO John Swainson, the former IBM vice president who joined CA to clean it up. He also confers regularly with the CEO and five other top officers on a new disclosure committee that meets to talk about SEC filings and news releases.

Source: Adapted from J. Weber, "The New Ethics Enforcers, *BusinessWeek*, February 13, 2006, pp. 75–77.

Each chapter has a "Management Is Everyone's Business" feature that centers on working as a team and that points out how the materials discussed in the chapter help *teams* operate more effectively. The first such feature is Management Is Everyone's Business 1.3 on page 13, summarizing the practical implications for teams of the concepts presented in this introductory chapter. As was the case for managers and individuals (Management Is Everyone's Business 1.1 and 1.2), these implications for teams will be discussed in greater depth in future chapters.

MANAGEMENT IS EVERYONE'S BUSINESS 1.1

Working as a Manager To become a successful manager requires that you learn how to be flexible and adaptable to be able to do a variety of things:

- Develop an appreciation for the big picture as well as how the details fit into the big picture.
- Be in touch with what is happening inside and outside your unit, as well as externally, with an eye toward setting goals that capitalize on opportunities and deal with potential threats.
- Plan activities to meet personal and organizational goals making best use of resources available to you.
- Treat your peers and those below and above you with respect.
- Energize subordinates to fully use their talents and provide them with an example to imitate of highly ethical behaviors.
- Be fair, honest, and consistent in your dealing with subordinates, but build on their unique strengths.
- Communicate clearly and persuasively, making effective and accurate use of all information available to you.
- Don't be afraid to make bold decisions, but be sure that these are made after careful consideration of all available data and the inputs of various parties who have a stake in these decisions.

MANAGEMENT IS EVERYONE'S BUSINESS 1.2

Working as an Individual To succeed in most modern organizations you will be asked as an individual to meet multiple expectations:

- *Show initiative*. Most successful firms value individuals capable of acting autonomously without close supervision. Some people refer to it as "self-leadership."
- *Show a capacity to become a leader*. This means that you should be able to influence others and not simply follow directions.
- *Learn to appreciate the organization's culture* and how you can work within that culture.
- *Be trusted*. This means that you are reliable, honest, loyal, and keep your word.
- *Show a capacity to keep on learning*. Challenging assignments most likely will go to individuals who can stretch their knowledge and skills and strive for personal growth.
- *Be willing to change your approach as situations change*. Inflexible people are unlikely to succeed in a rapidly changing environment.

MANAGEMENT IS EVERYONE'S BUSINESS 1.3

Working as a Team Most successful organizations nowadays strongly support the team concept, believing that employees with diverse skills working together on common problems are more likely to be innovative and that employees working as part of a team are more committed to doing a good job. This means that organizations that truly believe in the team concept should:

- Evaluate and reward team performance, not just the contribution of individual employees.
- Give sufficient autonomy for teams to make their own decisions.
- Select team members who are different yet complement each other.
- Form teams to deal with identifiable problems or issues, but also support teams whose task is to be creative and "think outside the box."
- Select and train managers capable of coordinating or linking the activities of various teams.

FIGURE 1.1

Key Aspects of Managerial
Success

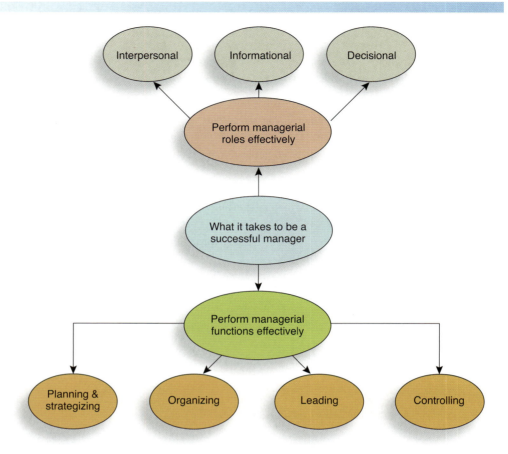

LOC-In

Gen-Art is a custom framing and art service boutique that is considering expansion into the surrounding regional market. The 20-person company has highly decentralized job authority and decision making. Instead of strict functional areas, the firm uses a team-based approach to satisfying client needs. Gen-Art avoids many levels of management in favor of a barebones approach to structure, with executives, project managers, and teams of technical staff. Ginny and Mercedes are two managers at Gen-Art.

1. *Ginny is the Vice President of Operations at Gen-Art. She helps make decisions regarding growth, goals, and longer-term issues. Ginny is a _____.*
   a. *strategic manager*
   b. *operational manager*
   c. *front-line manager*
   d. *tactical manager*
2. *As one of the project managers for Gen-Art, Mercedes operates at the _____ level. She is the direct link between the executive level of the firm and the technical staff she oversees.*
   a. *strategic*
   b. *controlling management*
   c. *tactical*
   d. *bureaucratic management*

The next sections of the chapter describe the critical aspects of most management jobs. Figure 1.1 above summarizes these aspects, namely, the ability to perform basic managerial functions (planning and strategizing, organizing, leading, and controlling) and the ability to perform major managerial roles (interpersonal, informational, and decisional). While the relative importance of each aspect may vary (for instance, strategic managers may be more involved in planning and strategizing than are operational managers), those capable of doing well on each of these job aspects are more likely to have a successful managerial career and be promoted to more responsible positions over time.

The Four Management Functions

More than once the question has been posed, "What do managers do?" Or perhaps more precisely, "What *should* they do?" Whether at the managerial, individual, or team level, the management process should include planning and strategizing, organizing, leading, and controlling. Some of these activities are typically performed at particular organizational levels; for example, planning and strategy making are core activities for senior executives. However, in most contemporary organizations, all employees are responsible for at least some aspects of the various management functions.

The four management functions are closely linked. For instance, the control system warns the organization when plans and strategies are not working and should be reconsidered. Inspiring leadership would quickly lead to frustration if people didn't know what their roles were or if there were no procedures to guide their actions. Grouping employees into teams may lead to much wasted time and confusion unless there is an overarching plan for unifying their efforts.

PLANNING AND STRATEGIZING Planning and strategizing are designed to lead the company to fulfill its mission. **Planning** includes setting future objectives and mapping out the activities necessary to achieve those objectives. To be effective, the objectives of individuals, teams, and management should be carefully coordinated.

Because no firm operates in a vacuum, reaching the firm's mission in spite of changes in the environment and competitive landscape is difficult. It involves a continuing assessment of the firm's strengths, weaknesses, opportunities, and threats (referred to as SWOT, to be discussed in detail in Chapter 7), so that appropriate strategies may be taken. Chapter 2, Managing in a Global Environment; Chapter 5, Managing the Planning Process; Chapter 7, Strategic Management; and Chapter 8, Entrepreneurship and Innovation, focus on issues related to planning and strategizing.

ORGANIZING Specifying how the firm's human, financial, physical, informational, and technical resources are to be arranged and coordinated is the process of **organizing.** This includes defining roles for all players, delegating tasks, marshalling and allocating resources, clarifying procedures, and determining priorities. Chapter 4, Managing Organizational Culture and Change; Chapter 9, Managing the Structure and Design of Organizations; Chapter 10, Human Resource Management; and Chapter 14, Managing Teams, describe various aspects of organizing.

LEADING Energizing people to contribute their best individually and in cooperation with other people is the **leading** function. This involves clearly communicating organizational goals, inspiring and motivating employees, providing an example for others to follow, guiding people, and creating conditions that encourage people from diverse backgrounds to work well together. Chapter 3, Managing Social Responsibility and Ethics; Chapter 6, Decision Making; Chapter 11, Managing Employee Diversity; Chapter 12, Motivation; Chapter 13, Leadership; and Chapter 15, Managing Communication, focus on various aspects of leadership.

CONTROLLING Measuring performance, comparing it to objectives, implementing necessary changes, and monitoring progress are the functions of **control.** Collecting quality feedback, identifying potential problems, and taking corrective

planning

The management function that assesses the management environment to set future objectives and map out activities necessary to achieve those objectives.

organizing

The management function that determines how the firm's human, financial, physical, informational, and technical resources are arranged and coordinated to perform tasks to achieve desired goals; the deployment of resources to achieve strategic goals.

leading

The management function that energizes people to contribute their best individually and in cooperation with other people.

controlling

The management function that measures performance, compares it to objectives, implements necessary changes, and monitors progress.

Giving the Boss the Big Picture

THEME: DEALING WITH CHANGE

Since the advent of the mainframe in the 1950s, companies have dreamed of using computers to manage their businesses. But early efforts came up short, with technology that was too costly or too clunky. Now, thanks to the Net and dashboards, those dreams are starting to come true. Forrester Research Inc. analyst Keith Gile estimates that 40 precent of the 2,000 largest companies use the technology. Some of the most prominent chief executives in the world are believers, from Steven A. Ballmer at Microsoft and Ivan G. Seidenberg at Verizon Communications to Robert L. Nardelli at Home Depot. "The dashboard puts me and more and more of our executives in real-time touch with the business," says Seidenberg. "The more eyes that see the results we're obtaining every day, the higher the quality of the decisions we can make."

The dashboard is the CEO's killer app, making the gritty details of a business that are often buried deep within a large organization accessible at a glance to senior executives. So powerful are the programs that they're beginning to change the nature of management from an intuitive art into more of a science. Managers can see key changes in their businesses almost instantaneously—when salespeople falter or quality slides—and take quick, corrective action. At Verizon, Seidenberg and other executives can choose from among 300 metrics to put on their dashboards, from broadband sales to wireless subscriber defections. At General Electric Co., James P. Campbell, chief of the Consumer & Industrial Division, which makes appliances and lighting products, tracks the number of orders coming in from each customer every day and compares that with targets. "I look at the digital dashboard the first thing in the morning so I have a quick global view of sales and service levels across the organization," says Campbell. "It's a key operational tool in our business."

Here are examples of what firms are doing with dashboard to monitor operations:

Microsoft

Steve Ballmer, Microsoft's CEO, requires his top officers to bring their dashboards with them into one-on-one meetings. Ballmer zeroes in on such metrics as sales, customer satisfaction, and status of key products under development.

Verizon

Managers can choose from more than 300 metrics to put on their dashboards, from broadband sales to wireless defections. Managers pick the metrics they want to track, and the dashboard flips the pages 24 hours a day.

General Electric

Many GE managers use dashboards to run their day-to-day operations, monitoring profits per product line and fill rates for orders. Immelt occasionally looks at a dashboard. But he relies on his managers to run the businesses so he can focus on the big picture.

---

action are crucial to long-term success. Organizations should use many approaches to detect and correct significant variations or discrepancies in the results of planned activities designed to meet the specific challenge of those activities.

As can be seen in Management Close-Up 1.3 above ("Giving the Boss the Big Picture"), technology is playing a key role in control systems that would have seemed impossible just a few years ago.

Chapter 16, Management Control; Chapter 17, Operations Management; and Chapter 18, Managing Information Systems, deal with specialized issues related to control.

Managerial Roles

The traditional management functions described above may give the false impression that day-to-day management activities are routine, orderly, and rational. A researcher named Henry Mintzberg studied a group of managers and came to the conclusion that the typical manager is not a systematic person who carefully decides how to plan, organize, lead, and control. Rather, managers face constant interruptions, make decisions based on limited data, change tasks frequently depending on shifting priorities, spend most of their time in meetings and informal

The newest Web-based management tool is the dashboard, a real-time display of critical information from corporate software programs arranged in easy-to-read graphics.

Oracle

Management at Oracle uses dashboards to track sales activity at the end of a quarter, the ratio of sales divided by customer service requests, and the number of hours that technicians spend on the phone solving customer problems.

Source: Adapted from S. E. Ante, "Giving the Boss the Big Picture," *BusinessWeek*, February 13, 2006, pp. 48–50.

discussions, and experience a hectic work pace that leaves little room for reflection. Using a method called "structured observation" that involved keeping track of the activities of top-level executives, Mintzberg summarized what managers do on a day-to-day basis by identifying a set of specific roles. A role consists of the behaviors expected of people who hold certain positions. These roles have been grouped by Mintzberg into three major categories, although managers often perform several of them simultaneously.

INTERPERSONAL ROLES Managers engage in a great deal of interaction, continually communicating with superiors, peers, subordinates and people from outside the organization. In doing so, a manager serves as a *figurehead*, or the visible personality representing an organization, department or work unit; a *leader* who energizes others to get the job done properly; and a *liaison* who links together the activities of people from both inside and outside the organization. Various chapters deal with the interpersonal role of managers, in particular Chapter 4 (Managing Organizational Culture and Change), Chapter 10 (Human Resource Management), Chapter 11 (Managing Employee Diversity), Chapter 12 (Motivation), Chapter 13 (Leadership), and Chapter 14 (Managing Teams).

INFORMATION ROLES   Managers obtain, interpret, and give out a great deal of information. These roles include being a *monitor* and *disseminator,* as well as the organization's spokesperson. While effective communication underlies almost everything discussed in this book, Chapter 15 specifically focuses on communication issues at work.

DECISIONAL ROLES   Managers are also asked to choose among competing alternatives. This includes balancing the interests of the various parties who have a stake in a decision. Four decisional roles include that of *entrepreneur*, who introduces changes into the organization; *disturbance handler*, who takes corrective action, provides damage control, and responds to unexpected situations or crises; *resource allocator*, responsible for assigning people and other resources to best meet organizational needs; and *negotiator*, reaching agreements and making compromises. These activities occur within and outside the firm when working with parties who control valuable resources, such as other organizational managers, suppliers, and members of various financial institutions. Four chapters are particularly relevant to the decisional roles of managers, namely Chapter 5 (Managing the Planning Process), Chapter 6 (Decision Making), Chapter 7 (Strategic Management), and Chapter 8 (Entrepreneurship and Innovation).

LOC-In

2   Learning Objective Check-In

1. *Zach is fairly satisfied with the way the past year has gone at his firm. Still, he engages in _____ in order to make sure that the goals of the firm are actually being achieved. He does this by measuring performance, comparing it to objectives, implementing necessary changes, and monitoring progress.*
   a. *leading*
   b. *organizing*
   c. *controlling*
   d. *planning*

The Evolution of Management Thought

Many of the key management ideas that blossomed in the 19th and 20th centuries are practiced by managers to this day. This section examines these early management ideas, from the operational perspective, the bureaucratic management approach, the administrative management approach, and the behavioral perspective, and contemporary management approaches. Systems theory, contingency theory, and the learning organization are part of the contemporary management perspective. These contemporary ideas represent recent thinking on sound management practices in the 21st century. We also present what we believe are emergent ideas in the management field during the latter part of this decade which are likely to influence management practices in the future, namely the modular organization and the intangible organization.

Niccolò Machiavelli (1469–1527) was imprisoned, tortured, and banished from Florence by the ruling Medici family, who believed he had conspired against them. While in exile he wrote *The Prince*, hoping it would win favor with the Medicis. Although Machiavelli eventually regained some prestige with them, *The Prince* was not published until 1532, five years after Machiavelli's death.

The following section is a rough chronology of the time period in which each particular management perspective originated. It is important to keep in mind that some of the "old" views are still being applied in varying degrees today. For instance, the operational approach with an emphasis on scientific management is still alive and well at Lincoln Electric in Cleveland, Ohio, and faithfully applied in countries that are industrializing rapidly such as China and India. Many of the principles of bureaucratic management, with its emphasis on rules and procedures, still ring true in the U.S. Postal Service and most government agencies. The military is still largely organized following the prescriptions of the administrative management school. You may find many of the ideas of the behavioral perspective, with its emphasis on human relations, present in "high-tech" firms such as Google and Intel. And you may even think of some modern organizations that follow a Machiavellian leadership style, in which tight control through fear and punishment is the norm.

FIGURE 1.2

Origin of Key Management
Perspectivers over Time

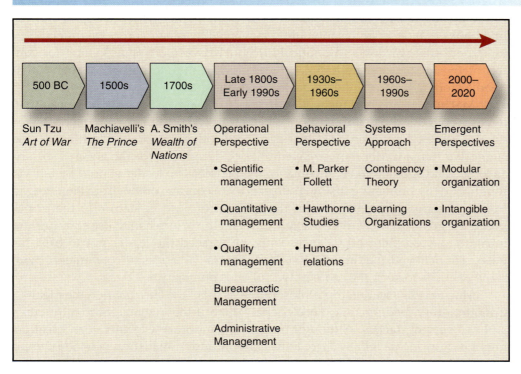

In other words, classical management insights are still valuable today even though the complexity and diversity of organizations have increased dramatically since most of these ideas were created (see Figure 1.2 "Origin of Key Management Perspectives over Time" above).

Early Management Thought

The art and practice of management have been present for many centuries. Designing and building such huge public works projects as the Great Wall of China, the pyramids of Egypt, and the aqueducts that provided water to cities in the Roman Empire required an understanding of management. For many years management was viewed as an art and was verbally passed on without documenting theoretical principles that could be used by future generations of managers. However, a few early thinkers laid the foundation for the classical and behavioral schools of management thought that arose during the last century. These thinkers include Sun Tzu in China, Niccolò Machiavelli in Italy, and Adam Smith in Great Britain.

EARLY IDEAS ABOUT MANAGEMENT STRATEGY Some of our earliest management concepts are found in *The Art of War*, written about 2,500 years ago by Sun Tzu, a Chinese general. Sun Tzu's ideas focus on developing military strategies that can lead to victory in battle. For example, he recognized that it is better to use intelligence and cunning to subdue an enemy than to rely on violence and destruction. Alliances and negotiated settlements allow a military leader to expand his empire without sacrificing soldiers or resources or destroying cities. Sun Tzu recognized that strategy involved a long-term perspective. He recommended attacking the enemy's weak points and taking advantage of one's own army's strengths. Sun Tzu's insights about dispassionately taking stock of strengths and weaknesses are still prominent features of strategic management.

Adam Smith (1723–1770), today regarded as the founder of classical economics, wrote during the earliest years of the Industrial Revolution. He regarded the personal interest of the individual and the human urge to seek advantage as the source of wealth and social progress.

EARLY IDEAS ABOUT LEADERSHIP Niccolò Machiavelli wrote *The Prince* during the Renaissance in 16th-century Florence, Italy. It was one of the first books that described leadership. Machiavelli was a government official during a period of warfare and political intrigue between city-states vying for control of the region, and he had a cynical view of human nature, believing that people were motivated by very narrow self-interests.

Machiavelli advised the leader or prince that it was better to be feared than to be loved. Love is a fickle emotion, whereas fear is constant. In other words, survival is a basic human instinct that dominates other emotions. Machiavelli also suggested that a leader may engage in lies or deceptions for the good of society, as long as he appears to be virtuous to the people. The leader should be fair yet tough, harshly punishing disloyal subjects to discourage others from engaging in treason. Machiavelli believed that the aristocrats close in stature to the prince posed the greatest threat to his welfare and that the prince had to use cunning and intrigue to keep them off balance. Thus, he warned the leader not to trust his peers. He believed that an effective leader forms alliances of convenience with some enemies to keep the more powerful ones off balance.

Machiavelli's leadership philosophy was that "the end justified the means." Contemporary leaders are called Machiavellian if they engage in manipulative and self-serving tactics. Although many contemporary executives and leaders might judge Machiavelli's advice to be extreme and unrealistic, even today rivals fight behind the scenes in highly politicized corporations, and sibling rivalry runs rampant in some family businesses.

EARLY IDEAS ABOUT THE DESIGN AND ORGANIZATION OF WORK The efficient organization of work has its roots in the classic 18th-century book *The Wealth of Nations*, written in 1776 by Adam Smith. As a professor of logic and moral philosophy at Glasgow University in Scotland, Smith was the first to recognize the principle of the **division of labor** in a manufacturing process. Division of labor converted production by craftsmen or artisans who were generalists into simple steps. Each worker became a specialist who repeated one step over and over, thereby achieving greater efficiencies in the use of time and knowledge. Smith showed how the manufacture of pins could be reduced to 18 steps done by 10 specialists who each performed one or two steps. Organizing the 10 laborers in a small factory made it possible to produce 48,000 pins in one day. When the pin makers operated independently as generalists, the total daily output was 200 pins. Smith observed that the division of labor was responsible for revolutionary gains in factory output. His work laid the theoretical groundwork for scientific management.

---

division of labor

The production process in which each worker repeats one step over and over, achieving greater efficiencies in the use of time and knowledge.

The Operational Perspective

operational perspective

The management perspective formed during the 19th and early 20th centuries when the factory system and modern corporations evolved to meet the challenges of managing large, complex organizations.

The **operational perspective** on management thought originated in the 19th and early 20th centuries. It coincided with the rise of the factory system and the formation of modern corporations, both of which provided challenges in efficiently operating and coordinating large, complex organizations. The operational perspective attempted to apply logic and the scientific method to management so as to discover and practice the one best way of doing a job.

Some of the legacy of the operational perspective is found today in a subfield called "productions and operations management" (see Chapter 17), although most contemporary management thinkers note the crucial role played by the human element of an organization. Three approaches fall into the operational perspective: scientific management, quantitative management, and quality management.

SCIENTIFIC MANAGEMENT   In the last half of the 19th century, organizations were unable to obtain increased productivity from employees despite making large investments in new technologies. Frederick Winslow Taylor (1856–1915) believed his life's calling was to change this situation. Born to a Philadelphia lawyer in 1856, Taylor learned the trades of common laborer and machinist in a small Philadelphia machine shop where he worked for four years. He was then hired by the Midvale Steel Company in Pennsylvania, where he moved quickly through the ranks while studying for a mechanical engineering degree at night. At Midvale, Taylor carefully documented the large amount of time that was wasted by workers who were ill equipped and poorly trained to perform the simplest tasks. Even shoveling coal was inefficient, because workers brought their own shovels with differing weights, sizes, and sharpness. No one had any idea which type of shovel worked best.

Taylor discovered that workers sometimes avoided doing their best work, a practice called *soldiering*, because they feared that management might raise quotas without increasing pay or that some employees would lose their jobs. Complicating the situation, there were no systematic rules to serve as guidelines for doing the jobs most efficiently. Workers learned their jobs by the use of rules of thumb and trial-and-error processes.

In response to the inefficiencies he observed in the steel industry, Taylor developed **scientific management**, which is summarized in Table 1.1 on page 22. The scientific method should be applied to determining the one best way to do a particular job. This optimal approach to work spares the worker from management criticism and provides managers and owners with the most output from each worker. Taylor encouraged management to share productivity gains with employees by using a piecework production system in which each worker's output would be measured against standardized productivity quotas. When workers reached or exceeded the quota, the financial gains would be shared. The result would be that workers could earn more by cooperating with management.

Next, Taylor supported the use of scientific selection methods to make the best matches between workers and jobs. At the time, seniority or the boss's preference was used to match workers with jobs. Taylor found this approach inefficient, and he suggested using measures of worker aptitudes, traits, and performance to scientifically determine the fit between person and job.

Finally, Taylor perceived a clear separation between the work of employees and managers. In Taylor's view, employees did the physical work, and managers planned, directed, and coordinated employees' efforts so that the goals would be reached. He believed that managers and employees should be dependent on each other to achieve desired output, which would encourage cooperation and result in fewer conflicts or strikes. Taylor also believed that the job of management was to inspire and motivate workers to fully cooperate and learn the scientific management principles applied to their job. Until his death in 1915, Taylor committed himself to what he termed a "mental revolution" in the practice of industrial management.

Following Taylor's footsteps Frank Gilbreth and Lillian Gilbreth introduced the idea of time and motion studies using the stopwatch and motion picture camera to improve workplace efficiencies. The Gilbreths analyzed each movement a worker performed during a particular task by filming the task actions and observing the film frame by frame. They then looked for better ways to perform each step to ensure that all the steps could be performed more efficiently with less time and effort.

Henry Gantt was a school teacher who felt that Taylor's piece rate incentive system placed employees under a great deal of stress. He introduced the notion of a "guaranteed day rate," in which employees knew the minimum

scientific management

A management method that applies the principles of the scientific method to the management process: determining the one best way to do a job and sharing the rewards with the workers.

table 1.1

table 1.1
Taylor's Four Principles of Scientific Management

1. Scientifically study each part of a task and develop the best method of performing the task.
2. Carefully select workers and train them to perform the task by using the scientifically developed method.
3. Cooperate fully with workers to ensure that they use the proper method.
4. Divide work and responsibility so that management is responsible for planning work methods using scientific principles and workers are responsible for executing the work accordingly.

Source: F. W. Taylor, *The Principles of Scientific Management*. New York: Harper, 1911.

Frederick Winslow Taylor (1856–1915), although born to a wealthy Philadelphia family, began his career as a machinist in a metal products factory. His observations there led to his 1911 work, *The Principle of Scientific Management*. His method timed tasks for both machines and workers—who often resented begin treated as machines.

income they would receive. When employees exceeded certain standards they were paid bonuses. Gantt also developed work scheduling charts which are still used today.

Scientific management had a profound effect on the captains of American industry. In one of the most famous applications, Henry Ford utilized scientific management in the production process of the factory that manufactured the Model-T Ford. The lasting contribution of scientific management was to transform management into a more objective, systematic body of knowledge in which best practices can be discovered for different jobs. It also gave managers and supervisors more active and clearly defined roles.

Despite these noteworthy contributions, scientific management had shortcomings. It did not appreciate the social context of work and the needs (beyond pay) of workers. It often led to dehumanizing working conditions in which every aspect of a worker's effort was measured, prohibiting employee initiative. Scientific management also assumed that workers had no useful ideas, and that only managers and experts were capable of coming up with good ideas or innovations.

A major problem that Taylor, the Gilbreths, and Gantt did not anticipate was that many firms would "pick and choose" what they wanted from scientific management while ignoring worker interests. For example, "some managers using scientific management obtained increases in performance, but rather than sharing performance gains with workers through bonuses as Taylor had advocated, they simply increased the amount of work that each worker was expected to do. Many workers experiencing the reorganized work system found that as their performance increased, managers required them to do more work for the same pay. Workers also learned that increases in performance often meant fewer jobs and a greater threat of layoffs, because fewer workers were needed."[2]

These problems have given scientific management a "bad name" in some circles, which continues to this day. They were at least in part responsible for the rapid rise in legislation designed to protect labor unions in the 1930s. They still provide some of the rationale for unions' existence in the 21st century. Workers continue to join together to defend their interests collectively as well as to prevent employers' abuses. Employment in manufacturing, where scientific management is most appropriate, as a percentage of the labor force has declined steadily over the years. The percentage of unionized workers has also been dropping, from about 35 percent of the workforce in the mid-1940s to less than 10 percent in the late 2000s.[3] In general, unions have not been able to repeat their success in organizing "blue collar" workers when they have tried to organize "white collar" workers in the service sector, that is, retail stores, banks, schools, and governmental agencies, which is where most new jobs are located.

QUANTITATIVE MANAGEMENT   The scientific management perspective later became known as the "quantitative management" school. The focus is on the development of various statistical tools and techniques to improve efficiency and allow management to make informed decisions regarding the costs and benefits of alternative courses of action. Four of these quantitative methods, which are still widely used today, include: (1) break-even analysis, (2) basic economic order quantity (EOQ) model, (3) material requirements planning (MRP), and (4) quality management. These are briefly described below and will be revisited in greater detail in Chapter 17, Operations Management.

Break-even analysis provides formulas which assess the total fixed costs associated with producing a product, the variable costs for each unit, and the contribution made by the sale of each unit to recovering both fixed and variable costs. The break-even point is the number of units which must be sold at a given price to recover all fixed and variable costs. At that point there is neither a profit nor a loss, but rather the company "breaks even." Additional sales result in profits and fewer sales result in losses.

The *economic order quantity (EOQ) model* dates back to 1915. The formula is generally credited to Ford W. Harris, who argued in his book *Operations and Cost* that effective management of inventories is critical to sustained profitability.[4] EOQ's objective is to minimize the total costs of inventory. The inventory holding costs include housing costs (building rent, taxes, and insurance), investment costs (interest payments), material handling costs (equipment and labor costs) and other miscellaneous expenses (pilferage, scrap, and obsolescence). The holding cost increases as the order quantity increases, because larger average inventories need to be maintained. On the other hand, as the quantity ordered increases, the annual setup or ordering cost per unit decreases (for instance, material handling and tooling may be made more efficient as the quantity purchased increases). Mathematically, the EOQ model demonstrates that the optimal reorder point occurs when the total setup cost is equal to the total holding cost.

Material requirements planning (MRP) is a set of tools designed to manage components where the demand for the items is linked to another demand. For example, the demand for TV antennas is linked to the demand for TVs. To determine the number of antennas needed, a TV manufacturer starts by determining the number of TVs that will be built and when. Once management forecasts the demand for TVs, quantities required for all other components such as antennas, knobs, and screens can be computed, because all components are dependent items. MRP helps a company reduce inventory costs and ensures that all items will be available when needed. Consider the following example: "Nancy Mueller turns quiche into cash. Her firm, Nancy's Specialty Foods, is designed for today's busy lifestyle, producing 750,000 prepackaged, frozen quiche hors d'ouvres each month. Material requirements planning (MRP) software has been key to her growing success. MRP is the primary management tool that keeps the ingredients and labor coming at the proper times and the schedule firm. Once Nancy's Specialty Foods knows the demand for her crabmeat quiche, she knows the demand for all of the ingredients from dough, to cheese, to crab meat, because all of the ingredients are dependent."[5]

QUALITY MANAGEMENT   The need for improved product quality emerged in the 1980s, when it became apparent that the United States was lagging behind some industrialized countries, most notably Japan, in the area of product quality. Many of the tools and techniques that were used to identify quality problems and take corrective action date back decades earlier. For instance, Walter A. Shewhart, a Bell Labs statistician, developed a set of methods in the 1920s that were designed to ensure standardization and reduce quality defects. His book *Economic Control of Quality*, published in 1931, is still considered a classic. Joseph M. Juran was a statistician who in the 1940s introduced the concept of "pareto analysis," which argues that 80 percent of all quality problems may be traced to a relatively small number of causes. Phillip Crosby spent his entire career at International Telephone and Telegraph. While there, Crosby documented the enormous costs of having to fix something that was not done right the first time. His ideas were later published in the 1970s in the business best seller *Quality Is Free* Arnand V. Feigenbaum developed the concept of *total quality control* in the 1940s, which argued for an integrated quality improvement effort across all functional areas (e.g., purchasing, finance, marketing) and not only in production and manufacturing. These ideas were later published in his 1951 book, *Total Quality Control*.

By now, most people are familiar with the concept "total quality management" popularized by W. Edwards Deming. Deming was an American statistician who advanced the use of statistics for constant quality improvement. Deming assisted many Japanese business leaders after World War II. His approach was to put quality first. Ironically, he was largely ignored in the United States for most of his professional life. Deming finally achieved recognition as a quality guru in the United States when he was well into his eighties, following the publication of his book *Out of the Crisis* in 1986. (See Table 1.2 on page 25.)

total quality management (TQM)

An organizationwide approach that focuses on quality as an overarching goal. The basis of this approach is the understanding that all employees and organizational units should be working harmoniously to satisfy the customer.

LOC-In

③ Learning Objective Check-In

Karen is a new production supervisor pondering her role as a part of management. She knows from her studies that it is important to take a long-term perspective toward strategy. She also knows that managers have to be crafty in order to survive against competition in the form of other companies. She was also thinking of how important the division of labor has been to productivity, and she could see the effects of this idea in her own work situation. Karen could not remember who, specifically, introduced these management ideas.

1. *Who recognized that management strategy meant taking a long-term perspective?*
   a. *Adam Smith*
   b. *John Maynard Keynes*
   c. *Niccolò Machiavelli*
   d. *Sun Tzu*
2. *_____ advised leaders to be cunning and crafty in order to survive against competitive rivals.*
   a. *Niccolà Machiavelli*
   b. *Adam Smith*
   c. *Sun Tzu*
   d. *John Maynard Keynes*
3. *_____ recognized the powerful effect that the division of labor could have on productivity.*
   a. *Winslow Taylor*
   b. *Adam Smith*
   c. *Sun Tzu*
   d. *Abraham Maslow*

Total quality management (TQM) is an organizationwide approach that focuses on quality as an overarching goal. The basis of this approach is the understanding that all employees and organizational units should be working harmoniously to satisfy the customer. Since the customer's needs are in constant flux, the organization must strive to continuously improve its systems and practices. The TQM perspective views quality as the central purpose of the organization, in contrast to the focus on efficiency advocated by the operational perspective. In TQM, quality is viewed as everybody's job, not just the role of quality control specialists, as in bureaucratic management (to be discussed below).

TQM reflects the thinking and practice of management in many of the world's most admired companies, including Toyota, Motorola, Xerox, and Ford. The key elements of the TQM approach are

- *Focus on the customer.* It is important to identify the organization's customers. External customers consume the organization's product or service. Internal customers are employees who receive the output of other employees.

table 1.2

Deming's 14 Points of Total Quality Management

1. Create constancy of purpose toward improvement of product and service, with the aim to become competitive and to stay in business, and to provide jobs.
2. Adopt the new philosophy. We are in a new economic age. Western management must awaken to the challenge, must learn their responsibilities, and take on leadership for change.
3. Cease dependence on inspection to achieve quality. Eliminate the need for inspection on a mass basis by building quality into the product in the first place.
4. End the practice of awarding business on the basis of price tag. Instead, minimize total cost. Move toward a single supplier for any one item, on a long-term relationship of loyalty and trust.
5. Improve constantly and forever the system of production and service, to improve quality and productivity, and thus constantly decrease costs.
6. Institute training on the job.
7. Institute leadership. The aim of supervision should be to help people and machines and gadgets to do a better job. Supervision of management is in need of overhaul as well as supervision of production workers.
8. Drive out fear, so that everyone may work effectively for the company.
9. Break down barriers between departments. People in research, design, sales, and production must work as a team, to foresee problems of production and in use that may be encountered with the product or service.
10. Eliminate slogans, exhortations, and targets for the work force asking for zero defects and new levels of productivity. Such exhortations only create adversarial relationships, as the bulk of the causes of low quality and low productivity belong to the system and thus lie beyond the power of the work force.
    a Eliminate work standards (quotas) on the factory floor. Substitute leadership.
    b Eliminate management by objective. Eliminate management by numbers, numerical goals. Substitute leadership.
11. Remove barriers that rob the hourly worker of his right to pride of workmanship. The responsibility of supervisors must be changed from sheer numbers to quality.
12. Remove barriers that rob people in management and in engineering of their right to pride of workmanship. This means, *inter alia*, abolishment of the annual merit rating and of management by objective.
13. Institute a vigorous program of education and self-improvement.
14. Put everybody in the company to work to accomplish the transformation. The transformation is everybody's job.

Source: From W. Edwards Deming, *Out of the Crisis*, MIT Press, 1986. Reprinted with permission of the MIT Press.

- *Employee involvement.* Since quality is considered the job of all employees, employees should be involved in quality initiatives. Front-line employees are likely to have the closest contact with external customers and thus can make the most valuable contributions to quality. Therefore, employees must have the authority to innovate and improve quality. In TQM workers are often organized into empowered teams that have the authority to make quality improvements.

- *Continuous improvement.* The quest for quality is a never-ending process in which people are continuously working to improve the performance, speed, and number of features of the product or service. Continuous improvement means that small, incremental improvements that occur on a regular basis will eventually add up to vast improvements in quality.

W. Edwards Deming, considered the father of TQM, outlined 14 points of quality, as listed in Table 1.2.

video: THE ENTREPRENEURIAL MANAGER

The McFarlane Companies

Summary

What do comics, sports, monsters, toys, and rock'n roll have in common? They all have benefited from the creative artistry of Todd McFarlane. He is responsible for the most successful comic books in history. He has produced a hit movie, directed music videos for Korn and Pearl Jam, won Grammys and Emmys, and runs one of the most successful toy companies in the world. He has licenses ranging from Shrek, Austin Powers, and The Beatles to Major League Baseball, the National Football League, and the NBA. McFarlane also owns part of the Edmonton Oilers hockey team.

McFarlane grew up playing baseball, and wanted to become a major league center fielder. He knew that was a long-shot, and that dream did not materialize for him. He developed an interest in comics late in high school. He wondered if he could make money drawing superheroes. He was self-taught through high school and college, and decided to send off samples to people in the business. He faced 300 rejection letters before finally getting a freelance job with Marvel Comics. They happened to be the biggest name in the industry. McFarlane worked his way up through the ranks, doing increasingly challenging characters with great success. By 1990, he was the highest paid comic book artist in the industry. McFarlane's success came with a downside, however. He was unsatisfied because he lacked ownership of the characters he was producing. He was also frustrated over creative differences. So he quit, started his own company, and took six other artists with him.

Had McFarlane taken only one or two people away from Marvel at a time, he says, they would each have been replaceable. When the seven members of what he calls the "dream team" of drawing left all at once, it had a significant impact within the industry. From artist to businessman to entrepreneur, McFarlane was expected to last about a year in the business. He never thought of failure, however. His first comic, Spawn, sold 1.7 million copies.

Entrepreneurship thrives on capitalism and innovation. The two factors for small business owners to do well are entrepreneurship and knowledge. Todd McFarlane's focus is having control over his life—even if it meant sacrificing wages at first. He has been very successful with the McFarlane Companies. Economics, technology, society, and the competitive environment have all had an impact on how the companies must be run. This is all within the context of the larger global environment and its associated pressures. Copyright laws, for example, are a crucial element of the economic and political environment that affects the McFarlane Companies.

Discussion Questions

1. In considering the competitive environment, McFarlane specifically addressed some things that his competitors were doing that he wanted to do differently—what were these? How does this related to Deming's idea of total quality management?

2. Consider what you already know about Maslow's theory of motivation. Based on this perspective, what needs were motivating McFarlane in his decision to start his own company? Do you think starting one's business is the only way entrepreneurs can achieve higher-level needs?

---

bureaucratic management

The management approach that examines the entire organization as a rational entity, using impersonal rules and procedures for decision making.

Bureaucratic Management

Another traditional perspective is **bureaucratic management**, which examines the entire organization as a rational entity. Max Weber (1864–1920), a German sociologist, introduced the concept of bureaucratic management as an "ideal" model that managers should try to emulate in order to operate an organization on a fair, rational, and efficient basis. According to Weber, the ideal bureaucracy should use impersonal rules and procedures for decision making rather than custom, family

table 1.3

Key Characteristics of Weber's Ideal Bureaucracy

1.	*Specialization of labor*	Jobs are broken down into routine, well-defined tasks so that members know what is expected of them and can become extremely competent at their particular subset of tasks.
2.	*Formal rules and procedures*	Written rules and procedures specifying the behaviors desired from members facilitate coordination and ensure uniformity.
3.	*Impersonality*	Rules, procedures, and sanctions are applied uniformly regardless of individual personalities and personal considerations.
4.	*Well-defined hierarchy*	Multiple levels of positions, with carefully determined reporting relationships among levels, provide supervision of lower offices by higher ones, a means of handling exceptions, and the ability to establish accountability of actions.
5.	*Career advancement based on merit*	Selection and promotion are based on the qualifications and performance of members.

Source: M. Weber, *The Theory of Social and Economic Organizations*, ed. and trans. A. M. Henderson and T. Parsons. New York: Free Press, 1947, pp. 328–337.

connections, or social class. Bureaucratic management challenged the aristocratic notion that authority should be based on birth and divine right. Instead, competence should be the criterion. For example, in the Germany of Weber's day only men of aristocratic birth could become officers in the Prussian army.

Table 1.3 above summarizes the important principles of Weber's bureaucratic management. Building on Adam Smith's early work on the division of labor, the ideal bureaucracy uses the principle of *specialization of labor* to break jobs down into well-defined tasks at which a person can become very competent. Formal rules and procedures are applied consistently and uniformly so that employees and customers can count on a rational and predictable environment. Weber opposed the idiosyncratic management style of bosses who lorded it over underlings in an unpredictable and arbitrary manner. He suggested that a well-defined hierarchy with clearly delineated reporting relationships was an effective way to maintain accountability. Thus the most appropriate organizational form was a pyramid structure with many reporting levels and a vertical downward chain of command. Finally, Weber strongly believed in career advancement based on merit, which stressed competency over nepotism and family connections.

Today bureaucracy is often associated with meaningless rules and red tape, but in fact Weber's bureaucratic management made positive contributions to management thought. The use of impersonal rules and procedures provides a fair and consistent way to deal with employee relations; for example, an employee handbook spells out the rules for employee discipline, performance appraisal, and work schedules rather than allowing management to handle employment policies in an arbitrary manner. Similarly, Weber's emphasis on merit as the basis of career advancement is now deeply embedded into the business culture of the United States and many other countries.

Other aspects of bureaucratic management are open to criticism. In particular, the need for a well-defined hierarchy has been challenged by the quality management viewpoint, which argues that hierarchies form barriers between employees and customers and result in reductions in quality and customer satisfaction. Current practice suggests that for firms facing rapid change and competing in markets that require constant innovation (for instance, the software industry) hierarchies should be minimized, moving away from a pyramid structure toward one that is flatter, with less direct supervision and more cooperation between workers and managers. On the other hand, the bureaucratic model developed by Weber still applies to organizations seeking to minimize deviations from standard procedures and norms. In other words, the bureaucratic approach to organizing is still advisable when reliability and efficiency are paramount.

table 1.4

Fayol's 14 Principles of Management

1.	*Division of work.*	Work should be divided into specialized tasks with responsibility for each task assigned to specific individuals.
2.	*Authority.*	Authority should be delegated along with responsibility.
3.	*Discipline.*	Clarify expectations and provide consequences for not meeting them.
4.	*Unity of command.*	Each employee should report directly to one supervisor.
5.	*Unity of direction.*	The organization's objectives should be the focus of the employee's work.
6.	*Subordination of individual interest to the general interest.*	The organization's interests should take precedence over individual interests.
7.	*Remuneration.*	Efforts that support the organization's objectives should be compensated.
8.	*Centralization.*	Superior and subordinate roles should be determined and their relative importance clarified.
9.	*Scalar chain.*	Communications among organizational areas should follow the chain of command.
10.	*Order.*	The organization of materials and jobs should support the goals of the organization.
11.	*Equity.*	Treat all employees the same, with justice and respect.
12.	*Stability and tenure.*	Employee loyalty and continuing service should be encouraged.
13.	*Initiative.*	Individual initiative of employees that supports the organization's objectives should be encouraged.
14.	*Esprit de corps.*	Employees and management should be encouraged to share the goal of achieving the organization's objectives.

Source: H. Fayol, *General and Industrial Management*, trans. C. Storres. Marshfield, MA: Pitman Publishing, 1949.

Administrative Management

administrative management

The management approach that examines an organization from the perspective of the managers and executives responsible for coordinating the activities of diverse groups and units across the entire organization.

The **administrative management** approach examines an organization from the perspective of the managers and executives responsible for coordinating the activities of diverse groups and units across the entire organization. It views management as a profession that can be learned by understanding basic principles. The key advocate was Henri Fayol (1841–1925), a French mining engineer and industrialist. In 1916, he wrote a book entitled *Administration Industrialle et Generalle* featuring what he considered to be practical guidelines for effective management based on his administrative experiences. Even though the book was not translated into English until almost four decades later, it had a significant impact on management thought and teaching.

Fayol identified five functions generic to all management activities: planning, organizing, commanding, coordinating, and controlling. He codified general principles of management that he thought could be applied to the management of any organization, as shown in Table 1.4 above. Conceiving of management as being made up of diverse functions is known as the *functional approach* to management.

Today, most organizations try to incorporate the following principles into policies and procedures:

- *Unity of command.* Each employee should be assigned to only one supervisor.
- *Unity of direction.* The employees' efforts should be focused on achieving organizational objectives.
- *Equity.* Employees should be treated with justice and respect.

Some other principles advocated by Fayol have not held up as well over time. For example, his principle that the *scalar chain of command* should define the path of communication in a top-down direction has been challenged. Both upward and horizontal communication can be equally important ways of communicating in organizations. In some situations, poor communication flows through the ranks have led to major mistakes, as documented by the investigations into what went wrong at the FBI and other government agencies before the September 11 terrorist attacks. Fayol could not have foreseen the revolution that has made the knowledge worker, who may be located at the base of the organization, a source of critical information and competitive advantage for organizational decision makers.

Still, as was the case for Weber's bureaucratic model, there may be some situations (such as the military) in which Fayol's administrative principles are still applicable. In general Fayol's main contribution to management was to specify the "best universal" way to organize by separating managerial tasks into interdependent areas of responsibilities or functions. Fayol's contention that these functions should flow in a logical manner from planning to controlling is still reflected in many modern management texts, even though they are often criticized for being too orderly and rigid to help the company adapt to a changing environment.

4 **Learning Objective Check-In**

1. *Nathaniel is trying to solve some management issues at his firm ABC International. He thinks that management can be learned by understanding some basic principles and functions. He believes that everyone should approach his or her role from the perspective of the managers and executives responsible for coordinating the activities of the organization. Nathaniel's approach has its roots in _____.*
   a. *bureaucratic management*
   b. *the behavioral perspective*
   c. *administrative management*
   d. *total quality management*

Behavioral Perspective

The **behavioral perspective** incorporates psychological and social processes of human behavior to improve productivity and work satisfaction. Operational theorists view management as a mechanical process in which employees would fit into any job or organization designed for optimum efficiency if given monetary incentives to do so. The behavioral perspective argues that human factors alone may affect workplace efficiency. The behavioral perspective traces its roots to the work of Mary Parker Follett and the Hawthorne studies, a series of long-term behavioral research experiments performed in an industrial setting. These works led to the human relations approach to management, which stresses the need for managers to understand the dynamics of the work group so as to positively influence employee motivation and satisfaction.

MARY PARKER FOLLETT Questioning much of the wisdom of scientific management, because it ignored the many ways in which employees could contribute ideas and exercise initiative, was Follett's primary contribution. She advocated increased employee participation, greater employee autonomy, and organizing the enterprise into "cross-functional" teams, composed of members of different departments working together on common projects. This would, in turn, foster upward and downward communication across various units. She also proposed that authority should rest with knowledge and expertise rather than with one's position in the hierarchy. "In other words, if workers have the relevant knowledge, then workers, rather than managers, should be in control of the work process itself, and managers should behave as coaches and facilitators—not as monitors and supervisors."[6]

THE HAWTHORNE STUDIES The Hawthorne studies were performed at the Western Electric Company's Hawthorne plant near Chicago from 1924 to 1932 under the direction of Harvard University researchers Elton Mayo and Fritz Roethlisberger. Their original purpose was to study the effects of physical working conditions on employee productivity and fatigue.

In the first set of studies, light was steadily decreased for an experimental group of employees, while illumination remained constant for the control group of employees working in a different area. Despite the different levels of illumination, the performance of both groups of employees rose consistently. This result

behavioral perspective

The management view that knowledge of the psychological and social processes of human behavior can result in improvements in productivity and work satisfaction.

Management's Historical Figures

Although individual workers perform specialized tasks on an assembly line, they work as a group rather than as individuals.

surprised the researchers, who expected the control group to outperform its experimental counterpart. They concluded that the special attention paid to the employees in the studies motivated them to put greater effort into their jobs. They labelled the phenomenon the **Hawthorne effect,** and suggested that when a manager or leader shows concern for employees, their motivation and productivity levels are likely to improve.

Later studies at Hawthorne revealed that the informal organization had a profound effect on group productivity. Mayo and Roethlisberger discovered that a work group would establish its own informal group performance norm, which represented what it considered to be a fair level of performance. Individuals who exceeded the group performance norm were considered "ratebusters," and those who performed below the norm were viewed as "chiselers." The work group disciplined both types of norm violations because ratebusters could speed up the pace of work beyond what was considered fair, while chiselers avoided doing their fair share of the work. The work group was likely to convince rate-busters to slow down and chiselers to work faster. These findings suggest that the influence of the work group may be as significant as the influence of the supervisor. Thus supervisors need the support of group members in establishing performance norms that converge with the work expectations of management.

The Hawthorne studies provided evidence that employee attitudes significantly affect performance in a manner which differs from the financial incentives championed by advocates of scientific management. Understanding the informal work organization made it possible to create cooperation between employees and management that resulted in a more productive organization.

HUMAN RELATIONS   The Hawthorne studies generated intense interest in the human side of various companies. Managers who previously concentrated on job design, work methods, or applications of technology to the task environment turned their attention to group behaviors, leadership, and employee attitudes. The **human relations approach** to management made relationships between employees and supervisors a vital aspect of management. Its advocates were people trained in the behavioral sciences, such as clinical and social psychologists, who emphasized building collaborative and cooperative relationships between supervisors and workers. Two key aspects of the human relations approach are focused on employee motivation and leadership style.

Employee Motivation   Abraham Maslow (1908–1970), a clinical psychologist who developed a theory of motivation based on a *hierarchy of needs,* assumed that unsatisfied human needs motivate behavior. The underlying assumption in Maslow's work was *humanism,* or the belief that the basic inner natures of people are good. This represented a stark contrast to Freudian psychology, which assumed the inner nature of personality was destructive, violent, and evil. This new, more positive view of human nature had a substantial impact on the fields of both psychology and management.

The hierarchy of needs model, explained in greater detail in Chapter 12, suggests that managers can motivate employees by providing an environment in which the employees can satisfy their most pressing needs. From a human relations perspective, this suggests that managers must develop positive relationships with subordinates in order to discover what their motivational needs are. For example, a manager who knows that employees are motivated by social relationships may be able to facilitate good coworker relations that will be nurturing to work group productivity. Maslow's ideas suggest that employee motivation is more complex than was assumed by the scientific management approach, which focused strictly on pay. Maslow assumed that pay can motivate only lower-level needs, and once those are satisfied it loses its power to shape employee behavior. Instead, nonmonetary factors such as praise, recognition, and job characteristics motivate human behavior.

Leadership Style   Douglas McGregor (1908–1964), a professor at MIT, used a human relations perspective to compare the assumptions leaders make about employees. He called them Theory X and Theory Y (see Table 1.5 on page 32).

Leaders and managers who operate under Theory X assumptions believe that employees are inherently lazy and lack ambition, and these managers use the external controls of punishments and rewards to drive employees to achieve organizational goals. They tend to supervise subordinates closely and deprive them of opportunities to show individual initiative and creativity. McGregor believed that highly controlling and autocratic supervisory styles based on Theory X assumptions would most likely be inefficient because they waste the human potential that could make substantial contributions to the organization.

LOC-In

5 Learning Objective Check-In

Iris from finance, Sampson from marketing, and Josephine from operations are on a cross-functional team of managers with the purpose of developing an approach by which to manage all three departments, which will be working together much more on client projects in the near future. In their first meeting, each manager offered his or her individual perspective on management. Iris said, "Employees are motivated by more than just pay. I find that when I praise my workers and tailor the job characteristics to their abilities, they work much harder." Sampson quickly pointed out that if he simply pays special attention to his employees, it motivates them to put greater effort into their jobs. Josephine recognized Sampson's point, and then offered her advice based on her own assumptions about employees. She said, "Employees are inherently lazy and lack ambition. We have to make sure we supervise them closely, or they will not work hard."

1. *Which management perspective best reflects what Iris initially proposed?*
   a. *Bureaucratic management*
   b. *Administrative management*
   c. *Behavioral perspective*
   d. *Human relations approach*
2. *Which management phenomenon was Sampson talking about?*
   a. *The Hawthorne effect*
   b. *Behavioral perspective*
   c. *Theory Y assumptions*
   d. *Total quality management*
3. *Josephine thought that employees are lazy and lack ambition. Which perspective was she demonstrating?*
   a. *Human relations approach*
   b. *Contingency theory*
   c. *Theory X assumptions*
   d. *Theory Y assumptions*

table 1.5

McGregor's Theory X and Theory Y Assumptions

Assumptions of Theory X

1. The average human being has an inherent dislike of work and will avoid it if he or she can.
2. People need to be coerced, controlled, directed, and threatened with punishment to get them to put forward adequate effort toward the organization's ends.
3. The average person prefers to be directed, wants to avoid responsibility, has relatively little ambition, and wants security above all.

Assumptions of Theory Y

1. The expenditure of physical and mental effort in work is as natural as in play or rest—the typical human being does not inherently dislike work.
2. External control and threat of punishment are not the only means for bringing about effort toward a company's goals. A person will exercise self-direction and self-control in the pursuit of the objective to which he is committed.
3. The average person learns, under the right conditions, not only to accept but to seek responsibility.
4. The capacity to exercise a relatively high degree of imagination, ingenuity, and creativity in the solution of organizational problems is widely, not narrowly, distributed in the population.
5. The intellectual potential of most people is only partially utilized in most organizations.

Source: Adapted from D. McGregor, *The Human Side of Enterprise.* New York: McGraw-Hill, 1960, pp. 33–48.

According to McGregor, leaders who hold Theory Y assumptions believe that most employees enjoy work and seek to make useful contributions to the organization. Employees are looking for ways to exercise creativity and initiative, and will most likely perform up to or even exceed job expectations when given responsibility. McGregor believed that managing on the basis of Theory Y assumptions allows the organization to utilize the human potential of all employees and become more productive. Sharing power and responsibilities with employees will make them more committed to organizational goals. McGregor's Theory Y assumptions fit with contemporary leadership styles that stress employee participation and empowerment, and they are often used in knowledge-based organizations where employee knowledge is a source of competitive advantage.

Contemporary Management Perspectives

Contemporary management perspectives include systems theory, contingency theory, and the learning organization perspective. Each of these contemporary viewpoints builds on the work of earlier management thinkers.

THE SYSTEMS APPROACH   The operational, bureaucratic, administrative, and behavioral approaches studied management by dividing it into elements or components such as work scheduling, motions, and functions, or employee needs and attitudes. While taking things apart is useful for analytical purposes, in reality all relevant parts of organizational activity interact with each other. System theorists warn us that "reductionism" in management thought may lead to simplistic prescriptions and may not help us understand why some firms perform at higher levels than others. In other words, system theorists believe that the whole is greater than the sum of the parts.

Chester I. Barnard's Early Systems Perspective   Barnard was a former president of New Jersey Bell Telephone Company. Based on his experience as a practicing executive, he believed that isolating specific management functions and principles may lead to the proverbial failing to see the forest for the trees. In his classic book, *The Functions of the Executive* (1938), Barnard depicted organizations as cooperative systems: "A cooperative system is a complex of physical, biological, personal, and social components which are in a specific systematic relationship by reason of the cooperation of two or more persons for at least one definite end."[7] He viewed organizations as complex, dynamic wholes where willingness to serve, common purpose, and communication are critical.

General Systems Theory From the perspective of **systems theory** an organization is a *system* consisting of interrelated parts that function in a holistic way to achieve a common purpose. The system takes *inputs* (resources) from the external environment and puts them through a *transformation process* (a technology) that converts them to *outputs* (finished products and services). The outputs are then put into the external environment.

The *environment* is the market, technological, social, and political conditions and forces that surround the system, critical factors that managers must consider as they seek to achieve organizational goals and objectives. The manner in which the outputs are received in the environment determines organization survival. If the environment rejects the outputs because quality is too low, the organization is likely to perish. The system receives **feedback,** information about how well the outputs were received, and uses the feedback to adjust the selection of inputs and the transformation process.

Systems theory has contributed some important concepts that affect management thinking. These include open and closed systems, subsystems, synergy, and equifinality.

Open and Closed Systems Open systems interact with the environment in order to survive. Closed systems do not need to interact with the environment. In reality, all organizations depend on the environment for inputs and for the purchase of outputs. The operational and bureaucratic perspectives on management treated the organization as if it were a closed system by overlooking the effect of the environment on management practice. Systems theory argues that the environment must always be taken into consideration in management decision making.

Subsystems Subsystems are interdependent parts of a system. A change in one subsystem affects the other subsystems. For example, when a company changes its reward system for sales representatives from salary to commission, the volume of sales revenues is likely to increase, which in turn, increases the level of output required from the manufacturing system. If the manufacturing system is operating at full capacity, an improved manufacturing process may be needed in order to satisfy the increased demand.

Synergy When the whole is greater than the sum of its parts, *synergy* exists. Management of organizational subsystems can result in synergies. For example, Microsoft sells more business applications software because all its applications software products are compatible with the Windows operating system. In other words, Microsoft's Windows operating system unit provides synergy for its business applications unit because the compatible products create value for the customer. Without the operating system unit, Microsoft would sell less business applications software.

Equifinality In an open system, equifinality means that an organization can reach the same goal though a number of different routes. Also, not every organization must begin from the same place or use the same tactics to achieve success.

systems theory

A modern management theory that views the organization as a system of interrelated parts that function in a holistic way to achieve a common purpose.

feedback

Information received back from the receiver, which allows the sender to clarify the message if its true meaning is not received.

Advocates of scientific management believed that management could be reduced to "one best way." By contrast, systems theory suggests that different inputs, sub-systems, and transformation processes can lead to similar outcomes.

CONTINGENCY THEORY According to **contingency theory**, what works for one organization may not work for another, because situational characteristics differ. The situational characteristics are called *contingencies.* Managers need to understand the key contingencies that determine the most effective management practices in a given situation. Thus, whether application of a management principle or rule (such as division of work and a well-defined hierarchy) leads to positive results depends on the particular conditions. Each situation has its own nuances and presents to the manager a unique set of problems. Lack of "fit," or a mismatch between management practice and what the situation calls for, leads to poor performance. Alternatively, high performance results when management practice is attuned to or congruent with the demands of the particular context being faced. Contingency theory strongly warns that managers must be flexible in order to apply those practices and techniques that are most appropriate to specific situations.

An example of an important contingency is the degree of change in the environment. Change can include the development of new technologies or the entry of new competitors to the market. When the environment is turbulent, managers are likely to select a *decentralized organization structure* in which authority is pushed to lower levels so that decisions can be made rapidly and flexibly. When the environment is stable and predictable, managers select a *centralized organization structure* in which decisions are made on a top-down basis to exercise more efficient control over resources. Contingency theory suggests that a manager should first identify and understand the contingency, then select the management practice that best fits the situation. Other contingencies include organization cultures, industry structures, and products and process or manufacturing technologies.

LOC-In

THE LEARNING ORGANIZATION The **learning organization** approach suggests that organizations that can "learn" faster than their counterparts have an advantage over competitors in the marketplace. Rather than *reacting* to change, which is a normal part of the business landscape, organizations need to *anticipate* change so they are well positioned to satisfy their customers' future needs with the most appropriate products and services. Therefore, a learning organization attempts to institutionalize continuous learning. This means that knowledge and information will be shared between employees and teams rather than controlled by an elite group of technocrats. Organizational structures should facilitate the sharing and transfer of information as broadly and quickly as possible. Flat structures with few management layers and cross-functional teams that bring together people from different business or scientific disciplines are examples of ways to break down barriers that keep people from sharing information and learning from each other.

FIGURE 1.3

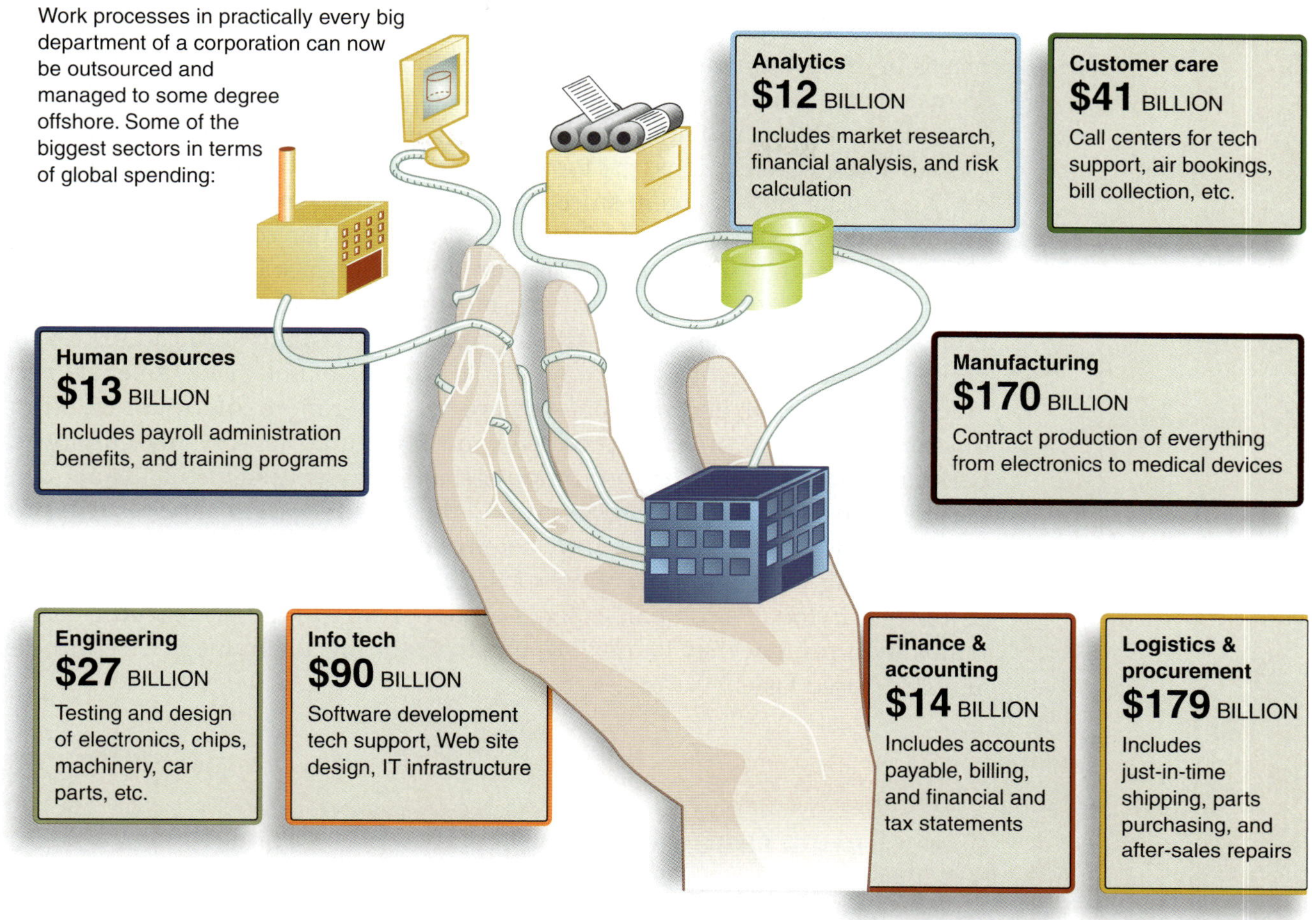

Work processes in practically every big department of a corporation can now be outsourced and managed to some degree offshore. Some of the biggest sectors in terms of global spending:

Analytics
$12 BILLION
Includes market research, financial analysis, and risk calculation

Customer care
$41 BILLION
Call centers for tech support, air bookings, bill collection, etc.

Human resources
$13 BILLION
Includes payroll administration benefits, and training programs

Manufacturing
$170 BILLION
Contract production of everything from electronics to medical devices

Engineering
$27 BILLION
Testing and design of electronics, chips, machinery, car parts, etc.

Info tech
$90 BILLION
Software development tech support, Web site design, IT infrastructure

Finance & accounting
$14 BILLION
Includes accounts payable, billing, and financial and tax statements

Logistics & procurement
$179 BILLION
Includes just-in-time shipping, parts purchasing, and after-sales repairs

The Modular Corporation

Source: P. Engardio, "The Future of Outsourcing," *BusinessWeek*, January 30, 2006, pp. 50–56.

Emerging Perspectives and Issues

There are two trends which are likely to influence management practice and theory in the foreseeable future, reflecting fundamental changes in how organizations create and deliver products and services: the modular organization and the intangible organization.

The Modular Organization

The classical organizational form with employees who work in departments that are housed within functional units (such as production, sales, human resource management, and so on), which are in turn housed within business units or divisions (corresponding, for instance, to product lines), which in turn report directly to corporate top executives, is being replaced in varying degrees by the so-called *modular corporation*, or what some people refer to as "disaggregated corporation." What this means is that every function not regarded as crucial is outsourced to an independent organization, often on a global basis (see Figure 1.3 above and Management Close-Up 1.1 on page 16). Hence, internal organizational forms are simplified since managers contract with and coordinate the activities of outsourcing partners rather than supervise long-term company employees who used to perform these tasks. This evolving organizational form is likely to have a major impact on most of the management issues discussed in this text (such as organizational culture, leadership, and motivation) but the effects are as yet not well understood.

The Intangible Organization

Technology is playing a dramatic role in how organizations function. The emphasis on innovation and creativity means that businesses are shifting their resources from tangible (such as plant and equipment) to intangible (such as know-how and product design) investments. For instance, according to *BusinessWeek*'s calculations, the top 10 biggest U.S. corporations have increased R&D spending by 42 percent since 2000 but they have increased capital spending on tangible goods by only 2 percent.[8] The modular corporation discussed above probably has something to do with this trend since factories and production facilities of outsourcing partners, mostly overseas, are replacing such investments in the United States. This is likely to have huge implications for the practice of management as we know it. In the words of one management expert, "Ideas, information, and relationships are becoming more important than production machinery, physical products, and structured jobs. Many employees perform much of their work on computers and may work in virtual teams, connected electronically to colleagues around the world. Even in factories that produce physical goods, machines have taken over much of the routine and uniform work, freeing workers to use more of their minds and abilities. Managers and employees in today's companies focus on opportunities rather than efficiencies, which requires that they be flexible, creative, and unconstrained by rigid rules and structured tasks."[9]

CONCLUDING THOUGHTS

In the chapter's introductory vignette, we posed some critical thinking questions regarding Toyota's success compared with the well-publicized recent problems of Ford and General Motors. Now that you have had the opportunity to learn about different management perspectives, let's look again at the questions.

First, while Ford and General Motors were pioneers in the use of scientific management techniques, they have lost much of their edge in efficiency and have suffered from a reputation for spotty quality. Toyota has been able to produce cars at lower costs and of better quality. Second, Ford and General Motors have not been able to adapt to change as well as Toyota. International competition has eroded much of the domestic market share Ford and General Motors used to enjoy, and these companies have not been able to make the necessary adjustments early on to prevent the slide.

Third, Ford and General Motors seem to have put in place strategies that have not led to a sustainable competitive advantage. These strategies appear to have missed the target in terms of what customers want. Toyota's strategy, on the other hand, has been customer driven during the past 30 years or so. Fourth, while starting from a position of overwhelming advantage 40 or so years ago (when they dominated the automobile market), General Motors and Ford appear to have made poor use of human, financial, and physical resources. Toyota, on the other hand, has become an exemplar of successful delegation of tasks, hiring and retaining highly committed workers, and marshalling and allocating resources in a timely and cost-effective manner. Toyota has beaten Ford and General Motors with low engineering costs, low manufacturing costs, and near-perfect quality. Toyota has been able to accomplish this with less hierarchy, which saves on middle-management costs and spurs greater worker initiative, since workers are expected to act on their own rather than follow orders under close supervision.

Fifth, Toyota has been able to manage environmental forces successfully by globalizing its operations, and it has become very flexible in its ability to respond to local conditions. Sixth, Toyota has been able to achieve its success while creating a lot of goodwill and cultivating a positive image as a great place to work, hiring hundreds of thousands of American workers and making billions of dollars of purchases from domestic suppliers. This means that Toyota has amassed a lot of political capital, making it difficult for Ford and General Motors to secure government protection on nationalistic "Buy American" grounds. Lastly, Ford and General Motors have not been able to break away from their confrontational bargaining relationships with labor unions, and their inability to meet prior commitments (for high wages, health care, retirement, and the like) is fueling an already negative labor relations climate.

Focusing on the Future: Using Management Theory in Daily Life

Your Management Career

Welcome to management! A degree in management offers you many career options. Five of the most common career tracks are described below. As you read this text and think about your skills, abilities, and interests, you may decide that one of these is right for you.

General or Operations Manager If organization is your strong suit, and you can move easily between the "big picture" and the smallest details, you may want to consider a career in operations. Students with an operations emphasis may end up in positions such as COO (Chief Operating Officer) or General Manager. These managers are responsible for improving the flow of the work process throughout the organization, and they need to be knowledgeable about everything "P"—production, pricing, people, profit, policy, and products. General or Operations Managers place a heavy emphasis on efficiency and effectiveness. Like most managers, Operations Managers spend a lot of their time in meetings—reviewing tasks and supplies for the day, checking on general project status, assigning and reassigning resources based on market projections, performance data, work flow, and personnel, coordinating with other departments to ensure that employees get the right resources at the right time and that schedules are coordinated, and handling administrative issues such as performance reviews, inventory, quality assessments, and changes to policies and procedures.

Accounting or Financial Manager If numbers are your playthings, and money matters most to you, you may want to consider a career in either accounting or finance. Accountants are the "detail people"—they handle the books for an organization, and they create and manage accounting records that conform to reporting regulations. They also prepare tax returns and reports, and ensure that taxes are paid in a timely fashion. Financial Managers look at "big picture" money issues—analyzing the financial status of the organization, preparing financial forecasts and budgets, assessing the risks of potential investments, and controlling risk and loss through insurance and other programs. Accounting and Financial Managers often work for consulting companies, and when they do, they must have sales and relationship management skills in addition to their mathematical and analytical abilities.

Human Resources Manager If problem solving is your gift, and people come to you for advice about everything from how to handle their personal relationships to what to do with their investments, HR may be for you. HR managers are responsible for the flow of people through the organization—everything from planning what types of people and skills will be needed, to recruiting and hiring, to training and development, to compensation and benefits, to retirement and/or termination. They spend a lot of their time resolving conflicts between employees, between employees and managers, and between the company and various outside vendors such as insurance agents and other benefits providers. Many students who "like people" think that they may want a career in HR, but be careful. The most successful HR managers have a firm grasp of finance and accounting principles, can think strategically in the interests of the organization, and have the ability to sell their programs and policies at all levels of the organization.

Marketing or Communications Manager   If you are a "creative type" and you are particularly good with either visual images or words, marketing may be the career for you. Marketing is all about getting an organization's products to the customer at a price that works for both buyer and seller, and encouraging people to buy using words and images. During this process you may have to develop pricing strategies, analyze market trends, work closely with product designers and distributors to match market trends with products or services, and create marketing campaigns with advertising and promotions managers. The other side of marketing is the Communication Manager, who presents the face of the company to the public. Communication Managers must be politically savvy—they know how to use words and the media to the best advantage of the company. They are responsible for writing press releases, drafting speeches for company executives, developing and maintaining the company's image through logos and signs, and managing special events to promote the company name, products, or services. The best Marketing and Communication managers are highly skilled interpersonally. They truly care about customer satisfaction and understand how others will interpret their words.

Entrepreneur   As a child, did you ever charge your friends to play your video games? Start your own Web site with an eye toward making a profit? Entrepreneurs often start creating businesses at a very early age. If you have a passion for hard work, a tolerance for taking risks, and a focus on the bottom line, you may want to consider becoming an entrepreneur. Successful entrepreneurs have skills in all aspects of management, and they know how to cover the skills they don't have by hiring the right people for their organization. They must be able to organize their business, plan tasks for themselves and others, handle the company's books and finances, sell their ideas to others, manage the people working for them, evaluate risks, take initiative, and develop new products, services, and processes for the business. Entrepreneurship is often lonely and undercompensated work, but it offers freedom and unlimited potential to those who are willing to risk everything.

A Note on Management Careers   Remember that all of the above are *managers* and as such, their jobs share certain similarities. For example, all managers have to get work done through others and that means that they have to know how to motivate and inspire their employees, which is different from doing the work yourself. In addition, managers have to be aware of more big picture issues—their job is to plan and organize the work for others, then to make sure that the work gets done, not necessarily to do the work themselves. In addition, most people find that as they move higher on their chosen career ladders, their jobs become more heavily focused on sales. A manager who cannot sell his or her ideas to others in the organization, or a manager who cannot bring new clients into the organization, is not likely to be successful. Finally, all managers are concerned about money—they create and approve budgets, and then must manage resources to fit within those budgets.

If you want to learn more about any of the jobs listed above, the best place to start is on the Internet. O*NET (http://online.onetcenter.org) is published by the U.S. government, and it contains a wealth of information on occupations, including tasks, abilities, work activities, knowledge, skills, work context, job zones, work styles and wages and employment trends. The Small Business Administration Web site (http://www.sba.gov) is a key resource for entrepreneurs—their "Starting Business" page (http://www.sba.gov/starting_business/index.html) covers start-up basics, planning, financing, marketing, employees, tax topics, legal aspects, and special interest topics for people considering starting their own business. Vault (http://www.vault.com) is a Web site devoted to providing career information—their "Day in the Life" reports can give you new insights on what life in various industries is really like (http://www.vault.com/nr/ht_list.jsp?ht_type=1.)

Now that you know a little about the different kinds of management jobs, you will probably want to know how these managers use the information you are learning in this class. Each of the managers described above uses the concepts and theories described in this text on a daily basis. Look for boxes like this one at the end of each chapter called "Focusing on the Future: Using Management Theory in Daily Life" to find out more.

summary of learning objectives

This chapter has provided an overview of the field of management and how it has evolved over time. The following are summaries of the chapter discussions for each of the learning objectives that we stated at the outset of this chapter.

1 Understand the challenges organizations face in the new millennium.

- *Be both efficient and effective*. This requires making the best use of resources and achieving goals that provide the firm with a sustainable competitive advantage.
- *Deal with key contemporary management issues*. Three key issues have been identified in this chapter: coping with and adapting to rapid change on a daily basis, satisfying the needs of demanding customers who have more choices than ever before, and making ethical decisions.
- *Be capable of managing new forms of organizations*. This requires coordination of different levels of managers (strategic, tactical, operational), employees who are expected to show initiative and enjoy high autonomy (empowerment), and teams composed of employees who cut across functional and disciplinary lines.

2 Specify the functions and roles of successful managers.

- *Managerial functions*. These are **planning** and strategizing (to assist the firm in meeting its mission), **organizing** (allocating of resources to meet the firm's mission), **leading** (energizing organizational members to contribute their most, both as individuals and as members of a team), and **controlling** (monitoring results and processes on an ongoing basis to detect deviations from the preferred state).
- *Managerial roles*. There are three major roles or behaviors expected of managers, namely an *interpersonal role* (engage in active communication with relevant parties), an *informational role* (obtain, interpret, and provide information to others), and a *decision-making role* (make choices and take responsibility for them).

3 Explain the origins of management as an academic discipline.

The earliest management thinkers include Sun Tzu, an ancient Chinese general who recognized that management strategy meant taking a long-term perspective; Niccolò Machiavelli, a Renaissance Italian who advised leaders to be cunning and crafty in order to survive against ambitious rivals; and Adam Smith, an 18th-century philosopher who recognized that the division of labor could have a powerful effect on an organization's productivity.

- **Scientific management**, represented by the ideas of Frederick Winslow Taylor, focuses on using experts to teach workers the best methods and techniques to do their jobs. Employees do the physical labor and managers provide the planning and organizing. It was assumed that employees would be willing to cooperate with managers, since employees were to be paid according to their level of output, and they could earn more pay this way.
- **Quantitative management** emphasizes the development of statistical tools and techniques to improve efficiency.
- **Quality management** focuses on approaches that may be used to improve quality and reduce the time and effort devoted to replacing what was done wrong in the first place. While originally concerned with manufacturing, many quality-management concepts have since been applied to the service sector as well.

4 Describe the bureaucratic and administrative approaches to the study of management.

These perspectives emerged during the early 20th century and were primarily concerned with the efficient use of organizational structures and processes. Many of the following ideas are still used today when deciding how to set up organizational hierarchies, reporting relationships, and policies and procedures.

- The idea of **bureaucratic management** was developed by Max Weber, a German sociologist. Bureaucratic management is governed by a set of impersonal rules and policies, including merit as a basis for career advancement. Weber believed that bureaucratic management was the most efficient way to organize and govern an enterprise.
- The **administrative management perspective**, advocated by Henri Fayol, assumes that general principles of management can be applied to any situation or circumstance. Fayol divided the activities of management into five functions that are still used today: planning, organizing, commanding, coordinating, and controlling.

5 Explain the behavioral perspective in analyzing management issues.

The **behavioral perspective** in management thought focuses on understanding how to manage human factors to improve workplace productivity. It traces its roots to the works of Mary Parker Follett and the Hawthorne studies performed at the Western Electric Company during the 1920s and 1930s. These studies suggested that leaders are able to positively influence employee motivation and productivity by showing concern for employee relationships.

Inspired by the works of Follett and the Hawthorne studies, the *human relations* approach to management emphasized work relationships as the key to a productive workplace. Abraham Maslow developed a theory of employee motivation based on a hierarchy of human needs. Maslow believed that managers need to view employees from a humanistic perspective, identify unfulfilled employee needs, and then show employees how these needs may be satisfied in the context of the workplace. The result should be a higher level of employee motivation and productivity. Douglas McGregor, another advocate of the human relations approach, examined the assumptions made by leaders. Theory X leaders assume that subordinates avoid work, whereas Theory Y leaders assume that subordinates want to do good work and are interested in taking on more desirable tasks, and they encourage employees to utilize more of their human potential for the good of the organization. While difficult to test empirically, with mostly conflicting results in academic studies, these human relations concepts are still very influential among management practitioners.

6 Interpret recent approaches to the study of management.

- Contemporary management perspectives that came to light in the mid-to-late 20th century include **systems theory**, **contingency theory**, and the **learning organization**. According to these perspectives, it is futile to search for "one best way" to manage a firm because organizations are in constant interaction with the external environment. Instead, managers must take the external environment into account so as to match the appropriate management practices to the surrounding circumstances for an effective outcome. The so-called learning organization is more concerned with problem solving than efficiency (which was the primary focus of the bureaucratic and administrative management perspectives).
- Some emerging management perspectives include the "modular organization" (where the firm becomes a shell, outsourcing many of its activities to separate independent organizations) and the "intangible organization" (where ideas, information, and relationships are critical to success).

discussion questions

1. Going back to the chapter's introductory vignette, do you think Ford and General Motors can reverse their fortunes in the foreseeable future? Why or why not? What should they do in order to improve their situation? Explain your answer.

2. Explain Machiavelli's advice to leaders that "it is better to be feared than loved." In the context of contemporary management, consider this modification of Machiavelli's advice: "It is better for a leader to be *respected* than loved." Would you agree or disagree with this statement? Discuss its implications.

3. What were the important contributions of scientific management? What were its limitations?

4. Examine the list of Fayol's 14 principles of management in Table 1.4. Which principles are still useful today? Which principles appear to be obsolete, according to contemporary management thinking?

5. According to the human relations perspective, leaders can influence certain factors within work groups that can result in improved performance and satisfaction. Describe how a leader would be likely to put knowledge of this perspective into practice and obtain increased performance from his or her subordinates.

6. Think of an example that illustrates an application of the following contemporary theories:

   a. Systems theory.

   b. Contingency theory.

7. How do the management perspectives discussed in this chapter relate to each of the chapter's Management Close-Ups ("How Outsourcing Is Transforming Whole Industries and Changing the Way We Work," "The New Ethics Enforcers," and "Giving the Boss the Big Picture")? Explain your answer.

Biz Majors Get an F for Honesty

management minicase 1.1

Research by the Center for Academic Integrity (RCAI), a think tank affiliated with the Kenan Institute for Ethics at Duke University, shows that undergraduate business students do more cheating than just about anyone else. The survey of nearly 50,000 students at 69 schools found that 26 percent of business majors admitted to serious cheating on exams, and 54 percent admitted to cheating on written assignments, including plagiarism and poaching a friend's homework.

The most honest group? Those in the sciences, where 19 percent reported cheating on tests. The results come from surveys conducted over the past three years by Donald McCabe, a management professor at Rutgers Business School and founder of RCAI. McCabe says cheating has increased since he began doing surveys 15 years ago. He partly blames technology for making cheating easier. Papers can be downloaded off the Internet, and answers text messaged to friends. But he adds that a "disturbing" number of students use recent corporate and political scandals to justify their behavior.

1. What do you think the survey results imply for people who are likely to become managers?
2. Do you think that the ethical climate is getting better or worse? Explain.
3. What can business schools do to promote ethical thinking among students?

Source: Reprinted from H. Oh, "Upfront," *BusinessWeek*, February 6, 2006, p. 14.

management minicase 1.2

Google: Using a Company's Culture to Conquer the World

Google is a company that has come from nowhere to become a 100-billion-dollar enterprise. Google is taking on the likes of Microsoft (desktop software), eBay (classified advertising), phone companies (the San Francisco wi-fi plan), and others. Google keeps a confidential list of the 100 top priorities under development. Specifics aside, what's certain is that Google will keep looking for new ways to organize and search for information. It will try to make money on most of them, primarily through advertising. It will expand more overseas (Google calculates that two-thirds of the world's Internet population speaks a language other than English), and it will form more global partnerships with content providers.

Sergey Brin and Larry Page, Google founders and top executives, set the tone at Google. They are businessmen who didn't go to business school, and they believe that gives them a creative edge. Their standard attire is black T-shirt, jeans, and sneakers (and lab coats for special occasions). They are at once playful—they used to take part in the regular roller-hockey games in the Google parking lot—and solemnly idealistic, as when discussing Google's new $1 billion philanthropic arm. Brin and Page are products of Montessori schools and credit that system with developing their individuality and entrepreneurship. They're often accused of being arrogant, but to the extent that they are, it may not be egotism as much as an insistence on doing things their way. (The pair sometimes celebrate big Google milestones by going out to Burger King.)

Brin and Page's creation is a company that is quirky and practically shouts about it. The lava lamps and electric scooters that replaced the original Segways at the "Googleplex" headquarters in Mountain View have become iconic. There is also a sand-volleyball court, a pair of heated lap pools, and, for some reason, a ball pit with dozens of brightly colored plastic balls, like the one you throw the kids into at Ikea. The dress code? "You have to wear something," says CEO Schmidt. And even he can't explain the (phoneless) London-style phone booth that stands in one hallway — "Who bought that?!" he wonders aloud, sounding like the sole sane person in a loony bin. Above all, there is Google's fetishistic devotion to food; the company serves three excellent meals a day, free, to its staff, at several cafes. One of their chefs, Charlie Ayers, once cooked for members of the Grateful Dead. At Google, we are not talking meat loaf and bug juice. For example, the executive chef from an acclaimed area restaurant recently prepared sugar-pie pumpkin lasagna and cedar spring lamb chops for Google employees.

What's intriguing is that this slightly goofy, self-indulgent culture has proved so adept at nuts-and bolts business. Schmidt says he intentionally propagated the perception of Google as a wacky place to allow the company to build up its business under the radar. "With the lava lamps and scooters, everybody thought we were idiots, the last vestiges of the dot-coms," he says. "It worked until it leaked out how well we were doing." Many details didn't become known until Google had to file its financials just before going public in 2004.

Unlike many competitors in Silicon Valley, Google tends to let engineers run the show. The company is almost allergic to marketing (name another $100 billion company that doesn't run TV ads). Innovation tends to bubble up from those bright young minds. The challenge is keeping them all happy. The free food and laundry and the heavily subsidized massages and haircuts all help, but there also has to be enough creative work to go around. Google came up with a formula to help ensure this. Every employee is meant to divide his or her time in to three parts; 70 percent devoted to Google's core businesses, search and advertising; 20 percent on pursuits related to the core; and 10 percent on far-out ideas. The San Francisco wi-fi initiative resulted from someone's 10 percent time; so did Google Talk, a system for instant and voice messaging.

Google is now getting ready to face its two big rivals. Google has aroused Microsoft by moving onto its turf and faces a lively battle with Yahoo!, which has a competing vision of the future of search.

Discussion Questions

1. What management aspects are unique to Google as described in this case? How and why have these aspects contributed to Google's success? Explain.

2. Do you see any downside to how Google is managed? Do you think Google can maintain its unique management approach well into the future?

3. To what extent do you think Google's management style may be effectively used by other organizations? Explain.

Source: Adapted from A. Ignatius, "In Search of the Real Google," *Time*, February 20, 2006, pp. 36–50.

Is the U.S.A. Falling Behind in Global Brain Race?

individual/
collaborative
learning
case 1.1

Science and technology are fundamental to a sustainable competitive advantage for companies across a wide range of industries. There is a growing controversy between those who believe the United States is about to be deposed as the world's leader in science and technology (which will undermine the competitiveness of U.S firms) and those who believe that the doomsayers are focusing on the wrong indicators. A summary of each perspective follows below.

We Are Falling Behind![1]

While the 20th century had the arms race, the competition in this century will be a brain race, says science policy analyst Michael Lubell of the American Physical Society. "Today's Sputnik? It's a little bigger. It's called China," he says. "The projected growth in high-technology products from there is staggering." The stakes are high. The United States now leads the world in spending on research and development—estimated to reach $328.9 billion this year—from both government and private sources. Innovation driven by such spending creates as much as 85 percent of the growth in economic productivity, according to a 2006 National Academy of Sciences report, "Rising above the Gathering Storm." And productivity growth determines who is the leader and who is a follower in the global economy. A 15 percent shortfall in British productivity from 1880 to 1990 transformed "the once proud empire to a second-rate economy in little more than a lifetime," in the words of economic writer Sylvia Nasar.

According to the National Academy report, "Although the United States continues to possess the world's stronger science and engineering enterprise, its position is jeopardized both by evolving weakness at home and by growing strength abroad." The report notes some "alarming" concerns:

- One U.S. chemist's or engineer's salary is enough to hire five Chinese chemists or 11 Indian engineers. Last year, China graduated 500,000 engineers; India, 200,000; and North America, 70,000. The training quality of a high proportion of Chinese and Indian engineers matches and in some cases surpasses that of U.S. engineers.

- The U.S. trade balance in high-technology goods fell from $33 billion in the black in 1990 to $24 billion in the red in 2004.

- U.S. funding of "research in most physical sciences, mathematics, and engineering has declined or remained flat—in real purchasing power—for several decades."

- Leadership in high-energy physics, a U.S. franchise since the Manhattan Project built the atomic bomb, is shifting overseas. Beginning in 2007, the most powerful particle accelerator on Earth will be outside the United States for the first time in decades. The atom smasher is now under construction at Europe's CERN lab in Switzerland. Similarly, U.S. scientists complain that fusion reactor tests and underground physics labs needed to stay ahead in the most cutting-edge areas are all overseas.

Don't Believe the Hype: We Are Still No. 1[2]

You can pick your statistics. Mine are that the U.S. leads the world by an immense margin in just about every measure of intellectual and technological achievement: Ph.D.s, patents, peer-reviewed articles, Nobel Prizes. But in the end, it's the culture. The economy follows culture, and American culture is today, as ever, uniquely suited for growth, innovation, and advancement. The most obvious bedrock of success is entrepreneurial spirit. The U.S. has the most risk-taking, most laissez-faire, least regulated economy in the advanced Western world. America is heartily disdained by its coddled and controlled European cousins for its cowboy capitalism. But it is precisely American's tolerance for creative destruction — industries failing, others rising, workers changing jobs and cities and skills with an alacrity and insouciance that Europeans find astonishing—that keeps its economy churning and advancing.

Some are alarmed that government R&D funding has fallen from a 60 percent to a 30 percent share of total funding. Does government necessarily make wiser investment decisions than private companies? The mistake of the Soviets, Japanese, and so many others was to assume that creativity could be achieved with enough government planning and funding. But the very essence of creativity is spontaneity. A society's creativity is directly proportionate to the rate of free interaction of people and ideas in a vast unplanned national chemical reaction. There is no country anywhere more given to the unencumbered, unfettered, unregulated exchange of ideas than the United States.

And not just ideas but also the people who give lift to them. America is uniquely socially mobile, ethnically mixed and racially tolerant. America is, in Ben Wattenberg's phrase, the first universal nation, indeed the only universal nation. Every street corner in New York City is a rainbow of humanity. The resulting interaction and fusion of cultures produce not just great cuisine and music and art but also great science and technology. Intel was co-founded by a Hungarian, Google by a Russian, Yahoo! by a Taiwanese. We are the world's masters of assimilation. Where else do you see cultures and races so at home with one another? In China?

Critical Thinking Questions

1. Which of the two positions presented above do you agree with the most? Explain your answer.
2. If you were the manager of a high technology organization, what would you see as the main consequences or implications to your firm of the contrasting points of view discussed above? Explain your answer.
3. Do you think the government should be the primary actor to spur technological achievement or should this responsibility fall on private firms? Defend your answer.

Collaborative Learning Exercise

Class is divided into groups of five. Half of the groups are asked to defend the first position described above ("We are falling behind!"). The other half of the groups are asked to defend the opposite position ("Don't believe the hype"). Groups can prepare their arguments outside class or during class, depending on time constraints and instructor's preference. Both "pro" and "con" teams are asked to present their arguments in class, with the instructor acting as moderator.

Sources:[1] Adapted with permission from D. Vergano, "U.S. Could Fall Behind in Global Brain Race," *USA Today*, February 9, 2006, p. D-1; [2] C. Krauthammer, " Don't Believe the Hype. We Are Still No. 1," *Time*, February 13, 2006, p. 41.

Lincoln Electric

Explore the Web site of Lincoln Electric (www.lincolnelectric.com), a leading producer of arc-welding products. Lincoln has dominated its markets by utilizing a management philosophy that is similar to the early 20th-century ideas of Frederick Winslow Taylor, the father of scientific management. Use the site's map feature to locate and read about the history of Lincoln Electric ("our history") and also learn what it is like to work at Lincoln Electric ("career opportunities"). Then answer the following questions:

1. What are the important features of the Lincoln Electric Performance System?
2. What do you think it would be like to work at Lincoln Electric? Would you enjoy working there? Why or why not?
3. What are Lincoln Electric's mission and vision? How does its Incentive Performance System support them?
4. Do you think Lincoln Electric is a well-managed company based on what you have read about it? On what information do you base your conclusion? Explain.

www.lincolnelectric.com.

Do You Fit in a Bureaucratic Organization?

Many organizations still exhibit the characteristics of a bureaucracy as described by Weber. Some people fit in well with highly bureaucratic organizations; others feel stifled and cramped by a bureaucratic organization. What is your preference? To determine your level of comfort with bureaucratic organizations, try the following exercise.

Instructions: For each statement, check the response that best represents your feelings.

	Mostly Agree	Mostly Disagree
1. I value stability in my job.	____	____
2. I like a predictable organization.	____	____
3. The best job for me would be one in which the future is relatively certain.	____	____
4. The federal government would be a nice place to work.	____	____
5. Rules, policies, and procedures tend to frustrate me.	____	____
6. I would enjoy working for a company that employed 85,000 people worldwide.	____	____
7. Being self-employed would involve more risk than I'm willing to take.	____	____
8. Before accepting a job, I would like to see an exact job description.	____	____
9. I would prefer a job as a freelance house painter to one as a clerk for the department of motor vehicles.	____	____
10. Seniority should be as important as performance in determining pay increases and job promotion.	____	____
11. It would give me a feeling of pride to work for the largest and most successful company in its field.	____	____
12. Given a choice, I would prefer to make $40,000 per year as vice president in a small company to $45,000 as a staff specialist in a large company.	____	____

		Mostly Agree	Mostly Disagree
13.	I would regard wearing an employee badge with a number on it as a degrading experience.	____	____
14.	Parking spaces in a company lot should be assigned on the basis of job level.	____	____
15.	If an accountant works for a large firm, he or she cannot be a true professional.	____	____
16.	Before accepting a job (given a choice), I would want to make sure that the company had a fine program of employee benefits.	____	____
17.	A company will probably not be successful unless it establishes a clear set of rules and procedures.	____	____
18.	Regular working hours and vacations are more important to me than finding thrills on the job.	____	____
19.	You should respect people according to their rank.	____	____
20.	Rules are meant to be broken.	____	____

Scoring and Interpretation

If you mostly agree with items 1–4, 6–8, 10–11, 14, and 16–19 that would mean that you have a high level of comfort with bureaucratic organizations. The opposite would be true if you mostly disagree with those items yet mostly agree with items 5, 9, 12–13, 15, and 20.

Sources: From *Human Relations: A Job Oriented Approach* by DuBrin, copyright © 1978. Reprinted by permission of Pearson Education, Inc., Upper Saddle River, NJ.

manager's checkup 1.2

Are You a Theory X or a Theory Y Manager?

Instructions: Circle the level of agreement or disagreement that you personally feel toward each of the following 10 statements.

SA = Strongly Agree
A = Agree
U = Uncertain
D = Disagree
SD = Strongly Disagree

1.	People need to know that the boss is in charge.	SA	A	U	D	SD
2.	Employees will rise to the occasion when an extra effort is needed.	SA	A	U	D	SD
3.	Employees need direction and control or they will not work hard.	SA	A	U	D	SD
4.	People naturally want to work.	SA	A	U	D	SD
5.	A manager should be a decisive, no-nonsense leader.	SA	A	U	D	SD
6.	Employees should not be involved in making decisions that concern them.	SA	A	U	D	SD
7.	A manager has to be tough-minded and hard-nosed.	SA	A	U	D	SD
8.	A manager should build a climate of trust in the work unit.	SA	A	U	D	SD
9.	If a unit is to be productive, employees need to be pushed.	SA	A	U	D	SD
10.	Employees need the freedom to innovate.	SA	A	U	D	SD

Global Giant: Wal-Mart

video summary

Summary

Since being one store in Arkansas in the 1960s, Wal-Mart has grown into the largest company in the history of the world. With annual sales larger than the economy of Saudi Arabia and profits greater than ExxonMobil, Wal-Mart's productivity is so high that it accounts for 10 percent of the U.S.'s total productivity growth. Its prices are so low that some 10 million customers shop at a Wal-Mart every week of the year. Critics claim that with such a fierce competitor as Wal-Mart, the communities, employees, and suppliers of the company become its victims, instead of its beneficiaries. Capitalism, they say, was not intended to work this way.

The video case presents evidence to suggest that the low prices that sustain Wal-Mart's popularity and growth actually sustain low worker wages and poor worker conditions for supplier firms and drive out competition from local shops and boutiques, like the flower shop that is mentioned. The workers, those critics claim, are entering the ranks of the working poor rather than the middle class. Wal-Mart counters these claims by saying that up to two-thirds of their employees are students, senior citizens, or second wage-earners who are seeking supplemental income, not primary means of subsistence. The firm says it recruits its workers accordingly. The fact remains Wal-Mart's typical employee is not paid a "living wage" by which he or she can afford, for example, health insurance or other necessities *if* that worker is a primary wage-earner. Other topics covered specifically in the case include the pressure to control costs for suppliers and the poor working conditions of those workers in foreign countries who produce low-cost goods sold in Wal-Mart stores.

Discussion Questions

1. From what you observed in the video, what can you say about Wal-Mart's commitment to human rights standards? What impression does this give you regarding the company's general management approach toward its workers?

2. At the end of the case, a customer said that she made the choice to buy low-priced bicycles from Wal-Mart, even if they were made by workers in China under inhumane conditions. How did she justify her decision? As long as consumers make decisions like these, why should Wal-Mart be concerned with human rights issues?

3. Wal-Mart is the largest company in the history of the world. Wal-Mart's representative in the video said that it recruits workers who are looking for supplemental income. What are the implications of an employer of this size and influence designing jobs that will provide only supplementary-standard incomes? Do all companies have a responsibility to offer comprehensive benefits packages, and if so, to which workers?

part two

The Culture of Management

An organization's external and internal environments are the context in which the practice of management takes place. Managers and nonmanagers alike must understand that effective business decisions take into consideration pressures from the external environment such as from global markets, technological changes, and the requirement to behave and be perceived as a socially responsible member of the community, as well as from internal factors within an organization such as the organizational culture and the expectation of ethical business conduct.

In Part Two we will begin by examining threats and opportunities firms face in the global environment. This will lead to a discussion of global business strategies and advantageous ways to enter foreign markets given a firm's unique characteristics. Next we analyze the nature of business ethics and the basis of ethical decisions. Then, we present the broader context of social responsibility and identify key stakeholders and ways to manage relationships with them. Finally, we examine organizational culture and how it helps an organization achieve its objectives. In Part Two, we also explain the forces that drive organizational change and describe ways to manage and counsel employees who resist the need for change.

2

chapter 2

Managing in a Global Environment

Learning Objectives

1. Describe the changing pattern of international business.

2. Identify major factors affecting international business.

3. Determine key decisions firms face when contemplating foreign expansion.

4. Differentiate the various ways firms can enter foreign markets.

5. Identify alternative ways of managing a foreign operation.

6. Recognize the key human resource policies that firms can develop to help expatriates succeed.

7. Understand the ethical and social responsibility implications of doing business in different countries.

Toys That Travel the World

Playmobil's sturdy little toys are popular in many countries around the world. In fact, they may now be more popular in other countries than they are in their native Germany.

The problem is not that German children don't enjoy the figures of farmers, policemen, knights, pirates, and soccer players, or the finely detailed ships, planes, castles, and other environments the toys inhabit. The award-winning play sets are designed to spark imaginative and independent make-believe play and are manufactured to last for generations. They appeal strongly to their primary audience: boys and, to a lesser degree, girls between 3 and 9. The problem is, German couples aren't having enough children to bring the toy business out of the four-year slump plaguing the German economy as a whole. Families are small, and spending on all sort of consumer goods is down, including cars, refrigerators, electronics—and toys.

Playmobil's manufacturer, the family-owned company Geobra Brandstätter, didn't wait for the bad news to arrive before it turned to overseas sales. Playmobil toys have already been popular abroad for many years and sell well in France, Italy, and Canada, in particular. The company earns nearly two-thirds of its $448 million in sales every year from countries other than Germany. CEO Andrea Schauer would like to expand sales in the United States, Latin America, and Asia, too. In fact, her strategy is one that many German companies are falling back on, sending German exports skyrocketing even as the unemployment rate, hammered by big layoffs at companies like Volkswagen, hovers around 12 percent. "You don't need a strong home base for sales anymore," says a Goldman Sachs economist in Frankfurt, Germany. "You just need Germany to be a good base for manufacturing."

For Playmobil, Germany remains a good manufacturing base despite high labor costs. With pay-per-hour rates quite a few times higher in Germany than in, say, China, where nearly three-quarters of the world's toys are now made, Playmobil still prefers to make most of its products in a factory a few miles away from headquarters. The reason is quality. "You can get any level of quality in China," says Schauer. "The question is, at what cost?" Changes in that policy may come, but Schauer doesn't see it happening for several years.

Another advantage of the decision to keep manufacturing at home is flexibility to adjust production quickly to meet demand. Still, Playmobil does outsource some of its manufacturing to Malta and some assembly work to the Czech Republic. And Germany remains important as a testing ground for new toy ideas, like World Cup soccer figures with moveable limbs and a Soccer Shoot-Out play set. Schauer plans still more new figures, including classic fairy-tale characters, and hopes the new products will appeal to more girls as well as to older boys. "It would be difficult if we had to learn that [Germany] is a market where we can't grow any longer," she says. "But we would find strategies to overcome that." Look for new toys coming soon to a store near you.

Sources: www.playmobil.com, accessed February 27, 2006; Mark Landler, "Selling Well Everywhere but Home," *The New York Times*, February 3, 2006, pp. C1 and C4; Natascha Gewaltig. "Can Germany Escape the Doldrums?" *BusinessWeek Online*, February 13, 2006, www.businessweek.com; "Coming Soon to a Rug Near You," *PR Newswire*, February 9, 2006, www.prnewswire.com.

CRITICAL THINKING QUESTIONS

1. *What international trends are exemplified by Playmobil's increasing dependence on foreign markets?*

2. *What social and economic trends within Germany have influenced Playmobil's corporate strategies?*

3. *What factors would influence Playmobil to change its strategy and decide to manufacture Playmobil toys abroad, say, in China?*

We'll revisit these questions in our Concluding Thoughts at the end of the chapter after you have had an opportunity to read the chapter material, which should give you a better understanding of the issues raised.

The Environment of International Business

global shift

A term used to characterize the effects of changes in the competitive landscape prompted by worldwide competition.

The world of international competition is one which eliminates companies that fail to adapt. The term **global shift** characterizes the effects of changes in the competitive landscape prompted by worldwide competition. Global shift means the international business environment is changing faster than ever. In industries ranging from automobiles to steel, banking to financial services, airlines to shipping, and low-technology manufacturing to R&D-intensive firms, each individual company faces a growing number of competitors for whom national barriers are almost irrelevant. In other words, the international business environment is forcing many firms to see the entire world as the stage for manufacturing, production,[1] and marketing. Old animosities must be replaced by a new, more global view, as described in the opening vignette about Playmobil. According to one observer, "We are moving away from an economic system in which national markets are distinct entities, isolated from each other by trade barriers and barriers of distance, time and culture, and toward a system in which national markets are merging into one huge global marketplace. . . . In many industries it is no longer meaningful to talk about the 'German market,' the 'American market,' or the 'Japanese market'; there is only the 'global market.'"[2]

The Changing Pattern of International Business

International competition is fierce in this new millennium. Successful firms survive by creating high-quality, competitively priced products and services. These goods must be well received both locally and globally. Some of the major developments in the global business community are a changing world output and world trade picture; lower trade barriers; integrated economic markets; global consumer preferences; technological innovation; globalized production; and management across cultures. See Figure 2.1 on page 54.

CHANGING WORLD OUTPUT AND WORLD TRADE PICTURE Four major changes in the world output and world trade picture occurred during the last few decades. This period corresponds to the time when most of the senior executives now in charge of major corporations were in low- to mid-level management positions.

First, the United States no longer dominates the world economy. World output attributed to the United States was almost 40 percent lower at the start of the new century than in the 1960s. Similarly, the percentage of world exports of manufactured goods represented by goods from the United States in the 1990s was about half what it had been in the 1960s.[3] In the first decade of this century, this trend seems to be accelerating. Since the U.S. economy grew at an average of approximately 3 percent annually during this period, this decline means that other economies, such as Germany's and those in Asia, grew even faster. While powerhouses such as Japan and Germany have not done as well in the 2000s, China has been making enormous strides and is quickly becoming a major economic world player (see Figure 2.2 "China's New Heights" on page 55).[4]

Second, large U.S. multinationals no longer dominate international business. In the mid-1970s, U.S. firms made up almost half of the largest multinationals, while Japanese firms accounted for only 3.5 percent of them. By the mid-1990s, Japan and the United States were nearly even, with Japanese firms accounting for 29.8 percent and U.S. firms for 30.2 percent.[5] Small and medium-sized businesses, many of them in rapidly industrializing Asian countries, are becoming "mini-multinationals" in the late-2000s. This trend is opening the door to greater participation in the world economy for countries that traditionally remained on the sidelines. For instance, Sainco is a relatively small high-technology firm focusing on electronic control devices. Located in Seville, Spain, Sainco was started from scratch about 30 years ago. Today, the company has facilities in more than 10 developing countries and does close to 70 percent of its business internationally.

Third, the centrally planned communist economies that made up roughly half the world suddenly became accessible to Western businesses during the late 1980s. Before that, their international dealings were often guided by political rather than economic considerations. Although the economies of formerly communist nations and the few remaining communist enclaves are not robust, most of these countries are committed to free market economics. Over time, they are likely to have a major effect on international trade. For instance, Shanghai and other Chinese provinces and cities have the fastest growing economies in the world and, if current trends continue, China's per capita income could approach that of southern European countries by the year 2020. China has almost a third of the world's population, so the global economic consequences would be enormous. In Europe, eight of the 10 new members that entered the European Union in 2004 (discussed in some detail below) are formerly communist countries that

Perhaps the single most important innovation affecting globalization has been the development of the microprocessor, shown here being manufactured by two technicians. Not only has it enabled the explosive growth of high-power, low-cost computing, but it has vastly increased the amount of information that can be processed by individuals and firms.

FIGURE 2.1

Major Global Business
Developments

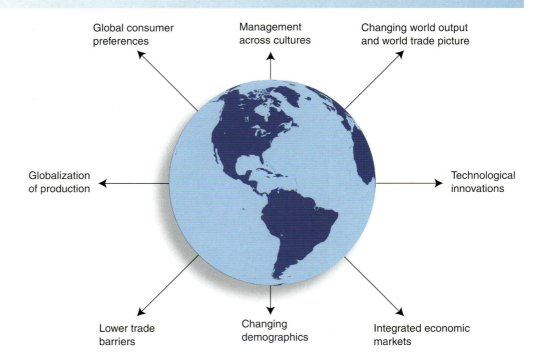

Global consumer preferences

Management across cultures

Changing world output and world trade picture

Globalization of production

Technological innovations

Lower trade barriers

Changing demographics

Integrated economic markets

used to have tightly controlled economies (Latvia, Estonia, Lithuania, Poland, Hungary, Czech Republic, Slovakia, and Slovenia). Most Europeans that form part of the 25-nation bloc of 450 million people also expect to expand the European Union in the future to include Russia and Romania, which were previous hard core communist nations.[6]

Finally, the global economy has become more knowledge-intensive and national barriers to labor markets are falling. This means that a growing number of firms consider the entire world their labor market, and companies now hire talent wherever it may be found. For instance, Delphi Automotive Systems (which filed for bankruptcy in the United States in 2005) had 66,000 employees in 51 plants around Mexico in 2006 (see www.maquilaportal.com). India, which graduates more than 200,000 lawyers a year, now provides litigation support for many law firms in the United States.[7] Foreign recruitment is no longer exclusively the province of companies in more developed nations. China's new companies are wooing away executives from such well-known multinationals as Microsoft, Morgan Stanley, Nokia, Procter & Gamble, and Motorola.[8] Japan, India, and to a lesser extent Mexico are also attracting European and American talent to some of their firms.[9]

CHANGING DEMOGRAPHICS   In general, the population is getting older in the industrialized countries. Western Europe would have actually dropped in population during the past two decades had it not received several dozen millions of immigrants, mostly from prior colonies (it is estimated that approximately 200 million people now live in countries other than their place of birth). In 2003, Estonia's president sounded an unusual warning to his 1.4 million countrymen: "Let us remember," said Arnold Ruutel in a live TV address, "that in just a couple of decades the number of Estonians seeing the New Year will be one-fifth less than today."[10]

That same downward trend in birth rates is apparently taking place in other parts of the world, although it is not as severe (see Table 2.1 on page 56). This means that both the business and government sectors must be more attuned to the needs of older people. It also means that the management of diversity (see Chapter 11) is likely to become more important in the future as richer countries experience rising levels of both legal and illegal immigration from poorer countries.

FIGURE 2.2

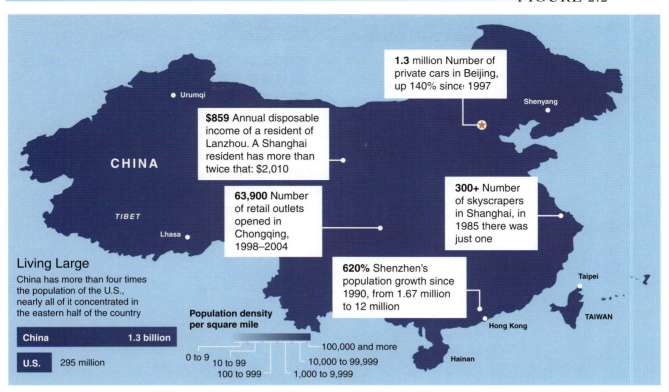

Living Large

China has more than four times the population of the U.S., nearly all of it concentrated in the eastern half of the country

China	**1.3 billion**
U.S.	295 million

1.3 million Number of private cars in Beijing, up 140% since 1997

$859 Annual disposable income of a resident of Lanzhou. A Shanghai resident has more than twice that: $2,010

63,900 Number of retail outlets opened in Chongqing, 1998–2004

300+ Number of skyscrapers in Shanghai, in 1985 there was just one

620% Shenzhen's population growth since 1990, from 1.67 million to 12 million

Population density per square mile

0 to 9   10 to 99   100 to 999   1,000 to 9,999   10,000 to 99,999   100,000 and more

China by the Numbers

- Mobile-phone text messages sent last year: 218 billion
- Percentage of the world's ice cream consumed: 20%
- Percentage of Chinese with a positive view of the U.S.-China relations: 63%
- Communist Party officials disciplined for corruption last year: 170,850

- Percentage of counterfeit goods seized at U.S. borders that come from China: 66%
- World ranking in automobile deaths: 1
- Percentage of urban Chinese with a college education: 5.6%
- Percentage of rural Chinese with a college education: 0.2%

- Estimated rural Chinese who have never brushed their teeth: 500 million
- Engineer graduates per year: half a million plus
- Smokers: 350 million

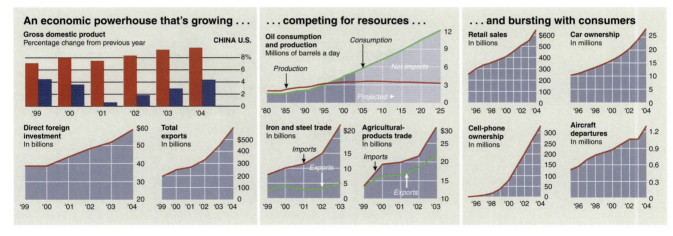

China's New Heights

Source: Adapted with permission from B. Hannah, E. Chaim, F. Mathew, J. Susan, K. Shannon, and E. Shannon, "Small World, Big Stakes," *Time*, June 27, 2005, pp. 30–44.

LOWER TRADE BARRIERS   For many years, most industrialized countries placed high tariffs on foreign goods in order to protect domestic producers. Countries such as West Germany, Italy, and Great Britain imposed tariffs that averaged about 25 percent of the value of the goods in the 1950s. Developing countries followed a policy of "import substitution" designed to stimulate domestic industry by establishing artificially high prices for foreign producers. These tariffs often exceeded 100 percent of the value of the product.

table 2.1

Malthus May Have Been Wrong

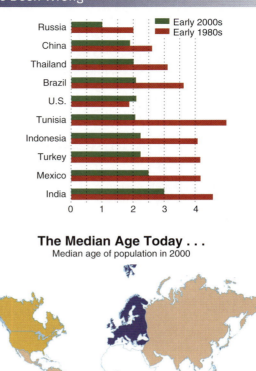

The chart shows fertility rates (children per woman), Early 2000s (green) vs. Early 1980s (red):

Russia	
China	
Thailand	
Brazil	
U.S.	
Tunisia	
Indonesia	
Turkey	
Mexico	
India	

The Median Age Today . . .
Median age of population in 2000

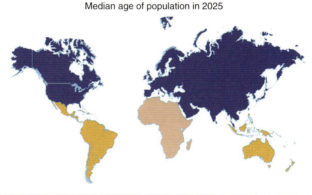

Up to 20 ▢   20 to 30 ▢   30 to 40 ▢   40 and up ▢

Increases in the Future
Median age of population in 2025

Source: From G. Naik, et al., "Malthus May Have Been Wrong," *The Wall Street Journal*, January 24, 2003, p. B-1. Copyright © 2003 by Dow Jones & Co., Inc. Reproduced with permission of Dow Jones & Co., Inc. via Copyright Clearance Center.

Most countries now realize that nationalistic trade policies do not work. Consumers pay higher prices for lower-quality goods when competition is curtailed. Also, countries are tempted to progressively raise trade barriers against each other, depressing world demand. This was a major factor behind the worldwide depression of the 1930s. As firms disperse production around the globe in search of cost efficiencies, identifying a product with a particular country has become increasingly difficult. A tariff on "foreign" products harms domestic firms and the citizens of the country that imposes the tariff because companies within that country miss out on global business opportunities. A University of Kentucky study credits Toyota's Georgetown presence with creating 22,000 jobs in the state, of which 6,500 were in the plant itself, and adding $1.5 billion to Kentucky's economy during its first eight years in operation.[11] Lower trade restrictions led to this economic windfall for the state.

Although protectionism is still popular in some quarters—including some U.S. politicians, industry associations, and union leaders who advocate "buy American" legislation—trade barriers continue their downward trend.[12] In the 2000s, tariff rates imposed by various countries are generally three to five times lower than in the 1950s. The goal of removing tariffs is embodied in the comprehensive **General Agreement on Tariffs and Trade (GATT)** treaty signed by 120 nations. Under GATT there have been eight rounds of negotiations, resulting in a lowering of trade barriers for manufactured goods and services. In 1993, the GATT negotiations in Uruguay, known as the Uruguay Round, created a **World Trade Organization (WTO)** to ensure compliance by member nations.

INTEGRATED ECONOMIC MARKETS Economic integration between groups of countries in a particular geographical area is gaining momentum, and today there are 33 such agreements, compared to 11 in the 1980s. The objective of economic integration is to reduce or eliminate barriers to the free flow of goods, services, labor, capital, and other inputs of production between member nations. The 25-member European Union (EU) has achieved the highest level of political and economic integration, allowing unrestricted movement of merchandise, people, and capital among member countries. The EU has also established a uniform set of product standards and financial regulations, a common central bank, and monetary union, although some management issues still remain unresolved. In 2004, the EU expanded by incorporating eastern European countries that were once behind the "iron curtain" as well as such "fringe" countries as Malta and Cyprus. Turkey is currently negotiating with the EU for future membership. One of the challenges facing the EU in the future is how to manage an increasingly diverse group of countries, some whose economies (such as Poland and Lithuania) are far behind those 15 EU members that formed the union up to 2004.

Attempts to pass a so-called European constitution failed in 2005, and glitches remain in the European Union that require companies to adapt their products to individual countries.[13] For instance, Kellogg, of Battle Creek, Michigan, has to manufacture four different varieties of corn flakes and other cereals at its plants in Manchester, England, and Bremen, Germany, to satisfy different vitamin and folic acid requirements set by countries such as Denmark, the Netherlands, and Finland.[14] Caterpillar Inc., which sells tractors throughout Europe, faces a similar situation. In Germany it must install a louder backup horn and locate lights in different places. The yield signs and license-plate holders on the backs of vehicles must be different, sometimes by just centimeters, from country to country. All this means that companies must still be flexible to respond to these political realities, even in one of the most economically integrated regions of the world.

In the Americas, the major economic alliance, **the North American Free Trade Act (NAFTA)**, is now more than 12 years old, and despite its controversial beginning (many feared it would lead to massive job losses), it is now viewed positively by most politicians and business leaders on both the American and Mexican sides of the border.

Ratified in 1994 by the United States, Mexico, and Canada, NAFTA eliminated tariff and most nontariff barriers among member nations in 2004. It also allows for the free flow of agricultural products between the United States and Mexico by 2009. Most experts agree that NAFTA has confounded many predictions by increasing U.S. employment rather than moving U.S. jobs to Mexico.

General Agreement on Tariffs and Trade (GATT)

A treaty signed by 120 nations to lower trade barriers for manufactured goods and services.

World Trade Organization (WTO)

Organization created in 1993 to ensure compliance with GATT.

NAFTA

The major economic alliance in the Americas.

FIGURE 2.3

Economic Communities:
Selected Economic Partnerships That Are Working to
Improve the Economic Conditions of Citizens

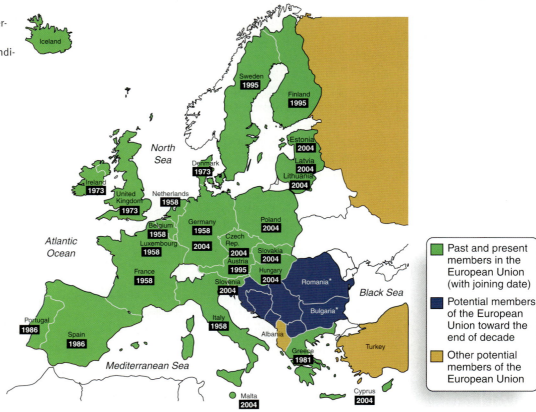

Similar to NAFTA, the Central American–Dominican Republic Free Trade Agreement was ratified in 2005 between the United States and five Central American Countries, Costa Rica, El Salvador, Guatemala, Honduras, Nicaragua, and the Dominican Republic. The six are home to 44 million people. The treaty (known as CAFTA) makes more than 80 percent of U.S. exports duty free immediately, with remaining tariffs phased out over 10 years. Other economic unions in the Americas, namely Mercosur (composed of Brazil, Uruguay, Paraguay, and Chile) and the Andean Pact (Boliva, Peru, Colombia, Ecuador, and Venezuela) do not involve the United States directly. Political winds at the time of this writing (2006) do not seem highly supportive of an expanded free-trade zone between the United States and these South American countries, but this could well change in the next few years. A major issue of contention appears to be agricultural subsidies in the United States (which is also an issue with European Union) to protect domestic farmers; South American countries see this as a problem since most of their exports are related to agriculture.

Two major regional economic groups are present in Asia. The oldest is the Association of Southeast Asian Nations, or ASEAN, formed in 1967. It includes Brunei, Indonesia, Laos, Malaysia, Myanmar, Philippines, Singapore, Thailand, and Vietnam. While its intent is to foster trade among its members and achieve greater economic cooperation, progress has been slow.

The second is the Asia Pacific Economic Cooperation (APEC) group, founded in 1990. This group of countries has the potential to become highly influential if it were to turn itself into a free trade area. Doing so would make it the world's largest trade bloc, because the 18 member states account for more than half of the world's GNP. The APEC group consists of countries such as China, Japan, and the United States. Several well-publicized meetings have been held among the heads of state with the intent of removing their trade and investment barriers by 2010 for the richest members and by 2020 for the poorest members. However, some members complain that the plan is vague and commits APEC members to doing little more than holding additional meetings.[15]

GLOBAL CONSUMER PREFERENCES Consumer tastes and preferences are converging, even though some national differences persist. The success of such firms as Coca-Cola, Levi Strauss, Taco Bell, Sony, and McDonald's illustrates this trend. Part of the reason for the development of worldwide tastes and preferences is the presence of the mass media, exposure to goods from various countries, and marketing strategies of multinational firms that tend to offer standardized products worldwide, because doing so costs less than customizing goods to local conditions.

GLOBALIZED PRODUCTION To be cost efficient, firms are increasingly splitting up production around the world to take advantage of other countries' ability to perform parts of the process better for less money. By establishing a global web of production activities, firms hope to achieve the highest quality standards at the lowest possible cost. For instance, of the $20,000 sticker price of a General Motors Chevrolet LeMans,

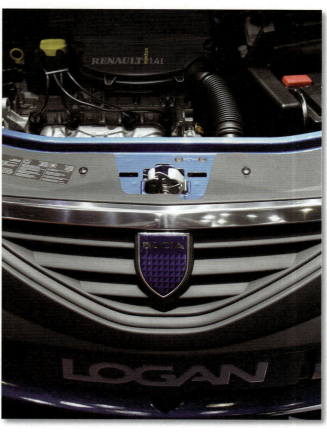

The French automaker Renault discovered how much consumer tastes are converging when demand for its new midsize sedan, the Logan, spilled over into other Western European countries such as Germany and Spain and generated a months-long waiting list. Renault had planned to produce a low-cost car for emerging markets like Poland and Romania and designed the stripped-down Logan to sell there for as little as $6,000. But utilitarian cars are the hottest trend in Western Europe, where, according to one French driver who bought a slightly upgraded version of the car, "The Logan is a genius idea."

- $6,000 goes to South Korea, where the car is assembled.
- $3,000 goes to Japan for sophisticated high-tech parts, including engines, transaxles, and electronics.
- $800 goes to Taiwan, Singapore, and Japan for small parts.
- $500 goes to Great Britain to cover advertising and marketing services.
- $1,000 goes to Ireland for data processing.
- About $7,600 goes to GM and to the lawyers, bankers, insurance agents, and consultants that GM uses in the United States.[16]

TECHNOLOGICAL INNOVATIONS Technology has made what was once impossible possible. In 1990, it would have been a logistical nightmare to build the Boeing 777 by outsourcing 132,500 parts to suppliers around the world. Now, Boeing outsources most of the components for the Boeing 777 commercial jet aircraft to 545 of the best suppliers around the world, and these companies produce the 132,500 engineered parts.[17]

Advances in communications, information processing, and transportation technology have made today's large international business feasible. Fiber optics, wireless technology, and the Internet and World Wide Web make it possible to process a vast amount of information at very low cost. For example, the cost of a three-minute phone call from London to New York fell from $13.73 in 1973 to about $4.30 by the late 1990s. By 2006 the cost had fallen to pennies.

Many firms depend on satellite technology to link worldwide operations and integrate plants and activities. Texas Instruments uses satellite technology to link 50 plants in 19 countries and to coordinate production planning, cost

Global Is Local in a New World Order of Business

A group of IBM computer programmers at Tsinghua University in Beijing writes software using Java technology. At the end of each day, the work is sent via the Internet to an IBM facility in Seattle, where programmers build on it during their workday. Then, the Seattle programmers send the working files another 5,222 miles to the Institute of Computer Science in Belarus and Software House Group in Latvia, which work on it and send it east to India's Tata Group. The Tata Group sends the software back to Tsinghua by morning in Beijing. The cycle continues until the project is done. "We call it Java Around the Clock," says John Patrick, vice president of Internet technology for IBM. "It's like we've created a 48-hour day through the Internet."

Communications technology has transformed the world into a single work place. As in the IBM programming cycle, workers collaborate in different locations using a computer network in ways they never could before. Caterpillar's global engineers in different countries simultaneously collaborate on tractor designs with a 3-D model over a computer network. ParaGraph International, a software company started by a Russian, Stepan Pachikov, links product development in Moscow and Campbell, California. The 50,000 employees at Schlumberger, a technology services company, work around the world but stay connected through the Schlumberger Information Network.

The Internet creates possibilities far beyond the phone or private data networks that used to be the backbone of international business. The Web is inexpensive and open to customers and suppliers worldwide, not just to the company's workers. Says Irving Wladawsky-Berger, head of IBM's Internet division, "The difference between Peoria and Romania on the Web is not very large."

In 2006, MCI was the world's largest provider of conferencing services, according to Telespan publishing. Its products include audio, video and Web conferencing, and related services, which help organizations worldwide to meet more productively without the time and costs associated with business travel. This enables companies such as Boeing, which has a multiyear agreement with MCI, "to create an efficient virtual collaboration environment."

The cost of doing business globally has also diminished thanks to technology. Eastman Chemical found the cost of three or four managers in the United States is the same as the cost of stationing one U.S. manager abroad; its U.S.-based managers can now use communication technology to manage by long distances. Of the company's 1,500 employees who work outside the United States, only 130 are Americans.

Sources: Adapted from MCI, Inc., "Boeing to Utilize MCI's Audioconfering Services to Speed Collaboration among Employees Worldwide," www.prnewswire.com, 2006; K. Maney, "Technology Is Demolishing Time, Distance," *USA Today*, February 28, 1999, p. A1; and special issue of *BusinessWeek* on globalization, February 3, 2003.

---

accounting, financial planning, marketing, customer service, and the personnel function.[18] Management Close-Up 2.1, "Global Is Local in a New World Order of Business" above, provides other examples of how technology is diminishing both time and distance challenges.

MANAGEMENT ACROSS CULTURES Culture still plays a major role in shaping consumer preferences and tastes. For instance, "Mattel's Barbie doll was a faltering product in Japan until marketing research determined that few Japanese identified with the Americanized doll. For the Japanese, Barbie was too tall, too long legged, and her blue eyes were the wrong color. Mattel produced a Japanized Barbie—shorter, with brown eyes, and a more Asian figure. Not surprisingly, 2 million Barbies were sold in two years."[19] When Arab satellite TV network MBC decided to introduce "The Simpsons" to the Middle East in 2005, Homer was called "Omar" and drank Coke, not beer.[20]

International firms often respond to local needs by customizing products and the marketing strategies which are designed to meet different consumer tastes. At the same time, successful firms try to create a need for their products without costly adaptations (even though management needs to be flexible to re-

Ikea Is Conquering the Global Furniture and Accessories Retail Market

Ikea, the Swedish retailer, has become a global cult brand around the world, with more than 230 stores in Europe, Asia, and Australia welcoming 410 million shoppers a year. What enthralls shoppers is the store visit — a similar experience the world over. The blue and yellow buildings average 300,000 square feet in size, about equal to five football fields. The sheer number of items — 7,000 products from kitchen cabinets to candlesticks — is a decisive advantage. "Others offer affordable furniture," says Bryan Roberts, research manager at Planet Retail, a consultancy in London. "But there's no one else who offers the whole concept in the big shed." The global middle class that Ikea targets shares buying habits. The $120 Billy bookcase, $13 Lack side table, and $190 Ivar storage system are best-sellers worldwide. (U.S. prices are used throughout this Close-Up.) Spending per customer is similar across different countries. According to Ikea, the figure in Russia is $85 per store visit — exactly the same as in affluent Sweden. To keep customers coming back, Ikea replaces a third of its product line each year.

Customer focus is so intense that even senior management must work behind cash registers and in the warehouse for brief stints every year. And the company maintains a close pulse on what customers want, asking suppliers and designers to customize Ikea products as necessary to make them sell better in local markets. For instance, in China, the 250,000 plastic placemats Ikea produced to commemorate the year of the rooster sold out in just three weeks. Julie Desrosiers, the bedroom line manager at Ikea of Sweden, visited people's houses in the United States and Europe to peek into their closets, learning that "Americans prefer to store most of their clothes folded, and Italians like to hang." The result was a wardrobe that features deeper drawers for U.S. customers.

The U.S. market poses special challenges for Ikea because of the huge differences within the country. "It's so easy to forget the reality of how people live," says Ikea's U.S. interior design director, Mats Nilsson. Recently, Ikea realized it might not be reaching California's Hispanics. So its designers visited the homes of Hispanic staff. They soon realized they had set up the store's displays all wrong. Large Hispanic families need dining tables and sofas that fit more than two people, the Swedish norm. They prefer bold colors to the more subdued Scandinavian palette and display tons of pictures in elaborate frames.

As Ikea has expanded its warehouse-style furniture and accessories stores worldwide, it's attracted millions of devoted consumers striving to enter the middle class. With over 225 stores in Europe, Asia, Australia, and the United States, including this one in Saudi Arabia, the store has hit on the right combination of mass-market products, like its best-selling Billy bookcases, and products customized for specific markets, like rooster placemats for China in the year of the rooster and more boldly colored showrooms for Hispanic neighborhoods in the United States.

Nilsson warmed up the showrooms' colors, adding more seating and throwing in numerous picture frames.

Ikea is particularly concerned about the United States since it's key to expansion — and since Ikea came close to blowing it in the 1990s. Beds were measured in centimeters, not king, queen, and twin. Sofas weren't deep enough, curtains were too short, and kitchens didn't fit U.S.-size appliances. "American customers were buying vases to drink from because the glasses were too small," recalls Goran Carstedt, the former head of Ikea North America, who helped engineer a turnaround. Parts of the product line were adapted (no more metric measurements), new and bigger store locations chosen, prices slashed, and service improved. Now U.S. managers are paying close attention to the tiniest details. "Americans want more comfortable sofas, higher-quality textiles, bigger glasses, more spacious entertainment units," says Pernille Spiers-Lopez, head of Ikea North America.

Source: Adapted from A. Sains, A. J. Palmer, J. Bush, D. Roberts, and K. Hall, "Ikea: How the Swedish Retailer Became a Global Cult Brand," *BusinessWeek*, November 14, 2005, pp. 95–106.

spond to customer desires). One good example is Ikea, the Swedish retailer, which in relatively few years has been able to establish a global cult brand around the world while remaining highly sensitive to local needs (see Management Close-Up 2.2, "Ikea Is Conquering the Global Furniture and Accessories Retail Market" above).

Lastly, firms establishing ventures overseas may need to adapt business strategies, structures, operational policies, and human resource programs to the culture. For instance, nepotism, or the hiring of relatives, is discouraged in Anglo-Saxon countries, but it is a common practice in many southern European, South American, and Asian countries.

Major Factors Affecting International Business

As firms internationalize to take advantage of global opportunities and to meet the competition, they need to consider factors that vary across countries and that are often very different from the familiar domestic setting. These factors include the general business environment, the legal system, economic conditions, and cultural norms.

GENERAL BUSINESS ENVIRONMENT   The general business environment of a country consists of all the factors that combine to affect the benefits, costs, and risks of conducting business in that country. Benefits are affected by the size of the market, the purchasing power of the population, and most important, the likely future wealth of consumers. Sometimes these factors can change unexpectedly. For example, Argentina was one of the eight wealthiest countries in the world until the 1940s, then fell below the top 40 by 2004 in part due to political instability, mismanagement of the economy, and widespread corruption. South Korea, on the other hand, was a very poor third-world nation in 1960. It is currently one of the 10 largest economies in the world and the fourth largest trading nation after Japan, the United States, and Germany.

The cost of doing business varies greatly from country to country. It may be necessary to make payments to the government or the political elite, or there may not be an appropriate infrastructure, or adherence to regulations may involve a major financial commitment. In some European countries, for example, it is necessary to give employees a month's paid vacation, numerous government-mandated holidays, and double pay for Christmas. McDonald's discovered that it had to develop dairy and vegetable farms, cattle ranches, and food-processing plants in Russia in order to serve food that met its quality standards in its Moscow outlet.

Operating in a foreign country also involves risk. Risks come in three forms and vary dramatically from nation to nation. *Political risk*, which is common in developing countries, may involve government changes (often by force), social unrest, strikes, terrorism, and violent conflict. Political risk may also come in more subtle forms, particularly in richer countries. For instance, both President Jacques Chirac and Prime Minister Dominique Villepin of France reacted to Hewlett-Packard Co.'s announcement in 2005 that it would lay off 1,200 workers in France by proposing that "companies might be required to sign a code of conduct limiting their ability to lay off workers if, as in HP's case, the government financed road works and other improvements benefitting their factories."[21] There are several well-known consulting and

Political risk is always present in overseas operations. French workers' fears that jobs are being lost to lower-cost countries in Eastern Europe and Asia sparked protests such as this one in Grenoble. These picketers were reacting to Hewlett-Packard's announcement that it would cut hundreds of jobs, or about half its French workforce. The French government is considering limiting the rights of foreign firms to lay of their French employees, particularly if the government has helped the firms establish their operations there.

publishing firms that provide up-to-date information on political risks country by country. These include:[22]

- Bank of America World Information Services
- Business Environment Risk Intelligence (BERI) S.A.
- Control Risks Information Services
- Economist Intelligence Unit (EIU)
- Euromoney
- Institutional Investor
- Standard and Poor's Rating Group
- Moody's Investor Services

A firm may also be exposed to *economic risk*. Some countries, such as Bolivia, have experienced annual inflation rates exceeding 26,000 percent, while others, such as Russia, make it difficult for foreign firms to get paid in hard currency (such as U.S. dollars) that can be repatriated to corporate headquarters, or may be riddled with corruption. Finally, firms may incur *legal risks.* For instance, some governments insist on local or government ownership of a percentage of equity of foreign firms. In other countries, intellectual property rights are not adequately protected. The illegal reproduction of CDs and software is a booming business in some Asian countries, and estimated annual losses exceed $2.2 billion.[23] And practices that are perfectly legal in the United States may be illegal overseas. For example, the European Union in 2005 banned Coca-Cola Co. from offering volume-linked rebates as well as from signing exclusivity deals with retailers (which is not uncommon in the United States). Coca-Cola now has to hand over as much as 20 percent of the room in its European coolers and vending machines to rivals such as Pepsi-Co Inc. to stock their own brands. If Coke is found in violation of this European Union order, "it faces the possibility of massive penalties of 10 percent of its worldwide revenue, the equivalent of 2.2 billion dollars."[24]

LEGAL SYSTEMS   The legal system of a nation consists of the rules defining what is permissible or illegal, the process for enforcing the laws, and the procedures available to redress grievances. A country's legal system reflects its culture, religion, and traditions. A firm must comply with the host country's legal system.

In general, there are three major types of legal systems. Countries with an Anglo-Saxon background or influence rely on **common law,** in which precedents based on past court decisions play a key role in interpreting the meaning and intent of legal statutes. This legal system is used in the United States and 26 other countries. **Civil law** relies on a comprehensive set of rules that form part of a highly structured code, and enforcement and interpretation of laws are made in reference to this code. About 70 countries, including most European nations and Japan, use a civil law system. **Muslim law,** based on religious beliefs, regulates behavior in approximately 27 Islamic countries, although interpretations and levels of enforcement vary significantly from country to country.

ECONOMIC ENVIRONMENT   Firms entering international markets are subject to unpredictable economic shifts that may have major effects on earnings. High inflation is one example, as in the Bolivian case noted above. The *exchange rate,* or the rate at which the market converts one currency into another, may also fluctuate. A devaluation occurs when more local currency is necessary to obtain a given amount of foreign currency, in effect making the local currency worth less outside the country. Companies are normally paid in local currency and later convert it into the currencies of their home countries. If the local currency is devalued relative to the company's domestic currency, the firm may receive less value for its products or services than was expected. To maintain profit levels, the firm must raise its prices, which may lead to fewer sales in the future.

Between late December 1994 and mid-January 1995, the value of the Mexican peso dropped 40 percent relative to the dollar, and U.S. firms in Mexico experienced an abrupt decline in revenues. Wal-Mart's Mexican stores were selling merchandise purchased with American dollars prior to the devaluation. Chrysler, Ford, and General Motors had imported parts from the United States and Canada to use in Mexican plants, and this caused the price of their automobiles to increase by 40 percent in early 1995, causing demand to drop between 30 percent and 50 percent below the levels attained in 1994.[25] Although the peso continued to fluctuate, by 2000 Mexico's car prices had recovered and demand had risen to almost their precrisis levels. As another example of the effect of devaluation, the French tourism industry suffered a 30 percent decrease in profits as the value of the dollar dropped up to 35 percent relative to the euro during 2003–2006 (which kept many American tourists home). After the riots that exploded in several French cities at the end of 2005, most severely in Paris, the euro dropped by approximately 10 percent almost overnight, negatively affecting U.S. firms that were repatriating European earnings back into the United States.[26]

Taxation represents another economic factor. Variations in tax policies are a major challenge to firms trying to minimize global tax liabilities. In Europe, the top corporate income tax rate ranges from 25 percent in Finland to 60 percent in Germany. An American manager sent to a subsidiary in Norway is exempted from domestic taxes for two years, but one sent to Spain must pay domestic taxes, which are far higher than in the United States, after a six-month stay. *Forbes* conducts an annual analysis of the tax burden in 47 countries

---

common law

The legal system in which precedents based on past court decisions play a key role in interpreting the meaning and intent of legal statutes.

civil law

The legal system that relies on a comprehensive set of rules that form part of a highly structured code; enforcement and interpretation of laws are made in reference to this code.

Muslim law

The legal system based on religious Muslim beliefs that regulates behavior; strict interpretation and enforcement varies significantly from country to country.

(including corporate income tax, personal income tax, wealth tax, social security, and sales tax); this annual report can be found on the Web at www.forbes.com/misery.

Also, firms that rely on technological innovations as a source of competitive advantage may have to deal with complicated licensing agreements and royalties. In Germany, royalties on patents are limited to 10 percent of sales, with the duration of patents and trademarks set at 20 years and 10 years, respectively. Egypt, on the other hand, places no limits on royalties, but only production processes may be patented and only for a maximum of 15 years.

More than 80 countries adhere to the International Convention for the Protection of Industrial Property (often referred to as the Paris Union), but the rules may be interpreted differently. What constitutes industrial espionage may also differ among countries, and firms face major risks in protecting their technology. A firm may find that its proprietary technology is copied by joint-venture partners, franchisees, licensees, and former employees who are hired by other firms, encouraged in part by lax enforcement of so-called intellectual property laws.

CULTURAL ENVIRONMENTS According to Hofstede, *culture* is the "collective programming of the mind which distinguishes the members of one group from another. . . . Culture, in this sense, includes systems of values; and values are among the building blocks of culture."[27] Culture reflects differences in the social structures, religions, languages, and historical backgrounds of various countries. **Culture shock** occurs when a person is exposed to a new culture with different norms, customs, and expectations and has difficulty adjusting.

To succeed internationally, businesses need to understand and be willing to make accommodations for cultural differences. Hofstede uses five dimensions to summarize different cultures:

1. **Power distance** is the extent to which individuals expect a hierarchical structure that emphasizes status differences between subordinates and superiors. For example, in countries that are high in power distance, such as the Philippines, Mexico, and most Arab nations, employees expect visible rewards that project power for people higher up in the organizational pyramid, such as a large office or an elegant company car.

2. **Individualism** is the degree to which a society values personal goals, autonomy, and privacy over group loyalty, commitment to group norms, involvement in collective activities, social cohesiveness, and intense socialization. In countries that are high in individualism, such as the United States, Great Britain, and New Zealand, employees believe they should look after their own interests.

3. **Uncertainty avoidance** is the extent to which a society places a high value on reducing risk and instability. Greece, Portugal, Italy, and other countries with high uncertainty avoidance have organizations with extensive rules and procedures and careful delineation of the work each individual is supposed to do.

4. **Masculinity/femininity** is the degree to which a society views assertive or "masculine" behavior as important to success and encourages rigidly stereotyped gender roles. Countries that are high in masculinity, such as Austria, Mexico, and the United States, value stereotypically male traits such as aggressiveness, initiative, and leadership.

culture shock

The reaction when exposed to other cultures with different norms, customs, and expectations.

power distance

The extent to which individuals expect a hierarchical structure that emphasizes status differences between subordinates and superiors.

Hofstede's Model of National Culture

individualism

The degree to which a society values personal goals, autonomy, and privacy over group loyalty, group norms, collective activities, social cohesiveness, and intense socialization.

uncertainty avoidance

The extent to which a society places a high value on reducing risk and instability.

masculinity/femininity

The degree to which a society views assertive or "masculine" behavior as important to success and encourages rigidly stereotyped gender roles.

Cirque du Soleil

Summary

Guy Laliberte started as a street performer, with the dream to take his group of jugglers, fire-eaters, stilt-walkers, and clowns on a world tour to have fun and entertain people. He had no idea that he was embarking on a journey that would revive the traditional circus and reinvent live entertainment, making him one of the most successful people in international business. Today, Cirque du Soleil has numerous shows playing worldwide. The troupe who originally formed Cirque in 1984 had to locate in a warmer climate, because performing under a tent in Canada year-round was not an option. So, they decided to go to Los Angeles in 1987, and were given the opportunity to do the opening show at the Los Angeles Arts Festival.

Guy hit the road around the same time that businesses around the world began moving toward globalization, taking regional businesses into the international markets. With the Cold War over, and trade barriers all over the world dropping for the first time in history, companies like Cirque found it much easier to penetrate new markets. The show was fortunately a press and public success immediately.

Cirque is not without significant challenges, however, that relate directly to globalization. First, Cirque must search the globe for specific talents in its shows. Cirque also looks to the Olympics to find talent. They do not approach an athlete until they are sure it is the athlete's last Olympics, which is an ethic the company upholds out of respect to the athletes and to their countries. Cirque faces a unique challenge because most global companies do not have to worry about the welfare of their employees during nonworking hours. Cirque concerns itself with employee welfare 24 hours a day for its traveling shows. This includes diet needs, dealing with language barriers, housing, and even homesickness.

Today, Cirque is successful as a truly global company and is giving back to the communities with which it interacts. Guy believes it is very important that the company remembers its roots and adhere to a code which emphasizes supporting the individual performers and their diverse communities.

Discussion Questions

1. How has the "global shift" contributed to the success of Cirque du Soleil? Why was this critical in the company's beginning? What about now?
2. How does management across cultures affect Cirque du Soleil? In your response, consider both consumers and employees.
3. Consider the various ways of staffing and managing international subsidiaries. Which method best resembles what Cirque does? What are the advantages and disadvantages of this system?

---

long-term/short-term orientation

The extent to which values are oriented toward the future as opposed to the past or present.

5. **Long-term/short-term orientation** is the extent to which values are oriented toward the future (saving, persistence) as opposed to the past or present (respect for tradition, fulfilling social obligations). Japan and China value employee seniority and believe that wisdom increases with age, which reflects a longer-term orientation.[28]

Figure 2.4 on page 67 shows the alignment of countries in terms of power distance and uncertainty avoidance. Latin, Mediterranean, and Far Eastern countries with relatively high masculinity and strong uncertainty avoidance make up the largest cluster, in the bottom right corner. The other clear cluster, in the top left corner, groups countries with low masculinity and weak uncertainty avoidance and includes mostly Anglo countries.

FIGURE 2.4

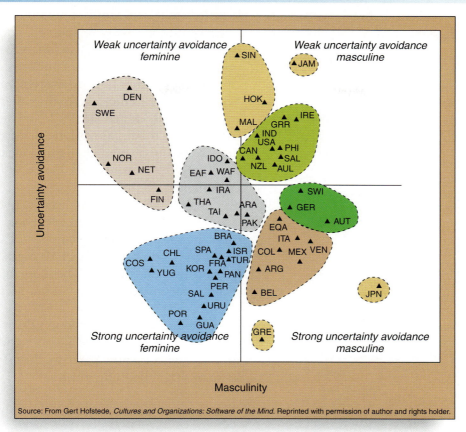

Source: From Gert Hofstede, *Cultures and Organizations: Software of the Mind.* Reprinted with permission of author and rights holder.

Abbreviations for Countries and Regions

ARA	Arab countries (Egypt, Lebanon, Libya, Kuwait, Iraq, Saudi Arabia, U.A.E.)	JAM	Jamaica
		JPN	Japan
ARG	Argentina	KOR	South Korea
AUL	Australia	MAL	Malaysia
AUT	Austria	MEX	Mexico
BRA	Brazil	NET	Netherlands
CAN	Canada	NZL	New Zealand
CHL	Chile	PAK	Pakistan
COL	Colombia	PAN	Panama
COS	Costa Rica	PER	Peru
DEN	Denmark	PHI	Philippines
EAF	East Africa (Kenya, Ethiopia, Zambia)	POR	Portugal
EQA	Equador	SAF	South Africa
FIN	Finland	SAL	El Salvador
FRA	France	SIN	Singapore
GBR	Great Britain	SPA	Spain
GER	Germany	SWE	Sweden
GRE	Greece	SWI	Switzerland
GUA	Guatemala	TAI	Taiwan
HOK	Hong Kong	THA	Thailand
IDO	Indonesia	TUR	Turkey
IND	India	URU	Uruguay
IRA	Iran	USA	United States
IRE	Ireland	VEN	Venezuela
ISR	Israel	WAF	West Africa (Nigeria, Ghana, Sierra Leone)
ITA	Italy	YUG	Yugoslavia

LOC-In

International Cultural
Diversity

As a general principle, management practices that conform to prevailing societal norms are more likely to succeed, and those that do not are more likely to fail. A firm with operations in two or more countries should carefully consider how management practices are likely to mesh with the other countries' cultural values. Table 2.2 on page 69 summarizes the organizational features and human resource management policies that work best in countries with high and low individualism.

Since 2005, there has been a noticeable trend for multinational organizations to hire executives from foreign countries, in the belief that they "can better affect change than a homegrown executive."[29] These organizations include, for instance, Sony, Nissan Motor, Renault, and Sanyo.[30]

Management Is Everyone's Business 2.1 on page 70 offers a set of recommendations for those who are now part of a cross-cultural team or might be in the future.

Entry Strategy

A firm contemplating foreign expansion faces three key entry decisions: (1) which countries to enter, (2) when to enter, and (3) scale of involvement. Each of these decisions is described in turn.

Choosing Foreign Countries

There are more than 180 countries in the world. Not all of them are equally attractive. Ultimately, the decision to sell products in a new country should be based on long-term profit potential considerations. While profit potential depends on the type of firm and what it looks for (for instance, a mining company may be most interested in the existence of certain minerals while a high technology firm may be more interested in the availability of scientific talent), in general there are some factors that most companies would consider. Other things being equal, the appeal of a particular country is likely to be greater when:

1. The size of the domestic market is large. For instance, Starbuck's has chosen China as a foreign location, even though the president of Starbuck's admits that "per capita consumption of coffee in China is very small." He quickly adds, however, that "what you have is a tremendous amount of people, so the market will grow".[31]

table 2.2

Cultural Characteristics and Dominant Values (Individualism, Organizational Characteristics, and Selected HR Practices)

DOMINANT VALUES	SAMPLE COUNTRIES	ORGANIZATIONAL FEATURES	REWARD PRACTICES	STAFFING/APPRAISAL PRACTICES
High Individualism				
Personal accomplishment	United States	Organizations not compelled to care for employees' total well-being	Performance-based pay	Emphasis on credentials and visible performance outcomes attributed to individual
Selfishness	Great Britain		Individual achievement rewarded	
Independence	Canada	Employees look after their own individual interests	External equity emphasized	High turnover; commitment to organization for career reasons
Belief in individual control and responsibility	New Zealand	Explicit systems of control necessary to ensure compliance and prevent wide deviation from organizational norms	Extrinsic rewards are important indicators of personal success	Performance rather than seniority as criterion for advancement
Belief in creating one's own destiny			Attempts made to isolate individual contributions (i.e., who did what)	"Fitting in" deemphasized; belief in performance as independent of personal likes and dislikes
Business relationship between employer and employee			Emphasis on short-term objectives	Attempts at ascertaining individual strengths and weaknesses and providing frequent feedback to employee
Low Individualism				
Team accomplishment	Singapore	Organizations committed to high-level involvement in workers' personal lives	Group-based performance is important criterion for rewards	Value of credentials and visible performance outcomes depends on perceived contributions to team efforts
Sacrifice for others	South Korea			
Dependence on social unit	Indonesia	Loyalty to the firm is critical	Seniority-based pay utilized	Low turnover; commitment to organization as "family"
Belief in group control and responsibility	Japan	Normative, rather than formal, systems of control to ensure compliance	Intrinsic rewards essential	Seniority plays an important role in personnel decisions
Belief in the hand of fate	Taiwan		Internal equity guides pay policies	"Fitting in" with work group crucial; belief that interpersonal relations are important performance dimension
Moral relationship between employer and employee			Personal needs (such as number of children) affect pay received	Limited or no performance feedback to individual to prevent conflict and defensive reactions

Source: From *Managing Human Resources* by Gomez-Mejia, et al. Copyright © 2007. Reprinted by permission of Pearson Education, Inc., Upper Saddle River, NJ.

2. The present wealth (purchasing power) of consumers in the market is high and projected to grow in the future. For instance, only about 40,000 people in the world can afford to buy a $300,000 Rolls Royce. Almost all of them are found in about 12 countries.[32] Wal-Mart is doubling its investments in Japan during 2006–2010. After years of being in the doldrums, the Japanese economy is starting to grow again. Its $1.2 trillion retail market is the world's largest after the United States.[33]

3. The needed resources are readily available. "British entrepreneur Richard Branson opened several of his Virgin Megastores in Japan despite its reputation as a tough market to crack. One reason for Branson's initial attraction to Japan was a cost of capital of only 2.5 percent—roughly one-third

Working as a Team   Many firms are entering joint ventures with companies in other countries. Joint ventures usually require that employees from different nations work in teams. Their success largely depends on the ability of international teams to work together in a climate of mutual respect. This requires not only a great deal of cultural sensitivity but also an understanding of the international context in which the firm operates. As a team member in a globalized economy you should:

- Be prepared to work closely, either physically or virtually, with employees who may be very dissimilar to you in terms of language, ethnic background, past experiences, and the like.

- Keep in mind that most other countries are far less individualistic than the United States and that the boundaries between "what I am supposed to do" and "what other specific members of the team are supposed to do" may not be as clear. In other words, as an American you might need to share more responsibilities with others than you may want to.

- Try to be humble and avoid an "ugly American" image of superiority. People in most foreign countries are very sensitive to that, and cross-national teams are quick to react to what they perceive as U.S. arrogance (even if they are all working for the same U.S. multinational).

- Be aware that social interaction, trust, and personal bonds that go beyond the particular technical issue or task at hand are important for effective teams, particularly in cross-national operations. You need to be patient and give sufficient time for those social ties to grow and strengthen, even if at first it seems like you are wasting too much time talking about nonwork related things.

- Be careful to avoid displays of wealth or discussions that might reflect your economic status (for instance, boasting about great fishing at your summer cottage or the SUV you drive). You are probably earning substantially more than locals that are part of the team, and this is likely to engender resentment.

- The team should develop procedures to ensure that everyone's ideas are considered, particularly when English proficiency may vary greatly from person to person (the individual with the best ideas may have the weakest English!).

its cost in Britain."[34] For many firms, a key factor is the availability of qualified labor at a cost that is lower than the firm would pay in the domestic labor market.

4. The firm's product offerings are suitable to a particular market. For instance, a sports firm specializing in baseball paraphernalia is likely to face an uphill battle in countries such as France and Italy, where baseball is practically unknown.

5. A positive business climate exists. Political risks, laws, business practices, and cultural norms all have a profound effect on the appeal of a particular location. A sudden change in a government may mean that contracts signed under a prior government may no longer be enforceable. Government regulations can restrict international firms from withdrawing profits. Cultural norms may influence the kinds of products that are sold and the extent to which they need to be adapted to suit local preferences. An accurate assessment of a nation's business climate is crucial when considering an international opportunity. While in the

FIGURE 2.5

Key Entry Decisions

Which country should we enter?

When should we enter?

How much should we commit?

What mode of entry should we use?

end there is some subjectivity involved in assessing the degree to which a business climate is favorable or not, firms have access to a great deal of information that can help them make this judgment. For instance, worldatlas.com (www.worldatlas.com) and the *World Factbook* (published by the CIA) provide detailed data on the sociopolitical and economic situations of most countries around the world, which is continually updated. Table 2.3 on page 72 shows a recent summary profile obtained from these sources of Mexico, China, and Japan, countries that are important to keep an eye on for many American firms competing in international markets.

When to Enter Foreign Countries

The timing of entry into a foreign market is a key consideration. Being the first to enter a market offers a *first-mover advantage* by preempting rivals, capturing demand by establishing a strong brand name, and in general making it difficult for later entrants to win business. For example, Gillette controls a large market segment in Latin America for razor blades, in part because it was the first international shaving company to move aggressively into that market. On the other hand, these advantages also have a downside. First movers face higher *pioneering costs,* such as the effort, time, and expense of entering a national market and educating consumers (particularly when the product or service is unfamiliar to local consumers). Late entrants may also learn from the experience of the first movers and perform better as a result. Kentucky Fried Chicken is generally credited with creating a market in China for American-style fast food, yet it was latecomer McDonald's which became most profitable in that market.[35] And many Western firms are learning that, in some markets, local companies can "learn the ropes" quickly from the foreign firm and become major competitors. For instance, India (which graduates more than 300,000 qualified engineers a year, and whose universities award 2.5 million more degrees) is quickly catching up with the likes of IBM and Microsoft, which have large investments there. India's annual software exports have gone from nonexistent to $42 billion in barely a decade and are likely to reach $87 billion by 2008.[36]

table 2.3

Select Country Profiles: The Cases of Mexico, China and Japan

Mexico

Mexico has a population of approximately 105 million. A third of the population is under the age of 14. Almost 90 percent of Mexico's exports go to the United States, and 75 percent of its imports come from the United States. Mexico is the largest U.S. trading partner. Gross domestic product per capita is $9,600 a year. Spanish is the official language but various Mayan, Nahuatl, and other indigenous languages are also spoken. Approximately 60 percent of the population is mestizo (Native American–Spanish), 30 percent Native American, 9 percent of European origin, and 1 percent from other ethnic groups.

The site of advanced Amerindian civilizations, Mexico was under Spanish rule for three centuries before achieving independence early in the nineteenth century. Ongoing economic and social concerns include low real wages, underemployment for a large segment of the population, inequitable income distribution, and few advancement opportunities for the largely Amerindian population in the impoverished southern states.

Mexico has a free market economy that recently entered the trillion-dollar class. It contains a mixture of modern and outmoded industry and agriculture, increasingly dominated by the private sector. Recent administrations have expanded competition in seaports, railroads, telecommunications, electricity generation, natural gas distribution, and airports. Per capita income is one-fourth that of the United States; income distribution remains highly unequal. Trade with the United States and Canada has tripled since the implementation of NAFTA in 1994. Mexico has 12 free-trade agreements with over 40 countries, including Guatemala, Honduras, El Salvador, the European Union, and Japan, putting more than 90 percent of its trade under free-trade agreements. The government is cognizant of the need to upgrade infrastructure, modernize the system and labor laws, and provide incentives to invest in the energy sector, but progress is slow.

China

China's population is almost five times greater than that of the United States even though its territory is slightly smaller (over 1.3 billion inhabitants). Mandarin is the official language of business, though there are many dialects. Twenty-one percent of China's exports are to the United States, while 10 percent of its imports come from the United States. Gross domestic product per capita is $3,600 a year.

In late 1978, the Chinese leadership began moving the economy from a sluggish Soviet-style centrally planned economy to a more market-oriented system. The system operates within a political framework of strict communist control; however, the economic influence of non-state managers and enterprises has been steadily increasing. China's authorities have switched to a system of household responsibility in agriculture in place of the old collectivization. The government has increased the authority of local officials and plant managers in industry, permitted a wide variety of small-scale enterprise in services and light manufacturing, and opened the economy to increased foreign trade and investment. The result has been a quadrupling of GDP since 1978. With its 1.3 billion people in 2006 but a GDP of just $5,600 per capita, China stands as the second largest economy in the world after the United States. Agricultural output doubled in the 1980s, and industry also posted major gains, especially in coastal areas near Hong Kong and opposite Taiwan, where foreign investment helped spur output of both domestic and export goods. On the darker side, the leadership has often experienced in its hybrid system the worst results of socialism (bureaucracy and lassitude) and of capitalism (windfall gains and stepped-up inflation). Beijing thus has periodically backtracked, retightening central controls at intervals.

Access to the World Trade Organization helps strengthen China's ability to maintain high growing rates, but at the same time it puts additional pressure on the hybrid system of strong political controls and growing market influences. China has benefited from a huge expansion in Internet use, with an estimated 98 million people online in 2006. Foreign investment remains a strong element in China's remarkable economic growth. As an indicator of this growth, Shanghai already has 4,000 skyscrapers, almost double the number in New York. And there are designs to build 1,000 more by the end of this decade. Shortages of electric power and raw materials may affect industrial output during 2007–2010. In its rivalry with India as an economic power, China has a lead in absorption of technology, rising prominence in world trade, and alleviation of poverty; India has one important advantage in its relative mastery of the English language, but the number of competent Chinese English-speakers is growing rapidly.

Japan

Japan's population consists of approximately 127 million inhabitants living in an area slightly smaller than California. Japan is a homogeneous country, with 99.4 percent of the population speaking Japanese, and little ethnic diversity. A third of Japan's exports are to the United States while 19 percent of its imports come from the United States. Gross domestic product per capita is $29,400 a year.

Government-industry cooperation, a strong work ethic, mastery of high technology, and a comparatively small defense allocation (1 percent of GDP) have helped Japan expand economically. Japan holds the rank of the second most technologically powerful economy in the world after the United States and has the third largest economy in the world after the United States and China. One notable characteristic of the economy is the cooperation between manufacturers, suppliers, and distributors in closely-knit groups called Keiretsu. A second feature has been the guarantee of lifetime employment for a substantial portion of the urban labor force. Both of these features are now eroding.

Japanese industry, the most important sector of the economy, is heavily dependent on imported raw materials and fuels. The much smaller agricultural sector is highly subsidized and protected. Crop yields in Japan are among the highest in the world. Usually self-sufficient in rice, Japan imports about 50 percent of its requirements of other grain and fodder crops. Japan maintains one of the world's largest fishing fleets and accounts for nearly 15 percent of the global catch.

For three decades, overall real economic growth had been spectacular: a 10 percent average in the 1960s, a 5 percent average in the 1970s, and a 4 percent average in the 1980s. Growth slowed markedly in the 1990s largely due to the aftereffects of overinvestment during the late 1980s along with contractionary domestic policies designed to wring speculative excesses from the stock and real estate markets. During 2001–2004 Japan is the only industrialized nation since the Great Depression that has experienced a sustained period of declining prices, or deflation. The crowding of habitable land area and the aging of the population are two major long-run problems. Robotics constitutes a key long-term economic strength, with Japan possessing 410,000 of the world's 720,000 "working robots." Recently the Japanese economy has been improving. At the same time, many Japanese firms have taken drastic measures to reduce labor costs, cut back on employment security guarantees, and increase productivity through managerial practices borrowed from the United States (such as widespread use of incentive systems and the hiring of employees at any level, not just at entry level). This is requiring a major adaptation for much of the Japanese workforce and managers who had become accustomed to permanent employment, strict promotion-from-within policies, pay pegged to seniority, egalitarian distribution of rewards, and weak ties between compensation received and individual contributions or performance.

Source: Adapted from www.CIA.gov, 2006, with further statistical updates by the authors obtained from various sources: J. McGregor, "One Billion Customers," *The Wall Street Journal*, October 18, 2005, p. B-5; J. Kanter, & K. Bradsher, "A Return to Quotas," *New York Times*, November 9, 2005, p. C-1; D. Jones, "Eatery Firm Goes East," *Arizona Republic*, November 6, 2005, p. D-4; L.T. Chang, "Hinterland Strives to Join China's Boom," *The Wall Street Journal*, April 27, 2005, p. A-12; L. Lee, P. Burrows, & B. Einhorn, "China, News Analysis and Commentary," *BusinessWeek*, November 7, 2005, p. 46; C. Chandler, "From Mart to Market," Fortune, May 16, 2005, p. 36; B. Brenner, & K. Kerwin, "Here Comes Chinese Cars," *BusinessWeek*, June 6, 2005, pp. 20–28; B. Bremner, "The Biggest IPO on Earth," *BusinessWeek*, October 312, 2005, pp. 30–35; J. Dean, "In China, English 101 Becomes a Booming Business," *The Wall Street Journal*, September 19, 2005, p. A-16; N. King, & J. Areddy, "U.S. Urges Chinese to Save Less, Buy More," *The Wall Street Journal*, October 14, 2005, p. A-14; D. Barboza, "China Builds Its Dreams and Some Fear a Bubble," *New York Times*, October 18, 2005, p. A-1; A. Browne, & K. Chen, "A Booming Coast Breathes New Life into China's Mainland," *The Wall Street Journal*, October 17, 2005, p. A-13; S. Power, "EU Lifts the Hood on Chinese Autos," *The Wall Street Journal*, October 7, 2005, p. A-14; *BusinessWeek*, special issue on China and India, August 29, 2005, pp. 50–84; D. Luhnow, "Competition Erodes Mexican Industrial Output," *The Wall Street Journal*, September 14, 2005, p. A-1.

Scale of Involvement

The firm must consider not only where and when to enter but also the magnitude of its commitment to the foreign location. For instance, Motorola has invested close to $30 billion in China between 2003–2006.[37] The decision to enter a foreign market on such a large scale is a major strategic commitment with long-term consequences for the corporation. It is also difficult to reverse. The scale of involvement decision is closely tied to mode of entry, to be discussed next. In general, scale of involvement is lowest if the firm simply decides to export its products to the foreign location and highest if the firm decides to have a wholly owned subsidiary in the foreign country.

Mode of Entry

The seven ways to enter foreign markets are exporting, turnkey projects, licensing, franchising, joint ventures, wholly owned subsidiaries, and strategic alliances. The advantages and disadvantages associated with each entry mode are summarized in Table 2.4 on page 76.

Exporting

Manufacturing firms typically begin globalization by **exporting** products to other countries and retaining production facilities within domestic borders. Exporting has two advantages. First, the firm may realize substantial savings through economies of scale. In other words, expanding the market creates greater demand, which requires increasing production, which results in fuller use of plant and equipment and improved learning as a result of practice, so unit costs tend to go down. Second, the firm avoids the expenses of establishing, controlling, and coordinating manufacturing operations on foreign soil. Japanese firms that have used this entry mode successfully, particularly in U.S. markets, include Sony, Matsushita, Honda, and Toyota.

The most obvious limitation of exporting is that foreign competitors may enjoy a cost advantage that far exceeds the economies of scale the company realizes. For instance, unskilled and semiskilled labor in most less-developed countries may be hired at a fraction of the cost of comparable labor in the domestic market. This is one reason why established and relatively simple products like bicycles, irons, and small domestic appliances are no longer manufactured in the United States. Moreover, bulk products, such as chemicals, may be expensive to transport

The vast Chinese market is hungry for goods of every kind, both imports and home-grown products. The country struggles with enormous contrasts, such as that between the growing wealth of its cities, like Shenzhen pictured here, and the continued poverty of its rural areas. Some observers say that technological innovation will be the key to continuing the increase in income for many of the country's 1.3 billion people, though with patent protection often tenuous, some multinationals are cautious about expanding their research and development efforts there.

LOC-In

3 Learning Objective Check-In

Film Café is a growing, national restaurant chain that features a dining experience where photographers circulate and take candid pictures, and then send them to an e-mail address provided by the patron after the dinner is over. Customers can order prints, share with friends online, etc. Film Café is considering foreign expansion.

1. *Which of the following represents the first key entry decision facing Film Café?*
   a. *When should we enter the foreign market?*
   b. *Which countries should we enter?*
   c. *What should our scale of involvement be?*
   d. *Should we consider licensing?*
2. *Because this service idea is unusual in other markets right now, Film Café could experience higher pioneering costs. Pioneering costs are associated with_____.*
   a. *timing of entry into foreign markets*
   b. *the present wealth of consumers in the foreign markets*
   c. *the firm's suitability of products to a particular market*
   d. *late entrance to the market*

exporting

A means of entering new markets by sending products to other countries and retaining production facilities within domestic borders.

from the home country to distant locations. Finally, imports are a politically sensitive issue in many countries, including the United States, and tariffs may be imposed on imported goods.

Turnkey Projects

turnkey projects

A specialized type of exporting in which the firm handles the design, construction, start-up operations, and workforce training of a foreign plant, and a local client is handed the key to a plant that is fully operational.

Turnkey projects are a specialized type of exporting. The selling firm handles the design, construction, start-up operations, and workforce training of a foreign plant, and a local client is handed the key to a plant that is fully operational. Turnkey projects are most often used in newly developed and less-developed countries. Limited access to complex, expensive production process technologies such as chemical production, pharmaceutical production, petroleum refining, and metal refining makes them more viable. A turnkey project allows a company to use its know-how to earn a profit in a foreign country without making a major, long-term investment. Some host countries, including many oil-rich nations, prohibit foreign ownership of an asset such as a petroleum refinery. In such cases, a turnkey deal may be the most attractive business option available.

Turnkey projects also have potential disadvantages. For one, the selling firm may be creating a competitor by giving away its technological superiority. For example, Saudi Arabia, Kuwait, and other Persian Gulf nations are using turnkey-built petroleum plants to directly compete with the Western firms that built those facilities. Also, the selling firm may lose a source of competitive advantage by transferring complex knowhow to actual or potential competitors.

Licensing

licensing

A means of entering new markets, primarily used by manufacturing firms, by transferring the rights to produce and sell products overseas to a foreign firm. In return, the licensing company receives a negotiated fee, normally in the form of a royalty.

In **licensing**, a company transfers the rights to produce and sell its products overseas to a foreign firm. In return, the licensing company receives a negotiated fee, normally in the form of a royalty. The typical licensing arrangement involves intangible property, such as patents, inventions, formulas, trademarks, designs, and copyrights. For instance, Xerox receives 5 percent of net revenues from Fuji-Xerox for allowing Fuji-Xerox to sell Xerox's photocopying technology in the Asian Pacific region.

An advantage of licensing is that the firm does not have to incur the expense and risk of opening a facility overseas. Instead, the licensee puts up most of or all of the capital necessary to start production. When a local government will not allow a firm to set up a wholly owned subsidiary, licensing may be the best alternative. This was why Xerox set up a joint venture with Fuji and licensed its technology to Fuji-Xerox. Also, a firm may own intangible property that has commercial value but may not wish to engage in manufacturing activities. For example, Bell Laboratories at AT&T invented the transistor in the 1950s but licensed the technology to other firms for manufacture.

A disadvantage of licensing is that the foreign firm may build on the technology and use an enhanced version to compete in global markets against the licensing firm that invented it. This happened to RCA when it licensed its color television technology to several Japanese firms, including Matsushita and Sony. Licensing also imposes constraints on the firm, limiting strategic flexibility on a global scale. Because each licensee establishes its own manufacturing operations, costs will go up, and increased prices will reduce demand for products using that technology (which would have an adverse effect on royalties). Licensing also greatly limits a firm's ability to use profits earned in one country to make bold competitive moves in other countries.

Franchising

Franchising is similar to licensing, except that it is mainly used by service companies, whereas licensing is primarily used by manufacturing firms. The franchisee pays a fee for using the brand name and agrees to strictly follow the standards and abide by the rules set by the franchise. McDonald's, for example, has over 3,000 locally owned franchises around the world. The menu, cooking methods, ingredients, and physical appearance of these restaurants must comply with McDonald's standards. McDonald's helps the stores obtain supplies and is closely involved in training managers to ensure that uniform quality standards are met.

Like licensing, franchising allows a firm to expand rapidly with relatively small capital investment and little risk exposure. The main drawback of franchising is that the firm depends on franchisees for quality control, and there is a risk that standards followed by the different stores may not be uniformly met by all the stores. Since the franchise name is intended to guarantee consistent product quality, a lack of uniformity hurts the reputation of the franchise.

Joint Ventures and Strategic Alliances

In a **joint venture,** two or more independent firms agree to establish a separate firm that is owned by the participating companies. The firms normally own equivalent shares of the joint venture and contribute a corresponding proportion of the management team.

Joint ventures are increasing in popularity. One major advantage is that foreign firms benefit by establishing a working relationship with a domestic firm that is familiar with the local labor market, political environment, competitive landscape, tastes and preferences, cultural norms, language, and legal systems. In return, the local partner receives access to the know-how, technology, and capital of the foreign firm. Further, the two firms gain by sharing development costs and risks, reducing the potential of unacceptably large losses in the case of poor results or business failure. Also, local equity partners may discourage a government from interfering with a multinational. Joint ventures are another way for companies to do business in countries that do not allow foreign firms to maintain fully owned subsidiaries.

Joint ventures have two serious drawbacks. First, the goals, strategies, culture, and personalities of the firms may conflict. Unless it is successfully resolved, conflict may lead to a dissolution of the union, with considerable cost to all involved. Second, the local partner may use the foreign firm's technology for its own competitive advantage.

International **strategic alliances** are cooperative arrangements between competitors or potential competitors from different countries. They may involve establishment of a formal joint venture as discussed above, such as the case of

McDonald's restaurants serve a varied, yet limited, value-priced menu in 120 countries around the world. Franchisees are independent entrepreneurs, typically local businesspeople.

franchising

A means of entering new markets similar to licensing, mainly used by service companies, in which the franchisee pays a fee for using the brand name and agrees to strictly follow the standards and abide by the rules set by the franchise.

joint venture

A means of entering new markets where two or more independent firms agree to establish a separate firm; the firms normally own equivalent shares of the joint venture and contribute a corresponding proportion of the management team.

strategic alliances

Cooperative arrangements between competitors or potential competitors from different countries, possibly to establish a formal joint venture or collaboration between firms on specific projects.

table 2.4

Advantages and Disadvantages of Various Modes of Entry Choices

MODE OF ENTRY	ADVANTAGES	DISADVANTAGES
Exporting	• Economies of scale • Lower foreign expenses	• No low cost sales • High transportation costs • Potential tariffs
Turnkey Project	• Access to closed markets	• Competition from local client • Loss of competitive advantage
Licensing	• Quick expansion • Lower expenses and risks • Lower political risk	• Loss of competitive advantage • Limited ability to use profits in one country to increase competition in another
Franchising	• Quick expansion • Lower development costs and risks • Lower political risk	• Loss of competitive advantage • Potential quality control problems • Limited ability to use profits in one country to increase competition in another country
Joint Venture	• Knowledge of local markets • Lower development costs and risk • Access to closed markets	• Potential for conflict of interest • Loss of competitive advantage
Strategic Alliance	• Access to closed markets • Pooled resources increase partner firm's capabilities • Benefit from complementary skills and assets	• Loss of competitive advantage • Potential overestimation of partner's capabilities
Wholly Owned Subsidiary	• Maximum control over proprietary knowledge/technology • Greater strategic flexibility • Efficiencies of global production system	• Large capital outlay • Lack of local knowledge • Increased risk

Source: T. S. Bateman and S. A. Snell, *Management: Competing in the New Era,* 5th ed. New York: McGraw-Hill/Irwin, 2005. Reproduced with permission of The McGraw-Hill Companies.

Fuji-Xerox, or collaboration between firms on specific projects. Strategic alliances have become extremely popular in recent years. Among the firms involved in these arrangements are

- *General Electric Snecma of France.* Joint venture to develop and manufacture a variety of low-thrust commercial aircraft engines.

- *Toshiba-IBM.* Sharing the $1 billion cost of developing a 64-megabyte and 256-megabyte memory chip facility, technology that will be transferred to a new IBM plant in Virginia.

- *Mitsui-General Electric.* GE's power-systems unit has picked up Asian contracts with Mitsui's well-connected bank. GE has the technology; Mitsui has the contacts and deep pockets.

- *GM–Daewoo.* To build 160,000 Buick Excells in Shanghai starting with the 2006 model, with the key parts for the car shipped from Korea.[38]

- *Texas Instruments – Compel Communications.* To build ultra-cheap cell phones to sell to people in developing nations starting in 2007.[39]

- *Canon–Hewlett Packard.* The two share laser printer technology. Hewlett-Packard buys engines from Canon, but they compete with end products around the world.

- *Mitsubishi-Caterpillar.* A long-time joint venture has become Cat's primary Asian manufacturing source. American and Japanese staff jointly designed a successful excavator line made in Japan, the United States, Indonesia, and China.[40]

Several advantages account for the recent growth of strategic alliances. First, "keeping pace with technological change and competing globally have stretched the resources of even the richest companies."[41] Pooling resources enables firms to accomplish tasks that neither can afford to do alone. Strategic alliances also allow firms to enter relatively closed foreign markets.

A strategic alliance means that firms can utilize complementary skills and assets. This was the case, for instance, in the alliance between Mitsui and GE noted above. Sharing core competencies can create synergies that enhance the competitive positions of both companies. Strategic alliances may result in the creation of technological standards for the industry, which would simplify the manufacturing process for the firms involved and also benefit the end user.

Strategic alliances have drawbacks similar to those of joint ventures. Most notably, the firm runs the risk of losing its competitive advantage by "giving away" proprietary know-how to the partner. The firm may also misjudge the partner's capabilities. The success of any strategic alliance depends on the interpersonal relationship between the managers of the firms. Lack of trust, misunderstandings, and opportunistic behaviors may cause the alliance to dissolve, which may result in writing off millions of investment dollars.

Wholly Owned Subsidiaries

When a multinational firm fully owns a company in a foreign country, the local company is a **wholly owned subsidiary** of the multinational. Wal-Mart owns all of its stores worldwide. This arrangement has several advantages. A wholly owned subsidiary offers a firm maximum control over proprietary knowledge and technology, so that competitors cannot gain access. In addition, the foreign company retains full discretion to move resources to other countries and thereby enjoys greater strategic flexibility. For instance, it may use profits from one country to move aggressively into other countries. A global production system may provide efficiencies because "the various operations must be prepared to accept centrally determined decisions as to how they will produce, how much they will produce, and how output will be priced for transfer to the next operation."[42]

On the other hand, wholly owned subsidiaries require large capital outlays, and ownership is thus the most expensive method of operating in foreign markets. The firm bears the full brunt of business risks, since these are not shared with a local partner. Corporate managers of a wholly owned subsidiary may not sufficiently understand local conditions. A firm that exclusively relies on wholly owned subsidiaries may be unable to operate in markets where legal or political imperatives require foreign firms to establish joint ventures with local partners.

wholly owned subsidiary

A means of entering new markets in which a firm fully owns its subsidiary in foreign countries.

LOC-In

4 **Learning Objective Check-In**

1. *Sim Squad, a successful business simulation company, is a service firm that has built a strong brand name in the United States. The company is considering entrance to new markets in foreign countries. Sim Squad's strategic managers plan to use _____ because they want to allow for rapid expansion in the foreign markets with relatively small capital investment and little risk exposure. The one drawback they face is concern over quality control in the various stores.*
   a. *licensing*
   b. *wholly owned subsidiaries*
   c. *joint ventures*
   d. *franchising*

2.1

OPENING A FACILITY ABROAD

AACC is a U.S. manufacturer of prosthetic devices, including canes, crutches, walkers, and other devices that help partially disabled people maintain some independence. All of AACC's management functions are located in the United States. Domestic sales account for 85 percent of its revenues, with the remaining 15 percent originating mostly in Canada and Mexico. AACC has decided to expand its international operations in order to remain competitive and increase its market share. CEO Ralph Solomon met with the firm's top executives and set up a committee within AACC to develop concrete proposals for internationalizing the company. Solomon has prepared the following memo that lists four areas that should be covered as part of the committee's recommendations.

TO: Members of AACC International Task Force

FROM: Mr. Ralph Solomon

SUBJECT: International Task Force

If we are to remain a strong and competitive firm, AACC must begin to exploit opportunities abroad. Several task forces will study alternative means of internationalizing AACC, including opening a manufacturing site abroad and moving aggressively into international markets.

I have appointed you to a task force to provide recommendations to guide future actions. Your analysis and recommendations must be clearly supported by facts. Any reasonable assumptions you make as part of your analysis should be justified in a clear and logical manner.

I am counting on you to develop a high-quality proposal, covering the following areas:

1. If AACC should be involved in overseas production, indicate where plants should be located and why.

2. AACC will entertain any of the following alternatives:

   - *Licensing of AACC Technology and Patents:* In this option, AACC would license its technology and patents to a foreign producer who would then produce products for AACC at a contracted price. AACC could purchase all or part of this producer's total output under this arrangement.

   - *Joint Venture:* AACC could invest funds in a new or existing company within a country with a partner in that country.

   - *Wholly Owned Facility:* Instead of having a host country partner, AACC could build or buy a production facility on a wholly owned basis.

   - *Strategic Alliance:* In this option AACC may develop a partnership with a foreign firm to conduct R&D on prosthetic devices and manufacture a variety of such products without formally setting up a joint venture.

   Analyze the pros and cons of each option. What alternative should be used for foreign manufacturing in the country you have selected? Justify your choice.

3. Develop a plan outlining how the foreign venture will be managed and the steps that should be taken to minimize potential problems that may emerge.

Exercise

Form committees, each consisting of four students, with the following roles assigned:

(continued on next page)

---

ethnocentric approach

An approach to managing an international subsidiary that involves filling top management and other key positions with people from the home country (expatriates).

polycentric approach

An approach to managing an international subsidiary in which subsidiaries are managed and staffed by personnel from the host country (local nationals).

Managing the Global Firm

The success of a foreign venture depends on who is in charge. If a manager does not perform up to par in a domestic unit, others can fill in. This is not the case in an overseas operation. The importance of choosing the right managers was underlined by CEOs of U.S. companies with revenues in the $300 million to $1 billion range who identified the choice of management for overseas units as one of their most crucial business decisions.[43]

There are three basic approaches to managing an international subsidiary: the ethnocentric, polycentric, and geocentric approaches. The **ethnocentric approach** involves filling top management and other key positions with people from the home country. These managers are known as *expatriates*. In the **polycentric approach,** international subsidiaries are managed and staffed by personnel from the host country, or local nationals. Nationality is deliberately down-

(continued from previous page)

Chairperson

- Coordinates team members' activities.
- Monitors team members' progress.
- Acts as a clearinghouse for information from various functional areas so that it can be easily understood and used by the entire team.
- Develops, proposes, and evaluates various scenarios, in close collaboration with other team members.
- Establishes agendas and protocol for team meetings, and controls any dysfunctional behavior, such as long monologues, personality clashes, and unfocused argumentation.
- Develops implementation and corporate strategy plans that integrate the team's functional areas.

Political/Legal Adviser

- Conducts political risk analysis for various countries under consideration.
- Provides legal support to the team including judicial interpretation of issues being discussed.
- Makes recommendations regarding the legal and political ramifications of various manufacturing arrangements overseas, such as joint venture versus wholly owned subsidiary.
- Analyzes government policies that may have an effect on AACC's operation, such as laws controlling profit repatriation to the United States.

Financial/Economic Adviser

- Provides the team with relevant data and recommendations concerning the general economic conditions of countries under consideration.
- Conducts research on the tax advantages and disadvantages in various countries.
- Analyzes business factors that may affect AACC's operations, such as inflation, devaluation, and convertibility of local currency into dollars.

Human Resources Adviser

- Analyzes human resources of those countries under consideration
- Works with the political/legal adviser in evaluating legal restrictions concerning expatriates.
- Estimates labor costs for AACC's foreign operation.
- Develops a resource plan for managing AACC's international venture.

Each committee will prepare a written report and make an oral presentation of an independent proposal covering the areas noted in the memo. The instructor will play the role of CEO and may ask questions of committee members to assess the soundness of the recommendations being offered.

Source: This exercise builds on an earlier simulation by L. R. Gomez-Mejia and J. E. McCann, *Meeting the Challenges of Foreign Expansion: An International Business Simulation*, Columbus, OH: Grid Publishing Co., 1985.

played in the **geocentric approach** as the firm actively searches on a worldwide or regional basis for the best people to fill key positions. Many of these individuals are likely to be **third-country nationals**—citizens of countries other than the host nation or the firm's home country.

Table 2.5 on page 80 summarizes the pros and cons of using local nationals and expatriates in foreign operations. It costs firms more than a third of a million dollars annually to transfer and compensate expatriates. Consequently, firms use them only for key positions, such as senior managers, high-level professionals, and technical specialists.

Twenty percent to 40 percent of expatriates return before completing their assignments, compared with fewer than 5 percent of Japanese expatriates.[44] Premature returnees cost $85,000 to $260,000 each, and the costs of business disruptions, lost opportunities, a leadership vacuum, and family hardships are probably many times greater. Six factors, which are summarized in Table 2.6 on page 80,

geocentric approach

An approach to managing an international subsidiary in which nationality is deliberately downplayed, and the firm actively searches on a worldwide or regional basis for the best people to fill key positions.

third-country nationals

Citizens of countries other than the host nation or the firm's home country.

table 2.5

Advantages and Disadvantages of Using Local and Expatriate Employees to Staff International Subsidiaries

ADVANTAGES	DISADVANTAGES
Locals	
• Lowers labor costs	• Makes it difficult to balance local demand and global priorities
• Demonstrates trust in local citizenry	• Leads to postponement of difficult local decisions (such as layoffs) until they are unavoidable, when they are more difficult, costly, and painful than they would have been if implemented earlier
• Increases acceptance of the company by the local community	
• Maximizes the number of options available in the local environment	• May make it difficult to recruit qualified personnel
• Leads to recognition of the company as a legitimate participant in the local economy	• May reduce the amount of control exercised by headquarters
• Effectively represents local considerations and constraints in the decision-making process	
Expatriates	
• Cultural similarity with parent company ensures transfer of business/management practices	• Creates problems of adaptability to foreign environment and culture
• Permits closer control and coordination of international subsidiaries	• Increases the "foreignness" of the subsidiary
• Gives employees a multinational orientation through experience at parent company	• May involve high transfer, salary, and other costs
• Establishes a pool of internationally experienced executives	• May result in personal and family problems
• Local talent may not yet be able to deliver as much value as expatriates can	• Has disincentive effect on local-management morale and motivation
	• May be subject to local government restrictions

Source: From *Managing Human Resources* by Gomez-Mejia, et al., Copyright © 2007. Reprinted by permission of Pearson Education, Inc., Upper Saddle River, NJ.

table 2.6

Why International Assignments End in Failure

Career blockage	Initially, many employees see the opportunity to work and travel abroad as exciting. But once the initial rush wears off, many feel that the home office has forgotten them and that their career has been sidetracked while their counterparts at home are climbing the corporate ladder.
Culture shock	Many people who take international assignments cannot adjust to a different cultural environment, a phenomenon called culture shock. Instead of learning to work within the new culture, the expatriate tries to impose the home office's or home country's values on the host country's employees, tending to internal conflict.
Lack of predeparture cross-cultural training	Surprisingly, only about one-third of multinationals provide any cross-cultural training to expatriates, and those that do tend to offer rather cursory programs.
Overemphasis on technical qualifications	The person chosen to go abroad may have impressive credentials and an excellent reputation in the home office for getting things done. Yet this person may lack cultural adaptability as an important trait to be effective overseas.
Getting rid of a troublesome employee	International assignments may seem to be a convenient way of dealing with managers who are having problems in the home office. By sending these managers abroad, the organization is able to resolve difficult interpersonal situations or political conflicts at the home office, but at a significant cost to its international operations.
Family problems	The inability or unwillingness of the expatriate's spouse and children to adapt to life in another country is one of the most important reasons for failure. In fact, more than half of all early returns can be attributed to family problems.

Source: From *Managing Human Resources* by Gomez-Mejia, et al. Copyright © 2007. Reprinted by permission of Pearson Education, Inc., Upper Saddle River, NJ.

account for most failures, although their relative importance varies by firm. Selection, training, career development, and compensation practices can deal with the factors that lead to failure.

Management Is Everyone's Business 2.2 on page 81 offers a set of recommendations that those who are now in or plan to be in management positions should consider in light of our discussion so far.

Working as a Manager Two major barriers preventing firms from capitalizing on business opportunities overseas are a lack of awareness about (1) how to enter foreign markets and (2) how to operate in diverse national settings. Managers can learn how to function well in foreign lands by developing a better appreciation of the unique challenges that may confront them. Few firms today have the luxury of avoiding globalization. New managers should be groomed to play a key role in internationalization.

As a manager you should:

- Be on the lookout for emerging business opportunities overseas, not only in your own backyard.

- Keep attuned to trends in international business that may have an effect on your company. These may involve changes in the law, exchange rates, trade pacts, political risks, and the like. Much of this information is readily available in business periodicals (such as *The Wall Street Journal*, *BusinessWeek*, and *The Economist*), on the Internet, and from trade, industry, and regional associations.

- Be sensitive to cultural differences among employees and customers but do not stereotype people.

- Try to attract and retain employees from various ethnic and cultural backgrounds, as this might help the company target its products and services to diverse foreign markets.

- Encourage subordinates to be involved in international efforts, and if appropriate, include this as part of the performance appraisal and merit pay/promotion review process.

- Actively develop external networks with influential people inside and outside the industry (for instance, by attending important international conferences), as this might help you establish personal contacts that could evolve into common projects, joint ventures, or strategic alliances with foreign firms. In most non–Anglo-Saxon countries business transactions tend to be very personal. Thus cultivating networks is critical for success.

- Make sure you do everything within your power to give the impression that as a manager you are fair, ethical, and socially responsible. A bad reputation, whether it is deserved or not, is almost certain to increase political risks for your company.

Selection

LOC-In

Choosing expatriate managers with the best odds of success means utilizing an effective selection process. Selection criteria should include cultural sensitivity. The selection board should have some expatriates. The company should require previous international experience and verify that the candidate's spouse and family are flexible, patient, and adaptable.

⑤ Learning Objective Check-In

1. *DigiShot is in the process of choosing managers to head its overseas operations. The firm plans to deliberately downplay nationality in the managers it selects. Instead, DigiShot is actively searching on a worldwide basis for the best people to fill the key positions. The company believes that this _____ approach to managing the subsidiary will determine its success.*

   a. bureaucratic
   b. geocentric
   c. ethnocentric
   d polycentric

Training

Cross-cultural training sensitizes candidates to the local culture, customs, language, and government. Table 2.7 on page 83 summarizes three approaches to cross-cultural training. More rigorous and lengthy training is generally reserved for key executives and those expected to

2.2

HOW WOULD YOU TRAIN EXPATRIATES TO GO OVERSEAS?

Assume that you are a human resource manager for a large energy firm with facilities in Colombia, Norway, Nigeria, and Saudi Arabia. In five months or so the company intends to send approximately 10 American expatriate managers to each of those locations. They are expected to stay at least a year.

You have been asked to develop a training program to help those expatriates and their families to adjust. Provide an outline of a training program, with key features that may be more appropriate for each of these countries such as security concerns and language training. (The instructor may decide to make this a team project by dividing the class into teams of five.)

be overseas for an extended period of time. Skills for Managing 2.2, "How Would You Train Expatriates to Go Overseas?" above asks you to develop such a program.

Career Development

Expatriates are more likely to complete foreign assignments and to be highly motivated to succeed when they believe that the assignments are instrumental to their future career opportunities. Unfortunately, this has not always been the case. Only 15 percent of the top 50 executives in U.S. corporations have worked abroad as compared with 35 percent of European executives and 27 percent of Japanese executives.[45] About 80 percent of executives posted abroad feel that employers do not value their international experience. Although 75 percent expect the move to benefit their careers, only 10 percent receive promotions when they return to the home office.[46] Female executives have less access to opportunities overseas than male executives, and the perceived value of international experience in their careers is also lower.[47]

At a minimum, successful career planning for expatriates requires firms to position international assignments as a step toward advancement within the firm. In addition, the home office should provide continued support to expatriates, such as by appointing a senior executive as a mentor, offering short sabbaticals in the home office, and bringing expatriates back to the home office occasionally.

One trend in the latter half of this decade is short-term expatriate assignments. Instead of relocating employees and their families for two years or more (a three-year assignment can easily cost $1 million) the stint overseas would last from several weeks to 12 months and leave the family behind.[48] There are several reasons for this trend, including cost savings, the high rate of expatriates who decide to renege on their contract and come home early if given a lengthy assignment, a belief that short-term assignments are less traumatic for the family, and the prevalence of dual careers (the spouse may continue to work at home when the expatriate is gone for a shorter time period).

On the other hand, there are also some problems to consider with short-term foreign assignments. One is that it takes time to learn about a foreign culture, and the expatriate may have to leave just when he or she feels comfortable with local

table 2.7

Three Approaches to Cross-Cultural Training

LENGTH OF STAY	LENGTH AND LEVEL OF TRAINING	CHARACTERISTICS
Impression Approach		
1–3 years	1–2 months + High	Assessment center Field experiences Simulations Sensitivity training Extensive language training
Affective Approach		
2–12 months	1–4 weeks Moderate	Language training Role-playing Critical incidents Cases Stress-reduction training Moderate language training
Information-Giving Approach		
1 month or less	Less than a week Low	Area briefings Cultural briefings Films/books Use of interpreters "Survival-level" language training

Source: Adapted from M. Mendenhall and G. Oddou, "Acculturation Profiles of Expatriate Managers: Implication for Cross-Cultural Training," *Columbia Journal of World Business* 21, no. 4 (1986), p. 78.

conditions. Often the "short-term" assignment needs to be extended to 18 months or more, which can be an unpleasant shock for families. And families may not be as happy with this approach as some companies seen to assume. The spouse left at home must do "your job plus 100 percent of the chores, plus filling in for your partner with the kids. The days are extremely long, tiring and mentally exhausting," writes one wife in a study of families involved in short-term assignments by Anne Copeland, director of the Interchange Institute, a Brookline, Massachusetts, nonprofit research concern.[49]

Management Is Everyone's Business 2.3 on page 84 offers a set of career recommendations that you might wish to follow in order to enhance your personal success in a globalized economy.

Compensation

In the international management setting, money makes the world go around. When salaries are inappropriately low, misgivings that the expatriate manager and spouse may have about foreign assignment rise. The cost of housing, food, and other consumer goods is far higher in many foreign locations than in the United States. For example, it is almost impossible to find decent accommodations in a 1,000 square foot apartment in a city like London, Paris, or Tokyo for less than $3,000 a month. Ninety-eight percent of companies offer some type of additional financial incentive and housing allowance for expatriates, but often this may not be enough to compensate for the cost disparity.[50]

LOC-In

6 Learning Objective Check-In

1. *Jared is going to become an expatriate manager at his company. He will be in the other country for about 12 months. Jared is in the middle of his four-week cross-cultural training sessions. He is learning the other language, studying cases, learning about stress-reduction techniques, and doing some role-playing to deal with critical incidents that may arise while he is in that country. Jared's cross-cultural training program is taking the _____ approach.*
   a. *information-giving*
   b. *affective*
   c. *impression*
   d. *experiential*

Planning expatriate compensation should follow two guidelines. First, the firm should provide the expatriate with a disposable income that is equivalent to what he or she would earn in the home office. This may require special allowances for housing, children's education, medical care, and so on. Second, the firm should provide an explicit "add-on" incentive, such as a sign-on bonus and a bonus at the end of the assignment for going overseas, and the bonus should be larger for less desirable locations.

Ethics and Social Responsibility

Globalization greatly increases the possibility that a manager will face an ethical dilemma. Different cultures have different notions of right and wrong. For instance, as noted in Management Close-Up 2.3, "Blow the Whistle—No, Wait: Ethics Hotlines May Be Illegal in Europe" on page 85, reliance on anonymous tips to identify unethical employee behavior is becoming common in the United States, but Europeans (who still have memories of authoritarian regimes in places like Spain, Italy, Germany, and much of Eastern Europe) find this practice appalling.

Blow the Whistle—No, Wait: Ethics Hotlines May Be Illegal in Europe

U.S. firms of all sizes are introducing "hotlines" so that any employee can anonymously report to company officials what he or she believes is an ethical problem (such as managers falsifying accounting numbers, lying to customers, short-changing safety requirements, committing or overlooking sexual harassment, overcharging the government, and the like). Many firms are trying to use these hotlines not only in the United States but also in their international operations. But they are encountering some unexpected opposition. For instance, France blocked McDonald's and Exide Technologies from using hotlines, asserting that they violate French privacy law because accusations can be anonymous. The ruling reflects concern that persons named by a whistleblower aren't told of the complaint and don't have a chance to prove their innocence.

Anonymity—a key feature of U.S. hotlines—raises hot button issues across Europe. In much of the European Union, notes London-based law firm Faegre & Benson LLP, "there is an historical unease over the concept of encouraging individuals to inform against others." Law firm Proskauer Rose LLP says that to Europeans—especially in Germany and France—anonymous reporting can "smack of WWII-era authoritarianism, neighbor spying on neighbor." The European priority is due process and a presumption of innocence for the denounced.

In Britain, Public Concern at Work, a U.K. charity focusing on the responsibility of workers to raise concerns about improper business practices, says "Generally, we do not recommend that workers raise their concerns anonymously," in part because "it is easier to get protection under the UK Public Interest Disclosure Act if the concerns are raised openly."

In an unrelated German case, a labor court refused to allow Wal-Mart to implement certain features of an ethics hotline program, finding that it violated codetermination rights of the local workers council—the policy hadn't been discussed with the employee body.

Beyond the French and German cases, Faegre & Benson notes, there are other concerns about personal data. EU Data Protection laws give individuals the right to know what data is being processed about them and that it has been processed fairly and lawfully, is kept secure, and is not transferred to a country that fails to protect privacy rights.

Some U.S. firms, such as Xerox, are trying to get around these objections by positioning the business ethics and compliance reporting system as "a helpline, not a hotline," where people "can ask general questions about policies; the focus isn't on snitching." It remains to be seen to what extent Europeans are likely to buy that story. In the meantime the French government has passed a more accommodating policy, although it still leaves much room for interpretation. According to this policy companies can "establish such hotlines as long as they restrict their use to collecting information on specific types of corporate malfeasance and place restrictions on how information collected through them is handled."

Source: Adapted from "Blow the Whistle — No, Wait: Ethics Hotlines May Be Illegal in Europe," *Business Ethics*, Fall 2005, p. 10. See also D. Reilly, "France Ends Impasse with SEC," *The Wall Street Journal*, November 21, 2005, p. A-8.

Another dilemma may be that a firm may lose business if it applies a stricter code of ethics than foreign competitors follow. A transaction that an American might perceive as bribery could be construed by others as a commission or as an incentive necessary to conduct business in a foreign country. While many Americans were disgusted by news reports in 1999 that Salt Lake City officials had bribed the Olympic Commission to select Salt Lake City as a future Olympic site, several of the officials defended the practice on the grounds that gifts were expected in that situation.

The U.S. Foreign Corrupt Practices Act of 1977 is a tough anticorruption law governing international business. The Act was passed as a result of United Brands's $2.5 million bribe to Honduran government officials to reduce the banana tax. The law expressly forbids substantial payments by American firms to foreign officials to influence decisions. Many businesspeople believed that the act would put U.S. firms at a disadvantage overseas, but there is little evidence that this has occurred. It is possible that the legislation created a better image for American firms internationally, counterbalancing any losses.

Many firms and industry groups have developed their own code of conduct for foreign operations. For example, the American Apparel Manufacturers Association (AAMA), whose members include Sara Lee, Jockey International, and VF, requires members to pay the existing minimum wage, maintain certain minimum safety standards, and avoid the use of child labor. In the fall of 2005, companies such as Nike, GAP, and Adidas formed the Joint Initiative on Corporate Accountability and Worker Rights, or JOIN, to monitor their foreign suppliers for abuses.[51] Nevertheless, firms continue to face many ethical issues when they go overseas in search of cheaper labor. These include child labor issues, gender discrimination issues, unsafe working conditions, and environmental contamination, among others.[52] At the same time that globalization continues to increase dramatically, abuses by some multinational firms and governments have given globalization a bad name for many, even though it has improved the economic conditions of many countries around the world.

7 **Learning Objective Check-In**

1. In theory, _____ means poor countries reduce unemployment, wealthy countries get cheaper labor, and workers earn far more abroad than they could at home. In practice, the brokers who make the labor deals have incentives and opportunities to gouge the workers they control. This is one element of globalization that demonstrates the need for firms to develop their own codes of ethical conduct for foreign operations.
   a. debt bondage
   b. foreign contract work
   c. uncertainty avoidance
   d. the U.S. Foreign Corrupt Practices Act of 1977

CONCLUDING THOUGHTS

At the beginning of the chapter we posed some questions pertaining to Playmobil's operations in Germany. Now that you have had the opportunity to read the chapter, it's time to revisit those questions. Playmobil's example shows that reliance on foreign markets is becoming increasingly necessary, and possible, as firms capitalize on opportunities beyond their borders. Firms without a global vision are more likely to experience a major competitive disadvantage. To earn profits, Playmobil has chosen to expand its markets beyond Germany and even Europe, and strengthen its sales presence in the United States, Latin America, and Asia as well. This globalization of business is fueling unprecedented economic growth in many parts of the world.

The competitive landscape is more complex than ever, and globalization presents many additional challenges. This chapter has dealt with the unique issues and problems firms face in the global environment, but the roots of many decisions that multinational firms make still lie at home. A stagnant or declining birth rate and a slowing economy in Germany have cut into the markets for many consumer products, forcing many German companies like Playmobil to look elsewhere for customers. Together, their decisions have helped make Germany the biggest merchandise exporter in the world, boosting corporate profits and the German stock market to new highs.

For Playmobil to consider making a deeper investment abroad, such as a licensing agreement or joint venture to move manufacturing to China, for example, the firm would want to be assured of quality control and the kind of logistical flexibility that management now wields over its domestic manufacturing operations. The cost of obtaining these safeguards would have to be outweighed by labor cost savings.

Focusing on the Future: Using Management Theory in Daily Life

Managing in a Global Environment

Bruce Humphrys serves in a general manager capacity for a nonprofit technical organization. As the Executive Director of Compatible Technology International (CTI), he must encourage his employees—a group of volunteer engineers, food scientists, and technicians—to create food processing tools that can be used in underdeveloped nations all over the world. To create products that will be used, rather than abandoned, Bruce has to take into consideration the general business environment, legal systems, the country's economic environment, and cultural environments. Take the case of the breadfruit dryer, for instance.

One of Bruce's senior food scientists, George Ewing, saw a need to give people in Haiti a way to dry breadfruit. Fresh, breadfruit is a vegetable similar to squash. It has a very short shelf-life; fruit lasts only a day or so after being harvested. But when breadfruit is dried, it can be turned into a flour which keeps well and enriches both the islanders' diet and their economy. Fortunately, Ewing met Camille George, a professor at the University of St. Thomas in St. Paul, Minnesota, at a political lunch. She had the expertise in heat transfer technology to help him create a simple breadfruit drying machine.

If Professor George and her students had been tasked with creating a food dryer for use in Minneapolis, their job might have been simple. But obviously, this was not the case. How could these engineers determine if their invention was meeting the needs of clients a half a world away? They knew that they would have to test their product extensively, and take the general business environment, the legal systems, the economic environment, and the cultural environment of their clients into account when doing so.

General Business Environment   Because Haiti is a country in turmoil, the general business environment was less favorable than it is in other parts of the world. The former President, Jean-Bertrand Aristide, resigned from office in 2004, which opened the door for the interim government to take steps to encourage foreign investments. But there is still a great deal of political turmoil in the area, and the Haitian government continues to be unstable. In fact, although a trip to Haiti was scheduled to test an initial food dryer design, it had to be cancelled. Instead, Professor George and her students traveled to the island of St. Vincent, where climate conditions were similar but the general business environment was much more stable.

Legal Environment   Like the general business environment, the legal environment in Haiti is difficult and complex. While on the surface, Haiti is a democracy, with a civil law system based on the Napoleonic Code, in practice, the Haitian legal environment is often chaotic. There is widespread corruption, and disputes are often resolved through bribery and favoritism. Steps are being taken to modernize the legal system and make Haiti more open to foreign investors, but at this time, changes are not fully in place. Fortunately for Bruce Humphrys, Compatible Technology International is a nonprofit organization, and therefore not bound by as many legal restrictions as a for-profit organization would be.

Economic Environment   Haiti is a developing country, with high levels of poverty and a poor infrastructure. Jobs are scarce, and the average Haitian worker supports up to six other people at any one time. If an invention is to benefit the Haitian people, it is imperative that it be simple, useful, and use few natural resources (such as fuel). For example, CTI developed a food grinder that is nothing more than a metal cylinder with a blade at the bottom and a crankshaft. Setting up the grinder is simple, and powering it requires nothing more than the ability to turn the crankshaft. The breadfruit dryer developed by CTI was solar powered and consisted of little more than wood and plastic sheeting, so it would be easy to build and transport.

Cultural Environment Culture, is the final, key ingredient in determining whether or not a CTI project will work. Humphrys tells the following story about how culture impacted a CTI project in Guatemala: "Our guys visited a group of Guatemalan women hand-shelling corn. They saw the hard time they were having, how labor-intensive the shelling was, and on the spot they developed a sheller. The sheller consisted of a piece of wood with a hole in the middle. The women pushed the ear of corn through the hole, shaving the kernels from the cob. When the engineers passed out their device, the women said thanks and put the sheller to work. But when the volunteers returned to that village several months later, they found the group still hand-cutting kernels from corn. The women told them, 'Thanks for your invention, it's much easier. But this is the time we use to talk about men, school, and kids, and your device makes our work too fast for that.'" Extensive conversations and tests with the women of St. Vincent showed that there were no obvious cultural problems with the breadfruit dryer, but interestingly enough, a different problem emerged.

George and her group of engineering students found that the dryer was not going to work in Haiti—it dried the outside of the breadfruit without drying the inside, causing the fruit to spoil. It turned out that breadfruit dried better when placed directly in the sun, where the island breezes provided continuous airflow. The good news was that during the testing process, the women of St. Vincent suggested another way to put the dryers to work making money for the islanders. It seems that Italian restaurants in the United States demand red pepper flakes that are just one color—a dark red. The dryers allowed flakes to uniformly dry to exactly that color, and the islanders in St. Vincent are now using them to improve their economy.

Source: Jean Thilmany, "Managing across Cultures," *Mechanical Engineering*, February 2005, http://www.memagazine.org/backissues/feb05/features/mngcult/mngcult.html; U.S. Department of State, *2005 Investment Climate Statement—Haiti*, March 2006, http://www.state.gov/e/eb/ifd/2005/42043.htm.

summary of learning objectives

Firms increasingly compete in a global market characterized by high uncertainty, many players, and great complexity. This chapter's discussion will help you in your future career as a manager, as a member of a work team, or as an individual to succeed in this new global environment. The material presented to meet each of the chapter's learning objectives stated at the outset of the chapter is summarized below.

1 Describe the changing pattern of international business.

- *Changing world output and world trade picture.* The United States no longer dominates the world economy. Large U.S. multinationals no longer dominate international business. Centrally planned economies are opening to Western businesses, and national barriers to labor markets are folding (particularly in knowledge intensive industries).
- *Changing demographics.* The population in industrialized countries is getting older, and immigration is growing worldwide.
- *Lower trade barriers.* While some protectionism is still present and perhaps receiving growing political support in some areas, lower trade restrictions are now the norm.
- *Greater market integration.* Economic integration between groups of countries is growing, and today there are 34 such agreements, compared to 11 in the 1980s. Of these, the greatest level of integration has been achieved by the European Union composed of 25 countries.
- *Converging global consumer preferences.* Consumer tastes and preferences are becoming more similar around the world.
- *More globalization of production.* A growing number of firms spread their production around the world in order to realize savings, particularly in labor costs.
- *Rapid technological innovations.* Advances in communications, information processing, and transportation are making it much easier to conduct business across geographical boundaries.
- *Greater cultural diversity.* To be effective, firms need to learn to adapt to an increasingly diverse set of customers, employees, and ways of doing business.

2 Identify major factors affecting international business.

- *General business environment.* You must consider of all factors that might influence the costs, benefits, and risks of operating in particular world areas or countries.
- *Legal systems.* The firm must be able to comply with vastly different rules and regulations around the world.
- *Economic environment.* The firm must consider a host of economic factors that can vary from one time period to another and across countries. These include differences in per capita income, inflation, exchange rates, taxation, licensing agreements, and royalties.
- *Cultural environment.* To succeed internationally, firms and their members must be sensitive to cultural differences and be willing to adapt products, services, and management practices to those differences. Some well-known cultural aspects that might influence management practices and that vary across countries include prevalent ideas about appropriate **power distance** between superiors and subordinates, degree of **individualism, uncertainty avoidance**, and **masculinity–femininity** in a culture, and whether a culture has a **long- versus short-term orientation**.

3 Determine key decisions firms face when contemplating foreign expansion.

- *Which countries to enter*. In general, countries are more attractive from a business perspective when the size of the domestic market is large, purchasing power is high or likely to increase in the future, the firm's products are appropriate for a particular country market, and there is a positive business climate.
- *When to enter particular countries*. There are both advantages and disadvantages to being one of the first ones in a particular market. Being first can help a firm solidify its position in that market. However, this also involves greater investment in opening a new market and there is greater uncertainty since the firm cannot benefit from the experience of other firms that were there first.
- *What the scale of involvement should be*. The magnitude of the commitment to a foreign country increases as the investment in that country rises. In general, the scale of involvement is lowest if the firm is only exporting products and services into a country and highest if the firm owns and operates a plant in that country.

4 Differentiate the various ways firms can enter foreign markets.

- **Exporting**. Used primarily by firms entering international markets for the first time. In this mode, all manufacturing takes place within the domestic borders, which may result in foreign competitors enjoying significant cost advantages.
- **Turnkey**. Used by firms that prefer to receive payment for designing and building a plant that is then handed over to locals.
- **Licensing**. The firm generates profits in the form of a fee or royalty by granting rights to manufacture and sell a product in another country.
- **Franchising**. Similar to licensing, except franchising is used primarily for services.
- **Joint ventures and strategic alliances**. This approach allows quick access to international markets by establishing new entities in conjunction with local firms.
- **Wholly owned subsidiaries**. The deepest level of foreign involvement, whereby the multinational finances and manages the foreign facility, gives the firm maximum control over the foreign facility, but also incurs all the costs and risks of the foreign venture.

5 Identify alternative ways of managing a foreign operation.

- **Ethnocentric approach**. Foreign subsidiary is managed by personnel sent from the home office or by expatriates.
- **Polycentric approach**. Foreign subsidiary is managed by hiring individuals from each country in which subsidiaries are located.
- **Geocentric approach**. Multinational recruits personnel regardless of nationality. Many of these individuals are likely to be **third country nationals** — employees who are not citizens of the multinational's home country nor the country where the foreign subsidiary is located.

6 Recognize the key human resource policies that firms can develop to help expatriates succeed.

- *Selection*. Choose expatriates who are sensitive to cross-cultural differences, including a consideration of how the candidate's spouse and family might respond to the foreign assignment.
- *Training*. Provide cross-cultural training that sensitizes candidates to what they may confront in the foreign assignments.
- *Career development*. Ensure that the expatriate perceives the foreign assignment as part of a long-term career path within the company.
- *Compensation*. Maintain parity with the standard of living at home and provide additional incentives if expatriate successfully accomplish the foreign assignment.

7 Understand the ethical and social responsibility implications of doing business in different countries.

- Norms vary by country and a major concern for firms operating internationally is defining ethical behavior.

- Although competitors may abide by a different set of rules, U.S. firms must comply with regulations that prohibit the payment of bribes.
- Firms develop their own codes of conduct or may follow codes drawn up by international organizations.

discussion questions

1. If you were CEO of a medium-sized U.S. manufacturing firm, which of the changing patterns of international business identified in this chapter would concern you most? Explain.

2. Do you think there should be a large common market from Alaska to Tierra del Fuego, similar to the European Union? Why or why not?

3. What do you think accounts for the success of Ikea (see Management Close-Up 2.2) around the world? Can other struggling U.S. retailers such as K-Mart and Sears imitate Ikea's success? Explain your answer.

4. Which of the two perspectives concerning the use of ethics hotlines described in Management Close-Up 2.3 seem more reasonable to you (i.e., the European versus the American perspectives)? Explain your answer.

5. If you were the owner of a small but rapidly growing high-tech firm making sophisticated computer chips for medical equipment, which mode of entry would you prefer for entering foreign markets? Explain.

6. Do you think an international firm should have local managers in all important posts? Why or why not?

7. Is a firm justified in paying a bribe if it believes a competitor will do so to win an important contract? Explain.

Sweatshop Swipe

management minicase 2.1

After years of relative quiet, the anti-sweatshop debate is heating up again. United Students Against Sweatshops (USAS) have mounted demonstrations on 40 campuses demanding that universities force companies that license and make their sports clothes and other apparel to use only suppliers that pay a living wage and respect unions. USAS wants clothing companies to agree to pay higher prices to overseas factories that make college goods, which have annual sales of about $3 billion. Factories would have to boost wages, now about $97 a month in China. Jim Wilkerson, Duke University's director of trademark licensing and stores, calls the idea "workable," adding: "It would raise prices, but only by about 25 cents on a $30 garment."

Discussion Questions

1. Do you think U.S. companies have the moral responsibility to offer a so-called living wage and to fight exploitative practices in foreign countries, even if doing so means putting the company at a competitive disadvantage? Explain your answer.

2. Do you think most consumers care about potential abuses of overseas contractors? Would most consumers be willing to pay slightly higher prices to improve the standard of living of foreign workers? Explain your answer.

3. Some believe that a company might actually increase business by convincing customers that it is socially responsible and that it values human dignity more than making an extra buck. Do you agree? Why or why not?

Source: Adapted from A. Berstein, "Sweatshop Swipe," *BusinessWeek*, October 10, 2005, p. 14.

management minicase 2.2

Drug Testing Goes Offshore

Patients can be recruited for clinical trials of drugs 10 times faster in Russia than in the United States, shaving precious time and millions of dollars off the drug-development cycle. From Azerbaijan to Nigeria, pharmaceutical companies are increasingly shifting clinical trials to emerging markets—as much as 40 percent of all drug trials in 2006, according to several pharmaceutical executives, up from about 10 percent in 1999. And they are doing it by outsourcing many of those trials to contract research organizations, which in turn subcontract the work of finding patients to local doctors. Merck's Vioxx and Zocor were tested in Russia and other developing countries, as were many of Pfizer's billion-dollar drugs, before gaining approval in the United States. While the vast majority of the trials are conducted without problems, there have been enough instances of ethical abuse and breakdowns in the scientific process to cause concern. A lawsuit still making its way through U.S. courts alleges that Pfizer tested a meningitis drug on Nigerian children in 1996 without their consent, resulting in five deaths. And there have been charges over the years that other trials have endangered patients or have been conducted without proper ethical review.

The shift of drug testing to poorer countries is largely being driven by economics. An average new drug costs $900 million to bring to market, and more than half the cost is tied to the four trial phases in which new medicines are tested on humans for safety and efficacy. Recruiting patients is the most expensive part of drug development, accounting for 40 percent of the trials' budget, according to published studies.

Working in countries such as Russia, says Pfizer senior vice president Adrain Otte, can cut three to six months off a trial, meaning a drug can get to market that much faster. And the trials are cheaper. GlaxoSmithKline CEO Jean Paul Garnier says that a third of his company's trials now take place in low-cost countries, and he aims to hit 50 percent within two years. Why? Running a trial in the United States costs about $30,000 per patient. He can do it in Romania for $3,000. "Globalization," says Garnier, "is the ultimate arbitrage for companies like GlaxoSmithKline."

Discussion Questions

1. Do you think it is appropriate for a pharmaceutical firm to conduct most of its clinical trials in less developed countries? Why or why not?

2. The Food and Drug Administration (FDA) in the United States requires that all trials submitted to it meet internationally accepted guidelines, known as Good Clinical Practice, that demand "the establishment of local review boards; ask government health ministries to approve all trials before they begin; warn against excessive payment to doctors; and outline how to obtain informed consent and avoid taking advantage of vulnerable patients." But as noted by Ward Cates, president of the research arm of nonprofit Family Health International. "How do you meet procedures required by the FDA in settings where electricity is going off two hours a day?" In your view, how can a pharmaceutical company ensure that clinical trials meet the FDA standards noted above? Is this realistic? Explain your answer.

3. Some companies argue that, cost savings aside, there are important benefits to more clinical trials overseas. From a mechanical standpoint, testing on ethnically diverse populations may offer more insight into the ways drugs can affect different people. And patients who would otherwise not receive any help get medication and treatment during the trials. Lastly, it helps drug companies penetrate new markets badly in need of new treatments. Russia's drug market is estimated at $5 billion this year, India's at $5.4 billion. Do you believe that these positive aspects outweigh potential problems with clinical trials overseas? Why or why not? Should the U.S. government become more involved in regulating these practices? Explain.

Source: Adapted from A. Lustgarten, "Drug Testing Goes Offshore," *Fortune*, August 8, 2005, pp. 67–72.

Got 5,000 Euros? Need a New Car?

In 2005, Renault launched a new car called "The Logan," originally planned for poorer countries, but which has became enormously successful around the world, including the richest European countries. The Logan, which sells for as little as 5,000 euros (at the time of this writing this would be just under $6,000), may soon be a major competitor in the U.S. market, putting additional pressure on struggling U.S. car companies such as GM and Ford.

No matter where the Logan sells, Renault has engineered a small miracle by making a car that is modern but stripped of costly design elements and superfluous technology. Its 1.4 liter, 75 horsepower engine and 1.6 liter 90 horsepower engine are very fuel efficient. Deutsche Bank pegs production costs for the Logan at $1,089 per car, less than half the $2,468 estimate for an equivalent Western auto. "The Logan is the McDonald's of cars," says Kenneth Melville, the Scot who headed the Logan design team. "The concept was simple: Reliable engineering without a lot of electronics, cheap to build and easy to maintain and repair."

The Logan was first produced in Romania, where gross pay for a line worker is $324 per month, versus an average $4,723 a month for auto workers in Western Europe. Now, Renault is ramping up production of the Logan from Russia to Morocco. A new Chinese plant is being built, which by 2010 may be producing as many as 700,000 units. "The investment in manufacturing is relatively low, so you can have factories that don't have to produce huge volumes to finance themselves," says Christoph Sturmer, senior analyst at researcher Global Insight in Frankfurt.

Renault expects sales of the sedan to climb from about 175,000 this year to 1 million by 2010, supplemented by the rollout of station wagon and pickup versions. By then, the Logan could add some $341 million to Renault's bottom line, according to Deutsche Bank auto analyst Gaetan Toulemonde. The company posted a profit of $4.26 billion on revenues of $49 billion last year.

Other companies are working on cheap cars, too. Volkswagen is considering building a $3,650 car for China. India's Tata motors is expected to debut a $2,000 car before 2008. But for now, the Logan is the one turning heads.

Critical Thinking Questions

1. How does a multinational firm benefit from seeing the entire world as its labor pool? Do you see any potential problem with this vision? Why or why not?

2. How does this case illustrate the changing pattern of international business discussed in this chapter? Explain your answer.

3. What are the implications of this case for U.S. car manufacturers' shareholders, managers, employees, and labor unions? Explain your answer.

Collaborative Learning Exercise

You have been appointed to a task force that advises the Chief Executive Officer of General Motors (GM) of the competitive implications to GM of Renault's planned expansion of the Logan during the next several years. The task force (composed of three to five students) will provide its recommendations and reasoning to the CEO (played by instructor).

Source: Adapted from G. Edmondson & C. Faivre de'Arcier, "Got 5,000 Euros? Need a New Car?" *BusinessWeek*, 2005, July 4, p. 49.

Colgate's Clean Sweep

Colgate was started in 1806 by an English immigrant who set up a starch, soap, and candle business on Dutch Street in New York. From these humble origins the company has become one of the largest multinational corporations with operations in almost all countries of the world, despite its "low-tech" product line of toothpaste, razor blades, soaps, and shaving creams. Visit Colgate's Web site as well as other related Internet sites to answer the following questions:

1. What accounts for Colgate's international success, despite the potential for intense competition in most markets?
2. Colgate boasts that its "Colgate Culture" has a worldwide basis. How can a company create such a culture despite operating in many different cultural milieus? What are the advantages and disadvantages of a company culture that transcends national culture?
3. Compare and contrast the structure of Colgate's executive team with another company's, which you can research on the Internet. Analyze the implications of your comparison from an international perspective.
4. After researching Colgate, would you advise the company to engage in licensing patents, joint ventures, or strategic alliances, or to establish wholly owned subsidiaries? Explain your answer.

manager's

checkup 2.1

Careers in Global Management

Given the substantial increases in global business over the last decade, it has become increasingly important for managers and companies to understand the career aspirations of young managers. This questionnaire allows you to increase your understanding of your own career aspirations.

What Are Your Career Plans?

The following section asks you a number of questions about your career plans. In the questions:

Home country is your country of citizenship.

An *international assignment* is one in which the company sends an employee for a single assignment of a year or more to another country.

A *global career* is a series of international assignments in various countries.

International travel is a business trip to another country without the employee moving there.

An *expatriate* is an employee who is sent by the company to live and work in another country.

For each of the following items, rate the extent to which you agree:

1 = Disagree

2 = Don't have an opinion

3 = Agree

How true is each of the following statements for you?

1. I am seriously considering pursuing a global career. _____
2. I would like my first job after school to be in another country. _____
3. If offered an equivalent position in my home country or in the foreign country of my choice, I would rather work at home. _____
4. While continuing to live in my home country, I would like to travel internationally more than 40 percent (approximately 20 weeks/year) of my time. _____

5. I would like to have an international assignment at some time in my career. _____

6. I would like to follow a global career in which I have a series of international assignments. _____

7. I had never thought about taking an international assignment until I read this questionnaire. _____

There are many reasons why people choose not to pursue a global career. Which of the following would discourage you from pursuing a global career or taking an international assignment?

1. I like living in my home country. _____

2. I do not want to learn another language. _____

3. I do not want to adjust to another culture. _____

4. My spouse or significant other would not want to move to another country. _____

5. It is not good to move children. _____

6. I want my children to be educated in my home country. _____

7. I do not want to live in:

    a. A country outside my home country. _____

    b. North America. _____

    c. Europe. _____

    d. Latin or South America. _____

    e. Asia. _____

    f. Africa. _____

    g. The Middle East. _____

    h My home country. _____

    i Other (specify). _____

8. International jobs involve too much travel. _____

9. If I live in another country, my children will not gain a sense of national identity. _____

10. My spouse or significant other would not want to interrupt his or her career. _____

11. I will lose my sense of identity, my roots. _____

12. International assignments put too much strain on a marriage. _____

13. When you are on an international assignment you become "invisible" to the company and tend to be forgotten for promotions. _____

14. It would be difficult to come back home after having lived and worked for a long time in another country. _____

15. I do not want to be exposed to political instability in some parts of the world. _____

16. I would be more socially isolated and lonely in another country. _____

17. I would be exposed to more personal danger in another country. _____

In comparing potential domestic and global careers, which do you think could give you the greatest professional opportunities? (Mark one)

	Domestic Career	About Same	Global Career
1. I could succeed faster in	_____	_____	_____
2. I could earn a higher salary in	_____	_____	_____
3. I could have greater status in	_____	_____	_____
4. I could be more recognized for my work in	_____	_____	_____
5. I could have a more interesting professional life in	_____	_____	_____
6. I could have a more satisfying personal life in	_____	_____	_____

In comparing women and men, who do you think will have the greater chance of being (Mark one)

	Women	Equal Chances	Men
1. Selected for an international assignment?	_____	_____	_____
2. Effective on an international assignment?	_____	_____	_____
3. Successful in advancing in a global career?	_____	_____	_____
4. Effective on domestic assignments?	_____	_____	_____
5. Successful in advancing in a domestic career?	_____	_____	_____
6. Socially isolated and lonely in another country?	_____	_____	_____
7. Exposed to personal danger in another country?	_____	_____	_____

In Your Opinion

1. What are the main reasons that would lead you to accept an international assignment? List three.

2. What are the main reasons why you would turn down an international assignment? List three.

3. What, if any, are the major challenges for women successfully pursuing global careers that include international assignments (which do not exist for men)?

Source: From *International Dimensions of Organizational Behavior,* 3rd edition, by N. J. Adler © 1997. Reprinted with permission of South-Western College Publishing, a division of Thomson Learning. www.thomsonrights.com. Fax 800-730-2215.

China Brands

Summary

Today, Japan leads the electronics market, with Korea a safe second. But the world's most populous country, China, is showing significant potential to explode in the electronics market. China is also making headway by marketing TsingTao beer as a global brand. China's brands are currently becoming successful by marketing to their billion and a half population at home. Xerox and Sony are already manufacturing within China, but it's the nation's own brands that are showing the potential to become global giants in the years ahead. One day China could have some of the world's most popular brands.

There has been a total quality management "revolution" in China, and Haier, a refrigerator manufacturer, is leading the way. The Chinese are placing an emphasis on the quality of their products; the next step, according to Berntt Schmidt of Columbia Business School, is to focus on building brands. Lenovo is the number one selling PC in China, is well known throughout Asia, and plans to launch internationally during its sponsorship of the 2008 Olympics in Beijing. In addition to these, SVA is a popular Chinese television manufacturer that has shelf space in Wal-Mart, Target, Sears, and other retail stores in the United States.

Discussion Questions

1. A company cannot succeed without applying as part of its strategy the technologies that have evolved (and continue to evolve), offering better products and better production techniques. How has China used technology to improve its position for success in the global economy?

2. New entrants into an industry compete with established companies that control the current market share. What are some barriers to entry for Chinese companies looking to expand in the electronics industry? The beverage industry? How might these firms overcome such barriers?

3. Customers purchase products and services and thus give brands legitimacy. Customers can influence pricing, quality, and service they demand from a company. How does China have an edge concerning its current customer base in China?

chapter 3

Managing Social Responsibility and Ethics

Learning Objectives

1. Apply the four key ethical criteria that managers and employees should use when making business decisions.

2. Explain why businesses establish codes of ethics as a method of guiding employee conduct.

3. Recognize ways to encourage ethical behavior in business.

4. Recognize morally challenging situations where ethical decisions should be made.

5. Identify important categories of stakeholders.

6. Recognize the influence of various stakeholders on a company's priorities, policies, plans and goals.

Eating for Credit

What does a former schoolteacher see when she travels between her home and her job every day and passes a blighted schoolyard? If she is Alice Waters, she sees an opportunity for her company to make a difference in kids' lives.

Waters, a former Montessori teacher, is the founder of Chez Panisse, a popular restaurant in Berkeley, California, that's been breaking new culinary ground for more than 35 years by serving local, seasonal, and sustainably grown foods. She has become a revolutionary force in the culinary world, championing organic food and helping popularize it from local farmers' markets all the way to the Clinton White House. The unused acre of the Martin Luther King Jr. Middle School's yard that lies between Waters's home and her restaurant had weeds poking through cracks in its cement several years ago when Waters was inspired to do something about it. With the school's approval, the help of some friends, and donated funds, Waters broke up and removed the cement, tilled and enriched the soil, and planted a bold swath of fruits, vegetables, herbs, and edible flowers. Students from the school worked with Waters and crew in planting, nurturing, and harvesting the organic garden. Then the idea really began to take off.

A kitchen was soon added, and the school's 1,000 students began to learn how to prepare the food they'd grown. "Give me any kid," says Waters today, "In six weeks, they'll be eating chard." Her project, known as The Edible Schoolyard, is now fully supported by the Chez Panisse Foundation, which Waters founded with a commitment to "transforming public education by using food traditions to teach, nurture, and empower young people." A new cafeteria where students and teachers will eat lunch together is under construction at the school. And not long ago, the Chez Panisse Foundation signed an agreement with the Berkeley Unified School District to create a new food curriculum for all the district's students in kindergarten through grade 12. The curriculum incorporates organic gardening, healthy cooking, and nutritious communal lunches for students and teachers alike. Lunch is an academic subject, and food-related activities permeate the curriculum, from math classes that measure garden beds to science classes that study drainage and erosion, while history classes look at the agricultural methods of pre-Columbian peoples. The program is beginning in five of the district's 16 schools with a $3.8 million grant from the foundation, and it has already become a model for other schools and organizations nationwide.

The foundation hopes its School Lunch Initiative will spearhead changes in the way parents, schools, and children everywhere think about growing and preparing food, beginning with "every public school child in Berkeley." Waters's concerns about rising rates of childhood obesity and diabetes are shared by many parents and educators, and she sees the Foundation's activities as a positive way to change consumers' dependence on the fast-food industry, unhealthy foods valued for their convenience, and wasteful methods of producing food. "These values are changing us," she wrote recently in *The New York Times*. "As a nation, we need to take back responsibility for the health of not just our children, but also our culture."

Will the Edible Schoolyard catch on? Will the School Lunch Initiative grow into a nationwide curriculum movement? Waters and the Chez Panisse Foundation hope so. "This is not just changing the food in the cafeteria and making that an educational experience," says Waters. "This is for every single child."

Sources: "Chez Panisse Foundation," www.chezpanisse.com, accessed February 27, 2006; Alice Waters, "Eating for Credit," *The New York Times*, February 24, 2006, p. A23; Karola Saekel, "Culinary Pioneers: Pioneering Garden Marks a Decade," *San Francisco Chronicle*, September 7, 2005, p. F2; Kim Severson, "Food Joins Academic Menu in Berkeley School District," *San Francisco Chronicle*, August 29, 2004, p. A1.

CRITICAL THINKING QUESTIONS

1. *What benefits does Chez Panisse receive by focusing attention on corporate social responsibility through the actions of its foundation?*

2. *Organizational stakeholders are groups that have an interest in how a company performs or uses its resources. Who are Chez Panisse's organizational stakeholders?*

3. *Which organizational strategy most closely corresponds to how Chez Panisse manages relationships with its stakeholders? Is it a proactive approach or an accommodation approach?*

We'll revisit these critical thinking questions regarding Chez Panisse in our Concluding Thoughts at the end of the chapter.

It's a tricky world out there. Consequently, ethics and social responsibility should be a high priority for every member of an organization. This chapter examines the nature of business ethics and the basis of ethical decisions. It presents codes of ethics and provides examples of ethical challenges you are likely to encounter as an employee or a manager in a business setting. Skills for Managing 3.1 on page 101 lists the management skills related to business ethics and social responsibility.

Next, the broader context of corporate social responsibility as well as the key stakeholders involved are examined. The goal is to help you gain a heightened awareness of the many ethical challenges that are present in the new millennium.

ethics

Principles that explain what is good and right and what is bad and wrong and that prescribe a code of behavior based on these definitions.

business ethics

Standards or guidelines for the conduct and decision making of employees and managers.

What Are Business Ethics?

Ethics are principles that explain what is right or wrong, good or bad, and what is appropriate or inappropriate in various settings. These ideas make it possible to prescribe a code of behavior for both work and one's personal life. **Business ethics** provide standards or guidelines for the conduct and decision making of employees and managers. Without a code of ethics, there is usually no consensus regarding ethical principles. Different people will use different ethical cri-

SKILLS FOR MANAGING ETHICS AND SOCIAL RESPONSIBILITY

What management skills are needed to make ethical decisions and to deal with the concerns of stakeholders with diverse interests in the company?

- *Ethical decision-making skills*. From time to time, every businessperson faces an ethical dilemma that is difficult to solve. Your solution may cause other people to become angry or resentful. You will need to be able to see beyond your own self interest. One decision can enhance your reputation as a manager or detract from it. Even if you do not engage in unethical practices, a co-worker or a subordinate may. How you deal with unethical behavior

will be likely to influence your reputation. In this chapter, guidelines for ethical decision making are discussed. You can practice these skills in various situations.

- *Analyzing stakeholder concerns*. Stakeholders are people with interests in how a company performs and how it uses its resources. It is important to be proactive in dealing with stakeholder issues. First, identify who the stakeholders are along with how they are affected by company policies and how they have been treated in the past, and then you will know how they can affect your ability to pursue business goals.

teria in determining whether a practice or behavior is ethical or unethical. For example, it is not unusual in all good conscience for a manager to exaggerate the positive accomplishments of an employee in order to promote the employee or provide a salary increase. But another manager may consider inflating an employee's performance record a distortion of the truth, and thus unethical conduct.

Business ethics are not the same thing as laws. Law and ethics are in agreement in some situations but not in others. For example, it is both illegal and unethical to steal merchandise from an employer, but often it is not illegal to engage in conduct that is unethical. While it may not be illegal to take credit for the work of a colleague, it is highly unethical. Unfortunately, more than a few individuals have engaged in such tactics in order to advance their careers. When an organization does not condemn such behavior, others are encouraged to imitate it. Soon the organization develops a culture of political back-stabbing that drives away the most talented people and drains the energies of those who remain.

Nearly half the workers surveyed in a recent study admitted to engaging in at least one unethical act during the previous year. The most frequent unethical behaviors included cutting corners on quality, covering up potentially damaging incidents, lying about sick days, and deceiving customers. The workers blamed such daily pressures as trying to balance work and family, being forced to work longer hours due to layoffs, and poor manager–worker communications. They felt that ethical dilemmas could be reduced by better communication and a serious commitment by managers to establishing ethical standards of conduct.[1]

Table 3.1 on page 102 lists some different categories of ethical issues in business. It suggests that many business relationships have the potential for unethical conduct, including those between employer and employee, company and customer, company and shareholder, and company and the community.

table 3.1

Selected Ethical Issues in Business

Employee–Employer Relations
- Petty theft of office supplies
- Cheating on expense accounts
- Distortion or falsification of internal reports
- Doing personal work while on company time

Employer–Employee Relations
- Sexual harassment
- Bullying and abusive treatment of employees
- Providing unsafe working conditions
- Unfair and dishonest performance evaluations
- Withholding recognition, appreciation, and other psychic rewards

Company–Customer Relations
- Deceptive marketing or advertising
- Unsafe or unhealthy products
- Uncivil treatment toward customers

Company–Shareholder Relations
- Excessive pay for top executives
- Mismanagement of corporate assets or opportunities
- Financial reports that distort actual performance

Company–Community/Public Interest
- Sponsoring activities that harm the environment
- Undue influence in the political process through lobbying
- Bribes given to influence public officials
- Taking resources out of the community without giving back to it

Source: Adapted from A. B. Carroll and A. K. Buchholtz, *Business and Society*, 6th ed., Mason, OH: Thompson, 2006.

Ethics Approaches

Different people utilize different ethical value systems. These systems are based on personal experiences along with religious, educational, and family training. One manager might consider it beneficial to downsize a company's workforce because the surviving employees, who make up the majority, will be employed by a more effective and efficient firm. Another manager might view a downsizing decision as unethical because the employees who lose their jobs are deprived of economic opportunities simply because it is cost effective. The different ethical value systems of the two managers lead them to place different judgments on the attractiveness or repulsiveness of downsizing.

Managers typically use one of four key ethical approaches when making business decisions. They are utilitarianism, individualism, the rights approach, and the justice approach. Each takes a different view of what is most important to individuals and society.

Utilitarianism

utilitarianism

A means of making decisions based on what is good for the greatest number of people.

Decisions should be made on the basis of what is good for the greatest number of people from a **utilitarian** perspective. To apply the utilitarian criterion, one would examine all the people affected by a decision and choose the solution that satisfies the most people. Utilitarianism is sometimes referred to as the "calculus of pain, because it tries to minimize pain and maximize pleasure for the greatest number of people." Although utilitarianism strives to attain the ideal of democracy by promoting good for the majority, it may overlook the rights or needs of a minority of individuals.

Individualism

People who base ethical decisions on **individualism** believe that personal self-interests should be promoted as long as they do not harm others. Individualism as a basis for making business decisions is derived from the principles of capitalism first expressed in the 18th century by Adam Smith. In *The Wealth of Nations*, Smith wrote that markets should be free, that they should be the basis of all transactions, and that they should be subject to a minimum of interference by other forces such as governments. All available information is utilized when individuals make economic choices. Lying and other unethical behavior are penalized because it is in people's self-interest to do business with ethical firms and individuals rather than with liars and cheats.

At the same time, the costs of obtaining information about individuals' or firms' motives may be steep, and there are differences in power between individuals bargaining in the market. In such cases, some individuals can take advantage of their power or access to information to the detriment of others. For example, American consumers of health care have less power than insurance companies and have little access to specific information on the implications of choosing one policy or one doctor over another. Citizens of France, Germany, and Sweden believe individualism has resulted in the lack of a national health care plan for U.S. citizens. Consequently, they believe, the weakest members of society are the ones who suffer the most.

individualism
The degree to which a society values personal goals, autonomy, and privacy over group loyalty, commitment to group norms, involvement in collective activities, social cohesiveness, and intense socialization; ethical decisions based on individualism promote individual self-interest as long as it does not harm others.

Rights Approach

The belief that each person has fundamental human rights that should be respected and protected is the **rights approach**. People have the rights of freedom of speech, privacy, and due process when charged with a crime or rule infraction. They also have the right to a safe and healthy environment. These rights make it possible for them to act in their own best interests, which in turn benefits society. According to the rights approach, a decision is unethical if it deprives an individual of fundamental human rights.

The rights approach provides specific criteria for judging the ethics of a decision; however, conflicting rights must often be sorted out when making business decisions. For example, a manager who shares negative information about personal problems experienced by a former employee with another employer who is considering hiring that individual exercises the right of free speech but may also have violated the employee's right to privacy. Whose rights should have priority?

rights approach
A means of making decisions based on the belief that each person has fundamental human rights that should be respected and protected.

Justice Approach

Treating all people fairly and consistently when making decisions is the basis of the **justice approach**. This includes considering both distributive and procedural justice. *Distributive justice* examines the fairness of rewards, punishments, and outcomes in an organization. It asks whether an employee received compensation equitable with performance or whether the employee was overpaid or underpaid. *Procedural justice* involves the fair and consistent application of rules and procedures. When an employee is disciplined for a safety rule infraction, the

justice approach
An approach to decision making based on treating all people fairly and consistently when making business decisions.

In 2005 former WorldCom CEO Bernard Ebbers was sentenced to 25 years in prison, one of the longest sentences ever received by a former chief executive. The stiff sentence stemmed in large part from the estimated $2 billion investor losses prosecutors attributed to Ebbers's fraud at WorldCom.

procedural justice standard would be violated if other employees who broke the rule were not similarly disciplined.

The justice approach is more flexible than other ethical approaches, because it recognizes that standards of fairness vary depending on the individuals involved in the decision. For example, unionized auto workers see equal raises for all workers as the fair way to distribute salary increases. Equality raises union solidarity. Managers consider rewarding people on the basis of individual performance as fair, because they believe rewards should be based on the workers' contributions to profitability.

Applications of Ethics Approaches

To see how the four approaches to ethical decision making differ, consider the policy of random drug testing. A utilitarian sees random drug testing as ethical because more employees and customers are protected from accidents caused by drug-using employees than are angered by having to submit to random drug tests. Random drug testing would also be perceived as ethical when applying the criterion of individualism: owners are free to enact policies that make the company more efficient, and employees are free to exercise their disapproval by quitting and seeking employment at a firm that does not require random drug testing.

On the other hand, a manager who applies the rights approach may consider random drug testing unethical because it violates an employee's right to privacy and the right of protection from searches without probable cause to justify the test. Similarly, random drug testing would be seen as unethical in the justice approach because it presumes that an employee is guilty of using drugs and makes employees prove that they are innocent based on the chemical analysis of body fluids. In American justice, a person is innocent unless proven guilty.

Comparison of Ethics Approaches

One way to compare the four approaches to ethical decision making is to view them on the basis of how well they satisfy two elements of a fair and just society: (1) the degree of economic freedom in society to earn and retain wealth compared to how wealth is redistributed and shared with the less fortunate; and (2) the degree of concern a society has for individuals compared to the degree of concern for the community. Notice that in some social systems concern for the community will take precedence over concern for individuals, while in other social systems concern for individuals will matter more. Similarly in some social systems economic freedom based on free enterprise takes precedence over having an equal distribution of the wealth in the society, while in other social systems a fair and equal distribution of the wealth produced in the society takes precedence over the freedom to accumulate individual wealth. For example, we would not be surprised if employees at a Wall Street investment bank had strong preferences for economic freedom and concern for individuals,

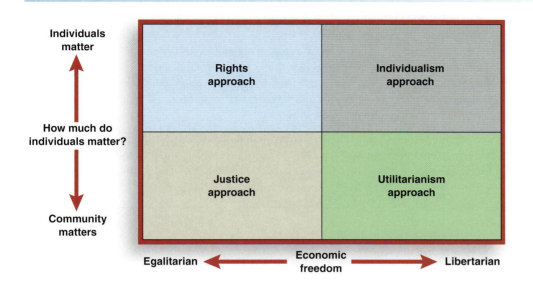

FIGURE 3.1

Comparison of Ethics Approaches

while employees who work for the Red Cross are likely to reflect strong preferences for equal distribution of wealth and concern for the community.

Figure 3.1 above compares the four approaches to ethical decision making by classifying them according to their degree of economic freedom and concern for individuals. The individualism approach to ethics reflects a high concern for individuals and high degree of economic freedom. The justice approach to ethics reflects a high concern for the community and for an egalitarian distribution of wealth. Similarly, the rights approach to ethics displays a high concern for individualism and for an egalitarian distribution of wealth. The utilitarianism approach to ethics reflects a high concern for the community and for economic freedom.

Codes of Ethics

When there is a void of ethical guidelines in a company, employees rely on personal value systems. Creating a more standardized approach can be accomplished by developing a code of ethics.

A **code of ethics** is a formal statement of ethics and values that is designed to guide employee conduct in a variety of business situations. It is particularly useful for giving employees ways to deal with conflicts of interest, gift giving and receiving, communicating with competitors, and making political contributions. More than 90 percent of large U.S. companies and almost half of smaller firms

LOC-In

① Learning Objective Check-In

Hillsdale Ceramics is reevaluating its approach to ethics. The firm has had problems in the past with inconsistent application of rules across different employees. Its managers also want to make sure that the decisions that are made affecting the entire company satisfy the greatest number of workers and cause "pain" to the fewest number. Lastly, the firm wants to make sure that the employees all enjoy a safe and healthy environment.

1. *The decision to apply rules consistently across worker situations is demonstrative of _____.*
   a. *distributive justice*
   b. *procedural justice*
   c. *individualism*
   d. *the rights approach*

2. *The approach used in making business decisions that benefit the greatest number of workers is called _____.*
   a. *individualism*
   b. *distributive justice*
   c. *the rights approach*
   d. *utilitarianism*

3. *The approach of making sure no business decision deprives an individual of the right to a safe and healthy environment is called _____.*
   a. *utilitarianism*
   b. *the rights approach*
   c. *individualism*
   d. *procedural justice*

code of ethics

A formal statement of ethics and values that is designed to guide employee conduct in a variety of business situations.

Working As a Manager It is critical for a manager to protect his or her reputation as an ethical person. Managers are role models for other employees and consequently are held to a higher standard of personal conduct. A tarnished moral reputation interferes with a manager's ability to influence employees and makes it difficult to serve as a communication link between executives and front-line employees.

Managers are responsible for creating an environment that supports ethical behavior and discourages unethical conduct. A manager should set ethical conduct goals. For example, a financial securities manager may set a goal of zero tolerance for dishonesty among stockbrokers.

have established codes of ethics.[2] Codes are typically published as either corporate credos or ethical policy statements. Also, many professions, such as doctors, lawyers, engineers, literary agents, and college professors, have codes of ethics. Managers should also be concerned with their reputation for ethical conduct as explained in Management Is Everyone's Business 3.1 above.

Corporate Credos

corporate credo

A formal statement focusing on principles and beliefs, indicating the company's responsibility to its stakeholders.

A **corporate credo** details a company's responsibility to its stakeholders. *Stakeholders* are groups or individuals with vested interests in the performance of the enterprise, including how managers distribute company resources. Stakeholders include employees, customers, and shareholders. The corporate credo focuses on principles and beliefs that can provide direction in a variety of ethically challenging situations.

The credo of Johnson & Johnson is reproduced in Figure 3.2 on page 107. As shown, the company identifies its responsibilities to consumers, employees, communities, and stockholders. This led to an extraordinary response to a difficult situation in the 1980s. When a criminal put capsules laced with cyanide in Tylenol bottles and some customers died as a result of taking the tainted medicine, Johnson & Johnson immediately took Tylenol off the market until it could be reissued in tamper-proof packaging. The credo was one factor that helped Johnson & Johnson effectively handle the crisis.

Ethical Policy Statements

ethical policy statements

A firm's formal guidelines that provide specific formulas for employees' ethical conduct.

Sometimes a credo is not specific enough for a large company that faces complex ethical challenges in many different markets and cultures. In such situations, more concrete guidelines on ethical conduct are needed. **Ethical policy statements** provide specific formulas for employee conduct. They answer such questions as whether a salesperson may offer a gift to a good customer, how much technical information can be shared with a competitor, whether an executive may purchase company stock in advance of a proposed merger, and whether the company can award a franchise to a relative of an employee.

Numerous companies have adopted ethical policy statements that inform employees of acceptable standards of conduct. Examples of such employers include:

FIGURE 3.2

Johnson & Johnson Corporate Credo

Source: Reprinted with permission of Johnson & Johnson, www.jnj.com.

Our Credo

We believe our first responsibility is to the doctors, nurses, and patients,
to mothers and fathers and all others who use our products and services.
In meeting their needs everything we do must be of high quality.
We must constantly strive to reduce our costs in order to maintain reasonable prices.
Customers' orders must be serviced promptly and accurately.
Our suppliers and distributors must have an opportunity to make a fair profit.

We are responsible to our employees,
the men and women who work with us throughout the world.
Everyone must be considered as an individual.
We must respect their dignity and recognize their merit.
They must have a sense of security in their jobs.
Compensation must be fair and adequate, and working conditions clean, orderly and safe.
We must be mindful of ways to help our employees fulfill their family responsibilities.
Employees must feel free to make suggestions and complaints.
There must be equal opportunity for employment, development
and advancement for those qualified.
We must provide competent management, and their actions must be just and ethical.

We are responsible to the communities in which we live and work
and to the world community as well.
We must be good citizens – support good works and charities and bear our fair share of taxes.
We must encourage civic improvements and better health and education.
We must maintain in good order the property we are privileged to use,
protecting the environment and natural resources.

Our final responsibility is to our stockholders.
Business must make a sound profit.
We must experiment with new ideas.
Research must be carried on, innovative programs developed and mistakes paid for.
New equipment must be purchased, new facilities provided and new products launched.
Reserves must be created to provide for adverse times.
When we operate according to these principles, the stockholders should realize a fair return.

Johnson & Johnson

1. St. Paul Companies, which specializes in commercial and personal insurance, and states that employees may accept gifts of inexpensive pens or appointment diaries, but not liquor, lavish entertainment, travel, or clothing.[3]

2. Eli Lilly and Company, a pharmaceutical firm, in which employees may not conduct business with a company with which they or their relatives are associated, unless Eli Lilly has given specific approval and authorization.[4]

3. General Dynamics Corporation, a defense-industry contractor, where employees may not use or share inside information that is not available to the general public for personal gain.[5]

4. J. D. Edwards and Company, a software firm, which prohibits profanity, as well as racial and sexual slurs. Instead, language should convey a loving, caring, and sensitive attitude toward other people.[6]

LOC-In

2 Learning Objective Check-In

1. *Markway is a high-end office supply company that often deals with upscale clients and establishes strong relationships with the communities it operates in. Sometimes, employees face conflicts of interest regarding gift giving and receiving, communicating with competitors, and making political contributions. The _____ at Markway is a formal statement of values that is designed to guide employee conduct at the company. It is especially useful in these conflicting situations.*
   a. *code of ethics*
   b. *vision statement*
   c. *mission statement*
   d. *ethical structure*

Managing Ethics

Is it possible to actually change the ways in which employees behave? Many organizational leaders, who are interested in creating more ethical climates, believe the answer is "yes." To do so means establishing a corporate culture in which ethical behavior is the norm. Among the approaches that are available are ethics training, ethical structures, and whistleblower policies.

Ethics Training

ethics training

A means of providing employees and managers practice in handling ethical dilemmas that they are likely to experience.

Ethics training gives employees and managers the opportunity to actually practice handling the ethical dilemmas they are likely to experience. More than 40 percent of large U.S. companies provide **ethics training** to their employees. Most courses contain the following elements:

1. Messages from top executives emphasizing ethical business practices.
2. Discussion of codes of ethics.
3. Procedures for discussing or reporting unethical behavior.

Ethics training at aircraft manufacturer Boeing provides an excellent model for other firms. Led by the business ethics adviser of the division involved, it includes a customized videotape with an opening message by the division's general manager and the presentation of dramatic and routine situations.

At Matsushita, a large Japanese consumer electronics company, ethics training emphasizes treating customers with dignity and respect. Manager's Notebook 3.1 (see page 109) on business ethics in Japan provides examples of ethical values instilled in Japanese employees at Matsushita.

Management Is Everyone's Business 3.2 on page 109 stresses that teams need to ensure that team members behave ethically, and one way to do this is to provide ethics training to team members.

Ethical Structures

ethical structure

The procedures and the division or department within a company that promotes and advocates ethical behavior.

Ethical guidelines are one component of an **ethical structure**. The other is the division or department that is assigned the responsibility of overseeing those guidelines. These two elements must be carefully coordinated.

One type of ethical structure uses an *ethics officer* with a title like "director of ethics compliance." This individual deals with potential ethical violations and advises decision makers regarding ways to comply with the company's code of ethics. This is the case at General Dynamics Corporation, which established an ethical structure in the 1980s after being sanctioned for overcharging the military for defense contract work. Currently 40 divisional ethics program directors report to the corporate director of ethics, and they operate 30 hotlines over which employees can request information or counsel and report incidents of potential misconduct.

Another ethical structure approach is to have senior-level managers from different functions and units serve on an *ethics committee* that provides ethical oversight and policy guidance for management decisions. Dow Corning's business conduct committee conducts ethical audits of company plants on a worldwide basis. An auditor from the committee interviews managers and other employees to determine whether the ethical code is being followed and the kinds of violations that are occurring. The auditor of a sales unit, for example, looks for kickbacks or inappropriate gifts given or received, while the auditor of a manufacturing unit focuses on environmental pollution. Universities also use ethics

BUSINESS ETHICS IN JAPAN: THE CASE OF MATSUSHITA

Business ethics have international dimensions. In large Japanese firms, business ethics blend Confucian philosophy—the basis of Asian values—with capitalist values. Here are some examples of ethical principles taught to employees at Matsushita, the world's largest consumer electronics company, with headquarters in Osaka, Japan.

- A corporation is a public entity and it can exist only if it receives the support of society and therefore must contribute to society.
- Treat people you do business with as if they were part of your family. Prosperity depends on how much understanding one receives from the people with whom one conducts business.
- After-sales service is more important than assistance before sales. It is through such service that one gets permanent customers.
- Don't sell customers goods that they are attracted to. Sell them goods that will benefit them.
- It is not enough to work conscientiously. No matter what kind of job, you should think of yourself as being completely in charge of and responsible for your own work.
- If we cannot make a profit, that means we are committing a sort of crime against society. We take society's capital, we take their people, we take their materials, yet without a good profit, we are using precious resources that could be better used elsewhere.

Source: Adapted from J. P. Kotter, "Matsushita: The World's Greatest Entrepreneur," *Fortune*, March 31, 1997, pp. 105–110; Corporate Citizenship at Matsushita, www.panasonic.co.jp/global/about/citizenship/index.html, 2005.

MANAGEMENT IS EVERYONE'S BUSINESS 3.2

Working as a Team   It is a good idea to provide team members some ethics training as part of the team development process. If a team tolerates unethical conduct from one member, others may also be influenced by the conduct of this team member. Tolerance of such unethical activities as inflating an expense account can lead to more serious breaches of conduct that damage the reputation of the entire team. A team is only as ethical as its "weakest ethical link."

committees, which focus on allegations of such unethical conduct as faking research data and situations in which a faculty member plagiarizes the work of students or colleagues.

Whistleblower Policies

Employees who are willing to disclose illegal, immoral, or illegitimate practices by their employer require the protection of a **whistleblower policy**.[7] Companies with whistleblower policies rely on individual employees to report unethical activities to the ethics officer or committee, which then gathers facts and investigates the situation in a fair and impartial manner. Whistleblower

whistleblower policies

A method by which employees who disclose their employer's illegal, immoral, or illegitimate practices can be protected; companies with whistleblower policies rely on whistleblowers to report unethical activities to the ethics officer or committee, which will then gather facts and investigate the situation in a fair and impartial way.

Enron Executive Sherron Watkins reported financial misconduct as a whistleblower.

policies protect these individuals from retaliation by executives or coworkers whose practices have been exposed. In situations in which whistleblower policies are not present, employees face many obstacles. For example, the quality control officers for the Trans Alaska Pipeline were threatened with actual physical harm and demotion, and were victims of spying, as other employees attempted to keep them from reporting problems that might lead to oil spills.[8]

While the federal government and some states have enacted laws to protect whistleblowers from retaliation, there is scant protection for those who report unethical activities that are not specified in the laws. The Sarbanes-Oxley Act, a federal law enacted in 2002 after the financial scandals at Enron and WorldCom, provides protection to whistleblowers who disclose financial fraud in publicly traded corporations. The law protects whistleblowers from retaliation from the company or its employees and those who violate the law are liable for both civil and criminal penalties.[9] However, this federal law does not protect whistleblowers who report unethical conduct not related to financial fraud. A whistleblower policy provides a communication channel to report unethical activities. Whistleblower policies should include the following key features:

1. The policy encourages reporting unethical conduct and sets up meaningful procedures to deal fairly with reported violations.

2. Those who report violations are protected from retaliation. Even if an informant is incorrect about the alleged wrongdoing, the protection is extended as long as the informant acted in good faith in making the complaint.

3. Alternative reporting procedures are provided in cases where those to whom the report must be given are involved in the wrongdoing.

4. A provision is made for anonymous reporting to an ethics officer or committee.

5. Feedback on ethics violations is provided to employees so that they are aware that the policy is being taken seriously and that complaints are being investigated.

6. Top management supports and is involved in the whistleblower policy.[10]

The financial scandals at Enron and WorldCom have put the whistleblowers, who tried to report the misconduct of executives at these firms, in the limelight.[11] In 2001, Enron executive Sherron Watkins wrote a blunt memo to Enron CEO Kenneth Lay warning him that the company might "implode in a wave of accounting scandals." Instead of thanking her, management factions tried to squelch the bad news and intimidate her for not being a team player. After the financial scandal broke and became a media event, Watkins was congratulated for her courage in confronting a CEO about Enron's controversial off-the-books partnerships and shaky finances. She serves as a positive role model for whistleblowers.[12]

Online **LearningCenter**
www.mhhe.com/gomez3e

What is Your Primary Conflict Handling Style?

Personal Ethics

Ethical decisions are among the most difficult decisions you will ever have to make. When one presents itself, allow yourself plenty of time to consider the alternatives. Examine the consequences as well as the proposed procedures established to arrive at the outcome. Think about how the decision would look if it were made public in the company newsletter. Make sure you consider all the people who are directly or indirectly affected by the decision. It is a good idea to get feedback from a trusted friend or colleague before you act.

Manager's Notebook 3.2 on page 112 lists eight steps you can take to make sound ethical business decisions.

The U.S. military has recognized the importance of having officers set examples for enlisted personnel and holds officers to a higher standard of conduct. Officers who disobey a command or act unethically face harsh sanctions. Managers set the tone for employees through their actions and by their examples. If a manager's behavior conflicts with the company's code of ethics, employees may decide to disregard the code of ethics.

Ethics

Managers can influence the ethical behavior of those within their units in the following ways:

1. Take actions that develop trust, such as sharing useful information and making good on commitments.

2. Act consistently, so that employees are not surprised by unexpected management actions or decisions.

3. Be truthful and avoid white lies and other actions designed to manipulate people by giving a false impression.

4. Demonstrate integrity by keeping confidences and showing concern for others.

5. Meet with employees to discuss and define what is expected of them.

6. Ensure that employees are treated equitably, giving equivalent rewards for similar performance and avoiding actual or apparent special treatment of favorites.

7. Adhere to clear standards that are seen as just and reasonable—for example, neither praising accomplishments out of proportion nor imposing penalties disproportionate to offenses.

8. Respect employees, showing openly that you care about employees and recognize their strengths and contributions.[13]

In addition, Manager's Notebook 3.3 on page 113 includes approaches for ensuring that a climate for ethical conduct is maintained on your team.

Next read the ethical dilemma in Management Is Everyone's Business 3.3 on page 113, and apply the ethics tests given there to the situation that is described.

LOC-In

3 Learning Objective Check-In

Susan believes it is possible to change the ways employees at her firm behave. She is interested in making the climate at her firm more ethical. She understands that the corporate culture will have to value ethical behavior and cultivate it as a company norm. Susan is currently discussing several approaches with the other strategic decision makers at the company.

1. *Susan's first idea is to give employees and managers the opportunity to actually practice handling ethical dilemmas that they are likely to encounter. This is part of the _____ approach.*
   a. *ethical code of conduct*
   b. *ethical structure*
   c. *ethics training*
   d. *whistleblower*

2. *Susan thinks it is crucial to specifically appoint an ethics officer to deal with potential ethics violations. The person would also help decision makers at the company with ways to comply with the code of ethics. This idea involves _____.*
   a. *ethical structure*
   b. *whistleblower policies*
   c. *ethics training*
   d. *personal ethics*

3. *Lastly, Susan wants to make sure that those who report violations are protected from retaliation as long as they act in good faith in issuing a complaint. She wants to make sure that _____ are protected at the firm.*
   a. *violators*
   b. *ethics officers*
   c. *administrators*
   d. *whistleblowers*

3.2
manager's motebook

EIGHT STEPS TO SOUND ETHICAL DECISION MAKING IN BUSINESS

1. *Gather the facts.* Avoid jumping to conclusions without having the facts available to you. Consider the following questions: How did the situation occur? Are there historical facts I should know? Are there facts concerning the current situation I should know?

2. *Define the ethical issues.* Identify the ethical values at stake in this problem. Sometimes two important values are in conflict. For example, the right to privacy may conflict with the right to expect a safe workplace. Is there a code of ethics that suggests which values have the highest priority?

3. *Identify the affected parties.* Start with the parties directly affected by the outcome of the decision. Next, think broadly and include other parties who may also be affected, such as employees in other units, people in the community, or customers. How would your decision affect all these parties?

4. *Identify the consequences.* Think about the consequences for all the parties that you have identified. What is the probability of each different consequence for each party? Do you see any highly negative consequences that must be avoided? What are the short-term and long-term consequences of the decision?

5. *Identify your obligations.* Identify the obligations you feel and the reasons for each. For example, did you make a promise to another employee that you could be in jeopardy of breaking? Is your duty at odds with keeping your word to this person? Can you justify making an exception for this decision? Since we each enact numerous roles (as employee, leader, parent, spouse, volunteer, etc.), we are bound to have role conflicts that force us to favor one role over another for a given situation. It is important to be aware of all our obligations when considering a decision.

6. *Consider your character and integrity.* How would others judge your character and integrity if they knew all the facts about the decision that you were about to make? Would you feel good about disclosing your decision to a newspaper that would be read by the members of your community? If you would be ashamed of disclosing your decision to others, perhaps you should rethink your decision so that you feel more comfortable with it when scrutinized by others.

7. *Think creatively about potential actions.* Perhaps there are limitations on your ability to develop good alternatives to your ethical problem. Are they caused by your own personal interest in the outcome of the decision, such as ego or the possibility of a reward? Are your motives honorable? Get the input of others when you perceive such limitations.

8. *Check your gut feelings.* After you make a decision, check your gut feelings. Intuition can be very useful in sorting out problematic decision alternatives. If you are uncomfortable, something is probably not right. Check your responses to the earlier steps in the decision process to make sure you did not skip a step or ignore some important information.

Source: Adapted from L. K. Trevino and K. A. Nelson, *Managing Business Ethics*, 3rd ed. New York: John Wiley & Sons, 2004, pp. 94–100. Reprinted with permission of John Wiley & Sons, Inc.

Here are some practical ways for improving the ethical climate governing the conduct of employees on your team:

1. Agree on a code of ethical conduct that the team expects from all members.
2. Require that all new team members learn the code of ethical conduct.
3. Integrate ethics into the team performance evaluations so that there is accountability for ethical conduct.
4. Recognize and reward ethical behavior in team members.
5. Ensure that unethical behavior is not tolerated by the team.
6. From time to time let team members explain how they handled an ethical dilemma so that others can benefit from this experience.
7. Use surveys to find out the ethical concerns of customers that the team serves.
8. Find the ethical concerns of other teams and units of your organization and share this information with your team members.

Source: Adapted From R. L. Daft, *The Leadership Experience*, 3rd ed., Mason, OH: Thomson, 2005, p.576. Reprinted with permission of South-Western, a division of Thomson Leaning. www.thomsonrights.com. Fax: 800-730-2215.

MANAGEMENT IS EVERYONE'S BUSINESS 3.3

Working As an Individual   Suppose you face an ethical dilemma that is putting your personal values to the test.

What would you do in the following situation?

> The company where you are employed has a very clear procedure for a task but you know a "better" way to do the job. Your productivity results are a bit low this month. If you use your new approach and violate the "rules," you can raise your results to a higher level.

It can be useful to check your choices against some ethical tests:

- *Front-page test*. How would I feel if my decision became a headline in a local newspaper? Would I feel comfortable describing my actions or decision to a customer or stockholder?
- *Golden rule test*. Would I be willing to be treated in the same manner?
- *Personal gain test*. Is an opportunity for personal gain clouding my judgment? Would I make the same decision if the outcome did not benefit me in any way?

Source: Adapted from F. Navran, *Ethical Dilemmas in the Everyday Workplace*, www.ethics.org/resources, 2005.

Ethical Dilemmas in the Workplace

The workplace presents a variety of ethical challenges to managers, teams, and employees. Four examples of ethical dilemmas at work are: (1) performance appraisals, (2) employee discipline, (3) romantic relationships, and (4) gift giving.

Performance Appraisal

Performance appraisal is a formal evaluation of an employee's performance provided on a recurring basis. Typically, an employee receives feedback regarding his or her strengths and weaknesses in a document summarizing the employee's performance over the period of evaluation, which is usually one year. In most cases, the individual providing the performance appraisal is the supervisor. More specific information about performance appraisals is presented in Chapter 10 (Human Resource Management).

In order to do an effective job at evaluation, the supervisor should devote substantial time to collecting accurate performance information. This feedback will be used to let employees know which skills they have mastered and those which require improvement. Performance ratings are also used as the basis for pay increases, future work assignments, promotions, and sometimes layoffs. So it is crucial to collect accurate and fair information. Managers who deliberately provide false or misleading information for reasons of vengeance, dislike of a subordinate, or racial or sexual discrimination are violating ethical and legal standards.

Employee Discipline

One tool that managers use to change an employee's behavior when it does not meet expectations or when it is inappropriate is the discipline system. An example of a behavior that fails to meet expectations is when an employee arrives late to work without a reasonable excuse. An illustration of inappropriate employee conduct requiring immediate intervention would be when a server in a restaurant uses profanity or verbally attacks a customer.

Supervisors can misuse discipline by making it a way to intimidate employees they do not like or for retribution when an employee makes a mistake. When a supervisor uses employee discipline for purposes of revenge rather than to correct an inappropriate behavior, the abuse of power is of course unethical. The following are examples of unethical employee discipline.

- Closely monitoring the behavior of a disliked employee, looking for the opportunity to use discipline to punish the employee, while giving more slack to employees who are not on the supervisor's "hit list."
- Using rumors and unsubstantiated evidence as a basis to apply discipline to a targeted employee without giving the employee an opportunity to defend his or her conduct.

Such examples suggest that the application of employee discipline requires some basic guidelines to protect employees from being victimized by supervisors. Here are some basic guidelines for giving employee discipline in a fair and impartial way.

1. *Notify* employees in advance of a company's work rules and the consequences for violating them. An employee who violates a work rule should be given the opportunity to correct the behavior without being punished.
2. *Investigate* the facts of an employee's misconduct before applying discipline. Give an employee the opportunity to give his or her side of the story before a decision is made about whether the misconduct actually took place.
3. *Be consistent* in the response to rule violations. Discipline should be administered consistently without favoritism or discrimination.

Office Romance

Romance often blossoms in the workplace. People who spend time together are likely to develop romantic feelings. Unfortunately, when a romantic relationship ends, as many of them do, one partner may feel angry and abandoned. A broken relationship can be highly disruptive to people who are simply trying to focus on work. Co-workers may even be drawn into the conflict which can strain working relations if the unit requires a high degree of collaboration between employees.

Further, when romantic partners are publicly affectionate in front of customers or other employees, it makes some people uncomfortable. Public displays of affection are almost always inappropriate. Jealousy or suspicion may result, if someone else has romantic intentions toward the co-worker involved, or if it is a boss involved in the romance. Subordinates may suspect that the boss is being manipulated by his or her romantic partner and showing favoritism as a result. The supervisor's credibility may be undermined in the eyes of subordinates.

Few companies actually ban romantic relationships in the workplace. However, many try to provide basic rules of conduct regarding office romances. Employees should be sensitive not only to the feelings of the partner in the relationship but also to co-workers and customers who may be affected by the couple's behavior. Here are two basic suggestions for ethical employee conduct in a romantic relationship at the workplace.

- Public displays of affection at the workplace should be discouraged.
- Employees should be prohibited from dating people they directly supervise. If a romance begins, one or the other partner should be transferred.

Giving Gifts in the Workplace

Gift giving routinely occurs in the workplace. Employees often exchange gifts with each other during the Christmas holidays, managers give flowers to their secretaries on special occasions, and vendors customarily give merchandise such as coffee mugs or pens to prospective customers. These situations represent constructive gift giving to build relationships between people by letting them know they are appreciated.

Sometimes, however, by accepting a gift from a vendor or employee a person faces an ethical dilemma. A test of the ethical appropriateness of accepting the gift would be to first think about how a manager or co-worker would perceive the gift and the person who gave it. If you would feel uncomfortable explaining the gift, the discomfort probably means it would be ethically problematic. Here are some examples of situations where it would be clearly unethical to give or accept gifts:

- A vendor seeking to develop a business relationship with a company may offer to provide lucrative financial opportunities to the executive in charge of purchasing, expecting to influence the executive to buy the vendor's product. The vendor is, in fact, using the gift as a bribe. The executive may be unduly influenced to purchase inferior goods. Closing deals with bribes probably means the products cannot compete in the marketplace. For example, several executives at Qwest, one of the major U.S. telecommunications companies, received valuable stock options from some smaller suppliers of Internet gear, and later steered large contracts to those companies. After the financial scandal was exposed, it became clear that Qwest executives made purchasing decisions based on who gave them stock options, not on the best equipment. One of the former members of Qwest's board of directors called the practice of suppliers giving stock options as an enticement an "ethical nightmare."[14]
- In part of a larger investigation of employee misconduct at A. T. Kearney Inc., a management consulting firm, it was revealed that CEO Fred Steingraber used funds from his personal expense account to

purchase gifts for family members. Steingraber used company funds to purchase a laptop computer for his son, and paid $37,000 for a lavish 50th birthday party for his wife, complete with a magician and surprise visits from her sisters, who were flown in from Germany. In defense of his spending for his wife's birthday, Steingraber stated that the party was also attended by executives from A. T. Kearney customers who would later purchase consulting services from the firm.[15] Inviting potential customers to a birthday party for the CEO's wife in order to influence their purchasing decisions is probably more than merely inappropriate. It may have been criminal.

LOC-In

4 Learning Objective Check-In

Marie has found that her job as a manager presents a variety of ethical challenges. She is often involved in determining whether employees should receive pay increases, certain future assignments, promotions, or even layoffs. While she does not particularly like one of her subordinates, she knows that she will have to collect accurate and fair information about him in order to help in the evaluation process. Another situation Marie has been dealing with involves two of her subordinates, one of whom is directly responsible for supervising the other as part of a work team. These two individuals have become romantically involved since Marie assumed her role in managing them, and she is debating whether or not to transfer one of them to another area of the company.

1. *Which of the following is a true statement about an ethical way for Marie to deal with the subordinate she does not like?*
   a. *Marie should devote substantial time to collecting accurate performance information about him.*
   b. *Marie does not have to let her subordinate know what skills he has or has not mastered and which require improvement.*
   c. *Marie may deliberately provide misleading information because she dislikes the subordinate.*
   d. *Marie should incorporate her personal feelings toward the employee into the evaluation so that he knows why she does not like him.*
2. *Marie wants to ensure that her employees conduct themselves ethically. She does not mind the idea of an office romance, but her firm does require that relationships cannot exist between employees and their direct supervisors. For this reason, _____.*
   a. *Marie will likely require both employees to transfer to new positions.*
   b. *Marie will likely require that the two individuals limit public displays of affection, but they may continue the relationship in their current work roles.*
   c. *Marie will likely require the transfer of one or the other of the two employees involved with each other.*
   d. *Marie will likely initiate an investigation into employee misconduct regarding the romantic relationship.*

A common approach companies use to avoid conflicts of interest in gift giving is to have a gift policy that limits the dollar value to a modest amount, such as $25. The policy may also require that each employee fully disclose each gift that is given and received along with its dollar value.

In cultures outside the United States, especially in developing economies, the laws and ethics related to giving gifts between parties as a business practice are highly diverse. In the African nation of Senegal, 40 percent of executives were reported to believe that bribery was necessary to obtain a public contract.[16] Managers seeking to do business within foreign cultures that are more tolerant of bribery and kickbacks may wish to avoid the temptation of using these practices, even if it means losing some business. Companies in countries with laws against giving bribes still face ethical challenges related to gift giving. For example, there is a tradition in the pharmaceutical industry of allowing sales representatives to give free samples of drugs to doctors. Police in Verona, Italy, opened an investigation of this practice by GlaxoSmithKline. They discovered a scheme that went beyond giving free samples to doctors. Company sales representatives gave gifts such as computers and lavish trips to doctors in exchange for writing of prescriptions for the company's drugs.[17] Such a "race to the bottom" of the ethical yardstick in order to win a foreign business contract is not worth the price, because public disclosure of this form of gift giving harms a company's reputation. A tarnished company reputation is nearly impossible to repair.

The Corruption Perceptions Index for 2005 displayed in Table 3.2 on page 117 indicates the perceptions of corruption that occur in the 10 least corrupt (with high index numbers) and the 10 most corrupt countries (with low index numbers). It was based on a survey of international managers and academics. As shown, the

table 3.2

The Corruption Perceptions Index 2005

LEAST CORRUPT COUNTRIES			MOST CORRUPT COUNTRIES		
COUNTRY	SCORE	RANKING	COUNTRY	SCORE	RANKING
Iceland	9.7	1	Pakistan	2.1	144
Finland	9.6	2	Angola	2.0	151
New Zealand	9.6	2	Cote d'Ivoire	1.9	152
Denmark	9.5	4	Equatorial Africa	1.9	152
Singapore	9.4	5	Nigeria	1.9	152
Sweden	9.2	6	Haiti	1.8	155
Switzerland	9.1	7	Myanmar	1.8	155
Norway	8.9	8	Turkmenistan	1.8	155
Australia	8.8	9	Bangladesh	1.7	158
Austria	8.7	10	Chad	1.7	158
United States	7.6	17			

Source: From Transparency International, www.tranparency.org. Reprinted with Permission.

United States is ranked as the 17th least corrupt country, behind countries with "cleaner" business practices such as Finland, Sweden, and New Zealand. There are a total of 158 countries ranked on corruption in the total survey. Countries ranked low on the Corruption Perceptions Index (most corrupt) are more likely to tolerate bribery as a business practice than countries with a high rank.

Social Responsibility

Do corporations have a responsibility to conduct their affairs ethically and to be judged by the same standards as individuals? Should a business be concerned with more than the pursuit of profits for its shareholders? **Social responsibility** is the duty a company has to conduct its affairs ethically in a manner that benefits both employees and the larger society. There are both benefits and costs associated with acting in a socially responsible manner.

social responsibility

The belief that corporations have a responsibility to conduct their affairs ethically to benefit both employees and the larger society.

The Benefits of Social Responsibility

Caring for the natural environment is one of several dimensions of social responsibility that must be considered in the allocation of a firm's resources. Companies that pollute the air, water, and land must consider the rights of people in the community to breathe clean air and drink clean water and must pay to help clean up the pollution or face government penalties. Companies spend billions of dollars each year in order to comply with laws that protect the environment.

Social responsibility ultimately leads to improved odds of long-term survival for the organization. A narrow focus on producing goods and services for profit only, without considering the ramifications of company activities, may impair company performance in the long run and result in a failure to survive. In fact, social responsibility can have a positive effect on company performance. Research indicates that it is related to higher financial performance and the ability to recruit better quality job applicants.[18]

Cleaning up the *Exxon Valdez* oil spill in Alaska.

Some recent examples of the problems that corporations have faced as a result of failing to address social responsibility include the following:

1. In 1999 the courts determined that tobacco companies had purposefully withheld from the public knowledge that nicotine in tobacco is an addictive drug. Phillip Morris, R. J. Reynolds, and other large U.S. tobacco manufacturers agreed to pay $246 billion over a period of 25 years to compensate victims of lung cancer and other fatal illnesses related to cigarette smoking.[19]

2. Merck, a giant pharmaceutical firm, suddenly recalled its blockbuster arthritis drug Vioxx from the market in 2004, with the release of new evidence that the drug raises the risk of heart attacks and strokes. This news immediately cut Merck's share price in half, lopping $30 billion off the value of the world's fourth-largest drug company. The lawsuits stemming from Vioxx users alleging harm from the product are estimated to range from a few billion dollars to as much as $20 billion.[20]

3. In 1989 the *Exxon Valdez* spilled 11 million gallons of oil and polluted 2,600 miles of shoreline along Alaska's Prince William Sound. Environmentalists, consumers, and local businesses mobilized and forced Exxon to pay $3 billion in damages and for the cleanup.[21]

4. Drexel Burnham Lambert, an investment bank that made huge profits financing junk bonds in the 1980s, pleaded guilty to six felony counts involving mail, wire, and securities fraud in 1989. The bank's officers, one of whom was Michael Milken, were singled out for their lack of concern for other stakeholders and Securities and Exchange Commission (SEC) regulations. The firm paid $650 million in penalties to the government and to the victims; Milken went to jail; and Drexel Burnham went out of business.[22]

5. Executives at Enron, a Houston-based energy company, approved risky financial investments with company resources in off-balance-sheet financial deals that lost billions of dollars. When these losses were disclosed in 2001, Enron stock suddenly collapsed. The stock lost 99 percent of its value within a few months, putting the company into bankruptcy, and forcing the layoff of thousands of employees as the

video: THE ENTREPRENEURIAL MANAGER

New Belgium
Brewery—
Environmental
Responsibility

Summary

Founded by a social worker and an electrical engineer, New Belgium Brewery has always found ways to operate efficiently and in a socially responsible manner. Embracing new technologies, seeking out alternative forms of energy, and reducing its waste, New Belgium strives to make smart decisions that do well by the environment each and every day. In the past, taking environmental issues to heart was considered contradictory to good business. You either helped business and killed the environment, or helped the environment, but killed business. New Belgium has shown that a company can be environmentally conscious and operate efficiently and effectively as a long-term, profit-seeking business.

Jeff Lebesch, one of the founders and an electrical engineer, thinks outside the box about what kinds of beers to make, how the company runs (including its unconventional start-up), and how the beer is actually produced. This alternative thinking about the operations aspect of the business allows Jeff and the rest of the firm to have an environmentally friendly perspective. The company realizes that as a manufacturing firm, it operates as a waste stream. The management of waste and focus on efficiency are good for the environment *and* for business.

At New Belgium, many innovative and environmentally friendly techniques are used in the beer-brewing process. The firm reduces the amount of resources that it uses, limiting the initial flow coming into the firm. The firm reuses resources and recycles what it can. It places an emphasis on being highly energy-efficient. Turning lights on and off automatically is a simple but very effective way to reduce energy consumption on a daily basis at New Belgium. This required an up-front investment in technology, but promises long-term cost-savings and is true to the environmental ethic the company embraces. Methane recaptured from the brewery's waste actually provides enough energy to fuel the brewery for 5 hours each day.

The company's workers are also its owners. When a decision to reduce carbon emissions was on the table, the entire firm was involved. A study revealed that the largest emissions came from the company's source of fuel—a coal plant at the time. The company voted unanimously to contract 100 percent of its energy from a wind farm nearby, which accomplished the environmental goal of reducing emissions and also allowed the wind plants to continue in operation. They voted to dip into their bonus pool in order to finance the deal. The firm even has a philanthropy committee, which demonstrates the firm's proactive stance toward social responsibility.

Discussion Questions

1. How is New Belgium's approach to social responsibility revolutionary? How does it contradict what you may have previously thought about social responsibility and effective business decision making?

2. Who are New Belgium's stakeholders? Give a few examples and explain the relationship between the stakeholders and the company, based on what you learned from the video.

3. What type of strategy does New Belgium use for managing its stakeholders? Use the example of environmental responsibility and the larger community as the stakeholder.

company struggled to survive the scandal that followed. The lack of transparency of the financial dealings of Enron meant that the company did not give an important stakeholder group, shareholders, the opportunity to know about how funds were invested.[23]

As these examples indicate, actions by such stakeholder groups as environmentalists, consumers, and the government may threaten the stability and existence of a company. When the management team takes the interests of key stakeholders into consideration, the threat of dealing with hostile interest groups is reduced. When a company's executives adopt a socially responsible approach

Ethos Water, a bottled water company recently purchased by Starbucks, donates 5 cents for every $1.80 bottle purchased to fund sustainable clean-water projects in underdeveloped regions such as Ethiopia, Honduras, Kenya, and Bangladesh. In 2005 the company contributed $250,000 from its sales to such efforts; its five-year goal is to raise and donate $10 million. The Earth Policy Institute points out that U.S. consumers' fondness for bottled water leads to the manufacture of enough plastic bottles to use up 1.5 million barrels of oil a year. But Jonathan Greenblatt, one of Ethos's founders, says the company's pitch appeals to those with a social conscience who ask, "How do I do more?" Is selling bottled water for a worthy cause an efficient way to be socially responsible?

that is aligned with the goals of an important stakeholder group, the stakeholder may reciprocate and influence its members to patronize the products of the company. For example, Anheuser-Busch, the largest brewer of beer, has worked hard to cultivate positive labor relations with its unionized workforce, an important stakeholder group. In return, the unions have encouraged their membership to drink Budweiser and Busch brands of beer made by Anheuser-Busch, rather than consume the beer of companies that treat unions harshly.

The Costs of Social Responsibility

There are essentially two aspects of being socially responsible. The first is avoiding illegal and unethical activities, such as discrimination, sexual harassment, pollution, and tax evasion. These negative activities should be avoided as part of the ethical structure of a company. Other activities associated with social responsibility have costs, because the company spends money to support a social good, such as a neighborhood cleanup program, giving money to the United Way, and other beneficial activities.

In these circumstances, social responsibility may be viewed by some as counter to the ethics of individualism, which suggest that individuals and companies should be able to pursue their own self-interests. Economist Milton Friedman argues that most managers do not own the businesses they operate and should act in the best interests of the stockholders, who are primarily interested in financial returns. Corporations should deploy resources to produce goods and services as efficiently as possible. Socially responsible firms that are less efficient may be driven out of business by more efficient competitors willing to singlemindedly pursue profits. These profit-maximizing firms are able to charge lower prices because social costs are not added to the cost of production.

Firms that give profits a low priority are more likely to fail and become a detriment to society because jobs and stockholders' investments are lost. In the late 1990s, when Levi Strauss lost market share to competitors Lee and Wrangler and profits decreased, some shareholders blamed the company's CEO, Robert Haas, for giving too high a priority to corporate social responsibility.[24]

A U.S. firm that has let social responsibility dominate its business strategy in a way that distracted management's attention from earning profits is Ben & Jerry's Ice Cream. Management Close-Up 3.1 on page 121 discusses some of the factors that have resulted in reduced profits for this company.

Rather than making social responsibility the top priority or ignoring it altogether, management should give corporate social responsibility a high priority without neglecting other important priorities, such as competing successfully in its markets. A thriving organization will have resources to support its social responsibility goals, while a failing organization is too involved in trying to survive and meet its basic business obligations. The challenge for managers is to strike a balance that responds to the concerns of both stakeholders and the general society, bearing in mind that responsible behavior is linked to long-term survival.

The benefits and costs of corporate social responsibility are summarized in Table 3.3 on page 121. As Table 3.3 suggests, in most cases the advantages of working toward the realization of corporate social responsibility goals outweigh the possible disadvantages.

Ben & Jerry Did Good While Their Business Didn't

Ben & Jerry's Ice Cream, founded in 1978 by two former Vermont hippies, Ben Cohen and Jerry Greenfield, had always given a high priority to integrating socially beneficial actions into the business. In 1993, it came out with a new flavor called Wavy Gravy, named after the musician who, according to Cohen, "symbolizes taking Sixties values, peace and love, and turning them into action in the Nineties." The company turned the proceeds from the flavor into action, too, by donating some of the proceeds to the musician's work with children.

The company gave away 7.5 percent of its pretax profits (three times the rate of the average U.S. corporation). For its brownie ice cream, it bought brownies that cost a little higher than average from a New York bakery that employed disadvantaged workers. The company had a pay policy that limited its CEO's salary to five times what the lowest-paid employee earned, a reflection of the founders' egalitarian philosophy. They stopped making Oreo Mint ice cream because the Oreo brand is part of tobacco giant RJR Nabisco. Ben & Jerry's paid Vermont dairy farmers extra for hormone-free milk, which cost the company $375,000 over other sources of milk.

The company profits declined and the stock price decreased, but the company continued its socially responsible style. In February 1995, the company moved from being founder-led to professional management when it hired Robert Holland as its CEO. Holland resigned less than two years later, following rumors that the co-founders opposed his support of the company's fat-free (and milk-free) sorbet products. Five years later the company became part of Unilever, a major multinational, which pledged to pursue and expand Ben & Jerry's social mission. Unilever paid $365 million and kept Cohen and Greenfield with the company, although they were not involved in the day-to-day operations.

In November 2000 Unilever ice cream veteran Yves Couette was appointed Ben & Jerry's CEO and vowed to build on Ben & Jerry's social mission. "Business has an important role to play in achieving social progress," said Couette, citing his earlier work for Unilever in Guadalajara, Mexico, where the company established an ice cream shop, run by a not-for-profit organization, to support disabled children. Perhaps more pragmatic than Cohen and Greenfield in viewing how a firm's social and economic missions need to work together, Couette said: "I firmly believe that the least socially responsible business is one that's out of business."

In 2004 Ben & Jerry's continued to put a high priority on being a socially responsible company. For example, it introduced a policy to purchase only "fair trade certified" coffee for its ice cream from coffee growers in developing countries who receive a fair price for their beans. However, four years of restructuring that followed the acquisition of Ben & Jerry's by Unilever, including hundreds of layoffs and the closing of two facilities, resulted in lowered employee morale for those who remained at the company, according to a 2004 companywide employee survey.

Sources: Adapted from A. Taylor, "Yo, Ben! Yo, Jerry! It's Just Ice Cream!" *Fortune*, April 28, 1997, p. 374; www.benjerry.com; "Consumer Group to Boycott Unilever Products," Reuters, December 6, 2000, available at http://dailynews.yahoo.com/h/nm/20001206/bs/unilever_benjerrys_dc_2.html; "Ben & Jerry's Social and Environmental Assessment," 2004, www.benjerry.com/our_company/about_us/

table 3.3

Benefits and Costs of Corporate Social Responsibility

SOCIAL RESPONSIBILITY BENEFITS	SOCIAL RESPONSIBILITY COSTS
1. Socially responsible companies are good corporate citizens to the community and to the environment. 2. Socially responsible company policies can enhance the image of a company as well as its product brands from the perspective of the consumers. 3. Socially responsible companies have fewer conflicts with stakeholder groups who disagree with the company over how it uses its resources. 4. Socially responsible companies are more likely to influence stakeholders to become loyal customers and become advocates of the company's products. 5. Research shows that corporate social responsibility is related to higher financial performance and the ability to recruit better quality job applicants.	1. Socially responsible companies may lose focus on the business goals while focusing on goals related to good corporate citizenship. 2. Socially responsible companies may divert needed resources for improving the business into social responsibility projects, which could put a company at a competitive disadvantage.

Organizational Stakeholders

stakeholders

The groups or individuals who have an interest in the performance of the enterprise and how it uses its resources, including employees, customers, and shareholders.

Organizations are, in many ways, political arenas in which various forces and coalitions compete. Organizational **stakeholders** are individuals or groups that have an interest in or are affected by a company's performance and the way it uses its resources. Stakeholders may be part of either the internal or external environment of an organization. The female employees of a company are an internal stakeholder group, for example, and an organization of consumers is an external stakeholder group.

Stakeholder groups tend to have more specific interests that may not always be in agreement with the interests of management or of other stakeholder groups. For example, shareholders may want a poorly performing company to close inefficient manufacturing plants and focus on more profitable product lines, while the labor union wants to protect worker jobs in all manufacturing plants. The management team must balance the interests of clashing stakeholder groups with its own interests. Compromises are necessary when important stakeholders have legitimate concerns that should be addressed. Management may decide to close some inefficient plants to satisfy the shareholders and invest resources in retraining displaced workers to satisfy the labor union.

A large company will have dozens of stakeholder groups exerting pressure on management. Table 3.4 on page 123 lists categories of stakeholders with whom a large firm is likely to deal. They are owners, employees, governments, customers, the community, competitors, and social activist groups.

Owners

Owners who have invested a portion of their wealth in shares of company stock want a reasonable financial return on their investment. If small investors are not satisfied with the financial performance of the company, they are likely to sell their stock. Large individual investors, mutual funds, and pension funds are more likely to be actively involved in influencing management through the board of directors or by voicing their concerns at meetings of shareholders. The CEOs of WorldCom, Enron, General Motors, IBM, and American Express lost their jobs when activist investor groups put pressure on the boards of directors to dismiss them because of disappointing financial performance.

Employees

Employees are largely focused on their jobs. They want to be treated fairly and with respect by the company. New employees are likely to want challenging work assignments that will advance their careers, while senior employees may be more interested in job security and retirement benefits.

Firms that neglect employee stakeholders may have to deal with angry labor unions, which can disrupt output through work stoppages or loss of the most valuable and marketable employees to competitors. This can disrupt the firm's ability to compete in its markets. In 1997 the truck drivers represented by the Teamsters Union organized a strike against United Parcel Service (UPS) because management refused to create full-time jobs for the part-time truck drivers represented by the union. More than half of all truck drivers at UPS were part-time employees, and the wait to become a full-time driver was about 10 years. UPS settled the strike with the Teamsters after losing about $700 million in revenues and some of its market share to its competitors. UPS agreed to create 10,000 new full-time jobs over a five-year period.

table 3.4

Some Categories and Specific Stakeholders of a Large Firm

OWNERS	EMPLOYEES	GOVERNMENTS	CUSTOMERS
Trusts	New employees	Federal	Business purchasers
Foundations	Senior employees	EPA	Government purchasers
Board members	Retirees	FTC	Educational institutions
Management owners	Female employees	OSHA	Consumers
Mutual funds	Minority employees	State	
Employee pension funds	Labor unions	Local	
Individual owners		Foreign governments	

COMMUNITY	COMPETITORS	SOCIAL ACTIVIST GROUPS
United Way	Domestic competitor	Sierra Club
Public schools	International competitor	American Civil Liberties Union
Residents in community		NOW (National Organization of Women)
Local media		MADD (Mothers Against Drunk Driving)
		Consumers Union

Source: Adapted from A. B. Carroll and A. K. Buchholtz, *Business and Society*, 6th ed., Mason, OH: Thompson, 2006.

Governments

The primary role played by the government is to make sure each company complies with regulations and laws. For example, automobiles must comply with Environmental Protection Agency (EPA) regulations that govern exhaust emissions. These regulations require auto manufacturers to invest in technologies such as catalytic converters to meet pollution regulations even though these investments add to the cost of manufacturing a car.

Companies' leaders will object when they believe that a proposed law will be detrimental. For example, McDonald's and other fast-food companies oppose hikes in the minimum wage because the cost structure of fast-food restaurants is highly sensitive to such increases. They may hire lobbyists to try to influence legislators to defeat proposed minimum wage increase legislation as a way of dealing with the threats in the political environment.

Customers

Many firms sell products to two types of customers: (1) individuals making purchases and (2) other businesses. Both types of customers are interested in purchasing quality products that are reasonably priced and safe to use. Customer groups sometimes organize to boycott companies that behave unethically or irresponsibly. Consumer pressure has protected old-growth forests from the timber industry's chainsaws, forced cigarette manufacturers to discontinue advertising on television, and generated international guidelines to reduce the production of ozone layer–depleting chlorofluorocarbons. On U.S. airlines, smoking is banned on domestic flights because of complaints from individual consumers and consumer groups. Consumer groups put market pressure on Volkswagen, the manufacturer of the Audi line of cars, to redesign the car's power train and transmission after a number of fatal accidents. Consumer opinion is influenced by periodicals such as *Consumer Reports* that judge the performance and reliability of consumer products and identify those that offer the best value and quality.

Community

There are local, national, and global communities. All types of communities expect corporations to be good citizens and to contribute to the quality of life. Firms that neglect or degrade their communities may be subject to pressure. When citizens in several communities in Maine opposed new Wal-Mart stores because of fears that they would hurt downtown businesses as they had done in other communities, Wal-Mart decided not to build the stores.

A business that operates in a local community pays taxes that support public services such as schools, police, and fire protection. It also creates jobs that may employ local people. Businesses can give the local community funds or equipment or can encourage employees to volunteer at community nonprofit organizations. IBM provides computer equipment to local colleges and encourages executives who qualify for sabbaticals (paid time off to pursue other interests) to teach in local public schools and to work with disadvantaged children. These investments in the community should pay off for IBM in the future because students trained on IBM equipment are more likely to purchase IBM products when they graduate from college.

Home Depot, the giant home improvement company, encourages its employees to build playgrounds for children in various local communities. It plans to build up to 1,000 playgrounds and has budgeted $25 million to do it. Nike has raised $20 million for cancer research through sales of its $1 yellow bracelets. Starbucks gives back to the community by sponsoring literacy programs as well as a holiday gift drive for seriously ill children.[25]

Competitors

Competitors expect a corporation to compete fairly in the market without engaging in such unethical business practices as industrial espionage, dumping products on the market at a below-cost price, and receiving unfair government subsidies. Competitor stakeholders can form economic coalitions to put pressure on any company that violates the principles of fair competition. They can also use the courts or the legislative branch of government to punish a corporate rule breaker. For example, competitors have charged Microsoft with unfair practices and have used the courts to break Microsoft into separate operating system and applications companies. Microsoft won its appeal of the court ruling to divide the company.

Globally, Airbus, the European manufacturer of commercial jets, threatened to lobby the European Union to boycott Boeing aircraft and successfully influenced Boeing to stop signing customers such as Delta, Continental, and American Airlines to 20-year exclusive contracts.[26]

Social Activist Groups

A business practice that runs counter to an important goal of a social activist group may result in negative media attention for the company or even a product boycott orchestrated by the social activist group. Although corporations cannot always satisfy such groups, it is often in their best interests to compromise with social activist groups to avoid being the focus of a campaign that can badly damage their reputation. Nestlé was the target of a national boycott led by the National Council of Churches because the infant baby formula it marketed to developing nations caused the sickness and death of thousands of babies. After seven years and millions of dollars unsuccessfully trying to resist the boycott, Nestlé altered some of its business practices.[27] People for the Ethical

Treatment of Animals (PETA) organized a boycott against L'Oreal and other cosmetics companies that tested their products on animals. After four years of futile resistance, L'Oreal promised that it would no longer conduct animal testing. The Rainforest Action Network (RAN) pressures large multinational corporations to halt economic development in poor countries that could pollute the global environment. It uses pressure tactics such as Internet campaigns, street theater, and celebrity endorsements on firms that it targets for change. RAN demanded that Citigroup, the global financial services company, stop lending money for logging, mining, and oil-drilling projects that destroy rain forests, threaten indigenous people, and accelerate global warming. It persuaded 20,000 people to cut up their Citi credit cards. Eventually these tactics resulted in Citigroup's coming to a common understanding with RAN on key global sustainable development issues.[28]

This is not to say that social activist groups prevail in all situations. For example, when the Florida Citrus Commission hired conservative talk show host Rush Limbaugh as a spokesperson, the National Organization for Women (NOW) and the National Education Association (NEA) asked consumers to avoid purchasing Florida orange juice. The boycott had no effect.[29]

LOC-In

5 **Learning Objective Check-In**

1. *Burton's is a textiles manufacturer that often gives money to support neighborhood programs for at-risk youth in the communities where it operates. While this does not contribute to the bottom line for Burton's, it is an important element of the company's value structure to give back to the communities which support it. The people who are affected by Burton's, including the local community, are collectively called its _____.*
   a. *business community*
   b. *stakeholders*
   c. *society*
   d. *ethics structure*

Strategies for Managing Stakeholders

Balancing the interests of a variety of groups is the managerial form of a juggling act. Managers must consider various stakeholder groups while preparing an overall business strategy. The approaches stakeholders use to get their point across to management range from making suggestions at shareholder meetings to threatening to withhold resources from the firm. The latter approach was used by consumer groups that threatened a boycott of StarKist products unless the company stopped purchasing tuna from foreign fishing fleets that caught and killed thousands of dolphins in their tuna nets.

When a stakeholder group makes demands on a firm, management should first perform an analysis by answering the following questions:

1. Who are the stakeholders?
2. How are the stakeholders affected by the company policies?
3. What are the stakeholders' interests in the business?
4. How have the stakeholders behaved in the past, and what coalitions are they likely to form around their issue?
5. How effective have the company's strategies been in dealing with these and other stakeholders?
6. What new strategies and action plans need to be formulated to deal effectively with the stakeholders?[30]

Once an analysis of the stakeholders has been accomplished the management team can develop strategies for dealing with the stakeholders by selecting one of the following four general approaches: confrontation, damage control, accommodation, or being proactive.

Confrontation

Management may select a **confrontation strategy** to deal with a stakeholder group whose goals are perceived to threaten company performance. This includes using the courts, engaging in public relations, and lobbying against legislation. For many years, the tobacco companies used a confrontation strategy to deal with antismoking groups and individuals who sued them. For example, tobacco companies spent millions of dollars lobbying state legislatures to pass "smokers' rights" laws. United Parcel Service selected a confrontation strategy to deal with the Teamsters Union when contract negotiations failed, and the confrontation resulted in the costly labor strike mentioned earlier.

Management must be very careful when it chooses to use a confrontation strategy. Typically, the company spends considerable time and money fighting a stakeholder group rather than focusing on more positive outcomes. The long-term outcome may be a negative image for the company unless it is able to mend its relations with its stakeholders and with customers critical of the company's actions.

Damage Control

The **damage control strategy** is often used when a company decides that it may have made mistakes and wants to elevate its public image and improve its relationship with the stakeholder. In 1999, after years of confrontation, the tobacco companies admitted to having deceived the public and paid $246 billion to settle the claims of people who contracted fatal illnesses related to tobacco smoking. Similarly, when a leak of poisonous gas resulted in the death of more than 2,000 people and serious injuries to 200,000 in Bhopal, India, in 1984, Union Carbide used a damage control strategy and initiated a settlement with the Indian government for $470 million to be divided among victims and their families.

Accommodation

The **accommodation strategy** is used when management decides to accept social responsibility for business decisions after pressure has been exerted by stakeholder groups. It may require changing business practices to better align with stakeholder goals. Long the target of environmental groups, McDonald's used the accommodation strategy when it changed its packaging from polystyrene foam to paper, which is less damaging to the environment. General Motors voluntarily recognized the United Auto Workers (UAW) union in the Spring Hill, Tennessee, Saturn manufacturing plant instead of forcing the union to undergo a formal election procedure. In return, General Motors obtained a labor agreement that allowed it to deploy its workforce more flexibly than is possible in other unionized auto plants.

Proactive

A company chooses a **proactive strategy** when it determines that it wants to go beyond stakeholder expectations. Proactive companies form partnerships with stakeholders and cooperate with them. These partnerships increase management's ability to predict and control the stakeholder environment and fewer crises emerge. For example:

- The Colgate-Palmolive Company "adopted" a failing junior high school in Harlem that needed its buildings and curriculum modernized. Colgate-Palmolive contributed funds and personnel for the renovation and

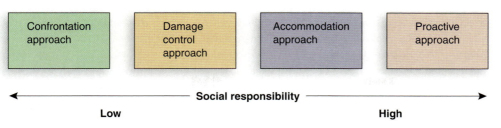

FIGURE 3.3

Approaches to Social Responsibility

restructuring of the school. Company personnel worked with school staff on budgeting, strategic planning, and management. Student reading levels and math competencies improved dramatically in the renovated school.

- The Coca-Cola Company sets ambitious goals for purchasing goods and services from minority- and female-owned vendors and puts a high priority on recruiting and developing minority and female employees. One woman and two members of minorities sit on the 14-member board of directors, and there are seven women and six minority members among the top 57 corporate executives. Coca-Cola also encourages its employees to volunteer in community programs such as Adopt-a-School and provides assistance to the United Negro College Fund and the National Hispanic Scholarship Fund.

- Merck, the pharmaceutical company, formed a partnership with the Costa Rican National Institute of Biodiversity. The institute provides Merck with plant and insect samples that may become the basis for new medicines, and Merck shares its pharmaceutical product royalties with the Costa Rican institute. Merck also provides funds for conservation efforts to preserve the Costa Rican rain forest.[31]

Figure 3.3 above shows how the different strategies for dealing with stakeholder concerns compare with respect to how they are related to an organization's commitment to social responsibility. The confrontation and damage control approaches reflect lower commitments to social responsibility and the accommodation and proactive approaches reflect higher commitments to social responsibility.

LOC-In

6 Learning Objective Check-In

1. *Pine Crest Linens has been manufacturing a variety of linens in the mid-sized town of Oakdale, Wisconsin, for over 20 years. The founders of Pine Crest view the manufacturer as a waste stream and realize they use resources and emit waste depending on how their operations are run and what kind of efficiencies are achieved at every stage. Despite good intentions, the company has a mixed political reception in the community—it provides above-average paying jobs, but also contributes to the local area's pollution problem. In order to limit its impact on the local environment, Pine Crest recently installed new technologies that allow it to recycle rinse water at least twice before drainage. This has lowered its water usage by almost 40 percent within the first two months of use. This represents a(n) _____.*
   a. *damage control strategy*
   b. *proactive strategy*
   c. *accommodation strategy*
   d. *confrontation strategy*

CONCLUDING THOUGHTS

In the chapter's introductory vignette we presented some critical thinking questions about Chez Panisse and the Chez Panisse Foundation. Now that you've had the opportunity to study ethical and social responsibility issues, you can reexamine those questions. First, one benefit that Chez Panisse derives from the attention it gives to a socially responsible cause is increased visibility for its retail business, the Chez Panisse restaurant in Berkeley. This recognition could help the restaurant attract more customers, as well as employees who admire its values and want to help it succeed. The Foundation's transformation of a blighted schoolyard also has produced goodwill in the neighborhood that might encourage people to patronize the restaurant or inspire donors to contribute to the Foundation.

Chez Panisse's stakeholders include its customers; its employees; parents, teachers, and children in the Berkeley school district; neighbors in the local and national communities; other school districts; competitors; and activist groups that value and support organic farming and sustainable use of Earth's resources.

Chez Panisse's stakeholder strategy is the proactive approach. Before setting up the Foundation, Waters used her own initiative and gathered donations in support of a worthy social cause. The Foundation's creation of and support of the School Lunch Initiative signals its cooperative relationship with the district school board for the benefit of all its students.

Focusing on the Future: Using Management Theory in Daily Life

Using Social Responsibility and Ethics in Daily Life

Barbara DeLong* was an HR Director at a medium-sized (900-person) telecommunications company when she used the "Eight Steps to Sound Ethical Decision Making in Business" to handle an ethics violation in her company.

The office manager came to Barbara one day and told her that she had noticed some irregular purchases on a bill from the company's office supply provider. Barbara handled the situation in the following way:

1. **Step 1.** *Gather the facts.* When Barbara asked to see the list, she was astonished to find items such as a vacuum cleaner, pocket thesaurus, lamps, cleaning supplies, and other items which over the period of about one month totaled more than $1,000. However, she knew that she also needed to find out the other side of the issue, so she asked the employee why she needed these items, whose response was they were job-related and she used them to clean the booth at campus recruiting.

2. **Step 2.** *Define the ethical issues.* Barbara used the company's purchasing policy to define the ethical issues involved, and also looked at the situation from a broader perspective. According to the purchasing policy, all purchases required approval from the HR Director—obviously this "legality" had been overlooked. However, Barbara also considered whether or not different issues were at play—for example, did the employee have a legitimate need for the items, and was she aware of the policy?

3. **Step 3.** *Identify the affected parties.* In this case, it was apparent that Barbara, the employee, and the company as a whole were affected. However, when Barbara reviewed company policy with the employee, the employee claimed that she had received permission from another manager to make the purchases, thereby bringing another party into the picture.

4. **Step 4.** *Identify the consequences.* In one way, the consequences in this case were clear-cut—if the employee was purchasing things for her personal use, she would be fired. However, Barbara also had to think about the consequences of losing a fully trained employee over what might have been a misunderstanding.

5. **Step 5.** *Identify your obligations.* As HR Director, Barbara had several obligations—first and foremost to do what was right for the company, secondly, to abide by all written corporate policies, and finally to treat company employees with respect. As noted

above, these obligations demanded that the situation be viewed in several different ways. As a result, Barbara pondered what she would do, taking all of her obligations into consideration.

6. **Step 6.** *Consider your character and integrity.* Barbara knew that if she let unauthorized expenses slip by, her own character and integrity could be called into question. She also knew that her decision would be scrutinized by other employees, company management, and her peers. More important, Barbara had firm convictions of her own about the importance of honesty in the workplace, and she was determined to live up to her beliefs.

7. **Step 7.** *Think creatively about your potential actions.* Barbara listened to the employee's side of the story, and took it seriously, but she also devised a plan for verifying that story. Since the employee claimed that another manager (the one she was recruiting for) had given her approval, Barbara offered to call that manager right then. At that point, the employee claimed that the manager would "probably forget that he gave me approval." Barbara balanced the company's need to retain the employee, her core values of honesty, and the importance she placed on respecting employees by allowing the employee to return the items purchased "for the campus recruiting booth" and letting the employee know that any similar behavior in the future would result in dismissal.

8. **Step 8.** *Check your gut feelings.* Barbara checked her gut feelings, which indicated that she should be somewhat lenient with the employee for a first offense, but to watch the employee carefully in the future. Sure enough, the employee was later terminated for a similar incident.

*Because of the nature of this incident, the manager involved has requested that her real name not be used.

summary of learning objectives

Business ethics are principles prescribing a code of behavior that explains what is good and right, and what is bad and wrong. They provide standards for conduct and decision making by employees and managers. **Corporate social responsibility** means that a company has a duty to use some of its resources to promote the interests of various elements of society. This chapter's discussion will help future managers, work teams and employees better understand the importance of ethics and social responsibility. The ideas presented in this chapter that meet each of the learning objectives stated at the start of the chapter are summarized below.

1 Apply the four key ethical criteria that managers and employees should use when making business decisions.

- **Utilitarianism** looks at what is good for the greatest number of people.
- **Individualism** sees individual self-interest as the basis of the greatest good as long as it does not harm others.
- The **rights approach** represents and protects fundamental human rights.
- The **justice approach** emphasizes treating all people fairly and consistently.

2 Explain why businesses establish codes of ethics as a method of guiding employee conduct.

- A **code of ethics** is a formal statement of a company's ethics and values, which guides employee conduct in a number of business situations.
- The code can be a **corporate credo**, which focuses on general values and beliefs, or an **ethical policy statement**, which provides specific rules for employee conduct.

3 Recognize ways to encourage ethical behavior in business.

- A company provides **ethics training** to its employees to develop skills to deal with ethical challenges in business.
- An **ethical structure** can be developed to monitor and audit ethical behavior.
- A company can have a **whistleblower policy** that encourages employees to disclose illegal or unethical practices of co-workers without fearing retaliation.

4 Recognize morally challenging situations where ethical decisions should be made.

- Morally challenging situations where ethical decisions should be made include: (1) *performance appraisals*; (2) *employee discipline*; (3) *romantic relationships* in the workplace; and (4) *gift giving*.

5 Identify important categories of stakeholders.

- **Stakeholders** are individuals or groups with an interest in the performance of the business and the way it uses its resources; companies should respond to their concerns.
- Important categories of stakeholders are owners, employees, governments, customers, the community, competitors, and social activist groups.

6 Recognize the influence of various stakeholders on a company's priorities, policies, plans and goals.

- Companies develop different strategies for managing stakeholder demands after analyzing the nature of the stakeholders' interests and the threats and opportunities that may result.
- The **confrontation strategy** challenges the stakeholder.
- The **damage control strategy** is used when management decides that it made a mistake in the way it treated a stakeholder and wants to minimize the damage to the company's reputation.
- The **accommodation strategy** is used when the company decides that it is in its best interest to accept the goals of a stakeholder.
- The **proactive strategy** is used by companies that want to go beyond meeting stakeholders' expectations in order to be a leader in social resonsibility.

discussion questions

1. Compare and contrast the four ethics approaches used for ethical decision making that are discussed in this chapter. Which criterion do you think is the best one? Which one would be the least useful? What is the basis for your selection? Now, suppose you were going to work at a business in China. Which of the four criteria would you be most likely to apply to an ethical business decision in China?

2. Why do you think companies invest resources in training their managers and employees in business ethics? Some people think that ethics should be learned within the family and by the time a person is a mature adult it is too late to learn about ethics. Do you agree or disagree with this statement? Explain.

3. Some sales organizations like to put their sales representatives on a straight commission pay plan, which means that they must successfully sell the product in order to receive any money at the end of the month. What type of ethical dilemmas or problems are likely to happen when the salespeople must operate under a straight commission plan? How might these ethical problems be managed?

4. Suppose you discover that your boss is embezzling funds from the company. Which of the policies described in this chapter would you use in deciding to disclose this situation to company officials who could take care of the problem before it becomes more serious? What kind of preparation should you make before you decide to disclose your boss's unethical conduct to the company authorities?

5. Is it possible for a business to do good for society and still make a reasonable profit? Explain.

6. In Germany, under the model of "stakeholder capitalism," employee representatives sit on company boards of directors. In the German model of business it is assumed that both labor (employee representatives) and capital (shareholder representatives) have important stakes in the enterprise and should work in harmony with each other. In the United States,

the board of directors usually represents only the owners of the business. What advantages to employees as stakeholders are available in Germany that are not provided to employees in U.S. companies? In the United States, how do employees let management know their stakeholder concerns?

7. What does it mean to be a socially responsible employer? What are the benefits for a company that decides to give a high priority to its social responsibility?

8. Is it possible for a small business to take an active role in social responsibility? What are some ways that a small business (for example, a family business or a local business you are familiar with) can be socially responsible?

management minicase 3.1

Starbucks Gambles that Encouraging Its Coffee Suppliers to Act Socially Responsible Is Good for Business

Starbucks, the fast growing coffee retailer with over $4 billion in annual sales, places a high priority on corporate social responsibility. It gives all its employees who work over 20 hours per week health insurance benefits and stock options. It strives to give back to the communities that it does business in by supporting local schools, literacy programs, and environmental activities. One of its newest social resonsibility initiatives is to cultivate and reward environmentally and socially responsible coffee suppliers, a practice it calls sustainable sourcing. Company executives reason that making sustainable sourcing an important cornerstone of its global growth strategy will help build the Starbucks brand. The impetus for Starbucks to start a program of social responsibility with coffee growers originally had been a way to respond to critics from the "fair trade" movement—which advocates fair payments to farmers in developing nations—that had accused Starbucks of underpaying coffee growers, a claim Starbucks denied after it opened its books to them to prove that was not the case.

There were sound economic reasons for the initiative as well. With an annual growth rate of 20 percent Starbucks executives wanted to make sure that the future supply of coffee would be predictable and reliable for its customers. If the supply of the specialty coffee beans that Starbucks uses were disrupted, its growth plans and quality of its coffee would be at risk. To protect its coffee supply, Starbucks realized it had to identify and nurture partners that could meet its quality standards and keep up with increasing demand. At the same time, to protect its brand, the company needed to be certain that its suppliers shared its commitment to corporate citizenship. Therefore in 2001 the company launched its preferred supplier program to attract and reward farmers committed to socially and environmentally responsible farming. The company assumed that the growers that took the best care of their employees and land would also be the most effective, responsible and responsible suppliers—the kind of partners it wanted to fulfill its aggressive growth plan.

To become a preferred supplier to Starbucks, coffee growers must apply to the program. Reviewers evaluate the applicants on 20 measures to determine how well they adhere to sustainable environmental practices (procedures that protect the scarce land on which high-quality coffee can grow) and responsible social practices (methods, for example, that reduce the risk that deliveries will be compromised by labor unrest, corruption, or legal violations).

Suppliers accepted into the program are awarded points for meeting environmental, social, and economic criteria. The more points they earn, the more Starbucks pays them for their coffee. Preferred coffee growers will receive a 5 percent premium on each pound of beans they sell. They can also earn long-term contracts to reduce market risk and receive credit to fund improvements that promote sustainability. Starbucks has a long-term goal that plans for 60 percent of its coffee to come from preferred suppliers.

Discussion Questions

1. How does Starbucks link its social responsibility goals of being a good corporate citizen with its business goals of aggressive growth?

2. What are the risks that Starbucks takes by attempting to influence how coffee growers treat their employees and use the land where they grow coffee?

3. Which strategy for managing stakeholders most closely corresponds to the way Starbucks responded to the criticisms it received from the "fair trade" movement? Be able to justify your choice.

Sources: E. Schrage, "Supply and Brand," *Harvard Business Review*, June 2004, pp. 20–21; C. Hymowitz, "Asked to Be Charitable, More CEOs Seek to Aid Their Business as Well," *The Wall Street Journal*, February 22, 2005, p. B1 ; A. Server, "Hot Starbucks to Go," *Fortune*, January 26, 2004, pp. 60–74; P. Argenti, "Collaborating with Activists: How Starbucks Works with NGOs," *California Management Review*, Fall 2004, pp. 91–116.

Employees' Retirement Savings Disappear in the Aftermath of the Enron Scandal

management minicase 3.2

Shareholders were not the only stakeholder group that suffered as a result of the dramatic collapse of Enron's stock price when its shady off-the-books financial dealings became public. Thousands of Enron employees experienced the nightmare of losing a large portion of their retirement savings. The average Enron employee had 62 percent of his or her retirement plan savings invested in Enron stock. Marie Thibaut, a 61-year-old Enron employee, saw her retirement savings in her employee retirement benefits go from $500,000 to $22,000 in the months following the Enron scandal. To make matters worse, Enron did not permit its employees to sell its Enron stock in retirement plans until they reached the age of 50.

Many companies, such as Enron, encourage employees to invest a significant portion of their retirement savings in company stock. It is common practice to give employees a 15 percent discount on the purchase of company stock when it is put into an employee's retirement savings plan. One of the motives used by a company that encourages its employees to own significant amounts of company stock is to give employees the "feel" of ownership by having a stake in the long-term performance of the company. Employees may also believe that the company stock is a good investment for their retirement because they have a long-term investment horizon of many years before retirement and expect the stock to be more valuable at the time of their retirement despite short-term variations in the price of the stock. At present there are no laws preventing employers from letting employees buy as much company stock as they want as a retirement savings investment. The question remains as to whether or not an employer is being socially responsible when employees are encouraged to buy large amounts of company stock as a retirement savings investment.

One common practice is to match an employee's retirement contribution to the plan with the employer's matching contribution made in the form of company stock. Procter & Gamble, Pfizer, General Electric, and McDonald's use company stock to match an employee's contribution to the 401(k) retirement plan in those companies. At other companies, the company stock is viewed as a "blue chip" stock, and employees are proud of the company and view the purchase of the stock as a valuable investment and a good way to show loyalty to company management. At Coca-Cola 81 percent of employees' retirement funds in the 401(k) retirement plan are in company stock.

Most students who have taken a course in business finance know that it is extremely risky to allocate a large portion of one's retirement funds to just one stock. A diversified portfolio of investments in a variety of different stocks representing different industries, as well as a portfolio containing a variety of different asset classes including bonds, cash, and real estate, help preserve the investment funds over the long run and minimize investment risk. With this insight, one wonders why so many companies continue the practice of letting their employees purchase large amounts of company stock to fund their retirement savings plans.

Discussion Questions

1. What are some possible approaches that a socially responsible employer could use with regard to the use of company stock as an investment for an employee's retirement plan? Do you think there should be a limit on the amount of stock as a percentage of overall retirement savings? Should the employer contribution match be made only in cash instead of stock? Should employees have more flexibility to reallocate their funds into different asset classes or stocks, rather than have long holding periods of many years when they are not permitted to sell their company stock within their retirement plans? Should the employer provide outside financial advice to an employee for making retirement plan investments that are neither too conservative nor too risky?

2. Why do you think so many Enron employees bought large amounts of Enron stock to fund their retirement? Do you think employees thought they knew something that other nonemployee investors were not aware of when they decided to buy large quantities of Enron stock?

Sources: C. Cropper, "The Ins and Outs of the New Tax Law: The Golden Years Get More Golden," *BusinessWeek*, January 28, 2002, pp. 110–111; J. Quinn, "401(k)s and the Enron Mess," *Newsweek*, January 21, 2002, p. 25; "When Labor and Capital Don't Mix: Enron's Demise Unmasks Conflicts in Company Pension Plans," *The Economist*, December 15, 2001, p. 60.

individual/ collaborative learning case 3.1

Do Sales Commissions Cause Sales Representatives to Behave Unethically?

Baker Electronics is an electronics appliance store in Columbus, Ohio, that puts its sales staff on a modest salary plus a commission based on the value of the electronics products sold in the store. The top salespeople at Baker generate about three-quarters of their take-home pay from sales commissions—only one-quarter comes from salary.

Baker frequently advertises specials on certain television models in the local Columbus newspaper, drawing people into the store asking about these models. Because these sale items have lower profit margins, the store also lowers the commission the sales staff receives on these models. The company prefers to sell higher-priced models but advertises the lower-priced ones to get customers into the store.

Baker offers little sales training. New salespeople spend a day or so working with the store manager and then are left to operate on their own. The store manager does not seem to care how sales are made as long as sales goals are achieved. The manager receives a significant bonus (as much as 100 percent of salary) based on the level of store sales.

Tom Pierce, one of the most successful salespeople at Baker Electronics, has developed some effective sales techniques that provide him a very good income on commissions. He is viewed as a role model by other salespeople at the store. Here are some examples of Tom's sales tactics:

> Tom points out to all customers the special features on the higher-priced televisions, and many go along with his advice and buy the more expensive model.

When customers are more interested in the sale-priced televisions, Tom will try to convince them that the added features on the more expensive models are very important, and some customers will buy a television with more features than they really need.

When a customer rejects Tom's advice and insists on purchasing a less expensive television, Tom adjusts some of the picture control switches when he demonstrates the model so that its picture is altered and appears fuzzier than the more expensive televisions. This tactic almost always results in the sale of a more expensive television.

Critical Thinking Questions

1. Do you think Tom's conduct toward the customers at Baker Electronics is unethical? Why or why not?

2. How do you think the sales commission policy influences Tom's treatment of customers? How might Tom behave differently if he were paid on a straight salary basis, with no sales commissions?

3. Will sales commissions always motivate salespeople to act in a greedy way and take advantage of customers? Can you think of examples of salespeople who received a sales commission but treated customers with respect and catered to their needs?

Collaborative Learning Exercise

With a partner or small group, assume you are marketing consultants brought into Baker Electronics to improve the sales process so that customers are treated ethically and responsibly by the sales staff. First diagnose what is wrong with the current reward system for sales staff, and then develop a recommendation for a new plan that should result in higher levels of customer satisfaction. Be prepared to present your analysis to the instructor and other members of your class.

Source: Adapted from L. K. Trevino and K. A. Nelson, *Managing Business Ethics*, 3rd ed. New York: John Wiley & Sons, 2004.

Social Responsibility at Levi Strauss

internet
exercise 3.1

www.levistrauss.com

Visit the Web site of Levi Strauss, the clothing company, and find its "Corporate Citizenship" section. Answer the following questions:

1. How do the giving programs support the social responsibility goals of Levi Strauss?

2. Some of the Levi Strauss giving programs might be considered controversial by some people, such as providing resources to fight AIDS or to achieve social justice. Why would Levi Strauss support programs that some of its customers may not agree with?

3. How can Levi Strauss employees become involved with the giving programs? Provide an example. If you were an employee at Levi Strauss, which giving program would you like to become involved with? Why?

manager's checkup 3.1

What Are Your Ethical Beliefs?

Instructions: Answer the following questions as honestly as you can. Circle the number between 1 and 5 that best represents your own beliefs about business.

		Strongly Disagree				Strongly Agree
1.	Financial gain is all that counts in business.	1	2	3	4	5
2.	Ethical standards must sometimes be compromised in business practice.	1	2	3	4	5
3.	The more financially successful the businessperson, the more unethical the behavior.	1	2	3	4	5
4.	Moral values are irrelevant in business.	1	2	3	4	5
5.	The business world has its own rules.	1	2	3	4	5
6.	Businesspersons care only about making profits.	1	2	3	4	5
7.	Business is like a game—one plays to win.	1	2	3	4	5
8.	In business, people will do anything to further their own interest.	1	2	3	4	5
9.	Competition forces business managers to resort to shady practices.	1	2	3	4	5
10.	The profit motive pressures managers to compromise their ethical concerns.	1	2	3	4	5

Scoring: Add the total number of points. The higher your score, the more cynical you are about ethical business practice.

Think about the reasons for your responses. Be prepared to discuss them in class.

Source: Adapted from L. K. Trevino and K. A. Nelson, *Managing Business Ethics*, 3rd ed., New York: John Wiley & Sons, 2004, p. 19. Reprinted with permission of John Wiley & Sons, Inc.

video summary

Good Deeds

Summary

What do British American Tobacco, McDonald's, Microsoft, and Nike have in common? They all may have had questionable reputations at some point or another, but they all also attended the Business for Social Responsibility convention last fall. McDonald's is criticized for contributing to an overweight society, but it has sworn off super-sizing at its restaurants. It also uses a tremendous amount of recycled goods in its packaging. Critics blame Microsoft for being monopolistic and cutthroat. Bill Gates, however, has become the world's foremost philanthropist. The company itself is also pushing social responsibility by making sure it has a diverse workforce, that it has happy employees, and that it treats its employees well.

Greyston Bakery goes so far as to "give anyone a chance" to prove themselves as good employees. The firm has hired ex-cons, drug addicts, and people from different walks of life on the premise that they want to work and succeed, and that with support, they can do that. How can any firm afford to be such a good guy?

If a firm's rivals are not acting in a socially responsible way, then those competitors' costs must be lower, and that must provide a competitive edge for those who do not take part in social responsibility—or does it? The idea that firms do well by doing good is becoming more common. The competitive edge may actually go to the firm that is socially responsible. Customers are often willing to pay a slightly higher price when they perceive that firms are operating in a socially responsible way. Certain workers will support the company's ethics, too, and are often willing to work for less. To be fair, not all socially responsible firms pay less. Some companies, like Eileen Fisher, offer much more comprehensive benefits and more competitive pay—and arguably get more out of their workers. In order to be seen as genuinely socially responsible, firms have to outdo other firms—something of a "race to the top."

Discussion Questions

1. In what ways can social responsibility have a positive effect on company performance? Cite an example from the video case.

2. What are the costs for a firm to be socially responsible?

3. Why is it important to understand who a firm's stakeholders are and what their interests are? How does this affect a firm's social responsibility?

chapter 4

Managing Organizational Culture and Change

Learning Objectives

1 Identify the three major aspects of organizational culture.

2 Apply a simple assessment tool to quickly gain a sense of the culture of an organization.

3 Describe the importance of organizational culture.

4 Identify the processes through which organizational culture can be developed and sustained.

5 Use classification systems to identify various types of organizational culture.

6 Identify the sources of resistance to change.

7 Apply models to effectively manage change efforts.

Working Out at REI

"The best comment that we get back from customers is about their interaction with our employees. They're the best at developing [the] relationships and the trust that build the loyalty that customers have for REI."—That assessment comes from Atsuko Tamura, a senior vice president at Recreational Equipment Inc., better known as REI, a retail cooperative with about 80 stores in the United States, many of them in the West and Northwest. Headquartered in Washington State, the outdoor-equipment retailer has grown steadily to reach $1 billion in sales and 7,500 employees. About 2.8 million of its customers are also members of the REI cooperative, who have input to corporate decisions and who share in its profits every year depending on how much they've purchased. CEO Sally Jewell credits the co-op structure with allowing the firm "to think in the long term," including planning concrete efforts to preserve and promote the environment for many years into the future. The company sets aside funds every year to support not just recreational programs but also local conservation and stewardship efforts like water clean-up and the construction of new trails. "One of our core values is authenticity, being true to the outdoors," Jewell says.

Authenticity is what brings adventure-seeking customers back to REI stores. The employees are carefully selected, experienced, and knowledgeable enthusiasts who are themselves deeply immersed in biking, running, yoga, camping, rafting, climbing, and the great outdoors. They live and understand the outdoors lifestyle. Thus their goal is not just to make a sale—they aren't paid commissions—but to help customers learn to experience and enjoy the outdoors as much as they do, using brand-name and REI brand equipment and supplies that the company sells. Climbing walls, indoor trails, and cold-weather rooms allow employees to help customers sample boots, parkas, and other equipment in many of the stores. Employees are also trained to lead workshops, classes, and recreational outings to make it even easier for inexperienced customers to get a taste of the outdoors. "That is our core purpose besides selling stuff," says Jewell. "We inspire, educate, and outfit for a lifetime of outdoor adventure."

REI employees have more in common with each other than their love of the outdoors lifestyle. The company's decision not to pay sales commissions was a conscious one based on the prevailing feeling among employees that commissions would introduce competition that didn't fit well with the organization's supportive culture. "As a culture, we said, 'No way,'" recalls Tamura. Stores are encouraged to compete, however, and each store's performance affects individual rewards in a new employee-bonus program.

The company knows the value of retaining its trusted sales force. It recently announced that all employees, even part-time and seasonal workers, will be eligible for health benefits. While other retailers are cutting back such benefits, REI stands out for its efforts to retain those who contribute so much to its success. "The customer really can't tell the difference between part-time and full-time staff," says Michelle Clements, REI's vice president of human relations. "Being able to retain an employee who is knowledgeable and enthusiastic about the outdoor experience is important."

One benefit of REI's carefully nurtured culture is an employee turnover rate of about 50 percent in an industry where 75 percent is average.

Sources: Barbara Clements, "It's Good to Be in the Co-op," *The News Tribune*, February 24, 2006; Anna Sowa, "REI Opens Outdoor Store in Bend, Ore.," *The Bulletin*, November 18, 2005; Dale Buss, "REI—Working Out," *BusinessWeek*, November 15, 2005, www.businessweek.com; and Barbara Clements, "Work Is Work, Says REI," *The News Tribune*, October 12, 2005.

CRITICAL THINKING QUESTIONS

1. *An organizational culture, like the culture at REI, might not be a good fit for everyone. Some people may prefer a more formal or a more competitive environment than REI's outdoor-lifestyle atmosphere of participation and cooperation. These people may not be hired, or they may leave an organization because they aren't comfortable with the culture. Do you think this is a problem for the organization? Why or why not? What, if anything, should be done to lessen any "misfit" problem?*

2. *In what ways do you think REI's outdoor-oriented culture contributes to its growth and profitability? What could other companies learn from this type of culture?*

3. *REI's CEO expects the company's role as a "facilitator for the outdoor recreation industry" will continue for hundreds of years. Do you think REI can maintain its culture over time? Should it?*

We'll think again about these questions about REI's culture in our Concluding Thoughts at the end of this chapter.

Understanding the Nature of Culture and Change

The concept of a culture in a company is complex. When trying to understand the culture of a firm, consider the many levels at which it operates. First, the physical location of the company plays a role. In the United States, company leaders are more likely to value risk taking, encourage competition, and exhibit several more individualistic tendencies. In contrast, managers in Japan and Mexico, in which cultures are more collectivist, tend to reward risk avoidance and cooperation. The second level is the company level. The culture at Microsoft, for example, is quite different from the culture in the Marine Corps. Even an individual department displays cultural characteristics. In other words, computer operators live in a world that is different from the one in the marketing department. This chapter focuses on the middle-level, companywide culture. It is designed to help you discover the nature of a culture and the impact the culture has on both individual employees and organizational performance.

In addition, this chapter examines organizational change. Change is addressed from two perspectives: (1) when it is a planned event, and (2) as an ongoing and dynamic environmental characteristic. When change is a planned event, such as when a company implements a new strategy, managers should expect resistance to change and find ways to overcome that resistance. In the case of ongoing and dynamic changes which routinely occur within and outside the organization, managers should develop approaches that are effective and offer employees a sense of stability. Effectively implementing or dealing with change often requires an understanding of the culture of the organization. Some changes can be relatively smooth if they fit well with the existing culture. Other changes can be anticipated to be more difficult and to take more management attention, particularly if the change involves alteration to the culture in the organization. Most organizations are now facing more turbulence than ever before. The ability to develop and maintain an effective culture and yet implement needed change is an important management skill. We next consider organizational culture and, in the following section, organizational change. Both culture and change are important topics to explore and manage in order to cope effectively with the turbulent world surrounding various organizations.

Section I: Organizational Culture

Organizational culture is a system of shared values, assumptions, beliefs, and norms that unite the members of an organization. Organizational culture reflects employees' views about "the way things are done around here." Culture gives meaning to actions and procedures within an organization[1] and may be considered to be the personality of the organization.[2] The culture specific to each firm affects how employees feel and act as well as the type of employee hired and retained by the company.

There are three aspects of an organization's culture, as shown in Figure 4.1 on page 142. The most obvious is the **visible culture** that an observer can hear, feel, or see. Aspects of visible culture include how people dress, how fast people walk and talk, whether there is an open floor plan without office doors or managers have private offices, and the extent to which status and power symbols are conspicuous. Assigned parking spots based on rank, differing cafeteria or eating arrangements based on organizational level, and the degree to which furnishings are plush and conservative versus simple and modern indicate the nature of power and status differentials.

The signs of a visible culture make it possible to study dominant cultural characteristics, such as whether the organization is competitive or easygoing, formal or informal, hierarchical or egalitarian, liberal or conservative. For instance, firms with *controlling* cultures often record and review their employees' communications, including telephone calls, e-mail, and Internet connections.

At a deeper level, **espoused values** are not readily observed but instead are the ways managers and employees explain and

organizational culture

A system of shared values, assumptions, beliefs, and norms that unite the members of an organization.

visible culture

The aspects of culture that an observer can hear, feel, or see.

espoused values

The aspects of corporate culture that are not readily observed, but instead can be perceived from the way managers and employees explain and justify their actions and decisions.

LOC-In

① Learning Objective Check-In

ATC Macros is a marketing consulting firm that has no office doors. There are not even private offices except on one floor, for client meetings. There are no reserved parking spaces, and the furnishings inside the office are modern yet simple. ATC encourages its employees to take risks and managers are encouraged to accept and tolerate employee mistakes when taking risks. At ATC, employees are treated well and receive liberal fringe benefits. Employees enjoy an on-site fitness center, flexible work schedules, and other family-friendly policies.

1. *The minimalist furnishings in the office, the lack of office doors, and the lack of private parking spaces all demonstrate part of ATC's*
   _____.
   a. *ethical code of conduct*
   b. *espoused values*
   c. *core values*
   d. *visible culture*

2. *ATC encourages employees to take risks. This is demonstrated by accepting and tolerating employee mistakes when other firms may not do so. This reflects ATC's _____.*
   a. *core values*
   b. *visible culture*
   c. *espoused values*
   d. *stability*

3. *ATC considers employees central to the firm's success, and therefore takes care of them by being flexible with their schedules and accommodating their family lives. Such policies at the center of ATC's organizational culture reflect its _____.*
   a. *core values*
   b. *espoused values*
   c. *visible culture*
   d. *ethical code of conduct*

FIGURE 4.1

Levels of Corporate Culture

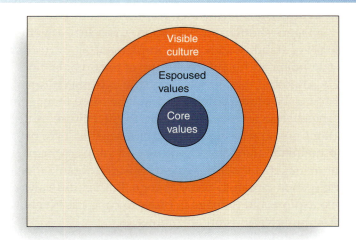

core values

A firm's principles that are widely shared, that operate unconsciously, and that are considered nonnegotiable.

A sweeping culture change is under way at Home Depot Inc., where CEO Robert Nardelli is using military analogies and models to try to reshape the chain of about 2,050 stores into a disciplined unit and reignite both its flagging growth rate and its once-enviable reputation for customer service. In addition to hiring hundreds of ex-military officers for the company's two-year management training program, Nardelli has tightened up performance appraisals and established tight financial, operational, customer, and people-skills goals for all employees. Of Home Depot's new challenges from competitors like Lowe's and Wal-Mart, one of Nardelli's top executives says, "It's as simple as warfare."

justify actions and decisions. For example, managers may justify layoffs primarily on the basis of a need to cut costs or to expedite decision making and improve response time by streamlining organizational levels. Other managers may say they tolerate mistakes because employees need to be encouraged to take risks or because it is better to treat workers with respect and provide them with second chances when necessary. Espoused values are those values that are expressed on behalf of an organization[3] or that are expressed as explanations for policies or actions.

People may not always give the real reason behind their actions. Employees are quick to spot hypocrisy. Managers who are not honest about why actions were taken may create an organizational culture full of cynicism, dishonesty, lack of credibility, and poor ethics, all of which eventually translate into poor firm performance.

Espoused values may vary substantially across organizations and this variability in expressed values can reflect real and important differences in these organizations. For organizations that have merged or been acquired it has been found that organizational performance after the merger is better for firms that had more closely matched espoused values to begin with.[4] This effect on postmerger financial performance illustrates the importance of espoused values.

Espoused values are generally consciously and explicitly communicated. At the center of organizational culture are **core values** that are widely shared, operate unconsciously, and are considered nonnegotiable. In some organizations, such as REI in the introductory vignette, a basic assumption may be that stability and commitment of the workforce are critical for success. Consequently, employees are well treated and receive liberal fringe benefits. At the other extreme, a basic assumption may be that employees are commodities and an expense that should be minimized in the business process, rather than an investment. Thus employees are tightly controlled, exceptions to established policy are kept to a minimum, there are detailed rules and procedures about what employees can and cannot do, and managers believe it is their duty to prevent deviations from the norms. Employees may be watching one another to ensure that no one breaks the rules, and people are trained to check with their superiors before making most decisions.

1. *What do we measure?*

   When performance is assessed, whatever is measured is what is truly important. Understanding what is actually measured reveals what the organization values. While there may be many statements about the importance of quality and customer service, if amount of sales is the only aspect of performance that is measured, the culture in the organization is more oriented to quantity than quality or customer service.

2. *What is celebrated, recognized, or rewarded?*

   What is held out in the organization as something to be celebrated or recognized? These things are the key to what is valued. Employees will be quick to pick up on this key to the culture in the organization.

3. *What data is used to assess the effectiveness of the organization?*

   Is productivity or amount of sales the sole measure focused on when making overall assessments of how well the organization is functioning? Or, are measures such as employee and customer satisfaction and loyalty also considered to be the most crucial? The data that is used as the principal means for taking the pulse of the organization reveals what is at the heart of the culture.

Source: Adapted from L. Larson, "A New Attitude: Changing Organization Culture," *Trustee* 55 (2002), pp. 8–14.

The basic underlying cultural assumptions create the lenses through which people perceive and interpret events. Someone sitting motionless may be seen as loafing in some firms, while at others, the employee would be perceived as pondering an important problem. When employees are absent from work, the organization's culture may lead managers to conclude they are shirking, and if an employee requests permission to perform some tasks at home, the request will probably be denied because the supervisor expects the employee will "goof off" rather than work. A simple and quick way of getting a handle on the type of culture that is operating in an organization is presented in Manager's Notebook 4.1 above.

LOC-In

2 Learning Objective Check-In

Raj Communications usually gives an award every quarter to the top performing teams in each of its three divisions. These awards are based on creativity and risk taking—not necessarily achievement of specific organizational objectives. In performance assessments, customer satisfaction is at the top of the evaluation list. Every division has customers, even if they are "internal"—meaning other divisions or departments.

1. *Which of the quick culture test questions speaks to the way Raj Communications treats its most creative teams?*

   a. *What do we measure?*

   b. *What data is used to assess the effectiveness of the organization?*

   c. *What is celebrated, recognized, or rewarded?*

   d. *How do we evaluate individual performance?*

The Importance of Culture

Organization culture can be a critical factor in determining the competitiveness of an organization. While culture may seem more of a concept than something that is physically real, the potential impact of culture can be very real and merits careful attention. Results from workplace studies indicate that organizational culture can be an even more important determinant of worker commitment and loyalty than pay.[5] Culture can also differentiate an organization in the labor market. For example, SAS, consistently one of *Fortune* magazine's "100 Best Companies to Work for in America," is a company that many

ORGANIZATIONAL CULTURE AS COMPETITIVE TOOL: SOME TIPS

1. Check whether your culture is strong or weak.
   - Do employees agree on the core values?
   - Do ceremonies, stories, and so on present a coherent and consistent message?
     - A strong culture should lead to greater cohesiveness and higher performance.
2. Is the culture consistent with the objectives of the organization?
   - Do the policies, practices, and employee beliefs and values line up with the strategy?
   - Does everyone know the mission of the organization?
     - A culture that is compatible with the strategy can reinforce the strategy and help to get everyone working together for the same purpose.
3. Want stability?
   - Emphasize trust, fairness, and personal development in the culture.
   - Offer public recognition of achievement.
   - Provide opportunities for personal growth and support for work/life balance.
     - An atmosphere of trust and opportunity for personal growth can be key to retaining and attracting the best workers.
4. Manage the culture!
   - Do you know what the culture is and what you want it to be?
   - What are the levers by which you can influence the culture?
     - If you don't manage the culture, it will evolve on its own (and in ways you may not want). If culture isn't managed, you will have lost a potentially important tool for achieving competitive advantage.
5. Analyze the cultures of other organizations before working with them.
   - Does a potential project with another organization make sense from a cultural perspective? Are the cultures compatible?
     - Incompatible cultures can lead to conflict and performance difficulty on joint projects. Also, to the extent that you are known by the company you keep, teaming with an organization with an incompatible culture could damage your own.

Source: Adapted from M. A. Mitchell and D. Yates, "How to Use Your Organizational Culture as a Competitive Tool," *Nonprofit World 20* (2002), pp. 33–34.

people seek out as a preferred employer. The employee- and family-friendly culture that has been carefully cultivated at SAS sets it apart and gives the organization a competitive advantage in the struggle to attract and keep the best workers. There are many ways in which organizational culture can be a key positive force in achieving organizational objectives. Manager's Notebook 4.2 above offers some tips to make sure the culture in your organization is a competitive asset.

Organizational culture can help managers achieve organizational objectives in several ways. As illustrated in Figure 4.2 on page 145, key functions performed by culture include employee self-management, stability, employee socialization, and supporting a firm's strategies. We now turn to a description of each of these effects of organizational culture. Each of these aspects points out how organizational culture can help or hinder the achievement of organizational objectives.

FIGURE 4.2

Key Effects of Organizational Culture

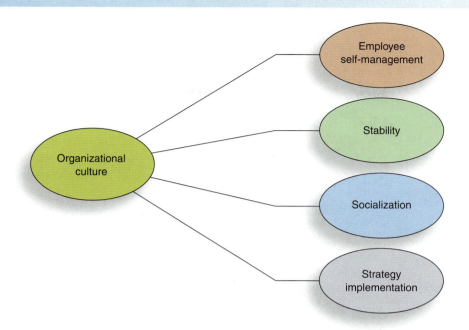

Employee Self-Management

"Keeping workers in line" consists of a variety of rational means to coordinate and control employees. Defining jobs with job descriptions; creating vertical levels and reporting relationships; drawing organizational charts; establishing departments, business units, and divisions; and developing work schedules are examples of rational controls. Still, no firm can function effectively unless employees choose to behave in the way the firm desires.

Organizational culture can induce employees to behave in a particular way without close supervision or formal control mechanisms. Most people like to feel that they belong; fitting into the culture and acting accordingly make it more likely that employees will be accepted by others. Conversely, failure to comply with cultural norms generates social pressures to conform; thus the individuals would either align with the cultural expectations or face ostracism and ridicule by their peers. Much of this process occurs informally and in an unspecified manner, filling in the gaps left by rational control systems.

Culture creates a sense of shared identity and facilitates commitment to something larger than individual self-interests. For instance, French biologist Nicolas Taquet left a state-controlled medical research lab in France because it was bureaucratic and constraining. Taquet immigrated to the United States to work as a researcher at the Baylor Institute for Immunology Research, where he was given the autonomy and the resources to pursue the development of anticancer compounds. He compared the two environments by noting that "I am so motivated here that I work weekends and nights. That wasn't the case back home."[6]

Stability

Culture provides a sense of continuity in the midst of rapid change and intense competitive pressure. In industries with "hyperturbulent environments" such as high technology, culture fulfills an important human need for predictability, security, and

comfort. It can take the edge off the stress caused by projects that change overnight, products that become obsolete in a matter of months, changeable work teams and reporting relationships, and frequent shifts in work methods and operations. The continuity provided by organizational culture has become increasingly valuable, as most organizations are experiencing ever more rapid rates of change. Likewise, as virtual connections and temporary alliances become commonplace, organizational culture can be the common understanding that both binds people together and facilitates their operations as a cohesive unit.[7]

Some organizations start socializing people to their culture when they recruit. Scottsdale, Arizona–based Cold Stone Creamery conveys its culture of fun and performing for customers by holding "auditions" for new workers.

socialization

The process of internalizing or taking organizational values as one's own.

prearrival

The first stage of socialization, consisting of the values, attitudes, biases, and expectations the employee brings to the organization when first hired.

encounter stage

The stage of socialization at which the individual begins to compare expectations about the firm's culture with reality.

metamorphosis stage

The stage of socialization at which the employee is induced to bring his or her values and ways of doing things closer to those of the organization.

Socialization

One key hurdle new employees face is finding out how to "fit in." Organizational culture subtly teaches employees the values of the organization. The process of internalizing or taking organizational values as one's own is called **socialization.** For example, the Marine Corps uses boot camps to socialize new recruits in "the Marine way." Sanyo requires new employees to live and eat together for five months at a company-paid resort to learn "how to speak to superiors [and acquire] proper grooming and dress. The company considers this program essential for transforming young employees, fresh out of school, into dedicated Kaisha Senshi, or corporate warriors."[8] Once accomplished, socialization helps the new individual feel he or she is part of the organization.

Socialization is a three-stage process. The first stage, **prearrival**, consists of the values, attitudes, biases, and expectations the employee brings to the organization when first hired. These may have been learned in the family, at school, in other organizations, or as members of a profession or discipline. Most organizations, some more deliberately than others, attempt to select employees who are most likely to fit into the company's culture. Even if the firm succeeds in hiring "the right type," however, the employee still has to learn the culture.

As the employee moves into the organization, the individual reaches the **encounter stage.** At this point, the individual begins to compare expectations about the firm's culture with reality. To the extent that there are discrepancies between cultural expectations and reality, the employee is induced to bring his or her values and ways of doing things closer to those of the organization during the **metamorphosis stage.** Unfortunately, in their rush to fill positions, companies often do not pay enough attention to this stage. Jeffrey Pfeffer, a noted management scholar, writes that a common myth is that "you build a great and effective company by hiring only great people. . . . I hate the 'war for people' imagery. It's a trend the companies have brought on themselves. They're paying people to switch jobs and wondering why they switch jobs so much."[9]

table 4.1

Entry Socialization Options

Formal socialization occurs when an employee's newcomer status is made obvious, through separate training or orientation away from the job.	*Informal socialization* happens when the new employee receives little special attention and begins working right away.
Individual socialization occurs when the new employee is trained or receives orientation individually.	*Collective socialization* occurs when a group of new employees receive training or go through orientation together.
Fixed advancement socialization happens when new employees undergo the same time period for each stage of training and are expected to spend the same amount of time in the position before being considered for the next level.	*Variable advancement socialization* occurs when the next stage of training or career advancement within a company is flexible and based on the employee's development.
Serial socialization takes place in firms that assign new employees to other staff members for specific training and mentoring in different areas.	*Random socialization* occurs when new employees are not expected to resort to specific staff members but determine how to handle things themselves.
Divestiture socialization removes new employees' individual characteristics so that the employees will fit into their roles and the company as it exists.	*Investiture socialization* assumes the new employees' individual traits and characteristics are valuable to the employees' and the firm's success.

Sources: J. Van Maanen, "People Processing: Strategies of Organizational Socialization," *Organizational Dynamics*, Summer 1978, pp. 19–36; E. H. Schein, "Organizational Culture," *American Psychologist*," February 1990, p. 116.

Table 4.1 above lists ways firms create a closer alignment between an employee's values and expectations and those of the firm. An organization can choose from among formal or informal, individual or collective, fixed or variable, serial or random, and investiture or divestiture socialization. Not all people are readily socialized. In extreme cases, an employee will feel disillusioned and decide that he or she is in the wrong place. Such an employee is likely to become disgruntled and/or leave the firm. Proper selection should reduce the probability of this happening.

Firms should also be wary of turning employees into conformists. A healthy organization tries to accommodate and take advantage of employee diversity, as discussed in Chapter 11, while maintaining cultural uniqueness.

Implementation of the Organization's Strategy

Organizational culture may contribute to firm performance by supporting implementation of the organization's strategy as well as desired changes in that strategy. In other words, if the firm's strategy and its culture reinforce each other, employees find it natural to be committed to the strategy. These shared values and norms make it easier for them to rally behind the chosen strategy.

Beware the Dark Side

Very few things in management are absolute. While a company's culture can be a major advantage in the marketplace, there is also the potential for negative outcomes. For instance, a firmly entrenched set of cultural values and norms may cause employees to resist any change, even one that is vital for survival. Further, a strong culture may

LOC-In

3 **Learning Objective Check-In**

At SMECO, organizational culture performs several important roles. Matthew works at SMECO and appreciates the sense of continuity that the culture seems to provide. When he joined the company, his contract helped in defining his role at the firm, but he has learned much more from the way others interact in his department.

1. *Providing a sense of continuity is one way that organizational cultures can _____.*
   a. *promote stability*
   b. *empower workers*
   c. *encourage self-management*
   d. *socialize workers*
2. *The most likely effect of the organizational culture defining Matthew's roles and expectations is _____.*
   a. *socializing workers*
   b. *creating cultural symbols*
   c. *self-management*
   d. *promoting stability*

The Columbia Accident Investigation Board concluded that the 2003 loss of the shuttle Columbia and its crew was caused as much by a "broken safety culture" as by damage to the shuttle's wing during launch. The board's report warned that if culture did not change, mistakes would continue to occur.

appear to some to be more like an exclusive club, causing valuable new employees or customers to feel like outsiders. Eventually these individuals may seek to work with other organizations. At the other end of the spectrum, there may be managers who neglect or fail to reinforce the key values present in a culture. This can lead to disregard for personal safety or little understanding and support for the firm's strategic efforts. Consequently, organizational leaders must continually assess the nature of an organization's culture, including what is valued and reinforced, or the problems associated with a culture that is too strong or too weak may emerge.

Managing Cultural Processes

The culture of an organization evolves gradually over time. It is normally strongly influenced by the beliefs and philosophy of the organization's founder. A firm's founder transmits his or her beliefs to a small group of close associates, often family members who already share the same values or at least know each other well. As the firm grows, the founder's values determine who is hired and who is retained and promoted. Selection and socialization processes tend to reinforce the founder's values. These values become firmly entrenched even after the founder is long gone. The Disney Company remains a close reflection of Walt Disney, even though he died four decades ago. Walt Disney strongly believed that every employee should present an ideal image to the public. This meant being impeccably groomed, cheerful, and friendly. Men were required to have no facial hair and to wear short hair.

Similarly, Jim Henson, creator of the Muppets, espoused beliefs that live on in his company. Henson "always wanted people to be creatively and emotionally invested in what they did. . . . He believed that projects worked best if they were a team effort. . . . He wanted people who were wildly and eccentrically different from himself at the company. He loved seeing what they could do and how they would surprise him."[10] "For many years, IBM was a reflection of J. Watson's personality. Southwest Airlines is made in Herb Kelleher's image. Mary Kay Cosmetics' culture reflects its founder's faith and beliefs. Microsoft's culture represents Bill Gates' intellectual, demanding, and perfectionist personality. Oprah Winfrey, the first African-American and the third woman to own a TV and film production studio, runs an organization that reflects her high-energy, nurturing style."[11]

A variety of things maintain and reinforce culture over time. Some may be deliberately imposed by management, as in the case of cultural symbols, rituals, and the choice of company heroes who best embody the firm's values. Others may be largely unconscious processes, such as the use of stories, language, and employee perceptions of the company's leadership style.

cultural symbols

The icons and objects that communicate organizational values, used by management to convey and sustain shared meaning among employees.

Cultural Symbols

People find it relatively easy to relate to or at least understand symbols or icons, such as flags, crosses, uniforms, or various logos (e.g., the Playboy Bunny). **Cultural symbols** are the icons and objects that communicate organizational values. Management uses them to convey and sustain shared meaning among employees. For example,

- Tandem Computers' corporate headquarters in Cupertino, California, looks and feels more like a college campus than a business facility. Small buildings are separated by green space. Jogging trails, a basketball court, a large swimming pool, a dance hall, and other amenities are provided on site. These symbols reinforce a company culture characterized by openness, participation, informality, and equality.

- The president of Nashville's Centennial Medical Center dramatically conveyed an open-door policy by removing the door to his office and hanging it from the lobby ceiling.

- To change their "stiff," conservative culture in order to attract new talent from freewheeling Silicon Valley firms and to appear more friendly to apprehensive customers, several leading brokerage houses, including Morgan Stanley Dean Witter, Lehman Brothers, and Goldman Sachs, introduced a policy of casual attire in 2000.

Company Rituals and Ceremonies

Organizations plan activities and events that offer all employees an opportunity to share cultural meanings. One example of a dramatic ritual occurs when police departments conduct ceremonies to honor bravery, community dedication, or acts of heroism. Ceremonies convey organizational values and display examples of outstanding performance. Medtronic, a producer of high-tech implantable medical products, holds an annual service day during which the production facility is shut down.[12] The purpose of the ritual is to provide Medtronic employees with the opportunity to contribute time and effort to a charitable cause for one day. The ritual helps to make real to employees the community-based values that are part of the Medtronic culture. Another example of a company that uses an annual event to underscore their culture is Johnson Controls. The company holds an annual meeting, called Team Rally, in which employee teams present how they improved a work process.[13] The presentations use skits and teams include how the improvements are disseminated to the rest of the organization. From a cultural standpoint, the Team Rally is a vehicle for Johnson Controls to emphasize the values of teamwork, continuous improvement, and sharing knowledge throughout the organization. Mary Kay Cosmetics Company bestows awards to high-achieving sales consultants in an auditorium filled with sales agents and their families. Glamorously dressed, they cheer as their most successful peers receive gold and diamond pins, furs, and pink Cadillacs.

Company Heroes

Organizations effectively communicate values by identifying individuals whose deeds best reflect what the organization believes in, so that other people can emulate their behavior. The police officers and firefighters who died at the World Trade Center on September 11, 2001, will long be remembered as organizational heroes.

Stories

Organizational culture is sustained by the narratives and legends that vividly capture the organization's values. At 3M, a commonly told story involves a worker who was fired for pursuing an idea that his boss asked him to drop. The former employee continued working on the idea without pay in an unused office. According to the legend, the product idea eventually became a big success, and the worker was rehired at the vice-president level. This story is used to communicate 3M's belief that perseverance is crucial to success.

Language

The language used by managerial employees may serve as a constant reminder of the organization's values. Language promotes both positive and negative values. For instance, the use of sexist language and ethnic jokes communicates to current and prospective workers that the company does not value diversity. Reliance on such euphemisms as "future enhancements" for "need to change a failing course of action," "reengineering efforts" instead of "layoffs," and "dehiring" for "termination" suggests the absence of an open, honest atmosphere in which issues can be discussed in a frank and candid fashion.

Firms often use slogans to succinctly express cultural values. For example, PepsiCo communicates the value of hiring the best people and teaching them to work together in its slogan, "We take eagles and teach them to fly in formation." Sequins International, a manufacturer of sequined fabrics and trimming, points out that "you don't have to please the boss; you have to please the customer."

Leadership

Employees infer a great deal about the organization from the leader styles they encounter. Effective leaders articulate a vision for the organization that employees find exciting and worth striving for. In addition, an effective leader provides a daily example of what the organization deems to be important. Employees make judgments about the underlying values of the organization not by what executives say, but by what they do. Many people attribute the survival of Chrysler in the early 1980s to its colorful CEO, Lee Iacocca. Iacocca negotiated a large loan from the federal government to save the company. He also served as an example by working for $1 a year plus Chrysler stock, which many analysts viewed as worthless. Within two years, Chrysler repaid the federal loan, and the value of its stock had skyrocketed. Iacocca showed Chrysler employees that perseverance, sacrifice, and commitment can overcome daunting challenges and can lead to personal success.

To reinforce an egalitarian and frugal image, Andrew Grove, CEO of Intel, the Silicon Valley manufacturer of computer chips, worked out of a cubicle similar in size to those of other engineers. Groves's cubicle was located on the main floor of the building for all to see. Grove insisted that all top managers fly coach class, rent subcompact cars, and avoid using company resources to bolster personal prestige. At Intel, offices were not to be elegantly furnished, and business meetings were not to take place at fancy restaurants.

Southwest Airlines has been profitable year after year, while most airlines struggle to survive and many have disappeared. Southwest's former CEO Herb Kelleher reinforced a culture of "be happy, enjoy your work, and make customers smile" through employee videos, "winning spirit" ceremonies, and speeches, and by serving as inspirational leader, kindly uncle, cheerleader, and clown.

Organizational Policies and Decision Making

Performance appraisals, budgets, new plans, and other policies and decisions clearly communicate company values, and therefore the company's culture. The criteria used for measuring success and the way they are used for control purposes tell employees what the organizational culture considers to be most important. For instance, some pharmaceutical firms measure innovation by the number of new patents, while others prefer to rely on the commercial value of existing or prospective patents. The former companies are signaling that they value many projects with small incremental changes to technology, risk aversion, a short-term orientation, and greater quantity. In the latter case, the signal is that focusing on fewer projects

Working as a Team   Just as with an organization, teams can develop their own cultures and ways of relating and doing things. The success of many organizations depends on effective team functioning, even if some team members have been newly assigned to the team or if the team primarily interacts in a virtual fashion. A key to effective team functioning is understanding and utilizing the culture of a team. As a team member, you can:

- *Help to assess the culture of your team* by using the questions in the Quick Organizational Culture Test presented in Manager's Notebook 4.1. These issues can be as relevant for team functioning as they are for organizational functioning.

- *Identify the key effects of the team culture.* Is the team culture clear enough so that it helps team members to manage themselves? Does the team culture help provide a sense of stability and socialize new team members? Is the team culture aligned with the strategic direction of the organization? If the team culture doesn't measure up in any of these areas, identify what you and the team can do to improve the culture.

- *Take steps to maintain and reinforce the team culture.* Within the constraints set by the organization, what symbols could the team put in place to effectively convey the culture? Similarly, ceremonies, rituals, stories, language, and team leadership could all be developed and refined so that an effective team culture is maximized. In addition, the ways in which the team operates and makes decisions can be a key means by which the team culture can be made apparent.

---

involving more radical technological changes and higher probability of large pay-offs is preferred. This is more likely to lead to fewer patents, greater risk taking, a long-term orientation, and a search for one home run rather than four singles.

Employees learn what the company truly values by watching where scarce resources are spent. For instance, the word *innovation* may be used repeatedly in speeches, in company brochures, and on plaques positioned next to each elevator. But if research and development expenditures are the first thing to be cut during hard times, employees receive the opposite message.

Cultural values are also communicated by the ways people are rewarded. For instance, despite lip service to the value of effective teaching, many universities determine faculty salaries and promotions largely on research productivity. This sends a strong message to faculty that what the university values are publications, not student success stories.

The importance of culture and managing culture (the topics of the previous two sections of this chapter) are commonly thought of at the organization level. However, culture can also have a central role at the level of teams in organizations. Management Is Everyone's Business 4.1 above offers suggestions for maintaining and developing culture as a team member.

LOC-In

④ Learning Objective Check-In

Mail One Corporation looks and feels like a college campus. There are jogging trails, open green spaces, small buildings, and recreation facilities. At Mail One, a common narrative told to new hires is about the founder's flying everyone at the firm to Dallas (from Idaho) at his own expense in order to give them a first-hand look at the shipping method the company was going to adopt. The trip proved more valuable to those employees than any on-site training in Idaho could have been. It reinforced the idea of personal sacrifice and the importance of sharing knowledge with employees.

1. *The fact that the Mail One headquarters is more like a college campus than a traditional office building demonstrates the use of _____.*
   a. *leadership*
   b. *storytelling*
   c. *cultural symbols*
   d. *rituals and ceremonies*
2. *The narrative of the founder's flying everyone to Dallas for a first-hand look at the new shipment method demonstrates _____.*
   a. *language*
   b. *storytelling*
   c. *rituals and ceremonies*
   d. *organizational policies*

Characteristics and Types of Organizational Culture

The cultures of organizations can differ in a variety of ways. For example, cultural uniformity, the strength of a firm's culture, the degree of formalization, and the extent to which organizational culture differs from national culture vary from one firm to another and can determine the extent to which organizational culture influences employees. In addition to these various external characteristics, the nature or type of culture varies widely across organizations. There are numerous typologies of culture. It is useful to be familiar with the types in order to recognize the type of culture that is present. In this section some of the dimensions along which organizational cultures can differ as well as individual types of cultures are identified.

Cultural Uniformity versus Heterogeneity

Organizations vary in the extent to which a uniform culture permeates the entire organization. In some large corporations, different subcultures may be found in different parts of the firm. This is the case at Motorola, where the culture varies among divisions. Some divisions are conservative, bureaucratic, and risk-averse and value seniority, while others are entrepreneurial, freewheeling, innovative, and risk-seeking and place little value on seniority. At 3M, on the other hand, the dominant culture, which emphasizes innovation, a focus on related products, and tolerance for failure, is evident in all parts of the corporation.

Neither uniformity nor heterogeneity is right or wrong. When divisions are largely autonomous and each has a different strategy for its own unique products or services, it makes sense for each division to have a different culture. On the other hand, subcultures could be problematic for a firm where all units are interdependent and employees must work closely together to implement the overall corporate strategy.

Strong versus Weak Cultures

The more employees believe in the espoused values, the more they act in accordance with those values and the more the culture plays a boundary-defining role, creating a distinction between the organization and others. A strong culture pressures people to do what the organization wants with less reliance on formal control mechanisms such as close supervision, hierarchies, rules, and procedures. It may also increase the level of intrinsic motivation because employees work hard for the right thing. On the other hand, a strong culture may become a liability if it presents a barrier to adaptation in a rapidly changing environment, makes some groups of employees feel unwelcome, or makes it difficult for the firm to work cooperatively with other firms.

Culture versus Formalization

In varying degrees, organizational culture can substitute for such formal systems of control and decision making as organizational structures, rules, procedures, policies, and direct supervision. A common destiny and shared meanings make it less necessary to create mechanisms to ensure compliance, predictability, orderliness, and consistency. To the extent that organizational culture increases trust among employees, it reduces the need for written documentation and monitoring of organization members.

National versus Organizational Culture

The workplace behavior of individuals is a function of various levels of culture.[14] A national culture can guide behaviors, such as Americans tending to be more independent while citizens of other countries may more positively value collaboration. Of course, cultural influences can go beyond national levels and include regional influences and ethnic and religious identification. There are times when organizations use employee selection and socialization to develop cultures that mute these broad cultural influences and that might be significantly different from a specific regional or national culture. Some multinational firms, such as Colgate, deliberately attempt to create a "global company culture" to circumvent the barriers to communication and understanding present in many multinational operations.

In most countries, there is a great deal of diversity in the workforce, and most cultural traits overlap across countries. For instance, while the typical U.S. worker may be an individualistic risk seeker and the typical Japanese worker may be team and security oriented, numerous people in both countries are more like the typical person in the other country than the typical person in their own country. Thus, a firm is able to attract and retain the type of employee that fits into its culture regardless of where it is located.

Types

An increasing number of culture typologies are being used to identify various kinds of cultures. No one typology is better or more correct than the others. Regardless of which is utilized, classifying the type of culture in an organization can be useful for identifying the kind of employees and the management characteristics that are present in a culture. For example, knowing the type of culture indicates whether or not employees who are risk takers are hired. Further, the type of culture present has implications for how people should be managed. Some of the basic types of organizational culture along with implications for employees and management are described next.

One simple but powerful classification differentiates between two basic organization culture types: (1) traditional control or (2) employee involvement.[15] A traditional control culture emphasizes the chain of command and relies on top-down control and orders. Control systems are put in place so that management can be assured that assigned projects and goals are being attained. In contrast, an employee involvement culture emphasizes participation and involvement. People work together to attain goals, not because they are externally coerced by rules and control systems, but because they are internally motivated. Table 4.2 on page 154 summarizes the key characteristics of these two basic types of organizational culture.

The traditional and involvement cultures have distinct differences in terms of understanding what types of employees are recruited and how the work environment should be managed. For example, employees that would be expected to be most successful in the traditional environment are more task and rule oriented. In contrast, the best performers in an employee involvement culture would be risk takers with strong interpersonal skills. Effective management in a traditional culture would emphasize task performance and careful measurement and control. Effective management in an employee involvement culture would need to be much "looser," and reward people for commitment and for taking risks, even though some of them may have failed.

table 4.2

Traditional Control and Employee Involvement Cultures

TRADITIONAL CONTROL: KEY CHARACTERISTICS	EMPLOYEE INVOLVEMENT: KEY CHARACTERISTICS
• Narrowly defined job duties	• Broadly defined job duties
• Top-down communication	• Lateral communication
• Centralized decision making	• Participative decision making
• Control systems	• Feedback systems

Source: Adapted from R. L. Heneman, M. M. Fisher, and K. E. Dixon, "Reward and Organizational Systems Alignment: An Expert System," *Compensation and Benefits Review 33* (2001), pp. 18–29.

baseball team culture

The fast-paced, competitive, high-risk form of corporate culture typically found in organizations in rapidly changing environments, with short product life cycles, with high-risk decision making, and dependent on continuous innovation for survival.

club culture

A type of organizational culture that seeks people who are loyal, committed to one organization, and need to fit into a group, and rewards them with job security, promotion from within, and slow progress.

Corporate Culture Preferences Scale

academy culture

A type of organization culture that seeks to hire people with specialties and technical mastery who will be confined to a set of jobs within a particular function and be rewarded by long-term association and a slow, steady climb up the organization ladder.

fortress culture

An organizational culture with the primary goal of surviving and reversing business problems, including economic decline and hostile competitors.

A second approach identifies four types of cultures using terms with which you are familiar: teams, clubs, academies, and fortresses. Each type calls for a particular kind of employee. A quality match increases the odds that an employee will be successful. Having employees whose personalities match the organizational culture tends to enhance the overall performance of a firm by reducing disruptive internal friction and employee turnover.[16]

A **baseball team culture** is present in an organization facing a rapidly changing environment, with short product life cycles, high-risk decision making, and dependence on continuous innovation for survival. Organizations like this are typically in such fast-paced, competitive, high-risk industries as advertising, software development, movie production, and biotechnology. The employee who best fits this culture tends to be a risk-taker, enjoys being a "free agent," shows little commitment to one employer, and thrives on time pressure and stress.

The **club culture** seeks people who are loyal, committed to one organization, and need to fit into a group. Organization members prefer to spend their entire careers in one organization. The organization, in turn, rewards them with job security, promotes from within, and allows them to prove their competence at each level. Employees in firms with club cultures grant "bonus points" for age and experience. Club cultures are present in companies such as United Parcel Service, Delta Airlines, the "Baby Bell" telephone companies, government agencies, and the military.

Like club cultures, an organization with **academy culture** prefers to hire individuals who are interested in a long-term association and a slow, steady climb up the organization ladder. Employees in academy cultures tend to be confined to a set of jobs within a particular function, so they should be people who enjoy becoming expert in one area. They should not expect broad individual development and intense networking with people from other areas. Specialization and technical mastery are the basis for rewards and advancement. Organizations that fit this mold include IBM, Coca-Cola, and Procter & Gamble.

Fortress cultures are obsessed with surviving and reversing sagging fortunes. These companies restructure and downsize to cope with the challenges of economic decline or a hostile competitive environment. Textile firms, savings and loans, large retailers, forest product companies, and natural gas exploration firms are found in this group. Fortress-type firms attract confident individuals who enjoy the excitement, challenge, and opportunities of a turnaround.

A final organizational culture typology is known as the *competing values framework*.[17] This framework is presented in Figure 4.3 on page 155. As shown, the competing values framework is based on two dimensions: focus and con-

FIGURE 4.3

Competing Values Framework

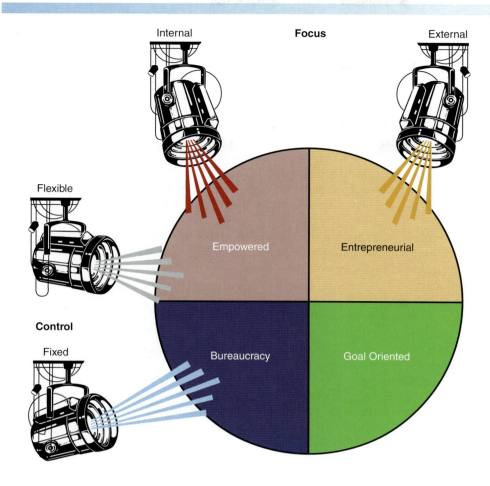

trol. The focus dimension refers to whether the primary attention of the organization is directed toward internal dynamics or directed outward toward the external environment. The control dimension represents the extent to which the organization is flexible or fixed in how it coordinates and controls activity. As depicted in the figure, the two ends of each continuum can be viewed as different colored spotlights. When the spotlights cross they form four unique colors that represent the four organizational culture models that make up the competing values framework. The purple quadrant depicts a bureaucratic culture which focuses internally and has a fixed approach to controlling the work process. A bureaucratic culture is concerned with maintaining stability and tries to achieve it with hierarchical control. The pink quadrant represents an empowered culture. The focus is internal, as it is with a bureaucracy, but the approach to control is looser and more flexible. The emphasis of an empowered culture is high morale and cohesiveness and it attempts to achieve these outcomes through development and support of the workforce. The light yellow quadrant depicts an entrepreneurial culture in which the organization is externally focused but flexible. The entrepreneurial organization seeks growth through being adaptable and agile. The green quadrant represents a goal oriented culture in which a focus on the external environment is paired with a fixed approach to control. A goal-oriented organization is paired with a fixed approach to control. A goal-oriented organization is focused on productivity and competing in the marketplace and it achieves this through careful planning and goal setting. Combining the types of focus and control leads to four

video: THE ENTREPRENEURIAL MANAGER

New Belgium Brewery— Organizational Culture

Summary

Jeff Lebesch and Kim Jordan, founders of New Belgium Brewery, are not typical business owners. Jeff and Kim think it is very important to have a culture at their firm where going to work every day is happy, where employees have a loving, open attitude toward one another, and where ownership in the firm is shared among co-workers. This is why they made the decision to make the company's finances transparent within the firm. This step was two-fold. First, it meant educating the company's workers on what the financial statements meant and how they impacted the business. Second, it meant sharing direct ownership of the firm with the employees.

While the primary objective of any firm is to achieve long-term profits, for Jeff and Kim, there is more to it than that: having fun is also important. By giving employees a say in the strategic direction of the business, the employees developed a vested interest in seeing the company progress further. Having employee-owners also helped enable the firm to grow from its small beginnings to its current state. As more employee-owners were brought on, an organizational culture began to form. The organizational culture includes the firm's shared values, beliefs, traditions, philosophies, rules, and role models for behavior.

The organizational culture directly affects New Belgium's costs and efficiency. While on a hike in Colorado, the employee-owners developed the New Belgium core values and beliefs: "to operate a profitable business which makes our love and talent manifest." A couple years into the firm's existence, 1996 began open book management at New Belgium. This is an important way that Jeff and Kim share responsibility, risk, *and* credit for getting beer out the door. Everyone at the firm has a stake in the firm's success and is trained to be financially literate so they can track progress, profitability, and other key measures.

From this organizational culture at New Belgium an organizational structure developed. The structure is the arrangement of positions within the organization. It is based on the nature of the relationships among people working at the firm. New Belgium's structure is largely functional, with departments composed of employees who deal specifically with issues pertaining to functional areas—wastewater reclamation or quality assurance, for example. Decision making is highly decentralized. Empowerment is high, and everyone is considered responsible for the interests of the firm.

Discussion Questions

1. Define one of New Belgium's espoused values or core beliefs. How is this different from a company you have worked for? Would you run your company this way?

2. Does New Belgium use much employee self-management? Support your response with what you learned in the video.

3. New Belgium introduced open book management in 1996. What tactics did top management employ for introducing this change? What reasons were given in the video for introducing open book management?

unique organizational cultures. Which type of culture is best depends upon the environmental situation and management's purpose for the organization. There is evidence, however, that the type of culture that is dominant in an organization can influence how effectively the organization performs. For example, it has been found that hospitals that maintain a more empowered culture for nurses tend to have nurses with greater commitment and job satisfaction and lower tendency to quit.[18] While an empowered culture may not work in all types of business, treating professionals, such as nurses, in a flexible and supportive manner makes sense and leads to improved patient care and lower turnover costs.

The competing values framework and the other typologies are useful for evaluating organizational cultures. These models help us to rationally think through and identify the employee and management practices that match a culture and lead to improved organizational performance. It is important to recognize that these frameworks depict pure types of culture. The reality is that most organizations do not have such coherent and internally consistent cultures.

5 **Learning Objective Check-In**

Jess tends to work better with a narrowly defined job description. She is familiar with top-down communication, and that is what she expects from her firm. Jess also expects centralized decision making, and does not necessarily expect to be involved in the decisions made at the company where she works. She does, however, want a long-term association with the firm and a slow, steady climb up the organizational ladder. Josh, on the other hand, prefers lateral communication. He works well with broadly defined job duties, and is flexible within them. Unlike Jess, Josh expects to be involved in the daily decision making at his firm.

1. *Which type of company culture would best suit Jess?*
   a. *Employee involvement culture*
   b. *Empowerment culture*
   c. *Entrepreneurial culture*
   d. *Traditional control culture*

2. *Which type of company culture would best suit Josh?*
   a. *Administrative culture*
   b. *Bureaucratic culture*
   c. *Employee involvement culture*
   d. *Traditional control culture*

3. *Based on what you have read, and using a quality match approach, which type of organizational culture would Jess thrive in?*
   a. *Baseball team culture*
   b. *Club culture*
   c. *Academy culture*
   d. *Fortress culture*

Managing Organizational Change

One of the more fixed aspects of a company is its culture. Employees tend to rely on the longstanding symbols, rituals, language, and values that provide a sense of continuity and stability. Unfortunately, the world surrounding the organization (and even the world inside the organization) is nowhere near as stable. In other words: Change happens! The second half of this chapter is devoted to the process of understanding and managing change. Only when managers effectively anticipate and execute change can the firm survive and succeed in the long term.

Types of Change

Change can be viewed as a planned event or as an unplanned and dynamic condition.[19] A planned change occurs when a change in an organization is anticipated and allows for advance preparation. In contrast, dynamic change refers to change that is ongoing or happens so quickly, such as with a crisis, that the impact on the organization cannot be anticipated and specific preparations cannot be made. For example, one organization may be in an industry in which government regulations will soon change. The change is known and can be anticipated and planned for. In contrast, a second organization may be in a field in which the market is volatile and fiercely competitive. Technological changes are the norm and difficult to anticipate. The change that this organization must contend with is dynamic and a continuous part of the organization's existence, rather than a discrete event, as with a planned change.

Whether facing a methodical shift required in a planned change or confronting a more dynamic change, many organizations have difficulty dealing with the need for change. AT&T was a regulated monopoly provider of local and long-distance telephone service for many years. When competition heated up due to government deregulation of the industry and the development of cellular phone technology, AT&T management decided to move away from its "monopoly culture," which valued security, to a "market culture," which valued high performance. Despite its efforts, AT&T management struggled to make this cultural change a reality, with only mixed results. One major reason for its struggle was that many senior and middle managers had been promoted through the ranks under a set of rules based on the culture of a monopoly. For many of these managers, embracing the new culture that challenges the values that led to their success proved difficult.

Forces for Change

Contrary to what many employees believe, companies simply do not make changes "just for the heck of it." Numerous internal and external forces can cause companies to make changes. In this section, an overview of the causes of change is provided.

ENVIRONMENTAL FORCES   A great deal of pressure on a company can emerge from relationships with customers, suppliers, and employees. Environmental forces include these business relationships as well as changes in technology, market forces, political and regulatory agencies and laws, and social trends.

Both technology and market forces were pressuring Merrill Lynch, the financial brokerage firm, to make changes. The pressure resulted from the low-cost online trading that was pioneered by the discount broker Charles Schwab. Customers grew to prefer using the Internet to do their own research rather than paying brokers for advice about financial investments. Unfortunately, Merrill Lynch's commissioned brokers feared losing profitable commissions from clients. Consequently, the management team resisted offering online trading for several years, resulting in large losses of clients and market share to Charles Schwab. Finally, when it was evident that the market for financial services had permanently changed, Merrill Lynch management offered online trading service to customers for fees similar to those charged by Charles Schwab. Lynch was then able to curtail its loss of market share and maintain a client base.

Barnes & Noble, the large bookstore chain, faced a similar technological threat. The company was losing market share to Amazon.com, which offered books on the Internet rather than in brick-and-mortar stores. Barnes & Noble effectively responded by changing its market distribution policy to include a Web site to distribute books.

Political and regulatory forces for change include local, state, and national laws and court decisions that affect business relationships. For example, a change in the minimum wage translates into increased labor costs for firms paying the minimum wage. Low-wage employers, such as fast-food restaurants, may have to change both wage structures and use of labor to comply with the law.

Carlos Lanz, president of Alcasa, a state-owned aluminum plant in Venezuela, is shown here with members of an employee cooperative. The Venezuelan government is offering cheap credit and debt reduction incentives to firms, like Alcasa, that adopt co-management policies allowing workers to make management decisions and even become owners. About 100 companies have so far accepted. "This is a new organizational culture," says Lanz.

Not all political forces that cause companies to change their work cultures are legally mandated. For example, after Supreme Court nominee Clarence Thomas was accused of sexual harassment, many companies added an explicit sexual harassment policy to employment policies to protect against allegations of harassment that could wind up in court. Similarly, as more women enter the workforce, companies have been changing rigid employment policies governing work schedules. More flexible work schedules enable employees who have dependent children at home to better juggle work and family responsibilities without neglecting either. The payoff is a more satisfied workforce with better morale, which translates into improved employee retention.

INTERNAL FORCES   Internal forces for change arise from events within the company. They may originate with top executives and managers and travel in a top-down direction or with front-line employees or labor unions and travel in a bottom-up direction.

In 1980, Jack Welch, CEO of General Electric (GE), decided to turn a mediocre collection of diverse and unrelated businesses into a world leader. He made each business-unit manager responsible for meeting high performance standards and reaching the ranking of first or second in market performance within the industry sector. Managers who failed to achieve this ambitious goal would lose their jobs, and their business units would be downsized or sold off. In the next several years, 100,000 of 400,000 jobs were eliminated. GE had the highest market valuation in the world by the year 2000.[20]

Employees who demand amendment of policies that affect the way they are treated can also be internal forces for change. For example, physicians have recently begun forming labor unions. They want to protect the ability to practice medicine and treat patients as they see fit rather than as managed care organizations dictate. Doctors are counting on the new unions to provide them with bargaining power to regain decision-making authority in areas such as patient loads, prescription choices, and treatment options for their patients.

FIGURE 4.4

Sources of Resistance to Change

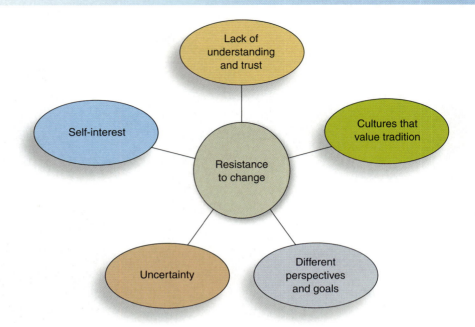

Resistance to Change

When change occurs, managers routinely encounter coalitions of employees or other managers who resist the proposed change. New work routines cause short-term anxiety as employees learn new ways of doing their jobs. Employees who thrived under one set of rules governing rewards have to adjust their efforts in order to meet a new set of performance expectations. Some of the reasons employees resist change include self-interest, lack of trust and understanding, uncertainty, different perspectives and goals, and cultures that value tradition.

Resistance to some changes is based on legitimate concerns. Consequently, these changes should be modified so that the concerns are dealt with.

Resistance to change can, in the extreme, involve acts of sabotage meant to undermine the change and to send a clear signal of firm resistance. For example, a large Massachusetts warehouse recently installed an automated conveyor system.[21] The project should have substantially improved company productivity. Instead, management encountered endless headaches and *reduced* productivity. Why? The workers feared that the change might cause them to lose their jobs. Various employees started jamming broomsticks into the conveyor system, an action that would shut the system down until a manager could track down the problem. If concern is great enough, resistance to a change can be fairly dramatic.

Some of the major reasons for resistance to change are described next. As illustrated in Figure 4.4 above, some of the major reasons for resistance to change include self-interest, lack of trust and understanding, uncertainty, different perspectives and goals, and cultures that value tradition. Understanding these causes can help you to manage resistance to change in others and even in yourself. We next turn to consideration of each of these reasons for resistance.

SELF-INTEREST Employees resist change when they fear losing something they value, such as economic benefits, status, or influence in the organization. Production employees may resist change in manufacturing technology because they fear having their jobs simplified and made more repetitive. A plant relocation from the city to the suburbs may mean that employees have a longer commute. As mentioned earlier, commissioned financial brokers at Merrill Lynch resisted online trading services because they would lose lucrative commissions from clients who switched to online trading.

LACK OF TRUST AND UNDERSTANDING   Employees may not trust the intentions behind a proposed change, or they may misunderstand its purpose. This type of resistance is most likely when previous changes were not well understood by employees or resulted in negative consequences. For example, some organizations launched Total Quality Management initiatives by telling employees that the objective of the quality initiative was to provide better service or product quality to the customer. The real goal was to use the quality gains to reduce the size of the workforce, but this was not disclosed to employees until later. Employees who embraced the initiative felt betrayed when the improved level of productivity was translated into layoffs. This deception has remained in the collective memory of the workforce, making it more difficult for management to obtain employee agreement to new changes.

UNCERTAINTY   Uncertainty results from fear of the unknown and lack of information about the future. It can be particularly threatening when employees' fears are based on negative consequences of previous changes in the organization. Between 1991 and 1997, employees at Apple Computer experienced three major layoffs that reduced the size of the workforce by more than a third. Many amenities that made working at the company special, such as wine and cheese parties on Friday afternoons and free bagels and cream cheese in the mornings, were also discontinued. As a result, employees feared losing jobs when projects ended, and many people substantially slowed their progress in anticipation of being discharged. Key technical and marketing personnel left for greener pastures, preferring to be in charge of their own destinies rather than waiting for the ax to fall. The uncertainty of continuing layoffs at Apple, coupled with changes that reduced the pleasant working conditions at the company, made employees more likely to demonstrate their resistance to change by quitting rather than resolving to cope with the change and uncertainty.

DIFFERENT PERSPECTIVES AND GOALS   A proposed change may be viewed through different lenses by employees with differing goals and perspectives. Even if a change is perceived as helping the organization, resistance may occur among employees who believe it will diminish the welfare of the unit to which they are attached. For example, the Saturn Division of General Motors in rural Tennessee represented a change from the way GM made automobiles in Detroit. Saturn was established to more closely follow the way the Japanese produced quality automobiles, and the improved manufacturing techniques perfected at Saturn were to be transferred to all other GM divisions to improve product quality and efficiency. Managers in the Chevrolet, Pontiac, and Oldsmobile divisions saw the Saturn Division as a rival that could threaten the flow of resources to their divisions. A coalition of division managers "ganged up" on the Saturn Division to ensure it would remain in the small-car niche, which began to shrink in the 1990s when customers switched their preferences to larger vehicles. Consequently, Saturn began to operate at a loss.

A recent survey found that 77 percent of workers go in to work when they are ill. Often the result is actually lost productivity because, although they are present, employees are unable to accomplish very much. Organizational cultures that frown on calling in sick are largely to blame, according to one human resource consultant. Employees in such environments say they fear for their jobs if they take time off for illness, particularly if the boss always comes in when sick. How can companies successfully change this kind of culture?

Assessing Your Flexibility

Working as an Individual   As the phrase goes, "the only constant is change," but the reality is that we all get comfortable with particular arrangements or ways of doing things. We often are then confronted with a change that somehow disrupts what we have gotten used to and it makes us uncomfortable … perhaps to the point of resisting the change. This resistance can result in our not getting on board with the new initiative or even privately or publicly being negative about the proposed change. These reactions can be normal human responses, but they can get in the way of our best intentions to add value to our organization and to move forward in our own careers. We need to understand and manage our own resistance to change in order to be as personally effective as we can be. Here are some things you can do as in individual worker to manage your resistance to change.

- Do you understand the reasons for the change? Maybe you are uncomfortable with the change because the reasons just don't seem to add up. Ask those who know to describe, as much as they can, the rationale for the change. Maybe there are strategic or confidential issues that can't be discussed in detail, but you might be able to clarify why the change is needed.

- It can sometimes seem that no one cares about your perspective. For example, you might see some problems with a proposed change, but your message doesn't seem to be getting through. It may be that the change is inevitable and that the change must happen despite short-term and operational problems. Your role, to be an effective employee, may be to find ways for the proposed change to work. Finding solutions and helping a change move forward can be good for the organization and for your career.

- You might be resisting a change because it seems to threaten your workplace situation. Maybe a proposed change will indeed mean that there will be risks and that the same old approaches won't get you ahead or get the paycheck amount you've been used to. While changes can involve risks, they usually bring opportunities as well. What is important is that you recognize and understand how the playing field has changed so that you can continue to be effective.

- You might be resisting a change due to the anxiety and stress that naturally comes along with any alteration to our routines. This anxiety can become a real stumbling block if you already feel stressed and overextended. The proposed change can then be viewed as just one more thing that you would just as soon not have to deal with. As individual workers, we need to remind ourselves that changes in the workplace are going to happen. Effective employees find healthy ways to deal with stress and find balance in their lives so that they can embrace changes with enthusiasm and a positive attitude.

CULTURES THAT VALUE TRADITION   Some organizational cultures are not supportive of change, valuing tradition and customary ways of doing things instead. Two organizations with strong cultures that resist change are the Catholic Church and the U.S. military. For years, the Catholic Church has refused to allow women to enter the priesthood despite the fact that there are not enough men entering seminaries to fill open positions. U.S. military leaders have resisted allowing openly gay and lesbian soldiers to serve in the military. Under the "don't ask, don't tell" policy, homosexual soldiers may serve only if they keep their orientation to themselves.

Resistance can be an important impediment to change in organizations, but it is an issue that occurs at a personal level. All of us, at times, experience discomfort with change in our working routines. Our resistance can signal a real problem with the change or it can get in the way of our own performance and advancement. Management Is Everyone's Business 4.2 above provides suggestions for dealing with resistance to change at a personal level.

Models of Organizational Change

Whatever the reason for change, an organization that effectively responds has a competitive advantage. The process begins when management recognizes and accepts the need for change. Once this is accomplished, other factors must be considered and possibly altered. There are three approaches which can help managers to effectively implement change and anticipate and deal with potential problems and resistance. These include the Star model, Lewin's three-step model, and the force-field analysis model.

THE STAR MODEL The Star model[22] identifies five factors that can be key to implementing a change. Further, the model is also a tool that can be used to help build and maintain an organization that is ready for change. The model was developed by noted management scholar Ed Lawler.

6 Learning Objective Check-In

Richard is one of the managers in charge of implementing change at his company. He often tries to overcome resistance by actually practicing the behaviors he has told his staff he will be expecting on a daily basis. One of his team members, Harry, has been resisting the changes Richard is trying to implement, claiming that the changes don't fit with the way the firm has always done things. Sarah, another team member, doesn't fully grasp the changes that are being implemented, and she is skeptical of the firm's and Richard's intentions in forcing change.

1. *What source of resistance to change is affecting Harry?*
   a. *Uncertainty*
   b. *Lack of trust and understanding*
   c. *Different goals*
   d. *Cultures that value tradition*
2. *Why is Sarah resistant to the changes being implemented?*
   a. *Different goals*
   b. *Lack of trust and understanding*
   c. *Self-interest*
   d. *Cultures that value tradition*

As illustrated in Figure 4.5 on page 164, a five-pointed star, with each point representing a factor important to change, represents the model. Each of the five factors is briefly considered below.

1. *Type of change.* What type of change, *evolutionary,* or *transformational,* is needed? Is the change an evolutionary progression of continuous improvements or alterations? Or is transformational change needed in which more dramatic alterations are needed, such as major changes in products or business models?

   A transformational change may require alteration in the remaining factors in the star model.

2. *Structure.* How are people grouped together and decisions made? Does the structure support the change or impede it?

3. *Reward systems.* What do people get paid and rewarded for? If team effort is needed, a reward system that recognizes individual performance isn't going to motivate people toward a team approach.

4. *Processes.* How is information communicated and behavior controlled in the organization? If the need for change is not well communicated and decisions are made in a hierarchical fashion, a change may be very difficult to implement.

5. *People.* What skills and capabilities are needed? Are the needed skills within the organization, or do they need to be trained or brought in from outside the organization?

In addition to the five factors, the Star model includes organizational culture. However, culture is portrayed as something that is derived from and influenced by the five factors. In other words, an organization doesn't simply have a culture that values employees; it develops that type of culture through the underlying factors. The challenge is to determine the mix of the factors that will create the culture needed to successfully implement and maintain the needed change. Skills for Managing 4.1 on page 165 provides you with the opportunity to apply the Star model and see if you think it is an effective change management tool.

FIGURE 4.5

Star Model

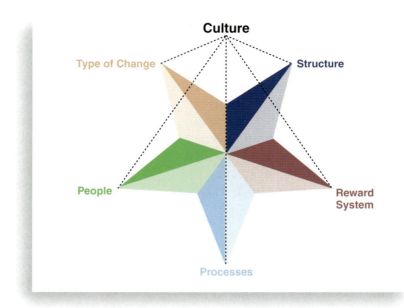

LEWIN'S THREE-STEP MODEL   Kurt Lewin, a noted social psychologist, developed the **three-step model** of organizational change shown in Figure 4.6 on page 165. The three steps are unfreezing, change (also called movement or transformation), and refreezing.

Unfreezing involves melting resistance to change by dealing with people's fears and anxieties so they can be more open to the change. People are given new information that makes them aware that the status quo is unacceptable and that some type of change is required.

The second step is the *change* itself, which is a departure from the status quo. Change can involve technology, people, products, services, or management policies and administration. It may be embodied in a new leader hired from outside the company to champion policies that were effective in another organization. Or, it may be represented by a new product that serves different customers and that requires new ways of selling and marketing.

The final step is *refreezing*, in which new management practices and employee behaviors become part of employees' routine activities. Coaching, training, and adopting appropriate reward systems facilitate the refreezing step.

For example, suppose management decides to change its corporate communication policy so that all company announcements are posted on a Web site instead of being distributed on paper. Step one would be to mobilize data to show employees that Internet communication is faster and more efficient than sending paper documents. Then the change would be made by setting up a Web site accessible to all employees (step two). In step three, employees who do not know how to read or post messages on the company Web site would receive training.

Lewin's three-step model of organizational change can be a useful framework when dealing with a planned event. As pointed out earlier in the discussion of types of change, not all change falls in the category of planned and discrete events. The three-step model would probably not be a useful framework when change is dynamic and ongoing. For example, some organizations, such as consulting firms, are organized around projects that constantly shift and con-

three-step model

A model of organizational change that features the three steps of unfreezing, change, and refreezing.

BE A STAR! APPLYING THE STAR MODEL

The Star model of organizational change focuses management attention on various factors that can be critical to a change effort. It is a tool that can help you identify key issues and determine where the organization needs to be in order for a change to be successful. The following exercises provide you the opportunity to use the Star model as a tool for effective change management.

1. Select an organization of your choice. It could be a real organization, one that you work for, or one that is fictional.

2. As an individual or team, identify a change that may need to take place in the organization that is of a transformational nature. Describe the forces leading to this need for change.

3. What should be done in order to adequately prepare the organization for change? Specifically use the Star model to identify the relevant areas. For each factor included in the Star model, assess where the organization is currently and the conditions that must exist in order for the change to be successful.

4. How would you propose to make the shift in each of the factors?

5. Share with the rest of the class:
   a. The need for change you focused on (and where it came from).
   b. Your assessment of the current status of the five star factors and where each needs to be.
   c. How you would propose to make the shifts on each factor.

Further Discussion Questions

1. How would you evaluate the Star model as a tool for identifying what needs to be done in order to successfully implement a change? Is the model too complex? Does it leave anything out?

2. Are there examples of transformational change in organizations that you are familiar with or have experienced? Were the factors of the Star model in place for the change to be implemented? Was the change attempt successful? Why, or why not?

FIGURE 4.6

Lewin's Three-Step Model of Organizational Change

---

front workers with different challenges. This project framework can mean change that is ongoing and that doesn't provide much opportunity for unfreezing, change, and refreezing.

FORCE-FIELD ANALYSIS The **force-field analysis** model of change, also developed by Kurt Lewin, states that two sets of opposing forces are at equilibrium before a change takes place. The forces consist of *driving forces*, which are pushing for change, and *restraining forces*, which are opposed to change. When the two forces are evenly balanced, the organization is in a status quo state and does not change.[23] Figure 4.7 on page 166 shows the restraining and driving forces when an organization is at status quo.

To implement change, the force-field model of change suggests that management can choose from one of three change strategies. Management can (1) *increase* the driving forces that drive the change, relative to the restraining

> **force-field analysis**
>
> A model of organizational change that states that two sets of opposing forces are at equilibrium before a change takes place and put at disequilibrium to make change come about: the driving forces, which are pushing for change, and the restraining forces, which are opposed to change.

FIGURE 4.7

Force Field Model of Change

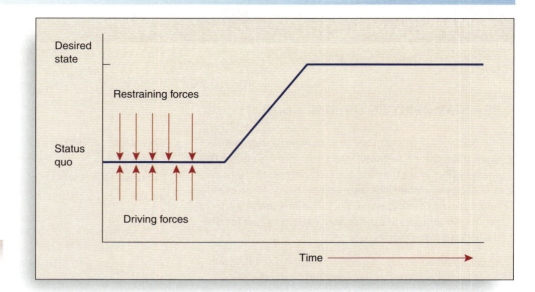

top-down change

Organizational change that is initiated by managers.

LOC-In

7 **Learning Objective Check-In**

Coolegra's management team is considering three alternative approaches for implementing changes at their firm. They want to effectively implement the changes, and want to make sure they can anticipate and deal with potential resistance or problems as they arise. Option A includes five factors that are key for implementation and is also meant to help build and maintain the organization that is ready for change. It involves looking at the structure of the firm, the reward systems, and the people's skills and capabilities as they exist and that are needed. Option B considers one of three strategies: increase the forces that drive change, relative to restraining forces; reduce the restraining forces, relative to driving forces; or do both. Option C involves dealing first with people's fears and anxieties, then pursuing the change, then reinforcing the new management practices and employee behaviors after the change. Coolegra's team must decide soon on a method of implementation.

1. *Option C above, which involves dealing with people's fears and anxieties so they can be more open to the change as the very first step is*
    a. *Lewin's three-step model*
    b. *Force-field analysis*
    c. *The Star model*
    d. *The negotiation model*
2. *Option A above, which would consider what skills and capabilities are needed and how people are grouped together and whether this structure supports or impedes change, is*
    a. *Lewin's three-step model*
    b. *Force-field analysis*
    c. *The negotiation model*
    d. *The Star model*
3. *Option B above, which involves potentially increasing the forces that drive change, relative to the restraining forces, is*
    a. *The Star model*
    b. *Lewin's three-step model*
    c. *Force-field analysis*
    d. *The negotiation model*

forces; (2) *reduce* the restraining forces that oppose the change, relative to the driving forces, or (3) do both.

Implementing Organizational Change

Practically every successful management activity requires someone to take charge. This is undoubtedly true when implementing change. In most cases, a change is led by the manager or executive who introduced it. Change that is initiated by executives is called **top-down change.** Top-down change can be implemented rapidly. It is often used to respond to a crisis. For example, when data were released in 2000 showing that the Bridgestone/Firestone tires used on Ford Explorers in the United States fell apart at freeway speeds, resulting in scores of fatal traffic accidents, Ford executives decided to absorb the cost of replacing the more than 6 million tires on vehicles that were still on the road. Some of the cost was to be reimbursed by Bridgestone/Firestone. Although they blamed Bridgestone/Firestone for supplying faulty tires, Ford executives acted proactively to manage the crisis. Unfortunately, later information indicated that Ford should have changed its dealings with the people to whom they sold Ford Explorers earlier; an investigation revealed that Ford executives were aware that design flaws in Bridgestone/Firestone tires had caused fatal accidents in Venezuela and Saudi Arabia, among other countries, prior to the publicity about accidents in the United States.

Taking Care of Patients and Your People Too!

Mercy Health System of Owensboro, Kentucky, was created by the merger between two hospitals. However, there was more involved than changing titles on two buildings. The change meant fear, resistance, and combining two distinct cultures. Rather than stating that one culture was correct and the model to follow, a 10-person "cultural design team" made up of hospital managers and staff was formed to help develop a new culture. The basic thrust of this effort was to develop a culture that got back to the basics of healthcare—helping people get better and stay well. The team surveyed over 1,000 employees regarding their perceptions of current practices, such as the hospital's reward system. Four groups were formed to follow up on the survey findings. Focus group members helped the culture team to identify core values of the organization: integrity, respect, service, teamwork, excellence, and innovation. A group of 50 employees from across the hospital was then formed. This group generated 100 behavioral examples of how those values could be demonstrated in the hospital. Each department then chose five or six of the behaviors as a basis for a cultural action plan for that department.

Next, an annual President's Award was instituted to recognize outstanding employees. An employee is nominated for this award by his or her co-workers through a report which describes how the person makes a difference in the hospital. An average of 15 staff members and three doctors, from a pool of 2,500 employees, win the award each year. Prizes include vacations, computers, and a month off with pay. CEO Greg Carlson shrugs off the cost of the program by pointing out that the gifts cost less than one-tenth of 1 percent of the $60 million dollar payroll. Further, it is an important tool that emphasizes the culture and increased loyalty.

Other features of the culture developed at Mercy Health System include empowering workers with unilateral control over a service-related budget. Specifically, employees can solve a patient problem by spending up to $200.00 without management approval. Nurses have, for example, chosen to use their budgets to purchase hats for chemotherapy patients and plane tickets for family members. The CEO stresses aligning personal values with the values of the Mercy culture. He has borrowed a framework from General Electric to send this message. As presented in Table 4.3 on page 168, the framework applied at Mercy Health System identifies four types of employees: (1) those who are committed to the organization's values and perform well, (2) those who are committed to the organization's values but don't perform well, (3) those who aren't committed to the cultural values but perform their tasks very well, and (4) those who aren't committed and don't perform well. As CEO Carlson points out, the workers who are aligned with the values but aren't performing at the desired level should be given additional chances. The tough group to deal with are those who perform well but aren't aligned with the organization's culture. Carlson's approach is that removing a person like that from the payroll sends an unmistakable message to everyone that the values of the organization are critically important.

Source: L. Larson, "A New Attitude: Changing Organizational Culture," *Trustee* 55 (2002), pp. 8–14.

People who act as catalysts and assume responsibility for managing change are called **change agents.** Change agents can be internal managers or outside consultants selected for their skill in dealing with resistance to change. Sometimes the change agents are the employees themselves.

A **bottom-up change** originates with employees. Bottom-up changes are put into effect more slowly than top-down changes. They generally begin with a series of meetings between employees and supervisors. Next, the change is discussed in meetings between supervisors and middle managers. Finally it is examined and approved or modified in meetings between managers and top executives. For example, an employee suggestion system may propose a change in a work practice that affects the whole company. After an employee-run suggestion committee approves the change, it is introduced to a policy committee composed of employees and managers for final approval and implementation.

Management Close-Up 4.1 above presents an example of an organization that proactively dealt with change. The approach used both top-down and bottom-up approaches in developing a new and better organizational culture.

change agents

People who act as catalysts and assume responsibility for managing change.

bottom-up change

Organizational change that originates with employees.

table 4.3

Four Types of Employees

		ALIGNMENT WITH CULTURE	
		NO	**YES**
Performance	**Low**	Worst	Give Another Chance
	High	Make The Tough Choice	Best

Tactics for Introducing Change

When a major organizational change occurs, it is advisable to expect both skepticism and resistance. Advance preparation is often the key to successfully making a change. As presented in Figure 4.8 on page 169, the choice of tactics for bringing about change in an organization include communication and education, employee involvement, negotiation, coercion, and top-management support.

COMMUNICATION AND EDUCATION One of the most effective ways to overcome resistance to change is to educate employees about why the change is needed. Information should flow in both directions. The individuals in charge should become aware of why people fear the change and provide information that eliminates some of the uncertainty. For example, Sun Microsystems, a California-based high-tech company, strives to be on the cutting edge of information systems technology by developing a steady stream of new software and hardware for its customers. Consequently, customer service managers must continually upgrade their technical skills in order to understand clients' problems and educate them about the latest product and service technologies. The company provides excellent educational support, so Sun employees are less likely to resist the relentless change that accompanies being a cutting-edge technology company.

EMPLOYEE INVOLVEMENT Involving potential resisters in the design and implementation of change can often help diffuse resistance. Employees who are active in a change process become more committed to the change. A common approach is to organize employees into teams that focus on providing solutions to change issues. To deal with the need to improve service to customers, the GTE unit of Verizon, a large U.S. telecommunications company, organized its employees into quality-improvement teams that design and implement changes in work processes. Employees receive recognition and rewards for changes that are successfully implemented by the teams. In a recent year, 90 percent of GTE employees participated in at least one such team.[24]

NEGOTIATION Many times a manager is in a situation where bargaining is involved in implementing a change. Negotiation includes making concessions

FIGURE 4.8

Tactics for Introducing Change

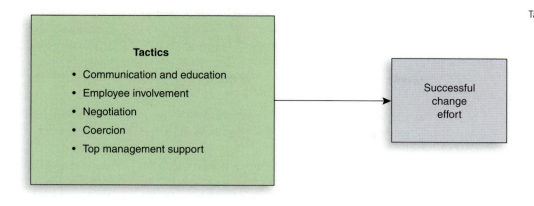

and giving resources or rewards to resisters in exchange for their cooperation. Individuals who have strong negative attitudes toward a change may be given the opportunity to take early retirement or to transfer elsewhere. In other cases, unions negotiate a labor contract to make trade-offs with management for their willingness to accept a proposed change. The negotiations could result in provisions that establish higher pay rates or more job security for union employees in exchange for their cooperation in plant closings, use of new technology, or mandatory overtime.

COERCION   Confronting and forcing resisting employees to change is the use of coercion. Resisters may be threatened with loss of jobs or rewards if they continue to hinder the implementation of a change. Coercion may be necessary in a crisis, when speed is essential, or changes will not be popular. For example, any employee who resists efforts to improve diversity and cultural tolerance will probably face termination.

TOP MANAGEMENT SUPPORT   The support of top management helps discourage resistance because it signals that the change is important. Change can require the collaboration of several organization units or departments, and some units may fare better than others, creating the potential for conflict over resources. In such cases, top management support can facilitate cooperation. For example, at Navistar International, a truck and heavy equipment manufacturer, top management supported the implementation of a new requisition process that affected maintenance, repair, and purchases of supplies and equipment. The goal was to reduce paperwork and increase the speed of purchasing of supplies while saving money by streamlining inventories. The change involved a redesigned requisition process, a computerized inventory control system, and a new procedure for analyzing vendor capability. An important reason for the success of the new requisition process was the support of top management.

Successfully introducing change is an important management skill. While resistance can be expected, successfully implementing change can be key to maintaining competitiveness or may even determine the survival of the organization. Management Is Everyone's Business 4.3 on page 170 provides suggestions for successfully introducing change.

Working as a Manager   Effectively introducing change is often part of the responsibility of management. Unfortunately, resistance to change is a common barrier faced by managers. Here are some ideas to help you, as a manager, to successfully manage change in your organization.

- *You must know what you want to accomplish with the change.* Before initiating a change, you should identify the desired results. Specifying these objectives is the means for determining if the change effort was a success.

- *Motivate workers to embrace the change effort.* Is there a competitive or strategic reason for the change? If so, sharing the reasons for the change with workers can develop a shared sense of urgency concerning the need for change. Explaining why a change is needed can motivate people to join the change effort.

- *Provide for employee involvement in the proposed change* as soon as and as much as possible. Announcing a unilateral change is a sure-fire way to generate resistance to change. However, providing opportunity for involvement can allow people to be part of the change effort.

- *Make sure you have feedback on how the change effort is proceeding.* Two-way communication with the workers can help ensure that you will know when corrective actions are needed. A change effort may be misunderstood or may lose steam. You need feedback loops so that explanations, motivation, or other needed actions can occur in a timely fashion.

- *Recognize that change can take time.* Workers may need time to understand and to learn new behaviors. Further, systems and policies may need to be changed. These changes can involve major adaptation and patience may be needed. Remember, personal resolutions usually involve changing only one behavior, yet most of them fail. Your change effort may involve much more than one behavior and this breadth and complexity can mean the change will take time.

CONCLUDING THOUGHTS

A set of critical thinking questions about REI was presented after the introductory vignette for this chapter. Now that you've read the chapter, you're ready to address the questions in more detail.

The first question asked about a possible "misfit" with a strong organizational culture, such as the one at REI. It's probably a good thing if an organization's culture is distinctive enough to lead someone to conclude that he or she would not fit in. A culture that stands out as much as REI's will also attract people to the organization and give them a reason to stay. Of course, the potential "misfit" problem could be lessened by actively recruiting and selecting the type of employee who does fit in.

The second critical thinking question asked about the link between culture and the bottom line. Certainly most organizations are in business to make a profit. However, directly linking everything that's done in the firm to its effect on the bottom line can lead to problems. Where would ethical concerns fit into this picture, for instance? Further, some organizations develop a particular type of culture not so much because it is instrumental in achieving a greater profit, but because it's important in its own right. REI's decision to forego the potential for increased sales by not paying its salespeople commissions is one example. The cultural values represented by this decision are what mattered to employees and managers, not the immediate impact of profit. How far would you go in supporting a local program, such as building a new bike trail or paying for the cleanup of a lake or stream, if there wasn't any evidence of an immediate influence on the bottom line?

With the help and example of its skilled and knowledgeable sales force, REI's culture influences its bottom line by actively encouraging customers to participate in the lifestyle the company promotes and supports. The culture also contributes to the bottom line through the generous human resource policies that keep such valuable people on staff.

The final question that followed the chapter's opening story about REI was whether a culture can be maintained over time, and whether it should be. Maintaining a culture requires understanding the organization and its underlying values, especially given changes in leadership. Since REI's culture is so important to its competitive position and success, its continuity and influence should not be left to chance as outside forces may dictate. It should be actively managed in order to preserve the sense of common purpose and shared lifestyle among its employees.

Focusing on the Future: Using Management in Daily Life

Managing Organizational Culture and Change

Shelley Bird is the Chief Communications Officer at NCR. From 2003 through 2005, she and her staff faced a daunting task: handling communications for a major restructuring program while at the same time the company was cycling through two new CEOs and an interim CEO. How did they do it? In a recent article for *Strategic Communication Management*, Bird outlines the six key lessons they learned in the process.

1. *Communicate the vision.* Shelley found that when a new CEO starts working, everyone watches closely, not only to see what changes will be made, but to assure themselves that the new executive is not going to stray from the core values of the organization. For this reason, she recommends quickly setting up meetings with influential groups so that the new CEO has an opportunity to make his position known. As she says, "If you can show that your new leader is creative and dynamic, yet embraces the company's core values, employees, customers, and other stakeholders will likely view any change objectively, rather than as an outright negative."

2. *Engage employees in the first 100 days.* Bird and her staff knew that it was imperative to communicate with employees frequently, especially in the early parts of a new CEO's tenure. Because any change of leadership is going to create concern and start rumors, Shelley publicized even small accomplishments and regularly communicated with employees "through a variety of channels—e-mail, frequent updates on our intranet, monthly breakfast meetings with small groups of employees, site visits and even broadcast voice messages." This empowered employees to act on the vision.

3. *Keep management in the loop.* In many organizations, the focus of communication is downward—the communication department is responsible for telling employees what managers want them to hear. But Shelley found that it was equally important to let managers know about problems, complaints and suggestions raised by employees. This enabled the managers to consolidate improvements and produce more change.

4. *Invite the community in.* Bird not only worked on communications within the company, but also outside the company. She worked hard to make sure community leaders were aware of planned changes, and that the effects those changes would make on the community were fully discussed. By doing so, she set up one branch of a powerful coalition of supporters of change.

5. In a similar fashion, Bird was also very *open with the press*—print, broadcast, and Internet. She knew that it was critically important to give the new CEOs time to delve into every aspect of the company they were managing, and that it wasn't possible

for a brand-new CEO to have very specific plans from his or her first day on the job. So, to give the CEOs time to work, while at the same time giving the media something to work with, Shelley crafted messages "at the 30,000 foot-level." She also made sure that the media got the same stories employees got, to avoid surprises in both groups. Again, these actions helped to build a coalition for change.

6. Finally, Bird recommends *measuring results*. Once results are measured and reported, new approaches can be institutionalized in the organizational structure. She monitored company performance, a substitute for looking at such "small picture" issues as employee satisfaction, corporate focus, etc. She found that at NCR, employees produced stronger than expected third quarter earnings. She backed this information up with survey results which showed that "employees around the world are engaged and have accessed the channels they are most comfortable with through the CEO communications Web site."

Source: Shelley Bird, "Communicating through Changes in Leadership at NCR," *Strategic Communication Management, 10* (1) (December 2005/January 2006), pp. 30–34.

summary of learning objectives

This chapter has addressed the topics of organizational culture and change. Organizational culture is a system of shared values, assumptions, beliefs, and norms that unite the members of an organization. Organizational culture reflects employee views about "the way things are done around here." Change is inevitable but can often meet resistance. Maintaining an effective culture yet implementing needed change is often a management balancing act in today's organizations. This chapter's discussion of its seven learning objectives to help you to effectively deal with culture and change issues as an individual worker, team member, and manager are summarized below.

1 Identify the three major aspects of organizational culture.

- **Visible culture**—things people can hear, see, or feel, such as formality or informality of employee dress.
- **Espoused values**—the expressed values of the organization.
- **Core values**—the fundamental values that drive what is important in an organization.

2 Apply a simple assessment tool to quickly gain a sense of the culture of an organization.

- What is measured when individual performance is assessed?
- What is celebrated, recognized, or rewarded?
- What is measured when organizational performance is assessed?

3 Describe the importance of organizational culture.

Organizational culture performs several important roles in organizations including:

- Encouraging employee self-management by defining roles and expectations.
- Promoting stability by providing a sense of continuity.
- Socializing workers by helping them fit in with the organization.
- Contributing to organizational performance by supporting the strategy of the organization.

4 Identify the processes through which organizational culture can be developed and sustained.

- Cultural symbols
- Rituals and ceremonies
- Stories
- Language
- Leadership
- Policies and decision making

All of the above can convey and sustain shared meaning and what is important in organizations.

5 Use classification systems to identify various types of organizational culture.

- *Control* versus *employee-involvement* culture.
- **Baseball team, club, academy,** or **fortress** cultures.
- *Competing values framework*—four types based on focus and control: empowered, entrepreneurial, bureaucracy, or goal oriented.

6 Identify the sources of resistance to change.
- Self-interest
- Lack of trust and understanding
- Uncertainty
- Different perspectives and goals
- Cultures that value tradition

7 Apply models to effectively manage change efforts.
- Star model
- Lewin's three-step model
- Force-field analysis

discussion questions

1. Think of a company you have worked at recently, either on a job or as an intern. What are the espoused values of this company? Did the managers or employees at this company behave consistently with those values? Give some examples if possible.

2. Pick one or more well-known companies that you are familiar with from media stories or firms that were discussed in some of your classes, such as Disney, General Motors, Microsoft, Apple Computer, Wal-Mart, Coca-Cola, or McDonald's. Give examples for each of the following approaches to sustain organizational culture for the company or companies that you have selected: (*a*) company rituals or ceremonies; (*b*) company heroes; (*c*) language; and (*d*) leadership. Does knowledge of these cultural activities reveal to you what it would be like to work at the company or companies you have selected? How might you use this information?

3. Compare and contrast strong and weak company cultures. What are the advantages of a strong company culture? What are the disadvantages of a strong company culture? In what circumstances is it preferable to have a weak culture?

4. Why do some people strongly resist change, a normal part of life in organizations?

5. What are the steps in Lewin's three-step model of organizational change? How can managers make use of this model? Are there situations in which the three-step model may not apply or be helpful? Describe.

6. Suppose you are a change agent and are planning to introduce a bottom-up change in an organization. Which implementation tactics are likely to give you the most effective results, with less resistance and better commitment to change? Justify your choices. Answer the same question for a top-down change. Again, justify your choices.

7. Under what circumstances would a coercive tactic to manage change be the most effective? Give an example. Which circumstances are more likely to produce strong resistance to change when a coercive tactic to change is attempted? If you can, give an example.

8. Consider the description of the actions taken at Mercy Health System (see Management Close-Up 4.1) to establish a new culture. How does the new culture lead to improved customer service? Identify the elements that contribute to the new culture (such as celebrations and stories). What other tactic might you recommend to Mercy Health System to further strengthen and maintain its culture?

How Is the Digital Age Changing Organizational Culture in Asia?

management
minicase 4.1

Thailand's Lamsam family maintained its business empire in a traditional way. The family kept a firm grip on its operations and discouraged taking risks that could rock the family business. For four generations, the clan elders—ethnic Chinese who own Thai Farmers Bank and the Loxley industrial group—had called the shots without much input from others.

Today Loxley's new philosophy is "try ten ideas and fail at seven—that's no problem," says executive vice president Chatikavanij Vasant, 43, who helped spearhead the change after studying and working for 14 years in the United States. "We have to make sure we are not dead." Nonfamily employees, for example, used to have to write deferential memos full of flowery Thai phrases if they wanted to be able to communicate with family members in the company's hierarchy. Since the company's massive overhaul, Loxley employees contact Vasant and his cousin, chief executive Dhongehai Lamsam, on the group's intranet.

Old-line family business dynasties across East Asia have come to the same conclusion. As one observer noted, "The Internet has become the answer for oligarchs who are questioning their business models as never before."

Discussion Questions

1. How do you think the Internet is affecting organizational culture? Explain.

2. Do you believe that a firm should actively promote open communication across management levels through the e-mail system? Why or why not?

3. Some people argue that the Internet is making it more difficult for firms to retain their own unique culture, forcing them to be more alike as information flows freely across organizational boundaries and even across national lines. Do you agree? Explain.

Source: Adapted with permission from B. Einhorn, "Look Who's Taking Asia Digital," *BusinessWeek*, February 21, 2000, p. 102.

How Jack Welch Changed Culture at General Electric

management
minicase 4.2

One way CEO Jack Welch reshaped and changed General Electric's (GE) culture was the Work Out program. Welch wanted to reach and motivate 300,000 employees and insisted that the people on the front lines, where change had to happen, should be empowered to create that change.

The Work Out began in large-scale offsite meetings. A combination of top leaders, outside consultants, and human resources specialists led them. Work Outs for each business unit followed the same basic pattern: hourly and salaried workers came together from many different parts of the organization in an informal three- to five-day meeting to discuss and solve problems. The events evolved to include suppliers and customers as well as employees. Work Out is no longer an event today but instead is the process by which work is done and problems are solved at GE.

The format for Work Out follows seven steps:

Choose a work process or problem for discussion.

Select an appropriate cross-functional team of 30 to 50 people, which may also include external stakeholders.

Assign a "champion" to follow through on recommendations.

Meet for several days and come up with recommendations to improve work processes and solve problems.

Meet with leaders, who are required to respond to recommendations on the spot.

Hold additional meetings as needed to implement the recommendations.

Start the process all over again with a new process or problem.

GE's Work Out process solves problems and improves productivity for the company, but the benefits go beyond these goals. Employees are able to openly and honestly interact with each other without regard to vertical or horizontal boundaries. Work Out is one of the foundations of what Welch called the "culture of boundarylessness" that is critical for continuous learning and improvement.

Discussion Questions

1. Which types of change implementation tactics did Jack Welch apply to the Work Out program at General Electric? Do you think coercion would have been an effective tactic? Why or why not?

2. Describe what the "culture of boundarylessness" at General Electric might be like. What might company rituals and ceremonies look like? How do you envision a company hero behaving in this kind of a culture? What do you think are the key cultural values in this changed culture at GE?

Sources: Adapted from R. L. Daft, *Leadership*. Fort Worth: Dryden Press, 1999, pp. 444–445; J. Quinn, "What a Work-Out!" *Performance*, November 1994, pp. 58–63; www.ge.com/news/leadership.html, accessed July 25, 2001.

individual/ collaborative learning case 4.1

Enterprise Resource Planning: An Example of Organizational Change

Being the champion of a change, or a change agent, isn't always easy. Enterprise Resource Planning (ERP), software that integrates information from accounting, manufacturing, distribution, and human resource departments, can give management a unified view of these processes in an organization. Unfortunately, the ERP software began gaining a reputation for being difficult to implement and often failing. The majority of these failures were attributed to software performance problems, but the reality was that in most of these situations the failure was due to inadequate attention to change. In other words, technology was not usually the problem; rather it was a lack of management recognition of ERP as an organizational change. An ERP system can add administrative tasks that may not seem needed, but without an overall understanding of the system, workers may not complete these tasks. Further, an ERP implementation may require a change in roles and increased technical expertise. The implementation of an ERP system at SI Corporation, a small manufacturer of industrial textiles, is an example of an ERP success story. SI expected the implementation of ERP to have a serious impact on its organizational culture.

After deciding to implement an ERP system, SI management created the position of "change management leader" with the responsibility of managing the human element of the implementation. The person hired for this new job, Patrick Keebler, started by assessing the environment for potential problem areas. He considered the levels of workers' computer skills and whether there were areas with a history of resistance to change. Keebler developed a change management strategy that focused on communication and training. As Keebler stated, if you unilaterally "announce that you've launched a new system, you'll get a lot of push back, but if you share your strategy and why it's important early on, people will embrace it."

Communication regarding the ERP implementation at SI included frequent meetings with departments and with shifts of workers. Surveys were also conducted. Based on the feedback at meetings and surveys, Keebler distributed a monthly newsletter about the ERP initiative. He provided information on why the company had chosen this tool and how it would work. Changes in the roles played in various positions were described. The flow of information reduced the amount of stress regarding the change and, argues Keebler, prepared the employees for the training that was needed.

After the ERP system was successfully launched, employees were offered refresher courses and self-paced tutorials on the Web. As the change manager noted "People will embrace a new system if you give them the skills and support to use it. Otherwise, you are just leaving it to chance!"

Critical Thinking Questions

1. Do you agree with the SI Corporation that implementing software such as ERP should be treated as an organizational change? Why or why not?

2. Assess what Keebler did regarding the implementation process. Do you think it was a good job or overkill? Support your judgment.

3. What other activities or approaches might you recommend to SI Corporation? (Hint: Revisit the models of organizational change described in this chapter.)

Collaborative Learning Exercise

Form a group with four or five of your classmates. Select a model of organizational change and describe how you would apply it to the issue of implementing an ERP system. Share your descriptions with the rest of the class. As a class, do you think there is one model that would seem to work best?

Source: Adapted from S. F. Gale, "For ERP Success, Create a Culture Change," *Workforce*, September, 2002, pp. 88–94.

Charles Schwab: Recommending Change as a Customer

Discount broker Charles Schwab provides online investing services and is an example of how the Internet has changed the way businesses provide services to their customers. Visit Charles Schwab's Web site and examine its features. Answer the following questions:

1. What features of Schwab's site do you like? Be specific.

2. Describe the advantages of making investments using the Web site of a company such as Schwab over the traditional method of working with a financial broker.

3. Describe the disadvantages of using the online investing services on the Schwab Web site. What improvements to its Web site would you recommend to Schwab for reducing them?

internet
exercise 4.1

www.schwab.com

Change: Making It Personal

Change is often forced on us in our work environment, were we are typically in a mode of reacting or adapting to different demands. However, we can all be more effective and valuable workers and managers if we are proactive and anticipate change for ourselves. The best managers take responsibility for keeping abreast of events and what they may mean for possible changes at a personal level and for the workgroup. You can use the following questions to guide you through the process of determining if a change may be in order.

manager's
checkup 4.1

Personal Level

1. Where do I want to be within the next three to five years? For example, what kind of position or career do I hope to be in?

2. Given my career aspirations, how is the business in this area changing? Are there new technologies or approaches that are emerging that could change how business in this area operates?

3. What, if anything, are other workers or managers with similar aspirations doing to prepare themselves?

4. What are the costs and benefits of my making a change? For example, if learning a new skill might be important to be competitive and achieve my career aspirations, what is the cost? Is the benefit worth the investment?

5. What opportunities do I have to make the change? For instance, learning a new skill could be done informally or through various workshops or courses. Weigh your options with recognition that costs and benefits might vary across your choices.

6. If the cost/benefit analysis is positive and you choose a particular opportunity, you need to plan for and execute the change. What resources will you need? This might, for instance, simply be money for tuition or workshop costs or might be the common but important problem of finding a babysitter on a regular basis.

Workgroup Level

1. Where is the business I work in heading in the next three to five years?

2. What influences are emerging that could change how this business operates? For example, is there new technology that could significantly alter the work process?

3. Who are the competitors and where are they heading? For instance, competition from overseas may be just starting but could be expected to quickly grow into a major issue.

4. What do employees need to do in order to meet the challenges identified in items 1, 2, and 3 above? Are the employees capable and willing to meet the challenges?

5. What are the costs and benefits of making the changes? Is it going to be worth it for your workgroup to make the needed investments? What payoffs can be expected? What are the costs if the changes aren't made?

6. What options for change might the workgroup choose from? For instance, becoming proficient with a new technology could be done with an independent consultant, a local college, or a representative for the new technology, among other options.

7. If the cost/benefit analysis is positive and a particular change option is chosen, you need to work with the employees to plan for and execute the change. What resources, such as time, money, or development support, will the workers need to turn the plan into reality?

Source: Adapted from P. Speer, "Managing Change Requires Diligence, Homework and a Systematic Approach to the CEO's Office," *Insurance Networking News: Executive Strategies for Technology Management*, 8(12) (2005).

video summary

Pike Place Fish Market

Summary

What makes a local fish market world famous? At Pike Place Fish Market, the attitude of making a difference for every person the company interacts with is just one of the ways the organization has become world famous. The company emphasizes trusting the workers, and empowering them to make decisions on the company's behalf. Building this culture took the decision to commit to change and took lots of time—after many meetings with a consultant, they began to get the idea that they could create their own futures. They use something called the power of personal responsibility—everyone has a choice and no one at Pike Place should be a victim of circumstance. This has led to employees who take responsibility for improving themselves, improving each other through coaching, and interacting well with the customers—or anyone. In hiring, Pike Place doesn't have "jobs available." Instead, it has "positions open" if the potential employee makes the "team." The team concept is very important at Pike Place.

In order to have a dynamic company full of people who are energized about their work, it is important to open up their creativity—open their eyes to "creating reality." The way to manage a group of people like that, according to the case, is to stay out of their way and let their creativity and eyes toward improvement develop the company further. Each person at Pike Place has personal goals. They ask "What is the next thing you want to master?" Everyone gives everyone else permission to coach each other. One person sees that he or she can possibly help another person based on personal experience. The key intention is empowerment—

not making someone else see how they are wrong. The results are unlimited. The flip side of all this creativity and inspiration—letting the company take a more "natural" course—is uncertainty, which can be uncomfortable. This risk taking, however, and willingness to deal with the sometimes uncomfortable aspects of change, has allowed Pike Place to improve drastically.

Discussion Questions

1. Briefly identify and describe some of the visible components of the organizational culture at Pike Place. Also describe some of the company's espoused values.

2. How does Pike Place use employee self-management as part of its organizational culture in improving the company?

3. Does Pike Place have a strong or weak organizational culture? How can you tell? Explain your answer.

part three

Management Strategy and Decision Making

Planning and the formulation of strategy establish broad objectives for an organization so that managers can set priorities and deadlines and marshall resources—people, financial, and physical—to accomplish short- and long-term goals. To think strategically, managers must scan the business environment for threats and opportunities. An important aspect of strategy formulation is being cognizant of the strengths and weaknesses of one's own organization. Then action must be taken based on the information gathered. The goal is to develop a competitive strategy in the market in light of the internal and environmental factors that anticipates the responses of one's competitors.

In Part Three we begin by examining the planning process. This leads us to the topic of decision making. The stages of decision making are presented followed by an analysis of two critical decision-making skills—time management and delegation. Next, we look at ways to formulate and implement a business strategy, including how to evaluate a firm's internal resources and capabilities. Part Three concludes with a discussion of entrepreneurship and one of the greatest management challenges—creating a new enterprise.

3

chapter 5

Managing the Planning Process

Learning Objectives

1 Identify the different elements of an effective plan.

2 Analyze the advantages and disadvantages of planning, and identify how planning pitfalls can be avoided.

3 Distinguish between formal and informal planning.

4 Recognize the features of well-designed objectives.

5 Identify the various types of action plans that managers can use to accomplish stated objectives.

Disney in Hong Kong:
Bad Luck, or Bad Planning?

5

Although it is by far the smallest of the company's 11 theme parks at just 299 acres, the brand-new Hong Kong Disneyland was the object of lavish care in the months before it opened in September 2005. Disney wants to make a flawless entry into the potentially enormous Asian tourism market and has dreams of opening other Asian Disneylands, so the company invested a great deal of planning in making sure it avoided the mistakes of the past.

Disneyland Paris, for instance, opened several years ago under the burden of culturally insensitive rules that offended French vacationers and cost Disney years of profit from the park. Employees were told to speak English only, wine was prohibited, and ticket and merchandise prices were set too high. Attendance sagged until major changes were made.

So in creating Hong Kong Disneyland, the company's managers planned to make the park as accessible to Chinese tourists as possible. Auspicious dates were chosen for the groundbreaking and completion of each of its buildings. Lucky numbers figured prominently in the layout and architecture of the facilities (one of the hotels features a main ballroom of 888 square feet, 8 being a lucky number), and unlucky numbers, like 4, were omitted from the elevator panels.

Signs in the park and explanations of the rides appear in both Chinese and English. The Jungle Cruise boats have names like Lijiang Lady (Lijiang is a region of China famous for its beautiful rivers) and guides who speak Mandarin. Food and souvenirs are reasonably priced, and instead of cotton candy and hot dogs, hungry visitors can find drumsticks in soy sauce and black sesame ice cream.

The American ambience that pervades the Disney experience elsewhere has been toned down in Hong Kong. The rides are tamer than Americans are used to, for one thing. Visitors from mainland China, the main target market for the park, appear more interested in taking photographs than in going on wild rides. And while there are fewer sightings of the life-size Disney characters like Donald Duck and Mickey Mouse that help to create the trademark fantasy experience at the company's other parks, cast members (as Disney employees are called) display plenty of Hong Kong's intrinsic warm friendliness.

Few stones were left unturned in Disney's planning process. Even the main entrance to the park was carefully thought out. With the guidance of local masters of *feng shui* (the ancient Chinese practice of placement and arrangement of space in pursuit of harmony with the environment), cash counters were set near corners or along walls to ensure prosperity. And Disney management shifted the entrance gate by 12 degrees to achieve the greatest possible harmony and success.

However, when success tried to come in the gate, harmony was in short supply, thanks to a last-minute slip-up in planning. Crowds of angry and disappointed visitors were turned away from the park during the Chinese New Year holiday, because of a marketing promotion that mistakenly failed to prevent the use of discounted tickets during the week-long celebration. Thousands of people, far more than Disney anticipated, were drawn by the combination of cheap tickets and a long holiday break. They lined up in the early morning hours to wait for entry, and when Disney began to turn them away due to overcrowding, closing the gates and halting ticket sales, police and security guards had to be called in to control the situation. Disney issued refunds and apologies, but public feeling ran so high that even the government of Hong Kong asked the company to improve its admission policies.

According to a Chinese newspaper, since then the park has operated well below its daily capacity.

Sources: Doris Ho, "Hong Kong Disneyland," *BusinessWeek Online*, www.businessweek.com, February 15, 2006; "Hong Kong's Tsang Hits Out at Disneyland Woes," *Forbes.com*, www.forbes.com, February 5, 2006; Keith Bradsher, "At Hong Kong Disneyland, the Year of the Dog Starts with a Growl," *New York Times*, February 4, 2006, p. A5.

CRITICAL THINKING QUESTIONS

1. *What did Disney do right in planning its latest theme park? What did it do wrong? Could its mistakes have been prevented?*

2. *At how many different levels did the company plan Hong Kong Disneyland?*

3. *How far into the future of its Asian operations does Disney seem to be planning? How many years should a company's plan encompass? Three years? Five? Ten?*

4. *What are some of the advantages and disadvantages a company may face when establishing long-term plans?*

We will revisit these questions in our Concluding Thoughts at the end of the chapter after you have had an opportunity to read the materials in this chapter.

What Is Planning?

planning

The management function that assesses the management environment to set future objectives and map out the activities necessary to achieve those objectives.

Does it make sense to plan in a world typified by rapid and dramatic change? The answer is a resounding "yes!" Planning programs identify what the organization wants to accomplish and how. **Planning** is a process that helps managers set objectives for the future and map out the activities and means that will make it possible to achieve those objectives.

There are both formal and informal planning processes. Most organizational leaders prefer to develop a formal written statement of future objectives and the approaches to reach them. The document can then be shared with those responsible for the execution of the plan, thereby reducing ambiguities and creating a common understanding. The written plan can be adjusted as necessary. As shown in Figure 5.1 on page 185, there are four key elements to a plan: objectives, actions, resources, and implementation.

FIGURE 5.1

Key Elements to a Plan

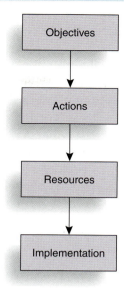

Objectives are goals or targets that the firm wishes to reach within a stated amount of time. One firm may wish to increase its return on investment from 8 to 14 percent in the next three years. Another may seek to increase market share from 5 to 10 percent over the course of five years. Setting objectives requires the firm to anticipate what is likely to happen in the future. A reasonable forecast allows a firm to set objectives that are both challenging and realistic. For instance, if a downturn is expected in the economy, ambitious profit objectives are less likely to be met. Likewise, if major players are entering the market, it will be more difficult to expand market share. A poor forecast may lead to objectives that are overly optimistic or that fall short of what the firm is capable of achieving.

Actions are the specific steps the firm intends to take to achieve the desired objectives. For instance, return on investment may be increased by downsizing, subcontracting some of the work, decreasing inventories, using technology to increase productivity, or developing new products. Company managers may also decide to increase advertising expenditures to expand its market share. Alternatively, it may be more efficient to undercut competitors by decreasing prices.

Planned actions cannot be carried out effectively without careful **resource allocation.** A quality plan states where resources will come from (for instance, borrowed versus internally generated funds) and how they will be deployed. The management team should be aware of the resource constraints the company faces so they can decide whether the company's goals can be realistically accomplished. As discussed later in this chapter, budgets are a way to allocate and control the resources committed to each step.

Finally, plans must be accompanied by **implementation guidelines** that show how the intended actions will be carried out. Implementation involves dividing tasks among the different actors, specifying reporting relationships, and establishing timelines.

For the sake of clarity, the four elements of planning are discussed individually in this chapter. In reality, they are closely intertwined. Objectives are not meaningful unless the firm can carry out the activities to achieve them and devote resources to support their implementation. An accurate assessment of the

objectives

The goals or targets that the firm wishes to accomplish within a stated amount of time.

Elements of the Planning Process

actions

The specific steps the firm intends to take to achieve the desired objectives.

resource allocation

The planning step that determines where the resources will come from (for instance, borrowing versus internally generated funds) and how the resources will be deployed to achieve the agreed-on objectives.

implementation guidelines

The planning step that shows how the intended actions will be carried out.

LOC-In

firm's resources provides an excellent starting point. Taking advantage of the firm's **core competencies** such as know-how, skills, brand recognition, and/or the company's reputation should clearly be considered in setting objectives and laying out action plans.

Planning occurs at every level within the organization. The plans made at higher levels direct and constrain the planning that takes place at lower levels. In general, planning at the top of the pyramid focuses on broad, long-term issues. For instance, a firm may decide to focus on a particular market segment, divesting itself of products or units that are unrelated to that market segment. Planning at lower levels tends to be primarily concerned with the operational details of the overall plan. Before going into details about the four elements of planning, it is important to keep in mind both the potential benefits and pitfalls of the planning process, to be discussed next.

The Benefits of Planning

Several important benefits are associated with planning. To begin with, planning requires managers to assess the external forces that affect the company. This helps the company respond to challenges present in the environment. The goals that are established as part of the plan give company members a sense of direction and purpose in that environment. Further, when planning is properly conducted, it helps the management team to establish priorities, coordinate activities, develop standards, and clarify forces that will contribute to success. Effective planning processes result in increased participation by lower-level members. This, in turn, leads to improved managerial skills for all of the members of the company. Next, planning is the basis of control. A well-designed plan sets the standards that will be used to assess performance at every level in the organizational hierarchy, both in the short term and over time. And finally, planning may help a firm reduce future uncertainty by anticipating what may happen in the future, forcing managers to think long term. These advantages are described in greater detail below.

Assessment of External Forces

One of the key aspects of planning is examining various environmental factors. This helps the firm deal with environmental uncertainty and identify both opportunities and threats present in the environment. Then, the management team can mobilize resources to neutralize potential threats as well as take advantage of opportunities.

For example, video stores, such as Blockbuster, have been forced to adjust to the beta format, VHS format, DVD format, and now the threat from direct pay-per-view delivery systems. Each time, the company has responded, most recently by creating a cooperative agreement with Direct TV to provide pay-per-view movies.

Developing a Sense of Direction and Purpose

A well-designed plan helps both managers and employees to understand what the organization is trying to achieve as well as the role that each plays in accomplishing those goals. Without a plan, managers and employees may not recognize how they share a common fate, even if they carry out the tasks they think are important. The lack of a clear sense of direction leads to multiple and often conflicting goals, and the ineffective use of resources.

Identifying the Factors That Affect the Organization

Properly conducted planning helps the organization focus on factors related to growth, renewal, and survival. Managers are able to reflect on issues that may not be obvious in the midst of day-to-day work pressures. For example, Pfizer is a leader in the development of new drugs, with some 60 drugs, for conditions ranging from diabetes to anxiety, in early stages of development. In its planning process Pfizer realized that it could take advantage of the opportunity to partner with the industry's smaller players to help them realize the potential of their own new medications. Consequently, Pfizer co-launched Lipitor, a cholesterol-lowering pill, in conjunction with Warner-Lambert. Pfizer's potent sales force, ranked no. 1 in physician surveys, helped the drug's sales smash an industry record in the late 1990s.[1]

Encouraging Participation

When workers participate in managerial activities, they tend to "buy in" and work much harder to see an effort succeed. They also experience stronger feelings of commitment to the organization. The planning process is an excellent place to encourage managers and employees to share inputs about the goals of the organization, and to find the best ways to achieve those goals. Participation is likely to strengthen the efforts dedicated to attaining those goals and increase goodwill toward their immediate supervisors and the overall company.

Coordination of Efforts

Managers who operate independently may not be aware of what other managers are doing. The planning process may help them coordinate efforts more effectively. For example, DaimlerChrysler Corporation created a joint German (Daimler is headquartered in Germany) and U.S. (where Chrysler is based) planning team of top executives to try to help Chrysler reduce its billion-dollar losses. One of the executives in the team is Dieter Zetsche, a German who is credited with Daimler's success in restructuring Mercedes-Benz and making it profitable again. In this manner DaimlerChrysler is trying to apply valuable expertise from one part of the organization in another.[2]

In companies in which operations are decentralized, each unit may use different performance criteria and resource allocation priorities. This became a major problem at Motorola in the late 1990s, leading to a significant decline in overall firm performance. A centralized planning process can help managers understand how actions or decisions in one area have consequences for other units as well as for the entire firm.

Establishment of Priorities

Planning can help a firm prioritize its major problems or issues. Lack of priorities can dilute the organization's efforts or make it susceptible to managers who take advantage of the confusion to impose their own agendas. Also, the failure to define priorities causes the firm to drift and prevents it from developing a clear strategic focus. This was a primary reason why Pepsi lost the "war" against Coke during the 1980s. Coke focused its energies on its core product, while Pepsi's efforts were dispersed across a variety of unrelated products such as restaurants, hotels, and retail outlets.

Focusing Attention on Different Time Horizons

Many business programs may take years to complete. Steps can be taken to achieve long-term objectives by balancing them with short-term goals. For instance, General Electric successfully competed against Roll-Royce, Pratt & Whitney, and Snecma (a French government–owned engine shop) for a 3 billion contract offered by the Chinese government for plane engines to build a fleet of 500 regional jets for the 2008 Beijing Olympics. General Electric won in large measure because it began to plan for the design and production of regional jet engines almost 10 years earlier. GE has been chosen as a "Worldwide Olympic Sponsor" for four Olympic games across various cities around the world during 2006–2012, which is likely to drum up additional business in the long haul.[3]

Understanding Circumstances Contributing to Past Success or Failure

It is vital for managers to learn from past successes and failures. Planning can bring the reasons for poor and good performance into sharper view, enabling the firm to draw on experience. For example, in 1997 Kodak lost $100 million when it introduced an advanced-photo-system camera and film, only to find that it did not have enough stock on hand to meet the demand. The company could not process the new film at enough locations. It finally responded by spending another $100 million on the system in a more focused approach. The management team also learned that most customers preferred less expensive models. As a result, Kodak introduced a new camera for under $50 that was a hybrid between digital and analog cameras. The new camera was soon responsible for 20 percent of Kodak's camera sales.[4] Kodak ran into serious trouble again later in the decade after facing a 49 percent decline in photo-finishing revenue and a 28 percent drop in traditional and single-use camera sales.[5] This time Kodak is betting on digital technology, hoping that digital profits will grow faster than the drop in film profits. A key reason for the confidence, according to Kodak's CEO, is that "Consumers are increasingly turning to retailers to make prints of their digital images, which is far more profitable than selling low-margin digital cameras."[6]

Ensuring the Availability of Adequate Resources

A well-designed plan leads to identifying the resources needed for the future. These resources may come from several sources. For example, the biotechnology firm Genentech reallocated 25 percent of its research staff to developing multiple products to achieve its new business objectives back in the early 2000s. Now Genentech is considered one of the top, if not the top, biotechnology innovator across a wide range of areas, including antibody engineering, bioinformatics, immunology, medicinal chemistry, molecular biology, pathology, biomedical imaging, and protein engineering.[7]

Establishing Performance Standards

The end result of any planning process is a series of statements regarding objectives to be met along with expected activities. These criteria define expected behaviors for organizational members and allow for the assessment of progress. As time passes, the relative contributions of individuals and groups can be assessed and rewarded.

A few years ago, General Electric (GE) established a tough quality standard called six sigma. Six sigma is equivalent to generating fewer than 3.4 defects per million manufacturing or service operations. To attain this goal, GE trained tens of thousands of employees in quality techniques. A reward system to support this quality initiative was also established. GE managers and employees who meet objectives may receive as much as a 25 percent increase in their annual base salaries without a promotion; cash bonuses can increase as much as 150 percent in a year to between 20 percent and 70 percent of base pay; and generous stock options are provided to 27,000 employees. As we enter the latter part of the 2000s, GE strongly believes that rewarding employees for achieving measurable quality objectives is fundamental to the continued success of its quality assurance plans.[8]

Kodak's decision to revamp its original advanced film imaging camera, although costly, resulted in a much more profitable product.

Supporting Organizational Control Systems

Organizations cannot be successful unless control systems are in place to ensure that objectives are being attained and that resources are being used appropriately. A *control* is "any process that helps align the actions of individuals with the interests of their employing firms."[9] A *control system* is "the knowledge that someone who knows and cares is paying attention to what we do and can tell us when deviations are occurring."[10]

Effective planning improves a company's control system by making it possible to compare target versus actual results. When a gap is detected between company goals and observed results, corrective actions are taken to modify activities for the future. In a few extreme cases, the existing plan may be completely abandoned. When company executives fail to abandon a plan after large resources have been spent on it even though all available evidence suggests that the plan is not working, the problem is called *escalation of commitment.* Some people believe, for instance, that the space shuttle disasters may be attributed to escalation of commitment to a space program that was doomed to failure from the beginning (see the Individual/Collaborative Learning Case at the end of this chapter entitled "Why Did NASA Stick with the Space Shuttle So Long?").

Developing "What If" Scenarios

Long ago, Ben Franklin suggested that "the only sure things in life are death and taxes." Organizations, like individuals, face a great deal of uncertainty. Planning can help managers deal with uncertainty by anticipating what may happen in the future. No firm has a crystal ball to accurately forecast the future. Planning can help identify different future scenarios and spell out what to do in each scenario. This is known as *contingency or scenario planning.* Ben Franklin recognized that uncertainty is inevitable but is still manageable. Another of his famous proverbs states that "chance favors the prepared mind." Management Close-Up 5.1 on page 190 offers

Planning for What If

There are five lessons that every company could apply to plan for the worst, particularly in a volatile and fast-changing world.

1. *Turbocharge your imagination*. The events that do the worst damage are the ones no one even conceived of. A perfect example is 9/11. The idea that a passenger jet might crash into the World Trade Center had been thought of; it was a fairly obvious possibility, especially since a plane had once crashed into the Empire State Building. What no one imagined was the combination of large planes with nearly full fuel tanks plus the impact of the crashes jarring fireproofing from the girders, and how this could bring the towers down. In retrospect, it obviously could have been imagined. It just wasn't.

2. *Build scenarios*. Shell managers created an Arab oil embargo scenario in the early 1970s. Because they had done the exercise, they could see how events might lead to one, and when it happened, they were much better prepared than their competitors to respond. They had seen this movie already, so they slowed refinery expansion and adapted their refineries to handle many types of crude oil while competitors vacillated. The common view in the industry is that Shell came through the oil shock far better than any other major producer.

3. *Think in probabilities*. If you can imagine an event, you can try to assign a probability to it, if not in absolute terms— 0.1 percent, 3 percent, 50 percent—then at least relative to other events. The problem is that it is excruciatingly difficult in real life because our brains aren't wired that way. Nassim Nicolas Taleb, in his book *Fooled by Randomness*, cites an example. Ask a sample of travelers at an airport how much they'd pay for an insurance policy that would give their beneficiary $1 million if they die from any cause on their trip. Then ask another sample how much they'd pay for a policy that would pay $1 million if they're killed by terrorists on their trip. People will pay more for the second policy, though that clearly makes no sense. We just do not think rationally about probabilities, a tendency every manager must fight.

4. *Use internal markets*. Using internal market is a forecasting technique in which employees bet small amounts of money furnished by the company to predict the likelihood of specific events. Hewlett-Packard has used internal markets to forecast sales more accurately than the marketing manager could; Eli Lilly has used them to predict the success of drug research with uncanny accuracy. Well-designed predictive markets can give managers new insight into specific risks and how they might affect the company.

Planning for the worst-case scenario is always easier in retrospect, but it is a process managers must train themselves to use. Understanding the effect of an airplane hitting the World Trade Center towers would have been a result of such planning. Another difficult planning task is accepting that the worst has happened and acting quickly in response, a flaw in many agencies' response to the flooding of New Orleans in the wake of Hurricane Katrina.

5. *Create a culture that insists on facing reality*. Prepare employees to respond quickly and effectively to the bolt from the blue, and the no. 1 impediment—incredible yet obvious—is failing to accept that the trouble has indeed happened. Even in New Orleans, immediately after Hurricane Katrina, TV showed images of people dancing in Bourbon Street; they thought everything would be okay.

Source: Adapted from G. Colvin,. "An Executive Risk Handbook," *Fortune*, October 3, 2005, pp.69–70.

DESIGN YOUR OWN CONTINGENCY PLAN

You are part of a five-member group of students planning to study in France two years from now. The five of you are planning to travel together and to save on housing costs by renting a three-bedroom apartment. Your plans call for a six-month stay. Let's assume that the current exchange rate is 0.85 euro per dollar, so it will cost each of you approximately 10,000 euros (or $8,500). You plan to save this amount of money by working in the evenings and during summers, although it will require a great deal of sacrifice (skipping movies, eating at home, not buying new clothes, and so on). At a typical student wage rate of $6.00 per hour, this will require 2,125 hours of work (at $4 per hour after taxes and transportation costs) exclusively devoted to save the $8,500. Of course, you will need money in the meantime to cover your daily expenses in addition to the money you are saving for the trip.

Engage in a contingency planning exercise under the following assumptions:

1. Two years from now the euro will be .95 on the dollar, meaning the cost will be $9,500.
2. Two years from now the euro will be 1.05 on the dollar, so the cost will be $10,000.
3. Two years from now the euro will be 1.15 on the dollar, making the cost $11,500.
4. Two years from now, the euro will be 1.25 on the dollar, or a total cost of $12,500.

The team (appointed by instructor) will develop a contingency plan to deal with each of the possible scenarios above. Keep in mind that this is a problem similar to what firms face in international markets when they engage in contingency planning for the future based on the strength of the dollar (see Chapter 2, Managing in a Global Environment). Note: During the period 2002–2007, the exchange rate has oscillated between 0.80 euro per dollar and 1.35 euro per dollar.

five lessons that companies should keep in mind to plan for unforeseeable circumstances such as 9/11, the Arab oil embargo, the outcomes of drug research and hurricane Katrina. The Skills for Managing 5.1 box above is designed to help you develop a contingency plan.

Management Development

Individual managers should play a major role in focusing the organization on the future. Planning helps managers to be proactive and forward-thinking rather than being reactive and just letting things happen. By considering future possibilities and developing a long-term vision, managers can become more committed to the firm and learn to convert abstract ideas or objectives into concrete actions. Including managers from every level of the organization in company planning processes is an effective form of "on the job" training. These planning experiences "season" managers, so they are able to move into more responsible roles in the future.

The Pitfalls of Planning

Company leaders will not realize the benefits of planning if the planning process itself is flawed. Future conditions can be forecasted incorrectly, reporting relationships can become overly hierarchical, planning can become a self-contained

Poor forecasts can result in poor results, as Blockbuster discovered when it did away with late fees but failed to reap any financial benefits.

activity, bureaucratization can become oppressive, and objectives and processes that are no longer optimal for the firm may be used. Each of these problems is described in greater detail in this section.

Poor Forecasts of Future Conditions

As you have seen, the business environment is changing faster than ever. Even the most sophisticated planning techniques may not predict accurately what is likely to happen in the future. The longer the time frame, the more likely that unforeseen circumstances will occur. This is one reason many firms became skeptical of the value of strategic planning in the 1980s. Major corporations such as the Adolph Coors Company, Campbell Soup, Exxon, General Motors, Oak Industries, Shaklee, Toro, and Wang Laboratories, among others, reported poor strategic decisions driven by inaccurate forecasts. Common problems included poor estimates of the demand for new products, miscalculation of the effect of international competition on main product lines, the inability to predict technological innovations, and changes in the economic and legal systems.[11] More recently,

- Blockbuster introduced a "never a late fee" program in the mid-2000s thinking it would attract new customers, but additional revenues and profits never materialized. Most observers believe that Blockbuster has lost money in this deal.

- General Motors provided generous discounts to car buyers in the mid-2000s, including a special "employee price" available to any customer, thinking it would take away market share from its rivals. This plan resulted in multibillion dollar losses for the car manufacturer without a corresponding increase in market share.

- Amway invested heavily in China between 1992 and 1998. In 1998, Beijing suddenly banned direct marketing, shutting down the $178 million-a-year China business of Amway Asia Pacific.

- At least 100 e-companies that received large investment capital in the late 1990s went bust during the first years of the new millennium, not long after many investors firmly believed forecasts stating that electronic commerce was the wave of the future.[12]

Plans Imposed from Above

The traditional approach to planning is from the top down, with the CEO and senior executives, and perhaps a planning department, establishing organizational objectives and laying out general business strategies. Managers at lower organizational levels then devise implementation methods and operational plans to support the objectives and strategies set at the top. Separating the plan generators from the plan implementers often leads to the development of plans that lower level managers begrudgingly try to put into practice. Such plans often do not benefit from the wisdom and experience of those at lower levels within the firm. Many "reengineering" plans have failed in part because they were imposed on the rest of the firm by the top of the hierarchy.

Planning as a Self-Contained Activity

There is a danger that the people engaged in planning will become so enamored of the process that they become a close-knit group divorced from the rest of the organization. Managers and employees may be cynical about objectives and suggestions for action emanating from specialized planning departments or units. Reflecting on this, one well-known consultant noted that "planning staff groups may gain much power and authority in organizations . . . [where they are] thrust into the role of proponent and doer of plans—too often, the real doers are pushed aside."[13]

Extensive Bureaucratization

When planning is conducted by specialists without the participation of other managers, there may be a tendency to generate volumes of paperwork accompanied by fancy oral presentations. In other instances, planning becomes overly quantitative and formula driven. As a result, the logic behind the recommendations may be difficult to understand and may lack common sense. In addition, the predictions of elegant mathematical models succeed or fail on the data and assumptions employed. Formulas that work relatively well in stable conditions may totally miss the mark in turbulent times.

Inflexible Adherence to Objectives and Processes

A firm may become overly committed to an outdated plan, ignoring clues that it is time to change direction. People tend to justify "sunk costs" by continuing to defend objectives in spite of disappointing results. For instance, for years Apple was obstinate in producing its Macintosh computers for loyal users in spite of continuing drops in sales that occurred largely because its software was incompatible with IBM, the market leader.

In another case, Detroit's Big Three automobile firms in the early 2000s continued their investment in SUVs, which fueled much of their earning growth during the 1990s, even though the market had become saturated over the preceding years. To spur sales the auto firms had to offer incentives; after five years of steadily increasing SUV incentive packages profit margins had disappeared in 2006. The sudden jump in oil prices following hurricane Katrina in 2005 only made matters worse, even though prices began to recede later on. Nevertheless, the auto firms have continued pouring more resources into a dwindling market, ignoring the data showing that previously established objectives were no longer viable.[14] In the case of General Motors, the response to this crisis seems to be drastic cost-cutting (at least 30,000 jobs are planned to be cut during 2006–2008), but it seems that the company still remains wedded to a business plan that has failed in the past.

LOC-In

② Learning Objective Check-In

DB&H contractors have firsthand experience with many planning pitfalls. For instance, within their company, planning is conducted by specialists without the participation of managers from the field. This tends to generate volumes of paperwork and fancy presentations, but can lack accurate recommendations. The planners are also a close-knit group who do not tend to associate with the rest of the organization's managers. This causes managers and employees elsewhere in the firm to look at "planning" with a cynical attitude and then dismiss the objectives. The senior executives at DB&H are always establishing organizational objectives and laying out general strategies, but the plan implementers are left to try to put those plans into practice without having had any input. The implementers' years of experience are repeatedly disregarded, and so many of the plans from the senior executives fail time and again for this reason.

1. *The lack of accurate recommendations at DB&H illustrates _____.*
   a. *plans imposed from above*
   b. *planning as a self-contained activity*
   c. *extensive bureaucratization*
   d. *inflexible adherence to objectives and processes*
2. *The cynical attitude some employees and managers have toward planning stems from_____.*
   a. *planning as a self-contained activity*
   b. *extensive bureaucratization*
   c. *plans imposed from above*
   d. *inflexible adherence to objectives and processes*
3. *Plans from the senior executives fail because they reflect _____.*
   a. *poor forecasts of future conditions*
   b. *extensive bureaucratization*
   c. *planning as a self-contained activity*
   d. *plans imposed from above*

Technology Is Fostering Bottom-Up Planning from the Inside and the Outside

THEME: CUSTOMER FOCUS

Corporate planners are starting to use the wisdom of online crowds to marshal the talents, resources, and ideas of millions of people worldwide. File sharing, blogs, and social networking services are connecting masses of people simultaneously. More companies are starting to understand the value of this technology to help them develop business plans for the short and long term. If they can get others to help them design and create products, they end up with ready-made customers—and that means far less risk in the tricky business of creating new goods and markets. So businesses are accessing the cyber swarm to target their efforts from research and development to marketing. Says Alpheus Bingham, vice president for Eli Lilly's e.lilly research unit, "If I can tap into a million minds simultaneously, I may run into one that is uniquely prepared."

Procter & Gamble's $1.7 billion-a-year R&D operation, for instance, is taking advantage of collective online brain trusts such as Lilly Company's InnoCentive Inc. in Andover, Massachusetts. It's a network of 80,000 independent, self-selected "solvers" in 173 countries who gang-tackle research problems for the likes of Boeing Co., DuPont, and 30 other large companies. One solver, Drew Buschhorn, is a 21-year-old chemistry grad student at the University of Indiana at Bloomington. He came up with an art-restoration chemical for an unnamed company—a compound he identified while helping his mother dye cloth when he was a kid. Says InnoCentive CEO Darren J. Carroll, "We're trying for the democratization of science."

And they're apparently succeeding. More than a third of the two dozen requests Procter & Gamble has submitted to InnoCentive's network have yielded solutions, for which the company paid upwards of $5,000 apiece. By using InnoCentive and other ways of reaching independent talent, Procter & Gamble has boosted the number of new products derived from outside to 35 percent, from 20 percent three years ago. As a result, sales per R&D person are ahead some 40 percent.

The online masses aren't just offering up ideas. Sometimes they all but become the entire production staff. In game designer Linden Lab's Second Life, a virtual online world, participants themselves create just about everything, from characters to buildings to games that are played inside the world. The 45-person company, which grossed less than $5 million last year, makes money by charging players for virtual land on which they build their creations. Second Life's 25,000 players collectively spend 6,000 hours a day actively creating things. Even if you assume only 10 percent of their work is any good, that's still equal to a 100-person team at a traditional game company. "We've built a market-based, far more efficient system for creating digital content," says Linden CEO Philip Rosedale.

Likewise, groups online are starting to turn marketing from megaphone to conversation. LEGO Group, for instance, brought adult LEGO train-set enthusiasts to its New York office to check out new designs. "We pooh-poohed them all," says Steve Barile, an Intel Corp. engineer and LEGO fan in Portland, Oregon, who attended. As a result, says Jake McKee, LEGO's global community-development manager, "We literally produced what they told us to produce." The new locomotive, the "Santa Fe Super Chief" set, was shown to

Keys to Successful Planning

The planning pitfalls described above can be avoided. Successful planning includes involving managers at different levels, using a combination of numerical and judgmental methods, viewing planning as a continuous activity capable of adapting to change, avoiding paralysis of the analysis, and concentrating planning efforts on a manageable set of issues.

Decentralizing the Plaining Powers

To one degree or another, every level of management should be involved in planning. Planning cannot be viewed as the province of staff specialists or senior managers living in ivory towers. In general, both the quality of the plan and commitment to it are likely to increase when key managers and employees at various organizational levels contribute to its formulation and implementation.

Customer groups are becoming a stronger voice in new-product planning at companies like LEGO Group, which recently collobarated with about 250 adult LEGO fans to produce its new Santa Fe Super Chief train set. The fans' enthusiasm quickly paid off in sales even without any other marketing.

250 enthusiasts, and their word-of-mouse helped the first 10,000 units sell out in less than two weeks with no other marketing.

In short, we may be entering the stage where companies routinely use Internet-powered services to tap into the collective intelligence of employees, customers, and curious outsiders to develop, implement, and adjust business plans "from the bottom up."

Source: Adapted from R. D. Hof, "The Power of Us: Mass Collaboration on the Internet Is Shaking Up Business," *BusinessWeek*, July 20, 2005, pp. 78–81.

One recent trend that seems to hold much promise is to secure the input of online groups to help develop, implement, and adjust business plans as necessary (see Management Close-Up 5.2, "Technology Is Fostering Bottom-Up Planning from the Inside and the Outside" on page 194).

Using Both Numerical and Judgmental Methods

Planning is as much an art as a science. An effective planning process requires a thorough understanding of interrelated environmental and organizational factors. These factors provide clues about where the firm should be moving in the future, the resources it has at its disposal, and the constraints it faces. While numerical data can be helpful, the numbers need to be carefully interpreted. There are situations in which numerical approaches are not suitable. Systematically tapping the knowledge of employees at different levels in the organization allows the firm to benefit from their experiences and to profit from the collective judgment of company employees.

Viewing Planning as Continuous and Capable of Adapting to Change

Company leaders must be flexible enough to respond to changes in technology, competitors' reactions, international trends, and industry conditions if the planning process is to be successful. Almost any objective and the steps to accomplish it are likely to become obsolete relatively quickly unless there are built-in mechanisms to consider and respond to change. Results should be monitored continuously to detect major deviations from initial assumptions and expectations. Planning should question future directions, chosen alternatives, and priorities. In particular, the firm needs to guard against escalation of a failing course of action, as noted earlier. Past choices and sunk costs should not entice the firm to continue investing in a plan when there is sufficient evidence to question the wisdom of that plan.

Firms use a variety of approaches to keep objectives and action plans attuned to changes in internal and external environments. These include scheduled retreats of key managers and employees, workshops led by consultants, environmental scanning (see Chapter 7 on strategic management), the use of two-way feedback between managers and employees in the performance appraisal process (see Chapter 10 on human resource management), and the creation of standing cross-functional committees composed of executives and key employees to monitor progress, identify current or emerging problems, and recommend corrective actions.

In some cases the firm must react quickly to deal with unforeseen circumstances. Even with the best-made plans, managers of successful firms are often called to act by "the seat of their pants" to confront crisis situations that seem to come from nowhere. (See, for instance, at the end of the chapter, Management MiniCase 5.2, "Disaster Planning: The Only Lifeline was Wal-Mart.")

Avoiding Paralysis of the Analysis

An obsession with paperwork, technical reports, statistical tables, and other supporting documentation causes paralysis by analysis. Plans only succeed when those responsible accept the plan and become devoted to seeing it implemented effectively. The key to successful planning is action, not becoming bogged down in overanalyzing every detail.

Concentrating on a Manageable Set of Issues

It is important to limit planning to key priority areas. As discussed in Chapter 7, a good way to identify these key areas is to focus on the firm's core competence or the resources that enable it to do things better than competitors. This keeps planning from being a "pie in the sky" exercise and anchors it to the firm's strengths. Beside simplifying the planning task, it will make plans easier to explain, since managers and employees will be cognizant of the problems, challenges, alternatives, and priorities being addressed. Moreover, the levels of risk and uncertainty are lowered since the plan is confined to areas about which the firm has information and experience, reducing the probability of unpleasant surprises. For example, Apple computers has been extremely successful at introducing a steady stream of new products (most recently Aperture for professional photographers, powerboooks with high resolution displays, IPOD, I Chat RV and IMaG5) by exploiting its core competence. Some of

FIGURE 5.2

Summary of Good and Bad Planning

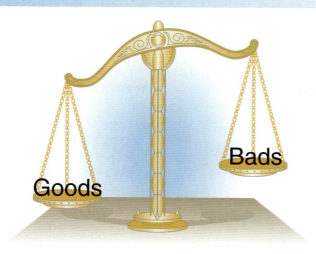

Decentralize planning process	Poor forecast of future conditions
Use numerical and judgmental methods	Plans imposed from above
Assess external forces	Planning as self-contained activity
Develop a sense of direction and purpose	Extensive bureaucratization
Identify factors that affect the organization	Inflexible adherence to objectives
Encourage participation	and processes
Coordinate efforts	
Establish priorities	

these products introduced in the mid-2000s were conceived as far back as 1987, when Apple decided that its future lay in merging the computing, communications, and entertainment industries.[15]

See Figure 5.2 above for a summary of good planning techniques and bad planning techniques and bad planning pitfalls.

Formal Planning and Opportunistic Planning

A dynamic world requires dynamic planning programs. **Formal planning** systems are designed to identify objectives and to structure the major tasks of the organization to accomplish them. Formal planning is what has been described thus far in this chapter. No matter how careful the formal planning process is, however, unexpected events can derail the plan. A second type of planning, referred to as **opportunistic planning,** should coexist with formal planning and can help the formal plan function more smoothly.

As its name implies, opportunistic planning refers to programmatic actions triggered by unforeseen circumstances. Resources that are not totally committed as part of the formal planning process may be used at the discretion of managers to deal with unexpected events. For example, since its inception Federal Express has viewed the U.S. Postal Service (USPS) as a direct competitor, predicating its growth on stealing market share from USPS by sending materials faster with almost perfect reliability. FedEx marketing and delivery plans quickly changed in 2001 when FedEx and the USPS became partners. The U.S. Postal Service now allows consumers to send FedEx packages directly from any U.S. Post Office using newly installed drop boxes, and FedEx now flies most of the Priority and Express packages for the Postal Service. This type of action as a result of "opportunistic planning" would have been unthinkable just a few months before.[16]

formal planning

A system designed to identify objectives and to structure the major tasks of the organization to accomplish them.

opportunistic planning

A type of planning that involves programmatic actions triggered by unforeseen circumstances; it can coexist with formal planning and can help the formal plan function more smoothly.

It is important to strike the proper balance between these two types of planning. Organizations that rely exclusively on formal planning can become too rigid, whereas firms that use only opportunistic schemes will be constantly reacting to external forces and will have no clear sense of direction. Formal planning should provide a structured framework without binding every action of the enterprise, while opportunistic planning should allow for creative responses within that organized framework. GE has a formal planning process, and its longtime CEO, Jack Welch, strongly promoted opportunistic planning during his tenure:

> *The story about GE that hasn't been told is the value of an informal place. . . . I don't think people have ever figured out that being informal is a big deal. . . . Making the company "informal" means violating the chain of command, communicating across layers, paying people as if they worked not for a big company but for a demanding entrepreneur where nearly everyone knows the boss.*[17]

The Formal Planning Process

As indicated earlier, the four elements of the formal planning process involve setting objectives, charting a course of action to meet the objectives, allocating resources to carry out the planned activities, and implementing the activities (see again Figure 5.1). Each of these steps is discussed in turn.

Setting Objectives

Objectives are the performance targets set during the planning cycle. Objectives provide the answer to the question: What are we trying to accomplish? Inappropriate or poorly defined objectives invalidate the rest of the planning process since there is no clear guide for organizational efforts.

Objectives are set at every level in an organization. The goals established at higher levels direct and constrain the objectives set at lower levels. In general, objectives are more general at the top and become more specific at lower organizational levels. Some people refer to this as a *cascading of objectives.* DuPont stated an overall corporate objective from 2003 to 2005 in which one-third of sales would come from products introduced in the last five years (up from 24 percent in 2003). To achieve this goal, DuPont's finance department set as its objective to increase the research and development (R&D) budget by 10 percent and to devote 65 percent of this budget to new product development (up from 33 percent in recent years). The objective of DuPont's 75 R&D centers distributed across 12 countries was to identify 75 projects (an average of one per center) to launch new products that have the highest revenue potential. For one particular team, called the Suprel Group, the objective became much more specific: to develop a lightweight and puncture-resistant fabric to be used in gowns for surgeons and nurses.[18] In other words, DuPont's product introduction goal that began at the top of the organizational pyramid filtered down to lower echelons, where they became more specific. The goals at each level should support the goals established at the next higher level.

The overall objectives of the organization reflect its *mission*, which is a statement of the organization's reason to exist (more on this in Chapter 7 regarding strategic management). DuPont's objectives for 2003–2005 were consistent with the mission of being "a science company, delivering science-based solutions in markets such as food and nutrition, health care, apparel, home and construction, electronics, and transportation."[19]

Specific and measurable objectives motivate behavior more than general and ambiguous ones. It is important to give employees a clear sense of direction. Unambiguous objectives allow managers to determine whether key outcomes are being reached and to take corrective action if they are not. By knowing exactly where the firm is trying to go, managers and employees can focus on the most important activities, thereby concentrating on achieving the best results. Worthwhile objectives include:

- Profitability targets, such as return on investment, return on assets, and earnings per share.
- Quality goals such as percentage of rejects, customer complaints relative to number of orders, or quality certification standards.
- Marketing objectives, such as market growth, market share, and international sales.
- Innovation outcomes, such as number of patents, percentage of sales attributed to new products, and return on R&D investments.

Further, managers should make sure that objectives are *challenging* and will "stretch" employees to work harder to use their full potential. Difficult goals must be achievable; otherwise employees will not believe that their efforts will lead to success.

Objectives should specify a *timetable* or *deadline*. This can serve to motivate individuals. A timetable can cause individuals to organize tasks, prompting them to monitor work to ensure that completion is on time. It also helps management evaluate individuals or units on the extent to which work was done in a timely fashion.

Finally, managers and employees are more likely to devote time and effort to the accomplishment of objectives that they perceive as more critical and whose achievement is associated with greater prestige, rewards, and future career opportunities. Deciding which objectives should have highest *priority* is an integral part of the planning process.

When firms have multiple objectives, scarce resources preclude pursuing them all with the same zeal. Frequently, desired objectives may work at cross purposes. For example,

- Managers may increase short-term profits by cutting back on capital expenditures, reducing R&D investments, and laying off employees. This may decrease future profits because of lost technological superiority, the introduction of fewer products into the market, and less employee commitment.
- A firm may reduce its overall level of risk by diversifying into different market areas so that downturns in one market segment may be counterbalanced by upturns in other segments. However, the overall profitability of the firm is likely to be lower, because it loses the competitive advantage of applying a core set of knowledge and skills to a focused product niche. For example, in the mid-1990s, Altavista began as an Internet search engine. By the late 1990s the company had decided to diversify its scope and to explore new market segments. Company executives invested $100 million to build the site into a multifaceted portal along the lines of Yahoo!. In the 2000s Altavista realized that expanding beyond its core knowledge had been a mistake and decided to return to its original mission.[20]

video: THE ENTREPRENEURIAL MANAGER

Joe-To-Go

Summary

Jerry Andrews found himself in quite a predicament one day as a soccer dad who had made a commitment to bring the coffee to the game the next day, assuming his wife would do it, only to find out his wife had other obligations. Realizing his commitment, and unwilling to break it, Jerry decided he would not break his promise to the other parents. He brainstormed that night and devised a way to take the coffee to the game—a disposable thermos. This is the idea that led to Jerry's creating and founding Joe-To-Go.

Jerry's example illustrates the value of the planning process, which includes writing a business plan, finding money to fund the enterprise, and contacting experts for advice or help early in the process. For Jerry, this meant, for example, finding an industrial designer who could turn Jerry's thought into a viable product. One of Jerry's main challenges was finding a disposable, thermoslike bag to keep the coffee warm. It took a lot of research, which translates to a lot of money. Entrepreneurs usually do not have the luxury of throwing money at projects, like large firms might. Instead, they have to be very careful about how they allocate their costs. Jerry used his limited resources to find a good engineer and a good patent lawyer.

Fortunately for Jerry, the partner he approached for financing also had a background in sales, and offered to help Jerry approach retailers for distribution. The initial response from the coffee industry and the packaging industry was encouraging. Four years into the business, the company had sold to a lot of "mom and pop" retail outlets, but did not have any national accounts. The business was not making enough money to survive, and Jerry lost his business partner to cancer. Jerry cut into his savings to continue the business. In the year 2000, Jerry's persistence paid off, and he got his first national account with Dunkin' Donuts, which licensed the product and has sold millions.

Discussion Questions

1. Planning programs identify what the organization wants to accomplish and how. What three areas were cited in the video as central to planning?

2. For entrepreneurs, business resources are typically personal resources. A few years into the establishment of the business, the resources began to dry up. How did Jerry deal with this circumstance? Do you think this action was part of his plan as an entrepreneur?

3. Joe-To-Go has found success through licensing the product to large national and international chains. While it is successful right now, what can Jerry do to ensure the company's continued success?

- A firm may pursue rapid growth to expand market share overseas, but company profits may suffer because it has to contend with diverse cultural milieus, is exposed to currency fluctuations, and is required to develop a management structure to deal with the complexities of a global operation (see Chapter 2).

- A firm may reduce costs by moving its manufacturing operations to a developing country where environmental regulations are lax. This would conflict with corporate social responsibility objectives.

As discussed in Chapter 3, a firm has many stakeholders, including employees, shareholders, consumers, and regulatory bodies. Each group may have different objectives. The planning process should identify the wishes of each of these groups and develop objectives that are clear, achievable, measurable, and prioritized so that they contribute to overall organizational performance.

FIGURE 5.3

Key Steps of the Typical Management by Objectives Cycle

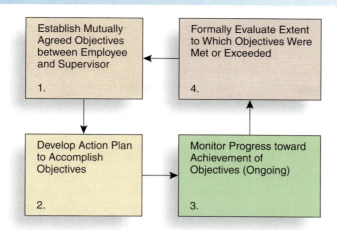

One planning technique that is widely used in the United States and abroad is *Management by Objectives* (MBO). MBO is a program in which objectives are mutually set between the employee and supervisor. The employee is held accountable for the accomplishment of those objectives at various intervals which are normally part of an annual performance appraisal. MBO programs are popular because they combine planning (through participatively set objectives) and control (employees are responsible for the attainment of measurable goals).

Figure 5.3 above shows the key steps of a typical annual MBO cycle. In step 1, objectives are agreed to between the superior and subordinate, and put in writing. Objectives such as companywide profitability targets are first established at the top of the organizational pyramid. These more general objectives then filter down through successively lower layers. For instance, overall profitability targets are broken down into objectives for divisions and product lines. While normally these objectives are established annually, it is possible to use a longer or shorter time horizon. In step 2, managers at each level develop action plans to accomplish the objectives set for them by their immediate superiors in step 1. As the plans are implemented in step 3, there are frequent checkups to ensure that things are on track and make any necessary adjustments. In step 4 (which normally takes place a year after objectives were set in step 1), the pairs of superior and subordinate who established the mutually agreed-upon objectives in step 1 meet to discuss the extent to which objectives were met. This feedback is normally put in writing in a formal document called the *performance appraisal form.* In the words of a human resource planning consultant, "Many managers struggle with feedback precisely because of a lack of planning. Without front-end planning, feedback has no context . . . the outcome of effective feedback is clarity—clarity regarding the performer's recent performance against previously agreed-upon criteria".[21]

Employees are usually rewarded with cash bonuses, stocks, promotions, and other suitable benefits when they accomplish or exceed the performance targets set in step 1. This performance information is then used as part of goal-setting for the next review cycle. Targets may be revised downward if they were deemed to be unrealistic in the prior MBO cycle, or made more difficult if the employee is ready for greater challenges.

Unfortunately, the very strength of MBO—measurability—often becomes its major weakness. Managers can manipulate the system to choose easier-to-reach targets and ignore intangible things that may be more difficult to measure, such as customer goodwill. They may also become reluctant to change priorities for fear of not achieving the agreed-upon objectives when the situation demands it. Worse yet, the setting of numerical objectives may lead to gaming on the part of managers to reach or exceed the quantitative targets set in step 1 (see Figure 5.3), tempting them to engage in unethical behaviors. In fact, many of the well-documented ethical lapses in the 2000s are attributed to top executives, managers, and even employees taking short cuts or manipulating numbers to reach challenging targets. In one of the most egregious cases, hospitals that were part of Tenet Health Care allegedly encouraged medical personnel to perform unnecessary medical procedures such as angioplasties, coronary bypasses, and heart catheterizations in order to meet or exceed profitability objectives.[22] Manager's Checkup 5.1 at the end of this chapter offers a set of ethical questions that all managers and employees should ask themselves from time to time to address ethical dilemmas that may arise at any phase of the planning process.

For an MBO system to be effective in the long run, the system must be flexible and allow for subjective judgments when assessing whether or not objectives are being achieved. The greater the volatility of conditions faced by the firm (rapid changes in technology, markets, competitors and the like) and the more its products and services change frequently, the greater the need for flexibility in the MBO system.

Management Is Everyone's Business 5.1 above offers a set of recommendations that should help you develop personal plans to make you a more effective employee.

FIGURE 5.4

Charting a Course of Action

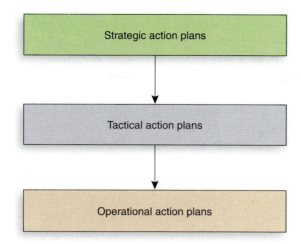

strategic action plans

Management plans based on macro approaches for analyzing organizational features, resources, and the environment and establishing long-term corporatewide action programs to accomplish the stated objectives in light of that analysis.

Charting a Course of Action

LOC-In

Once objectives have been established, the next step in the planning process (see again Figure 5.1) is to determine the actions necessary for producing orderly results. Three types of actions are normally planned: strategic, tactical, and operational. See Figure 5.4 above.

STRATEGIC ACTION PLANS Top executives are normally responsible for developing strategic action plans. At times divisional managers and the board of directors are also involved. **Strategic action plans** are based on overall organizational features, resources, and the environment. They establish long-term, corporatewide actions designed to accomplish the company's mission and major objectives. An important emphasis at this level is linking the action plans of different organizational functions and units so that they reinforce the strategies adopted by the entire organization.

To be effective, a strategic action plan should meet the following criteria:

1. *Proactivity,* which is the degree to which the strategic action plan takes a long-term view of the future and actively moves the company forward in the desired direction.

2. *Congruency,* or the extent to which the strategic action plan fits with organizational characteristics and the external environment (see Chapter 7).

3. *Synergy,* or the integration of the efforts of various organizational subunits to better accomplish corporatewide business objectives.

4 Learning Objective Check-In

Hickory, Norman & Schultz (HN&S) have various objectives that they want to pursue. For example, the firm wants to achieve a 15 percent increase in profitability on all new products in the next three years. This, in conjunction with rapid market share growth in China and parts of Africa, represents the most important objective for the firm. HN&S is concerned over the method it used to develop these objectives and which it plans to use to achieve them. Its concern is that 15 percent is too conservative a profitability increase and things like customer goodwill—intangibles—will be ignored throughout this process.

1. *The 15 percent increase in profitability on all new products in the next three years represents _____ in the objectives.*
   a. *priority*
   b. *quality*
   c. *specificity and measurability*
   d. *challenge*

2. *The profitability increase and market share growth in China and Africa represent _____.*
   a. *quality*
   b. *priority*
   c. *challenge*
   d. *specificity and measurability*

3. *Based on what you know about the concerns the company has about the method it is using to develop and implement the achievement of these objectives, the company is likely using _____.*
   a. *Total Quality Management*
   b. *Management by Objectives*
   c. *the Balanced Scorecard Approach*
   d. *the Strategic Action Plan Approach*

TACTICAL ACTION PLANS   **Tactical action plans** are developed at the division or department level. They specify the activities that must be performed, when they must be completed, and the resources a division or department will need to complete the portions of the strategic action plan under its purview. The primary criterion of effectiveness for tactical action plans is the extent to which they contribute to the achievement of the company's strategic objectives. In general, tactical action plans cover a period of one to two years. Two important aspects of tactical action plans are division of labor and budgeting.

The formal assignment of authority and responsibility to job holders is referred to as **division of labor.** This helps ensure that tasks of job holders are appropriate for accomplishing the overall plan of the division or the department, which in turn should support the organization's strategic action plans. Common ways to change organizational design to achieve strategic action plans include:

- Assigning more job positions in the organization to work crucial to the attainment of strategic objectives.
- Creating specialized job positions that emphasize work crucial to the attainment of strategic objectives.
- Assigning work crucial to the attainment of strategic objectives to high-level job positions.[23]

division of labor

The production process in which each worker repeats one step over and over, achieving greater efficiencies in the use of time and knowledge; also, the formal assignment of authority and responsibility to job holders.

By controlling and allocating funds, **budgeting** becomes an integral part of tactical action plans. Budgeting provides information about the strategic direction of the firm, makes clear the contribution to strategic objectives, forces budget committees to carefully ponder strategic perspectives to decide whether to accept or reject each proposal, and creates monitoring devices to examine the extent to which the projected contribution to strategic objectives is actually realized.

Managers and/or employees may also be asked to participate in the budget-setting process. Involving them promotes better understanding of the tactical action plan by those who will be carrying it out. It can also improve acceptance of decisions and commitment to them. Employee involvement may take a variety of forms, including:

- Creating budget forecasts.
- Preparing budget proposals.
- Allocating the overall budget to various activities.
- Developing significant rewards for reaching budgetary targets, such as bonuses, pay increases, and recognition at special events.
- Transferring resources from one activity to another in the event of unforeseen circumstances.

budgeting

Controlling and allocating the firm's funds; *variable budgeting* allows for deviations between planned output and actual output by considering the fact that variable costs depend on the level of output, whereas fixed costs do not; *moving budgeting* creates a tentative budget for a fixed period of time and then revises and updates it on a periodic basis to take changes into account.

Budgets are based on forecasts, which in turn depend on assumptions about the future. For example, a production budget for a two-year period is projected by estimating the costs of materials, labor, and capital equipment required to produce an expected sales level. The assumptions made about both sales levels and the required resources could be wrong. The sales volume could be higher or lower than expected. Market demand, competitors' pricing, shifts in consumer tastes, and interest rates all affect sales. The resources needed depend on such factors as economies of scale, efficiency of production, introduction of new technology, and the cost of supplies. For instance, using copper instead of aluminum to make microchips cut IBM's and Intel's production costs of microchips almost in half in the late 1990s. On the other hand, the cost of wood almost doubled in 1995 and 1996, greatly increasing construction costs for home builders.

table 5.1

An Example of a Variable Budget

Output (units)	2,000	2,200	2,400	2,600
Sales (at $10.00 per unit)	$20,000	$22,000	$24,000	$26,000
Variable costs (at $6.00 per unit)	12,000	13,200	14,400	15,600
Fixed costs	2,000	2,000	2,000	2,000
Total costs	14,000	15,200	16,400	17,600
Planned profit	$ 6,000	$ 6,800	$ 7,600	$ 8,400

Two budgeting techniques are designed to be more flexible: variable budgeting and moving budgeting. *Variable budgeting* accounts for deviations between planned output and actual output because variable costs depend on the level of output, whereas fixed costs do not. For instance, plant and equipment are fixed costs, because the firm pays principal, interest, and maintenance on those assets even when they are not being utilized at full capacity.

Variable budgets take into account the dependance of anticipated profits on the expected relationship between costs and output. A variable budget recognizes that planned profit and total costs do not vary proportionately with sales. The hypothetical variable budget in Table 5.1 above shows how an increase in output of 30 percent, from 2,000 units to 2,600 units, can produce an increase in profits of 40 percent. To be accurate, variable budgeting also needs to consider how the cost of different inputs co-vary as a function of output level. For example, as output increases, administrative office support decreases as a percentage of total operating costs.

In contrast to variable budgeting, *moving budgeting* creates a tentative budget for a fixed period of time, normally a year. The budget is then revised and updated on a periodic basis to take changes into account. Reexamining the premises, assumptions, and estimates made when the tentative budget was initially created allows the budget to be a living, flexible document.

One downside of moving budgets is that they demand frequent revisions, requiring employees to spend additional time on the budgeting process. Also, some managers attempt to secure more resources by arguing that the financial resources originally received were inadequate.

Firms need to be careful that managers do not become obsessed with numbers and dollars, ignoring more "intangible" aspects of performance that in the long run are critical for financial success. For example, quality, customer service, employee commitment, innovation and creativity, reputation, consumer loyalty, and ability to attract and retain top talent may suffer if managers only receive pay raises and positive performance evaluations for strictly adhering to the budget.

OPERATIONAL ACTION PLANS   Line managers and employees directly responsible for individual tasks or activities are the ones who create **operational action plans.** These plans tend to be narrowly focused on resources, methods, timelines, and quality control issues for a particular kind of operation. In general, the time frame for operational action plans is shorter than for tactical action plans.

Figure 5.5 on page 206 illustrates a typical operation. Inputs (human, financial, raw materials, and other resources) are transformed (through assembly, chemical treatment, combination with other elements) into outcomes (products or services). The control component includes information about the required characteristics of

operational action plan

A management plan normally created by line managers and employees directly responsible for carrying out certain tasks or activities.

FIGURE 5.5

A Typical Operating System

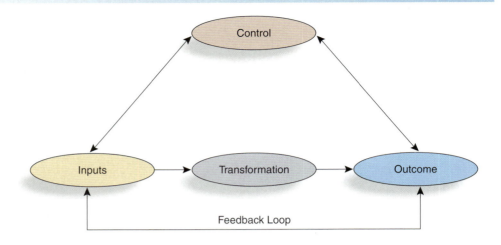

Control

Inputs → Transformation → Outcome

Feedback Loop

Few companies had operational plans as flexible as FedEx's proved to be in the aftermath of Hurricane Katrina. One senior technical adviser in the firm was even able to mobilize enough spare parts to repair a nine-foot FedEx radio antenna atop a 54-story New Orleans building, allowing not just FedEx but also the Army and other rescue groups to restore vital basic communications in the days after the storm. Still, FedEx took lessons away from its Katrina experience: Arrange in advance to house employees displaced by a disaster, and stock up on satellite phones, not cellphones.

Project Planning

inputs and outputs and how inputs must be modified to produce outputs. It ensures that the quantity and quality of inputs and outputs fall within certain parameters and that costs remain within a stipulated budget. Feedback is returned from output to transformation and input, so that continuing improvement may be achieved by using resources more efficiently. Any activity creating an output that affects tactical action plans and that uses significant resources can be analyzed using this general model.

The main challenge of operational planning is using resources most efficiently. For instance, when the primary resource of an operation such as an R&D facility is people's know-how, operational plans may focus on how to transform employees' knowledge to produce an innovation (outcome). The goal should be to use these resources efficiently to generate innovations that add value to the company's overall operation.

When the relationship between resources and outcomes is uncertain, the control function must allow substantial latitude for failure. This is the case, for instance, in most pharmaceutical firms. There is typically less than a 10 percent chance of getting a therapeutic protein that works in the animal-disease model to market. The human testing required for approval takes at least six to eight years to complete. A particular drug may be dropped out during any of the three phases of clinical trials for reasons ranging from lack of efficacy to high toxicity.[24]

If properly conducted, operational planning offers several benefits to organizations, including:

- The opportunity to use feedback for continued incremental learning.
- The ability to visualize alternative types of operations—that is, alternative ways to use resources to create a product or service.
- The ability to predict the effects of modifications in operations on the efficiency of operations.
- The ability to evaluate the effectiveness of operations.

A more specific set of operational planning techniques have been developed in an area called *project management*. As the name implies, a project is a set of tasks designed to achieve certain objectives. In most cases, projects are completed by teams. Project management planning techniques allow one to identify specific tasks to be done, when they need to be completed, the resources required, and to document what has been accomplished so far. There are now many powerful Web-based programs that managers and team members can use to schedule project tasks, monitor them from start to finish, and report variances from expected results. Figure 5.6 on page 208 shows a description of one program, called Intuit QuickBase.

Implementation

Planning is meaningless unless it can be carried out successfully. The implementation phase is a critical part of the planning process. Implementation involves defining tasks to be accomplished, assigning individual responsibilities for those tasks, and managing individuals to ensure that the tasks are appropriately completed.

One distinction that is often made is between *standing plans* and *single-use plans*. **Standing plans** regulate situations that occur repeatedly. That is, they are plans created to help the organization deal with issues that come up on a regular basis. Organizations implement standing plans using a programmed approach that includes policies, rules, and standard operating procedures. A **policy** is a general guide for managers and employees to follow. For instance, an organization with a flexible work hours policy provides employees with the opportunity to choose when to come to work and when to go home. A **rule** is a formal, written statement that states the general permissible bounds for the application of particular policies. For instance, a rule might be that employees need to arrive at work between the hours of 7 and 9 in the morning and work for nine consecutive hours, including a half-hour lunch and two 15-minute breaks. A standard operating procedure (SOP) describes in detail the precise steps to be followed in a specific situation. For instance, an SOP may specify that each employee must punch a time clock upon arriving at work, check with the supervisor, file a work plan for the day, and complete a computerized report at the end of the day that documents the percentage of time devoted to each major task and what he or she accomplished. In other words, employees are expected to show up for work regularly so standing plans may be developed to provide work scheduling flexibility and ensure that employees are there when they are supposed to be, do what they are supposed to do, and provide enough information to others so that supervisors and co-workers know the status of various tasks assigned to them.

5 Learning Objective Check-In

Nalgen, a chemical engineering firm, knows the value of developing action plans. It has several criteria for different levels of action plans at the firm. First, the top executives develop plans that are proactive, that fit with the external environment, and that actually integrate the efforts of various subunits. The action plans developed at the department level have to specify what activities are to be performed, when they are to be completed, and what specific resources will be required to complete the tasks involved. One very important facet of the departmental planning includes controlling and allocating the firm's variable costs, which depend on the level of output. The last areas where action plans are needed are mainly in product conversion.

1. *At Nalgen, the top executives are designing _____ to fit with the external environment.*
   a. *operational action plans*
   b. *budgets*
   c. *strategic action plans*
   d. *tactical action plans*
2. *The departmental plans specifying resources required can also be referred to as _____.*
   a. *strategic action plans*
   b. *tactical action plans*
   c. *operational action plans*
   d. *unit action plans*
3. *Controlling and allocating variable costs is part of _____.*
   a. *operational action plans*
   b. *variable budgeting*
   c. *moving budgeting*
   d. *the division of labor*
4. *Which type of action plan is involved with product conversion?*
   a. *Operational action plans*
   b. *Tactical action plans*
   c. *Unit action plans*
   d. *Strategic action plans*

standing plans

Plans created to help the organization deal with issues that come up on a regular basis.

policy

A general guide for managers and employees to follow.

rule

Written statement of the general permissible bounds for the application of particular policies.

FIGURE 5.6

Intuit QuickBase

Source: www.quickbase.com/.

> *"With our company, 'QuickBase' has crossed over from a noun to a verb."*
> —*Dr. Scott Friedman*
>
> *Got a vital project? Now you can QuickBase it.*
>
> *Project managers—those busy conductors of the office orchestra—now have a powerful Web-based solution that is simple enough for the whole team to use. QuickBase lets managers create a central online home for all their project data: project schedules, documents, issue lists, team rosters, information of all kinds. Everyone on the team can see and update current versions, so they're always on task and in sync.*
>
> *Now you can manage your project to success with our dedicated <u>Project Manager</u>* application, which puts all the tools you need in one simple-to-use solution. Suddenly, life for the project manager just got easier.
>
> With <u>Project Manager,</u> you get:
>
> - **True accountability.** Everyone can see what's due and when. Updates and changes are available immediately. No more excuses.
>
> - **Better collaboration.** Critical documents are never trapped on anyone's hard drive. Since QuickBase is Web-based, everyone on your team can use it anytime and anywhere they have Web access.
>
> - **More time saved.** The familiar Web interface makes using QuickBase as easy as clicking a mouse. Your team spends less time e-mailing documents and more time on the job.
>
> - **Immediate results.** Get your team up and running in minutes—no need to order, distribute and install new software. With QuickBase, everything you and your team need is instantly available on the Web.

single-use plans

Plans implemented for unusual or one-of-a kind situations.

Single-use plans are implemented for unusual or one-of-a-kind situations. For example, one of NASA's major goals was to reach the moon, which involved the design and construction of a lunar module to take astronauts to the moon and bring them back to earth safely.

Keep in mind that effective planning is not a lonely activity carried out by experts or by a few executives at the top of the organizational pyramid. Most successful business plans require a team effort with a great deal of coordination and integration across departmental and organizational levels. Management Is Everyone's Business 5.2 on page 209 provides a set of recommendations that teams should consider when involved in the planning process.

In the end, all plans must be implemented by people. Plan implementation requires thinking about four major issues: the means of implementation, a process for organizational problems solving, the linking of planning with organizational control systems, and mechanisms for dealing with organizational change.

MEANS OF IMPLEMENTATION   Managers must find a way to induce people to take the necessary steps to accomplish the planned actions. Four major approaches may be used: authority, persuasion, policy, and feedback mechanism.

Authority   Authority is formal power. It is accorded to the position rather than the person. As part of plan implementation, the employee at each position is vested with the authority to make certain decisions and is held accountable for those decisions. Subordinates are expected to comply with the requests of people in positions of authority unless they are asked to do something that is unethical or illegal.

Persuasion   While most firms rely on some form of authority structure to ensure employee compliance with planned actions, a plan that is acceptable to employees increases commitment to that plan. Persuasion is an important aspect of

Working as a Team   Teams require a great deal of coordination and integration to function effectively. Otherwise, many hours may be lost in activities, meetings, and communication that lead nowhere. This not only wastes time, but it can also result in frustration, poor morale, lack of credibility, and high employee turnover. A sound planning process can help teams define what they are trying to accomplish and develop mechanisms to achieve objectives in a more efficient manner, keeping confusion to a minimum. As part of the planning process, teams should:

- Ensure that work done by the team fits with overall organizational objectives and those of other pertinent teams and units within the firm.

- Set up an effective communication system to keep others informed of what the team is trying to accomplish and any particular issues that are relevant to other teams and units within the firm (for instance, unexpected glitches that may make it difficult to meet deadlines and hence affect other teams whose work is interdependent). An inexpensive Web-based log can be very helpful in this regard and does not require a lot of time and paperwork.

- Allow for emergence of spontaneous teams that were not part of the original plan but which may offer innovative insights or come up with creative solutions to unexpected roadblocks found along the way.

- Establish a clear reason for the team's existence, including goals to be accomplished, timelines, means to evaluate attainment of team objectives, and "sunset" rules to determine when it might be a good time for the team to disband.

- When appropriate, create planning teams whereby planning experts (who might be planning specialists who report directly to top executives or hired outside consultants) work with groups of managers and key employees from major divisions or departments to come up with their own goals or plans. This tends to foster creativity yet helps ensure coordination of decentralized plans so the efforts of the entire organization move in the same direction.

effectively implementing plans. Employees who are convinced of the merits of a plan are more likely to respond enthusiastically to directives of managers who have formal authority and to "go beyond the call of duty" in finding better ways to effectively execute the plan.

Persuasion in most companies requires employee involvement rather than a manager simply making a speech extolling the virtues of a particular plan. For example, to become a change agent during Kellogg's conversion from cereal company to snack-foods company in the first decade of the century, CEO Carlos Gutierrez (who later became U.S. Commerce Secretary) encouraged communication instead of Kellogg's traditional top-down approach. Previously, new product ideas had been presented only at monthly meetings and only by the head of research and development. Gutierrez opened himself up to hearing from people, and now technicians from the company's three-year-old, $75 million W. K. Kellogg Institute for Food and Nutritional Research can bring their ideas directly to him.[25]

Policy   Both formal authority and persuasion must operate within a general institutional context that governs the relations and actions of individuals responsible for implementing the plan. To this end, organizations develop policies that define appropriate and inappropriate behavior. These guidelines usually appear in a formal document to ensure that relevant policy information is communicated to all individuals involved. Effective policies are flexible, comprehensive, coordinated with subunits whose actions are interrelated, ethical, and written clearly and logically.

Feedback Mechanism   Successful plan implementation requires a continuous flow of information that is used to determine to what extent the plan is being carried out as expected. It is also important to assess how and why individual activities are helping attain company objectives. If the information sought is threatening to people, then knowledge sharing, constructive analysis, and a spirit of open inquiry are inhibited. Active employee involvement includes initiative, honest discussion of ideas, and generation of inputs or suggestions from the "bottom up." The learning that occurs is a crucial part of problem solving during the plan implementation phase.

A PROCESS FOR ORGANIZATIONAL PROBLEM SOLVING   Plan implementation seldom, if ever, occurs smoothly. Many unknowns must be dealt with. Part of an effective implementation program is establishment of a system that allows for a careful diagnosis of problems so that individuals responsible for carrying out the plan can learn from their mistakes. A six-stage approach may be used to facilitate this problem-solving process:[26]

1. *Identify performance gaps.* A diagnosis begins with a manager and a team defining the difference or shortfall between objectives and achievements. This step must not become part of such personnel decisions as merit pay, performance appraisal, and promotion. Doing so dampens people's willingness to be self-critical and openly share information.

2. *Identify tasks and work processes necessary for accomplishing the plan.* This requires defining what each individual is expected to do, the sequence of tasks, and the degree of interdependence or integration among the critical tasks needed to ensure successful execution of the plan. For instance, some key managers faced the following tasks:

    At Medtek, Torrance realized that if he were to be successful at developing innovative new products, his laboratory would have to be world-class in chemical and hydraulic technologies and be able to link these technologies to manufacturing and marketing requirements. For Chow at BOC, a critical task identified for delivering customized service to global customers was close integration across geographically dispersed organizations. With the Grenzach team's goal of reducing costs, the critical tasks were to maintain the functional excellence within the plant as well as to increase integration across the functional areas.[27]

3. *Check for organizational congruence.* Once the tasks and work processes have been identified, it is necessary to determine the extent to which other organizational elements support or hinder their attainment. In other words, it is important to know if the planned activity is aligned or fits with organizational structure, culture, human resource policies, and individual competencies and motives. If these organizational building blocks are incongruent with task requirements, the planned activities are likely to fail.

4. *If any incongruencies or inconsistencies are found, intervene to create alignment in order to effectively implement the plan.* In general, incremental changes, such as modifying the incentive system, can be accomplished without

PLANNING AND PERFORMANCE

Browse through several issues of major financial newspapers or business periodicals that provide in-depth coverage of firms, such as *The Wall Street Journal*, *BusinessWeek*, *Fortune*, or *Forbes*. Select five to ten firms that are in the news. Research these firms' recent activities and answer the following questions.

1. How did the planning process affect these companies' performance?

2. How could better planning have helped their performance?

actually reconsidering the feasibility of the plan itself. But if there is systemwide lack of congruence that requires extensive changes in formal organizational arrangements, culture, and people, it probably means that the plan is impractical. In such a case, the entire plan needs to be reconsidered and better adjusted to organizational realities.

5. *Execute the plan.* At this stage, managers and employees take actions targeted at achieving the key milestones of the plan, ideally reinforced by congruent organizational arrangements, culture, and people who facilitate the execution of those actions.

6. *Learn from the consequences.* This is an ongoing process during plan implementation. It is used to diagnose the causes of performance gaps, anticipate what may cause problems in the future, and reveal better ways of doing things. Skills for Managing 5.2 above asks you to select five to ten firms that are in the news and analyze how the planning process may have affected their performance and how their planning process may have been improved.

LINKING OF PLANNING WITH ORGANIZATIONAL CONTROL SYSTEMS

Planning and the organizational control system should go hand in hand. As noted above in the section regarding operational action plans, an effective control system alerts managers when something is going wrong and provides them the opportunity to respond. Once plans are formulated and carried out, an effective control system allows the organization to compare planned objectives with observed results. If there is a significant discrepancy between expected and actual results, then managers should take corrective action in order to improve future plans and make modifications to those plans being implemented. It is wise to leave open the possibility of abandoning existing plans and replacing them with new ones when the control system indicates that there is a high deviation of expected versus actual results.

MECHANISMS TO DEAL WITH ORGANIZATIONAL CHANGE

Most plans require changes in the way things are currently done. This is particularly true if the firm is attempting to shift direction or is operating in a turbulent

5.1

manager's notebook

- *Participation involvement co-optation.* The most positive method of getting powerful individuals on board is to solicit their involvement in planning and directing the change effort. The greater their degree of involvement, the more chance they have to put their own stamp on the change, and the more they own and become committed to it.

- *Incentives.* Rewards and punishments are another powerful way to shape desired behaviors. To the extent that participants see no incentive (or worse, are penalized) for supporting the change, it is reasonable for them to resist. So it is critical to be clear about current versus future rewards.

- *Exchange.* Like political systems, organizations are filled with exchange relationships: I do you a favor, you do me a favor. Indeed, reciprocity exists worldwide and tends to balance out over time. All managers need to have a bank account of favors owed them. These favors can be called in during times of change.

- *Isolation.* To the extent that key individuals continue to resist the change, they can be either socially or physically isolated.

- *Removal or transfer.* Key antagonists who cannot be converted to supporters may have to be removed. If politically powerful opponents are permitted to actively or passively resist the change, they may encourage others to resist and form coalitions to blunt the change.

Source: Adapted from M. L. Tushman and C. A. O'Reilly III, *Winning through Innovation: A Practical Guide to Leading Organizational Change and Renewal.* Boston: Harvard Business School Press, 1997.

environment. There are three major challenges in trying to simultaneously implement a plan and manage change associated with its implementation: (1) dealing with power and politics, (2) reducing individual anxiety and resistance, and (3) maintaining control during the transition period. If managers can successfully handle these challenges, employees are likely to be eager to implement the plan and to make accommodations to ensure a smooth transition. If ignored, these three factors can stop the successful implementation of even the most carefully drawn plans.

Managing the Political Dynamics of Change Practically every significant change results in politics and resistance. Managing politics can be accomplished in a number of ways, including enlisting the support of key players, being consistent, and ensuring stability.

It is important for managers to mobilize the support of key players. First, the manager must identify the people who have the power to make or break the change and who control critical resources or expertise. Once the pivotal individuals are identified, it is necessary to ascertain how the change will likely affect each of them, how each is likely to react to the change, and the methods available to influence them. As shown in Manager's Notebook 5.1 above, managers can use a variety of approaches to influence key players. In descending order of desirability, these include active participation of all affected by the changes, rewards and punishment, reciprocity, and isolation and/or removal of those who continue to resist the change.

In managing the dynamics of change, managers must attempt to ensure consistency in words and actions. To prevent cynicism among those responsible for implementing the plan, what managers say is important must be congruent with the actions taken or being reinforced. If a plan calls for close cooperation among individuals and units, rewarding only individual actions would generate mixed messages, and employees might resist the change. Managers can use a number of symbolic activities and mechanisms to influence planned actions, including how they spend their time, the types of questions they ask, what they follow up on, what they discuss at meetings, the types of things they choose to summarize, how they use language, the type of special events they provide, and the new heroes and myths they create to illustrate the change in standards and direction.[28]

Finally, managers must build in stability. People can absorb only so much change at once, and it is necessary to create stability during the implementation. This requires sending consistent messages—signals—to lessen uncertainty:

> *Part of this signaling is to be clear about what is not changing—what people can hold onto in the future. If some aspects of culture, physical location, and staffing patterns will not change, these anchors to the past need to be communicated and reinforced early on. At Alcoa, even in the context of wholesale change, managers made it clear that the glorious Alcoa engineering heritage and its commitment to high-quality aluminum would not change. As Kodak [has refocused], George Fisher has reemphasized the firm's commitment to the photographic market and signaled an end to diversification. Clarity about what will not change helps moderate fears of the future.[29]*

Managing Individual Resistance   Organizational change can generate individual anxiety and stress. Up to a point this energizes employees, and their attentiveness and motivation increase. Too much stress, however, causes individuals to oppose change, leading them to try to block the plan or to leave in search of better employment prospects elsewhere. Dysfunctional anxiety can be reduced by showing people why the change needs to occur, making them stakeholders in the change effort through active participation, recognizing and rewarding the new behaviors required by the plan, and providing opportunities to disengage from the past at public events such as lunches, ceremonies, and employee skits.

Maintaining Control during the Transition   The turbulence and uncertainty associated with the change should not be allowed to result in chaos. Both for operational and political reasons, it is important for managers to convey the idea that the situation is under control during the transition period. This can be done by communicating a clear idea of the future state, using multiple methods to promote change, designing transition management structures, setting transition milestones, and measuring progress on a continuing basis.[30]

To close this chapter, we'll note that while the planning process should not be a top-down exercise, managers still play a key role in mustering planning efforts so that these can be shepherded in an orderly fashion. Management Is Everyone's Business 5.3 on page 214 offers a set of suggestions that managers should follow to help fulfill this role.

Working as a Manager   Managers are expected to collaborate with employees to define objectives for their units and to clearly communicate the relative importance of those objectives. Once the objectives are established, managers need to develop a plan to accomplish them and lay out the steps of implementation. This process provides a frame of reference that can facilitate orderly change and avoid unnecessary disruptions and turmoil when unexpected changes occur. In other words, a quality planning process is useful to the manager precisely because it smooths the way change is conducted and gives employees a sense of confidence and continuity even in the midst of rapid change. As a manager engaged in planning you should:

- Keep a pulse on what customers want and be on the lookout for changing consumer desires that might affect your company's business. The best of plans are useless if these are not designed to meet certain objectives that are important to those who are likely to invest in the company's products and services.
- Ensure that planning in your area of responsibility is closely linked with the rest of the organization.
  - If you are a top manager, planning emphasis should be on broad objectives to guide the entire organization and overall allocation of resources to support accomplishment of those objectives.
  - If you are a middle manager, emphasis should be on tactical plans that allow you to best utilize people and resources under your control to support the firm's general plan.
  - If you are a first-line supervisor or a lower-level manager, emphasis should be on drawing specific action steps to complete assigned objectives of your unit, including precise scheduling, concrete tasks to be accomplished, budgeting, assigning responsibilities to each subordinate and the like.
- Establish an effective goal-driven plan.
  - Goals should be specific and measurable so that people know what is expected and how success or failure will be evaluated.
  - Goals should be prioritized to ensure that most important ones are given greatest attention.
  - Goals should be challenging but attainable.
  - Goals should have a time horizon in order to facilitate scheduling and motivate individuals to have a sense of urgency.
  - Goal achievement should be evaluated and rewarded, with appropriate feedback given to all employees who were involved in the process.
- Ensure that planning does not become a straightjacket.
  - Plans are seldom carried out as originally intended because of the unexpected. Hence, you need to think about "what if" and have backup plans just in case.
  - Be ready for a rapid response that may be needed under changing circumstances (for example, priorities may need to be readjusted quickly in response to a competitor's move).
- Engage others in plan design and implementation.
  - Plans are a poor motivational tool unless managers and employees truly believe that such plans are a good idea and become committed to them. Unfortunately, many business plans end up collecting dust in drawers because plan designers never secured the necessary "buy in" from those supposed to carry them out.
  - Encourage spontaneous inputs from employees and outsiders that might help you develop a more realistic plan, and perhaps reconsider the wisdom of a particular plan.

CONCLUDING THOUGHTS

Now that you've had the opportunity to learn about the benefits and pitfalls of planning, as well as the elements that contribute to a successful plan, let's revisit the critical thinking questions raised at the beginning of this chapter. Disney could have prevented the fiasco of the New Year's holiday in Hong Kong by looking more carefully into the length of the holiday and making sure its discount tickets were void for the entire week. Nevertheless, the company got many things right in creating the park, including learning from the mistakes it made in Paris and giving cultural sensitivity a much higher priority when moving abroad. Local language, customs, food, and customer preferences for entertainment were studied and honored, with the help of input from local residents and experts.

The new park was planned on many levels. A strategic decision was made to enter the Asian market and Hong Kong was chosen as the first site. Tactical plans probably governed the design of the park, its size, features, and attractions. Finally, operational plans covered such individual issues as hiring policies and the issuing of discount tickets.

Disney is planning far into the future when it anticipates expanding its Asian operations. The longer the time period, the greater the uncertainty. Promising opportunities today may dry up in a few years. For instance, competitors characteristically move in quickly and the market for a new product or service can quickly become saturated. For this reason, company leaders must anticipate future opportunities so that the organization can take advantage of them when the time comes. If the company anticipates threats and opportunities, Disney's massive investment in the Chinese market may provide impressive payoffs in the years ahead.

The setting of long-term objectives, such as for continued growth in Asia, gives the firm concrete targets that outline the steps needed to accomplish them. Objectives also provide criteria against which to assess whether or not actual performance was satisfactory or unsatisfactory so that corrective steps (and perhaps a redefinition of objectives) may be undertaken. This is what Disney was forced to do in Paris. On the other hand, the setting of objectives can be dangerous if it robs the firm of flexibility to make necessary changes and if managers believe that they have to play a "numbers game" to meet numerical targets.

Focusing on the Future: Using Management Theory in Daily Life

Managing the Planning Process

Mary Kelley thought that she was just going for an informational getaway when she attended an Esalen seminar on brainwave biofeedback in 2002. Instead, she met Robert deStefano, and Sleep Garden, Inc., was born. Today, Mary handles public relations, operations, accounting, fulfillment, and a multitude of other tasks in her role as entrepreneur. Robert acts as creative director, advertising manager, and chief salesperson for the company. Together, they produce noningestible sleep aids (typically CDs and DVDs) which are clinically proven to help people fall asleep and stay asleep without drugs.

When creating her company, Mary followed the four key elements of a plan: objectives, actions, resources, and implementation.

Objectives   In their early conversations, Mary and Robert spent a lot of time trying to decide exactly what the company was supposed to do. They developed three key objectives. Sleep Garden exists to: (1) Provide a natural alternative to drugs and ingestibles (herbs, melatonin, etc.) used in promoting sleep; (2) Make these alternatives available and accessible to a mass market; and (3) Deliver a high quality product. While their objectives have stayed the same over time, Mary and Robert must frequently reevaluate how to achieve those objectives. For example, they have changed their packaging and price structure to more effectively deliver products to consumers. Sometimes, however, they know that what they're doing is exactly right. One of the first

300 products they sold went to Beulah Mae, a lady in Louisiana who never would have had the opportunity to attend a seminar on California's central coast. Clearly, Sleep Garden products are now accessible to a mass market.

Actions   Mary and Robert based their actions on the results of an environmental scan (described in Chapter 7) to see if their venture might work. Once they had convinced themselves that Sleep Garden was a marketable idea, they set about enhancing their product for delivery to customers. The first step was to conduct clinical trials—could a CD with music designed to alter brainwaves actually help induce sleep? Tests showed that their product was viable, and the next step was packaging. Sleep Garden's first product was a 3 CD/book set that retailed for $59.95. While initial sales were good, they were not spectacular, and feedback from retailers gave the entrepreneurs important information. First, the product was 8 inches by 8 inches by 1.5 inches—too big for most retail shelves. Second, the box containing the product was not completely full, so it crushed in the warehouse. Finally, the $59.95 price was too high for consumers who might be interested in the idea, but not willing to invest over $60 for something they had never encountered before. Mary and Robert learned that they needed to talk with retailers in addition to end consumers when designing their product; and that was the action they took next.

Advertising the new products was another important action. Mary describes their different advertising strategies—everything from an Internet Web site to mass advertising in print, radio and catalogs. Some worked, and others were expensive failures, but each advertising campaign taught the duo important lessons. Each creative, packaging, production, distribution, and advertising decision required that Mary and Robert reassess and reallocate their resources—the third element of a successful plan.

Resource Allocation   Like most entrepreneurs, Mary and Robert were their own most important resources. Each of them brought different skills to the company. Robert, with his background in advertising, was a creative driving force whose contributions included everything from package design to video direction and postproduction. Mary, whose background was in areas as varied as ancient Mesopotamian art, business, and technology, brought funding and a willingness to tackle databases, scientific sleep research, public relations, operations, accounting, and order fulfillment. She even answered the Sleep Garden 800 number for a time. According to Mary, the most important resources the team brought to the project were their respective networks—the contacts each of them had built up over 20-year careers.

Despite their skills, Mary and Robert knew that they would have to outsource some work if their company was to be successful. They invested in artists (a composer and a yoga instructor), product development advisors, packaging printers, advertising placement, and CD/DVD manufacturers—all of whom had a role to play in getting their product to market.

Implementation   During the implementation process, Robert and Mary divided the tasks of running the business. Robert, with his strong graphic design and copywriting skills, worked on product development and copy for everything from packaging to advertising to Web site content. He also used his background in producing commercials to direct and do postproduction work on the yoga video that was to become one of Sleep Garden's biggest products. Mary did proofreading, because even the most creative artist needs a second pair of eyes. In addition, she created a direct marketing database and the Sleep Garden Web site, while at the same time handling accounting. Because of her previous experience in academic and marketing research, she was responsible for scouring the Web to find information on the latest sleep research and technologies. She also oversaw all of the clinical trials to determine whether or not Sleep Garden products actually worked.

Mary set up task lists for every phase of the business. Using project planning software, she created Gantt charts that let the partners know when they were dangerously overcommitted and helped them to see what could realistically be done in any given amount of time. Despite the charts, Mary and Robert soon learned the critical need for flexibility when implementing their plans. After the production of their first CD set, they parted ways with the person who had performed on those CDs—leaving them to find new artists who could help them to move their company forward.

Mary stresses that the implementation of their objectives has gone more smoothly because she and Robert have complementary, not similar, skills. While they don't always agree, the two partners know that their perspectives can be merged to give a more complete picture of any business issue. Together, they are turning Sleep Garden into a growing concern with good prospects for the future.

summary of learning objectives

1   Identify the different elements of an effective plan.

- **Objectives**. Goals or targets to be accomplished.
- **Actions**. Specific steps needed to achieve the stated objectives.
- **Resource allocation**. Necessary financial and human resources to carry out the planned activities.
- **Implementation guidelines**. A description of how intended actions will be executed.

2   Analyze the advantages and disadvantages of planning, and identify how planning pitfalls can be avoided.

- *Benefits of planning*. These include assessing external forces, developing a sense of direction, identifying the factors that affect the organization, encouraging participation, coordinating efforts, establishing priorities, focusing attention on different time horizons, understanding circumstances contributing to past success or failure, ensuring the availability of adequate resources, establishing performance standards, supporting organizational control systems, developing "what if" scenarios, and management development.
- *Pitfalls of planning*. These include poor forecasts of future conditions, plans imposed from above, planning as a self-contained activity, extensive bureaucratization, and inflexible adherence to objectives and processes.
- *Avoiding planning pitfalls*. Managers can overcome disadvantages of planning by involving different organizational levels, using both numerical and judgmental methods, viewing planning as continuous and capable of adapting to change, avoiding paralysis of the analysis, and concentrating on a manageable set of issues.

3   Distinguish between formal and informal planning.

- **Formal planning**. A well-defined set of objectives, action plans, resource allocation procedures, and implementation guidelines, usually in a written document.
- **Opportunistic planning**. Programmatic actions to respond to unforeseen circumstances.

4   Recognize the features of well-designed objectives.

- *Cascading of objectives*. In general, objectives are broader at the top of the organization and become more specific at lower organization levels.
- *Specificity and measurability*. By knowing what is expected and how expectations will be measured, managers and employees can focus on the most important actions, thereby concentrating on achieving the best results.
- *Difficulty*. Challenging yet achievable objectives induce employees to work harder to use their full potential.
- *Milestones*. Timetables and deadlines serve to motivate individuals to try harder.
- *Priorities*. Ranking of objectives in order of importance.

5   Identify the various types of action plans that managers can use to accomplish stated objectives.

- **Strategic plans**. The primary purpose is to link the action plans of different organizational functions and units so that they can help support the business strategy adopted by the entire corporation.
- **Tactical plans**. Divisions or department leaders must decide what activities should be performed, when those activities should be completed, and what resources to allocate to accomplish them. This includes defining the responsibilities of jobholders and controlling and allocating resources through the budgeting process.

- **Operational plans**. Employees directly responsible for carrying out activities should develop systems to transform resources into products or services, including a control component to ensure that quantity and quality of inputs and outputs meet established criteria within budget constraints.

discussion questions

1. What types of firms are most likely to benefit from a formal planning process? What types are most likely to face the planning misfires discussed in this chapter?

2. Of all the planning benefits discussed in this chapter, which ones do you think are most important? Why?

3. How would you rank the relative difficulty of carrying out the five approaches to successful planning discussed in this chapter? Explain your choices.

4. Take a look at the list of ethics-related questions pertaining to planning in Manager's Checkup 5.1. Can you think of any specific situations (for instance, a plan that might involve extensive layoffs) where these issues become very important? Explain.

5. Based on Management Close-up 5.2, how do you think technology is likely to change strategic, tactical, and operational action plans in the future? Explain your answer.

6. Among the four means of implementation discussed in this chapter, which are easiest to use? Which are most difficult? Why?

7. Which of the six steps in the organizational problem-solving scheme presented in this chapter is most likely to fail? Why? What should a firm do to prevent this potential failure?

8. Some people argue that managing the political dynamics of change is likely to backfire, since employees may see it as an attempt to manipulate. Do you agree? Why or why not?

management minicase 5.1

Newspapers: A Plan That Seemed like a Godsend Is Turning Sour

The latest circulation figures for U.S. newspapers show a continued decline in the number of readers at almost all major publications, such as *USA Today*, *The Wall Street Journal*, the *Los Angeles Times*, *Washington Post*, and *Houston Chronicle*. Weekday circulation of more than 700 newspapers nationwide has showed almost a 20 percent drop during the past 10 years or so. Circulation figures are important because they are used to set advertising rates, a major revenue generator, apart from the actual income derived from sales of newspapers. Some newspapers thought they had an answer to this problem in the mid-2000s after developing and implementing what appeared to be an innovative business plan called "sponsored sales." These are newspapers sold in bulk to hotels, airlines, and other outlets. By getting a captive audience (for instance, airline passengers or hotel guests) and a guaranteed front-end contract from a buyer (such as a large hotel chain), circulation numbers increased significantly at much lower cost (in comparison, for example, to individual home delivery). Unfortunately, to the newspapers' dismay, most advertisers now consider such circulation less valuable and have lowered their fees to newspapers which invested heavily (and became successful) in sponsored sales plans. Newspapers are now required to show sponsored sales figures so that advertisers can adjust their payments accordingly.

Discussion Questions

1. What do you think accounts for the trend of declining sales among newspapers? Could newspapers have planned for this? Explain your answer.

2. If you were responsible for corporate planning at one of the major newspapers, what process would you put in place to forecast what is likely to happen in the future? What types of plans would you put in place to ensure the newspaper remains profitable? How would you handle the unpredictable? Explain your answer.

3. What should firms do when they realize that their customer base, such as subscribers and advertisers in the case of newspapers, seem to be dwindling year after year? Can you think of another industry where a similar situation is occurring? Explain your answer.

Source: Adapted from J. Hagan, "Circulation Continues to Decline at Most Major Newspapers," *The Wall Street Journal*, November 8, 2005, pp. B7–B8.

Disaster Planning: The Only Lifeline Was Wal-Mart

management minicase 5.2

Wal-Mart, America's biggest company, is many things to many people—discounter extraordinaire, union buster, guardian of small-town virtues, wrecker of small-town shops—but one thing most people agree on is how well it responded to Katrina. Wal-Mart's truckers hauled $3 million of supplies to the ravaged zone, arriving days before the Federal Emergency Management Agency in many cases. The company also contributed $17 million in cash to relief efforts. Wal-Mart demonstrated how efficient it can be. As of September 16, 2005, all but 13 of the Wal-Mart facilities that Katrina had shut down were up and running again. The company had relocated 97 percent of the employees displaced by the storm and offered them jobs at any Wal-Mart operation in the country.

Wal-Mart began its response to Katrina on August 23—six days before the storm rampaged through New Orleans. That was the day Jason Jackson, Wal-Mart's director of business continuity, noticed that a storm off the coast of Florida had become a tropical depression and was headed for the state's southern tip.

Jackson's drab title belies his importance. He oversees Wal-Mart's Emergency Operations Center (EOC) down the road from the home office in Bentonville. You'd expect the Emergency Operations Center at the nation's largest company to be a high-tech war room. In reality, it is just another chamber of blue cubicles at a company whose executives proudly disdain spending time or money on anything so frivolous as design. But what takes place in the EOC is truly artful.

Every day, it seems, Jackson and his crew get a call from a Wal-Mart with a crisis. In August 2005, someone shot two workers in the parking lot of the Wal-Mart in Glendale, Arizona. The EOC immediately alerted surrounding stores, in case the shooter showed up on their doorsteps to inflict more harm. (He was apprehended at his house near the crime scene.) The same day, a terrified employee phoned from a store in Melbourne, Florida, where somebody had just tossed a Molotov cocktail. Jackson's team kept employees calm as a manager wrestled the suspect to the ground.

Hurricanes, for the folks at the EOC, are practically run-of-the-mill—last year Jackson and his staff responded to four hurricanes in five weeks in Florida. With Katrina looming, Jackson, a fast-talking 33-year-old who was once an assistant fire chief in Sylvan Hills, Arkansas, followed his normal procedure. Using data culled from the National Weather Service and private meteorologists, he plotted the storm's likely path across southern Florida. He alerted company officials to begin shipping crucial items to Wal-Mart distribution centers near stores in the area before Katrina could pay them a visit. "It's like a giant game of chess," Jackson says.

There was little guesswork involved. Wal-Mart has studied customer buying patterns in hurricane-prone areas. Some of the company's findings are obvious: When a storm is on the way, customers stock up on bottled water, flashlights, generators, and tarps. Afterward, they buy chain saws and mops. But there have been surprises too. Customers also load up on

Strawberry Pop-Tarts. Why is that? "They are preserved until you open them, the whole family can eat them, and they taste good," says Dan Phillips, Wal-Mart's vice president, information systems division.

The EOC also made sure the needs of Wal-Mart store managers in the area were addressed. Jackson alerted the company's trucking division to ship backup generators and fuel to Florida stores so they would be prepared for power losses. Trucks also delivered dry ice, so if the generators failed, frozen food could be kept from thawing for 72 hours.

Before the winds died down, Wal-Mart had dispatched members of its "loss prevention" team—people deployed to protect stores against everything from shoplifting to vandalism. The team was amazed at what it discovered. Looters had cleaned out the Tchoupitoulas Street store in New Orleans. Elsewhere, though, local Wal-Mart employees fended off looters and gave away items to the truly needy.

Discussion Questions

1. Based on what you have learned in this chapter, what did Wal-Mart do that many other firms and government officials did not do to deal effectively with the hurricane? Explain your answer.

2. How should corporate planners handle situations such as Katrina before they actually occur? Explain your answer.

3. Another company that was praised for its work in the aftermath of Katrina was Federal Express. It has a policy called "flexibility planning." Long before Katrina, FedEx conducted disaster drills several times a year—for everything from big earthquakes to bioterrorism to a monster typhoon hitting the company's hub in the Philippines. Do you think most companies should engage in this sort of planning exercise? Why or why not? Explain your answer.

Source: Adapted from D. Leonard, "The Only Lifeline Was the Wal-Mart," *Fortune*, October 3, 2005 pp. 74–80; and, E. F. Xratz, "For FedEx, It Was Time to Deliver," *Fortune*, October 3, 2005, pp. 83–84.

individual/
collaborative
learning
case 5.1

Why Did NASA Stick with the Space Shuttle So Long?

The core problem that lay at the heart of the Challenger tragedy in the mid-1980s applies to the Columbia tragedy in 2003 as well. That core problem may be the original plan for the space shuttle itself. For 20 years, the American space program has been wedded to a space-shuttle system that is expensive, risky, and too big for most of the ways it is used, with budgets that monopolize funds that could be invested in an alternative system that would make space flight cheaper and safer.

The space shuttle is three decades old. The shuttle's main engines, first tested in the late 1970s, use significantly more moving parts than do new rocket-motor designs. The fragile heat-dissipating tiles were designed before breakthroughs in materials science. Until recently, the flight-deck computers on the space shuttle used 8086 chips from the early 1980s, the sort of pre-Pentium electronics no self-respecting teenager would dream of using for a video game.

More important, the space shuttle was designed under the highly unrealistic assumption that the fleet would fly to space once a week and that each shuttle would need to be big enough to carry a 50,000-lb. payload. In actual use, the shuttle fleet has averaged five flights a year; in the year of the Columbia's disaster (2003), flights were to be cut back to four. The maximum payload is almost never carried. Yet to accommodate the highly unrealistic initial goals, engineers made the shuttle huge and expensive. The Soviet space program also built a shuttle, called Buran, with almost exactly the same dimensions and capacities as its American counterpart. Buran flew to orbit once and was canceled, as it was judged to be expensive and impractical. Originally projected to cost $5 million per flight in today's dollars, each shuttle launch instead runs to around $500 million.

In two decades of use, shuttles have experienced an array of problems—engine malfunctions, damage to the heat-shielding tiles, and other difficulties that have nearly produced other disasters. Seeing this, some analysts proposed that the shuttle be phased out, that cargo launches be carried aboard by far cheaper, unmanned, throwaway rockets and that NASA build a small "space plane" solely for people, to be used on those occasions when men and women are truly needed in space. NASA, however, has remained faithful to the original plan of using the shuttle to send people into space even though in financial terms and safety terms the results have been disappointing, to say the least. The more money that has been invested in the shuttle, the harder it has been for NASA to walk away from it. In fact, NASA renewed its shuttle program after the 2003 Columbia tragedy, and in 2006 the shuttle was grounded again after additional problems were discovered with the tiles, which almost caused another serious accident in 2005.

Critical Thinking Questions

1. Why do you think NASA has been staunchly committed to the space shuttle program, more than three decades after the initial plans were drawn up, with a technology that had its origins in the 1960s? Was NASA justified in this long term commitment to the space shuttle program, even after the Challenger disaster in the mid-1980s? Explain your answer.

2. Based on what you have learned in this chapter, what does the space shuttle program tell us about the pitfalls of planning? In retrospect, what should NASA have done differently in its planning process to prevent the problems discussed in this case? Explain.

3. Can planning help an organization better deal with uncertainty? What does the space shuttle case discussed above teach us about the difficulties of dealing with uncertainty? Explain.

Collaborative Learning Exercise

You have been appointed as part of a five-member independent panel to determine why the results of the space shuttle program differed from the objectives that were established in the original plans drawn up decades ago. Using the materials you have learned in this chapter, analyze whether the gap between objectives and results may be attributed to faulty objectives, or problems with the actions, resources, and implementation used to achieve the objectives. Based on this analysis, develop the outline of a plan to prevent past problems from happening again in the future. Carefully justify your recommendations.

Source: Adapted from C. Easterbrook, "The Space Shuttle Must Be Stopped," *Time*, February 10, 2003, pp. 46–47; J. Kluger, "Why NASA Can't Get It Right," *Time*, August 8, 2005, p. 25.

E-Business Goes E-Bankrupt but Survivors Are Doing Well

internet exercise 5.1

The so called "dot-com" firms were supposed to be the wave of the future in the late 1990s until the bubble burst in early 2000. Hardly any dot-com firms made any money, meaning investors had received little, if any, returns. The Web site F**Kedcompany. com keeps track of the death struggles of troubled dot-com companies. Very few of them have survived. Surprisingly, four years later, most of those that survived are showing healthy profits. These include the autoshopping Web site Autobytel Inc., financial news site Marketwatch.com, Web search site Ask Jeeves, online loan site Lendingtree, software management firm Digital River Inc., bookseller Amazon.com, jewelry retailer Blue Nile Inc., and e-Bay Inc. Research some of the dot-com firm successes and failures on the Internet and answer the following questions using the materials discussed in this chapter:

1. What reasons can you find for their success or failure? Is there a pattern? Explain.
2. Would better planning have averted the demise of those which failed? Why or why not?
3. Should the planning process be different for brick-and-mortar companies vis-à-vis dot-com firms?

Ethical Checklist

Circle the appropriate
answer on the scale: "1" =
not at all; "5" = totally yes

		1	2	3	4	5
1.	**Relevant Information Test**. Have I/we obtained as much truthful information as possible to set reasonable targets and a realistic action plan?	1	2	3	4	5
2.	**Involvement Test**. Have I/we involved all who have a right to have input and/or to be involved in this plan?	1	2	3	4	5
3.	**Consequential Test**. Have I/we anticipated and attempted to accommodate for the consequences of this plan any individuals who are significantly affected by it?	1	2	3	4	5
4.	**Fairness Test**. If I/we were assigned to take the place of anyone of the people affected by the plan, would I/We perceive the plan to be essentially fair, given all the circumstances?	1	2	3	4	5
5.	**Enduring Values Test**. Does this plan uphold important values of mine in a way that the plan leaves my conscience at peace?	1	2	3	4	5
6.	**Universality Test**. Am I/we convinced that this plan does the most good to most people, not only to myself/ourselves?	1	2	3	4	5
7.	**Light-of-day Test**. How would I/we feel and be regarded by others (peers, friends, family members) if the details of this plan were disclosed for all to know?	1	2	3	4	5

Total Ethical Analysis confidence Score. Place the total of all circled numbers here ____ ____ ____ ____

Confidence Score of Planning Ethics

7–14	Not very confident
15–21	Somewhat confident
22–28	Quite confident
29–35	Very confident

Source: Adapted from copyright holders: Dough Wallace and Jon Pekel, Twin Cities based consultants in the Fulcrum Group (651-714-9033; e-mail at jonpekel@atti.com).

video summary

Wal-Mart's Public Image

Summary

In Aurora, Colorado, a propeller helps power a highly publicized, brand-new, eco-friendly Wal-Mart. Plus there are signs powered entirely by solar cells; the store is heated with the help of reused frying oil; low-energy lights shoppers trigger on and off when they walk by. It might seem to be evidence of a new, kinder, gentler Wal-Mart. Spokesperson Mona Williams says that's because the company is listening to its critics. Williams says, "We've talked to environmentalists, we've talked to NGOs, we've talked to people in neighborhoods. We've really reached out to say: 'What should we be doing differently? What can we do to be a better citizen? What can we do to be a better company?' And we've listened to those folks, and that's why, I think, you're seeing a lot of the changes that you're seeing right now. What if we were that good in every aspect of our business and also reaching out with social responsibility, what kind of company could we be? Could that take us to the next level?"

Some think that the eco-store is just another element of "offensive charm" that the company uses. Others stand committed to the firm and what it has done to help improve their lives. Customers love low prices, and so they consider their personal savings on consumer goods to be the most important factor in their shopping at Wal-Mart. Never mind the litany of complaints lodged against the firm for driving out small business, squeezing suppliers, exploiting foreign and domestic workers, and abusing illegal aliens. The debate continues, with Wal-Mart serving as both corporate example and a symbol of these negative images.

Discussion Questions

1. What is the objective of Wal-Mart's current campaign? How is this campaign a plan by which to achieve the company's desired changes?

2. What is the Wake Up Wal-Mart campaign? How do you think this will affect planning for the company?

3. Specifically, what are some benefits of planning that Wal-Mart is enjoying at this point in time? Consider external forces, direction and purpose, and growth-related factors.

chapter 6

Decision Making

Learning Objectives

1 Recognize the nature of management decisions: programmability, uncertainty, risk, conflict, decision scope, and crisis situations.

2 Utilize the six steps of decision making.

3 Apply the criteria of quality and acceptance to a decision.

4 Reap the benefits and avoid the problems of group decision making.

5 Develop time management skills to generate adequate time to make decisions.

6 Know when to delegate, and how to do so wisely.

Google Decides about China

6

Some management decisions are not only difficult; they are risky and even uppopular, as Yahoo! and Microsoft found when they entered the Internet market in China. To obtain licenses to conduct business there, both companies agreed to the many demands and restrictions placed on their operations by the Chinese government. They have withstood a storm of criticism from rights groups, the media, and a Congressional subcommittee, most of it springing from the results of their decisions. At the request of the Chinese government, Microsoft shut down the blog of a popular and outspoken writer in Beijing. The company also censors words the government considers sensitive, using its blog-hosting software. Yahoo! gave Chinese authorities information about a journalist who had sent outspoken e-mails to a U.S. human rights organization. He and two other dissidents have since been jailed based on the information.

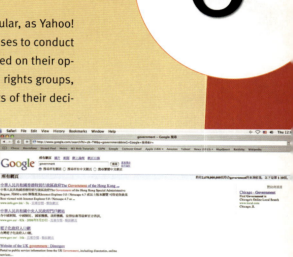

In this uncertain environment, the belated decision by Google, the world's biggest search engine, to finally follow Yahoo! and Microsoft into the Chinese market was a difficult one that entailed a great deal of uncertainty, risk, and conflict. Wall Street analysts approved of the decision, given that with 130 million users, China is second only to the United States in its rate of Internet use and is expected soon to be first by a wide margin. To ignore such a huge market is, many feel, out of the question. Others argue that some material restricted by Western companies slips by the censors and so does reach Chinese Internet users despite the government's efforts. The companies themselves say that they are less than enthusiastic about the restrictions placed on them, but that human rights conditions in China will not improve without widespread communication. But in spite of these defenses, and the argument that it is providing a service Chinese consumers would not otherwise have, Google has come in for its share of criticism for its decision as well.

Like Yahoo!'s and Microsoft's offerings, Google's Chinese search engine includes a build-in censor to prevent access to content that might be considered politically sensitive by the Chinese government, such as "Falun Gong" (the name of a spiritual movement banned in China) and "multiparty elections." Google also restricts certain news sites and information about democracy. Unlike its competitors, however, Google already hosts a Chinese-language site from a location outside China that it does not censor, though the Chinese government has tried to limit access to it from within the country. Google is also alone in notifying users when search results have been filtered out, whether by censorship or for any other reason (such as copyright laws). Google has chosen not to introduce e-mail or blogging services, which the Chinese government insists must be heavily controlled when based in China. These products, says Google's senior policy counsel Andrew McLaughlin, "will be introduced only when we are comfortable that we can do so in a way that strikes a proper balance among our commitments to satisfy users' interests, expand access to information, and respond to local conditions."

Although its decision remains controversial, some feel that Google has chosen a defensible compromise, in which, according to a Columbia University law professor, at least "won't be put in a compromising situation where [it's] actually providing information that puts someone in jail."

Sources: Nicholas Kristoff, "China's Cyberdissidents and the Yahoos at Yahoo," *New York Times*, February 19, 2006, p. WK13; Tom Zeller, Jr., "Web Firms Questioned on Dealings in China," *New York Times*, www.nytimes.com, February 16, 2006; Steven Levy, "Google and the China Syndrome," *Newsweek*, February 13, 2006, accessed at http://msnbc.msn.com; and Ben Elgin, "Google's Dicey Dance in China," *Business Week Online*, www.businessweek.com, January 25, 2006.

CRITICAL THINKING QUESTIONS

1. *How would you characterize the nature of Google's decision to enter China in terms of programmability, uncertainty, risk, conflict, and decision scope?*

2. *Did Google approach its decision differently from the way Yahoo! and Microsoft did? What might account for any differences?*

At the end of the chapter in our Concluding Thoughts, we will revisit the critical thinking questions regarding the decisions made at Google, Yahoo!, and Microsoft.

The world of management in the new millennium is filled with risk and uncertainty. Most of the time, there is a lack of information and a limited amount of time available for managers to make decisions. In some cases, procrastinating and not making a decision (thus sustaining the status quo) takes on greater risk than a proactive change. Each management decision can contribute to or hinder the success of an enterprise. This chapter examines the characteristics of managerial decisions. It identifies the stages that decision makers move through from the beginning to the implementation of the decision. An explanation of group decision making is also provided. Finally, the chapter examines time management and delegation, two skills helpful in the decision-making process. Skills for Managing 6.1 on page 227 lists the skills managers need to develop for the decisionmaking process.

Characteristics of Management Decision Making

decision making

The process of identifying problems and opportunities and resolving them.

Decision making is the process of identifying problems and opportunities and resolving them or taking advantage of them. Company decisions are made by managers, teams, and individual employees, depending on the scope of the decision and the design and structure of the organization. Organizations with decentralized structures delegate more decisions to teams and front-line employees.

DECISION MAKING

- *Time management skills*. To make good decisions, managers need time to understand the problem and develop creative solutions. They need to be proactive by planning activities and priorities so that enough time is budgeted for the important decisions to be made, and also to become aware of activities that waste time.

- *Delegation skills*. Managers who know how to delegate are able to accomplish more than those who feel the need to be involved in every decision, no matter how trivial. Many managers mistakenly believe that subordinates are not able to make effective decisions. Managers unable to delegate find themselves with too many tasks and decisions and too little time to do everything well.

This definition of decision making emphasizes *both* identifying *and* resolving a problem. At Intel, for example, Andy Grove determined that the problem was that competing in the memory chip market was draining resources that could be better deployed in the microprocessor chip market. He made the decision to withdraw from the memory chip market, which entailed closing plants and selling off assets, and to concentrate on microprocessors, which involved investing in expanded facilities.

The characteristics of management decision making include programmability, uncertainty, risk, conflict, scope, and crisis.

Programmability

Many times, there are established routines and procedures for resolving company problems. These are **programmed decisions.** For example, the job of a retail sales clerk consists primarily of making programmed decisions about stocking shelves, taking sales orders, operating a cash register, and constructing sales displays that attract customers. Well-developed procedures are established for each of these tasks in sales policy and procedure manuals developed by the marketing unit.

A **nonprogrammed decision** occurs when the situation is unique and there are no previously established routines or procedures that can be used. Situations that require nonprogrammed decisions are poorly defined and unstructured, yet they have important consequences for the organization. Managers and professionals who have more knowledge and experience make most nonprogrammed decisions. For example, an outside sales representative with a sales territory and the responsibility for calling on new and continuing customers has a job that requires nonprogrammed decision making. The sales representative must find and call on potential customers, develop rapport with them, determine whether they need the product, and close the sale. Since each customer's needs and financial situation are different, the sales representative must make a series of nonprogrammed decisions.

Nonprogrammed decisions tend to be more important than programmed ones because they are more complicated and difficult to make and are likely to have a greater effect on organization performance. Managers are likely to delegate programmed decisions to subordinates, which frees up more time to make the more difficult nonprogrammed decisions.

programmed decision

Identifying a problem and matching the problem with established routines and procedures for resolving it.

nonprogrammed decision

The process of identifying and solving a problem when a situation is unique and there are not previously established routines or procedures that can be used as guides.

Nonprogrammed decisions are the province of top management. Executives at Coca-Cola had decided to market a new diet soda to be called Coke Zero, sweetened with aspartame. But Wal-Mart Stores, the country's largest food retailer, accounts for a large portion of Coca-Cola revenues every year. Wal-Mart wanted to sell a new drink sweetened with Splenda, an artificial sweetener that was selling briskly in its stores. So Coke shelved the aspartame-based drink and developed Diet Coke with Splenda instead. The company later used the name Coke Zero on a different product.

Uncertainty

If all the information needed is available, a decision may be made under a condition of **certainty.** An automobile manufacturer plans for annual employee labor costs because the company has a contract with a labor union and knows with complete certainty what employee wage rates will be. Of course, not all the factors affecting businesses can be controlled by a contract. And when contracts expire, there will be uncertainty until the terms of the new contract are finalized.

Most management decisions are made under varying levels of uncertainty. **Uncertainty** means that incomplete information is available to make a management decision. The decision maker does not know all the alternatives, the risks associated with each, or the outcomes associated with the alternatives. Many important management decisions must be made under high levels of uncertainty. When a company launches a new product, there is uncertainty about whether consumers will buy it. New Coke was rejected by consumers, even though market research gathered prior to the decision revealed that most consumers liked cola that tasted sweeter than traditional Coke.

In the network television industry, there is about a one in ten chance that a new prime-time television program will generate sufficient viewer ratings to make a profit. Sometimes television executives must rely on gut instincts because there is little information available. The situation comedy *Seinfeld* generated poor ratings in its first two seasons, but a few executives championed the show and ultimately it became one of NBC's profitable programs.

Risk

The degree of uncertainty about the outcome of a management decision is the degree of **risk.** Under a state of risk, the availability of each alternative and its outcome are associated with probability estimates. For example, medical research provides probability estimates for the risk of survival or mortality after five years of a medical diagnosis of a patient for lung cancer. Risk has both positive and negative aspects. When a manager of mutual funds tries to maximize

certainty

The condition when all the information needed to make a decision is available.

uncertainty

The condition when the information available to make a management decision is incomplete.

risk

The level of uncertainty as to the outcome of a management decision.

the profit potential of the fund stock portfolio and minimize the loss potential when the market is falling, the manager copes with both aspects of risk. Many mutual fund managers select some stocks from countercyclical industries, which move in opposite directions in response to market fluctuations, in order to balance the risk by ensuring that all the fund's stocks do not lose value when the economy is declining.

Decision environments for risk vary depending on company culture and size. People who work in entrepreneurial firms must be more comfortable with making risky decisions than people who work in large corporations with established procedures. A high-technology company that must deliver cutting-edge products is likely to promote a culture of risk taking, while a U.S. government agency that can plan cash flow for 25 years into the future based on demographic forecasts, such as the Social Security Administration, is more likely to support a culture of risk avoidance. Companies with risk-taking cultures encourage decision makers to take moderate risks. Such companies even tolerate some failures as part of the learning process. Organizations with risk-avoidance cultures are less tolerant of decision outcomes that result in failure.

Management Is Everyone's Business 6.1 above provides some examples of how individuals deal with decision-making risk in everyday life.

Conflict

It is always difficult to get everyone to agree about what to do. Management decision making is often characterized by conflict over opposing goals, utilization of scarce resources, and other priorities. To ensure that the implementation of the decision will go smoothly, effective managers consider many different stakeholders. Otherwise, individuals or groups who are forced to accept a choice they oppose will not be committed to the decision and may even try to undermine it.

An important criterion for choosing a decision alternative is its acceptance by key employee groups such as executives, managers, and front-line employees. This is discussed later in the chapter.

Conflict can enhance the quality of a decision by sharply focusing attention on diverse ways of thinking about the consequences of the decision from diverse agendas of the people involved. In other words, various people consider how the decision will affect them. Conflict is managed when individual perspectives are taken into consideration in fashioning the solution. Conflict is examined in greater detail in Chapter 14.

When a decision is being made about research and development funding, the chief financial officer may favor reducing funding because basic research is not expected to produce profits for the firm for six to eight years. At the same time, this executive may prefer to fund applied research that will pay off in two or three years. The chief technical officer in charge of research may strongly disagree with this "short-term" investment perspective and may seek to sustain funding for basic research so that the research pipeline for new products will not dry up. The conflict in this decision is over short-term versus long-term profits.

People who have different stakes and perspectives in a decision related to the expenditure of scarce resources should have a voice in the decision process. In most cases, involving them in the process and working through the differences makes it more likely that they will be committed to the decision outcome, even if it is not one they favored.

Decision Scope

decision scope

The effect and time horizon of the decision.

strategic decision

Decisions that have long-term perspective of two to five years and affect the entire organization.

tactical decisions

Decisions that have a short-term perspective of one year or less and focus on subunits of the organization, such as departments or project teams.

operational decisions

Decisions with a short time perspective, generally less than a year, and that often are measured on a daily or weekly basis.

The effect and time horizon of the decision are what is meant by the **decision scope.** The effect of a decision includes who is involved in making the decision and who is affected by it. The time horizon of a decision may range from a single day to five years or more. **Strategic decisions** encompass a long-term perspective of two to five years and affect the entire organization. They include decisions about which product markets should be entered and left, as well as determinations of appropriate firm growth and profitability goals. Top executives are responsible for making strategic decisions.

Tactical decisions have a short-term perspective of one year or less and focus on subunits of the organization, such as departments or project teams. They include determining the distribution of departmental resources for various activities in the departmental budget. Middle managers are most likely to make tactical decisions. Tactical decisions should take into consideration the broader, strategic direction of the firm and be supportive of it.

Operational decisions cover the shortest time perspective, generally less than a year. They are often made on a daily or weekly basis and focus on the routine activities of the firm such as production, customer service, and handling parts and supplies. Supervisors, teams, and frontline employees are involved in operational decisions. Operational decisions must take into consideration both the long-term perspective of the strategic decisions and the shorter-term perspective of tactical decisions.

Crisis Situations

Decision making during crisis is more challenging and difficult than under ordinary conditions. Crisis situations include: (1) highly ambiguous circumstances in which causes and effects are not known, (2) rare and extraordinary events that can threaten the survival of an organization, (3) an event in which

How UPS Managed to Deliver During the 9/11 Crisis

THEME: CUSTOMER FOCUS Many crisis decisions were made following the September 11, 2001, terrorist attacks at the World Trade Center in New York City and at the Pentagon in Arlington, VA. As the attacks took place, airborne aircraft were advised to land at the nearest airport and subway trains that were headed toward the World Trade Center were halted, thereby saving thousands of lives. Thousands of people were evacuated from buildings close to ground zero. United Parcel Service (UPS), the package delivery service company, went into crisis management mode shortly after the attack. With all air traffic grounded, Joe Liana, UPS's Manhattan district manager, called in all employees to report to UPS's package sorting facility to identify high-priority packages such as medical supplies that were time sensitive. He ordered drivers to make 200 truck deliveries to hospitals, doctors, and pharmacies. Joe and other district managers had been given a great deal of autonomy to make decisions in their districts by UPS top management.

During the days immediately after the attacks UPS set up a crisis management plan to deliver more packages by truck because air travel was prohibited, and nobody knew when air transportation would resume. UPS vice chairman Michael L. Eskew decided to transfer packages designated for aircraft to trucks when they met certain criteria. A package needed to be able to be delivered within three days by truck in order to avoid overwhelming the truck operations' ability to deliver. Eskew gambled that aircraft operations would be resumed within one week. This turned out to be a correct assumption. As a result of UPS's crisis-management decisions, the company was able to resume package delivery operations quickly, without losing market share.

The key decisions made at UPS were: (1) empowering local district managers to handle a crisis on their own, and (2) holding back from the ground delivery system any air packages that would have taken more than three days to deliver.

Sources: Adapted from C. Haddad, "How UPS Delivered through the Disaster," *BusinessWeek*, October 1, 2001, p. 66; J. Bram, J. Orr, and C. Rappaport, "Measuring the September 11 Attack on New York City," *Economic Policy Review*, November 2002, pp. 5–20.

---

there is a small amount of time to respond, (4) a surprise to organizational members that takes place, or (5) dilemmas in need of decisions that will result in change for better or worse.[1] A decision during crisis is likely to have the characteristics of risk, uncertainty, and nonprogrammability. Examples of crisis would include a hostile takeover of a company, a product defect discovered that is harmful to consumers, a work stoppage by organized labor, a natural disaster that disrupts the company's ability to provide service to customers, or a terrorist attack—such as what happened in New York City on September 11, 2001. See Management Close-Up 6.1 above for a description of decisions made by UPS after 9/11.

After Hurricane Katrina struck the Gulf Coast in August 2005, there were shortages of food and fresh water and outages of power and telephone communication affecting millions of residents. Despite suffering shutdowns of 126 stores in the Gulf Coast region due to this disaster, Wal-Mart used its Emergency Operations Center at its Bentonville, Arkansas, headquarters to oversee the distribution by its company trucks of hundreds of thousands of cases of bottled water, food, and emergency generators into the stricken region to spearhead relief

Wal-Mart was able to respond promptly and effectively to the crisis that followed the path of Hurricane Katrina in New Orleans. The company trucked hundreds of thousands of cases of food, water, and other supplies to stricken areas, often days ahead of federal agencies.

LOC-In

efforts. The Wal-Mart trucks arrived days ahead of the relief efforts of the Federal Emergency Management Agency (FEMA), which was criticized for its slow response to the crisis caused by Hurricane Katrina. The company donated $17 million in cash to support these efforts. Wal-Mart also offered jobs to 97 percent of the employees who were displaced and jobless due to the storm, and they were offered employment at any Wal-Mart store in the country.[2]

Making a decision in a crisis situation can make or break the career of a manager. When he became the CEO of IBM in 1993, Lou Gerstner, decided to focus IBM on providing services to customers at a time of crisis when the survival of the company was at stake. The decision to change IBM's strategic focus by shifting its emphasis from making hardware to delivering services proved to be successful and a career-making move for Gerstner.[3]

Stages of Decision Making

Decision making is a six-step process. The stages, which are summarized in Figure 6.1 on page 233, are (1) identifying and diagnosing the problem; (2) generating alternative solutions; (3) evaluating alternatives; (4) choosing the best alternative; (5) implementing the decision; and (6) evaluating the results. The six-step decision-making process we present assumes a *rational process* with abundant information available to the decision makers. Later in the chapter we will add complexity to the decision-making process by relaxing the assumption of rationality.

Identifying and Diagnosing the Problem

The first stage of decision making is identifying and diagnosing a problem or opportunity. An *opportunity* is a special type of problem that requires committing resources in order to improve company performance. A *problem* occurs when performance is below expected or desired levels of performance. Typical problems include:

- A high level of employee turnover.
- A reduction in firm profits.
- Unacceptable levels of "shrinkage" in a store (employee theft).
- Low-quality finished goods.
- An increase in workplace injuries.
- The invention of a new technology that would increase the productivity of the workforce.

Once a problem has been recognized, the decision maker begins to look for the causes of the problem. This requires gathering information, exploring possible causes, eliminating as many causes as possible, and then focusing on the most probable causes. For example, a manager who observes a high level of employee

FIGURE 6.1

The Stages of Decision Making

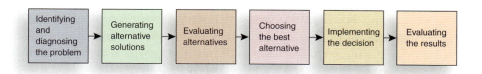

turnover first gathers information to diagnose the problem and then attempts to understand why the turnover is occurring. Some possible causes of turnover are job dissatisfaction with unchallenging and repetitive work, below-market pay rates, job stress, opportunities for better jobs in the labor market, and conflicts between work and family obligations. It is important to fully diagnose the problem before attempting to solve it. If the real cause of turnover is work and family conflicts due to inflexible work schedules and the manager assumes that it was caused by inadequate compensation and raised employee pay as a solution, the manager may not have solved the problem.

Generating Alternative Solutions

The second step is to generate possible solutions to the problem based on the perceived causes. Some problems can be solved using programmed solutions, when there are ready-made answers. Novel situations require non-programmed decisions because there are no policies or procedures available to provide direction.

In the case of nonprogrammed decision making, it is important to come up with creative alternative solutions and to suspend judgment of their worth until all possible alternatives have been developed. If solutions are evaluated too soon during the second stage of decision making, creativity can be stifled, resulting in lower-quality solutions. Many companies use groups to generate solutions for nonprogrammed decisions because they provide a greater diversity of opinions and more innovative solutions than do people working individually. Consequently, group decision making is often used to develop continuous improvements in customer service to generate novel solutions to customer needs.

LOC-In

2 Learning Objective Check-In

1. *Write Smart Co. has a very specific decision-making process that it follows for handling client problems that has been quite successful for the firm. The first stage, in which the team members at Write Smart help the client figure out exactly what the problem is that it faces, is _____.*
   a. *identifying and diagnosing the problem*
   b. *evaluating the results*
   c. *generating alternative solutions*
   d. *implementing the decision*
2. *Then, based on the perceived causes of the problem, the firm _____.*
   a. *chooses the best alternative*
   b. *evaluates the results of the decision*
   c. *generates alternative solutions*
   d. *identifies and diagnoses the problem*
3. *After making a decision, the final, and perhaps most important, step for Write Smart is to help clients recognize ways to _____. Based on this, the client may choose to pursue some modifications, which Write Smart can also help them do.*
   a. *choose the best alternative*
   b. *generate alternative solutions*
   c. *implement the decision*
   d. *evaluate the results of the decision*

Evaluating Alternatives

The third stage requires the decision maker to examine the alternative solutions using a set of decision criteria. The decision criteria should be related to the performance goals of the organization and its subunits and can include costs, profits, timeliness, whether the decision will work, and fairness.

A practical way to apply decision criteria is to consider quality and acceptance. **Decision quality** is based on such facts as costs, revenues, and product design specifications. For example, a technical engineering problem can be solved by gathering data and using mathematical techniques. **Decision acceptance** is based on people's feelings. Decision acceptance happens when people who are affected by a decision agree with what is to be done.[4]

Decisions can be classified by how important quality and acceptance are to their effectiveness. Some technical decisions require a high degree of quality but low acceptance, since people may be indifferent to the outcome. Buying raw materials at the best price is an example of a decision where quality is important but acceptance is not. An expert buyer of raw materials can make this decision. Other decisions place a high emphasis on acceptance, while quality is not important. High-acceptance, low quality decisions involve fairness issues, such as: Who will work the overtime hours? Who gets the office with the window? The important point in such decisions is not who gets to work overtime, but how people feel about the outcome and if they are willing to accept it.

The most difficult decisions require high quality and high acceptance. The decision to close an automobile assembly plant and lay off employees is an example. Decision quality requires a reduction of labor costs, but acceptance requires the support of the labor union so that it will not call a strike to protest the layoff, resulting in even greater losses to the firm. The decision maker must find ways to balance conflicting goals in this type of problem. Figure 6.2 on page 235 presents a *decision tree*, a diagnostic tool that can be used to evaluate different decision alternatives. The figure shows a decision that is evaluated according to three decision criteria that must be satisfied: *feasibility*, quality, and acceptance. Decision feasibility seeks an answer to the question: Is it *practical* to make this decision? All decisions must first of all pass the test of *feasibility*. For example, a decision alternative in the example of the automotive plant that might meet all other criteria to fire the CEO and replace him with another person might not be feasible. In the decision tree presented in Figure 6.2, satisfactory levels of both quality and acceptance are needed once feasibility is determined. The decision to close an automobile plant and lay off the workforce could be evaluated with the help of the decision tree in Figure 6.2.

LOC-In

Choosing the Best Alternative

The next stage of decision making is the selection of the best alternative by either optimizing or satisficing. **Optimizing** involves selecting the best alternative from among multiple criteria. For example, assume the decision criteria used to select an individual to fill a vacancy consists of technical job knowledge, previous work experience, and leadership skills. Further, assume that it will take six months to be able to generate a large enough applicant pool to be able to find the best person to fill the job. The optimizing solution is available when the benefits of reaching the solution outweigh the costs. However, most of the time, the costs of keeping a job vacant for six months to find the optimizing

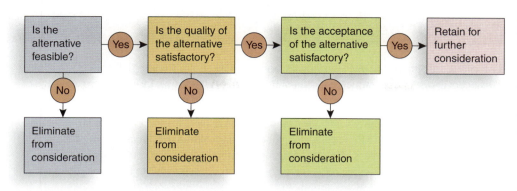

FIGURE 6.2

Evaluating Alternatives in the Decision Making Process: Managers must thoroughly evaluate all the alternatives, which improves the probability that the alternative that is selected will be successful. Failure to evaluate an alternative according to all the decision criteria can result in a bad decision. The *decision tree* shown here is a diagnostic tool that aids the process of evaluating alternatives.

solution are not worth the effort. Therefore, the optimizing approach would not be applied. Also, many important decisions must be made under conditions of risk, which constrain the ability of the decision maker to optimize.

Satisficing involves selecting the first alternative solution that meets a minimum criterion. Decision makers satisfice when complete information is not available or gathering it is too expensive. Satisficing means that the decision maker has found an acceptable if not optimal solution. For example, when selecting a new employee to fill a job vacancy, many organizations make a job offer to the first person who meets the basic selection criteria, rather than engaging in an extensive search for the best possible candidate, which takes more time and money.

Trader Joe's, the quirky and highly popular retailer of unusual foodstuffs like antioxidant trail mix, wild blueberry juice, and dark-chocolate covered espresso beans, extends its mystique by keeping many of its business practices under wraps. But a special tasting panel at the company's California headquarters meets regularly to evaluate new products, tasting several different varieties of each and offering frank opinions. Doug Rauch, company president, credits the process with helping Trader Joe's sell products that are "addictive" rather than just good.

Implementing the Decision

Putting the alternative solution into practice and making sure it works is the next step of decision making. Implementation requires the decision maker to put the solution into practice. Decision making without implementation is simply an intellectual exercise.

Implementation is a critical step because it requires the support and cooperation of executives, managers, and employees who may have different interests and goals. For example, a manager's decision to hire a minority group employee to fill a job vacancy under a corporate diversity plan may not be effectively implemented if other employees resent and avoid working with the employee. An important aspect of managing and implementing diversity is to train employees to value diversity so they are supportive of the plan's goals. The omission of training could lead to poor implementation. (See Chapter 11 for more information on implementing a corporate diversity plan.)

Several factors help make implementation successful. They include:

- Providing resources, such as staff, budgets, and office space, that will be needed for successful implementation.
- Exercising leadership to persuade others to move the implementation forward.

satisficing

Selecting the first alternative solution that meets a minimum criterion.

PITFALLS IN THE DECISION-MAKING PROCESS

Here are some pitfalls that decision makers need to know about. These pitfalls can result in low-quality decisions or poor implementation of the decision alternative. By following each stage of decision making in the correct sequence, managers can avoid many of them.

1. *Solution focus.* Time pressures often lead decision makers to shoot from the hip without taking enough time to thoroughly diagnose and understand the management problem in all its complexity. Unless all factors causing a system to be out of control are identified, proposed solutions to the problem are not likely to be responsive to the true problem.

2. *Premature evaluation.* The temptation is always present to evaluate and judge alternatives as they are being developed and expressed by peers, subordinates, or the decision maker. Idea generation is a creative process that can be stifled and frustrated by managers who pronounce early judgment when an alternative solution is suggested. A deeply flawed idea can inspire others to come up with novel solutions that may not be expressed unless people feel free to think creatively, without worrying about others judging them for their creative ideas.

3. *The "If it isn't broke, don't fix it" syndrome.* This bias favors programmed solutions based on what worked in the past, even though that may no longer be relevant to the present or future. In a business environment of changing customer needs, decisions that favor what satisfied customers in the past are not likely to meet current and future customer expectations.

4. *Bias toward objective data.* In environments of high uncertainty, decision makers may give a high priority to objective data. For example, data on viewer behavior is collected by market research analysts for a pilot television program. Such data, however, are not likely to be useful for making accurate predictions of program success when the new program is very different from others, such as *Seinfeld* and *The Sopranos.*

5. *Overlooking important constituencies.* The decision maker should identify the diverse groups within (and sometimes outside) the organization that are likely to have strong feelings about the decision outcome and solicit their input.

- Developing communication and information systems that enable management to know if the decision alternative is meeting its planned objectives.
- Considering ways to recognize and reward individuals and teams that successfully put the decision alternative into practice.[5]

Evaluating the Results

The final stage in the decision-making process is to evaluate the results. Decision makers gather information and try to learn if the implemented decision achieved its goals. The availability of accurate and timely information and feedback permits the decision maker to make a thorough evaluation and to determine whether modifications are needed.

Decision makers need to establish reasonable goals and benchmarks to make sound judgments about the effectiveness of the decision. It is also important to allow enough time for a decision to take effect. An executive collecting productivity data on a new manufacturing plant would be foolish to immediately judge its effectiveness without giving plant management time to eliminate the production bottlenecks that are typical in new manufacturing plants. It would be better to suspend judgment until plant personnel learn the best ways to operate the equipment and develop routines to work well together. The pitfalls associated with decision making are summarized in Manager's Notebook 6.1 above.

video: THE ENTREPRENEURIAL MANAGER

The Debbie and Les Busfield Story

Summary

Strongfield Trimco, Inc., is more of a high-end framer, which frames more expensive—between $300,000 – $3 million—homes. Les and a partner started the company in 1981. In the beginning, they did not have the same focus that the company has today. They would take on jobs building any range of things for the customer—from carports to apartment buildings. That lack of specialization meant the firm was doing a lot of work, but was not making any money. After about eight years, the partners went their separate ways. Les and his wife Debbie, however, saw the future of the company in framing. Debbie and Les bought out Les's partner, and formed a new partnership. Framing became the focus—it was what they were good at and what they "knew" as a firm. For a number of years, they did strictly custom homes and gained much new business through word of mouth.

According to Debbie, an entrepreneur has to be unafraid to make mistakes. She credits Les with the ability to make decisions. He knows the value of making a decision because "you need a decision" and do not always have the luxury of taking weeks to make that decision. His method is to make the best decision he can, learn from the mistakes he makes, and not to beat himself up over wrong decisions or not making the best choices all the time. For him, it is often more important to choose in a timely way than to delay the choice and consider every single angle involved. Les and Debbie complement one another in their skills and abilities in handling the business itself. Les often defers to Debbie to deal with personnel or organizational issues, whereas Debbie usually defers to Les for dealing with daily operational issues or details of running the actual business. Debbie also credits a willingness to take risks and to deal with failures as critical to success as an entrepreneur.

Debbie also explains that "you can't do it all—you have to have good people." As an entrepreneur, doing the hiring herself is very personal. Each person hired is representative of Les and Debbie, as well as the company they have created. She says that the hiring decisions are very important and while she may want to hire a person she "likes," it is more important to hire someone who will work well in a particular position. She says that they find it very important also to reward their workers and involve them in the decisions that concern them directly, including ways that can improve their time at the company. Not only do they ask the employees about their ideas, they then get back to them with what they are doing about those particular ideas. Strongfield enjoys a very low turnover rate in employees, something Debbie and Les are very proud of.

The final critical point Debbie makes is that Les and she do not know everything there is to know about running their own business. Tapping into external resources and being willing to pay for other people's specialized knowledge can take an entrepreneur very far in being successful at having his or her own business. The price paid for the business advisors' efforts and advice were returned several times over, according to Debbie.

Discussion Questions

1. How do Debbie and Les deal with uncertainty, risk, and conflict as elements of their decision-making processes? How are the methods for dealing with these factors different for an entrepreneur than for a large, established firm?

2. Discuss the stages of human resources decision making used at Strongfield Trimco, Inc. Give some context to your answer based on specific examples from the video.

3. What is delegation? How do Debbie and Les Busfield use delegation in their management of the company?

The Limits of Rational Decision Making

It is a major leap of faith to assume that all decision making is rational. It is not. This is because rational decision making is based on the following assumptions:

- The problem is clear and unambiguous.
- There is a single, well-defined goal that all parties agree to.
- Full information is available.
- All the alternatives and their consequences are known.
- The decision preferences are clear.
- The decision preferences are constant and stable over time.
- There are no time and cost constraints affecting the decision.
- The decision solution will maximize the economic payoff.[6]

Many decisions are complex and are made in situations where these assumptions do not apply. There are several factors that limit rational decision making. They include organization politics, emotions and personal preferences, the illusion of control, intuition, and escalation of commitment. By being aware of these biases, decision makers can improve the quality of their decisions.

Organization Politics

coalitions

Political alliances between managers who agree on goals and priorities.

organization politics

The exercise of power in an organization to control resources and influence policy.

Organizations are likely to have **coalitions,** which are political alliances between employees who agree on goals and priorities. Various coalitions may disagree about alternatives for a decision, and an executive or leader may need to exercise power and influence to build a consensus between diverse coalitions. **Organization politics** involves the exercise of power in an organization to control resources and influence policy. Organization politics is more likely to be present in firms with democratic cultures where power is decentralized and decisions are made through consensus.

Decisions based on political coalitions do not always favor the most rational solution. Sometimes they favor the solution that sustains the power of the top executive or dominant individual or group. For example, an executive may provide resources to a coalition of managers to obtain their support on an important decision. Still, there are times in which organization politics can lead to a successful decision, as shown in Management Close-Up 6.2 on page 239.

Emotions and Personal Preferences

Decision makers are not robots choosing alternatives without emotion or passion. Many times a poor decision is reached because the decision maker is having a bad day. The two emotions which are the most disruptive to quality decision making are anger and depression. An angry person is not going to look at an issue clearly, nor is someone who is depressed.

Personal preferences include a variety of individual quirks. For example, a manager who hates the idea of going into debt, both personally and in his or her company, will make decisions which may or may not benefit the company. Or the opposite may be true. The same is true for someone who enjoys taking risks as opposed to someone who is risk-averse. It is vital to make certain the person or group making a decision is not swayed by an individual agenda or pattern of decision making.

The Decision to Build the Sensor Razor at Gillette

THEME: CUSTOMER FOCUS

Organization politics can influence key company decisions and affect a firm's welfare, for better or worse, as in Gillette's development of its Sensor razor. Although the Sensor was fabulously successful when it was released to the market, it came close to being a very different product due to a disagreement over its product design.

The Gillette Company's British research facility spent 13 years developing the idea behind the Sensor razor. The idea was to create a thinner razor blade that would make Gillette cartridges easier to clean. The cost for the product's research and development reached $200 million.

The technical demands of building a razor with thin blades and floating parts that could follow the contours of a man's face led researchers up several blind alleys. They tried established techniques, but none filled the bill. They tried innovative ideas, such as setting the blades on tiny rubber tubes, perhaps filled with fluid, but these ideas proved too costly and complicated to manufacture. Eventually Gillette came up with a prototype. The 500 men who tested it liked it, and the product was put into production.

The Sensor's next problems involved manufacturing and product placement. Because of the razor's innovative design, an entirely new manufacturing process was needed to laser-weld each blade to a support. Gillette management approved developing the new manufacturing equipment, but two groups of executives disagreed on the final product. One group wanted to produce and market a razor that was lightweight, expensive, and disposable; the other faction thought the product should be a heavier, more permanent razor with replaceable blades. When Gillette was threatened by an outside takeover, it reduced the resources allocated to the Sensor project. A new executive vice president made the decision to deemphasize razors that were disposable, so the Sensor's final form was determined.

The Sensor razor has been an unqualified success. It was quickly embraced by consumers, and Gillette recovered its huge investment in record time.

Gillette's decision process for the Sensor began because executives became aware of the potential for a new razor with floating, thin blades. Leaders proceeded with a trial-and-error custom design. When some alternatives were found unacceptable, Gillette returned to earlier steps until a workable product was created.

At Gillette, there is no such thing as getting ahead of oneself. New products go on the drawing board as much as a decade before they are introduced. Months before the Sensor was launched in 1994, the company already was working on its successor: the Mach 3 shaving system, a blend of leading-edge technology and relentless consumer testing, took seven years and $750 million to develop.

Sources: Adapted from R. L. Daft, *Leadership: Theory and Practice*, Fort Worth: Dryden Press, 1999, pp. 467–468; G. Rifkin, "Mach 3: Anatomy of Gillette's Latest Global Launch," *Journal of Strategy and Business*, 2nd quarter, 1999, www.strategy-business.com.

Illusion of Control

Another limitation of rational decision making results from the **illusion of control,** which is the tendency for a decision maker to be overconfident of his or her ability to control activities and events. Top executives are especially susceptible to this problem, because they can be isolated from the rank and file employees and may be surrounded with "yes men."

A good example of the illusion of control was the decision by President Richard Nixon to cover up a break-in of Democratic party headquarters in the Watergate building by Republican party operatives during the 1972 presidential election. Nixon assumed he could control public perception of the incident because he was the president. The cover-up turned out to be a disastrous error and ultimately led to talk of impeachment and Nixon's resignation from office in 1974.

illusion of control

The tendency for decision makers to be overconfident of their ability to control activities and events.

Intuition and Escalation of Commitment

Intuition and escalation of commitment are two other factors that limit the rational decision-making process.

intuition

When a decision maker depends on gut feelings or innate beliefs as a basis for making a decision.

INTUITION   When a decision maker depends on a gut feeling or innate belief about something and acts on it, then **intuition** is the basis for the decision. The feelings that lead to intuition are based on years of experience in making decisions in similar situations. These repeated occurences form patterns that are recognized by the decision maker when a new situation occurs that matches an earlier experience and is recognized to have similar properties. For example, a pilot of a commercial jet airplane who experiences a pocket of severe air turbulence may depend on intuition for his decision on how to maneuver the aircraft based on pattern recognition from previous experiences in dealing with turbulence.

In a recent book titled *Blink: The Power of Thinking without Thinking*, author Malcolm Gladwell explains that decision makers who must make quick decisions depend on their intuition by using a process called *thin slicing* which focuses attention on a few factors to make a critical decision while filtering out a lot of other data that may be present.[7] A police officer who encounters a person in a dark alley that he suspects of committing a crime will depend on interpreting a few key factors such as body posture (is it aggressive or submissive?), facial expression (friendly or hostile?), position of hands (out in open or going for something in the pocket?) that influence how the officer responds to the situation. An officer's intuition based on previous experience related to how a threatening suspect would act affects whether an officer will draw a firearm and shoot the suspect or not. A mistake at reading the signals of the key variables could be tragic for the suspect and the officer. Sometimes useful data has been filtered out of the decision process when intuition is the basis for a decision resulting in a poor outcome. In the example of the police officer who encounters a suspect that matches the profile of a dangerous criminal, the officer may give a verbal command to the suspect to put his hands in the air, which the suspect may ignore, which may trigger an intuitive response from the officer to take out his gun and fire. The reason for the suspect's not responding to the officer's command might in fact be that he did not speak English and did not understand the police officer's order. If the officer does not somehow check out this fact, the officer's intuition may lead him to make a bad decision.

When a victim of a car crash is brought into the emergency room (ER), the doctor depends on intuition to quickly size up the patient's prognosis for survival by focusing on monitoring a few of the patient's vital signs such as blood pressure, temperature, or control of blood flowing from an open wound, and then must make a quick decision regarding which medical procedure to use to improve the patient's chance for survival. Medical training requires that a resident ER physician spend many hours at the hospital to build a reservoir of experience that can be used as basis for making intuitive medical decisions that require quick interventions.

Intuition depends heavily on there being a correspondence between a manager's past experiences and the current situations that require decision making. Intuition is less reliable for managers who lack experience or find themselves in a situation that is so unique that it cannot be compared to past experiences.

escalation of commitment

The refusal to abandon an earlier decision even when it is no longer appropriate, which happens because the decision maker is highly committed to a course of action and wants to stay the course.

ESCALATION OF COMMITMENT   When a decision maker has made a past choice, and in hindsight it no longer appears to be valid, the decision maker may be in denial of new information that could lead to a different course of action. The refusal to abandon a choice from an earlier decision even when it is no longer appropriate from a rational decision-making perspective is called **escalation of commitment**, sometimes referred to as a *sunk-cost trap*.[8] This happens when a decision maker becomes so committed to a course of action that she or he decides to stay the course even when it appears to have been wrong. All this

Working as a Manager A major barrier to decision making is procrastination. Managers wait until the last minute to make decisions because of inertia, too many interruptions, improperly classifying a decision as simple and low priority, hoping that the need for the decision will go away, or having insufficient information and being afraid of deciding to do the wrong thing. As a manager you need to establish *clear priorities* and determine which of your activities produces the greatest value. Then you should set dates for the completion of these activities. Setting priorities forces you as a manager to make decisions and helps control procrastination.

may do is make things worse when the decision maker allocates more resources to a goal that is not likely to pay off.

In banking, escalation of commitment shows up in decision making with disturbing regularity and can have dire consequences. A borrower's business can run into trouble, and the banker who made the loan will often advance additional funds in the hopes of providing the business with some extra time to recover and pay back the loan. If the business has a good probability of being turned around, this may be a sound decision. Otherwise, it is just throwing good money after bad.[9]

The harmful effects of escalation of commitment on decisions can be managed by having trusted advisors who were uninvolved with earlier decisions give honest views to the decision maker. Also cultivating a company culture that tolerates mistakes when it is possible to learn from them reduces the fear decision makers have of exposing their mistakes to the criticism of others.

Management Is Everyone's Business 6.2 above explains how to avoid another barrier to the decision-making process, which is procrastination.

An agreement between Snapple and New York City to sell Snapple in city-owned buildings, including City Hall pictured here, fell far short of its goal to generate $66 million in cash and $60 million worth of marketing and tourism promotion. In spite of the deficit, the city agreed to renegotiate the innovative but widely criticized agreement, lowering its sales goals and investing more funds in promoting the partnership.

Nonrational Decision-Making Models

The actual conditions for most decisions tend to be complex and most decisions occur under conditions of uncertainty, often falling short of satisfying the assumptions of rational decision making. *Nonrational decision-making* models have been developed for these situations. Nonrational decision-making models assume that information-gathering and processing limitations make it difficult for managers to make optimal decisions. Two nonrational decision-making approaches are the administrative model and the garbage can model.

Administrative Model

Herbert Simon, a Nobel prize–winning economist, points out that even if all the necessary information is available to make a decision, many managers cannot completely absorb and evaluate the information appropriately.[10] The *administrative model* of decision making, developed by Herbert Simon, describes how decisions are actually made by managers and assumes the information available is incomplete and imperfect, a condition that most managers experience in reality. These insights led to his concept of *bounded rationality.* Bounded rationality means that the ability of a manager to be perfectly rational is limited by factors such as cognitive capacity and time constraints. A decision maker's perceptions about the relative importance of various aspects of data may cause him or her to overlook or ignore some important information.[11] Moreover, the human memory can retain and process only a limited amount of information at one time. Consequently, decision makers apply *heuristics,* or decision rules, that quickly eliminate alternatives. For example, when a manager says, "We can't afford to hire any more people," that manager has applied a decision rule that eliminates a variety of options.

As a result, managers do not assess every potential alternative. Instead, by using the heuristic known as *satisficing,* a manager seeks out the first decision alternative that appears to be *satisfactory.* Satisficing is an accurate representation of many management decisions. This is because the cost of delaying a decision or searching for a better solution is outweighed by the benefits of quickly finding a satisfactory solution. For example, a home owner is satisficing when she makes a decision to sign a contract with a company to paint her house after taking only three bids. The decision rule is to consider only the quality of materials, cost, and time needed to complete the job. Choosing a satisfactory bid to paint the house without seeking the optimal solution (the best of all possible painters) is satisficing.

Garbage Can Model

Managers often behave in a random pattern when making decisions. The *garbage can* model suggests that managers have a set of preestablished solutions to problems located in "garbage cans."[12] If such a solution to a problem appears to be satisfactory or appropriate, it is applied to the problem.[13] This means that managers have some preselected solutions or skills for which they are searching for problems to "fix."

The garbage can model is likely to be used when decision makers are undisciplined and have no clear immediate goals. As a result, the decision-making process lacks structure. While the garbage can model can sometimes result in a desirable outcome, it can also lead to serious difficulties. For example, for several generations the Bronfman family owned and managed Seagram's, a highly profitable manufacturer and distributor of whiskies and other alcoholic drinks. Edgar Bronfman, the son of Seagram's CEO, persuaded his father to buy Universal Pictures, a Hollywood movie studio, because Edgar had previously financed and produced a few independent movies and had friends in the entertainment industry. Bronfman assumed he possessed the skills to run a major studio. Ultimately, neither Edgar Bronfman nor Seagram's management displayed the ability needed to effectively operate a movie business. The company was forced to sell the studio while taking a huge loss which resulted in a dramatic reversal of fortune for the Bronfman family.

Personal Decision-Making Styles

Managers go about making decisions in different ways. The differences between how managers approach problems and make decisions are referred to as personal *decision styles.* There are four categories of decision styles: directive, analytical, conceptual and behavioral.[14]

1. The *directive style* is used when a manager perceives a clear and simple solution to a problem. It is used when a manager prefers to avoid dealing with a lot of information and may consider only a few alternatives. The decision maker using this style tends to be efficient and rational and relies on existing rules and procedures for making decisions.

2. The *analytical style* is used by managers who prefer to gather as much data as possible before they make a decision. The decision maker considers more alternatives than a directive style and bases the decision on a rational and objective analysis of data gathered from different sources in order to make the best possible decision from the information that is available.

3. The *conceptual style* is used by managers who tend to be very broad in their outlook and examine many alternatives. Unlike the analytical style, the person who uses the conceptual style prefers to discuss the problem and alternatives with other people. Decision makers using this style rely on information from both people and systems and prefer to solve problems creatively.

4. The *behavioral style* is used by managers who place a high priority on other people's concerns and talk to them about how they feel about the problem and the effect of the decision on them. The decision maker is also concerned about the personal development of other people and how involvement in the decision process may help them achieve their goals.

Managers are most likely to choose among different decision styles depending on the type of decision that is being made. For example, with a programmed decision such as filling out a customer's product order, a manager is likely to select a directive style, and for a nonprogrammed decision a manager could choose from among the analytical, conceptual, and behavioral styles. However, most managers have a dominant decision style. For example, former U.S. President Bill Clinton enjoyed sifting through a lot of data and considered many alternatives before making a decision, which suggests an analytical style, while former U.S. President Ronald Reagan liked to make decisions according to his values and intuition by considering fewer alternatives, which resembles the directive style of decision making.

Decision Making in Groups

When employee acceptance of a decision is important, it is usually necessary to involve a group of employees in the decision-making process. For example, the department chair organizes a recruitment committee to participate in the decision to hire a new professor in a university department. This is done because acceptance by colleagues is critical; all promotions and performance evaluations are performed by committees of peers in universities. Hiring decisions at law, accounting, and consulting firms also require input from groups of junior and senior colleagues. These professionals often work in cooperative teams to serve clients and expect to have a voice in selecting new organizational members. Committees, task forces, or teams can be the basis for a group decision.

The Benefits and Problems of Group Decision Making

Group decision making has several advantages as well as problems, which are displayed in Table 6.1 on page 244. Group decisions can improve both the quality and the acceptance of a decision. By involving people in the process,

table 6.1

Benefits and Problems of Group Decision Making

BENEFITS	PROBLEMS
Increased acceptance. Those who play an active role in group decision making and problem solving tend to view the outcome as "ours" rather than "theirs."	*Social pressure.* Unwillingness to "rock the boat" and pressure to conform may combine to stifle the creativity of individual contributors.
Greater pool of knowledge. A group can bring much more information and experience to bear on a decision or problem than an individual acting alone.	*Minority domination.* Sometimes the quality of group action is reduced when the group gives in to those who talk the loudest and longest.
Different perspectives. Individuals with varied experience and interests help the group see decision situations and problems from different angles.	*Logrolling.* Political wheeling and dealing can displace sound thinking when an individual's pet project or vested interest is at stake.
Greater comprehension. Those who personally experience the give-and-take of group discussion about alternative courses of action tend to understand the rationale behind the final decision.	*Goal displacement.* Sometimes secondary considerations such as winning an argument, making a point, or getting back at a rival displace the primary task of making a sound decision or solving a problem.
Training ground. Less experienced participants in group action learn how to cope with group dynamics by actually being involved.	*"Groupthink."* Sometimes cohesive "in-groups" let the desire for unanimity override sound judgment when generating and evaluating alternative courses of action.

Source: From *Organizational Behavior* by R. Kreitner and A. Kinicki. Copyright © 2007. The McGraw-Hill Companies, Inc. Reproduced with permission.

management allows them to examine all the alternatives and criteria, opening the door for deeper understanding of the rationale for the alternative that was selected, and increasing the likelihood that they will accept and be committed to the decision. Groups tap a greater pool of knowledge and provide more diverse perspectives than any single individual could generate acting alone. Group decision making is also beneficial because it provides the opportunity for employees with less experience with group activities to learn how to cope with group dynamics by actually being involved.

The problems associated with group decision making arise from bringing people with different interests together. Dominant individuals or factions may intimidate others into agreeing with their goals. The group may be unwilling to deal with conflict and come to a quick settlement in order to keep the peace. Hidden agendas (such as self-promoting individual's using the group as a captive audience), political deal making, and **groupthink** (valuing social harmony over doing a thorough job) can all lead to low-quality decision outcomes unless the group decision process is managed by a leader who can protect the group from these problems.

groupthink

Valuing social harmony over doing a thorough job.

One of the limiting factors in group decision making is time. The group requires sufficient time to go through all six stages of decision making in sequence. If time for decision making is limited, it may be better for a manager to make the decision alone and then attempt to persuade others to abide by it. Management Is Everyone's Business 6.3 on page 245 suggests how teams can be more productive in their use of time devoted to team meetings.

Managing Group Decision Making

A leader must work to minimize the potential problems listed in Table 6.1 above. Some ways to ensure that quality decisions are made by groups include adapting leadership style, assuming the devil's advocate role, and using various decision-making techniques to stimulate creativity.

Working as a Team   Teams can rely too heavily on team meetings to make decisions, resulting in wasted time. Although meetings are important for building trust in the early stages of team formation, they can be an inefficient way to use time and frustrate people if they are used indiscriminately. By assigning tasks to subgroups or individual team members and giving them responsibility for decision making associated with these tasks, a team should be able to manage its workflow so that meetings are reserved for critical decisions or events that genuinely require the presence of all members.

table 6.2

Leader Decision-Making Styles

DECISION-MAKING STYLE	CHARACTERISTICS	AMOUNT OF SUBORDINATE PARTICIPATION
Decide and persuade	Leader solves the problem and makes decision with available information	None
Discover facts and decide	Leader gathers facts from subordinates and then makes the decision	Very little; indirect involvement
Consult and decide	Leader consults with individual subordinates, obtaining their ideas and opinions, and then makes the decision	Modest amount of participation through being presented with the problem by the leader
Consult with group and decide	Leader consults with group of subordinates, gathering their collective ideas, and then makes the decision	Substantial amount of participation by being engaged in the group discussion of the problem
Group decision	Leader shares problem with group and accepts the decision made by the group, acting as a coach to the group decision-making process	High involvement of subordinates in the decision-making process

Sources: Adapted from V. H. Vroom and A. G. Jago, *The New Leadership: Managing Participation in Organizations,* Englewood Cliffs, NJ: Prentice Hall, 1988; R. L. Daft, *Management,* 7th ed., Mason, OH: Thomson, 2005, p. 324.

LEADERSHIP STYLE   A group leader can adapt his or her style to the requirements of the problem. Table 6.2 above shows five different decision-making styles that leaders may select from, depending on the need for decision quality and acceptance, the time available, and leader and subordinate skills and competencies.

When a manager places a high priority on agreement among the group members about what is fair, the leader should focus on allowing each person to voice an opinion. The leader should try to involve all group members and discourage dominating individuals from monopolizing the discussion.

A manager who places a high priority on quality and acceptance must manage the decision process by carefully framing the problem and putting constraints on decision alternatives that are too risky or uncertain. In such cases, the leader may allow for some participation by group members but reserves the right to make the decision. A leader can frame the same problem as either a threat or an opportunity, which can influence how the group perceives the problem.

Research in the social sciences has shown that groups tend to take greater risks than individuals because responsibility for the outcome can be diffused over the entire group. The leader can remind the group to avoid considering decision alternatives that could lead to disastrous results. For example, the group responsible for deciding whether to go ahead with the launch of the *Challenger* space shuttle in 1986 would have made a different decision if NASA's leadership had examined the risk that a critical component would shrink when exposed to cold temperatures and cause the space shuttle to explode immediately after the launch.

Problems that involve technical or specialized knowledge are best solved alone by the decision maker. For example, if an important instrument malfunctions in the middle of an intercontinental flight, a commercial aircraft pilot may decide to land the plane at the nearest airport rather than continue to the original destination. Obviously, time is a critical factor in this situation, and the decision is best handled by the captain of the aircraft.

DEVIL'S ADVOCATE ROLE

Social pressures to conform in groups can lead to the problem of groupthink, in which group members withhold critical comments or unpopular views in order to sustain social harmony in the group. If groupthink is not managed, it can reduce decision quality.

One way to reduce the threat of groupthink is to assign a group member the role of **devil's advocate.** The devil's advocate is expected to criticize and challenge decision alternatives that are agreed on by other members of the group. This person may (1) develop scenarios in which the majority-sponsored decision alternative could fail or (2) promote alternative solutions that challenge the one supported by the group. In this way, the devil's advocate introduces creative conflict and tension into the group decision-making process. This may ultimately lead to a better solution or one that is more deeply understood by members of the group. The payoff is likely to be stronger group commitment to the decision.

DECISION-MAKING TECHNIQUES TO STIMULATE CREATIVITY

Introducing criticism into the group decision-making process too early can stifle creativity. **Brainstorming** is a technique that is designed to generate creative decision alternatives verbally by interacting with members of a group. Critical and judgmental reactions to ideas from group members are not allowed during a brainstorming session. Instead, the group is encouraged to come up with the greatest number of ideas, and especially ideas that are wild and unusual. Group members are also asked to build on and extend earlier ideas, to increase the possibility of a truly innovative solution. The rules of brainstorming prohibit criticism of any ideas until all the ideas have been expressed. In the entertainment industry, teams of writers and other content creators make widespread use of brainstorming sessions. For example, brainstorming is used by the group of comedy writers who develop jokes for the "Tonight Show with Jay Leno."

For more complex problems, a variation of brainstorming called **storyboarding** is used. Storyboarding begins with group members jotting down ideas on index cards and posting them on a bulletin board or on conference room walls. Group members can shuffle, rewrite, or even eliminate cards. The technique is useful for examining complex processes involving technology in order to improve efficiency. At the Xerox corporate research laboratory in California's Silicon Valley, researchers sketch ideas onto a large white wall to begin discussions of ideas with other researchers.

The **nominal group technique (NGT)** helps a group generate and select solutions while letting group members think independently. NGT is a structured group meeting in which the following steps take place:

---

devil's advocate

The role of criticizing and challenging decision alternatives that are agreed on by other members of the group, to induce creative conflict and possible alternative better solutions.

brainstorming

A technique to generate creative ideas for solving problems by reducing critical and judgmental reactions to ideas from group members.

storyboarding

A variation of brainstorming in which group members jot down ideas on cards and then can shuffle, rewrite, or even eliminate cards to examine complex processes.

nominal group technique (NGT)

A decision-making technique that helps a group generate and select solutions while letting group members think independently; group members are given the problem and each presents one solution without discussion; then all solutions are discussed, evaluated, and ranked to determine the best alternative.

1. Group members meet and are presented with a problem. Prior to any discussion, each member independently writes down solutions to the problem.

2. Next, each group member presents one of his or her ideas to the group. The idea is listened to and recorded on a flip chart or blackboard without any discussion or criticism.

3. After all the ideas have been presented and posted, discussion and evaluation begin.

4. At the conclusion of the evaluation, the group members anonymously vote and rank their top choices. The decision alternative that receives the highest ranking from the group is selected.[15]

NGT allows the group to discuss alternatives without inhibiting group members from engaging in independent critical thinking. NGT is often used in the strategic planning process, such as in the development of the corporate mission statement.

Creativity in solving problems often is fostered in a group situation, where members can build on each other's ideas and solutions by *brainstorming*.

Another approach to group decision making is called the **Delphi technique,** which was originally developed by the RAND Corporation for technological forecasting. The Delphi technique is similar to NGT, but it does not involve face-to-face meetings of group members. Group members are presented with a problem and receive a questionnaire soliciting solutions. Each group member anonymously completes the questionnaire and sends it to a central location, where responses are tabulated and summarized. The results are then returned to the group members, and each is asked again for solutions. Having the input of all the other group members may inspire some group members to modify their positions or develop new ideas, while others may stick with their original ideas. Questionnaires are completed a second time and tabulated. The cycle of giving and receiving anonymous feedback continues until a consensus is reached on the best decision alternative.

Assessing Your Creativity Quotient

Delphi technique

A decision-making technique in which group members are presented with a problem and complete an anonymous questionnaire soliciting solutions; the results are tabulated, summarized, and returned to the group members, and each is asked again for solutions; the process continues until a consensus decision is reached.

The application of computer software provides for an electronic approach to the Delphi technique. The Leeds School of Business at the University of Colorado uses an electronic meeting room with 20 computer terminals with software that allows each person in a group to view his or her input to a decision posted anonymously on the computer screen along with all the other inputs from other group members. The software handles the complexity of bringing ideas together quickly, displaying them, and helping groups analyze them. The software lets the group go through several rounds of generating and evaluating decision alternatives until a consensus is reached. The electronic meeting room is useful for making controversial decisions when highly opinionated or high-status individuals should be kept from dominating the decision process, which means shy people are better able to participate in the process.

The Delphi technique is particularly useful when experts who are geographically separated need to make a decision. For example, a Wall Street investment bank may select a panel of 30 economists from different universities around the world to use the Delphi

LOC-In

4 Learning Objective Check-In

1. *Laura is in charge of facilitating group decision making regarding some proposed sales approaches within her company. The group members cannot gather together physically. Laura will have the group members complete a questionnaire, the results of which Laura will tabulate and return to the group. This cycle repeats with the group members modifying answers based on the feedback from the group as a whole. Laura is using _____.*
   a. *nominal group technique*
   b. *storyboarding method*
   c. *Delphi technique*
   d. *brainstorming*

technique to forecast macroeconomic indicators such as interest rates, growth in the economy, and rate of inflation as a basis for thinking about future investment opportunities.

Decision-Making Skills

Effective managers know one of the most important things they will be asked to do is make quality decisions. Time management skills and delegation skills can improve the quality of those decisions. These skills are described next.

Time Management

A decision maker must have enough time to make effective decisions. Adequate time makes it possible to understand the problem, develop several suitable alternatives, evaluate the decision in light of goals and priorities, and establish a workable approach to implement the decision.

Not having enough time is stressful and puts the decision maker in a reactive mode. A **reactive manager** is always dealing with the most urgent problem and putting out fires. Decisions made this way are likely to be haphazard and to have major flaws in either quality or execution. For example, it may be necessary to have employees work overtime to satisfy an urgent customer demand. The reactive manager may feel pressured to randomly assign employees to work overtime, rather than involving the group in the decision. It is likely that working overtime will conflict with family or personal plans of at least some of the employees, which leads to resentment and resistance.

Reactive managers tend to lose control of their time and lose sight of the "big picture." Always dealing with crises means living on an emotional roller coaster. Those who skip planning their daily and weekly schedules because of looming crises have no time to think about goals and priorities.

Crises can be avoided by anticipating and dealing with problems when they are smaller and more manageable. A **proactive manager** anticipates problems before they become pervasive and "works smarter, not harder." Proactive people manage time. Time is set aside on both a daily and weekly basis to set goals and priorities. Proactive managers jealously protect this time from interruptions. This way, they can complete their work, deal with important decisions, and enjoy life outside of work with family and friends. They are able to lead more balanced and less stressful lives than reactive managers.[16]

One way to manage time is to eliminate or minimize "time wasters," activities that squander time. These include

- Television (the average American watches about four hours of television per day).
- Internet and e-mail messages.
- Lengthy telephone conversations.
- Random errands and waiting in lines.
- Interruptions by people who stop in to chat.
- Meetings (managers are often expected to attend many meetings to coordinate activities of their units).

Manager's Notebook 6.2 on page 249 lists helpful ways to avoid time wasters and practice effective time management.

EFFECTIVE TIME MANAGEMENT PRACTICES

The following practices help managers eliminate or reduce time-wasting behavior and allow them to be more proactive.

1. *Make a list of things that need to be done today.* Write your daily plan during quiet time the night before, rather than at the office in the morning when urgent matters may get in the way of writing your list.

2. *Plan weekly, monthly, and annual schedules of activities.* Weekly schedules allow you to organize work, school, personal, and family activities. Longer term schedules let you plan time for nonwork facets of your life. For example, monthly plans may include travel that requires advance purchase of tickets. Annual plans also give an opportunity to consider your values and long-term objectives.

3. *Schedule difficult and challenging activities when you are at your highest level of energy and alertness.* For example, if you are a "morning person," schedule demanding activities in the morning and reserve afternoons for less difficult things such as returning phone calls or doing routine record keeping.

4. *Set deadlines.* Deadlines improve your use of time. Work always expands to fill the time available—if you don't specify a termination time, tasks tend to continue longer than they need to.

5. *Answer phone messages and e-mail in batches during a lull in your work schedule.* Phone calls and e-mail can interrupt your train of thought on important projects. Returning them all at one time allows you to use your time more efficiently.

6. *Have a place to work uninterrupted.* When a deadline is near, you can concentrate on the task at hand. Trying to refocus on a task or project after interruptions wastes a lot of time.

7. *Do something productive during nonproductive activities.* Try to multitask (accomplish multiple tasks at the same time). Listen to educational or personal improvement tapes while driving to and from work or class. Read the newspaper or balance your checking account while you're waiting in line. When watching television, take care of household tasks such as cooking, cleaning, and doing laundry.

Source: Adapted from D. A. Whetten and K. S. Cameron, *Developing Management Skills,* 6th ed., Upper Saddle River, NJ: Prentice Hall, 2005. Adapted by permission of Pearson Education, Inc.

Delegation

LOC-In

The transfer of decision-making authority from a manager to a subordinate or a team at a lower level in the organization is **delegation.** It should not be confused with participation, in which the group *shares* decision-making authority with management. When a manager delegates decision-making authority, the subordinate makes the decision.

Managers delegate decisions for several reasons. The most important is that delegation gives the manager more time to spend on the most important tasks and decisions. For example, the chief executive officer (CEO) of a large corporation can focus on the overall direction and coordination of the corporation and delegate operational responsibilities for profits and losses to the general managers who report to him or her. Another reason to delegate is that it teaches subordinates how to make their own decisions and to deal with the consequences of those decisions. The

5 Learning Objective Check-In

1. *Arthur works in the transportation industry, where technology is rapidly evolving and the work pace is very fast. Arthur anticipates problems before they become pervasive. He makes time on both a daily and weekly basis to set goals and priorities. Arthur is a _____.*
   a. *reactive manager*
   b. *consequential manager*
   c. *proactive manager*
   d. *behavioral manager*

delegation

The transfer of decision-making authority from a manager to a subordinate or a team at a lower level in the organization.

Delegating the responsibility for resolving customer complaints to the front-desk staff has resulted in satisfied customers and empowered employees for the Hampton Inn firm.

subordinates receive feedback on the quality of their decision making and develop new skills that prepare them for future promotions. Finally, delegation may lead to higher quality decisions that result in greater customer satisfaction, because lower-level employees are closer to actual customers and therefore are more aware of their needs.

During the past decade, many corporations have relieved middle management of decision-making authority and have given it to teams of front-line employees, attempting to eliminate unnecessary layers of management in the process. Hampton Inn, a national hotel chain, has delegated authority to deal with customer complaints to desk clerks and housekeepers. Desk clerks can decide whether a complaint is justified and provide an immediate refund to a dissatisfied customer. This delegation of authority is part of Hampton Inn's "100% Satisfaction Guarantee," developed to gain a distinctive advantage in the highly competitive hotel industry, and it has resulted in higher levels of both customer and employee satisfaction, since Hampton employees feel more committed and motivated by being trusted to make important decisions involving guests.

Effective delegation involves the following steps:

1. Determine what you want done. Writing it down can be helpful.
2. Match the desired task with the most appropriate employee.
3. Be sure you communicate clearly when assigning the task. Follow up to make sure the task is fully understood. Set clear deadlines.
4. Keep communication channels open. Make it clear that you are available for consultation and discussion.
5. Allow employees to do the task the way they feel comfortable doing it.
6. Trust employees' capabilities. Do not hold such high expectations that they can only fail.
7. Check on the progress of the assignment, but do not rush to rescue the employee at the first sign of failure.

BARRIERS TO EFFECTIVE DELEGATION

How do barriers keep managers from effectively delegating responsibilities to their subordinates and using their full capabilities? This exercise presents some ways managers can avoid these barriers.

After reading the following justifications managers use to explain why they have not delegated responsibilities to subordinates in their work units, form groups of four or five people to discuss them.

Discuss each justification and consider what you believe are the underlying causes for a failure to delegate. Finally, work together to answer the group discussion questions that appear at the end of the exercise.

1. I feel uncomfortable asking subordinates to do some of the tasks I normally do.
2. My subordinates lack the appropriate knowledge to do the task I would like to delegate to them.
3. I can do some tasks more quickly than I can explain them to my subordinates.
4. My subordinates lack the appropriate skills and experience, so I can do the task better than they can.
5. My subordinates are already too busy.
6. If someone else does a task, it may weaken my control.
7. If someone else makes a mistake, I am responsible.

8. I feel better if people see me as an extraordinarily hard worker.
9. I feel uncomfortable relying on the judgment of subordinates around delegated tasks.
10. I no longer know what is going on.

Discussion Questions

1. What reasons or arguments could you give to counter each of the 10 objections to delegation that are listed above? Is failure to delegate a symptom of a more fundamental management problem? Why or why not?
2. How could you get a manager to overcome the fear of delegating work to subordinates?
3. Are there some tasks that cannot be delegated to subordinates? If so, give some examples. Is there any type of work that you would recommend that managers not delegate? Explain.
4. Describe a situation that would be highly favorable to delegating work to subordinates. Describe a highly unfavorable situation.

Source: From *Becoming a Master Manager*, 3rd ed., edited by R. E. Quinn et al. Copyright © 2003 John Wiley & Sons, Inc. Reprinted with permission of John Wiley & Sons, Inc.

---

8. Hold the employee responsible for the work and any difficulties that may emerge, but do so as a teacher, not a police officer. Explore what is going wrong, and help employees develop their own solutions.
9. Recognize what the employee has done, and show appropriate appreciation.[17]

Some *barriers* to delegation of responsibilities by managers and ways to surmount these barriers are shown in Skills for Managing 6.2 above.

LOC-In

6 Learning Objective Check-In

1. *Marco is a manager at a software engineering firm in Los Angeles. In the past, Marco has made all the decisions regarding his team and some of the more technical implementation decisions on a case-by-case basis. Because the group he oversees has more combined experience than he does in several matters relating to software development, he has recently transferred decision-making authority from himself to the entire team. Because of the effective team dynamics already in place and his confidence in the team's expertise, Marco believes this _____ will prove very successful.*
   a. *proactive management*
   b. *reactive management*
   c. *nominal group technique*
   d. *delegation*

CONCLUDING THOUGHTS

At the end of the chapter's introductory vignette we presented some critical thinking questions about decisions made by top executives at Yahoo!, Microsoft, and, in particular, Google. Now that you've had the opportunity to learn about decision making in the chapter, consider those critical thinking questions again.

Google's decision to enter the Chinese Internet market was clearly nonprogrammable, and it was high in uncertainty and risk. Entering any huge and growing market, even at home, is always a risk, but the Chinese government's restrictive control of Internet operations based within its borders adds another layer of potential hazard that Google's executives had to carefully calculate. The decision clearly brought conflict to, and probably within, the company, as debates about the possible outcomes of its choice continue. The scope of the decision is vast, with China poised to become the world's largest Internet market in a very short time, and its effects will extend far into the future if Google's offerings in China gain prominence.

Google's decision differed from Yahoo!'s and Microsoft's in coming a few years later, after the first two companies had gained some experience in the Chinese market. Google had the opportunity to learn from its competitors' mistakes and has so far chosen to base only one of its Chinese-language operations in China, where it must operate under government scrutiny. Google's executives also had a shorter time horizon in which to make their decision than the other companies did, since competition from them and from Chinese Internet providers will continue to grow with the market.

Focusing on the Future: Using Management Theory in Daily Life

Management Strategy and Decision Making

A new variant on the job of marketing is the *creative director* position. Companies as diverse as Marvel Enterprises (the publisher of Marvel Comics), Leo Burnett, and Bang and Olufsen all have creative director or chief designer positions. At Burger King, the "chief concept officer" is Denny Marie Post, a 48-year-old executive with more than 25 years of marketing experience behind her. Prior to working at Burger King, she was the chief innovation officer for KFC, Inc.[1]

Post points out the importance of combining creativity with a more formal decision-making process when she describes the development of the Enormous Omelet Sandwich. This sandwich, a combination of two eggs, sausage, cheese and bacon, boosted Burger King breakfast sales by 20 percent when it was introduced in March, 2005.[2]

The idea for the sandwich occurred during a brainstorming session in the Burger King test kitchen. Three or four of the creative staff were looking at a new mold for eggs. The mold was rectangular rather than circular, and as Post tells it, "I said, 'What if we put something between it and made it like an omelet? Like bacon.' Somebody else said we could use a bun from lunch and dinner, and before you know it, about three or four of us had built it."[3] But just having a good idea and building on it wasn't enough for Post. She knew that before Burger King invested money in a new product, there had to be some proof that the product would work. Getting the Enormous Omelet Sandwich into the hands of consumers required that Post use all four of the last stages of the decision-making process.

Evaluating Alternatives   Post uses a "concept screening process" to separate good ideas from the bad. Every food idea is run past a group of Burger King's most devoted customers. They evaluate each idea, just by looking at a description and a picture of the proposed food item. In this way, Post can tease out the good alternatives from the ones that are less likely to sell. She points out that of the 500 ideas run past the group in a given year, only 120 will receive further consideration. So, the first step in evaluating the Enormous Omelet Sandwich was to see how it fared with this important group of evaluators.

Choosing the Best Alternative   It isn't always easy to settle on one or two ideas for implementation. Post points out that when Burger King was testing the Enormous Omelet Sandwich, they were also testing a breakfast sandwich which included a biscuit and pepper-jack cheese. Although the other sandwich made it through several rounds of testing, in the end, evaluators decided that most people's taste buds weren't ready for pepper-jack anything at breakfast. Post used an optimizing strategy to select the best product, based on multiple criteria.

Implementing the Decision   Implementing the decision involved not only getting stores ready to produce the new product (which required the special egg molds discussed earlier), but also getting customers ready to buy the new product. Burger King started by targeting a specific market—16-to-24-year-old males who want to be "satisfied" after eating a sandwich, and who don't care much about calorie content or nutrition. They then commissioned their advertising agency, Crispin Porter + Bogusky, to create new commercials featuring "The King," a Burger King advertising mascot.[4] Finally, they created print and other media advertising to support the television ads designed to appeal to their target demographic.

An important part of implementation is being willing to stand up for decisions, even when those decisions are questioned by others. Denny Marie Post appeared on multiple television news and talk shows in 2005 to defend Burger King against charges that it was contributing to a growing obesity crisis in the United States. At 730 calories per sandwich with 47 grams of fat, the Enormous Omelet Sandwich was characterized by one ABC reporter as a "gut buster" and other reporters pointed out that the sandwich was basically a heart attack waiting to happen. Post countered these claims by informing the media that Burger King also offered low fat food options, and that consumer choice was the most important thing in the long run.[5]

Evaluating the Decision   Denny Marie Post watched sales carefully after the introduction of the new sandwich. As noted above, they were up for the first two months by 20 percent. They remained high throughout the year, and Burger King credits the Enormous Omelet Sandwich with helping to save the company.[6] In fact, the sandwich was so successful, that a second sandwich, the Meat'normous Omelet Sandwich, was introduced in the fall of 2005.

Source: [1] Burger King Company Information Web site, http://www.bk.com/CompanyInfo/bk_corporation/executive_team/post.aspx, April 13, 2006;
[2] Bruce Horovitz, "Restaurant Sales Climb with Bad-For-You Food," *USA Today*, May 12, 2005;
[3] Michael Prospero, Fast Talk: Creative to the Core, *Fast Company*, December 2005, p. 30
[4] *South Florida The Business Journal*, "'Enormous' Launch Adds to Burger King Breakfast Menu," March 28, 2005, April 13, 2006, http://www.bizjournals.com/southflorida/stories/2005/03/28/daily1.html;
[5] Amy Menefee, "Networks Hound Burger King for Launching 'Enormous Sandwich,'" Free Market Project, April, 1, 2005, April 13, 2006, http://www.freemarketproject.org/news/2005/news20050401.asp;
[6] *QSR Magazine*, "Best of 2005," http://www.qsrmagazine.com/issue/84/best/menu.phtml, April 13, 2006.

summary of learning objectives

Decision making is the process of identifying and resolving problems and taking advantage of opportunities. It involves understanding the underlying causes of a problem or nature of an opportunity and implementing an effective plan or solution. This chapter's discussion will help future managers, work teams, and employees make better, more effective decisions. The ideas presented in the chapter to meet each of the learning objectives is summarized below.

1 Recognize the nature of management decisions: programmability, uncertainty, risk, conflict, decision scope, and crisis situations.
- **Programmability** refers to whether the problem is well defined based on past experience or whether there are no established procedures for making a unique decision.
- **Uncertainty** means that incomplete information is available to make a decision.
- **Risk** varies with the level of uncertainty associated with the decision outcome. Under a state of risk, the availability of each alternative and its outcome are associated with a probability estimate.
- **Conflict** occurs when there are disagreements about goals and priorities that affect the selection of the solution. Conflict is a normal part of the decision-making process when diverse interests are competing to control the outcome.
- **Decision scope** involves the effect and time horizon of the decision.
- In a **crisis** situation there is a small amount of time to make a decision that can impact the survival of the organization.

2 Utilize the six steps of decision making.
- Decision making involves a step-by-step process that unfolds in sequential stages:
- *Identify and diagnose the problem*. Understand the underlying causes of the problem before attempting to form possible solutions.
- *Generate alternative solutions*.
- *Evaluate the alternative* solutions in light of the decision criteria. The decision criteria should be related to performance goals.
- *Choose the best alternative* solution by either **optimizing** (selecting the optimally best solution) or **satisficing** (selecting the first alternative that meets the minimum criteria).
- *Implement the decision*. This means putting the solution into practice and establishing controls to make sure it works the way it is expected to work.
- *Evaluate the results*. Decision evaluation involves gathering information and learning if the decision is on target to reach its goals. If not, modifications should be made to ensure the goals are reached.

3 Apply the criteria of quality and acceptance to a decision.
- **Decision quality** is based on factual information such as costs, revenues, or profits.
- **Decision acceptance** is based on people's feelings. Decision acceptance happens when people who are affected by a decision agree with what is done.

4 Reap the benefits and avoid the problems of group decision making.

- The decision-making process is likely to reside within a group when employee commitment to the decision outcome is critical to the successful implementation.
- Group decision-making can be beneficial to the *quality* of the decision by involving more people who have a greater diversity of ideas and opinions, and it can enhance decision *acceptance* by giving more people a voice in the decision.
- Disadvantages of group decision making are having to deal with dominant individuals or forceful factions and **groupthink**, where the group avoids meaningful critical evaluation of solutions in favor of maintaining social harmony and cohesion.

5 Develop time management skills to generate adequate time to make decisions.

- One way to manage time is to eliminate or minimize "time wasters," activities that squander time.
- Another way to manage time is to be proactive and anticipate problems before they become pervasive by "working smarter, not harder."

6 Know when to delegate, and how to do so wisely.

- When a manager **delegates** decision-making authority, subordinates make decisions.
- The most important reason for a manager to delegate is that it gives the manager more time to spend on more important tasks and decisions.

discussion questions

1. What is the difference between a programmed and nonprogrammed decision? Consider a programmed decision and a nonprogrammed decision you have made recently. Compare and contrast the approaches you used to make these two decisions.

2. Can you teach people to make decisions? What types of decisions are useful for giving people experience in decision making? What types of decisions should be avoided in teaching trainees about decision making?

3. What are the advantages of delegating decision making to front-line employees and teams? Are there any disadvantages to this approach to decision making?

4. Should only top executives, such as the CEO, be involved in making strategic decisions? Can you think of a tactical or operational decision that could benefit from the involvement of the CEO or another top executive? What are the drawbacks of involving CEOs in tactical and operational decision making?

5. How can electronic communications such as the Internet and e-mail be used to improve the decision-making process? Give some examples.

6. Define the following decision-making errors and identify ways to correct for them:

   a. Poor problem identification.

   b. Solution focus.

   c. Premature evaluation.

   d. Groupthink.

   e. Overemphasis on objective data without considering gut feelings.

   f. Omission of a way to monitor and control the decision.

7. Think of a decision in which you used an optimizing criterion for selecting the best decision alternative, and another decision in which you used a satisficing criterion. What factors influenced you to optimize instead of satisfice? Which ones affected your choice to satisfice instead of optimize?

8. Under what conditions is it better to involve a group of employees in decision making, rather than an individual manager? What roles should a manager or leader take in the group decision-making process?

management minicase 6.1

US Airways Escapes a Near Death Experience

US Airways hit a double whammy in 2001 when the Justice Department rejected its proposed merger with the larger United Airlines and travel declined following the September 11 terrorist attacks. In the spring of 2002, US Airways filed for Chapter 11 bankruptcy protection, which gave the company protection from its creditors while it restructured its debt and tried to attract new capital. By the spring of 2003, US Airways was ready to emerge from bankruptcy as a viable airline. Much of the credit for this amazing escape from a near death experience should be given to the crisis management skills of David Siegel, the CEO. Siegel was a seasoned veteran airline executive who had most recently worked at Continental Airlines during its turnaround.

Shortly after Siegel was hired, he quickly implemented a new strategy at US Airways. First, he refocused the airline route structure so that the profitable short-hop routes between major East Coast cities were retained, while some of the longer routes between smaller, second-tier cities were abandoned. This route reconfiguration allowed the company to get rid of some larger jet aircraft with more expensive operational costs and replace them with cheaper and smaller regional jets.

Next, Siegel forged new ties with the pilots. His "jobs for jets" program (he let displaced pilots of large aircraft have first chance to fly regional jets) and his willingness to open the company's books induced pilots to agree to pay cuts of at least 26 percent. That cut in labor costs helped the company win conditional approval of $900 million in federal loan guarantees.

When the airline's mechanics wouldn't join other unions in making voluntary sacrifices, Siegel took the carrier into Chapter 11—a status that gives companies the ability to void labor contracts with a judge's approval. That leverage helped Siegel bring the unionized mechanics around. Siegel also got the unionized pilots to agree to major work-rule changes that increased labor cost efficiency. Finally, Siegel terminated the pilots' pension plan which eliminated a $2 billion shortfall and cleared the final hurdle for the company to move out of Chapter 11. While the pilots were grumbling about the loss of their pension plan many others were cheering. "David Siegel knows where he's going, and he's tough," says Frank Jay, a Houston-based executive recruiter for the airline industry.

Discussion Questions

1. David Siegel made some critical decisions to turn US Airways around under conditions of risk. What are the sources of risk with respect to the decisions made by Siegel? For example, what are the risks associated with taking the company into Chapter 11 bankruptcy? What are the risks of taking away benefits from the unionized pilots and mechanics?

2. David Siegel was an "outsider" who was hired to take US Airways out of a difficult financial situation that was threatening its survival. What decision-making advantages does an "outsider" such as Siegel have over an "insider" who is promoted from within to be the new CEO, when it comes to making tough decisions that can improve a distressed company's ability to survive?

Source: Adapted from J. Helyar. "A Tale of Two Bankruptcies," *Fortune*, February 17, 2003, pp. 68–69.

Merck's Decision to Withdraw Its Vioxx Drug from the Market

management minicase 6.2

By the time Merck, a leading pharmaceutical firm, withdrew its pain relief drug Vioxx from the market in 2004, more than 100 million prescriptions had been filled in the United States alone. Researchers estimate that Vioxx may have been associated with as many as 25,000 heart attacks and strokes, and more than 1,000 claims have been filed against the company. Evidence of the drug's risks was available as early as 2000, when the *New England Journal of Medicine* reported evidence that linked Vioxx to a greater risk of heart attacks and strokes. In one of Merck's own reports to federal regulators it showed that 14.6 percent of Vioxx patients suffered from cardiovascular problems while taking the drug and 2.5 percent developed serious problems including heart attacks. So why did so many doctors keep prescribing it?

The answer is that without realizing it, decision makers ignore certain critical information due to a phenomenon called *bounded awareness*—when cognitive blinders prevent a person from seeing, seeking, using, or sharing highly relevant, easily accessible, and readily understandable information during the decision-making process. Doctors that prescribed Vioxx, for example, in many cases received positive feedback from the patients. So, despite having access to information about the risks, physicians may have been blinded to the actual extent of the risks. To make matters worse, Merck heavily advertised Vioxx to customers by using media such as television to stimulate the demand for the drug so that by 2004 it became one of the firm's most profitable products. One must also wonder why Merck's executives allowed the drug to remain on the market for several years after the published research reported that there were problems with the drug.

Bounded awareness, an impediment to effective decision making, can occur at three stages in the decision-making process. First, decision makers may fail to see or look for important information that is needed to make a sound decision. Second, they may fail to use the information that they do see because they are not aware of its relevance. Third, decision makers may fail to share information with others, which limits the organization's awareness.

When making decisions in which a bad decision can have disastrous consequences, it is a good idea for executives to broadly collect information from many sources and share information with diverse people who bring different perspectives to the decision-making process. Had this approach been taken, disasters such as the terrorist attack on the World Trade Center or the *Challenger* space shuttle explosion might have been avoided because in both these situations decision makers had information that predicted these events yet in the decision-making process this information was not used.

Discussion Questions

1. Why do you think the decision makers at Merck failed to use the information that indicated the Vioxx pain relief drug was linked to increased risk of heart attacks and strokes?

2. What practices should Merck develop to improve its decision-making process in order to avoid future product recalls such as the situation with Vioxx, which is likely to cost the company billions in legal costs to settle with customers as well as tarnish its reputation as a leading drug company?

3. Why do you think so many doctors failed to use the published information about the risks to their patients of using Vioxx and instead continued to prescribe this drug? What should doctors do to improve their decision making when it concerns prescribing drugs to patients?

Sources: Adapted from M. Bazerman and D. Chugh, "Decisions without Blinders," *Harvard Business Review*, January 2006, pp. 88–97; M. Watkins, and M. Bazerman, "Predictable Surprises: The Disasters You Should Have Seen Coming," *Harvard Business Review*, March 2003, pp. 72–80; and M. Bazerman, *Judgment in Managerial Decision Making*, 6th ed. New York: Wiley, 2005.

individual/ collaborative learning case 6.1

Intel Recalls the Pentium Chip

In the fall of 1994, cofounder Andrew Grove was riding high as CEO of Intel, the largest and most profitable semiconductor company in the world. Intel's chips were found in 80 percent of the personal computers in the world. In its twenty-sixth year of making computer chips, it was anticipating a record $10 billion dollars in sales and 30 percent growth.

Intel was beginning full-scale production of the Pentium, its newest microprocessor chip. This chip's superior performance promised a bright future for the company. In the previous year, Grove began a massive advertising campaign for Intel chips, which elevated public awareness of Intel and differentiated the products that contained its chips.

In the midst of these positive circumstances, a troubling event occurred. A bug was discovered in the Pentium chip that could cause mathematical errors during processing. The bug caused a division error once every 9 billion times. At this rate a typical user of spreadsheet software on a Pentium-controlled computer would run into the problem once every 27,000 years of use. Intel scientists were aware of this error in June 1994, but because it would cause an error so infrequently, they did not consider it to be a material flaw and put the problem on the back burner, while the company continued to ship the Pentium chip.

When individual users encountered the error and turned to Intel for help, however, they were not happy with Intel's response to the problem or to their requests for replacement chips. The company's policy was to replace chips only after assessing each individual's problem. Customers who claimed their computers handled a lot of division functions were given replacement chips, while others might or might not have their chips replaced.

Users affected by the chip's flaw began posting information about the error on the Internet in late October; it was picked up by a trade newspaper, which ran a story about it on the front page; other trade papers ran the story as well. Three weeks later when CNN, the cable news network, wanted to question Intel executives about the bug on television, a media frenzy occurred. Stories appeared in major newspapers with headlines such as, "Flaw Undermines Accuracy of Pentium Chips."

The crisis mushroomed in mid-December, when IBM announced that it would stop shipments of all Pentium-based computers. Because IBM was a key player in the computer industry, its action attracted a lot of attention. Intel customers clamored to find out what Intel was going to do with the Pentium chips that it had already sold to them.

After the events of the fall, Grove knew he had to make a decision on the Pentium chip. Should Intel spend millions of dollars to replace the flawed chip for all users, or should it counter what the company felt were overly negative reports from the media with a more moderate response?

Critical Thinking Questions

1. Why do you think the media paid so much attention to the error in the Pentium chip, which occurred only once in every 9 billion divisions? Was the margin for accuracy high enough for the typical customer of a personal computer? Explain.

2. Why would Intel release the flawed Pentium chip to the market instead of delaying its introduction until the flaw was fixed?

3. Why do you think Intel treated early customer complaints about the Pentium error by relying on standard Intel customer complaint procedures—a programmed approach to decision making?

Collaborative Learning Exercise

Assume it is 1994. With a partner or small group, identify the true nature of the problem Intel CEO Andrew Grove faced. Recommend a course of action to Grove, considering the following alternatives. Should all the Pentium chips be replaced at a cost of $500 million? Or should he run an aggressive media campaign to tell Intel's side of the story, spelling out how trivial the flaw is and trying to convince customers that they are highly unlikely to be affected by it? Support your recommendation.

Source: Adapted from A. Grove, *Only the Paranoid Survive*. New York: Currency Doubleday, 1996, pp. 11–16.

Decision Making at Coca-Cola

Coca-Cola CEO Roberto Goizueta acted decisively after making a mistake with the launch of the New Coke product in 1985. In this exercise you will learn more about the Coca-Cola Company and what it stands for. Visit the Coca-Cola Web site and explore the "Our Company" and "Investors" areas there, and then answer the following questions:

1. What are the key values at Coca-Cola? What do these values reveal about the Coca-Cola Company?

2. Coke sponsors many sporting events, such as World Cup Soccer, National Football League, National Basketball Association, Tour de France bicycle race, Rugby World Cup, and the Olympic Games. Why is Coke so involved with sponsoring these events? What benefits do you think Coke receives from these sponsorships?

3. Who is the current CEO of Coca-Cola? How has Coke's market valuation changed since 1997, when it was valued at $180 billion?

internet
exercise 6.1

www.cocacola.com

Determining Decision Risk and Uncertainty Preferences

How likely are you to take risks in making decisions? Consider the following statements and mark each "True" or "False" to indicate whether you agree or disagree.

_____ 1. I get my hair cut at the same place every month because I know it will always be cut the same way.

_____ 2. If I need to hire an engineer, I know that if I hire the job candidate who has a master's degree in engineering she'll have the knowledge to do the job.

_____ 3. With the growing consumer market in China, products should sell well there.

_____ 4. A new computer is expensive, but it will help generate enough business to cover the cost in just four months.

manager's
checkup 6.1

_____ 5. If two auto shops are equally reliable and say they can repair my car tomorrow, I'll take my car to the one that says it can do the same repairs for $25 less.

_____ 6. If a company doesn't jump into the service sector of its market, it will miss a golden opportunity.

_____ 7. If I know someone always gets to the office by 8:30 in the morning, I know I can call him there at 8:45.

_____ 8. One health-insurance policy would cost me less in premiums but charges a higher deductible; another policy has higher premiums but a lower deductible. Since I'm generally healthy, I'll buy the first policy.

_____ 9. Switching to environmentally responsible packaging will appeal to our customers, even though the packaging is not as attractive, so we should switch.

_____ 10. One hardware store opens at 7:00 in the morning and another at 9:00, but only the latter store carries the brand of batteries I prefer. I can go to either store. Since I don't need the batteries first thing in the morning, I'll wait until the second store opens.

Scoring: "True" answers to statements 1, 5, 7, and 10 indicate a preference for certainty. "True" answers to statements 2, 4, and 8 indicate an acceptance for risk. "True" answers to statements 3, 6, and 9 indicate an acceptance of uncertainty.

Source: From _Management of Organizations_, by P. M. Wright and R. A. Noe: Copyright © 1996 The McGraw-Hill Companies, Inc. Reprinted with permission.

video summary

Economic Rebuilding in New Orleans

Summary

A commission called "Bring New Orleans Back" is charged with helping struggling business owners get back on their feet after much of their property and the city's tourist industry were damaged by Hurricane Katrina. In the middle of a famous historic district, flooding ruined the kitchen in John Tsatsoulis' Market Cafe, and he's in the process of installing $200,000 worth of new equipment, including a truckload of pieces for a new walk-in freezer. Tsatsoulis decided that all the equipment would need to be replaced because "everything stunk" and it may have been contaminated by the rotten food and floodwaters. Still, he is making the investment to refurbish his restaurant from his personal savings, and says he doesn't anticipate retirement anytime soon. He is in it for his children, he says. One of his current challenges is getting workers to return to the city to work for him again. Some of them have moved away to find other jobs; others have children who may not have a school to come back to if they were to decide to return. For the city, these are just some examples of the problems New Orleans faces. The city thrived on tourism, yet today there are precious few tourists to patronize local shops or restaurants. One business owner, who ran a meat market before the hurricane, says if he does reopen, he will cater to the construction workers—selling hot meals, cigarettes, and, possibly, some alcohol. "That's it," he says, considering that the company would likely have great trouble sustaining itself in its previous form. If the tourists are not there spending money, there's no income for the businesses, workers, or tax base for the city. The normally crowded sidewalks are dormant and the carriages are running empty. Many businesses say they're doing about 20 percent of what they normally do this time of year.

Many people agree that housing will be the key to economic recovery for the city. Anthony Patton sits on an economic development commission that is studying how to revitalize the economy. He is particularly critical of the federal Small Business Administration, which grants low interest loans. He says that both types of loan application processes that apply in this situation to businesses in New Orleans seeking to rebuild are too slow. The SBA says they have increased the number of staff who deal with loan applications from 800 before Katrina to 4,000 today. Most of the business owners say they are hanging on by their financial fingernails, hoping the city, state and federal governments can find a way to bring people back to the Crescent City to live, to work and to play—because without all three, New Orleans commerce cannot recover.

Discussion Questions

1. What is *decision acceptance*? Name some decisions in the video case that affect various stakeholders in New Orleans. Do you think there is decision acceptance among the business owners of New Orleans?

2. What will business owners have to do differently once the city is restored? How will market conditions there be different, and how will this affect their decision making?

3. A common criticism of the government in its response to the disaster in New Orleans is that it spent too much time planning and did not respond soon enough. What factors are involved here that demonstrate the nature of management decisions? Name at least two and describe them.

chapter 7

Strategic Management

Learning Objectives

1. Explain how the firm's external environment should be examined as part of the strategic management process.

2. Explain how the firm's internal environment should be examined as part of the strategic management process.

3. State the meaning and purpose of the firm's strategic intent and mission.

4. Understand how the strategy formulation process helps the firm achieve its mission.

5. Describe the issues that should be considered in strategy implementation.

6. Understand how the outcomes of the strategic management process should be assessed.

iPod Universe

7

It's not unusual these days to spend a few hundred dollars on an iPod. In one recent year Apple sold 32 million of its digital music players, or one every second. But as good as that news is, the story of the iPod universe may be even better for Apple and for the dozens of firms licensed to create accessories for its hottest new product.

For every $3 spent on an iPod, at least $1 is spent on an iPod accessory, which means that each player spins off about three or four additional purchases. Accessory makers are happy because they're shipping new products as fast as they can make them. Retailers—not just electronics stores but even Urban Outfitters and auto dealerships—are happy because their profit margins on accessories are about twice as high as on the iPod itself. And although little of the $850 million spent on accessories every year goes into Apple's coffers, Apple is happy too. In this case, Apple's strategy is not really about the revenue—it's about helping support the iPod's dominant position as the coolest music player you can own.

With sales of accessories projected to soon soar past $1 billion annually, the iPod is looking very secure. "For us it's great because the decision to buy an iPod is reinforced when consumers see all the accessories," says Greg Joswiak, Apple's vice president for worldwide iPod marketing. And one manufacturer of about a dozen iPod accessories agrees: "I've never seen anything like it in my career."

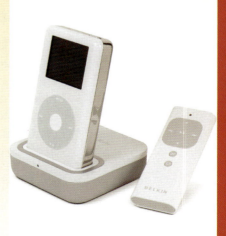

Unlike Disney and Mattel, which have tightly controlled the huge market for Mickey Mouse and Barbie accessories by licensing the brand or creating the accessory products themselves, Apple has encouraged other manufacturers to freely enter the fray with products that complement the player's sleek and simple design. The iPod almost begs to be personalized, and there's no shortage of ways to do so, starting with a $10 nylon case and ranging all the way up to a Kolcraft baby stroller with an iPod slot built in. More than half of all accessory sales are for cases, car chargers, transmitters, speakers, and docking stations. The number of accessories on the market has doubled in less than a year, and even the markets for headphones and for the lowly clock radio are enjoying a renaissance thanks to the iPod. "You throw an iPod in there and you have a growth category again," said on industry analyst.

As happy as Apple is with the success of its strategy, it does plan to become more active in the accessory market in the near future. "We've chosen to participate in the [accessory] market, not overwhelm it," Joswiak says, but that's changing. Apple will be adding to its line of products, which now features mostly an assortment of colorful cloth sleeves it refers to as "socks." One recent Apple entry was an iPod hi-fi home stereo system.

Its savvy in the accessories market may be one of the reasons Apple isn't hurting very much from the effects of one of its other strategies: providing minimal customer support.

Sources: Laurie J. Flynn, "Apple Offers Hi-Fi System to Use ipod in the Home," *New York Times*, *www.nytimes.com*, March 1, 2006, Joe Nocera, "Good Luck with That Broken iPod," *New York Times*, February 4, 2006, p. C1; Damon Darlin, "The iPod Econsystem: Add-Ons Have Become a Billion-Dollar Bonanza," *New York Times*, *www.nytimes.com*, February 3, 2006.

CRITICAL THINKING QUESTIONS

1. *How has Apple's strategy of encouraging the manufacture of iPod accessories helped boost the success of the iPod player?*

2. *What role does strategic management play in Apple's decision to encourage other manufacturers to ride on the iPod's success?*

3. *What will be the result of Apple's more aggressive entry into the accessory market?*

We'll revisit these questions at the end of the chapter in our Concluding Thoughts, after you've had a chance to read about strategic management.

The Strategic Management Process

It is the job of top-level management to chart the course of the entire enterprise. The strategic management process includes analysis of the internal and external environment of the firm, definition of the firm's mission, and formulation and implementation of strategies to create or continue a competitive advantage. These efforts steer the organization in a particular direction and require large resource commitments, which is why strategic management is generally the responsibility of top executives.

Reversing strategic decisions can be costly, so most firms take a long-term perspective when making these choices. For instance, in the mid-1990s, Ford CEO Alex Trotman announced "Ford 2000," a new strategic direction for the firm. The strategy spelled out all the new cars and trucks Ford would manufacture in the following 10 years and the resources required to produce them. It called for reducing the number of basic designs or platforms from 24 to 16 and increasing the number of models produced from them by 50 percent. To save on costs and increase quality, Ford would revamp its design and manufacturing process on a worldwide basis. All North American and European engineering operations were consolidated in five vehicle development centers, each of which had a global mission.

Five years later, Ford realized that although centralized worldwide responsibility for functions such as product development, purchasing, design, and manufacturing generated significant cost savings, it also resulted in less customer responsiveness at the local level. Jacques A. Nasser, who became CEO following Trotman, made significant adjustments to Trotman's plan by restoring much of the power that had been stripped away from regional Ford managers: "The central idea is to create bite-size, highly accountable regional brand units that can get to their target customers' tastes and needs."

Yet Nasser lasted only two years on the job. According to his successor, Bill Ford (whose great-grandfather was Henry Ford), Nasser was fired by the Ford family (which still controls one-third of Ford's shares) for "pursuing strategies that were either poorly conceived or poorly timed." Bill Ford decided to centralize many of Ford's activities in order to avoid duplication and focus the company's attention on launching new products, saving on costs, and eliminating low-margin vehicles. Unfortunately, by 2006, it had become evident that this strategy was not producing the intended results. Ford's market share dropped precipitously and its U.S. auto sales have been declining about 5 percent a year, much faster than General Motors' (which has also been suffering lately). In late 2006, Bill Ford stepped down as Ford's situation continued to deteriorate. Besides planning a reduction in workforce of about 30,000 employees by 2012, Ford announced a new strategy for 2006–2010 to emphasize production of cars that run on ethanol (which is distilled from corn and grain)—a market niche with little competition from Japanese car makers—and "nostalgia" cars (such as the Mustang) to appeal to baby boomers.[1] It remains to be seen at the time of this writing if this strategy will work; if not, Ford may need to once again revise its strategic plans.

The experience at Ford demonstrates another key attribute of strategic management: For a strategy to be successful, a firm must be flexible and make changes to the plan based on experience. Strategic management involves both long-range thinking and adaptation to changing conditions. However, each change also carries risk. Some of these issues are explored in greater detail in Chapter 8.

Strategies should be designed to generate a sustainable competitive advantage. This means that competitors will be unable to duplicate what the firm has done or will find it too difficult or expensive. When competitors ultimately learn how to copy the strategy, the firm should modify or reformulate the strategy to stay ahead. American Express was a pioneer in the credit card business in the 1950s. The card charged an annual fee and all purchases had to be repaid within a month of billing. For almost 25 years, the American Express card was a worldwide symbol of prestige. American Express posted high earnings year after year. Soon, competitors such as Visa and MasterCard entered the industry with card features that were more convenient to customers, such as no annual fees, installment payment plans, air travel insurance, and extended warranties on purchases. These cards were also differentiated based on prestige, with different-colored cards for varying credit limits. American Express began to lose its competitive advantage. In the late 1990s, American Express's CEO, Harvey Golub, and president, Kenneth Chenault, launched a fierce counterattack against Visa and MasterCard, introducing a wide variety of cards for different market segments with many features that matched or surpassed those of the competitors. American Express has launched about 20 new cards including a consumer-friendly "Blue card" with an electronic smart chip embedded in it that could contain account information. In 2006, American Express summarized its new strategy as "to earn 100 percent of plastic spending of all target U.S. individuals and their households by providing a wide range of payment options (charge and lending cards) . . . offering a portfolio of products tailored to the needs of specific customer groups."[2]

In the automotive sector, the truck and SUV segments were General Motors' golden goose, bringing in almost twice as much profit per vehicle as compared to cars. Asian manufacturers such as Nissan and Honda quickly entered this attractive market and have already conquered more than a third of the light truck and SUV market in the United States. GM's profits have dropped accordingly. A major challenge facing GM is how to modify or reformulate its strategy now that its golden goose has been stolen by competitors capable of producing these vehicles at much lower costs.[3]

As a last example of how imitation by competitors tends to erode profits, and why firms must be on constant alert to be able to respond, Whole Foods (a supermarket chain) has increased its earnings at a nearly 20 percent annualized clip since the early 1990s, at a time when most other chains were stagnant or making modest profit gains. It has done so by targeting a growing market niche of consumers willing to pay more for organic food (for instance, chicken without hormones and bananas without pesticides). But by 2006, other supermarket chains, such as Safeway and Fry's, were beginning to copy the Whole Foods approach. Investors are currently wondering how Whole Foods will be able to respond to this competitive challenge in years to come.[4] What investors think of a company's competitive strategy is a critical issue for most firms, since in the long run, a firm must earn at least average returns if it hopes to stay in business. Investors are likely to withdraw their funds from firms with below-average earnings.

In this chapter, we discuss the major aspects of the strategic management process and how this process affects the firm's competitive advantage. Figure 7.1 on page 267 shows the interdependent parts of the strategic management process that firms must manage to win battles in a global marketplace that grows more ferocious every year. First, the firm needs to analyze its external and internal environments. Second, information gathered from this analysis serves as a basis of a statement of strategic intent and mission. Next, company leaders formulate and implement strategies that will allow the firm to achieve sustained superior performance in light of its strategic intent and mission. Last, the executive team should periodically assess the outcomes of strategic plans. *Strategic outcomes* refer to intended and unintended results. Intended results can include higher profits, more focus on products or services, and increased stock price; unintended results can be lower customer responsiveness, higher cost, and improved productivity. The strategic outcome information in turn feeds into the analysis of the internal and external environment, which may lead to redefinition of strategic intent and mission, strategy formulation, and implementation.

As indicated in the case of Ford Motor Company, strategic management is a dynamic process. Adjustments may be necessary after examining strategic outcomes. For the sake of clarity, each step in Figure 7.1 is discussed separately, but it is important to remember that the various components of the strategic management process are closely linked to one another.

FIGURE 7.1

Components of the Strategic
Management Process

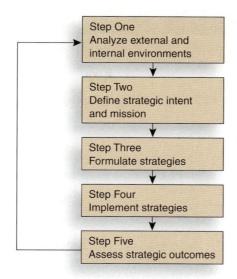

Step One
Analyze external and
internal environments

Step Two
Define strategic intent
and mission

Step Three
Formulate strategies

Step Four
Implement strategies

Step Five
Assess strategic outcomes

Step One: Analyzing External and Internal Environments

One commonly used strategic tool is a **SWOT (strengths-weaknesses-opportunities-threats) analysis**. The objective is to analyze factors from both within and outside the organization that may influence success. The external and internal factors to be considered in the SWOT analysis are discussed next. SWOT enables managers to identify organizational strengths (S) and weaknesses (W), and environmental opportunities (O) and threats (T). A properly conducted SWOT analysis generates information which helps a firm respond to various strategic challenges. SWOT does not tell the firm what strategies to pursue; instead it provides input for strategic decisions. Skills for Managing 7.1 "Will Harley-Davidson Hit the Wall?", on page 268, shows a summary of a SWOT analysis for the motorcycle manufacturer. Based on this SWOT information, executives at Harley-Davidson must consider whether or not to redefine the company's strategic intent and mission. For instance, the management team should consider broadening the firm's mission to incorporate a wide array of two-wheel vehicles, not only large motorcycles, reformulating strategies to diversify its product mix, and changing strategy implementation protocols such as opening franchises in newly developing markets.

Figure 7.2 on page 268 summarizes the factors that should be considered in an analysis of the firm's external and internal environments. Each of these is discussed in turn next.

SWOT analysis

A strategic management tool to evaluate the firm, which is accomplished by identifying its strengths and weaknesses and identifying its opportunities and threats.

SWOT Analysis

The External Environment

In strategic management, the world around the company must be considered as carefully as the world inside the company. Company leaders must study the external environment in order to identify opportunities and threats in the marketplace, avoid surprises, and respond appropriately to competitors' moves. CEO Bill Gates's observation may explain why Microsoft controls 93 percent of the world market for PC operating systems: "Why have we doubled our R&D on Windows in the last three years? Because we know that unless we do that we will

7.1

WILL HARLEY-DAVIDSON HIT THE WALL? IDENTIFYING STRENGTHS, WEAKNESSES, OPPORTUNITIES AND THREATS

Wearing black leather and riding huge Harleys, a motorcycle gang thunders through northern Georgia as if on the way to a rumble. But the only rumble for this gang—the Atlanta Harley Owners Group (HOG)—is the one in their stomachs. It's another Sunday ride in the country for the group, and as usual it ends with a feast. "We live to ride, and we ride to eat," says club assistant director B. K. Ellis, a systems analyst.

Ellis is one of 55 HOG members on the outing, mostly white-collar types with secret lives as bikers—and total devotion to their Harleys. "It's the imagery, the mystique," says Ellis. Every year, Harley owners around the country get together for rallies, with up to 20,000 bikers at some events. In 2006, for instance, there were local and national rallies to celebrate Elvis' birthday, sports events, and unveiling of new Harley-Davidson racing bikes. Some would be hard-core guys with big tattoos and bad tempers, the sort who once typified the Harley customer. But most would be playing hooky from $78,000-per-year jobs (the average salary of today's Harley customer), riding $16,000 motorcycles (the typical cost of Harley's biggest bike, a cruiser), and pledging fealty to an open-road cult that doubles as a highly profitable $4 billion-a-year company.

This is the motorcycle world that Harley-Davidson has reinvented, one that seems—and is—a century removed from the Milwaukee shed where William Harley and Andrew Davidson first collaborated in 1903. To continue riding this success in the new millennium, top executives at Harley-Davidson believe that the time has come to analyze the com-

pany's strengths, weaknesses, opportunities, and threats (SWOT) in order to formulate and implement future strategies. The results of the SWOT analysis are summarized below.

Strengths

- *Customer Loyalty.* Harley today is more of a fraternity than a producer of machinery. Buying a Harley makes you part of a ready-made motorcycle gang consisting of 600 U.S. HOG chapters, operated under the dealers' aegis. Style is as important as speed. On dealer floors, leather-draped mannequins outnumber the bikes. Harley has artfully parlayed the romance of the road and the independence of the biker to capture baby-boomers. The company's core customers have reprised their 1960s rebelliousness through a product that bespeaks their middle-aged success.

- *Brand Recognition.* Even though it sells a niche product, Harley consistently ranks among the 10 best-known American brands, in the company of Coca-Cola and Disney.

- *Top Growth Stocks.* Harley ranks among America's top growth stocks since its 1986 IPO. Its 37 percent average annual gain runs just behind the 42 percent pace of another 1986 debutant: Microsoft.

- *Strong Dealer Networks.* The people who catch Harley fever will be directed to a hometown dealer. A Harley dealer is never too far away. Many offer "Rider's Edge" courses for novices.

(continued on next page)

FIGURE 7.2

Step One of the Strategic Management Process: Analyze External and Internal Environments

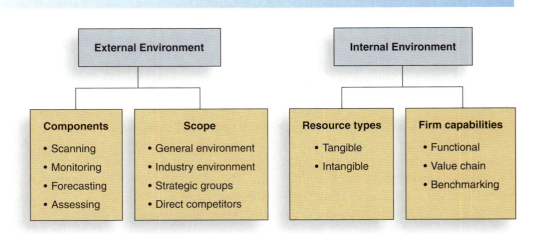

(continued from previous page)

Weaknesses

- *Limited Product Line.* Most of the company's revenues are tied to the big cruiser bike.
- *Quality.* Harley hasn't built better bikes than its four main Japanese competitors and the company once had persistent quality problems. There is still room for improvements in quality.
- *Limited Cross-Cultural Appeal.* The firm has been primarily USA-centric and is strongly associated with the American culture. This has limited its international sales.

Opportunities

- *International Markets.* As foreign markets continue to expand, primarily in developing countries such as India and China with a growing middle class, there may be an excellent outlet for the firm's products.
- *Youth Market.* Harley-Davidson appeals primarily to those over 45. Thus, there is an excellent market opportunity if the firm can develop products that appeal to prospective younger buyers.

Threats

- *Narrow Market Niche.* As the customer base has grayed, the average age of a Harley rider has risen from 38 to 46. Yet, the prime age for motorcycle customers is 35 to 44.

In addition, 91 percent of buyers are males, further limiting the customer base.

- *Generation Gap.* Harley's appeal still lies more in image than in performance, but fashion-driven companies are vulnerable to changes of fashion and generation. The future of Harley's business is in the new generations, not exactly the forte of a company attuned to baby-boomer rhythms and values. Naturally the boomers' kids want to ride anything but the old man's model. They may be drawn to machines that are the anti-Harley.
- *Customer Resistance to Change.* Making changes is tricky for a company with Harley's cult following: They risk alienating current customers. The V-Rod's water-cooled engine is a big departure from Harley's traditional air-cooled one, and to some uneasy riders a portent of additional unwelcome changes to come. "If they ever do anything with that [roaring] sound, they've lost their customer base," according to an industry consultant.
- *Strong Signs of Weakening Demand.* The customer waiting list for new motorcycles has shrunk from as much as two years to a matter of months. Dealer premiums that used to range between $2,000 and $4,000 have disappeared for most models.

Source: Adapted with permission from J. Helyar, "Will Harley-Davidson Hit the Wall?" *Fortune*, August 12, 2003, pp. 120-124. Updated by authors in 2006 using information obtained from www.harley-davidson.com.

be replaced. . . . Somebody makes something better? The demand can shift to that person overnight."[5] A major challenge for company executives is to gather accurate market intelligence in a timely fashion and transform it into usable knowledge that may be used to gain a competitive advantage.

Components of External Analysis

Studying the external environment requires managers to tap into a variety of sources, including the media, online information, journals and trade magazines, and other sources. There are four components of an external analysis: scanning, monitoring, forecasting, and assessing.

SCANNING   Analysis of general environmental factors that may be relevant to the firm's future is referred to as **scanning**. The primary objective is to identify

scanning

The analysis of general environmental factors that may directly or indirectly be relevant to the firm's future.

Managers at Coke and Pepsi must now consider a new threat to soda's dominance as the quintessential American drink. Sales of soda have begun to decline as alternatives like bottled water and sports drinks like Red Bull, Gatorade, Powerade, and Full Throttle have grown in popularity. The shift comes about as consumers begin to worry about the problem of obesity and look for healthier and more varied choices.

monitoring

Observing environmental changes on a continuous basis to determine whether a clear trend is emerging.

forecasting

Predicting what is likely to happen in the future, the intensity of the anticipated event, its importance to the firm, and the pace or time frame in which it may occur.

assessing

Evaluating the environmental data received to study the implications for the firm.

early signs of emerging trends and changes in the environment that may result in an opportunity or a threat. For instance, when there were fewer college-age students, many private universities stayed afloat by targeting senior citizens, foreign students, and working adults. Colgate-Palmolive also looked at changing demographics before launching Total, which in 2006 became the top-selling toothpaste in the United States. It contains triclosan, a broad spectrum antibiotic (effective against bleeding gum disease, making it a hit among aging baby boomers).[6] Also, many corporations have adapted products and marketing campaigns to segmented markets to take advantage of ethnic diversity. The Internet is having a major effect on the way firms sell their products and services worldwide. It can also change the competitive landscape almost overnight.

MONITORING Observing environmental changes on a continuous basis to determine whether a clear trend is emerging is referred to as **monitoring**. For example, recent data appears to contradict the belief that the future of North American business lies in design and innovation, while less developed countries will compete primarily through less skilled, lower-cost operations. In fact, countries such as India, China, and Brazil are quickly becoming "first world" in some high technology industries, showing high degrees of creativity, design, and innovation.[7] Monitoring can reduce the firm's level of uncertainty by interpreting current or past environmental information that is consequential to strategic decisions and that might require a response. Monitoring can reduce the level of uncertainty by keeping them aware of such events as elections, currency stability, lower inflation, and savings rates.

FORECASTING In **forecasting**, the firm attempts to predict what is likely to happen in the future, the intensity of the anticipated event, its importance to the firm, and the pace or time frame in which it may occur. Some firms routinely delay investing in new information technology based on forecasts of lower costs relative to the amount of computer power that may be purchased. However, these investments can only be postponed for so long before the firm is at a disadvantage. As discussed in Chapter 2, firms that expand internationally attempt to predict a host of variables that may have a direct effect on return on investments. These variables include political and legal change, economic conditions, and currency convertibility.

Forecasts can be wrong, so a firm needs to retain strategic flexibility to make necessary adjustments. Continuous scanning and monitoring of the environment can provide valuable feedback about whether a firm needs to reconsider its position.

ASSESSING Evaluation of environmental data received to study the implications for the firm is the process of **assessing**. Without an accurate assessment of consequences, the firm can make major blunders. For instance, when the cost of resin, a key raw material, increased, the management team at Rubbermaid thought that the company's well-recognized brand name and strong market presence would allow it to pass the increased costs on to customers. To their surprise, relatively unknown competitors such as Sterilite did not increase prices and quickly took away some of Rubbermaid's market share. Wal-Mart, which accounted for more than 15 percent of Rubbermaid's total household product sales, deleted Rubbermaid from its promotional materials and replaced it with Sterilite.

Rubbermaid is not alone.[8] Extended warranties represent the most profitable line of business for Best Buy and Circuit City. Unfortunately for these two firms, Wal-Mart is putting a big dent in their earnings by offering warranties that are 50 percent less expensive on average. Wal-Mart, with its over $300 billion in sales and approximately 1.5 million employees, is the biggest employer in 21 states, with more people in uniform than the U.S. Army. And Wal-Mart "is pressuring everyone from Bloomingdale's to Banana Republic to compete on price as well as image."[9] But there is one company that even Wal-Mart eyes warily these days: Google, a seven-year-old business in a seemingly distant industry. "We watch Google very closely at Wal-Mart," says Jim Breyer, a member of Wal-Mart's board. "In Google, Wal-Mart sees both a technology pioneer and the seed of a threat. The worry is that by making information available everywhere, Google might soon be able to tell Wal-Mart shoppers if better bargains are available nearby."[10]

Scope of the External Analysis

Analysis of the environment requires thinking on several levels. Managers can examine the environment at four different levels, including the general environment, the industry, strategic groups, and direct competitors.

THE GENERAL ENVIRONMENT Broad environmental forces may have an impact on a firm even though their consequences may not be apparent or the effect may not be immediate. For instance, most population growth is occurring in third world countries. This means that a huge middle class is developing in such poor countries as India and China. This may represent a market opportunity for some Western firms.[11] The population of the United States and many Western countries is aging rapidly as a result of increasing life expectancies and declining birth rates. Some automobile manufacturers anticipate that the demand for trucks, sport utility vehicles, and vans has peaked, because older people prefer more comfortable cars with a plush feel to them. This has implications for R&D investments, car design, and manufacturing processes.

Sometimes changes in the general environment may be abrupt and unpredictable. For instance, Boeing expected to earn $2.6 billion on sales of $47 billion by the end of 1997. Boeing ended up losing $348 million, in large measure because of a sudden economic crisis in Asia, where it had 35 percent of its backlogged orders. A few years later, Boeing had almost recovered. Then came the terrorist attacks of September 11, 2001. Once again, profits plummeted as most airlines in the United States and abroad were faced with empty flights. By 2006, Boeing was entering a boom period after booking a record order for 1,002 new planes[12] and landing a big new commercial satellite customer (Mobile Satellite Ventures) with an order valued at between $500 million and $1 billion.[13]

The general environment may be broken down into individual segments. These segments include demographic trends, economic conditions, political/legal forces, sociocultural conditions, technological changes, and globalization. Each of these is discussed next. They are not independent segments. A change in one, such as globalization, is likely to affect others, especially sociocultural conditions.

Demographic Trends The study of population characteristics and trends is demographics. Some may have a direct impact on both current and future business opportunities. These include population size, age distribution, ethnic mix, levels of labor force participation by women and the size and composition of families.

A Shine on Their Shoes

THEME: CUSTOMER FOCUS Most dot-com firms have failed, yet Zappos.com's blue-ribbon customer service is rapidly winning market share. Zappos, which was launched by a young entrepreneur named Tony Hsieh, sells shoes online, differentiating itself by its selection—some 90,000 styles and more than 500 brands, from Bass to Givenchy—and a near-fanatical devotion to customer service. Shipping and return shipping are free; most repeat customers get upgrades to free overnight or second-day delivery. The company has a 365-day return policy and promises to pay 110 percent of the difference if a customer finds a better price for the same item elsewhere. "With Zappos, the shoe store comes to you," says Pamela Leo, a customer in Montclair, New Jersey. "I can try the shoes on in the comfort of my own home. I can tell if the shoes I want will really work with a particular suit. It's fabulous." Hsieh, loath to advertise, has relied on such word of mouth to help double Zappos' sales every year for the past six years, to a projected $500 million in 2007. At the time of this writing (2006), Zappos had almost 2 million items in stock ready to be shipped.

At Zappos, a customer-service team makes sure that every customer e-mail gets a response. Customer-service employees don't use scripts and aren't pressed to keep calls short. Hsieh says customer loyalty is so important to the company culture that the call center and headquarters have to be in the same place—Las Vegas. Every new hire spends a week in the Kentucky warehouse before starting work. Staff is treated well: Health insurance premiums are 100 percent company-paid (though employees contribute to dependents' premiums). All 650 employees, from execs to warehouse workers, get a free lunch every day.

The warehouse is open 24/7, so customers can order shoes as late as 11 p.m. and still get next-day delivery. "If customers know that they're going to get the best service from Zappos and they're going to get it overnight, then anytime we're going to add a product category, our customers will be loyal to us," says Hsieh.

Zappos tries to treat its vendors equally well. The company's extranet lets vendors see which shoes are selling and how profitably. "I can see my business from their point of view," says Tom Austin, who manages the California and Nevada territories from Clarks Companies North America. "Fred [Mossler] just says, 'I don't want to run out of shoes, you take care of us.' You can't believe how pleasant they are to work with." Zappos even holds a vendor appreciation party before the big industry trade show each year. And yes, the call center staff are all invited.

Source: Adapted from K. Weisul, "A Shine on Their Shoes." *BusinessWeek*, December 5, 2005, p. 84. Updated by the authors in 2006 by consulting Zappos' Web page (www.zappos.com).

Subway's "Eat Fresh" and dieter Jared Fogle helped propel the fast food restaurant past the big guys—namely McDonald's and Burger King. By recognizing the changing environment of its consumer—the desire for healthier fast food—Subway has become a number one franchise.

A full chapter in the book (Chapter 11) is devoted to population diversity issues both in the United States and overseas. Demographic information can be useful when formulating strategies. For instance, electronic commerce was touted by many as the wave of the future in the late 1990s. Numerous investors rushed to pump money into Internet stores only to see the majority of them go bankrupt in less than two years. Surprisingly, by the middle of this decade electronic commerce is flourishing as exemplified by the case of Zappos, a shoe online retailer (see Management Close-Up 7.1 above, "A Shine on Their Shoes"). A major reason for this turnaround is that the demographic characteristics of those using the Internet have changed considerably in the past five years. There are now more women who are Internet users than men. This trend is relevant for e-commerce because women do most of the household shopping. Other firms that have taken advantage of demographic changes include Cochlear Ltd. (which produces ear implants to improve hearing)[14] and condo developers (which have seen condo values rising twice as fast as single family homes).[15] How? By targeting a rapidly graying population (more on this when we discuss diversity in Chapter 11). Skills for Managing 7.2 on page 273,

BUSINESS IMPLICATIONS OF AN INCREASINGLY OLDER POPULATION

In the richest countries of the world such as in North America and Western Europe, the population is aging rapidly. By 2020, it is estimated that approximately 35 percent of the population will be over 65, and about half will be 50 and older. A recent survey (Wiles, 2003) shows that various age groups have different attitudes toward life, including the willingness to take risks with investments or try new things. While 43 percent of those under 40 are willing to take substantial or above average risk, only 18 percent of those 58 or older are willing to do so.

In this exercise, the class is divided into groups of five. Each group chooses a well-known firm for analysis. It could be an investment bank, a brokerage house, a retailer, an educational institution, or a high-technology organization, for example.

1. Each group should first assess how the aging of the population is going to affect the business in the next 20 years.

2. Then each group must provide recommendations for dealing with any anticipated population effects they have identified.

3. A spokesperson from each group should then present the results of the group deliberations to the entire class.

"Business Implications of an Increasingly Older Population," challenges you to assess the effects of a rapidly aging population on business and the strategies firms may adopt to deal with that demographic change.

Economic Conditions   The economy of a region surrounding a company has a major impact on the strategic success of that company. Local companies are affected by local economic conditions, regional firms by regional conditions, and national companies by both national and international economic concerns. A sharp economic downturn in Asia during 1999–2003, for instance, had a major negative effect on financial institutions in the United States as well as most larger American manufacturing firms. Also, the 40 percent rise of the euro currency against the U.S. dollar between 2002 and 2007 created a substantial hardship for European exporters because it meant that their products had become much more expensive for Americans to buy.

In the modern world, most firms are highly interdependent. The ups and downs in one economic sector are likely to have a ripple effect on other sectors. For this reason, company leaders should be attuned to changes and trends in the economic environment.

Political/Legal Forces   The segment of the environment in which government policies and actions take place also has major effects on firms. Local, state, and federal governments along with the judicial system constantly issue a flurry of new regulations or reinterpretations of past regulations. Some of these produce dramatic effects. For instance, the Maryland legislature in 2006 passed a law whereby companies in the state with 10,000 or more employees must spend at least 8 percent of their payroll on health insurance, or else pay the difference into a medical fund. Many other states are considering similar legislation. This is likely to have a major cost impact on Wal-Mart's bottom line, which currently does not meet this threshold.[16] Regulatory changes introduced by sovereign governments overseas compound the complexity of political/legal forces. When

President George Bush decided to impose a 30 percent tariff on imported steel, other countries quickly responded with a tariff of their own on select American products. Mexican truck drivers are unable to enter the lucrative U.S. transportation market (as stipulated in the NAFTA accords drawn up about a decade ago; see Chapter 2) mainly due to political pressure on the part of the American Teamsters Union, which claims that Mexican trucks are unsafe.

Technological changes are occurring so fast that the legal system is having a hard time keeping up. Company leaders seek to develop political strategies to influence evolving legislation that covers new technologies. For instance, there is still no answer to a seemingly simple question: If a consumer buys an item on the Internet, which government entity has the right to collect a sales tax on that item, the state government, local government, or perhaps even a foreign government? As another example, a 120-year-old body of antitrust legislation, including the Sherman Act, designed to prevent monopolies, seems to be outmoded in the Digital Age. This became clear when Microsoft was charged with antitrust violations in the late 1990s under the Sherman Act for monopolizing computer operating systems, thereby engaging in unfair competition against competitors such as Netscape Communication Corp. and Intuit. At least for now Microsoft has won the legal battle, and its dominant position in the operating systems arena has strengthened considerably. Microsoft now controls 93 percent of new PC operating systems, up from 86 percent in 1997, and 96 percent of browsers, up from 67 percent in 1999. As noted by one observer, "From its inception, this case was supposed to prove that trustbusting is still relevant in the Digital Age. When the Justice Department sued the company in 1998, it argued that the century-old Sherman Antitrust Act could be applied swiftly and predictably to police high-tech monopolies. These claims now look pretty dubious."[17]

Part of the reason Microsoft was able to influence the court was a strong consumer preference for a common operating system. In other words, isn't it nice to send and open an attachment in the same manner in Washington, D.C., as you would in Moscow? As the digital economy evolves, antitrust legislation may need to change accordingly in order to accommodate these "natural monopolies" in which consumers have reasons to prefer unified technical standards. But how well a company fares under various political/legal forces also depends on a firm's strategy. For instance, almost 10 years after it was charged with antitrust violations, a poll of 940 senior executives in 68 countries ranked Microsoft as one of the top three most innovative companies around the world.[18] In the end, favorable public perceptions are likely to shelter a firm from political interference.[19]

Sociocultural Conditions   This part of the environment consists of the norms, values, and preferences of a society. These change over time, and vary by country or even by geographical area within a country. In general, firms are more likely to succeed if they can adapt products and services to prevalent sociocultural conditions. For instance, McDonald's has recently surprised many of its competitors by being able to crack the fastidious French market by adapting its menu and the look of its restaurants to French taste. Ironically, McDonald's has suffered declining sales in the United States, because many people are becoming leery of unhealthy fried fast food. McDonald's is trying to adapt in the United States by introducing upscale organic coffee, healthier menus, leather sofas, soft lighting, and wireless internet access.[20] As of 2007, these changes seem to be having a favorable impact on McDonald's bottom line.

Barbie Dolls, which are produced by Mattel, became a hit in the 1950s by capturing children's imaginations through what American society considered universal signs of beauty at the time: blond hair, blue eyes, large breasts, pale white skin, long legs. As the civil rights movement took hold in the 1960s, large numbers of non-European immigrants entered the United States, and international markets became more diverse, Mattel had little choice but to change Barbie or see its market slowly disappear. Barbie now comes in all colors and ethnic types, appealing to a wider variety of prospective buyers.

Technological Changes The segment of the environment in which new knowledge is created and transformed into innovative products, services, or inputs is the technological environment. As the knowledge base increases, it is easier to create new knowledge or recombine existing knowledge to develop new products, processes, and materials. It took society thousands of years to create the first computer. Yet, it wasn't long ago when mainframe computers in 4,000 square feet of floor space could do less than a contemporary 2×2, one-pound personal computer can do now. In some product lines, such as software, the life cycle is measured in months, because new software quickly makes prior software obsolete.

By increasing productivity, technology can greatly decrease production costs. This, in turn, is reflected in product prices. DVD players were considered a luxury around the year 2000 with prices generally exceeding $1,000 dollars each. They now are priced as low as $35, and many have better features than their more expensive predecessors. A similar downward price trend is expected for the flat, widescreen TVs which not long ago sold in the $4,000–$12,000 range and can now be purchased for $1,200 or less.

Technological changes have had a tremendous impact on the newspaper industry. Managers have seen the newspaper medium grow old before their eyes as readers and advertisers turn to television, Webcasts, and podcasts for news and entertainment, just as the costs of printing and distribution have risen.

More than ever before, firms must keep abreast of technological changes to remain competitive. For instance, for more than 100 years AT&T drew most of its revenues from residential landline phone businesses. But since the mid-1990s, this source of revenue has steadily declined due to cell phones and the Internet. A reborn AT&T now aims to deliver TV, Web, and wireless services hoping that these items will account for 80 percent of its revenues by 2010.[21] Bill Gates, the founder of what is possibly the most economically powerful business organization in history, is fond of saying that "Microsoft is three months away from bankruptcy." As noted earlier, he is referring to the constant fear that a competitor will develop a better and cheaper technology that will quickly replace Microsoft's market dominance. While this is unlikely to happen any time soon, it is not as far-fetched as it may seem. For instance, the free Linux operating system, an alternative to Microsoft's software, is rapidly catching on and threatening Microsoft as a result.[22] As another case in point, Google seems to have come out of nowhere to put enormous pressure on its main competitor, Yahoo, quickly surpassing it on advertising sales.[23]

Globalization In a world that continues to get smaller, firms are becoming increasingly dependent on foreign markets for raw materials as well as for processing and the sale of products and services (see Chapter 2). In many cases, it is difficult to define what is "domestic" and what is "foreign," as companies divvy up production processes and other essential activities, such as R&D and marketing, across different countries. These borderless strategic alliances and joint ventures with various ownership configurations are increasingly more common even among firms that are fierce competitors (such as the alliance between Japan's Sony, headed by Welsh-born executive Sir Howard Stringer, and Korea's Samsung to produce flat panel technology during 2006–2010).[24] For

video: THE ENTREPRENEURIAL MANAGER

Developing a Golden Parachute

Summary

Not much has changed about parachutes in the last 500 years, but a New York entrepreneur named Daniel Preston has revolutionized the product and its capabilities—and is now doing business with the U.S. government as a top client. His inspiration to work on the parachute came from an accident he had with a faulty parachute that resulted in a broken neck. The technology he has developed for parachutes involves integrating GPS and other applications into a computer within the chute itself, which constantly recalculates algorithms to determine its proper position and adjust for any inaccuracies—actually activating motors that guide the parachute to return to its targeted path. These motors guide the item or person being parachuted from a height of 3,000+ feet to within 1,000 feet. At that point, a regular parachute opens and the item sails to the ground in the typical fashion. He is an avid parachutist who set out to make a better parachute.

One obvious application for a "smart parachute" is in the military. Preston says that in the first few months in the war in Afghanistan, U.S. planes were doing airdrops that entirely missed the country's border, let alone specific targets. Because planes could easily be shot down by relatively inexpensive missiles if they flew below 1,000 feet, it is much safer—if less efficient—to fly higher and drop loads from there. Preston's robotic parachute allows an uncompromised solution: fly high and stay secure, but also have accuracy in the drops using the guided parachutes, equipped with motors, gyroscopes, altimeters, and computers.

Preston has also created an entirely new bonded composite fabric to make the chutes themselves. Replacing the nylon ripstop fabric that has been the standard for decades, Preston's new synthetic fabric is much stronger and lighter than nylon. All the products are handcrafted with old-style Singer sewing machines. The company also has capabilities to test the products in-house, particularly the strength of the stitches in each chute.

Discussion Questions

1. Consider technological changes as part of the general environment. How did current technological changes affect Preston's success as an entrepreneur?

2. What barriers to entry did Preston have to overcome in order to make it in the parachute industry? Give one example from the video case and explain.

3. Describe the type of internal resources that give Preston's business its advantage over competitors.

---

instance, is Mazda a Japanese firm even though Ford Motor Company is its major shareholder and Ford's executives play an active role in managing the company? Did DaimlerChrysler become a German or an American firm after Daimler from Germany bought Chrysler, even though most of Chrysler's facilities are in the United States and Mexico? Should Toyota's plants in Kentucky be considered Japanese or American even though they are completely staffed by Americans?

THE INDUSTRY ENVIRONMENT An industry is composed of a group of firms with products that can substitute for one another. In the computer industry, the consumer may substitute an IBM PC for an Apple Macintosh. The industry environment has a direct effect on a firm's strategic competitiveness. This input is greater than the general environment, because firms within an industry are competing for a share of the same market.

Online **LearningCenter**
www.mhhe.com/gomez3e

Porter's Five Forces

The best-known framework for analyzing the industry environment was developed by Harvard professor Michael Porter.[25] According to this framework, the Five Forces within an industry are: the threat of new entrants, the threat of substitutes, suppliers, customers, and intensity of rivalry among competitors.

The Threat of New Entrants New competitors can change an industry overnight. Unless product demand is increasing, a new entrant is likely to take away part of the market and earnings enjoyed by existing firms.

The threat of new entrants decreases as barriers to entry and fear of retaliation by current industry participants increase. Obstacles that serve as roadblocks to prevent new companies from becoming part of an industry are called *barriers to entry*. Examples include the following.

- The government can restrict entry. For instance, trucking and liquor retailing are regulated. The costs of complying with government regulations discourages some potential entrants, and requirements such as liquor licenses may serve to limit the number of operating establishments a governmental body will allow.

- Intellectual property that is legally protected may keep firms out of the industry. For instance, Kodak could not enter the field of instant photography until the basic patents held by Polaroid had expired.

- Capital requirements may be so high that few firms have the resources to enter and few, if any, financial institutions are willing to lend them money. This would be the case for a new firm trying to enter the automobile manufacturing industry.

- If strong brand identification already exists within the industry, prospective entrants would have to spend heavily in marketing to overcome a consumer's natural inclination to purchase familiar brands.

- New entrants may not enjoy the cost advantages that help existing firms remain profitable. These include economies of scale from large size, favorable locations, and existing plants and equipment.

- New entrants may find it difficult to enter established distribution channels. For instance, they may have to use costly marketing campaigns, price breaks, and easy credit to get space on supermarket shelves.

1 Learning Objective Check-In

Marketway is a company whose purpose is to deliver the latest information about firms' environments—essentially, they contract jobs to perform external analyses for other firms. Marketway advises many manufacturing clients, as well as service-based firms. For instance, it recently worked with a car manufacturer to consider the impact of declining birth rates and an aging population on the types of cars it should begin designing in the near term.

1. *From an external analysis perspective, the aging population in Western countries demonstrates a _____.*
   a. demographic trend
   b. political/legal force
   c. sociocultural condition
   d. technological change

2. *The example in the scenario above focuses on an issue that is part of the car manufacturer's_____.*
   a. immediate environment
   b. industry environment
   c. general environment
   d. tactical environment

By opening franchises around the world, McDonald's has been successful in its global expansion strategy, but can it continue to guarantee (relatively) that a Big Mac anywhere in Taipei is the same as a Big Mac in the United States?

Competitors may also be reluctant to enter a market if they believe that existing firms will react strongly. For instance, a new airline has low probability of surviving for very long because existing airlines use fare wars, premiums for passengers flying certain routes, and easy upgrades to first class to beat the competition. New airlines still enter the market from time to time, but many entrepreneurs and investors have probably been dissuaded from launching a new carrier because of fears of retaliation.

At the same time, the Internet is eroding barriers to entry by allowing new firms access to a global customer base. One observer notes that the Web is making high-end fashion as accessible to shoppers in Peoria as to those in Paris.[26]

The Threat of Substitutes Technological changes may lead to the discovery and manufacturing of new products that supplant existing products. Higher quality, lower costs, more features, and safety considerations may induce consumers to shift preferences from the old to the new as shown in the following examples: Cheaper hardened plastics can now be used for automobile chassis in place of metal, posing a major threat to steel and aluminum companies that depend on the automobile industry for a substantial portion of their revenues. Likewise, cellulose, Styrofoam, and rock wool are increasingly replacing traditional fiberglass as insulation. Kodak has never recovered from the change from operating in a world of film where profit margins were high and product cycles were lengthy to living in the low-margin digital world where products continually change.[27] As a last example, people's music-buying habits have increasingly shifted toward musical downloads and as a result CD sales have dropped from 730 million units in 2000 to an estimated 550 million units in 2006.[28]

Suppliers It is almost impossible to find a self-sufficient firm. Firms purchase inputs from suppliers and transform them to create products or services. Human resources are supplied by universities, trade schools, and other firms; raw materials are obtained from distributors, wholesalers, trading houses, and mining companies; and capital is supplied by banks, individual investors, and venture capitalists.

Suppliers can affect the cost of inputs, such as when a strong union sets a high wage for a particular craft. Dependence may pose a major threat to the firm if the skills are essential to the firm's production process. In other words, greater dependence on a particular supplier increases the power of that supplier to impose terms on the buyer. This dependence increases if the buyer has few other sources of supply, the supplier has many other buyers, satisfactory substitutes for the input are not available, or the cost of changing suppliers is significant.

Customers Another major force in the industry is customers, who look for higher quality and the best service at the lowest price. Customers enjoy more bargaining power and negotiate better terms when they purchase a large portion of the firm's output, the product is important to them, close substitutes are easily available, and the products are relatively standardized or undifferentiated.

Intensity of Rivalry among Competitors Firms use price, product differentiation, and product innovation to improve their market positions. Product differentiation includes extended warranties, "free" options, customer service, and user friendliness. Product innovations are new features that competitors don't yet offer. Typically one firm's action causes a reaction from other firms. A firm that makes a bold move to capture more of the market can expect retaliation from other players in the industry. Airlines, for instance, almost always match the price cuts of competitors, and they are quick to imitate any differentiating features of competitors. For example, Independence Air was launched in 2004 as a discount airline flying 50-seat jets but had to close down in 2006 as rivals such as United, Delta, and US Airways added flights and dropped ticket prices to combat the upstart.[29] Investors in Independence Air lost about $300 million in its short history and its 2,700 employees ended up in unemployment lines. When Continental credited triple miles rather than actual miles flown as part of its frequent-flyer program, most major airlines promptly followed suit. Robert Crandall, CEO of American Airlines, summarized the competitive environment of the industry as "intensely, vigorously, bitterly, savagely competitive."[30]

The intensity of competitive rivalry increases with the number of competitors. Other factors that cause competitive rivalry to increase are slow industry growth, unused productive capacity, undifferentiated services, and high exit barriers, such as major costs incurred by a firm in purchasing specialized plant and equipment.

STRATEGIC GROUPS The management team must also examine the opportunities and threats in the external environment by focusing on the moves of competitors that follow similar strategies. A *strategic group* consists of a cluster of firms within an industry that tend to adopt common strategies of technological leadership, quality standards, prices, distribution channels, and customer service.[31] Ford, Chevrolet, and Toyota are in a different cluster than Mercedes, BMW, and Rolls-Royce. Similarly, Wal-Mart and Target are more likely competitors to Kmart than to Dillard's and Macy's. Such groups may be difficult to identify, and firms may have products that could belong to different strategic groups. However, many managers find it useful to closely track the behaviors of their closest competitors within the industry.

COMPETITOR ANALYSIS It is helpful to conduct a detailed study of each company that management considers a major competitor. Company leaders obtain data from a variety of sources including trade fairs, court records, annual reports, and competitor brochures. These data may be used to make educated inferences about competitor's goals and objectives, current strategies, strengths and weaknesses, and possible competitive moves. Deloitte & Touche estimates that 58 percent of firms have a formal process for obtaining competitor intelligence information, and that the rest use informal methods.[32]

Skills for Managing 7.3, "Conducting an Environmental Analysis," on page 280 challenges you to identify the external factors that are most likely to impact the success of a business of your choice.

The Internal Environment

Have a look back at Figures 7.1 and 7.2. We now turn to analysis of the firm's internal environment, the second component (see Figure 7.2) of Step One of the strategic management process outlined in Figure 7.1. Every company has something that it does well. These are called "core competencies." Along with an analysis of the external environment, company executives should identify the internal resources, capabilities, and knowledge the firm has that may be used to exploit market opportunities and avoid potential threats. The **resource-based view** argues that basing a business strategy on what the firm is capable of doing provides a more sustainable competitive advantage than basing it on external

resource-based view

A strategic management viewpoint that basing business strategy on what the firm is capable of doing provides a more sustainable competitive advantage than basing it on external opportunities.

CONDUCTING AN ENVIRONMENTAL ANALYSIS

A firm uses an environmental analysis to explore the nature of the environment relevant to the firm and to relate the characteristics of the external environment to the firm's internal environment.

Assume you are about to start a new business that will offer a wide range of products and services to clients around the globe. You are in the process of putting together your business plan and are thinking about the challenges that your business will face. The better prepared you are for the competitive challenges, the more likely your business will succeed.

You have just read that organizations are open systems, which means that they are affected by the characteristics of their business environment. This makes sense to you, but you aren't quite sure with which characteristics of the environment you should be concerned.

Form groups of three to five members. Each group chooses a particular type of business that it would like to start. Be as specific as possible about the business; for example, a fast-food restaurant selling Mexican food, or a retailer of imported boutique clothing. Team members work together on the following questions:

1. Discuss your perceptions of the business environment for your business. Determine environmental characteristics you believe will have an impact on it. Consider the business environment with respect to these characteristics, how these areas are changing, and how they affect the way your group would manage the business. The characteristics might include (but aren't limited to)

   a. Competition (e.g., intensity, competitors, tactics).
   b. Customers (e.g., demands, needs, loyalty, location).
   c. Events that affect your business (e.g., predictability, certainty, obviousness).
   d. Political/technological forces.
   e. Knowledge (e.g., pace of obsolescence, complexity, requirements, learning).
   f. Change (e.g., pace, controllability, predictability, obsolescence).

2. Determine the four environmental characteristics that your group feels will have the most impact on the success of the business. List each characteristic, explain why your group believes it is an important force affecting your business, and describe how the internal environment should be molded to deal effectively with those forces (such as its resources, capabilities, core competencies, control mechanism).

Source: Janet Wohlberg, Gail Gilmore, and Steven Wolff, *OB in Action: Cases and Exercises*, 5th Ed. Copyright © 1998 by Houghton Mifflin Company. Used with permission.

opportunities. This is so because "customer preferences are volatile, the identity of customers is changing, and the technologies for serving customer requirements are developing rapidly, [so] an externally focused orientation does not provide the constancy of direction to act as a secure foundation for formulating long-term strategy."[33]

Since 1948 Honda has successfully used its expertise in the design and development of engines to manufacture and sell motorcycles, cars, and such gasoline-based engines as ground tillers, lawn mowers, pumps, and chainsaws. Likewise, 3M has used its knowledge of adhesive and thin-film technology for more than three generations to produce a broad range of successful products including Scotch Tape, magnetic tape, Post-it Notes, and adhesives that help heal minor cuts.

While a thorough understanding of company resources and capabilities can help the management team select a strategy that exploits these internal assets, no company can remain in business for very long unless there is a market for its products and services. Thus, even firms that base strategies on the internal environment must continuously monitor the external environment to devise appropriate responses to external opportunities and threats. Firms such as Sony, Black & Decker, Marks & Spencer, BMW, Motorola, and Intel attribute much of their long-term success to the ability to link information from the external environment, such as changing consumer tastes, shifting demographics, competitor's intelligence information, and new technologies, to internal resources and capabilities.

Resource Types

Many ingredients must be combined effectively to create an advantage for the company. These resources include a wide spectrum of inputs that firms use to deliver products and services. Capital, equipment, talents of employees and managers, patents, and brand names are key resources that may be *tangible* or *intangible*.

TANGIBLE RESOURCES   Financial resources, physical assets, and workers are all **tangible resources** which can be observed and quantified. A strategic assessment of tangible resources should enable management to efficiently use them to support the company and to expand the volume of business. The management team may also be able to find more profitable uses for tangible resources.

INTANGIBLE RESOURCES   Items which are difficult to quantify and include on a balance sheet often provide the firm with the strongest competitive advantage. These **intangible assets** are invisible and not obvious, and are difficult for competitors to purchase or imitate. The three most strategically important intangible resources are the firm's reputation, technology, and human capital.

Reputation   Other things being equal, consumers tend to buy products or services from a firm that is held in high regard. Many customers are even willing to pay more for that firm's recognizable brand. Reputation reduces uncertainty and risk. For years, IBM was able to sell personal computers at prices which were 50 percent more than competitors because the IBM name was synonymous with reliability and excellent customer service. When Nestlé acquired the British chocolate manufacturer Rowntree in the late 1980s, the bid price exceeded the book value of Rowntree's assets by more than 500 percent, an indication of the value of Rowntree's brand names Kit Kat and After Eights. Harley-Davidson stock went up faster than competitors' during the 1990s because the Harley name supported a price premium of about 40 percent above that of comparable motorcycles. Some of the most widely recognized brands around the world include Coca-Cola, Microsoft, IBM, GE, and Nokia.

Technology   Valuable patents, copyrights, and trade secrets that competitors don't have are all examples of the various technological advantages companies can enjoy. Also, the ability to create new technology faster than competitors or to make more efficient use of existing technology creates a sustained advantage. For example, Affymetrix, Inc., based in Santa Clara, California, pioneered a technology that allows up to 60,000 gene sequences to be scanned in one step. Licensing this technology to pharmaceutical companies enabled them to more precisely

Some U.S. automakers are hoping their internal resources will help them meet the continuing stiff competition from Japan. *Consumer Reports* recently named all Japanese cars as its top picks for the year, but Dodge, for one, still believes in the appeal of its classic models like the Charger and Challenger, which it's selling for top dollar in record numbers. "The Japanese can't manufacture this kind of heritage," says an auto industry analyst. "But if you have it and can bring it forward, it can be a game changer."

tangible resources

Assets that can be quantified and observed, including financial resources, physical assets, and manpower.

intangible resources

Resources that are difficult to quantify and include on a balance sheet, which often provide the firm with the strongest competitive advantage.

target certain drugs to meet the needs of the patient; and it may fundamentally alter the treatment of many types of cancer.[34] Firms that produce approximately 1,500 or more patents each year include Sony, Toshiba, Hitachi, Intel, Samsung Electronics, Micron Technology, Hewlett-Packard, Canon, Matsushita Electric, and IBM.[35]

Human Capital   The skills, knowledge, reasoning, and decision-making abilities of the workforce which support a firm's innovation and productivity reflect the value of the human capital present in the company (more on this in Chapter 10). Human capital can provide a very strong core competence that other firms cannot imitate in the following ways:

- Knowledge resides in people's minds, so it is unique to the employees in each firm.
- The ability to harness human resources depends on the integrated achievement of interdependent individual employees and their willingness to collaboratively use their talents to support the firm's mission. That is, capabilities are created from teams of people working together, which represents an asset that is specific to the firm.
- It takes a long time to develop a core competence. Competitors are unlikely to assume the cost and risk of trying to duplicate it.
- The organization's culture may play a key role in how well people work together to achieve organizational objectives. Culture is idiosyncratic to each organization, which means it is a unique competitive factor.

Analyzing the Firm's Capabilities

Successful organizations excel or have the potential to excel in a specific activity. The Federal Express guarantee of next-day delivery anywhere within the United States is such a competitive advantage. British retailer Marks & Spencer ensures a high and consistent level of product quality across a wide range of merchandise through meticulously managed supplier relationships. General Electric reconciles control, coordination, flexibility, and innovation in one of the world's largest and most diversified corporations.

Company leaders can choose from three approaches to examine their capabilities. The first analyzes organizational capabilities for each of the major functional areas of the business. Table 7.1 on page 283 is an example of how a **functional analysis** is conducted. This type of approach is easy for most people to understand, and provides the basis for meaningful discussion of the firm's strategy.

The second method breaks the firm down into a sequential series of activities and attempts to identify the value-added of each activity. Professor Michael Porter refers to it as a **value-chain analysis**. Porter distinguishes between primary activities, concerned with the transformation of inputs and outputs (such as materials handling, purchasing, inventory holding, machining, and packaging), direct customer contact (such as sales, marketing, and customer service), and support (such as administrative assistance and human resource management). In other words, rather than analyzing the firm's capabilities in terms of what different functions contribute, Porter suggests that it is better to identify those activities that create value and those that do not. This approach has the distinct advantage of focusing the analysis on value creation. That is, it can help managers determine the extent to which the value created by a particular activity is greater than the cost incurred to create that value. This is referred to as "margin."

functional analysis

A strategic management approach that establishes organizational capabilities for each of the major functional areas of the business.

value-chain analysis

Strategic management analysis that breaks the firm down into a sequential series of activities and attempts to identify the value-added of each activity.

table 7.1

Analyzing Capabilities by Functional Areas

FUNCTIONAL AREA	CAPABILITY	EXAMPLES
Corporate management	Effective financial control systems	Hanson, Exxon
	Expertise in strategic control of diversified corporation	General Electric, ABB
	Effectiveness in motivating and coordinating divisional and business-unit management	Shell
	Management of acquisitions	ConAgra, BTR
	Values-driven, in-touch corporate leadership	Wal-Mart, FedEx
Information management	Comprehensive and effective MIS network, with strong central coordination	American Airlines, L. L. Bean
Research and development	Capability in basic research	Merck, AT&T
	Ability to develop innovative new products	Sony, 3M
	Speed of new product development	Canon, Mazda
Manufacturing	Efficiency in volume manufacturing	Briggs & Stratton
	Capacity for continual improvements in production processes	Toyota, Nucor
	Flexibility and speed of response	Benetton, Worthington Industries
Product design	Design capability	Pinifarini, Apple
Marketing	Brand management and brand promotion	Procter & Gamble, PepsiCo
	Promoting and exploiting reputation for quality	American Express, DaimlerChrysler
	Responsive to market trends	The Gap, Campbell Soup
Sales and distribution	Effectiveness in promoting and executing sales	Microsoft, Glaxo
	Efficiency and speed of distribution	FedEx, The Limited
	Quality and effectiveness of customer service	Walt Disney Co., Marks & Spencer

Source: From R. M. Grant, *Contemporary Strategy Analysis*, copyright © 2001. Reprinted with permission of Blackwell Publishing.

While theoretically useful for understanding competitive advantage, the value chain concept is difficult to apply in practice. For one thing, it may be impossible to meaningfully assess the net value added (margin) of singular activities. Company activities tend to be so intertwined that they are seldom carried out in isolation. For instance, customer service, which is a primary activity, is unlikely to be superior if product quality is deficient (a production issue, which is also a primary activity) or if recruits are poorly trained (a human resource issue, a support activity). Making those comparisons in relation to competitors is even more difficult because this information is very hard to obtain.

A third approach assesses capabilities by comparing the firm's activities or functions with those of other firms. This approach, normally referred to as **benchmarking**, has four stages:

1. Identifying activities or functions that are weak and need improvement.

2. Identifying firms that are known to be at the leading edge of each of these activities or functions.

3. Studying the leading-edge firms by visiting them, talking to managers and employees, and reading trade publications to ascertain how and why they perform so well.

4. Using the information gathered to redefine goals, modify processes, acquire new resources, and engage in other activities to improve the firm's functions.

benchmarking

A strategic management approach that assesses capabilities by comparing the firm's activities or functions with those of other firms.

Benchmarking has been used as an important strategic tool by a number of well-known companies. It played a central role in the revitalization of Xerox during the 1980s. Detailed comparisons of Xerox copiers and those of competing manufacturers revealed that Japanese rivals made copiers at half the cost in half the time and with half as many workers. Xerox's defects per thousand in assembly were 10 to 30 times greater than those of Japanese competitors. The result was the establishment of a continuous program of benchmarking in which every Xerox department is encouraged to look globally to identify "best in class" companies against which to benchmark. Similarly, ICL, the British computer subsidiary of Fujitsu, benchmarks against the manufacturing processes of Sun Microsystems and the distribution system of the retailer Marks & Spencer. As a last example, in 2006 Volkswagen was losing about $1.2 billion a year in its North American operation, a huge amount putting the survival of VW in question. A benchmark analysis by VW identified what might be a major reason behind these appalling losses. Wolfang Bernhard, head of the German automaker's Volkswagen brand, summarized the results of the study as follows: "Volkswagen takes twice as many hours to assemble a car as its most productive rivals, and it labors at a cost disadvantage of a couple thousand dollars per vehicle in the U.S. market."[36]

In the end, all approaches used to analyze the firm's capabilities have advantages as well as disadvantages. And while there is no model or rule that is clearly best for every situation, having an understanding of all of these perspectives (functional, value chain or benchmarking) can help strategists make better decisions and form higher quality strategies.

Step Two: Strategic Intent and Mission

The second component of the strategic management process (following the analysis of the external and internal environments) consists of formal statements of strategic intent and mission. (See Figure 7.3 on page 285.) **Strategic intent** is internally focused, indicating how the firm will use its resources, capabilities, and core competencies. It guides future actions and focuses employees' attention on using their talents to outdo competitors. Several large firms express their strategic intent as follows:

strategic intent

The firm's internally focused definition of how the firm intends to use its resources, capabilities, and core competencies to win competitive battles.

- Unocal Corporation: "To become a high performance multinational energy company—not the biggest, but the best."
- Eli Lilly and Company: "It is our strategic intent that customers worldwide view us as their most valued pharmaceutical partner."
- Intel: "We intend to become the premier building block supplier to the computer industry."
- Microsoft: "To provide the Yellow Pages for an electronic marketplace of online information systems."[37]

strategic mission

The firm's externally focused definition of what it plans to produce and market, utilizing its internally based core competence.

A firm's **strategic mission** flows from its strategic intent, defining the company's external focus in terms of what will be produced and marketed, utilizing the firm's internally based core competence. Figure 7.4 on page 286 reproduces Chevron's strategic mission statement, which is distributed to all employees.

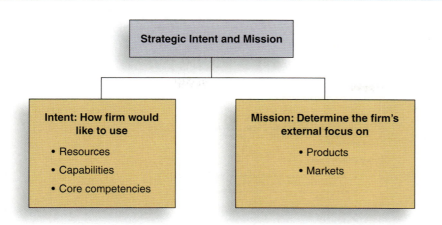

This is a good point to remind you again that even though the components of the strategic management process have been presented one step at a time (following the model in Figure 7.1), they are not completely separate from each other nor do they cover every element. This is particularly true in the case of the firm's strategic intent and mission. For a brand new entrepreneurial firm being built from the ground up, the strategic management process is fairly straightforward. First, the entrepreneur looks for opportunities in the environment, and then defines strategic intent and mission to take advantage of those opportunities. For instance, according to legend, Kenmons Wilson became irate at shoddy accommodations during a family vacation in the early 1950s, and sitting at night in a hotel room he dreamed up a new business whose mission would be "to provide comfortable, child-friendly, inexpensive lodging." This led to a motel chain offering customers high-quality accommodations anywhere in the world. Wilson built the first Holiday Inn in Memphis in 1952. At the time of his death in 2003 there were 3,000 motels worldwide bearing the Holiday Inn name.[38]

As firms mature, however, the strategic management process is not as clear-cut. Why? Very few firms can radically change their strategic intent and mission in search for new opportunities in the external and internal environment. Most established companies have invested large sums of money in plant, equipment, and human resources to accomplish a mission. Thus, they are more likely to focus on those aspects of the environment that are relevant to their already existing strategic intent and mission. Another way of looking at it is that the firm's strategic intent and mission restrict how managers view the environment. Over the long term, however, a firm whose strategic intent and mission are incongruent with the environment is unlikely to continue to be successful, and may face extinction. Think of what would have happened to DuPont had it remained faithful to its original mission in the 19th century: the production of dynamite for use in coal mines. Instead, by diversifying into a variety of chemicals, DuPont seized on new opportunities as they became available and grew and prospered as a result.

LOC-In

③ Learning Objective Check-In

1. *Adriatics is a software development firm that specializes in research and intense-weather data gathering tools. For example, their highly sensitive tools can be used in tornadoes or hurricanes, or in underwater environments. Adriatics' _____ is to develop the most advanced intense-weather data gathering tools in the industry, whereas its _____ is to make marketable the tools and research software it develops and offer them to the world at the best value possible.*

   a. *strategic mission; strategic intent*
   b. *vision statement; strategic mission*
   c. *strategic intent; vision statement*
   d. *strategic intent; strategic mission*

FIGURE 7.4

A Strategic Mission Statement:
The Chevron Way

Source: Reprinted with permission of Chevron Corporation.

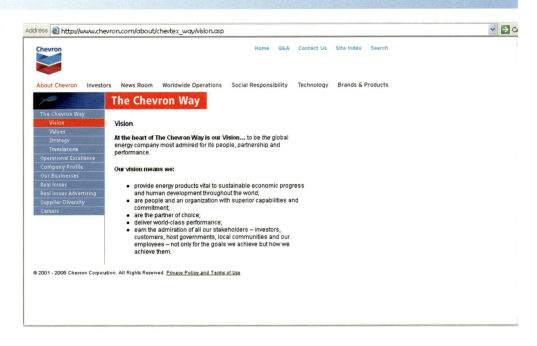

Step 3: Strategy Formulation

strategy formulation

The design of an approach to achieve the firm's mission.

Strategy formulation, the third component of the strategic management process (see again Figure 7.1), is the design of an approach to achieve the firm's mission. An effectively formulated strategy integrates, marshals, and allocates the firm's internal resources and makes appropriate use of external environmental information. The idea is to formulate a mission-consistent strategy that will lead to sustained superior performance. For instance, as shown in Management Close-Up 7.2 on page 287, a growing number of firms use innovation labs as a strategy to stay ahead of competitors in a rapidly changing environment. Strategy formulation takes place at the corporate and business-unit levels (see Figure 7.5 on page 287).

Corporate-Level Strategy

corporate-level strategy

The corporation's overall plan concerning the number of businesses the corporation holds, the variety of markets or industries it serves, and the distribution of resources among those businesses.

Strategy formulation begins with an overall approach to the direction of the organization. A **corporate-level strategy** encompasses the number of businesses the corporation holds, the variety of markets or industries it serves, and the distribution of resources among those businesses. For instance, the Wm. Wrigley Jr. Company focused almost exclusively on the chewing gum market. Seagram, on the other hand, diversified from its core beverage business by acquiring MCA in the entertainment industry. This is called a **diversification strategy**.

diversification strategy

A firm's strategic plan to create and manage a mix of businesses owned by the firm.

Corporate diversification strategy addresses two questions: (1) What business are we in? (2) What businesses should we be in? Corporate diversification may be analyzed in terms of portfolio mix, diversification type, and diversification process. Each of these is discussed in turn.

portfolio analysis

An approach to classify the processes of a diversified company within a single framework or taxonomy.

PORTFOLIO ANALYSIS   The basic idea of **portfolio analysis** is to classify the businesses of a diversified company within a single framework or taxonomy. Two of the most widely applied techniques are the McKinsey–General Electric Portfolio Analysis Matrix and the Boston Consulting Group's Growth-Share Matrix.

Innovation as a Key Part of Strategy Formulation

Not long ago traditional R&D labs required that scientists and engineers toil away privately for years in the pursuit of patents, then hand their work over to product developers, who in turn dropped it onto designers' and marketers' laps for eventual shipment out to the public. The likes of Bell Labs and RCA Laboratories could take years to develop transistors and color TVs, knowing they would enjoy protected markets for years more. But today's rapacious competition means innovations grow stale fast. Companies must churn out updates far more quickly.

The need for speed in innovation in order to achieve a company's mission stretches beyond high-tech companies. Outfits as varied as Mattel, Steelcase, Boeing, Wrigley, Procter & Gamble, and even the Mayo Clinic now use so-called innovation labs to shatter bureaucratic barriers that have grown up among inventors, engineers, researchers, designers, marketers, and others. In these labs, teams of people from different disciplines gather to focus on a problem. They brainstorm, tinker, and toy with different approaches—and generate answers that can be tested on customers and sped to the market.

A central tenet of the innovation lab movement is that layout and design are crucial. Mattel Inc.'s preschool toy unit, Fisher-Price, has its center at company headquarters in East Aurora, New York, but it's clearly a separate part of the operation. Called "the Cave," the center boasts bean-bag chairs, comfy couches, and adjustable lighting that make people feel as if they are far from the office. Teams of staffers from engineering, marketing, and design meet there with child psychologists or other specialists to share ideas. After observing families at play in the field, they return to brainstorm—or "sketch-storm," as they call it. Then they build prototypes of toys from foam, cardboard, glue, and acrylic paint.

Companies that use innovation as part of their strategy often find it helpful to create a place where it can happen. At Fisher-Price headquarters, staffers enjoy the quirky comforts of "the Cave," a place designed for meeting and sharing ideas.

Already, Fisher-Price staffers can point to successes. After observing babies as they learned basic skills, innovation lab participants realized that while the company could boast about toys that make noise or flash lights, it was short on real-world practical stuff. Fisher-Price solved the problem with Laugh and Learn Learning home, a $65 model home made of plastic, where kids can crawl through a front door and explore the alphabet, numbers, music, speech, and different sounds. A smash hit in its 2004 debut, it's now a full line of toys. Several other forthcoming products are the result of a consideration of problems moms had feeding kids, which came up in one of the lab sessions.

Source: Adapted from J. Weber, S. Holmes, and C. Palmeri, "Mosh Pits of Creativity," *BusinessWeek*, November 7, 2005, pp. 98–101. Updated with information obtained from www.fisher-price.com (2006).

FIGURE 7.5

Step Three of the Strategic Management Process: Formulate Strategy

```
                    Strategy Formulation
                   /                    \
        Corporate Level          Business-unit Level
        • Portfolio analysis      • Cost leadership
        • Diversifiation type     • Differentiation strategy
        • Diversification process
```

McKinsey–General Electric Portfolio Analysis Matrix This model has two sides, and classifies all businesses held by a diversified corporation (see Figure 7.6 on page 289). The horizontal side refers to the health of the business unit in terms of markets (using indicators such as the domestic or global market share of the business, its competitive situation, and its level of profitability). The vertical side reflects the attractiveness of the industry of the business unit along the dimensions of market size, market growth, and industry profitability. This two-dimensional matrix is used to classify all the business units of a diversified corporation. Then the matrix is used as a diagnostic tool to make recommendations, such as:

- When a business unit ranks high on both dimensions (see quadrant 9), it means that it has an excellent future and should be "grown" (i.e., more resources should be allocated to it).

- When a business unit ranks low on both dimensions (see quadrant 1), it means that future prospects are poor and should be "harvested" (i.e., the corporation should squeeze all the possible profits out of it without doing much in terms of additional resources devoted to it).

- When a business unit falls in the middle (see quadrants 3, 5, 7), it becomes a candidate for a "hold" strategy (corporation adopts a "wait and see" attitude, but continues to allocate sufficient resources to maintain current level of activity).

Boston Consulting Group's Growth-Share Matrix This approach (also known as the BCG Matrix) applies a similar method to that of the McKinsey–General Electric Portfolio Analysis Matrix except that the horizontal axis refers to the business unit's market share and the vertical axis refers to the annual real rate of market growth (see Figure 7.7 on page 289). The strategic recommendations of the BCG Matrix approach are also quite direct and simple:

- A business unit that is both low in market share and low in market growth (a "dog") should be divested as soon as possible.

- If a business unit has a high market share in a market with low growth potential (a "cow"), it should be "milked" as much as possible with only limited additional resources devoted to it.

- If a business unit has both a high market share and operates in a growing market (a "star"), the corporation should greatly invest in it to fuel additional growth.

- If a business unit has a low market share but operates in a growing market (a question mark), additional analysis is necessary to decide whether or not more responses should be channeled its way.

The main advantage of the portfolio approach (which includes both the McKinsey–GE Matrix and the BCG Matrix) to examine the businesses a diversified corporation holds is that it can combine several elements of strategically useful information in a single framework. This simplicity also has its downside. Portfolio models assume that each business unit operates independently. Often business units are not "stand-alone" profit centers. Many do (or should) share valuable resources. Corporate executives may also acquire or sell business units without considering the effects this may have on the rest of the corporation's core business. Within each business unit, managers may have an incentive to "play by the numbers" to avoid their unit's being placed in the "harvest" or the "dog" categories.

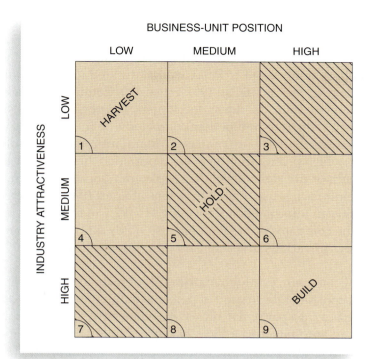

FIGURE 7.6

The McKinsey–General Electric Portfolio Analysis Matrix

Source: From R. M. Grant, *Contemporary Strategy Analysis*, copyright 2001. Reprinted with permission of Blackwell Publishing.

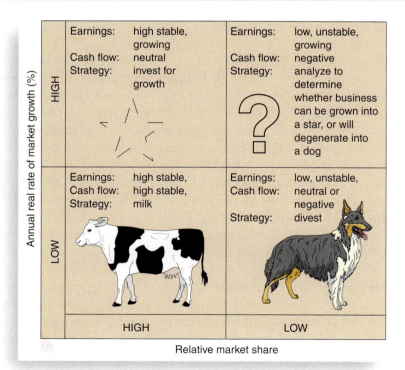

FIGURE 7.7

The Boston Consulting Group's Growth-Share Matrix

Source: From R. M. Grant, *Contemporary Strategy Analysis*, copyright 2001. Reprinted with permission of Blackwell Publishing.

Canon suffered from most of the problems noted in the previous paragraph. The company was managed with a typical corporate portfolio mentality. Canon had a dozen major independent divisions, or profit centers with a great deal of duplication of activities that could have been shared (such as R&D and purchasing). Canon divisions "operated like individual fiefdoms, obsessed with building sales numbers at any costs."[39] Fujio Mitarai decided to change this portfolio scheme upon taking over as CEO in 1997. Since then Canon has done remarkably well. Now, there are four key divisions: copiers, printers, cameras, and optical equipment. Each cooperates rather than competes with the others. To underscore that all divisions are part of one company, Mitarai introduced consolidated balance sheets, in which profits and losses are reported at the corporate level, not at the business unit or divisional level. To keep communication flowing across divisions and reinforce a sense that all divisions are part of one company, Mitarai frequently holds an informal board meeting at 7:45 A.M. to have division executives debate the company's direction. He also holds daily lunch meetings with senior managers of various divisions and monthly meetings for 800 lower-level managers.

As a final comment, portfolio matrices may create the illusion of objectivity when in fact a considerable amount of personal judgment is involved when classifying businesses into particular boxes. As noted by one observer, "Is BMW's North American auto business a 'dog' because it holds less than 1 percent of a low-growth market or a cash 'cow' because it is market leader in the luxury car segment?"[40]

TYPES OF DIVERSIFICATION Firms may be classified according to the mix of businesses owned by the firm. Four major types of business mix are concentration strategy, vertical integration strategy, concentric diversification strategy, and conglomerate diversification.

concentration strategy

A form of diversification strategy that focuses on a single business operating in a single industry segment.

Concentration Strategy A firm following the **concentration strategy** focuses on a simple business operating in a single industry segment. A firm is classified as a single business if 95 percent or more of its total sales come from that business. A concentration strategy allows the firm to become the best at a particular competency, which may provide a sustained competitive advantage. For example, Research in Motion, Ltd. (RIM) has been a leader in the wireless e-mail gadget, with all of its profits derived from one highly successful product: The BlackBerry. The disadvantage of a concentration strategy is that a firm assumes a higher degree of risk when most earnings come from a single source. In the case of RIM, Motorola, Nokia, Palm, Inc., Samsung Electronics, Hewlett Packard Co., and Siemens are quickly entering the BlackBerry's market, introducing an array of inexpensive wireless e-mail devices with beefed-up features.[41]

vertical integration strategy

A form of diversification strategy in which a firm integrates vertically by acquiring businesses that are supply channels or distributors to the primary business; producing its own inputs is backward integration, and distributing its own outputs is forward integration.

Vertical Integration Strategy Another method to grow quickly is to buy the company that sells you supplies. Or set up retail outlets to sell your own goods and services, rather than going through others. In **vertical integration**, a firm acquires businesses that are supply channels or distributors to the primary business. Producing its own inputs is called *backward integration*, and distributing its own outputs is *forward integration*. Either may give the firm greater control and allow it to reduce costs and uncertainty. For instance, Time Warner acquired Turner Broadcasting in part to help distribute Turner's classic movies and also so that the Turner cartoon network would show Warner Brothers cartoons. A potential disadvantage of a vertical integration strategy is that the firm may be unfamiliar with the business of suppliers or distributors, and make mistakes as a result.

Concentric Diversification Strategy   In **concentric diversification**, the firm expands by creating or acquiring new businesses related to the firm's core business. This would be the case, for instance, in the recent purchase of Compaq by Hewlett-Packard. Concentric diversification strategies offer two advantages. First, it may be possible to reduce costs, because two similar businesses may share HR departments, shipping processes, inventory systems, or other activities. Second, the core competency of the original company can be transferred to the newly acquired company. Two potential disadvantages of this strategy are that business-unit managers do not always cooperate with one another and that corporate headquarters may not be able to effectively manage the interrelationships among the business units.

Conglomerate Diversification   **Conglomerate diversification** involves managing a portfolio of businesses that are unrelated to each other. For instance, Union Pacific Corporation's original focus was building and managing railroads. It has now expanded into oil and gas exploration, mining, microwave technology, fiber optic systems, waste disposal, trucking, and real estate. One advantage of conglomerate diversification is that risks are spread across different markets and industries so that potential downturns in one business segment may be offset by higher earnings from other business units.

Research suggests that as a whole conglomerates are not as profitable as the other types of corporate diversification strategies.[42] The main problems appear to be that conglomerate diversification does not build on a firm's core competencies and that corporate executives do not have sufficient knowledge to effectively manage disparate business units.

PROCESS OF DIVERSIFICATION   A firm's corporate diversification strategy may also be examined in terms of the way it diversifies. Diversification occurs by acquisition and restructuring, and by internationalization.

Acquisition and Restructuring Strategies   The primary means for conducting a diversification strategy are through **acquisition**—purchasing other firms—and **merger**—integrating two firms. Firms engage in mergers and acquisitions to gain greater market power, move into new markets, avoid the cost of new product development, and spread business risks. Among the problems that can arise are failure to integrate different corporate cultures, overvaluation of the target firm, inability to achieve successful synergies between the firms, and increased inefficiencies and poor cost controls attributed to large size. For example, a recent survey suggests that companies that are merging often focus on cost-cutting, not consumer service.[43]

International Strategy   Firms are increasingly moving some manufacturing operations overseas. Even small companies seek to secure access to markets outside domestic borders. Firms internationalize for a variety of reasons, including a desire to increase market size, share resources and knowledge between units, lower costs, and spread business risks across diverse markets. Internationalization issues were discussed at length in Chapter 2.

Business-Level Strategy

Once company leaders determine a diversification strategy, they must decide how to compete in each business area or market segment. This is referred to as *business-level strategy*. For instance, Kmart and Wal-Mart have traditionally emphasized the

concentric diversification strategy

A form of diversification strategy in which the firm expands by creating or acquiring new businesses that are related to the firm's core business.

conglomerate diversification

A form of diversification strategy that involves managing a portfolio of businesses that are unrelated to each other.

acquisition

The process of purchasing other firms.

merger

The process of integrating two firms.

Southwest Airlines has been able to successfully differentiate itself from its competitors by way of no-frills, low-price fares, and a highly diversified workforce. But Southwest also is known for its humorous flight crews, who often crack jokes and pull gags on passengers.

low-cost end of the retail market while Dillard's and Dayton's have focused on high-quality, higher-priced leading-edge fashion.

There are two basic choices when selecting an industry position. One is to try to achieve lower cost than rivals. The other is to try to differentiate products and command a premium price. Providing products and services that are less expensive than those of competitors is referred to as **cost-leadership strategy**. Delivering products and services that customers perceive to be different and better is a **differentiation strategy**.

A cost-leadership strategy requires the firm to carry out its activities more efficiently than competitors, passing along cost savings to consumers in the form of lower prices. Firms may reduce costs through large-scale efficient facilities, low overhead, fast turnover of inventories, volume buying of needed inputs, state of the art technology, plants located in low-wage countries, and "build to order systems." Because their profit margins are low, such firms need to sell large volumes to earn acceptable returns. For example,

- Toys 'R' Us secured a large market share in the toy retailing industry in the United States and overseas by charging 10 percent to 15 percent less than competitors. Its efficient distribution system, volume purchasing, and large stores have given the firm the necessary cost advantage to undercut the competition.

- Unifi, Inc., one of the most efficient producers of filament polyester and nylon fiber, dominated its market by being a leader in manufacturing technologies, allowing it to underprice its competitors.

- Southwest Airlines was able to maintain high profitability in an industry where being in the red is not uncommon. It specializes in no-frills, low-price fares on selected "short-hop" routes and a highly versatile workforce willing to perform multiple jobs. A single employee may serve as a bag handler, front desk representative, ticket collector, and steward. Southwest maintains its low-cost strategy while outperforming all other U.S. carriers in terms of on-time performance, baggage handling, and number of complaints.

A differentiation strategy requires a firm to continuously invest in the creation of new products or add new features to existing products so that customers believe the products are different and better than those offered by competitors. The challenge for these firms lies in selling products at a price that customers are willing to pay. For instance, at a time when most airlines have cut back on frills (Northwest, for example, does not even offer free pretzels anymore) and try to fit as many passengers as possible in a plane, United has made a conscious decision to go the other way by keeping onboard blankets and pillows, making seating more spacious, and designing new services for both the high and low end of the market. "United is determined not to be another clone of low-cost, low-fare juggernaut Southwest airlines . . . United is making an all-out effort to raise revenue by pampering travelers."[44] This also means accepting higher costs, so it remains to be seen to what extent United can generate greater profits through its differentiation strategy. Commonly recognized differentiated products include:

- Toyota's Lexus: the relentless pursuit of perfection.
- Ralph Lauren's and Tommy Hilfiger's clothing lines: image.
- Caterpillar: a heavy equipment manufacturing firm committed to providing rapid delivery of spare parts to any location in the world.
- Maytag appliances: product reliability.
- McKinsey & Co: the highest priced and most prestigious consulting firm in the world.
- Rolex watches: prestige and image.
- Gateway: low-cost PCs for home use.
- Yahoo: comprehensive Web surfing.

LOC-In

④ Learning Objective Check-In

Sing Brand Foods is a corporation that has six different business units, including Gregory's, an upscale chain of restaurants popular throughout the Midwest.

1. *Executives involved in _____ most likely work at the corporate level.*
   a. differentiation strategy
   b. cost leadership strategy
   c. restaurant staffing decisions
   d. the diversification process
2. *Executives involved in _____ make decisions regarding the strategy formulation at Gregory's.*
   a. portfolio analysis
   b. differentiation strategy
   c. diversification type decisions
   d horizontal diversification strategy

Step 4: Strategy Implementation

An idea is nothing until it becomes an action. The fourth key component of the strategic management process is strategy implementation (see Figure 7.1). Even the best conceived strategies are of little value if they are not implemented effectively. For instance, recently Blockbuster Inc. ditched late fees to compete more effectively with video-by-mail chains such as Netflex Inc., which allows consumers to pay a flat monthly fee and retain movies for as long as they want. But the wisdom of Blockbuster's move is now in doubt since those late fees accounted for $250–300 million a year (or about 15 percent of Blockbuster's annual revenue). "With the company's finances in tatters and its stock price down by more than 60 percent . . . some investors and analysts are arguing for a companywide return of the fees for tardy customers."[45]

To implement formulated strategies successfully, company executives must consider strategic leadership, organizational structure and controls, cooperative strategies, global strategies human resource strategies, and corporate entrepreneurship and innovation (see Figure 7.8 on page 294).

Strategic Leadership

Effective leadership plays a fundamental role in the relative success or failure of a firm (see Chapter 13 on leadership). This is particularly true for top executives who are responsible for charting general implementation plans, making key resource allocation decisions, and delegating day-to-day operations. In the opinion of three well-known management authors, "By word and/or personal example and through their ability to dream pragmatically, effective strategic leaders meaningfully influence the behaviors, thoughts, and feelings of those

FIGURE 7.8

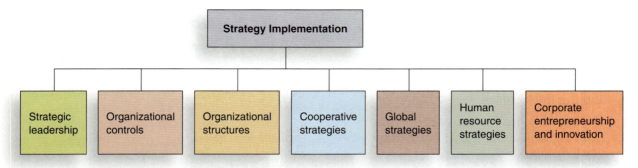

Step Four of the Strategic
Management Process:
Implement Strategy

with whom they work."[46] Management Is Everyone's Business 7.1 on page 295 provides a set of recommendations for those who are expected to play a managerial role as part of the strategic management process.

Organizational Controls

A company's board of directors is expected to monitor the actions and decisions of top executives to ensure that they act in the best interest of the firm. Until recently, boards of directors operated freely, with little government supervision. The Sarbanes-Oxley Act of 2002 has changed most of that. Crafted by Congress in the aftermath of financial collapses at corporations like Enron, Global Crossing, and WorldCom, the act outlines a set of accountability standards by public companies in the areas of financial reporting and disclosure, audits, conflict of interest, and governance. While differences of opinion abound, particularly when it comes to the added compliance cost for companies (paying for auditors, paperwork, administrative expenses and such) most observers believe that Sarbanes-Oxley has had positive effect by preventing some of the worst corporate abuses.[47] A whole chapter of this book (Chapter 16) is devoted to organizational control issues.

Organizational Structures

Below the top-executive level, firms have many choices for organizing the work that needs to be done to implement a particular strategy. Implementation begins with defining roles for different individuals and establishing procedures, reporting relationships, chains of command, decision-making processes, and organizational forms (collectively known as organizational structures). Chapter 9 is entirely devoted to managing the structure and design of organizations.

Organizational structure is critical to strategy implementation because "through structure, managers largely determine what a firm does and how it completes that work, given its chosen strategies. Strategic competitiveness can be attained only when the firm's selected structure is congruent with its formulated strategy."[48]

While organizational structures help in providing for an orderly execution of strategies, most successful firms tap the collective knowledge of employees through the use of teams that might cut across job titles, departments, functional areas, business units, levels, and the like. The strategic management process should be an organizationwide effort rather than a top-down exercise. Management Is Everyone's Business 7.2 on page 296 provides a list of recommendations that teams should consider as part of their role in the strategic management process.

Cooperative Strategies

Cooperative strategies involve establishing partnerships or strategic alliances with other firms. For instance, Procter & Gamble and General Electric cooperated to develop a jet engine for Boeing's new jumbo jet. Although the companies were fierce competitors over the years, senior executives indicated that "neither of us [was] prepared to make the enormous financial, personnel, and technical investment required to develop an all-new engine in an uncertain environment." Additionally,

cooperative strategies

Establishing partnerships or strategic alliances with other firms.

Working as a Team   The strategic management process generally involves teams of managers and employees from different areas who bring their perspectives and expertise to bear on the issues facing the firm. An important factor in the success of the strategic management process is how well the firm can mobilize and integrate the efforts of managers and employees to identify relevant environmental trends, define or redefine firm strategies, and support the successful implementation of those strategies.

This all means that organizations should:

- Form strategy-making teams either on a continuous basis or from time to time by bringing together employees from different functional areas (marketing, manufacturing, human resources), background (technical, managerial, sales), organizational levels (for instance, top executives as well as first-line supervisors), and various parts of the organization (departments, business units, divisions). Such diverse teams can bring to bear a wide field of vision on the strategic challenges facing the organization.

- Create scanning and monitoring teams that gather, filter, and interpret environmental information and what this might mean to the organization. Ideally, such teams should be composed of individuals akin to different parts of the environment (for instance, customer needs, global trends, technological innovations).

- At any level within the organization, teams should be created as needed to analyze strengths–weaknesses–opportunities–threats affecting the unit in question (the unit might be the entire organization at one extreme or a specific department at the other extreme). The broader the unit in question, the greater the need to increase diversity within the team to ensure that multiple perspectives are part of the process.

- Ensure that strategy formulation leads to proper implementation by securing the collective commitment of employees to the adopted strategy. The more employees work in teams as part of this process, the more likely they will accept and fully support strategic decisions, particularly those requiring significant changes affecting their lives. Teams can also offer top managers a better sense of limitations or constraints being faced, as well as information about resources they might not be aware of.

- Blend cultures of units involved in mergers and acquisitions by creating teams that can effectively draw bridges across disappearing organizational boundaries. Mergers and acquisitions often fail because financially driven executives tend to ignore or underestimate the difficulties involved in managing cultural integration.

according to a Boeing executive, "using our complementary skills and resources we can produce an engine that meets the requirements of Boeing and our airline customers in a more timely fashion and at lower cost and risk."[49] Recently many major airlines have been sharing ticket sales to make travel easier.

Strategic alliances can serve a number of purposes. Firms may combine resources, capabilities, and core competencies to gain market power, overcome trade barriers, learn from each other, pool resources for expensive and risky projects, compete more effectively in a particular industry, and speed up entry into new markets. Strategic alliances also allow a firm to create and disband projects with minimal paperwork.

Human Resource Strategies

The policies and practices of the human resource department should also support the firm's overall strategy (see Chapter 10 on human resource management). Who gets recruited, how performance is evaluated and rewarded, how training is conducted, and how career advancement is managed should be consistent with the

Working as an Individual   Individual employees are more likely to make greater contributions to the firm if they engage in activities that have strategic value. If the firm's strategic objective is to increase market share by underpricing competitors, the employee can suggest easy-to-cut costs or easy-to-reduce inefficiencies. The employee can also be attuned to changes in his or her areas of expertise and advise management on the strategic implications of those changes. Lastly, employee success depends on the ability to adapt to the firm's strategic change.

This means that you as an individual should:

- Learn about the strategies of your entire organization and how your unit fits into it. Much of this information may be obtained through company publications, business media, and the Internet. You can also ask your supervisors directly. If you do so with a sincere "I want to contribute more" attitude, they are likely to respond to you positively.

- Develop skills attuned to the strategy of the organization and strategic redirections that might be taking place. This will make you more valuable as an employee.

- Behave in a manner consistent with the strategy of the organization and the role of your unit as part of the big picture.

- Volunteer with a positive attitude to participate to the extent you can in your firm's strategy formulation and implementation. Many firms now encourage technology employees to use Web technology to provide input and ideas that may be valuable to those who make strategic decisions.

strategic mission of the firm. For example, a company that wants to be innovative in various markets would want to develop human resource policies that stimulate rather than dissuade employees from taking risks. This may require greater tolerance for failure, more subjective assessment of performance, more incentives for taking risks, and the hiring of managers with track records of making risky but prudent decisions. These policies are likely to influence how individual employees see their role as part of the strategic management process. Management Is Everyone's Business 7.3 above offers a set of tips that an individual employee might consider to become a contributor to the implementation of his/her firm's strategy.

Corporate Entrepreneurship and Innovation

Competitive pressures require firms to be innovative (see Chapter 8 on entrepreneurship and innovation). High returns and investments in innovation tend to go hand in hand. Innovation contributes to a sustainable competitive advantage if (1) it is difficult or costly for competitors to imitate, (2) customers can see a value in the innovation, (3) the firm enjoys a time advantage over the other company, and (4) the firm is capable of commercializing the innovation.

Research and development is necessary for firms in high-technology markets such as computers, electronics, and pharmaceuticals. However, firms also need to encourage entrepreneurship, supporting employees who are willing to take risks and be aggressive, proactive, and creative and can see opportunities where others perceive problems.

LOC-In

⑤ Learning Objective Check-In

1. *There is a fairly strict hierarchy at Pierpont Stores. The board of directors, for example, monitors the actions and decisions of all the top executives in the company to make sure they are acting in the best interest of the firm and its various stakeholders, particularly shareholders. Below the board, there are certain chains of command that can appear stifling to some on the outside, but actually prove quite effective for this particular company. The purpose of the board of directors and the internal chains of command is to _____.*
    a. *implement strategy effectively*
    b. *safeguard against competitive influence*
    c. *develop the best alternatives for developing strategy*
    d *evaluate the effectiveness of strategies used in the past*

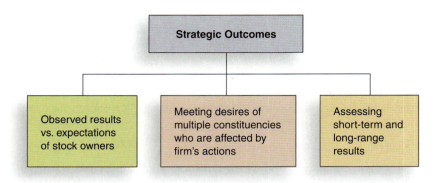

Step 5: Strategic Outcomes

The fifth and final step of the strategic management process is an analysis of the strategic outcomes, or the end result of the entire process. (See Figure 7.9 above which corresponds to the last stage shown in Figure 7.1.) Company leaders should periodically assess whether the outcomes meet expectations. This information should be used to determine whether or not company strategies are successful.

A firm must first and foremost cater to the desires of its primary stakeholders. **Stakeholders** are the individuals and institutions who have vested interests in the performance of the firm. In a capitalist system, the main stakeholders are the people who own stock in the company and who are the major suppliers of the firm's capital. These stakeholders expect to earn at least an average return on their investment, although they would prefer the return to be as high as possible. If lenders are dissatisfied, they can make it more costly for the firm to raise capital and may increase the number of restrictions on the company's borrowing. Shareholders who are unhappy with the firm's stock performance can sell stock and invest their money in other firms. Because the firm depends on investors and stockholders, its highest priority when analyzing strategic outcomes is the needs of those constituencies.

At the same time, the firm's managers should consider the desires of other people who are affected by a firm's actions. At times, the interests of these other stakeholders may conflict with those of shareholders. For instance, customers prefer products with great reliability, more features, and low price. Employees would like a greater share of the company's profits. The community may want the firm to invest in projects of social interest. That is, what appears to be a good outcome for some stakeholders may have negative consequences for other stakeholders, and this might raise important ethical concerns. This would be the case, for instance, of patients who benefit from low complication rates and shareholders who receive higher returns in certain hospitals at the expense of difficult-to-treat patients who might be denied treatment (see Management Close-Up 7.3, "Making It Easy to Size Up a Hospital" on page 299). The firm should try to find

---

stakeholders

The groups or individuals who have an interest in the performance of the enterprise and how it uses its resources, including employees, customers, and shareholders.

Making It Easy to Size Up a Hospital

THEME: ETHICS   Few decisions are more important than what hospital you should choose to treat a serious illness. But most Web resources that rate the quality of care at hospitals dole out data through the sites of health plans or big employers. This has changed in 2006 as Chicago-based Subimo opened myhealthcareadvisor.com to the public at $12 for a six-month subscription. The company says the launch is a reaction to a good review *BusinessWeek* gave Subimo's employer-distributed ratings back in 2005, which produced thousands of requests for a public site. Subimo ranks hospitals from 1 to 100 on factors such as complication rates, cost, and use of technology. For many diseases, it also summarizes research so patients can explore new treatments. "As people pay more of their health-care costs, there's a place for tools that will help them manage their own care," says Subimo Vice President Joe Donlan.

Not everyone agrees that this is a good idea. Many doctors feel that such systems may inadvertently induce hospitals to compete in less than ethical ways in order to appease potential investors and shareholders. For instance, a hospital may be tempted to refuse difficult-to-treat patients to reduce reported complication rates. And hospitals which accept the most critically ill patients may be penalized since they are likely to score lower on complication rates and expenses.

Source: Adapted from T. J. Mullaney, "Making It Easy to Size Up a Hospital," *BusinessWeek*, September 5, 2005; www.myhealthcareadvisor.com/testimonials, 2006.

---

win–win situations for as many stakeholders as possible. For instance, higher quality products at a lower price may benefit investors if the firm's market share increases. Employees may also benefit if the company enjoys greater ability to pay and offers them greater job security.

Some of the standard measures of strategic success include:

- Profits
- Growth of sales/market share
- Growth of corporate assets
- Reduced competitive threats
- Innovations that fuel future success

It is vital for the executive team to assess both the short term and long range when assessing strategic outcomes. Long-term success should be the ultimate criterion when studying strategic outcomes.

LOC-In

6 **Learning Objective Check-In**

ARTRON is a publicly held company. It has upwards of 1,500 investors who hold a direct interest in the firm's performance and profitability. ARTRON has manufacturing facilities in eight different locations on the West Coast. It provides an average of 130 jobs in each of those communities and gives back to the community through direct philanthropic investments in important causes, like education.

1. *Those investors who have an interest in the firm's profitability are called _____.*
   a. *stakeholders*
   b. *shareholders*
   c. *activists*
   d. *interested parties*

2. *The children and adults who benefit from the philanthropic efforts of ARTRON in different communities are considered the company's _____.*
   a. *shareholders*
   b. *social activists*
   c. *administrators*
   d *stakeholders*

CONCLUDING THOUGHTS

At the beginning of the chapter you read about Apple's strategy for helping the market for iPod accessories to thrive through the effort of outside manufacturers and marketers. Now that you've had a chance to read the chapter, let's revisit the questions posed there.

Apple's strategy to allow the manufacture of all kinds of iPod accessories has helped other manufacturers earn revenue, but it has also helped Apple itself by keeping the sleek little player at the peak of coolness among its customers. Already valued for its design appeal as well as its functionality, the iPod now stands at the center of a universe of affordable products to personalize it and broaden its use. Apple's decision to foster the creation of that universe has proved a wise one, since the existence of covers, speakers, ports, headphones, and other gear clearly plays into the iPod purchase decision, giving it an advantage no other music player has.

Apple's own entry into the accessories market could well prove quite successful, since the company has waited for other manufacturers to establish the market and carry some of the initial risk of introducing a whole new product category. Now it's time for Apple to capitalize on its own resources.

Focusing on the Future: Using Management Theory in Daily Life

Strategic Management

In Chapter 5, you saw how Mary Kelley and Robert deStefano used the action planning model to start their business, Sleep Garden, Inc. Now let's look at how Mary and Robert used Porter's Five Forces for analyzing the industry environment of their new venture.

Threat of New Entrants   Fortunately, Sleep Garden faced few threats to entry. Almost all government regulation of sleep aids centers on ingestibles—drugs are highly regulated, and herbs, while they have not been regulated in the past, are coming under more scrutiny now. By contracting with their own yoga instructor and composer, Robert and Mary avoided intellectual property constraints, although they have to be careful that their creative properties are not imitated or duplicated by others. Mary has provided the funding for the new venture, and that was a constraint—if she had not had the money available to keep the company going for the past several years, it could easily have folded. While drug products like "Ambien" and "Lunesta" have strong brands, they do not directly compete with such Sleep Garden products as "zMusic" or "zYoga." As a new, small company, Sleep Garden did not have things like existing plants or economies of scale, but they leveraged the resources they had. For example, they found manufacturers who were willing to produce short runs of their products and stores which saw the products as natural tie-ins to their existing customer base.

Threat of Substitutes   Sleep is big business today, and there are many products on the market designed to help people sleep. Fortunately for Mary and Robert, most of the products are either scientific (drug based) or artistic (white noise or new-age music CDs) but virtually none combine both scientific research and art. The uniqueness of a nondrug, clinically tested product set them apart from their competitors. However, the two entrepreneurs still faced the challenge of clearly defining their target market, and then identifying the best channels for reaching that market. While one of their original objectives was to make their products available to a mass market, they found that mass market advertising in print and radio did little for them. Instead, they found that their products sold well in upscale, natural (organic) food stores such as Whole Foods. People in these stores responded to the idea of a "natural" sleep aid. A different marketing channel involved positioning their products as an in-room spa experience, and for this, they contacted high-end resorts and hotels. Clients in these places are looking for pampering and expect a product that comes with "extras" and attractive packaging.

Suppliers There are many companies that manufacture CDs and DVDs in the United States today. Because of this, Mary and Robert were able to keep their manufacturing costs relatively low, a boon for a new business. However, postproduction editing, scoring, and rerecording can make or break a video product. While there are many postproduction studios, Robert felt that only one offered the quality of services that would make their "zYoga" DVD stand out. For that reason, the postproduction supplier had more power and was able to command a higher price than a less skilled supplier. Similarly, Robert and Mary had to pay more to a supplier that designed the merchandising units used to display Sleep Garden products, because there are few companies which produce this type of "product furniture."

Customers One of the most important things Mary and Robert learned as they built their business was the power not only of end customers, but of intermediate customers—the brokers and distributors who actually get product into the hands of consumers. Many stores will deal only with brokers, and each broker used shaves a bit of profit off a given product. End users have little power over price or packaging, but retailers have a great deal of power, and the bigger the retailer is, the more power they have. For example, it is an entirely different process to get product into an individual grocery store than it is to get product into an entire chain of stores such as CVS or Wal-Mart. The bigger the chain, the more power they have over products, packaging, and pricing. But even small retailers can impact the way a product is sold. For example, Robert and Mary purchased merchandisers so that retailers wouldn't have to move other products off store shelves in order to get Sleep Garden products in stores.

Intensity of Rivalry among Competitors While rivalry is intense in the drug segment of the sleep market, Mary and Robert were relieved to find that they had few head-to-head competitors in their side of the industry. This made a friendlier environment for their business.

By analyzing industry forces prior to incorporating their business, Robert and Mary had a clear picture of the challenges that would face them in getting their product to market. While these challenges evolved and changed over time, continual monitoring enabled the Sleep Garden executives to modify their strategy accordingly.

summary of learning objectives

1 Explain how the firm's external environment should be examined as part of the strategic management process.

- There are two important considerations when examining the external environment. Analysis *components* are scanning (tracking the environment for changes), monitoring (observing environment to determine if clear trends are emerging), forecasting (trying to predict what is likely to occur in the future), and assessing (evaluating consequences of environmental data to the firm).
- Environmental forces may be examined at different levels of specificity, or *scope*, including the general environment (such as demographic changes, economic forces, and sociocultural conditions which might impinge upon the firm), the industry environment (tracking groups of firms with products/services that can serve as substitutes for one another), strategic groups (observing the behavior of cluster of firms within the industry that tend to adopt common strategies), and direct competitors (studying the moves and countermoves of select sample of firms believed to be key competitors).

2 Explain how the firm's internal environment should be examined as part of the strategic management process.

- *Resource analysis*. Focuses on the tangible and intangible resources that provide the firm with core competencies that are difficult for competitors to imitate.
- *Capabilities analysis*. Focuses on what the firm can do better than competitors, which might be analyzed by *function* (such as marketing and human resources), value added of various activities (**value-chain analysis**), and **benchmarking** (comparing the firm's activities and/or functions with those of firms known for best practices).

3 State the meaning and purpose of the firm's strategic intent and mission.

- **Strategic intent**. Statement of how the firm would like to use its resources and capabilities.
- **Strategic mission**. A definition of the firm's external focus in terms of what it will produce and market.

4 Understand how the strategy formulation process helps the firm achieve its mission.

- **Corporate-level strategy** refers to strategic decisions concerning number of businesses, the variety of markets or industries in which the firm operates, and the distribution of resources across those businesses. Analysis can proceed in three ways:
  - *Portfolio analysis*. Creation of a taxonomy to classify various businesses owned by the corporation by their revenue potential (for instance, those which are low in market share and low in market growth versus those which are high in market share and that operate in a growing market).
  - *Diversification type*. The company may choose to hold a single business competing in one industry segment (concentration strategy), diversify by setting up or acquiring firms that serve the primary business (vertical integration strategy), create or purchase new businesses related to the core business (concentric diversification), or manage a portfolio of unrelated businesses (conglomerate diversification).
  - *Diversification process*. Focuses on how the firm should diversify such as purchasing other firms (acquisition), integration of two firms (mergers), and internationalization (moving some of its operations overseas).
- **Business-level strategy** involves decisions on how to compete in a given industry. The two major choices are competing with price (by being a low cost producer or *cost leader*) and on special features that command a price premium (*differentiation*).

5 Describe the issues that should be considered in strategy implementation.

- The formulated strategy must be implemented effectively, and feedback from the implementation process should be used to adjust the formulated strategy.
- Effective strategy implementation requires a corporate governance system (to ensure that executives make decisions that are most beneficial to the firm), a system for completing the necessary work (organizational structure and controls), functional strategies (to support the overall strategy), and strong leadership at the top as well as entrepreneurial activities at lower organizational levels.

6 Understand how the outcomes of the strategic management process should be assessed.

- An analysis of how the firm's *shareholders* are being served; at a minimum shareholders should earn an average return on their investment.
- A consideration of the extent to which the needs of other **stakeholders** who might be affected by the firm's actions are being satisfied.
- An analysis of short-term and long-range results.

discussion questions

1. Some argue that the business environment changes so quickly that we are entering a period of "hypercompetition," which will make it difficult to establish long-term strategic objectives. Do you agree? Identify five major forces that accelerated environmental change at the turn of the century.

2. Scan business publications such as *BusinessWeek, The Wall Street Journal,* and *Fortune*. From these publications' articles, select a firm that has been affected by each of the following: the general environment, the industry, strategic groups, and direct competitors. Explain the reason for your choice and show how that particular segment of the environment affects the firm you have chosen.

3. Why should most firms develop their strategic mission following a rational process that incorporates internal and external environmental data? Explain.

4. Going back to Management Close-Up 7.3, if you were a hospital administrator, how would the availability of "hospital performance" data affect your behavior? Explain.

5. In what situations do you believe that strategy formulation leads to strategy implementation? In what situations do you believe that strategy implementation plays an equal role with strategy formulation as a source of competitive advantage? Explain.

6. In what situations do you believe that the external environment of the firm is more important than the internal environment as a determinant of the firm's profitability? Explain.

7. In 2006, Norway passed a law that a minimum of 40 percent of members of boards of directors must be women.[50] This represents a dramatic change as only a handful of women were on such boards prior to the passage of this law. Why do you think Norway passed such a law? Based on what you have learned in this chapter, is this a good policy? Explain your answer.

management minicase 7.1

For Every Xbox, a Big Fat Loss

Despite all the hype surrounding the new Xbox 360 video game console, Microsoft won't make money on the machine itself. A tear-down analysis by market researcher iSuppli of the high-end Xbox 360, which contains a hard drive, found that the materials cost Microsoft $470 before assembly. Chips alone account for 72 percent of that. The console sells at retail for $399, for a loss of $71 per unit. Other items in the box, such as the power supply, cables, and controllers, add $55 more to Microsoft's cost, pushing its loss per unit to $126.

That is slightly higher than what Microsoft swallowed on the first Xbox console. iSuppli analyst Chris Crotty says efficiency gains eventually should shave $50 off chip costs, which with other reductions over time could get Microsoft closer to breakeven. A spokeswoman says Microsoft expects that including sales of its own game software, the Xbox line should start out "gross margin neutral"—breakeven—and turn a profit in 2007. Will this classic razor-blade strategy work? It hasn't so far. In 2005, Microsoft's home entertainment division lost $391 million on sales of $3.3 billion. Xbox 360 added to this problem since initial production fell awfully short of demand, missing large potential sales during the critical Christmas season in 2005, and much of 2006.

Discussion Questions

1. Based on what you have learned in this chapter, why would a company such as Microsoft develop, produce, and sell a product at a loss? Do you think this is a deliberate strategy? If so, is it rational? Explain your answer.

2. Do you think demographic trends are likely to support or hinder the market for this type of product? More broadly, what do you see as opportunities and threats in this market? Explain your answer.

3. From a resource-based perspective, do you think Microsoft's core competencies are likely to give the company a competitive advantage in the game consoles market in the future? Explain your answer.

Source: Adapted from A. Hesseldahl, "For Every Xbox, a Big Fat Loss," *BusinessWeek*, December 5, 2005, p. 13. Updated by authors in 2006.

management minicase 7.2

The Great Rebate Runaround

Mail-in offers are everywhere these days. Shoppers hate collecting all the paperwork, filling out the forms, and mailing it all in to claim their $10 or $100. But no matter how annoying rebates are for consumers, the country's retailers and manufacturers love them.

From PC powerhouse Dell to national chains Circuit City and OfficeMax to the Listerine mouthwash sold at Rite Aid drugstores, rebates are proliferating. Nearly one-third of all computer gear is now sold with some form of rebate, along with more than 20 percent of digital cameras, camcorders, and LCD TVs, says market researcher NPD Group Inc. Hal Stinchfield, a 30-year veteran of the rebate business calculates that some 400 million rebates are offered each year. Their total face value is $6 billion, he estimates. Office-products retailer Staples Inc. says it and its vendors alone pay $3.5 million in rebates each week.

Why the rage for rebates? The industry's open secret is that fully 40 percent of all rebates never get redeemed because consumers fail to apply for them or their applications are rejected, estimates Peter S. Kastner, a director of consulting firm Vericours Inc. That translates into more than $2 billion of extra revenue for retailers and their suppliers each year. What rebates do is get consumers to focus on the discounted price of a product, then buy it at full price. "The game is obviously that anything less than 100 percent redemption is free money," says Paula Rosenblum, director of retail research at consulting firm Aberdeen Group Inc.

The quest for buyers who don't end up collecting a rebate has spawned special industry lingo. Purchases by consumers who never file for their rebates are called "breakage." Wireless companies that pay 100 percent rebates on some cell phones, for example, rely in part on "breakage" to make money. Rebate checks that are never cashed are called "slippage."

The impact on a company's bottom line can be startling. Consider TiVo Inc. The company caught Wall Street off guard by sharply reducing its first-quarter loss to $857,000, from $9.1 million in the same period last year. One reason: about 50,000 of TiVo's 104,000 new subscribers failed to redeem mail-in-rebate offers, reducing the company's expected rebate expense by $5 million. TiVo says it generally sees lower redemption rates during the Christmas shopping season, when consumers may be too distracted to file for rebates on time.

Credit this bonanza for retailers and suppliers partly to human nature. Many consumers are just too lazy, forgetful, or busy to apply for rebates: Call it a tax on the disorganized. Others think the 50¢—or even $200—is just not worth the hassle of collecting. But many consumers and state and federal authorities suspect that companies design the rules to keep redemption rates down. They say companies count on complex rules, filing periods of as little as a week, repeated requests for copies of receipts, and long delays in sending out checks to discourage consumers from even attempting to retrieve their money. When the check does arrive, it sometimes gets tossed in the trash because it looks like junk mail.

Discussion Questions

1. Do you think that use of rebates offers a company a cost-leadership advantage? Why or why not? Explain your answer.

2. How would you analyze the expanding use of rebates from a competitive dynamic perspective? Explain your answer.

3. Do you think that heavy reliance on rebates to drum up customers may be considered an unethical business strategy? Should federal law regulate use of rebates in the future? Explain your answer.

Source: Adapted from B. Grow, "The Great Rebate," *BusinessWeek*, December 5, 2005, pp. 34–39.

Drug Wars: Can Walgreen Co. Survive?

individual/
collaborative
learning
case 7.1

Almost half of all Americans live within two miles of a Walgreen store (the density of its stores can reach Starbuckian levels—downtown San Francisco has 21 stores within a one-mile radius)!

Walgreen is the only Fortune 500 company other than Wal-Mart to have increased both sales and earnings every year for the past 30 years. Its share of the $221 billion prescription-drug market is 14 percent and growing. Between the end of 1975 and 2000, its shareholder returns exceeded GE's and Intel's. The stock peaked in 2000 and sputtered for a couple of years, but Walgreen consistently outperformed the S&P 500, surpassing its previous peak by a wide margin in 2006.

But as they say with mutual funds, past performance is no guarantee of future results, and Walgreen faces some vicious multifront battles in the future. First, there is Walgreen's biggest traditional rival, CVS, which has been expanding rapidly. It recently acquired 1,268 Eckerds to push its total store count to 5,415. Scarier still are the supermarkets and mass-merchandisers that have been moving emphatically into the pharmacy business. Wal-Mart, which already has 3,144 stores with pharmacies, is testing 24-hour pharmacies and offers eye exams in many stores.

The most dangerous threat of all—and one to which Walgreen was late to respond—is the rise of low-cost mail-order prescriptions, which represents a profound shift in the way Americans buy their medicines. The problem for Walgreen is that all the operational excellence in the world is useless if customers have no compelling reason to enter your store. Mail order is now the fastest-growing sales channel for prescription drugs. Last year drugs by mail grew 18 percent, to $33.9 billion, according to IMS Health, accounting for 14.4 percent of the total U.S. prescription market—up from 11.8 percent in 2001. Meanwhile, drug sales at chain stores grew only 6 percent. Mail order threatens not only the chains' bread-and-butter prescription business (which in Walgreen's case makes up 63 percent of total sales) but also the higher-margin "front-end" general merchandise. That is because customers who receive drugs in their mailbox are less likely to visit their local drugstore to shop for things like film, cosmetics, candy, and small appliances.

Critical Thinking Questions

1. Using the material presented in the chapter, how would you explain Walgreen's success story in the past? Do you think Walgreen can overcome the challenges discussed in this case? If so, how? Explain your answer.

2. If you were asked to analyze Walgreen's capabilities, how would you go about conducting such a study? What kind of data would you obtain? Explain your answer.

3. Describe Walgreen's industry environment using Porter's Five Forces framework as discussed in this chapter.

Collaborative Learning Exercise

You have been appointed to an advisory task force of the board of directors at Walgreen to provide a set of recommendations to help the company overcome the challenges discussed in the case. Each task force will have approximately five students and meet for approximately 20 minutes. Each task force is then expected to justify its recommendations to the chairman of the board (represented by the instructor of your class).

Source: Adapted from M. Boyle, "Drug Wars," *Fortune*, June 13, 2005, pp. 25–36.

internet exercise 7.1

Internet Strategies

Dot-com firms and an increasing number of bricks-and-mortar companies rely on the Internet as a normal part of their operations. Many of these have discovered, however, that the Internet is no panacea. Choose any five firms and analyze how they use the Internet to achieve their strategic objectives. Answer the following questions:

1. After comparing and contrasting the different firms, how effectively do you think they use the Internet from a strategic perspective?

2. Is the Internet an appropriate medium to achieve a sustainable competitive advantage? Support your conclusions using the materials discussed in this chapter.

Big Problems with the Big Dig

Summary

Last December, a ceremony was held to celebrate the opening of the massive highway tunnel running underneath Boston affectionately dubbed the "Big Dig." The project has been riddled with cost overruns and project setbacks from the beginning. A few months ago, however, the worst setback of all happened: Leaks from the tunnel walls are pouring hundreds of gallons of water onto the roadways. The Massachusetts Roadway Authority estimates it could take up to another 10 years to fix the leaks. They say that the contractor who was hired to do the work, Bechtel and Modern Continental, will be held responsible. Bechtel says seepage is inevitable, but the tunnel is structurally sound. Modern says they completed the work satisfactorily to specifications and the leaks are not their fault. The Big Dig officials, however, have documents showing that the contractors knew that the materials were not up to specifications as far back as 1999. All parties involved agree the tunnel is safe. However the project officials are angry that the tunnel leaks.

Discussion Questions

1. The Big Dig officials said they hired the biggest contractor in the world to do the project, and if they could not do it right, "they [are] going to pay for it." What is the importance of reputation as an intangible resource for a given firm?

2. The video shows that project officials have documentation showing that the contractors knew the slurry used in the tunnel was not up to specifications. If the materials are not sound, it makes sense that the tunnel is now leaking. At which stage in the strategic management process do you think decision makers could have done things differently to possibly prevent the problems they are facing today?

3. Consider the points of view that were represented in the video. Who were the participants in the Big Dig and what are their perspectives? Now consider the problem and the idea of accountability. Is there an emergent strategy in this crisis? What do you think the project managers should do to resolve the situation?

See the Online Learning Center at www.mhhe.com/gomez3e for updates to this video.

chapter 8

Entrepreneurship and Innovation

Learning Objectives

1 Explain the economic importance of entrepreneurship.

2 Identify the key characteristics and skills of entrepreneurs.

3 Recognize the basic ingredients needed to effectively start and manage an entrepreneurial venture.

4 Differentiate among the legal forms of organizing an entrepreneurial venture.

5 Identify alternative forms of entrepreneurship.

6 Describe innovation and demonstrate why it is important for business success.

7 Apply the "Five C" management tactics to maximize innovation.

Nothing to Sneeze At

It might be common wisdom that doctors or scientists know best how to fight colds, but a surprisingly successful new cold product was created by a schoolteacher, and that's part of its widespread appeal.

Airborne, with its "natural formula of 17 ingredients" and sly cartoon-character packaging, is the runaway hit of the cold-and-flu aisle. The company recently logged annual sales over $120 million, and Airborne is now supported by venture capital, an experienced CEO, and a $10 million ad campaign. In some markets it outsells even Sudafed and Tylenol Cold tablets, and children's versions called Airborne Jr. and Sore Throat Gummies have been added to the product line. CEO Elise Donahue claims the product has "consumer loyalty like nothing I've ever seen before," citing product-referral rates of more than 60 percent among first-time users and nearly 100 percent among regular users.

All this success sprang from a second-grade teacher's distress at the constant colds she was picking up from the students in her Carmel, California, classroom. "All winter, I'd be sick, from one cold to the next," says Airborne's inventor and company founder Victoria Knight-McDowell. "I decided children's germs must somehow be more virulent than adults' germs."

Searching for an answer, Knight-McDowell began brewing up experimental remedies in her kitchen with vitamins C, E, and A, zinc, selenium, forsythia, ginger, isatis root, and Echinacea. When two years of using her self-treatments went by without a cold, she decided she was on to something, and she sold her first package of fizzy tablets to a local drugstore. Then she and her husband cashed out their savings to combine them with his check for writing a television screenplay and invested the money in Airborne, starting out by giving away samples in malls. "Our families thought we had gone round the bend," says Knight-McDowell. "They wanted us to do something responsible, like buy a house. They thought we were mad." But orders came in, and distribution grew. Soon the couple were leasing a warehouse and couple of order-fulfillment centers to meet demand. Knight-McDowell quit her teaching job and appeared on the "Dr. Phil" show, actor Kevin Costner endorsed the product, and the company was on its way.

Because it's marketed as a dietary supplement, Airborne did not have to be tested or approved by the Food and Drug Administration. None of its ingredients, including popular "remedies" like Echinacea and vitamin C, have been scientifically proven to prevent colds. And the packaging states that Airborne "is not intended to diagnose, treat, cure, or prevent any disease." The instructions are to take it "at the first sign of a cold symptom or before entering crowded environments," echoing the Web site's claim that "workers within our highly technological society now spend close to 90% of their time indoors" where, it warns, the EPA estimates "our exposure to pollution may be as much as five times greater . . . than outdoors!"

Controversial in some scientific circles because it's not backed by any proof of its effectiveness, Airborne nonetheless remains an extremely popular product. Positioned as a mainstream product and proud to be invented by a nonexpert, it bases its appeal on consumers' growing distrust of the very establishment that won't endorse it. "We have letters from over 40,000 consumers a year saying they swear by it," says Donahue. "People trust a schoolteacher."

Sources: www.airbornehealth.com, accessed March 13, 2006, Dana Wechsler Linden, "Nothing to Sneeze At," *Forbes* March 13, 2006, p. 41; Rob Walker, "Cold Call: Airborne," *New York Times Magazine*, www.nytimes.com, January 8, 2006; Rachel Konrad, "Out with the Cold: Teacher Serves Up Possible Remedy," *Los Angeles Daily News*, www.dailynews.com, April 24, 2003.

CRITICAL THINKING QUESTIONS

1. *What leads people to become entrepreneurs?*

2. *How can people face the risk involved in starting a new business?*

3. *Where do the ideas come from for starting a new business?*

We'll look at these questions again at the end of the chapter in our Concluding Thoughts, after you've had a chance to learn about entrepreneurs and Innovation.

Creating a new enterprise can be one of the most exciting management challenges. Numerous entrepreneurs have built successful companies by discovering and meeting unmet needs. Many kinds of people start businesses. Men, women, minorities, immigrants—all can and do become entrepreneurs. As a result, entrepreneurship is becoming a popular field of study for many university business students.

Like Lillian Vernon, Arthur Blank, Bernard Marcus, and Michael Dell, today's entrepreneurs face a variety of challenges. They must find answers to such questions as: Do I have the right skills and abilities to become a successful entrepreneur? What type of business should I start? How can I raise capital to grow the business? Which markets should my business compete in? How much growth and what rate of growth is desirable? Manager's Notebook 8.1 on page 311 presents the basic entrepreneurial skills needed to successfully launch a new business venture. This chapter explores questions and issues about starting and growing a business. The first issue is describing what entrepreneurship is and is not.

entrepreneurship

The process of creating a business enterprise capable of entering new or established markets by deploying resources and people in a unique way to develop a new organization.

What Is Entrepreneurship?

The process of creating a business enterprise capable of entering new or established markets is **entrepreneurship**. Successful entrepreneurship requires deploying resources and people in unique ways to develop a new organization. An **entrepreneur** is an individual who creates an enterprise that becomes a new entry to a market. Broadly stated, an entrepreneur is anyone who undertakes some project and bears some risk.[1]

entrepreneur

An individual who creates an enterprise that becomes a new entry to a market.

Entrepreneurship Myths

Entrepreneurs have received considerable attention from the business and popular press in recent years. Still, many misconceptions remain concerning entrepre-

SO, YOU WANT TO BECOME AN ENTREPRENEUR? KEY SKILLS FOR ENTREPRENEURIAL SUCCESS

- *Opportunity Recognition Skills*. Entrepreneurs are able to identify opportunities when they develop or exist. To be successful, an entrepreneur must scan the environment, searching for opportunities and ideas. Sometimes an entrepreneur may discover a problem to be solved or find a market need that is not being filled. Other times, a person may be committed to becoming an entrepreneur and then looks for a potential business opportunity. In either case, the entrepreneur must be aware that an opportunity exists and be able to take advantage of the situation.

- *Opportunity Fit Assessment*. Not everyone can succeed at everything. To be successful, an entrepreneur must be able to evaluate whether or not his or her personality, skills, and leadership style match with the opportunity. This includes the technical and business skills that are required in addition to personal preferences and needs.

- *Implementation Skills*. Successful entrepreneurs tend to have a high need for achievement, have an internal locus of control, be risk takers, and be confident in their ability to master unforeseen challenges.

- *Networking Skills*. Networking skills are critical to obtaining financial capital, business and technical knowledge, retail shelf space, and other resources required to start a business.

Source: N. Lindsay and J. Craig, "A Framework for Understanding Opportunity Recognition: Entrepreneurs versus Private Equity Financiers," *Journal of Private Equity* 6 (2002), pp. 13–24.

neurs and what they do in order to succeed. We next consider some of these myths and contrast those with the common reality faced by most entrepreneurs.[2]

MYTH 1: ENTREPRENEURS ARE BORN, NOT MADE One common belief is that entrepreneurs possess certain innate traits that are different from regular people. In fact, many types of people with different personality characteristics have become successful entrepreneurs. Many of them studied entrepreneurship as a discipline before launching a business. Business schools offer courses in entrepreneurship that provide opportunities to learn and practice skills that are useful to entrepreneurs.

MYTH 2: IT IS NECESSARY TO HAVE ACCESS TO MONEY TO BECOME AN ENTREPRENEUR A second common myth is that only wealthy people, or those who have access to wealthy people, can start businesses. The truth is, however, that many companies have been started by people with few resources. These entrepreneurs accumulated capital by putting in long hours without pay and reinvesting the profits of the business into expansion. For example, Hewlett-Packard, the giant electronics company, was started in a Palo Alto, California, garage in 1940 by two Stanford University students with a few hundred dollars and an order for sound equipment from the Walt Disney Company.

MYTH 3: AN ENTREPRENEUR TAKES A LARGE OR IRRATIONAL RISK IN STARTING A BUSINESS Risk is part of any business venture and this reality certainly applies to entrepreneurial ventures. The costs of embracing an entrepreneurial vision in terms of personal funds and family relationships can be tremendous. However, in terms of absolute amount of financial risk, most entrepreneurs

Like many design-conscious parents, Michael and Ellen Diamant (shown here with their son Spencer) were unhappy with the clunky shapes and bland designs of the baby gear they found on the market when their son was born several years ago. Says Michael, "We decided to take products that are under the radar and turn them into objects that are beautiful to look at." So their baby-gear company Skip Hop was born. It now grosses several million dollars a year from trendy diaper bags; new products designed by award-winning professionals are already in production.

small business

Any business that is independently owned and operated, that is small in size, and that is not dominant in its markets.

have little to risk at the outset of a new business venture. It is usually later, when trying to grow the business into a larger enterprise, that the entrepreneur can face larger risk. At this later time, the business may have developed substantial value, which means there is more to lose.

MYTH 4: MOST SUCCESSFUL ENTREPRENEURS START WITH A BREAKTHROUGH INVENTION Contrary to the idea that entrepreneurs capitalize on revolutionary change, most entrepreneurs start a new business with only a moderate or incremental change that is designed to serve a market need. Certainly, innovation and being able to distinguish your product or service from others in the marketplace is important for a start-up business. Rather than revolutionary change, however, great execution, being first in a market, or a small innovation/improvement is often enough for an entrepreneur to be successful.

MYTH 5: ENTREPRENEURS BECOME SUCCESSFUL ON THEIR FIRST VENTURE People tend to remember entrepreneurial successes. Many times, however, failure is a key part of the learning process. By failing, entrepreneurs learn lessons that eventually lead to the creation of successful ventures. Nolan Bushnell, the entrepreneur who is best remembered for starting the videogame company Atari, failed at several different businesses but he persisted and learned from his mistakes. Likewise, initial business ventures of Richard Branson, founder of Virgin Records, include a failed magazine launch.[3]

A Distinction between an Entrepreneurial Venture and a Small Business

A **small business** is any company that is independently owned and operated, is small in size, and does not dominate its markets. For research purposes, the U.S. Small Business Administration defines a small business as employing fewer than 500 employees. Small businesses do not always grow into medium-sized or large businesses. Some small-business owners prefer to keep their operations modest.

One of the most important goals of an entrepreneur, on the other hand, can be growth. An entrepreneurial venture may be small during its early stages, but the goal may be to become a medium-sized firm of 100 to 499 employees or a large firm with 500 or more employees. Giant firms like Wal-Mart, Home Depot, Microsoft, and Intel started as entrepreneurships with the goal of becoming dominant companies in their markets. At the start, however, a small business and an entrepreneurial venture may be hard to tell apart. For a small business owner, stability and profitability are the ideal situation. For the entrepreneur, growth and a greater presence in the market can be important objectives.

The Importance of Entrepreneurship

According to the latest figures compiled by the U.S. Census bureau, the number of U.S. businesses increased by 10 percent between 1997 and 2002, with approximately 23 million businesses operating in the United States by the end of 2002.[4] Over 550,000 new businesses opened up in 2002.[5] The economies of the United States and many other countries depend on the creation of new enterprises. Entrepreneurship creates jobs, stimulates innovation, and provides opportunities for diverse people in society.

Job Creation

Entrepreneurship and the creation of small businesses have surprising impacts on the creation of new jobs. According to the most recent data, small businesses created three-quarters of the net new jobs in the 1999–2000 year. Over the decade of the 1990s the net job creation by small business varied between 60 and 80 percent. Young start-ups, businesses in the first two years of existence, account for nearly all of the net new jobs in the U.S. economy.[6]

Innovation

Entrepreneurships are responsible for introducing a major proportion of new and innovative products and services that reach the market. They are often started by visionary people who develop an innovative way to do something faster, better, cheaper, or with improved features. Entrepreneurships often pioneer new technologies designed to make older technologies obsolete. This was the case when Apple Computer pioneered the first commercial personal computer and challenged the computing technology of the 1970s, which was based on centralized, mainframe computers. Eventually, the personal computer became the dominant technology and spawned a huge market for computer components, software, systems, and services.

Opportunities for Diverse People

People of diverse backgrounds who have experienced frustration and blocked career paths in large corporations can improve their economic status and develop interesting careers by becoming entrepreneurs. Entrepreneurship provides an attractive alternative for women who bump up against the glass ceiling in male-dominated firms. Many female corporate executives have left their firms to become entrepreneurs to: (1) balance work and family responsibilities; (2) obtain more challenge and autonomy; and (3) avoid unpleasant organization politics.

Similarly, increasing numbers of blacks, Hispanics, and Asian Americans have launched successful entrepreneurial efforts. Entrepreneurship can provide anyone, particularly in the United States, an alternative to the corporate career path. The most recent U.S. Census Bureau data indicates that business ownership by minorities and women has increased significantly.[7] For the period 1997 to 2002, the number of black-owned businesses increased by 45 percent, Hispanic-owned businesses increased by 31 percent, and Asian-owned businesses increased by 24 percent. Female-owned businesses for the period increased by 20 percent.

LOC-In

1 Learning Objective Check-In

Jess, Carol, and Kate are all women entrepreneurs. Jess has three kids and is a single mother. Kate was a former corporate manager who worked in a male-dominated firm and was not advancing to top executive status despite years of hard work. Carol, diplomatic to a fault, simply wanted to remove herself from the cutthroat environment of the corporate world in which she worked previously to start her own company and still serve top clients.

1. *Jess removed herself from the corporate world to enter entrepreneurship in order to _____.*
   a. *make strategic decisions at a firm*
   b. *avoid unpleasant organization politics*
   c. *balance work and family responsibilities*
   d. *obtain more autonomy*
2. *Carol chose entrepreneurship because she wanted to _____.*
   a. *make strategic decisions at a firm*
   b. *obtain more autonomy and challenge at work*
   c. *balance work and family responsibilities*
   d. *avoid unpleasant organization politics*
3. *Kate chose entrepreneurship because she wanted to _____.*
   a. *avoid unpleasant organization politics*
   b. *advance beyond the "glass ceiling"*
   c. *obtain more autonomy and challenge at work*
   d. *achieve personal fulfillment through innovation*

Earl G. Graves, Sr., chief executive officer of Earl G. Graves Ltd., founded Black Enterprise in 1970. His vision was to create a link of commerce and communication between the black professional class and American industry.

Characteristics of Successful Entrepreneurs

internal locus of control

A strong belief in one's own ability to succeed, so that one accepts responsibility for outcomes and tries harder after making mistakes.

external locus of control

A strong belief that luck, fate, or factors beyond one's control determine one's progress, causing feelings of helplessness and decreasing intensity of goal-seeking efforts in the face of failure.

Entrepreneurial Characteristics and Skills

There are many motives for starting a new business. Some entrepreneurs learn from successful family role models. A few stumble onto an entrepreneurial career path by inventing a new product and building a business around it, as did Steven Jobs and Steve Wozniak with the first prototype of the Apple computer. Others become dissatisfied with corporate careers and discover that entrepreneurship provides an attractive set of challenges and rewards.

Manager's Notebook 8.2 on page 315 presents basic categories that have been used to segment entrepreneurs into various types. Whatever the type of entrepreneur, there appear to be common characteristics important for success. As depicted in Figure 8.1 on page 315, key entrepreneur characteristics underlying success can be divided into categories of *personal characteristics* and *skills*. We first discuss the characteristics.

Characteristics of Entrepreneurs

Some key characteristics associated with entrepreneurship are a high need for achievement, an internal locus of control, the willingness to take risks, and self-confidence.

People with a *high need for achievement* have a strong desire to solve problems on their own. They enjoy setting goals and achieving them through their own efforts, and like receiving feedback on how they are doing. These characteristics help entrepreneurs to be more proactive and anticipate future problems, needs, or changes.

An entrepreneur is likely to have an **internal locus of control**, with a strong belief in his or her ability to succeed. When a person with an internal locus of control fails or makes a mistake, the individual is likely to accept responsibility for the outcome and try harder, rather than searching for external reasons to explain the failure. Entrepreneurs are persistent and motivated to overcome barriers that would deter others. People with an **external locus of control** believe that what happens to them is due to luck, fate, or factors beyond their control. When people with an external locus of control fail, they are more likely to feel helpless and are less likely to sustain or intensify their goal-seeking efforts.

An entrepreneur takes on some level of risk when trying to start a new venture. In some cases, entrepreneurs may risk a substantial portion of their own capital as well as funds contributed by family, friends, and other investors. The entrepreneur may leave the security of a corporate career and still be uncertain that the new venture presents a better opportunity. However, entrepreneurs, as a group, may not face quite as much risk of failure as previously thought. A widely held belief has been that 90 percent of entrepreneurial efforts fail in the first year of operation. Current data indicates that 67 percent of new ventures are successful after four years.[8] While this percentage is certainly far from a guarantee, it is not nearly as gloomy as the high 90 percent failure rate that had been previously suggested.

AN ENTREPRENEURIAL CLASSIFICATION SYSTEM

- *The Craftsperson*—has trade or skill or overwhelming desire to do a craft.
- *The Opportunist*—commits to the entrepreneurial effort because it makes business sense.
- *The Inventor*—likes to create and bring new products to market.

These categories are not always mutually exclusive. Many entrepreneurs fit into more than one category. These general categories can still be useful for understanding the basic motives and approaches used by entrepreneurs. A craftsperson may not have a good handle on the financial realities of his/her new business venture. Likewise, an opportunist may have little understanding or concern for the skill and care that might be needed to produce the product or provide the service. Still, both have certain drives which may enable them to succeed.

Source: R. J. Kuntze, "The Dark Side of Multilevel Marketing: Appeals to the Symbolically Incomplete." Dissertation at Arizona State University, 2001.

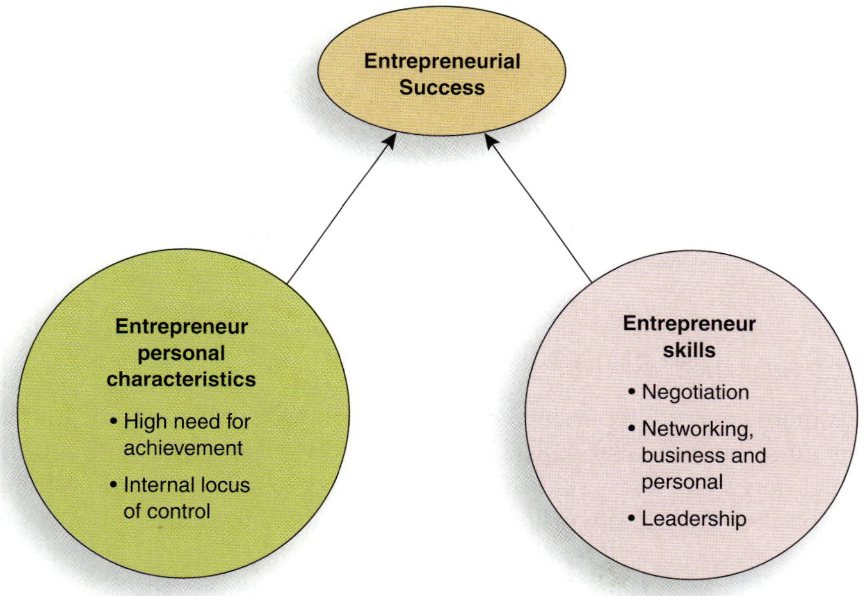

FIGURE 8.1

Key Entrepreneur Characteristics for Success

Entrepreneurs feel certain they can master the skills needed to run a business and that they can overcome unforeseen obstacles. This self-confidence can be used to energize and motivate others. Self-confidence enables entrepreneurs to improvise and find novel solutions to business problems that might discourage people who are more self-critical.

Michael Dell, the entrepreneur who founded Dell Computer, exhibits all of these characteristics. His background and reasons for launching his company are described in Management Close-Up 8.1 on page 316.

Entrepreneurs acquire these characteristics in various ways. Some learn them from family role models. Others are exposed to entrepreneurs in school, work, or social activities. Most people have opportunities to develop entrepreneurial characteristics by imitating others who have these characteristics.

Michael Dell, Founder and CEO, Dell Computer Corporation

THEME: CUSTOMER FOCUS

Michael Dell is founder and CEO of Austin-based Dell Computer Corporation, a widely recognized U.S. computer company with over 61,000 employees and over $40 billion in revenues for 2005. With a net worth of $17 billion, he is the wealthiest person in Texas. Dell's idea was to sell computers directly to the customer by telephone, avoiding costly middlemen and saving the customer money. Rather than building computers to distribute to retail outlets and carrying large inventories of finished computers and parts to build them, he built computers to order. The company saved money by having a lean, just-in-time inventory of parts from suppliers. Michael Dell pioneered the use of the Internet as a distribution channel for selling computers, and Dell now sells more computers on the Internet than any other company.

Dell was born into a Houston family of high achievers. His father was an orthodontist, his mother a stockbroker. When Michael was 8 years old he applied for a high school equivalency exam, and by age 13 he started a mail order stamp-trading business. When Dell was 16 he started selling subscriptions to the *Houston Post* by phone and became salesman of the month shortly after. A year later he was earning $18,000 annually supervising fellow high school students as they sold subscriptions.

At a young age Dell became very interested in computers. While spending a lot of time around computer retail stores, he realized that these stores were charging up to a 40 percent markup on their products. Even though these stores were charging a high amount for their computers, their service was not very good. Dell realized that he could buy the products directly from the manufacturer, sell them cheaply to the customer, provide better service, and completely eliminate the retail store.

Dell decided to start his computer business when he was just a freshman at the University of Texas at Austin. Working out of his dorm room, Dell sold computers built to order to interested buyers. Three months later, Dell had racked up sales of $181,000. Two years later, when Dell turned 20, the company reached $34 million in sales.

Michael Dell has remained at the helm of Dell Computer from the start, becoming one of the youngest CEOs of a major U.S. corporation while still in his twenties.

Sources: A. Serwer, "Michael Dell Rocks," *Fortune*, May 11, 1998, pp. 59–70; A. Serwer, "Michael Dell Turns the PC World Inside Out," *Fortune*, September 8, 1997, pp. 76–86; D. F. Kuratko and R. M. Hodgetts, *Entrepreneurship*, 2nd ed., Fort Worth: Dryden Press, 1992, p. 72; www.dell.com.

Entrepreneurial Skills

Just as there are certain personal characteristics that are likely to be found in entrepreneurs, there are also skills which are related to success. An entrepreneur utilizes a variety of business skills to create and operate an enterprise. Among these are negotiation skills, networking skills, and leadership skills.

NEGOTIATION SKILLS Whenever an exchange of goods or services between two or more parties takes place, quality negotiation skills are helpful. A party who applies negotiation skills effectively ensures favorable terms for both parties by finding common ground. This problem-solving style of negotiation, also referred to as *win–win* negotiating, requires the individual to act in good faith to forge a relationship based on trust and cooperation. This makes it easier to discover a basis of exchange that is attractive to both parties. More information on negotiation skills is provided in Chapter 14.

Entrepreneurs use negotiation skills to obtain resources needed to launch and maintain a company. Among the situations that require negotiation skills are:

- Borrowing money from a bank at good terms to finance business expansion.
- Locking into an attractive, long-term lease to control office space expenses.
- Obtaining a low price on raw materials from a supplier to gain a cost advantage over competitors.
- Negotiating employment contracts to attract and retain key executives.

Scott Jochim turned a high school paper on auctions into his first business. He has established three successful companies since then and finds entrepreneurship to be empowering. He is currently president of Digital Tech Frontier, a technology company he started at age 23. The company provides virtual-reality technology for education, entertainment, and therapy. Scott's company has built a revenue in the six-figure range, but he says, "If I can get a cancer patient to write me and say I made chemo more bearable, that makes everything I've done worth it."

NETWORKING SKILLS   Gathering information and building alliances requires quality networking skills. These are applied to both personal and business networks.

A **personal network** is based on relationships between the entrepreneur and other entrepreneurs, suppliers, creditors, investors, friends, former professors, and others. These personal contacts can help an entrepreneur make effective decisions by providing information that reduces uncertainty for the business. For example,

- A fellow entrepreneur can help locate a wealthy interested private investor (sometimes referred to as a "business angel") to provide scarce capital.

- A former professor may provide free technical consulting advice and student volunteers to help develop a marketing strategy for the new venture.

- A banker may be able to locate a skilled executive who could provide complementary management skills to the entrepreneurship at a critical stage of growth.

- Talks with fellow entrepreneurs who have been through the process of building a business from the ground up can provide invaluable feedback and emotional support.

Entrepreneurs build personal networks by actively seeking out individuals with similar interests, staying in touch with them, and looking for opportunities to make the relationship mutually satisfying. By being responsive to the needs and interests of the people in their personal networks, entrepreneurs build trust and goodwill. A personal network can be formed through participation in professional societies, business clubs, charitable organizations, trade fairs, and networks of entrepreneurs. Skills for Managing 8.1 on page 318 presents an opportunity to analyze and improve your networking skills.

personal network

The relationships between an entrepreneur and other parties, including other entrepreneurs, suppliers, creditors, investors, friends, former colleagues, and others.

8.1

NETWORKING SKILLS

Reflect on a meeting of a professional student club or organization that you have recently attended.

1. What was your purpose for attending this meeting?
2. Did you have any specific goals in mind in terms of the kinds of people you hoped to meet and how you hoped to benefit from the meeting?
3. How many people did you meet at the meeting?
4. How many of these new acquaintances did you connect with so that there was a possibility for a relationship to emerge?
5. How many people did you follow up with a phone call after the meeting?
6. What was the basis of your relationship with these new contacts?
7. Have you continued to keep in touch with these new contacts? If not, why not?

Instructions: Answer the preceding questions individually. Then form small groups of four to five students. Share your experiences in networking with each other. Then work together to answer the following questions. If time permits, attend a professional meeting after developing some network strategies and report back to the group with your experiences.

Discussion Questions

1. What are some effective practices that can be used to network with other people?
2. How can you avoid getting entangled in too many fruitless network relationships that are not mutually beneficial?
3. What are some ways to keep your network vital so that you can feel free to tap your network for opportunities when the time comes and you are in need of help?

Source: From *Entrepreneurship*, by M. J. Dollinger. Copyright © 1995 The McGraw-Hill Companies, Inc. Reprinted with permission.

---

business network

A firm's alliances formed with other businesses to achieve mutually beneficial goals.

Networking skills can come in handy in developing useful business alliances. A **business network** is a set of alliances forged with other businesses to achieve mutually beneficial goals. A larger company may enter a partnership with a small entrepreneurship in order to gain some of the benefits of the new and innovative product or service the entrepreneurship is developing. Through licensing agreements that provide limited access to the technology or strategic alliances to pool resources, a new company may gain access to a larger corporation's marketing and finance professionals or may obtain capital to help enter markets that are difficult to reach. This includes acquiring shelf space in Wal-Mart or having a national direct sales force call on customers.

Microsoft entered a strategic alliance with IBM in 1980 to provide DOS-based operating systems for the new IBM personal computer. This strategic alliance ensured the success of Microsoft and greatly enabled it to set the technology standard for personal computer operating systems, which resulted in huge profits for Microsoft.

LEADERSHIP SKILLS Quality leaders provide a shared vision for others to work toward common goals. As leaders, entrepreneurs inspire and motivate employees to do what is good for the enterprise, even when it is not in their short-term interests. For example, employees in a start-up company are likely to work extremely long hours for modest pay. The entrepreneur depends on leadership skills to bolster employee morale and guide the enterprise toward the objectives, overcoming obstacles that stand in the way.

Starting a business is a difficult prospect. In addition to possessing certain personal characteristics and skills, there are steps that an entrepreneur should take to help assure the success of the new business. Management Is Everyone's Business 8.1 above offers some simple but important recommendations that should enhance your success as an individual entrepreneur.

Starting and Managing an Entrepreneurial Venture

An entrepreneurial venture begins with an idea. The next steps are developing a business plan, selecting the most appropriate type of legal structure to operate under, obtaining financing, and dealing with growth and expansion. Many entrepreneurial ventures are new businesses, rather than being franchises or spin-offs.

LOC-In

② Learning Objective Check-In

Patrick is opening his own business. He believes that he has the ability to succeed and he takes responsibility for how his life turns out. Patrick has an overwhelming desire to practice woodworking.

1. *According to the classification system of entrepreneurship, we saw in Manager's Notebook 8.2, we would say that Patrick is a(n) _____.*
   a. *craftsperson*
   b. *opportunist*
   c. *investor*
   d. *inventor*
2. *Patrick's _____ tells us that he believes he has personal responsibility for the outcomes in his life.*
   a. *entrepreneurial spirit*
   b. *negotiation skills*
   c. *external locus of control*
   d. *internal locus of control*

New Business Ideas

Entrepreneurs get ideas for new businesses from many different sources, including

- Newspapers, magazines, and trade journals that identify market trends.
- Inventions or discoveries that provide products or services faster, better, cheaper, or with more features. Corporations like the 3M Company give technologists unstructured time to experiment, hoping for the discovery of the next Post-it Notes.

Of Kids and Mice: Making Mice Work for Children

THEME: CUSTOMER FOCUS

Many kids are being exposed to computers at a very young age. Unfortunately their fine motor skills aren't always up to the task. Moving a mouse around that is too big for your hand can be very frustrating. Why not make a mouse that fits a child's hand and is cute and engaging at the same time? That's exactly what Susan Giles thought when she saw the frustration of her 4-year-old granddaughter trying to operate a computer. Giles created a rounder and smaller mouse. She decorated each one to look like a cute bug or dinosaur and gave them cute names. The venture turned out to be so successful that she devoted herself full time to running Kidz Mouse. How successful is the company? Giles keeps numbers concerning the business to herself. She did however sign a contract with Nickelodeon to make mice based on network characters such as SpongeBob Square Pants and Blues Clues. Another indicator of success is that the mice can now be found at outlets such as CompUSA and Best Buy, among others.

Source: M. Cassidy, "Creative Marketing: The Mouse Tap," *Detroit Free Press*, December 5, 2002, accessed February 19, 2003, at www.freep.com/money/tech/mice5_20021205.htm; www.kidzmouse.com, accessed December 28, 2005.

- Trade shows and exhibitions, where new products and innovations are displayed.
- Hobbies, such as jogging, bicycling, or skiing, as was the case with new companies that marketed running shoes (Nike), mountain bicycles (Cannondale), and snowboards (Burton).
- Family members, including children, such as in the design of video games, educational toys, and the baby jogger that lets people combine jogging with taking the baby out. (See Management Close-Up 8.2 above for an example of an entrepreneur whose business was inspired by her children.)
- Entrepreneurship courses in business schools. Babson University in Wellesley, Massachusetts, sponsors a business plan contest between teams of business students who compete for prize money. Student entrepreneurs with promising business plans are likely to attract the attention of investors.

Why Entrepreneurs Fail

Entrepreneurial ventures can fail if the business idea is poorly implemented. The most common reasons for business failure include:

- *Lack of capital.* When an entrepreneur underestimates the need for capital and assumes more debt than can be repaid, the new business is in trouble. Many businesses fail because investors do not purchase enough stock during the initial public offering to cover accumulated debts.
- *Poor knowledge of the market.* An entrepreneur can miscalculate the appeal of the product or service. This often occurs when an inventor "falls in love" with an invention and expects consumers to do so as well.
- *Faulty product design.* Design or other features of a product can be rejected by consumers. This was the case with word processing products sold by Wang Computer, which were linked to mainframe computers and were

much more expensive than rival products that were driven by personal computers. Wang was unable to sell enough of its products and went out of business.

- *Human resource problems.* Entrepreneurs may select employees who do not support the goals of the business. In a family business, there is the potential for divorce or sibling rivalry to divide workers into feuding factions.

- *Poor understanding of the competition.* Entrepreneurs should study their competitors and try to understand their interests. Firmly entrenched businesses may react aggressively and use price cuts or special discounts to try to drive new competitors out of business. Any time a new grocery store opens, local competitors will make dramatic efforts to keep customers.

Sometimes businesses exit the market for reasons other than failure. An entrepreneur may sell the business to a competitor for a good price or close it because a more attractive business opportunity has come along.

LOC-In

3 **Learning Objective Check-In**

1. *Carlita has always had trouble using the standard adjustable headphones that come with electronic devices she has purchased in the past. They are either too stiff or too loose, or else they do not adjust to be small enough. Carlita has an idea for developing easily adjustable audio and video equipment for adults and children for use with standard electronic equipment, including video game equipment. She thinks that she might be able to turn her idea into a new business venture. The source of Carlita's idea is _____.*
   a. *newspapers, magazines, and trade journals*
   b. *inventions or discoveries*
   c. *trade shows and exhibitions*
   d. *personal hobbies or discoveries*

Business Plan

Once an entrepreneur develops an idea for a new business venture, the next critical step is to prepare a **business plan**, which is a blueprint that maps out the business strategy for entering markets and explains the business to potential investors. A business plan details the strategies and tactics needed to minimize the enterprise's risk of failure, which is highest during the early stages.

Key components of the business plan include:

- A description of the product or service.
- An analysis of market trends and potential competitors.
- An estimated price for the product or service.
- An estimate of the time it will take to generate profits.
- A plan for manufacturing the product.
- A plan for growth and expansion of the business.
- Sources of funding.
- A plan for obtaining financing.
- An approach for putting an effective management team in place.

A detailed outline for creating a business plan appears in Figure 8.2 on page 323.

business plan

The business's blueprint that maps out its business strategy for entering markets and that explains the business to potential investors.

Legal Forms

Entrepreneurs can select from three different legal forms when launching a new enterprise. The legal forms are a proprietorship, a partnership, and a corporation. An entrepreneur should consider tax implications, willingness to accept personal liability, and the ease of raising capital for the business before making this important decision.

video: THE ENTREPRENEURIAL MANAGER

Auntie Anne's

Summary

Auntie Anne's began in Lancaster, Pennsylvania, often called the "Heart of Amish Country." In almost 15 years, the company has opened over 800 franchises worldwide. It began in the Downingtown Farmer's Market in 1988. Having no money, but wanting to help her husband open a free family resource and counseling center, Anne Beiler borrowed $6,000 to buy a concession stand in that farmer's market, selling the original Auntie Anne's pretzels, lemonade, and other goodies. Anne tasted the soft pretzel recipe and decided it just wouldn't do at first. Her husband, Jonas, helped her modify the recipe, and they were an instant success. Eventually they eliminated pizza and ice cream and focused on pretzels. At first, friends and family asked if they could sell the pretzels at other locations. By the time there were 40 different locations, Anne decided they needed to turn what they had into an official business. They considered several options, including a sole proprietorship, a partnership, and a corporation. The alternative they settled on, however, was the franchise.

The Beilers looked to outside help in setting up an official franchise. A franchise is an arrangement where there is less risk for the potential partners. The marketing assistance is another advantage. Additionally, the ownership advantages are virtually unlimited. There is high brand recognition cultivated by the franchise company. There is also good training which is managed by the larger company. Disadvantages to franchising include large start-up costs, shared profits, management regulations (also seen as an advantage for Auntie Anne's because of quality control support), coattail effects (not an issue for Auntie Anne's), restrictions on selling (owners cannot just sell the franchise to anyone), and fraudulent franchisers. Luckily for Auntie Anne's, there have been only two litigation issues in 30 years of operation.

Diversity, e-commerce, technology, and international markets are important factors for business owners today. Anne is an inspiration for many women because she serves as a good example of how to develop a company oneself and be successful. For Auntie Anne's, e-commerce is a growing area of the business, if not a very large one right now. The company operates franchises in all areas of the world.

Discussion Questions

1. How did Anne Beiler start her pretzel business? How did she get the idea to turn it into an entrepreneurial venture?
2. What legal form was right for Auntie Anne's? What are the pros and cons of this arrangement?
3. How is the company using technology to advance the business?

---

proprietorship

A form of business that is owned by one person.

PROPRIETORSHIP   Many new businesses are owned by single individuals. **Proprietorships** are easy to form and require a minimum of paperwork. The owner keeps all of the profits and makes all of the important decisions without having to get the approval of co-owners.

A proprietorship is limited to one person, which restricts the owner from obtaining more than limited amounts of credit and capital. Another drawback is that the sole owner has unlimited liability, which means that the personal assets of the owner may be at stake in a lawsuit. About 74 percent of all U.S. businesses are proprietorships, though revenues and profits are relatively small compared to other forms of ownership.

partnership

A form of business that is an association of two or more persons acting as co-owners of a business.

PARTNERSHIP   An association of two or more persons acting as co-owners of a business creates a **partnership**. Each partner provides resources and skills and shares in the profits. A partnership can raise more capital than a proprietorship

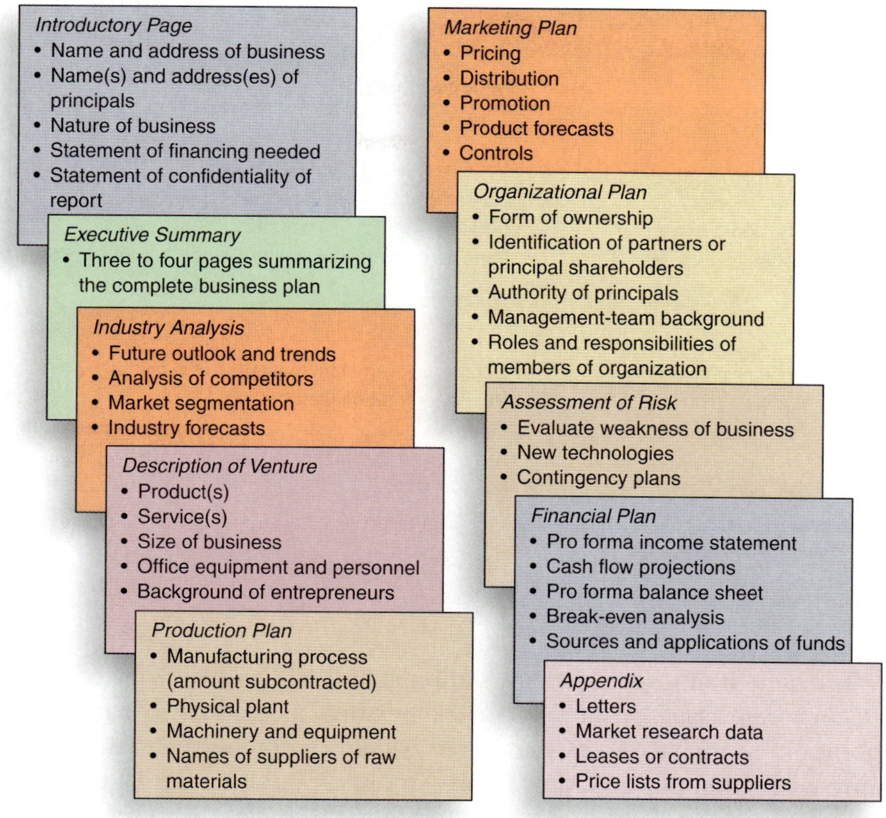

FIGURE 8.2

Outline of a Business Plan

Source: From *Entrepreneurship*, 4th ed., by R. Hisrich and M. Peters. Copyright © 1998 The McGraw-Hill Companies, Inc. Reprinted with permission.

Introductory Page
- Name and address of business
- Name(s) and address(es) of principals
- Nature of business
- Statement of financing needed
- Statement of confidentiality of report

Executive Summary
- Three to four pages summarizing the complete business plan

Industry Analysis
- Future outlook and trends
- Analysis of competitors
- Market segmentation
- Industry forecasts

Description of Venture
- Product(s)
- Service(s)
- Size of business
- Office equipment and personnel
- Background of entrepreneurs

Production Plan
- Manufacturing process (amount subcontracted)
- Physical plant
- Machinery and equipment
- Names of suppliers of raw materials

Marketing Plan
- Pricing
- Distribution
- Promotion
- Product forecasts
- Controls

Organizational Plan
- Form of ownership
- Identification of partners or principal shareholders
- Authority of principals
- Management-team background
- Roles and responsibilities of members of organization

Assessment of Risk
- Evaluate weakness of business
- New technologies
- Contingency plans

Financial Plan
- Pro forma income statement
- Cash flow projections
- Pro forma balance sheet
- Break-even analysis
- Sources and applications of funds

Appendix
- Letters
- Market research data
- Leases or contracts
- Price lists from suppliers

and can provide complementary skills that can create more opportunity for the enterprise. For example, one partner of a small Los Angeles law firm is skillful at generating new clients from his extensive networks in the local bar association, while the other is skilled at providing meticulous legal research that results in a high court success rate. The synergy between these two law partners results in more profits than would be possible if each were operating alone.

While partnerships are easy to start and are subject to few government regulations, they do have some drawbacks. Each partner is responsible for the acts of the other partners. If one partner makes a bad business decision, the other partners are liable. In other words, each owner's personal assets are at risk in a lawsuit or to pay off debts. If the partners disagree about important goals of the business, the firm may become paralyzed or fail. If one of the partners dies, a partnership will be in jeopardy unless provisions for the other partners to buy out the deceased partner's share have been made. Nonetheless, some large and successful businesses use the partnership legal structure. Large accounting firms such as Arthur Andersen have more than 1,000 partners in offices around the globe.

CORPORATION A **corporation** is a legal entity separate from the individuals who own it. A corporation receives limited rights to operate from the state or government that provides its charter. A corporation is more complex and costly to form and operate than a proprietorship or a partnership. Since its activities are regulated by the government, many records must be kept and regularly filed with the government.

corporation

A form of business that is a legal entity separate from the individuals who own it.

table 8.1

Partnership and Corporation Forms of Ownership

ADVANTAGES	DISADVANTAGES
Partnership	
Ease of formation	Unlimited liability for firm's debt
Direct share of profits	Limited continuity of life of enterprise
Division of labor and management responsibility	Difficulty in obtaining capital
More capital available than in a sole proprietorship	Partners share responsibility for other partners' actions
Less governmental control and regulation	
Corporation	
Owners' liability for the firm's debt limited to their investment	Extensive government regulation of activities
Ease of raising large amounts of capital	High incorporation fees
Ease of transfer of ownership through sales of stock	Corporate capital, profits, dividends and salaries double-taxed
Life of enterprise distinct from owners	Activities limited to those stated in charter

Sources: Adapted from W. Megginson et al., *Small Business Management*, 2nd ed., New York: Irwin/McGraw-Hill, 1997, pp. 74, 78; D. F. Kuratko and R. M. Hodgetts, Entrepreneurship, 2nd ed., Fort Worth: Dryden Press, 1992, p. 208.

The benefit of forming a corporation is limited liability. If the corporation is sued, corporate assets are at risk, but the personal assets of the owners are not. A corporation is separate from the owner. When the owner dies, the corporation continues. Corporations are able to raise more capital than any of the other legal forms of enterprise. Corporations are able to raise capital through the sale of shares of stock to the public or through loans and bonds.

Besides incorporation fees and the additional record-keeping expenses, many corporations are doubly taxed by the government. The corporation pays taxes on its profits, and the owners pay taxes on their dividends. Some other countries do not have this double taxation system, and some firms find it attractive to incorporate in countries that offer advantageous tax treatment. The advantages and disadvantages of partnerships and corporations are summarized in Table 8.1 above.

Sources of Financial Resources

Entrepreneurships require capital to get started. The two principal means of obtaining the resources to fund a new business are debt financing and equity financing. Factors favoring one type of financing over the other include the value of the firm's assets, the interest rate, and the availability of investor funds.

DEBT FINANCING Commercial loans are a common form of **debt financing**. Company leaders must set up a plan to repay the principal and interest. The schedule to repay the loan may be short term, lasting less than one year, or long term. Commercial banks are the principal source of debt financing.

The bank establishes a repayment schedule for the loan and secures the loan with company assets such as inventories, equipment, and machines or real estate. Failure to make the scheduled loan repayments can lead to **bankruptcy**, a legal procedure that distributes company assets to creditors and protects the debtor from unfair demands of creditors. Bankruptcy can hurt the reputation of an entrepreneur and make it difficult to obtain future business loans.

debt financing

A means of obtaining financial resources that involves obtaining a commercial loan and setting up a plan to repay the principal and interest.

bankruptcy

A legal procedure that distributes company assets to creditors and protects the debtor from unfair demands of creditors when the debtor fails to make scheduled loan repayments.

An entrepreneur must be careful not to take on too much debt. Excessive debt will result in most of the company's positive cash flow going to retiring the debt rather than growing the business. New ventures that have uncertain cash flows during start-up may not be able to qualify for debt financing.

Other sources of debt financing for more specific purchases are:

- Equipment manufacturers (for example, a computer firm may debt finance a computer system).
- Suppliers (credit may be given on supplies for a fee).
- Credit cards (some businesses were started by overextending several of an owner's credit cards, an expensive way to obtain financing).

EQUITY FINANCING   As a business grows, an entrepreneur will most likely combine a mix of debt and equity sources of capital. **Equity financing** is raising money by selling part of the ownership of the business to investors. In equity financing, the entrepreneur shares control of the business with the investors. Equity financing does not require collateral. Sources of equity financing include private investors, venture capitalists, and public offerings in which shares of stock are sold.

Early in the growth of a business, the risk of failure may be great. At this stage, private investors and venture capitalists may be willing to provide equity financing. **Venture capitalists** specialize in making loans to entrepreneurships that have the potential for rapid growth but are in high-risk situations with few assets and would therefore not qualify for commercial bank loans.

equity financing

A means of obtaining financial resources that involves the sale of part of the ownership of the business to investors.

venture capitalists

Financial investors who specialize in making loans to entrepreneurships that have the potential for rapid growth but are in high-risk situations with few assets and would therefore not qualify for commercial bank loans.

Venture capitalists manage pools of money provided by wealthy individuals and institutions seeking to invest in entrepreneurships. High-technology businesses such as software, telecommunications, and biotechnology are particularly attractive to venture capitalists because they anticipate high financial returns from their investment. Microsoft, Compaq Computer, and Intel were started with venture capital financing and made fabulous returns for early investors. Venture capitalists also provide management knowledge, contacts to hire key employees, and financial advice.

public offerings

A means of raising capital by the sale of securities in public markets such as the New York Stock Exchange and NASDAQ.

Public offerings raise capital by selling securities in public markets such as the New York Stock Exchange and NASDAQ. A public offering can provide large infusions of cash to fuel rapid internal growth or to finance a merger or acquisition. One drawback of a public offering is that publicly traded companies must disclose a great deal of information, including quarterly reports on income, balance sheet assets, and use of funds. Competitors can exploit weaknesses that are disclosed in these reports. After a public offering, management decisions are under a higher level of public scrutiny. There is a lower tolerance for management mistakes, and there is increased shareholder pressure for dividends and predictable quarterly profits. Unhappy shareholders can sell their shares, driving down the value of the company. Public offerings generally do not take place until an entrepreneurship achieves a critical mass of about $10 million to $20 million in annual revenue.

Managing Growth

Entrepreneurs manage business growth by establishing benchmarks based on market data and a thorough analysis of the firm's ability to handle increased demand without sacrificing quality. A business plan is an invaluable tool for planning growth targets. These milestones can be used to pace company expansion. The growth of a business reflects the success of the entrepreneurial effort, but can also place stress on the entrepreneur to become an effective manager. Management Is Everyone's Business 8.2 on page 327 provides some suggestions to help you successfully make the shift to managing your business.

Too much growth can put an unbearable strain on the operations of a business. A company that grows too quickly may experience the following:

- The company spends most of its available cash on expansion and has difficulty meeting obligations to creditors. The result is a cash flow crisis.

- Employees are likely to experience stress from such rapid changes as moving to new jobs without training, adjusting to new supervisors and colleagues, and making frequent changes in office locations.

- Accounting and information systems that worked well when the firm was smaller must be replaced with more complicated and sophisticated systems. Current personnel may not be capable of operating these systems, and information may not be available when it is needed.

- Management may no longer be competent to manage a larger or more diverse portfolio of business units or product lines. The board of directors may replace the chief executive officer or other key executives with more experienced managers. To make matters worse, the founder may resist stepping down. In 1985 Steve Jobs, the founder of Apple Computer, was asked to leave by its board, which felt his leadership style was not appropriate for the large company that Apple had become. (Jobs,

Working as a Manager   As an entrepreneurial business grows, the entrepreneur must adapt and manage an increasingly complex enterprise. Here are some key ideas to help make this transition a success.

- Delegation is a good thing! Many people who start a business like to be in control and it can be difficult for them to share responsibilities and duties. However, delegation is not giving away power or responsibility. It is a way to develop others and to demonstrate your trust and provide opportunity for loyal workers. In addition, delegation can free up needed time for the entrepreneur: time for the work he or she is best at and time for family and needed leisure. An entrepreneur cannot be in all places at once. The inability to delegate can actually be detrimental to the growth of the business.

- Develop formal, consistent, and fair policies for dealing with recurring business issues. As the business grows, management can't be done on an ad hoc basis any longer. Systematic approaches need to be developed so that the entrepreneur won't have to "reinvent the wheel" each time an issue comes up. Processes, such as hiring and performance appraisal, may need to be formalized so that these functions can be done effectively and fairly.

- Consider establishing a board of advisors. As the business grows, advisory board members can provide valuable advice and guidance. The board can provide a sounding board to deal with issues that arise as the business grows.

always the entrepreneur, started another company. In 1997 he returned to Apple—by then under different leadership—with the technology he had developed in the interim and sold it to Apple for $400 million.)

Unchecked growth can threaten the survival of a business venture. For example, James L. Bildner, the founder of J. Bildner & Sons Inc., a specialty food business, expanded rapidly from a single store to a chain of 20 stores after a public offering in 1986. The company ran out of cash because it had built too many stores. Employees started leaving and operations became chaotic. Too many new stores, ineffective new products, attempts to hire too many new people at once, and lack of controls made everything worse. The company experienced large losses, inventory control problems, and the departure of loyal customers. This crisis could have been avoided if the management team had pursued less aggressive growth. Sometimes managers should turn down growth opportunities in an expanding market rather than lose control of the operation.

LOC-In

4 Learning Objective Check-In

Janet's Scallops is a new business that Janet Phillips wants to start within the coming year. She will own the business herself, keeping all the profits and assuming all the risk personally. Furthermore, Janet will obtain a short-term commercial loan and will repay the principal and interest on that loan. If the company grows as she hopes it does, Janet plans to entertain the idea of another type of financing by which she will sell part of the ownership of the business to investors.

1. *Which of the following best describes the type of legal form that Janet's business will assume?*
   a. *Proprietorship*
   b. *Corporation*
   c. *S-Corporation*
   d. *Partnership*

2. *Which of the following best characterizes the type of financing Janet plans to use in the beginning of her business?*
   a. *Equity financing*
   b. *Public offerings*
   c. *Venture capitalists*
   d. *Debt financing*

3. *Which of the following represents the type of financing option Janet will entertain if the business is successful and grows in the future?*
   a. *Debt financing*
   b. *Venture capitalists*
   c. *Equity financing*
   d. *Public offerings*

Alternative Forms of Entrepreneurship

This chapter has focused on *independent entrepreneurship*. Alternatives to this form of entrepreneurship are intrapreneurship, spin-offs, and franchising. In general, these alternative forms involve smaller risks than independent entrepreneurship.

Intrapreneurship

intrapreneurship

A form of business organization in which new business units are developed within a larger corporate structure in order to deploy the firm's resources to market a new product or service; also called corporate entrepreneurship.

The development of new business units within a larger corporate structure in order to deploy the firm's resources to market a new product or service is **intrapreneurship**, or *corporate entrepreneurship*. Some large companies develop cultures that foster innovation and the nurturing of new businesses. The 3M Company maintains a corporate goal that requires over 30 percent of corporate sales to come from products less than four years old. The technical staff is encouraged to devote 15 percent of its time to experimentation in new product designs that are peripheral to the projects they have been assigned to work on. These policies support a culture of innovation that has resulted in a steady stream of internally developed new products at the 3M Company.

When Apple showed the world that there was a large market for personal computers, IBM saw the need to design its own personal computer to challenge the Apple computer. The IBM Personal Computer was developed in a separate business unit located in Florida and isolated from the rest of the company. To build, test, and market launch the IBM PC in only 12 months, the IBM Personal Computer unit used standard electronic components and systems, rather than using all-IBM manufactured components as was typical in the company.

In the 1990s the National Broadcasting Company (NBC), the television network owned by General Electric, launched CNBC, a cable television network that provided financial news 24 hours a day. The launch coincided with the 1990s bull market that generated a large demand for televised financial news. Within a few years CNBC was profitable and successful, attracting a highly desirable audience of wealthy executives and investors.

An advantage of intrapreneurship is that the company provides funding and corporate resources that an independent entrepreneur cannot gather. The intrapreneuring corporate engineer or manager does not have to abandon a corporate career to manage the new venture. On the other hand, a successful *intrapreneur* within a corporation usually does not receive the financial rewards that might be generated by an independent entrepreneurship.

Spin-Offs

spin-off

An independent entrepreneurship that produces a product or service that originated in a large company.

Sometimes a new product developed by a corporation does not fit with the company's established products. A group of managers may decide to create a new business for this product rather than forgo the opportunity to market it. A **spin-off** is an independent entrepreneurship that produces a product or service that originated in a large company. Spin-offs are typical of technology companies, which must develop a steady stream of new products to keep up with competitors. Some of the new technologies do not fit with the company's core competencies, providing the opportunity for spin-offs.

Xerox's Palo Alto Research Center (PARC) is a laboratory located in California's Silicon Valley that develops new optical imaging products that fit with the core competencies of Xerox. Occasionally, new technologies that do not fit with other Xerox products are spawned in this research laboratory. Xerox encourages

From Outsourcing to Franchising: Capitalizing on the Entrepreneurial Spirit

Yorkshire Electricity is an electric utility company located in the U.K. As with many utility companies around the globe, Yorkshire experienced great pressure to reduce costs and increase productivity. Government shareholder pressure resulted in the top management at Yorkshire cutting staff and looking for reengineering options. Maintenance was a major cost in the utility company since 15,000 operational sites were being maintained by a department that couldn't compete with the external marketplace in terms of productivity and cost. The immediate solution appeared to be outsourcing the maintenance function. However, there were many skilled people employed by the utility that were the best in their trade. It did not seem advisable to lose that valuable resource. Instead, the management team developed a novel approach to achieving private sector productivity and costs: They set up a franchise model.

Yorkshire Electricity established an organization called Freedom Maintenance in which people still work for the utility, but as franchisees, not as employees. It took two years to gain the approval of the board of directors and the union. Freedom Maintenance started with 55 franchises in 1996 and now has approximately 500 franchises.

The franchises are responsible for their own tools, vehicles, and materials. The Freedom organization helps out by handling some administrative work, such as invoicing and collection, on behalf of the franchises. The process has created hundreds of new businesses that work independently, but with some assistance from the overall organization. The model has allowed some former Yorkshire employees to exercise their skills along with an entrepreneurial spirit. One franchiser now employs eight people and relies on his former employer for less than 50 percent of his business. The self-employment model has worked well for Yorkshire Electricity. The company has realized a 20 percent savings in maintenance costs since establishing the franchise model. The model has worked so well in the United Kingdom, Freedom is promoting the approach in the electric utility industry in the United States.

Source: B. Mottram, S. Rigby, and A. Webster, "The Freedom to Call Your Own Shots," *Transmission & Distribution World* 55 (January 2003).

the formation of spin-offs when the technology has commercial potential. In some cases, Xerox forms a partnership with the managers who start the spin-off. For example, when a security product that encrypts messages for cellular phones was developed in the PARC laboratories, Xerox created a spin-off called Semaphore Communications to manufacture and market the device.

Franchises

When a business with an established name and product is sold to additional owners along with the rights to distribute the product, a franchise operation is created. Franchising is particularly prevalent in the retail service sector of the economy, such as in the restaurant, hotel, and retail businesses. McDonald's, Taco Bell, Subway, Quality Inn, Dunkin' Donuts, Radio Shack, and Midas are well-known franchises. Franchising can also occur in unexpected situations. See Management Close-Up 8.3 above for a description of franchising in the public sector that proved effective and saved jobs from being outsourced.

In franchising, an entrepreneur assumes fewer risks because the franchise can provide: (1) a product or service with an established market and favorable image; (2) management training and assistance in operating the business; (3) economies of scale for advertising and purchasing; (4) operating and structural

Dippin' Dots franchises sell tiny beads of "flash-frozen" ice cream in many flavors and colors. In January 2005, Dippin' Dots ranked 93rd on *Entrepreneur Magazine's* Franchise 500 list. A Dippin' Dots franchise currently costs $12,500 plus other costs.

5 **Learning Objective Check-In**

1. *Walton's is a large corporation in which new business units are developed within the larger corporate structure in order to deploy Walton's resources to market new products and services. This is an example of _____.*
   a. *proprietorship*
   b. *intrapreneurship*
   c. *spin-offs*
   d. *a franchise*

controls; and (5) financial assistance. The franchising company sells the distribution rights for a limited geographic area to the entrepreneur for a fee plus a share of the revenues.

Sometimes franchising companies fail to provide promised services. The franchise company may oversell franchise rights in a geographic location, making it difficult for an entrepreneur to profit. Such conflicts of interests can result in lengthy courtroom battles.

Innovation

Innovation is a key to long-term success. Exploring and developing new technologies and new ways of doing things are vital to the future viability of an organization.[9] Entrepreneurs often pursue innovative ideas in their new business ventures. They may come up with ideas and pursue them when an organization decides that the time and cost of development are just too great.

However, as pointed out earlier, entrepreneurship is often about rather modest and incremental change to a product or service, rather than a radical change. Further, larger organizations may embrace and encourage innovation. While innovation and entreprenuership are related concepts, they are basically separate and distinct issues. Whether you have entrepreneurial aspirations or want to work in a corporate environment, you are likely to find yourself in situations that call for *innovation*.

What Is Innovation?

Fundamentally, innovation is doing something differently. As Michael Tushman, professor of management at Harvard Business School, describes it,[10] innovation can involve *radical* or *incremental* change. Radical innovations often make prior technologies obsolete. For example, digital compact discs have all but replaced cassette tapes and require a compact disc player to use them. Alternatively, incremental innovations are generally improvements of existing products that usually do *not* render prior products or technologies obsolete. Examples include smaller cell phones or even Caffeine-Free Coke. So while it may be difficult to find cassette tapes in your local record store due to the radical innovation of the CD, both Coke and Caffeine-Free Coke can easily be had at your local supermarket.

Whether a change is radical or incremental, it is not just the change that is important or that defines an innovation. Certainly, the change or invention is a critical component, but an invention, by itself, does not make for innovation. A description of innovation used by 3M, a company known for innovation, is a new idea together with action or implementation that has a bottom-line impact.[11] As illustrated in Figure 8.3 on page 331, an innovation requires both a change, such as a new product or service, and implementation that results in positive impact. In other words, an innovation is more than just a novel idea or product; an innovation has to add value and somehow result in positive gain or improvement. Without adding value, a new idea or product could be just a novel invention, but would not qualify as an innovation. To be an innovator, you must find a way to

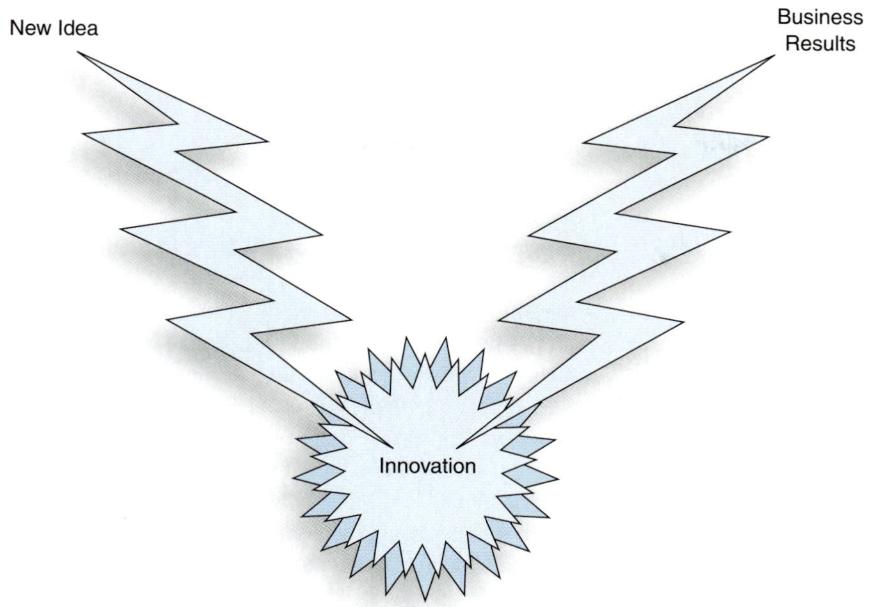

FIGURE 8.3

Innovation Requires Two Key
Ingredients

implement your idea as a cost-effective or commercially viable product or service. Consider, for example, the Segway people mover. It is, no doubt, a novel invention, but a couple of years after its creation, can it be considered an innovation? At the time of its creation, Segway supporters envisioned cities being redesigned to accommodate the machine and the use of the Segway as a replacement for the automobile for short trips.[12] Today, Segways are being used in only limited situations and, chances are, you do not see any of them in regular use. The Segway is a neat invention, but it hasn't had a socioeconomic impact—it hasn't changed people's lives or what they buy. Novelty without a tangible return is not an innovation. In contrast, going from diapers to disposable diapers may have been a mundane and simple change, as inventions go, but it has proven to be major innovation.[13]

So, having ideas without the ability to execute them isn't of much business use. Management Close-Up 8.4 on page 332 presents an invention that would seem to have great innovation potential. However, the commercial viability of the product has yet to be proven. Skills for Managing 8.2 on page 333 invites you to take a closer look at the innovation and consider its current status as a potential product.

LOC-In

6 Learning Objective Check-In

1. *William thinks he has developed a composite material that could replace glass windows in houses where tornadoes are prevalent. While the material is more expensive than glass, it is 100 times more durable, and is practically shatter-proof. As an added bonus, it is naturally UV-resistant due to one of the chemicals used in producing the product. Given what you know about William's material, what kind of innovation do you think it represents for people living in tornado areas of the country?*
   a. *Incremental*
   b. *Distributive*
   c. *Radical*
   d. *New generation*

The Importance of Innovation

Innovation is playing a more important and central role in many organizations. A recent survey of senior executives from around the world concluded that innovation has become essential to success in their industries.[14] The importance

Electronic Ink: The Next Big Thing?

THEME: DEALING WITH CHANGE E Ink is a Massachusetts Institute of Technology spin-off that, in 2002, received $25 million in fourth-round venture funding from Toppan Printing. At the end of 2005, E Ink corporation received the "Best of Small Tech" award, an honor given to companies that have made particularly noteworthy achievements. What was E Ink working on that merited that kind of investment and recognition? Electronic ink—a product that promises fundamental change in how we communicate. Electronic ink is a new way to form characters that can be presented on paper-thin screens. Monitors and handheld devices using electronic ink displays would have screens that are five times brighter and use 90 percent less energy than current displays. Perhaps the most wide-ranging application for electronic ink is a new form for books and newspapers.

Just what is electronic ink? Electronic ink is composed of millions of microcapsules, each about the diameter of a human hair. Within each microcapsule are positively charged white particles and negatively charged black particles suspended in a clear fluid. When a negative electric field is applied, the white particles move to the top of the microcapsule where they become visible to the user. At the same time, an opposite electric field pulls the black particles to the bottom of the microcapsules where they are hidden. By reversing this process, the black particles appear at the top of the capsule, which now makes the surface appear dark at that spot. E Ink laminates these microcapsules to a plastic sheet which is then sold to customers as a film product called Imaging Film.™

Because the film developed by E Ink is inherently flexible, E Ink is part of an effort by the leading electronics manufacturers to develop flexible thin-film transistors. By combining E Ink's Imaging Film with flexible TFTs, the dream of flexible electronic paper that would mimic the pages of newspapers or books can be realized.

The vision that E Ink hopes to bring to reality is the contents of books and newspapers being delivered electronically. A newspaper subscription could, for example, mean an electronic delivery of the newspaper via a radio frequency receiver attached to the electronic ink pages. The content of the paper would appear on the plastic pages until the new edition of the "paper" was delivered. Note, reading the newspaper or book would not involve scrolling down a monitor and the content would be highly portable, just as with a paper-based product. Further, the electronic paper can be reused indefinitely without cutting down any trees to make paper.

Sources: Adapted from C. T. Heun, "New 'Ink' Veers Display toward the Good Old Look," *Informationweek*, February 11, 2002, p. 18; B. Schmitt, "Growth Signs for New Ink," *ChemicalWeek* 164 (February 27, 2002), p. 46; www.eink.com, accessed December 29, 2005.

being placed on innovation may reflect a shift in the economic paradigm. In recent years the focus has been on quality and consistency of execution. However, business success may now be more tied to providing innovations that respond to customer needs. In broad terms, you might think of the current situation as shifting from quality and price as key drivers to creativity.[15] It is not that quality and price are irrelevant; it is that they are assumed. What can differentiate and underlie success in the marketplace is innovation. One of the best examples of a company that is succeeding based on creativity and innovation is Apple. The company is continually bringing new innovations to its iPod, reducing size and increasing capability to include video.

ELECTRONIC INK: FROM COOL INVENTION TO COMMERCIAL PRODUCT?

As described in Management Close-Up 8.4, electronic ink has the potential to replace paper, save trees, and disseminate information immediately. These possible outcomes, among others, as well as the potential market have probably been key to enticing venture capital to E Ink.

Discussion Questions

1. Is electronic paper a radical or incremental change? Defend your judgment.

2. Evaluate the potential market for electronic paper. Do you think it is a commercially viable innovation? Why or why not?

Internet Research Questions

1. The market for electronic paper has some competitors (such as Gyricon media applying the technology to signs and Dow Chemical working on plastic light-emitting diodes). Look for current information on these competitors and on E Ink. Do you think the market is differentiated enough that each company will have its own niche or do you think that there will be a competitive struggle for dominance in the market?

2. A key to successfully launching a new innovation is protecting the idea from possible competitors. How did E Ink protect the electronic paper technology? Do you think protecting an innovation is a necessary expense?

3. Assess the current status of E Ink. Does the company seem close to making electronic paper a commercial reality? What accomplishments/products has the company achieved to date? What recommendations, if any, would you make to E Ink?

Managing for Innovation

If innovation is a key to success, how can an organization be managed so that innovation is encouraged and maximized? Some notable organizations that have recently embraced innovation as a key strategy provide some lessons. First, if you want to maximize innovation, there must be measures of innovation. For example, top leaders at General Electric are being measured on how imaginative they are.[16] For GE, that means characteristics such as the courage to fund new ideas, leading teams to discover better ideas, and encouraging educated risk taking. Second, you need to get close to the customer. For example, Procter & Gamble sent out teams of people to observe how they cleaned bathrooms. In South Africa, women were observed using brooms to clean walls and showers. This customer observation resulted in the development of the Mr. Clean MagicReach, a new product with a four-foot detachable pole that was introduced to the marketplace in 2005. In terms of service, customer observation is also crucial to innovation. For example, The Gap Inc. has found social shopping, shopping in pairs or threesomes, is common in its stores. As a result, the company is making its dressing rooms bigger.[17]

The preceding examples and the lessons that can be drawn from them are general and probably leave you without a good sense of how to actually manage to increase innovativeness. There are no guaranteed and simple management

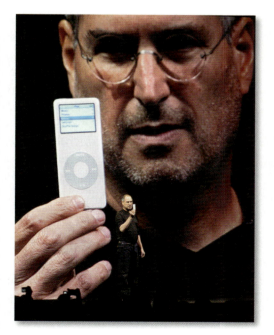

Stephen Jobs, CEO of Apple which he cofounded in 1976, is widely credited with nurturing the company's distinctive brand of creativity and innovation, blended with sleek and groundbreaking product design.

table 8.2

Management Tactics to Maximize Innovation—The Five Cs

TACTIC	FOCUS
Capability	People
Culture	Balance
Cash and recognition	Rewards
Customer orientation	Trends
Cut losses	Manage investments

techniques, but there are things that can be done to give innovation a chance to flourish.[18] We refer to these management tactics as the "Five Cs." They are summarized in Table 8.2 above.

The first management tactic listed in Table 8.2 is *capability*. Capability means having people with the skills and interests needed to generate innovative ideas. People who are smart and open and who like to try new things are more likely to create new ideas. In addition to capitalizing on these preexisting person characteristics, capability of employees can be increased by encouraging and providing opportunities for creativity. For example, the software company Intuit holds weekly free-association sessions as a means to get people to generate ideas and think about marketable changes.[19]

In addition to having the capability to generate innovation, the organizational environment should foster creativity. In most situations, organizational leaders devote most company resources to current services or products. On the other hand, giving all of the resources to the current business means that the organization may be trapped in the past. What is needed is a *culture* (the second "C") that balances routine work and innovative efforts. The appropriate *balance* depends upon the industry and on the type of managers in the organization. Whatever the balance point is, the trick is to maintain control and structure within the core process, while encouraging risk taking and experimentation outside of the everyday service or production process. Disney Corporation, for example, insists on a strict script in terms of how visitors are greeted, how rides are operated, and so on. The company also holds a monthly competitive and fun opportunity for any employee to attend and present a new idea.[20] On one side of their operation, the organization may need to limit variation. On the other side, it needs to be encouraged. It is a question of balance and making sure that people understand when each approach is appropriate. Google manages this balance with a 70/20/10 formula: 70 percent of time should be spent on the core business; 20 percent on side but related-to-the-core projects; 10 percent on unrelated new business.[21]

Establishing a culture supportive of innovation can require more than balance in terms of resources and time allocation. Innovation can sometimes be thwarted because people aren't willing to open up and risk criticism. This problem can be particularly pronounced in team settings. Management Is Everyone's Business 8.3 on page 335 offers suggestions for how team members can cultivate innovation.

The third "C" represents the tactic of *cash and recognition*. If you really want to encourage new ideas and creativity, then there should be recognition and reward for those who can deliver. Organizations can offer cash prizes for ideas

Working as a Team Teams are common in workplaces and it is therefore often the case that innovation is expected to happen at the team level. The success of a business may hinge on the innovativeness of its teams. As a team member, here are some key suggestions/questions to maximize innovativeness.

- *Know your customer.* Whom does your team serve? Are there internal customers, external customers, or maybe both?

- *What do your customers need, expect, and want?* If possible, team observation and discussions with its customers can help identify needs and possible innovations. How well does your team provide products or services to customers? If you try an innovation, can you quickly get customer feedback on the effectiveness of the change?

- *Establish team time-lines to roll out innovations.* Also establish measures and review sessions so that the effectiveness of a change can be assessed and corrections can be made.

- *Support team creativity.* Sharing ideas in a team setting can be difficult for some, particularly if criticism, or even good-natured kidding, might result. Brainstorming, a technique for generating ideas, should occur without any criticism or editorial comments from others. This rule may need to be enforced so that all possible ideas are generated and shared with the team. A way to enforce the no-comments rule is to use an object as a prop. All team members can be told that during brainstorming they must hold the "idea object" in order to speak. Only the person with the object can speak and no other comments, no criticism, analysis, negotiation, and so on can take place. Needing the object to speak can be a simple but effective technique to set aside politics, egos, and other possible stumbling blocks to the creative process.

LOC-In

that are implemented and might even offer stock or other *rewards* to recognize particularly noteworthy innovations. Given incentives, people will quickly recognize that the encouragement to "think outside the box" is more than empty rhetoric.

As already discussed, *customers* are another important resource with regard to innovation. Listening to customers can provide a wealth of beneficial information. Critical customers may be the key to identifying improvements or new *trends* in products or services.

The last "C" stands for *cutting losses.* Often individuals or teams become emotionally committed to an innovative idea they have been working on. While this personal investment can increase the effort put into the project, it can also cloud judgment about what is reasonable. A process of checkoffs by people not directly involved in the project can make for an objective decision as to whether to continue investment.

 7 Learning Objective Check-In

Gillian is a manager who wants to maximize innovation at her firm. She is trying to apply several ideas to accomplish this. For instance, she has balanced the distribution of business resources among current uses and innovation efforts. This is one way of encouraging risk taking and experimentation at the firm. On the other hand, she wants to avoid clouded judgment about what is reasonable among people who are personally invested in projects. Once individuals or teams are emotionally committed to an innovative idea they have been working on, it is difficult for them to see when they should step away from that idea. She has put in place a process that helps teams separate themselves personally from their projects and remain objective.

1. Which of the following "Cs" represents Gillian's first idea above, "balance" in the distribution of resources?
   a. Culture
   b. Customers
   c. Cash and recognition
   d. Cutting losses
2. Which of the following "Cs" represents the second idea above, keeping objectivity about a project?
   a. Customers
   b. Cash and recognition
   c. Capability
   d. Cutting losses

CONCLUDING THOUGHTS

After the story about the successful cold medicine invented by a nonexpert that opened the chapter, we posed some critical thinking questions about entrepreneurial ventures and new business ideas. Now that we have explored the topics of entrepreneurship and innovation, it's time to revisit those introductory questions. First, while some personal characteristics, such as an internal locus of control, are important, anyone with the motivation can become an entrepreneur. Victoria Knight-McDowell was motivated at first by little more than the desire to be free of cold germs! Entrepreneurs need a deep well of motivation, in addition to abilities and personal characteristics relevant to the business they would like to pursue. The source of motivation is often an internal commitment to an idea or process. The practical reality is that motivation often comes from necessity and external obstacles. For example, many people have become entrepreneurs because they were laid off or were frustrated as members of a large organization.

Second, the risk involved in entrepreneurial effort isn't as great as is typically think. The initial financial investment an entrepreneur makes might be relatively modest. It is later, when the business has grown, that the entrepreneur may have more dollars at risk. Nonetheless, in terms of psychological risk, the entrepreneur may be putting in an incredible investment at the start of a new venture.

Finally, the basis for a new business idea doesn't have to be radical change. On the contrary, entrepreneurs often capitalize on modest incremental changes to a product or service. Whether an incremental change or a radical innovation, the ideas often come from the particular skills and experiences of the entrepreneur. What may be more important than the particular idea is how it is implemented. The lack of a viable business plan can be the ruin of even a great idea.

Focusing on the Future: Using Management Theory in Daily Life

Entrepreneurship and Innovation

Dave Moore is the pastor of the New Summit Presbyterian Church—not someone most people would think of as an entrepreneur. And yet, in bringing a new church from zero members to over 300, in an environment where two-thirds of all new churches fail, he has had to use each of the five management tactics (Five "Cs") to maximize innovation described in this chapter.

Capability   When Dave arrived in Lee's Summit, Missouri, he found 10 people who were interested in being part of a new church. A few of these people had been asked to be part of the new church by the Presbytery—they were "doing their duty to the denomination." Others wanted to start a new church in the area where they lived. Regardless of their initial reasons for joining, Dave recognized that he needed to build on the capabilities of each of these 10 people if the endeavor was to succeed. As he puts it, "I wanted to honor the gifts and passions of everyone involved—the first members, our emerging church leaders, and everyone else who would become part of our organization."

Based on a demographic study of the area, Dave determined that people who were likely to consider joining a new church would look at three key areas: (1) overall environment, including the structure of services and teaching; (2) music; and (3) child care. With these in mind, he asked people to consider where they could best contribute. Responses came in quickly. One member offered to do all the publicity for the new church, another to handle the technology needed in the church office and during services, another to run the day care center, and another to set up seating for services. In addition to these somewhat obvious tasks, Dave found that his other members could contribute expertise on financing and real estate development, accounting and budgetary controls, marketing, planning and the other business functions related to running any organization. One critical area remained understaffed—music. To handle this issue, Dave and the members of the church decided to hire a part-time Music Director.

As New Summit grew, new needs for people with specialized capabilities emerged. Over time, Dave and the other members of the church created a new full-time position for a church secretary. They also identified four primary "quadrants" for church activities: gather (evangelism), inspire (worship), equip (training), and send (mission work). These quadrants (and their associated teams) were developed as a direct result of Dave's reading and study of Margaret Wheatley's book *Leadership and the New Science*—a theoretical work which proposes that the "core identity" of any person or organization is more important than having policies or procedures. Each of these activities now has a leadership position associated with it. The vision for the future is that as the church grows, these leadership positions will be staffed with full-time people. Finally, 10 elders of the church serve as a "board of directors" and handle major financial and managerial decisions.

Culture

Balancing innovation and tradition is not an easy job in any church, and it can be especially difficult when the church is a new venture. At first, the church services were held in a rented school auditorium. As the congregation grew, they were able to acquire a large piece of land on which to build their sanctuary. But what kind of building should go up? Tradition called for a steepled structure where people would congregate on Sundays for an hour or two. But since caring for one another and the community were integral parts of the New Summit vision and mission statements, after much deliberation, a different kind of structure was raised—a large, open space that could accommodate child care and after school activities as easily as traditional worship.

This issue was recently faced again, as the church members and elders started the process of putting up a second building. Cognizant of the fact that new buildings cost $100 to $150 a square foot in their area, the group again had to weigh the traditional with the innovative. They found that while stained glass and an organ "spoke to" people in earlier times, today's congregants speak a different language—one that is more digital and visual. Money that might have been spent on pews is now being spent on projection systems, and rather than stained glass, people respond to images of classic paintings projected on blank walls. The interesting thing about this new technology is that it allows for a marriage of tradition and innovation. For example, in one recent service, classic paintings of the crucifixion were blended with images from a current movie—Mel Gibson's "The Passion."

Dave says that he is constantly seeking ways to "talk to people in their own language." But he also realizes that this new language may not appeal to everyone. His research shows that his church is more likely to appeal to people who do not normally go to any church. It is harder to get past the expectations and past experiences of people who are "traditionally churched" because they have a different image of what church "should be." Dave challenges congregants who want a more traditional service to take responsibility for putting it together, but he also reaches out to them by trying to include at least one more traditional hymn in each service, and by retaining key elements of the service that can act as a touchstone for traditionalists.

Cash and Recognition

Dave and the other leaders of New Summit have a large number of volunteer workers to motivate, and they need to be creative with rewards for those workers. While the tasks themselves can be rewarding, and there is always the promise of an eternal reward, it can be a challenge to sustain day-to-day motivational levels. Recently, Dave instituted a new program called "Kingdom Assignments." This program, created by Pastor Dennis Bellesi at the Coast Hills Community Church in Aliso Viejo, California, challenges congregants by providing them with $100 to "further the Kingdom of God" in any way they see fit. As Dave points out, the purpose of the exercise is to let people know that "the ministry that you are going to participate in has yet to be discovered, and you have a significant part in discovering it." The program is motivating both because of the recognition people receive in the church for their projects, and also because it gives people the opportunity to have complete control over a project of their own choosing. This is a key component of intrinsic motivation.

Customer Orientation

Lee's Summit is a "bedroom community" of 80,000 people. Some demographers classify it as a "hopes and dreams" community. People in Lee's Summit want a meaningful career, a meaningful marriage, good relationships with friends, financial security, and a good education for their children. It is a safe community where people rarely worry about crime and drugs. But it is also a community in which people do not go to church on a regular basis. Dave asked his staff at New Summit to survey every church in the area and find out how many people the sanctuary could hold when filled to capacity. They estimated that if every sanctuary was filled to capacity twice every Sunday, there would still be 50 percent of the people in Lee's Summit who would not have a place to sit.

The survey indicated a need for a new church, but Dave had to take his customers' needs into account to attract them to that church. As he puts it, "We wanted to attract people to our services, so we said, 'Come as you are. We'll accept you, we'll speak your language, we'll take care of your kids, we'll have topics that are relevant to you, and we'll provide a place to enrich all of the relationships in your life.'" He soon found that it wasn't just Sunday morning services that attracted people, but activities they could enjoy, both as adults and as a family. Soon the new church was buzzing with everything from small group meetings to building Habitat for Humanity houses— anything and everything that might attract people and draw them away from Sunday morning soccer games and other competitors for their time and efforts.

Cut Losses   When is it time to pull the plug on an innovative idea? While Dave learns as much from ideas that work as those that don't work, he watches carefully to be sure that he is not committing too many resources to a failed innovation. For example, New Summit hired a youth director at one point. It made sense at the time, because of the number of growing families, and it was a popular decision with the congregation, but it was also fraught with problems. Nationally, most youth directors are underpaid and do not stay in their jobs for more than two years. Despite Dave's best efforts to anticipate and deal with these problems, the new youth director simply didn't work out, and left after one year of service. Dave used the opportunity to reevaluate the position and decided that it would be better to put the church's resources into a full time "equipping minister" whose focus would be on training people of all ages to help them to discover their gifts.

summary of learning objectives

Entrepreneurship and innovation are critical to the continued competitiveness and economic vitality of any developed economy that hopes to remain a player in today's global marketplace. Entrepreneurship refers to the process of creating an enterprise capable of entering new or established markets. Innovation refers to the translation of knowledge into products or services that add value. Both the opportunities created through entrepreneurship and the new value and bottom-line impact of effective innovation are needed for long-term economic prosperity. This chapter's discussion should help you to promote entrepreneurship and innovation as a manager, team member, and individual employee. The chapter's learning objectives and the related chapter discussion points are summarized below.

1 Explain the economic importance of entrepreneurship.

- Entrepreneurship is responsible for much of the job creation in the U.S.
- Innovation and entrepreneurship go hand in hand bringing new products to market.
- Entrepreneurship brings opportunities to minorities and women.

2 Identify the key characteristics and skills of entrepreneurs.

- Entrepreneur's have an **internal locus of control**—a belief in one's own ability to succeed.
- Negotiation skills, networking sills, and leadership skills are critical to successful entrepreneurs.

3 Recognize the basic ingredients needed to effectively start and manage an entrepreneurial venture.

- New business ideas can come from a variety of sources.
- The business plan maps out the business strategy.
- Selecting the right form of business is crucial—**proprietorship, partnership, corporation**.
- Obtaining financing is often **debt financing** or equity financing.
- Growth must be managed.

4 Differentiate among the legal forms of organizing an entrepreneurial venture.

- Proprietorship—owned by one person.
- Partnership—association of two or more persons acting as co-owners.
- Corporation—a legal entity separate from individual owners.

5 Identify alternative forms of entrepreneurship.

- Intrapreneurship—new business units developed within a larger corporate structure.
- Spin-offs—independent entrepreneurship that originated in a large company.
- Franchises—an established business that sells distribution rights to additional owners.

6 Describe innovation and demonstrate why it is important for business success.

- Innovation
  - New Idea
  - Business Results
- Key to success in creativity-driven market

7 Apply the "Five C" management tactics to maximize innovation.
- Capability
- Culture
- Cash and recognition
- Customer orientation
- Cut losses

discussion questions

1. How does an entrepreneurial business differ from a small business? What are the similarities?

2. What are the differences between an entrepreneur and a manager?

3. What is the significance of entrepreneurship to the U.S. economy?

4. Identify the important personal characteristics of entrepreneurs. Do you think only people with these characteristics should become entrepreneurs? What problems does this approach present? What alternatives could be used to encourage people to choose an entrepreneurial path?

5. Compare and contrast debt financing and equity financing as ways of starting a new business. Does one have an overall advantage over the other? What situation is more favorable to the use of debt financing? Which situation favors equity financing?

6. Why is growth important to an entrepreneurial business? How can rapid growth be detrimental to its survival?

7. Can an individual be an entrepreneur yet work within a large corporation? Explain your answer.

8. What are the advantages of starting a franchise business (such as a McDonald's) instead of an independent entrepreneurial business? What are the disadvantages?

9. What is the purpose of a business plan for an entrepreneurial effort? Some successful businesses are started without any business plan and operate according to the gut instincts of the entrepreneur. What do you think accounts for the success of businesses that are run "by the seat of the pants" without any formal planning?

10. Describe what is meant by the statement that an invention is not necessarily an innovation. Can you provide any examples of inventions that may not be innovations?

11. Describe how you would go about setting up conditions to maximize innovativeness. Put yourself in the place of a manager and use the "Five Cs." How would you assure quality while at the same time encouraging the chaos of experimentation and creativity?

Innovation: Core Competitive Advantage or Fair Game for Outsourcing?

Innovation has been a key to U.S. productivity and, therefore, a key to our economic strength. Further, there seems to be a belief that innovation is our forte and future. Operational details, such as executing a new design with low cost and high quality, might be left to India and China, but we will have the competitive edge in generating the innovations. This somewhat romantic belief also means that the United States will remain the home of the prestigious and high-paid professionals who create and design innovative enhancements to products and services. Unfortunately, this belief is increasingly at odds with reality.

While other countries, such as India and China, have significant cost advantages over the United States, that doesn't mean that these markets are static. U.S. companies cannot count on these countries to cheaply produce the innovative products we design. Quite to the contrary, India and China are also ramping up their ability to compete on innovation. For example, employees at a variety of Indian organizations receive training on topics such as creative thinking, customer service, managing change and innovation, and prototyping new solutions. These training topics clearly indicate that the organizational systems in other countries are not simply waiting for the next innovative development from the United States so that it can be cheaply produced. Global competition is coming, not just on price and quality, but on innovation.

Despite the competitive threats to the American capability to innovate, some organizations seem to be giving away their claim on this competence. Companies are outsourcing not just their manufacturing capabilities, but their innovation capabilities. For example, Boeing is working with India's HCL Technologies to jointly develop software for one of its upcoming jets. Procter and Gamble has an objective of increasing new product ideas generated outside of the company from the current level of 20 percent to 50 percent by 2010. Other companies are taking a more measured approach to outsourcing innovation. For example, Motorola might outsource the entire design process for its cheapest phones, but may keep in-house the development of its high-end phones.

Discussion Questions

1. Do you think innovation can be a source of competitive advantage for organizations? Why or why not?

2. If innovation can be important to organizational success, how can U.S. companies maintain a competitive edge over foreign competition?

3. Why would firms outsource innovation? What advantages could they gain? What costs or risks might they experience? (Hint: Motorola outsourced the design and manufacture of a mobile phone to a Taiwanese company. The Taiwanese company then sold the phone in the huge China market under its own brand name.)

4. Some managers contend that a line must be drawn that separates "commodity" work (that can be outsourced) from core or "mission-critical" work (that should not be outsourced). How can this line be drawn and enforced? (Hint: Motorola has a policy that limits the outsourcing of innovation. Many other approaches may be possible.)

5. Consider the following statements:

   a. Outsourcing innovation means giving away your competitive advantage.

   b. Outsourcing innovation allows you to maximize performance by capturing the creative skills of workers around the world.

   Which statement do you agree with? Explain.

6. Using the two statements in Question 5, divide into opposing teams and argue the two positions. Summarize the discussion and any resolution with the rest of the class.

Sources: Adapted from W. R. Brody, "What Happened to American Innovation?" *Chief Executive, 214* (2005), pp. 22–24; P. Engardio, B. Einhorn, M. Kripalini, A. Reinhardt, B. Nussbaum, and P. Burrows, Outsourcing Innovation, *BusinessWeek Online*, March 21 2005; R. L. Martin, "India and China: Not Just Cheap," *Business WeekOnline*, December 13, 2005.

management minicase 8.2

Nice Threads: High Tech Gets into the Fabric of Things

Fabric is gaining more capability than you may be aware of. Some of the changes include the inclusion of silver in fabrics that gives the fabric antibacterial properties. For example, Noble Biomaterials makes x-static, a silver laden fabric, that it has put into various pieces of clothing for its antibacterial properties. However, it found that an attractive feature for customers is that the material doesn't get smelly, no matter how long it is worn. In 2004 every U.S. soldier was wearing x-static socks, T-shirts, and gloves. The company will achieve approximately $50 million in sales in 2005. There are also companies that are adding microcapsules containing skin conditioners or scents that are bonded to the fibers of clothing.

While the inclusion of silver and microcapsules may be interesting developments in the fabric world, the real eye-popping changes that may be on the horizon are in an area often referred to as e-textiles. E-textiles are traditional fabrics integrated with electronics. The combination of electronics and textiles is taking a variety of forms, from garments that simply hold electronic devices to electronic devices that can be temporarily attached to special fabrics. Some of this work is at the laboratory stage, but some smart fabrics are already hitting the market. For example, Elek-Tex, an e-textile, conducts electricity when compressed. The material is being used to incorporate iPod controls into ski jackets. Textronics makes an elastic material that conducts electricity and could be used for heating or to monitor vital signs, among other possibilities. The company has just developed a sports bra that monitors heart rate and displays the information in a wrist-worn receiver. In France, a cinema has experimented with a pressure-sensitive textile on seats as a means for tracking occupancy levels. Yet another e-textile, Luminex, incorporates fiber-optic strands and has been used to make safety garments that glow.

The e-textiles or smart fabrics are taking a variety of forms and not all may prove commercially viable. Approximately 200 companies are estimated to be involved in developing e-textile products. So far, only a few companies are making a profit in this new field.

Discussion Questions

1. Lower-tech fabrics, such as x-static and the inclusion of microcapsules, are much closer to commercial reality than are e-textiles. As an entrepreneur, would you prefer to try to bring a lower-tech fabric or an e-textile to market? Why?

2. Given the discussion of innovation in this chapter, do you consider e-textiles to be inventions or innovations?

3. To the extent that e-textiles are currently more in the category of invention, what would it take to move them into the category of innovation?

4. Smart fabrics, or e-textiles, seem technologically feasible. However, e-textiles will not be commercially successful unless they serve a customer need. Can you identify customer needs that might be met with e-textiles?

Sources: V.S. Borland, "New directions for Apparel and Home Fabrics," *Textile World, 155* (2005), 53–55; F. Byrt, "Clothes Get Wired at Digital-Edge Design Shops: Textronics Foresees T-Shirts That Monitor Heart Rates, but Market Not Yet Certain," *The Wall Street Journal*, November 17, 2005, p. B4; D. I. Lehn, C. W. Neely, K. Schoonover, T. L. Martin, M. T. Jones, "E-TAGs: e-Textile Attached Gadgets," paper presented at the Communication Networks and Distributed Systems Modeling and Simulation Conference, January 2004; S. Schubert, "The Ultimate Silver Lining: How Bill McNally turned His Idea for an Antibacterial Fabric into $50 Million Sensation," *Business 20, 6,* (2005), 78; *The Economist*, "Threads That Think," December 10, 2005.

Running a Sole Proprietorship

The most common form of business ownership in the United States is the sole proprietorship. One such business was L. A. Nicola, a Los Angeles restaurant owned by Larry Nicola. Located away from diners' row, the restaurant attracted clientele for one major reason: great food. As with his later restaurants, Nicola made the menu choices and, in his role as chef, saw that the food was cooked to perfection. He kept on top of new industry trends and knew how to change the menu to reflect the emerging tastes of customers. For example, before health foods became a fad, L. A. Nicola had cut down on sauces and fatty foods and was offering leaner cuisine.

Nicola gets out into his restaurants and works the crowd. He ensures that everything is running smoothly, greets old customers, and welcomes new ones. From his L. A. Nicola venture he went on to open other California restaurants.

What does Nicola like best about being a sole proprietor? He says it is the freedom of choice to do things his own way. If he sees something going wrong, he can correct it. If a customer is not getting proper service, Nicola will intervene and help the waiter out or assign a second waiter to the area. If a customer's food has not been cooked to his or her taste, Nicola can send it back to the kitchen and personally supervise the preparation.

Nicola is not alone in his desire for freedom in running things his own way. In recent years more and more sole proprietorships have been formed by individuals who used to work for other companies and have now broken away and started their own businesses. In the restaurant industry, chefs with an entrepreneurial spirit often first learn the business through experience and then open their own restaurants. Since chefs are usually the people who know the most about restaurants, they have a distinct advantage in starting a new business—the operation cannot succeed without them.

Critical Thinking Questions

1. Why is the sole proprietorship business form so popular with people who want to start a business?
2. What type of liability do sole proprietors have if their business suffers a large loss?
3. If Nicola decided to raise $1 million and expand his restaurant, could he do this as a sole proprietor or would he have to form a partnership or corporation? Explain.

Collaborative Learning Exercise

One of the drawbacks of a proprietorship is that the responsibilities of operating the business are the proprietor's alone. It is difficult to take vacations, and sole proprietors tend to be workaholics who average 61 hours of work per week. Stress, burnout, and neglected families are occupational hazards. Further, there is no one in the business to provide guidance, since the business is owned and operated by one person. The business owner may make a serious blunder in the business strategy and may not become aware of it before it is too late to recover. Meet in a small group to develop tactics that would be useful to entrepreneurs for dealing with these challenges for sole proprietors.

Sources: Adapted from D. F. Kuratko and R. M. Hodgetts, *Entrepreneurship*, 2nd ed., Fort Worth: Dryden Press, 1992, pp. 220–221; R. R. Roha, "Home Alone," *Kiplinger's Personal Finance Magazine*, May 1997, pp. 85–89.

internet exercise 8.1

Freedom!

Management Close-Up 8.3 focused on the Freedom Maintenance franchise model set up in the U.K. Freedom Franchising Services has a Web site that further describes the franchising model. Explore the Freedom Franchising Web site and any related Web sites regarding this franchise.

1. What services are offered by the Freedom franchises?
2. What is needed to be a Freedom franchise? What skills or other characteristics would a franchise owner need to have in order to be successful?
3. What is the current status of the Freedom Franchise organization?
4. Would you recommend the franchise concept to U.S. electric companies? Why or why not?
5. Could the concept be successfully implemented in other industries?
6. Can you find any information on Freedom applying its franchise model in the United States?

manager's checkup 8.1

Customer-Based Innovation

A starting point for generating useful innovations, especially in regard to customer service, is to reflect on our own experiences as a customer. Try answering the following questions regarding your own experience as a customer.

1. How did I feel about the service experience (special, appreciated, annoyed, frustrated, ignored, etc.)?
2. What happened, or didn't happen, that led me to feel this way?
3. What did I learn from that service experience about what affects how a customer feels?
4. Can I apply what I learned, or some portion of it to my organizations's service?

As a manager:

5. To what extent do you encourage your workers to ask themselves the same questions?
6. Are your workers empowered to try to make innovative and positive changes to how customer are served?

Source: Adapted from D. Riddle, "Training Staff to Innovate," *International Trade Forum*, 2, (2000), pp. 28–30. Published by the International Trade Center.

video summary

Powering a Creative Economy

Summary

When you think of creativity, Corporate America is probably not the first thing that comes to mind, but that's changing, and it's changing fast. With millions of manufacturing jobs being outsourced, and millions of knowledge-based jobs following steadily behind them, America is turning to creativity and innovation for its new competitive edge. Companies like Procter & Gamble and General Electric are trying to model themselves more after successful innovators like Apple, which struck it rich recently with the iPod "experience," including iTunes and an array of devices that make music and video entertainment portable and interactive. The thrust of this "movement" is to generate big ideas that will give firms big margins and generate big profits. This will likely be a difficult road for these companies, because the people who work in these firms are largely engineers or process-oriented people who are used to small, incremental changes. They are now being told to take risks and think creatively, in the face of a 96 percent failure rate for all innovation attempts. However, there are ways to improve the odds of successful innovations, including cultivating the culture for innovation within a company. Consumer-centric innovation is another method by which companies can spur innovation.

Discussion Questions

1. The case presents the argument that the U.S. economy will sustain itself on innovations developed in companies like Apple, GE, and P&G. Do you think firms like P&G can change their culture to emphasize innovation, rather than just accommodate it? Why will this be difficult?

2. Is innovation "safe" from outsourcing? Can the task of innovation be outsourced to other countries, like manufacturing and knowledge-based jobs have been?

3. There is currently a 96 percent failure rate among new innovation attempts. What can managers do to maximize innovation efficiency within their firms?

part four

Organization Management

A successful organization doesn't just happen! Resources need to be arranged and the right people brought together in order for an organization to function effectively and efficiently. Organizing people in an ineffective way or treating them inappropriately can undermine even the greatest hopes and efforts for effective performance. The manager has responsibility for setting the stage by arranging a structure for the organization and by setting policies and practices that bring together the best skills and efforts of people.

In Part Four we will examine various choices for how an organization might be structured. We will also look at policies and practices for managing people as a means of bringing together and maintaining an effective workforce. People bring with them a variety of skills and experiences and there are many ways in which contributions to the organization can be made. The effective manager can orchestrate the variety of talents in ways that contribute to organizational success. Finally, in this part we will also examine managing diversity in the workplace.

4

chapter 9

Managing the Structure and Design of Organizations

Learning Objectives

1. Identify the vertical and horizontal dimensions of organization structure.

2. Apply the three basic approaches—functional, divisional, and matrix—to departmentalization.

3. Develop coordination across departments and hierarchical levels.

4. Use organization structure and the three basic organization designs—mechanistic, organic, and boundaryless—to achieve strategic goals.

5. Develop an awareness of strategic events that are likely to trigger a change in the structure and design of an organization.

Daimler Shifts Gears

The new CEO of DaimlerChrysler, Dieter Zetsche, stepped into an ailing, strife-ridden company. In-fighting among managers and neglect of the flagship Mercedes division, along with a long list of costly global acquisitions that failed to live up to their promise, had led to nagging problems with quality, declining sales, and dramatic financial losses for the venerable $173 billion firm. Costs were rising, and rivals BMW and Audi passed Mercedes in European sales. Finally the company posted an operating loss of over $600 million in 2005.

So Zetsche, an engineer who had been the head of product development for Mercedes and chief of the Chrysler division, acted almost immediately upon assuming the CEO's role in 2006 to realign the company and start turning things around. He cut 6,000 jobs at the company's Stuttgart (Germany) headquarters, or 20 percent of its administrative and management workforce, and in a dramatic ploy he moved senior executives from their luxurious corporate offices to an old engine factory on the other side of town, a location he calls "the cradle of the Daimler organization."

A consultant close to the company agrees that the move is more than symbolic and will force executives and engineers to work closely together again: "Zetsche is going back to where the real stuff is happening—in the car factory." "It's a very strong signal," says one Daimler manager. "It goes far beyond cost cutting."

Not that the new CEO is overlooking cost cutting, however. To put the company back in the black as fast as possible, Zetsche plans to trim $1 billion a year from the German automaker's costs, and job cuts may total 30,000 around the world over the next several years in areas like finance, human resources, and strategic planning. "Our earnings are not where we want them to be," he says. "We need to get to work."

Zetsche is also determined to make Mercedes the core of the business, and a symbol of top quality, again. To achieve that he has begun a massive restructuring designed to streamline group operations, speed problem solving, and eliminate redundant functions. The goal is to make both Mercedes and Chrysler faster, more responsive, and more focused on their basic business processes of development, production, and sales. From now on, one executive will run the administrative functions of finance, human resources, communications, and strategy across all divisions. Mercedes' research and technology unit has been folded into the development unit to reduce the time it takes to bring new technologies to market, to share technology more effectively between Mercedes and Chrysler, and to give Mercedes customers the innovations they want. Change isn't confined to the auto side. Zetsche is splitting the commercial vehicle division in two, with vans and buses in one new division and trucks in another.

The new CEO has even cut the company's management board from 12 to 9 members, and he and other top managers are taking on extra workloads. Say one analyst, "Zetsche is flattening anything that smacks of corporate overlayers. Mercedes and Chrysler will now share not just technology and a small slice of production, but also the electronic architecture for the vehicles and such administrative tasks as purchasing."

Zetsche turned the Chrysler Group around in 2001, staving off bankruptcy. Now that he heads the company and oversees its flagship division, can his restructuring do it again?

Sources: Gail Edmondson, "On the Hot Seat at Daimler," *BusinessWeek Online*, www.businessweek.com, February 17, 2006; Carter Dougherty, "Cost-Cutting at Daimler to Eliminate 6,000 Jobs," *New York Times*, www.nytimes.com, January 25, 2006; Gail Edmondson, "Daimler Shakeup: Realignment in the Auto Industry," *BusinessWeek Online*, www.businessweek.com, January 25, 2006.

CRITICAL THINKING QUESTIONS

1. *How do the structural changes being made at Daimler respond to the company's new goals?*

2. *Why was the former structure no longer useful for reaching strategic goals?*

---

organizing

The management function that determines how the firm's resources are arranged and coordinated; the deployment of resources to achieve strategic goals.

organization structure

The formal system of relationships that determines lines of authority and the tasks assigned to individuals and units.

vertical dimension

The element of who has the authority to make decisions and who supervises which subordinates.

At the end of the chapter in our Concluding Thoughts, we will revisit the critical thinking questions regarding the decision to change DaimlerChrysler's structure.

Many strategies and key business decisions have profound effects on the structures and designs of various organizations. A change in strategic direction due to a merger or acquisition or a change in competitive strategy requires the management team to rethink how to deploy company resources. **Organizing** is the deployment of resources to achieve strategic goals, and is reflected in: (1) the organization's division of labor that forms jobs and departments, (2) formal lines of authority, and (3) the mechanisms used for coordinating diverse jobs and roles in the organization.

Organizing follows the formulation of strategy. While strategy indicates *what* needs to be done, organizing shows *how* to do it. This chapter begins by examining the vertical and horizontal dimensions of organization structure. It then examines ways to coordinate organizational units so that they move in the same direction toward meeting organization goals. Finally, it identifies different approaches to organization design.

Skills for Managing 9.1 on page 351 lists the key skills for managing organizing.

The Vertical Dimension of Organization Structure

Organization structure is a formal system of relationships that determines lines of authority (who reports to whom) and the tasks assigned to individuals and units (who does what task and with which department). The **vertical dimension** of organization structure indicates who has the authority to make decisions and

ORGANIZATION STRUCTURE AND DESIGN

- *Understanding the chain of command.* Some organizations are structured in a hierarchical fashion. In these organizations, employees are expected to respect and follow the chain of command, that is, the directives of top managers. Other organizations are less hierarchical and permit individuals in the lower ranks to initiate and implement ideas without the approval of their bosses.

- *Understanding the dimensions of organization structure.* Some of the factors that affect the design of an organization include size (large or small), emphasis on teams or individuals, degree of change in the work environment, and broad versus narrow spans of supervisory control. By understanding the key dimensions of organization structure, you can get an idea of what it would be like to work in an organization so that you can choose a work environment in which you can make your most valuable contributions.

---

who is expected to supervise which subordinates. **The horizontal dimension** is the basis for dividing work into specific jobs and tasks and assigning those jobs into units such as departments or teams.

horizontal dimension

The element of dividing work into specific jobs and tasks and assigning jobs into units.

Unity of Command

The concept of **unity of command** is based on one of Fayol's 14 principles of management (see Chapter 1): a subordinate should have only one direct supervisor. Multiple bosses may give a subordinate conflicting instructions or goals. In unity of command, a decision can be traced back from the subordinates of the manager who made it.

unity of command

The management concept that a subordinate should have only one direct supervisor.

Exceptions to the unity of command principle are sometimes necessary. For example, computer programmers in software firms are often assigned to different projects as the need arises. They are supervised by a project manager who coordinates the people and resources on the project and by a functional manager, the manager of information technology (IT), who supervises the IT department. This violation of the unity of command principle makes it critical for both managers to coordinate goals and priorities to avoid causing confusion.

Authority, Responsibility, and Accountability

Managers, teams, and employees have varying amounts of authority, responsibility, and accountability based on where they are in the vertical structure of the organization. **Authority** is the formal right of a manager to make decisions, give orders, and expect those orders to be carried out. A manager is an agent of the owners of the business. The role of the manager encompasses decision-making authority to manage the workforce, resources, and assets of the business in the owners' best interests. Authority is given to the position of the manager, not the person. It originates at the top of the organization based on the property rights of

authority

The formal right of a manager to make decisions, give orders, and expect the orders to be carried out.

the owners and flows down the vertical organizational hierarchy from top executives to middle managers to supervisors and operative employees. Consequently, positions at the top of the hierarchy have more authority than positions at lower levels.

responsibility

The manager's duty to perform assigned tasks.

Responsibility is the duty to perform assigned tasks. All employees are expected to accept these responsibilities as a condition of employment. Ideally, a manager's responsibilities are matched with the appropriate amount of authority so that the manager is in "control" of the task. The manager may *delegate*, or transfer responsibility to a subordinate or team, but the manager is still in control because the subordinate or team is subject to his or her authority. Managers delegate decision-making authority for some tasks in order to give themselves more time to focus on the most important tasks and decisions. Chapter 6, on decision making, listed the steps that lead to effective delegation skills. Management Is Everyone's Business 9.1 above offers some advice on how you can manage your work responsibilities more effectively given a limited amount of time to do them.

New York City Mayor Michael R. Bloomberg promised voters an overhaul of the city's troubled public school system, but his subsequent dismantling of the system's central bureaucracy was controversial. The principals' union opposed the mayor's plan on the grounds that it stripped principals of their authority. "In any organization," responded the mayor, "the line managers are the ones that really make things work. In schools, we call a line manager a principal."

Sometimes managers are given responsibility without equal levels of authority. This situation is common in organizations in which managers must work with managers of other units or with customers outside of the organization. For example, the vice president of global learning solutions at Lucent Technologies, a manufacturer of telecommunications equipment, is responsible for disseminating employee development courses to various business units throughout the large corporation. This executive does not have the authority to control whether or how business-unit managers use the training services with their own employees. Instead, the executive must "market" the training courses to various business units in order to effectively fulfill the responsibility of the position.

A manager may delegate responsibilities to subordinates, but he or she remains accountable for the actions of subordinates. Managers hold the ultimate responsibility for tasks they delegate. **Accountability** means that a manager or other employee with authority and responsibility must be able to justify results to a manager at a higher level in the organizational hierarchy. One way managers are held accountable for the performance of their units is in periodic performance appraisals. For example, a **management by objectives (MBO)** program can be used to compare planned goals with achieved results. Employees receive rewards based on meeting or exceeding expected results.

There are two distinct types of authority: line and staff authority. **Line authority** entitles a manager to directly control the work of subordinates by hiring, discharging, evaluating, and rewarding them. It is based on superior–subordinate authority relationships that start at the top of the organization hierarchy and extend to the lowest level. This provides what is called the **chain of command. Line managers** hold positions that contribute directly to the strategic goals of the organization. For example, the line managers of a manufacturing firm include production managers and sales managers who contribute directly to the bottom line.

accountability

The expectation that the manager must be able to justify results to a manager at a higher level.

management by objectives (MBO)

A goal-setting program for managers and subordinates.

line authority

The manager's control of subordinates by hiring, discharging, evaluating, and rewarding.

chain of command

The superior–subordinate authority relationship.

line managers

The management level that contributes directly to the strategic goals of the organization.

FIGURE 9.1

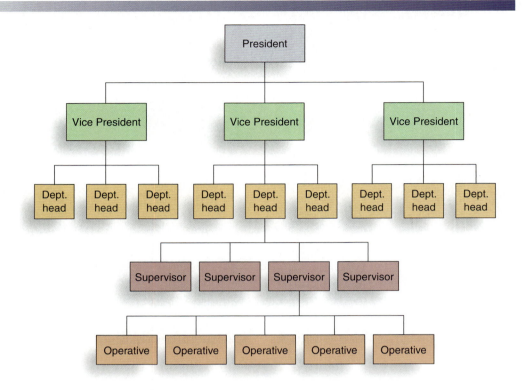

staff authority

Management function of advising, recommending, and counseling line managers.

staff managers

The level of management that directs line managers.

organization chart

A graphic depiction that summarizes the lines of authority in an organization.

span of control

The feature of the vertical structure of an organization that outlines the number of subordinates who report to a manager, the number of managers, and the layers of management within the organization.

Staff authority includes giving advice, making recommendations, and offering counsel to line managers and other members of the organization. Staff authority is based on expertise and is not directly related to achieving the strategic goals of the organization. **Staff managers** help line managers achieve bottom-line results, but they contribute only indirectly to outcomes. For example, the accounting, legal, and human resource management staffs of a manufacturing firm provide specialized advice on cost control, federal regulations, and staffing requirements to line managers.

The key to knowing whether a position has line or staff status is the organization's strategic objectives. In an accounting firm, the accountants have line authority since their work directly contributes to the bottom line, whereas accountants in a manufacturing firm are used in an advisory capacity and thus are classified as having staff authority.

An **organization chart** summarizes the lines of authority in an organization. In the organization chart seen in Figure 9.1 above, authority flows in a vertical downward direction starting with the president, who has authority over the vice president, who in turn supervises several department heads. The department heads manage the supervisors, who have authority over the operatives. Each box represents a position in the organization occupied by one person. Each horizontal level of boxes represents a level of authority in the organization. Management Is Everyone's Business 9.2 on page 355 shows you how you can influence your boss despite the fact that authority flows in a vertical downward direction in an organization's formal structure.

Span of Control

A critical feature of the vertical structure of an organization is the number of subordinates who report to a manager. This is called the **span of control**, and it determines the number of managers and number of levels of management in an

Working as an Individual   While formal power and influence in an organization are often structured to flow in a top-down direction, this does not mean that you cannot influence your boss by managing your relationship with him or her. For example, you can

- Make yourself indispensable by anticipating your boss's need for support and by providing it without being asked.
- Look for ways to show loyalty by speaking well of your boss to others.
- Develop a trusting relationship by being dependable, consistent, and honest. Do your work well and look for ways to exceed your boss's expectations.
- Keep your boss well informed.

organization. A manager with a small span of control supervises a small number of subordinates (about five or six on average) and can closely monitor the work of each subordinate. Small spans of control are usually associated with many levels of management, which gives rise to a tall vertical organization structure.

A tall vertical structure may have too many levels of management separating front-line employees from top executives. It may cause the organization to perform inefficiently because the company is not being responsive to the needs of customers. When a top executive is required to go through numerous intermediaries to learn what is happening at the operational level of the business, information often gets distorted and poor decisions result.

Larger spans of control (ranging from 10 to 20 or more subordinates) mean more responsibility is pushed to lower levels. A manager with a large span of control may not be able to directly monitor the behavior of all subordinates. However, using management information systems, which provide systematic feedback on employee performance, and work teams, in which monitoring activities are performed by peers on the team, managers can effectively supervise many subordinates.

Large spans of control result in fewer management levels. Executives at well-managed companies such as General Electric and Nucor (one of the most productive steel companies in the world) take pride in having fewer levels separating top management from first-level operative employees who deal with customers or produce the product. A large span of control works best when there are routine tasks, highly trained subordinates, competent managers, similar jobs with comparable performance measures, and subordinates who prefer autonomy.

Centralization and Decentralization

Centralization and decentralization are related to the degree of concentration of decision authority at various levels of the organization. **Centralization** means that decision-making authority is located at the top of the organization hierarchy. Centralized companies can coordinate activities in a consistent way across diverse units or departments of an organization.

With **decentralization** decision-making authority is pushed to lower levels in the organization. Decentralization is often more effective in rapidly changing environments where it is necessary to be responsive to changing

centralization

The location of decision authority at the top of the organization hierarchy.

decentralization

The location of decision authority at lower levels in the organization.

When Sir Howard Stringer took over as CEO of the Sony Corporation, he quickly announced a series of important changes designed to stem losses at the huge Japanese electronics maker. The biggest change was the creation of 13 product-category units intended to centralize control of product development. The new units are empowered to cross-fertilize ideas and communicate across Sony's famously autonomous divisions. The computer and entertainment subsidiary will build new PlayStation consoles, for instance, with microprocessors co-produced in the semiconductor division and content from Sony's movie and music units.

customer needs and tastes. Decentralized decision-making authority spurs innovation and risk taking by allowing individuals to control resources and engage in experimentation without having to obtain the approval of higher authorities.

In recent years decentralized decision authority has become relatively common in organizations. Decentralization permits greater utilization of the talents and abilities of managers and teams of employees and makes it possible to be more responsive to the needs of customers. By maintaining a highly decentralized structure, the 3M Corporation has become one of the world's most innovative companies with more than 60,000 diverse products such as Scotch Tape, Post-it Notes, video recording tape, reflective highway signs, and computer storage diskettes. One of the keys to the high rate of innovation at 3M is its 40 autonomous product divisions and other business units that are purposely kept small. Managers of these divisions and units have the authority to run their establishments as they see fit.

There is a trade-off between centralization and decentralization. Centralization allows management to coordinate the various parts of the organization in a consistent manner. Decentralization provides greater flexibility to respond to change. IBM used a centralized structure for many years because building mainframe computers required the expenditure of vast sums of money and the coordination of units that built and designed hardware and software components. However, IBM moved significantly in the direction of decentralization as its dependence on mainframe computers diminished and as its consulting services began to provide a significant portion of its total revenues. Decentralized decision authority made IBM more flexible and responsive to customers.

Formalization

The degree of written documentation that is used to direct and control employees is the level of **formalization** present. An organization with high formalization provides employees with many documents that specify the "right way" to conduct business with customers or interact with other employees. These documents include policy manuals, job descriptions, procedures, memos, and rule books. A high degree of formalization encourages employees to do their jobs in standardized and predictable ways.

Other organizations choose a low degree of formalization, with few rules and regulations, which encourages employees to improvise. This is especially useful when customer needs and conditions are subject to change. For example, Nordstrom, a retail store that serves affluent customers, has an employee handbook that consists of a single page with one rule: "Use your good judgment in all situations."

LOC-In

1 **Learning Objective Check-In**

Ballard Company has a strict management philosophy that each subordinate in the firm—at any level—should have only one direct supervisor. Ballard also uses a goal-setting program, wherein managers and subordinates compare planned goals with achieved results. When the employees meet or exceed expectations, they receive appropriate rewards.

1. *The concept that a subordinate should have only one direct supervisor is called _____.*
    a. *unity of command*
    b. *unity of management*
    c. *span of control*
    d. *accountability*
2. *Ballard Company's goal-setting program can also be called _____.*
    a. *line authority*
    b. *control-based management*
    c. *management by objectives*
    d. *staff authority*

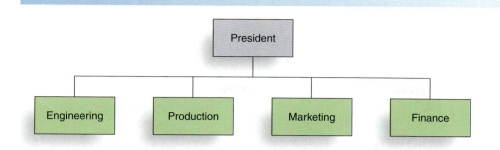

FIGURE 9.2

Functional Departmental
Structure

The Horizontal Dimension of Organization Structure

The horizontal basis for organizing jobs into units in an organization is called **departmentalization**. The three basic approaches to departmentalization are functional, divisional, and matrix.

Functional Structure

A **functional structure** places similar jobs into departments. For example, the departments in Figure 9.2 above are engineering, production, marketing, and finance. The president integrates the activities of these departments so that each department's efforts are aligned with organizational goals and objectives.

The functional approach works best in small to medium-sized companies operating in somewhat stable business environments without a great deal of change and uncertainty. The functional structure has several advantages. Decision authority is centralized at the top of the organization hierarchy. Career paths foster professional identity with the business function. Because this approach permits employees to do specialized tasks, it creates a high degree of efficiency.[1] A functional form of structure causes employees to develop specialized expertise in a functional area of the business, such as finance or marketing.

In a company with a functional form of structure, an employee in the finance department of a telecommunications company, for example, can specialize in providing financial assistance to small-business clients who purchase small phone systems. The employee can advance within the finance department by building a depth and breadth of knowledge in finance and identifying professionally with the field. The individual may be promoted to a position that provides financing to corporate clients who purchase larger, more sophisticated phone systems. The result of serving a variety of clients is that the employee eventually becomes a financial expert.

The disadvantages of the functional departmental structure include communication barriers and conflicts between functional departments. It may be difficult to coordinate products and services, which could result in diminished responsiveness to the needs of customers. When employees are assigned to functional departments, they tend to identify with the functional departmental goals rather than with organizational goals or customer needs. This could lead to departmental conflict. Anyone who has called a large corporation looking for service only to be put on hold and transferred several times by indifferent employees has experienced one of the disadvantages of a functional organization.

Engineers who work in an engineering department may provide a "state of the art" technical design that is difficult to manufacture and that contains features that are not desired by the targeted customer. In this case, engineering goals are at odds with production and marketing goals. If the top executive

formalization

The degree of written documentation that is used to direct and control employees.

departmentalization

The horizontal basis for organizing jobs into units in an organization.

functional structure

A departmentalization approach that places similar jobs into departments.

FIGURE 9.3

Divisional Organization
Structure

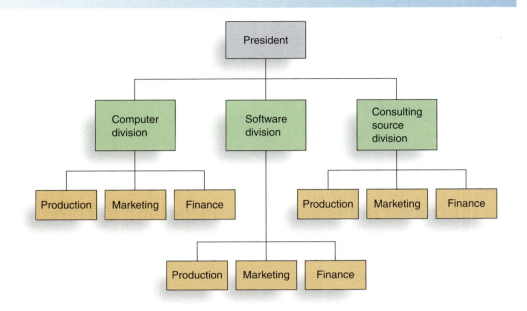

does not have time to manage the conflict among the engineering, marketing, and production departments, the product development cycle may slow down as the departmental managers try to work out their differences. By the time these differences are ironed out the product may be late to market and potential sales revenues are lost.

Divisional Approach

divisional approach

A departmentalization approach, sometimes called the product approach, that organizes employees into units based on common products, services, or markets.

The **divisional approach**, sometimes called the *product approach*, organizes employees into units based on common products, services, or markets. The divisional approach is used when a company produces many products or provides services to different types of markets, such as regional, domestic, and international markets, that require specialized knowledge. In the divisional approach key functional activities are present in each division and are coordinated by a general manager responsible for generating divisional profits.

Figure 9.3 above shows a hypothetical computer company structured into three divisions: computer, software, and consulting services. The division structure allows employees to develop expertise in both a function and a line of products or services. A salesperson in the computer division can develop specialized product knowledge in selling computer systems without knowing about software or consulting services. The salesperson is likely to produce more sales revenues by focusing on computer systems rather than trying to sell software and consulting.

General Motors was one of the companies that pioneered the division structure, creating divisions based on its different automobile brands (Chevrolet, Pontiac, Buick, and Cadillac). Hewlett-Packard has used the division structure to reinforce its entrepreneurial culture so that employees identify with smaller units within the large company. Hewlett-Packard expects that keeping the divisions small will encourage employees to innovate new products. Large consumer products companies such as PepsiCo, Procter & Gamble, Johnson & Johnson, and Colgate-Palmolive also use the division structure to create opportunities for managers to learn the skills of operating a unit of the company from a profit-and-

FIGURE 9.4

Geographic-Based Organization
Structure

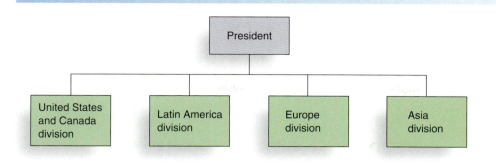

General Motors broke its corporate structure into several divisions based on automobile brands, each with its own management.

loss perspective. The most successful division managers (judged by the profitability of their divisions) are identified as likely candidates for executive leadership roles.

GEOGRAPHIC-BASED DIVISIONS   A variation of the product-based divisional structure organizes divisions by geographic region. **Geographic-based divisions** allow an organization to focus on customer needs that may vary by geographic region or market. In this approach to organizing, the functional business activities are coordinated by a division manager, who is responsible for products or services provided to a specific area. Figure 9.4 above shows the organization of a fast-food company with United States and Canadian, Latin American, European, and Asian divisions. This structure allows each division manager to satisfy customer tastes and preferences in the region. Thus, American and Canadian menus may focus on hamburgers, a favorite North American food; the menu may add chicken burgers in India, since beef is a forbidden food for many Indians, and noodle soup in China; and the European menu may make wine available to French, Italian, and Spanish customers who customarily drink wine with meals.

CUSTOMER-BASED DIVISIONS   Another variation of the product-based divisional structure organizes divisions by particular types of customers or clients. Customer-based divisions allow an organization to focus on customer needs within a basic functional structure. With customer divisions, each department contains employees who perform functional tasks for a specific type of customer. The division manager coordinates the business activities for a specific type of customer. Figure 9.5 on page 360 shows the organization of a bank that organizes its banking services into divisions that serve personal banking customers, small business banking customers, and corporate banking customers. Each customer division

geographic-based divisions

A variation of the product-based departmentalization structure in which divisions are organized by geographic region.

FIGURE 9.5

Customer-Based Organization
Structure

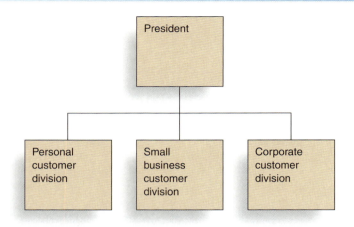

provides a different array of services that are relevant to it. For example, Wells Fargo Bank, a large San Francisco–based commercial bank, has organized its banking services into a customer-based structure.

CONGLOMORATE The *conglomorate* is another variation of the product-based divisional structure and is made up of a set of unrelated businesses. Each business is run independently from the other businesses by a general manager who has profit and loss responsibility. Figure 9.6 on page 361 shows a conglomorate that consists of four business groups: aircraft engines, medical systems, financial services, and plastics. Companies that use the conglomorate structure include United Technologies Corporation (helicopters, air conditioners, aircraft engines, and elevators), Honeywell (aerospace, automation and control solutions, specialty materials, and transportation systems), ITT (electronic components, defense electronics and services, fluid technology, and motion and flow control), and General Electric (financial services, media, health care, industrial products and infrastructure technologies). The executives in the company headquarters oversee all the businesses and make decisions concerning allocating corporate resources to businesses and decisions related to buying and selling businesses.

Dow Jones & Company recently merged its print and online operations in order to reorganize the company around its three big markets: consumer media, enterprise media, and community media. The company had been organized by distribution method: print, online, and community newspapers.

ADVANTAGES AND DISADVANTAGES OF THE DIVISIONAL APPROACH The divisional approach has several advantages, including:

- Coordination among different business functions.
- Improved and speedier service.
- Accountability for performance.
- Development of general manager and executive skills.[2]

Bringing all the functional areas together to focus on a line of products reduces barriers that inhibit coordination among marketing, finance, production, and other functions. Employees identify with products and customers rather than with professional business disciplines. This allows the company to provide better quality products and services and employees are more responsive to customers. Division managers have bottom-line profit responsibility, which prepares

FIGURE 9.6

Conglomorate-Based Organization Structure

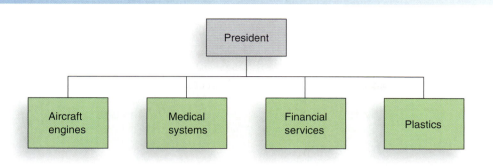

them to operate larger units or assume higher level corporate responsibilities. In a sense, the division managers are running a smaller company within the company, which motivates them to meet performance goals for the unit.

The disadvantages of the divisional approach include:

- Duplication of resources by two or more departments.
- Reduced specialization in occupation skills.
- Competition among divisions.[3]

The price an organization pays for the better coordination of the functional areas within the division is that some efficiencies are lost due to the duplication of employee roles within divisions. For example, each division may have its own direct sales force, which is more costly to support than a single sales force serving the entire organization. Further, employees operating within the division structure may not be able to specialize in their functional areas to the degree needed to provide specific competencies. Thus, each division may employ one or two human resource management generalists who know a little bit about payroll, benefits, and basic employment policies but are incapable of designing specialized performance appraisal systems for supervisory personnel. Consequently, each division may hire expensive outside consultants to perform this activity. Finally, coordination and cooperation between divisions may be problematic, resulting in further inefficiencies. When divisions compete for corporate resources, office politics may inhibit cooperation or sharing of information between divisions. At General Motors, auto sales gains in the new Saturn division came at the expense of some lost sales in the Chevrolet division. Executives in the Chevrolet division engaged in politics at the corporate level to make sure their Saturn "rival" did not receive corporate funds to produce a proposed Saturn minivan or sport utility vehicle, currently the hottest growth segments in the auto industry.

In general, the divisional structure is best suited to medium to large-size firms with a variety of products in environments with moderate to high levels of uncertainty. The divisional structure provides flexibility to allow an organization to respond to rapidly changing market conditions. However, provisions for integration between the divisions must be developed to take full advantage of the division structure. Methods to integrate across divisions are discussed later in this chapter.

Matrix Approach

The **matrix approach** superimposes a divisional structure over a functional structure in order to combine the efficiency of the functional approach with the flexibility and responsiveness to change of the divisional approach. Each employee in a matrix unit reports to two bosses—a functional manager and a product or project

matrix approach

A departmentalization approach that superimposes a divisional structure over a functional structure in order to combine the efficiency of the functional approach with the flexibility and responsiveness to change of the divisional approach.

FIGURE 9.7

Matrix Organization Structure

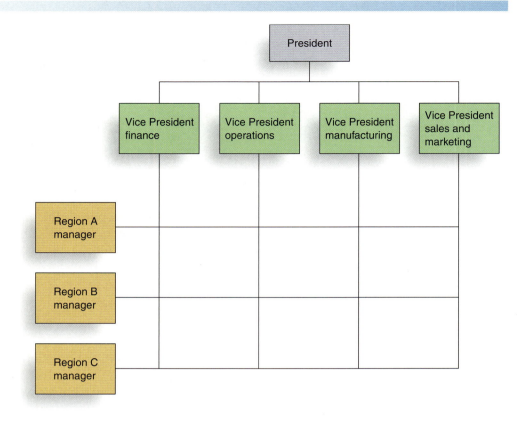

manager. This means that there are dual lines of authority in the matrix organization. As seen in Figure 9.7 above, there is a vertical chain of command for the functions of finance, operations, manufacturing, and sales and marketing. There is a lateral chain of command for the three regions. An engineer who is assigned to work in region A will report to both region manager A and the vice president of engineering applications.

The matrix approach originated in U.S. defense companies so that employees with scarce technical skills could work on one or more projects that were under time pressures for completion. The project manager is responsible for coordinating budgets, personnel, and resources in order to bring the project in on time and within budget. The functional manager is responsible for allocating specialists to projects, making sure their skills are current, and evaluating their performance according to professional standards. The National Aeronautics and Space Administration (NASA) has used matrix structures to assign space scientists to various projects such as weather satellite or space shuttle programs. Dow Corning has used matrix structures to give marketing specialists broader exposure to different products.

The advantages of the matrix approach include:

- Efficient utilization of scarce, expensive specialists.
- Flexibility that facilitates starting new projects and ventures quickly.
- Development of cross-functional skills by employees.
- Increased employee involvement in management decisions affecting project or product assignments.[4]

The key advantage is that flexibility makes it easier to start new projects or business ventures quickly with a minimum of bureaucratic inertia. Further, talented specialists can be utilized more efficiently under this approach.

Identify Your Preferred
Organizational Structure

The disadvantages of the matrix form include:

- Employee frustration and confusion as a result of the dual chain of command.
- Conflict between product and functional managers over deadlines and priorities.
- Too much time spent on coordinating decisions in meetings.[5]

One of the main problems with the matrix structure is that the product manager and functional manager may not agree on priorities or resource allocations, leading to conflict. Employees who have two bosses with different priorities may feel stressed and powerless to please both. The result may be another disadvantage, too much time devoted to meetings to coordinate various agendas and resolve conflicts.

2 Learning Objective Check-In

1. *Janet, Trina, and Jim work in the finance department at SamCo, a utility company. Janet specializes in capital credits, while Trina works in remittance, and Jim works on projects dealing with business clients. While the finance department is specialized, it is also somewhat isolated from the other departments, despite the fact that they affect the entire business's operations. What kind of departmentalization does SamCo use?*
   a. *Matrix structure*
   b. *Divisional structure*
   c. *Functional structure*
   d. *Conglomerate structure*

Coordination Mechanisms

No matter whether the functional, divisional, or matrix approach to horizontal structure is selected, each requires **coordination** to link activities so that diverse departments or divisions work in harmony and learn from each other. For example, an innovation in customer service in one division can quickly be diffused throughout the organization so that gains in customer satisfaction spread throughout the entire organization. The Wal-Mart "greeter" who welcomes customers entering the store began as an experiment in one store and spread throughout the organization when customers responded positively to being greeted. Coordination also allows units to align departmental goals with organizational goals so that interdepartmental goal conflicts are avoided or resolved. Coordination mechanisms include meetings, organizationwide reward systems, teams and task forces, liaisons, integrating managers, and the organization's culture.

coordination

Linking activities so that diverse departments or divisions work in harmony and learn from each other.

Meetings

To achieve harmony in pursuing organizational goals, individual employees must "be on the same page" as their leaders and their co-workers. One way to achieve this harmony is to organize a **strategic meeting** to synchronize plans and objectives. Representatives of each unit attend the meeting and participate in the formulation of policies that are designed to align the activities of the various departments. Such meetings may occur at the division level (involving functional managers) or at the corporate level (typically involving division managers). They provide opportunities for face-to-face contact so that managers can learn to trust and collaborate with one another. For example, McGraw-Hill/Irwin, the publisher of this text, holds a marketing strategy meeting twice a year to discuss sales and marketing policies and strategies for marketing its textbooks to colleges. Editorial, production, marketing, and sales managers exchange information about books and ideas for new projects that may serve unmet needs in the market. Chapter 15 examines meetings in greater detail.

strategic meeting

Bringing people from different departments or divisions together to synchronize plans and objectives and to coordinate activities.

Organizationwide Reward Systems

Another approach to coordinating activities of people from different departments is to provide a reward based on organizationwide profits. **Profit-sharing** plans pay a share of the company's profits to the employees in the form of a bonus. In a typical plan, the size of the bonus check is tied to quarterly profits.

Profit sharing creates a "we're in this together" mentality, which nurtures collaboration between departments. As a result of profit sharing at Hewlett-Packard, for example, new technologies developed in one division can be shared with other divisions and fashioned into new products. Profit sharing bonuses have averaged around 15 percent of base salaries at Hewlett-Packard. An employee earning an annual salary of $50,000 may earn an additional $8,000 in a typical year. Profit sharing can also be used to encourage cooperation between people at different levels of the hierarchy. For example, pay raises of both union and management personnel at Ford are tied to a profit-sharing plan. The result has been better labor relations and a total absence of work stoppages in recent years.

Task Forces and Teams

One of the keys to an effective workforce is teamwork. A **task force** is a temporary interdepartmental group formed to study an issue and make recommendations. The issue typically has organizationwide implications, and the task force gathers input from different departments. For example, the University of Colorado's diversity task force consists of representatives from all nine colleges. The group provides recommendations on how to make the culture of the university welcoming to people from diverse backgrounds.

A **problem-solving team**, sometimes called a *parallel team*, is a special type of group. A representative group from different departments is formed to solve problems such as quality improvement, workplace safety, and employee grievances. A problem-solving team can operate either on a temporary or a continuing basis. A problem-solving team at Federal Express improved the process of package sorting, providing savings in labor costs. At Ford, problem-solving teams made improvements in the quality of employee work life, which ultimately resulted in improved product quality. For more information, see Chapter 14, "Managing Teams." Management Is Everyone's Business 9.3 on page 365 offers some advice on how you can coordinate the efforts of two or more teams working in parallel to solve a complex problem.

Liaison Roles

A **liaison role** is used to facilitate communications between two or more departments. Liaisons are useful in situations where it is necessary to continuously coordinate between departments in order to improve the quality of communication and resolve misunderstandings and conflicts.

A software systems specialist from the information technology (IT) department may be assigned to coordinate contact between the IT and the marketing departments. When the IT department makes a decision involving the purchase of new computer software or decides to get rid of old software, the IT liaison meets with the marketing department to obtain input. Without the IT liaison, the IT experts may unknowingly discard software in the middle of a critical task, or they

Working as a Team There are occasions when several teams are working in parallel to solve a complex problem and will need to have their efforts coordinated. For example, one of the authors of this text is familiar with a university that developed an honesty policy for students and formed a number of different student teams to work on different aspects of the honesty policy. Different teams were assigned to (1) develop a code of ethical student conduct, (2) write an honesty policy for students that they are expected to sign as a condition of admission to the university, (3) scan the external environment to learn from other universities' experiences with administering an honesty policy, and (4) set up a mechanism to enforce the honesty policy run by the students to hear cases of alleged student dishonesty and determine how infractions of the policy will be treated. Here are some coordinating mechanisms that would be useful when several teams are working in parallel on a complex problem:

- Form a steering committee composed of representatives from each team. The *steering committee* oversees the overall process of managing the entire problem. Team representatives are selected for the steering committee. These individuals report the progress of their specific team to the entire steering committee so that this information can be brought back to the other teams. Useful knowledge or best practices that are used by one team can be shared with all the teams.

- When only a few teams are working in parallel it may be useful to assign a *boundary spanning role* to an individual who is a member on both or several teams. The person in the boundary spanning role tells the members of a specific team what the other teams are doing and helps to coordinate their efforts. This helps to reduce redundant efforts and share information that all teams may find beneficial to achieving their goals.

The Alabama Church Fires Task Force was a special investigative team of law enforcement officers from the federal firearms bureau that worked with the FBI, state fire marshals, and local sheriffs to track down suspected arsonists in a series of suspicious fires at 10 rural churches. Three students were later arrested.

may purchase software that is not "user friendly" for the marketing people. Liaison roles reduce the likelihood of making decisions that do not represent the interests of other departments.

Integrating Managers

integrating manager

A management position designed to coordinate the work of several different departments: the integrating manager is not a member of any of the departments whose activities are being coordinated.

Many times the job of coordination is assigned to a specific individual. For example, an **integrating manager** position may be created to coordinate the work of several different departments. The integrating manager is not a member of any of the departments whose activities are being coordinated. These managers have job titles such as project manager, product manager, or brand manager. They use negotiation and persuasion skills to influence functional managers to provide resources and to influence employees to be committed and motivated to achieve the product or project goals on time and within budget.

project manager

A management role that coordinates work on a scientific, aerospace, or construction project.

A **project manager** coordinates work on a scientific, aerospace, or construction project. When the Denver International Airport was being built, a project manager coordinated construction in each of five project management areas: site development (earth-moving, grading, and drainage); roadways and on-grade parking (service roads, on-airport roads, and off-airport roads connecting to highways); airfield paving; building design (baggage handling, concourses, terminal, and parking); and utility systems and other facilities (electrical transmission, oil and gas line removal and relocation).

product managers

A management role that coordinates the development of new products.

Matrix organization structures utilize **product managers**. These individuals coordinate the development of new products. They also negotiate with various functional managers for resources (people, finances, technology) and keep the product moving so it can be released to the market on time. The product manager must be a champion for the new product during the budget planning process, so that the product receives the resources needed to finish the project. New products without champions are vulnerable to critics who support diverting resources to areas that offer more immediate cash returns.

LOC-In

3 **Learning Objective Check-In**

1. *Carolina Company pays its employees bonuses depending on quarterly company profits. Also, because management and staff pay raises are both tied to profits, Carolina has seen better cooperation between people at different hierarchical levels. What is the term used for this type of compensation arrangement?*
   a. Dissemination of funds
   b. Profit sharing
   c. Strategic pay
   d. Management integration

brand managers

A management role that coordinates the ongoing activities of branded consumer products.

Brand managers coordinate the ongoing activities of branded consumer products such as food, soap and cleaning products, toiletries, and over-the-counter medicines. A brand manager coordinates the activities of marketing, advertising, sales and pricing, production, accounting, control, packaging, and product research. The brand manager makes sure the work of people in these different functional areas is aligned with the strategy for the product.

Organizational Culture

organizational culture

A system of shared values, assumptions, beliefs, and norms that unite the members of an organization.

The system of shared values, assumptions, beliefs, and norms that unite the members of an organization is the company's culture. It reflects employees' views about "the way things are done around here." **Organizational culture** influences people to share values, and that translates into a commitment to working together to achieve important goals. Culture gives employees an internal gyroscope that directs them to do things that make the entire organization more effective.[6] For more information see Chapter 4, "Managing Organizational Culture and Change."

video: THE ENTREPRENEURIAL MANAGER

Destination CEO—
Jim McCann

Summary

Jim McCann grew up on the tough streets of New York. He was the son of a small businessman, and, like many other young Irish kids in his generation, he wanted to be a cop. He stumbled into the flower business—literally stumbling into a friend of a friend who was selling his local flower shop for $10,000. McCann went to high school in Brooklyn, went to John Jay College of Criminal Justice, and went to work as a social worker. He married and started a family in his 30s, and so he suddenly had more mouths to feed.

He always had odd jobs on the side, but decided the flower business was for him. He kept his job at St. John's, a group home for boys in New York, and did social work, but also went into business selling flowers. He opened up another shop or two (or three) each year after that for the next 10 years. The company introduced 24 hour/day ordering in their industry. They could not afford to have someone work overnight every night, so the family took the orders themselves, waking up in the middle of the night to jot down an order.

At this point, McCann had decided this was the business he wanted to devote all his energies to. Formerly called Flora Plenty in New York, the company expanded, acquiring 1-800-FLOWERS in Dallas. They established a Web site with the new name and were the first merchant of any kind on AOL when the Internet was just becoming popular, in 1994. They also offered 24 hour/day service nationwide and took credit card orders over the telephone—before anyone else in the industry. The company is expecting sales to reach $650 million this year, up 8 percent from last year.

Discussion Questions

1. After Jim McCann started Flora Plenty in Manhattan, what key strategic events triggered a change in the structure and design of that organization?

2. Describe some ways that 1-800-FLOWERS, and its predecessor, Flora Plenty, were cognizant of environmental factors and their role in shaping the business.

3. Consider organizational culture and its role in coordinating departments and vertical levels within an organization. Describe the organizational culture of 1-800-FLOWERS as you perceive it from the video and explain what effect this can have on the company.

Organization Design

The structure of a company must match the firm's strategies in order to operate at peak levels. **Organization design** is the selection of an organization structure that best fits the strategic direction of the business. The three basic organization designs are mechanistic, organic, and boundaryless (see Table 9.1 on page 368). These designs incorporate the vertical and horizontal structural elements covered earlier in this chapter.

Before the most appropriate design can be selected, management should determine how to best deploy the organization's assets and develop a strategy for the business. (For more information on how organizations develop strategies that improve firm performance, see Chapter 7.) As the strategic direction changes, so do the structural elements that make up the design. The opening vignette of this chapter shows how changes in strategy can affect organization structure and design.

Strategic factors that affect the choices of organization design include:

1. *Organization capabilities*. The activities that the company does best are likely to be retained, while under certain strategic conditions (for example, a cost leadership strategy) the activities that are peripheral to the core mission of the business may be contracted out to more efficient suppliers.

organization design

The selection of an organization structure that best fits the strategic goals of the business.

table 9.1

Mechanistic, Organic, and Boundaryless Designs

MECHANISTIC	ORGANIC	BOUNDARYLESS
Rigid hierarchical relationships	Collaboration (both vertical and horizontal)	Collaboration (vertical and horizontal, as well as customers, suppliers, and competitors)
High formalization	Low formalization	Same as organic
Top-down communication	Informal communication	Same as organic
Centralized decision authority	Decentralized decision authority	Same as organic
Narrowly defined specialized jobs	Broadly defined flexible jobs	Same as organic
Emphasis on individuals working independently	Emphasis on teams	Emphasis on teams that also may cross organization boundaries

Sources: Adapted from S. P. Robbins and M. Coulter, *Management*, 8th ed. Upper Saddle River, NJ: Prentice Hall, 2005, p. 245; L. R. Gomez-Mejia, D. B. Balkin, and R. L. Cardy, *Managing Human Resources*, 5th ed. Upper Saddle River, NJ: Prentice Hall, 2007, p. 47.

2. *Technology.* The type of technology the firm uses to produce its product or service has an effect on the organization design. For example, an electronic components company that utilizes mass production technologies for manufacturing its integrated circuits in an expensive fabrication plant is likely to be structured on a centralized basis to take advantage of plant efficiencies while a fast food company utilizing service technologies will be structured on a decentralized basis in order to respond to local customer tastes and needs. Here are some different categories of technology that can affect the choice of organization design:

   - *Manufacturing technology* converts products from raw materials. One type of manufacturing technology is *small-batch technology*, which produces custom-made products for customers or products produced in small quantities. Luxury pleasure boats or women's high fashion clothing uses this type of technology. *Mass production technology*, another type of manufacturing technology, produces standardized products using an assembly line with a heavy reliance on automated machines such as robots. Automobiles and consumer electronics use this type of technology. The most sophisticated and complex form of manufacturing technology is *continuous process technology* in which the entire work flow is automated. The manufacturing process runs continuously and employees simply monitor the machines that control the process. Chemicals manufacturing and petroleum refining use this type of technology.[7]

   - *Service technology* provides services to customers, which makes contact with the customer a critical feature of this technology. Service firms tend to be structured on a decentralized and flexible basis in order to respond to each customer's needs. Consulting, medical firms, law firms, hotels, restaurants, and banks utilize service technologies in order to provide service to their customers.[8]

   - *Digital technology* uses the Internet to provide a customer with faster service, at a lower price, and with more choices. Businesses that use digital technology include search engines such as Google, booksellers such as Amazon.com, and trading communities such as eBay. Organizations that use digital technology tend to be structured on a decentralized and flexible basis in order respond quickly to a customer's needs.[9]

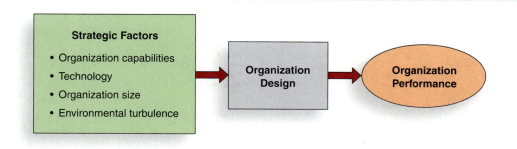

FIGURE 9.8

Strategic Factors That Influence
Organization Design

3. *Organization size*. As organization size increases, so do work specialization
   and the need to coordinate the work of diverse employees. Large organizations need more coordinating mechanisms than small ones.

4. *Environmental turbulence*. Organizations that operate in turbulent environments require different designs than organizations that operate in more
   stable environments in which change happens gradually. Turbulent environments are characterized by dynamic change due to market, technological, political, and regulatory or social forces.[10] Under conditions of rapid
   change, on-the-spot decisions are made, and lower level employees need
   the authority to make decisions. Decentralized structures that delegate
   authority to lower-level employees are used in turbulent environments to
   enable decisions to be made by those who are closest to the customer or
   the source of change.[11] An organization with a predictable and stable environment is more likely to have a structure with greater centralization.
   Figure 9.8 above shows that the strategic factors that influence the choice
   of organization design ultimately affect organization performance.

Mechanistic Organizations

A **mechanistic organization design** emphasizes vertical control with rigid hierarchical relationships, top-down "command and control" communication channels, centralized decision authority, highly formalized work rules and policies,
and specialized, narrowly defined jobs. It is based on many of the classical management principles that were described in Chapter 1. The organization has a tall
pyramid shape with numerous levels of management. Managers have small
spans of control and closely supervise subordinates.

A mechanistic organization design is best suited to a stable and relatively
predictable environment. It depends on managers making decisions and front-
line workers executing the decisions by doing repetitive tasks. While industry is
moving away from this design, it is still applied in government agencies, labor
unions, and some family businesses.

Organic Organizations

A focus on change and flexibility requires a more **organic organization design**.
Such a design emphasizes horizontal relationships involving teams, departments, or divisions and provisions to coordinate these lateral units. Organic organizations are relatively decentralized and low in specialization, formalization,
and standardization. Employees have more leeway in dealing with changing customer needs or technological challenges. The span of control is larger than in a
mechanistic organization, and managers are less inclined to closely supervise

**mechanistic
organization design**

A management design
based on the classical
perspective of
management, emphasizing
vertical control with rigid
hierarchical relationships,
top-down "command and
control" communication
channels, centralized
decision authority, highly
formalized work rules and
policies, and specialized,
narrowly defined jobs;
sometimes called a
bureaucratic design.

**organic organization
design**

A management design that
is focused on change and
flexibility, emphasizing
horizontal relationships
that involve teams,
departments, or divisions,
and provisions to
coordinate these lateral
units.

HBO's hit programs like the Emmy-award winning *The Sopranos* and *Sex and the City* were made possible by flexibility and decentralization at Home Box Office and parent company AOL-Time Warner.

Mechanistic versus Organic Organizational Structures

subordinates. The organic design has fewer levels of management separating front-line employees from the executives. Its shape is flatter in appearance.

An organic organization design is most effective in turbulent and uncertain environments. Organic designs are beneficial for nurturing creativity and innovation, where employees are more likely to spend their time thinking and planning. Organizations that use organic design include high technology, entertainment and media, financial services, and consumer goods companies. Many entrepreneurships adopt organic designs from inception because management anticipates future growth in a highly uncertain environment. As deregulation has heated up the competitive landscape, public utilities, airlines, and telecommunications companies are also moving toward the use of organic designs.

Home Box Office (HBO) plays movies and produces programs with adult topics. HBO has benefited from the flexibility and decentralization of an organic design. Its corporate parent, AOL-Time Warner, has given HBO writers creative and artistic freedom of expression. With the organic design, HBO is physically removed from the rest of the AOL-Time Warner corporation, which also contains the larger Warner Brothers operating under the pressure of ratings-driven broadcast schedules.[12] HBO programs, on the other hand, are directly paid for by subscribers. This allows HBO to produce more controversial and cutting-edge television content than is possible under traditional television broadcasting constraints. Partly due to the independence provided within an organic design, HBO programs such as *The Sopranos* and *Sex and the City* have won many Emmy television industry awards for quality. Moreover, HBO has also become a highly profitable business for AOL-Time Warner.

Some organizations have a hybrid design in which mechanistic and organic designs are used in different parts of the organization. For example, McDonald's utilizes a mechanistic design at its Chicago-area headquarters, where corporate functions such as training, marketing, and advertising are centralized. Managers are arranged in a hierarchy with an emphasis on vertical reporting relationships. However, within the geographical regions of McDonald's, the company applies an organic design so that divisions can be more responsive to changing customer tastes. Figure 9.9 on page 371 arranges the basic types of organization structures from highly mechanistic to highly organic.

Boundaryless Organizations

boundaryless organization design

A management design that eliminates internal and external structural boundaries that inhibit employees from collaborating with each other or that inhibit firms from collaborating with customers, suppliers, or competitors.

Recently, a newer form of organizational structure has emerged in response to changing technologies and evolving marketplace relationships. **A boundaryless organization design** eliminates internal and external structural boundaries that inhibit employees from collaborating with each other or that inhibit firms from collaborating with customers, suppliers, or competitors. This design has many of the features of organic design, but it uses a flexible structure that makes it possible to overlap with other organizations so that seamless cooperation between organizations results in better service to the customer. By using teams that span organization boundaries, a boundaryless organization may share employees with a supplier through a joint venture; use its sales force to sell a partner's products; share a patented manufacturing process with a customer through a licensing agreement; or buy a large block of a competitor's stock to gain the right to use the

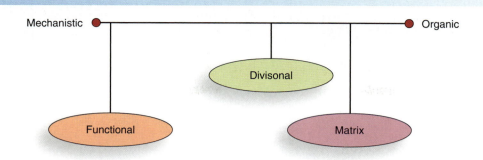

FIGURE 9.9

Organization Structures: From Mechanistic to Organic

competitor's technology. Such cooperative arrangements enable a boundaryless organization to improve the speed with which it reacts to change and uncertainty in the environment.

One of the first executives to use the boundaryless organization design was Jack Welch, the former CEO of General Electric. Welch was the architect of a bold plan to redesign General Electric, a large, diversified corporation, so that each of its divisions would operate with a minimum of bureaucracy. Hierarchies were flattened and vertical functional silos were broken down.

- At its locomotive division in Erie, Pennsylvania, GE formed a partnership with a paint supplier to improve the consistency of the paint used on its locomotives. Team members from GE and the paint supplier collaborated to reduce painting time and improve quality.

- GE Capital's Global Consumer Finance business worked with top global retailers such as Wal-Mart to deliver financial services to their customers.

- GE signed a 10-year maintenance agreement with British Airways in 1998. GE and British Airways maintenance crews work together on maintenance and overhaul projects.

Other companies have followed GE's lead. Boundaryless designs have been used to: (1) enter foreign markets, (2) manage the risk of developing new technologies, and (3) pool resources to compete in an industry with high financial entry barriers. For example,

- Airbus Industries utilizes a boundaryless design that consists of a partnership of four firms from France, Germany, England, and Spain that collaborated to market and develop commercial jet aircraft. The group competes with Boeing, the world's leading producer of passenger jets.

- Paramount and Twentieth Century Fox combined to produce, market, and distribute the enormously expensive epic movie *Titanic*, which broke box office records in the late 1990s. The production costs of the movie were higher than any single film company could risk alone.

- General Motors has formed partnerships with two Japanese auto manufacturers, Suzuki and Isuzu, to build and market small cars for the North American market.

- Northwest Airlines and KLM (the Dutch national airline) formed a partnership merging air routes and customer sales processes to facilitate better service on international flights.

A type of boundaryless design that has been adopted by many multinational firms in recent years is the network design. The *network design* consists of a series of strategic alliances or relationships that a company develops with suppliers, distributors, or manufacturers in order to produce and market a product. A *strategic*

WHERE CAN YOU DO YOUR BEST WORK?

Different types of organization design provide different environments for working and managing. This exercise lets you assess your preferences with respect to different structural dimensions of an organization.

First answer the following questions individually. Then, in groups of four to five people, share your responses with each other. Finally, complete the group discussion questions that appear at the end of the exercise and be ready to share your group's answers with the class.

1. Would you rather work in a large (more than 1,000 employees) or small (fewer than 100 employees) organization? Why?

2. Do you prefer to have frequent (on a daily basis) interactions with your boss, or would you prefer infrequent (once or twice per month) interactions with your boss?

3. Do you prefer to work primarily as part of a team or as an individual?

4. Do you prefer to be a specialist in a company (knowing a lot about a highly specialized function or business process), or do you prefer to be a generalist (having a broad scope of knowledge of different facets of the business, but not specializing in any of them)?

5. Do you prefer a job that is constantly changing and requires continuing training and education to keep pace

with change, or do you prefer a job with stable content that lets you develop work routines that are predictable after you master the job skills?

6. Do you prefer working cross-functionally with people you have no line authority to influence, or do you prefer working in vertical relationships with people who are either subordinates or superiors, located up or down the chain of command?

Discussion Questions

1. What are the advantages of working in a mechanistic organization, an organic organization, and a boundaryless organization? You may want to refer to Table 9.1.

2. What are the disadvantages of working in a mechanistic organization, an organic organization, and a boundaryless organization?

3. Do group members agree or disagree that one design is superior to the others for providing the best work environment? Does organization design matter when it comes to choosing a company to work for? Are there certain designs that one should avoid when searching for a job?

4. What conclusions about your career path and goals can you draw from this discussion?

LOC-In

4 Learning Objective Check-In

1. *Tip Tops, Incorporated, is an external marketing consulting firm whose industry is always changing. In addition, it never has two clients who are exactly alike, and while it can apply some of the same techniques across clients, there is no "template" for the way it provides services. Lastly, the technological climate also changes rapidly in this industry. Given what you know about Tip Tops, which type of organization design would be most appropriate for this firm?*
   a. *Mechanistic organization*
   b. *Organic organization*
   c. *Boundaryless organization*
   d. *Task-based organization*

alliance is an agreement between two or more companies to collaborate by sharing or exchanging resources to produce and market a product (see Chapter 2 for more on strategic alliances). For example, Hewlett-Packard and Canon formed a network design to produce laser printers that has endured for over 15 years. Hewlett-Packard provides its computer technologies and know-how which is combined with Canon's knowledge of imaging and laser technology. By sharing the knowledge and technologies, the laser printers that are marketed by Hewlett-Packard own a dominant share of the market.

How do you know if your organization has the optimal design? Manager's Notebook 9.1 on page 373 provides some important symptoms to let managers become aware of a malfunctioning organization design.

IS YOUR ORGANIZATION DESIGN FUNCTIONING EFFECTIVELY?

Managers should be aware of symptoms that indicate a malfunctioning organization design. Here are some of the most important. If one or more of these exist, managers are advised to consider making changes to the organization's structure.

- *The organization design focuses employees on work that uses noncritical skills rather than emphasizing the opportunity to use their strengths.* The design should provide the opportunity for highly skilled employees to do the work that they do best, rather than being bogged down by less critical tasks of lesser value. For example, sales and marketing people may be spending too much time attending required staff meetings to coordinate with others on projects within a matrix structure. Disappointing sales results may be the result of using a structure that keeps salespeople away from their customers by forcing them to attend regular meetings. The matrix structure may be diverting salespeople from making their most valuable contributions to company performance.

- *The organization design has too many levels in the hierarchy.* Too many management levels inhibit the responsiveness of employees in an organization. Consequently they do not serve customers, because they are oversupervised and do not have enough autonomy. Employees' contacts with customers are limited, because they must obtain management approval to take action. Instead, the structure should help them show initiative and adopt standardized procedures in order to please a customer. A good rule to use is to ask if the managers at higher levels are adding value to or taking value away from the business activity. Value is added when they improve quality or consistency. Managers take value away by slowing down the process of giving service to the customer or by taking away the initiative of lower-level employees to better serve customers. By giving additional authority to lower-level employees who have direct contact with customers, organizations provide better service. The executive team may also learn that they need fewer levels of managers to supervise employees.

- *The organization design is not flexible enough to accommodate changes in strategy or the environment.* A well-designed structure should allow the organization to be innovative and adapt to changing circumstances. For example, if a new product takes off unexpectedly and is in high demand in a fast growing market, this market jolt is likely to result in a reallocation of company resources devoted to producing the successful new product. The current organization design should be able to accommodate a decision made to reallocate capital, people, and technology to satisfy the surging demand for the new product. A flexible design, like a tree bending in the wind, should be able to deal with an unexpected jolt from the environment.

Source: Adapted from M. Goold and A. Campbell, "Do You Have a Well-Designed Organization? *Harvard Business Review*, March 2002, pp. 117–124.

Redesigning Organizations

As a firm's strategy changes, organization structure and design also change to support the implementation of the new strategy. In a sense, organization design can be considered a continuous work in progress. An organization is *redesigned* to enable the firm to more effectively use its technology, assets, and human resources to accomplish strategic goals. The key strategic events that are likely to trigger change in the structure and design of an organization are mergers, acquisitions, and divestitures.

MERGER When two independent companies agree to combine their assets and form a single organization a **merger** has taken place. In many cases, companies that compete in the same industry merge to create a larger entity with greater economies of scale. Redundant facilities such as corporate headquarters or back-office operations can be disposed of to create a more efficient operation.

There were numerous bank mergers in the 1990s. California-based Wells Fargo and Midwest-based Northwest Banks merged operations and decided to use the Wells Fargo name for the emergent organization. Citicorp, the largest U.S. Bank, merged with Travelers Group, a leading insurance company, to create a global financial giant called Citigroup.

ACQUISITION An **acquisition** takes place when a firm buys all or part of another business. The acquiring firm may use cash or trade some of its stock to purchase the acquired firm. In the 1980s, many companies acquired businesses in unrelated industries as part of a strategy of diversification, as when Phillip Morris, a tobacco company, acquired Kraft and General Foods.

In the corporate applications software industry Oracle, the world's second largest software company, spent $10.3 billion to acquire PeopleSoft Inc. in 2004 and $5.8 billion to acquire Siebel Systems Inc. in 2005. These acquisitions enabled Oracle to realize a strategy that will allow it to help its corporate clients run everything from accounting and sales to customer relations and supply-chain management with its software.[13]

DIVESTITURE A **divestiture** occurs when an organization sells a business in order to generate cash. The goal is to better deploy the funds elsewhere, or to refocus on a core business which is better understood by management. General Electric divested many business units that did not fit with its boundaryless organization strategy and high performance expectations. GE acquired others (such as the NBC television network) that better fit with the company's strategy. The redesign helped General Electric become a flatter and more competitive company and increased its market value from $12 billion in 1981 to $346 billion in 2006.

Many corporations that increased their size through mergers and acquisitions in the 1970s and 1980s found that the complexity of managing the new business units led to disappointing earnings. In the late 1980s and the 1990s, many corporate divestitures took place, and **downsizing** (a strategy used to reduce the scale and scope of a business to improve its financial performance) became common. Management Close-Up 9.1 on page 375 shows how Sara Lee adopted a strategy of divestiture to add value.

---

merger

The process of integrating two firms.

acquisition

The process of purchasing other firms.

divestiture

The corporate process of selling a business in order to generate cash, which the corporation can better deploy elsewhere, or to refocus on a core business which is better understood by management.

downsizing

A management strategy used to reduce the scale and scope of a business to improve its financial performance.

LOC-In

5 Learning Objective Check-In

Scottsdale Company, a producer of high-end lawn and garden equipment, including some chemical products, is anticipating one of two alternatives that will be affected by its near-term strategy, which is to expand the company. The first alternative is to agree with Pro-Gene, a fertilizer company, to combine the assets from both companies and form a single organization. If this alternative is chosen, the new firm will be able to eliminate some of the administrative operations and even consolidate manufacturing facilities in some cases. The second alternative is to actually purchase some smaller firms along Scottsdale's supply chain, particularly at the back end.

1. *If Scottsdale chooses the first option, it would be engaging in _____.*
   a. *acquisition*
   b. *a divestiture*
   c. *task forces*
   d. *a merger*
2. *If Scottsdale chooses the second option, it would be engaging in _____.*
   a. *a divestiture*
   b. *acquisition*
   c. *a merger*
   d. *centralization*

Deverticalizing Sara Lee

Many large consumer goods companies have embraced outsourcing. For example, Nike doesn't make any shoes. Pillsbury's Green Giant line of canned vegetables are not actually canned by the Minneapolis, Minnesota, food company—Seneca Foods does it for Pillsbury. Outsourcing lets companies concentrate on sales, marketing, and improving their brands while the actual manufacturing of their products is done by other companies.

In 1949 a Chicago baker perfected cheesecakes that kept their quality after being frozen. Charles Lubin, the baker, named his shop after his eight-year-old daughter, Sara Lee. Today Sara Lee is a top multinational corporation whose products are sold in over 140 countries. Globally, the company is first in the packaged meats industry, and it is ranked first in the United States for frozen baked goods, intimate apparel, and socks.

Since 1997, however, Sara Lee has sold or closed more than 100 plants while maintaining its position in its markets. The corporation surprised everyone with its decision to sell its manufacturing operations and outsource the work. The corporation wanted to focus on developing new products and promoting its brands instead of manufacturing them. Senior management called the divestiture action "deverticalizing" the company's organization, with its brands being made by suppliers according to Sara Lee's specifications.

Sara Lee will be focusing on marketing brands in the baked goods and packaged meats categories, which include the Sara Lee brand cheesecakes and other desserts, Jimmy Dean sausages, Ball Park franks, and Earth Grains breads. It plans to divest other products that do not fit into its targeted product categories. In 2005 it announced that it had put its brands in the intimate apparel products category up for sale, including Hanes underwear, Wonderbras, and Playtex panties. By narrowing its focus on branded food products Sara Lee expects that it will be better able to innovate and boost profit margins.

Sources: Adapted from "Sara Lee: Chock full o' Brands," *The Economist*, November 12, 2005; P. Eogoi, "Sara Lee: No Piece of Cake," *BusinessWeek*, May 26, 2003, pp. 66–68; "Separate and Lift," *The Economist*, September 20, 1997, p. 69.

CONCLUDING THOUGHTS

In the introductory vignette at the beginning of the chapter we presented some critical thinking questions related to aspects of organization structure at Daimler. Now that you have had the opportunity to learn about managing organization structure and design in the chapter, let's reexamine the questions that were raised in the vignette.

First, there is a strong and direct relationship between the new organizational structure at Daimler and the changing marketplace. The changes in organizational structure and strategic direction were designed to allow the company to move faster and be more flexible in response to competitive threats, as well as to resume its preeminent position in automotive quality and innovation. The new structure was also intended to cut costs, an important goal for the firm as it suffered staggering losses.

The reason the structure at Daimler was no longer working was that it allowed for duplication of administrative functions, which was not only costly but also invited destructive conflict among division, and it separated management from the company's core functions of engineering, research, and design that fuel innovations and quality. Unifying the streamlined firm under a leaner management team and emphasizing cooperative functions between and across divisions is intended to refocus the firm's energies on getting back to the basics and reclaiming its place at the top of the luxury car market.

Managing the Structure and Design of Organizations

Andy Bryant, the CFO of Intel, manages Finance, Information Technology (IT), and Human Resources (HR) for his company. His integrated role mirrors the team roles he assigns to his Finance personnel. They now work in cross functional teams with employees from Operations. Together, Finance and Operations employees have developed a business partnership, and both departments are involved in the development of new products, improving the efficiency and effectiveness of operations and increasing productivity and profitability.[1]

Under Bryant, the Finance Department underwent an organizational redesign. The first step in the process was to develop a strategic vision for the department that mirrored the strategic vision of Intel as a whole. Intel's Finance Vision and Charter is as follows:

Vision: Intel Finance is a full partner in business decisions to maximize shareholder value.

Charter:

- Maximize profits by providing effective analysis, influence, leadership, and control as business partners.
- Keep Intel legal worldwide while maintaining high standards of professionalism and integrity.
- Protect shareholder interests by safeguarding the assets of the Corporation.
- Deliver world-class services and productivity.
- Develop effective leaders and partners through career opportunities that foster improved performance and professional growth.[2]

This strategic vision highlights several key points: (1) Finance has an interest in the business, and they take the "bottom line" seriously; (2) Finance expects to partner with others in the corporation for the betterment of the company as a whole; and (3) employees in finance are professionals, and they need to be on the cutting edge of their industry as well as being involved in the overall business of the company. These points brought Bryant to the next step in the organizational design process—setting up an organizational structure that matched the strategy. Bryant chose a modified matrix for his organizational structure.

To address the first and second points, Bryant made sure that each Finance employee was assigned to a particular project or area of operations. Financial professionals working in a specific operational unit are expected to know everything about that unit—from understanding the manufacturing process to learning how the unit markets and sells its product or products.

In acknowledgment of the third point, all Finance employees report to a Finance Manager, along with an operations manager. In most organizations, financial staffers are embedded in operating units. Intel's structure allows Finance employees to gain an overview of the company's entire financial picture, and have access to financial competencies that they would not get in a standard decentralized structure.

In setting up this new organizational design, Bryant also paid attention to corporate culture. He knew that the role of the Finance employees was an advisory one—the final decision on any operational issue had to stay with operations or general managers. To avoid the conflicts inherent in such a structure, he insisted that his Finance employees understand not only finance, but also the business of the group they were supporting, how to influence and persuade others without a command position, and when and how to proactively address issues. The bottom line was that if Finance was to be considered to be a true partner, and to be included in the strategic decision-making process, Finance employees had to be able to provide information to operations that was useful in running a business, not just interesting. Operations managers want bottom-line information, presented succinctly and clearly. They don't want huge piles of reports, and they don't want financial analysts to do every report that is requested—just those that will really add value to the operation. Operations managers expect Finance professionals to have an opinion and to express that opinion in a way that brings both groups closer to agreement.

A key component of any organizational design intervention is to measure results. At Intel, Finance measures results based on whether they have effectively changed business practices, and whether or not those changes increase corporate savings and/or profitability.

Interestingly, Andy Bryant's own leanings toward the operations side of the business may have prompted his desire to create better relations between his team and operations. As he notes in a recent interview, "I have tried three different times to leave Finance for operations.[3] He also points out that ex-CEO Andy Grove prevented that move each time, finally telling Andy, "you need to do what's in the best interest of the company."

Sources: [1] PriceWaterhouseCoopers, "Global Best Practices," http://www.globalbestpractices.com/Home/Document.aspx?Q=273,4537,205,D39F085F-3BCD-4C5C-B6FC-685918BC21B6; [2] R.R. Boedecker, and S.B. Hughes, "Best Practices in Finance: How Intel Finance Uses Business Partnerships to Supercharge Results," *Strategic Finance*, October 2005, pp. 26–34; [3] Don Durfee,"Intel's Andy Bryant," *CFO*, November 2005, pp. 48–51.

summary of learning objectives

Organizing is a process that involves the deployment of resources to achieve strategic goals. **Organization structure** is the development of a formal system of relationships that determine lines of authority and the tasks assigned to individuals and units. This chapter's discussion will help future managers, work teams and employees better understand the importance of organizing. The content presented in this chapter to meet each of the learning objectives we set out at the start of the chapter is summarized below.

1 Identify the vertical and horizontal dimensions of organization structure.

The **vertical dimension** of organization structure is concerned with who has the authority to make decisions; it involves

- **Unity of command**: each subordinate should have only one supervisor.
- **Authority**: the formal right of a manager to make decisions and give orders that are carried out by others.
- **Responsibility**: the duty to perform a task that has been assigned.
- **Delegation**: a transfer of responsibility to a subordinate or team subject to the authority of the manager.
- **Line authority**: direct control over the work of subordinates.
- **Staff authority**: advising, recommending, and counseling other managers and personnel in the organization.
- **Span of control**: the number of subordinates who directly report to a manager.
- **Centralization**: decision authority concentrated at the top of the organization hierarchy.
- **Decentralization**: decision authority pushed to lower levels in the organizational hierarchy.
- **Formalization**: the amount of written documentation that is used to direct and control employees.

The **horizontal dimension** of organization structure is **departmentalization,** which is the basis of the deployment of employees into jobs in units that are called departments.

2 Apply the three basic approaches—functional, divisional, and matrix—to departmentalization.

- The **functional structure** of departmentalization assigns people with similar skills to a department such as accounting or marketing. It is highly efficient because it permits employees to do specialized tasks.
- The **divisional approach** organizes employees into units based on common products, services, or markets. It improves coordination between different business functions and allows for faster services to customers.
- The **matrix approach** combines the efficiency of the functional approach with the flexibility and responsiveness of the divisional approach. The matrix approach greatly facilitates starting new projects and ventures, and it efficiently utilizes the talents of scarce specialists.

3 Develop coordination across departments and hierarchical levels.

As organizations grow and become more complex, there is a greater need for **coordination** mechanisms to link activities between departments. Some key coordination mechanisms include the following:

- **Strategic meetings:** face-to-face gatherings of departmental or division managers to coordinate overarching organizational objectives.
- **Organizationwide reward systems:** rewards that are based on organizationwide results that strengthen collaboration between departments.
- **Task forces:** ad hoc interdepartmental groups that are formed to study a specific problem and make recommendations.
- **Problem-solving teams:** groups representing different departments that solve problems on either a temporary or permanent basis.
- **Liaison role:** a position held by an individual that is used to facilitate communications between two or more departments.
- **Integrating manager:** a manager who is responsible for the success of a project or product and who coordinates the work of people from different departments.
- **Organization culture:** a system of shared values, assumptions, beliefs, and norms that give the members of an organization a common understanding about "the way things are done around here."

4 Use organization structure and the three basic organization designs—mechanistic, organic, and boundaryless—to achieve strategic goals.

Organization design involves selecting an organization structure that best fits the strategic goals of the business. Managers can design organization goals that are mechanistic, organic, or boundaryless.

- **Mechanistic designs** emphasize vertical structure and use top-down "command and control" communication channels with a high level of formalization.
- **Organic designs** emphasize horizontal relationships involving teams and rely on coordination mechanisms to keep everything under control. There is more flexibility and less formalization in an organic design than in a mechanistic design.
- **Boundaryless designs** eliminate structural boundaries between organizations and units within them so that employees can develop collaborative relationships with customers, suppliers, and sometimes competitors. While sharing some similarities with the organic design, the boundaryless design uses teams to span oragnizational boundaries with other firms to more quickly respond to change and uncertainty in the environment.

Develop an awareness of strategic events that are likely to trigger a change in the structure and design of an organization.

5 The key strategic events that are likely to trigger a change in the structure and design of an organization are mergers, acquisitions, and divestitures.

- A **merger** takes place when two independent companies agree to combine their assets and form a single organization. In many cases these merging firms compete in the same industry and achieve efficiencies based on size.
- An **acquisition** takes place when a firm buys all or part of another business. The acquisition may be in the same industry or a different one than that of the acquiring firm.
- A **divestiture** occurs when an organization sells a business in order to generate cash.

discussion questions

1. What would it be like to be a department manager in a functional organization structure? In a divisional approach to organization structure? In your comparison discuss responsibilities, skills, competencies, and decision-making authority.

2. How do responsibility, authority, and accountability differ? What happens to responsibility, authority, and accountability when a manager delegates work to a subordinate?

3. What are the advantages and disadvantages of centralization and decentralization? You are the CEO of a diversified food company with four divisions that produce breakfast cereals, cookies, salty snack foods, and fruit juices under different brand names. Give an example of a situation where centralized decision authority would be more effective to use. Give an example where decentralized decision authority would be more effective to use. Justify your answers.

4. What issues or problems would an organization encounter with a matrix structure? Would you like to work in a matrix organization structure? Why or why not?

5. Your organization is organized with functional departments. It has encountered the following problems. What coordinating mechanism would you select to manage each problem? Justify your selection.

   a. The number of workplace accidents has increased greatly in all the departments.

   b. Departments are competing with each other for budgets and other scarce resources, resulting in dysfunctional conflict.

   c. The research, engineering, manufacturing, and marketing departments disagree on product specifications and performance features, and new products are being delivered too late to market as a result.

6. How are teams used in the organic design? What about in the boundaryless design?

7. Does an organization in a turbulent environment require more horizontal relationships than one in a stable environment? Explain.

8. Why does the structure of an organization follow the development of the organization strategy, rather than the strategy following the development of the structure?

---

management minicase 9.1

Microsoft Reorganizes in Order to Reignite Entrepreneurial Fires

Microsoft's CEO, Steve Ballmer, announced in 2005 a major reorganization of the company in an attempt to compete more aggressively against nimble upstarts such as Google Inc. and Salesforce.com. The purpose of the reorganization is to trim Microsoft's growing bureaucracy. Microsoft, the world's largest software company, which now has 60,000 employees, has had difficulty in releasing upgrades of its products on time. Its next version of Windows has fallen way behind its scheduled release date due to glitches in new software features that have not performed up to expectations.

The reorganization represents a drastic streamlining of Microsoft's structure. The corporate structure is collapsing from seven product divisions to three. The newly formed divisions consist of (1) platform products and services, which includes the Windows operating system; (2) business, which includes the Office suite of business software products such as Word, Powerpoint, and Excel, and (3) entertainment and devices, which includes the Xbox game-machine and Microsoft TV. A new position of president was established for each of these three product divisions, which reflects the critical importance placed on leadership in the divisions.

It is hoped that the reorganization will let Microsoft respond more quickly to opportunities in the market and take advantage of its strength in resources and deep pool of talent. Product groups that depend on similar technology are put under the same organization and under chiefs who know how to get things done.

Discussion Questions

1. Recently Microsoft has lost some key software designers to Google and some other smaller software companies. Will the reorganization help Microsoft retain its top technical employees?

2. What do you think was the reason that Microsft combined seven divisions under its previous organization structure into only three divisions in the reorganization?

3. How can large companies such as Microsoft manage their structure to remain innovative and remain close to the customer? Are there other practices that the company should consider?

Source: Adapted from J. Greene, "Less Could Be More at Microsoft," *BusinessWeek*, October 3, 2005, p. 40.

Restructuring the 3M Company for Growth and Profitability

management
minicase 9.2

The 3M Company of 2003 bore a resemblance to the "old IBM" of the 1980s, which was a place of lifetime employment for tinkerers, coddled from postgraduate life to the grave, and who might or might not eventually turn out commercial products. They read the company's weekly newspaper that provided features about cooking classes, stamp collecting, and volunteerism. In other words, life at 3M was cushy and undemanding for its employees.

Complacency begat financial disappointments. Between 1992 and 2002 sales crept ahead at an average of 1.6 percent and profits increased 4.9 percent a year. The 3M Company generated $16 billion in sales in 2002. The 3M Company's product lines focused on industrial and consumer goods such as abrasives, glues, and various types of tapes with adhesive qualities. Starting in 2001, CEO James McNerney formulated a strategy of diversification to refocus 3M on faster-growing markets that could provide better performance in terms of growth and profitability to investors. McNerney used a two-pronged approach to realize these goals. First, he reduced operating expenses by $500 million, mostly by laying off 6,500 of 3M's 75,000 workers. He slashed inventories and accounts receivable by $675 million and trimmed debt. Profitability jumped 38 percent to $2 billion due to these efforts.

Second, CEO McNerney decided to reposition 3M as more of a health care company, building on the health unit's 22 percent of revenue and 27 percent of operating income. Until now, 3M's medical products have been mostly low tech, such as skin patches or inhalers, or service based, including software used to code medical procedures for Medicare reimbursement. Scientists in 3M's laboratories are developing medications to treat respiratory, cardiovascular, skin, and sexually related diseases. The company is an important supplier of materials to repair and replace teeth, and the CEO wants to branch into such areas as fluoride treatment and products to stem periodontal disease. With the U.S. population aging, the $12 billion restorative dental care market is expected to reach $21.5 billion in 10 years.

McNerney is also looking for acquisitions in expanding industries. He recently completed a $680 million acquisition of Corning's precision lens business, which makes parts for projection TVs.

The 3M Company had 148 plants in 60 countries with 53 percent of sales outside the United States. At any given time there were 1,500 products in development. Many never made it further. The company's organization chart was bewildering. Mixing faster-growing businesses with low-tech slowpokes made it impossible to evaluate performance, a frequent complaint from the investment community. McNerney has asked researchers to focus the $1 billion they spend annually on their best ideas, ones that have a sales potential of $100 million or more in annual sales. He is also asking 3M employees to think more like their customers—a novel idea in this organization.

Discussion Questions

1. The CEO at 3M has formulated a new strategy of diversification with increased growth and profitability. In what ways will the new strategy affect the organization structure at 3M? How will it affect the vertical dimension of organization structure? Will it be flatter or taller? How will it affect the horizontal dimension of organization structure? Will 3M need to change the basis for its allocation of departments?

2. The CEO is asking the scientists at the research laboratories at 3M to focus on research projects that could result in $100 million or more annual sales. Will this new policy result in a more centralized or decentralized research and development unit at 3M?

3. With the changes in structure that are likely to follow the diversification strategy that calls for higher performance in terms of growth and profitability, what type of coordination mechanisms do you think will best enable 3M management to link activities between diverse departments or divisions. Do you think that the portfolio of 3M products and services is becoming more diverse or less diverse? Justify your answers.

Source: Adapted from M. Tatge, "Prescription for Growth," *Fortune*, February 17, 2003, pp. 64–66.

individual/
collaborative
learning
case 9.1

Fast Food's Yummy Secret

It is one of the biggest companies in one of the biggest industries in America. Its brand names are viewed from highways and city streets throughout the world. From its base in Louisville, Kentucky, it oversees the opening of three new restaurants, one of them in China, every day. It does over $10 billion in annual sales and yet few customers have ever heard of it.

However, if they know KFC (previously Kentucky Fried Chicken), or Pizza Hut, or Taco Bell, then they know Yum! Brands. The parent of those three fast-food chains, it has 34,000 restaurants around the world, 2,000 more than McDonald's. With 1,378 KFC restaurants and 201 Pizza Huts in China in 2005, Yum! owns two of the best-known brand names in the world's most populous market. This is not bad for a company that Pepsi-Cola got rid of in 1997 in a spin-off because it did not fit with Pepsi's beverage and snack foods units.

A spin-off occurs when the corporate parent, Pepsi in this case, decides that the businesses in the proposed spin-off could be better managed as an independent company rather than as a unit within the structure of a larger corporation. It is expected that the spin-off will produce more wealth for shareholders as an independent firm and so the shareholders could potentially benefit from the spin-off. Pepsi shareholders received shares in Yum! Brands after the spin-off was completed.

After the spin-off the morale of the franchise owners of the restaurants at Yum! increased substantially—one of the reasons was that restaurant managers received stock options. The managers treated the restaurant crews better too. Kitchen employees were retained on average twice as long after the spin-off, reducing training and recruiting costs. Under Pepsi, the three restaurants acted more like rivals, with each buying its own advertising through different agencies. After the spin-off the restaurants collaborated by using a single ad agency and gained better deals by leveraging Yum!'s greater size.

Critical Thinking Questions

1. What is the difference between a spin-off and a divestiture?
2. Why do you think that Pepsi management decided it would be more beneficial to spin off the fast-food restaurant businesses from the rest of the company? How does the fast-food restaurant business differ from the business of producing beverages such as Pepsi-Cola or selling snack foods such as corn chips?

Collaborative Learning Exercise

With a partner or a small group try to develop additional ways that collaboration between the three fast-food restaurants, KFC, Pizza Hut, and Taco Bell can be beneficial to Yum! Brands. How can collaboration achieve more customers for the restaurants? Save costs with supplies? Enter new markets? Achieve better relations with employees? Generate higher levels of brand awareness? Offer better service and food to the customers? Why do you think there was less collaboration between the restaurants when they were organized within the Pepsi corporate structure before the spin-off was completed? Be prepared to share your findings with other members of your class.

Source: Adapted from *The Economist*, "Special report: Yum! Brands: Fast Food's Yummy Secret," August 27, 2005, pp. 60–62.

PepsiCo: A World Leader in Food and Beverages

PepsiCo is a world leader in convenient foods and beverages. It has organized a powerful portfolio of branded foods and beverages based on developing some brands internally and through acquiring other brands and managing them effectively as assets. Visit the PepsiCo Web site and click on the "company" and the "history" features in order to answer the following questions:

1. What are the important brands that PepsiCo owns? Which ones did they acquire? Which ones did the company develop internally?
2. How are the beverages organized into groups?
3. How are the convenient foods organized into groups?

internet
exercise 9.1

www.pepsico.com

Do You Follow the Chain of Command?

Would you fit into the traditional hierarchical structure of a corporation? Would an organization that puts a low priority on hierarchical relationships be more your style? This exercise can indicate your ability to manage within an organization that expects allegiance to the chain of command.

Consider the following statements and mark each as "True" or "False" to indicate whether you agree or disagree.

_____ 1. When something bothers me at work, I go straight to top management.

_____ 2. The only way to get what you need is to talk to the owner of the company.

_____ 3. If my supervisor behaved in a way that offended me, I would speak directly to his or her boss.

manager's
checkup 9.1

_____ 4. Although I feel comfortable delegating responsibility to my employees. I follow up to make certain they have accomplished the tasks they were assigned.

_____ 5. If I suspected my boss were engaging in unethical behavior, I would speak to someone in the human resources department in strict confidence.

_____ 6. I will not mention a potential promotion to my star employee until I have received approval to do so from upper management.

_____ 7. If I wait for the required approval from human resources to begin interviewing candidates for the new position that is open, it will be months before I can get anyone on board to help with this project. So I am going ahead with the interviews.

_____ 8. If I suspected my boss were having emotional problems, I would speak to his or her best friend, who also works at the company.

_____ 9. If a customer made a special request I did not have the authority to approve, I would politely explain that I'd get back to him or her as soon as possible.

_____ 10. If a friend of mine wanted to apply for a job at my organization, I'd sneak her past human resources to speak with my boss.

Scoring: "True" responses to statements 4, 5, 6 and 9 indicate an ability to follow the chain of command. "True" responses to statements 1–3, 7–8 and 10 indicate an inability to follow the chain of command.

Source: From _Management of Organizations_, by P. M. Wright and R. A. Noe. Copyright © 1996 The McGraw-Hill Companies, Inc. Reprinted with permission.

video summary

One Smooth Stone

Summary

One Smooth Stone is a business-theater company that businesses contract with to help deliver a particular message for items such as a new product launch, a businesswide initiative, or a special sales event. At One Smooth Stone, everyone in the company works together to meet client needs, which are often changing with regard to time, competition, and other factors. Therefore, there are no divisions or departments which might pigeonhole a client. The company does not "pretend to have a prepackaged solution," but instead works with each client individually to determine the perfect idea and then deliver on it. One Smooth Stone hosts a diverse clientele whose needs vary widely. Clients can arrange to have preproduced videos, impersonators, celebrities, rock stars, or the company's in-house entertainers to help deliver the intended message. One Smooth Stone does contract out to other companies or freelance contractors for particular needs. The company is highly selective about whom they contract with, because while those workers may not be under the same roof as One Smooth Stone, in the clients' eyes they still represent the company. For this reason, everyone, including contractors, are held to a very high standard regarding basic principles and values.

A very important factor in the success of One Smooth Stone and everyone who works there is that the company works together to achieve goals and all be a part of the organizational culture. Everyone in the company is held to the same guiding values, summarized in three words: smart, fast, and kind. If the company works together to deliver on these three principles, delivering smart work, doing each task on time or faster, and being kind to each other and to the client, then the results and financial success will come naturally.

Discussion Questions

1. Mark Ledogar attributes the success of One Smooth Stone to the great relationships the company has with its clients and the great structure within the organization itself. What are the key elements of One Smooth Stone's organizational structure? What classification does this indicate?

2. Ledogar said that the company does not pretend to have a prepackaged solution for each client, but instead relies on the client's needs or specifications to tailor the presentation design to that client's goals. Constant flexibility and adaptation are one of the most important elements of success for the company on a client-specific level. What are some other values that describe not only the culture of the business organization but also the way One Smooth Stone delivers quality to its clients?

3. Clients who use One Smooth Stone to head up the production and presentation of their events need to receive a measurable return on investment (ROI), first from the event, and therefore also from One Smooth Stone. What methods does One Smooth Stone use to deliver that ROI to their clients?

chapter 10

Human Resource Management

Learning Objectives

1. Explain the role of human resource management in achieving a sustainable competitive advantage.

2. Identify the key factors in the environment affecting the management of human resources.

3. Describe the human resource planning process.

4. Explain the key components of staffing and their importance.

5. Describe how training and career development provide employees with tools to succeed once they are hired.

6. Identify the purposes of performance appraisal and how it might be conducted.

7. Describe the key objectives of the compensation system and its components.

Hire a Hero

Every employer wants to hire the right people for the right jobs. One company that's finding a lot of the right people lately is Toyota, whose Hire-a-Hero program helps returning soldiers find jobs. Members of all the U.S. military branches can search a special Toyota Web site for job opportunities at more than 1,400 Toyota and Lexus dealerships anywhere in the country and at the automaker's corporate and manufacturing facilities. Army, Navy, Air Force, Marines, Coast Guard, and National Guard personnel can search job information on the Web site by city and state and then contact the hiring dealers or managers directly. Web sites associated with the military branches are cross-linked to the Toyota and Lexus Web sites as well, making it easy for military men and women to find the hundreds of jobs that are listed there.

Skill, discipline, commitment, and leadership ability are only a few of the advantages Toyota hopes to gain by hiring veterans. Many military personnel return from the service with specialized techni-cal training that's highly sought after in the automotive industry and that translates readily into the civilian workplace. Don Esmond, senior vice president of Toyota Motor Sales, U.S.A., and a Vietnam veteran, says, "Our dealers have found that the men and women of the U.S. military make up one of the best talent pools in America."

Launched a few years ago when Esmond decided to develop a hiring program in California for guardsmen and reservists returning from service in Iraq and Afghanistan, Hire-a-Hero earned Toyota the federal government's 2005 Secretary of Defense Freedom Award. Since its beginning, Hire-a-Hero has expanded to in-clude veterans of all branches and now also includes a $1.25 million scholarship program for children of current and former Marines.

Besides hiring veterans, Toyota also looks out for those who become employees first, soldiers next. While some reservists called to active duty have lost their em-ployment benefits or even their jobs while serving in the military, "that's some-thing that will not happen at Toyota," said a company spokesperson. "The company makes up the difference in their citizen-soldier's pay, maintains their health care benefits and continues paying into their pension plan." Care packages for the wounded, specially equipped vans for the Paralyzed Veterans of America, and an ombudsman to help Guard and Reserve employees' families are other Toyota initiatives for its military employees.

Toyota's largest concentration of veterans—70 of 523 employees—are at work at the North American Parts Center in Ontario, California. In the Torrance, California, facility where the program began, 202 of 5,500 associates are veterans.

"The Hire-a-Hero program is a tool to make members of the military aware of job opportunities available at independently owned Toyota and Lexus dealerships," Toyota's spokesperson says. "The company benefits by hiring a diverse group of individuals who have typically demonstrated commitment and responsibility and have attained skills and leadership abilities while on military duty."

Bill Lester, who races a Toyota Tundra with a Hire-a-Hero logo at NASCAR, echoes the thought. "All of these men and women are heroes to me," he says, "and it's an honor to help inform them about Toyota and Lexus job opportunities when they decide to return to civilian life."

Sources: www.etoyota.com/joblink/main.asp, accessed March 16, 2006; Rudi Williams, "Toyota Helps Guards, Reservists Find Jobs," www.americasupportsyou.mil, February 27, 2006; "Toyota's Hire a Hero Program Debuts at Richmond," www.theautochannel.com, September 8, 2004; "Toyota's 'Hire a Hero' to Aid Veterans' Return to Civilian Workforce," Toyota press release, n.d., www.glassbytes.com, accessed March 16, 2006.

CRITICAL THINKING QUESTIONS

1. *How does the Hire-a-Hero program help Toyota attract and retain skilled employees despite a shortage of technically trained and committed labor?*

2. *Why is effective management of human resources critical to achieving a sustainable competitive advantage?*

We'll revisit these questions in our Concluding Thoughts at the end of the chapter, after you have had a chance to read about the challenges of human resource management.

The Importance of Human Resource Management

The heart and soul of practically every company is its employees. Human resource issues are crucial at every level of the organization. Even entry-level supervisors play a vital role in HR practices. They are part of the selection process, and then train, coach, and evaluate employees.

The Human Resources Department supports managers in carrying out HR responsibilities. The HR department may conduct a pay survey to determine a salary range for a given position, inform managers about changes in employment law, develop a form to evaluate employees, or determine if applicants meet minimum position requirements. But in the end, it is managers who determine a prospective employee's salary subject to budget constraints, ensure that the law is being applied correctly, assess a subordinate's performance, and make final hiring decisions. For this reason, there is an old saying among HR professionals: "Every manager is a personnel manager." Management Is Everyone's Business 10.1 on page 389 shows some of the implications of this for those with managerial responsibilities. And as we have discussed in prior chapters, teams of employees are playing a larger role in most organizations. This is particularly true in HR decisions as outlined in Management Is Everyone's Business 10.2 on page 389.

MANAGEMENT IS EVERYONE'S BUSINESS 10.1

Working as a Manager   Many if not most management problems are a result of poor human resource practices. Indicators that something is wrong with HR practices include inability to recruit top talent, loss of key employees to competitors, costly lawsuits, internal conflicts that sap the organization's time and energy, low innovation by employees afraid of taking risks or with outdated skills, and little concern for quality. By diagnosing the cause of these problems, managers may be able to design and implement appropriate HR programs in collaboration with the HR department or external consultants to help the firm gain or maintain an edge against its competitors. As a manager you should:

- Ensure that human resource practices in your unit are congruent with overall organizational strategies.
- Be attuned to major changes in the law at federal, state, and local levels which might affect human resource practices in your unit. Remember, ignorance of the law is no excuse!
- Try to be consistent in your treatment of employees when it comes to discipline, appraisals, pay decisions, and so on.
- Make sure that personnel decisions concerning selection, training, appraisals, compensation, and so forth are job-related. This is important both legally and in order to maintain employee morale.
- Help employees grow in their jobs by giving them helpful/constructive feedback and challenging assignments.

MANAGEMENT IS EVERYONE'S BUSINESS 10.2

Working as a Team   Employees working in teams often take over HR functions that have traditionally come under the purview of supervisors. For instance, peers may evaluate each other, allocate rewards, decide who should be on the team, interview candidates, and organize their own work flow. The firm needs to provide adequate support so that teams are able to perform these HR functions. Ultimately, the firm is responsible for the team's actions. For instance, the firm is liable for discriminatory practices or sexual harassment within teams even if managers do not condone such practices. Team members should:

- Play a major role in supporting each other through training, information exchange, helpful feedback and such.
- Comply with all pertinent laws pertaining to sexual harassment, various forms of discrimination, violation of overtime laws (for instance, by expecting hourly workers to meet after they have complied with a 40-hour week), and so on.
- Be aware and try to reduce biases that might make certain team members uncomfortable (for instance, cracking jokes about people from other disciplines or backgrounds) and that could even lead to unfair judgments in appraisals, assignments, and incentive allocation.
- Seek assistance from the Human Resource Department if there are issues within the team that might benefit from professional advice and intervention (for instance, members who are perceived to be freeriders).

This chapter describes the human resource skills you will need to help an organization become more productive, comply with legal requirements, and gain or maintain a competitive edge in the marketplace.

Environment of Human Resources

Managers need to constantly monitor the external environment for opportunities and threats affecting human resources and be prepared to react quickly to these changes. Major environmental considerations include workforce diversity, legislation, globalization, competitive forces, and labor unions.

Workforce Diversity

The U.S. workforce is rapidly becoming more diverse. Company leaders can take advantage of diversity in order to succeed. African Americans, Asian Americans, Hispanics, and other minorities make up approximately one-third of the U.S. workforce. At least 11 million undocumented workers are also estimated to be working in the United States. In large urban centers where most business activity takes place and corporate headquarters are usually located, the workforce is often 50 percent to 75 percent nonwhite. Women represent almost half of the workforce, and women with children under six years of age are the fastest growing segment. The workforce is aging, includes a larger proportion of disabled employees, and a growing number are openly homosexual.

In 2006, the proportion of the U.S. population that is foreign born reached almost 11 percent. This historic high is more than double what it was in 1970 and a third higher than it was in 1990.[1] Unlike early immigrants who came from Europe, recent immigrants come from every corner of the world.[2] Clear-cut racial distinctions are also blurring as intermarriage of different groups has steadily increased. The resulting large population of biracial children "view the world from the wondrous, troubling perspective of insider/outsider."[3]

Employees and managers need to work effectively with people who are different from them. The HR department is responsible for facilitating this process. Many HR departments organize diversity training workshops for managers and employees to enable them to better relate to customers and one another. Some HR departments hire a manager of diversity who is responsible for dealing with the day-to-day issues of managing a diverse workforce.

Globalization

In order to grow, many firms enter the global marketplace as exporters, overseas manufacturers, or both. Even those that choose to remain in the domestic market are not insulated from foreign competition. Human resources plays a central role in this process. A firm may restructure the top-management team and decentralize operations to meet the global challenge, use cheaper foreign labor to reduce costs, or promote managers with foreign experience and

table 10.1

Key Legislation Affecting Human Resources

LAW	YEAR	DESCRIPTION
Workers compensation laws	Various	State-by-state laws that establish insurance plans to compensate employees injured on the job
Social Security Act	1935	Payroll tax to fund retirement benefits, disability, and unemployment insurance
Wagner Act	1935	Legitimized labor unions and established the National Labor Relations Board
Fair Labor Standards Act	1938	Established minimum wage and overtime pay
Taft-Hartley Act	1947	Provided protection for employers and limited union power; permitted states to enact right-to-work laws
Landrum-Griffin Act	1959	Protects union members' right to participate in union affairs
Equal Pay Act	1963	Prohibits unequal pay for the same job
Title VII of Civil Rights Act	1964	Prohibits employment decisions based on race, color, religion, sex, or national origin
Executive Order 11246	1965	Same as Title VII, also requires affirmative action
Age Discrimination in Employment Act	1967	Prohibits employment decisions based on age of persons aged 40 or older
Occupational Safety and Health Act	1970	Establishes safety and health standards for organizations to protect employees
Employee Retirement Income Security Act	1974	Regulates the financial stability of employee benefit and pension plans
Vietnam-Era Veterans Readjustment Act	1974	Prohibits federal contracts from discriminating against Vietnam-era veterans
Pregnancy Discrimination Act	1978	Prohibits employers from discriminating against pregnant women
Job Training Partnership Act	1982	Provides block money grants to states to pass on to local governments and private entities that provide on-the-job training
Consolidated Omnibus Budget Reconciliation Act (COBRA)	1985	Requires continued health insurance coverage paid by employee following termination
Immigration Reform and Control Act	1986	Prohibits discrimination based on citizenship status; employers required to document employees' legal work status
Worker Adjustment and Retraining Act (WARN)	1988	Employers required to notify workers of impending layoffs
Drug-Free Workplace Act	1988	Covered employers must implement certain policies to restrict employee drug use
Americans with Disabilities Act (ADA)	1990	Prohibits discrimination based on disability
Civil Rights Act	1991	Amends Title VII; prohibits quotas, allows for monetary punitive damages
Family and Medical Leave Act	1993	Employers required to provide unpaid leave for childbirth, adoption, illness

Source: From *Managing Human Resources* by Gomez-Mejia, et al. Copyright © 2007. Reprinted by permission of Pearson Education, Inc., Upper Saddle River, NJ.

language skills. The HR department can organize international training programs, offer financial incentives for managers to export the company's products, and identify the appropriate mix of foreign (or *expatriate*) and local managers in overseas operations.

Legislation

Over the past 40 years, federal, state, and local governments have passed many laws to protect employees and ensure equal employment opportunity. Company leaders must deal effectively with applicable government regulations. The HR department plays a crucial role by monitoring the legal environment and developing internal systems such as supervisory training and grievance procedures to avoid costly legal battles. Key legislation and executive orders are summarized in Table 10.1 above.

Most work-related laws are designed to prevent **discrimination**, the unfair treatment of employees because of personal characteristics that are not job-related. Title VII of the Civil Rights Act of 1964 is considered the most important legislation on this matter. Title VII prohibits firms from basing "compensation,

discrimination

The unfair treatment of employees because of personal characteristics that are not job-related.

table 10.2

Central Provisions of Title VII, Civil Rights Act of 1964

Section 703. (a) It shall be an unlawful employment practice for an employer— (1) to fail or refuse to hire or to discharge any individual, or otherwise to discriminate against any individual with respect to his compensation, terms, conditions, or privileges of employment, because of such individual's race, color, religion, sex, or national origin, or (2) to limit, segregate, or classify his employees or applicants for employment in any way which would deprive or tend to deprive any individual of employment opportunities or otherwise adversely affect his status as an employee, because of such individual's race, color, religion, sex, or national origin.

Source: Title VII, Civil Rights Act of 1964.

---

protected class

The legal definition of specified groups of people who suffered widespread discrimination in the past and who are given special protection by the judicial system.

affirmative action

A federal government-mandated program that requires corporations to provide opportunities to women and members of minority groups who traditionally had been excluded from good jobs; it aims to accomplish the goal of fair employment by urging employers to make a conscious effort to hire members of protected classes.

disparate treatment

A form of discrimination that occurs when an employer treats an employee differently because of his or her protected class status.

adverse impact

A form of discrimination, also called disparate impact, that occurs when one standard that is applied to all applicants or employees negatively affects a protected class.

terms, conditions, or privileges of employment" on a person's race, color, religion, sex, or national origin. The central provisions of Title VII appear in Table 10.2 above.

Interpretations of the Civil Rights Act led to a legal definition of a **protected class** of groups of people who suffered widespread discrimination in the past and who are granted special protection by the judicial system. These include African Americans, Asian Americans, Hispanic Americans, Native Americans, and women. **Affirmative action** aims to accomplish the goal of fair employment by urging employers to make a conscious effort to hire members from protected classes. In affirmative action programs, employment decisions are made at least in part on the basis of demographic characteristics such as race, sex, or age. These programs are controversial because some people believe that only "blind" hiring practices are fair and that the programs may result in hiring quotas that hurt people who are not members of protected groups. This, in effect, penalizes them for the errors of their parents and grandparents. A series of Supreme Court decisions indicate that employment decisions cannot be made solely on the basis of protected class status; people should be "essentially equally qualified" on job-relevant factors before protected class status is permitted to play a role. The Supreme Court in a 2003 ruling reaffirmed the notion that protected class status may be considered in retention decisions but prohibited the use of such explicit criteria as quotas or added points in an exam based on a person's race, ethnic status, or gender.

Two forms of discrimination are considered illegal and may result in substantial fines and penalties for employers and/or in a court-imposed affirmative action plan. The first form of discrimination, **disparate treatment,** occurs when an employer treats an employee differently because of his or her protected class status. The second form of discrimination, **adverse impact** (also called *disparate impact*), occurs when the same standard is applied to all applicants or employees but that standard affects a protected class more negatively. For instance, a minimum height requirement for police tends to automatically disqualify more women than men. If a protected class suffers from adverse impact, then the firm may be required to demonstrate that the standards used were job-related and that alternative selection methods were too costly or unreliable.

The Equal Employment Opportunity Commission (EEOC) was created by the Civil Rights Act of 1964 to initiate investigations in response to discrimination complaints. An individual bringing a complaint to court must prove that there is *prima facie* ("on its face") *evidence* of discrimination. In the case of disparate treatment, a plaintiff can establish prima facie discrimination by showing that he or she was at least as qualified for the job as the person who was hired. In the case of an adverse impact lawsuit, the EEOC has established the *four-fifths rule* for prima facie cases. This means that the hiring rate of a protected class should be at least four-fifths of the hiring rate of the majority group. For example, a firm may hire 50 percent of all its white male job applicants but only 25 percent of all African-American male job applicants. Using the four-fifths rule, there is prima facie evidence of discrimination because four-fifths of 50 percent is 40 percent, which exceeds the 25 percent hiring rate for African-American men.

Once a plaintiff has established a prima facie case, the accused organization must demonstrate that illegal discrimination did not occur. This can be difficult to prove. There are three basic defenses that an employer can use:

1. **Job relatedness** is the most compelling defense. Here the firm shows that decisions were made for job-related reasons. The HR department can help demonstrate job relatedness by preparing written documentation to support and explain the decision.

2. The organization may claim a **bona fide occupational qualification (BFOQ),** a personal characteristic that must be present to do the job. An example is the need for a female actor for a woman's part in a movie. This option is severely restricted as a justification to discriminate.

3. The final basis to justify disparate impact is **seniority.** In companies with a well-established seniority system, more senior workers may receive priority, even if this has an adverse impact on protected class members.

As illustrated in Table 10.1, other federal legislation influences HR decisions. For instance, the **Drug-Free Workplace Act** requires employers to implement policies that restrict drug use, and the **Family and Medical Leave Act** requires employers to provide unpaid leave for childbirth, adoption, and illness. In most large firms, the HR department is responsible for keeping track of changes in legislation that affects human resources and for developing steps to comply with various laws. This role is crucial because the law may be enforced differently for each firm. For example, many firms require drug testing of all employees, but some require testing only at the time of hiring or at random times. Organizations must also be flexible to respond to changing circumstances in enforcing the law. For example, the Air Force used to randomly test 65 percent of its cadets for drug use. The Air Force has recently decided to increase that percentage and do more testing on weekends, because some of the new recreational drugs, such as Ecstasy, pass through the body quickly.[4]

Sexual harassment, a violation of the Civil Rights Act, has become a highly visible issue. There are two forms of sexual harassment. The first involves sexually suggestive remarks, unwanted touching, or any other physical or verbal act that creates what is called a "hostile environment," for either gender. The second type is called *quid pro quo* harassment, in which sexual favors are sought and/or granted in exchange for company rewards, such as pay raises, promotions, or more choice job assignments. To avoid liability, a company must develop an explicit policy against sexual harassment and a system to investigate allegations. Managers must be made aware that this type of behavior will not be tolerated and may result in severe penalties, including termination. They must also be educated about sexual harassment policies, for instance, in special workshops.

job relatedness

A defense against discrimination claims in which the firm must show that the decision was made for job-related reasons.

bona fide occupational qualification (BFOQ)

A defense against discrimination in which a firm must show that a personal characteristic must be present to do the job.

seniority

A defense against discrimination in which companies with a well-established seniority system can give more senior workers priority, even if this has an adverse impact on protected class members.

Drug-Free Workplace Act

Federal legislation that requires employers to implement policies that restrict drug use.

Family and Medical Leave Act

Federal legislation that requires employers to provide unpaid leave for childbirth, adoption, and illness.

sexual harassment

A form of discrimination that is broadly interpreted to include sexually suggestive remarks, unwanted touching, any physical or verbal act that indicates sexual advances or requests sexual favors, a promise of rewards or hidden threats by a supervisor to induce emotional attachment by a subordinate, and a "hostile environment" based on sex.

NINE DON'TS OF INTERVIEWING

1. Don't ask applicants if they have children, plan to have children, or have child care arrangements made.
2. Don't ask an applicant's age.
3. Don't ask whether the applicant has a physical or mental disability that would interfere with the job. (Employers can explore the subject of disabilities only after making a job offer that is conditional on the applicant's satisfactory completion of a required physical, medical, or job-skills test.)
4. Don't ask for identifying characteristics, such as height and weight.
5. Don't ask marital status, including asking a female candidate her maiden name.
6. Don't ask applicants about their citizenship.
7. Don't ask applicants about their arrest records (employers may ask whether a candidate has ever been convicted of a crime).
8. Don't ask applicants if they smoke (employers can ask whether applicants are aware of legislative restrictions against smoking and whether they are willing to comply with them).
9. Don't ask applicants if they are HIV-positive or have AIDS.

Source: From *Managing Human Resources* by Gomez-Mejia, et al. Copyright © 2007. Reprinted by permission of Pearson Education, Inc., Upper Saddle River, NJ.

---

employment at will

A very old legal doctrine stating that unless there is an employment contract (such as a union contract or an implied contract), both employer and employee are free to end the employment relationship whenever and for whatever reasons they choose.

Many state and local governments have also passed laws that restrict organizational discretion in the use of human resources. An important law is a limitation on **employment at will,** a longstanding legal doctrine stating that unless there is an employment contract (such as a union contract or an implied contract), both employer and employee are free to end the employment relationship whenever and for whatever reasons they choose. Most states have written employment laws that allow terminated employees to sue if they can show that they have been wrongfully discharged. One common ground is lack of good faith and fair dealing, such as firing a worker shortly before he or she becomes eligible for a retirement plan.

Manager's Notebook 10.1 above lists some interview questions that, if asked, could be interpreted as violating employment law.

Unions

In 1945, about 35 percent of the labor force belonged to unions. Since then, union membership has been declining steadily, reaching a low of approximately 13 percent in 2006.[5] If the present trend continues, this percentage will drop to approximately 8 percent by 2012. Strong employer challenges to unions, plant closures, international competition, and a shrinking manufacturing sector have all contributed to the decline in union membership. Unions are still influential in some sectors, such as automobile manufacturing; even there, however, unions have been more willing to work closely with management in such areas as quality control, cross-training, and innovative compensation systems to meet global challenges.

U.S. employees generally seek representation from a union for one or more of the following reasons:

video: THE ENTREPRENEURIAL MANAGER

The Hiring Game

Summary

If you've walked into a business or store recently and thought the workers were a little older than usual, you're right. At Pitney Bowes, over 25 percent of workers are above age 50. In fact, the AARP has partnered with firms like Pitney Bowes, Home Depot, MetLife, and Johns Hopkins Medical Center to meet established standards for recruitment, hiring, and retention of senior workers. Today, working past age 65 is a necessity for many people. Rising health costs and the rising cost of living means that pensions are not enough for most workers, and they must seek at least part-time work elsewhere before retiring for good. The wages they can earn help supplement the pensions they are already collecting.

The workers themselves are a great deal for many companies. They tend to cost less than their younger counterparts because, if they are entering the workforce, or just entering a new field, they only require new training in order to be capable of doing a particular new job. On the other hand, younger workers may require training, but also require health benefits to include health insurance as well as pensions or fringe costs that older workers simply do not need. Older workers have Medicare and Social Security to draw on, and that cuts costs for firms, who can thus benefit from older workers.

People are living longer, too, and many say that retirement just isn't an option, or they are not ready for it yet, even if it were a financial option at age 55 or 65. Work can be a social event as much as a productive act, and can help those who are widowed later in life.

In order to stay on the AARP list, companies must demonstrate a real dedication to helping retain the older workers they recruit in the first place. Many say, however, that it is just as beneficial to the companies as it is to the workers. In 2010, one in three workers is anticipated to be over age 50. There will be a shorter supply of young workers to take jobs, and employers will increasingly turn to older workers to help sustain production.

Discussion Questions

1. How does an aging population affect the management of workforce diversity? Give examples from the video case to support your explanation.
2. How will aging worker demographics continue to affect labor supply? How can older workers be a good alternative to hiring younger workers for some companies?
3. How do firms get on the AARP list of top employers for older workers? Discuss the staffing process in your response.

- Dissatisfaction with certain aspects of their job (such as poor working conditions or pay that is perceived to be low).

- A belief that as individuals they lack influence with management to make needed changes, and that by working together through concerted action they can put greater pressure on management to make concessions.

- A belief that the union can equalize some of the power between workers and management, so that the company cannot act unilaterally.

- Job insecurity and the conviction that unions can protect workers from arbitrary layoffs by establishing a set of rules that management will abide by. For instance, a unionized firm may stipulate that layoffs will be done in order of seniority.

- The need to establish formal grievance procedures, administered by both the union and management, whereby individual workers can appeal managerial decisions that they believe are unfair.

The agreement between the union and management is written in a document called the **labor contract.** In addition to specifying pay schedules, fringe benefits, cost of living adjustments and the like, the labor contract gives employees specific rights. If an employee believes his or her rights have been violated under the contract, the individual can file a grievance against the company. For instance, an employee who believes that he or she was overlooked for promotion may try to remedy this perceived unfairness by filing a grievance, hoping to be reconsidered for the promotion.

Although union membership has been declining around the country, the nearly 100 workers in a tiny chain of stores have formed a union. Employees of Footco, which runs 10 sneaker stores, relied on the help of local churches and other community groups, as well as New York State Attorney General Eliot Spitzer, to get the chain to agree to accept the Retail, Wholesale and Department Store Union after a yearlong struggle. "Now I will make the same money working 45 hours a week that I used to make working 55, 60 hours," said one employee, an immigrant from Mexico. Said the company's owner, Young B. Cho, "It's the right thing to do. Everybody is happier. The workers are happier."

Labor unions were largely unprotected by law in the United States until 1935. Crafted by Congress during the Great Depression, the Wagner Act (1935), also known in union circles as the "Magna Carta of Labor," facilitated the establishment and expansion of unions. The Wagner Act created the National Labor Relations Board (NLRB), which is responsible for supervising union elections through secret ballots by workers. The NLRB also determines whether or not a union or management group has engaged in unfair labor practices. For example, firing union sympathizers is an unfair practice, as is a union's calling for a strike while a labor contract is still in effect. The Wagner Act tried to equalize the power of unions and management. After World War II, however, there was a widespread perception that unions had become too powerful, and in some cases corrupt.

The Taft-Hartley Act (1947) specified a set of unfair labor practices by unions along with the remedies that the National Labor Relations Board may take if the union is found guilty of engaging in those practices. Unfair union practices include causing an employer to pay for services that are not performed (a practice often called *featherbedding*) or refusing to bargain in good faith for a new contract.

Twelve years later, The Landrum-Griffin Act (1959) allowed the federal government, through the Department of Labor, to regulate some union activities. Landrum-Griffin was enacted because a few unions experienced problems with corrupt leadership and had misused union funds. Among other things, Landrum-Griffin requires each union to report its financial activities and the financial interests of its leaders to the Department of Labor.

Labor relations tend to be country specific and reflect the sociocultural and historical milieu of each nation. For instance, in the United States labor relations are characterized by:

labor contract

A written agreement negotiated between union and management.

business unionism

Unions that focus on "bread and butter" issues such as wages, benefits, and job security.

job-based unionism

Unions that are organized by type of job.

collective bargaining

Negotiations between union and management with little, if any, government involvement.

- **Business unionism.** Unlike most other countries where unions are ideological and often tend to pursue political goals, U.S. unions focus on "bread and butter" issues such as wages, benefits, and job security.

- **Job-based unionism.** In contrast to unions in many other countries, which tend to be organized according to political persuasion, U.S. unions tend to be organized by the type of job. Truck drivers are often members of the Teamsters Union and many public school teachers are members of the National Education Association. This is in line with the American notion that interest groups represent the desires of particular constituencies.

- **Collective bargaining.** Under the U.S. collective bargaining system the government takes a neutral or nonintervention role, allowing the players to make the rules that govern their particular workplace. In most other countries, the government is closely involved in labor-management relations. For instance, for almost 70 years the Partido Revolucionario Institucional (PRI) governed Mexico, and unions were an integral part of the government machinery.

- **Voluntary contracts.** Because both parties enter into the labor contract voluntarily, in the United States one party can use the legal system to enforce the terms of the contract if the other party does not fulfill its responsibilities. In many other countries, such as Italy and Sweden, working conditions and employee benefits are codified into labor laws. These laws are enforced by the central government and labor unions often put direct pressure on the government to modify legislation affecting workers. General strikes to force the government's hand are common around the world, but unheard of in the United States. Recently, unions in France called for a general strike to force the government to pass a 35-hour working week. Likewise, unions in Spain recently called for a general strike to force the government to pass legislation that would make it costly for firms to lay off workers.

- **Adversarial relations.** U.S. labor laws view management and labor as natural adversaries who want to have a larger share of the firm's profits and who must reach a compromise through collective bargaining. When asked about the objectives of the labor movement, Samuel Gompers (considered the founder of the AFL-CIO) responded with one word: More! For this reason, rules have been put in place so that the pie can be divided peacefully through orderly negotiations. In some other countries, the labor relations system stresses cooperation rather than competition between management and labor. For instance, the German system uses work councils and codetermination to involve workers in decisions at all levels of the organization. Even a company's board of directors generally will include union members. This would be seen as a conflict of interest in the United States. In Japan, enterprise unions work closely with companies for mutual benefits and the union generally has complete access to the company's financial records.

LOC-In

② Learning Objective Check-In

Hillary, an Asian American, comes from a group of people who suffered widespread discrimination in the past. She has suffered some discrimination from her previous employer, who treated her differently because of her ethnicity. For example, he never assigned her to work with clients, and gave her most of the "backroom" assignments. Hillary is a very capable worker, who has benefited from a government-mandated program that required her new employer to give a conscious effort in hiring Asian Americans, among others.

1. *Hillary is a member of a _____ in the United States.*
   a. *protective class*
   b. *protected class*
   c. *control group*
   d. *direct hire program*
2. *Hillary's previous employer was practicing _____.*
   a. *disparate treatment*
   b. *adverse impact*
   c. *disparate impact*
   d. *legal discrimination*
3. *Hillary is a beneficiary of _____.*
   a. *protective class status*
   b. *adverse impact*
   c. *affirmative action*
   d. *discrimination in the workplace*

The Human Resource Management Process

Figure 10.1 on page 398 introduces the key components of the human resource management process. The input that drives the entire process is **strategic HR planning (SHRP),** which is the development of a vision about where the company wants to be and how it can utilize human resources to get there. By forcing managers to think ahead, SHRP can help a firm identify the difference between

Genentech: Supporting Innovation with HR Practices

Genentech—a biotech company with over 8,000 employees located in San Francisco—was recently chosen (2006) as "The Best Place to Work" by *Fortune* magazine. People at Genentech are driven by a passion to find new drugs for millions of patients who need them, particularly cancer patients. Genentech makes it clear that improving the lives of its customers—those with serious illness—is its primary goal. At Genentech, using market data or return-on-investments analysis to drive the science is strictly taboo. "At the end of the day, we want to make drugs that really matter," says CEO Art Levinson. "That's the transcendent issue." Not that this company considers itself a philanthropy. By decade's end, it aims to be the leading U.S. oncology company in terms of sales and a leader in both immunology and tissue-growth disorders, setting ambitious new product goals in each of those categories.

Human resource strategies at Genentech are designed to accomplish the firm's mission: serving the sick through revolutionary drug discoveries. These HR strategies are summarized below:

- Genentech has created a university-style working environment that facilitates interaction, and this in turn fosters creativity. With its storybook view of San Francisco Bay, the place feels more like a college campus than a pillar of the Fortune 500. Signs point to the North Campus, down by the water, and the South Campus, up on the hill. Employees don't get assignments, they get "appointments." They traverse the grounds by shuttle bus and bicycles provided by the company. Every Friday night there's at least one "ho-ho"—Genentechese for kegger—a tradition that began in the 70s when the workforce was

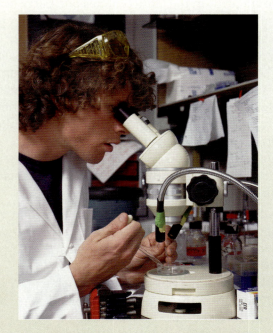

Genentech scientists enjoy the collaborative, nonhierarchical work atmosphere. The San Francisco biotech lab was recently chosen as *Fortune* magazine's #1 best place to work in the United States. Ninety-five percent of employees are company shareholders, and no one wears a tie.

mostly a handful of rowdy postdocs barely out of grad school. At Genentech, every milestone calls for a party and a commemorative T-Shirt—and on very big occasions, very big celebrity bands. A year and a half ago, after an unusual run of FDA approvals, the parking lot in front of

FIGURE 10.1

The Human Resource Management Process

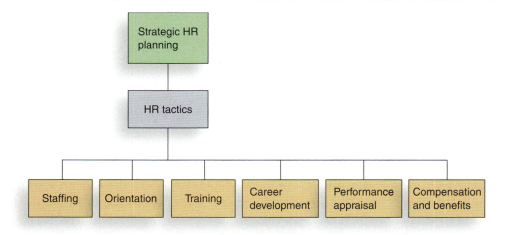

Building 9 became the site of a rock concert featuring Elton John, Mary J. Blige, and Matchbox 20.

- Genentech minimizes power differentials and symbols of authority that create barriers among employees. For instance, at Genentech nobody dresses up, except on Halloween. This even includes CEO Levinson, often seen in tennis shoes and a black "CLONE or DIE" T-shirt. There are no fancy titles, all offices look alike and regular employees as well as top executives use low-end, metal office furniture.
- Genentech gives employees substantial freedom to pursue their own interests in order to foster creativity and reinforce a "can do" mentality. For example, it tells scientists and engineers to spend fully 20 percent of each work week pursuing pet projects.
- Genentech encourages employees to take risks. As it often happens, what look like promising projects have to be canceled because they don't work or other priorities take their place. In those cases, not only are the researchers not fired; they usually have a say in their next assignments.
- Genentech awards sabbaticals to employees to avoid burnout.
- Genentech has been extremely generous in sharing its success with employees. Ninety-five percent of workers are shareholders, and they have benefited handsomely from the soaring stock.
- Genentech invests a lot of time, effort, and money in its orientation program to acculturate the rookies. New-hire orientation includes patient lectures, history

lessons by old-timers, in-depth sessions on the company's goals, its science—and the fact that the place works "because of all the thousands of little decisions that are made very day," says HR Vice President Denise Smith-Hams.

- Genentech polls its workers weekly to ferret out complaints and monitor any problem areas that might need attention before these grow worse.
- Lastly, Genentech pours tremendous energy into hiring people with the kind of passion it feels it needs to accomplish its strategic goals. In fact, it can take five or six visits and 20 interviews to snag a job. The process is meant partly to screen out the free agents—people preoccupied with salary, title, and personal advancement. If candidates ask too many such questions, "Boom, wrong profile," says CEO Levinson. The gauntlet is also designed to let job candidates know exactly what they're getting themselves into. "We're extremely nonhierarchical," Levinson tells new hires. "We're not wearing ties. People don't call us doctor. We don't have special dining rooms." (They aren't even assigned parking spaces, and it's hell in the morning to find a spot.) Executive job seekers from Big Pharma, especially, find that a jolt, he says. "A lot of them say, 'But I like being different! I like being special!' Well, you're not going to be special here. If that's important to you, that's fine. But you won't be happy here."

Source: Adapted from B. Morris, "No. 1 Genentech". *Fortune*, January 23, 2006, pp. 80–86.

"where we are today" and "where we want to be," and to implement human resource programs (often referred to as **HR tactics**) to achieve its vision.

The ultimate objective of SHRP is creating a *sustained competitive advantage*. A common view held by HR managers is based on the **contingency theory** notion that no HR strategy is "good" or "bad" in and of itself but rather depends on the situation or context in which it is used. According to this approach, the consistency or compatibility between HR strategies and other important aspects of the organization, which is known as *fit*, leads to better performance. The lack of a fit creates inconsistencies that reduce performance. Management Close-Up 10.1 on page 398 shows how HR strategies fit with the overall business strategy of Genentech.

Human Resource Planning

Human resource planning (HRP) is the process organizational leaders follow to ensure that the company has the right number and the right kinds of people to meet output or service goals. Figure 10.2 on page 400 summarizes the HRP process.

HR tactics

The implementation of human resource programs to achieve the firm's vision.

contingency theory

The management theory that there is no "one best way" to manage and organize an organization because situational characteristics, called contingencies, differ; also, the view that no HR strategy is "good" or "bad" in and of itself but rather depends on the situation or context in which it is used.

FIGURE 10.2

Human Resource Planning

Source: From *Managing Human Resources* by Gomez-Mejia, et al. Copyright © 2007. Reprinted by permission of Pearson Education, Inc., Upper Saddle River, NJ.

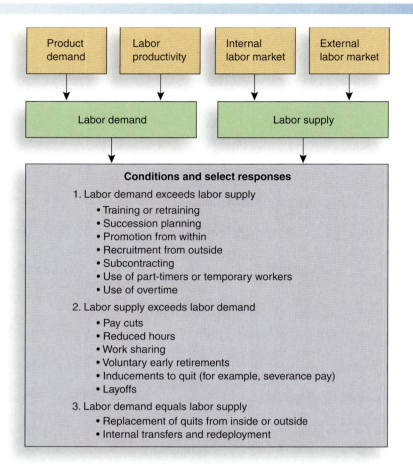

Stages of the Strategic HRM Planning Process

---

labor demand

The forecast of how many and what type of workers the organization will need in the future.

labor supply

The availability of workers with the required skills to meet the firm's labor demand.

skills inventory

A human resource inventory that keeps track of the firm's internal supply of talent by listing employees' education, training, experience, and language abilities; the firm can use this information to identify those eligible for promotion or transfer before trying to fill the position from the external market.

The first step is forecasting **labor demand,** or how many and what type of workers the organization will need in the future. Labor demand is likely to increase as the demand for the company's products increases and to decrease as productivity increases, since fewer labor hours will be needed to produce the same level of output. However, the demand for various types of workers (for example, factory versus clerical) may not increase or decrease at the same rate, so this forecast must be performed for various employee groups.

The second part of the HRP process entails estimating the **labor supply,** or the availability of workers with the required skills to meet the firm's labor demand. The labor supply may come from the internal labor market inside the firm or from the external labor market outside the firm. Many firms keep track of the internal supply of talent by generating a human resource inventory called a **skills inventory.** Employees are asked to list their education, training, experience, and language abilities. This information is used to identify those eligible for promotion or transfer before trying to fill the position from the external market. Such a process can reduce recruitment costs and increase employee commitment to the firm.

As shown in Figure 10.2, the HR planning process may lead to very different organizational responses. If labor demand exceeds supply, the firm may invest in training workers, promoting from within, and actively recruiting employees to meet projected needs. On the other hand, if there is an excess labor supply, the HR department may plan cutbacks in the workforce through work sharing, voluntary early retirements, and layoffs.

Through careful planning some firms develop creative means to avoid or minimize layoffs, which are costly in terms of employee morale and loss of human capital. For example, these firms have been able to minimize layoffs in past recessions by using alternative ways to save money:

- Hewlett-Packard delayed employee raises for several months and awarded no bonuses for its top executives.

- First Union asked employees to limit the number of color copies they make and restricted first-class travel to red-eye flights.

- Charles Schwab cut salaries for senior executives and gave smaller bonuses to the rank and file. The brokerage firm also rationed travel and entertainment dollars and reviewed advertising contracts.

- Xerox grounded corporate jets and cut back on catered food and free coffee to prevent more layoffs.[6]

LOC-In

3 **Learning Objective Check-In**

Morristown Motors usually recruits from the four regional trade schools to fill its entry-level certified mechanic positions. In recent years, the company has been experiencing higher levels of service orders from its clients and has even expanded its client base by about 15 percent every two years. The firm is considering hiring more entry-level mechanics in future years than it has in the past. Fortunately for the firm, this profession has grown popular in the region, and the schools are turning out more qualified applicants each year.

1. *Because the firm is expanding, Morristown's hiring manager can forecast an increase in the firm's _____.*
   a. *cost of new hires*
   b. *labor demand*
   c. *labor supply*
   d. *contingency theory*

2. *Because the region's schools are turning out more qualified applicants each year, Morristown's hiring manager can forecast an increase in the firm's _____.*
   a. *cost of new hires*
   b. *labor demand*
   c. *labor supply*
   d. *cost of recruiting workers*

Staffing Process

Human resource planning guides the staffing process, or the hiring of employees to meet the firm's labor needs. The staffing process has three components: recruitment, selection, and socialization, or orientation.

RECRUITMENT   Generating a pool of qualified candidates for a particular job is the **recruitment** component of staffing. It requires a **job specification,** which identifies the qualifications necessary for effective job performance. Most firms conduct a **job analysis** in which they systematically gather and organize information about the tasks, duties, and responsibilities of various jobs. While there are many job analysis techniques, virtually all of them lead to a **job description,** which is a formal document that identifies, defines, and describes the duties, responsibilities, and working conditions associated with a job. A properly conducted job analysis ensures that the hiring process is job-related in case of a legal challenge.

Once the qualifications for effective job performance have been identified, the HR department looks for recruitment sources that are most likely to produce the best candidates. Most searches start with current employees, utilizing skill inventories if available. The second major source of recruits is referrals from current employees. Both sources give HR more information about applicants than would going outside. One disadvantage is that the firm may not attract a diverse pool of applicants, creating potential equal employment opportunity (EEO) problems. Other sources of recruits include former employees, advertisements, employment agencies, colleges, and customers. Recruitment over the Internet is becoming more prevalent and occurs at broad job search engines such as Monster.com, which includes all types of positions. Specialized job search engines

recruitment

The process of generating a pool of qualified candidates for a particular job.

job specification

The knowledge, skills, and abilities needed to successfully perform the job.

job analysis

The systematic gathering and organizing of information about the tasks, duties, and responsibilities of various jobs.

job description

A formal document that identifies, defines, and describes the duties, responsibilities, and working conditions.

such as Dice.com target information technology professionals; Dice.com is advertised as "a high-traffic job board with over 350,000 IT professionals searching every week."[7]

One way to increase recruitment effectiveness is a *realistic* **job preview** in which potential applicants are provided with honest information about the positive and negative aspects of the job. It can reduce selection expenses because individuals can "self-select" into or out of positions based on realistic job information.

An emergent trend to attract potential recruits without incurring additional costs (such as higher salaries) is to offer prospective candidates greater work flexibility than offered by other employers. This approach is being used by Best Buy, apparently with great success (see Management Close-Up 10.2, "Reworking Work" on page 403).

SELECTION   An effective recruitment effort should create a pool of qualified applicants. As the word implies, **selection** is the screening process used to decide which individuals to hire. The ultimate objective is to hire people who will perform well based on the criteria the firm uses to evaluate employees. No selection process is foolproof. Some hires will turn out to be mistakes and other candidates who would have made good employees may be rejected. An organization with a high proportion of individuals who fall into these categories, as shown in Figure 10.3 on page 404, is likely to see much lower job performance on average than an organization that consistently makes the right hiring decisions.

Valid and reliable selection techniques help reduce the proportion of errors and increase the proportion of correct hiring decisions. **Validity** is how well a technique used to assess candidates is related to performance in the job. A technique that is not job-related is useless and, as noted earlier, is also illegal if it results in discrimination. In fact, documenting validity is essential to a legal defense of job discrimination.

Validity can be demonstrated in two ways. **Content validity** means that the selection process represents the actual activities or knowledge required to successfully perform the job. Many firms require applicants to perform tasks similar to those they will carry out on the job if hired. For instance, if a minimum requirement for a job is possession of a valid pilot's license, a flight simulator may be used to select the best pilot. **Empirical validity** means that there is statistical evidence that the selection method distinguishes between higher and lower performing employees. For instance, a selection method that consistently predicts which individuals fall into boxes 1 and 4 in Figure 10.3 would have high empirical validity. Lack of empirical validity means that the selection method cannot predict who is going to be a better or worse performer.

Reliability   It is important to measure the consistency or **reliability** of results of the selection method. For instance, if multiple interviewers reach entirely different conclusions about each job applicant, the method is not reliable. Or if test scores for the same applicant vary dramatically from one day to the next, the test is not reliable. In other words, reliability is an indicator of how much random error there is in the measure being used. Lack of reliability is equivalent to a speed indicator on a car that is 10 to 30 miles per hour above or below the actual speed. Because the reading is unreliable, the position of the speed needle is not helpful in assessing how fast the car is traveling.

---

job preview

Information about the positive and negative aspects of the job that is provided to potential applicants.

selection

The screening process used to decide which job applicant to hire.

validity

The measurement of how well a technique used to assess candidates is related to performance in the job.

content validity

The measurement that the selection process represents the actual activities or knowledge required to successfully perform the job.

empirical validity

Statistical evidence that the selection method distinguishes between higher and lower performing employees.

reliability

The consistency of results from the selection method.

Online **LearningCenter**
www.mhhe.com/gomez3e

Reliability and Validity

Reworking Work

Jennifer Janssen is having one of those days. She works in the finance department of Best Buy, and one of the company's electronics suppliers is furious because he claims he has not been paid. "He told me, 'I'm not going to ship any more product to your company unless I get this issue resolved,'" she says. She has to fix the problem by the end of the day, but the 35-year-old mother of 5-year-old twins also has to pick up her children from day care. What happens next? Perhaps she makes a sheepish call to her husband asking if he could skip out early while she puts out the fire at work. Maybe she scrambles madly to find someone who can clean up the mess in time for her to sneak out at four. Or perhaps, after another late night, she spends the car ride home wondering whether she should just quit.

Instead of "swarming around all over the place, trying to find a body" who can cover for her, Janssen is calm. As she figures out what happened to her vendor's check, she knows that she will walk out of the office at four—without guilt, without looking over her shoulder—because even if a solution isn't found by then, she can keep working on it from her laptop at home. No one whispers that she's leaving. In fact, no one notices. That's because Janssen is part of an ambitious new experiment to solve the problems of overwork and work–family balance. Like many other U.S. companies, Best Buy has struggled to meet the demands of its business—how to do things better, faster, and cheaper than its competitors—with an increasingly stressed-out workforce.

The freedom, employees say, is changing their lives. They don't know if they work fewer hours—they've stopped counting—but they are more productive. That's welcome news for a company that hopes its employees will give it a competitive edge. And employees have adapted well to the new system.

Let's take the case of Traci Tobias. When Tobias needs to find people, she checks the whiteboards hanging outside their cubes, where she and her co-workers write down where they are on any given day: "In the office today," "Out of the office this afternoon, available by e-mail." The impromptu meetings are gone, but business done by cell phone is way up. Because she no longer assumes that everyone is around, Tobias makes more of an effort to catch up with her colleagues by phone or e-mail instead of just dropping by someone's office. "You can still have those conversations," she says, just

The flexible nature of Jennifer Janssen's job in the finance department of Best Buy demonstrates the company's commitment to an experiment in turning around its former high-stress culture. Flexible hours, working from home, increased autonomy, and goals that focus on accomplishments rather than time spent at the desk are transforming the lives of the electronics retailer's employees.

not always in person. She noticed that e-mails have gotten more concise and meaningful, with much less "FYI." And as everyone started to rethink their priorities, guess what fell to the bottom of the list? "We spend a lot less time in meetings," Tobias says. "They used to have a two-hour weekly staff meeting that often devolved into chit-chat. Now, if they don't need to meet, they don't."

Best Buy uses its new work flexibility approach as a major selling point to convince people to apply for jobs and get those who pass the selection screening to sign up.

Source: Adapted from J. Thottam, "Reworking Work," *Time*, July 5, 2005, pp. 50–55.

FIGURE 10.3

Performance Consequences of
Selection Decision

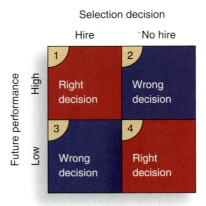

Selection decision

Selection Tools as Predictors of Job Performance   An organization may use a variety of selection tools to screen out applicants and attempt to increase the proportion of good performers, as shown in Manager's Notebook 10.2 on page 405. The quality of different selection tools as predictors of performance is shown in Table 10.3 on page 406.

If properly conducted, interviews can provide useful information and help select the best candidates. Skills for Managing 10.1 on page 406 provides an exercise to sharpen your interviewing skills by applying a set of good interviewing practices.

Interviews are the most often used screening tool, but they, too, have a variety of problems, which are shown in Table 10.4 on page 407.

To avoid some of these shortcomings, many organizations are turning to a particular type of interviewing technique known as the *situational* or *behavioral interview*. This type of interview requires that the applicant role-play a particular situation—for instance, calming down an irate customer. Behavioral interviews seem to do a much better job of predicting future performance than other selection methods. On the other hand, when professionally conducted with the help of a consultant, these interviews can be rather expensive, costing between $245 and $500 per interview. Yet, the investment may be worthwhile for many critical positions. Skills for Managing 10.2 on page 407 asks you to practice developing and conducting this type of interview.

Another recent trend in personnel selection in the United States is allowing the applicant to display his or her skills by performing certain jobs, often for little or no pay. The performance is used as the basis for hiring instead of written paper-and-pencil exams or other types of tests. This selection practice is routine in some countries. For instance, German firms have long relied on apprenticeships (roughly similar to what are called "internships" in the United States) to make hiring decisions; the firm keeps only those who performed well during the trial period.

LOC-In

4 Learning Objective Check-In

Sydney Corp.'s engineering department conducts analysis in which they systematically gather and organize information about the tasks and responsibilities of each of its engineering positions. This is meant to help develop a formal document that identifies and defines these duties and responsibilities, as well as any working conditions associated with each job. These factors help Sydney Corp. in generating a pool of qualified candidates for each of these jobs.

1. *In the example, the _____ systematically gathers and organizes information about the tasks and responsibilities of each position.*
   a. *HR strategy*
   b. *job specification*
   c. *job description*
   d. *job analysis*
2. *The _____ is the formal document discussed in this example.*
   a. *contingency plan*
   b. *job specification*
   c. *job analysis*
   d. *job description*
3. *_____ involves generating a pool of qualified applicants for a particular job.*
   a. *Contingency planning*
   b. *Recruitment*
   c. *Job analysis*
   d. *Job placement*

- *Application forms* are used almost universally. They provide information that shows whether the candidate meets minimum qualification requirements as identified in the job analysis. Firms can also use information from application forms to determine whether the applicant would qualify for other openings when they occur. A *biodata form* asks a series of specific questions about the candidate's background, experiences, and preferences. Biodata have been found to have moderate validity in predicting job performance.

- *Letters of recommendation* typically are very positive—most people are reluctant to put negative information in writing. Their value thus is limited as a predictor of future performance, but they still may be helpful, particularly in finding a job match for the employer.

- *Ability tests* measure a wide range of abilities, from manual dexterity to verbal skills. *Cognitive ability tests* measure reasoning skills in a particular area, such as math or writing, and may be a good predictor of job performance. *General cognitive ability* tests measure general intelligence or ability to learn. Ability tests can be valid, but they may also be culturally biased and result in a disproportionate number of minorities being rejected.

- *Performance simulation tests* attempt to mimic the job experience and are based on actual job behaviors or *work samples*. These tests are particularly helpful for hiring managers. An *assessment center* is a set of simulated tasks, such as making business decisions with limited information. *In-basket exercises* provide memos, reports, requests, data, and messages for candidates to work through. Candidates can then be evaluated by the quality of their decisions and of their process. Performance simulation tests are highly predictive for managerial jobs and may identify hidden strengths and weaknesses.

- *Personality tests* are used to measure enduring traits, such as extroversion, that can affect how applicants relate to others and their basic outlook on life.

- *Psychological tests* gauge an individual's values, motivation, attitudes, and so on. These tests ask questions such as, "To what extent do you agree that luck plays a key role for success in life?" These types of tests are used to select employees who presumably are more motivated, more open to new experiences, and more capable of working independently without close supervision. The validity and reliability of a particular test or situation may not have been established, however, and the firm must be careful not to delve into applicants' personal lives.

- *Honesty tests* are growing in use among retail chains, banks, and other service-sector companies to screen out applicants who may steal from the employer.

- *Interviews* are the most frequently used selection technique. Ironically, the interview is often unreliable and a poor predictor of job performance. Interviews are subject to many overt and subtle biases, but they can be a useful selection device. Excellent guides are available to help managers be objective during the interview process and keep it job-related. For example, the National Federation of Independent Business and the Atlantic Legal Foundation recently developed a handbook on federal employment laws, including a list of questions managers should never ask in job interviews.

- *Physical exams* once were widely used, but their use has declined. Employers cannot discriminate on the basis of disability. Furthermore, social attitudes toward the disabled have changed dramatically in recent years. Employers are more willing to hire employees with overt physical problems that are easily spotted in a cursory physical exam. The cost of physical exams has increased enormously, and employer health insurance programs such as health maintenance organizations typically do not exclude prior conditions that may be uncovered during a physical examination.

Sources: C. J. Russell et al., "Predictive Validity of Biodata Items Generated from Retrospective Life Experience Essays," *Journal of Applied Psychology* 75 (1990): 569–580; P. M. Muchinsky, "The Use of Reference Reports in Personnel Selection," *Journal of Occupational Psychology* 52 (1979): 287–297; M. G. Damodt, D. A. Bryan, and A. J. Whitcomb, "Predicting Performance with Letters of Recommendation," *Public Personnel Management* 22 (1993): 81–90; J. E. Hunter, "Cognitive Ability, Cognitive Aptitudes, Job Knowledge, and Job Performance," *Journal of Vocational Behavior* 29 (1986): 340–362; G. M. McEvoy and R. W. Beatty, "Assessment Centers and Subordinate Appraisal of Managers," *Personnel Psychology* 42 (1989): 37–52; L. R. Gomez-Mejia, D. B. Balkin, and R. Cardy, *Managing Human Resources,* Upper Saddle River, NJ: Prentice Hall, 2007; www.nfib.com/legal.

10.1

INTERVIEWING SKILLS

The objective of the interview is to elicit information from applicants so that the company can choose the applicant who is best qualified to perform the tasks the job requires. This exercise helps you develop interviewing skills for selection purposes.

In this exercise, an interviewer for a large retail store is on campus to recruit students for management trainee jobs after graduation. There are several job openings. The exercise proceeds through the following steps:

1. The class is divided into pairs of students. One student in each pair will act as interviewer and the other will play the role of applicant. The applicant should create a curriculum vitae (either real or fictitious) before class and provide a copy to the interviewer.

2. The interviewer from each pair interviews the applicant for 10 minutes in front of the entire class.

3. The class rates each pair using the interviewer skills checklist. For each item in the checklist, assign a rating of 0 (very poor) to 10 (outstanding).

4. At the end of each interview, the class discusses how effective it was by answering the discussion questions at the end of this exercise.

Interview Skills Checklist

Rate each of the following skills demonstrated by the interviewer on a 0 (very poor) to 10 (outstanding) scale. Maximum = 100.

_____ Was the interviewer prepared? (Lack of preparation is the most common, and costly, mistake interviewers make. Use the interviewee's résumé to create an interview agenda and review it before the interview.)

_____ Did the interviewer put the applicant at ease? (Few things are more unsettling to an applicant than being ushered into an office and waiting for the interviewer to be ready. Greet applicants, and put them at ease with some pleasant small talk before moving on to the interview questions.)

_____ Did the interviewer make snap judgments or treat the applicant as a stereotype? (Stereotyping is bad for the manager and bad for the company. Curb your tendency to rush to judgment. Always keep in mind that you are dealing with an individual, not a type.)

_____ Did the interviewer ask results-oriented questions? (Ask questions that will uncover not only what the job candidate has done but also what the results of the person's actions have been.)

(continued on next page)

table 10.3

Quality of Selection Tools as Predictors

	POSITION			
TOOL	SENIOR MANAGEMENT	MIDDLE AND LOWER MANAGEMENT	COMPLEX NONMANAGERIAL	ROUTINE OPERATIVE
Application form	2	2	2	2
Written tests	1	1	2	3
Work samples	—	—	4	4
Assessment center	5	5	—	—
Interviews	4	3	2	2
Verifying application data	3	3	3	3
Reference checks	1	1	1	1
Physical exam	1	1	1	2

Note: Validity scale is 5 at the highest and 1 as the lowest.

Source: From *Management* by Robbins. Copyright © 2003. Reprinted by permission of Pearson Education, Inc. Upper Saddle River, NJ.

(continued from previous page)

_____ Did the interviewer allow the applicant to pause? (Many interviewers jump in during any pause in the dialogue to discuss their own views on management and the company. The applicant may be absorbing information before forming a question or comment, which the interviewer should wait for.)

_____ Did the interviewer stick to job-related issues? (The interviewer's questions should be directly relevant to the tasks the employee is expected to carry out in the future.)

_____ Did the interviewer avoid questions that may increase the risk of being sued for discrimination in hiring? (Litigious questions include queries about children, disabilities, age, and maiden name, as well as seemingly innocent questions such as, "Are you originally from this area?" which may be misused or misinterpreted.)

_____ Did the interviewer ask simulated questions? (These are questions that try to elicit from candidates how they would respond to particular work situations.)

_____ Did the interviewer establish two-way communication? (The applicant should be given a chance to ask questions about the job, the company, and the long-term career prospects within the company.)

_____ Did the interviewer close definitively? (Don't let the session drift on until both parties begin to flounder about or lose interest; don't close it abruptly when interrupted by a phone call or a colleague. Plan a time limit and bring the interview to a natural close rather than letting an outside event terminate the conversation prematurely.)

Discussion Questions

1. Assess the effectiveness of the interviewing approach used by various interviewers. How well did the applicants handle the questions raised by the interviewers?

2. Use the skills checklist total to determine whether a particular interviewer was better than others. Did one applicant handle the interview questions better than the others?

Source: Reprinted from *88 Mistakes Interviewers Make and How to Avoid Them* by Auren Uris. Copyright © 1988 AMACOM Books. Reprinted with the permission of AMACOM Books, via Copyright Clearance Center.

table 10.4

Common Problems with Selection Interviews

1. Interviewers may not agree on their assessment of a candidate—their evaluation thus may say more about the interviewers than their subject.

2. The interviewer may form an overall impression of the applicant in the first two or three minutes of the interview. Snap decisions reduce the validity of the interview, because judgments are made based on very limited information.

3. Interviewers may hold a stereotype of the ideal candidates and give lower assessments to individuals who don't fit it.

4. The interview may proceed haphazardly depending on the applicant's response to open-ended questions, such as "Where would you like to be 10 years from now?" and "Tell me about yourself." The applicant's answers may trigger questions different from those asked of other candidates, with different information thus available for evaluating them.

5. The interviewer may view more favorably those candidates who are like himself or herself in terms of background, attitudes, gender, ethnicity, and so on.

6. The order in which applicants are interviewed may affect the evaluation.

7. What an interviewer perceives as negative information, such as an applicant revealing an upcoming marriage to someone who works in a different state, may outweigh the positive information.

8. The interviewer's style may affect the applicant's responses. For instance, an aggressive interviewer may intimidate an individual who is shy, even if this trait is not job-related.

9. The interviewer may not make careful written notes of the information provided by the applicant and may just have a global perception of the applicant after the interview has concluded.

Source: From *Managing Human Resources* by Gomez-Mejia, et al. Copyright © 2007. Reprinted by permission of Pearson Education, Inc., Upper Saddle River, NJ.

10.2

CREATE AND CONDUCT YOUR OWN BEHAVIORAL INTERVIEW

Assume that you are part of a team of four managers asked to develop a situational or behavioral interview for the following positions:

- Customer representative
- First-line supervisor of a clerical pool
- Human resource director
- Marketing director

Once you develop a behavioral or situational interview for each, you are asked to role-play one or two interviews for each position. The instructor will then assign students to serve as interviewees. At the end of the exercise, the entire class will discuss the effectiveness of the behavioral interview.

ORIENTATION An *orientation program* helps new employees to learn more about the company and what is expected of them in the job. The program should also be designed to help reduce the initial anxiety of the transition into the company. An orientation program should also familiarize employees with co-workers and provide the opportunity to systematically learn about work rules, personnel policies, benefits, equipment, location of the copy room, as well as how to get supplies.

Several studies show that most people find starting a new job to be stressful. Stress may be compounded by other changes in a person's life, such as having lost a previous job, going through a divorce, or moving into a new town. One important function of orientation is to help employees cope with stress. John Wanous, a well-known researcher, suggests using the Realistic Orientation Programs for New Employee Stress, or ROPES, which provides realistic information about the job and the organization, gives general support and reassurance, demonstrates coping skills, and identifies potential stressors. This program helps employees become fully functional more quickly and reduces turnover.[8]

Employee Training

Training is a planned effort to provide employees with specific skills to improve their performance. Effective training can also improve morale and increase an organization's potential. Poor, inappropriate, or inadequate training can be a source of frustration for everyone involved. Unfortunately, training programs often are affected by passing fads. For example, many firms in the late 1990s sent key employees to newly developed e-commerce programs that were offered in business schools at Carnegie-Mellon in Pittsburgh, Old Dominion in Norfolk, Virginia, Stanford in Palo Alto, and dozens of other colleges and universities. By 1999, these schools were earning at least $24.3 million in revenue from such courses. In 2001, many of the programs were struggling and companies doubted their value as Internet business faltered. Companies also suspected that e-commerce training, instead of being something new or unique, was really a principles-of-marketing course in a different format.[9] As of 2006 there is renewed interest in Internet-based training but there is greater

FIGURE 10.4

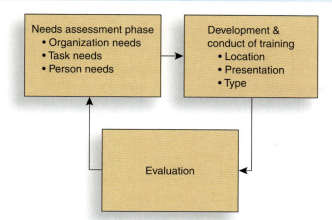

The Training Process

Source: From *Managing Human Resources* by Gomez-Mejia, et al. Copyright © 2007. Reprinted by permission of Pearson Education, Inc., Upper Saddle River, NJ.

sensitivity as to when it might be appropriate (for instance, a step-by-step technical training course) and when it might not (for instance, human relations training for supervisors).

For a training program to be effective, it must encompass the entire training process, which consists of three major phases. As shown in Figure 10.4 above, the first phase is **needs assessment,** a determination of whether training is needed. This requires an examination of the organization's plans to expand, diversify into new products, establish an overseas joint venture, or undertake other activities that may require employees with additional skills.

Next is the **development and conduct of training phase.** Making sure that training solves an organizational problem or need is critical to ensuring that it will be beneficial to the company. The first major decision is the location of the training. **On-the-job training (OJT)** takes place in the actual work setting under the guidance of an experienced worker, supervisor, or trainer. Job rotation, apprenticeships, and internships are all forms of on-the-job training. For instance, new hires at Baptist HealthCare wear an ID badge sticker for the first 90 days so that co-workers can offer a helping hand.[10] At Sherwin Williams about 600 new college hires receive training in different divisions and functions each year. **Off-the-job training** takes place away from the employment site. Common examples are formal courses, simulations, and role playing. One major advantage of off-the-job training is that employees can concentrate on the training without the interruptions that are likely to occur on the job, which facilitates learning and retention. A variety of presentation techniques and approaches may be used for off-the-job training:

- *Slides* and *videotapes* are relatively inexpensive. They can be an excellent way to stimulate discussion and raise questions. An HR representative should be available to offer more detailed explanations.

- *Computer-assisted instruction (CAI)* lets trainees learn at their own pace—the computer is always available and never becomes tired, bored, or irritable. CAI programs will limit flexibility in that the computer cannot answer questions that have not been preprogrammed, and some employees may not be comfortable or well versed in using computers effectively.

- *Classroom lectures* provide specific information and raise issues for group discussion, facilitating problem solving. However, people may forget what they learn in a lecture unless they practice it.

needs assessment

A training tool that is used to determine whether training is needed.

development and conduct of training phase

A stage in the training process that ensures training will solve an organizational problem or need; this step is critical to ensuring that training will be beneficial to the organization.

on-the-job training (OJT)

Training that takes place in the actual work setting under the guidance of an experienced worker, supervisor, or trainer.

off-the-job training

Training that takes place away from the employment site.

- *Simulations* duplicate tasks or activities normally encountered on the job. Firms use simulations when the information to be mastered is complex, the equipment used on the job is expensive, and the costs of making the wrong decision are high.

- *Virtual reality* provides three-dimensional electronic environments for tasks that require rehearsal and practice or the visualization of objects and processes where many factors need to be monitored simultaneously.

- *Vestibule training* provides training on the same equipment the employees will use at work. They can learn how to use the equipment without disrupting ongoing operations at the workplace.

- *Cross-functional training* trains employees to work effectively with employees in other areas. Two commonly used forms of cross-functional training are *team training,* which helps employees learn to work effectively in groups, and *brainstorming,* which helps employees learn creative problem solving by encouraging them to generate ideas openly, without the fear of judgment.

On-the-job training is more appropriate in certain situations. Manager's Notebook 10.3 on page 411 lists some situations when OJT should be used.

evaluation

The organization's reexamination of whether training is providing the expected benefits and meeting the identified needs.

The final phase of the training process is **evaluation.** From time to time, an organization should reexamine training methods to determine whether they provide the expected benefits and meet the needs identified in phase I. Effectiveness may be measured in monetary terms (e.g., dollars saved by reducing the number of defects) or nonmonetary terms (e.g., fewer employee complaints). The most important consideration is that the evaluation criteria should reflect the needs that the training was supposed to address.

In recent years, many companies have introduced ethics training programs or require that prospective hires, particularly middle- and top-level executives, show evidence that they have undergone such training. This is clearly one of the most rapidly growing areas in executive training programs, whether conducted in-house or by educational institutions. For instance, one such program requires that the trainee actually visit with executives who are in prison to learn firsthand what landed them there.

Career Development

Career development is a long-term effort in which the organization helps employees utilize their full potential. It is not a one-shot training program or a series of workshops. Instead there are three major phases—assessment, direction, and development—as shown in Figure 10.5 on page 411.

assessment phase

A career development step in which employees are helped to choose personally fitting career paths that are realistically attainable and to determine any obstacles they need to overcome to succeed.

ASSESSMENT   The **assessment phase** involves helping employees choose career paths that are realistically attainable and fit with the employee's temperament and personality. The assessment phase includes determining what obstacles they need to overcome to succeed. Some companies use a combination of tools to accomplish this, including performance appraisal data from supervisors, psychological tests, assessment centers, interest inventories, and skill inventories.

direction phase

The step in career development that involves determining the steps employees must take to reach their career goals.

DIRECTION   The next phase, the **direction phase,** includes determining the steps employees must take to reach their career goals. Appropriate direction requires understanding of the *sequence* of jobs employees are expected to fill over time—that is, identifying jobs that are logically connected and that offer increasing responsibility. A job analysis may provide a sound basis for creating

Ask these questions when deciding whether on-the-job training should be undertaken. If your answer is "yes," the training generally should be done on the job.

1. Is participatory learning necessary?
2. Is one-on-one training called for?
3. Does only a small group of employees need training?
4. Is the cost of training the employees away from the job more than the benefit expected from the training?
5. Is the training not appropriate for a classroom setting?
6. Are safety factors and equipment requirements not available away from the job site?
7. Does the training have to be done immediately?
8. Does the training have to be done to meet new safety requirements that have just been implemented?
9. Is disrupting ongoing work by pulling employees away from the job too costly?
10. Is the training designed for an infrequently performed task?
11. Does the employee have to meet defined standards to obtain certification or qualification?
12. Is the equipment needed for training too large to move or not moveable?
13. Is the equipment needed for training too fragile or carefully calibrated to move?
14. Are the materials required for training also part of the overall job site?
15. Are the training procedures or equipment too dangerous to use off site?
16. Does the training involve sensitive information that must be kept in a secure environment?

Source: From C. A. Mullaney and L. D. Trask, "Show Them the Ropes," *Technical & Skills Training,* October 1992, pp. 8–11. Reprinted with permission.

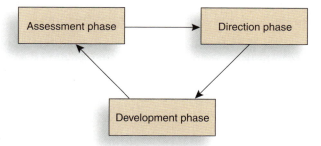

FIGURE 10.5

The Career Development Process

Source: From *Managing Human Resources* by Gomez-Mejia, et al. Copyright © 2007. Reprinted by permission of Pearson Education, Inc., Upper Saddle River, NJ.

a logical career path so that skills learned on a job prepare the employee for the next higher level of responsibility. The **career path** presents the steps and a plausible time frame for accomplishing them.

Firms use a variety of approaches to assist employees in the direction phase, including:

- *Promotability forecasts,* judgments by managers about the advancement potential of subordinates.
- *Succession planning,* the identification and development of replacements for jobs that are expected to open up.

career path

The steps for advancement to a career goal and a plausible time frame for accomplishing them.

---

development phase

A career development step in which actions are designed to help the employee grow and learn the necessary skills to move along the desired career path.

---

mentoring

Developmental activities carried out by more seasoned employees to help those who are learning the ropes.

Mentoring

---

coaching

Ongoing, mostly spontaneous, meetings between managers and their employees to discuss career goals, roadblocks, and available opportunities.

---

job rotation

A formal program in which employees are assigned to different jobs to expand their skills base and to learn more about various parts of the organization.

---

tuition assistance programs

Support by the firm for employees' education and development by covering the cost of tuition and other fees for seminars, workshops, and continuing education programs.

- *Individual career counseling,* one-on-one sessions to examine the person's present and possible next career stages.
- *Job posting systems,* in which all vacancies are listed on a bulletin board, in a company newsletter, or in a phone recording or computer system.
- *Career resource centers,* where career development materials such as workbooks, tapes, and texts are located in a central location, such as the HR department.

DEVELOPMENT   The final phase, the **development phase,** outlines actions designed to help the employee grow and learn the necessary skills to move along the desired career paths. Some common programs include:

- **Mentoring,** or the developmental activities carried out by more seasoned employees to help those who are learning the ropes. Mentoring takes many forms, including role modeling, sharing contacts, bouncing ideas, advising, and giving general support. It may be formal or informal. Most firms expect senior employees, particularly those in managerial positions, to act as mentors.
- **Coaching,** which is the ongoing, mostly spontaneous, meetings between managers and employees to discuss career goals, roadblocks, and opportunities.
- **Job rotation** is a formal program in which employees are assigned to different jobs to expand their skills base and to learn more about various parts of the organization.
- **Tuition assistance programs,** which support the employee's education and development by covering the cost of tuition and other fees for seminars, workshops, and continuing education programs.

Management Is Everyone's Business 10.3 above offers a set of recommendations that individual employees might wish to follow to enhance their career success within the organization.

Performance Appraisal

One of the keys to both individual and organizational success is providing quality feedback about individual performance. Performance appraisals have three important objectives. First, they open two-way communication channels so that supervisors may convey to employees what is expected of them and employees have an opportunity to tell supervisors what is on their minds. Second, they provide constructive feedback to employees so that positive steps may be taken to capitalize on strengths and reduce weaknesses; performance appraisal is an integral part of the career development process. (See Skills for Managing 10.3 on page 415.) Finally, a performance appraisal helps the manager decide who should be paid more based on individual contributions. The numerous techniques that measure performance can be classified by the type of judgment required (relative or absolute). They can also be classified by the focus of the measure (trait, behavior, or outcome).

JUDGMENT APPROACHES TO PERFORMANCE APPRAISAL

Performance appraisals may use relative judgment or absolute judgment approaches.

In **relative judgments,** employees are compared to one another. Supervisors may be asked to rank subordinates from best to worst, or they may be asked to create a *forced distribution* by classifying a given percentage of employees into various groups, such as exceptional, standard, room for improvement, and not adequate.

The advantage of the relative judgment approach is it requires supervisors to make difficult choices. Supervisors who want their subordinates to like them typically prefer to rate most as excellent, which may not be valid. The relative judgment approach has serious disadvantages, however. Performance distributions may vary among units: the performance of a person at the top in one unit may rank at the bottom of another. These systems can force managers to make unrealistic performance distinctions, which creates dissatisfaction in the workforce. They may also reduce cooperation among workers, which will have a negative impact on the performance of the entire unit.

Appraisal methods using **absolute judgments** evaluate the performance of employees against performance standards, and not in comparison to other employees. There are several advantages to this approach. The evaluation data are comparable from one unit to another. Employees are more likely to cooperate with one another since individual ratings that are high are not a threat to the other workers. From a developmental perspective, the supervisor can provide more constructive feedback since the evaluation is centered on job requirements. Absolute judgments are also easier to defend legally than relative judgments; the firm can show that each employee's evaluation is based on performance dimensions that measure success on the job.

Absolute judgments are based on the performance appraisal interview, which also provides a manager the opportunity to help employees deal with behavioral

5 Learning Objective Check-In

Gene is a manager who works in the HR department. He helps coordinate various programs for his firm. For instance, he coordinates a program that familiarizes workers with the firm by providing them the opportunity to learn about rules, policies, benefits, and which resources are available in a particular job. Gene also coordinates programs with each functional department whereby new hires or veteran workers who are entering new phases in their careers with the organization can learn job-specific methods for completing assigned tasks. Lastly, Gene helps consult with employees, one-on-one, in determining the steps they must take to reach their career goals.

1. *What is the first type of program Gene is involved in coordinating?*
   a. *Bureaucratic management*
   b. *Orientation*
   c. *On-the-job training (OJT)*
   d. *Assessment*

2. *The _____ program allows each functional department to ensure that workers are up to date with job-specific methods for completing their work.*
   a. *contingency plan*
   b. *training*
   c. *orientation*
   d. *career development*

3. *Gene's consultation with individual workers is part of the _____ phase of career development.*
   a. *performance appraisal*
   b. *assessment*
   c. *development*
   d. *direction*

relative judgments

A performance appraisal approach in which employees are compared to one another.

absolute judgments

A performance appraisal approach in which the performance of employees is evaluated against performance standards, and not in comparison to each other.

Margin definitions

trait appraisal instruments

Performance appraisal tools that evaluate employees based on consistent and enduring worker characteristics.

Appraisal Methods

behavioral appraisal instruments

Performance appraisal tools that assess certain employee behaviors, such as coming to work on time.

behavioral anchored rating scales

Performance appraisal tools that assess the effectiveness of the employee's performance using specific examples of good or bad behaviors at work.

outcome appraisal instruments

Performance appraisal tools that measure workers' results, such as sales volume, number of units produced, and meeting deadlines.

Potential Errors in the Rating Process

problems that make them less effective. An estimated 19 million U.S. citizens suffer from depression each year, and most receive no treatment.[11] The regularly scheduled appraisal interview may provide the supervisor with a mechanism to help depressed employees seek professional help without the employees feeling that they are being singled out.

MEASUREMENT APPROACHES TO PERFORMANCE APPRAISAL

Performance appraisals may also be based on focus of the measures approaches. These appraisals assess different aspects of employee characteristics and focus on specific data.

Trait appraisal instruments evaluate employees based on characteristics that tend to be consistent and enduring, such as decisiveness, reliability, energy, and loyalty. Because people routinely make trait judgments about others, they can be a powerful way of describing people. This type of appraisal instrument also has several disadvantages, such as ambiguity (what does it take to be loyal?) and propensity for conscious or unconscious bias (the supervisor may feel that women are more emotional than men and therefore rate the trait differently). It is also difficult to defend legally, given that assessment of traits focuses attention on the person rather than on job performance.

Behavioral appraisal instruments assess certain employee behaviors, such as coming to work on time, completing assignments within stipulated guidelines, and getting along with co-workers. A *behavioral observation scale* is one type of behavioral appraisal instrument in which various behaviors are listed and supervisors record the frequency of their occurrence.

Behavioral anchored rating scales assess the effectiveness of the employee's performance using specific examples of good or bad behaviors at work, often referred to as *critical incidents*. The main advantage of this approach is that it is closely focused on concrete aspects of job performance. Employees may more clearly understand why they received a particular rating and what they need to do to improve their performance. This approach is easier to defend legally. One drawback to using this approach is that the instrument is expensive to develop. They become more difficult to apply in companies with a wide variety of jobs, especially if those jobs frequently change.

Outcome appraisal instruments measure results, such as sales volume, the number of units produced, and meeting deadlines. Setting quantitative measures of performance for most jobs is subjective. The most prevalent outcome-oriented approach focuses on goals agreed to by the employee and supervisor. Management by objectives (MBO) is one technique widely used for this purpose (see the planning chapter, Chapter 5, for a more extensive description of these programs). In MBO programs, employees and supervisors agree on a set of goals to be accomplished for a particular period. Performance is then assessed at the end of the period by comparing actual achievement against the agreed-upon goals. This approach provides clear direction to employees, reduces subjectivity, and allows individual goals to be established (for instance, objectives for new workers may be less challenging than those set for senior employees). As we saw in Chapter 5, MBO also has drawbacks in that it can be manipulated—employees and managers may set conservative goals to lessen the risk of not reaching the target. Some aspects of a job that are difficult to measure quantitatively, such as cooperating with other units or departments, may not be made part of the evaluation and thus may be ignored by the employee.[12]

LOC-In

6 Learning Objective Check-In

1. *Phil evaluates his employees by comparing them to one another. This can be difficult for him, but he realizes that it forces him to make choices regarding who really contributes the most or the least to the team. This _____ method sometimes calls for the use of a forced distribution.*
   a. *absolute judgment*
   b. *relative judgment*
   c. *trait appraisal*
   d. *behavioral appraisal*

PERFORMANCE APPRAISAL FEEDBACK SKILLS

Constructive feedback is critical to effective performance management, with evaluative communication directed at the employee's performance and not at the person. Skills in providing feedback can help you uncover reasons for a performance problem and create an effective solution and performance improvement. This exercise, which helps you develop feedback skills, begins with the following steps:

1. The class is divided into pairs of students. One student in each pair will act as supervisor and the other will play the role of the employee.

2. Each student pair will meet outside class to prepare and discuss a performance problem, based on any personal work experiences, experiences heard from other people, or personal observation.

3. In front of the class, the supervisor and employee in each pair discuss the performance problem for 10 minutes. The class rates each of the supervisor–employee pairs using the performance feedback skills checklist. For each item in the checklist, students in class will assign a rating of 0 (very poor) to 10 (outstanding).

4. At the end of each pair's meeting in front of the class, the class discusses the feedback approaches used and then answers the discussion questions at the end of this exercise.

Performance Feedback Skills Checklist

Rate each of the following skills demonstrated by the supervisor-employee pair from 0 (very poor) to 10 (outstanding). Maximum = 100.

_____ Did the pair present perceptions, reactions, and opinions as such and not as facts?

_____ Did the pair refer to the problem relative to performance, behavior, or outcomes, not to the individual as a person?

_____ Did the pair provide feedback in terms of specific, observable behavior, not general behavior?

_____ Did the pair talk in terms of established criteria, probable outcomes, or possible improvement, as opposed to being good or bad?

_____ Did the pair discuss performance and the specific behaviors that appear to be contributing to or limiting full effectiveness?

_____ Did the pair avoid overload terms (for example, *crabby, mess-up, rip-off,* or *stupid*) that can produce emotional reactions and defensiveness?

_____ Did the pair concentrate on things that the employee or supervisor can control, and focus on ways the employee can use the feedback to improve performance?

_____ Did the pair react defensively or emotionally rather than trying to convince, reason, or supply additional information?

_____ Did the pair give each other feedback in a manner that communicates acceptance of the employee as a worthwhile person and of that person's right to be an individual?

_____ Was feedback tied to specific development plans that could capitalize on strengths and minimize performance weaknesses?

Discussion Questions

1. Describe the feedback approach used by various supervisors. Was there an approach that you felt was particularly effective or ineffective? Why?

2. Use the checklist to determine if a particular pair was more effective than others. If there is significant disagreement in the class, discuss the reasons why.

Compensation

The three key objectives of any compensation system should be to attract high-quality workers from the labor market, retain the best employees the company already has, and motivate employees to work harder and to help the company achieve its strategic goals.

As illustrated in Figure 10.6 on page 416, an employee's total compensation package is made up of three components. The first is **base compensation,** or the fixed amount of money the employee expects to receive in a weekly or monthly

base compensation

The fixed amount of money the employee expects to receive in a paycheck weekly or monthly or as an hourly wage.

FIGURE 10.6

Components of Total Compensation

Source: From *Managing Human Resources* by Gomez-Mejia, et al. Copyright © 2007. Reprinted by permission of Pearson Education, Inc., Upper Saddle River, NJ.

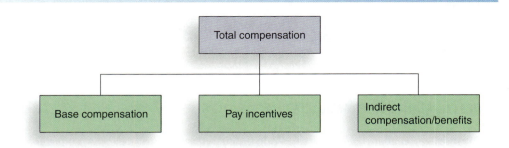

Offering additional compensation can be profitable to the firm in the long run, such as Boeing's bonus to its employees for their work in meeting a major deadline.

pay incentives

Compensation that rewards employees for good performance, including variable pay and merit pay.

benefits

A compensation component that accounts for almost 40 percent of the typical total compensation package and includes health insurance, pension plans, unemployment insurance, vacations, sick leave, and the like.

strategic compensation

Compensation practices that best support the firm's business strategy.

paycheck or as an hourly wage. The second is **pay incentives,** or the compensation that rewards employees for high performance. Incentives may be based on employees' own contributions or the performance of the team, business unit, or entire company. They are generally paid out as a percentage of base compensation. Pay incentives are often referred to as *variable pay* because the amount is contingent on or varies according to changes in performance. Incentive plans include one-time-only bonuses, pay raises (*merit pay* increases), profit sharing, and company stock or stock options. For instance, 19,000 engineers and technical workers at Boeing each recently received a $1,000 bonus after meeting a deadline for delivery of Boeing's 491st commercial jetliner.[13] The third component of total compensation is **benefits,** or *indirect compensation,* which accounts for almost 40 percent of the typical total compensation package. Benefits include health insurance, pension plans, unemployment insurance, vacations, and sick leave.

Compensation is a major cost for most firms. Labor costs may be as high as 60 percent in some manufacturing environments and even higher in service organizations. For instance, personnel costs reach 80 percent of the total budget of the U.S. Postal Service. This means that how well compensation dollars are allocated is likely to have a significant effect on firm performance. The design of the compensation system should fit with the firm's strategic objectives, the firm's unique characteristics, and the company's environment. Pay should also exhibit internal equity and external equity, and match employee contributions.

FIT WITH THE FIRM'S STRATEGIC OBJECTIVES The reward system should help implement the firm's strategy. A firm trying to expand its market share may pay the sales force on commission in order to generate more sales, while a firm trying to create customer loyalty in a narrow market segment may pay the sales force primarily on salary to focus on existing customers as well as on new business. This requires strong collaboration between top executives, who are responsible for strategy formulation, and the HR department, which designs the compensation program.

Compensation practices that best support the firm's business strategy are called **strategic compensation.** For instance, Ford, a pioneer in quality improvements since the 1980s, made it a core of its business strategy and summarizes it in its motto: "Quality Is Job One." A rash of quality-related problems surfaced in 2000, however, culminating with the recall of Firestone tires used in Ford vehicles and safety concerns with Ford Explorer. To prevent these problems from recurring, Ford executives' bonuses were tied to improving customer satisfaction more quickly than its rivals in the industry, based on consumer surveys and other data.[14]

Firms should be aware that incentives can help support strategic objectives but they may raise potential ethical issues, if employees and managers try to manipulate the system to get the incentives. Or there may be unintended consequences. This is a fear expressed by some with the incentive plan being introduced by some hospitals to have doctors share in cost savings (see Management Close-Up 10.3, "To Fight Costs, Hospital Seek Allies in the Operating Room" on page 418).

FIT WITH THE FIRM'S UNIQUE CHARACTERISTICS AND ENVIRONMENT Company leaders must consider the organization's needs along with the firm's environment when designing a compensation program. A labor-intensive company with a highly unstable demand for products may provide more incentives and less in base pay to reduce financial risks, because base pay requires a fixed financial commitment.

What is important to one firm may be almost irrelevant to another. A high-tech firm that provides generous compensation to managerial and marketing personnel and underpays its research and development staff may lose the ability to innovate because competitors have stolen the company's best talent. On the other hand, a manufacturing firm producing a standard commodity that has changed little over the years, such as coat hangers, may not need to pay a premium for innovative talent.

INTERNAL EQUITY The perceived fairness of the pay structure within a firm is termed **internal equity.** A common procedure called **job evaluation** is intended to provide a rational, orderly, and systematic judgment of how important each job is to the firm. The key input to job evaluation is the job analysis, which was discussed earlier. Most firms use committees (which may include manager, employees, consultants, and union members) to examine the job analysis data to make that judgment. After applying a set of evaluation criteria called **compensable factors,** such as responsibility, educational requirements, and problem-solving potential, the committee develops a hierarchy of jobs in terms of their relative importance. To simplify matters, some firms group jobs into grade levels, where jobs at higher grade levels are considered to be more important than those at lower levels. Table 10.5 on page 419 is an example of the pay structure of a large restaurant that uses grade levels.

EXTERNAL EQUITY The perceived fairness of the compensation employees receive relative to what other companies pay for similar work is termed **external equity.** HR departments often use market surveys to study external equity. An organization may conduct its own salary surveys, but most purchase commercially available surveys. Information about these surveys may be obtained over the Internet. HR.com offers timely information on compensation and benefit surveys available to employers. The purpose of these surveys in most job-based compensation systems is to determine pay ranges for each grade level.

internal equity

The perceived fairness of the pay structure within a firm.

job evaluation

A rational, orderly, and systematic judgment of how important each job is to the firm and how each job should be compensated.

compensable factors

A set of evaluation criteria used in job evaluation.

external equity

The perceived fairness of the compensation employees receive relative to what other companies pay for similar work.

To Fight Rising Costs, Hospitals Seek Allies in the Operating Room

THEME: ETHICS

It is a war on rising hospital costs, being fought one tiny balloon at a time. And as with most wars, some of the tactics are controversial.

Until recently, some cardiologists at the Pinnacle Health System hospital group in Pennsylvania would inflate a new artery opening balloon each time they inserted a stent into a patient's clogged arteries. Now, if they can, these doctors will use a single balloon throughout a patient's procedure.

That simple step, which the doctors say poses no additional risk to patients, saves at least a couple of hundred dollars a procedure. And—here lies the controversy—the doctors share in any money they save the hospital (the program is called "gainsharing"). While the new approach gives them a financial incentive to be more cost conscious, it also fundamentally recasts the traditional arm's-length relationship between a hospital and the doctors who practice there.

PinnacleHealth says it saved 5 percent last year in cardiology supplies by conserving on balloons and getting cardiologists to agree, when feasible, to use stents. pacemakers, and other cardiac devices that it buys at a negotiated volume discount. Those savings equaled about $1 million, which the hospital split with doctors. "This is just common sense," said Dr. Ken May, whose 17-doctor cardiology practice is among the groups involved.

Hospital administrators and consultants say getting doctors to agree to use certain brands or waste fewer supplies can be difficult. The only way to make doctors cost sensitive, the hospital says, is to pay them to pay attention.

TOTAL HIP IMPLANTS	DR. SMITH	DR. JONES
Vendor	Contract	Non-contract
Additional training	None	Yes
Gainsharing percentage	15%	20%
Total number of surgeries	20	30
Average savings per surgery	$1,200	$1,200
Total savings	$24,000	$36,000
Gainsharing received	$3,600	$7,200
Total hospital savings:	**$60,000**	
Total physician gainsharing:	**$10,800**	

Regulators and other still worry that such programs, if not designed properly, could induce doctors to put money matters ahead of the interests of patients. Representative Pete Stark, a California Democrat, has described Congressional enthusiasm for "gainsharing" as "not only misguided" but "potentially dangerous." Gainsharing's critics include device makers, whose profits are threatened if hospitals are able to demand better prices.

"We believe that gainsharing would have an immediate and significant negative effect on public health by encouraging the use of the least expensive option without consideration of long-term effects or overall health economics," said Martin J. Emerson, chief executive of American Medical Systems, a maker of pelvic devices based in Minnetonka, Minnesota.

Source: Adapted from R. Abelson, "Dr. Saves-a-Lot," *The New York Times*, November 1, 2005, pp. C-1 and C-5.

Gainsharing is one of the ways in which hospitals are teaming up with doctors to save costs in ways that don't affect patient care. While the idea, which splits the cost savings between the doctors and the hospital, has its critics and potential downsides, it does appear to be gaining support.

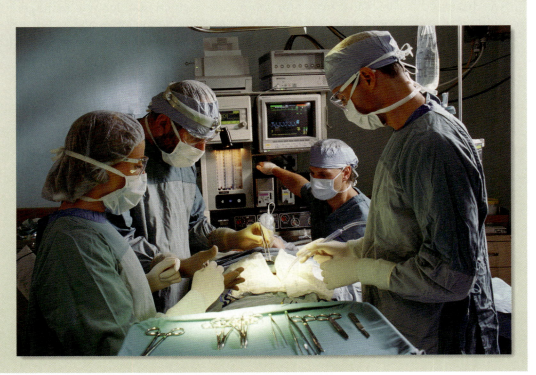

table 10.5

Determining Pay Structure Using a Job-Based Approach

GRADE	JOB TITLE	NUMBER OF POSITIONS	HOURLY PAY
6	Chef	2	$21.50–32.50
5	Manager	1	12.50–22.00
5	Sous chef	1	12.50–22.00
4	Assistant manager	2	8.50–13.00
4	Lead cook	2	8.50–13.00
4	Office manager	1	8.50–13.00
3	General cook	5	7.50–9.00
3	Short-order cook	2	7.50–9.00
3	Assistant to lead cook	2	7.50–9.00
3	Clerk	1	7.50–9.00
2	Server	45	7.00–8.00
2	Hostess	4	7.00–8.00
2	Cashier	4	7.00–8.00
1	Kitchen helper	2	6.50–7.25
1	Dishwasher	3	6.50–7.25
1	Janitor	2	6.50–7.25
1	Busser	6	6.50–7.25
1	Security guard	2	6.50–7.25

Source: From *Managing Human Resources* by Gomez-Mejia, et al. Copyright © 2007. Reprinted by permission of Pearson Education, Inc., Upper Saddle River, NJ.

EMPLOYEE CONTRIBUTIONS One important element of an employee's level of contribution to the company is the job he or she holds.

As discussed earlier, employees with more responsible positions generally contribute more to the organization, which is why they get paid more. Another key factor is how effectively employees perform their tasks. To attract, retain, and motivate high performers and to be fair to all workers, a company should reward employees based on their relative levels of performance.

Most firms reward employees based on their individual contributions. Companies may use piece rates, special awards, stock, bonuses, and merit pay. Merit pay increases, which are based on the supervisor ratings of employee performance and normally given once a year, are by far the most popular and are used by almost all companies.

LOC-In

7 Learning Objective Check-In

Jeff's firm pays him $84,000 per year, up to $500 per quarter in quarterly performance bonuses, and a prearranged set of factors like 80 percent of health insurance costs, a fully matched 401(k), various work-associated insurances, and 20 days of personal leave to include vacation or sick leave.

1. What does the $84,000 represent in terms of Jeff's total compensation package?
   a. Pay incentives
   b. Benefits
   c. Base compensation
   d. Company goodwill

2. What does the potential $500 per quarter represent in terms of Jeff's total compensation package?
   a. Pay incentives
   b. Profit sharing
   c. Benefits
   d. Base compensation

3. What does the range of fringe components, including personal leave and health insurance, represent in terms of Jeff's total compensation package?
   a. Base compensation
   b. Pay incentives
   c. Benefits
   d. Company goodwill

CONCLUDING THOUGHTS

Thinking back to the introductory vignette and the questions raised at the beginning of this chapter, Toyota benefits from its Hire-a-Hero program because it creates a direct line of communication with returning veterans who have many of the types of technical skills and training the company is looking for in its employees. Leadership and commitment are other pluses that many veterans bring to the workplace, and Toyota makes a practice of supporting and rewarding its military and ex-military employees in return for their dedication and expertise.

If Toyota does better, so will its employees. In the end, nothing will make a company more successful than carefully selecting and placing the right people for the right jobs, ensuring that employees learn their jobs well, seeing to it that they will all have futures in the company, treating them fairly, and compensating them well.

Focusing on the Future: Using Management Theory in Daily Life

Human Resource Management   Brendan Geary is the Director of Compensation and Benefits at Panalpina, a freight forwarding and logistics services company. The company, which has headquarters in both Switzerland and the United States, is truly global, operating 500 branches in 80 countries, with partnerships in an additional 60 countries. In addition to freight forwarding, Panalpina offers supply chain management advice based on over 100 years of intercontinental air freight and ocean freight experience. With 13,000 employees scattered worldwide, Brendan is acutely aware of factors influencing the environment of Human Resources, and the compensation and performance management programs he designed contain many of the "best practice" features described in Chapter 10.

Human Resource Environment   Two factors of the Human Resource environment that influence Brendan's work with Panalpina on a daily basis are globalization and legislation.

Globalization. Panalpina managers often take on assignments in other countries, and Brendan must structure their benefits and compensation accordingly. Compensation strategies vary by geographic area. In Europe, for example, managers typically receive less take-home pay, but their pensions and health benefits are strong, in part due to the high taxes that support socialized medical programs. In the United States, less money is spent on pensions and health benefits, but take-home pay is much higher. Brendan must determine whether an executive is making a permanent move or a temporary one when setting up that employee's compensation package. If the move is permanent, he tries to bring compensation in line with local practices as quickly as possible, but if the move is temporary, he adopts a compensation strategy which is consistent with practices in the executive's home country.

Legislation. In terms of legislation, Brendan spends the majority of his time dealing with issues related to the Fair Labor Standards Act (FLSA) and the Family Medical Leave Act (FMLA.) The FLSA distinguishes exempt from nonexempt employees and establishes guidelines for minimum wages. In 2004, the law was amended, and new guidelines were established to clarify the duties associated with jobs that are exempt from being paid overtime. In the last year, Brendan has had to deal with one lawsuit (settled out of court) and three labor commissioner hearings about overtime issues. He finds that the bottom line for determining if an employee is exempt is whether or not that person "regularly makes independent judgments in their work."

The Family Medical Leave Act presents a different challenge for Brendan, one that is primarily related to reporting requirements. Because the FMLA requires that employees be given up to 12 weeks of unpaid leave a year to care for themselves or a family member, and because that leave can be taken in daily and/or hourly increments, Brendan finds that it is critical to monitor FMLA leave closely. Employees who request time off must clarify whether they are taking FMLA time and when they are planning to return to work. By law, an employee's job must be held open for him or her for the 12 weeks he or she is on FMLA leave. Unfortunately, some employees abuse the FMLA guidelines and try to take far more than the 12 weeks to which they are entitled. To deal with this issue, Brendan utilizes a third party administrator who tracks FMLA leaves throughout Panalpina.

Compensation   Obviously, as Director of Compensation and Benefits, Brendan must create compensation programs that will attract high quality applicants, retain the best employees the company already has, and motivate employees to work harder and help the company achieve its strategic goals. Brendan recently changed the sales compensation program, keeping in mind the following key design components.

Fit with the Firm's Strategic Objectives. One of Panalpina's primary strategic objectives is organic growth—expanding the company's overall revenues in a natural fashion. In a freight forwarding company, this means utilizing existing trade lanes whenever possible, and bringing in business that fills identified trade lanes to capacity. When Brendan was hired, all Panalpina sales personnel received their incentive compensation based on simple incremental gross profit on different product lines. But Brendan knew that some sales were more in line with the company's strategic objectives than others. Therefore, he created a sales compensation plan that offers increased rewards for selling to clients on existing trade lanes, for selling to larger rather than smaller clients, and for identifying clients who can "fill out" cargo planes and ships to capacity.

Fit with the Firm's Unique Characteristics and Environment. As noted above, the global character of Panalpina makes it imperative that compensation programs are designed with regional standards in mind. For the sales compensation program, this means adjusting salary and commission components to fit with local norms. Salaries differ depending on geographic location.

Internal Equity. The salary component of sales compensation is adjusted so that all sales personnel receive equivalent starting salaries. This means that salaries have to be adjusted using geographic pay differentials to reflect the underlying economic conditions of the area in which the salesperson is working. This keeps perceptions of pay equitable across the organization. On the incentive side of the mix, pay is tied directly to results, so it is easy for salespeople to see how their inputs relate to outcomes and see the overall fairness of the system. Rather than spending a lot of time on job evaluation studies, Brendan allows the market to determine the value of jobs to the organization.

External Equity. Panalpina does not do traditional job evaluation studies—instead, Brendan focuses his compensation strategy on external market data and works to ensure that all salaries in the company are market driven. Job salaries are benchmarked by participating in sponsored compensation surveys or purchasing compensation survey information from a consulting company like Watson Wyatt.

Employee Contributions. All compensation systems at Panalpina are tied to employee contributions. As noted above, sales personnel receive incentive compensation which is directly linked to the amount of money they bring into the company in sales. Salaried employees participate in an annual review process, where their performance is rated based on goal setting and competency components. This rating is incorporated into a merit pay program, which uses a merit matrix to establish the rate of salary increase associated with each performance rating level. High potential and especially talented employees receive extra compensation reviews to be sure that they are being paid for their contributions to the company.

summary of learning objectives

1 Explain the role of human resource management in achieving a sustainable competitive advantage.

- The business strategy of the firm should guide human resource strategies, which in turn provide the basis for HR programs in effectively implementing those strategies.
- All managers are responsible for making human resources decisions, while the human resource department provides the necessary support so that managers can hire the best talent, train employees, assess performance, and reward contributions.

2 Identify the key factors in the environment affecting the management of human resources.

- The workforce is becoming increasingly diverse in terms of race, ethnicity, gender, age, and such.
- Globalization is widening the labor market from which firms recruit and requires greater HR involvement in preparing employees to compete in that environment.
- Legislation that affects human resource management, primarily discrimination issues, is constantly being interpreted at federal, state, and local levels.
- Labor unions have been declining in strength in the United States but still remain strong in certain industry sectors and in many countries around the world.

3 Describe the human resource planning process.

The process involves two steps:

- Forecast of **labor demand**: An estimate of how many and what kinds of workers will be needed in the future.
- Forecast of **labor supply**: An estimate of the availability of employees with required skills.

4 Explain the key components of staffing and their importance.

- **Recruitment**. Firms can greatly improve the quality of the workforce by generating a good pool of applicants.
- **Selection**. Firms can hire better employees by developing selection programs that are job related and capable of predicting who is most likely to be a good performer.
- The *orientation program* can ease the entry of employees into the company so that they become fully functioning in the shortest time possible.

5 Describe how training and career development provide employees with tools to succeed once they are hired.

- *Training* provides employees with specific skills to enhance their job performance.
- *Career development* offers long-term growth so that employees can use their abilities to the maximum during their employment with the firm.

6 Identify the purposes of performance appraisal and how it might be conducted.

- *Developmental purpose*. The performance appraisal system can help identify employee weaknesses that should improve through training and career development as well as strengths that may be channeled to better utilize the employee's talents.

- *Recognition purposes.* The appraisal system may provide important input to reward employees (for instance, through promotions and salary adjustments) based on their relative contributions.
- *Appraisal means.* Employees' performance may be judged by comparing them to one another or by evaluating performance relative to an establishment performance standard. The focus of the appraisal may be traits (such as decisiveness and reliability), behaviors (such as using examples that illustrate good or bad behaviors at work), and outcomes (measuring observed results). All approaches have advantages and disadvantages so it is important to be aware of their pros and cons as discussed in this chapter.

7 Describe the key objectives of the compensation system and its components.

- A well-designed compensation system should serve to attract, retain, and motivate good employees.
- The compensation system allocates pay based on the importance of the job, how well employees perform their assignments, and the pay for similar positions in the labor market.
- The compensation package is made up of three components: **base compensation** or salary, **pay incentives** (amounts may vary by year, usually depending on performance), and **benefits** (such as health insurance, pension plans, unemployment insurance and so on).

discussion questions

1. Many firms today subcontract to external consultants part of the work that traditionally was conducted in the HR department. Why do you think this is happening?

2. What do you foresee as the major forces affecting human resources in the future? Do you see those forces as threats or opportunities for firms? Why?

3. A cynic might argue that most firms do not hire employees following the practices outlined in this chapter (job analysis, realistic job previews, and the like), but they still manage to have an effective workforce. Some go even further and argue that those practices tend to create an expensive bureaucracy with doubtful benefits. Do you agree? Why or why not?

4. Going back to Management Close-Up 10.2, do you think the flexible work plan developed by Best Buy may be used in most firms? What are some of the challenges employers are most likely to face if they implement such programs?

5. Should a firm use an objective or a subjective performance appraisal system? What factors determine which type of system a company should use? Explain.

6. Going back to Management Close-Up 10.3, do you believe that gainsharing programs such as the one described should be used in the medical industry? Why or why not?

management minicase 10.1

Rewards for Good Teaching?

Over the objections of the teachers' union, the Houston Board of Education unanimously approved the nation's largest merit pay program, which calls for rewarding teachers based on how well their students perform on standardized tests.

The $14.5 million program, which immediately replaces a model with lower incentives, would distribute up to $3,000 annually per teacher and up to $25,000 for senior administrators.

Abelardo Saavedra, the Houston superintendent of schools, praised the vote, saying that it "will ensure that the academic growth of each child is important and will be compensated." Houston business leaders also supported the change.

But Gayle Fallon, president of the United Federation of Teachers, which represents about 40 percent of the district's 12,300 teachers, condemned the program as misguided. In its place, Ms. Fallon called for across-the-board raises to lift Houston from what she said was the low-paying end of area school districts.

"No one has been able to show us one ounce of research that paying teachers for test scores improves performance," she said.

The pay incentives are to be based on three components, or "strands." One will reward teachers based on how much their school's test scores have improved compared with the scores of 40 other schools with similar demographics around the state. Another will compare student progress on the Stanford 10 Achievement test and its Spanish-language equivalent to that of students in similar classrooms in the Houston district. The third measure will be student progress on the statewide Texas Assessment of Knowledge and Skills test, as compared with that in similar Houston classrooms.

About half the district's teachers will be eligible for stipends in all three categories, for a maximum total of $3,000. The system's 305 principals with the best-achieving teachers could earn as much as $6,000 in merit pay, and the 19 executive principals and five regional superintendents will be eligible for up to $25,000.

Discussion Questions

1. What are the pros and cons of rewarding teachers for student test results? What side do you mostly agree with (pros or cons?). Explain your answer.
2. Do you think it is fair to pay teachers a stipend up to $3,000, principals up to $6,000, and executive principals/regional superintendents up to $25,000? Explain your answer.
3. If you were to suggest a performance appraisal system for teachers, how would you do it? Would you tie the resulting appraisals to pay and if so, how would you do it? Explain your answers.

Source: Adapted from R. Blumenthal, "In Houston, Teachers Get Merit Pay," *New York Times*, January 13, 2006, p. A-12.

management minicase 10.2

Handling Family Issues in the Office

As kids' fall school sports, clubs, and activities get into full swing, these extracurricular activities are encroaching on parents' office life. Many youth activities, it seems, require ever-intensifying travel, fund raising, and competition. To manage it all, parents are jamming their volunteer roles into the workday using company copiers, faxes, phones, and computers to print schedules, send e-mails, and make calls, budgets, and flyers.

Working parents say integrating extracurricular pursuits with office life is the only way to get everything done, and communications technology enables them to do both work and personal tasks both at home and the office. Still, the trend can cause problems for co-workers and employers, calling in some cases for more thoughtful time management.

No one tracks parents' extracurricular use of office resources. But 82 percent of kids ages 6 to 17 take part in extracurricular activities, says Child Trends, a nonprofit Washington, DC, research group.

A recent survey conducted by the Ethics Resource Center, a nonprofit Washington, DC, research and advocacy group, suggests that multitasking often raises co-workers' ire over abuses of employers' e-mail and Internet access.

More than three-fourths of employers have written policies on monitoring personal use of company computers and e-mail, and more than half monitor phone use, says a survey of 336 human-resource managers by Society for Human Resources Management, an Alexandria, Virginia, professional group. Many of the policies prohibit personal use of office gear. However, many employers tend to turn a blind eye to parental transgressions that don't interfere with work.

Many working parents justify the extracurricular distractions by pointing out that they do as much or more office work at home. A survey of 501 adults shows employees spend an average 3.7 hours a week doing personal tasks online at the office. But they spend 5.9 hours working their paid jobs from home.

"People who are running copies of soccer schedules on the company copiers do not give it a second thought, because they're also using their home resources to do work—the home PC, the phone, a room in the house, paper, and personal time," says Jeff Saltzman, chief executive officer at Sirota Survey Intelligence, Purchase, New York, which surveys 1.5 million employees annually on work issues. Thus, if a big project for a sports team or dance troupe needs a graphic design or photocopying, parents may opt to do it at the office because the technology often is better.

Discussion Questions

1. Should employers have explicit policies on family-related uses of time and equipment while at work or should this issue be handle informally on a one-to-one basis? Explain.

2. Should employers give employees credit for work done at home even if this is very difficult, it not impossible, to monitor? Explain your answer.

3. Some people argue that employees' performance should be assessed and rewarded based on outcomes or what they get done rather than time at the office. Do you agree? Explain your answer.

Source: Adapted from S. Shellenbarger, "Work and Family," *The Wall Street Journal*, October 20, 2005, p. D-1.

How to Reduce Turnover

individual/
collaborative
learning
case 10.1

Applebee's International Inc. is trying to infuse a bit of General Electric Co. into the restaurant business. In a bid to reduce high turnover rates among restaurant employees, Applebee's, the U.S.'s biggest casual-dining chain by number of restaurants, reviews and ranks its hourly employees and then rewards managers for retaining their better workers.

The tactic is an unusual combination of two more-common techniques: employee-ranking systems popularized by some large corporations such as GE and retention bonuses paid to managers in high-turnover industries such as retail and restaurants. In those industries, turnover rates among hourly workers can run as high as 200 percent, meaning that the average worker leaves after six months. For other mid-size and large companies, annual employee turnover is typically about 10 percent to 15 percent.

At Applebee's, Overland Park, Kansas, managers must divide hourly workers into "A" players, the top 20 percent; B, the middle 60 percent; and C, the bottom 20 percent. The managers then are eligible for merit raises and bonuses based on how well they retain employees in the top 80 percent. The practice is unusual in the restaurant industry, where managers tend to worry more about staffing the next shift than career development and performance evaluation.

Applebee's says the system is time-consuming, but worth the effort. Before introducing the system, Applebee's measured overall turnover but didn't use the numbers to evaluate managers. Then, executives realized, "there is a different value if you lose a top-20 person than if you lose a bottom-20 person," says John Prutsman, who is in charge of human resources for the restaurants. In order to reward managers for keeping the best people, the company had to develop a system for reviewing hourly workers, including the grading criteria.

Today, Applebee's evaluates all hourly employees twice a year on nine counts, including reliability, attitude, guest service, and teamwork. First, employees complete a self-evaluation. Then, managers grade employees. Since employees can work for more than one manager, determining a final grade requires meeting to reconcile differing opinions. A typical Applebee's has about 60 hourly workers, one general manager, and three or four lower-level managers.

Critical Thinking Questions

1. Do you think Applebee's approach to reducing employee turnover is fair and reasonable? Explain your answer.

2. Some people believe that the key to retaining good workers in low-paying jobs is to offer them flexibility in scheduling rather than financial incentives. Do you agree? Explain your answer.

3. Do you think a system such as that used by Applebee's should be adopted by other fast-food restaurants such as McDonald's, Burger King, Taco Bell, and others? Why or why not? Explain your answer.

Collaborative Learning Exercise

A large hotel and restaurant chain has been experiencing turnover rates of 250 percent a year, on average. You are part of a consultant group (consisting of 4–6 students selected by the instructor) responsible for developing a proposal to identify the causes of the problem and to develop a set of suggestions to try to reduce turnover. After each team meets for about 20 minutes, class will reconvene and each team will present its recommendations to the instructor. This should be followed by an open class discussion.

Source: Adapted from E. White, "How to Reduce Turnover," *The Wall Street Journal*, November 28, 2005, p. C-3.

internet exercise 10.1

www.hr.com

Help on the Web

HR.com provides extensive and current information, updated almost daily, on all facets of human resource management, including compensation and benefits, staffing, legal issues, training and development, and labor relations. Explore the Web site and answer the following questions.

1. How can you use this information to become more effective as a manager? As a team member? In managing your own work? Explain.

2. What specific examples can you draw from this Web site that illustrate how this information may be beneficial to you in these different roles?

Patagonia

Summary

For every one hire at Patagonia, about 900 résumés come in for the position. The people who work at Patagonia are passionate—about something—and they know that in their own way they are making a difference. Yvon Chouinard started the business with the "Let my people surf" philosophy. This means that when the surf is up, the surfers in the company are allowed—even supposed—to go surfing. You can't schedule surfing or skiing next Tuesday at 2:00, because nature isn't predictable that way. The employees are encouraged and expected to stay current in whatever it is they do at the company. If they make skis, for instance, then they are expected to ski themselves. In the same light, the employees are expected to stay current in grassroots issues and bring what they learn about these issues back to the company so that the firm itself is current and responsive. Patagonia even pays employees for a 90-day internship to work for nonprofit grassroots efforts. Sometimes, employees even leave the company to go to work full time for these environmental organizations. That's okay with Patagonia, because the environment is the ultimate beneficiary. The child care facility at Patagonia was started in 1985. It has always been an integral part of Patagonia. Children are an integral part of the campus. Not only are they present at lunchtime, they are always a part of the day-to-day activities—running around the area. Work and family are not separate at the company. This increases job satisfaction tremendously at the company because people do not have to choose between their work and family obligations—they can check in on their kids when they need to.

Discussion Questions

1. What does workforce diversity mean at Patagonia?
2. Describe Yvon Chouinard's philosophy of "Let my people surf." How is this an effective HR policy for Patagonia?
3. How does the Patagonia grants council contribute to employee satisfaction?

chapter 11

Managing Employee Diversity

Learning Objectives

1 Explain the meaning and benefits of employee diversity.

2 Develop an awareness of the unique perspectives, problems, and issues of diverse employee groups.

3 Understand demographic trends in the labor force and their managerial implications.

4 Describe the challenges firms may face in the management of diversity.

5 Describe various approaches that managers may use to enjoy the benefits of employee diversity and meet the challenges associated with diversity.

Eleven Decades of Ensuring That Employee Diversity Equals Corporate Success

11

From its inception more than a century ago, at a time when employee diversity was an alien concept, IBM has embraced workforce diversity as a fundamental value. IBM's commitment to workforce diversity can be traced back to 1899, when it hired its first female and black employees—20 years before women's suffrage, 10 years before the founding of the NAACP, and 36 years after the signing of the Emancipation Proclamation.

In the early 1950s, when racial discrimination was perfectly legal and the norm in the South, Thomas Watson, IBM founder and CEO, wrote a policy statement stating IBM's commitment to fairness and inclusion. During negotiations with the governors of two southern states regarding the building of IBM plants, Watson said there would be no "separate but equal" racial policies at IBM. To ensure the governors took him seriously, he wrote a letter to his management team in 1953 and made the letter public. As a result, he said, both governors responded by choosing payroll and tax dollars over bad social policy. Almost five and a half decades later, IBM continues at the forefront of diversity. According to IBM's Chairman and CEO, Sam Palmisano, "diversity policies lie as close to IBM's core as they have throughout our heritage. Today, we're building a workforce in keeping with the global, diverse marketplace, to better serve our customers and capture a greater share of the on demand opportunity."

Commitment to diversity is far more than a public relations act for IBM. This is exemplified by the following:

- IBM purchases about $1.3 billion in supplies from minority-owned firms.
- IBM has eight task forces designed to make diverse employees feel welcomed and valued at IBM and to focus on the various constituencies as customers. These include Asian, Black, Gay/Lesbian/Bisexual/Transgender, Hispanic, men, Native American, people with disabilities, and women.
- IBM invests heavily in supporting initiatives to ensure all of its employees use their full potential. These initiatives include "Black Executive Forums" (to mentor black managers), "Multicultural Techies Inside Track" (to reduce voluntary attrition of minorities at IBM), "Women Perfectly Suited to Fulfill IBM's On Demand Strategy" (to prevent subtle ways women can be

excluded in the corporate environment), and the "Hispanic Task Force to Bridge Digital Divide" (to facilitate the recruitment, training, and mentoring of Hispanics).

- IBM has an extraordinarily extensive corporate Web site dedicated to diversity issues, which is continually updated. At the time of this writing (2006), 25 densely packed Web pages fall under the IBM diversity icon. Diversity information is divided into 11 areas (Asians, Blacks, Gay/Lesbian/Bisexual/Transgender, Hispanic/Latino, mature adults, people with disabilities, and so on).

- IBM has received over 150 national and international prestigious awards for successful management of diversity during the past decade, including the "Top Ten Best Companies for Asian Americans," "National Society of Black Engineers Employee of Choice," "Business Leadership Award from Equality Forum," "Top Five Companies in terms of Lesbian/Gay, Friendliness," "Society of Hispanic Professional Engineers Employer of the Year," "National Science Foundation—Diversity Award," "American Society on Aging—Business of the Year Award," and "Top Company for Women Executives," plus many, many others.

Source: Adapted from T. Childs, "Managing Workforce Diversity at IBM," *Human Resources Management*, 114 (1) (Spring 2005), pp. 73–77; www.ibm.com (2007).

CRITICAL THINKING QUESTIONS

1. *Why do most executives believe that effective management of diversity is critical to business success?*

2. *What are the most difficult challenges firms face in managing employee diversity? What can they do to deal with those challenges?*

We will be revisiting these questions again in our Concluding Thoughts at the end of the chapter after you have had an opportunity to read the following discussion on managing diversity.

The Meaning of Diversity

diversity

The wide spectrum of individual and group differences.

Appreciating and Valuing Diversity

The term **diversity** describes a wide spectrum of differences between people. On an individual level, a person's sexual preference, disability status, or many other characteristics may cause the individual to be perceived as different. Groups of individuals share characteristics that distinguish them from other groups. Some of the characteristics, such as race, age, and gender, cannot be controlled by the individuals involved. Others, such as occupation, political party membership, and religion, may be changed through conscious choice and deliberate effort.

The crucial fact to bear in mind about diversity, however, is that although the attitudes, life interests, expectations, and norms of behavior of groups may differ on average, the differences between groups are smaller than the differences within groups. Classifying people into such typologies as black or white, male or female, and gay or straight often leads to false stereotypes because it incorrectly assumes that group averages or characteristics apply to every individual in the group.

In Figure 11.1 on page 431, the curve for veterans shows that people who have been in the armed forces tend to be more accepting of an authoritarian management style than nonveterans. However, the figure does not prove that a particular veteran is more accepting of an authoritarian management style than a particular nonveteran. About half the veterans—those below point D on the curve—are less accepting of authoritarianism, and there is a great deal of overlap

FIGURE 11.1

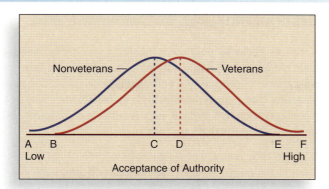

Group versus Individual Differences on Acceptance of Authoritarian Leadership

Source: From *Managing Human Resources*, by Gomez-Mejia, et al., copyright © 2007. Reprinted by permission of Pearson Education, Inc., Upper Saddle River, NJ.

between veterans and nonveterans on this trait. This is true of almost all psychological traits.[1] In other words, only a relatively small amount of employee diversity is explained by group membership. This is an important point to keep in mind. While managers need to be alert to diversity in their employees, the effective manager views employees as individuals, not as members of a particular group.

Currently, American-born white males constitute only 15 percent of new entrants to the workforce. The rest are women, immigrants, and minorities. Women now represent about half of the workforce, and nonwhites comprise about a third of the working population. In many parts of the country, the numbers are even more striking. Almost a third of New York residents are foreign-born, Miami is two-thirds Hispanic, San Francisco is one-third Asian, and 80 percent of Detroit residents are African Americans. The Hispanic community in the United States is increasing by 1.7 million a year. In seven of the largest states (including California, Texas, Florida, and New York) 20 percent or more of the population speaks a foreign language at home; in an additional 16 states, the proportion of nonnative English speakers exceeds 10 percent.[2]

In this chapter, you will be able to develop some skills that will positively affect your ability to relate to employees of different backgrounds. While these skills are important for everyone, they are crucial for those with managerial responsibilities, as summarized in Management Is Everyone's Business 11.1 on page 432.

One in 10 Americans is of Hispanic origin.

FIGURE 11.2

Benefits from a Heterogeneous Workforce

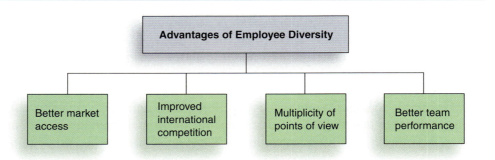

Advantages of Employee Diversity

As noted in Figure 11.2 above, a firm can derive many benefits from a heterogeneous workforce. First, however, company leaders must help employees avoid misunderstandings, ill feelings, and marginalization of those who do not fit into the dominant groups. Some of the most important potential benefits of diversity are better market access, global competitiveness, greater creativity, and improved team performance.

MARKET ACCESS   A diverse employee base allows a firm to tap into profitable markets. Utilizing employees who are attuned to these markets gives the firm a competitive edge. Women, older Americans, African Americans, Hispanics, and Asian Americans have more buying power than in the past. They expect businesses to provide products and services that meet their needs. As Deborah Yarborough, a manager at Silicon Graphics, points out, if they "don't feel respected and listened to, they will take their business elsewhere."[3]

Tapping a Market That Is Hot, Hot, Hot

When National City Corp. bank decided to roll out 78 new branches in Chicago two years ago, it went in knowing its market. With Hispanics expected to account for virtually all of the city's population growth over the next decade, the bank hired dozens of Spanish-speaking staffers and printed thousands of glossy pamphlets, hawking savings accounts to new immigrants and explaining the benefits of IRAs to more established Latinos. This year, the nation's 10th largest bank will double its Hispanic marketing budget, targeting middle-class Latinos with direct mail offering mortgage financing and money-market accounts, all written in Spanish. "A simple hello in Spanish," says Christian Sandoval, vice president of Hispanic marketing at National City, "can open the door to a Hispanic better than a product with a 4.5 percent interest rate." Spanish-speaking employees are always available to assist customers.

From Bank of America Corp. to Banco Popular, tapping into the growing Hispanic market is increasingly key for U.S. financial institutions. Indeed, U.S. banks may soon go on a shopping spree in search of smaller regional players with ties to Latino communities.

Foreign banks such as Spain's Banco Bilbao Vizacaya Argentaria have already snapped up banks in Texas, California, and Florida. "Now," predicts Jack M.W. Phelps, senior financial analyst for the Federal Deposit Insurance Corp., "we'll see domestic banks buying small Hispanic-oriented banks to acquire their skills."

Hispanics' wealth is rising three times faster than the U.S. average although 56 percent of them have never held a U.S. bank account. The FDIC predicts Hispanics will account for more than 50 percent of the U.S. retail banking growth over the next decade. That amounts to more than $200 billion in new businesses. Those numbers mean that banks are hiring all the talent they can get to take advantage of this Hispanic business boom, and branch managers are often provided incentives for programs designed to achieve a strong footing in this small but rapidly growing ethnic market. The result is a flurry of innovative marketing approaches being introduced by these branches. For example, in California, Wells Fargo & Co. is redecorating its branches with Mexican themes. That helped spur holders of matricula consular, the Mexican ID cards often used by illegal immigrants, to open 700 new accounts per day last year. At Bank of America; Spanish-language advertising brought in 1 million new checking accounts from Hispanics last year, fully 25 percent of the new accounts opened. And Banco Popular, a fast-growing bank based in Puerto Rico, now sends trucks outfitted with teller booths to U.S. construction sites so Latino laborers can deposit their checks directly into banking accounts. Wherever Latinos live and work, banks can no longer afford to be far behind.

Source: Adapted from B. Grow, "Tapping a Market That Is Hot, Hot, Hot," *Business Week*, January 17, 2005, p. 36.

Many companies have successfully tapped into diverse markets. Hispanic, Asian, and female community development officers from First Community Bank Boston present seminars to diverse communities in order to develop market opportunities. The bank also provides translation, advertising, an 800 line for people who do not speak English well, and modification of loan application procedures to make them less threatening to non-Anglo groups.[4] As described in Management Close-Up 11.1 above, other banks are targeting services to minority groups. These companies are able to develop those market niches to attain a sustainable competitive advantage. Avon has a workforce that is almost a third minority. The marketing team at Avon discovered a niche in an industry. that had been largely ignored: the beauty needs of women of color. The company introduced a highly profitable cosmetic line for black women back in 1999 which is still selling well almost a decade later.[5] At both American Express Co. and Merrill Lynch & Co., African-American female employees attempt to attract black investors by holding workshops and networking receptions in such venues as African-American museums. Within two years of launching the program, 68 percent of new business at American Express has come from African-American clients.[6] Upon the advice of several older employees approaching retirement, in the mid-2000's Motorola decided to romance the rapidly growing over-55 market by making phones with features that aging consumers like, such as a zoom function to bump up the font size on the tiny screen and internal speakers that can be connected to hearing aids.[7]

INTERNATIONAL COMPETITION   As discussed in Chapter 2, success increasingly depends on a firm's ability to compete on an international stage. A growing number of U.S. firms have established joint ventures with foreign companies, and many workers are employed by foreign companies and work for foreign managers. Japanese cars are produced in Kentucky, Swedish pharmaceuticals are made in Italy, and U.S. software is developed in India. Phillip Morris and Intel operate in more then 200 countries and employees speak more than 100 languages.

Firms with employee diversity in their home offices are likely to display the cultural sensitivity, understanding, and awareness that will help them succeed in the global arena. An observer has noted that "there is a growing consensus that U.S. managers are more . . . able to adapt to other cultures and environments than managers from other countries. Experts suspect that's because U.S. managers grow up leading a more diverse workforce at home."[8]

Bank of America has taken advantage of its employee diversity in a global context. The organization does business in 37 countries, and the California customer call center staff speaks more than 13 languages. This is possible because 32 million Americans speak a language other than English at home, and 8.6 million of them live in California.[9] Similarly, the Du Pont Company uses its 100-plus ethnic and gender networks as a source of internal resource for global access. As a senior manager explains, "Network members have provided important insights regarding ethnic markets here in the United States as well as in other regions of the world. For example, the company recently test marketed a new hosiery fiber with women in its Asian network. In addition, African American networks helped our agricultural products business build a closer relationship with black farmers in South Africa, a major customer base for DuPont."[10]

MULTIPLICITY OF POINTS OF VIEW   People from different backgrounds bring a variety of experiences, skills, abilities, and information to bear on the tasks at hand. This allows them to examine issues and problems from different angles. Research on group dynamics suggests that groups with members from a variety of backgrounds are likely to come up with more ideas and solutions than groups whose members are homogeneous.[11] Diversity is an important source of innovation that helps fuel creativity and improve a firm's competitive position in the marketplace. For example, "diverse groups of employees conceptualized product development, manufacturing and the marketing strategies" for Saturn Corporation.[12] American-born physicists are in the minority at Bell Laboratories, and the first language of biochemists at Schering-Plough's research labs is less likely to be English than Korean, Hindi, Chinese, Japanese, German, Russian, Vietnamese, or Spanish. Effective management of diversity has helped these firms become highly successful in their efforts to be innovative.

TEAM PERFORMANCE   Groups consisting of people with different personality types, attitudes, ethnicity, and gender also make better decisions. A diverse team may be able to find better solutions because of the divergent thinking processes characteristic of a more diverse group of people. Diversity minimizes the phenomenon called *groupthink*, in which a homogeneous group agrees on a mistaken solution because members share a similar mindset. The presence of team members who view the problem differently may stimulate others in the team to discover novel approaches that they would not have considered, thereby leading to better decisions. Moreover, diverse group members may learn from, emulate, and internalize the different strengths of other team members. This allows the team to conceptualize problems in a more comprehensive manner, avoiding simplistic solutions that may prove to be unsatisfactory.

The Challenges of Diversity

As summarized in Figure 11.3 on page 436 potential problems can emerge when there is increasing employee diversity. These problems include pressures toward homogenization, lower cohesiveness, interpersonal conflict and tension, and confusing employee diversity with affirmative action. Firms must effectively manage these challenges in order to derive the benefits noted above.

Management Minicase 11.2 at the end of this chapter discusses how this is a particularly serious issue in some parts of the economy such as Wall Street.

PRESSURES TOWARD HOMOGENIZATION There is a natural tendency for organizations to become demographically homogeneous because people are attracted to others they believe are similar to themselves. Indeed, as employee diversity increases, individuals segregate into groups composed of people like themselves, and dissimilar co-workers may feel pressure to leave the organization. Turnover of dissimilar employees tends to produce a **monoculture** within the firm, causing the organization to become more homogeneous. As a firm becomes more monocultural, the job satisfaction of minority employees and women decreases, which translates into higher resignation rates. On average, at all organizational levels and among all age groups, the turnover rate of minorities is 40 percent higher than that of whites, and the turnover rate of women is more than twice that of men.[13]

Dissimilar employees who stay may be segregated within the firm and kept out of the mainstream. **Ethnocentrism** may become prevalent among various groups of employees, meaning that they believe that their way of doing things, their values, and their norms are inherently superior to those of other groups and cultures. To the extent that managers are white males, their values, beliefs, motivations, and attitudes may prevent dissimilar employees from being promoted, because they do not look, act, and think in what are considered appropriate ways for individuals who aspire to responsible managerial positions. Although the exclusion of women and minorities may not be malicious or deliberate, ethnocentrism at the top makes it difficult for dissimilar groups to participate at all organizational levels. This creates a **glass ceiling,** an intangible barrier that prevents women and minorities from rising to the upper levels. Only about 3 percent of senior executives in Fortune 500 firms are women.

The prevalence of segregated groups may also lead to **segmented communication** channels within the firm. This means that communication flows are far greater within groups than between groups. For example, one study indicates that a surprising amount of communication occurs only among individuals

Minorities make up 15 percent of the Ohio State Highway Patrol, which actively recruits its diverse workforce through campus recruiting and employee referrals and promotes minority officers to leadership positions.

monoculture

The homogeneous organizational culture that results from turnover of dissimilar employees.

ethnocentrism

A belief that may become prevalent among majority-group employees, meaning that they believe that their way of doing things, their values, and their norms are inherently superior to those of other groups and cultures.

glass ceiling

The intangible barrier that prevents women and minorities from rising to the upper levels in business.

segmented communication

Flows of information within the firm that are far greater within groups than between groups.

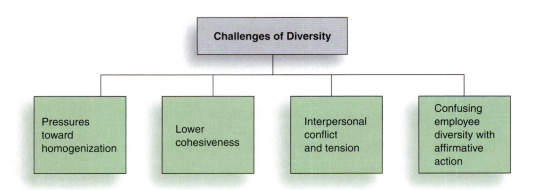

of the same sex and ethnic status. This was found to be true among all professional groups and at all organizational levels, even at the executive level where there are few women and minorities.[14] When employee viewpoints and ideas remain confined to employees' own groups, it is difficult to establish common ground across various groups. Unfortunately, this also means that dissimilar employees may not be attuned to mainstream communication networks or be able to share their unique experiences with the rest of the company.

LOWER COHESIVENESS A measure of how emotionally close group members are and how supportive they are of each other is the degree of **cohesiveness.** Diversity may lead to a fragmented workforce with little cohesion. In the extreme, it may lead to a lack of commonality of organizational values and goals. Taylor Cox, a respected academic and consultant on diversity issues, noted that "a core of similarity among group members is desirable. Members must share some common values and norms to promote coherent actions on organizational goals. The need for heterogeneity, to promote problem solving and innovation, must be balanced with the need for organizational coherence and unity of action to provide competitive advantage."[15] Management Is Everyone's Business 11.2 on page 437 includes a set of recommendations that teams should consider in order to effectively deal with these issues.

INTERPERSONAL CONFLICT AND TENSION As organizations become more diverse, mistrust, lack of understanding, and lack of mutual respect may lead to decreasing cooperation among employees and poor integration of individuals who are supposed to work closely with each other. Diversity may also cause stress and interpersonal friction, making it difficult to reach agreement on issues. In extreme cases, open conflict and other problems may ensue. In countries where there is high "power distance" (see discussion of this cultural dimension in Chapter 2) it may be difficult for low power employees to participate and hence diversity may not be used as an asset.[16] Attempts to do so may even be counterproductive. On the other hand, in countries, such as the United States, where power distance is low, there is a greater likelihood of individuals' overcoming cultural barriers to communication and achieving the potential advantages in diversity.

CONFUSING EMPLOYEE DIVERSITY WITH AFFIRMATIVE ACTION
Affirmative action and employee diversity are not the same thing. As we discussed in the preceding chapter, **affirmative action** is a government-mandated

cohesiveness

The emotional closeness group members feel toward each other and how supportive they are of each other.

Comparing Affirmative Action, Valuing Diversity, and Managing Diversity

affirmative action

A federal government–mandated program that requires corporations to provide opportunities to women and members of minority groups who traditionally have been excluded from good jobs; it aims to accomplish the goal of fair employment by urging employers to make a conscious effort to hire members of protected classes.

Working as a Team   Despite management's best intentions, employee diversity may lead to interpersonal problems within and between teams unless all employee groups and group members learn to work effectively with one another in a climate of mutual respect. Interpersonal friction can lead to open conflict, wider mistrust and loss of respect, even chaos, and overt or subtle discrimination by those who control organizational resources. If groups become dysfunctional or segregated, the problem-solving and innovation benefits of diversity will be reduced or lost. Team members should:

- Strive to listen to the viewpoints of different individuals within the team and consider those as valid as yours.

- Resist temptation to relate primarily to people who are similar to you, disregarding the rest of the team.

- Actively seek to bring people into the team who are different, and value some degree of heterogeneity as a good thing.

- Be careful with verbal and body language that other team members may find offensive.

- Ensure the participation of all members of the group, even those who might be shy, quiet, or afraid, and enable then to bring their ideas to the table.

- Strive to create a win/win environment within the team so that all participants, regardless of background, develop a sense of common fate within the group.

program that requires corporations to provide opportunities to women and members of minority groups who traditionally here been excluded from good jobs. Introduced more than 35 years ago, affirmative action programs are controversial. Some members of groups not covered by the programs have complained that affirmative action programs lead to "reverse discrimination," in which opportunity is denied to majority-group members. There is also a belief that affirmative action programs lead to lower self-esteem among beneficiaries by creating the perception that they received undeserved special treatment.

It would be difficult to prove what the real effect of affirmative action has been. It is clear that women and minorities have had more advancement opportunities since the programs were implemented. For instance, the percentage of women managers increased from 27 percent to 44 percent between 1981 and 2007. The number of African-American officials, managers, technicians, and skilled craftspeople has tripled since the mid-1960s, while the number in clerical positions has quadrupled and the number in professional jobs has doubled. In 2006, 15 Hispanics occupied top executive spots among Fortune 1000 companies. Three black executives were listed as CEOs in the Fortune 500 (www.fortune.com/sections). At some of the largest blue-chip firms the progress has been remarkable. For instance, almost half of the 50 highest paid employees at Xerox in 2006 were minorities, and a third of board members at General Motors are minorities.

It may be logical to assume these changes are the consequence of affirmative action. On the other hand, diversity is a fact of life as well as work life. Unlike affirmative action, a *diversity program* recognizes that, as a *de facto*

A diverse workforce is a key component of highly regarded firms.

consequence of demographic changes in the workforce, organizations need to employ women and minorities in order to succeed. Whereas affirmative action is a political solution to societal ills, a diversity program is a human resource program that focuses on performance and competence to ensure equal opportunities in a manner blind to ethnicity and sex. Unfortunately, some employees, particularly white males, believe that *diversity* is simply another name for affirmative action. A survey found that twice as many white men as women and minorities believe that promotions of women and minorities are a result of affirmative action.[17]

Diversity programs present four related challenges to HR managers and companies. First, white males may view a program as a threat to their own opportunities for advancement. When white male executives develop a cynical view of diversity management, the program is unlikely to provide competitive advantage to the firm. Second, the perception of special treatment may undermine the formal procedures, policies, and enforcement mechanisms of the diversity program. Third, women and minorities in positions of authority may not receive as much respect from their subordinates and colleagues as do white men. Finally, the organization may not reap the benefits of employee diversity described earlier.

It is probably true that a generation ago many business leaders launched affirmative action programs somewhat begrudgingly. Government pressure and the fear of losing costly class action suits were probably their primary motives. Today, there is strong support for the idea that creating an environment of inclusion of diverse groups is a competitive business necessity. Indeed, a quick look at the Web pages of most of the Fortune 1000 firms today shows that diversity is at the forefront of policy statements made by CEOs. For instance, according to the chairman and CEO of PricewaterhouseCoopers, LLP, "we must promote diversity and inclusion to attract and retain the best talent, to maintain meaningful client relationships, to win continuously in the marketplace."[18] Business leaders are quick to stress that diversity policies are not intended to encourage what may be perceived as preferential quotas for particular groups.[19] Rather, the intent is to provide opportunities to employees of different backgrounds. Nevertheless, debate on these issues is likely to continue for years to come. Most Americans, including a majority of women and minority group members, reject quotas that set aside a proportion of job openings for "protected classes."[20] At the same time, most successful firms hold managers accountable for achieving diversity goals.[21]

LOC-In

1 **Learning Objective Check-In**

1. *Jeanne is a U.S. manager who has always led a diverse workforce, ever since she began working at an aerospace engineering firm as a project manager in 1986. Today, that firm is highly successful versus other firms from Japan, Italy, and Canada. Jeanne suspects that this _____ is attributable to the firm's ongoing emphasis on diversity.*
   a. *multiplicity of points of view*
   b. *international competitiveness*
   c. *market access*
   d. *team performance*

Diversity Today

The U.S. workforce has been a mosaic of diverse cultures at least since the 1880s. When large contingents of immigrants arrived from southern Europe, Poland, Ireland, and Russia, they were considered outsiders because they had different customs, did not speak English, and were not Protestants. Immigrants from

Asia and from eastern and southern Europe were largely excluded under the Immigration Act of 1929 because they were considered intellectually inferior based on their performance on standardized tests during Army recruitment drives in World War I. Women were largely missing from the workforce except in elementary-school teaching, nursing, and sewing. Most clerical administrative work was performed by men. Many of the largest companies considered hiring southern Europeans, Catholics, Jews, and Irish to be a poor business practice.

Throughout successive generations, many ethnic barriers eroded, and the diverse European groups entered the mainstream. This created the myth of the "American melting pot," a belief that the United States was a country of immigrants and that diverse groups would assimilate and blend into the American culture over time. However, "in real life many ethnic and most racial groups retained their identities—but they did not express them at work. Employees often abandoned most of their ethnic and cultural distinctions while at work to keep their jobs and get ahead. Many Europeans came to the United States, Americanized their names, perfected their English, and tried to enter the mainstream as quickly as possible."[22]

Today the prevalent thinking is that rather than making everyone fit a common corporate mold, organizations should support, nurture, and utilize people's differences in a way that both respects employees' unique perspectives and promotes a shared vision. If a firm is going to succeed, company leaders must learn to manage a diverse workforce.

A good place to start is to be cognizant of the unique perspectives, problems, and issues of various groups. It is important to keep two things in mind. First, as discussed earlier, characteristics overlap between any two groups. Second, employees have multiple identities, some of which are more strongly felt at different moments in their lives and in different contexts. For instance, a female black Hispanic engineer from Cuba who is 50 years old and disabled may identify most strongly with women under some circumstances and with Cubans under others.

Each person's self-concept reflects a web of identities: sex, race, ethnic origins, place of birth, religion, age, sexual orientation, occupation, socioeconomic status, and so on. Seeing individuals in terms of multiple identities permits a better appreciation of their personalities in more subtle, less stereotypical, and ultimately more realistic ways. Many of the social and legal barriers that have kept ethnic groups apart have come down because there are millions of people with mixed identities. For this reason, the Census Bureau now allows Americans to classify themselves into multiple racial categories. The evidence seems to suggest that airtight racial distinctions are slowly disappearing. Currently, approximately one-fourth of blacks and more than half of Hispanics marry people outside their racial or ethnic group.[23] At the same time, specific employee groups certainly have concerns that still remain. The following is a presentation of some of these groups' concerns. Obviously, they should be considered carefully as general trends rather than the stereotyping of every member of the category. Skills for Managing 11.1 on page 440 will help you counteract negative stereotypes that often exist between groups of people who perceive themselves to be different. The Management Is Everyone's Business 11.3 on page 441 provides a set of recommendations that you should apply to yourself as an individual when dealing with people who are different from yourself.

COUNTERACTING STEREOTYPES

Racial or ethnic prejudice takes many forms. German Americans were often discriminated against during World War I, Japanese Americans were put into concentration camps during World War II, African Americans are often targeted by police for routine traffic violations, and Hispanic Americans often have to deal with immigration raids. Within five months of the terrorist attacks of September 11, 2001, there was a 150 percent increase in the number of "bias incidents" reported by the police against Arabs, Muslims, and others who may look like them, such as some East Indians. The American-Arab Anti-Discrimination Committee logged more than 440 hate crimes and cases of discrimination and harassment against Arabs and Muslims within two months of Sept. 11. Such claims again increased following the Gulf War II in 2003 and disclosures in 2006 that the federal government without warrants was tapping phones and checking e-mails of those who might be suspected of terrorist connections.

Racial or ethnic prejudice is generally based on crude stereotypes that are as old as mankind itself. The earliest records of stereotyping are Egyptian hieroglyphs about Assyrians and Babylonians. The Lydian tablets (from present day Izmir), which are just being translated, speak harshly of piratical seamen called Achaeans (Greeks). Or think of the Old Testament and the Israelite stereotyping of Philistines. The Greeks referred to all aliens as "barbarians" because they couldn't speak Greek but went "baa-baa," like sheep. The Scots and the French have, through history, been England's favorite stereotype targets. The Scots have been seen as "wild" ever since their James VI became James I of England in 1603 and brought south thousands of "thuggish" Scots on the make. Suspicion of France has been rampant ever since the Norman Conquest.

A common thread in stereotyping is that particular groups make themselves feel better by looking down on other tribes and having a laugh at their expense. The English mock the "stupid" Irish, who in turn make jokes about the Western Irish Paddies, seen to be doltish bumpkins. East Coast Americans look down on Kansans, perhaps, or Appalachian mountain dwellers. New yorkers look down on everybody. The French have attitudes toward "boorish" Germans, the Germans have attitudes toward "backward" Turks, and the British (and Americans) joke about the "arrogant" French. Old European attitudes toward people from the Orient (Asia) speak of cruelty and too much lust.

Team Exercise

As noted above, humans have a tendency to lump together people who are different from them into categories, ascribing certain characteristics (often negative) to those who fit into those categories. One way to break down stereotypes is to meet people who presumably should share characteristics associated with their category (not only ethnic or tribal, but old or young, male or female) but in fact are individuals (some who might somewhat fit the stereotype, some who are the opposite of the stereotype, and many others who might fall anywhere in between). Your class will be randomly divided into groups of five. Each group will make a list of commonly held stereotypes for any one category of your choice. Please choose only one category (or one pair of opposites). Categories may include gender, age—older versus younger workers, geographic origin (for instance, those from specific states, or those from the North, South, Midwest, West, and East), urban versus rural, occupational groups (such as lawyers, teachers, or taxi drivers), university majors (such as accounting, music, or physical education majors), union versus nonunion members, public versus private sector employees, fraternity or sorority members, those who come from high and low family incomes, blue collar versus white collar employees—as you can see your possiblities are almost endless. Then after listing the stereotypes, each team should think of examples of individuals they have known from the category or opposing categories and the extent to which those individuals differ from or fit the stereotypes.

After meeting for approximately 15–20 minutes, each group should post or write their results, and the instructor will then mediate discussion.

Source: Adapted from T. Varadarajan, "At Least It Is OK to Back Away with Stereotypes," *The Wall Street Journal*, February 21, 2003, p. W-15.

Working as an Individual It is important to learn to work with people who are different from you. Employees who can relate effectively to members of other groups are more likely to be favorably noticed by management and placed in positions of responsibility. One of the most fundamental management skills is the ability to get work done through others. However, even those who are not interested in a managerial role will benefit from relating well to people of diverse backgrounds; support from peers will make their work easier to accomplish. As an individual employee you should:

- Show respect for other people in the organization no matter how different they are from you.

- Develop a reputation for relating well to all sorts of people; this is almost certain to help your long-term career prospects within and outside the firm.

- Avoid being overly sensitive to perceived "slights" by other employees who are different from you; perhaps you might unwittingly be blowing things out of proportion.

- Go out of your way to work with people who are different from you; you may be surprised how much you can learn and grow from the experience.

- Develop insights into your way of thinking and why you respond to certain people the way you do; perhaps you may be unaware that you are reacting to them based on prejudice and stereotypes without considering all the relevant factors.

- Volunteer to participate in diversity initiatives (such as diversity training) offered by your organization.

African Americans

African Americans constitute 11.3 percent of the population and 11.8 percent of the workforce in the United States. Prior to the Civil War, most African Americans were enslaved. Since then this group has suffered the most blatant forms of discrimination. Discrimination has resulted in poverty, segregated housing, fewer educational opportunities, and severe underrepresentation in managerial and professional jobs.

Until the 1960s, it was legal in the United States to segregate African Americans and create company policies that automatically eliminated them from employee selection and promotion decisions. Prestigious universities refused to admit them, creating a vicious cycle of low educational achievement, little opportunity for career advancement, and little chance to enter professional, technical, and managerial jobs. Institutionalized racism is now illegal. But many blacks believe that discrimination is still present in the corporate world today.[24]

Unfortunately, many whites do not realize that bigotry against blacks in the workplace is still a serious problem. For instance, one survey showed that half as many whites as blacks believe that there is a lack of fair treatment in promotion decisions. The discrepancy between white and minority perceptions of equal opportunity in the workplace was larger among African Americans than among any other ethnic group surveyed, including Hispanics and Asian Americans.[25] In fact, a 2006 report concluded that "a new wave of

Asian Americans fight many preconceptions in the workplace. Suzette Won Hass struggled with her Korean heritage as a child and felt embarrassed to speak the language. Now she regrets not knowing it better.

race-discrimination cases is appearing in the workplace: African Americans who feel that they are being passed over for Hispanics."[26] Bias is not always intentional; unintentional bias has been reported at numerous companies and organizations, including Amtrak, Coca-Cola, and the New Jersey State Police.

Asian Americans

Asian Americans make up 3.6 percent of the U.S. population. People designated as Asian Americans include a wide variety of races, ethnic groups, and nationalities including people of Japanese, Chinese, Korean, Indian, and Pakistani descent. Asian Americans are well represented in technical fields, but despite high educational achievements, they are severely underrepresented in managerial positions and seldom make it to the upper echelons. Those Asians who head high-tech companies are often the founders of the companies. Asian Americans have been held back by the stereotype that they are too reserved to lead others and that they have limited verbal skills. Other characterizations of Asians as hardworking and deferential can end up relegating them to roles as corporate workhorses—not leaders—and keep them segregated in technical areas. Asian Americans are also subject to bigotry; in the mid-1990s, 40 percent of African Americans and Hispanics and almost a third of whites saw Asian Americans as "unscrupulous, crafty, and devious in business."[27] A survey reported by *Time* in 2006 suggests that many Asian Americans feel alienated even when they were born in the United States. They are often seen as what sociologists call "forever foreigners . . . their looks lead to a lifetime of questions like 'no, where are you really from?'"[28] As of this writing, all Asian American households, on average, have an annual median household income that is 16 percent greater than that of whites, and those Americans who trace their roots to India enjoy an income advantage over whites of more than 42 percent.[29] The perception that Asian Americans are already successful paradoxically makes some managers insensitive to their needs and problems.

Disabled Americans

According to the United States Census 2000, approximately 50 million Americans have some form of disability. Among people with disabilities between the ages of 16–64, the employment rate is 55.8%. People with disabilities are subject to unwarranted discrimination when supervisors resist hiring them for fear that they require special equipment, training, and support. They may also be perceived as being less capable and less flexible than non-disabled employees. Once hired, co-workers may feel uncomfortable around them, making disabled employees feel isolated or patronized so that they are unable to fully integrate into a work group.

In fact, accommodating employees with disabilities is less expensive than people think. According to the 2005 report issued by the Job Accommodation Network, the typical cost of accommodating a disabled employee is $600. Disabled employees are also less prone to absenteeism and turnover than other employees.[30]

Some progress has been made over time in the hiring of people with disabilities. The National Organization on Disability/Harris Survey of Americans with Disabilities reports that in 2003 56 percent of this group was gainfully employed, compared to 46 percent in 1986 (www.fortune.com/sections). However, this same survey indicates that there are many more disabled people (two out of three) who are unemployed but would prefer to be working. One promising development is the use of telecommuting to increase employment of people with disabilities. The Equal Employment Opportunity Commission (EEOC) has issued a set of guidelines to encourage the hiring of disabled employees on a telecommuting basis (see www.eeoc.gov/fact/telework.html). According to an EEOC officer, "for some people with disabilities, telework may actually be the difference between having the opportunity to be among an employer's best and brightest workers and not working at all."[31] Some organizations are also starting to provide assistance for parents of children with disabilities.[32]

Foreign-Born Americans

It is estimated that 10 percent of Americans are foreign born. The statistics are not reliable, because they do not account for at least 11 million undocumented immigrants. About 820,000 immigrants enter the United States legally every year.[33]

Immigrants tend to be relatively young, ambitious, and upwardly mobile. Some business sectors view them as a remedy for the relatively small generation of native-born Americans now entering their thirties. Immigrants form 250,000 new households every year, fueling demand for the services of builders, brokers, bankers, and department stores, among other businesses. In Los Angeles, about a quarter of home buyers aged 25 to 44 are foreign born. More than two-thirds of California's population growth in the past 15 years can be attributed to immigrants. New York State would have lost population were it not for 475,000 newcomers.

The United States is still the land of opportunity for most of the world. At any given time, there are more than half a million foreign students in American universities. A high proportion of them choose to remain in the United States after graduation, particularly those majoring in engineering and technical fields, where they often outnumber native-born Americans.

The United States has had a love–hate relationship with immigrants for much of its history. Periodically, immigrants are denounced for taking jobs away from native-born citizens and for not assimilating into the proverbial American melting pot. Established immigrants have worried that they might have to compete with new immigrants for jobs. Such beliefs have generally been unfounded, but they have often resulted in restrictive legislation. They also expose the foreign born to resentment and discrimination, complicating other factors, such as language, culture, and race, that create barriers to their full participation at work.

Nonetheless, the United States continues to provide upward mobility for people coming to its shores. One study revealed that the earnings of the more than 25 million immigrants who arrived since the mid-1970s had reached the average income of the native-born population within 15 years of arrival. Also, the poverty rate of those who are in the country for 15 to 20 years is lower than that of people born in the United States.[34]

Another study suggests that most foreign-born immigrants do not create an economic threat to those who are native born. According to 2002 figures, the income differential between a household led by a foreign-born and a native-born resident in the United States is only about 12 percent ($36 thousand versus $41 thousand dollars annually). This is amazingly low considering the additional hurdles an immigrant faces in learning a new language, adapting to a new culture, coping with employment discrimination, and so on.[35]

It is important to note that large-scale immigration is not the exclusive province of the United States. World migration has increased dramatically during the past 25 years in many parts of the planet.[36] All one has to do is to stroll through the streets of Paris, Vancouver, Amsterdam, Johannesburg, London, Madrid, Kuwait, or San Jose to see the mix of people from different nationalities who live and work there, often with dubious legal status. During the 10-year period 1996–2006, the United States received 27 percent of the world's international migrants, yet Western Europe received almost as many (21 percent).[37] While the United States has always been a nation of immigrants, firms in many other countries are now having to adapt to such demographic changes rather abruptly.

Hispanic Americans

Nearly 28 million people, or one in ten Americans, consider themselves to be of Hispanic origin. This figure, which is based on census data, is probably a conservative estimate. Many Hispanics are afraid to identify themselves for fear of the Immigration and Naturalization Service and a general distrust of the government. A widely quoted figure is that the actual number is closer to 40 million and in some areas such as California, New York, southern Texas, and southern Florida, the proportion reaches close to one-fourth of the population.[38]

According to census figures, roughly 60 percent of Hispanics have roots in Mexico, 12 percent in Puerto Rico, and 5 percent in Cuba. Fifty-eight counties in the United States have a Hispanic majority. The largest number of Mexican Americans (2.6 million) live in Los Angeles County. The largest concentration of Puerto Ricans (900,000) live in the five boroughs of New York City. Dade County, Florida, where Miami is located, has the most Cuban Americans (600,000). However, a recent study using census figures found that Hispanics are not staying in segregated areas but rather moving to areas with few from their ethnic group such as Ford (Kansas), Texas (Oklahoma), Prince William (Virginia) and Crawford (Iowa).[39] The portion of the U.S. economy that is Hispanic is bigger than the gross national product of most Spanish-speaking countries, with 772,000 Hispanic-owned firms.[40]

"Hispanic" is not a term for a race but a label encompassing a wide variety of groups. It includes American Indians of the Southwest, whose homelands became Spanish colonies more than four centuries ago and who adopted Spanish surnames and customs, as well as immigrants from Spain, Mexico, Guatemala, Argentina, Cuba, and other Central and South American countries. At least 70 million Latin Americans are of European descent, 25 million are of African descent (mostly from the Spanish Antilles and the Caribbean basin), 10 million or so are of Asian descent from various countries, 60 million are Native Americans, and a high proportion are individuals of mixed ethnic background. Hispanic groups are diverse within their own countries as well as within the United States in terms of race, history, and economic status. What they have in common are the Spanish language, which Hispanic families tend to maintain across generations, the Catholic religion, which plays a key role in people's lives and values, and a high regard for extended family. Hispanic people tend to be family-oriented. Some cultural attributes, such as humor, a more laid-back style, chivalry, and freedom to express emotions, may also be present.

Language and skin color can pose problems for Hispanics in the workplace, particularly for recent immigrants. Many Hispanic immigrants come from an agrarian background and have limited formal education. Value differences may also cause problems. "Some Latinos see non-Latino North Americans as unemotional, insensitive, self-centered, rigid, and ambitious to the point where they live to work rather than the other way around."[41] For their part, non-Hispanics often complain that Hispanics' "punctuality, absenteeism, planning, and scheduling can be a lot more loose than one would expect."[42] Clearly these negative stereotypes do not apply to most people of either group.

Homosexuals

Estimates of the percentage of the population that is homosexual vary between 1 and 10 percent. Homosexuals are sometimes referred to as an "invisible minority" because an individual's status is not obvious unless the person declares his or her sexual orientation. Unlike race, gender, national origin, age, and disability, there is no federal antidiscrimination law protecting homosexuals, and only a handful of states offer such protection at the state level. The military has a controversial "don't ask, don't tell" policy that allows dismissal from the military only if an individual discloses his or her homosexuality.

Understandably, most gays and lesbians keep their homosexuality secret for fear of jeopardizing their careers. Declared homosexuals may face intolerance and scorn from co-workers, bosses, and even clients. However, company attitudes are changing in a way that was unthinkable even a decade ago. For instance, General Motors of Canada, Hewlett-Packard, Intel, American Express, IBM, and the Walt Disney Company now make health benefits available to same-sex partners of employees. Likewise, public policy regarding homosexuals is likely to become more tolerant in the future. For instance, starting in 2005 the state of California grants state-registered domestic partners all of the same rights, protections, benefits, obligations, and duties as married spouses.

Older Workers

The U.S. workforce is growing older each year. The average age of the workforce is expected to reach 42 by the year 2010, and the proportion of employees between 50 and 65 is currently increasing at twice the rate of the overall population. Negative stereotypes of older workers as being inflexible, resistant to learning new skills, and coasting until retirement are pervasive.

Contrary to stereotypes, older workers, particularly those in jobs requiring little physical exertion, function as well as they did 20 or 30 years earlier. They also have more wisdom and seasoned judgment. Many successful companies have

Many older workers feel vulnerable to layoffs and other cost-cutting measures. Bob Miller, 55, of Chicago, lost his job at an insurance company despite 20 years of experience and looked for work for more than two years afterwards.

implemented programs to share the knowledge and wisdom of older workers with younger employees through mentoring. In the words of an HR consultant, "these companies are striking gold in a silver mine by leveraging senior workers as knowledge champions."[43] Because the service sector has been growing more rapidly than manufacturing, physical strength and health are less important for successful performance than they were in the past. Nevertheless, older workers often suffer from discrimination in hiring and promotion decisions. Also, unlike countries in which the wisdom of older people is respected, the input of older workers in U.S. firms is often not accorded the consideration it deserves. (See Management Close-Up 11.2, "When Grey Heads Roll," on page 447.) Another serious problem older workers encounter is the rising cost of health insurance and the increasing reluctance of firms to provide any sort of job-based coverage. Indeed, this has become a considerable topic of debate in the latter half of this decade, and from all indications both state and federal governments are likely to become more heavily involved in health care.[44] The United States is the only industrialized country that does not offer public health insurance. This lack of coverage can be catastrophic to elderly workers.

LOC-In

③ Learning Objective Check-In

1. *Harry is a 64-year-old worker who works in an office environment. He is very good at dealing with clients and has more wisdom than the average younger worker. Harry has been passed over three times in the last three years, however, and he suspects his age plays the biggest role in the decision, especially since he has the most experience, the best record, and intends to continue working well past age 65. Which of the following statements is true regarding older workers?*
   a. *The U.S. workforce is growing younger each year, with the average age expected to fall to 40 by 2010.*
   b. *The proportion of workers between 50 and 65 is increasing at twice the rate of the overall population.*
   c. *The manufacturing sector has been growing faster than the service sector, making older workers less useful today.*
   d. *Older workers seldom suffer from discrimination in hiring and promotion decisions.*

Religious Diversity

Many, if not most, Americans trace their roots to immigrants who fled religious persecution and wars in Europe. Apart from those of the Jewish faith, the United States has been traditionally and overwhelmingly Christian. In recent years, however, there has been a growing non-Christian minority, with approximately 4 million Americans now professing Islamic, Hindu, Taoist, or other non-Christian beliefs. This went largely unnoticed until America's tolerance toward people of different religious backgrounds was severely tested by the terrorist attacks of September 11, 2001. A survey by the Society for Human Resource Management (SHRM) revealed that so-called "ethnic religions" such as Islam now come just after race and gender in American perceptions of "otherness."[45] Security fears due to terrorist threats have led to many complaints of "racial profiling" and discrimination by Arab Americans, as well as those who may be confused as Muslims, such as some people of East Indian descent.[46] Religious tolerance has been most severely tested in Europe in recent years, culminating with the Paris riots in 2005 and widespread protests by Muslim believers in 2006 against what they see as Western insensitivity to their faith.[47]

Many firms are now developing policies concerning tolerance for religious diversity. These policies cover such issues as permissible garments at work, religious holidays, potential harassment or ridicule based on one's faith, and the display of religious symbols on company premises.

Undocumented Workers

There are at least 11 million workers in the United States who are here illegally or without immigration papers. Approximately 57 percent come from Mexico, and the remaining 43 percent from various countries around the world. In many

When Grey Heads Roll

THEME: ETHICS

One of the growing ethical issues this decade is whether organizations systematically terminate older employees in what is perhaps a short-sighted attempt to save money as these employees typically enjoy higher salaries and increased health premiums. In recent years there has been a flurry of allegations by older employees that they are easy prey of cost cutters in corporate America. Below you will find several recent examples. Keep in mind, however, that the firms involved deny that age was a factor in layoffs and the "smoking gun" needed to prove deliberate age discrimination is hard to find.

Best Buy: Layoffs According to Age?

Several weeks after being laid off last spring by Best Buy, the consumer electronics retailer, Lynette M. Steuck, a software project manager, showed up for a résumé-polishing "outplacement session" of the sort commonly offered to employees recently shoved out the door. As Ms. Steuck, 51, a divorced mother, surveyed the sparely furnished conference room, she was struck by something. "It was shocking," she recalled recently. "There were probably 25 to 30 people in the session. And there were only three or four people under the age of 40."

By the end of December, when Ms. Steuck and 45 other laid-off Best Buy workers sued the company in federal court, accusing it of age discrimination, she and her lawyer had concluded that almost two-thirds of recently terminated employees—82 out of 126 were at least 40 years old. The plaintiffs contend that this was out of proportion with the ages of Best Buy's workforce over all, citing a newspaper interview in which the woman who leads the company work-life programs said the average age of its 5,000 employees was 29.

The risk of being laid off from Best Buy rose with age, said Stephen J. Snyder, the lawyer representing the former employees. "The people in their 30s were at greater risk of termination than those in their 20s, the 40s more than the 30s, the 50s more than the 40s," said Mr. Snyder, a partner at Gray, Plant, Mooty, Mooty & Bennett, a Minneapolis law firm. "And the people in their 60s and up were at the greatest risk of all."

One Best Buy plaintiff, Hugh F. Juergens, said he was let go by Best Buy even though the company had given him a rating of 4 out of 5 in the previous performance review. Best Buy defines a grade of 4 as "exceeds expectations." In that review,

his most recent before termination, Mr. Juergens's manager wrote: "Hugh is an exemplary associate who goes beyond what is expected of his role." Yet when he asked why he was fired the company replied in a letter: "Your employment was terminated due to your failure to meet the expectations of your position."

Sprint: Legitimizing Age Discrimination through Performance Appraisals?

"It's not the blatant: 'Jones, you're too old. We're firing you,'" said Tom Osborne, a senior attorney at AARP and a co-counsel for plaintiffs in a case against Sprint. Instead, he said, companies might adopt new employee-evaluation systems that happen to reverse the career-long high performance ranking of older employees.

In the Sprint case, 2,300 people who were recently laid off contend that a subjective and arbitrary new ranking system was used to weed out older workers. Known as "forced ranking," the system requires individual departments to apply bell-curve ratings in which 30 percent of workers must be classified as subpar. "We can show statistically that when it came to rankings, those over 40 did worse than those under 40," said Mr. Egan, the lead attorney for the Sprint plaintiffs. One of the people let go, Sharon L. Louk, who was fired days shy of her 53rd birthday, contended in an affidavit that her boss said at one point, "We need to get young people." Another former Sprint employee, Bonnie L. Hooes, 49, said that several months before she was let go, she received an e-mail message from her new supervisor describing the ideal worker as having among other qualities, "lots of runway ahead of them."

3M: Systematic Bias in Favor of Younger Workers?

Arbitrary management decisions are all a central assertion in the lawsuit against 3M. "We are alleging that older people are more likely to be put into the lower-ranking groups" when evaluated by managers, said Susan M. Coler of Sprenger & Lang, a law firm in Minneapolis, who represents the 3M plaintiffs. The suit also contends that younger workers were more likely than their older colleagues to receive training that led to promotions and raises.

Source: Adapted from N. Alster, "When Grey Heads Roll," *New York Times*, January 3, 2005, p. B-3.

Undocumented workers provide needed services but their presence creates tension in many communities. These day laborers are seeking work from a Long Island employer in a parking lot that serves as an informal gathering place for such workers.

sectors (particularly construction, agriculture, services, and parts of manufacturing) undocumented employees do much of the work.[48] Let's take, for instance, the case of Chesapeake Bay seafood processors. These processors claim that they would face catastrophe if they did not have access to alien workers: "These workers have come to dominate shellfish processing over the past decade, doing dirty, repetitive work that machines can't and Americans won't. The work is unpleasant. Picking crabs, for instance, requires scraping off the gills, cleaning out the organs, breaking off the mouth, and prying meat out of tiny cavities. All that must be repeated up to 600 times a day, yielding a daily wage that might reach $120 on a good day."[49]

The U.S. "love-hate" relationship with immigration is nothing new, although this contradiction has become more pronounced in recent years as so-called illegal immigration has greatly outpaced legal immigration. Part of the problem is that immigration laws have become so restrictive that it is nearly impossible for a prospective unskilled or semiskilled immigrant to obtain a working visa in the United States (unless married to a U.S. citizen). But on the other hand, there is undoubtedly a huge demand for their services in many sectors. This creates a situation of increasing tension and potential abuses.[50] Also, children of these undocumented workers are often born and raised in the United States, so they are "full blown" Americans, yet face an uncertain future because of their parents' legal status.[51]

This is an issue that will loom large in public debate for years to come. At the core of this debate lies the need to balance humanitarian concerns, employer demand for labor, potential incentives for American firms to export jobs overseas (which might occur if U.S.-based firms did not have access to a supply of cheap labor at home), inflationary pressures (prices of basic commodities and services are likely to rise if this alien workforce were to disappear), the question of fair versus expedient application of immigration laws, border security, and the desires of various political constituencies. Certainly, this is not an easy feat! What almost everyone agrees on, however, is that the current system is not working, creating a lot of frustration on all sides.[52]

Women

As noted earlier, the labor force is half female, and 40 percent of the U.S. workforce consists of families in which both spouses are working. In recent years women have successfully entered many occupations previously reserved for men such as law, medicine, police, and even firefighting (see Management Close-Up 11.3 on page 449). However, women continue to face several problems at work. Those who want families may be seen as not being committed to their careers. Firms in the United States, unlike much of the industrialized world, are not required by law to provide maternity leave. Women continue to have primary responsibility for child rearing and most household duties. Only a tiny percentage of firms offer day care, job sharing, and reduced hours for employees with young children. This situation causes many women in their 20s and 30s to withdraw from the workforce or curtail their work-related activities at crucial times in their careers. For instance, only 38 percent of women who graduate from Harvard Business School are expected to be working full time in professional careers 20 years after graduation (based on historical records from the early 1980s to the 2000s).[53]

On Engine 22, Women Who Answer the Bell

THEME: DEALING WITH CHANGE

When the crew from Fire Engine Company 22 raced off at 7:50 a.m. the other day for the first call of their 24-hour shift, a woman reporting chest pains, their big red rig was primed for action but missing a typical feature: a man.

The four members of Engine 22, Division A, a captain, an engineer, a firefighter-paramedic, and a firefighter, protect the Point Loma neighborhood of San Diego, an affluent peninsula on the Pacific Ocean. They are one of the few crews in the nation made up entirely of women, winding up together last October, as the captain, Joi Evans, said, because of "the way the cards fell."

Together they work, cook, shop, train and sleep in small dorm rooms in the station house, around the clock for 10 days a month, at a time when women are making some inroads into the fire service nationwide but are still only a sliver of the front line in one of the most physically grueling and male-dominated professions. With women accounting for about 8 percent of the 880 uniformed firefighters assigned to its station houses, compared with the national average of 2.5 percent, the San Diego Fire-Rescue Department, which has a female assistant chief, is considered one of the best departments for women to work, according to Women in the Fire Service, and advocacy group based in Madison, Wisconsin.

With an even higher number of women, Minneapolis had its first female fire chief sworn in a year ago, and 17 percent of its 380 uniformed firefighters are women, the fire department there says.

On the other end of the spectrum, in the New York City Fire Department, the nation's largest, and long considered by critics to be a backwater for women in firefighting, only 36 of the 11,430 uniformed firefighters are female, according to that department's latest figures.

In the San Diego station house, male firefighters contend with friendly pranks by the women. Though many men in the fire service are known as excellent chefs, Ms. Cleary (a female firefighter) pasted a strip of yellow police tape across Divisions B's refrigerator: "Danger: Men Cooking."

Even though these women carry 75 pounds of gear on their backs as they fight fires, their performance on the job is just as good as that of their male counterparts.

Source: Adapted from S. Kershaw, (2006, Jan. 23). "On Engine 22, It Is Women Who Answer the Bell, *New York Times*, January 23, 2006, p. A-14.

The glass ceiling makes it hard for women to move beyond a certain level in the corporate hierarchy. Women have limited access to the "old boys' network," the informal relationships that exist among managers and executives in which much important communication occurs. Significant decisions, such as who will be promoted, are often made through loose coalitions that are part of this informal network.

Women face sexual harassment at work far more often than men. Unwanted sexual advances, even if they are not overt, may cause women to quit their jobs. When a woman refuses, resists, or challenges such pressures, she often jeopardizes her future with the department or company. Sexual harassment is discussed in more detail in Chapter 10.

Finally, men and women may have somewhat different communication styles. They may attach a meaning that is different from the one that a person of the opposite sex intended to convey (see Figure 11.4 on page 450). This increases the odds of miscommunication and conflict. Since more men are in powerful positions than women, this works against a woman's upward advancement.

LOC-In

4 Learning Objective Check-In

1. *Chris, Kim, and Jamal were co-workers in the finance department. Chris and Jamal often went to lunch together, shared information, and coordinated with one another on difficult or complementary projects. Yet Kim often wondered why she was not a part of the _____. Eventually, Kim resigned from her position in the department. It became clear to her, from daily experience and tensions and discussions with previous employees, that women were not a welcome part of the finance department.*
   a. *diversity resources*
   b. *management structure*
   c. *communication flow*
   d. *negotiation process*

FIGURE 11.4

Men and Women, Divided by Language

Source: Adapted from R. D. Bucher, *Diversity Consciousness* (Upper Saddle River, NJ: Prentice Hall, 2000), p. 130.

Deborah Tannen is a professor of linguistics, the science of language. In her research, Tannen has focused on the different communication styles of men and women. She has written extensively on this subject. Her books, entitled *You Just Don't Understand, That's Not What I Meant,* and *Talking from 9 to 5,* offer examples of gender differences:

- Men tend to engage in report talk, women in rapport talk. Report talk is a way of showing one's knowledge and skill. Rapport talk allows one to share with others and develop relationships.
- When making requests, women tend to be indirect. A female supervisor might ask: "Could you do this by 5 PM?" Something more direct and to the point is more typical of a male supervisor: "This needs to be done by 5 PM."
- Women have a greater information focus. They do not hesitate to ask questions in order to understand something. Men have more of an image focus. Even though men may be unclear about an issue, they may forgo asking questions, to preserve their image or reputation.
- Women often say "I'm sorry" to express concern about something. Men, on the other hand, may interpret this to mean that women are accepting blame or responsibility. This is not at all what women have in mind.
- People tend to judge men for what they say and do. Women are often judged by how they look and dress.
- For women, tears may be a way of expressing valid emotions. For men, they are a sign of weakness and immaturity.

Tannen makes the point that these differences do not apply to all men or women in all situations. By realizing that differences such as these may exist, we lessen the chances of miscommunication and conflict.

Building on Diversity

Organizations can choose from a number of strategies for improving the management of diversity. Several of these, which are summarized in Figure 11.5 on page 452, are discussed next.

Top Management Commitment

Lower-level managers and employees are unlikely to take diversity seriously if they believe that senior executives are not giving the management of diversity a high priority. Some CEOs take active and visible roles in diversity management, attending multiple meetings on diversity issues, while others merely make an internal announcement about the program. At Sara Lee, top executives played a major role in a three-day conference on diversity, launching several diversity initiatives. Similarly, the top nine officers of Bank of America attended a three-day off-site meeting on how to improve the management of diversity. The meeting involved all of the bank branches and was attended by a cross-section of employees from various geographic areas, job levels, racial groups, ages, and sexual orientations. Attendees examined the following issues:

1. How can we develop all employees so that they are ready for opportunities that arise in the company?

2. How can we be sure that minorities and women gain access to better jobs, as they become available?

3. How can we make sure that we give minorities and women opportunities without discriminating against white men?

4. How can we show all employees that we value their contributions?

5. How can we change attitudes of both employees and customers?

6. Will the same approach work for new employees and those with many years of service?[54]

video: THE ENTREPRENEURIAL MANAGER

Gender Pay Gap

Summary

There have been great strides in equality in the workplace—just look inside today's surgery rooms, Senate sessions, and corporate offices. There are female CEOs, lawyers, presidential advisors, and professors. Equality, however, may have taken one giant step backwards. Government data pegs women's wages at 77 percent of men's compensation today, but the true figure may be a lot worse. Despite an increase in the number of women graduating from college, there still remains a gap in pay between men and women.

According to a study by the Institute for Women's Policy Research and consulting firm Macro International, three-quarters of women dip in and out of the workforce at some point in their working lives, and that results in much lower wages—as low as 38 percent of men's wages. Just one year out of the workforce, and women's total earnings decrease by 32 percent. After three years out, total earnings decrease by 56 percent. Men's rates were slightly lower.

Family responsibilities weigh more heavily on women than on men. The lack of day care and flexible work hours may prompt women making less than their husbands to stay home with the children, facing few if no options. There is, fortunately, an upside to all of this news. Women have been outnumbering men in college since the mid-1980s. The graduation rate has also exceeded men's for the past few years. This is good news, since it takes women earning bachelor's degrees, on average, to earn what men with high school degrees can earn.

Discussion Questions

1. What were the results of the study cited in this video case? Are federal statistics consistent with these results?

2. According to the Institute for Women's Policy Research, when do women's wages fall? What determines by how much they fall?

3. According to the study, what work-life issues are different for women than for men? How do they affect women's careers and wages?

Linking Diversity Initiatives to Business Strategies and Objectives

If diversity management is perceived only as a program emanating from the Human Resource Department with lip service support from top management, it is unlikely to be effective. Announcing a diversity program without giving it corporate support could give employees the impression that the company is simply going through the motions, which would be counterproductive. This was alleged to be the situation at Texaco in 1996 before the firm had to make drastic moves in response to public scandal.

Employee diversity objectives should be key components of corporate mission statements and company strategies. Companies whose leaders have incorporated management of diversity into their mission statements include Inland Steel, FMC Corporation, Digital Equipment Corporation, and NASA. Hewlett-Packard has a comprehensive diversity model that considers external and internal forces and that includes corporate objectives and diversity goals and objectives. FMC has produced a *Diversity Handbook for Managers*, with guidelines and examples to create a tight link among business strategy, human resources strategy, and the management of diversity. Topics covered include new management orientation, diversity briefings for senior management, networking groups, developmental assignments, linking diversity performance to other corporate objectives, and benchmarking with other companies.

FIGURE 11.5

How Organizations May Build
on Diversity

Management Responsibility and Accountability

People tend to invest time and effort in things that are measured and rewarded. "Diversity is not likely to become part of management and employee priorities without real accountability for specific objectives."[55] General Electric, Inland Steel, Hewlett-Packard, and other companies hold their managers accountable for employee diversity by making it part of their performance appraisals and merit pay. Some companies link a significant amount of a manager's financial reward to effective handling of diversity issues. For example, one-fifth of managers' annual bonuses at Harvard Pilgrim Health Care is directly tied to meeting measurable diversity objectives.

Firms use a variety of accountability tools to ensure the implementation of diversity strategies. These include written and verbal **360-degree feedback** (multirater feedback from peers, suppliers, other levels of management, and internal and external customers), employee surveys, performance appraisals, and self-evaluations. General Electric has managers assess their own performance on key diversity practices, including recruitment objectives, support of work/life balance programs, and involvement in outreach programs.

360-degree feedback

Multirater feedback from peers, suppliers, other levels of management, and internal and external customers.

Diversity Audits

Before launching a new diversity initiative or designing an intervention to fit a situation, it is important to ascertain why things are the way they are, which things should stay the way they are, and which should be changed. A diversity audit can help reveal possible sources of bias, and the indicators or factors used in the audit can also be used to measure whether corrective actions have the desired effects. For instance, if the percentage of women who quit each year in a particular division is twice as high of that of men, this could indicate that there is a problem that should be examined further.

- Diversity is about each person coming to terms with his or her attitudes, beliefs, and expectations about others and gaining comfort with differences.
- Diversity is big enough to include everyone: young and old, homeless and affluent, immigrant and native, white and black. Diversity goes beyond race and gender.
- No one is or should be the target for blame for current or past inequities. All human beings have been socialized to behave in certain ways, and all of us are at times both perpetrators and victims of discrimination and stereotypes.
- Human beings are ethnocentric—they see the world through their own narrow view and judge the world by what is familiar to them.
- The human species resists change. This makes the constant adaptation required for diversity difficult for people already overwhelmed by staggering transitions in today's organizations.
- Human beings find comfort and trust in likeness. There is a tendency to seek the company of those most similar to ourselves.
- It is difficult for people to share power. History shows that it is rarely done voluntarily and without a reason that will somehow benefit those dominating the pool of wealth.

Developmental Activities

Besides measuring and rewarding diversity efforts, companies also offer developmental opportunities to managers and employees to improve diversity management. The most common activities are diversity training, senior mentoring, apprenticeships, and diversity learning labs.

DIVERSITY TRAINING   Many programs can improve awareness of diversity issues. Managers and employees should learn about specific cultural and gender differences to help them respond in the workplace. At the information services company EDS, for example, employees attend diversity awareness workshops that focus on working together with people of different race, sex, religion, age, and social status, people with disabilities, and so on. Besides improving customer satisfaction with the company, these workshops have increased the pool of applicants for the company.[56] However, any firm using diversity training programs needs to be very careful that these are not perceived as a medium to reinforce stereotypes or as an opportunity to vent hostility toward a particular group, such as white males. Figure 11.6 above shows a list of issues, according to the Society for Human Resource Management, that should be considered in diversity training.

SENIOR MENTORING   Some firms have implemented senior mentoring programs in which managers and senior employees are encouraged to identify women and minorities with promising careers. The mentor is responsible for coaching the employee, offering a nurturing environment, and facilitating the employee's career progress. Marriott, for instance, has made senior mentoring available to disabled employees for many years. Honeywell and 3M team up experienced executives with young women and minorities to give them advice on career strategies and corporate politics. General Electric recently introduced a buddy system to assist new employees with their transition to GE.

APPRENTICESHIPS   Apprenticeship programs groom prospective employees before they are hired on a permanent basis. For instance, General Electric provides scholarships and internships to minority students, many of whom become a permanent part of GE's workforce at a later date.

LOC-In

5 **Learning Objective Check-In**

Poston Company conducts on-site programs that improve the employees' awareness of diversity issues. These programs help managers and employees learn about specific cultural and gender differences to help them respond better in the workplace. Another method Poston Company uses to manage diversity internally is programs that groom prospective employees before they are hired on a permanent basis. They achieve this by providing internships to a variety of targeted student groups, many of whom become a permanent part of the workforce following the internships.

1. *The programs employees attend that help them with the awareness of and appropriate responses to cultural and gender differences are collectively called _____.*
   a. *diversity training*
   b. *administrative management*
   c. *behavioral training*
   d. *apprenticeships*

2. *The internships at Poston Company that groom prospective employees before they are hired on a permanent basis at the company represent _____.*
   a. *senior mentoring programs*
   b. *apprenticeships*
   c. *diversity learning labs*
   d. *diversity training sessions*

DIVERSITY LEARNING LABS Diversity learning labs improve knowledge and insight about market niches of diverse client populations. American Express has established 15 diversity learning labs that "receive concentrated funding, resource and training support from the region and corporate office. They are focused on diverse segments in the African-American, gay and lesbian, Hispanic, and women's market. The labs are not only experiencing increased diverse client acquisition but are also surfacing key learning such as strong project management experience in diverse segments."[57]

Encouraging Diversity Networks

The corporate environment can be insensitive, cold, or even hostile to the needs of many women and minorities. Support groups offer a nurturing environment to employees who otherwise may feel excluded from the corporate mainstream or lost in a bureaucracy run by people dissimilar to them. Companies with support groups for women, homosexuals, and/or racial and ethnic minorities include Allstate, Avon, Digital Equipment, and Xerox. DuPont is reported to have more than 100 such networks. Apple headquarters in Cupertino, California, has a Jewish cultural group, a gay/lesbian group, and women's groups.

Microsoft has a large number of support groups representing a variety of constituencies, such as Attention Deficit Disorder, Deaf and Hard of Hearing, Single Parents, and Working Parents, in addition to various ethnic groups.[58] Despite their potential value in promoting diversity, it is important to make sure that these support groups do not become "self-contained units" that separate particular kinds of employees from the rest. This inadvertently creates conflict and a "we versus them" mentality.

Company leaders may actively encourage or even require employees, particularly those in responsible professional and managerial positions, to become part of international teams. The growing global economy and increasingly diverse customers and markets justify such added expenses as travel, long-distance calls, and extra time. Intel Business Practices Network makes use of global teams. "Teams are multicultural/multifunctional, often involving people across three to five geographies—domestically and internationally. . . . The global team approach has paid off in a short time to market innovative ideas and product design."[59]

Accommodating Family Needs

Although 8.7 million single mothers and 1.4 million single fathers are in the workforce, as are more than half of women with young children, most companies are not family-friendly. Men as well as women find it difficult to balance family and career. Being responsible for child care results in less opportunity for advancement for employees of both sexes.

This is starting to change. Many executives now realize that the benefits of accommodating employees' family needs can exceed the cost and inconvenience. Family-friendly policies expand the pool of applicants so that the firm can recruit better employees, improve morale, and reduce turnover and absenteeism. Because workers have fewer worries and distractions, they can concentrate on their jobs and better use their talents.

Some of the options available to organizations to help employees handle family and career simultaneously include:

1. Day care assistance—for instance, Merck and Campbell Soup have day care centers at the workplace. One company, Massachusetts–based Bright Horizons Family Solutions, runs round-the-clock child care facilities for Toyota in Kentucky and S. C. Johnson in Wisconsin and two Ford Motor Co./United Auto Workers Family Service Learning Centers, and is currently developing child care facilities for 11 more firms.[60]

2. Flexible work schedules and arrangements.

3. Compressed work weeks—for example, working four 10-hour days instead of five 8-hour days.

4. Job sharing—two part-time workers share one full-time job. A survey of more than 1,000 companies in 2002 by consulting firm Hewitt Associates indicates that 28 percent of the organizations surveyed offer job sharing, up from just 12 percent in 1990.[61]

5. Telecommuting—full- or part-time employees work at home, maintaining their connection to the office via fax, phone, and computer.

6. Care assistance for elderly dependents.

7. Paid time off to care for family members who are ill.

8. Paid parental leave.

9. Keeping relocations to a minimum.

10. Giving a high priority to finding a position for a spouse within the company.

11. Providing job search assistance to relocated spouses.

Though much remains to be done, some companies are trying to help employees meet the needs of work and family by providing child care and other support services such as special help to parents of disabled children.

CONCLUDING THOUGHTS

At the beginning of the chapter, we asked why most executives believe that effective management of diversity is critical to organizational success. This belief IBM has put into practice since the 19th century, even though the term "employee diversity" was probably coined for the first time in the 1980s. Besides the moral argument that it is the right thing to do, most executives now believe that effective management of diversity is "all business" and that it represents a pragmatic response to demographic changes. These executives argue that effective management of diversity is good as well as necessary for business because (1) changes in technology and competition make diverse thinking a necessity; (2) minorities make up a majority of the labor market in many parts of the country, and, to be competitive, firms need to retain and motivate minority employees; and (3) companies are wooing customers from all corners of the globe, and they need the help of executives who can function in different cultures.

A major challenge organizations face is how to balance the need for greater workforce diversity with the perception that this diversity comes at the expense of the dominant group. In other words, it is important to actively support employee diversity in such a way that everyone sees it as a win–win situation. Managers should devote considerable time and resources to ensuring that diversity efforts are inclusive rather than exclusive and that employees come to appreciate and respect the contributions of other employees who may not be like or look like them.

Managing Employee Diversity

Roxana Carbajal is a Human Resource Director at an Embassy Suites Hotel, which is owned by the Hilton Hotel Corporation. She currently serves approximately 145 employees, of whom only 3–4 percent are "nonminority." Eighty percent of the employees speak Spanish, 7 percent Mandarin, 3 percent Cantonese, 8 percent Tagalog (Filipino), 1 percent Hindi, and 1 percent German. Roxana was hired in part because she is bilingual—and also because she knows how to maximize the performance of a diverse workforce.

The Hilton Hotel Corporation has a wide variety of diversity initiatives and policies, ranging from a formal mission statement through diversity training programs, mentoring, and even diversity performance measurements at the hotel level. Roxana's job is to be sure these programs and policies are carried out in the day-to-day activities of her hotel.

The Workforce Diversity Mission Statement is "to create and maintain a diverse work place culture that strengthens the business value of the corporation and affirms Hilton Hotels Corporation as an industry leader in the global market."[1] In Roxana's world, this means that she must attract and hire a diverse workforce, and then create an environment in which everyone focuses on creating a first-class destination for world travelers. Put in a different way, it is the responsibility of the Human Resource Director to create "a workforce that reflects diversity of our hotel guests, appreciates uniqueness of each guest, and values contributions of all fellow team members."[2] Roxana starts this process by advertising open positions widely and using Equal Employment Opportunity agencies such as the California Employment Development Department to get the news of job openings to a diverse set of applicants. When interviewing new applicants, Roxana uses a structured interview process, which is less likely to be unfairly discriminatory than an unstructured interview.

Once they are hired, Roxana ensures that all new employees receive orientation training that incorporates information on working with diverse co-workers and serving a diverse clientele. One of the most important messages of the program is to communicate the "Embassy Way." Every employee is expected to recognize guests promptly, use their first names, and smile at them. This form of homogenization helps to ensure a consistent experience for guests, and it also brings diverse co-workers closer together. In addition to diversity training, all hotel employees and managers go through "Harassment Free" training, as well as additional customer service training. Again, all training serves to make employee behavior more consistent and to make employees and managers aware of diversity issues.

One of Roxana's jobs is collecting diversity information to monitor the Affirmative Action Plan in her hotel. This information, which is similar to a diversity audit, serves two purposes. First, it is provided to the Federal Government to demonstrate that the standards of the Equal Employment Opportunity Commission are upheld in the hotel's Affirmative Action plan. Second, it is used to demonstrate that the hotel is in compliance with the diversity guidelines from the Office of Federal Contract Compliance (OFCCP). Since the hotel is used by government employees, it is considered to be a federal contractor, and must therefore undergo regular reviews at the discretion of the OFCCP.

On a daily basis, Roxana uses many of the diversity practices outlined in the text to be sure that her hotel retains their talented employees. For example, when an employee does not have a good command of English, a translator will be brought in to help meetings between employees and their managers go more smoothly. The hotel provides time off and leaves of absence on an as-needed basis so that employees can care for their families. Managers receive behavioral training, so that they administer policies fairly, regardless of race, and so that they can set an example for their employees of how to work with diverse clients. One of the things Roxana understands is that discrimination does not occur only between majority and minority groups. She also needs to be sure that people in one minority group do not discriminate against people in other minority groups. She does this by helping managers establish criteria for hiring and performance reviews that are job related and by counseling individuals who seem to be having difficulty meeting diversity standards.

Sources: [1] Hilton Hotels Corporation, "Diversity Programs" https://cvmsolutions.com/hilton, accessed 4/30/06; [2] ibid.

summary of learning objectives

1 Explain the meaning and benefits of employee diversity.

- The term diversity refers to differences among people that are either inborn (such as race and gender) or chosen (such as occupation and religion).
- The benefits of employee diversity include better access to differentiated markets, greater competitiveness on a global scale, more creative problem solving within the firm, and enhanced team performance.

2 Develop an awareness of the unique perspectives, problems, and issues of diverse employee groups.

- African Americans, Asian Americans, the disabled, the foreign born, homosexuals, Hispanics, older workers, those who hold different religious views, and women often face unique problems in the workplace, and firms need to take their problems into account to improve the management of diversity.
- Managers should avoid making inferences about a specific individual based on demographic group characteristics because there is a great deal of overlap between groups on most psychological traits.

3 Understand demographic trends in the labor force and their managerial implications.

- The U.S. workforce is increasingly diverse in terms of gender, race, ethnicity, expressed sexual orientation, age, and so on. Currently, American-born white males constitute only about 15 percent of new entrants to the workforce and by the middle of the 21st century more than half of the workforce is likely to be non-white.
- Firms that can manage employee diversity effectively, and do it better than other firms, are likely to enjoy a competitive advantage.

4 Describe the challenges firms may face in the management of diversity.

- Some people erroneously believe that effective management of employee diversity means that minorities and women receive special treatment.
- If not properly managed, diversity may negatively result in pressures to induce dissimilar employees to leave the firm, segregating them, limiting communication flow, and preventing their career advancement.
- When diverse employees do come together, a firm's cohesiveness may diminish while interpersonal conflict and tension could intensify if this is not understood and headed off.

5 Describe various approaches that managers may use to enjoy the benefits of employee diversity and meet the challenges associated with diversity.

- Improving the utilization of employee diversity includes obtaining top-management commitment, linking diversity initiatives to business strategies and objectives, holding managers responsible for diversity results, conducting diversity audits, implementing a variety of developmental activities, fostering the establishment of employee diversity networks, and offering family-friendly programs to help employees accommodate work and family life.
- It is important to actively support employee diversity in such a way that everyone sees it as a win-win situation.
- Managers should devote considerable time and resources to ensure that diversity efforts are inclusive rather than exclusive and that employees come to appreciate the respect the contributions of other employees who may not be or look like them.

discussion questions

1. Look back at Management Close-Up 11.1 on tapping the Hispanic market for banking services. How would you develop a plan to take advantage of employee diversity in order to sell *your* product or services to particular market segments? Explain your answer.

2. Going back to Management Close-Up 11.2, what ethical responsibilities if any should a company have with older employees? Explain your answer.

3. Look back at Management Close-Up 11.3 on women firefighters. Why do you think women are still severely underrepresented in many fields (even though much progress has been achieved in the last 20 years or so)? Explain your answer.

4. Of all the challenges of diversity discussed in this chapter, which do you think is the most serious? Explain why.

5. What do you see as the connection between affirmative action and the management of employee diversity? How are they similar? How are they different?

6. How would you know whether your firm was doing a good or a bad job of managing employee diversity? What type of data would you need to answer this question?

7. Of all the initiatives for improving the management of diversity discussed in this chapter, which do you consider the most important? Why?

management minicase 11.1

We Are All Getting Older!

A rapidly aging workforce in the developed countries has become a key concern as expressed by the labor ministers of the United States, Canada, United Kingdom, France, Germany, Italy, Japan, and Russia, who recently met in London. Here is how some countries and organizations are trying to meet this challenge.

The Graying Baby Boom Generation around the World

Jenny Francois doesn't have the world's most glamorous job. For 20 years she has commuted 45 minutes to the office of insurer Macif in Agen, France, where she punches data into a computer. But in the not-too-distant future, Francois and hundreds of millions of people like her in the industrialized world could look back at the early 21st century as the beginning of the end of a wonderful era, when even average workers could retire in reasonable comfort in their still-vigorous 50s. Thanks to France's pension system, Francois, 58, is in "pre-retirement." For three years, she has worked two days a week and still collects 1,500 a month—over 70 percent of her old full-time salary. Her pay will dip only slightly when she reaches 60. "The system is great for me," Francois says. "I think it should be every worker's right.

It's already clear that the system will be far less generous to future retirees in France and elsewhere. And the message isn't going down easy. Despite a national wave of strikes, France has enacted new rules requiring people to work longer to qualify for the benefits to avert a fiscal crunch. Italy, Germany, Japan, Finland, South Korea, Brazil, and Greece all have moved to or proposed to trim benefits, raise retirement ages, and hike workers' pension contributions. To counter the pension crisis. China is likely to gradually boost the retirement age, now 55 for women and 60 for men, to 65 by 2030. It might further loosen the one-child policy. Meanwhile, even those with two children, like Ms. Wang, worry. "I'm considering finding another job," says Wang. "I might work as a cook for construction workers, but I know that will be very tiring." For now, too many of China's wannabe retirees may have to labor on into their golden years.

Help Wanted: Older Workers Please Apply

In a push to recruit older workers, Home Depot, the hardware chain, now offers "snowbird specials" winter work in Florida and summers in Maine. Borders bookstores lure retired teachers to sales jobs with discounts and the promise of reading and discussion groups. Pitney Bowes, the business services company, pays tuition for courses in computer programming as well as spare-time skills like golf and flower arranging. Some companies like Wal-Mart are making their pitches at senior centers and others are sending company brochures to churches and community libraries and posting their attractions on Web sites. AARP, the advocacy group for older people, recently put on its Web site links to 13 "featured employers" including MetLife, Pitney Bowes, Borders, Home Depot, Principal Financial, and Walgreen that are recruiting older workers with offers of health benefits, training, and flexible work schedules. More than 71,000 people have used the Web site in a recent month to seek job information.

In industries with labor shortages, like nursing, older workers already have an edge. Nurses, who typically retire at 53, are being recruited at high rates, says Peter Buerhaus, associate dean of the school of nursing at Vanderbilt University. "They are probably the fastest-aging work force in the country." More than 70 percent of nurses hired in recent years are over 50.

Battling the Brain Drain

As older workers retire in droves, organizations are trying to find ways to prevent their crucial knowledge from leaving with them.

Consider the chilling example of the National Aeronautics and Space Administration. Way back in the 1960s, it spent $24 billion (in 1969 dollars) and at one point employed 400,000 people—to send 12 astronauts to the moon. But in the 24 years since the Apollo program ended, the engineers who carried crucial know-how in their heads, without ever passing it on to colleagues, have retired or died (or both). At the same time, important blueprints were catalogued incorrectly or not at all, and the people who drew them are no longer around to draw them again. So to fulfill NASA's desire to return to the moon in the next decade, NASA is essentially starting all over again. Estimated cost to taxpayers in current dollars: $100 billion.

Now more and more organizations—among them General Electric, Dow Chemical, and Northrop Grumman—are working on ways to capture their oldsters' knowledge and disseminate it to younger workers before it's too late. Defense contractor Northrop Grumman has created what are called communities of practice—companywide groups that meet, in person and online, to share information. "Social networks, people building connections across divisional boundaries, are where the breakthrough innovations are coming from," Schaffar says. "We're seeing a crop of young, emerging leaders coming out of these groups."

Still another mechanism for transferring expertise is something General Electric calls "action learning teams." Action learning teams put people together from several disciplines—manufacturing, sales, marketing, legal, finance—to solve particular problems. The handpicked young managers who participate, along with older and presumably wiser colleagues, "get exposed to very big projects and issues, but with a safety net. You learn by doing, and you get continuous feedback on your performance." One advantage of the teams, says Bob Corcoran, GE's chief learning officer, is that they "encourage people to learn a lot about a lot of things, not just their own jobs. It reduces the likelihood that when boomers do retire, you'll be left saying, 'Gee, old Alex was the only person here who knew how to do this.'"

There is another approach companies are taking: pooling resources. For example, four years ago, Procter and Gamble started worrying that boomers retiring in masse would decimate their R&D department. Eli Lilly, with which P&G had done some joint research projects, had the same concern. So the two companies formed Yourencore.com, an online network of retired and semiretired research scientists and engineers that matches available brains with short-term R&D projects. Two more employers, Boeing and National Starch & Chemical, recently joined the group, which draws on a database of 470 scientists. The folks who sign on with Yourencore are paid an hourly rate for their project work and often do their own consulting and teaching on the side.

Discussion Questions

1. What are some of the common issues in the scenarios described? Explain.

2. What do you see as the key implications of a population that is getting older to the practice of human resources? Explain.

3. Some people argue that the United States is a "youth loving" society and that for this reason organizations often do not value the wisdom of older workers. Do you agree?

Sources: "Chao Addresses Challenges of Aging Workforces at Conference," *Newsline*, April 27, 2005 http://resourcespro.worldatwork.org/; P. Engardio, C. Matlack, G. Edmondson, I. Rowley, C. Barraclough, G. Smith, "Global Aging: Now, the Geezer Glut," *BusinessWeek*, January 31, 2005, pp. 44–47; M. W. Walsh, "When Your Pension Is Frozen," *New York Times*, January 22, 2006, p. A-1; M. Freudenheim, "Help Wanted: Older Workers Please Apply," *New York Times*, March 23, 2005, P. A-1; A. Fisher, "How to Battle the Coming Brain Drain," *Fortune*, March 31, 2005, pp. 21–128; J. Helyar, "50 and Fired," *Fortune*, May 10, 2006, pp. 78–86.

management minicase 11.2

Despite Past Cases, Wall Street Has Yet to Shake a Boys' Club Image

Six women who are senior bankers at Dresdner Kleinwort Wasserstein services have sued the investment bank for $1.4 billion on behalf of 500 women who work at Dresdner Kleinwort, contending that they were denied equal bonuses and promotions that went to men with less experience.

The complaint, brought by three directors and three vice presidents—all still working at the bank—also cites instances of lewd behavior toward the women, entertainment of clients at a strip club, and repeated examples of scaled-back opportunities for women after they returned from maternity leave.

In one case, Katherine Smith, a director in equity sales trading in London who has worked at the bank or at its predecessors since 1996, was referred to as the "Pamela Anderson of sales/trading" by her supervisor, according to the lawsuit. And while Ms. Smith has been among the group's top producers in terms of commissions generated for stock sales, she was awarded progressively lower bonuses and denied a promotion to managing director, the most senior rank on Wall Street, "because she is a woman and because she has a child," the suit contends.

Another woman complained of a male managing director who routinely brought prostitutes to the office during his lunch hour, according to the lawsuit. In recent years, sexual harassment cases have plagued Wall Street, which has yet to shake its reputation as something of a boys' club. Saleswomen and female traders, investment bankers and private wealth managers at firms like Merrill Lynch, Morgan Stanley and Salomon Smith Barney have sued, claiming discriminatory treatment, unequal pay and promotion, and demeaning work conditions.

Morgan Stanley recently agreed to pay $54 million to settle a sex discrimination case covering as many as 340 women. The settlement awarded Allison K. Schieffelin, a successful bond saleswoman who brought the case, $12 million. Merrill Lynch and Smith Barney have paid more than $200 million combined to women who worked in their brokerage operations.

Like many banks on Wall Street, Dresdner Kleinwort has a low percentage of women in senior positions. According to May 2005 data cited in the lawsuit, women account for less than 2 percent of managing directors in Dresdner Kleinwort Wasserstein's worldwide capital markets division. Only 13 percent of directors, the next level down, are women. Of the 500 women in the capital markets division, about 60 percent are associates, the second-lowest rank, or below.

The six plaintiffs have been at Dresdner "for a total of 50 years," said their lawyer, Douglas H. Wigdor of Thompson Wigdor & Gilly in New York.

One plaintiff, Jyoti Ruta, a director in structured finance who has worked with the firm since 1994, said: "I have heard so many women at DrKW who tell me the things that their male managers and colleagues have done to them. It saddens me. They love their work, they are building their careers and they believe in the firm, but they are treated in such a way that they will never advance."

According to the suit, Ms. Ruta was stripped of revenue-generating opportunities, left out of critical client events, and generally relegated to the sidelines after she returned from maternity leave. She is currently pregnant with her second child. She said the firm had retaliated against her for taking action against it by issuing false performance reports and scrutinizing activities like lunch breaks.

Discussion Questions

1. Why do you think in some industries such as the one discussed women are so under-represented in managerial positions? Explain.

2. If you were an executive in another Wall Street firm and saw these data and allegations being made against Dresdner Kleinwort, what steps if any would you take to ensure this does not occur at your company? Explain.

3. Some people argue that overt discrimination is a thing of the past and that a company trying to make money has no reason to discriminate. Do you agree? Explain.

Source: J. Anderson. "Six Women at Dresdner File Bias Suit," *New York Times*, January 10, 2006, p. C-1.

Approaching a Demographic Milestone

The Census Bureau estimates that with a baby being born every 8 seconds, someone dying every 12 seconds, and the nation gaining an immigrant every 31 seconds on average, the population is growing by one person every 14 seconds. At that rate, the total is expected to exceed 312 million by 2009. Compare this to a total population of 200 million 30 years earlier!

Demographers do know that the United States, which ranks third in population behind China and India, is still gaining people while many other industrialized nations are not. (Japan, officials there announced in 2006, has begun shrinking.) Driven by immigration and higher fer-

**individual/
collaborative
learning
case 11.1**

Approaching a Milestone

The Census Bureau estimates that the population of the United States reached 300 million in Fall 2006. Here is a look at how the country's population has changed over the years.

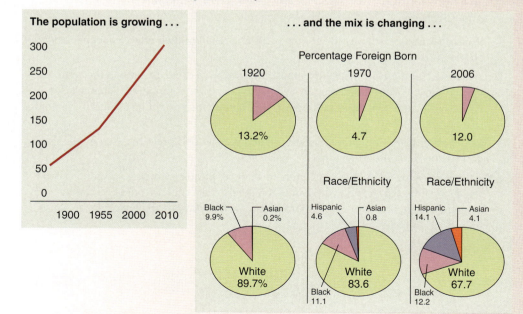

The population is growing . . .

. . . and the mix is changing . . .

Percentage Foreign Born

1920 — 13.2%
1970 — 4.7
2006 — 12.0

Race/Ethnicity

1920: Black 9.9%, Asian 0.2%, White 89.7%
1970: Hispanic 4.6, Asian 0.8, White 83.6, Black 11.1
2006: Hispanic 14.1, Asian 4.1, White 67.7, Black 12.2

*Data on Hispanics not available for 1920. Totals do not add to 100 because of rounding.
Sources: Census Bureau; William H. Frey, University of Michigan.

tility rates, particularly among newcomers from abroad, the United States' population is growing by just under 1 percent annually, the equivalent of the entire population of Chicago (2.8 million).

Given the demographic changes recorded in the 20th century, the 300 millionth American, born in the same year the first baby boomers turn 60, will be a very different person from the paradigm in 1915, when the population passed 100 million, or even in 1967, when it topped 200 million. The nation is becoming more diverse and has been doing so much faster since the 1970 census than in the 50 years after the 100 millionth American registered in 1920. Somewhere along mid-century the word majority will disappear.

Critical Thinking Questions

1. What do you see as the main implications for U.S. firms of the trends discussed above? How are they likely to affect the practice of management? Explain.

2. Do you think that most Americans in general and U.S. firms in particular have handled the changing demographics well during past decades? How about the future? Explain.

3. Some people strongly argue that increased workforce diversity gives American firms a global competitive edge. Do you agree? Why or why not?

Collaborative Learning Exercise

The class is divided into groups of five. Each group is expected to develop a set of recommendations that companies should consider in light of the trends discussed above. After meeting for approximately 15–20 minutes, groups will reconvene and present their conclusions to the entire class with the instructor as moderator.

Source: S. Roberts. "Come October, Body Count Will Make 300 Million or So," *New York Times*, January 13, 2006, p. A-1.

internet exercise 11.1

Managing Employee Diversity

Choose four or five of the companies listed in *Fortune*'s "America's Best Companies for Minorities," published annually (www.fortune.com). Search the Internet for information about them. Use the companies' Web sites and other sites. Use this information to answer the following questions:

1. What advantages have accrued to the firms as a result of their effective management of employee diversity?

2. Are there common approaches to managing employee diversity among the companies you've chosen? What strategies are unique to any of the companies? What reasons, such as industry, geographical location, size, and history, might lie behind these unique strategies?

3. Could other firms apply the diversity-related policies and practices used by the firms you've chosen? Why or why not?

4. *Fortune* rates the firms "the best" in their diversity efforts following specified criteria which are noted in the published annual report. What criteria would you use to evaluate a company's diversity efforts? How would you rate the firms you've chosen to investigate based on your criteria?

Bully Broads

Summary

"Bully Broads" is a program designed by Jean Hollands for women executives who are over-aggressive, intimidating, and most likely sent by their employers for "reform." The two-year-old program in Silicon Valley has been gaining popularity among today's top women chiefs—CEOs, VPs, entrepreneurs, and various other higher-ups. Many of the women openly admit that they often think "other people are idiots" or they are simply "incompetent." The aim of the school is to change those attitudes. Hollands's program options peak at $18,000, which buys these women one-on-one executive coaching, group therapy, and role playing designed to simulate real office problems. The program is not without controversy. Kim Gandy of the National Organization for Women (NOW) detests the program, and says it sets women back years. She says the women are results-oriented, achieve their goals, are aggressive, and are being punished for the same behaviors that men are lauded for. Hollands does not deny there is a double standard. In fact, she says that because of it, women must operate within that double standard to accomplish their goals. Women, she says, must be friendlier, appear more approachable, and be less intimidating and aggressive.

Discussion Questions

1. Jean Hollands says that people have a primal reaction to the word "Bully Broads." What was your first reaction to the term? Do you think that the term stereotypes women executives, and, if so, do you think that stereotyping stalls their progress up the corporate ladder?

2. The women in the video are obviously different from what the general business climate expects of women today. They are also, however, talented, high-achieving, and have proven themselves in order to get to their high-ranking positions. How does the Bully Broads program affect a company's ability to retain motivated executive employees as well as attract and retain motivated employees in general?

3. The companies that send women to Bully Broads are paying up to $18,000 per person. This is a significant investment for an executive that may or may not stay with the company. Do you think the companies that participate in this program are making a direct investment in diversity training, or does Bully Broads have a different focus? Explain.

part five

Leadership in Management

Designing an appropriate organizational structure and bringing together a workforce with the needed talent doesn't guarantee an effectively performing organization. People need to understand and identify with a vision for the organization and they need to see a link between their performance and the outcomes they obtain. Further, employees often work in a team context and team dynamics need to be managed so that performance is facilitated, not inhibited. In other words, effective management involves more than simply determining what needs to be done and finding the talent to do it. How things are done and conveyed to the workforce is critical to obtaining effective performance.

In Part Five we will examine the tools that managers can use to motivate employees. We will also consider approaches to being an effective leader and why integrity in leadership is critical to maintaining an effective and ethical organization. We will also consider managing people in a team context and how to effectively communicate with others in the organization. In sum, in this part we will examine the process, or the "how," of effective management.

5

chapter 12

Motivation

Learning Objectives

1 Differentiate between extrinsic and intrinsic motivation.

2 Describe the need theories of motivation and their implications for managing.

3 Generate steps that can be taken to improve performance by applying the various process models of motivation.

4 Apply reinforcement principles to manage performance.

5 Identify causes of low performance and how they could be improved using the expectancy model.

6 Understand the basic approaches to motivation.

7 Identify features of job design that can affect worker motivation.

8 Apply the job characteristics model to link job design to motivation.

Trouble in the Valley

For those who enjoyed the high-flying creativity and laid-back corporate culture of Silicon Valley and who loved to play, invent, and troubleshoot blockbuster video games, it might have seemed that there was no better place to work than Electronic Arts, Inc. (EA), the world's largest independent video game maker. Its luxurious modern campus in Redwood City, California, included a big gymnasium that could rival a private health club, a well-stocked cafeteria, pool tables, basketball courts, a masseuse and acupuncturist, and flexible work schedules that let employees make use of all these amenities. Like other software and game companies in the Valley, EA based its compensation policies on the entrepreneurial spirit on which technology workers thrived. It paid its employees salaries, stock options, and bonuses that could amount to 5 to 30 percent of annual salary. When the company did well, everyone shared in the rewards.

But life at EA wasn't all fun and games. As the industry grew, so did the stakes, and EA, as well as other tech employers, began asking more and more of its artists, animators, designers, programmers, and engineers. Overtime hours were common, and even though they were sometimes excessive during the "crunch" times leading up to release of a new game, they were unpaid hours. Some workers routinely put in six or seven long days a week over a period of months, adding up to as much as 60 to 80 hours with no breaks and no additional pay.

Many of these employees had started out when the game business consisted of relatively small, often privately owned, companies, in which everyone was motivated by the great pride they took in the games they built. Now, however, the consolidation of the video game business into only a few big publicly-owned companies meant that a $10 to $20 million investment rode on each new title developed. Deadlines were tighter and shareholders' profit expectations grew. And in the meantime, employees found themselves entering their 30s, 40s, and 50s, some with families. For many, the long hours, unpaid overtime, and minimal benefits were growing more painful. The amenities at the office could not take the place of tangible rewards like family-friendly schedules and fair pay. Some employees were reluctant to speak out about their unpaid labor, and about unremittingly stressful conditions that some called "a sweatshop," because they liked the creative and dynamic atmosphere of the industry and were unwilling to give management a reason to look abroad for cheaper labor, as other industries have done.

But finally a class-action suit was filed against EA, claiming that the company required its employees to work overtime without compensation. Two other suits and a rash of negative publicity about working conditions soon followed.

The original suit was eventually settled for $15.6 million, and EA announced that it would begin to pay some workers overtime, but they would no longer be eligible for options or bonuses. The company also promised to restructure project management of new video games so that critical deadlines could be met earlier in the process, relieving the "crunch" period. Finally, a trade association was formed to establish ethical work standards for game industry developers.

Sources: Brooke A. Masters and Amy Joyce, "Suits on Overtime Hitting Big Firms," *Washington Post*, www.washingtonpost.com, February 21, 2006; John Gaudiosi, "Gaming Industry Gets Trade Group," Reuters, www.localnewsleader.com, February 21, 2006; Matt Richtel, "Fringes vs. Basics in Silicon Valley," *New York Times*, March 9, 2005.

CRITICAL THINKING QUESTIONS

1. *What did Electronic Arts employees want to get from their jobs?*

2. *Was their motivation the same over time, or did it change?*

3. *Is the key to motivation simply getting paid?*

We will return to these questions in our Concluding Thoughts at the end of the chapter, after you have had an opportunity to read the chapter material.

Motivation: An Overview

Motivation is seen by an increasing number of organizations as a key consideration when it comes to company success. Today's competitive environment requires a workforce that is motivated and committed to reaching work-related goals. This chapter focuses on two central questions: First, what motivates people, and second, how can you keep employees engaged and enthusiastic about their work? In the following sections we will consider the answers to these questions by examining two categories of theories about motivation: *content* and *process*. Content theories of motivation seek to understand *what underlies and drives motivation* in order to effectively motivate people. The process theories of motivation seek to understand what steps can be taken *to improve and maintain motivation.*

Before reviewing specific theories and concepts concerning motivation, it may be worthwhile to consider the theories and the concept of motivation more broadly and explain their value. First, it is not that some theories are right and some are wrong. Rather, no single theory captures everything of importance or applies in all situations. Having a broad understanding and the ability to apply various models can give you a much more versatile set of tools with which to manage motivation. Second, the motivation theories, or models, as with most theories, can seem academic, but they have great *applied value.* The models can help you understand motivation, what affects it, and, therefore, how to effectively manage motivation. The models give you frameworks for organizing and thinking through motivation problems.

We may not be consciously aware of it, but models often guide how we assess situations and what actions we take. For example, our personal beliefs can lead us to make assumptions and act in certain ways, even though we may not be aware of our internal models. What accounts for your friend not doing well on a midterm exam? Does the fault lie with the test, the instructor, or with your friend? Was the test too hard, the material not adequately covered by the instructor, or did the friend not study or lack the needed ability? Your personal beliefs will lead you, perhaps without conscious awareness, to conclusions about the source of the poor grade and what may solve it. Similarly, your beliefs about motivation can guide your understanding of a workplace motivation issue and lead you to choosing particular ways to manage the issue.

Finally, while motivation is an internal and unseen force, it is useful to recognize two basic types of motivation: intrinsic and extrinsic. **Intrinsic motivation** comes from the personal satisfaction of the work itself while **extrinsic motivation** comes from the rewards that are linked to job performance, such as a paycheck. An example of intrinsic motivation could be someone volunteering in community efforts, such as helping feed and clothe the homeless. The motivation for doing this is not the explicit rewards linked to the task because the involvement is voluntary. In other words, it is not about the money. Rather, community involvement is typically driven by the task itself: the experience and personal satisfaction of helping others and the knowledge that your efforts can help make a meaningful and positive difference. In contrast, a summer job at a local restaurant is probably something done more for extrinsic than intrinsic reasons. For instance, car payments and money for school may be reasons for working at the summer job. In other words, it's all about the money! The summer job itself may even be something that is disliked, such as strenuous manual labor, busing tables, etc. Yet, there is motivation to perform the job because of the monetary rewards that it is linked to. If someone asked why a student was working at the summer job, the answer would most likely emphasize the money, not characteristics of the job that were positive and satisfying. In most work situations, however, today's workers are seldom driven solely by extrinsic rewards. Today's workers want to derive meaning and satisfaction from their work, not only money. A recent survey of health care workers found intrinsic factors to be more important than extrinsic factors in determining career satisfaction and the desire of workers to stay with their current job.[1]

All these factors are important to keep in mind as we seek to understand what underlies and drives motivation (content theories) and how to improve and maintain motivation (process theories).

Dean McDermott, who has held management positions for several different companies over 30 years, is an example of intrinsic motivation. Now looking into starting a wholesale seafood business, he says of his expectations from working, "You can go to work, and it doesn't seem like a job. You can have fun."

intrinsic motivation

Motivation that comes from the personal satisfaction of the work itself.

extrinsic motivation

Motivation that comes from the rewards that are linked to job performance, such as a paycheck.

Content View of Motivation

People's needs are the content that drives or energizes their efforts. Content theories attempt to look inside people and better understand what energizes action. Fundamentally, all of these theories share a common emphasis on *needs* as the origin of motivation. They conclude that if there were no needs, there would be little basis for energizing any activity. Understanding the needs that motivate people can be a valuable aid to managers. If you know the needs of your workers, you can align organizational characteristics and rewards to meet the needs when employees achieve organization goals. Knowing the needs that drive your workers can help you to provide the types of outcomes and work settings that those workers will find rewarding and satisfying.

Maslow's Hierarchy of Needs

MASLOW'S HIERARCHY OF NEEDS According to Abraham Maslow, people experience needs in a specified order, from the simple physical needs to complex psychological needs, as shown in Figure 12.1 on page 471. In ascending order, the needs are:

1. *Physiological needs,* such as food and shelter.
2. *Safety or security needs,* such as danger avoidance, a steady job, and a healthy work environment.
3. *Social needs,* such as friendships, supervisory support, a sense of belonging, and affection.
4. *Esteem needs,* such as personal pride, a positive self-concept, and status.
5. *Self-actualization,* or the desire to use one's potential to the maximum.

Maslow argues that each lower level need has to be satisfied before the next higher level need becomes salient or motivating.[2] For instance, a hungry person is highly motivated to do whatever it takes to secure food, even taking actions that jeopardize safety, such as accepting a dangerous job or stealing the food. A person who is deprived of nourishment is not likely to be overly concerned with social status.

One central management implication of Maslow's hierarchy is that providing additional rewards to meet a need will motivate a person only if the need has not already been satisfied. Also, when lower level needs are not satisfied, providing for higher levels will not motivate people. According to Maslow, the only need that can never be fully satisfied is *self-actualization,* which is at the top of the hierarchy. People can keep developing and learning as long as they have the opportunity to do so. Interesting and challenging work will continue to promote personal growth.

LOC-In

On the whole, there is only questionable empirical research support for the notion that needs operate in the precise sequence that the steps imply. However, there is general agreement about two important points: (1) a dominant or salient need will motivate people more than a less important or weaker need, and (2) managers should strive to provide employees with opportunities for self-actualization, since personal growth is likely to keep them interested in learning and developing their talents over time. Rewards associated with lower level needs (e.g., higher pay) only go so far in motivating people unless the work itself is stimulating and exciting. In other words, extrinsic motivation is not sufficient for the long haul. People want more from work than a paycheck or a bonus. They also want personal growth and meaningfulness in their jobs.

ALDERFER'S ERG THEORY Clayton Alderfer revised Maslow's theory to make the needs and the sequence of needs less rigid. Alderfer's revised need hierarchy is called **ERG theory,** referring to three groups of core needs: existence, relationships, and growth.[3] The *existence group* is concerned with material requirements for survival, corresponding to the physiological and safety needs in

FIGURE 12.1

Maslow's Hierarchy of Needs
Theory

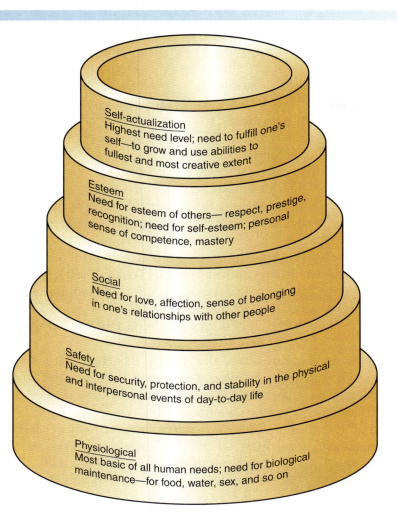

Self-actualization
Highest need level; need to fulfill one's
self—to grow and use abilities to
fullest and most creative extent

Esteem
Need for esteem of others— respect, prestige,
recognition; need for self-esteem; personal
sense of competence, mastery

Social
Need for love, affection, sense of belonging
in one's relationships with other people

Safety
Need for security, protection, and stability in the physical
and interpersonal events of day-to-day life

Physiological
Most basic of all human needs; need for biological
maintenance—for food, water, sex, and so on

Maslow's hierarchy. The *relationship group* of needs involves people's desire for social support, interpersonal relationships, and favorable recognition by others. These needs roughly correspond to Maslow's social and ego (or esteem) needs. Alderfer describes a third set of needs related to personal *growth,* or the intrinsic desire to use and develop one's talents. This set closely overlaps Maslow's self-actualization category, although it also includes some elements of the ego category such as the drive to achieve.

The key difference between these two theories is not that Alderfer collapses five needs to three. Rather, Alderfer does not assume a rigid hierarchy in which one need has to be satisfied before other needs emerge. Instead all three categories can operate simultaneously. Also, Alderfer claims that if a higher order need is not being met, people may demand more rewards to satisfy lower level needs. Cross-cultural evidence suggest that Alderfer's more flexible view of needs is more realistic than Maslow's perspective. For instance, workers in Spain and Japan are likely to place social needs before physiological requirements.

McCLELLAND'S NEEDS David McClelland also identified a set of important needs that serve as motives.[4] The most important needs for managers are the needs for achievement, power, and affiliation. The **need for achievement** is a drive to accomplish things, in which the individual receives great satisfaction from personal attainment and goal completion. Most U.S. managers believe that

need for achievement

The drive to accomplish things, in which the individual receives great satisfaction from personal attainment and goal completion.

the need for achievement is important to success, and visible signs that a person is achievement-oriented are important in upward movement within organizations. Ironically, some research suggests that effective general managers do not typically have a high need to achieve because people with high achievement needs are more interested in personal gains than in helping others do well.[5] Instead, high achievers tend to be more successful at entrepreneurial activities such as running their own businesses, launching new projects, or leading self-contained units within a large firm. McClelland claims that people can be trained to increase the need for achievement.

The **need for affiliation** is the desire to be liked by others, to receive social approval, and to establish close interpersonal relationships. Research suggests that a low need for affiliation is associated with managerial success.[6] This is so because an important part of the manager's job is to make tough decisions that will displease some people.

The **need for power** is the desire to influence or control other people. Managers have a strong drive to have an effect, to be in charge, and to compete against others. To the extent that an individual does not want power purely for the pursuit of personal goals and does not place prestige and influence ahead of effective performance, the strength of this need is an important predictor of success in managerial jobs.

One particularly controversial part of this theory is that a high need for achievement in a national population is necessary to launch and sustain a high level of economic development. However, empirical data suggest that a high achievement need is not universal among industrialized nations.[7] For instance, security is a more important motivator among many Greek and Japanese managers, and social needs are often paramount in Scandinavian countries. In most

Dan Ross works for Covance, a pharmaceutical company, where he supervises a number of younger employees. He likes to provide them with plenty of feedback. "Going three weeks without telling someone how they are doing is less likely to keep them in that position," he says. "You've got to give them the challenge of some things to change."

Latin countries, an important part of achievement is the ability to reward friends and families, practices that may be viewed as corrupt in Anglo-American countries. The point is that needs and their importance vary significantly from one society to another.

HERZBERG'S TWO-FACTOR THEORY   Two-factor theory focuses on characteristics that motivate and reduce motivation at work.[8] Frederick Herzberg developed this theory based on interviews with workers regarding what led them to be satisfied and motivated at work and what resulted in being dissatisfied and unmotivated. His key findings, and the heart of two-factor theory, is that two separate sets of characteristics affect motivation and, thus, employee performance.

The first set, which Herzberg labeled *hygiene factors,* corresponds to the lower level needs in Maslow's theory. Hygiene factors are contextual or extrinsic aspects of jobs such as salaries, fringe benefits, company policies, working conditions, and interpersonal relations with co-workers and supervisors. They can cause dissatisfaction if they are inadequately met. Unfortunately hygiene factors also *do not* motivate people to do a good job.

To achieve higher levels of worker effort, first the hygiene factors must be well managed. Next, the key is to provide workers with *motivators,* or intrinsic rewards derived from the work itself, that provide continuous stimulation to strive for the best possible performance level, as shown in Figure 12.2 on page 473.

FIGURE 12.2

Motivators	Hygiene factors
Achievement	Pay
Challenge	Supervision
Responsibility	Physical work conditions
Recognition	Rules, Regulations, Policies
Autonomous decisions	Benefits

Low   Hi   Low   Hi

Satisfaction   Dissatisfaction

Herzberg's Two-Factor Theory

Source: From J. M. Ivancevich, P. Lorenzi, S. J. Skinner, and P. B. Crosby, *Management: Quality and Competitiveness,* McGraw-Hill/Irwin, 1997. Reprinted with permission of J. M. Ivancevich.

According to Herzberg, such motivators include the nature of the work, responsibility for a task well done, feedback and recognition, opportunities for personal growth and learning, and feelings of achievement derived from task completion. Herzberg contends that these motivators increase job satisfaction, and that removing dissatisfying characteristics from a job does not necessarily make the job satisfying.

The notion that the two sets of factors are distinct and the statement that only intrinsic factors motivate people are controversial. A raise is an extrinsic reward, or a hygiene factor, and it may also be a strong form of recognition (an intrinsic reward, or a motivator factor). Although the pure form of the theory has not been supported by most studies, Herzberg's work has been widely

FIGURE 12.3

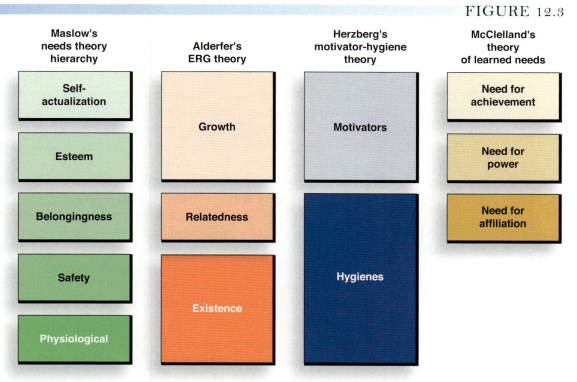

Content Theories of Motivation Compared

LOC-In

2 Learning Objective Check-In

Melissa has a strong desire to be liked by others and to establish close interpersonal relationships with her co-workers. She also has a strong drive to accomplish things and has considered starting her own business someday. Melissa is competitive and has a strong drive to be in charge.

1. *Melissa's strong _____, as evidenced by her desire to be well liked, would indicate she might not be a good fit in management of other people.*
   a. *need for affiliation*
   b. *need for achievement*
   c. *need for power*
   d. *existence need*
2. *How should Melissa's strong drive to accomplish things be classified? Do managers typically have this?*
   a. *High need for achievement; yes*
   b. *High need for achievement; no*
   c. *High need for power; yes*
   d. *High need for power; no*
3. *Melissa's strong competitive nature and drive to be in charge indicates a strong _____.*
   a. *need for achievement*
   b. *need for power*
   c. *need for affiliation*
   d. *need for acceptance*

Assessing How Personality Type Impacts Goal-Setting Skills

read. Many managers believe that the theory is a helpful method for analyzing motivational problems at work. It reminds managers that intrinsic rewards are too often ignored.

The content theories emphasize the importance of needs as motivators. Figure 12.3 on page 473 summarizes and contrasts the needs that were focused in the content theories.

Process View of Motivation

A second approach to motivation revolves around the study of the processes that lead to changes in behavior. These process models provide a map of what determines a person's level of motivation. The question is, regardless of the content of a need for a person, how is that motive transformed into performance? The process that changes an internal state to a behavior or activity is the focus of these models.

GOAL-SETTING THEORY Hundreds of studies demonstrate that people are more motivated when there are concrete objectives or targets to achieve.[9] These studies suggest that three important aspects of goals energize people to try harder. First, employees must believe that the goals are good. That is, they should "buy into" the goals. One effective way to increase goal acceptability is to have employees and supervisors jointly set the goals in a participative fashion. Second, the targets set should challenge people to "stretch" their abilities, but they should also be realistic. Unattainable goals frustrate and demoralize employees. Third, goals should be specific, quantifiable, and measurable to give people clear direction on how to focus their efforts so they can concentrate on meeting or exceeding the established targets. The goal-setting process is illustrated in Figure 12.4 on page 475. As depicted in the figure, setting goals in a participative fashion and identifying goals that are challenging, specific, and measurable will help lead workers to accept the goals. In turn, acceptance of a goal energizes the worker to put forth the needed effort. This motivation results in improved performance and attainment of the goal, setting the stage for another round of goal setting.

Goal setting must be carefully done. In most jobs, successful performance depends on the accomplishment of intangible tasks or duties that cannot be quantified or translated into a neat set of targets or objectives. The evaluation and reward system should be flexible enough to prevent employees from single-mindedly focusing on the achievement of measurable performance objectives at the expense of other key elements of the job. Consider the following goal-setting failures:

1. In the late 1980s, several airlines experienced deteriorating customer relations and a large number of no-shows when their sales representatives' pay was based on the number of bookings.

2. In a midwestern state, paying snowplow operators on a per-mile basis resulted in many roads packed with snow and ice because it was easier to cover more miles and get paid more by disengaging the snow-removal equipment.

FIGURE 12.4

The Goal-Setting Process

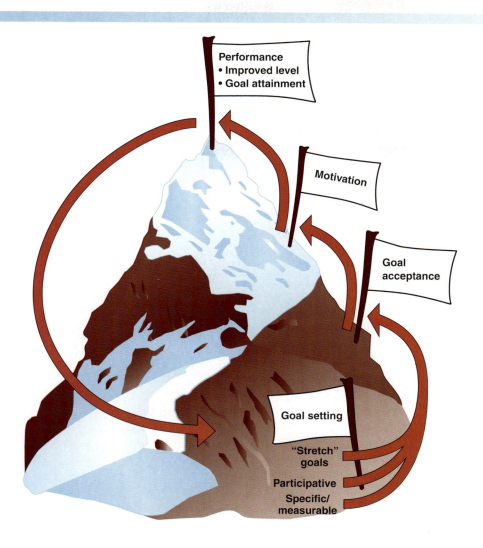

3. In some academic departments, faculty may be poor teachers because pay, promotion, and tenure are based only on having research published in leading journals.

4. Top executives are frequently accused of maximizing short-term gains to trigger larger annual bonuses at the expense of long-term performance.

One well-known approach to implementing goal theory is management by objectives (MBO). In an MBO system, employees and supervisors agree on a set of measurable goals to be accomplished within a certain amount of time. MBO allows the firm to implement overall organizational objectives by breaking these down into specific objectives assigned to different units and individuals in the firm. As depicted in Figure 12.5 on page 476, the objectives for the entire firm "cascade down" to the divisional, departmental, and individual levels.

The cascading feature of the MBO approach means that goals at each level of the organization are aligned with the overall objectives of the organization. Thus, goals that might be pursued by a division, department, or even an individual, must be justified in terms of serving to achieve higher-level goals. The cascading nature of the MBO process helps to assure that all levels of the organization are aligned and working together to serve a common purpose. For example, an overarching goal of low cost should result in very different types of goals throughout the organization than would, say, an overarching goal of innovativeness or quality. However, to be most effective, goals shouldn't simply be

FIGURE 12.5

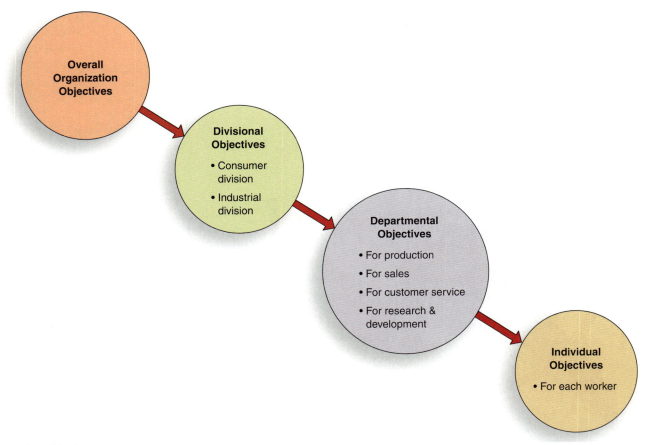

Cascading Objectives

handed to workers. A participative approach can allow workers to have their input into the process and to formulate objectives that best fit with their interests and skills, while contributing to the organization's goals.

Management by objectives has several advantages. First, it results in a hierarchy of objectives that links specific objectives with each succeeding organizational level. Second, each person knows exactly what is expected of him or her. This makes it easier to evaluate and reward employee contributions by comparing them to agreed-on goals. Third, because employees and managers jointly participate in the goal-setting process, MBO facilitates the flow of work-related information from the bottom up as well as the top down.

One drawback of MBO has already been discussed: in many jobs the most important tasks cannot be easily quantified. By emphasizing what can be measured, an MBO system may cause people to lose sight of crucial behaviors that have no clear metrics, such as being patient and friendly with customers. Another drawback is that MBO systems may encourage people to play it safe by choosing less challenging goals that are more easily attainable. This risk-reduction strategy makes sense from the employee's perspective if job security and organizational rewards are contingent on the achievement of agreed-on goals.

Another issue to consider is, "Where do goals come from?" Goal setting is a proven motivational technique, but who should define the goals that employees are working toward? Skills for Managing 12.1 on page 477 examines the customer as the source that should drive performance goals.

LINKING MOTIVATION TO THE CUSTOMER

Motivation is often thought of as working harder, but to what end? Exactly what should be maximized? Where do performance expectations come from? Are they meaningful to the workers? Performance goals often reflect company expectations, but goals based on customer expectations can have an immediate impact on a business. Goals or performance expectations that are customer driven can increase motivation because of the link workers can see between their efforts and a meaningful outcome: customer satisfaction. Goals that lack meaningfulness create a sure-fire recipe for loss of motivation and failure.

Discussion Questions

1. How could you develop performance expectations from the customer perspective? Identify the major steps you would take to develop customer-based performance goals.

2. Do you think customer-driven performance goals will inspire increased motivation? Why or why not?

3. What else might be needed in addition to customer-based goals that would maximize performance?

4. Are there potential drawbacks to focusing solely on customer-based goals? For example, employees might work hard to satisfy customer-based goals, but ignore other aspects of the job that don't directly involve customers. Identify any other potential problems with customer-based performance goals. How could you reduce or eliminate those problems?

EQUITY THEORY   At work, people develop beliefs about the fairness of the rewards they receive relative to their contributions.[10] **Equity theory** suggests that people's perceptions of fairness depend on their personal assessment of outcomes and inputs. *Outcomes* are rewards such as recognition, promotions, and pay. *Inputs* are contributions such as effort, education, and special skills. Employees have a general expectation that the outcomes or rewards they receive will be proportionate to the inputs they provide. People make this judgment not in an absolute sense but by using others as a reference point. A comparison person may be a co-worker inside the firm or a friend who works for a different company. The relationship is summarized by the ratio:

$$\frac{\text{Personal outcomes}}{\text{Inputs}} \quad \text{versus} \quad \frac{\text{Others' outcomes}}{\text{Inputs}}$$

equity theory
The view that people's perceptions about the fairness of the rewards they receive relative to their contributions affect their motivation.

Fairness is achieved when the ratios are equivalent. Ratios that are not equivalent produce a psychological state called *cognitive dissonance,* which creates dissatisfaction and results in attempts to bring the ratios back into balance.

People who perceive that they are being inequitably treated can use one of four methods to attempt to change the ratios, or they can mentally reassess the situation and decide that it is equitable after all. One option is to reduce inputs by cutting back on the level of effort, and if the imbalance becomes too great, to leave the firm. A second option is to influence the outcomes. For instance, the employee may document what he or she has accomplished to persuade the boss to provide a raise or a promotion. Third, a person can decrease others' outcomes. For instance, a dissatisfied employee may spread rumors about people in order to reduce their outcomes. Finally, a person who feels that he or she is getting more than deserved may increase effort levels to reduce the dissatisfaction resulting from guilt.

Reinforcement Theory

Equity theory contains two important concepts. First, motivation largely depends on a perception of fairness in the exchange process between what the person contributes and what the person receives. Second, people are constantly comparing themselves to others. The way they see their input–outcome exchange relative to others affects their behaviors. The direct implications of these two concepts for managers is that workers pay attention to fairness of the exchange and to other workers. As a manager, you might like to think that a worker will pay attention to only their own "deal" regarding the exchange of inputs to outputs, but you would only be fooling yourself. The reality is that people are always looking at the exchanges enjoyed by others and making comparisons to their own arrangements. Further, when employees make these comparisons, they tend to overestimate the compensation of others.[11] As a manager, you can avoid this bias and the downward adjustment of inputs that can result by making public general compensation levels. You may not want to post names and salary levels, but having established pay grades for jobs is a good way to avoid the overestimation that can occur when workers make exchange comparisons with other workers. In addition, you can help to put exchanges in balance by recognizing that outputs can include more than financial outcomes. For example, even if you don't have control over financial outcomes, as a manager you could offer recognition, flexibility, and other nonfinancial rewards as a means to achieving equitable exchanges.

Understanding equity theory as well as needs theories and goal setting also helps team members manage their own motivation levels. Management is Everyone's Business 12.1 above offers some suggestions to help you manage motivation as a team member.

LOC-In

③ Learning Objective Check-In

1. *Don sees that his staff are constantly chatting and comparing the fairness of different individuals' compensations. Don manages factors like fairness according to _____, which suggests that his staff's perceptions of fairness depend on their personal assessments of their recognition and rewards as well as their contributions, backgrounds, and education.*
   a. *strategy theory*
   b. *MBO*
   c. *goal-setting theory*
   d. *equity theory*

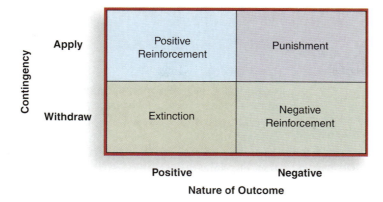

FIGURE 12.6

Types of Reinforcement
Conditions

Source: From J. M. Ivancevich, P.
Lorenzi, S. J. Skinner, and P. B.
Crosby, *Management: Quality and
Competitiveness*, McGraw-
Hill/Irwin, 1997. Reprinted with
permission of J. M. Ivancevich.

positive reinforcement

A pleasurable stimulus or
reward following a desired
behavior that induces
people to continue the
behavior.

REINFORCEMENT THEORY One clearly established principle in the social sciences is called the *law of effect*, which was formalized by psychologist Edward Thorndike. The law of effect states that behaviors are encouraged or discouraged depending on the consequences which follow.[12] Four key consequences, as seen in Figure 12.6 above, are:

1. **Positive reinforcement** is a pleasurable stimulus or reward following a desired behavior that induces people to continue the behavior. For instance, people are likely to spend more time in the office if they feel it will help them earn promotions even though it may not increase their overall productivity. One common use of positive reinforcement in the workplace is performance contingent pay, such as merit pay and bonuses. Performance contingent rewards can be powerful motivators but, as illustrated in Management Close-Up 12.1 on page 480, these same practices can be the source of problems if they don't work the way people think they should.

2. **Negative reinforcement** is the removal of unpleasant conditions following desired behavior, resulting in an increase in the frequency of that behavior. For instance, a worker may be subjected to close scrutiny and loud direction from an authoritarian foreman. However, the boss may remove this negative condition once the worker demonstrates that he/she can correctly perform the task.

3. **Punishment** is an aversive or unpleasant consequence following an undesired behavior. This leads to a decrease in that behavior. However the avoidance of undesired behaviors through punishment does not mean that people will engage in desired behaviors. For instance, a boss who yells at people for being late may provoke employees to show little initiative to try their best once they clock in. In fact, they may resent the boss and try to get even whenever they can. The threat of punishment for undesired behaviors may be more effective than the actual use of punishment because punishment decreases undesirable behaviors only temporarily and may create anger and resentment, which hurt communication and undermine

Positive reinforcement is a successful motivator at Imre Communications, a Baltimore marketing firm, where employees are awarded extra vacation time during the Christmas holiday for helping the company meet its financial goal of revenue growth reaching 19 percent or more. President David Imre (left), shown here with an employee, says, "I don't think people would have been as gung-ho if I had simply offered extra cash."

negative reinforcement

The removal of unpleasant consequences associated with a desired behavior, resulting in an increase in the frequency of that behavior.

punishment

An aversive or unpleasant consequence following undesired behavior.

Motivation and the Disappearing Carrot

THEME: ETHICS

Bonuses. Merit pay. Money tied to performance. The idea of making some portion of pay contingent on performance has long been a key motivational tool of Western management. Performance-contingent pay is meant to provide an incentive to workers. The practice is certainly consistent with reinforcement and expectancy theories in which money is the reinforcer. The merit pay system points out exactly how task performance is instrumental to getting a reward. There are also volumes of studies of white lab rats which demonstrate that contingent reinforcement works as a great motivator. Rats, however, do not know what performance contingency plan they are on and whether the terms of it might have been violated. Lab rats can't charge unfairness or file lawsuits. Employees, on the other hand, do have the capacity to examine the provisions of their merit pay plan and draw conclusions about whether or not what they received in bonus pay was fair.

The experience of Cory White, a senior manager, provides an all-too-real example of how the effective motivation principle of performance contingent rewards can go awry. White worked for Idea Integration Corporation, an e-business consulting unit of MPS Group Inc. He managed the PeopleSoft consulting practice. Similar to his staff, White was on a plan in which he would be paid bonuses based on meeting perfor-

mance goals, including revenue targets and business development. Under White's management, the PeopleSoft practice grew 22 percent and profitability increased 211 percent in the second quarter of 2001. However, Mr. White did not receive a bonus that quarter or for any quarter in 2001. By his calculation, he had accumulated $120,620 in unpaid bonuses and an additional $53,000 for stock options that were promised but never granted. Idea Integration Corporation claims that the problem with White is an isolated event, but White claims the organization had a pattern of not paying bonuses. White left Idea Integration in 2002 and filed a suit against his former employer for fraud and breach of employment contract—an outcome far different from the positive motivation outcome that would be hoped for with the use of performance-contingent pay.

White's case may not be an isolated incident. Six other employees of Idea Integration claimed similar experiences and state that their incentive plans were changed after they earned most or all of the bonuses. The proverbial carrot was there, but they weren't allowed to reach it.

Source: T. Reason, "Incentive Confrontation: A Bitter Dispute over Bonuses Highlights the Hazards of Incentive Pay," *CEO: The Magazine for Senior Financial Executives* 19 (2003), pp. 46–51.

---

goodwill and personal initiative. Management Close-Up 12.2 on page 481 explores the negative approach to motivation.

extinction

Withholding of a positive consequence following desired behavior.

4. **Extinction** is withholding of a positive consequence following desired behavior. Eventually, faced with never being reinforced following a behavior (that used to be followed by a reward), the frequency of the behavior will decrease to the point where it disappears, or is extinguished. For example, a worker may have been rewarded on the basis of quantity. However, the emphasis in the organization may have shifted to quality. Out of habit, the worker may, for a while, still focus on quantity of production. Behaving in ways to maximize quantity, maybe sometimes at the expense of quality, will soon extinguish when the worker realizes that the behavior is no longer rewarded.

Reinforcing Performance

Reinforcement theory indicates that managers should link desirable outcomes (such as pay raises or promotion) to the behaviors they want to encourage. They should also try to reduce undesirable outcomes associated with the behav-

Crack the Whip!

THEME: ETHICS
As vice president of a New Jersey auto dealership, Charles Park doesn't always throw things at his workers. He had, however, been known to do it occasionally. In one instance, when he was a manager at an auto dealership, he was confronted with a consistently low level of performance of one of his auto salesmen. Park had a discussion with the salesman but nothing improved. The salesman was older and treated Park as a son. Out of frustration, Park threw a binder at him. Either ironically or because of Park's action, the salesperson actually sold a couple of cars that day. Doling out this form of negative treatment is not the way to treat employees. Park, however, contends that ". . . if you do it once in a while, it works." Even if the statement is correct, being violent with employees invites trouble.

Jeff Leafy, a sales executive at a Washington, DC, software company, had a promising young salesperson on his staff. He thought she had the capacity to become a superstar in sales, but her productivity had been declining. Leafy decided to get her attention with a little negative feedback in the attempt to kickstart her back toward the right performance path. He firmly told her that she needed to pick up the pace if she expected to move up with the company. Of course, this message was threatening and negative in just its content, but it was also likely delivered in a fairly bombastic and loud manner. His speech ended up pushing the salesperson over the edge and she wound up in a fetal position on his office floor by the conclusion of the interaction. The company attorney

Even though negative treatment works sometimes, it frequently backfires.

came to his office and ambulance personnel took the salesperson to the hospital. Unbeknownst to Leafy, the salesperson was going through a period of particular difficulty in her personal life. Leafy's negative approach only made the problem worse.

Source: J. Chang, "Cracking the Whip: In a Perfect World, Sales Managers Would Use Only Positive Incentives to Get the Best Performance from Their Teams. But in Less-than-Ideal Situations, Is There a Time and Place for Negative Motivation?" *Sales & Marketing Management* 155 (2003), pp. 24–27.

---

iors they wish people to exhibit. For instance, providing day care facilities may prompt more women to accept jobs that require frequent travel and unpredictable schedules.

It is important to recognize that, based on reinforcement theory, motivation does not reside in the worker. Rather, motivation is in the contingencies that exist between behaviors and rewards. From the reinforcement theory perspective, whether someone is motivated is simply a handy but inaccurate reference. Motivation exists in the contingencies between behaviors and outcomes and there is no need to make any inferences about what is going on inside of the person. Thus, from the reinforcement theory perspective, motivation is largely, if not entirely, due to the contingencies set up by management.

video: THE ENTREPRENEURIAL MANAGER

Be Your Own Boss

Summary

Have you ever dreamed of quitting your job, cutting out of the cubicle, and starting a business all your own? There were nearly 600,000 start-ups last year alone—and nearly that number of failures. Two brothers found success, however, with the Darien Sport Shop in Darien, Connecticut, after refusing to take no for an answer. Two years ago, Shep and Ian Murray left their corporate jobs in New York City to make ties. They had little experience, and even less money, but they had a strong passion for what they had set out to do. Their company, Vineyard Vines, is expected to post $20 million in sales this year. The brothers started out peddling their ties off their boat in a harbor at Martha's Vineyard, out of backpacks, or out of Tupperware containers to local store owners. They were met with much resistance, but finally got store owners to agree to try selling the ties, once they offered the store owners an unconditional risk-free return policy by which the brothers would buy back any unsold goods.

The company has since expanded from neckties to many other products—belts, shirts, totes, and scarves. The brothers started with their passion for the idea, and built relationships with people with whom they did business. The company has since grown, but the relationships, they say, have stayed the same. Ian says they have learned that relationships are keys to success for them as entrepreneurs.

Clifford Schorer, of the Columbia Business School, says they are seeing a lot more student-entrepreneurs today pinning their hopes on the service industry as opposed to selling a particular product. These are smaller-scale businesses that require less capital. They are more personality driven to some degree. Pure passion, he says, is the first step. Lots of people get excited about ideas, but few people have the drive and passion to carry those ideas through to fruition and actually become successful in their businesses.

Discussion Questions

1. Which of Maslow's needs were met by both the brothers' corporate jobs in New York *and* the entrepreneurial venture in Connecticut? Which job satisfied the brothers' higher-level needs?

2. Apply McClelland's needs theory to Ian and Shep Murray. On which needs do they rank high? On which ones do they rank low?

3. Do you think entrepreneurs like Ian and Shep are motivated more by intrinsic factors or extrinsic factors? Explain your response.

LOC-In

4 Learning Objective Check-In

1. *Dave comes into work about 15 minutes early every day. Even though it is not part of his everyday responsibilities, he answers the phone, which always manages to ring before operating hours. He only lives 5 minutes from the office, whereas the others in his department all commute at least 30 minutes and have to fight traffic. Dave's time sheet reflects "8:00," the same as everyone else's, but his managers notice his presence, and he knows it. Dave knows that one of his managers will be seeking a replacement in two more months. If Dave were to get this job, for which he is qualified now, it would represent _____.*
   a. *contingent reinforcement*
   b. *equity theory*
   c. *behavioral theory*
   d. *positive reinforcement*

Thus, managers should link carefully selected rewards to the behaviors they desire. In essence, the goal is to concentrate on behaviors rather than private employee feelings, thoughts, or "motives."

As individual workers, we do not need to wait for management to find and set up the right contingencies to motivate us. Reinforcement theory has important implications for managers, but is also a powerful motivation tool for workers. Management Is Everyone's Business 12.2 on page 483 offers suggestions for applying reinforcement theory to manage our own behaviors.

Working as an Individual   All of us sometimes have things we would like to do differently and aspects of our work performance that we know we could improve. Reinforcement theory provides a simple but powerful means for motivating and managing our own work behavior. Here are some suggestions, based on reinforcement theory, for managing your own work behavior. You can generate your own suggestions to add to this initial list.

- Are there aspects of your performance that you could improve? *Pick a behavior* and define it. For example, if you want to be more effective at making work-related presentations, a relevant behavior might be a tendency to say "um" that detracts from your message.

- *Measure the behavior* you want to change. You can't apply reinforcement principles and manage performance, even your own, unless you have a good measure of the behavior. Take a baseline measure so you have an idea of your current performance level. In the case of a behavior such as saying "um," you can keep track of the number of occurrences with a simple frequency counter (such as a wrist device that can be used to record occurrences).

- *Identify a reward* and a contingency framework. For example, you might want to offer yourself a reward of a new DVD, dinner with a friend, the purchase of new music, and so on as a reward. Once you identify a reasonable but effective reward, you need to establish the link between the desired behavior and the reward. One way to do this is to simply tie the reward to the desired behavior: You get to make a purchase when you make three work-related presentations without saying "um."

- Another approach that can be more effective is to *use points* as a basis for earning rewards. For example, if your baseline frequency is 20, you might earn 5 points when the frequency is down to 10 and another 5 points when it reaches 5. You might associate a zero frequency with 20 points. Further, you can associate different point levels with various rewards, such as 5 points to download a song but 25 points for the new DVD you want. This point approach provides interim reinforcement and motivation until you reach the desired goal. Reaching zero frequency for a habitual behavior, such as saying "um," can be a long-term process that is best accomplished with the point system approach.

EXPECTANCY THEORY   One of the most widely accepted explanations of motivation is Victor Vroom's **expectancy theory.**[13] According to this theory, the strength to act in a particular way depends on people's beliefs that their actions will produce outcomes they find valuable and attractive. For instance, employees work harder if they believe that hard work will lead to better performance appraisals and promotion. Fundamentally, expectancy theory is a model about choice. That is, the amount of effort that is put forth on a task is something that people choose. As illustrated in Figure 12.7 on page 484, that choice is based on three critical factors:

- *Expectancy:* The link between effort and performance on a task. It is the belief that a given level of effort will lead to success on the task.

- *Instrumentality:* The perceived link between task performance and rewards.

expectancy theory

The view that having the strength to act in a particular way depends on people's beliefs that their actions will produce outcomes they find valuable and attractive.

FIGURE 12.7

Expectancy Theory of
Motivation

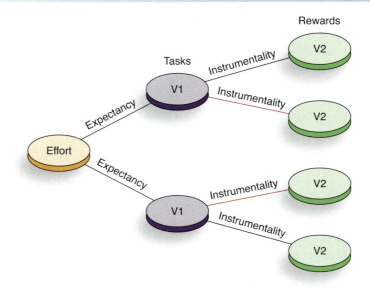

- *Valence:* The value placed on task performances and rewards.

  V2: The value placed on rewards.

  V1: The value placed on task performance. It is a function of the links (instrumentalities) seen between task performance and rewards, and the value placed on those rewards.

While the expectancy model might appear complex at first, it is a fairly simple and rational model. The basic statement made by the model is:

> The effort put forth on a task will be determined by the value the person places on the task and on the belief that he or she can perform the task.

That's the essence of the expectancy model! In other words, the model states that people will be motivated to perform well on a task only if the reward has value to them and if they believe they can be successful. Does task performance have value to your workers? Do they believe they can succeed? According to the expectancy model, these are critical questions and the answers will determine the level of motivation of workers.

The question of whether the person believes they can succeed is the expectancy link in the model. The expectancy link may be stronger for some people than for others simply because they have greater self-confidence. In addition, expectancy levels would likely be influenced by ability levels and the degree of training on performing the task. If someone hasn't been trained on a task and feels that he or she does not have the skills needed to adequately perform the task, his or her expectancy level would be expected to be low. Another set of factors that can influence expectancy levels, and probably the most important factors in the typical work situation, are situational constraints on performance. *Situational constraints,* or system factors, are barriers to performance. For example, a worker may feel that the materials aren't of sufficient quality or that tools are inadequate for the job. Other system barriers perceived by a worker might include insufficient time, conflicting demands, uncooperative co-workers, or unsupportive management, among others.

The question of whether task performance has value has to do with valence and instrumentality. Workers will place a high value on succeeding at a task if they see a strong link (instrumentality) between task performance and rewards that they desire. Workers might not see a strong tie between performance and rewards because, for example, they think that managers distribute rewards based on politics, not performance. Further, the rewards that good task performance leads to may not always be viewed so positively by all workers. For example, rewards such as more travel and increased authority and responsibility may be viewed as negative, rather than positive, outcomes by some workers. According to the expectancy model, in order for task performance to have a positive value, workers need to see positive outcomes and a strong link between their task performance and those rewards.

Expectancy theory helps explain why some people merely do the minimum necessary to get by while others seem to put all they have into their jobs. First, expectancy theory recognizes that there is no universal way to motivate people, because personal beliefs and perceptions play a major role in how people see the linkage of effort, performance, and outcomes, and the attractiveness of those outcomes. These beliefs may be influenced by the organization (for instance, through training and incentive programs), but factors such as family background, culture, educational level, and personality are likely to play a role. Second, many employees may not give a maximum effort because they don't think it will be properly assessed by the organization. For instance, supervisors often don't differentiate high from low performers or may include personal factors in their evaluations (see Chapter 10). Third, organizations are often afraid to reward people based on performance because measuring performance is difficult and because people disagree about the accuracy of the performance assessment, particularly when it is not favorable. Finally, rewards that are individualized are more motivating. Not all employees want the same thing. A working mother may place a high value on a flexible work schedule and may work harder to obtain flexibility. The hope of a better retirement package may induce a 55-year-old to be a key contributor at a time when other people are slowing down. Unfortunately, many managers are limited in the rewards they can provide, and few organizations allow rewards to be tailored to meet individual needs. Manager's Notebook 12.1 on page 486 presents a calendar of person motivators that could be used in most situations.

LOC-In

5 Learning Objective Check-In

Tim believes that iron welding is a very important and valuable task. However, he does not believe that he is qualified to do the task on his own, and therefore he does not think he can do a good job at it. Because he does not believe he can accomplish the task, he does not believe he will be rewarded if he tries.

1. *For Tim, there is a high _____ for iron welding.*
   a. *V2 valence*
   b. *V1 valence*
   c. *expectancy of success*
   d. *reinforcement*
2. *Based on the expectancy model, we should expect Tim to _____.*
   a. *perform well at iron welding*
   b. *lack the motivation to perform well*
   c. *place a particularly high value on rewards*
   d. *place a low value on task performance*

LOC-In

6 Learning Objective Check-In

1. *Brooke seeks to understand what steps can be taken to improve and maintain motivation. She is an operating manager who wants to influence her work crew. Brooke's focus indicates she should consider the _____.*
   a. *content theories of motivation*
   b. *goal theory of motivation*
   c. *process theories of motivation*
   d. *self-actualization theories of motivation*

MOTIVATION BY THE MONTH

Often it's the little things that add up and make more of a difference than the big things. Motivation is no exception. While incentive plans and goals are critically important, it can be at the level of day-to-day activity that managers have the opportunity to change the culture regarding motivation. Personal steps that a manager takes to recognize and motivate performance can be more meaningful and energizing to people than an impersonal reward system with rules set up by the organization. Below are some personal motivation ideas for each month of a year. This calendar is simply a starting point. You may decide to create your own motivation calendar.

- **January** Hold a performance contest and give prizes. For example, give a $50 gift certificate for the salesperson who makes the most in sales in a two-hour period.
- **February** Ask your top performer to lead a training session for the staff.
- **March** Ask a member of your staff to anonymously suggest what he or she would do differently as manager.
- **April** Walk around the work area and distribute prizes such as T-shirts, mugs, or cash to those you catch doing positive things.
- **May** Take the top performer to lunch and invite your boss to go along.
- **June** Ask your staff for anonymous input on obstacles that inhibit performance and how they might be eliminated.
- **July** Pair your top person with someone who is having performance problems. Provide lunch on the day they work together.
- **August** Write a personal thank-you note to each of your workers recognizing them for their efforts.
- **September** Start a wall of fame on which accomplishments of your staff (letters from customers, recognition, awards, etc.) are posted.
- **October** Take the worker you know least to lunch. Ask the employee about his or her long-term career goals. Commit to helping the employee reach those goals.
- **November** Provide a long weekend to your staff after they hit a major performance target.
- **December** Designate one day as "work at home" day and encourage people to do shopping and other holiday activities with the time they save commuting.

Source: "Little Carrots, Big Results," *Sales & Marketing Management* 155 (2003), p. 36.

Motivation by Design

Are there ways to structure jobs to maximize motivation? This basic issue is the focus of a field of study called *job design*. Job design is the structure of work such that performance and worker satisfaction are maximized. Chapter 9 focused on organizational structure and job design. In this chapter we focus on the aspects of job design that are associated with motivation.

Job Enlargement

Jobs often become specialized, narrow, and routine. Job enlargement tries to reverse this trend. Job enlargement combines tasks into a larger job. The intent of job enlargement is to make a job more varied and interesting by expanding the scope of the job. A single task may quickly become repetitive and boring, but being responsible for more tasks can make the work more interesting. Job enlargement can have a positive effect on motivation and performance if the enlarged job makes a meaningful whole. However, if the job enlargement simply consists of separate routine and unrelated tasks, the enlarged set of tasks will have no greater meaning than the separate tasks. In this case, the enlarged job quickly becomes routine and repetitive, albeit consisting of more tasks than before.

Job Rotation

Job rotation is another approach designed to reduce boredom and monotony. Job rotation moves workers from one task to another, thus increasing the overall complexity and variety of the job. For example, General Electric has a rotation program for entry-level human resource management staff,[14] in which participants might shift from labor relations, to compensation, to staffing, and then to other functions such as auditing and finance. GE found that the rotation program can take some people out of their comfort zones, but even that is viewed as positive. The program provides participants with a broader understanding of the business as well as building connections across the organization. In addition to these benefits, job rotation can also be useful for lowering accident and injury rates.[15] Continuously performing one task can lead to boredom and fatigue, which can then lead to accidents or other injuries, such as muscle strains. Job rotation lowers this risk by introducing variety and changing the worker's activities.

Job Enrichment

Job enrichment involves giving employees greater opportunity to plan, organize, and control portions of their jobs. The intent of the enrichment approach to job design is to provide employees with greater involvement in their work, improved meaningfulness of the work, and a greater sense of accomplishment. Job enrichment is not meant to be simply giving people more work. It is giving people greater responsibility and more work that requires a higher level of knowledge and skill.[16] Skills for Managing 12.2 on page 488 presents the job design concept of a cell as a means to introduce job enrichment as well as gain greater efficiency.

General Electric's job rotation program helps Human Resources staff understand the entire organization.

LOC-In

7 **Learning Objective Check-In**

Lauren suspects her workers are getting bored from monotony on the job. She is considering moving the workers to different tasks, periodically, to increase the overall complexity of their jobs, and to add some variety to their tasks. In addition to this, she intends to expand the scope of their jobs by giving workers responsibility for more tasks. Once the workers have more tasks to work on, Lauren knows there will be a greater need for day-to-day planning and organization of these tasks. She knows her workers well and trusts their ability to organize their own work to a great degree. This is why she intends to allow them greater involvement in the way they organize their schedules.

1. *The decision periodically to move workers to different tasks reflects _____.*
   a. *job rotation*
   b. *job enrichment*
   c. *job enlargement*
   d. *job empowerment*

2. *The decision to expand the scope of workers' jobs reflects _____.*
   a. *job enrichment*
   b. *job rotation*
   c. *job enlargement*
   d. *job empowerment*

3. *The decision to give workers more control over the increased number of tasks they will have responsibility for reflects _____.*
   a. *job enrichment*
   b. *job enlargement*
   c. *job rotation*
   d. *job development*

12.2

JOB ENRICHMENT AND EFFICIENCY: TAKING THE MANUFACTURING CELL TO THE OFFICE

Many organizations in the manufacturing sector have focused on improving the structures of company factories so that production is completed as efficiently and effectively as possible. One of the techniques used in these improvement efforts has been the manufacturing cell. A manufacturing cell puts together people and equipment that are involved with similar parts of products. The approach of creating these "families" has worked well in the manufacturing environment. The manufacturing cell does away with separate departments for functions such as design, manufacturing, production planning, sales, and finance. Instead, people involved in similar products are put together in a cell and communication, efficiency, lead times, and production can all be improved. The cell design may also be applied to office operations.

Office cells group together people that are involved in handling or producing the same information. While people may be in separate functions, they may all process the same paperwork. Putting all of these people together can eliminate department-to-department handoffs that can take time and introduce errors in communication. For example, Ingersoll Cutting Tool Company created an office cell to handle special customer orders. Before creation of the cell, the special orders went through 12 departments and it took as long as four weeks before an order made its way to the factory floor. The office cell included two workers whose jobs were enriched and included multifunctional duties. After implementing the cell design, the average time to process the special orders decreased from 10 days to 2 days. Similarly, a Finnish manufacturer, Ahlstrom, utilized the cell design to combine different functions. The organization created three office cells with each focusing on a geographic region. The cell design collapsed 10 separate operations into 5 broader jobs. The team of workers in each cell created their own guidelines and op-

erating procedures. The result? After implementation of the cell design, the average time to process an order fell from one week to one day.

Discussion Questions

The following items can be addressed individually or in small groups. The major conclusions can then be shared with the rest of the class.

1. Diagram a traditional organizational design in which people are separated into functions or departments. Use shapes to convey your conception (boxes, arrows, etc.).

2. Diagram a cell design.

3. Distinguish between the two designs. What makes them different? Is one way of designing work better than another? Why? Which design do you think you would rather work in? Why?

4. How do you think it would be best to structure work so that it is motivating and done efficiently? Diagram your suggested design.

5. Shifting to a cell design can be a significant workplace change. How would you implement this change?

Internet Research Questions

1. Can you find examples of organizations that have put the cell design in part of their operation? How has it worked?

2. Are there other examples of designing work that, either through job enrichment or some other means, are meant to improve motivation and performance? Describe these alternative designs.

Source: Adapted from N. L. Hyer and U. Wemnerlow, "The Office That Lean Built: Applying Cellular Thinking to Administrative Work," *IIE Solutions* 34 (2002), pp. 37–42.

---

job characteristics model

According to this model, the way jobs are designed produces critical psychological states which in turn affect key personal and work-related outcomes.

Job Characteristics Model

The **job characteristics model,** summarized in Figure 12.8 on page 489, proposes a view of the relationship between job design and employee motivation. According to this model, the way jobs are designed (for instance, variety of skills required, autonomy, and feedback) produces critical psychological states (such as experienced meaningfulness of the work), which in turn affect key personal and work-related outcomes.[17]

FIGURE 12.8

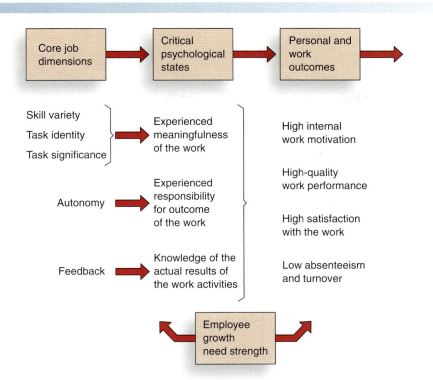

The outcomes include high internal drive to succeed, attention to quality, satisfaction with the work itself, and low rates of absenteeism and turnover. For these outcomes to occur, employees must feel that their jobs are meaningful, that they can accept personal responsibility for a job well done, and that they receive accurate feedback that tells them how well they do their jobs. The job characteristics model refers to these conditions as *psychological states* and indicates that these states are more likely to be present when jobs are designed so that employees utilize a greater variety of skills; are responsible for completion of a whole, identifiable piece of work; have an opportunity to perform tasks that have a positive effect on the lives of others; enjoy autonomy and discretion in decision making; and can learn where they stand by receiving accurate information about job performance. Providing all five of these core dimensions in a single job results in *job enrichment*, which allows a person to grow and develop.

A supportive leadership style is necessary for job enrichment to work. The leadership notion of *empowerment* (see Chapter 13) is consistent with the idea that enriched jobs created conditions most likely to motivate employees to achieve favorable results. Management Close-Up 12.3 on page 490 shows how Wal-Mart has used enriched jobs to empower employees. Managers who empower employees give them greater responsibility, freedom, and influence to set performance standards, reducing the need to monitor and control their behavior through close supervision.

LOC-In

8 Learning Objective Check-In

Candace gets good feedback at work. She also enjoys a high degree of autonomy in what she does. In addition to these factors, Candace's job is never boring; she knows that what she does is important, and there is something new to tackle every day.

1. *The* autonomy *Candace enjoys can reasonably lead to which critical psychological state, according to the job characteristics model?*
   a. *Experienced meaningfulness of the work*
   b. *Experienced responsibility for outcome of the work*
   c. *Knowledge of the actual results of the work activities*
   d. *High satisfaction with the work*

2. *The* feedback *Candace enjoys can reasonably lead to which critical psychological state, according to the job characteristics model?*
   a. *Experienced meaningfulness of the work*
   b. *Experienced responsibility for outcome of the work*
   c. *High satisfaction with the work*
   d. *Knowledge of the actual results of the work activities*

3. *The* skill variety and task significance *Candace enjoys can reasonably lead to which critical psychological state, according to the job characteristics model?*
   a. *Experienced quality work performance*
   b. *Experienced responsibility for outcome of the work*
   c. *Knowledge of the actual results of the work activities*
   d. *Experienced meaningfulness of the work*

I'm Proud of What I've Made Myself Into

THEME: ETHICS

In the midst of shoppers, three dozen employees get together in a suburban St. Louis Wal-Mart for the motivating pep talk that management holds every morning. The store manager gives them the good news that the men's department sales have increased almost 20 percent over the previous year, and the employees break into boisterous applause. Nancy Handley, the 27-year-old manager for the men's department, is thrilled. She is the one who makes sure that enough stock is available to customers, that sales items are marked for shoppers, and that the clothes are presented attractively. Handley works more hours at her Wal-Mart job than she would in a manufacturing position and earns less per hour. A widow with a seven-year-old child, Handley finds the recognition and responsibility that come with her job give her more satisfaction. "I'm proud of who I've made myself into, and the department I've created," she says.

Although Handley's day includes running around to keep clothes hung up and folded as well as being sure prices are marked clearly, she doesn't find her job mindless. It is up to her to decide things such as how many shirts, socks, and undershorts the store should stock. She also has some control over pricing and displays, and she secretly checks on the competition to see what their prices are.

"I used to be scared of having such responsibility," she says, and she doesn't always order the right thing. One year, for example, the St. Louis Rams mittens she ordered didn't sell well; she hadn't realized that most men don't wear mittens. "Nowadays, I make pretty good decisions," she adds.

Wal-Mart's treatment of workers and managers as partners—all employees are called "associates"—has meant that almost all attempts at unionization at the company have failed. Handley herself might be expected to embrace unionization considering that many members of her family belong to unions. Not so—for Wal-Mart, with its responsive and accessible managers, she feels unionization would be "useless" and sees no need to "pay someone to argue for me."

Sources: Adapted from L. Lee, "I Am Proud of What I Have Made Myself Into—What I Have Created," *The Wall Street Journal*, August 28, 1997, p. B1; S. Chandler, "Stumbling Sears Seeks to Launch Second Revolution," *Arizona Republic*, October 17, 1999, p. D1; T. Arango, "Weekly Sales on Plan at Wal-Mart, Below Plan at J. C. Penney," *The Street.Com*, January 29, 2001.

MANAGEMENT IS EVERYONE'S BUSINESS 12.3

Working as a Manager   Maintaining and increasing motivation is an important management skill that can determine your success as a manager. It can be difficult to motivate people and energize them to work toward some outcome. However, good managers understand that motivating others is part of the job and that it is a doable task. The following are motivation suggestions for you as a manager.

- Be familiar with the motivation theories covered in this chapter. The ability to apply motivation theories to the workplace in order to analyze and solve motivation difficulties can help any manager improve performance. Effective managers understand the factors that influence motivation and use them as levers to energize employees toward organizational goals.

- Consider the various types of needs of your workers and align rewards, as much as you can, with employee needs.

- Make sure that workers understand the overriding objective they are working toward. Understanding of a common goal can bring people together and transform the situation from a collection individuals to a cohesive and energized team of workers.

- Remove barriers to performance that can demotivate and demoralize workers.

- Are the right contingencies and rewards in place to encourage the desired behaviors?

- Structure the environment so that workers derive meaningfulness, responsibility, and feedback from their jobs.

Motivating workers is a major part of being an effective manager. This chapter provides you with an overview of the main approaches to motivation. These models can be important tools for you as a manager that can be keys to improving and maintaining performance. Management Is Everyone's Business 12.3 above provides suggestions to help you to effectively manage motivation.

CONCLUDING THOUGHTS

At the opening of the chapter we considered the working conditions at Electronic Arts and posed some critical thinking questions about motivation. Now that you have seen the basic approaches to motivation, revisit those introductory questions. First, it seems that EA employees enjoyed the creative and dynamic work they did and the entrepreneurial, risk-taking atmosphere the company maintained. Employees felt reasonably well compensated by their pay, their bonuses, and their stock options, as well as by the many perks or amenities of the workplace. Eventually, however, they grew less motivated by risk and sacrifice and wanted a chance to establish a work-life balance for themselves, along with pay that was tied more directly to their hours (the overtime pay) and less to the company's general health and profitability (the stock and bonuses).

The key to motivation involves much more than simply pay. In terms of the two-factor theory, intrinsic motivators might have been operating for many EA employees in the early days of their employment in Silicon Valley. To some extent the work was its own reward. Later, when their life circumstances and the nature of the industry changed, the balance for many employees seems to have tipped in favor of extrinsic rewards like a predicable compensation model and manageable working conditions. As noted in the chapter, other factors such as needs and equity perceptions can be crucial determinants of motivation. Effective motivation of people requires broader consideration and skill than simply applying one motivation model to work performance or failing to acknowledge that motivation can change over time.

Focusing on the Future: Using Management Theory in Daily Life

Motivation

Managers don't often talk about using expectancy theory or equity theory when motivating employees. But a recent article in the *Harvard Business Review*[1] shows that much of the "motivational advice" given by leaders stems directly from the theories presented in Chapter 12.

Intrinsic Motivation   Christopher Bangle, the Global Chief of Design at BMW in Germany, describes how he got his board of directors to approve work on a display he designed for the Pinakothek der Moderne, Munich's modern art museum. At first, Bangle himself vetoed the project—it would not bring in any revenue at a time when he and his team were working hard to design new cars. But when he saw the space, he suddenly could imagine working on a grand idea—in other words, he created a vision that others could accept as their own. This is the first step in inspiring intrinsic motivation. Next, he looked for a way to make his board feel personal satisfaction about the project. By describing the project as a "once-in-a-lifetime cultural opportunity with the newest, largest design museum in Europe," he appealed not only to the directors' appreciation of art, but also to their desire to do something lasting. In the end, the board not only approved the work, but eagerly supported it.

Positive Reinforcement and Maslow's Hierarchy of Needs   Liu Chuanzhi is the chairman of Leveno (formerly the Legend Group of Beijing). You may know Leveno as the company that purchased IBM's personal computer division.[2] He knows the power of incentives (positive reinforcement), but he also knows that different people need different types of incentives (Maslow's Hierarchy of Needs). For example, he gives his executive team members stock, because they want to have a sense of ownership in the company (meeting self-actualization needs). In addition, he gives his most senior executives opportunities to talk with the media, which provides them with the recognition they want for doing their work (meeting esteem needs).

Mid-level managers are given opportunities to stand out on the basis of performance and chances to improve their skills. This gives managers the recognition and promotion opportunities they crave (meeting esteem needs). In addition, mid-level managers are encouraged to "participate in strategic processes, designing their own work, and in making and executing their own decisions" (meeting esteem needs). All of these things increase intrinsic motivation, but it is only when managers achieve results that they are rewarded (positive reinforcement).

Finally, Chuanzhi suggests that line employees are most motivated by security (meeting safety needs). For this level of employee, bonuses are tied to responsibility and conscientiousness, but also to team performance. In addition, teams are given the option of allocating part of the team bonus back to individuals, as long as it is approved by corporate (meeting social needs). The important things are that the rewards are linked directly to performance (positive reinforcement) and individuals and teams are involved in the decision-making process (intrinsic motivation).

Goal Setting Theory   Hank McKinnell, the Chairman and CEO of Pfizer, says, "You motivate people by moving quickly toward a goal, especially if getting to the goal involves pain. Knowing that the organization is committed to quick, decisive action frees people to think creatively and work in concert."

When McKinnell took over Warner-Lambert in 2000, he set ambitious goals for the combined companies. In particular, he wanted both companies to operate as a unit only five months after the merger. Because the merger was a contentious one, Warner-Lambert employees did not feel comfortable with Pfizer. But McKinnell established one unifying goal for all employees, then gave people the freedom to do what they had to do to meet the goal. He managed the potential drawbacks of goal setting by telling people that anything they did needed to be consistent with the core values of the company. These include respect for people, integrity, and performance. The result, in McKinnell's words, was "a nearly seamless new Pfizer that was totally operational just a few hours after signing the contract."

Equity Theory   Herb Baum retired as the Chairman, President, and CEO of the Dial Corporation in 2005. His advice on "Care for the Little Guy" reflects an innate understanding of equity theory. Baum compared his salary to the salaries of his most poorly paid employees and took steps to balance out the inequity in the situation. At Quaker State, Baum gave up his company car after listening to line employees describe how they had to budget every dollar, even for something as basic as buying shoes for their children. At Dial, Baum gave $155,000 of his own bonus (in $1,000 increments) to 155 of the lowest-paid employees in his company. These steps may not have evened out pay inequity completely, but they provided employees with personal outcomes beyond pay—the feeling that a senior executive cared for them. Improved personal outcomes led to improved inputs. Baum says, "Right now, we're experiencing our lowest level of attrition in 11 years, and we're tracking toward another banner year because people are happy."

Sources:[1] C. Fiorina, "Start with the Truth," *Harvard Business Review* 81(1) (2003), p. 42. Retrieved May 20, 2006, from the Business Source Premier database; [2]*Shenzhen Daily*, "Liu Chuanzhi: The Man Who Acquired IBM PC." Retrieved May 21, 2006, from http://www.china.org.cn/english/NM-e/115844 htm.

summary of learning objectives

Motivation is a key variable in determining performance. Developing your knowledge and skills to understand and solve motivation problems can make you a highly effective and successful manager, individual, and team member. This chapter's discussion can help assure that you develop the needed knowledge and skills. The chapter material related to each of these learning objectives presented at the start of the chapter is summarized below.

1 Differentiate between extrinsic and intrinsic motivation.

- Extrinsic motivation comes from the rewards that are linked to job performance.
- Intrinsic motivation comes from personal satisfaction derived from the work itself.

2 Describe the need theories of motivation and their implications for managing.

- Maslow's Hierarchy of Needs—People experience needs in a particular order.
- Alderfer's ERG Theory—Three groups of core needs (relationship, existence, growth) that are not ordered.
- McClelland's Needs—Identifies needs for managers to consider (need for achievement; need for affiliation; need for power).
- Herzberg's Two-Factor Theory—Hygiene factors (extrinsic factors) and motivators (intrinsic factors).
- General implication of need theories is that needs energize action, and knowing the needs of your workers can help you to align rewards so that motivation and desired performance are maximized.

3 Generate steps that can be taken to improve performance by applying the various process models of motivation.

- Goal-Setting Theory—Maximize goal acceptability by taking a participative approach to setting goals; set challenging, but realistic, goals; goals should be specific, quantifiable, and measurable.
- Equity Theory—Make outputs proportionate to inputs; establish fairness in outcome/impact ratios so that comparisons with others results in the conclusion that treatment is equitable.
- Reinforcement Theory—Apply the law of effect and make sure that appropriate consequences closely follow work behaviors.
- Expectancy Theory—Remove barriers so that employee expects that s/he can perform the tasks if they put in the effort; establish clear links between task performance and rewards; offer rewards that are positively valued by workers.
- Job Characteristics Model—Design enriched jobs
  - Skill variety
  - Task identity
  - Task significance
  - Autonomy
  - Feedback

4 Apply reinforcement principles to manage performance.

- Positive reinforcement—follow desired behavior with rewards.
- Negative reinforcement—remove negative condition following desired behavior.
- Punishment—follow undesired behavior with unpleasant consequence.
- Extinction—withhold a reward that used to be linked with the behavior.

5 Identify causes of low performance and how they would be improved using the expectancy model.

- Low expectancy—provide needed training and remove situational constraints.
- Low instrumentability—define and measure performance using clear and unbiased measures. Link rewards to performance.
- Poor second level valence—determine what workers want and offer these characteristics as rewards.

6 Understand the basic approaches to motivation.

- Content theories of motivation
- Process theories of motivation

7 Identify features of job design that can affect worker motivation.

- Job enlargement
- Job rotation
- Job enrichment

8 Apply the job characteristics model to link job design to motivation.

- Design jobs so that psychological states (meaningfulness, responsibility, knowledge of results) lead to maximized motivation.
- Key design characteristics include skill variety, task identity, task significance, autonomy, and feedback.

discussion questions

1. Use the expectancy model framework to analyze factors which might influence motivation. Specifically, what might influence expectancy levels? Likewise, what might influence instrumentality linkages and valences?

2. Given your answers to question 1, what could be done to improve the levels of expectancy, instrumentality, and valence?

3. Why might someone be motivated to perform poorly or to be a disruptive or negative influence in the workplace? Use the motivation models to analyze the issue. What could be done to improve such a situation?

4. Consider a time when you were highly motivated to do your best at something (such as a particular task, a job, a course). Based on the theories discussed in this chapter, analyze what made you feel that way. Would the same motivation affect you in a different situation?

5. Some people argue that employees are either highly motivated or they are not, and there is little the firm can do to change that predisposition. Do you agree? Why or why not?

6. If you were forced to choose, which of the motivational theories discussed in this chapter do you think is most likely to account for employee motivation? Explain your rationale.

7. On average, U.S. workers spend about 20 percent more time at work and devote less time to leisure in comparison with other industrialized countries such as Japan, Great Britain, France, and Germany. This gap seems to be increasing.[18] How would you explain this phenomenon? Support your answer in light of the material discussed in this chapter.

Recognize Your Employees

Money can be an important general motivator, but managers often have limited control over the amount of pay received by workers. Certainly, there are things that a manager can and should do to maximize motivation. For example challenging and measurable goals should be set and good working conditions should be provided. These are effective and highly recommended motivation approaches. However, managers can supplement these with an approach that closely ties rewards to desired performance. Specifically, a recognition program can energize a workplace and motivate workers.

If you doubt the bottom-line impact of *recognition* consider the results of a recent survey. Firms whose employees indicated that they did the best at recognizing performance were also the most profitable. The firms who were best at employee recognition were found to have on average a 6.1 percent return on assets while firms with the poorest employee recognition had an average return on investment of 1.7 percent. Recognition is an important motivational tool, and the survey results indicate that it can have an important bottom-line financial impact.

Discussion Questions

1. Which motivation theory most closely fits the use of employee recognition as a motivational tool?

2. Why do you think employee recognition has an impact on performance and the bottom line? That is, why does recognition work?

3. Many organizations have recognition programs, such as employee of the month plaques. However, these awards are often rotated among workers. Similarly, some organizations recognize workers on important dates, such as anniversaries or birthdays. Do you think these types of recognition programs would be effective at motivating improved performance? Why or why not?

4. To be effective, what characteristics should a recognition program have? Describe the key characteristics and provide rationale for their need.

Sources: S. L. Rynes, B. Gerhart, and K. A. Minette, "The Importance of Pay in Employee Motivation: Discrepancies between What People Say and What They Do," *Human Resource Management* 43 (2004), pp. 381–394; L. Grimaldi, "Study Proves Recognition Pays Offs," *Meetings & Conventions* 40 (2005), p. 32.

The Give and Take of Motivation: Give Them What They Need and Take Away the Obstacles

Motivation often involves more than simply pushing someone harder. Motivation can be critically influenced by (1) ability and (2) the presence of situational constraints.

Ability

If a worker doesn't believe that he or she has the ability to adequately perform a task, motivation will surely suffer. An industry consultant points out that the key to workers having the ability they need is training. The emphasis must be on more than formal training sessions. People need the kinds of hands-on experience that gives them the confidence they need to succeed. From employee orientation to learning details about products and services offered by the organization, knowledge can fan the flames of motivation since employees know they have the information they need to perform the job.

Employees should all be familiar with the products or services offered and with the work processes. While this statement may seem obvious, consider the last time you looked for a product or service, only to find that the salesperson really couldn't help. Perhaps there was only one person who had expertise in the area you were looking at (and, of course, that person wasn't available at the time)—or maybe you even found that you knew more than the salesperson. Similarly, not all employees are equally familiar with work processes. For example, some workers may not completely understand or be comfortable with a computerized order process or a phone system.

What happens when there is lack of knowledge of products or services or of work processes? The worker can't have, in expectancy model terms, a high level of expectancy. Even if he or she tries hard, if the individual does not have the knowledge needed, it is impossible to perform well. Poor knowledge can, however, motivate workers to avoid what they don't know. They will try to avoid areas of the operation which make them uncomfortable. These workers are behaving out of fear that their deficiencies will be uncovered. Unfortunately, this doesn't lead to maximum performance. Both workers and the organization are worse off as a result.

Constraints

Motivation to perform can also be influenced by the presence of situational constraints. For example, the red tape of bureaucracy and unnecessary time and steps to get the job done often act as obstacles to job performance. When enough obstacles pile up, workers see that performance is hopelessly constrained by the system. Motivation to improve performance can be quickly choked out by red tape and other obstacles. This problem won't be solved by rousing motivational speeches or by offering training and incentives. Solving this type of motivational problem requires removing the obstacles to performance that are in the work system.

Discussion Questions

1. One way to improve worker knowledge and ability to perform is to institute a "shadow" program. In a shadow program, a less experienced or poorer performing worker is assigned to an effective worker. The shadow program might last a day or a week, depending on the complexity of the job and how quickly the necessary information can be absorbed. The inexperienced or poorer performing worker follows the experienced worker, observing and working alongside him/her. The shadow program gives workers familiarity, experience, and tips on how to effectively perform the job.

    a. Assess a shadow program. Do you think it is a good way to eliminate lack of ability as an obstacle to job performance? Why or why not?

    b. What other techniques or approaches might work to improve worker knowledge of products/services and work processes? Which do you think would be most cost effective?

2. Pick a job with which you are familiar. Are there unnecessary bureaucratic obstacles that can hinder performance? Describe.

3. What could be done to eliminate or reduce bureaucratic obstacles?

4. Bureaucratic obstacles are just one example of obstacles that weaken motivation. Generate examples of other obstacles. Provide your recommendations for how each of them could be eliminated or reduced.

5. While adequate ability and lack of obstacles are key to maximizing motivation, they certainly aren't the only important factors. What other factors do you think are key to maximizing motivation?

Sources: Adapted from H. Darlington, "People—Your Most Important Asset," *Supply House Times* 45 (2002), pp. 113–114; E. Spragins, "Unmasking Your Motivations," *Fortune Small Business* 12 (2002), pp. 86–87.

individual/
collaborative
learning
case 12.1

Motivating Low-Wage Workers

Mini Maid Inc., a chain of more than 100 franchises in 24 states offering residential maid service, is owned by Leone Ackerly. In the 24 years since she started the firm, Ackerly has developed a philosophy of mutual respect that motivates a low-wage workforce and improves customer service and productivity.

Most Mini Maid employees are women who grew up on welfare, according to Ackerly. They typically are in their twenties and have little education or skills; many have been abused. Ackerly learned that many of her workers felt they were not respected, but when given respect, they changed for the better. Ackerly doesn't care that previous employers looked down on her workers. Even though most of them start working at Mini Maid just for the paychecks, "We ask them to look at us as their partners in a team effort. We tell them, 'this is what we give you; this is what you give us.' Right off the bat, the new employee feels that she is an important part of our company. What happens at this point is that they begin to listen."

Ackerly checks applicants' backgrounds before hiring them—a police record or history of drug use means they won't be offered a job. She presses charges against any maid caught stealing. She expects her employees to be punctual, clean and neat, and polite, and she gives them discipline, standards, and structure.

She has found that fair and honest dealings with employees are returned in kind. If they respect their manager, they do a better job representing the company. Ackerly provides workers with an attendance bonus each pay period for coming to work every day, on time, and in uniform. The extra motivation and reward encourage good work habits. The results go beyond the job. Over the years, Ackerly's workers have learned to apply the concept of mutual respect to their family lives.

Besides respect, low-wage workers need to feel recognized, says consultant Rosalind Jeffries. The self-esteem of a low-wage worker typically is very low, and the pat on the back and expression of thanks go a long way as motivators. Fine Host Corp., a food service in Greenwich, Connecticut, hires contract workers to bus tables and cook and serve food, and has found that recognition is key to keeping them motivated. Fine Host president and CEO Richard Kerley understands that the employees are the ones who can drive customers away, and he knows that recognition is relatively easy to give. "Though there may be economic restraints on what we pay them, there are no restraints on the recognition we give them." His company gives employee awards and puts their names on company buildings in recognition of good work. Also, the employees receive framed certificates when they complete training courses. Kerley believes companies like his must show people they are appreciated.

Irving Edwards is CEO of All Metro Health Care in Lynbrook, New York, a company that employs home health aides. The company sponsors an award for caregiver of the year and occasionally sponsors essay contests for its workers, complete with prizes. Gifts such as watches and blenders are given to employees when they score high in a quarterly training game. Health aides who are asked to work on holidays know the company will serve them food at the office, too.

Critical Thinking Questions

1. How would you describe the motivational techniques used by these firms in light of the theories discussed in this chapter? Explain.

2. One critic argues that a growing trend is for firms to try to motivate workers the "cheap way"—a pat on the back or an inexpensive certificate—but that these actions make employees more cynical rather than more highly motivated? Do you agree with this assessment? Why or why not?

3. Do you believe that workers can be motivated for the long haul with nonfinancial rewards that appeal to their self-esteem? Why or why not?

Collaborative Learning Exercise

Students form groups of four or five and assume the role of manager for Mini Maid. The task is to outline a short speech to be given to new employees that explains "what we give you, and what you give us." Special attention should be paid to ways to sustain motivation. Post or display completed outlines and compare.

Sources: Adapted from R. Maynard, "How to Motivate Low Wage Workers," *Nation's Business*, May 1997, pp. 35–40; "The Pay Is in the Bank," *BusinessWeek*, January 29, 2001, p. 10.

Go for the Goal!

Goal setting has proven to be an effective approach for motivating and improving performance. Mygoals.com is a Web site devoted to helping people achieve their goals. Explore the free portion of this Web site (much of the site is accessible without registering) and address the following questions.

1. How could you use the information on this site to help you as a college student? As a businessperson? In your personal life?

2. Select a goal on the Web site and choose one of the "pre-made" goal plans. What types of obstacles were identified for your consideration? Why are obstacles an important topic in the goal-setting arena?

3. Select one of the "featured types" on the Web site (such as "success in business"). Draft responses to each of the suggested steps and share these with the rest of the class.

manager's

checkup 12.1

Expectancy Theory and Your Motivation to Manage

How effective are you, or do you think you will be, as a manager of other people? Some managers embrace the role of managing others and some managers never seem to get comfortable with or perform well with the "people" aspect of their management position. Expectancy theory provides a framework for understanding your performance as a manager and can help you to identify actions you might take to improve your management performance.

Instructions: For each statement, check the response that best represents your judgment.

	Mostly Agree	Mostly Disagree
1. I believe that I can be an effective manager.	____	____
2. I can do a good job of managing people.	____	____
3. It will be hard for me to deal with worker problems.	____	____
4. I am comfortable dealing with nonpeople issues, such as accounting or supply issues.	____	____
5. It is not clear to me how the effectiveness of managing others can be measured.	____	____
6. How good you are as a manager depends on who you have as workers.	____	____
7. Being a good manager is key to my getting ahead in my career.	____	____
8. Getting things done through others is how you build a great career.	____	____
9. Developing others is fundamental to personal and organizational success.	____	____
10. Developing a team of committed workers is a key to success.	____	____

Scoring. The first six items are focused on your *expectancy level. For items 1, 2, and 6:* give yourself 1 point for each "mostly agree" response and 0 points for "mostly disagree" responses. *For items 3, 4, and 5:* give yourself 0 points for "mostly agree" responses and 1 point for each "mostly disagree" responses.

You can calculate your expectancy score by simply totaling the points you scored on the first six items. The higher your score (up to a maximum of 6), the higher your expectancy level. The lower your expectancy score, the more you see barriers to being effective at people management.

Think about steps you might take if you have a lower expectancy score. Be prepared to discuss them in class.

Items 7 through 10 are focused on your *instrumentality perceptions*. Give yourself 1 point for each "mostly agree" response. Your instrumentality score is the total number of points you obtained. The higher your score (up to a maximum of 4), the stronger the link you see between effectively managing people and achieving successful outcomes.

Think about the steps you might take if you have a lower instrumentality score. Be prepared to discuss these suggestions in class.

The Container Store

video summary

Summary

What does it take to be one of the best at what you do? Just ask the employees and management members working at The Container Store. Time and time again this business has been voted as one of the best companies to work for in America by *Fortune* magazine. This operation is known within the retail industry today as being a world-class organization. Its product lines include over 10,000 items designed to simplify and streamline the lives of its customers.

The company's culture is grounded on the guiding principle of hiring great people. It patiently waits for just the "right" applicant before filling any of its vacant positions. The Container Store staunchly holds a strong belief in the success of its operating philosophies. This organization proudly claims to possess the happiest and most empowered employees in the retail industry today. It is renowned for the exemplary customer service that is provided by each employee, no matter whether they are working in full or part-time positions.

The various theories of management, which have evolved over the years, have decidedly impacted the organization's employees and how they are motivated to optimum performance levels. The managers at this company follow the philosophy that a good manager will not just utilize a single management theory, but will instead tailor management efforts around several theories at once in order to achieve maximum effectiveness. They believe the best employee motivation strategy is derived through the job itself and feel that by addressing the needs of their people and the job, the best possible performance achievements will result.

Discussion Questions

1. Identify and discuss Abraham Maslow's Need Hierarchy theory. How does The Container Store attempt to satisfy the physiological needs of its employees?

2. Discuss the concept of job enrichment. How does The Container Store utilize this concept? Explain how this has proven advantageous to this organization.

3. The employees of The Container Store state that they love their jobs. Each worker is proud of his or her job performance and contributions to the organization. They exhibit strong organizational commitment in every action they undertake. Describe organizational commitment given the context of The Container Store. Discuss how job satisfaction is related to employees' commitment to the organization and its goals.

4. Do the employees at The Container Store seem to be motivated intrinsically or extrinsically? Explain.

5. Which of the theories in the process view of motivation seem to be applicable at The Container Store?

chapter 13

Leadership

Learning Objectives

1. Distinguish between management and leadership.

2. Recognize how leaders use different power bases to exercise influence.

3. Identify effective leader characteristics based on person-based theories and recognize the limitations of these approaches.

4. Recognize how different contexts call for different leadership qualities, using situational theories of leadership.

5. Identify ways to engender leadership through organizational characteristics or employees by applying dispersed theories of leadership.

6. Understand, through the exchange theories, how to implement leadership through relationships with others.

7. Describe and apply the concept of authentic leadership.

Leadership at Nissan: Key to Transformation

Nissan Motors was near bankruptcy in the 1990s. The company's turnaround has been principally credited to the skillful leadership of Carlos Ghosn. Ghosn was educated as an engineer in France. He worked for Renault, quickly rising to an executive level position. Renault acquired Nissan in the 1990s, but the operations and brands of the two organizations have been kept separate. Ghosn was sent to Japan and charged with turning around Nissan and remaking it into a profitable automaker. How did Ghosn succeed? First, he broke down barriers and brought people together, despite their differences in functional training and in business styles. He brought them together to focus on what would make the company successful. In other words, he had enough courage and focus on achieving success that he jumped in and broke cultural barriers. He interacted with employees and listened to their ideas about how performance could be improved. Ghosn also challenged traditional Japanese business relationships that hindered performance and profitability. Under Ghosn's direction, some plants were closed while others were opened, costs were cut, and automobiles were redesigned.

Carlos Ghosn did not make these changes unilaterally. He formed cross-functional teams of workers and asked them to review the company's performance. The teams identified a number of problems including lack of a profit orientation, not enough focus on customers, and lack of a sense of urgency, among other issues. The diagnoses provided by the teams led to a three-year improvement plan, the "Nissan Revival Plan," that included goals of a return to profitability by 2000 and an operating profit of 4.5 percent of sales by 2002. The goals were achieved within two years and a new three-year plan was put in place in 2002. One of the company's goals was to achieve an 8 percent operating profit margin. In 2005, Ghosn was able to state that the company had achieved all of the plan's goals, including maintaining an operating profit of 10 percent, beating its own goal in every year of the plan. Nissan is now embarked on achieving the objectives of another three-year plan that will guide the company through 2007. The plan includes objectives for profit, sales volume, and return on investment. If the past can predict future performance, Nissan will likely achieve, if not surpass, all of its goals.

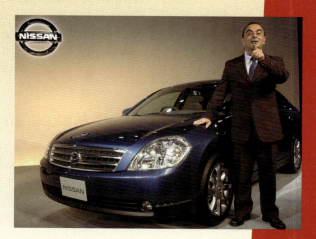

What accounts for Carlos Ghosn's success as the leader of Nissan? Ghosn is clear about what he believes accounts for his success in leading Nissan. While he has an engineering background, by his own admission he is not a top-rate engineer and he didn't graduate from the best engineering school. Ghosn attributes his success as a leader of Nissan to his talent for managing people. He considers his effectiveness as a leader to be much more a function of his capability to gather people together and get things done than of his technical skills.

It took confidence, tenacity, and vision to achieve a successful turnaround. Ghosn saved the company from bankruptcy by taking on the organization's culture as well as Japanese traditions. He involved people, listened to what they had to say, and helped Nissan workers to create a new vision for the company.

Source: G. S. Vasilash, C. A. Sawyer, and K. M. Kelly, (2005). "Nissan: The Extraordinary Happens Every Day," *Automotive Design & Production* 117, p. 48; D. Magee, *Turnaround: How Carlos Ghosn Rescued Nissan* (New York: Harper Business/Harper Collins, 2003).

CRITICAL THINKING QUESTIONS

1. *What makes someone a good, or even great, leader?*

2. *How much of a difference does leadership make? Can one person really make that much of a difference?*

3. *Is there one leadership type that works best?*

4. *Ethics in organizations has recently become a focal topic. What can leaders do to avoid ethical problems in their organizations?*

We will have another look at these questions in our Concluding Thoughts at the end of the chapter after you have read the following discussion of leadership.

Leaders are not just top executives or powerful CEOs. Anyone can be a leader, even if their sphere of influence is limited to their own immediate area or work team. There is increasing realization that leadership is important at all levels of an organization. Organizations are looking for leadership from all employees and are recognizing leadership to be critical to the performance and very survival of the organization. This chapter examines what makes a person an effective leader and how managers can make a difference and bring about improved performance and effective change in organizations. There are a variety of approaches to leadership. Leaders can employ different styles and still be successful. Further, a leadership approach that is successful in one situation may not succeed in other situations. In this chapter we will identify the major theories of leadership and explore the models of effective leadership that each of these theories lead to. The intent is to describe the skills needed to lead people to accomplish organizational objectives and help them use their talents effectively.

What Makes an Effective Leader?

Almost everyone agrees that strong leadership is necessary to ensure organizational success. At the same time, there is no simple, universally agreed upon definition of *effective leadership*. Some think that such personal characteristics as charisma, perseverance, and strong communication skills cause people to follow a leader. Thomas Watson of IBM, Alfred Sloan of General Motors, and former presidents Ronald Reagan and John F. Kennedy are seen by many as the embodiment of these traits. Others think of effective leadership as "being at the right place at the right time," where there is a fit between the leader's message and the situation. In the business community, Lee Iaccoca's authoritarian, brassy, and opinionated style contributed to his image as a savior of bankrupt Chrysler Corporation in the early 1980s. After Chrysler became the U.S. auto company that earned the most profit per vehicle, these same attributes were seen by many as egotistical, capricious, and unresponsive to the needs of employees and consumers. Ironically, in 2001 many Chrysler employees, union members, and investors wished Iaccoca would come back from retirement—Chrysler had lost a whopping $1.7 billion during a six-month period and expected to lay off more than 26,000 employees from 2001 through 2003, almost a quarter of its workforce.[1]

One essential aspect of effective leadership is the ability to influence other people. A leader should have vision—ideas or objectives that clarify to others where they should be headed. The vision may be ill conceived, inaccurate, or selfish, or it may identify opportunities that others have failed to see. Although it can take years to assess whether the vision is "good" or "bad," without vision there is little hope of energizing people to act. The leader must "sell" the vision by articulating it in a compelling and persuasive manner that inspires people to overcome obstacles and keep moving toward the ideal future. The leader encourages followers to establish appropriate implementation activities to support the accomplishment of the vision and to induce them to use their personal initiative and talents in achieving the vision. Stephen M. Case, former AOL Time Warner's CEO, noted, "In the end, a vision without the ability to execute is probably a hallucination."[2]

Management versus Leadership

Not all leaders are managers; not all managers are leaders. According to one observer, "Management is about coping with complexity. Good management brings about order and consistency by drawing up formal plans, designing rigid organizational structures, and monitoring results against the plans.[3] In other words, the role of management is in the area of implementation and control. In contrast, leadership involves developing a vision and inspiring people to achieve that vision.[4] Leadership often requires altering the status quo and getting people to commit to the strategy. Management is most likely to be oriented toward maintaining the status quo along with monitoring and measuring to make sure that the right things are getting done in the trenches.

The distinction between leadership and management is more than semantics. It is important to understand the distinction so that the appropriate role can be applied in each situation. While there is a distinction between leadership and management, the two roles are not mutually exclusive. As graphically depicted in Figure 13.1 below, leadership and management can be overlapping roles. For

Jim McNerney, new CEO of Boeing, will need to demonstrate persuasive leadership skills in order to change the culture at the aircraft manufacturer, which has suffered from bitter internal rivalries and embarrassing ethical scandals. "If we can get the values lined up with performance," McNerney says, "then this is an absolutely unbeatable company." He has already won praise within the firm for leading by example, with a management style that respects and values co-workers and underlings.

Assessing Your Leader-Member Exchange

Do You Have What It Takes to be a Leader?

FIGURE 13.1

Management and Leadership Separate and Combined Roles

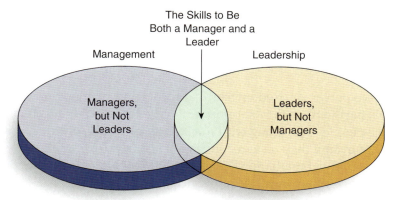

table 13.1	
Typical Characteristics of Effective Management and Leadership	
MANAGEMENT CHARACTERISTICS	**LEADERSHIP CHARACTERISTICS**
Control	Inspiration
Implementation	Strategy
Narrow	Breadth
Consistency	Change
Measurement	Establish Direction
Get the Job Done	Changing What the Job Is

many people, however, the separate personal characteristics and skills needed for each role mean that they can be effective at either managing or leading, but not both. Table 13.1 above summarizes some of the typical contrasts between leadership and management and spells out the skills and characteristics needed for each. Managers who balance both sets of characteristics can enact either role in an organization. Successful business careers and wider choices and opportunities are often the result of having a combination of these characteristics. Sometimes, management skills aren't important while leadership is, and vice versa. Still the capacity to be both a manager and a leader can increase your value and effectiveness in an organization. Taking steps to develop skills in each of these areas can lead to a long-term payoff in your career. Manager's Notebook 13.1 on page 505 presents the practical skills needed to be an effective leader, according to a best-selling author and consultant.

While management can be differentiated from leadership, most management positions provide opportunities to engage in leadership. Table 13.2 on page 505 presents leadership practices that managers can typically engage in.

POWER Managers and leaders can influence other people through their use of power. For a manager, one source of power comes from the position in the organization. Many leaders, however, have the power to influence others more as a function of who they are than because of their positions. For example, people might follow the orders of a manager because he/she has the authority to reward and punish workers. On the other hand, people might follow a leader because they find him/her to be inspirational and charismatic. In a well-known work on power, J. French and B. Raven proposed five ways in which people may be induced to follow a leader (or manager):[5]

1. **Coercive power** is based on fear that the leader/manager may cause people harm unless they support him or her. Intimidation and anxiety may induce people to go along with the actions, attitudes, or directives of a superior even if they disagree. Even if a leader does not use overt threats, the possibility of retaliation such as a poor recommendation to a prospective employer may induce compliance.

Online LearningCenter
www.mhhe.com/gomez3e

Sources of Power

coercive power

Power based on the fear that the leader may cause people harm unless they support him or her.

LEADERSHIP SKILLS: LET'S GET PRACTICAL

Jeffrey Gitomer, a sales and customer service expert, is a best-selling author of books such as *The Sales Bible* and *Customer Satisfaction Is Worthless . . . Customer Loyalty Is Priceless*. Gitomer holds over 100 seminars a year and consults with companies such as BMW, Cingular Wireless, IBM, Hyatt Hotels, among hundreds of others. He is out there interacting with front-line people and leaders and sees all manner of leadership styles and work problems. He gets rankled by prescriptions for leaders that are broad, ambiguous, and difficult to implement. His work puts him in a position to see the importance of practical and doable suggestions. Here is a sample of his practical skill suggestions for anyone wanting to be an effective leader.

- Let your people share their goals with you and modify them together. When people start with their own goals, they are more committed to them and believe they can achieve them.
- Create a workplace environment that is fun and challenging, not oppressive and stressful.
- Make sure pay is at a fair level, benefits are good, and that there is security.
- Praise your people often. Praise them for ideas, efforts, and accomplishments.
- Be a role model. If you want your people to be ethical and dedicated, they need to see those characteristics in your actions and words.
- Be someone whom your people like and respect. Respect without liking will eventually get you high turnover. People want to work for leaders they like and respect.

Source: www.gitomer.com; J. Gitomer, "Define Leadership: Now Redefine It in Terms of You, *Business Record (Des Moines)*, April 18, 2005, pp. 23, 31.

table 13.2

Practices Associated with Leadership by Managers

Planning and organizing	Determining long-term objectives and strategies; allocating resources according to priorities; determining how to use personnel and resources efficiently to accomplish a task or project; determining how to improve coordination, productivity, and effectiveness
Problem solving	Identifying work-related problems; analyzing problems in a systematic but timely manner to determine causes and find solutions; acting decisively to implement solutions and resolve crises
Clarifying	Assigning work; providing direction in how to do the work; communicating a clear understanding of job responsibilities, task objectives, priorities, deadlines, and performance expectations
Informing	Disseminating relevant information about decisions, plans, and activities to people who need the information to do their work
Monitoring	Gathering information about work activities and external conditions affecting the work; checking on the progress and quality of the work; evaluating the performance of individuals and the effectiveness of the organizational unit
Motivating	Using influence techniques that appeal to logic or emotion to generate enthusiasm for the work, commitment to task objectives, and compliance with requests for cooperation, resources, or assistance; setting an example of proper behavior
Consulting	Checking with people before making changes that affect them; encouraging participation in decision making; allowing others to influence decisions
Recognizing	Providing praise and recognition for effective performance, significant achievements, and special contributions
Supporting	Acting friendly and considerate; being patient and helpful; showing sympathy and support when someone is upset or anxious
Managing conflict and team building	Facilitating the constructive resolution of conflict; encouraging cooperation, teamwork, and identification with the organizational unit
Networking	Socializing informally; developing contacts with people outside of the immediate work unit who are a source of information and support; maintaining contacts through periodic visits, telephone calls, correspondence, and attendance at meetings and social events
Delegating	Allowing subordinates to have substantial responsibility and discretion in carrying out work activities; giving them authority to make important decisions
Developing and mentoring	Providing coaching and career counseling; doing things to facilitate a subordinate's skill acquisition and career advancement
Rewarding	Providing tangible rewards such as a pay increase or promotion for effective performance and demonstrated competence by subordinates

Source: From Garry Yukl and David Van Fleet, "Theory and Research on Leadership in Organizations," *Handbook of Industrial and Organizational Psychology*, 1992, Vol. 3, pp. 149–197, L. M. Hough and M. D. Dunnette (eds.). Reprinted with permission of the authors.

2. **Reward power** means that the leader/manager can provide something that other people value so that they trade their support for the rewards. Rewards may be financial (such as promotion with higher pay) or psychological (such as greater status from being perceived as close to the leader).

3. **Legitimate power** comes from the legal or formal authority to make decisions subject to certain constraints. For instance, in most universities the chair of an academic department has the legitimate power to write an annual evaluation of each faculty member to be used to allocate merit pay, assign teaching schedules, and establish differential teaching loads. Few department chairs have the legitimate power to hire or terminate full-time faculty without approval from others.

4. **Expert power** derives from the leader's/manager's unique knowledge or skills, which other people recognize as worthy of respect.

5. **Referent power** is based on the satisfaction people receive from identifying themselves with the leader/manager. They are willing to grant power to the leader because they see him or her as a role model.

These power bases are not independent. Employees may comply with the wishes of a person they admire (referent power) who is a division head (legitimate power) with formal authority to promote (reward power) or terminate employees (coercive power) and who has expertise about a particular product line (expert power). Leaders typically prefer to emphasize some of these sources of power more than others. For instance, some supervisors motivate subordinates by serving as an example (referent power) even if they have the authority to induce compliance through punishment (coercive power) or financial incentives (reward power).

LOC-In

② Learning Objective Check-In

1. *Andy tries to cultivate a close professional relationship with his staff in the engineering department. A certain clique has even been established as a result of this. Either workers are close to Andy, or they are not. Those who are close often feel a sense of higher status in the office because they are "in" with the boss. Andy is exercising _____.*
   a. *expert power*
   b. *reward power*
   c. *legitimate power*
   d. *coercive power*

Leadership Theories

Over the years there have been many attempts to understand what makes a leader effective. Can leadership skills be learned or are people just "born" with them? These and other questions have led to the development of a variety of leadership theories. There is probably not one theory that is the best and most accurate. Still, much can be learned about being an effective leader from an understanding of all of the theories. These leadership theories can be roughly divided into the categories of (1) person, (2) situation, (3) dispersed, and (4) exchange. Theories in the person category note the characteristics and behaviors of effective leaders. Situational theories emphasize that what makes for effective leadership depends on the situation. Leadership theories in the dispersed category suggest that leadership comes from sources other than an individual leader. Finally, the exchange theories view leadership from the perspective of relationships with others. Examples of leadership theories in each of these categories appear next.

Person-Based Theories

TRAIT THEORY What sets Napoleon Bonaparte, Franklin Delano Roosevelt, Mohandas Gandhi, Cesar Chavez, and Nelson Mandela apart from the crowd? When we think about leaders, certain traits or personal characteristics may come to mind, such as self-confidence, determination, and communication skills. Researchers have tried to create a personality profile or set of characteristics that distinguishes leaders from nonleaders. It has become clear, however, that personality traits do not tell the whole story of what makes for an effective leader. Certainly, factors such as the needs of followers, cultural norms, prior group history, and other situational variables come into play. Nevertheless, cumulative research suggests that certain traits increase the likelihood of being an effective leader, although they don't guarantee it. These include ambition; energy; the motivation or desire to lead; intelligence; integrity, or high correspondence between actions and words; a "can-do attitude," or self-confidence; the ability to grasp and interpret large amounts of information; and the flexibility to adapt to the needs and goals of others.[6]

The trait approach never resulted in a list of personality characteristics present in all effective leaders. This led to a loss of popularity of the trait approach to leadership in the 1960s. There has recently, however, been more attention directed at the importance of the personal characteristics of leaders. A major survey of managers in the 1980s revealed that 87 percent identified honesty as a trait associated with effective leadership.[7] Honesty was a trait leaders admired more than competence, being inspirational, and intelligence. The importance of honesty was underscored by the ethical scandals involving the top leadership of organizations such as Enron and WorldCom. Management Close-Up 13.1 on page 508 presents a summary of some corporate ethical scandals that changed the importance that many people place on integrity in leadership.

The promise of the trait approach is to provide a profile of the effective leader. This profile can then serve as a map to people who aspire to be leaders and guide their efforts to be effective in the leadership role. While such a profile would be instructive, traits are typically considered to be fairly fixed and difficult to change. Thus, leadership theorists began turning their attention to leader behaviors, rather than traits. We next consider the behavior-based approach to leadership.

BEHAVIORAL THEORIES   Behaviors are observable and tend to be under our direct control. In contrast, personality traits are internal and inferred characteristics that are presumed to be difficult to alter since they are a product of history and genetics. Taking a behavioral approach to leadership thus offers the advantages of focusing on characteristics that are observable and can be changed by people. Behavioral theories attempt to identify what good leaders *do*. Broadly speaking, these theories either map out the behavioral dimensions of leadership or describe leadership styles.

Behavioral Dimensions   Two classic studies were conducted at Ohio State University and the University of Michigan in the 1940s and 1950s. The studies revealed two dimensions that summarize how subordinates describe most leadership behaviors.[8] The first dimension is the concern that the leader has for the feelings, needs, personal interest, problems, and well-being of followers. This dimension was called **consideration** at Ohio State and *employee-oriented behaviors* at the University of Michigan. The second dimension, which refers to activities designed to accomplish group goals, including organizing tasks, assigning responsibilities, and establishing performance standards, was labeled **initiating structure** at Ohio State and *production-oriented behaviors* at the University of Michigan. The consideration and initiating structure dimensions are often portrayed using a simple 2 × 2 matrix, as presented in Figure 13.2 on page 509.

Using these two dimensions, researchers R. R. Blake and J. S. Mouton developed a tool to classify managers based on leadership behaviors in a model called the **managerial grid**.[9] As illustrated in Figure 13.3 on page 509, the vertical

consideration

The behavioral dimensions of leadership involving the concern that the leader has for the feelings, needs, personal interest, problems, and well-being of followers; also called employee-oriented behaviors.

initiating structure

The behavioral dimension of leadership that refers to activities designed to accomplish group goals, including organizing tasks, assigning responsibilities, and establishing performance standards; also called production-oriented behaviors.

managerial grid

A system of classifying managers based on leadership behaviors.

Ethical Poverty at the Top: High Profile Cases

THEME: ETHICS

Executives being led away in handcuffs. CEOs taking the fifth amendment when being questioned by U.S. senators. These are not images that promote faith in business leaders. Unfortunately, incidents involving the lack of integrity, unethical behaviors, and corruption of business leaders have become all too common. Here are summaries of some recent ethical scandals.

- Enron, once a giant in the energy industry, filed for bankruptcy at the end of 2001. That year, Kenneth Lay, then CEO of Enron, received $152.7 million in payments and stock. The company collapsed after a $1 billion loss. Enron's management and accounting leaders had inflated profit numbers by $600 million and hidden debts and exaggerated revenues in order to continue to attract investors. This allowed Lay and other top executives to continue to receive and sell the lucrative Enron stock. Lay's compensation in the year that the company collapsed was 11,000 times the amount of severance paid to the approximately 4,000 workers who were laid off as a result of the collapse. Lay invoked the fifth amendment and declined to answer questions in a congressional hearing regarding improprieties at Enron. He and other former Enron executives are facing a variety of fraud charges. The court cases are still continuing. Also, the Arthur Andersen accounting firm was convicted in a Texas court in June 2002 for obstruction of justice in the Enron case. Enron was a client of Arthur Andersen and paid approximately $27 million per year in consulting fees and a similar amount in auditing fees. Arthur Andersen's leaders claimed that Enron withheld vital information, but was still found guilty of obstruction for shredding Enron documents.

- Bernard Ebbers was the CEO of WorldCom, a telecommunications firm. Ebbers borrowed $408 million from the company, but the company improperly accounted for $9 billion and was forced into bankruptcy. Ebbers had pledged company stock as collateral, but the shares became worthless after the collapse of the company. Investors and former workers with little money in their retirement funds were left to compare their financial outcomes with that of Ebbers.

- John J. Rigas was the CEO of Adelphia Communications until his indictment for stealing billions from the organization. Rigas is suspected of conspiring with four other executives to take money from the company.

Sources: J. Biskupic, "Why It's Tough to Indict CEOs," *USA Today*, July 24, 2002, pp. A1, A2; B. Foss, "Corporate Image: Greed, Deceit, Handcuffs," *The Arizona Republic*, December 30, 2002, p. D4.

In May 2002, members of Enron's board of directors were questioned by the U.S. Senate. Their CEO at the time, Kenneth Lay, chose to invoke the fifth amendment.

FIGURE 13.2

	Low	High
High	Leader focuses efforts on employee well-being, such as group cohesiveness, employee satisfaction, and development.	Leader's behavioral efforts are focused on maximizing performance and on employee well-being.
Low	Leader is not focused on either task performance or people. The leader's behaviors might be termed ineffectual or passive.	Leader focuses his/her efforts on productivity, with little concern for employee satisfaction or development.

Consideration (vertical axis)

Initiating Structure (horizontal axis)

FIGURE 13.3

The Managerial (Leadership) Grid

Source: From *Grid Solutions*, by Robert R. Blake and Anne Adams McCanse (formerly *The Managerial Grid Figure* by Robert R. Blake and Jane S. Mouton), Houston: Gulf Publishing Company, p. 29. Copyright 1991 by Scientific Methods, Inc. Reproduced by permission of Grid International, Inc.

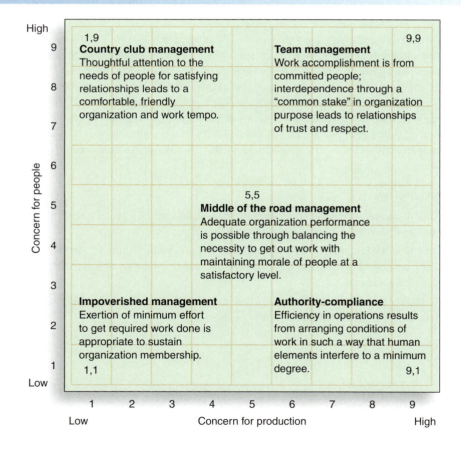

1,9 Country club management
Thoughtful attention to the needs of people for satisfying relationships leads to a comfortable, friendly organization and work tempo.

9,9 Team management
Work accomplishment is from committed people; interdependence through a "common stake" in organization purpose leads to relationships of trust and respect.

5,5 Middle of the road management
Adequate organization performance is possible through balancing the necessity to get out work with maintaining morale of people at a satisfactory level.

Impoverished management
Exertion of minimum effort to get required work done is appropriate to sustain organization membership.
1,1

Authority-compliance
Efficiency in operations results from arranging conditions of work in such a way that human elements interfere to a minimum degree.
9,1

Concern for people (vertical axis): Low to High, 1–9

Concern for production (horizontal axis): Low to High, 1–9

video: THE ENTREPRENEURIAL MANAGER

Dale Gray

Summary

Communications Services, Inc., began as Gray and Associates, but they didn't have any associates. The firm started in the front bedroom of Dale Gray's house with two weeks' worth of vacation pay that had been saved up from a prior job. There were no outside investors, and the firm didn't take on any debt to get its start. Today, the company has grown into Communication Services, Inc., and there are over 100 people in the company across six offices in the Southwest and one office in Portland, Oregon. The firm is one of the top 20 companies in telecommunications infrastructure development. Gray started out as a geologist, and now he has built telecommunications systems across the country and on five different continents.

Gray says he is used to making the decisions at a company, and has been his own boss for 17 years. He would be a "lousy employee," he says, and when he was one—back in his 20s—his boss told him to "slow down" because he was making his co-workers look bad. That's when Gray recognized that he had a drive about his work that other people didn't have. He had a passion and commitment to achieving his goals that would help him in becoming a successful entrepreneur. Other skills that helped him were less glamorous, like making a commitment to teach himself the things others would not teach him and becoming disciplined in the way he managed the business once it was larger. For instance, once the firm became successful and started to grow, it required a business plan with specific organization and financial goals and strategy.

Gray recommends hiring the right people in the first place rather than hiring someone, then finding out the firm has made a compromise, invested money in training the individual, and then has to let them go anyway. It costs more up front to finance the personnel search and find the people who share the passion and goals of the firm than it does to simply train them; however, Gray looks at this as an investment and has seen it work for his firm. The company has arrangements with all of its suppliers—with whom it spends millions—for them to come to the firm and offer free training in order to keep CSI up to speed on new product developments or applications. CSI's clients also participate in this training at no cost, according to the arrangement.

Discussion Questions

1. Dale Gray discusses some elements of management and leadership. Distinguish between these two and provide an example of each from the video.

2. Using the Initiating Structure by Consideration Matrix presented in Figure 13.2 in the text, classify Dale Gray according to these behavioral dimensions. What does his classification into each dimension mean?

3. Do you think entrepreneurs like Dale Gray feel stifled when they work as employees of other firms? Discuss the concept of power in your answer.

axis of the managerial grid is a scale of 1 to 9 for concern for people, and the horizontal axis is a scale of 1 to 9 for production. Presumably, the "ideal" behaviors fall in the 9,9 quadrant. Leaders who are high on concern for production and high on concern for people tend to achieve optimal subordinate performance and satisfaction. Simply stated, the most effective managers relate well to their followers and can efficiently delineate what needs to be done. The managerial grid is used by practitioners and management trainers because of its simplicity and intuitive appeal.

Leadership Style A classic study defined two behavioral leadership styles or decision-making approaches: the autocratic style and the democratic style.[10] Leaders using the *autocratic* style make decisions on their own and announce them as a done deal. A *democratic* leader actively tries to solicit the input of subordinates, often requiring consensus or a majority vote before making a final decision. This early study suggested that a democratic style resulted in higher subordinate satisfaction with the leader but that an autocratic approach resulted in somewhat higher performance. The performance advantage associated with an autocratic style tends to disappear when the leader is not present to monitor subordinates. A *laissez-faire* style, in which a leader avoids making decisions, results in both low satisfaction and low performance.

LOC-In

③ Learning Objective Check-In

Kathy tends to emphasize the characteristics and behaviors of successful leaders in developing her own leadership style at work. She bases important promotions from within the company on how effective the candidate was at accomplishing group goals, organizing tasks, and assigning responsibilities. Just as important, she looks at the concern that the leader-candidate had for the feelings, needs, and problems of his or her previous work team.

1. *Generally, Kathy's theory on leadership is one of the _____.*
   a. *dispersed theories*
   b. *situation theories*
   c. *exchange theories*
   d. *person theories*
2. *Specifically, Kathy's method for choosing candidates for promotion shows a preference for the _____.*
   a. *behavioral theories*
   b. *trait theory*
   c. *contingency model*
   d. *path-goal theory*

Situational Theories

Subsequent research on leadership questioned the "one best way" approach suggested by the behavioral theories. A situational, or "it depends," approach began to replace the simplistic view that a particular set of behaviors or decision-making style separates good from bad leaders. The key point of the situational approach is that leadership success depends on the fit between the leader's behavior and decision-making style and the requirements of the situation. One author illustrated how leadership effectiveness was dependent on the situation as follows:

> *Bob Knight, the men's head basketball coach at Indiana University, consistently uses an intense, task-oriented leadership style that intimidates players, officials, the media, and university administrators. But his style works with the Indiana teams he recruits. Knight has one of the most impressive win–loss records of any active major college basketball coach. But would this same style work if Bob Knight was counsel-general of the United Nations or project manager for a group of Ph.D. software designers at Microsoft? Probably not![11]*

Bob Knight's leadership style ultimately resulted in his being asked to resign by the university in 2000 because of numerous complaints about his behavior, indicating that the fit between him and the university was no longer acceptable.

Several theorists have attempted to isolate critical situational factors that affect leadership effectiveness. The resulting theories include Fiedler's contingency model and the path–goal model.

FIEDLER'S CONTINGENCY MODEL According to Fiedler, three aspects of a situation determine which leader behavior or style is most suitable:[12]

- *Leader-member relations:* The extent to which the leader is well liked and enjoys the trust, support, and respect of subordinates.
- *Task structure:* The extent to which the leader delineates which "what, how, and why" work tasks are performed.
- *Position power:* The degree to which the leader has the authority to reward and punish subordinates.

Fiedler's Contingency Model

According to Fiedler, the better the leader–member relations, the more highly structured the job, and the stronger the position power, the more control or influence a leader enjoys.

Fiedler identified two major leadership styles. **Task-oriented leadership** emphasizes work accomplishments and performance results; **relationship-oriented leadership** focuses on maintaining good interpersonal relationships. Fiedler contends that task-oriented leaders are more effective in situations that are either highly favorable or highly unfavorable. The most favorable situations are categories I, II, and III in Figure 13.4 on page 513 where at least two of the three determinants noted above are positive, and the most unfavorable situation is category VIII, where all three determinants are negative. For situations in the middle categories, which are of moderate difficulty, a relationship-oriented leader performs better.

As a whole, there is some empirical evidence for this model.[13] However, the implication that a leader must be assigned to a situation that suits his or her style makes the model somewhat problematic, because it implies that leaders cannot change their styles. The emphasis on a fit between the leader and the situation makes it difficult to translate the theory into practice. Work environments change often, and there is no easy way to assess on an ongoing basis how good the leader-member relations are, how structured the task is, and how much position power the leader actually enjoys.

Despite these warnings, this contingency model provides a useful analytical tool to better understand when and why particular leadership styles appear to be most effective.

PATH–GOAL THEORY   Another contingency model of leadership that has gained wide acceptance and enjoys substantial empirical support was developed by Robert House. **Path-goal theory** focuses on how leaders influence subordinate perceptions of work goals and paths to achieve those goals.[14] The crux of the theory is that it is the leader's job to help followers achieve their goals and to influence followers to ensure that their goals are consistent with the overall objectives of the group or organization.

The theory specifies four leadership behaviors, as shown in Figure 13.5 on page 513. A *directive leader* establishes expectations for followers, determines targets to attain, organizes tasks, sets deadlines and schedules, and closely monitors progress. These behaviors are similar to the initiating structure and the autocratic styles discussed earlier. For instance, Thomas M. Siebel is the brash CEO of Siebel Systems Inc., a Silicon Valley maker of software used to manage customer relations. Siebel is almost obsessed with inspecting everything to make sure it is done right. His philosophy is, "No software gets written until customers weigh in. Outside consultants routinely poll clients on their satisfaction, and [employee] compensation is heavily based on those reports." Siebel's direct approach is unusual for Silicon Valley, but his firm has a third of the market for customer-management software, a market Siebel shares with Oracle.[15]

A *supportive leader* is warm and friendly and shows concern about the problems and needs of subordinates. This is the same as consideration. A *participative leader* actively elicits subordinate input and opinions and uses them when making decisions that affect the group. This is similar to a democratic leadership style. A

David Packard (left) and William Hewlett, co-founders of Hewlett-Packard, in an early photo.

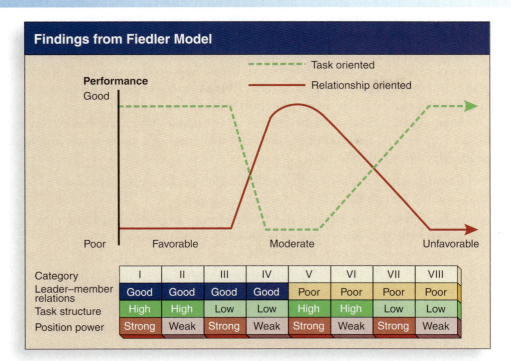

Fiedler's Contingency Model of Leadership

Source: From *Organizational Behavior*, 7th ed., by Robbins. Copyright © 1996. Reprinted by permission of Pearson Education, Inc., Upper Saddle River, NJ.

Findings from Fiedler Model

Category	I	II	III	IV	V	VI	VII	VIII
Leader–member relations	Good	Good	Good	Good	Poor	Poor	Poor	Poor
Task structure	High	High	Low	Low	High	High	Low	Low
Position power	Strong	Weak	Strong	Weak	Strong	Weak	Strong	Weak

classic example of a highly successful participative leader was William Hewlett, the Silicon Valley and computer-age pioneer who cofounded Hewlett-Packard in a garage in 1938. Shortly before his death in 2001 at age 87, he said that he was proudest of his personal relationship and camaraderie with employees. One observer recalled, "Despite his position and wealth, Hewlett delighted in working side-by-side with employees or playing penny-ante poker with them."[16]

An *achievement-oriented leader* is primarily concerned with motivating people by setting challenging goals, coaching subordinates to perform at the highest level, and rewarding those who meet or exceed their targets. House believes that leaders are flexible enough to exhibit all four of these behaviors and that their effectiveness depends on their ability to use the behavior appropriate to the particular circumstances.

Path–goal theory proposes two key factors that determine which leadership behaviors are most appropriate. The first, the **situational context**, refers to factors outside the control of the subordinate, such as the tasks defining the job,

situational context

The factors that are outside the control of the subordinate such as the tasks defining the job, the formal authority system of the organization, and the work group.

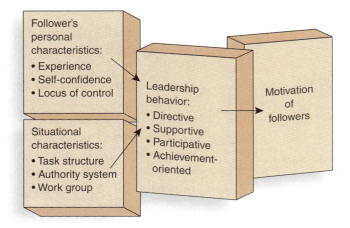

FIGURE 13.5

The Path–Goal Framework

Source: From *Management of Organizations*, by P. M. Wright and R. A. Noe. Copyright © 1996 The McGraw-Hill Companies, Inc. Reprinted with permission.

the formal authority system of the organization, and the work group. The second, the personal characteristics of the follower, are the attributes of the subordinate such as experience and perceived ability or self-confidence. Effectiveness is defined in terms of the performance of subordinates and the extent to which followers perceive a leader's behavior as increasing their present or future satisfaction. A leader's behavior is more effective if it is congruent with the situation and the personal characteristics of subordinates.

Many propositions have been derived from this theory and have been supported empirically. Based on personal characteristics of followers, the following leadership styles are effective:

- Subordinates who are highly authoritarian prefer a directive leadership style because to them this commands respect.

- Subordinates who believe they control their own destinies are more satisfied with a participative leadership style because it gives them more opportunity to influence decisions that affect their lives. Those who believe their destiny is in the hands of others prefer a more directive style.

- Supportive and participative leaders improve satisfaction and enhance group performance of subordinates with high perceived ability who don't wish to be told what to do and those with considerable experience who are capable of offering valuable input.

Based on fit with the situational context, the effective leadership styles are as follows:

- Directive leadership improves followers' satisfaction when the tasks are ambiguous and stressful because it helps clarify the situation.

- Supportive leadership increases subordinate satisfaction when the tasks are clearly structured and laid out. Employees see directive leader behavior as patronizing or insulting when they already understand what needs to get done.

- Achievement-oriented leadership increases subordinates' satisfaction and group productivity when the organization can provide rewards contingent on the performance of the group.

LOC-In

④ Learning Objective Check-In

Caroline tailors her leadership style to the situation at hand. She operates fairly consistently around all the people in her department. Caroline operates very effectively when there is an important deadline that needs to be reached by the group, especially if it represents a serious challenge or opportunity for the team to do well.

1. *Caroline best demonstrates _____.*
   a. *path–goal theory*
   b. *trait theory*
   c. *Fiedler's Contingency Model*
   d. *Maslow's hierarchy of needs*
2. *In the example above, Caroline is a _____.*
   a. *relationship-oriented leader*
   b. *task-oriented leader*
   c. *supportive leader*
   d. *participative leader*

The leadership behaviors suggested by path–goal theory can be utilized by anyone. The behavioral choices can be particularly effective tactics for you in the role of team member. Management Is Everyone's Business 13.1 on page 515 offers suggestions for applying the leader behaviors from path–goal theory as a team member.

The situational contingency theories described in this section suggest that the leader's style that will be most effective depends on the situation. Thus, situational factors determine the effectiveness of a leader's actions. The situational and contingency theories assume that the source of leadership is the leader. Other approaches emphasize sources of leadership besides the leader. These approaches to leadership are labeled "dispersed" and are considered next.

Working as a Team   Many organizations rely on teams as the principal operating unit. Teams often are empowered and expected to somehow achieve their performance targets. The teams may not have a formal team leader, but rely on informal relationships and team skills to get the work done. An empowered team setting such as this is a situation which could benefit from a team member willing to apply the path–goal theory of leadership. The following are some suggestions for applying the path–goal leader behaviors as a team member:

- *Directive behaviors*. When things are unclear or people are distracted, it can be helpful for a team to have a member that, perhaps gently, helps to organize and schedules tasks.
- *Supportive behaviors*. Supportive behaviors in the form of concern for other team members can be helpful for team performance. Supportiveness may be particularly appropriate and effective when team members are experiencing some difficulties or a team member is new to the team.
- *Participative behaviors*. Pushing for a democratic process or taking steps to assure that all team members' voices are heard can be an important contribution to a team.
- *Achievement-oriented behavior*. Helping a team to set new or higher goals can be important for keeping a team producing at a high level.

Dispersed Theories

Leadership can sometimes come from sources other than the leader of the organization, which is the main point of the dispersed approach. Leadership can come from various aspects of the system in an organization, or it can come from the workers themselves. These two possibilities are the focus of the substitute leadership and self-leadership theories, respectively.

SUBSTITUTE LEADERSHIP   Substitute leadership theory might be considered the opposite of the person-based approach to leadership. The person-based approach emphasizes the importance of a leader's traits and behavioral style. The substitute leadership theory downplays the importance of the leader and emphasizes characteristics of the situation. Substitute leadership theory is based on the idea that, at least in some situations, leadership is not only ineffective, it is irrelevant. People tend to romanticize leadership and attribute more importance to leaders than may actually be merited.[17] Substitute leadership theory takes the contrary perspective and emphasizes the importance of the situation.

Substitute leadership theory attempts to identify workplace characteristics that can substitute for leadership or neutralize efforts made by a leader. For example, if workers are highly trained and professional, a leader will likely not be needed or have that much impact. In that situation, the workers know what needs to be done and will follow through and perform their function. On the negative side, an inflexible organizational culture may operate to neutralize any attempts to bring change to the organization.

Substitute leadership theory reminds us of the importance of situational factors. Depending on the situation, leaders may make less difference than they think they might. Further, wise leaders can capitalize on substitutes for leadership, putting in place, for example, a highly trained and cohesive workforce so that consistent leader presence and direction isn't needed. However,

Business Ethics: It Takes Leadership and a System

THEME: ETHICS

Several recent corporate scandals have led to distrust of business and heightened the perception that businesspeople are crooks. How can an organization assure that honesty and integrity permeate its people and operations? It is now more important than ever that organizations demonstrate to investors and customers that integrity and honesty are their top priorities. The following are examples of organizations that are noted for their strong ethics with leaders who promote and maintain the company's ethical reputation.

Set the Example

Ethical standards have to be established and implemented from the top. Gary Kelly, CEO of Southwest Airlines, takes the position that integrity is revealed in how you deal with customers, vendors, buyers, and employees. In other words, what really matters are the behaviors of leaders, not what they say in speeches and policies. As a leader, if your behavior indicates lack of ethical standards or you condone unethical behavior, you cause irreparable damage to your credibility. Interestingly, Southwest Airlines does not rely on manuals containing layers of policies and procedures to instill and maintain integrity. It relies on a strong culture and trusts employees to do the right thing.

Establish a System

Leadership is important for setting the example of high ethical standards. At the same time, simply setting a good example isn't necessarily sufficient to convey the importance of ethical conduct and to maintain it. FedEx uses multiple media of communication such as e-mail, fax, and voice mail, to emphasize integrity. Gene Bastedo, vice president of internal audit at FedEx, also states that the company emphasizes that it will not tolerate impropriety of any kind. If there is any wrongdoing, swift action is taken. Unethical or inappropriate behavior is not tolerated regardless of the dollars involved. Two employees at FedEx recently learned that the company is serious about its strong stance on ethics. The individuals were found to be embezzling and were promptly fired and turned over to authorities for prosecution.

Darden Restaurants Inc., the largest casual dining restaurant in the United States, provides written rules for how employees should conduct themselves. The chain includes over 1,200 restaurants and has developed specific guidelines ranging from acceptance of gifts to dealing with financial information.

Microchip Technology Inc. is also pursuing a written code of conduct for its employees. It is a young, fast-growth company that has relied on a brief statement of ethics that was a part of its original guiding principles. However, the organization is finding that it needs more specifics and clarification of how these ethical values apply to everyday activities. The company is now working on developing a written code of conduct.

In sum, driving ethics through an organization requires leadership that exemplifies those standards. Setting an example is not enough. Clear specification of values and expected conduct can take the form of various communications and policy and procedure statements. These systems can act as leadership substitutes to help develop and maintain the desired ethical performance of the organization.

Source: D. Blank, "A Matter of Ethics: In Organizations Where Honesty and Integrity Rule, It Is Easy for Employees to Resist the Many Temptations Today's Business World Offers," *Internal Auditor* 60 (2003), pp. 26–31.

---

self-leadership

Leadership that stresses the individual responsibility of employees to develop their own work priorities aligned with organizational goals; the manager is a facilitator who enhances the self-leadership capabilities of subordinates, encouraging them to develop self-control skills.

can putting in place even extensive system upgrades ever totally substitute for effective leadership? Management Close-Up 13.2 above looks at business ethics and takes the position that it can be both the person and the system that are important for performance. Skills for Managing 13.1 on page 517 also considers ethical performance and addresses whether situational factors can really replace leadership.

SELF-LEADERSHIP   **Self-leadership** stresses the individual responsibility of employees to develop their own work priorities aligned with organizational goals. The manager is a facilitator who enhances the self-leadership capabilities of subordinates, encouraging them to develop self-control skills. As summarized in Table 13.3 on page 518, this leadership approach is far more decentralized than traditional leadership, which focuses on the supervisor as the pivotal figure.

Leadership and Ethical Excellence: Obedience or Internalized Values?

The ethical scandals that rocked corporate America, including the high-profile Enron and WorldCom cases (see Management Close-Up 13.1), resulted in a tightening of accounting standards and greater governmental oversight of corporate finances. The purpose for these additional rules and controls is to assure that organizations function ethically. Such controls and reporting requirements can serve as substitutes for leadership and may provide the structure and incentives needed to assure ethical behavior. Controls, policies, and procedures are tools that can help guide ethical conduct, but like all tools, they have limits.

Guidelines cannot make us honest nor can they provide us with integrity. They can lay out a path to follow. They can also be ignored, circumvented, or undermined. Even if there is no unethical intent, what happens when a worker confronts a situation that isn't exactly covered by the guidelines? What will a worker do when there may be great temptation and possibility of personal gain and no one is observing? Harry Jansen Kraemer, CEO of Baxter International Inc., a global health care company, points out that workers in every corner of the world make ethical decisions in the course of conducting business. Kraemer notes that you simply cannot be everywhere looking over every employee's shoulder. The only way to be sure that workers try to make the right decisions and take the right actions is to know that each of them has the right values. It is not enough to provide external rules to be followed. The only way to be sure about ethical conduct is to know that the workers share the same values that guide conduct.

Discussion Questions

1. Do you think guidelines are sufficient to assure ethical conduct in a business. Why or why not?
2. As a business leader, which would you rather have, ethical conduct due to obedience or due to internalized values? Why?

3. How can a leader instill the desired values in the workplace? That is, how could culture based on those values be developed?
4. Consider the following matrix.

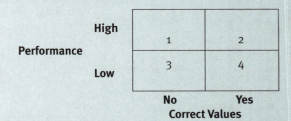

Assume that there are workers in each of these four cells. What do you think should be done about workers who perform their jobs but really don't embrace the ethical values of the organization (cell 1)? What do you think should be done about workers who aren't performing so well, but have the right values (cell 4)? Defend your answers.

Research Questions

1. Identify organizations that have suffered some sort of ethical scandal. Does it appear that the ethical problems are due to a lack of guidelines or due to a lack of shared ethical values?
2. Identify organizations that are noted for their high level of ethical conduct. What appears to most account for their positive ethical performance, the use of specific guidelines or the development of common ethical values?
3. How would you recommend an organization go about improving its ethical performance? Specifically, what steps should be taken to improve and maintain ethical conduct of its employees?

Source: H. M. J. Kraemer, "Do the Right Thing: Practice Values-Based Leadership," *Executive Excellence* 20, pp. 5–6.

There are two important mechanisms to foster self-leadership within the firm. The first is **empowerment,** or the process of transferring control of individual work behavior from the supervisor to the employee. Employees must be provided with skills, tools, support, and information so that authority and responsibility can be successfully delegated to them. The second key vehicle is

empowerment

The process of transferring control of individual work behavior from the supervisor to the employee.

table 13.3

Characteristics of Traditional and Self-Managing Behaviors

TRADITIONAL LEADER BEHAVIORS	SELF-MANAGING LEADER BEHAVIORS
Organization. Structures own and subordinates' work	Encourages self-reward
Domination. Restricts or limits the discretion of individuals or groups	Encourages self-observation
Production. Sets standards for task performance	Encourages self-goal setting
Recognition. Expresses approval or disapproval of behavior	Encourages self-criticism
Integration. Promotes group cohesion and reduces group conflict	Encourages self-rehearsal
Communication. Provides, seeks, and exchanges information with group members	Acts as a role model by exhibiting appropriate behavior
	Fosters the development of a culture that nourishes and supports self-leadership

Source: From J. M. Ivancevich, P. Lorenzi, S. J. Skinner, and P. B. Crosby, *Management: Quality and Competitiveness*, McGraw-Hill/Irwin, 1997. Reprinted with permission of J. M. Ivancevich.

---

role modeling

The leadership mechanism in which managers serve as examples of the behaviors they would like employees to emulate.

LOC-In

5 **Learning Objective Check-In**

James is a very effective manager who consistently has a capable and effective staff. He encourages his subordinates to develop self-control skills and is a firm believer in the empowerment of his staff. His subordinates often say that they look to James as a successful role model whose goals are aligned well with the goals of the organization.

1. *Which leadership perspective best reflects James' attitude?*
   a. *Transformational leadership*
   b. *Substitute leadership*
   c. *Self-leadership*
   d. *Transactional leadership*
2. *James pursues a(n) _____ in his approach to his role at work.*
   a. *dispersed theory of leadership*
   b. *person-based theory of leadership*
   c. *exchange theory of leadership*
   d. *situational theory of leadership*

role modeling, whereby managers serve as examples of the behaviors they would like employees to emulate. Role modeling is more likely to be effective if workers can see a link between adopting the desired behaviors and positive outcomes, such as higher pay, a promotion, and public recognition.

All of us can exercise our self-leadership and take increased responsibility for our work performance. As long as we have sufficient empowerment, and empowerment has become a common organizational practice, we can apply the principles of self-leadership to our own work. Management Is Everyone's Business 13.2 on page 519 offers suggestions for applying the self-leadership approach.

The dispersed approaches to leadership emphasize leadership that comes from sources other than the leader. Other perspectives emphasize that leadership is an interaction and the source of leadership comes from the relationships that are developed between a leader and his/her workers. We next turn to the exchange approach to leadership.

Exchange Theories

The exchange perspective on leadership emphasizes the importance of the relationship between a leader and employees. It is the exchange, the nature of the relationship, that underlies a leader's ability to direct and be effective. The following are some of the major leadership theories that fit in the exchange theory category.

---

transactional leaders

Leaders who use legitimate, coercive, or reward powers to elicit obedience.

TRANSACTIONAL AND TRANSFORMATIONAL LEADERSHIP Most classical leadership theories are concerned with **transactional leaders,** who use legitimate, coercive, or reward powers to elicit obedience. Transactional leaders may not generate passion and excitement, and they do not empower or inspire individuals to transcend their own self-interest for the good of the organization. However,

Working as an Individual   Being a responsible and proactive employee who actively manages his/her performance can set you apart from many other employees. Organizations are on the lookout for people who can manage themselves and continually improve their contribution in the workplace. Applying the self-leadership tactics listed in Table 13.3 provides a systematic and practical way to manage your own performance. Application suggestions include the following:

- *Identify your own rewards*. What is it that you would find motivating? No one knows the answer to this question better than you.

- *Observe your own performance*. What would you like to work on to develop yourself or to get ahead in the organization? Perhaps there are things you want to learn or areas where you could improve. Your organization might not offer any formal rewards for you to make these improvements (that is why you need to identify your own rewards, as suggested in the first bullet point), but you may be convinced that your learning or improvement will pay off down the road. If this is the case, you have identified a great focus for your self-leadership activities.

- *Set your goal*. What do you want to achieve in terms of learning or improvement? As we learned in Chapter 12, the more specific and measurable your objectives, the better.

- *How are you doing?* What is your current performance level or how is your performance improvement plan progressing? It can be helpful to have sources of feedback other than your own assessment (which could be unduly harsh or forgiving). Make use of any objective measures (such as measures of amount or frequency) and/or ask for input from others who are familiar with your work.

- *Practice* so that you can achieve your desired level of performance. You can practice mentally by rehearsing, or visualizing, what steps you will follow and how your resulting performance will be maximally effective. You can also look for others who perform effectively well and use them as role models.

transactional leaders can get the job done and keep people focused on the tasks at hand. **Transformational leaders,** on the other hand, attempt to instill in followers the ability to question standard modes of operation. They are capable of revitalizing organizations by tapping people's reservoir of creativity. While transformational leaders are charismatic, they also inspire people, provide them with intellectual stimulation, and give followers individualized consideration. Table 13.4 below compares the characteristics of transactional and transformational leaders.

transformational leaders

Leaders who revitalize organizations by instilling in followers the ability to question standard modes of operation.

table 13.4

Characteristics of Transactional and Transformational Leaders

TRANSACTIONAL LEADER	TRANSFORMATIONAL LEADER
Contingent reward. Contracts exchange of rewards for effort, promises rewards for good performance, recognizes accomplishments	*Charisma*. Provides vision and sense of mission, instills pride, gains respect and trust
Management by exception (active). Watches and searches for deviations from rules and standards, takes corrective action	*Inspiration*. Communicates high expectations, uses symbols to focus efforts, expresses important purposes in simple ways
Management by exception (passive). Intervenes only if standards are not met	*Intellectual stimulation*. Promotes intelligence, rationality, and careful problem solving
Laissez-faire. Abdicates responsibilities, avoids making decisions	*Individualized consideration*. Gives personal attention, treats each employee individually, coaches, advises

Source: Reprinted from *Organizational Dynamics*, Winter 1990, B. M. Bass et al., "Transactional to Transformational Leadership: Learning to Share the Vision," p. 22. Copyright © 1990, with permission from Elsevier.

LOC-In

6 Learning Objective Check-In

Joyce knows how to get at her workers' creativities. She is charismatic, but she also drives other people to question the status quo and challenge themselves and the company. Joyce provides her workers with intellectual stimulation and is always consistent and dependable.

1. Which theory best represents what Joyce believes about leadership?
    a. Exchange
    b. Dispersed
    c. Situational
    d. Person-based
2. Which of the following best classifies Joyce?
    a. Transactional leader
    b. Transformational leader
    c. Achievement-oriented leader
    d. Substitute leadership

In addition to articulating a vision and communicating that vision to subordinates, transformational leaders build trust by being dependable, consistent, and persevering. "They do not feel self-important or complacent: rather, they recognize their personal strength, compensate for their weaknesses, nurture their skills and continually develop their talents, and know how to learn from failure. They strive for success rather than merely trying to avoid failure."[18] Overall, transformational leadership is more likely than transactional leadership to reduce turnover rates, increase productivity, and improve employee satisfaction.[19]

Recent work indicates that transformational leadership has a positive impact on performance by lowering frustration and increasing optimism.[20] In other words, it is not characteristics of transformational leaders, per se, that have a direct influence on performance in an organization. Rather, it is the influence on levels of worker frustration and optimism that, in turn, leads to improved performance.

AUTHENTIC LEADERSHIP   Authentic leadership theory[21] is an approach that emphasizes the importance of a positive directive force, particularly in an environment of increasing complexity, change, and uncertainty. Authentic leadership is a recent development that is meant to go beyond transformational leadership. Transformational leadership may be viewed as instrumental leadership. That is, the task of the leader is to facilitate the attainment of organizational goals through the effective leadership of the workforce. The transformational leader may embrace certain values and ways of doing things because they are instrumental in obtaining desired performance outcomes.

Judy McGrath's management style in her role as CEO of MTV demonstrates a transformational leader's commitment to inspiration and stimulation. Says McGrath of the creative, take-chances spirit she fosters at MTV, "The smartest thing we can do when confronted by something truly creative is to get out of the way."

In contrast, authentic leadership emphasizes a terminal value approach. An authentic leader is true to his/her values and portrays those values and positively influences employees. The primary goal is not portraying whatever facade of values or emotions that might facilitate achieving a performance goal. Rather, the authentic leader provides a positive influence and role model in the organization. Management Close-Up 13.3 on page 521 presents a tool that authentic leaders can use to effectively convey their values. Authentic leadership theory will likely be further developed. Here we provide only a brief description of the authentic leadership approach as it currently exists.

Authentic leadership theory suggests that effective leaders are guided by doing what is right for constituents, not their own self-interests. Authentic leaders focus on making a positive difference and on developing others to be leaders. What may best describe the authentic leader is the profile of characteristics of authentic leadership, as summarized in Table 13.5 on page 521.

Tell Us a Story

Rational arguments, statistics, and facts are often the tools of a manager. However, effective leaders may know what recent research has revealed: storytelling is much more convincing and memorable than facts. For example, Mary Contratto, CEO of Little Company, a health care organization, believes storytelling is a leadership skill. She tells the story to employees in the organization of how a trainer at a gym assigned to her 13-year-old son became an emergency room nurse. Contratto and the trainer were discussing her son's goals when Contratto learned that the trainer had given up on being a nurse and was about to switch occupations. The CEO was able to provide the support and motivation that was needed. The trainer is now a dedicated nurse. Contratto shares the story to convey to employees that each of them can make a difference. They can be recruiters and promoters for the organization when interacting in their communities.

Contratto also encourages employees to share their stories of best and worst service. The organization emphasizes service as a critical aspect of the company's mission. They plan to use stories to make real the importance of service to patients, the families of patients, and doctors. Stories can engage employees and be far more effective than a statement that service is part of the mission. Storytelling is memorable, effectively conveys values, and feels more authentic.

Source: Adapted from B. Kaufman, "Stories That Sell, Stories That Tell: Effective Storytelling Can Strengthen an Organization's Bonds with All of Its Stakeholders," *Journal of Business Strategy* 24 (2003), p. 11+.

table 13.5

Profile of Authentic Leadership Characteristics

CHARACTERISTIC	DESCRIPTION
1. Value Driven	Motivated by doing what's right and belief that everyone has something positive to contribute.
2. No Gap between Internal Values and Actions	Authentic leader understands his/her own core values and projects them with consistency.
3. Transparent	Open about weaknesses and open to suggestions for improvements and changes in direction.
4. Influence by Inspiration	Authentic leaders portray confidence, hope, and resiliency.
5. Developmental Focus	Authentic leaders view development of people as important as task accomplishment.
6. Moral Capacity	Authentic leader can judge unclear issues and dilemmas. They may change their mind, but not to shift with popular opinion, but to be consistent with their values and current analysis.

As shown in the list of authentic leadership characteristics in the table, the emphasis of authentic leadership is on people and making a positive difference. Trust, credibility, integrity, and inspiration can be far more powerful for motivating performance than can coercion and deceit. Authentic leadership places values and integrity at the forefront of effective leadership, the kind of leadership model that is crucial in the wake of various legal and ethical scandals in organizations.

Assessing Emotional Intelligence

Working as a Manager Managers serve a critical role in organizations. We have distinguished between the roles of manager and leader in this chapter, but the reality is that the two roles are often blended. For example, tasks need to be completed on time, but workers may also need to be inspired. The job of being manager often requires that the leadership be infused with the management responsibilities. The following suggestions offer ideas for adding leadership to the job of manager.

- Be a role model for the key values and ethical principles you want your workers to live up to.
- Consider the situation before taking action. An effective leader adapts to the situation and chooses a course of action that will be most effective.
- Task completion is important but remember so too are your workers. You need to balance task and relationship concerns.
- Empower your workers and give them the knowledge and support they need to become self-leaders.
- Situations of uncertainty or difficulty can call for you to inspire and offer a vision to give your workers meaning and purpose in their efforts.
- Be true to yourself. People will quickly see through someone who is simply acting and is not truly committed to a course of action.

LOC-In

7 Learning Objective Check-In

1. *Illyana works for a full-service software development company as the director of contracts and procurement. Illyana is a truly positive influence on the employees in her unit. She is a role model who is always doing what is best for others and does not worry about her own self-interests in her work decisions. In her 17 years at the company, her moral character, internal values, and actions within the organization have all been in sync. Which of the following best characterizes Illyana?*
   a. *Transformational leader*
   b. *Transactional leader*
   c. *Authentic leader*
   d. *Employee-oriented leader*

The leadership theories discussed in this chapter provide different frameworks for understanding leadership. Further, your familiarity with these models can help you to transform them into your personal tools for increasing your leadership effectiveness. Management Is Everyone's Business 13.3 above offers some suggestions for applying the leadership framework when you are in the role of manager.

CONCLUDING THOUGHTS

At the beginning of this chapter, some critical thinking questions were posed. After covering some of the basics of leadership, we now return to these issues. First, there is no standard set of characteristics that make for a great leader. A variety of personalities have developed into great leaders. There are also a variety of situational demands and constraints. Great leadership is more likely to occur when the characteristics of a person fit the situation. The person-based leadership approaches outline the characteristics of the leader that make a difference. However, situational theories indicate that company circumstances are important as well.

Second, leadership can make a critical difference. As noted at the beginning of this chapter, without Carlos Ghosn at the helm, it is possible that Nissan Motors might not even exist. However, there does seem to be a tendency to focus on a leader and attribute greater causal significance to him/her than is merited. As discussed in the description of substitute leadership, it is possible to overly romanticize the role of a leader. The best leaders realize that they can't be in all places at all times. Instead, they rely on their people being aligned with the interests of the organization and on effective systems being in place.

The issue of leadership style was raised in the chapter. As with personal characteristics, no one style always works best. A style may resonate or be a better natural fit than others for a leader. Some situations may call for an autocratic style or a task-oriented leader. Other situations may be better suited to a leader with a more people-oriented style. Thus, any given style is not always the best.

Finally, ethics are a central issue when considering leadership. A leader must make ethics a central concern of the organization and not just rhetoric that can be ignored. Going beyond "ethics as window dressing" means the leader communicates the importance of ethical conduct, acts as a role model, and assures that everyone in the organization shares ethical values. Ethical conduct doesn't just happen, nor can it always be assured through compliance. People need to understand and align themselves with the values of integrity and ethics and know what those values mean in terms of actual behaviors. Leaders can make a positive ethical difference, but it takes an active and concerted effort.

Focusing on the Future: Using Management Theory in Daily Life

Leadership

Many of the managers profiled in the "Focusing on the Future" boxes throughout this text talk about leadership during their interviews. Like motivation, "leadership experience" often mirrors leadership theory, whether managers know it or not!

Task-Oriented versus Relationship-Oriented Leadership   "Barbara DeLong," the HR Director whose story about an ethical decision-making process appears in Chapter 3, explains the necessity of using relationship-oriented leadership skills in addition to task-oriented leadership skills. As she tells it:

> When I took over a department, I wanted to know how things worked. I asked questions with regard to processes and procedures for performing tasks within the department. I also asked what was working, what was not working, and where we could eliminate repetitive tasks. My "task-oriented" approach was perceived as a threat by two of the junior members of our group, because they thought I was trying to eliminate their positions. As a result, two good employees left the company. Be careful of how you approach job redesign or job simplification! You have to think about people's feelings as much as you think about how to get the information you need to make design decisions.

Exchange Theories   Mark Hasting, the Target Group Vice President who talked about operations and information technology in Chapters 17 and 18, believes that every leader has to remember three things: (1) You're a boss; (2) You're a subordinate; and (3) You're a peer. His view of leadership is that it's all about these relationships or exchanges. When he talks about working with the people who report to him, you can see a transformational leader at work:

> As a boss, you have to take care of those who take care of you, but also take care of those who don't. Your job is to create an environment that encourages people to be part of it. I respect the associates who work with me—I give them autonomy and listen to their needs and suggestions. When I make a mistake I admit it—that's how the team knows that I'm

accountable to them. You have to be real and admit when you've done something wrong. A boss doesn't have to have all the right answers, but you do need to know where to go to find answers. Sometimes, if an associate comes to me with a question I can't answer, I'll ask, 'How would we go about looking that up?' Then I'll say, 'Let's look it up together.' That gives me the chance to help the employee learn how to find answers for him or herself, while at the same time giving me an answer that I might need in the future.

Mark's comments about his relations with his bosses and his peers demonstrate authentic leadership at work. It is clear that Mark is working for the good of the group, not just his own group. As a subordinate, Mark feels strongly that it is his job to make his boss look good. It can be hard sometimes, because Mark doesn't always agree with his boss's point of view, but as he says, "I have an obligation to submit my ideas constructively. If I can't do that, I should be doing it the boss's way."

As a peer, Mark says, "You've got to play a supporting role, a devil's advocate role, and an honest role. Good peers are completely honest with you, and expect you to be completely honest with them." Mark has a pact with some of his most trusted colleagues—he shares anything he hears about their performance with them, and he expects that they will do the same for him. All of this is done confidentially, and for the end purpose of challenging each other to do more, better, differently. Mark notes, "As peers, we can have real conversations without agendas, and those are critical to our success."

Path–Goal Theory   Mary Molacavage, the lab associate whose stories about control systems appear in Chapter 16, gave a good example of managers using the path–goal theory to lead people when she talked about feedback control. Both of the scientists to whom Mary reports asked her what kind of feedback she would like—one by asking if Mary wanted to be watched while she did a procedure, and the other by asking Mary how many of the procedures Mary was learning she wanted the manager to watch. By involving Mary in the decision-making process, both managers exhibit a participative style of motivation. In Mary's case the participative style is especially appropriate because Mary is a highly trained individual who does believe that she controls her own destiny. By involving Mary in the decision-making process, Mary's managers make it more likely that Mary will be satisfied with her work, and also increase Mary's overall performance.

summary of learning objectives

Organizations need leadership in order to survive and prosper. This chapter has covered the major leadership theories so that you can use your understanding of these approaches as tools to develop your own leadership skills. The chapter material relevant to each of the learning objectives presented at the start of the chapter is summarized below.

1 Distinguish between management and leadership.
- Management is about implementation and control.
- Leadership is about vision and inspiration.

2 Recognize how leaders use different power bases to exercise influence.
- Coercive power
- Reward power
- Legitimate power
- Expert power
- Referent power

3 Identify effective leader characteristics based on person-based theories and recognize the limitations of these approaches.
- Person-Based Theories
  - Trait Theory
  - Behavioral Theories
    - consideration and initiating structure
    - managerial grid
    - leadership style
- Limitations
  - Best leadership approach may depend on situation

4 Recognize how different contexts call for different leadership qualities, using situational theories of leadership.
- Fiedler's Contingency Model
- Path-Goal Theory

5 Identify ways to engender leadership through organizational characteristics or employees by applying dispersed theories of leadership.
- Substitute Leadership
- Self-Leadership

6 Understand, through exchange theories, how to implement leadership through relationships with others.
- Transactional Leadership
- Transformational Leadership

7 Describe and apply the concept of authentic leadership.
- Authentic leadership
  - terminal value approach
  - Ethical behavior and commitment to organizational values requires more than direction and compliance. Leaders need to be proactive in regard to ethics and values and be role models for people in the organization.

discussion questions

1. Do you agree that managers and leaders are different kinds of people? Why or why not?

2. Some people argue that organizations need to put in place mechanisms to prevent informal leaders from imposing their own agenda on others. Do you agree? Why or why not?

3. Think about some people you have met who are excellent leaders and some who have been entrusted with a leadership position yet are highly ineffective. Use the theories discussed in this chapter to analyze what made those individuals effective or ineffective as leaders.

4. Develop your own leadership theory. It can be a combination of the approaches covered in this chapter or you can bring in something entirely new. Why do you think your approach is an effective way to lead?

5. When are the substitutes for leadership most important. Is the need for substitutes decreasing or increasing in today's work environments? Why?

6. How much of a difference do you think a leader can make? Explain your judgment.

7. Differentiate between the major types of leadership theories (person, situation, and so on). Which type do you think offers the best approach?

8. Are there instances when each of the major types of leadership theories would be best? Can you identify the type of situation that would call for each type of leadership approach?

management minicase 13.1

Put It on the Card: What's Your Leadership Message?

Lee Enterprises, Inc., is led by Mary Junck, the company's first woman CEO. Lee owns 44 daily newspapers in 18 states and more than 175 weekly newspapers, shoppers, and specialty publications. The company also has book-publishing, commercial printing, and online operations. Junck took the helm in 1999. The organization sold all of its TV stations that year and has since seen its revenues soar 58.9 percent and its daily circulation increase by 75 percent. By all measures, the organization is doing very well. What accounts for this positive performance?

When asked about what drives the continued high performance at Lee, many employees point to a tool developed by Mary Junck—a card about the size of a business card. Officially known as the "Priorities Card," the card succinctly lists Junck's most important goals. Some of the goals are:

- Growing revenue—creatively and rapidly.
- On-time delivery—meet deadlines and get it there on time.
- Focus coverage on real people.
- Strong local news.

The goals of the Priorities Card are simple and everyone in the organization has one. Greg Veon, a vice president at Lee, says that he always carries a Priorities Card with him. The card brings priorities into focus for everyone in the organization. Kathleen Rutledge, an editor for Lee, points out that the card puts things in black and white, which she finds to be supportive and comforting. For example, including "strong local news" in the set of goals makes a priority that may have always been implicit into an explicit priority.

Discussion Questions

1. The Priorities Card is a very simple tool. Why do you think it is effective?

2. What leadership theory would best capture the Priorities Card approach?

3. Other organizations use cards as well. Find examples of these cards. Are they different from Junck's approach?

4. Would you use a priorities card if you were a leader in an organization? Why or why not?

5. If you were a leader in an organization, what goals would you list on a priorities card?

Adapted from: Anonymous, "All a Matter of Priorities," *Editor & Publisher*, February 10, 2003.

Where Having Fun Really Pays

management minicase 13.2

Garrett Brown, 32, a desktop support specialist for DWL Inc., recently spent the day in simulated dogfights in a World War II Spitfire replica. Even better, he gets an extra $1,000 each year to do it.

DWL is a privately held Toronto customer-relationship management consulting firm founded in the late 1990s, with clients such as Body Shop International and National Life Insurance. Being sure people have fun is part of DWL's day-to-day management. Top executives believe encouraging fun helps morale and retention among the 300 employees, and the company is spending about $500,000 a year on this belief. The company offers $1,000 annually to each employee to do something fun. Trips and cruises are common uses for the money. One employee surprised his father with a trip to a favorite fishing camp. Another bought a guitar, and still another signed up for cooking lessons.

At year's end, the company posts photos of the activities—the more colorful, the better. Sometimes the photograph tells it all. For example, one employee's wife coaches high school girls' volleyball. The employee used his money to tag along on one of his wife's trips to the Caribbean with the girls. His photo of 15 volleyball players carrying him on the beach impressed the panel of five employees voting on who had the most fun during the year.

The winner is awarded $5,000 for next year's activity; two runners-up each receive $2,000. Last year's winner used the money for his avocation: video art. Though he enjoys producing videos, there isn't much local interest in it, so the employee used the money to produce a video and travel to its showing in Amsterdam.

Mark Mighton, VP of Sales Operations, invented the program and earned the informal title of Director of Fun. He reviews the employees' applications for the annual grant, which are usually informal e-mails. About 90 percent of the applications are accepted immediately; the other 10 percent usually are approved on the second try. The typical reason for rejection is that the idea didn't involve having enough fun—a new TV, a mortgage payment, a new bathroom sink, and anything job-related will be rejected. Mighton sets an example with his own choices—in 2001, his African safari was paid for in part by the fun fund.

Justin La Fayette, DWL's CEO and founder, wants everyone to participate to keep work in perspective and to offset the "north of 50-plus, 60-plus hours a week for extended periods" so many employees put in. He sees the fun fund as a way of keeping work and leisure balanced and believes that it is a key factor in the 98 percent retention rate the company boasts as well as a powerful employee motivator. Workers themselves make decisions on how they can best contribute to the company's success and are rewarded both by jobs that are more exciting and by the opportunity and the means to enjoy their time outside the office.

Discussion Questions

1. Based on the material you read in this chapter, how would you characterize the leadership approach used by DWL Inc.'s top management? Explain.

2. Do you think that the leadership style at DWL Inc. would be successful in most situations? Why or why not? If not, explain under what situations it may work better.

3. The focus on fun in some organizations, such as DWL and Southwest Airlines, may seem paradoxical. The more the focus is on fun the greater the performance seems to be. How would you explain this paradox?

Source: D. R. Khurallah, "Where Having Fun Really Pays," *Information Week*, January 15, 2001, p. 87.

individual/ collaborative learning case 13.1

Leaders: Made, Not Born

Leadership positions are often given to people whose performance stands out. Unfortunately some high performers do not have the skills needed to be effective leaders. While some people might appear to be natural leaders, for most people, leadership requires learning a key set of skills. Organizations take a variety of approaches to developing leadership skills.

Targeted Training

Training is aimed at people recently promoted to leadership positions. The management team at Appleton Papers, a manufacturing company in Appleton, Wisconsin, saw too many untrained new supervisors making costly mistakes. The HR department implemented a new supervisor training program that focused on communication, interpersonal, and performance management skills. Company leaders believe the training has returned many multiples of its cost.

Not all such training is equally effective. It is not just an issue of covering content, but how the content is covered. Small nibbles are often better than a big bite. For example, offering brief sessions focused on an aspect of effective leadership provides new leaders the opportunity to practice and apply the skill in the workplace. A month-long full-time leadership course, on the other hand, can be overwhelming. Trainees can have difficulty remembering all of the content.

Training for new leaders may not always be immediately available. Southwest Airlines counters this problem by providing new supervisors with an on-the-job survival guide. The guide is customized to each position and is available online to all new supervisors.

Leadership training isn't just needed by new supervisors. Mid- and upper-level managers sometimes need to improve their leadership skills. General Physics, a training and development company headquartered in Elkridge, Maryland, noted the need for leadership improvement in its operations. According to one of the directors at General Physics, there were difficulties in communication networks, establishing goals, empowerment, and managing performance. In an attempt to make a targeted and positive change in their level of leadership skills, management at General Physics instituted a leadership boot camp. Participants in the boot camp included managers who had been identified as having some difficulty on a leadership skill through a 360-degree evaluation program. Officers of the organization were also included as participants and were expected to learn the materials and act as role models following the program.

The boot camp was meant to both convey material and shock and grab people, thereby convincing them of the importance of effective leadership. The boot camp included an overnight stay, a 5:30 A.M. wake-up call, physical exercise, a gruff presentation by "Sergeant Death," and training activities that continued until 10:00 P.M. The boot camp was effective at General Physics. People proudly hung their boot camp diplomas on their walls and dog tags were made into key fobs. Most importantly, a follow-up study revealed a 17–25 percent improvement in leadership competencies. General Physics now requires the boot camp experience for anyone promoted to a supervisory position.

Diffuse Training

Leadership skills can be important for anyone in an organization. A person may not be in a formal leadership position, but need leadership skills as part of a team or project. In these situations, leadership skills are helpful to everyone. Unisys Corporation, an information technology company headquartered in Pennsylvania, takes a broad-based approach to leadership training. Employees from all ranks are encouraged to take advantage of the program. The goal of Unisys is not to develop 25 key leaders, but to develop 2,500 leaders throughout the organization. Larry Weinback, CEO of Unisys, started the program and acts as its dean. He is a champion for the program and a frequent class speaker. He contends that the leadership training program has had a powerful impact on the Unisys culture.

Critical Thinking Questions

1. Do you think that effective leadership can be learned, or are some people simply born to it?

2. Which approach to leadership training would you recommend, targeted or diffuse? Why?

3. What advantages are there to the diffuse approach? What costs are associated with this approach? Do you think the benefits would be worth the cost?

Collaborative Learning Exercise

Form groups of four or five students. The task for each team is to develop the basics of a leadership training program. Specifically: (a) What leadership competencies would you focus on? (You might research the topic of leadership competencies to generate a comprehensive list to choose from.) (b) What criteria would you use to identify program participants? That is, who would be selected to attend the training? (c) Would your program be targeted or diffuse? Share the essentials of your program with the rest of the class.

Sources: Adapted from K. Tyler, "Sink-or-Swim Attitude Strands New Managers," *HRMagazine* 48 (2003), pp. 78–83; J. Ronan, "A Boot to the System: How Does a Training Company Shake Up Its Leadership Style? It Marches the Managers Off to Boot Camp," *T & D* 57 (2003), pp. 38+; S. F. Gale, "Building Leaders at All Levels," *Workforce* 81 (2002), pp. 82–85.

internet
exercise 13.1

www.businessweek.com

Leading the Pack

In January of each year *BusinessWeek* identifies top managers and entrepreneurs as exemplary leaders and justifies its choices. Visit the *BusinessWeek* Website (www. businessweek.com) and enter "Top 25 Managers" as a search term to access articles from the January issue. Use the results of your search to answer the following questions:

1. Develop a list of 3–10 characteristics that these people have in common.
2. How do differences in leadership style contribute to success?
3. How did the firm's context or situation affect the leadership style among *BusinessWeek*'s top leaders?

manager's
checkup 13.1

Power and Influence

This exercise can help you discover your attitudes toward different kinds of power and influence. Each student should complete the worksheets independently and then meet in groups of three to five students to discuss their answers. Each group also should answer the questions at the end of the exercise and then report their ideas to the entire class.

A. Power Worksheet

Following are some statements about power. Indicate how you feel about each of the statements by circling the corresponding number.

		Strongly Disagree	Disagree	Neutral	Agree	Strongly Agree
1.	Winning is everything.	1	2	3	4	5
2.	Nice guys finish last.	1	2	3	4	5
3.	There can only be one winner.	1	2	3	4	5
4.	There's a sucker born every minute.	1	2	3	4	5
5.	You can't completely trust anyone.	1	2	3	4	5
6.	All power rests at the end of the gun.	1	2	3	4	5
7.	Power seekers are greedy and can't be trusted.	1	2	3	4	5
8.	Power corrupts; absolute power corrupts absolutely.	1	2	3	4	5
9.	You get as much power as you pay for.	1	2	3	4	5

B. Influence Worksheet

1. On the following table, list the first names of people who influenced you during the past week or so according to the kind of power that person used. If a person used multiple power bases, put the name next to all that apply. Indicate whether the influence was positive (+) or negative (−).

Social Power Base	Name	(+ or −)
Coercive	_____	_____
Reward	_____	_____
Legitimate	_____	_____
Expert	_____	_____
Referent	_____	_____

2. Answer yes or no to the following questions about the list in question 1.
   a. Is anyone listed next to several power bases with + after his or her name?
   b. Is anyone listed next to several power bases with − after his or her name?
   c. Do most of the people marked + fall under the same power bases?
   d. Do most of the people marked − fall under the same power bases?

3. From your answers to questions 1 and 2, list which social power bases you found to be positive (+) and which you found to be negative (−). Do you prefer to use those power bases you listed under + when you try to influence people? Do you actually use them?

C. Power and Influence Worksheet

Use the table in the influence worksheet to identify the person having the strongest positive influence on you (Person 1) and the person having the strongest negative influence (Person 2). These persons' names usually appear most frequently in the worksheet.

For each statement that follows, circle the number that indicates how you think Person 1 would respond to it. In a different color, circle the number that indicates how you think Person 2 would respond to it.

		Strongly Disagree	Disagree	Neutral	Agree	Strongly Agree
10.	Winning is everything.	1	2	3	4	5
11.	Nice guys finish last.	1	2	3	4	5
12.	There can only be one winner.	1	2	3	4	5
13.	There's a sucker born every minute.	1	2	3	4	5
14.	You can't completely trust anyone.	1	2	3	4	5
15.	All power rests at the end of the gun.	1	2	3	4	5
16.	Power seekers are greedy and can't be trusted.	1	2	3	4	5
17.	Power corrupts; absolute power corrupts absolutely.	1	2	3	4	5
18.	You get as much power as you pay for.	1	2	3	4	5

Compare your responses in Part A to those in Part C. Do you more closely resemble Person 1 or Person 2? Do you prefer to use the kinds of power that person uses? Which kinds of power do you use most frequently? Which do you use least frequently? When do you feel you have the greatest power? When do you have the least power? How do these answers compare to what you found in Part B?

video summary

Financial Troubles at GM

Summary

General Motors has stood as a "rock of Gibraltar" for the American economy for decades. The company manufactured parts and weapons to carry the United States through World War II. After the war, and the Depression, Americans indulged in new cars—at least half of which were built by GM. Today, GM doesn't even have a quarter of the American automobile market. Its managers are accused of not listening to customers, not listening to employees, and generally turning a blind eye to the needs and trends driving the business.

Pensions, health care benefits and a costly jobs bank are continuing to create steep cost disadvantages for General Motors compared to foreign car manufacturers. GM has worked with the UAW from the organization's beginning. "What was good for the country was good for General Motors, and vice versa" its chairman said in 1953 because, in part, the first corporation to make a billion dollars a year was forced by the United Auto Workers to share its bounty with labor. Between World War II and Vietnam, the real incomes of GM's blue collar workers doubled. Today, health costs are perhaps the biggest burden for the firm: for health insurance costs, current workers pay nothing out of pocket, and retirees pay very little. When you add the jobs bank to the pensions and health care tab, GM has a total cost disadvantage, compared to non-U.S. rivals, of $2,500 or more per car—before it even starts making one.

"The bottom line is, they're paying themselves, their workers and their management more than the value they're creating in the marketplace. They can't sell their cars for a price that will permit them to cover their costs." According to economist Peter Morici, "consumers won't pay a premium for poor GM quality." The big news, according to GM, is that it's finally cutting costs: closing unprofitable plants, negotiating a cheaper health care deal with the union. In addition, GM's become the number one producer of cars in China. So there seem to be some signs of hope.

That former GM chairman once said, what's good for General Motors is good for America. Unfortunately what's happening is what's bad for General Motors is terrible for America. It's disrupting the entire Midwestern economy, and it has broad consequences for the industrial competitiveness of American manufacturing.

Discussion Questions

1. The words *manager* and *leader* often are used interchangeably. Managers, however, are not always effective leaders. Do you think that, with the right leadership, GM can achieve a successful turnaround?

2. Of Fiedler's two major leadership styles, which do you think would go the furthest toward accomplishing the company's new goals and competing with foreign auto makers? Explain your response.

3. What is the basis for path–goal theory? How does that relate to GM's current situation with the UAW?

chapter 14

Managing Teams

Learning Objectives

1. Translate the benefits teams provide into competitive advantages.

2. Identify the different types of teams—self-managed, parallel, project, and virtual.

3. Track the stages of team development that occur over the life of a project and help the team perform effectively.

4. Recognize the key roles that team members must play to ensure high performance.

5. Master the skills to detect and control team performance problems.

6. Manage team conflict through negotiation.

Rapid-Response Teams Save Lives at Tenet Healthcare Corporation www.tenethealth.com

Rapid-response teams avert life-threatening medical catastrophes by aggressively deploying experienced clinical staff to the bedside if a patient's condition becomes ambiguous enough to raise concerns. The teams provide assistance before a situation escalates into a critical event that could lead to serious complications, days in an intensive-care unit (ICU), or even death. Although the teams operate in various modes at hospitals across the country, they often include an ICU nurse, a respiratory therapist, and a hospital staff person. Rapid-response teams are one of six interventions that have been recommended as practices that should be used to reduce thousands of avoidable deaths at American hospitals each year.

In addition to saving lives, rapid-response teams are credited with helping hospitals increase nursing job satisfaction by taking away a layer of stress. At Tenet Healthcare Corporation the teams have provided a strong morale boost for nurses, according to its senior vice president for clinical quality and chief medical officer. Aproximately 80 percent of Tenet's 69 hospitals have rapid-response teams on one or more units.

One research study has reported that rapid-response teams in hospitals produced substantial cost savings by reducing by 75 percent the number of patients admitted to the ICU, which has resulted in savings of millions of dollars.

Source: C. Becker, "Fast Start for Hospitals," *Modern Healthcare*, December 19–26, 2005, pp. 8–9.

CRITICAL THINKING QUESTIONS

1. *What are the benefits of using rapid-response teams to provide medical services to patients in a hospital? How does the use of rapid-response teams compare to a more traditional approach to providing care to patients who have problems with their vital medical signs?*

2. *What type of team most closely matches the rapid-response teams at Tenet Healthcare Corporation? There are four types of teams to choose from: self-managed teams, project teams, parallel teams, or virtual teams. Justify your choice.*

At the end of the chapter in our Concluding Thoughts we will revisit these critical thinking questions regarding the use of rapid-response teams at Tenet Healthcare Corporation.

Many U.S. companies that employ knowledge workers are increasingly using teams to fully engage and empower workers to take advantage of their specialized knowledge. As more work is being performed by teams, the ability to manage them has become an increasingly important skill. This chapter examines the management of teams, beginning with the reasons companies use teams and the different types and design aspects of teams. Key topics include the behavioral issues that must be identified and administered, problems that need to be addressed along with ways to deal with them, and the critical skills needed to effectively manage teams such as those outlined in Skills for Managing 14.1 on page 537.

The Benefits of Teams

In this new millennium, many tasks are far too complex to be completed by a single individual. As a result, the success of various teams and groups directly affects the success of the overall organization.

A **team** is a small number of people with complementary skills who are committed to a common purpose, a set of performance goals, and an approach for which they hold themselves mutually accountable. Team members interact with each other on a regular basis. A team can be as small as two people, such as a telephone company's sales team, composed of a customer service representative and a customer service engineer. Larger teams may be responsible for taking charge of core business processes such as order fulfillment, customer service, or procurement of raw materials and supplies. When the size of a team exceeds 25 members the individuals have difficulty interacting intensively. The range of team size for high-performing teams is between 5 and 12 members. This range in size allows for teams to be large enough to take advantage of the different skills of members and small enough to provide a feeling of community and cohesion among the team members.[1]

Teams share performance goals. Individuals on teams are mutually responsible for end results. The teams at the hospitals discussed in the opening vignette are responsible for patient care. If one person on the team is negligent, all team members are responsible for and affected by the poor care given to the patient.

A quality team environment produces **synergy,** which results when individuals blend complementary skills and talents to produce a product that is more valuable than the sum of the individual contributions. Teams can energize and motivate individuals to perform at consistently high levels, another aspect of synergy.

A **work group** differs from a team. Members of a work group are held accountable for individual work, but they are not responsible for the output of the entire group. For example, a group of accountants in an accounting firm may meet occasionally to discuss auditing procedures. Still, each accountant works individually with clients, and the firm holds the accountant responsible only for that work. The accountants are part of a group, not a team.

Table 14.1 on page 537 lists the differences between a team and a work group. Team members hold themselves mutually accountable for team goals, and leadership responsibilities are shared among the members of the team. They openly discuss goals and procedures with each other until they reach a consensus. A work group is more likely to have a strong, directive leader who seeks input from group members and then delegates work to various individuals to complete.

---

team

A small number of people with complementary skills who are committed to a common purpose, a set of performance goals, and an approach for which they hold themselves mutually accountable.

synergy

When individuals blend complementary skills and talents to produce a product that is more valuable than the sum of the individual contributions.

work group

A group whose members are held accountable for individual work, but are not responsible for the output of the entire group.

SKILLS FOR MANAGING TEAMS

- *Conflict management skills*. Conflict is a natural part of the growth and development of a team. Team members need to be able to recognize the difference between functional conflict, which stimulates team performance, and dysfunctional conflict, which can undermine effectiveness. Different situations call for different approaches to managing conflict.

- *Negotiation skills*. The win–win approach to negotiation is a way to develop a solution that satisfies the needs of both parties. This type of negotiation is particularly effective when it is important to maintain long-term relationships, which is the case with teams.

- *Skills for handling difficult team members*. In cases in which a team member is preventing the team from performing to potential, it is crucial to deal with and motivate the difficult person. Two types of difficult people you are likely to encounter on a team are the "free rider," who tries to get away with doing as little work as possible, and the "nonconforming high performer," who performs well as an individual but does not work well with other people.

table 14.1

Not All Groups Are Teams

CHARACTERISTIC	WORKING GROUP	TEAM
Leadership	Strong, clearly focused leader	Shared leadership roles
Accountability	Individual	Individual and mutual
Purpose	Same as the broader organizational mission	Team purpose that the team itself delivers
Work products	Individual	Collective
Meeting style	Efficient	Open-ended discussion, active problem-solving
Performance measurement	Indirectly, by its influence on others (e.g., financial performance of the business)	Directly, by collective work products
Decision-making process	Discusses, decides, and delegates	Discusses, decides, and does real work together

Source: Reprinted by permission of *Harvard Business Review*. Excerpt from "The Discipline of Teams," by J. R. Katzenbach and D. K. Smith, March–April 1993. Copyright © 1993 by the Harvard Business School Publishing Corporation. All rights reserved.

Effectively managing teams makes it possible for companies to achieve important strategic business objectives, which may result in competitive advantages. The benefits of using teams include lower costs and higher productivity, quality improvements, speed, and innovation. Each is described next in further detail.

Costs and Productivity

When a company delegates management work to teams, team members do many of the things that were formerly carried out by the supervisor, and the organization needs fewer supervisors. Companies can save on the labor cost of surplus supervisors and middle managers. In addition, cross-training team members to have a broad set of competencies allows a significant reduction of the total number of employees required.

Before organizing its auto assembly plants into teams, Ford Motor Company hired more skilled production workers than needed in order to have substitutes available. Using teams meant that cross-trained workers were available to cover for absent employees, making the plants more productive. This allowed Ford to abandon the practice of stockpiling employees.

Quality Improvements

The responsibility for quality now rests with team members who assemble the product or provide the service rather than on an inspector who judges quality after the product is completed. This self-inspection, or "do it right the first time," approach to quality has several advantages. It saves the company money on defective products and wasted raw materials. It can also greatly reduce the labor cost of hiring quality specialists who inspect the work of others.

Quality management experts such as W. Edwards Deming recommend using teams that include employees who deal directly with customers. The goal is to achieve continuous quality improvements.[2] "Small wins" in quality delight customers. These new work methods and practices can be rapidly disseminated throughout the company by quality teams that inform other organizational members about them. Levi Strauss, the manufacturer of casual clothing, used teams to reduce defects in its clothing by 25 percent. The Saturn division of General Motors used self-managed teams to achieve one of the highest levels of customer satisfaction of any U.S. auto manufacturer.[3]

Speed

The responsiveness of a company to the needs of the customer is a vital area of concern. Improved speed reduces the time it takes to fill a customer order. It can shorten the time required to develop a new product. Speed can also improve the responsiveness of a company, such as how quickly an electric company restores service when a power transmission line is downed in a severe storm.

Teams can reduce the time needed to respond to customers. When teams are organized around important business processes, the time to complete the processes can be greatly reduced. A **business process** is a value-adding, value-creating activity such as product development or order fulfillment. Teams reduce barriers between departments that slow the flow of work. An example of such a barrier is the handoff from a bank loan officer to a credit analyst who then lets the paperwork sit for many days before examining the creditworthiness of the customer.

Many companies have taken advantage of improved speed. Kodak cut product development process time in half by using concurrent engineering teams composed of employees with cross-functional skills. Motorola used multiskilled production teams to manufacture a custom paging device within two hours of placement of an order. Southwest Airlines turns around an aircraft from landing to takeoff in 20 minutes by using customer service teams to unload, service, and load the aircraft. This is one-third the time it takes competitors to load and unload planes.

business process

A value-adding, value-creating activity such as product development or order fulfillment.

Teams Give AES Corporation a Competitive Advantage

THEME: CUSTOMER FOCUSED

The AES Corporation is a successful global developer and operator of electric power and steam plants. Company sales are more than $10.8 billion per year and AES has over $29 billion in corporate assets across 26 countries. The company has never formed corporate departments or assigned officers to oversee project finance, operations, purchasing, human resources, or public relations. Instead, these functions are handled at the plant level, where plant managers assign them to volunteer teams.

The front-line employees on teams at AES develop expertise in domains such as finance. They also receive the responsibility and authority to carry out required tasks. While mistakes are sometimes made while learning, the overall results are impressive. The AES team structure saves on management costs because the company has only five managerial levels. This allows AES to optimize the time of specialized staff members such as financial experts. For example, when the company developed a $400 million plant in Cumberland, Maryland, a team of just 10 people obtained more than 36 separate permit approvals and negotiated the complex financing, including tax-exempt bonds and contracts with 10 different lenders. Normally, projects of this scope require hundreds of employees, each with narrow and specific tasks to perform. The savings, increased speed, and flexibility of the AES team-

AES volunteer teams perform tasks that might normally be handled by traditional departments.

based approach are clear and constitute a key source of the company's competitive advantage.

Sources: "AES Corporation: The Global Power Company," www.aes.com (2006); J. Pfeffer, *The Human Equation: Building Profits by Putting People First.* Boston: Harvard Business School Press, 1998, p. 77.

Innovation

The ability to create new products and services can be enhanced with the use of teams. Teams allow companies to innovate more quickly. In high-technology industries, being first to market with a unique or improved product provides a powerful competitive advantage. A cross-functional team composed of people who have knowledge of the market, technologists, and experts in production reduces the cycle time for product development. It is no coincidence that companies known for innovation such as Microsoft and Hewlett-Packard intensively utilize teams in their product development processes. Moreover, recent research reveals that teams composed of members with diverse work experience backgrounds are more innovative and more likely to share information than teams composed of people with similar kinds of work experience.[4]

When engineers at Boeing designed its innovative 777 aircraft, the company's management group relied exclusively on more than 200 teams to design and build major components of the plant. The teams included representatives from nearly every function, including customers and suppliers. They made it possible for the company to build the aircraft right the first time and not incur the cost of altering the configuration after the fact.

Management Close-Up 14.1 above explains how AES Corporation employs teams to achieve and sustain a position as a leading power company.

FIGURE 14.1

Team Characteristics

Source: Based on material from *Compensation for Teams: How to Design and Implement Team-Based Reward Programs* by Steven E. Gross. Copyright © 1995 The Hay Group, Inc. Adapted with the permission of the publisher, AMACOM Books, a division of American Management Association International, New York, NY. All rights reserved. http://www.amacombooks.org.

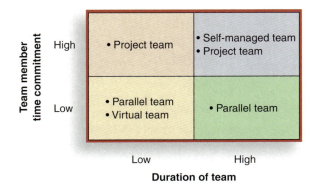

Types of Teams

Just as a mechanic looks for the right tool to do a job, management must identify the right type of team to complete a task or project. The four types of teams normally found in organizations are self-managed teams, project teams, parallel teams, and virtual teams. Each differs in terms of duration (a few months or less compared to several years or more) and the amount of time members are expected to commit to the activities of the team (full-time or part-time). Figure 14.1 above shows where each of these teams fits in terms of duration and time commitment.

LOC-In

① Learning Objective Check-In

1. *Guard Smart Inc. has a matrix structure with a highly developed workforce. The employees receive training to ensure they are current in their respective specialties. To maximize their effectiveness, the employees are all committed to common purposes, depending on which people they are working with at a particular time. The performance goals and approach for achieving them are common among workers, and, perhaps most important, they hold themselves mutually accountable for reaching these goals. Guard Smart employees operate in _____.*

   a. *SDWTs*
   b. *teams*
   c. *work groups*
   d. *focus groups*

self-managed team (SMT)

Sometimes called a *process team*, a group that is responsible for producing an entire product, component, or service.

Self-Managed Teams

A **self-managed team (SMT)**, which is sometimes called a *process team*, is responsible for producing an entire product, component, or service. These teams are formalized as part of the organization's structure. Employees are assigned to them on a full-time basis and they have a longer duration. SMTs utilize employees whose jobs are similar but who may have different levels of skill. Team members combine skills to produce an important organizational outcome, such as an automobile engine (production process) or the installation of a computer system for a customer (customer service process).

Self-managed teams have authority to make many decisions traditionally reserved for supervisors or managers. For example, team members at General Motors's Saturn facility in Spring Hill, Tennessee, schedule work, hire new team members, select appropriate work methods, manage budgets, schedule delivery of raw materials, and maintain quality standards for the work output. There are no supervisors. Each team literally manages itself. Other SMTs utilize a supervisor or manager to direct the work, but this supervisor is a coach rather than a traditional boss who tells subordinates what to do. The SMT or process team concept requires empowerment in order to engage each worker's best mental and physical efforts.

Working as a Team   It takes time for a team to earn the right to manage itself. It is not realistic to expect a team to start out with the ability to manage itself. Here are some indicators that show that a team is moving in the direction of becoming a self-managed team.

- A team is being given more and more responsibilities by management as it proves itself capable of handling every responsibility that it receives.
- Team members have developed processes for working out their differences so that most of the team's time can be devoted to performing its work.
- The style of the team leader is changing from that of being a directive leader who monitors and controls the work of team members to that of a coach who provides feedback and encourages team members to be proactive and make their own decisions.
- The team has many capable team members who each have the potential to lead the team if called upon to do so.

SMT members need to be trained in a variety of skills to become fully functional. These include:

1. *Technical skills.* Team members must be cross-trained to rotate between different tasks or workstations. Cross-training team members offers the SMT greater flexibility to provide speed, efficiency, and quality.

2. *Management skills.* Members of the SMT have the authority to make management decisions. Therefore, they need training in such skills as budgeting, scheduling, time management, planning, goal setting, and judging the performance of peers.

3. *Interpersonal skills.* Team members need effective interpersonal skills to form the team and sustain its performance. They must be able to communicate ideas persuasively, negotiate when there are differences of opinion, and manage conflict when emotions are aroused over important differences in goals. Two important interpersonal skills necessary for all types of teams, conflict management and negotiation, are examined later in this chapter.

Management Is Everyone's Business 14.1 above shows how to know when a team is making progress in becoming a self-managed team.

Saturn retains a high level of customer satisfaction by using self-managed teams.

Project Teams

A **project team** works on a specific project that has a beginning and an end. Team members work full-time until the project is complete and then disband to work on other projects, possibly with different team members. A project team is composed of members from different functions (such as marketing, production, and finance) or different technical disciplines (such as biology, chemistry, and mathematics). Members collaborate to complete the project. A key criterion for judging project team performance is meeting or exceeding deadlines or important milestones leading to completion.

project team

A group that works on a specific project that has a beginning and an end.

David Waxman (standing) goes over potential ad storyboards with his creative team at Spot Runner, an ad agency dedicated to producing inexpensive ads that clients customize. Project teams like this take an assignment from start to finish.

parallel teams

Sometimes called *problem-solving teams* or *special purpose teams*, groups that focus on a problem or issue that requires only part-time commitment from team members.

virtual teams

Groups that use interactive computer technologies such as the Internet, groupware (software that permits people at different computer workstations to collaborate on a project simultaneously), and computer-based video-conferencing to work together regardless of distance.

Project teams have many uses. The Mobil energy company used project teams to reengineer key business processes in order to bring employees closer to the customer. At Massachusetts General Hospital in Boston, the trauma center uses a project team composed of doctors, nurses, interns, and technicians to treat accident victims. The speed at which the trauma center team can respond to the patient's medical condition can make the difference in saving a life.

Parallel Teams

Parallel teams are sometimes called *problem-solving teams* or *special-purpose teams*. These teams focus on a problem or issue that requires only part-time commitment from team members. The employee spends a few hours per week with the parallel team. The remainder of the time is spent working as an individual contributor in a functional department such as accounting. The parallel team does not alter the structure of the organization. Instead, a team is formed to solve a specific problem. When the problem is solved the team is likely to be disbanded. The team may be of short or long duration.

Parallel teams can make important contributions to organizations. *Suggestion teams* offer work method improvements or find new ways to please and delight customers. *Safety teams* reduce accidents and such common work maladies as back injuries or repetitive motion strain. *Selection committees* recruit and select job applicants for professional organizations such as law, accounting, or consulting firms. *Grievance committees* settle employee relations problems.

American Airlines involves nearly the entire workforce in parallel teams. Its 3,500 seven-person suggestion teams have proposed better ways to satisfy customers and save money for the company. In one three-month period, these suggestion teams developed 1,600 suggestions that were adopted, resulting in more than $20 million in cost-saving or revenue-generating improvements.

Virtual Teams

In order to take advantage of interactive computer technologies such as the Internet, groupware (software that permits people at different computer workstations to collaborate on a project simultaneously), and computer-based videoconferencing to enable distant people to work together, **virtual teams** may be formed. These teams are similar to problem-solving teams in that they require only a part-time commitment from team members. Virtual team members interact electronically, rather than engaging in face-to-face interaction typical of problem-solving teams.

Virtual teams permit organizations to link individuals who would otherwise be unable to work together. The most talented technical staff can work on problems that require their special skills. This can be a strategic advantage. Accenture, a global firm that provides information technology (IT) consulting services, can deploy a top IT consultant in the Chicago office and Accenture colleagues from the London and Amsterdam offices to work for a client in Belgium. Using the virtual team saves valuable time and the costs of travel, lodging, and downtime.

Virtual teams also make it possible for companies to cross organizational boundaries by linking customers, suppliers, and business partners to improve the quality and increase the speed with which a new product or service is brought to the market. For example, textbook authors who are university professors form a virtual team with the publishing company's editors and self-employed specialists who design the book and create the graphics.

Because members of virtual teams interact with each other via computers and other forms of electronic communications technology there can be a greater potential for misunderstandings to occur than with other types of teams that have the benefit of face-to-face communication. Therefore several management practices for virtual teams are suggested:[5]

2 **Learning Objective Check-In**

Mr. Fisher has been considering some changes to make the team setup at his company more effective. Right now, teams are used only when there is a specific project that has a beginning and an end. Mr. Fisher sees the need for a different type of team that could operate on an ongoing basis with part-time commitment from certain employees. For example, one team would be tasked with focusing on safety issues, which have had an increasing impact on the firm since its recent expansion. It is important that these employees be on-location so they can assess risks and observe safety issues at the site in person.

1. Mr. Fisher's company currently uses a(n) _____ structure.
   a. parallel team
   b. project team
   c. virtual team
   d. SWT
2. A(n) _____ would be appropriate for addressing the safety issues that the company has been facing recently.
   a. project team
   b. virtual team
   c. parallel team
   d. SWT

- There should be clear team goals and team roles provided that are not in conflict with commitments to other organization units.

- There needs to be a careful implementation of efficient communication and collaboration processes that prevent misunderstandings and conflict between team members.

- It is important to have orientation workshops and other forms of training offered to those who are expected to work in virtual teams as a way to prepare them for the challenges of this type of work.

Managing Team Performance

Team performance requires vigilant management. Teams do not always perform effectively, possibly because of a lack of team spirit, a disruptive team member, or a lack of commitment to team goals. Factors that need to be taken into account in managing effective team performance are the stages of team development, the roles of team members and leaders, and team member behaviors.

Stages of Team Development

Before a team can get started, planning and organizing must take place so that all members understand their roles and how they contribute to achieving team objectives. There are five stages of development: forming, storming, norming, performing, and adjourning.[6] These stages occur in sequence, although they may occur rapidly when a team is under strong time pressure.[7]

Philip Evans and Bob Wolf (pictured) of the Boston Consulting Group worked with Linux, the open-source software community, to protect BCG's system against an encroaching computer virus. The virtual team that assisted them consisted of about 20 people in a dozen different companies and many time zones, most of whom had never met. The team solved the problem in a little over a day.

Seagate Technology, which makes computer storage hardware, flies about 200 employees to New Zealand each year for an annual week of intense team-building exercises that climax with a day-long race in which team members kayak, hike, ride bikes, swim, and rappel down a cliff. CEO Bill Watkins says the exercises break down barriers and make better team players. He urges participants, "Just get involved. Don't be too cool to participate. Some of you will learn about teamwork because you have a great team. Some of you will learn because your team is a disaster."

forming stage

The first stage of team development, which brings the team members together so they can get acquainted and discuss their expectations.

storming stage

A stage in team development in which team members voice differences about team goals and procedures.

norming stage

A stage in team development that is characterized by resolution of conflict and agreement over team goals and values.

FORMING When team members meet for the first time to get acquainted and discuss expectations the group is in the **forming stage.** Basic ground rules are established: What is the purpose of the team? How often will it meet? Should everybody expect to participate?

It is important for team members to begin to develop social bonds during the forming stage. Team leaders may organize a social activity to help members interact and build relationships.

STORMING Team members voice differences about team goals and procedures during the **storming stage.** Differences may involve goal priorities, the allocation of team resources, fair work procedures, role expectations, or the selection of a team leader. These are important issues. All team members must be comfortable with the decisions before the team can perform its task.

Conflict is a normal part of team development. It should be out in the open and not suppressed. Coalitions often form during the storming stage. These subgroups may compete for dominance in setting the team agenda. Such conflict must be managed so that the team can move forward. If it is not properly managed, conflict can halt team development, leading to failure. Team leaders play an important role by defusing the negative aspects of conflict and tapping creative energies so that harmony and cohesion are achieved.

NORMING Conflict resolution and agreement over team goals and values emerge in the **norming stage.** Team members finally understand their roles and establish closer relationships, intensifying the cohesion and interdependence of members. At this point, the members begin to develop a team identity rather than seeing themselves as individuals. The team is in agreement about how to deal with and sanction members who violate important team rules and procedures.

PERFORMING The **performing stage** is characterized by a focus on the performance of the tasks delegated to the team. Team members collaborate to capture synergies between individuals with complementary skills. When situations change and new tasks and priorities emerge, the team adjusts its tactics. When the team receives critical feedback, it has the flexibility to learn from mistakes and make improvements.

The performance stage of team development can be viewed as the payoff of the investment of time and effort by team members. Forcing a team to perform before it has its house in order (by skipping some stages or spending too little time on the earlier stages) is likely to result in a malfunctioning group that is unable to achieve performance expectations.

ADJOURNING   Teams that are designed to disband reach the **adjourning stage** in which the team has completed its work. Team members feel satisfaction about the completion of the team's goals, but they are also anxious about possible new assignments and about separating from friends they made while on the team.

It is a good idea to have a ceremony to celebrate the end of the project or mission when the adjourning stage is reached, especially if the team's work was successful. Team members benefit from feedback on lessons learned that they can apply to future assignments. Teams and outstanding contributors can be recognized in various ways:

1. When a team completed an important project, the owner of Five Star Speakers, a training company in Kansas, closed the office for a half day and took the entire staff to a movie and to a restaurant for coffee afterward.

2. After a team successfully achieved an important deadline at The Gap, headquartered in San Bruno, California, the manager gave a gift certificate for a facial or massage at a spa to each team member.

3. Team members at Naval Publications and Forms Center in Philadelphia preserve the memory of a completed team project with a specially designed pin.[8]

LOC-In

③ Learning Objective Check-In

Bryan, Jackie, and Jenna are members of a virtual team. In April, the team members established ground rules for the team and developed a specific purpose they all agreed on. They went to dinner and got to know one another's professional backgrounds more completely. At the third meeting, in July, Bryan voiced some concerns about the priorities that had been established at the April meeting. Based on what they learned in May, he reasoned, they really should reconsider their priorities, at least for the short term.

1. *Which of the following stages represents the April period in which the members had their first meeting, where they established ground rules?*
   a. *Adjourning*
   b. *Norming*
   c. *Performing*
   d. *Forming*
2. *In which stage did Bryan voice his concerns to the team?*
   a. *Forming*
   b. *Norming*
   c. *Storming*
   d. *Performing*

Roles of Team Members

Roles are expectations regarding how team members should act in given situations. Effective team performance requires the enactment of two roles, the task-facilitating role and the relationship-building role. It is difficult to enact both of these roles equally. Most team members emphasize one or the other.

The **task-facilitating role** places a priority on helping the team accomplish its task goals such as improving quality, satisfying customers, or developing new ideas. Some of the ways team members enact the task-facilitating role include:

1. *Direction giving:* Identifying ways to achieve goals and providing goal clarification.

2. *Information seeking:* Asking questions, identifying knowledge gaps, and requesting other members' opinions.

3. *Information giving:* Providing facts and data, offering judgments.

4. *Coordinating:* Pulling ideas together and helping others understand team members' suggestions and opinions.

5. *Summarizing:* Combining ideas made by team members and drawing conclusions.

The **relationship-building role** focuses on sustaining harmony between team members. This role facilitates improved interpersonal relationships and sustains team morale. The relationship-building role involves:

1. *Supporting:* Praising team members' ideas and recognizing their contributions.
2. *Harmonizing:* Mediating the differences between team members and identifying compromises.
3. *Tension relieving:* Using humor to put others at ease.
4. *Energizing:* Exuding enthusiasm and good spirits to motivate others.
5. *Facilitating:* Acting as a catalyst to smooth interactions between individuals who have difficulty communicating with each other.

Both the task-facilitating and relationship-building roles must be enacted. Some team players must focus on team objectives while others concentrate on maintaining team morale. If they do not, the team is likely to perform inadequately. If all members select the task-facilitating role, for example, the team will not develop past the norming stage because it will not get past the interpersonal conflicts that arise at this point of development.

The Role of the Team Leader

Most teams have leaders who help the teams progress through the stages of development and reach their objectives. Leaders help teams balance task-facilitating and relationship-building roles. They also deal with individuals who cause problems, such as people who dominate discussions, take unrealistic positions, or are so critical they stifle creativity. Their style of leadership is typically similar to that of a coach who: (1) provides feedback to team members ("I like how you answered that customer question"); (2) expresses a shared vision for the team ("Let's see if we can make zero defects for the entire week"); and (3) supports team members ("Tell me what resources you need to achieve our goal, and I will find them for you"). Manager's Notebook 14.1 on page 547 lists ways to be a successful team leader.

Some teams are led by supervisors or managers, who are expected to adjust their leadership style to work effectively with a team composed of subordinates. Parallel teams and project teams are likely to have a manager or supervisor in the role of the team leader. Other teams, especially self-managed teams, may have leaders selected from the ranks. This "lead employee" may be chosen by peers or by management. Some teams are "leaderless," generally those composed of highly motivated and experienced employees. In a sense, all team members are leaders on a leaderless team. Each of the four musicians who make up the Tokyo String Quartet, one of the world's finest chamber music ensembles, is a skilled virtuoso soloist, and the quartet operates more or less as a leaderless team. The automobile manufacturing plants at both Saturn and Chrysler use self-managed teams in their manufacturing process. Table 14.2 on page 547 lists the sim-

LOC-In

4 **Learning Objective Check-In**

Averly is a team member who happens to work in the records department. So he is responsible for providing facts and data that pertain to issues of importance to the company's employees and, sometimes, offering an interpretation of the data. Jenny is another team member, who understands the varied personalities within the team. She is always smoothing the interactions between several of the individuals who have difficulty communicating with each other.

1. *Averly is demonstrating the _____ of team members.*
   a. *team leader role*
   b. *relationship-building role*
   c. *task-facilitating role*
   d. *energizing role*
2. *Jenny is demonstrating the _____ of team members.*
   a. *relationship-building role*
   b. *task-facilitating role*
   c. *team leader role*
   d. *supporting role*

EFFECTIVE WAYS TO ENACT THE ROLE OF TEAM LEADER

How can a team leader positively influence team processes and outcomes?

- *Take care of team members*. Set an example of how you want team members to treat one another and customers. If the leader is self-focused, the resulting negative example for other team members will make the team less effective. Be a strong advocate for team members with management when it is justified, even when it may mean taking the heat for their mistakes or the mistakes of the team as a whole. Your loyalty to the team members will be paid back when they need to make personal sacrifices to reach team goals in high-pressure situations.

- *Communicate with team members*. Effective team leaders are good communicators. Include the entire team in the communication loop by letting team members know what other managers want them to know. Listen to the concerns of team members as well, and communicate their ideas or comments to higher level managers who can respond to these concerns by making changes. Facilitate good feedback and participation from all team members so that effective team decisions can be made.

- *Share power with the team*. Effective team leaders embrace the concept of teamwork in deeds as well as words. Share the power, information, and responsibility with the team members. Have faith in their decisions, even when they might not be the ones you would have made.

- *Learn to relax and admit your ignorance*. Team leaders aren't expected to know everything, and they cannot always be in control. Overcome the fear of looking vulnerable by not knowing the answer to a question—leaders who admit and learn from mistakes earn the respect of team members faster than those who act as if they were always in control. Being open and vulnerable also serves to build trust and improve team relationships. Team members will respond by opening up to each other, which will strengthen team members' bonds with each other.

Source: From *The Leadership Experience*, 3rd ed., by R. L. Daft. Copyright © 2005. Reprinted with permission of South-Western, a division of Thomson Learning: www.thomsonrights.com. Fax 800 730-2215.

table 14.2

Team Leaders at Saturn and Chrysler

TEAM CHARACTERISTIC	SATURN	CHRYSLER
Size	6–15 members	20–25 members
Election of leader	Yes	Yes
Term of leader	3 years	1 year
Premium pay of leader	None	$0.50/hour
Supervisor	None	Yes

Source: From H. Shaiken, S. Lopez, and I. Mankita. "Two Routes to Team Production: Saturn and Chrysler Compared," *Industrial Relations* 36 (1997), pp. 17–45. Copyright © 1997 Blackwell Publishers. Reprinted with permission.

ilarities and differences between these teams. In particular, the self-managed teams at Saturn do not have a direct supervisor, while at Chrysler a supervisor acts as a "facilitator" or coach.

Management Is Everyone's Business 14.2 on page 548 explains why it is important for managers to consider the size of the team when forming teams to do specific tasks.

Marissa Mayer oversees Google teams that look for ways to keep innovation bubbling up at the search engine's headquarters. In her role as leader she meets with teams several times a week to review plans and offer help and support.

Behavioral Dimensions of Effective Teams

Members of effective teams share several behavioral characteristics. They are cohesive with each other, select high performance norms, cooperate, exhibit interdependence, and trust one another.

team cohesiveness

The extent to which team members feel a high degree of camaraderie, team spirit, and sense of unity.

COHESIVENESS   The extent to which members feel a high degree of camaraderie, team spirit, and sense of unity is the degree of **team cohesiveness.** Individuals who are part of a cohesive team are concerned about the welfare of teammates as well as the team as a whole. When teams lack cohesion, individu-

Navy SEALs Are Highly Cohesive and Effective Teams

Some examples of high-performing teams occur outside the world of business in fields such as sports, medicine, and the military. The U.S. Navy SEALs are an elite team of individuals in the military who perform dangerous missions for the Navy. For example, one team of Navy SEALs went behind enemy lines recently to rescue Private Jessica Lynch who was captured during the war between the United States and Iraq in 2003. Other teams of Navy SEALs advanced on Taliban strongholds in Afghanistan during the 2001 war and called in devastating jet bomber firepower that blasted enemy troop concentrations.

While the first four weeks of Navy SEAL training is grueling, they pale in comparison with the fifth week known as hell week. During hell week, recruits swim many miles in cold water in the Pacific Ocean, they row rubber boats for hours on end, they run obstacle courses over and over, they perform grueling calisthenics using 300-pound logs, and they sustain personal insults from trainers. During the entire hell week, recruits sleep perhaps four hours.

About 30 percent of the recruits drop out during the five-day, hell-week experience. This commitment is needed because hell week is followed by months of rigorous underwater training, weapons training, explosives training, parachute training, and a six-month probationary period. The ultimate success rate for recruits is about 30 percent.

Highly cohesive teamwork is essential because SEALs never operate on their own and team members identify totally with the group. Navy SEALs will never leave the battlefield if a fallen SEAL remains. The SEALs show us that rigorous training and a strong sense of cohesion among team members can produce highly effective outcomes.

Sources: J. Morse, B. Bennett, S. Donnelley, and M. Hequet, "Saving Private Jessica," *Time*, April 14, 2003, pp. 66–67; S. Foster, *Managing Quality* (Upper Saddle River, NJ: Prentice Hall, 2001) pp. 333–334; K. Labich and E. Davies, "Elite Teams Get the Job Done," *Fortune*, February 19, 1996, pp. 90–98.

als are less likely to enjoy meetings or social events and to work toward team goals. Members of teams that display cohesiveness are more likely to communicate with and influence each other. This is particularly beneficial when members have a strong attachment to high team performance.

There are ways to positively influence team cohesiveness:

1. Provide ample opportunities for team members to interact with each other during the early stages of team development. Social activities such as ice breaker exercises help stimulate interaction.

2. Ensure that all team members have a voice in determining team goals. When the goals are attractive to all members, individuals are more motivated to participate in activities that intensify team cohesion.

3. Celebrate successful team outcomes with rewards for team members or recognize outstanding individual contributions to the team with an awards ceremony. These celebrations build team spirit.[9]

A good example of a highly cohesive team is given in Management Close-Up 14.2 above, which examines the rigorous training experienced by the Navy SEALs, an elite military unit.

NORMS The shared beliefs that regulate the behavior of team members are its **team norms.** They represent the values and aspirations of the members and are likely to be formed during the forming and norming stages of development. Teams enforce norms with rewards and sanctions.

It is important for teams to develop and enforce norms to govern the behavior of employees who avoid doing their fair share of the work. When a team is cohesive but has weak performance norms, members are likely to tolerate

team norms

Shared beliefs that regulate the behavior of team members.

loafers rather than confront them, making failure more likely. A cohesive team with high performance norms has low tolerance for poor performance and is more likely to be effective. A shirker will feel that all team members are monitoring his or her behavior just as a supervisor would, making it uncomfortable to resist improving performance.

One way to ensure that team members have high performance norms is to select high-performing individuals as members of the team. Students in a management course that required team projects took this approach when they asked their professor to let them form their own teams so they could avoid conflicts with students who expected the rest of the team to do most of the work.

Team performance norms vary according to the mission of the team. At Microsoft, teams of software developers expect to work 80 or more hours a week to complete projects on time. A software developer insisting on a 40-hour weekly schedule would not last very long at Microsoft. Team performance norms influence quantity, quality, attendance at meetings, and open discussion of topics. Teams prohibit taking phone calls at meetings. And norms indicate that the team is more important than any individual, so it is better to be a team player than a star.[10]

cooperation

Team behavior that is manifested in members' willingness to share information and help others.

competitive behavior

Team behavior that views other people as rivals for a limited pool of resources and focuses on individual goals, noncollaboration, and the withholding of information.

interdependence

The extent that team members depend on each other for resources, information, assistance, or mutual support to accomplish their tasks.

pooled interdependence

Team behavior where team members share common resources such as fax and copy machines, supplies, and secretarial support, but most of the work is performed independently.

sequential interdependence

A series of hand-offs of work flow between team members in which output of one team member becomes the input of the next team member, and so forth.

COOPERATION   The willingness to share information and help others reflects the level of **cooperation** in the team. Team members who help achieve goals exhibit useful cooperative behaviors. These behaviors are sometimes at odds with **competitive behaviors,** which view other people as rivals for a limited pool of resources and focus on individual goals, noncollaboration with other employees, and the withholding of information. It is up to the team to nurture cooperative behavior by enforcing norms that reward cooperation and sanction competitive behavior. Rewarding team outcomes can help raise the level of interdependence among team members.

INTERDEPENDENCE   The extent to which team members depend on each other for resources, information, assistance, or mutual support to accomplish their tasks[11] is the degree of **interdependence** present. Tasks that involve teams of musicians giving an orchestral concert or actors giving a theatrical performance require a high degree of interaction and exchange—consequently these tasks are highly interdependent. On the other hand, tasks that involve a dock team unloading boxes of fresh fruit from a large trailer truck require lower levels of interaction, exchange, and interdependence. Three types of interdependence affect teams: pooled, sequential, and reciprocal.

Pooled interdependence is found in teams requiring the lowest amount of reliance on other members. Team members have significant aspects of their jobs where they are relatively independent from one another. With pooled interdependence, team members share some common resources such as fax and copy machines, clerical supplies, and secretarial support, but most of the work is performed independently. Real estate agents in the same branch office may share office space, supplies, copy and fax machines, and the same clerical person, but nonetheless do most of their selling activities independently. Teamwork still matters when pooled interdependence is present. Anyone who has experienced an urgent need to copy an important document for a customer and found the copy machine in a state of disrepair due to the harsh treatment it received from the last user will attest to the need for teamwork.

Sequential interdependence is a series of hand-offs of work flow between team members in which the output of one team member becomes the input of the next team member, and so forth. Each team member in the sequence of exchanges depends on all previous team members to do their portion of the work correctly or else the entire team performance falls short of expectations. For example, automobile insurance companies often organize claims adjustment processes as a sequence of steps acted on by different claims specialists. An insurance team handles an automobile accident claim starting first with the insurance agent who collects accident information from the customer. The agent hands the accident claim over to the accident investigator who inspects the damage to the car and writes a claims report. Finally the case is sent to an accident claims adjuster who coordinates the claims of other parties involved in the accident and determines the payout to the customer. A mistake assessing the damage to the car by the accident investigator diminishes the performance of the entire claims adjustment team, because either an over- or underpayment will be made.

The greatest amount of interdependence, **reciprocal interdependence,** occurs when team members interact intensively back and forth with each other. The output of team member X becomes the input of team member Y, and the output of team member Y returns as the input to team member X. This series of reciprocal exchanges of work between team members continues until the work is judged to meet performance standards. Projects involving research and scientific work are often organized with teams that are characterized by reciprocal interdependence. Software development teams consist of: (1) software design experts that create the computer code, (2) software testing experts that test the software for bugs that reduce the reliability of the software, and (3) technical writers that create technical manuals that explain to customers how to use all the different applications that are built into the software. Software designers, testers, and writers are reciprocally interdependent, as can be demonstrated when software bugs are discovered by testers. The presence of a software bug is a flaw in the code which results in a need to make a modification to the code by the designers. The software code modification may in turn result in the need for revisions to be made to the computer user manual by the technical writers. Each time a software bug is located, this cycle of change is repeated until all the bugs are eliminated.

Research on team performance has revealed that high levels of task interdependence which require interactions between team members to obtain critical resources correspond to higher levels of performance. Team members that are highly dependent on one another develop solutions more quickly, finish more tasks, and perform better than those on teams whose members are not highly dependent upon one another.[12] Figure 14.2 on page 552 illustrates the three types of interdependence between three employees, X, Y, and Z doing tasks that result in producing an output that is dependent on their collective efforts.

TRUST Team members are mutually accountable. If one member makes a serious error, it reflects on the performance and reputation of all team members. **Trust** is the willingness of one person to increase his or her vulnerability to the actions of another person whose behavior he or she cannot control.

All teams require trust between members. Self-managed teams require the highest degree of trust. Supervision of a self-managed team is performed by team members who are mutually vulnerable. They evaluate, reward, and even discipline each other. When trust is present, there is a much greater likelihood that team members will cooperate to complete critical tasks.

Trust can be created among team members by:

1. *Communicating openly.* At team meetings and in face-to-face conversations, strive to be open and honest. Share thoughts and feelings with team members when they relate to the business of the team.

reciprocal interdependence

The greatest amount of interdependence that occurs when team members interact intensively back and forth with each other until their work is judged to meet performance standards.

trust

The willingness of one team member to increase his or her vulnerability to the actions of another person whose behavior he or she cannot control.

FIGURE 14.2

Types of Interdependence

Pooled Interdependence

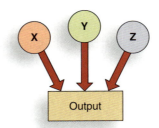

Sequential Interdependence

Reciprocal Interdependence

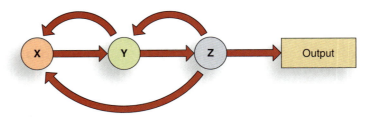

2. *Sharing credit with others.* Do not take credit for more than your fair share of the team's success. Be generous with praise and recognition for the contributions of other teams.

3. *Reciprocating help from teammates.* Look for ways to help teammates, and reciprocate goodwill so teammates feel that their efforts are appreciated.

4. *Avoiding acting purely out of self-interest.* Find ways to align your needs with the interests of the team and other team members.

Team Performance Problems

Several problems within teams make it difficult to succeed. Trust and cooperation are absent or weak in malfunctioning teams and performance suffers. Managers and team members must try to determine the cause of poor team performance and implement changes to improve it. Manager's Notebook 14.2 on page 553 identifies typical team performance problems a manager can expect to encounter. Three of the most challenging problems are free riders, the nonconforming high performer, and the lack of rewards for teamwork.

Free Riders

free riders

Individuals who find it rational to withhold effort and provide minimum input to the team in exchange for a full share of the rewards.

Individuals who find it rational to withhold effort and provide minimum input to the team in exchange for a full share of the rewards are known as **free riders,** which is also called *social loafing* or *shirking*. It takes place because individuals can hide behind the collective effort of the team and get "lost in the crowd." When free riders are tolerated, other members may reduce their efforts ("Why should I work hard when free riders profit at my expense?") and team productivity suffers as a result.

THREATS TO EFFECTIVE TEAM PERFORMANCE

1. *Free riders*. Free riders do not participate in team efforts, but they expect to take credit for team success and receive a full share of team rewards. Free riders can quickly reduce team morale and productivity if their behavior is tolerated.

2. *Dysfunctional team conflict*. Teams can become dysfunctional if some members take a personal dislike to others or engage in political maneuvers and games. Factions within the team that compete for power by rewarding friends and punishing enemies are often the result. Infighting among these factions redirects team energies to political goals of the factions rather than the performance goals of the team and the organization.

3. *Groupthink*. Groupthink is a malady that happens when the team is intolerant of a healthy diversity of opinions—teams come to value agreement and consensus and avoid the functional conflict over real differences that can positively influence the team's performance. Groupthink undermines the purpose of most teams: the combination of people with different skills and experiences to create something more valuable than what the individual could have accomplished alone.

4. *Self-management opposition*. Team members may not want to be self-managed. Some teams are composed of individuals who prefer to have leaders direct and inspire them and who prefer less involvement in the actual decision making. Teams that desire a strong leader but who are forced to become self-managing typically will not be successful.

5. *Insecure supervisors*. Many team initiatives are derailed by supervisors and managers who feel threatened by any proposed change. Some supervisors may feel that self-managed teams reduce their status when the teams take on some of the supervisor's responsibilities. These supervisors may resist and undermine the success of self-managed teams. Unless supervisors have a reason to support teams, they may meet this approach with strong resistance.

6. *Disruptive high performers*. A high-performing team member may demand special treatment and treat other team members disrespectfully. Disruptive high performers often cost the team more in terms of cohesiveness and total outcome than their special talents warrant.

7. *Lack of teamwork rewards*. An organization that expects people to work productively in teams might nevertheless reward employees based on their individual contributions. This bias toward individual performance rather than team performance reinforces competition among team members to be seen as individual achievers rather than cooperative workers. It creates strong disincentives for teamwork to take place.

Sources: Adapted from A. Sinclair, "The Tyranny of Team Ideology," *Organization Studies* 13 (1992): 611–626; L. R. Gomez-Mejia and D. B. Balkin, *Compensation, Organizational Strategy, and Firm Performance*. Cincinnati: South-Western, 1992.

Free riders take advantage of the difficulty managers face in separating out each team member's contribution to the overall outcome. Fortunately, there are a number of ways to deal with free riders before they undermine team morale. The best approach is to make it difficult for individuals to profit from free riding:

- Empower team members to have control over the recruitment and selection of new members. Front-line employees have more opportunities than managers to observe co-workers and know their work habits.

- Empower team members to have a voice in evaluating and disciplining peers who are not performing up to expectations. This makes it more difficult for free riders to loaf without consequences. For example, Unisys, a computer information systems company, requires that performance reviews be carried out by the team leader and three peers chosen by the employee. A poor evaluation may result in a diminished team bonus for the poorly performing member.

- Ensure that high performance norms are established early in the life of the team so that each member clearly understands performance expectations. Social controls, such as shunning those who violate performance norms, are more effective at eliminating free riding than monitoring by the supervisor. Managers can influence the development of norms by articulating a shared vision and mission that captures the imagination of the team and that spells out the expectation that each individual must provide a high level of effort.

The Nonconforming High Performer

nonconforming high performer

A team member who is individualistic and whose presence is disruptive to the team.

Teams have procedures to deal with poor performers and individuals who violate a norm. These include disciplining the offending party through peer group pressure and giving the individual strongly worded critical feedback during a performance evaluation. A greater challenge is dealing with a high-performing team member who is individualistic and whose presence is disruptive to the team.

Sports teams and the entertainment industries have many examples of high-performing individuals with outsized egos who expect star treatment. Allen Iverson, an all-star guard on the Philadelphia 76ers professional basketball team and the league's most valuable player in 2000–2001, has been a difficult player to manage. Despite being an excellent player in games, Iverson had missed team practices as well as flights to games with team members. He also recorded songs that are disrespectful to women. Iverson's behavior had a negative impact on the team's morale, his coach, and the team's fans. In the 1990s, television actresses Roseanne, of the "Roseanne" show, and Brett Butler, the star of "Grace Under Fire," drove out a succession of writers and producers. The executive producers for these popular programs, Marcy Carsey and Tom Werner, were sometimes criticized for caving in to the stars' demands and for being inhospitable to writers. Carsey and Werner brushed aside the criticism. Such stars "have a lot on the line," says Carsey. "And any kind of nervousness, insecurity on their part is totally natural and very healthy."[13]

Must high performers conform and be treated like everybody else on the team or be asked to leave? The answer is, "it depends." Japanese corporations have a motto that "the head that sticks out gets pounded," which means that there is little tolerance for nonconforming behavior on Japanese teams. Those who ignore norms cause other members of the team to lose face, the personal dignity that is vitally important in Japanese culture. The United States has a more individualistic culture and is more tolerant of quirky behavior, even on teams.[14]

Sometimes it is better to channel the star's creative energies into the work of the team. A high performer who deserves special recognition should receive it. Some high performers simply want recognition for their contributions. Sports has most valuable player awards, and film has the Oscars. There's no reason why a business cannot have a recognition event for high contributors to team success.

Some teams are less cohesive and more individualistic than others. These teams can better tolerate a nonconformist.[15] Nonconforming high performers can succeed on problem-solving teams, virtual teams, and project teams where the intensity of team interactions is low compared to self-managed teams. A nonconformist is less likely to upset other team members on a virtual team because they are interacting via computer terminal, while an egotistical team member may quickly get on the nerves of others on a self-managed team because there are many more opportunities for face-to-face interactions.

Working as an Individual   It is important to know how to cope with disruptive team members. Since team members are mutually dependent on each other for shared outcomes a direct confrontation with another team member can quickly escalate into a conflict and harm the performance of the team. Here are some suggestions for how to cope with team members who have annoying habits.

- Use supportive communication and collaborative approaches to deal with team behaviors that are problematic. For example, if a team member habitually arrives late and interrupts team meetings, it is a good idea to announce an odd starting time (9:43 A.M.) for the meeting to emphasize the need for promptness and establish a "latecomer kitty" for refreshments.

- A positive way to handle the "silent distractor" who reads a newspaper, rolls their eyes, or fidgets while other people are speaking is to ask the person questions and draw him or her into the conversation.

- A useful approach to deal with an individual who tries to dominate a team meeting by talking excessively would be to establish rules that allow each team member to express their input and limit the time for discussion for each item on the meeting agenda. These rules have some similiarities with the nominal group technique described in Chapter 6. A team member can be assigned a role as a timekeeper to keep the agenda moving so that the meeting does not take more than the alloted amount of time.

Management Is Everyone's Business 14.3 above offers some suggestions on how you can deal with disruptive team members in a positive way.

Lack of Rewards for Teamwork

A problem common to many organizations that utilize teams is that there are few if any rewards for teams that meet or exceed performance goals. These same organizations provide merit pay and other rewards for individual performance. When the only rewards are for individual performance, employees are likely to compete with each other for the incentive pay. This undermines the willingness to collaborate and team cohesiveness. For example, scientists at the National Institute of Standards and Technology (NIST), a U.S. government research laboratory, are expected to work on project teams with scientists from different disciplines. However, the main reward is merit pay, which rewards individual scientific contributions such as publishing research in leading scientific journals or making presentations at prestigious scientific conferences. Managers determine which scientists receive merit pay by comparing all the scientists and ranking them. These same managers have found it difficult to motivate the scientists to work on team projects that produce results for the good of the laboratory.

The lesson is that teamwork must be rewarded to strengthen and sustain team effort. Rewards can be monetary (such as a team bonus) or nonmonetary (such as a recognition). Other ways to reward teamwork include:

- Develop a "reward and recognition" committee that has a budget to recognize outstanding team performance with monetary or nonmonetary rewards that are meaningful to the team members. The committee should be composed of representatives from various teams and managers. It should design team reward policies and then administer rewards to deserving teams.

(5) Learning Objective Check-In

1. *Karyn is a team member who consistently performs above expectations on an individual basis. Her role as a team member is very important but Karyn is constantly seeking special recognition because she thinks she is doing more than her fair share. The other members tell her that the work she is doing is good but not always necessary and even disruptive. Karyn's team is highly cohesive and shuns expressions of individuality, putting team recognition ahead of personal status. Which of the following characterizes Karyn?*

   a. *The nonconforming high performer*
   b. *The free rider*
   c. *The loose cannon*
   d. *The insecure supervisor*

- Involving customers in the team reward process. For example, customers could nominate a team for a cash bonus or recognition reward. Xerox recognizes its customer service teams in this way.

- Using team rewards to complement pay policies that reward employees for their work as individuals. Team-based pay does not have to replace merit pay. Employees will be less likely to neglect their team responsibilities because they will be motivated to focus their best efforts on both individual and team goals in order to realize their total potential earnings.[16]

Team Management Skills

Teams must advance through stages where conflict and differences between members are normal. If members get stuck on important issues because of conflict, the team fails to achieve its potential, and performance suffers. Two management skills—conflict management and negotiation—are critical for team members and team leaders.

Conflict Management Skills

Conflict arises when members disagree over team policies, goals, or the motives and values of other team members. People are always going to have differences of opinion. Conflict is a normal part of the work of teams. But if conflict is not managed effectively, team members will focus on the dispute rather than on team performance. The first step in managing conflict is determining whether the conflict is functional or dysfunctional.

functional conflict

Conflict that stimulates team and organizational performance.

FUNCTIONAL CONFLICT There are times when conflict stimulates team and organizational performance. We refer to this as **Functional conflict**. As suggested in Figure 14.3 on page 557, moderate levels of conflict can have a positive influence on the team and the organization, because:

- *Creativity is stimulated.* Various positions can be contrasted when team members advocate differing approaches to achieving a goal. The debate can engage each member to express an opinion and even come up with a creative compromise that was not obvious until the conflict put the issues into perspective. Teams in creative fields such as advertising or consulting rely on the tensions embedded in conflict to develop innovative solutions for clients.

- *Poor solutions are avoided.* People often become emotionally attached to their ideas. Disagreements over a goal or a decision alternative may lead to conflict. If the conflict is over an issue that affects team performance, the conflict is functional. When team members feel free to openly express their opinions and disagree with others, poor choices are avoided.

Online **LearningCenter**
www.mhhe.com/gomez3e

Styles of Handling Conflict

FIGURE 14.3

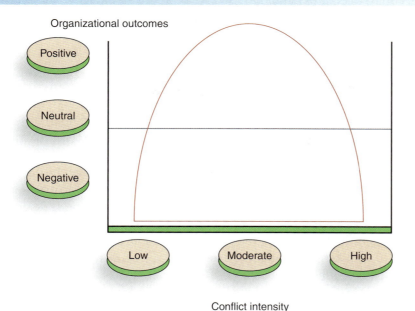

FIGURE 14.3

Intensity of Conflict and Organizational Outcomes

Source: From L. David Brown, *Managing Conflict at Organizational Interfaces*, 1983. Reprinted with permission of L. David Brown.

- *Team members are energized.* Conflict excites and arouses individuals. Moderate conflict can energize people to exert more effort toward team goals. Debates are an excellent way to motivate students to learn about a topic in economics such as capitalism or markets. When students take sides in a highly charged debate, their motivation to learn about the topic increases.

When team members have a disagreement over ideas, plans, and projects, referred to as *task conflict*, the differences between individuals tend to be depersonalized. In many cases task conflict is functional to the team because it can stimulate creativity by forcing people to rethink problems and come up with solutions that everyone can be satisfied with.[17]

DYSFUNCTIONAL CONFLICT   Some forms of conflict have negative effects on team and organizational performance. This **dysfunctional conflict** occurs when the intensity of the conflict is high, which is disruptive to team performance, or when the intensity is pervasive but too low, which results in lack of stimulation. When individuals on a team develop a personal dislike for each other based on personality clashes, anger, or interpersonal tension, there exists a *relationship conflict* within the team. Relationship conflict is dysfunctional and interferes with the team's productivity because team members are focused on reducing tension between the conflicting individuals and improving cohesion rather than working on the task at hand. Relationship conflict can appear to be a dispute over goals or resources when in reality the conflict is between people whose personalities are in conflict. Individuals in a relationship conflict may try to keep their personal dislike of each other hidden from other team members, which only allows it to simmer. It is important for the team to discover the nature of a relationship conflict so that it can find ways to manage it so that it does not disrupt team performance.

Manager's Notebook 14.2 (see item no. 3 there) introduced the idea of **groupthink,** which occurs when team members prefer to avoid conflict rather than tolerate a healthy diversity of opinions. This results in traditional and

dysfunctional conflict

Conflict that has a negative effect on team and organizational performance.

groupthink

Team behavior that occurs when members prefer to avoid conflict rather than tolerate a healthy diversity of opinions.

conservative decisions which are likely to be unsatisfactory and even danger-ous. It is important to find ways to manage groupthink, which may be thought of as dysfunctional *avoidance* of conflict.

People tend to have different *conflict management styles*, based on placing dif-ferent emphasis on concern for their own needs and concern for the needs of oth-ers. The various styles of conflict management include integrating, obliging, dominating, avoiding, and compromising. Each is appropriate in different situa-tions. It helps to have a repertoire of conflict management styles to draw upon.

The **integrating style,** or *problem-solving style*, is used when the manager or team member can frame the issue as a problem and encourage the parties to iden-tify the problem, examine alternatives, and agree on a satisfactory solution. The solution depends on the negotiating skills of the parties. This style enables each party to achieve its interests. The integrating style provides effective long-term solutions to conflicts, enabling the parties to come to a consensus and get on with the work. It is also time-consuming and does not work when immediate conflict resolution is needed.

An **obliging style,** or *smoothing style*, may be used when the party manag-ing the conflict is willing to neglect his or her own needs in order to accommo-date the needs of the other party. The individual decides to smooth over the conflict and focus on similarities with the other party. This style creates a win for the other party and a loss for the individual making the accommodation. It pro-vides a short-term resolution to conflict, but the solution may give rise to resent-ment that may later cause a new conflict.

A **dominating style,** or *forcing style*, may be used when the manager or team member acts in an assertive and forceful way and persuades the other party to abandon his or her objectives. The dominating style is a top-down approach to managing conflict. When time is critical and there is an emergency, this style may be the most effective way to proceed. When a verbally aggressive team member uses it to intimidate another team member during a discussion of values, the style is inappropriate and intensifies rather than mitigates conflict.

An **avoiding style** is used when the individual decides it is better to avoid the conflict rather than deal with it. It can be effective when the issues are trivial and avoiding can be used to buy time. The avoiding style will be ineffective when applied to more serious issues. If all team members have a tendency to use the avoiding style, the team is highly likely to suffer from groupthink and lag in performance.

A **compromising style** may be used when the manager or team member makes some concessions to the other party and the other party is willing to re-ciprocate. When this happens, a give-and-take resolution is reached. The com-promising style requires the parties be able to "split the difference" over the issues in dispute. This style may be effective when resources can be shared. It may be inappropriate when values or principles are the source of the conflict. In some cases, compromise results in a solution that is of low quality and unacceptable to all team members.

APPLYING THE PROBLEM-SOLVING STYLE OF CONFLICT MAN-AGEMENT
The problem-solving style of conflict management offers the best opportunity for both parties in a dispute to achieve their interests. It can be used when the parties are willing to communicate openly and disclose their interests to each other. They must be able to explore different ways to reach mutually sat-isfying solutions. In many cases, the interests of a party may be different than that party's stated position. While a party's stated position may focus on competition

---

integrating style

Conflict resolution demonstrated by framing the issue as a problem and encouraging the interested parties to identify the problem, examine alternatives, and agree on a solution.

obliging style

Conflict resolution demonstrated when the party managing the conflict is willing to neglect his or her own needs in order to accommodate the needs of the other party.

dominating style

Conflict resolution used when the manager or team member acts assertively and forcefully and persuades the other party to abandon his or her objectives.

avoiding style

Conflict resolution used when the individual decides it is better to avoid the conflict rather than to deal with it.

compromising style

Conflict resolution used when the manager or team member makes some concessions to the other party and the other party is willing to reciprocate.

over a limited resource or opportunity that each party wants, a party's interest may be reached by other means. For example, an employee's stated position in a conflict over her work schedule with a manager could be to avoid working overtime hours in order to be able to coach her daughter's soccer team which plays games late in the afternoon. The employee's interest, which is to spend time with her daughter in the late afternoon, may be achieved with a more flexible work schedule, allowing her to do some of the work at home, which may also satisfy her manager's need for overtime work to be performed.

Applying the problem-solving approach to conflict management, a meeting should be convened at the right time and place when both parties are feeling motivated to resolve the conflict. After the problem-solving discussion between the parties gets under way, there may be times when one or both parties become angry or frustrated with each other. Time out may need to be taken at these points to allow the parties to cool down. Later, after the cooling-off period, discussions can resume until a workable resolution is achieved.

Becky, an advertising account executive, used the problem-solving style of conflict resolution with her team. Becky managed an account team at a busy advertising agency. The team worked hard and played hard. In return Becky was flexible about time off for team members. Recently, Becky felt that they were prioritizing their social lives above meeting work deadlines. Having stayed late to finalize urgent jobs for clients, she felt angry that tasks had been left for her to complete. Becky called a team meeting and calmly and assertively stated how she felt about the team's behavior. She explained that in taking on their work, her own work had not been completed on time, putting potential new business at risk. Becky asked the team for ideas to solve the problem. They all agreed that with privileges on time off came responsibilities for seeing jobs through. The result of this problem-solving discussion with the team was that Becky was able to complete her work and rely on her team to take their responsibilities seriously. Becky was able to resolve the conflict because she was able to state how her team's behavior had affected her. She explained what she wanted to happen instead and was willing to explore ideas to overcome the problem with her team.[18]

Unfortunately the willingness of both parties in a conflict to communicate openly is not always present, and this is needed for the problem-solving style to be effective. For example, at times parties in a conflict may not want to reveal their interests to each other because they have hidden agendas. The hidden agendas may be to "get even" with the other party because of real or imagined causes attributed to the other person. Problem solving in this case is pointless, because one or both of the parties are not willing to cooperate to solve the problem. In this hidden agenda situation, a different conflict management style such as the avoiding approach will be more appropriate.

SELECTING A CONFLICT MANAGEMENT STYLE   A useful approach to selecting a conflict management style is to examine the conflict situation according to the chart presented in Figure 14.4 on page 560. The figure matches a person's combined level of assertiveness and cooperativeness to one of the five conflict management styles: problem solving, smoothing, dominating, avoiding, and compromising. Assertiveness means a person is willing to satisfy his or her own concerns. Cooperativeness occurs when a person attempts to satisfy the other party's concerns. Since conflict management is a dynamic process, a party that behaves in an uncooperative fashion is likely to be treated the same way by the other party. Therefore, styles that depend on cooperativeness such as the problem-solving and smoothing styles cannot be used. The mutual uncooperativeness enacted by the parties would result in the use of either the dominating

FIGURE 14.4

Five Conflict-Handling Styles

Source: Adapted from K. Thomas, "Conflict and Conflict Management," in *Handbook of Industrial and Organizational Behavior*, ed. M. D. Dunnette. New York: John Wiley, 1976, p. 900.

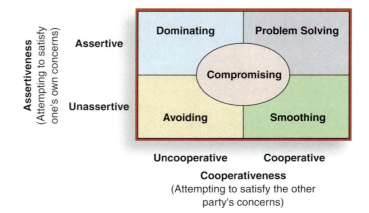

or avoiding styles of conflict management. An assertive party will select the dominating style while a less assertive party will select the avoiding style.

When the parties strive to be cooperative with each other, they can select the problem-solving or smoothing styles, but not the dominating or avoiding styles. The problem-solving style provides the most promising opportunity to reach long-term solutions because both party's concerns are likely to be met. However, if a party in the conflict does not behave in an assertive way the smoothing style may be selected to reach a resolution. Smoothing solutions may provide a short-term conflict resolution for the unassertive party, but it will not be satisfying to this party in the long term since one's concerns were not satisfied. Finally, if the parties in the conflict are only moderately assertive and cooperative as shown in Figure 14.4, a compromising style of conflict management is selected. In the compromising style the parties have moderate concern for their own interests and those of the other party. Compromises can be effective in some situations and not in others, since the compromise produces solutions that partially satisfy the concerns of each party but do not fully satisfy the concerns of either party.

Negotiation Skills

Negotiation skills are used in situations where people attempt to exchange goods and services and to find a fair price or solution. The problem-solving style of conflict management relies heavily on negotiating skills. Negotiation skills can also be used in negotiating a raise, settling on the price of a house, or agreeing on a fair procedure to allocate overtime hours.

win–win style

Negotiating style requiring all interested parties to convert a potential conflict into a problem-solving process in which each party seeks to identify common, shared, or joint goals.

One of the most useful negotiation skills is the **win–win style** of negotiation, which is also referred to as *integrative bargaining*, as it employs the *integrative* problem-solving style discussed in the previous section. The win–win negotiating style requires the parties to convert a potential conflict into a problem-solving process in which each party seeks to identify common, shared, or joint goals. In a sense, each party is looking for solutions that are good for everyone. This is particularly important when they are involved in a long-term working relationship. (See Skills For Managing 14.2 on page 561.)

To make use of the win–win negotiating style:

1. Prepare for negotiation by understanding your own needs and strengths and weaknesses. Determine your own bottom line.

2. Attempt to understand the other party's real needs and objectives. Engage in a dialogue in which both parties disclose their true preferences and priorities, rather than disguise and manipulate them.

NEGOTIATION FOR A PAY RAISE

This exercise applies win–win negotiation skills in a business situation that is common to many managers and employees—negotiating a pay raise.

Many managers are faced with the situation where one of the employees under their supervision asks for an increase in pay. The negotiation can be sensitive. The manager and employee are likely to be in a long-term employment relationship, and if one party "wins" at the expense of the other in the context of negotiation, it could strain their working relationship. A win–win negotiation style seems to be most appropriate for this situation.

Instructions: Find one partner to work with in this exercise. One person takes the role of the employee seeking a pay raise, and the partner takes the role of the manager. Together, explore ways to turn a request for a pay raise into a win–win negotiation where the outcome is a settlement that is satisfactory to each party. Following are the constraints of the negotiation situation:

1. The manager must follow the salary guidelines provided by the policy and cannot make a special exception for this employee.

2. The employee has already received a pay raise this year but feels it is inadequate and is not due for another pay raise until next year.

3. The manager wants to preserve the motivation of this employee, who is a good performer in the unit.

Discuss how you and your partner would approach the salary negotiation and answer the following questions.

Discussion Questions

1. How should the employee frame the request for a pay raise to the manager to get a more favorable outcome? What kind of information should the employee focus on?

2. How should the manager frame the answer to the request to the employee to get a more favorable outcome? What kind of information should the manager focus on?

3. What are the areas of agreement between the two parties? What are the areas of disagreement between the two parties?

4. What are some possible solutions that would be acceptable to both parties?

---

3. Emphasize the commonalities and minimize the differences between the parties. Reframe goals as part of a larger collaborative goal. For example, the team goal of providing customer satisfaction is a common goal on which both parties agree, although they may differ on specific approaches to achieve it.

4. Search for solutions that meet both parties' goals and objectives. When parties are combative or competitive, they are more likely to focus on their own objectives and ignore those of the other party. A win–win negotiation is successful only when the needs of both parties are met.

5. Focus on building a relationship in a negotiation rather than making a one-time deal.[19]

One other style of negotiation that can be used in limited situations is the **win–lose style** of negotiation, sometimes referred to as *distributive bargaining*. The win–lose negotiating style is typically used when there is a single issue that consists of a fixed amount of resources in which one party attempts to gain at the expense of the other. Therefore, the win–lose negotiation is concerned with who will receive the most beneficial distribution of a fixed amount of goods. A negotiation between a buyer and seller of a used car may take the form of a win–lose negotiation regarding the car's price. The seller is interested in obtaining the highest price and the buyer is interested in obtaining the lowest price for the car.

win–lose style

Negotiating style used when there is a single issue that consists of a fixed amount of resources in which one party attempts to gain at the expense of the other.

Win–lose negotiating styles have limited applications on teams because team members are mutually accountable and interdependent on each other to achieve their common goals. Moreover, parties involved in a win–lose negotiation are most likely to use the dominating style of conflict management. Successful win–lose negotiation outcomes depend on a party's ability to impose its will and convince its opponent that the costs of disagreement with its terms are high. The party that can impose the highest costs of disagreement to its position achieves the most concessions from the opposing party.

Behaviors typical of a win–lose style include deception, exaggerating one's strengths, threats, bluffs, and withholding information that would be helpful to the other party. A job applicant who is desperate for a job may enter into a win–lose negotiation with an employer who may use his ability to impose high costs (the threat of no job offer) on the job applicant and pressure her to take a job offer at a much lower salary than she wants. As this example shows, success in win–lose negotiation depends on the ability of each party to take advantage of and exploit the weaknesses of the other party. Win–lose negotiating styles should be used sparingly and only in exceptional circumstances. Most management processes require developing effective, collaborative, long-term relationships between employees, customers, and other parties. These relationships will be impaired when win–lose negotiating styles are used. The party that "loses" the negotiation is not likely to have positive feelings toward the "winner."

Finally, there are three common mistakes that inexperienced negotiators should be aware of and try to avoid making:

- *Do not assume that a negotiation must always result in a settlement.* When a person assumes that a negotiation must result in a settlement, the other party can take advantage by threatening to end the negotiations. This can result in unnecessary concessions being made to facilitate a settlement. It is a better practice to enter a negotiation with a resistance point in mind. The resistance point represents one's minimum acceptable position for a settlement. If the other party refuses to at least meet your resistance point in negotiations then it is better to walk away and end the negotiations.

- *Avoid becoming fixated on one particular issue in the negotiation.* Some issues are easier to settle than others in a negotiation. If the parties get stuck on an issue and find their positions frozen and lacking a settlement, it is best to move on. Settle other issues that are less difficult to agree on. In many cases the goodwill that is established between the parties when they can resolve the easier issues provides the momentum that enables the parties to collaborate and finalize the difficult issues that remain.

- *Do not assume that the other party has all the power due to greater levels of experience.* If you assume that you are powerless in a negotiation, there is a good chance you will act as if that assumption were true. You will be less apt to reach your goals. In truth, each party to a negotiation has some power— otherwise the negotiation would not take place. People negotiate because each party perceives that its counterpart controls something that it wants in an exchange. By being aware of both your interests and those of the other party, you can negotiate more confidently and increase your chances of reaching a satisfying settlement.

LOC-In

6 **Learning Objective Check-In**

1. *Harry believes that James is receiving way more money than he should out of the team budget. Harry's reasoning is that his work is more essential to the long-term success of the team and that James's work can wait until next year to get funded. Harry and James disagree, but they agree that it is important for only one of them to proceed with the bulk of funding and that resolution must be achieved before the next disbursement of funds occurs. In this situation, it would be appropriate to use the _____ of negotiation to solve this problem.*
   a. *bureaucratic management style*
   b. *lose–lose style*
   c. *win–win style*
   d. *win–lose style*

CONCLUDING THOUGHTS

After the introductory vignette at the beginning of this chapter we presented some critical thinking questions related to the use of rapid-response teams at Tenet Healthcare Corporation. Now that you have had the opportunity to learn about teams and managing teams, look back at these questions at the beginning of the chapter. The rapid-response teams provide several critical benefits to patients in a hospital. The teams provide medical intervention in time to prevent life-threatening catastrophes. The teams also boost the morale of nurses who work long hours in demanding working conditions. They reduce the level of stress experienced by nurses, who are able to provide better care to patients when their stress level is under control. Traditional approaches without the teams may have resulted in a higher mortality rate for patients and higher levels of stress and lower morale for nurses.

The type of team that most closely matches the rapid-response teams at Tenet Healthcare Corporation is the self-managed team. Tenet's rapid-response teams are given responsibility to make decisions regarding offering immediate help or seeking further medical assistance to support a patient whose vital signs are deteriorating. Characteristic of self-managed teams, there are no supervisors on the rapid-response teams and they manage themselves.

Focusing on the Future: Using Management Theory in Daily Life

Managing Teams

Anne Roth is the Research Manager for the Marketing Department of a large financial-services institution. She heads a staff of four Market Research professionals. She describes her primary job as "providing customer information to my company."

Recently, Anne needed to use the win–win style of negotiation to convince her manager, the Director of Research, to authorize a study requested by Human Resources (HR). The Director had concerns because the study was being done for HR, and he did not see how the study would benefit the Marketing Department. The study was an expensive one, and he knew that it would take a large chunk of the resources he had budgeted for his department.

The requested study had two major components: a Hiring Managers Study and a New Hire Study. Both components look at the "onboarding" process in the organization—what happens in the first 90 days after a new employee is hired, and how satisfied both new employees and managers are with HR services during that time. Anne was able to work with her Director to create a study that met both the needs of the HR Department as well as the needs of the Marketing Department by using the five steps of win–win negotiations:

1. *Prepare for the negotiation by understanding your own needs and strengths and weaknesses.* Anne understood the delicacy of a situation that had multiple stakeholders and the fact that she would have to meet the needs of several parties simultaneously if the research was to be authorized. On the one hand, she knew that the research had the potential to uncover important information about how her company was incorporating new employees. She was excited about the idea of measuring and improving the flow of intellectual capital throughout the organization. She also knew that she had the resources to complete the project, once it was authorized. However, she was also conscious of her tendency to take on too much work and to not delegate work as fully as possible.

2. *Attempt to understand the other party's real needs and objectives.* Anne understood that her boss was worried about a number of things: the way the Market Research Department was perceived throughout the rest of the company, the resources available for all of the projects the Market Research Department was pursuing, and concerns about the professional status of the Market Research employees (for example, would

they still be able to publish in American Marketing Association publications?). Not only did Anne have to understand her boss's perspective, but she also had to understand the needs and objectives of a number of other parties, including the Human Resource Department and the employees in her organization. The Human Resource Department wanted data from the surveys quickly, but employees were concerned about privacy, and wanted to be sure that their survey responses could not be individually identified. Anne had to take all of these needs into consideration if the project was to work.

3. *Emphasize the commonalities and differences between the parties.* Fortunately for Anne, there was one major goal shared by all of the people concerned—everyone wanted to contribute to the bottom line of the organization, and everyone agreed that getting and keeping good employees would increase their company's profitability.

4. *Search for solutions that meet both parties' goals and objectives.* In working with her boss, Anne pointed out that the research she was proposing would be seen and used throughout the organization, thereby increasing the visibility of the Market Research Department. More importantly, research costs could be justified because study results could be directly linked to increased retention, thereby demonstrating a return on investment for the monies spent on gathering the information. Finally, Anne was able to show that the research methodology used was of interest to the Market Research professional community and that internal customers were as valid a sample base as external customers. This helped to assuage her boss's professional concerns.

    To deal with the needs of the HR Department, Anne proposed a three-tiered reporting structure. For jobs that had a large enough sample size (for example tellers), research results would be reported once a month. For jobs with smaller sample sizes (for example, mid-level management), results would be reported once every six months, and for jobs with the smallest sample sizes (for example, senior executives) results would be reported once a year. While HR wanted results quickly, they also wanted those results to be accurate, and Anne convinced them that if employees thought they could be individually identified, they would not give accurate results. In a similar fashion, she was able to work with employee groups to assure them that the research would not identify them individually and to let them know that the research results would be distributed widely enough that the company would take action on the information employees shared.

5. *Focus on building a relationship in a negotiation rather than making a one-time deal.* Throughout the research process, Anne built relationships at all levels of the organization. Because the research is ongoing, she has been able to let HR know whether or not their onboarding processes are working, both from the perspective of managers and from the perspective of employees. As the research results are reported throughout the company, the Market Research Department is receiving very favorable reviews—they are now seen as the place to go for research that is cost effective, relevant, and practical. Anne's boss is impressed by the retention results in the departments where the research has been done. The company is clearly doing a better job keeping its most important asset—its employees. Finally, employees are pleased with the research outcomes because they see the company taking their opinions seriously and taking action on their concerns.

summary of learning objectives

A **team** is a small number of people with complementary skills committed to a common purpose, set of performance goals, and approach for which they hold themselves mutually accountable. This chapter's discussion will help you in your future as a manager, as a member of a work team or as an employee to better understand teams and how to manage teams. The material in this chapter to meet each of the chapter's learning objectives that were presented at the outset of the chapter is summarized below.

1 Translate the benefits teams provide into competitive advantages.
- The benefits of using teams include lower costs and higher productivity, quality improvements, speed, and innovation. All of these benefits translate into competitive advantages in markets because they allow organizations to provide products and services at lower cost, higher quality, and with faster service—all sources of competitive advantage.

2 Identify the different types of teams—self-managed, project, parallel, and virtual.

Teams can be classified according to the expected duration of the team and the time commitment that team members can be expected to provide. Based on these two factors, the types of teams include:
- The **self-managed team** is responsible for producing an entire product, component, or service.
- The **project team** works on a project until completion and then disbands.
- The **parallel team** works on a particular problem that requires only part-time commitment.
- The **virtual team** works on a problem in which the members collaborate via computer.

3 Track the stages of team development that occur over the life of a project and help the team perform effectively.
    There are five stages in the development of teams.
- The first stage is the **forming** stage, when people get acquainted and establish ground rules.
- Second is the **storming** stage, when team members discuss differences in goals, priorities, and values and strive to manage conflicts over these issues.
- Third is the **norming** stage, characterized by resolution of important differences in goals and values and establishment of norms governing the behavior of team members. The norms enable the team to sanction individuals who violate important team rules and procedures.
- Fourth is the **performing** stage when the team focuses on performing its important tasks.
- The last is the **adjourning** stage, the process of disbanding the team when the team's purpose is completed.

4 Recognize the key roles that team members must play to ensure high performance. Effective team performance requires team members to play different roles to enable the team to realize its potential.
- The **task-facilitating** role puts a priority on helping the team accomplish its task goals.
- Some team members play the **relationship-building** role, which focuses on sustaining harmony between people on the team.
- The **team leader** helps the team strike a balance between the task-facilitating and relationship-building roles, and the lender must deal with deviant individuals who frustrate the team's ability to perform effectively.

5 Master the skills to detect and control team performance problems.

One of the challenges of managing teams is dealing with problems that can undermine the focus of the team. Three of the most challenging issues are:

- Dealing with **free riders**, who take credit for the team efforts while providing minimal work.
- Getting the best efforts from **nonconforming high performers**, who perform well as individuals but are difficult to work with in collaborative endeavors.
- Working around the lack of rewards for teamwork in contrast to individual performance so that the motivation of team members can be sustained.

6 Manage team conflict through negotiation.

An effective way to manage team conflict is by framing the issue as a problem and encouraging the parties to collaborate together to develop a solution that they can agree on jointly. This problem-solving approach to conflict resolution depends on the negotiating skills of the parties, which include the following:

- Understanding your strengths and weaknesses as well as those of the other party.
- Attempting to understand the other party's real needs and objectives so that the parties can enter into a dialogue and disclose their true preferences and priorities.
- Framing goals and objectives so that commonalities are emphasized and differences are minimized.
- Searching for solutions that meet the goals and objectives of each party.
- Focusing on building a relationship as a result of the negotiations rather than aiming to achieve a one-time deal.

discussion questions

1. Based on your personal experiences, what do you think are the advantages of teams? Which situations in a business are most likely to be most favorable for teams to perform effectively?

2. Again drawing on your own personal experiences, indicate what you think are the disadvantages of using teams. Which situations in a business are least suitable for team performance?

3. What is the role of the team leader? Should teams always have leaders? When might it be reasonable for a team to purposely leave out the role of team leader?

4. How do teams deal with individuals who violate important norms, for example, by engaging in negative conflict? Which do you think is a more effective way to sustain team performance: (*a*) the use of peer group pressure or (*b*) a supervisor who monitors and controls the behavior of team members?

5. Suppose you are working on a class project with five students, and one of the team members never shows up for your weekly meetings. Soon your project is due to be turned in to the professor. You and other team members are getting concerned about this "free rider." How should the team deal with this problem?

6. Suppose you are on a project team similar to the one in Question 5. One of the team members is very abrasive—using foul language and having a negative attitude—and is highly critical of the work of all the other team members, including you. This person also has an A (3.95) grade point average and wants to do the whole project alone and is willing to turn it in to the professor and share the credit with the whole team. The team is divided about how to respond to this offer, because this team member could quite possibly achieve a better grade on the project than the team. How should the team deal with this individual?

7. Can too little conflict be a problem for a team? What are the effects on team performance of little or no conflict? In cases where there is an absence of functional conflict, how can conflict be stimulated? Which role(s) are most likely to stimulate the conflict?

Companies Use Different Approaches to Encourage Teamwork

management minicase 14.1

In the business world companies often develop their own unique practices to encourage their employees to treat each other as team members rather than as competitors for pay and promotions. They encourage this teamwork because it is profitable to do so. They find that when employees are collaborative the customer receives better service, resulting in more business for the company and bottom-line rewards for all. Companies develop different approaches to get their employees to collaborate with each other based on the nature of the business.

At Thrive Networks, an IT outsourcing company in Concord, Massachusetts, management decided to redesign its reward system for salespeople to reduce barriers for sales staff to collaborate. Previously each salesperson was paid almost entirely on a sales commission directly linked to individual sales performance. Individual sales commissions stimulate competitive instincts in members of the sales force so that they treat each other as competitors for customers. Interestingly, the three people in the sales force at Thrive Networks each had different strengths. Jim Lippie was a proven lead generator, a master networker who brought in a dozen potential customers a week. John Barrows's talent was meeting with prospective clients and generating compelling proposals. Nate Wolfson's greatest skill was as a closer, the guy who could soothe last-minute concerns and make sure the papers were signed. Management reasoned that by eliminating the competition between the three members of the sales force and integrating their talents, the resulting collaborations would produce the opportunity for more deals and more rewards for all concerned.

To encourage teamwork between the sales staff the reward system was redesigned so that all sales commissions were pooled collectively and shared so that each salesperson received an equal share of the commissions once a monthly team goal was achieved. Under this team reward scheme each salesperson contributed what he did best to the overall team goal of selling IT services to customers. The results have been promising. Sales have gone up and the time to close a deal has been reduced by 30 percent.

A different approach to encouraging team behaviors among employees was adopted at Intel, the manufacturer of integrated circuit chips that power desktop and laptop computers. Intel employed many scientists and engineers that were expected to collaborate with each other on projects that would lead to the development of new products. Employees were under challenging time pressures to deliver products to market ahead of competitors. Conflicts between employees occurred with regularity causing disruptions to project schedules. Intel developed an approach suited to their needs which taught employees how to resolve conflicts by training them to use a variety of tools for handling discord. The implementation of these conflict resolution skills resulted in significant time savings on projects because little time was wasted in figuring out the best way to handle a disagreement or trading accusations of "not being a team player" since there was a clearly defined process set up that people could follow to handle the conflict.

Discussion Questions

1. The redesign of the reward system for salespersons at Thrive Networks strengthened teamwork. What factors were operating in the sales environment that supported the use of team rewards?

2. Do you think servers at a restaurant would respond the same way that the sales force did at Thrive Networks and become more collaborative if management decided to pool everybody's tips from customers and give each server an individual share of the tips? What would be the ideal set of conditions at a restaurant for servers to give better customer service under a system of shared tips?

3. Why did Intel decide to teach its employees a common set of conflict resolution skills as a way to improve teamwork among its employees?

Sources: J. Weiss and J. Hughes, "Want Collaboration? Accept—and Actively Manage—Conflict," *Harvard Business Review*, March, 2005, pp. 93–101; C. Cannella, "Kill the Commissions," *Inc.*, August 2004, p. 38.

management minicase 14.2

Whole Foods: Using Teamwork as a Recipe for Success

Whole Foods Inc. is the nation's number one chain of natural foods supermarkets. The company has more than 181 stores under the names of Whole Foods Market, Bread & Circus, Bread of Life, Fresh Fields, Merchant of Vino, and Wellspring Grocery. These stores are complete supermarkets with an emphasis on organically grown produce, fresh-baked bread, wholesome deli foods, and other health-food products. Conspicuously absent at Whole Foods stores are soft drinks in plastic containers, coupon dispensers for laundry detergent, salted potato chips, sugared cereals, and other high-sugar or high-fat products.

In the turbulent supermarket industry, Whole Foods has created a new approach to managing its employees—an approach based on teamwork and employee empowerment. Each Whole Foods store is an autonomous profit center composed of an average of 10 self-managed teams. A separate team operates each of the departments of the store, such as produce, canned goods, or the bakery. Each team has a team leader and specific team goals. The teams function as autonomous units. Members meet monthly to share information, exchange stories, solve problems, and talk about how to improve performance. The team leaders in each store form additional teams. Store leaders in each geographical region are a team and the leaders of each of the company's six regions are a team.

Why teams? Two primary benefits result from the company's emphasis on teamwork. First, teams promote cooperation among the store's employees. The teamwork approach facilitates a strong sense of community. This fosters pride and discipline in the work ethic of employees. An example of this is found in Whole Foods' hiring practices. The teams, rather than the store managers, have the power to approve new hires for full-time jobs. The store leaders provide the initial screening, but it takes a two-thirds vote of the team, after what is usually a 30-day trial period, for the candidate to become a full-time employee. This type of approval helps a team bond, which in turn facilitates a cooperative atmosphere. Another example of the ways in which teamwork promotes cooperation is evident in Whole Foods' team meetings. Each team holds a team meeting at least once a month. There is no rank at the team meetings. Everyone is given an equal opportunity to contribute to the discussion.

The second benefit that Whole Foods realizes from its emphasis on teamwork is an increased competitive spirit among its employees. The individual teams, stores, and regions of the company compete against each other in terms of quality, service, and profitability. The results of these competitions determine employee bonuses, recognition, and promotions. To facilitate competition, the company is extraordinarily open in terms of team performance measures. At a Bread & Circus store in Wellesley, Massachusetts, a sheet posted next to the time clock lists the previous day's sales broken down by team. A separate sheet lists the sales numbers for the same day the previous year. This information is used by the teams to determine "what it will take" to be the top team for the store during a particular week. This type of competition also exists at the store level. Near the same time clock, a weekly fax is posted listing the sales of each store in the New England region broken down by team with comparisons to the same week the previous year. One note of caution has emerged from these experiences: Competition between teams can become too intense. The company had to "tone down" the intensity of the competition between teams and stores on a few occasions.

The overall results of Whole Foods' management practices have been encouraging. The company has grown from one store in 1980 to 181 stores in 2005. The profitability of the company has been strong. In 2005 Whole Foods Inc. reported $4.70 billion of sales with $135 million net income, which was a 5 percent increase in net income over the previous year. This is a strong level of performance in the competitive grocery store industry, in which low profit margins are common. Whole Foods' decision to use teamwork as a "recipe for success" represents a novel and innovative approach to management.

Discussion Questions

1. Do you think Whole Foods' emphasis on teamwork could be applied to other companies in the grocery store industry such as Safeway, Kroger, or Albertson's? Why or why not? Do you think it would make a difference if the company's employees were represented by a union?

2. What are your thoughts about the Whole Foods practice of sharing team performance data with all company employees? Do you think that this practice risks creating an "overly competitive" spirit among the firm's teams and employees? Explain your answer.

Sources: Adapted from S. T. Foster, *Managing Quality*, Upper Saddle River, NJ: Prentice Hall, 2001, pp. 346–347; "Whole Foods Market," www.wholefoodsmarket.com/company/, 2006; D. Mc Ginn, "The Green Machine," *Newsweek*, March 21, 2005, pp. E8–E12.

Managing Rewards for Teams

individual/
collaborative
learning
case 14.1

The following are three different reward situations you may encounter as a manager or a team member. Think about the type of reward and how it should be administered in each of these situations.

Parallel teams at Colorado General Hospital. Colorado General Hospital is a large hospital in Denver, Colorado. Employees are organized into traditional departments based on medical services: emergency room, intensive care, surgery, and so on. Support services include building maintenance, food services, and administration. Employees work in departments as individuals reporting to functional line managers. They are also placed on parallel teams or committees, such as the quality committee, safety committee, and the public relations committee. Employees spend about two hours per week on committee assignments and can expect to be a member of the committee for a two-year period before being replaced by new members. The output of the committees can be very significant, such as productivity-enhancing suggestions that result in labor or materials savings to the hospital.

Process teams at Universal Insurance. Universal Insurance provides automobile, property, and casualty insurance to its customers. The company recently underwent a major reengineering effort. The firm was restructured into core business processes, including claims administration, new product development, marketing services, and financial investment, focusing on processes that add value to the needs of the customer. Information systems technology software is applied to each process, requiring employees to learn new application software (and periodic software upgrades) that enhance employee productivity. The company has a strong culture that values quality and applies customer satisfaction as a criterion for success. Employees are given permanent assignments to self-managed process teams that are responsible for providing a core business process.

Project teams at Speedy Software. Speedy Software is a Seattle, Washington, software company that provides applications software that operates on the Internet. The market for this software is highly competitive. New products are released every year and upgrades on existing software appear even more frequently. If the company misses announced product release dates, the potential for lost profits is substantial because market share can quickly be captured by competitors who are first to market with software with better features. Therefore, time to market is a critical factor for company success. The software engineers are organized into different project teams according to the type of software product. Engineers may work on a project very intensively for a period of 6 to 24 months and then can be reassigned to a new product. Sometimes project priorities change and a talented software designer may be shifted to a hot project before the other product is completed.

Critical Thinking Questions

1. In each of the team reward situations, what size reward, measured in dollars, do you think is most appropriate? For example, should any of the teams receive a substantial reward (worth thousands of dollars)? What about more frequent small rewards ($25–$100)? In which situations would monetary rewards work most effectively? What about nonmonetary rewards, such as tickets to a sports event or dinner for two at a nice restaurant?

2. What should be the criteria for the team reward in each of the three situations? Justify your choice.

3. Should team members each receive equal amounts of the reward, or should the reward be based on each individual member's contribution to the team? Should team members who leave in the middle of a project or reward period (for example, during the middle of the fiscal year) be eligible for a full share of the team reward? How should newcomers to the team be rewarded?

Collaborative Learning Exercise

The instructor organizes the class into five- or six-member teams, each assigned to one of the team reward situations. The team develops a policy for rewarding teams in its situation which includes the following: eligibility to receive reward, basis of dividing the reward between team members, size of reward, the frequency of giving the reward to the team, and performance criteria for the reward. The teams present their policies to the class and compare the policies. The class and the instructor develop a list of conclusions that represents the best practices for providing rewards to teams.

Teamwork at Taco Bell

Internet
Exercise 14.1

Taco Bell, the Mexican fast food restaurant chain, expects its employees to work in teams starting as front-line restaurant employees serving customers and all the way up the career ladder into management. Visit the Taco Bell Web site and view the career path at Taco Bell so that you can answer the following questions. Once you are at the home page of Taco Bell you will want to click onto "careers" and next click onto "career path."

1. What type of skills for managing teams discussed in this chapter would be needed to perform as a "team member" at Taco Bell?

2. What type of skills for managing teams would be needed to perform as a "shift leader" at Taco Bell?

3. What type of skills for managing teams would be needed to perform as an "area coach" at Taco Bell?

www.tacobell.com

What Is Your Primary Conflict-Handling Style?

manager's
checkup 14.1

For each of the 15 items, indicate how often you rely on that tactic by circling the appropriate number.

	Conflict-Handling Tactics	Rarely				Always
1.	I argue my case with my co-workers to show the merits of my position.	1	2	3	4	5
2.	I negotiate with my co-workers so that a compromise can be reached.	1	2	3	4	5
3.	I try to satisfy the expectations of my co-workers.	1	2	3	4	5
4.	I try to investigate an issue with my co-workers to find a solution acceptable to us.	1	2	3	4	5
5.	I am firm in pursuing my side of the issue.	1	2	3	4	5
6.	I attempt to avoid being "put on the spot" and try to keep my conflict with my co-workers to myself.	1	2	3	4	5
7.	I hold on to my solution to a problem.	1	2	3	4	5
8.	I use "give and take" so that a compromise can be made.	1	2	3	4	5
9.	I exchange accurate information with my co-workers to solve a problem together.	1	2	3	4	5
10.	I avoid open discussion of my differences with my co-workers.	1	2	3	4	5
11.	I accommodate the wishes of my co-workers.	1	2	3	4	5
12.	I try to bring all our concerns out in the open so that the issues can be resolved in the best way possible.	1	2	3	4	5
13.	I propose a middle ground for breaking deadlocks.	1	2	3	4	5
14.	I go along with the suggestions of my co-workers.	1	2	3	4	5
15.	I try to keep my disagreements with my co-workers to myself in order to avoid hard feelings.	1	2	3	4	5

Scoring

Integrating		Obliging		Dominating		Avoiding		Compromising	
Item	Score	Item	Score	Item	Score	Item	Score	Item	Score
4	____	3	____	1	____	6	____	2	____
9	____	11	____	5	____	10	____	8	____
12	____	14	____	7	____	15	____	13	____
Total	____	Total	____	Total	____	Total	____	Total	____

Your primary conflict-handling style is _____
(The category with the highest total.)
Your backup conflict-handling style is _____
(The category with the second highest total.)

video summary

Delta Force

Summary

Colonel Lee Van Arsdale has a history that is centered around 25 years of exemplary military service with such prestigious operations as the Green Berets and Delta Force. Now retired from active military duty, Arsdale currently owns a corporate consulting firm. This firm offers protection and security services to executives in need. It is his past military experience which has enabled him to move forward with his present-day business endeavor. His experience in handling stressful and dangerous situations serves as the guiding force for his own business operations. Colonel Arsdale says he developed his leadership capabilities through his experiences in the military. He states this skill development and growth is now serving him well within the private sector today.

Arsdale openly acknowledges there are strong similarities that exist between the world of business and the military. For instance, he indicates that each operates in an attempt to fulfill an established mission. He indicates the most valuable members to either group are those who are self-motivated, mature, and willing to accept responsibility. He also points out that team operations should be driven by a cohesive mission. In a typical military situation, planning is top-down; however, in this special elite force, the mission comes from the top, but the planning is done from the bottom up. Individuals operate in teams that are very independent and have few rules.

He stresses that it requires active recruiting to secure the best available members for either military or business endeavors. Colonel Arsdale staunchly believes in the achievements that can be derived through effective teamwork. Arsdale states that the leader, whether military or business, must be able to effectively motivate his or her followers in order to realize complete success in their mission.

Discussion Questions

1. The terms *work group* and *team* are often used interchangeably. Modern managers sometimes use the word *teams* to the point that it has become a cliche; they talk about teams while skeptics perceive no real teamwork. Thus, making a distinction between groups and teams can be useful. Why is Delta Force a good example of a real team? What elements of teamwork are present in this example?

2. Which type of team best describes Lee Van Arsdale's teams? Which leadership styles does he subscribe to, and how do they affect his team leadership?

3. Can you find similar levels of commitment to Delta Force in the business world?

chapter 15

Managing Communication

Learning Objectives

1. Understand the communication process.

2. Eliminate barriers that distort the meaning of information.

3. Recognize the basic patterns of organizational communication.

4. Understand how to organize and run effective meetings.

5. Master electronic forms of communication.

6. Work with an organization's informal communication system.

Call Center Jobs Are Outsourced to the Home Thanks to Broadband Communications Technology

15

More and more companies are moving customer service jobs out of high overhead call centers and into what is possibly the lowest-overhead place in the United States: workers' homes. The widespread availability of broadband communications linked to the Internet has made it possible for people who want to work out of the home, such as stay-at-home parents, the disabled, retirees, and those caring for adults or children with special needs, to have a job that does not interfere with their lifestyle. JetBlue Airways is perhaps the most famous practitioner of using home workers—all of its 1,400 reservation agents work from home. But they are employees. Many of the new call center jobs for home workers are independent contractor positions offered by outsourcing companies. The difference is that independent contractors are expected to pay for their own health care, computer equipment, and training.

The home workers, sometimes called cyberagents, are often educated, stay-at-home workers who were previously unable to engage in paid employment because they lived in rural areas, could not afford child care, were unable to work at a job that required mandatory face-time schedules, or had retired. More than 75 percent of home agents have some college education versus only 25 percent of employees who work in call centers. Home agents also appreciate saving money on gas and car expenses and not having to deal with commuting in traffic before starting work.

The call center work of cyberagents also provides a flexible just-in-time workforce. Shifts can last as little as 15 minutes. Agents are paid only for the time spent on the phone. Within the United States a call center worker onsite costs about $31 per hour versus $21 per hour for a home agent. Home agents can earn $8 to $13 or more an hour and are also more productive. Willow, an outsourcing company that employs cyberagents, indicates that its home agents make sales that are up to 25 percent higher than in call centers; their customer satisfaction rates are often 40 percent better. Customers appreciate being able to have a native English speaker to communicate with. Outsource providers of call center services such as Willow expect the number of home agent jobs to increase from its current level of 112,000 in 2006 to 330,000 by 2010.

Source: M. Conlin, "Call Centers in the Rec Room," *BusinessWeek*, January 23, 2006, pp. 76–77; S. Armour, "Cost-Effective 'Homesourcing' Grows," *USA Today*, March 13, 2006.

1. *What are the advantages to companies of using home workers who respond to customer inquiries compared to the practice of using a centralized call center staffed by employees who work onsite at the company?*

2. *What challenges do companies face managing employees who work at home providing call center services to customers?*

We will revisit these critical thinking questions in our Concluding Thoughts at the end of the chapter.

Communication is the glue that holds social organizations together. This chapter begins with a simple model of communication between two people. We then explain why it is important for the communication process to be managed to avoid misunderstandings. Next, the ways communication processes operate in organizations are described. Effective methods to manage different forms of communication in organizations and useful communication skills are also provided. This chapter will help you learn and develop skills to improve your ability to communicate with other employees, as outlined in Skills for Managing 15.1 on page 577.

The Process of Communication

Communication is the process of transmitting meaningful information from one party to another through the use of shared symbols. Communication is successful when meaning is understood. Two forms of information are sent and received in communication: facts and feelings.

Facts are bits of information that can be objectively measured or described, such as the retail price of a new product, the cost of raw materials, the defect rate of a manufacturing process, or the number of employees who quit during a year. Facts can be communicated verbally or in written documents and can also be transformed into digital symbols and stored in computer databases. **Knowledge workers** are employees who manage information and make it available to decision makers in the organization. They are the most common type of worker in the 21st century organization, and they depend on the process of communication to obtain appropriate information to do their jobs effectively.

Feelings are an individual's emotional responses to decisions made or actions taken by other people. Although feelings can be communicated verbally or in written documents, they are more likely to be communicated as nonverbal facial expressions, tone of voice, or body postures. To be effective, managers and employees must know how to interpret the feelings of others. Since managers achieve results through the actions of employees, it is important for them to take emotional reactions into consideration.

Organizations require diverse communication channels to facilitate communication among employees, managers, and customers. When messages with strong emotional content are to be received and understood, these channels must allow for face-to-face communication. Despite advances in computer technology that have created powerful ways to store, retrieve, and manipulate information, company leaders must still make provisions for communication on an interpersonal basis in order to develop trust and cohesion among organization members.

---

communication

The process of transmitting meaningful information from one party to another through the use of shared symbols.

facts

Bits of information that can be objectively measured or described, such as the retail price of a new product, the cost of raw materials, the defect rate of a manufacturing process, or the number of employees who quit during a year.

knowledge workers

Employees who manage information and make it available to decision makers in the organization.

feelings

An individual's emotional responses to decisions made or actions taken by other people.

SKILLS FOR MANAGING COMMUNICATION

- *Assertive communication skills.* Assertive communication skills enable you to communicate in ways that meet your needs while at the same time respecting the needs and rights of others. Developing assertive communication skills allows you to send a message directly to other people while avoiding many barriers that may distort the message. A manager who can communicate a request for assistance assertively to an employee is more likely to motivate the employee to provide the needed support.

- *Presentation skills.* Presentation skills help you inform or persuade customers or other employees. Because there is limited time to communicate with a client or an executive, having strong presentation skills allows you to make the best case for your ideas.

- *Nonverbal communication skills.* Nonverbal communication skills are invaluable for understanding the emotional state of the people you are dealing with. An employee who can understand the boss's nonverbal messages will know when it is a good time to ask for a pay raise. Lack of ability to understand nonverbal communication makes it more difficult for managers to know whether a strategy or policy is working according to plan.

- *Listening skills.* Listening skills are as important as verbal communication skills because they help employees and managers frame messages to meet the needs of the intended audience. Employees who possess listening skills are more effective at forming positive working relationships with other team members. Managers with listening skills are better able to understand and counsel subordinates.

A Model of Communication

Figure 15.1 on page 578 is a simple model of the communication process. Although the model illustrates communication between two people, it also applies to more complex communication situations. As the figure indicates, communication begins with a **sender**, who has a message for the **receiver**. The sender *encodes* the message and selects a **communication channel** that will deliver it to the receiver. Encoding is selecting appropriate symbols such as written words, numbers, digital symbols, sounds, or body language that can be correctly *decoded* by the receiver. The sender must anticipate the decoding skills of the receiver. For example, when a businessperson from the Netherlands does business with a U.S. executive, it is likely that all conversations and documents will be in English, because most Americans do not speak or understand Dutch, the language of the Netherlands, whereas the Dutch businessperson is very likely to speak English.

The communication channel influences the quantity and quality of information that is conveyed to the receiver. Communication channels include face-to-face conversations, group meetings, memos, policy manuals, e-mail, voice mail, videotapes, and computer printouts. Factors that influence the choice of a communication channel include the complexity of the message, the time available to compose and distribute it, the size and proximity of the audience, and the skill of the sender in using various channels. For example, some professors rely on traditional blackboard lectures because they do not have enough preparation time to create multimedia overheads.

sender

Individual or party that initiates communication with another individual or party.

receiver

Individual or party that receives message from sender.

communication channel

Influences the quantity and quality of information that is conveyed to the receiver. Channels of communication include face-to-face conversations, group meetings, memos, policy manuals, e-mail, voice mail.

FIGURE 15.1

The Communication Process

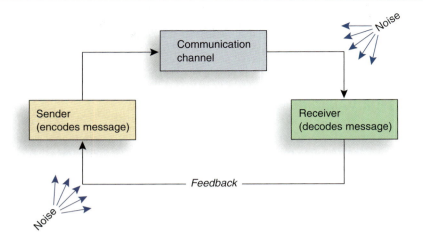

decoding

Translating the symbolic verbal, written, or visual symbols into an undistorted, clear message.

For communication to be effective, the receiver must be able to decode the message and understand its true meaning. **Decoding** means translating the symbolic verbal, written, or visual symbols into an undistorted, clear message. The receiver may misinterpret the message if unable to decode it, perhaps because the receiver does not have the necessary skills in language or culture. For example, a U.S. buyer may insist on a written contract before agreeing to do business with a Mexican supplier. However, in Mexico, business deals are based on oral agreement, and contracts represent a lack of good faith. There are cultural differences within the United States. A simple example is the fast-talking New York sales representative who is trying to sell life insurance to a potential client in Monroe, Louisiana. The New Yorker may interpret the slower speech of the southerner as unsophisticated and less intelligent. The southerner may interpret the New Yorker's accent and fast speech as rude and untrustworthy. Other decoding problems include the use of technical jargon and the ambiguity of English words with multiple meanings. A communication channel that is rich in information, with opportunities for visual as well as verbal cues, provides a context to help the receiver select the appropriate meaning of a word with several different meanings. On the other hand, lean communication channels provide a limited context from which to select the true meaning of an ambiguously worded message.

feedback

Information received back from the receiver, which allows the sender to make sure the true meaning is received.

Important messages should include opportunities for feedback from the receiver. **Feedback** allows the sender to make sure the true meaning is received. For example, if a company decides to change the basis of sales representatives' pay from salary to straight commission, communicating the change to the sales team at a face-to-face meeting is more effective than sending a memo or e-mail message because there are more opportunities for feedback and clarification. Many management problems can be avoided by using communication channels with feedback, especially when individuals are likely to feel strongly about the content of the message.

two-way communications

Communication channels that provide for feedback.

one-way communications

Communication channels that provide no opportunity for feedback.

Channels that provide for feedback are called **two-way communications**, because they allow the sender and receiver to interact. Communication channels that provide no opportunity for feedback are **one-way communications**. Although interactive communication is ideal, it is not always possible when information must be disseminated to many employees in a short period of time. IBM informs employees about the promotions of top executives in its corporate newsletter (a one-way communication channel). However, the sales force is informed about new products at a sales meeting (a two-way communication channel). As this example suggests, two-way communication channels are required for important and complex information.

Another important condition of effective communication is overcoming noise. **Noise** is anything that interferes with sending or receiving the message. Noise can distort the true meaning of the message. Sources of noise include the sender (whose accent may be difficult to understand); the communication channel (if the telecommunications system lacks bandwidth, an Internet message may be slow and frustrating); the receiver (who may have poor vision and be unable to read a memo); and the environment (time pressures may reduce availability to listen to a message). A manager at the Houston distribution center of Baxter International, a medical and health products company, receives more than 60 voice mail messages a day from customers and employees. Having many customers to satisfy and employees to supervise makes it difficult for the manager to respond to all messages promptly. However, by using some of the communication options in the voice mail system, the manager can respond to queries that require only short, direct answers.

noise

Anything that can interfere with sending or receiving a message.

LOC-In

1 **Learning Objective Check-In**

Gina wants Jerry to understand that she is no longer interested in pursuing a particular client's project. Based on the way Gina gestures to Jerry while she describes the project itself, he clearly understands what she is trying to communicate.

1. *In this example, Gina is the _____.*
   a. *decoder*
   b. *receiver*
   c. *sender*
   d. *noisemaker*
2. *The personal conversation between Gina and Jerry represents the _____.*
   a. *communication channel*
   b. *control factor*
   c. *model of communication*
   d. *vertical communication*
3. *Gina's gesturing during the conversation is one way of _____ the message.*
   a. *decoding*
   b. *controlling*
   c. *encoding*
   d. *giving feedback to*

Barriers to Effective Communication

The model of communication presented in Figure 15.1 suggests that barriers can disrupt the accurate transmission of information. These barriers take different forms:

1. *Sender barrier*. The sender may send a message to an audience that is not interested in the content of the message.

2. *Encoding barrier*. The sender uses a vocabulary that is too technical for the audience.

3. *Communication channel barrier*. The sender selects a communication channel that is too lean to provide the richness of information receivers need to decode the message. For example, a written memo is inadequate for explaining a change in the employee retirement plan.

4. *Decoding barrier*. The receiver does not have the decoding skills necessary to understand the message. For example, poor reading skills can prevent employees from using manuals and other reference materials.

5. *Receiver barrier*. The receiver is too busy focusing on other things to be able to accurately listen to and understand the verbal or nonverbal content of the message.

6. *Feedback barrier*. The organization has few formal communication channels with feedback loops to give lower echelon employees the opportunity to communicate their true feelings about policies.

Online
LearningCenter
www.mhhe.com/gomez3e

Barriers to Effective Communication

7. *Noise barrier.* The receiver does not understand how to use time-saving features of e-mail and voice mail, resulting in message overload and unacceptable delays in responding to messages of customers and co-workers.

8. *Perception barriers.* Perception barriers occur when two individuals experience the same message differently because their mental images of the message are not identical. A receiver will fit a message into an existing pattern of experiences to make sense out of it. Sometimes the message becomes distorted during this sensemaking process. One type of perception barrier is **selective perception**, whereby the receiver focuses on the parts of the message that are most salient to his or her interests and ignores other parts that are viewed as not relevant. For example, an employee interested in a job vacancy may use selective perception to discount the fact that the job requires more work experience than the employee currently has accumulated. The result is a personal disappointment when the employee is not chosen for the job.

Another important type of perceptual barrier is **prejudgment**, which involves making incorrect assumptions about a person due to membership in a group (based on age, race, gender or ethnicity) or about a thing (such as performance evaluation) based on earlier positive or negative experiences. For example, a manager who has a negative earlier experience with an older employee may generalize this experience to other old people. The manager may become resistant to hiring an older job applicant even if positive information is available, because the manager has already negatively prejudged the applicant. It is important to be aware of these perceptual barriers and avoid them. Prejudging older people (over 40 years of age) negatively is an illegal practice that can have costly legal implications.

Large, complex organizations are likely to have many barriers. These barriers can be managed by using various management practices. Senders should be educated about the necessity of learning the background of intended audiences and should gain firsthand familiarity with audiences prior to initiating communication. All members of the organization should be trained in the effective use of communication technologies to manage the flow of information. There should be a diverse mix of communication channels from lean (memos or policy manuals) to rich (videoconference and multimedia) so that senders can match the channel to the complexity of the message. The management team must make sure employees have appropriate communication skills. Key skills include listening, public speaking, and nonverbal communication skills. HR departments can either screen applicants for evidence of these skills or provide on-the-job training programs which give employees opportunities to practice and improve their communication skills.

---

selective perception

Type of perception barrier whereby the receiver focuses on the parts of the message that are most salient to his or her interests and ignores other parts that are not relevant.

prejudgment

Type of perceptual barrier which involves making incorrect assumptions about a person due to membership in a group or about a thing based on earlier positive or negative experiences.

LOC-In

② Learning Objective Check-In

1. *Steve is trying to teach a group from the company's China subunit how to use the latest phase of the software implementation that he is in charge of. While the Chinese team has learned very good spoken English from their meetings and phone conversations with the U.S. team, several among them do not know how to read and write the language very well. Steve's pamphlets, then, are useless in delivering an immediate message to the people he is trying to teach, and he will have to rely on his other presentation skills and direct training methods. Which of the following is depicted in this example?*
   a. *Decoding barrier*
   b. *Directional barrier*
   c. *Communication channel barrier*
   d. *Sender barrier*

video: THE ENTREPRENEURIAL MANAGER

Managing
Communication

Summary

These days, mothers are the mothers of invention—fathers, too. There is a new breed of successful inventors who have one thing in common—they are parents. You might say that creativity is born out of frustration. Ellen Diamant just wanted a diaper bag that would clip onto the stroller when she was pushing her new son, Spencer. She started sketching an idea when her husband said it would be perfect for a new business. Prior to that, she hadn't thought of its implications. She thought she would be making something for her personal use, at most. The couple decided to pursue the "Skip Hop" bag as a full-fledged business, and, after about $100,000 in up-front investment, they have become profitable and highly successful, selling their unisex stroller bag in numerous retail chain baby stores, and planning to continue improving the product.

The ideas, they say, were the easy part. The execution and followthrough is where many a well-intended inventor loses out. Tamara Monoseff is founder and CEO of Mom Inventors, which helps moms through the process step by step; she is also an inventor herself. She says that communication is very important. The first step, she advises, is research. Moms should go to the retail buyers themselves and ask them if they think the product would sell, if it should be changed, how much they think it could sell for, and so on.

First, make sure the product doesn't already exist and get feedback from informal focus groups. Second, evaluate the cost of a patent. It is not always cost-effective to get one, and they are not always necessary. Next, find manufacturers online, including at USchamber.com for the United States, and Alibaba.com for Chinese manufacturers. Many retailers actually have their own departments to handle the pitches for a lot of these products.

Discussion Questions

1. Describe the model of communication that Tamara Monoseff recommends in the video for would-be inventors and moms. Is this one-way or two-way communication?

2. If an entrepreneur set up a focus group for evaluating a potential product, what elements of communication would be important for that entrepreneur to consider and plan for?

3. How did the Diamants use communication to their advantage in securing retail buyers for their product?

Patterns of Organizational Communications

Communication patterns in organizations are complex. Possible barriers to organizational communication include: (1) differences in employee status and power, such as communication between a subordinate and a supervisor; (2) diversity, such as cross-gender communication; and (3) differences in interests, such as a manufacturing unit focused on quality and efficiency of output and an engineering unit focused on executing a technically elegant design that may be difficult to manufacture. Organizational communication patterns operate downward, upward, and horizontally. Each direction poses specific management challenges.

Downward Communication

Downward communication frequently occurs between managers and subordinates, when the manager provides direction, feedback, and critical information to help subordinates perform at expected levels. Examples include employee performance evaluations, job descriptions, orientation of new employees, praise and recognition, company business strategies and goals, and company policies and procedures.

Upward Communication

In **upward communication**, a message is sent from a position lower in the hierarchy to a receiver higher in the hierarchy. It lets managers know how individuals, teams, and units of the company are performing. When performance deviates from expected standards, managers can make corrective adjustments.

One of the most important components of upward communication is feedback to managers about employee feelings about company policies. Organizations are likely to have barriers that filter information from subordinates before it is received by managers. Employees are well aware of the tendency to punish the bearer of bad news. It is also considered disloyal for employees to take a problem "over the head" of the boss to a higher echelon manager. Therefore, it is necessary to design special communication channels that encourage employees to express their true feelings or provide unfiltered information. Hewlett-Packard has an open-door policy that encourages employees to bring problems to any manager in the company and requires managers to resolve problems within a specified period of time. Toyota is well-known for effectively using employee suggestion systems to improve product and process quality. Besides suggestions, upward communication includes employee grievances, information about the unethical behavior of managers, accounting information, and information about the defect rate of the product.

Horizontal Communication

When a sender and a receiver are at a similar level in the organization **horizontal communication** takes place. This includes communications between team members, between different teams, and between employees in different units, such as when a safety specialist and a quality control inspector discuss proposed changes in the manufacturing process. Horizontal communication is becoming increasingly important in organizations because it involves collaboration between employees with different skills and competencies. A high proportion of communications between knowledge workers consists of horizontal communication in which information is shared. Figure 15.2 on page 583 provides an illustration of the three different patterns of organizational communication: downward, upward, and horizontal.

Downsizing and reengineering have resulted in slimmer organizations with fewer levels and a greater emphasis on teams. Horizontal communication plays an important role in this environment. Interactive electronic communication tech-

Direction and feedback from manager to employee is a form of downward communication.

downward communication

Sending a message from a high position in the organization to an individual or group lower in the hierarchy.

upward communication

Sending a message from a position lower in the hierarchy to a receiver higher in the hierarchy.

horizontal communication

Communication between a sender and a receiver at a similar level in the organization.

FIGURE 15.2

Organizational Communication Patterns

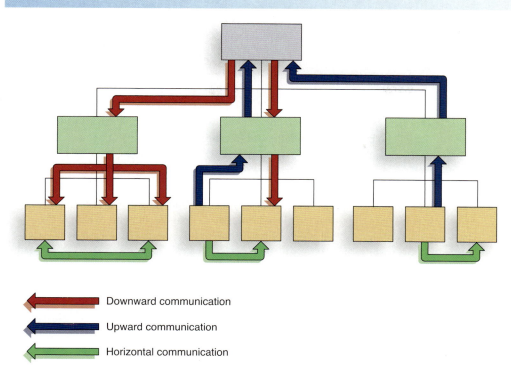

Downward communication

Upward communication

Horizontal communication

nologies such as e-mail greatly facilitate horizontal communication by making it possible to establish learning communities and virtual teams of employees who work together even when separated geographically. Other examples of horizontal communication are peer performance, cross-functional new product development team meetings, self-managed work team meetings, suggestion committee meetings, and diversity task forces.

Managers and team members should have the ability to give feedback to subordinates or peers. Feedback may be communicated either horizontally (from peer to peer) or vertically (from supervisor to subordinate). All employees need feedback to improve their skills. Positive feedback lets them know they are progressing toward their goals and can be used to strengthen behaviors that are already learned. Negative feedback tells employees which behaviors should be modified to improve performance. Tips for providing feedback can be found in Manager's Notebook 15.1 on page 584.

LOC-In

3 Learning Objective Check-In

Olin heads up the catalog division of a major camp gear supplier. His phone operating staff tells him that they have gotten lots of feedback from customers about a particular product, and they think that it might be worth looking into a couple of changes that could make the product better for a wider range of their customers. Olin then tells his counterpart, Joe, in the product development division what complaints were filed most frequently about the product and in what time frame they were received since the product's launch.

1. *When the staff tells Olin about the complaints, this is _____.*
   a. *downward communication*
   b. *upward communication*
   c. *horizontal communication*
   d. *external communication*
2. *When Olin passes the information on to Joe in product development, this is _____.*
   a. *upward communication*
   b. *downward communication*
   c. *horizontal communication*
   d. *sideways communication*

HOW TO PROVIDE CONSTRUCTIVE FEEDBACK TO OTHERS

Here are some useful suggestions about giving constructive feedback to peers or subordinates.

1. *Focus your feedback on specific behaviors* that were successful or that were unsuccessful. You will help motivate the employee to continue the successful behaviors and to improve the unsuccessful ones. Instead of saying "You did a great job on this project," tell the employee, "Your careful checking and rechecking caught several errors."

2. *Keep personality traits out of your feedback* by focusing on "what" rather than "who." Specify what results the person achieved or failed to achieve. Instead of saying "You don't work hard enough," tell the employee, "You used outdated figures in your report."

3. *Investigate whether the employee had control over the results* before giving feedback about unsuccessful behaviors. For example, the employee who used outdated figures in a report may have been given them by corporate headquarters and had no way of knowing they were outdated. Ask questions of the employee to find out whether unsuccessful behavior is something the employee can control. Be very cautious before offering negative feedback.

4. *Feedback should be given as soon as possible;* don't save up your feedback about both successful and unsuccessful behaviors for an end-of-the-quarter meeting, for example. Feedback given shortly after an event occurs is the most effective at changing or sustaining an employee's behaviors.

5. *Ensure privacy when giving feedback about negative behaviors;* giving it in public will cause a reaction against you by any observers. *Feedback about positive behaviors can be given in public* to recognize an employee's success. It can help motivate the employee and others.

Source: Adapted from S. P. Robbins and P. L. Hunsaker, *Training in Interpersonal Skills*, 2nd ed. Upper Saddle River, NJ: Prentice Hall, 1996, pp. 73–75.

Managing Organizational Communications

Organizations can improve the quality of communications by providing a diverse mix of lean to rich communication channels that provide opportunities to communicate in upward, downward, and horizontal directions. Managers and employees must be trained to use the communication channels appropriately. Because communication technologies are rapidly changing, upgrading the communication skills of employees should be considered a process of continuous improvement.

Communication channels vary according to **information richness**, the potential information-carrying capacity of data. Rich communication channels provide opportunities for feedback, provide a full range of visual and audio information, and personalize the message for the receiver. Rich communications channels are best for nonroutine, ambiguous, and difficult messages. Face-to-face communication provides the richest channel of communication, as displayed in Figure 15.3 on page 585. Lean communication channels provide no opportunity for feedback, have a limited mix of information, and are impersonal. A mass-produced bulletin or flier is an example of a lean communication channel.

information richness

The potential information-carrying capacity of data.

FIGURE 15.3

Communication Channels Ranked by Information Richness

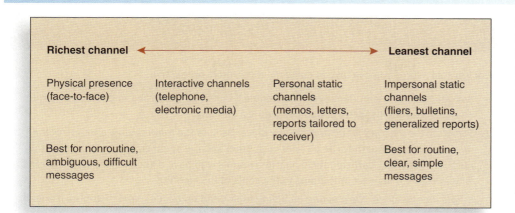

Richest channel ←			→ Leanest channel
Physical presence (face-to-face)	Interactive channels (telephone, electronic media)	Personal static channels (memos, letters, reports tailored to receiver)	Impersonal static channels (fliers, bulletins, generalized reports)
Best for nonroutine, ambiguous, difficult messages			Best for routine, clear, simple messages

Sources: Robert H. Lengel and Richard L. Daft, "The Selection of Communication Media as an Executive Skill," *Academy of Management Executive* 2 (August 1988): 225–232; and Richard L. Daft and Robert H. Lengel, "Organizational Information Requirements, Media Richness, and Structural Design," *Managerial Science* 32 (May 1986): 554–572.

Face-to-Face Communication

Rich information content is possible in face-to-face communication, because there is a high level of interactivity between the sender and the receiver. Job interviews are likely to be done face-to-face. One of the most important types of face-to-face communication is the meeting.

Meetings, or gatherings of organizational members, are held to inform and train participants, solve problems, monitor and coordinate activities, delegate tasks, and create social bonds between diverse organization members. *Staff meetings* allow managers to coordinate activities with subordinates. *Corporate or business-unit meetings* address strategic issues and involve executives who formulate long-range goals. *Task force meetings* are held to discuss goals that affect a broad range of employees such as diversity in the workplace or safety. *Team meetings* are used to coordinate the work activities of members of a self-managed team, including performance goals, training new members, scheduling work, and suggesting improvements in work methods. The application of multimedia technologies that transmit video, voice, and text over satellite networks have made face-to-face meetings with globally dispersed people possible.

Face-to-face communications, such as meetings, provide an opportunity for feedback and personalized messages for receivers.

15.2

manager's notebook

Here are some steps you can take to make meetings more productive:

1. Ask yourself if it's important even to schedule a meeting. If you can handle the issue with an e-mail or a memo instead, don't schedule a meeting.

2. *Schedule the meeting for an appropriate place*. Be sure the room is large enough for the participants and that they can all hear each other and the speaker. Be careful to limit the number of meeting participants to only individuals who have a good reason to attend and who are able to make contributions to the goals of the meeting.

3. *Create an agenda for the meeting* including topics and time limits, and distribute it ahead of time. The meeting participants will be able to plan their own contributions. Keeping the meeting to the agenda will ensure that all topics are covered. Plan to take careful notes during the meeting as each topic is covered.

4. *Establish rules for participation*. All participants need to have an opportunity to contribute; determine an order so that a few participants don't dominate the meeting.

5. *Follow the agenda's time limits* for each topic. Keep an eye on the clock; if a topic exceeds its allotted time, you should return to it later and go on to the next topic.

6. *Leave some open time* for topics that may not have been included on the agenda. If discussion of additional topics is expected to take more time, add them to the next meeting's agenda instead.

7. *End the meeting with a plan of action*. Discuss the steps that will be taken as a result of the meeting. Distribute a written report of the meeting and the steps to be taken based on your notes.

Sources: Adapted from P. Sauer, "Quick Show of Hands: Who Hates Meetings?" *Inc.*, May 2004, pp. 73–78, 112; R. Volkema and F. Niederman, "Planning and Managing Organizational Meetings: An Empirical Analysis of Written and Oral Communication," *Journal of Business Communication* 33 (July 1996): 275–293.

Managers can spend as much as 60 percent to 80 percent of their time in meetings. A sales manager is likely to hold regular meetings with sales representatives, attend management meetings with other sales managers, and participate in committee meetings with marketing, advertising, and promotion employees on new product development or brand management. Employees who are asked to spend more time in team-based work units require periodic meetings to form a consensus on how the team should conduct its activities. Meetings can waste time and become frustrating. It is important to manage them effectively. Manager's Notebook 15.2 above lists techniques to run a meeting effectively.

LOC-In

4 **Learning Objective Check-In**

1. *Jeremy needs to delegate several tasks among his work staff, which has a busy schedule with other projects already. It is important that he does not waste time in communicating the new project's work, but it is equally important that he makes sure everyone on the staff understands his or her role. Which of the following would be appropriate for Jeremy to conduct?*
   a. *Corporate meeting*
   b. *Staff meeting*
   c. *Team meeting*
   d. *Task force meeting*

Choosing the Best Communication Medium

Written Communication

Written communication includes memos, policy manuals, employee handbooks, company newsletters, bulletin boards, letters, and fliers. Written documents have an advantage over face-to-face communication, because messages can be revised, stored and made available when needed, and disseminated in identical copies so the same message is received by all. Written communication can be personalized for a small audience or written in a generic style that accommodates a larger audience. The limitations of written communication are that there are no provisions for feedback, and the sender may not be certain if the message was received, read, and/or understood. Two popular forms of written communication are memos and company newsletters.

MEMOS   Short business messages that provide information to employees are sent in memos. They can be used to inform employees about the agenda, time, and place of a meeting; to schedule work; or to describe a change in an employment policy. A memo should be brief and to the point. Also,

- Make sure that the heading indicates: (1) the intended audience; (2) the subject of the memo; (3) the name of the sender; and (4) the date that the memo was written.

- Revise and edit the memo to eliminate misspellings and poor grammar. Make sure the message is clear and unambiguous. If the sender catches an error after the memo is distributed, it may be necessary to send a follow-up memo to tell the audience to disregard the previous memo. This can annoy receivers.

- Add the names of people who need to be aware of the communication to a copy list at the end of the memo. Copied individuals may not be the focus of the memo, but they need to know about it. For example, the controller who schedules a meeting of staff accountants to discuss a new way to expense research and development costs may copy the vice president of finance.

- Avoid sending memos to people who do not need to know about the content. Employees should not waste time reading memos that are not important.

COMPANY NEWSLETTERS   Many companies have short monthly or quarterly publications designed to keep employees informed of important events, meetings, and transitions and to provide inspirational stories about employee and team contributions to the business. Newsletters help foster community spirit by keeping everybody informed about what others are doing. Desktop publishing software has made the production of newsletters feasible for even the smallest companies.

A newsletter can be a one-way or interactive form of communication depending on the goals established by management. In the one-way form, a newsletter is an official downward communication from management to inform employees about company policies, procedures, and other information. In its two-way form, the newsletter is a communication channel for all directions of communication (upward, downward, and horizontal), allowing each member of the workplace to voice opinions and contribute stories of interest. Large corporations are likely to have several newsletters, with the corporate-level news from headquarters presented in a one-way version and business-unit or plant newsletters containing employee input.

Electronic Communication

Advances in electronic technology make interactive communication possible between senders and receivers, even when they are separated by physical distance and busy schedules. Electronic communication channels vary in the richness of the information that is transmitted and can include text, voice, graphics, or video. Two important forms of electronic communication are voice mail and e-mail.

VOICE MAIL A detailed audio message that is recorded electronically and can be played back when convenient is a voice mail. Employees can play back all messages at once and answer them in a concentrated block of time so that redundant "telephone tag" calls can be avoided. Voice mail also allows a sender to set up a menu of responses to commonly asked questions, which saves additional time. Routine calls can be routed to a recorded message, and more attention can be paid to callers with nonroutine questions. Vanguard, one of the largest U.S. mutual fund companies, uses a voice mail menu to answer commonly asked questions about investments. Each customer has a special code to obtain daily mutual fund account balances and market prices of funds and to make financial transactions.

Voice mail is not always used effectively. Many organizations, including such government offices as the Social Security Administration, present a long menu of options that waste the caller's time. Some people use voice mail to screen phone calls, avoiding callers they do not want to talk to. Screening too many calls can annoy customers and block internal company communication. The following suggestions can help managers use voice mail appropriately:

- Update your personal greeting regularly. Let callers know when they can expect your return call.

- Include information in the greeting about how to reach a co-worker who can help callers if you are unavailable or if the call is urgent.

- Try to answer your phone while at your desk. Use the voice recording only for good reasons, such as being in the middle of an important meeting with a colleague.

- Check messages regularly and return calls promptly.

- Set the message capacity for one or two minutes to discourage callers from leaving overly verbose messages. For long conversations other communication channels are preferable to voice mail.[1]

e-mail

Electronic mail via computers.

ELECTRONIC MAIL **E-mail** allows employees to communicate via written messages through personal computer terminals linked to a network. It is a fast way to distribute important business results to a large number of employees. Virtual teams of employees can work simultaneously on a document even though they may be separated geographically using e-mail attachments. E-mail is often used to exchange information (such as coordinating project activities and scheduling meetings), for social reasons (such as keeping in touch with colleagues), and to post general information that can be of use to many employees (for example, the time and place of the company picnic). The use of e-mail creates an upward communication channel for employees to gain access to executives who previously may have been inaccessible to them. For example, Bill Gates, the chairman of Microsoft, makes his e-mail address known to all Microsoft employees. He reserves several hours each day to send and reply to messages.

Despite its advantages, e-mail creates challenging problems. It can contribute to information overload; numerous e-mail messages are sent to large lists of people when the message may be of interest to only a few. E-mail should not be considered private. Recent court decisions state that U.S. companies have a right to monitor the e-mail of employees.[2]

When using e-mail,

- Scan the subject heading at the beginning of the message. If the topic is of no interest to you, delete the message without reading it.

- Create electronic files to store important messages so they can be quickly retrieved when needed.

FIGURE 15.4

Selected Smilies Used to
Convey Emotion in e-Mail

Source: D. Brake, *Dealing with e-
Mail* (London: DK, 2003), p. 46.

Smiley	Meaning
:-)	The basic smiley—usually indicates happiness.
;-)	Winking—usually indicates a joke or (sometimes) flirtatiousness.
:-(	Frowning—usually indicates sadness or disagreement.
:-I	Indifferent—usually indicates apathy or disinterest.
:->	Sarcastic—usually indicates insincerity or cynicism.

- Set up electronic lists of people who should receive the same message. For example, the project team leader should set up a list of all team members and send messages to the list rather than to each individual member.

- Assume that your e-mail will be read by management. Use other communication channels for private or controversial messages.

- Protect sensitive documents with encryption software so that private information is not accessible to hackers or other unintended receivers.

- Use e-mail to transmit factual information, and avoid using it to criticize colleagues or to communicate messages with content that will cause strong emotional reactions from the receiver.

- Avoid sending messages written in all-capitals, which is like screaming.[3]

In some companies e-mail is the dominant form of communcation because the employees may be spread out geographically and rarely if ever are able to meet on a face-to-face basis. That is the case at Alpine Access, a provider of outsourced call-center services based in Golden, Colorado.[4] One way to attempt to communicate emotion within an e-mail message is with the use of a *smiley*, also called an *emoticon*, which consists of a sequence of ordinary characters found on a computer keyboard that symbolize a face expressing some kind of emotion. The classic smiley shows a smiling face with a colon representing the eyes, a dash represents the nose, and a right parenthesis represents the mouth as shown in Figure 15.4 above and is used at the end of a sentence to convey happiness. Other smilies as shown in the figure can represent joking around, frowning, indifference, or sarcasm. However some people find these symbols to be childish, and, unfortunately, they are not universally understood.[5]

LOC-In

5 Learning Objective Check-In

Ryan likes to stay in touch with his clients and co-workers constantly throughout the day. Sometimes, however, he has meetings to attend or other work to accomplish, and so he cannot spend all his time communicating with these important people. He wishes he could set aside a block of time to devote to using the phone and talking to clients or catching up on important internal news at the company. This would allow him to be more productive with his time.

1. _____ is one option for Ryan that would allow him to set up and record messages that could be played back when convenient.
   a. E-mail
   b. Voice mail
   c. The grapevine
   d. Informal communication

2. Which of the following would be the most appropriate way for Ryan to catch up on important company happenings throughout the day?
   a. Voice mail
   b. Team meetings
   c. E-mail
   d. Memos

Krispy Kreme's Web Portal Makes Franchises More Profitable

It turns out that a combination of doughnuts and Internet can be highly profitable. Krispy Kreme is a national doughnut franchise with headquarters in Winston-Salem, North Carolina. The wildly popular Krispy Kreme doughnuts are sold in 278 locations in the United States and Canada. The company sells over 2.7 billion of these sweet treats each year. Each franchise store makes between 4,000 and 10,000 doughnuts per day. Managers must have all the necessary tools to keep the 24-hour production process running smoothly. One of the critical tools that the Krispy Kreme Company uses is a customized Web portal, mykrispykreme.com. It is an Internet-based communication device used to take the guesswork out of managing a doughnut franchise. Local owners are able to connect directly with Krispy Kreme Company headquarters.

When a franchise manager logs on, the opening screen offers weather news, because people buy more doughnuts and coffee when the weather turns. These weather updates have paid big dividends to the franchises by allowing managers to better forecast the number of doughnuts to make, says Frank Hood, the company's chief information officer. Ordering supplies and doughnut mix is performed online, eliminating costly errors. The Web portal even has a virtual help desk. Need to know how to calibrate a coffee grinder? Fix a fryer? It's all there,

By using information from its Web portal, franchise store managers at Krispy Kreme can run the doughnut machines more efficiently to meet the daily demand of customers.

with streaming video and audio and graphics on what to do. The videos called "Hot Topics" are available 24 hours a day. Owners have seen healthy increases in store profitability since the Web portal has become available to them.

Source: Adapted from C. Skipp, "Hot Bytes, by the Dozen: Krispy Kreme's Web Portal Keeps Franchises Humming," *Newsweek*, April 28, 2003, p. 42.

Internet

A computer network with multimedia communication capabilities, allowing a combination of text, voice, graphics, and video to be sent to a receiver; a network of networks, connecting hundreds of thousands of corporate, educational, and research computer networks around the world.

The **Internet** is a computer network with multimedia communication capabilities. A combination of text, voice, graphics, and video can be sent to a receiver over the Web. Companies' sites on the World Wide Web are places where potential customers can learn about products and services and place orders. The use of the Internet makes it possible for companies to serve international customers. Many universities advertise MBA programs on their Web sites to attract international students. Electronic commerce over the Internet has created many new business opportunities. Amazon.com sells books and other merchandise over the Internet. Charles Schwab, the discount broker, lets customers buy and sell stocks online. Management Close-Up 15.1 above describes how the Krispy Kreme Company uses its Web portal, an Internet-based communication device, to display valuable information to the managers of the franchise stores so they can more accurately forecast and produce fresh doughnuts for their customers.

Management Is Everyone's Business 15.1 on page 591 explains why virtual
teams should plan to schedule periodic face-to-face meetings in order to build team spirit and trust. The payoff is a more productive team.

Informal Communication

grapevine

Informal communication that takes place at the workplace.

Informal communication, sometimes referred to as the **grapevine**, is used when there are gaps in or barriers to formal communication and employees do not receive information they desire. It takes place at the water cooler or in the hallway, in the company cafeteria, in employees' offices, in the parking lot, in restaurants, and at trade shows. Job opportunities, who is being considered for a big promotion, the likelihood of downsizing, the features of a competitor's new product, and the unethical behavior of a manager are typical topics on the grapevine.

Informal communication can be a source of creative ideas. Sun Microsystems, a Silicon Valley manufacturer of computer workstations, schedules occasional Friday afternoon parties so that technical employees can visit with business-oriented employees. Ideas for new products sometimes start out as informal conversations over a beer.

Some gossip and rumors are harmful to employee morale. If employees fear that the company will soon downsize, rumors that exaggerate the true state of affairs are likely to be exchanged. This makes employees fearful of losing their jobs and negatively affects company performance. Negative rumors that disrupt employee motivation must be managed with other forms of communication.

One effective way to manage rumors and misinformation is **management by wandering around (MBWA)**, dropping in unannounced at a work site and engaging employees in spontaneous conversations. MBWA can improve the level of trust between employees and management by opening up new channels of communication. Sam Walton, the founder of Wal-Mart, visited stores weekly and used MBWA to learn what front-line employees were thinking about and to see if they needed help with problems. General managers at Hewlett-Packard use MBWA to develop personal rapport with all the employees in their business units. Business units at HP contain fewer than 500 employees, to facilitate informal communication. MBWA permits the general manager to deal with potentially harmful rumors before they spread. It also helps sustain an entrepreneurial company culture that allows HP to be an innovator and technology leader. Management Close-Up 15.2 on page 593 shows how companies can utilize different types of communication to develop a trusting work environment with open communications.

A pattern of informal communication that managers should be aware of occurs when employees form informal social groups called *cliques*, which may disrupt the flow of communication between employees by excluding those

management by wandering around (MBWA)

Dropping in unannounced at a work site and engaging employees in spontaneous conversations.

Blogs, or Web-based journals, are becoming more prevalent as a means of communication both within and outside the company. Cannondale has recently set up room on its corporate Web site for 15 members of its sales and marketing staff to file updates, press releases, photos, and news about the bike racing teams the company sponsors. "We're transferring our corporate content management system to blogs," says the company's Webmaster.

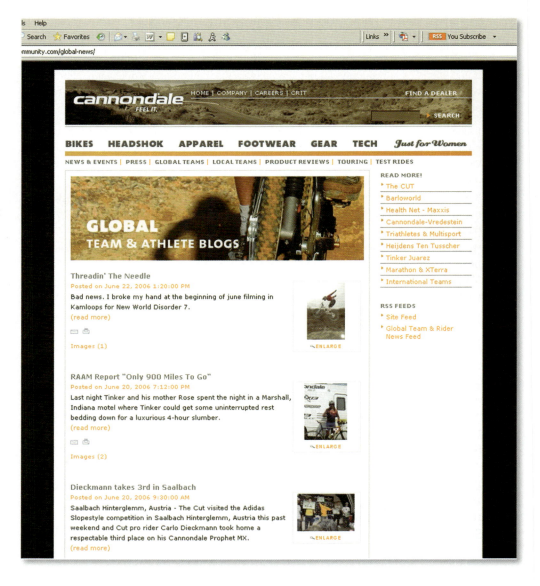

who are not part of the clique. Cliques form because of friendships between employees, who are often similar to each other, which can result in the exclusion of those are are different in age, race, gender, or ethnicity. You may have seen cliques in your high school days when athletes ate lunch at one table and intellectual students ate lunch at a different table and neither group mixed with the other. The social tension between the members of the clique and the excluded employees can negatively affect team or unit performance.[6] One constructive way to deal with a clique once it is proven to be disruptive to employee morale is to reassign employees within the clique to different projects where they can form new working relationships with diverse members of the organization. Company-sponsored social events may also open up new channels of communication so that more information is shared, which may reduce some of the ways cliques block the sharing of information.

LOC-In

6 **Learning Objective Check-In**

1. *Serena is a sales manager who likes to stay in close proximity to all the sales representatives so she is available to help them as problems arise. She likes to put the sales reps at ease and make sure they know she is available by dropping in on them unannounced and engaging in spontaneous conversations with them. This reminds them that she is always there to help and that it is all right to have casual conversations with her about their needs and concerns. This method of communication is _____.*
   a. *using the grapevine*
   b. *management by wandering around (MBWA)*
   c. *formal communication*
   d. *a low-richness method*

How Companies Communicate to Build Trust

THEME: ETHICS

Open communication is essential to building trust between employees and management, which leads in turn to improved sharing of information—upward, downward, and horizontally. Following are some methods that companies have used in creating a trusting environment with open communication:

1. *Communicating across borders*. Ciba Specialty Chemicals uses a satellite conference meeting to distribute its quarterly results to 5,000 employees in 14 corporate regions around the world. Employees of the specialty chemical firm can fax questions back to the board during the meeting.

2. *Using focus groups and teams to understand and resolve employee concerns*. S. C. Johnson & Son, the household cleaning goods company, holds employee focus groups and forms teams to discover and resolve issues that concern employees. The company, which employs 12,500 people around the world, also has business councils for special interest groups within the company, such as minorities, that meet and present their concerns to management.

3. *Sharing company information in meetings*. Family-owned industrial valve and seal manufacturer A. W. Chesterton holds quarterly meetings with its employees, and CEO Jim Chesterton answers questions. The company's departments, divisions, and subsidiaries also meet regularly and exchange information openly.

4. *Using a bulletin board for suggestions*. Dana Corporation employees are encouraged to post two suggestions a month on the company's bulletin board. Other workers add comments to them, and 80 percent of them are then implemented or acted on. The suggestions help the industrial manufacturer understand employee concerns and also provide valuable input for improving quality.

Source: Adapted from J. C. McCune, "That Elusive Thing Called Trust," *Management Review*, July/August 1998, pp. 10–16.

Communication Skills

One of the best ways to ensure effective communication is to provide opportunities for employees to develop communication skills. Skill in sending and receiving messages greatly reduces the possibility that a distorted message will be transmitted. Four key communication skills are assertive communication skills, presentation skills, nonverbal communication skills, and listening skills.

Assertive Communication Skills

Assertive communication skills enable an individual to communicate in ways that meet her or his own needs while at the same time respecting the needs and rights of others. A person who displays these skills states exactly what is wanted or needed from individuals being targeted for the message. The communicator holds himself or herself personally accountable for meeting needs. At the same time, the individual respects the needs of others and does not intrude or act childishly or manipulatively. Speaking calmly, directly, and confidently without instilling fear or anger in the other person is being assertive. The goal is to respond directly and outwardly to a problem.

A person who communicates assertively sticks to the facts, and does not communicate in a critical, subjective way. Assertive communication involves giving facts, feedback or information that makes clear the communicator's wishes, needs, wants, beliefs, or feelings. Here are some examples of speaking directly in a factual manner:[7]

- "I would like you here by eight o'clock."
- "I am quite pleased with the way the situation has been resolved."

Assertive communication includes obtaining honest feedback from others. The individual will ask direct questions or make direct statements to find out the other person's views, needs, wants, and feelings to make sure there is no misunderstanding between the two parties. Here are some examples of ways to receive direct feedback:

- "What would you prefer to do?"
- "I would like to hear your views on this."
- "What are the pros and cons on this idea from your point of view?"

There are several less effective communication styles that people use in the workplace. This is because the communicator is either indirect or is not mindful of the needs of others or of her or his own needs. These dysfunctional communication styles include: (1) passive, (2) aggressive, and (3) passive-aggressive communication.[8] An individual who engages in **passive communication** does not let others know directly what he or she wants or needs. A passive communicator hopes that his or her needs will be met without asking. Others are expected to figure out what is needed, and, if they fail, the passive communicator becomes resentful and pouts. Passive communicators often worry about what others think about them. They do not disclose their feelings or needs for fear of offending others. Not surprisingly, passive communicators are often frustrated and moody, making them difficult to work with.

An **aggressive communication** style is a forceful approach to communicate with others which expresses dominance and even anger. An aggressive communicator ignores the needs and rights of others, and loudly proclaims what he or she wants. The aggressive communicator may coerce others by using threatening words until he or she gets what is wanted. The individual who uses this style intimidates others. The cost is damage to relationships with others, who are not likely to trust an aggressive communicator. In the long run, others begin to resent and avoid the aggressive communicator.

A **passive-aggressive communication** style avoids giving direct responses to others' requests or feedback. Instead the passive-aggressive communicator tries to "get even" with others later for real or imagined injustices. This individual fears giving direct feedback to others for the same reasons that the passive communicator does. On the other hand, the passive-aggressive communicator uses sarcasm, sniping, and indirect criticism to express anger and aggression. Often the passive-aggressive communicator manipulates others by playing on their fears or insecurities to obtain what is wanted or needed. Needless to say, passive-aggressive communication is dishonest and does not foster positive working relationships.

If a person becomes aware of a tendency to communicate in one of these three dysfunctional styles, he or she should learn and practice honest, assertive communication skills.

Presentation Skills

Presentation skills are critical in almost every job. Salespeople must present products in convincing ways to potential clients. Engineers need to present ideas persuasively to the managers who control funding. Managers must present performance results to executives, and team members may need to present ideas for quality improvement at staff meetings. Managers and team leaders of-

---

passive communication

Style of communication whereby individual does not let others know directly what he or she wants or needs.

aggressive communication

A forceful style of communication with others that expresses dominance and even anger. The needs and wants of others are ignored.

passive-aggressive communication

Style of communication whereby individual avoids giving direct responses to other's requests or feedback.

Online **LearningCenter**
www.mhhe.com/gomez3e

What is Your Communication Style under Stress?

ten need to persuade the team or employees to do something or to accept a new policy. Basic guidelines for developing effective presentation skills include the following:

- *Prepare objectives* for your presentation. Know what you want the audience to do. Do you want them to buy a product? Invest in a new technology? Implement a new policy that controls travel expenses?

- *Organize the presentation* into several key ideas, no more than five, that will persuade the audience to act in the way you want them to. Organize your ideas in a logical sequence based on the relative importance of each idea. Use a mix of information to support your ideas, including publications, statistics, quotes from famous people, and personal anecdotes that you share with the audience.

- *Structure the presentation* into three parts: introduction, body, and conclusion. The *introduction* tells the audience what the presentation is about and what benefits they should get out of it. It should begin with a good opening, such as a story or declarative statement that grabs the audience's attention and sustains it through the rest of the presentation. The *body* is the main message and idea of the presentation. The *conclusion* summarizes the key takeaway points that the speaker wants to emphasize so that the audience will be persuaded to act.

- *Tailor the presentation* to the needs of the audience. Find out in advance who will be attending the meeting, anticipate the motivations and interests of the audience, and design the presentation to meet some of those needs and interests.

- *Establish your credibility* if the audience is not familiar with your credentials. An effective leader will introduce the speaker to establish the speaker's credentials.

- *Speak in a responsive and conversational style* that engages listeners. Nobody wants to hear a speaker read aloud or make a programmed presentation that sounds like it was memorized. Treat the audience as if you developed the presentation just for their benefit.

- *Use visual aids* such as overhead slides, charts, exhibits, or colorful posters that reinforce the verbal message. Computer programs that combine text, graphics, and color to make overhead slides are a basic part of the professional's toolkit.

- *Practice your presentation skills*, which, as all performance skills, improve with effort and practice. Look for opportunities to make presentations and receive feedback. Making a presentation to a school group or a social organization or teaching a class is a good way to get additional experience.

- *Restate the key ideas* you want the audience to remember when concluding the presentation. Summarize the objectives and purpose of the talk. End the presentation with an audience appeal for action if appropriate. Also, it is always a good idea to leave some extra time at the end of the presentation for answering questions. This lets the speaker clarify any misunderstandings that members of the audience may have had concerning the message the speaker wants them to receive.

Management Is Everyone's Business 15.2 on page 596 provides some suggestions on how to tell a story that makes a strong connection between the speaker and the audience so that they want to give their full attention to the presentation.

Nonverbal Communication Skills

nonverbal communication

The sending and decoding of messages with emotional content. Important dimensions include body movements and gestures, eye contact, touch, facial expressions, physical closeness, and tone of voice.

Effective communication involves more than words. **Nonverbal communication** is sending and decoding messages with emotional content. Friendliness, respect, acceptance, rejection, dominance, submissiveness, anger, fear, and humor are conveyed primarily by nonverbal signals. When the verbal and nonverbal messages disagree, the receiver is likely to discount the verbal message and believe the nonverbal message. For example, a sender who verbally promises to act in good faith but does not make eye contact and keeps glancing at a wristwatch is indicating lack of respect for the receiver. Important dimensions of nonverbal communication include body movements and gestures, eye contact, touch, facial expressions, physical closeness, and tone of voice.

BODY MOVEMENTS AND GESTURES   Posture can indicate attentiveness or lack of interest in a conversation. In a job interview, an interviewee should lean slightly forward to indicate that he or she is attentive to the interviewer. Gestures can add or detract from the verbal message. Hand gestures help emphasize points, but fidgeting sends the message that the speaker is nervous and lacks confidence. Different cultures place different meanings on gestures. In the United States, holding the thumb and first finger in a circle means OK. In Brazil it is an insult and may provoke a fight.

EYE CONTACT   Attentiveness or lack of interest on the part of the sender or receiver in face-to-face communication is conveyed by eye contact. In business communication, it is important for both parties to make some eye contact, but prolonged eye contact may be interpreted as aggressiveness or inappropriate intimacy. Use eye contact carefully in business conversations.

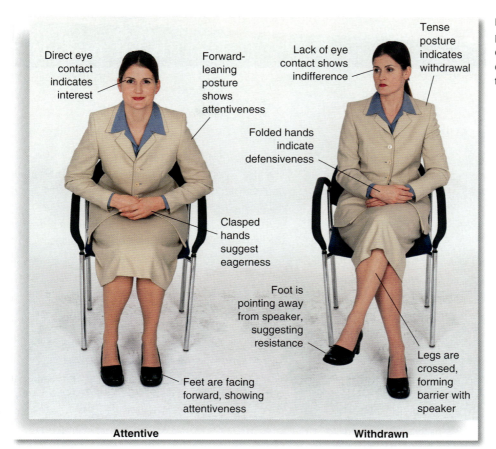

Direct eye contact indicates interest

Forward-leaning posture shows attentiveness

Clasped hands suggest eagerness

Feet are facing forward, showing attentiveness

Attentive

Lack of eye contact shows indifference

Tense posture indicates withdrawal

Folded hands indicate defensiveness

Foot is pointing away from speaker, suggesting resistance

Legs are crossed, forming barrier with speaker

Withdrawn

By having a forward leaning posture and making direct eye contact with a speaker (photo on far left), one conveys attentiveness to the other person.

TOUCH   A firm handshake is an enthusiastic greeting, but a weak handshake sends a negative signal, indicating low enthusiasm. Touch signals liking, acceptance, and friendship. Even more than eye contact, touch should be used sparingly in business situations. Unwanted touching in the U.S. workplace is a form of sexual harassment. Some other cultures are more permissive about touching. For example, in France it is not uncommon for employees who are good friends to greet each other with a kiss on the cheek.

FACIAL EXPRESSIONS   Emotions such as happiness, satisfaction, anger, fear, and confusion are signaled by facial expressions. A confused look is feedback that the verbal message was not clearly received. Smiling conveys happiness and warmth. Along with the handshake, a smile is probably one of the most effective ways to establish a positive connection with a new acquaintance.

PHYSICAL DISTANCE   Individuals regulate the physical distance between themselves and others, reserving the smallest distance (from touching to two feet away) for close, intimate friends and family, and the greatest distance (4 to 12 feet) for business and casual social acquaintances.[9] Violating an individual's expectations of an appropriate social distance causes discomfort and high probability of a miscommunication.

Physical distance expectations vary between cultures. Some cultures permit closer physical distances than others. Venezuelans have much smaller distance zones for business acquaintances than U.S. workers and might consider it rude if one backs away. A public speaker who understands how to use physical distance can create a strong bond with the audience. Oprah Winfrey, the television talk show host, bonds with her audience by reducing physical distance and going into the audience to speak with audience members up close.

NONVERBAL COMMUNICATION

Most nonverbal communication deals with feelings. Although feelings may be hidden, they are typically very potent. This exercise illustrates common nonverbal signals and explores their potency compared to verbal communication.

Form groups of four to five students. Each team works together as follows.

1. Each member of the group writes down three feelings ("happy," "irritated," and so on).

2. Each group member takes a turn trying to communicate nonverbally one of the feelings to the rest of the group. After about a minute, group members guess at the feeling. After each person's turn, he or she records how many group members guessed the correct feeling.

3. The entire class then reviews the overall level of accuracy and briefly discusses the typical accuracy of nonverbal communication.

4. In the small groups, again, step 2 is repeated except that while the person is giving the nonverbal message, he or she also gives a different verbal message. (The verbal message need not be opposite to the nonverbal, but it must be different.)

5. The entire class group discusses the difference between the two nonverbal communication approaches.

Discussion Questions

1. How accurately were people able to understand the first round of nonverbal signals? Were more subtle or less common feelings harder to identify?

2. What happened to the level of accuracy when a different verbal signal was present?

3. When you see this happen in a real situation—different verbal and nonverbal messages are sent—which are you most likely to believe? Why?

Source: From *Organizational Behavior* by Sashkin and Morris. Copyright © 1984. Reprinted by permission of Pearson Education, Inc., Upper Saddle River, NJ.

Oprah Winfrey's strong verbal communication skills are enhanced by her use of nonverbal communication, including touch and facial expression, with her audiences.

TONE OF VOICE Emotions such as attentiveness, friendliness, anger, or fear are transmitted by the tone in a voice. Aspects of the tone of voice that communicate different emotional states include pitch, loudness, speed, clarity of speech, and inflection. In a business setting, it is important to communicate confidence in order to establish credibility. Therefore, it is a good practice to speak clearly, emphasize key words, and use variable speed and inflection at appropriate times to keep the audience interested. Avoid talking in a monotone, which conveys lack of interest to the audience and reduces their motivation to listen.

Listening Skills

Listening is a fundamental communication skill for understanding both the verbal content and the underlying feelings embedded in the message. Listening is an active, not a passive, activity. It requires the listener to be involved in the communication process. The listener should try to avoid judging the speaker or the message being given. Instead, the listener should focus attention on trying to understand the content of the message. An active listener indicates both verbally and nonverbally that he or she is engaged in the conversation. When the speaker is communicating a feeling, the listener can restate what the speaker is expressing, asking for confirmation. The speaker will either confirm the impression or clarify it. In either case, the speaker will be encouraged to continue the conversation. Also, by using nonverbal indicators of listening—making eye contact, nodding the head, and leaning forward, for example—the listener is encouraging the speaker to continue. Lack of feedback from the listener can discourage the speaker from sharing opinions or feelings. Passively listening may unintentionally short-circuit a conversation.

When listening to another person, the speaker's tone of voice often discloses his or her emotional state, which helps the listener understand the feelings behind the words. Aspects of the speaker's tone of voice to listen for include the pitch, loudness, and speed of the verbal message. By decoding the meaning of the speaker's tone of voice, the listener can provide feedback to the speaker that can improve the quality of communication between the two parties. Here are some examples of how to interpret and respond to a speaker's tone of voice.

- If a speaker's pitch of voice is high and strained, it indicates feelings of nervousness. A calm, reassuring response from the listener encourages the speaker to proceed speaking. On the other hand, a quick, jerky response from the listener may cut the speaker short and disrupt the speaker's train of thought. Speaking in a lower pitch that is unstrained indicates the speaker is feeling confident and has emotional composure.

- If the speaker's tone of voice is shaky and hesitant with numerous pauses, it indicates a lack of confidence and doubt. By maintaining eye contact and offering reassuring gestures such as nodding one's head, the listener encourages the speaker to go on and complete the message.

- When the speaker's voice is too loud, or on the other hand the speaker mumbles the words quietly, the listener will have difficulty understanding the message. In either case the listener has a duty to ask the speaker to reduce or increase the voice volume depending on the situation. If the speaker's voice is too loud, the listener should calmly ask the speaker to reduce the volume to a more comfortable level. This should be done in a nonjudgmental way. If the speaker speaks too softly and mumbles, making it difficult to hear the words, the listener should ask the speaker to increase the volume. In both instances the focus should be on conveying the desire to understand the speaker.

Listening is an invaluable skill for managers. By actively listening to another individual, the manager shows empathy for and understanding of the speaker's perspective, even if it is different from the manager's own position. This is critical when managers negotiate with each other or with customers to find solutions acceptable to both parties. Employees or other managers are unlikely to bring

GUIDELINES FOR ACTIVE LISTENING

You can show a speaker you are actively listening to the ideas and feelings that are being communicated by observing the following dos and don'ts.

Do create a supportive atmosphere.

Do listen for feelings as well as words.

Do note cues, such as gestures, tone of voice, and body posture.

Do occasionally test for understanding by asking, "Is this what you mean?"

Do demonstrate acceptance and understanding verbally and nonverbally.

Do ask exploratory, open-ended questions.

Don't try to change the other's views.

Don't solve the problem for the speaker.

Don't give advice, no matter how obvious the solution may seem.

Don't pass judgment.

Don't explain or interpret others' behavior.

Don't give false reassurances.

Don't attack if the speaker is hostile to you (try to understand the source of any anger).

Don't ask questions about the "why" of feelings.

Source: From *Effective Behavior in Organizations*, by Cohen, et al. Copyright © 1976 The McGraw-Hill Companies, Inc. Reprinted with permission.

MANAGEMENT IS EVERYONE'S BUSINESS 15.3

Working as a Manager   As a manager you are occasionally likely to deal with an employee who has a problem that is highly sensitive or emotional in nature. This is the time to use your listening skills.

- First, seek to understand the nature of the problem and the perspective of the employee before telling him or her what you think about the issue or passing judgment on it. Hearing the employee out lets the person know that you are being supportive and are concerned.

- The use of listening skills lets you understand the problem from the employee's perspective so that both of you can develop a mutually beneficial solution.

- If it is necessary to give critical or negative feedback, make sure that the behavior being criticized is one that the employee is able to control. There is little value in communicating a shortcoming to a person if he or she has no control over it.

- For example, a dyslexic employee might have difficulty writing memos that are free of spelling errors. Rather than criticizing the dyslexic employee's spelling skills, a manager could encourage the employee to use the spell-checking function on a computer before distributing memos. The dyslexic employee is better able to control the spell-checking function on the computer than to correctly spell all the words in a written message.

problems to managers who have weak listening skills. This is likely to undermine a manager's credibility and limit effectiveness. Manager's Notebook 15.3 above presents specific ways to improve active listening skills. Management Is Everyone's Business 15.3 above explains how a manager can apply listening skills to deal with an employee who is experiencing an emotionally sensitive problem.

CONCLUDING THOUGHTS

After the introductory vignette at the beginning of the chapter we presented some critical thinking questions related to the practice of using broadband communications technology to enable home workers to provide customer support services via the Internet. Now that you have had the opportunity to learn about managing communication in the chapter, let's discuss the critical thinking questions. First, one of the advantages of using home workers who respond to customer inquiries is that it opens up opportunities for workers who are highly educated, have chosen to be at home for their children, or other family members, yet have valuable skills that employers can put to good use. Home workers usually serve customers better at a lower cost than onsite call center employees, who tend to be younger, less educated, and less reliable. Home workers are more motivated and productive because they can combine work and family responsibilities without the role conflicts of traditional jobs and their inflexible schedule of work on the company premises.

Second, companies must deal with some challenges when managing employees who work at home. Supervising, coaching, and mentoring home workers can be difficult to do well. While the customer service work of home workers can be monitored electronically and corrected, an employee's need for coaching and feedback to improve performance may require face-to-face communication that can be difficult to schedule if an employee lives far from the company office. A home worker can feel islolated and detached from the company if there is no opportunity to interact with other employees. Occasional meetings organized by the company where home workers can share ideas and best practices with each other could help reduce feelings of isolation and detachment as well as improve their job skills.

Focusing on the Future: Using Management Theory in Daily Life

Managing Communication

At first, you might not think that a chief financial officer would put a lot of emphasis on communication, but Todd S. Thomson, formerly the CFO of Citigroup, and now the CEO of its Global Wealth Management Division, sees communication as one of the three most critical parts of the CFO's job. Todd not only knows the power of communication for himself, but he used his knowledge of communication theory to transform the way information flowed throughout Citigroup.

In an interview with Michael Useem, the director of the Wharton Center for Leadership and Change Management, Todd suggests that there are three essential roles for a CFO. The first is to act as the "conscience of the organization"—the CFO is responsible for making sure the finances of the company are handled in the best interests of the shareholders. The second is to make sure that costs are reined in—that the organization is spending money on things that will pay off, not just on "good ideas." Finally, and perhaps most importantly, the CFO needs to be sure that he or she is "bringing the right information to the right people at the right time to make the right decisions."

Todd's communication strategy revolves around facts—identifying them, analyzing them, and getting them where they will do the most good. He recognizes the importance of horizontal, downward, and upward communication. Senior managers at Citibank engage in horizontal communication every week when they gather for their "business heads" meeting. The result of their weekly communication session is a "management information report." That report is used every week for downward communication, and it carries important messages to managers at lower levels of the organization. The emphasis of the report changes from week to week—one week it might be about cross-selling, and the next it might present an expense analysis—but the report always gives managers the information they need to assess and improve their department's performance, and it gives them a direction to emphasize in their activities for the week.

Todd places as much emphasis on upward communication as he does on downward communication. Quarterly conference calls and an annual gathering ensure that his employees have a time and space for upward communication. Like the downward communication from the business heads meeting, all information Todd gets from his employees is expected to be based on facts, not opinion. If an employee brings opinions to Thomson, he or she is sent back to "do their homework," and told to return with facts. Employees who cannot produce specific details after getting this kind of feedback do not last long in the organization.

By focusing all communications on facts, Todd is attempting to minimize both receiver and perception barriers. Todd knows his audience, and he recognizes and respects their need for getting crucial information in a form that supports business decision making. He knows that an impassioned plea will hold less weight with CEOs than a logical argument supported by detailed information. At the same time, he knows that too much irrelevant detail can also derail a presentation or report. For these reasons, he makes sure that his communications are models of targeted reporting—they focus on specific business issues, and use facts to drive discussion.

Todd further reduces receiver barriers by tailoring his presentations to his audience. For example, in the past he worked with two Citigroup CEOs who had very different styles—Sandy Weill and Charles Prince. As he explains it,

> Sandy is a "people person" and tends to manage through people. Sandy would wander around into offices—including mine—on a regular basis, and we would sit down and start talking about the business. Chuck tends to structure more formal reviews as opposed to informal discussions.

By understanding the style of each CEO and giving them information in their preferred format, Todd Thomson was able to build a good working relationship with both of them.

Useem notes that Thomson's latest job change (moving from CFO to CEO) involved a huge leap. The amount of money alone is staggering—as CFO, Todd was responsible for managing annual revenues of over $100 billion, but as CEO, he is responsible for over one *trillion* dollars worth of revenues. Likewise, the number of employees supervised jumped—from 6,000 under the CFO to 30,000 as CEO. How, then, did Todd approach such a challenging assignment?

Todd's response emphasizes another aspect of communication—listening. He points out that both jobs require one thing—getting people to believe in your vision for the company and motivating them to take action to make the vision reality. This process starts with listening—meeting people, getting them to tell you what they know about the business, and probing them for information about opportunities and issues. It is only after he has heard what his employees have to say that Thomson sets out his expectations for where the business will go and presents a strategy for getting there. The result, in his words, is,

> I find that people will follow that kind of direction. They appreciate the fact that you are listening, the fact that you set your expectations out very clearly up front, and that you have taken some time to put a strategy in place and communicate it.

Source: Knowledge@Wharton, "The CFO as Company Conscience," http://leadership.wharton.upenn.edu/ digest/05-05.shtml, accessed May 7, 2006.

summary of learning objectives

Communication is the process of transmitting information from one party to another through the use of shared symbols. The information may take the form of facts, objective information, or feelings. This chapter's discussion will help future managers, teams, and employees better understand the importance of managing communication. The discussion in this chapter that meets each of the learning objectives set out at the start of the chapter is summarized below.

1 Understand the communication process.

- The process of communication includes a **sender** and a **receiver**. The sender encodes the message in symbols and the receiver must decode the message to receive the intended meaning.
- The sender selects a **communication channel** that can vary from rich to lean in terms of the amount of content that can be transmitted. Communication channels include face-to-face conversations, written memos, videotapes, and voice mail.
- Communication channels that provide feedback should be utilized when the content of the message is complex and important. **Noise** may interfere with the receiver's ability to accurately decode the message. Communication channels with **feedback** provisions can reduce the threat of noise-distorted messages.

2 Eliminate barriers that distort the meaning of information.

- Differences in employee status and power, diversity, and self-interest create communication barriers that must be managed for effective organizational communication to take place.
- An organization that designs a communication system with multiple communication channels and that develops communication channels that provide opportunities for feedback help the sender to clarify whether the message's content was accurately received by the receiver, which can reduce barriers to communication.

3 Recognize the basic patterns of organizational communication.
   Patterns of communication in organizations include:

- **Downward communication** in which the sender is at a high level in the organization and the receiver is at a lower level.
- **Upward communication** in which the sender is at a lower level in the organization and the receiver is at a higher level.
- **Horizontal communication** in which both the sender and receiver in the organization are at similar levels.

4 Understand how to organize and run effective meetings.
   Some ways to make meetings more effective include the following practices:

- Make sure there is a good reason for a meeting. If one can use other ways to communicate that can be substituted for a meeting such as a memo, do not schedule a meeting.
- Select a meeting place that allows everyone to hear each other and the speaker.
- Create a meeting agenda and distribute it in advance of the meeting so that everyone knows what topics the meeting will cover.
- Keep the meeting on time so that all the agenda topics are covered and if possible leave some time to cover other topics that may not be on the agenda.
- End the meeting with a plan of action.

5 Master electronic forms of communication.
   Electronic forms of communication such as e-mail let employees exchange text messages and documents coded into digital symbols and transmitted over

the Internet. Employees should use good judgment in deciding what kinds of messages to send with electronic communication.

- Messages with highly emotional content have a better chance of being accurately received with face-to-face communication, which provides a richer channel for sending emotional content.
- Messages that have content that is of a highly sensitive, controversial, or personal nature should not be sent over electronic communication channels because the employer has the legal right to monitor electronic communications and hold an employee responsible for the content that is sent.

6 Work with an organization's informal communication system.

Informal communication occurs in organizations when there are gaps in or barriers to formal communication and employees do not receive the information they desire.

- An effective way to work with an organization's informal communication system is with the application of **management by wandering around (MBWA)**, which consists of dropping in unannounced at a work site or office to engage in spontaneous conversations with employees. MBWA can open new channels of communication between managers and employees and can also help to dispel rumors and gossip that may be harmful to employee morale.

discussion questions

1. Why is it important for a communication channel to have provisions for feedback? Can you think of a situation in which it may be useful to have communication without any provisions for feedback? Describe this situation.

2. What communication barriers could distort the communication between you and your professor? What are some approaches you could use to overcome these communication barriers?

3. Why are organizations today placing a greater emphasis on horizontal communications?

4. Is e-mail superior to older forms of electronic communications such as the telephone or voice mail? What are the advantages of e-mail? What are the disadvantages of e-mail? How can we manage a large volume of e-mail messages so that we are not spending too much time responding to messages each day?

5. Assume you are a manager and you overhear two employees exchanging harmful gossip about the personal life of another employee. Why do employees gossip and spread rumors about each other? How can this type of informal communication be managed? How would you handle this situation?

6. As a team leader, suppose one of the employees on your team has poor listening skills and continuously interrupts others who are speaking, becoming a source of frustration for the other team members. How would you improve this situation?

7. Research shows that in a job interview, the interviewer is likely to be strongly influenced by first impressions of the interviewee. In many cases a decision is made within the first minute of the interview. Assuming you want to make a positive impression in a job interview, how would you communicate nonverbally to create a favorable impression?

8. What is the difference between communicating assertively and communicating aggressively?

Employee Blogs Are Becoming the New Virtual Watercooler

A recent trend in communications is the rapid proliferation of employee blogs, which are Web sites that let employees voice their opinions and feelings about the company where they are employed. Employees offer opinions on the blog that would not be possible on official company communication channels such as newsletters or the company e-mail system. Because the blogs are stored on the Internet, employees can express controversial opinions and remain anonymous.

A proprietor of a blog called Mini-Microsoft has been a thorn in the side of the giant software company by posting a stream of anonymous critiques of the company, the employer of the blogger. The blog pulls no punches, calling Microsoft a "passionless, process-ridden, lumbering idiot" in a recent posting. Yet the blog is also chock full of humor, intelligence, and earnest suggestions for fixing Microsoft.

While Mini-Microsoft is just one among an estimated 2,000 blogs operated by Microsoft employees, it has become a virtual watercooler for employees. Hundreds anonymously vent their frustrations there without fear of retribution. Mini has emerged as something of a folk hero. Visitors to the site and other bloggers describe Mini as both the employee most likely to save Microsoft—and most likely to be fired. Mini-Microsoft provides a fascinating example of a phenomenon that is sweeping the nation. Employee bloggers are shining a bright light on the inner workings of their companies and thrusting all sorts of bottled-up frustrations out in the open. Whispered conversations suddenly become broadcast publicly. That puts newly found power in the hands of employees for doing either good or ill to their employer. Analyst Charlene Li of Forrester Research advises companies not to try to suppress their bloggers. "You can keep it hidden, or get those voices out there and deal with the problem," she says.

There are limits to what an employee can share in a blog, however. Posting confidential employer information on a blog such as trade secrets, business strategies, or private personnel information can be prohibited by state and federal laws that protect employer rights to intellectual property and employee rights to privacy.

Discussion Questions

1. Do you agree with the advice of the analyst from Forrester Research in the case who said that companies should not try to suppress bloggers? Justify your opinion.

2. What benefits can a company derive from the information posted on employee blogs by monitoring them at regular intervals?

3. Why do you think the Mini-Microsoft blog is so influential both inside and outside the company?

Sources: Adapted from J. Greene, "Mystery Blogger: A Rendezvous withi Microsoft's Deep Throat," *BusinessWeek*, September 26, 2005, p. 104; *The Economist*, "Blogging: Outreach and Outrage," March 11, 2006, p. 77; N. Vonk, "A Blogger's Guide to Blogging," *Campaign*, February 17, 2006, pp. 28–29; C. Wilson, "The Blogger at Work," *T + D*, March 2006, p. 15.

Actions Speak Louder than Words All around the World

"He wouldn't look me in the eye. I found it disconcerting that he kept looking all over the room but rarely at me," said Barbara Walters after her interview with Libya's Colonel Muamar el-Qaddafi. Like many people in the United States, Walters was associating eye contact with trustworthiness, so when Qaddafi did not make eye contact, she felt uncomfortable. In fact, Qaddafi was paying Walters a compliment. In Libya, *not* looking conveys respect. Looking straight at a woman is considered nearly as serious as physical assault.

Nonverbal communication varies widely between cultures and even between subcultures. The differences strongly affect communication in the workplace. Whether you are trying to communicate with a new Asian-American assistant, the Swedish managers who recently bought your company, the young African-American college student who won a summer internship with your firm, or representatives from the French company you hope will buy your firm's new designs, your efforts will depend as much on physical cues as on verbal ones. Most Americans aren't usually aware of their own nonverbal behaviors. They have trouble understanding the body language of people from other cultures. The list of differences is endless:

- In Thailand it is rude to place your arm over the back of a chair in which another person is sitting.
- Finnish female students are horrified by Arab girls who want to walk hand in hand with them.
- Canadian listeners nod to signal agreement.
- Japanese listeners nod to indicate only that they have understood.
- British listeners stare at the speaker, blinking their eyes to indicate understanding.
- People in the United States are taught that it's impolite to stare.
- Saudis accept foreigners in Western business attire but are offended by tight-fitting clothing and by short sleeves.
- Spaniards indicate a receptive friendly handshake by clasping the other person's forearm to form a double handshake.
- Canadians consider touching any part of the arm above the hand intrusive, except in intimate relationships.

It may take years to understand nonverbal communication in other cultures, but there are resources to help you prepare. Books and seminars on cultural differences are readily available, as are motion pictures showing a wide range of cultures. You can always rent videos of films and TV shows from other countries. Examining the illustrations in news and business magazines can give you an idea of expected business dress and personal space. Finally, remaining flexible and interacting with people from other cultures who are visiting or living in your country will go a long way toward lowering the barriers presented by nonverbal communication.

Discussion Questions

1. Explain how watching a movie from another country might help you prepare to correctly interpret nonverbal behavior from that culture.
2. Assume that one of your co-workers is originally from Saudi Arabia. You like him, and the two of you work well together. However, he stands so close when you speak with him that it makes you very uncomfortable. How would you communicate your discomfort to this co-worker?

Source: Adapted from C. Bovée and J. Thill, *Business Communication Today*, 6th ed. Upper Saddle River, NJ: Prentice Hall, 2000, p. 38.

individual/
collaborative
learning
case 15.1

Selecting the Most Effective Form of Communication

You are a sales representative for a leading pharmaceutical company, which produces a full range of drugs for medical treatments to patients. You communicate on a regular basis with other sales representatives within and outside your sales region, the sales manager and the district manager, and many clients within your sales territory who are primarily physicians and directors of managed care health organizations. Since you work primarily out of an office in your home, you must depend heavily on electronic communication to stay in touch with customers, colleagues, and management. Here is some information about e-mail, voice mail, and fax to help you select the most appropriate electronic communication channel.

E-mail has the following advantages:

It is fast and inexpensive and provides easy access to others.

It facilitates communication with busy executives and managers.

It provides documented evidence that a message was received.

It is less intrusive than other forms of communication. Recipients can respond when time permits.

Senders can communicate with large numbers of people quickly and simultaneously.

It facilitates global communication where time zones create communication barriers.

E-mail also has disadvantages:

Not all offices have e-mail.

Some people are uncomfortable or inexperienced with e-mail.

It may be awkward to use when the message contains emotional content or when a relationship of trust has not yet been established between the parties.

It is not suitable for private or confidential messages.

Here are some tips for users of e-mail:

Check e-mail three or four times per day.

Assume e-mail is not private.

Check spelling and grammar, because e-mail represents you and your organization.

Voice mail has the following advantages:

It is the most personal form of electronic communication.

It allows the receiver to give a quick response.

Your voice can convey sincerity that the written word cannot. It can ease a problematic situation.

Voice mail also has disadvantages:

It can be frustrating to listen to a long prerecorded message with a menu of choices that may not apply to the caller's needs.

It cannot replace a handwritten thank-you note.

Here are some tips for using voice mail:

Anticipate that you may be leaving a recorded message. Before you make the call, prepare what you want to say and avoid rambling.

Avoid leaving the same message several times.

The greeting you prepare on your own voice mail should communicate your availability and tell the caller how to reach a live person in case of an emergency.

Avoid cute and humorous greetings.

Fax has the following advantages:

It quickly delivers a close approximation to original documents.

It is useful when a relationship is new or formal.

It is sometimes important to use stationery with the company name on the letterhead.

It is useful when a document requires a signature.

Fax also has disadvantages:

Many people share fax machines and waiting is sometimes necessary.

Confidential information may be disclosed because faxes can rarely be sent privately.

Faxes sometimes get lost.

Here are some tips for users of fax machines:

Always use a cover sheet that has your fax and telephone numbers.

Avoid reading other employees' faxes.

Critical Thinking Questions

1. You want to let the sales manager know which clients you will be visiting within your territory next week. Which communication channel would you select and why?

2. One of your clients complained about a late delivery of a shipment of drugs that was promised by a certain date. You must provide a response to the problem. Which communication channel would you select and why?

3. You will be attending the annual sales convention at Las Vegas, and while there you want to meet a colleague who works in the Australian subsidiary of your firm who will also attend the meeting. Which communication channel would you select to set up your meeting in advance and why?

Collaborative Learning Exercise

With a partner or small group, rank e-mail, voice mail, and fax from best to worst according to the following characteristics: richness of information, ease of use, availability, level of privacy, and speed of communication. Did everyone in your group agree on the rankings? What accounts for any differences in your rankings of these communication channels?

Source: Adapted from B. Pachter, "Tips for Technological Correctness," *HR Focus*, November 1996, p. 21; D. Brake, *Dealing with e-Mail*. London: DK, 2003.

internet exercise 15.1

www.wholefoodsmarket.com

Whole Foods, Whole Philosophy

Visit the Web site of Whole Foods Market, click on the "company" button, and explore the "whole philosophy" section, including the "core values," "quality standards," and "declaration of interdependence" sections of the company philosophy. Then answer the following questions:

1. What message does the Whole Foods Market company philosophy communicate to the consumer about the food products it sells?
2. What message does the Whole Foods Market company philosophy communicate to employees and job applicants about the work environment at the company?
3. Do the graphic and visual images on the Web site communicate the same or a different message to you as the text (the words) describing the company philosophy?
4. Suppose the text gave a different message to the reader than the visual images do. Which message would most likely be received by the reader? Explain your answer.

manager's checkup 15.1

Listening Self-Inventory

How good are you at listening? Consider the following statements and check yes or no next to each. Be as truthful as you can in light of your behavior in the last few meetings or gatherings you attended.

		Yes	No
1.	I frequently attempt to listen to several conversations at the same time.	____	____
2.	I like people only to give me the facts and then let me make my own interpretation.	____	____
3.	I sometimes pretend to pay attention to people.	____	____
4.	I consider myself a good judge of nonverbal communications.	____	____
5.	I usually know what another person is going to say before he or she says it.	____	____
6.	I usually end conversations that don't interest me by diverting my attention from the speaker.	____	____
7.	I frequently nod, frown, or whatever to let the speaker know how I feel about what he or she is saying.	____	____
8.	I usually respond immediately when someone has finished talking.	____	____
9.	I evaluate what is being said while it is being said.	____	____
10.	I usually formulate a response while the other person is still talking.	____	____
11.	The speaker's "delivery" style frequently keeps me from listening to content.	____	____
12.	I usually ask people to clarify what they have said rather than guess at the meaning.	____	____
13.	I make a concerted effort to understand other people's points of view.	____	____

	Yes	No
14. I frequently hear what I expect to hear rather than what is said.	____	____
15. Most people feel that I have understood their point of view when we disagree.	____	____

Scoring: The correct answers according to communication theory are as follows: "No" for questions 1, 2, 3, 5, 6, 7, 8, 9, 10, 11, 14. "Yes" for questions 4, 12, 13, 15. If you missed only one or two questions, you strongly approve of your own listening habits, and you are on the right track to becoming an effective listener in your role as manager. If you missed three or four questions, you have uncovered some doubts about your listening effectiveness, and your knowledge of how to listen has some gaps. If you missed five or more questions, you probably are not satisfied with the way you listen, and your friends and co-workers may not feel you are a good listener either. Work on improving your active listening skills.

Source: From *Supervisory Management*, by Florence M. Stone. January 1989. Copyright © 1989 American Management Association/Amacom. Reproduced with permission of American Management Association/Amacom via Copyright Clearance Center.

Privacy in the Workplace

video summary

Summary

Is your boss reading your private e-mails and instant messages (IMs)? If so, he or she has every right to according to the law today. There is a privacy battle going on right now that is getting bigger every day. On the one side, companies' e-mails can be subpoenaed in a court setting if the firm is sued, for instance, and companies' interests are at stake depending on the e-mails' contents. On the other side, a worker often assumes e-mails are private and are off-limits for anyone who doesn't have the password he or she set up in the first place. E-mails can actually be read, archived, and used against workers by their boss or even the government.

Twenty-five percent of companies have fired someone because of an e-mail. At least 40 percent of companies have someone on the staff to monitor what goes across computer screens. Internet sites visited, e-mails sent, and even every keystroke can be monitored. Everything is fair game, and it is almost impossible to actually delete anything. Nancy Flynn, founder of the E-Policy Institute, consults with companies about e-mail monitoring and instant messaging and policies regarding them. She has written several books on the topic. She likens e-mail and archived computer data to DNA that can make or break a case for an employee.

Not only can employers track and archive e-mails and messages on a work computer and listen to and record phone conversations, they can also keep track of how much time employees spend goofing off. This includes playing "solitaire" or surfing the Net. In fact, many companies have written policies concerning how much time a person can spend goofing off before getting into trouble.

One of the biggest offenses related to e-mail is saying damaging remarks about the boss in the e-mail. Above all else, Nancy Flynn recommends that workers take a look at and become familiar with the e-mail policy. It is important to actually ask someone in HR to see the policy if it is not readily available elsewhere. Her advice is to comply with that policy to the letter.

Discussion Questions

1. Do you think employers should have the right to access the personal e-mail communications sent by their workers using workplace computers? Why or why not?

2. What are some ways to avoid getting into trouble with e-mail at work? How can employees use e-mail appropriately?

3. Where can employees find information regarding their company's e-mail or Internet policies? Would you behave differently if there was no written policy regarding e-mail at your company?

part six

Operations and Information Systems Management

Establishing and adhering to standards is critical for safety and customer satisfaction. Regardless of the talent and motivation in an organization, errors can occur and performance can only be as good as the information it is based on. To assure continued high performance and survivability of the organization, managers need to be able to determine what should be done and whether their decisions are being adequately executed. Responsible management requires standards, good information, and the means to quickly bring any deviant performance back to the standard level.

In Part Six we will examine how managers can assure that performance meets expectations. We will consider how managers can control performance and whether the focus of control efforts should be on people or on systems. We will also consider how production processes can be assessed and deviations from standards eliminated. The old adage that knowledge is power is now truer than ever. We will therefore look at how information can be utilized for effective management.

6

chapter 16

Management Control

Learning Objectives

1 Describe management control and understand the importance of control systems.

2 Identify the four basic management control approaches.

3 Describe the steps a manager would take to apply a bureaucratic control process.

4 Identify the major types of bureaucratic control.

5 Generate the basic framework for a balanced scorecard.

6 Differentiate between market and financial control.

7 Distinguish between system and person factors as the focus of control.

Looking for Your Luggage?

16

Airlines worldwide lost a record 30 million bags last year, a number boosted by a global surge in travelers, a recent study says.

According to the study from SITA, a Switzerland-based technology consultant for the airline industry, in 2005, the world's airlines boarded about 2 billion passengers, who checked 3.7 billion bags. The airlines mishandled about 1 percent of bags.

Neither the rate of baggage mishandling nor the average length of time it takes for mishandled bags to catch up with their owners—about 31 hours—has changed much in recent years, SITA executive Rich Fiorenza says. About 240,000 of the lost bags in 2005 never reached their owners. Fiorenza says the sheer number of people flying is pushing the number of mishandled bags and the sums spent to reunite bags with owners to new levels.

Although a 99 percent success rate might be considered outstanding in many fields, Fiorenza says, airlines need to meet a tougher baggage-handling standard because of the huge number of customers affected. "It remains that 30 million bags were mishandled last year," he says. "And if one of them was yours, you don't care that 99 percent were handled right."

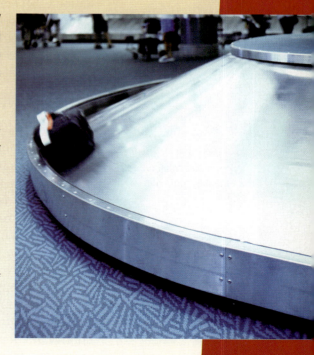

Mishandled bags are a major customer service issue that can undermine a carrier's corporate image, Fiorenza says. And mishandled bags carry a huge cost for airlines. Last year, airlines spent an estimated $2.5 billion returning lost bags to their owners or on compensation to owners of bags that were never returned. That's up from the $1.6 billion that airlines spent in 2004 dealing with mishandled bags. "That's right off the industry's bottom line, a totally needless cost," Fiorenza says.

About 61 percent of all mishandled bags in 2005 got lost during the process of transferring them from one flight to another, SITA says. As a result, passengers on nonstop flights have a significantly smaller chance of having their bags mishandled than do passengers with connecting itineraries.

About 15 percent of mishandled bags in 2005 the airlines failed to load on the proper flight in the first place. Another 9 percent of mishandled bags had encountered ticketing errors, passenger mistakes, or security delays.

Source: Dan Reed, "Airlines Lost Record Number of Bags Last Year," *USA Today*, March 21, 2006, p. 5B.

CRITICAL THINKING QUESTIONS

1. *The airline industry experiences only a 1 percent mishandled baggage rate. Why are industry consultants calling for new standards?*

2. *What kind of appropriate standards can airlines set for allowable numbers of lost-luggage incidents?*

3. *How will the industry know when its standards have been achieved?*

We will revisit these questions about management control in our Concluding Thoughts after you have read this chapter.

Control is an important management function. Control ensures that standards are met, errors are limited, quality is acceptable, products are safe, and the company is performing at the highest possible level. When control is missing or inadequate, management cannot know if standards are being adhered to or if outcomes are acceptable or safe. Inadequate controls lead to poor or unsafe products, shoddy service, or, in the introductory feature on the airlines, lost luggage along with substantial direct and indirect costs. One key management role is making sure that the process and outcomes of the business meet expected standards. Without having data that provides this assurance, management is hoping for the best but really can't know or promise customers what they will get in terms of a product or service.

In this chapter we examine the concept of management control. The major management control tools are reviewed and a variety of issues regarding control are examined. Several questions are considered, such as: What should be the focus of control efforts—people or the system? What steps are needed for effective control? Is there a downside to control, and can it be eliminated/minimized? First, however, this chapter begins with a consideration of the nature of management control.

What Is Management Control?

control

The process of comparing performance to standards and taking corrective action.

Control is the process of comparing performance to standards and taking corrective action, if needed. In other words, control involves measurement and regulation. It is the means by which management assures that desired objectives are being achieved.

Control is closely associated with the management function of planning. People often refer to "planning and control" in one phrase, as if the two were almost one function. Control complements planning because it is the means by which management assesses whether or not plans are being appropriately carried out. Corrective actions get the organization back on track and help managers achieve their intended goals.

There are a variety of ways to categorize the various types of control approaches. Figure 16.1 on page 615 is a framework of management approaches to control. As depicted in the figure, control approaches can be categorized according to two factors: type and focus. The *type* factor is divided into formal and informal approaches to control. Formal control systems consist of written rules.

FIGURE 16.1

Control Approaches as a
Function of Type and Focus

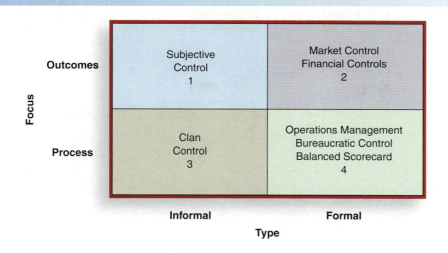

They specify explicitly and in detail the processes, standards, and steps to be followed. In contrast, informal control relies on unwritten expectations regarding performance. For example, work groups are likely to develop norms for performance. Employees who fail to perform at those levels receive quick and certain feedback that they need to improve. Even though they are unwritten, informal controls can be a powerful source for regulating performance.

The *focus* factor refers to whether a control tool is directed at the outcome or the process. An outcome approach focuses on the results of a business process, such as number of units sold, amount of market share, or financial outcomes, such as profits. In contrast, a process approach focuses on how the work is actually performed. A process control tool centers on the steps involved in a process and the standards that should be followed in carrying out these steps.

The framework in Figure 16.1 will be used to organize our discussion of management control techniques. Remember that the framework may oversimplify the reality of control as it is practiced in organizations. First, both factors (type and focus) are, in reality, more of a matter of gradation than of a choice between two levels. For example, an organization may employ a control strategy that is in the range of informal to formal. Second, and related, the control techniques are not necessarily "pure." That is, an organization may employ multiple control approaches, some of which may be more formal and others more informal, and some more focused on process and others on outcomes. Nonetheless, in most organizations, there is a primary, or dominant, approach to control.[1] Company executives may use control techniques that focus on both process and outcomes, but outcome control may clearly be the primary focus, while process is only a secondary concern. With these caveats in mind, control techniques from each of the four cells of the framework are examined next.

LOC-In

Informal and Outcome-Focused Control

An informal approach and a focus on outcomes is a combination labeled in Figure 16.1 in cell 1 as **subjective control**. Subjective controls are not guided by objective standards. Rather, outcomes are subjectively considered and actions are

subjective control

Informal approach based on global assessment of outcomes.

Steve Harden used a training program originally created for FedEx and safety lessons from the aviation industry to craft a new company called LifeWings that teaches doctors, nurses, and technicians how to perform well under pressure as a team. Each medical team is taught to create a standardized checklist of activities for every procedure, to speak up if variations occur, and to hold regular briefings to ensure consistent patient care. Says Harden, "Human beings will eventually make errors. But you can equip them with communication behaviors that help detect and correct those errors before they become serious."

taken based on those assessments. For example, a company may rely on feedback from customers regarding the quality of their products or services. If no complaints are heard, it is assumed that things are fine. When given a complaint, the company will try to satisfy the customer. The subjective control approach does not typically utilize explicit standards or a standard process for adjusting outcomes. Instead, the approach employs more global, or broad-based, assessments, such as "Are you satisfied with the product?" or "Are there any problems?" if there is any assessment at all. When assessments are not systematic, customers are asked different questions in different ways. The subjective approach also does not specify how deviations from an acceptable level of performance (whatever it is or however that may be defined by individual customers) should be handled. For example, if quality is claimed not to be acceptable, the organizational leaders may try to do something, but what should be done isn't specified beforehand.

The subjective control approach is common particularly in smaller businesses and in service settings. Smaller and start-up organizations may not have the time or resources needed to establish more systematic control systems. In service settings, it can be more difficult to establish standards. In manufacturing settings, products can be exactly measured to determine if they are within quality tolerances. While measuring the quality of a service interaction is not straightforward, it is possible to systematically measure service outcomes. It is also possible to specify various corrective steps that should be taken in the event quality is not achieved. The subjective control approach simply is not as specific about corrective actions, as compared to other methods of control.

The subjective control approach might be summed up with the description that "We aren't really sure how we are doing, but we hope you like our diligent efforts." Control efforts in this approach might be considered as an example of management-by-exception. That is, if there is a complaint, action will be taken. Otherwise, management approaches the issue of control based on the old adage, "no news is good news." The subjective control approach is not a professionally acceptable or effective management control technique; however, it is common. You may have encountered this approach in any number of situations.

Formal and Process-Focused Control

Another set of control techniques, found in cell 4 of Figure 16.1, are formal and focus on the process. These approaches are probably the most widely known and used. They occur when the focus is on the work process and impose established standards, or rules, for how this process should be carried out. Operations management and, in particular, the quality approach, are examples of a formal and process-focused approach. Remember, however, that operations management is not simply a control technique; it is a means for increasing efficiency and effectiveness in production processes. Since Chapter 17 is devoted to a consideration of operations management, it is not covered here. The following are some well-known and newer emerging control approaches from the formal and process-focused category.

LOC-In

2 Learning Objective Check-In

1. *Maguire Labs uses a control approach that is largely informal and is based on the quarterly outcomes of their product quality. If customers do not complain explicitly or submit warranty claims on a product, the firm assumes that the quality is fine. If there are problems, customers who have them are dealt with on an individual basis so that the relationship is positively maintained. This example illustrates _____.*
   a. *subjective control*
   b. *objective control*
   c. *clan control*
   d. *bureaucratic control*

Bureaucratic Control

Bureaucratic control is likely what most people think of when they think of management control. Bureaucratic control techniques are characterized by written guidelines or controls. While these standards can apply to outcomes, bureaucratic controls routinely focus on work processes. Bureaucratic control techniques apply standards to assess performance and apply corrective actions to regulate performance and bring it back to the level of the standards. The focus of bureaucratic control techniques is to detect discrepancies between performance and standards and to take systematic action to remove any deficiencies.

THE CONTROL PROCESS Bureaucratic control techniques are composed of a cycle of steps, including (1) establishing standards; (2) performance measurement; (3) identifying gaps; and (4) corrective action. Each step is considered next.

Establishing Standards Standards are the benchmarks against which performance is compared. Standards can take a variety of forms and be derived from a variety of sources. For example, standards could take the form of goals or could consist of professional guidelines or legal or financial procedures. Standards can also be based on statistical analysis and what is considered to be acceptable variance in performance (see the discussion of the quality approach in Chapter 17). Standards can also be derived from the practice of benchmarking, examining the performance of other organizations. No matter how standards are derived and whatever types they are, they form the requirements of the job. The standards are the criteria against which performance will be compared.

A critical issue is how the standards are developed. While it can be relatively quick and easy to take a top-down approach and unilaterally develop standards, this approach may not work well in practice. A participative approach to creating standards takes longer but yields standards that are understood by everyone. When employees participate in creating standards, they are likely to be more committed to the standards and will work harder to achieve the desired results.

bureaucratic control

A formal control approach involving a cycle of (1) establishing standards, (2) performance measurement, (3) identifying gaps, and (4) corrective action.

Categories of Managerial Control

Performance Measurement   Levels of performance can be assessed in a variety of ways. The data used to determine performance levels can be classified as objective or subjective. Objective performance data includes measures such as number of pieces produced, amount of downtime, amount of waste, time to complete a task, and so on. The advantage of objective data is that it is typically free from error and bias.

Subjective performance data includes measures that involve human judgment. A supervisor's judgment of overall performance levels, a worker's judgment of the quality of materials, or a manager's assessment of the safety level of the work environment are all subjective assessments. The subjective nature of the data reflects the fact that it involves human judgment, thus opening the door to possible error and/or bias. However, subjective data is not constructed out of thin air—it is based on the work environment, albeit as perceived and assessed by people. These perceptions and assessments can sometimes make for subjective data that is superior to objective performance data. Consider, for instance, objective data that lists the number of accidents in a plant. For a given time period, there may be no accidents and the lack of mishaps might lead top management to conclude that the operation is safe. At the same time, subjective data from supervisors or employees might tell a much different but more accurate story. Supervisors might judge the work environment as too cluttered and conclude that the work practices of many workers emphasize speed over safety. In other words, the environment might be an accident waiting to happen. Management control based on objective data may completely fail to recognize how hazardous the work environment might be. Objective data by itself often fails to tell the whole story—it is often deficient. Subjective data can sometimes provide a more complete picture.

Whether performance data is subjective or objective in nature, it is important that adequate measures be devised and data collected. An old adage states that if you don't measure it, you can't manage it. Skills for Managing 16.1 on page 619 looks at the importance of performance measurement in the domain of personal hygiene and food safety.

Identifying Gaps   After developing standards and performance measures, the next step in the control cycle is to compare the two in order to identify any deficiencies. This step points out gaps between actual and intended performance levels. At times the task is not quite as simple as it may seem. It is important to recognize that there is always some amount of variation in any process, and not every deviation from a standard is meaningful. In other words, the problem in identifying gaps is determining how big a difference makes a difference. Figure 16.2 on page 620 presents a control chart, a tool commonly used in the quality approach (see Chapter 17). The control chart is helpful for determining whether deviations are meaningful gaps between performance and standards.

As presented in Figure 16.2, control charts include upper and lower control limits. Where these limits are set depends upon how variable a process is and how important deviations are to quality or safety. It is common to set control limits at the levels of 2 standard deviations above or below the average performance level. Consider the performance levels depicted in the example control chart as representing the amount of time taken by each of three teams to respond to calls for service. Team 2 tends to perform the best, with response times even quicker than the standard. Team 3 tends to have the slowest response times, but all teams exhibit appreciable variance on this performance measure. Are any of the deviations from the prescribed or preferred level of meaningful size? The answer, according to the control chart approach, is "no."

"DID YOU WASH YOUR HANDS?"

Handwashing is recognized as one of the most effective ways to reduce the occurrence of foodborne illness. Unfortunately, people in the foodservice industry estimate that handwashing frequency is about half of what it should be, even in schools and hospitals. This subjective estimate is about as good as the performance data gets. In most organizations, many things get measured, but handwashing is seldom one of them. This lack of objective measurement may be coming to an end.

Various models of handwashing stations are being developed to improve and better manage this simple but important activity. One model uses scanning technology to identify each employee who washes his or her hands. The system even includes a minimum scrub time in the handwashing process.

Discussion Questions

1. Do you think that objective measurement of handwashing is important to a food safety control system? Or do you think subjective self-report (yes—I washed my hands!) is sufficient? Explain your answer.

2. Measurement is needed to manage. However, simply measuring something can also convey its importance. Do you think this will work for handwashing? If not, what else could be done to increase handwashing frequency?

3. How could the scanning technology be used to not only record but also reward frequent handwashers? Do you think the motivational component could be important to a food safety control system? Explain.

Research Questions

1. To what extent does lack of handwashing seem to be implicated in episodes of foodborne illness? Is there any

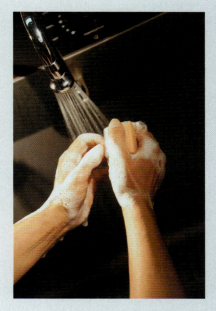

Are you washing your hands as often as needed?

data that you can find that provides some assessment of the extent to which lack of handwashing is a problem?

2. Can you find information on technology being applied to measure handwashing frequency? Do you think technology and objective measurement are the solution to handwashing problems? Why or why not?

Source: J. Mann, "Handwashing: Technology Adds a Measure of Management," *Foodservice Equipment & Supplies* 56 (2003), pp. 39+.

The upper and lower control limits on a control chart set the limits of acceptable, or normal, variation. Deviations from standard levels that fall within those limits are simply normal variation. To treat those deviations as a meaningful gap in performance is making the proverbial mountain out of a molehill. Deviations that fall outside the range defined by the control limits are, however, meaningful gaps between performance and the expected levels of performance.

Corrective Action   The final step in the control process is taking corrective action. Based on the previous step, what should management do? One option is to do nothing. Doing nothing is appropriate, and actually preferable, when no meaningful gaps in performance are found. If management takes action based on

FIGURE 16.2

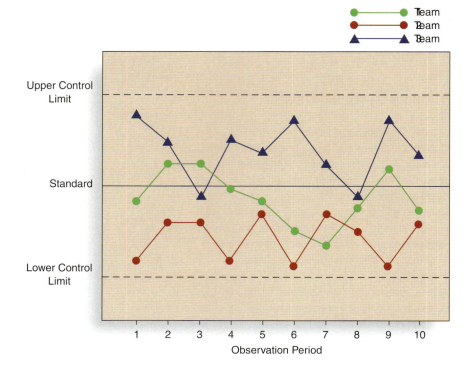

deviations that are within the acceptable range, meaningful performance improvement will not occur. Quite the contrary, management intervention when performance is within the range of the control limits may actually lead to increased variance in performance.[2] For example, a poor performance episode, but one that is within the acceptable range, might lead a vigilant manager to take action. Depending on the situation and the type of performance being examined (perhaps response time, as in our example, or the amount of sales, amount of waste, etc.), a manager might focus on motivating workers and tell them they need to work harder or decide to provide additional training. The manager might also look for ways to change the work situation, methods for arranging tools or materials, or advertising programs. The problem is that these interventions are not called for based on the control limits. The changes may upset normal work processes and end up increasing variability in performance. Taking no action can be the best approach, particularly when deviations from a standard are not of meaningful size.

When deviations from a standard are meaningful gaps in performance, a manager should take action. If corrective action is appropriate but isn't taken, the control process becomes simply a measurement exercise. The question is, what corrective action should be taken? While performance is typically thought of as the focus of corrective actions, there is another possibility; the standards themselves. When performance levels are systematically and significantly better or worse than the standard level, it is possible that the problem lies with the criteria and not with the performance. The standards may be too easy or unduly harsh. This means the problem lies with the standards, not with performance.

Managers must first be certain that the standards are reasonable and defensible. Then, management action can be directed at performance. The goal of the action is to improve performance and eliminate the gap from the standard level. But how best to do that? To say that action should be directed at performance still begs the question of what actions should really be taken. What should a manager do?

Working as an Individual   Our own work performance is the critical factor in determining our pay level, promotion opportunity, and career success, yet we typically leave the management of our performance to others. The bureaucratic control process is a practical tool that can be used to manage your own performance levels. Taking this systematic and proactive approach can result in improved performance as well as increased benefits and opportunities that are linked to job performance. The following are suggestions for using the bureaucratic control process as a tool to manage your own performance.

- *Establish standards for your performance.* You can do some informal benchmarking by observing others in your line of work and considering your own expectations. Also, consider the standards used in your workplace. In the end, you need to settle on clear and realistic standards for your performance.

- *Measure your performance.* How are you doing? Using the standards you set, assess yourself and ask others for their judgments as well.

- *Identify gaps.* How does your performance compare to the standards you set? Are there aspects of your work where your performance far exceeds or comes up short in comparison to the standards? Don't make the proverbial mountains out of molehills. Instead, focus your attention where it's needed—on real gaps.

- *Take corrective actions.* What can you do to eliminate the gaps? In the case of greatly exceeding a standard, removing the gap might call for reallocation of your time and effort away from that area of your work to areas needing improvement. If your performance is significantly below a standard, removing the gap might call for training or the application of a motivational technique (see Chapter 12). Whatever the direction of the deviation from the standard, you first need to determine the cause of the gap. Determine if the gap is due to personal factors, such as ability or motivation, or due to system factors, such as equipment or the social context. Only after careful consideration of causes can you take corrective actions that can be successful.

Simply stated, corrective actions need to be directed at the cause(s) of the deficiencies. Corrective actions directed at aspects of the performance system that aren't the cause of the problem will fail to correct anything meaningful. For example, directing action to employees to motivate them to work harder will not remove a deficiency if the cause is poor materials or supplies. The cause(s) of performance deficiencies need to be carefully identified so that corrective action can be effective and lead to improvement. Taking action without first carefully determining the cause of the deficiency can easily lead to workers questioning the quality of management and can erode respect for the manager.

The bureaucratic control process is typically used by managers to improve and maintain the process of others. However, the process can be applied to your own work performance. Management Is Everyone's Business 16.1 above offers suggestions for using the bureaucratic control process as a self-management tool.

LOC-In

③ Learning Objective Check-In

Dan has been on a work team that is developing limits that act as performance standards on the number of accidents incurred by linemen, electrical field workers, on the job. This is the first in a series of steps that Dan's company will be taking in order to actually achieve an acceptable minimum number of accidents per year.

1. *The above example illustrates which of the following steps in the control process?*
   a. *Performance measurement*
   b. *Establishing standards*
   c. *Taking corrective action*
   d. *Identifying gaps*

2. *The team receives data that was collected by linemen about the number of accidents reported over the last two years. The data includes causes and frequency of types of accidents. What is the next step once this data is collected?*
   a. *Monitor*
   b. *Identify gaps*
   c. *Allocate resources*
   d. *Take corrective action*

FIGURE 16.3

Types of Control

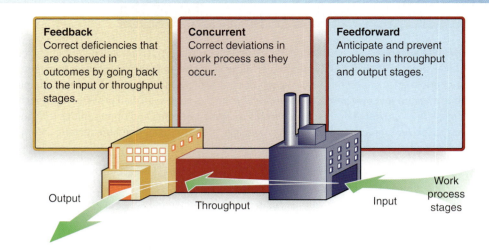

Feedback
Correct deficiencies that
are observed in
outcomes by going back
to the input or throughput
stages.

Concurrent
Correct deviations in
work process as they
occur.

Feedforward
Anticipate and prevent
problems in throughput
and output stages.

Output

Throughput

Input

Work
process
stages

TYPES OF BUREAUCRATIC CONTROL   There are three basic types of control
that managers can exercise: feedforward control, concurrent control, and feedback
control. These types of bureaucratic control are summarized in Figure 16.3 above.

Feedforward Control   Feedforward, or preliminary, control is designed to prevent problems before they occur. Preventive maintenance on aircraft is an example of control that is meant to avoid problems. Rules and procedures must be
strictly followed in aircraft maintenance to maximize safety and reduce the
chances of an accident. Feedforward control is also represented by rules and procedures that are to be followed so that ethical and performance problems are minimized. When an organization estimates market demand for a product and
examines whether or not sufficient supplies of materials are available and adequate production capacity exists to meet demand, feedforward control is being
used.[3] Management Close-Up 16.1 on page 623 presents an example of a company
that restructured the production process to more efficiently meet market demand.
Feedforward control can also be based on models of past work processes. This approach has been used at a sophisticated level to predict and control various characteristics of chemical reactions used in the energy industry.[4] The same principles
can be applied to other areas of business. Models can be developed to predict demand for a product or service by taking into account factors such as seasonal and
cyclical economic conditions. The resulting prediction is then used to determine
the amount of supplies and staffing levels that are needed.

Concurrent Control   Concurrent control takes place as the work process is being carried out. A simple but effective form of concurrent control is supervisory
oversight of the work process. A knowledgeable manager observes the work
process and quickly corrects problems as they occur. Advances in information
technology have dramatically increased the possibilities for concurrent control.
For example, remote and real-time access to production and budgetary data allow managers to take concurrent control over processes that were not previously
possible. Further, new technologies provide the opportunity for concurrent control to be carried out automatically. Wyandot, Inc., is an example of a company
that has embraced technology as an aid to concurrent control of the production
process. Wyandot, located in Marion, Ohio, enjoys approximately $100 million in
annual sales of its tortilla chips, corn chips, corn snacks, and caramel corn.[5] The
company produces 2,000 pounds of corn chips per hour and 5,000 pounds of tortilla chips per hour. The baking and frying processes are central to Wyandot's

Medtronic: Moving to a Pull-Based System

THEME: CUSTOMER FOCUS

Medtronic Inc.'s Xomed plant is located outside Jacksonville, Florida. The plant produces medical devices for ear, nose, and throat surgery and for ophthalmology. Between mid-2000 and the end of 2002, the production lead time decreased from 253 days to 129 days and productivity (measured as annual sales per employee) increased 40 percent. How did Medtronic do it?

The Xomed plant was the typical production facility, with production occurring in batches. Customers would receive orders depending on what batches were being run, how many, and in what order. Plant management set a goal to become more flexible and lean so that production would be more responsive to customer requests. A technique called value-stream mapping was used to make the production process more efficient and responsive to market demand.

Value-stream mapping is the process of documenting the process flow from suppliers through to the delivery of final products to customers (in Xomed's case, doctors, hospitals, and surgery centers). In the Xomed system, this included the flow of physical components as well as the flow of information. The mapping helped management identify bottlenecks and waste. It also helped them to change their view of production from batches prepared on separate "islands" to a stream of connected processes.

The improvements that the mapping process made were dramatic, such as a 40 percent reduction in production lead time. Further, weekly production meetings and production plans

Medtronic's Xomed plant implemented value-stream mapping and has improved its ability to deliver its products on time.

are now a thing of the past. Now, a doctor's order that pulls a product from the finished goods inventory sends a signal to the production process. Even for intricate surgical tools and devices the plant's on-time delivery rate (based on the date the customer requested) is 96 percent. Management of Xomed now boasts that the production process has become flexible, fluid, and pull-based, being driven by customers rather than capacity.

Source: J. S. McClenahen, "Mapping Manufacturing: Remarkable Results at Medtronic's Medical-Devices Plant Flow from Value-Stream Mapping," *Industry Week* 251 (2002), pp. 62+.

Wyandot's cooking processes are carefully and automatically controlled with sensors and computers.

Employee Theft: Feedback from an Annual Inventory Just Doesn't Cut It as a Control System

THEME: ETHICS

The location is a large East Coast distribution center that will remain anonymous. The manager of the facility was confident that the annual inventory would come out fine. However, the inventory report revealed a loss of $800,000. The manager told the corporate office that he simply did not believe the report. Another complete inventory was scheduled for 90 days later. That report confirmed the loss and showed that additional losses had occurred since the prior inventory. The manager thought it was impossible to have $1 million dollars of inventory walk out the door without him knowing about it. What was going on? Corporate headquarters instructed the manager to bring in assistance. A team of security experts was retained.

What the security experts found was, in short, employee theft. There were control systems in place, but they had been circumvented or were not effective. The following describes how theft was taking place.

A truck driver signed in at the distribution center and backed his truck up to the appropriate door. There he counted the cases of product to assure that he had the correct amount. The driver was just going through the motions because his accomplice, an employee at the distribution center, had already called him by cell phone and told him 12 extra cases of inventory would be included in the load. The truck driver told the forklift driver that the load was correct and to put it on the truck. The trucker was waved through a gate by a security guard who wrote down the license plate number of the truck. The guard looked at the load, but didn't know how much product the trucker had when he arrived or how much he should be leaving with. After leaving the facility, the trucker dropped off the $9,000 worth of goods at a rented storage facility. The items had already been negotiated to be sold for 30 percent of their value. A few days later, the trucker returned to the distribution center and shared the proceeds with the shipping employee. The security team brought in by the manager found that this pair of thieves had repeated the scam more than 50 times in 16 months, accruing an inventory loss of $1 million.

The general manager of the facility had always assumed that the company's inventory was well protected. The facility had 24-hour guard service and a state-of-the art perimeter alarm system, and more than two dozen closed circuit television cameras constantly videotaped the facility. Obviously, these employees had found a way to get around the safeguards. While the inventory feedback came too late to prevent the $1 million loss, at least the problem was finally brought to light. Management was then able to work on control systems that were more effective.

Source: B. Brandman, "How $1.2 Million of Inventory Vanished into Thin Air," *Transportation & Distribution* 42 (2001), pp. 31+.

---

business. Consequently, the management team developed automated concurrent controls over the processes. Sensors are used to constantly measure the temperature at the fryer inlet and outlet. This data results in an automatic adjustment that maintains the optimal temperature. Similar controls are used throughout the production process, based on the 156 miles of wire that run through the facility and connect everything to two computer systems.

Feedback Control Feedback control occurs after a process has been completed. Feedback control uses data from past performance to improve future performance. Timeliness is a serious concern with feedback. The longer feedback is delayed, the less useful it becomes. A long delay makes it more difficult to identify the causes of performance problems. Further, the delay may have allowed poor service to continue or defective or unsafe products to be made and distributed. Delay in feedback is often not helpful to workers. People want feedback. Feedback can be motivational if provided in a timely fashion. Feedback that is not timely is less helpful, because workers are already focused on different tasks or projects. Motivation and performance can be improved with feedback, but only if it is timely. Management Close-Up 16.2 above presents a real-life example of delayed feedback that proved to be costly to a company. Skills for Managing 16.2 on page 625 further explores this situation and consid-

EMPLOYEE THEFT: GOING BEYOND FEEDBACK CONTROL

As described in Management Close-Up 16.2, employee theft was a serious problem at a distribution center. The following is additional information gathered by the security team.

- The alarm system was not fully operational. Several motion detectors were blocked by inventory or had been repositioned to point at the ceiling. Magnetic contacts on two doors were found to be deliberately defeated so that the alarm would not operate.

- Closed-circuit cameras provided broad views of the docks and storage areas, but details of the number of cases being shipped or received couldn't be seen clearly on the videotape. Further, no one monitored the camera system or reviewed the videotape.

- Security guards made routine patrols and were instructed to keep an eye out for anything. However, security guards couldn't detect the kind of collusion that was going on between employees and truckers.

Discussion Questions

1. A number of theft control systems were not working or had been deliberately defeated. Aside from trying to steal from an employer, why else might employees take steps to defeat alarm systems?

2. Given your response to the previous question, how would you recommend this company go about developing more effective theft control procedures? Would a participative approach be useful? Why or why not?

3. Alarm and tracking systems offer concurrent control. How could this company take steps toward preventing the theft problem, not just detecting it and then dealing with it? (Hint: Could background checks on new hires be helpful for prevention? Explain.)

Research Question

Locate security recommendations (a number of companies offer security suggestions on their Web sites). Can you classify these suggestions as either feedforward, concurrent, or feedback control techniques? Which approach do you think is best for purposes of controlling theft? Why?

LOC-In

ers control techniques that could be implemented that would prevent the problem or provide more timely performance measures.

The Balanced Scorecard

The **balanced scorecard**[6] is a technique designed to control and improve performance in the four areas of: (1) customer service, (2) learning and growth, (3) finance, and (4) internal business processes. While bureaucratic control typically focuses on how internal business processes are carried out, the balanced scorecard takes a much broader approach. An important function of the scorecard is to link strategy to action.[7] For instance, strategic direction can be used to derive goals for each of the four areas of the scorecard. While the balanced scorecard takes into account a broad range of factors, it is included here as an example of a formal technique focused on the work process. The reason for this is because the broad and future-oriented approach of the scorecard is meant to influence behaviors and actions on a day-to-day basis. In other words, it is typically the work process, priorities, and how things are done that remain the focus of the balanced scorecard.

4 **Learning Objective Check-In**

1. *Aaron is a manager at a retail store in California that sells outdoor equipment. The company has recently been trying to use its resources, including capital, more appropriately throughout the year based on fluctuations in demand from season to season. Specifically, it feeds budget data to a central database where it can be analyzed by strategic planners and functional managers, which allows the company's managers such as Aaron to take control over processes while they are occurring. This is a system of _____.*
   a. *feedforward control*
   b. *feedback control*
   c. *task central control*
   d. *concurrent control*

balanced scorecard

A technique designed to control and improve (1) customer service, (2) learning and growth, (3) finance, and (4) internal business processes.

FIGURE 16.4

A General Balanced Scorecard Format

	Objectives	Measures	Targets	Initiatives
Financial What we need to do to succeed financially				
Customer What we need to do to excel at customer service				
Internal Business Processes What we need to do to have world class processes				
Learning and Growth What we need to do to change and increase our potential and effectiveness				

FIGURE 16.5

Southwest Airlines Scorecard

Source: Adapted from G. H. Anthes, "Balanced Scorecard," *Computerworld* 37 (2003), pp. 34+.

Area	Objectives	Measures	Targets	Initiatives
Customer	On-time flights Lowest prices	FAA on-time annual meeting	No. 1	Quality management
		Customer ranking (survey)	No. 1	Customer loyalty program
Internal	Fast ground turnaround	Time on ground	30 minutes	Cycle-time optimization program
		On-time departures	90%	
Learning	Ground-crew alignment with company goals	% ground-crew shareholders	Year 1: 70% Year 3: 90%	Employee stock option plan
		% ground-crew trained	Year 5: 100%	Ground-crew training

Figure 16.4 above presents a basic framework that is commonly used for balanced scorecards. Balanced scorecards can, however, take a variety of forms. Some scorecards use different weights to reflect the importance or priority of each of the four domains of finance, customers, business process, and learning and growth. Scorecards generally share the focus on these four areas as well as specify goals, targets, or standards in each area. The balanced scorecard directs activities in various strategic directions and then provides a means of control by assessing performance attained in each of the four areas against the stated standards or goals. Figure 16.5 above presents an example of a portion of a balanced scorecard from Southwest Airlines. As shown in the Southwest Airlines scorecard, the approach can be applied to an entire organization. Balanced scorecards can also be at the level of units, teams, and individuals.

IMPLEMENTATION SUGGESTIONS FOR THE BALANCED SCORECARD: GET IT DONE!

Get Top Management Commitment

If the balanced scorecard is to be successfully driven through the organization in a timely fashion, there must be top management support. Start with a half-day workshop on the balanced scorecard for top management and anyone who would need to lead the implementation initiative. If top management isn't sold on the concept, implementation is bound to flounder.

Focus on the Priorities

Identify the key priorities and measures in the organization. It may be effective to have two levels of balanced scorecards: (1) a governance level that includes 5 or 6 high-level measures and (2) a management level that includes up to 20 priority areas and measures.

Select a Small Team

Pick 2–4 committed and fearless leaders who won't procrastinate and can implement the scorecard approach.

Don't Get Too Flashy

A number of organizations are offering specialized software for the development of balanced scorecards. However, most data needed to set up an initial scorecard framework should already be readily available in-house. Investment in expensive consulting and software shouldn't be needed!

Balanced Scorecards Are an Art, Not a Science

There is no one best way. Things can always be changed or improved later on. Don't let perfectionism derail implementation of a value-added system.

Source: D. Parmenter, "Balanced Scorecard," *Accountancy Ireland* 35 (2003), pp. 14–17.

The balanced scorecard has become a widely used management tool. Many organizations have implemented some version of the approach. As originally conceived, it should be possible to implement the balanced scorecard in 16 weeks. However, a number of managers have found that time frame to be difficult.[8] Manager's Notebook 16.1 above presents suggestions for quickly and effectively implementing a balanced scorecard approach.

Bureaucratic control typically focuses directly on the work process and directly regulates how the process is carried out. The balanced scorecard takes a broad look at the directions and priorities of the organization. However, the thrust of the technique is to regulate actions taken in the workplace. The initiatives in the balanced scorecard identify the process, or how the objectives will be achieved. The process embodied in these initiatives may not be part of the balanced scorecard, but these guidelines and standards are likely in the bureaucratic controls that are in place for those initiatives. There are formal approaches to control that focus on outcomes, not the process that might be used to achieve those outcomes. The following section reviews outcomes-focused control, the techniques in cell 2 of Figure 16.1.

LOC-In

5 **Learning Objective Check-In**

1. *Anthony plans to use the balanced scorecard approach to improve company performance. He has read about how it is a good way to link strategy to action and evaluate the results. In rank order, customer service is the most important, followed by finance and internal business processes. Based on what you know about the balanced scorecard, which of the following is the factor that will receive the least emphasis in Anthony's application of the technique?*
   a. *Learning and growth*
   b. *Internal business processes*
   c. *Behavior of customer service representatives*
   d. *Increased customer awareness*

Formal and Outcome-Focused Control

Formal and outcome-focused control techniques regulate performance by applying standards or guidelines to the outcomes of a process. The details of how a work process should be carried out are not the concern of this approach to control. Rather, outcomes are regulated and processes must then be adapted to achieve or comply with the requirements. Here are some of the better-known approaches to formal outcome-focused control.

Market Control

Market control is the use of indicators of market values as standards for regulating performance. For example, an organization may use profits as the means for evaluating the performance of a business unit. Poor profit levels may result in corrective actions, from various improvement efforts to closing or selling the unit. Market control does not necessarily rely on financial measures of value in a market. For example, the dean of a business school at a university uses market control when assessing the performance of the doctoral programs of the various departments. Specifically, allocation of budget dollars is driven, in part, by how many doctoral students the department places and the quality of the jobs they take. Those departments whose doctoral students get jobs at the best places are rewarded with larger budgets.

Financial Controls

Financial controls use various monetary measures to regulate performance. While market controls rely on external measures of the value of products or services, financial controls focus on internal monetary values, largely regarding revenues and expenses in the organization. A business unit could, for example, be doing very well in terms of the market value of its products or services, but may not be in good financial health internally. This outcome can occur due to mismanagement of funds, poor investments, and other problems. A thorough consideration of the various financial control techniques is beyond the scope of this chapter. However, some of the basic financial control approaches will be considered, beginning with the most common financial control approach—the budget.

BUDGETARY CONTROL   Budgets are used to specify amounts to be expended for various activities or events. Budgets are frequently stated in monetary terms, but they can take other forms. A production budget might specify the number of units to be produced and a labor budget might specify the number of hours of labor that will be available along with dollar amounts. Normally, however, budgets are stated in monetary terms. Whatever the unit of measurement, budgets provide quantitative measures. These measures provide the yardstick by which performance can be judged. Further, budgeting allows management to control and allocate its resources. Without budgetary control, the best of business ventures can easily run into financial trouble and even bankruptcy.

Budgeting helps managers control and predict costs. Recently, there has been a growing amount of criticism directed at the practice of budgetary control. These critics suggest that budgets amount to "managing by the numbers" and do not allow the flexibility needed to pursue other potentially valuable options. For example, a business opportunity may arise that is promising and fits with the strategic direction of an organization. However, if the budget is fixed, there may be no resources available to pursue the opportunity. The fixed and limiting nature of budgets can simultaneously be both an advantage and a disadvantage.

FINANCIAL STATEMENTS   In addition to budgets, financial statements are also tools that are used to assess and control the financial health of an organization. Two of the most commonly used are balance sheets and profit and loss statements.

Balance Sheets   The balance sheet provides a financial picture of an organization by listing assets and liabilities at a particular point in time. The balance sheet is a "snapshot" of how an organization is doing in financial terms.

Profit and Loss Statements   A profit and loss statement provides a listing of income and expenses over time. A profit and loss statement may cover a period of years and offers a picture of trends in the organization.

Balance sheets and profit and loss statements can be used to identify problem areas and take corrective actions, if needed. The overall performance of an organization or business unit can be summarized and evaluated using data from financial statements. The data can be combined to create key financial ratios that reflect various aspects of bottom-line, financial performance.

FINANCIAL RATIOS   Financial ratios provide a quick overall check of company performance. Many types of financial ratios are available. For example, *liquidity ratios* reflect an organization's ability to pay short-term debt. *Leverage ratios* reflect the amount of funds available in an organization from shareholders and creditors. *Profitability ratios* indicate the amount of financial return from an investment, with return on investment (ROI) as probably the most widely recognized example of a profitability ratio. There are standards, or at least rules of thumb, regarding acceptable ranges for the financial ratios. The values of the financial ratios relative to the standard levels or the change in the ratios over time can help management to assess and control the business. Financial information, such as profit levels and return on investment, is commonly after-the-fact information that is averaged over the work process. However, Management Close-Up 16.3 on page 631 describes how some innovative organizations are pushing financial outcome control into the work process.

ACTIVITY-BASED COSTING   Activity-based costing is another financial control technique. Traditional accounting approaches separate costs into discrete functional categories, such as purchasing, human resources, and maintenance. Activity-based costing, in contrast, associates costs associated with tasks that are performed. As an example, consider the costs that might be associated with producing a particular product. Costs are traditionally divided into categories such as labor salary, labor fringe benefits, supplies, and fixed costs. However, costs could also be calculated for tasks such as receiving and processing sales orders, expediting supplies, expediting production, distribution of finished products, and resolving errors and problems. The latter way of breaking out costs is much more useful for management. It is difficult to control or lower fixed costs. It is much easier to try to manage costs associated with the various tasks that are part of the production process. That is the reason for organizations to be attracted to the use of activity-based costing.

video: THE ENTREPRENEURIAL MANAGER

The Syl Tang Story

Summary

Syl Tang is an entrepreneur who is based in New York City. She developed HipGuide.com in 1998. The multimedia style and city guide covers nine cities, including Boston, Chicago, Las Vegas, London, Paris, Los Angeles, San Francisco, New York, and Miami. The information covered ranges from bars, clubs, hotels and restaurants to beauty salons, shopping, and local services. Tang says as an entrepreneur, she thinks about "the money" every day. Revenue for HipGuide comes in two fashions. Primarily, it comes through branded content, meaning Hipguide produces branded content for magazines or other entities that need it. The secondary revenue source is product marketing.

Tang says one of the most important things for an entrepreneur starting out is to remember to listen first. She says that so many other people are actually experts on the range of topics the entrepreneur will need to use or be familiar with. Entrepreneurs themselves, however, do not know all the answers all the time, and so they need to surround themselves with those experts and take in all they are willing to share.

Many people say that a business plan is the most important thing. Most of the people who say that, however, are financiers or bankers or the "financial people." They want to have security, to see where you're going, and to know the finer print. While Tang acknowledges that successful entrepreneurs have to have a plan and have to have the end in mind, they also have to be prepared to be very flexible depending on what happens with the business. The details are important, but they can change quickly.

As an entrepreneur and a manager, there is typically a lot more diversity in the type of decisions you are going to have to make. You have to decide on HR decisions, for instance, as well as what to do when people don't pay you what they owe. Hiring decisions play a very important role in the company's success, especially in a small company where the entrepreneur feels the benefits or repercussions of a good or poor choice in candidates.

Discussion Questions

1. If Tang wanted to implement a control method for HipGuide.com that was focused on the company's operations and processes, but was more formal in nature, what would you recommend? Support your answer based on what you learned from this chapter.

2. Entrepreneurs like Tang have to balance the intangible and market-driven successes of the firm with financial responsibility and solvency. What methods would be appropriate for evaluating the financial performance of HipGuide.com?

3. In Syl Tang's industry, the environment is dynamic and change is driven by customer service. Based on what you learned in the video, and given this caveat, what type of control method might be appropriate? What are its advantages over more formal types of control?

Formal control measures regulate performance by applying standards to outcomes. In other words, this approach to control is the application of external standards to which people in the organization need to comply. In the case of outcome-focused control techniques, the standards have to do with financial or market-based measures. With process-focused control approaches, the standards have to do with how work is carried out. In either case, formal control mechanisms rely on imposing external standards and putting in place the possibility of

Profit Velocity: Financial Control Meets the Work Process

Profit is a straightforward measure, as represented by the function:

$$Profit = Revenues - Expenses$$

In many organizations, profits are often taken at face value. If profits are up, everything is good. If profits are down, it's time to cut costs. That's about as sophisticated as it gets in many organizations. However, competitive pressures are pushing organizations to find new ways to maximize financial outcomes. New technologies now provide the means for financial data to be introduced into the work process itself. One emerging approach is called "profit velocity."

To understand the concept of profit velocity, consider the example of Ondeo Nalco, an Illinois-based maker of water treatment chemicals. The company is using software to track the velocity with which product flows through key production and supply-chain bottlenecks. Factors such as product price, rate of production, the amount of scrap, and others are all considered. The sales force can then take the information and push sales of products that maximize profits. Profit isn't necessarily maximized by selling the highest-priced or most complex products. It may be that those products have the highest error rates and greatest amounts of waste. In essence, the profit velocity approach shows the sales force that they could be maximizing revenues but are getting nowhere on profits if they are pushing the wrong products.

In addition to marketing implications, Ondeo Nalco has applied the profit velocity concept into the work process itself. The approach highlights the areas that must be closely managed or improved if profits are to be maximized. Further, the company has gotten to the point where a line operator knows that turning a screw on a variable feed pump to the right would mean making $780 per hour while turning it to the left would mean profit would go down to $650 per hour. The approach makes profit a highly visible and real concept on the plant floor. It gives workers a direct sense of impact and ownership in the organization.

U.S. Steel is another company that uses software and the profit velocity concept to guide production and sales. The profit velocity measure has given everyone in the organization a common metric to work with. Normally, production people often want to produce quantity while the sales force wants to maximize revenues. Instead, profit velocity provides the information both sides need to maximize profits. The focus for production becomes making products that maximize profits, not just making more product. For sales, the focus becomes selling products that maximize profits, not just revenues.

Source: D. Drickhammer, "Goosing the Bottom Line," *IndustryWeek* 251 (2002), pp. 24–28.

corrective actions to assure compliance with those standards. However, there may be situations in which internalizing standards would result in better performance control. These are found in another approach to control.

Informal and Process-Focused Control

Informal and process-focused control emphasizes an implicit sense and common understanding of how things should be done. This control approach does not rely on explicit guidelines and standards. Instead, it assumes that people have an internal set of standards that will appropriately guide how they do their jobs. This approach has been termed clan control. (See again Figure 16.1, cell 3.)

Clan Control

Reliance on corporate culture and the norms it develops as an informal means for regulating the work process is **clan control**. In essence, with clan control, employees control themselves. A strong culture can influence performance levels

clan control

Culture-based control.

At the factory in central Italy where Tod's luxury leather shoes are made, leather specialists check the thickness of cowhides before shoe parts are cut from patterns. Each pair of shoes is cut from a single hide to ensure that the grain of the pair is consistent, and each pair is made by hand. Says Vice President Andrea Della Valle of the company's craftspeople. "This is really the heart of the company. Without them, without their expertise and the soul they put into this craftsmanship, we would not have a product."

and how work is carried out. Chapter 4 was devoted to a consideration of culture and how to develop or change the culture of an organization. It is recommended that you revisit that chapter for details concerning culture and how it can control behaviors in organizations.

Culture-based control offers an advantage of not overspecifying how a work process should be performed. The reason for this being an advantage, at least in many of today's organization settings, is the degree to which work environments are dynamic and driven by customer service. Change in many work environments has become the norm. Given this dynamic nature, explicit guidelines and standards might be obsolete by the time they are put in place. Likewise, a customer-driven strategy means that the work process can't be overly structured. Discovering customer needs and finding ways to best satisfy customers are difficult, and change from one customer to the next. Given today's dynamic and customer-focused work environments, an internalized means of control is more effective. Culture may not specify operational details, but it can provide a clear set of values that guide workers, even when explicit rules or standards are not available.

Your performance as a team member can be enhanced by recognizing and applying clan control. Management Is Everyone's Business 16.2 on page 633 offers suggestions for utilizing clan-based control as a team member.

What Is Management Control (Revisited)?

This chapter began with a description of control as principally involving measurement and regulation. While the *process* of control is clear in this description, what should be the *content* of its focus? In other words, control should involve the measurement and regulation of *what?* Specifically, should control efforts be directed at people, systems, or some other aspect of the company?

People versus Systems

Control mechanisms are, fundamentally, directed at performance. However, the question remains as to what is the best way to improve and control performance—with measures and corrective actions focused on people or on systems? This question is simple to state but it is an issue fundamental to management philosophy. The traditional Western management approach has been to assume that workers are the critical factor in determining performance. Thus, motiva-

LOC-In

6 Learning Objective Check-In

Graham, a strategic manager, is attempting to develop a viable control method for his firm. The company operates in a highly competitive marketplace where technology is rapidly changing and the cost of research and development is very high across the industry. Specifically, he is keeping his eye on one business unit which he suspects has been falling short of its profit potential for several years in a row, despite a market upturn.

1. *Which of the following would be appropriate in evaluating research and development as a cost driver for the company's various products?*
   a. *Market control*
   b. *Clan control*
   c. *Activity-based costing*
   d. *Bureaucratic control*
2. *Which of the following would be useful in evaluating and possibly confirming the underperforming business unit?*
   a. *Balance sheets*
   b. *Activity-based costing*
   c. *Market control*
   d. *Budgetary control*

Working as a Team   Many organizations are empowering teams to accomplish objectives. The performance control mechanism in many of these teams is the implicit norms of clan control. The following suggestions are meant to help you as a team member to respond to and enhance the clan control that operates in a team.

- *Learn the norms of your team.* What do others on your team expect? What is viewed as good or exceptional performance: What things might you do that would irritate the team or be viewed as negative by team members? You don't want to take the time or risk of finding out the answers to these questions by trial and error. You should, however, get a sense of these norms by your own observation and by asking team members. If you are unclear about some performance norms, you could ask team members for examples of performance or generate your own and ask how team members would evaluate or feel about that kind of performance.

- *Take steps to establish or clarify your team's clan control.* Many times teams have not developed norms or don't have a shared sense of norms for the team. You could assist your team in developing its clan control through steps such as:

    Establish a team mission statement. What does the team view as its central purpose and what values does it view as most important? Some team meetings with team members on this topic could yield not only a mission statement, but an improved sense of a shared purpose and common norms.

    Ask people to share their favorite stories about good or poor performance. These stories can be the core of clan control and convey key team values and norms.

    Ask your team members to help generate team member characteristics that any future team hires should have. These characteristics will likely bring out and clarify the norms of the group. Further, the characteristics could prove useful in selecting new team members.

---

tional programs and close supervision are viewed as the best ways to control and improve performance. In contrast, other nationalities and cultures have different views about control and how it should be focused and used.[9] For example, the quality perspective, developed mainly in Japan, emphasizes the importance of the system as a determinant of performance.[10] Thus, quality advocates emphasize control over systems as key to performance improvement. This issue is not easily resolved. It is safe to say that in most situations, both person and system factors make a difference when it comes to performance. But where should control efforts be directed?

There are differing opinions on this issue,[11] but we recommend that control efforts be focused on systems and on performance, rather than on people. Focusing on people can result in resistance and negative reactions, problems commonly associated with control efforts. For example, workers may not like the increased monitoring or reporting required by the control system. They may resist and find fault with the system if they don't see it as improving, or somehow necessary to, performance. If they feel that the control system is overly intrusive (for example, involves unneeded videotaping of back office operations), they may do their best to undermine the control system.

Working as a Manager   The very term *control* implies power, and people can negatively react to the use of power. On the other hand, management has a responsibility to assure that performance is adequate and that objectives are being achieved. The following are some recommendations for you as a manager to develop and apply management control in ways that will reduce the chances of negative reaction from employees.

- *Separate performance from people.* When applying control techniques, be careful to focus on performance, not on workers or characteristics of those workers. It may be that a worker is not sufficiently detail-oriented, but the control efforts should focus on, for example, quality or error measures. To directly focus on the personal characteristic of the worker would invite emotional and negative reaction.

- *Determine what needs to be measured and controlled.* Person factors may actually be less important than system characteristics in determining performance.

- *Engage workers in developing effective and fair control procedures.* Taking a participative approach to management control offers the opportunity to develop a partnership with workers. Bringing workers into the development and application of control systems conveys trust and a common goal of solving problems and improving performance.

- *Share control system information with workers.* The only way performance improves is with feedback. Your workers likely understand the work systems and problems better than anyone. Empowering the workers and sharing control system information with them can result in far greater commitment and performance improvement than would ever result from unilateral control.

LOC-In

7   Learning Objective Check-In

1. *Mike is an employee at Zip Lite, a company that specializes in small but useful items like specialty flashlights, utility knives, and tools. The firm's management has implemented a control method that solicits input from the employees. The thrust of the control initiative is to achieve better quality in customer service and the way that the customer sets up an account with the firm. Often, this setup process can be cumbersome to both the customer and the employees because much of the information collected is never used by the firm, yet the forms are tedious and thorough. Mike thinks he will tell his manager what he thinks about the system and some ways to improve it. At Zip Lite, the focus of the management control is on _____.*

   a. *people*
   b. *performance and systems*
   c. *processes only*
   d. *finances*

Control is a necessary management function. It is important to focus on both performance and the system. Focusing external control on people conveys the message that management distrusts them. Focusing control efforts on performance and system characteristics and involving and empowering workers can convey that management views workers as partners in the effort to maximize performance. How the control system is developed and implemented is also critical. Management Is Everyone's Business 16.3 above offers further suggestions for you, as a manager, regarding the application of management control.

CONCLUDING THOUGHTS

After the introductory feature of this chapter on airlines' lost luggage, we posed some critical thinking questions regarding management control. Now that you have read about approaches to control, let's revisit those questions. First, organizations often put control systems in place because of a problem with performance or safety. However, effective managers know that control is not an option to be employed only if it is needed to fix mistakes. Control is central to effective management. If managers clearly understand the role of control, they know that (as in the air travel industry) even a small percentage of failures can result in high costs or high levels of customer dissatisfaction.

Second, the airline industry can set standards based on objective performance criteria like the number of pieces lost, the number of lost pieces returned to owners, the length of time required to return lost pieces, and so on, all of which should be as low as possible. Subjective factors will have little bearing on these standards because the performance measures are all quantifiable.

Finally, if the industry sets new standards, it can track its achievement of those standards by measuring the same data on a regular basis—by day or week, by flight, by airport terminal, and so on—and comparing against past numbers. Consistent monitoring and assessment will reveal whether gaps between standards and performance are being diminished.

Focusing on the Future: Using Management Theory in Daily Life

Management Control

Mary Molacavage is not your average manager. Her first undergraduate degree was a B.A. in speech pathology, and she spent many years as a teacher of the deaf, getting her M.Ed. in education of the deaf along the way. When she decided it was time to move on from teaching, she got her M.B.A. with an option in marketing, and then took courses in biotechnology at a local community college. Now she is working as a lab associate in a start-up genetic engineering company. Her long-term plan is to stay in the biotech industry, but with an emphasis on marketing rather than lab work.

One of Mary's primary jobs as a lab associate is to mix the media used to grow bacteria in the lab. This process requires precisely mixing a special broth with agar and other ingredients such as antibiotics in Petri dishes. Once prepared, these plates provide a surface on which researchers can test growth patterns of cells. Because each experiment requires different proportions and dilutions, Mary uses feedforward, concurrent, and feedback controls to make sure that she is providing the highest quality materials to the scientists working in her lab.

Feedforward Controls Mary's lab courses in college offered her a preliminary form of feedforward controls. By mastering basic training that included learning how to measure, weigh, pour, and mix ingredients, use an autoclave, and monitor temperatures, Mary ensured that she would be able to create usable plates of material in the lab. While these things may seem simple, Mary suggests that training is critical. For example, when an experiment calls for one liter of solution made with a powder, you can't just take powder and add it to a liter of water, because that would make more than a liter. Instead, you have to pour a little water, mix the powder into it, then fill the flask to get exactly one liter.

Another type of feedforward control occurs in the lab. Every process has a protocol that tells lab associates things like what proportions of different ingredients should be used, how long the mixture should be autoclaved, what antibiotic should be added, and how long to cool mixtures between adding ingredients. Mary says,

> Every detail is important. If a mixture is too hot when an antibiotic is added, the antibiotic will be killed, but if a mixture cools down too much, the agar will solidify and make it impossible to add additional ingredients.

> Protocols are extremely detailed. For example, one line might read: "Pellet the cells by centrifugation for 1' at 13,200 rpm in the microfuge. **Discard the supernatant** carefully and completely then resuspend the cell pellet in 200ml of Solution A. Let sit for 5'."[1]

The scientists/managers in Mary's company also use feedforward control when they decide what they are going to research based on market demand for drugs. For example, as consumers become more concerned with avian flu, more and more biotechnology companies will start searching for a vaccine for the disease.

Concurrent Controls   As noted above, each lab uses protocols to establish what must be done in any given procedure. In addition to protocols, larger labs have Standard Operating Procedures—SOPs—that clarify the exact processes used whenever protocols are followed in the lab. For example, some labs require that each time a chemical is weighed, another person must be present to verify that the correct amount of the substance has been measured. These SOPs serve as concurrent controls to standardize the quality of work outcomes. One SOP in Mary's lab involves marking every prepared Petri dish with a symbol indicating what is in the dish. That way, researchers know that they are getting the right materials, even when the dishes have been prepared in advance.

Mary relies on the scientists in the lab to provide her with another form of concurrent control—information about how long different parts of the procedure will take. This helps her to plan her time more effectively. For example, if it is going to take two hours for agar to harden, she can do something else, but it must be done within the exact time frame of the protocol. When Mary was first starting in the lab, she learned the dangers of trying to multitask without exact time guidelines. She knew that it would take awhile for her plates to harden, so she started to create a batch of cells that would later be recombined by the scientists in her lab. Unfortunately, without clear timelines, she missed critical timing marks on both projects, and had to throw out her work.

Another concurrent control is writing everything down so that an experiment can be repeated exactly in another lab or by another scientist. Mary keeps detailed notes of all her work. In addition, she writes down procedures as she is discussing them with other researchers in the lab, and then uses those notes to double check and be sure she has understood the process prior to starting her work (a form of feedback control).

Feedback Control   Mary uses feedback controls from both her managers and her work as she completes tasks. She can tell if she has prepared a plate correctly when she looks at it several days later. The plate should be smooth with no bubbles or lumps, the lid should show no signs of splashed agar or broth, and the dish should not contain any evidence of bacteria other than those being tested in the experiment. If Mary sees any extraneous bacteria, she knows that the plate has not been prepared using aseptic conditions, and she modifies her procedures accordingly.

Because the company is small, and people are moving fast, Mary says that she doesn't have a lot of feedback control from her managers. The feedback control she receives is a combination of concurrent and feedback control. For example, a scientist will go over a protocol with her and then say, " Do you want me to watch you doing it, or do you feel comfortable doing it on your own?" If Mary says she is comfortable, the researcher will say, "I'll be back in ten minutes to check with you, and see if everything is going okay."

Another scientist asks the question in a different way. When teaching Mary new protocol, the researcher will say to Mary, "How many of these do you want me to watch you do?" In this way, she shows that she is available for feedback control, but she still gives Mary the opportunity to determine how much feedback she needs.

[1] "Mini-Prep Protocol for Purification of Plasmid DNA from Bacteria," http://people.morehead-st.edu/fs/d.peyton/protocols.html, accessed on May 20, 2006.

summary of learning objectives

Control is an essential central management function. There are distinct approaches that can be taken to management control. This chapter has provided you an overview of these approaches to control. The material in the chapter that addresses each of the chapter's learning objectives is summarized below.

1 Describe *management control* and understand the importance of control systems.

- Control is the process of comparing performance to standards and taking any needed corrective actions.
- Control is the means by which management assures that desired objectives are being achieved.

2 Identify the four basic management control approaches.

Crossing the dimensions of *type* and *focus* results in four basic approaches to management control:

- Informal and outcome-focused
  - **Subjective control**
- Formal and process-focused
  - **Bureaucratic control**
  - **Balanced scorecard**
- Formal and outcome-focused
  - Market control
  - Financial control
- Informal and process-focused
  - Clan control

3 Describe the steps a manager would take to apply a bureaucratic control process.

- Establishing standards is the first step to gaining control.
- Performance measurement is essential because if you can't measure it you can't control it.
- Identify gaps between the standards and actual performance.
- Take corrective action to fix the problem.

4 Identify the major types of bureaucratic control.

- Feedforward control is designed to anticipate any problems before they occur.
- Concurrent control takes place as the work process is going on.
- Feedback control uses past data to improve future performance.

5 Generate the basic framework for a balanced scorecard.

- The balanced scorecard is a broad approach that focuses on control and performance improvement.
- The technique usually addresses four areas: (1) Financial, (2) Customer, (3) Internal business processes, (4) Learning and growth.

6 Differentiate between market and financial control.

- Market control relies on external measures as standards for regulating performance.
- Financial control relies on internal monetary values to regulate performance.

7. Distinguish between system and person factors as the focus of control.
- Performance is a function of both person and system factors.
- Focusing control on people can have a negative reaction and it may be more effective to focus on performance and the system.

discussion questions

1. What are the four categories of control techniques? Which of the four categories do you think is the best approach? Why?

2. Differentiate among feedforward, concurrent, and feedback control. Can you provide an example of each?

3. Standards are critical to control efforts. How do you think they should be developed?

4. Identifying gaps between performance and standard levels is an important step in the bureaucratic control process. Describe situations in which it is not beneficial to take corrective action in response to every gap.

5. Describe the balanced scorecard approach. It does not offer tight operational guidelines or standards, so what advantage(s) does it offer? Would you recommend using it? Why or why not?

6. Differentiate between market and financial controls. In what type of organizational situations do you think each approach would be best to use? Describe.

7. What is clan control? Under what organizational circumstances do you think it would be an effective control technique?

8. Do you think control efforts should be directed at people or at systems? Why?

management minicase 16.1

Standards for Quality Control: Don't Forget the Customer!

Control systems are often developed from an internal and functional perspective. For example, production may develop standards regarding product features and quality based on common practice and guidelines in the industry. However, these standards and features may be irrelevant to customers. The same disconnect can occur in the services sector. For example, the police department of a large metropolitan area had a self-imposed standard of responding to a burglary call within 5 minutes. However, they treated cases of missing children as a standard missing person case and took no action for 24 hours. Focus groups with citizens quickly revealed that the standards did not translate into effective performance from the public's perspective. Citizens really didn't care about timeliness in response to a burglary since it had already occurred. A police response within the day would be nice, but a dramatic and quick response just wasn't needed or useful. On the other hand, citizens wanted an immediate and serious response to a missing child case. As a result of listening to constituents, the police department dropped its 5 minute standard for burglaries. In addition, it will now call out police officers on bikes, cars, and even helicopters in response to cases of missing children.

A number of organizations check on their service levels by collecting customer feedback. Of course, it is best to integrate the customer perspective into the development of standards right from the start. For example, the development of quality standards for Motel 6 and Red Roof Inn included customer focus groups across the country.

Discussion Questions

1. Does including the customer perspective reduce the control of management over work processes or outcomes? Explain.

2. Do you think customer feedback is a sufficient way to involve the voice of the customer in setting standards?

3. Other than focus groups, can you think of other ways to include customers in the development of standards?

4. Are there other ways in which customers could effectively be included in a control system? For example, would it be worthwhile to include customers in the performance measurement step? What about in other steps?

Sources: R. L. Cardy, *Performance Management: Concepts, Skills, and Exercises* (Armonk, NY: M. E. Sharpe, 2004); R. A. Nozar, "Guest's Input Helps Develop Standards," *Hotel and Motel Management* 216 (2001), pp. 36+.

Outcomes or Process?

management minicase 16.2

A focus on measuring and managing the process is a common approach to control. As discussed in this chapter, process-focused control typically involves strict guidelines and detailed procedures to follow. Some organizations, however, are discovering that focusing on outcomes can offer advantages over a process focus. For example, Drew, a water treatment company, shifted to an outcome-based control system to regulate chemical levels. Specifically, the common approach to regulating chemicals in water treatment focuses on measuring the flow of chemicals themselves. Drew moved to a system in which chemical levels are regulated by monitoring their effects. Such a system reduces the use of corrosion control chemicals by monitoring the occurrence of the corrosion effect. The result can be less chemical usage and a less negative environmental impact.

Water can't talk back or resist control efforts, but people can! Some hotels are finding that focusing on outcomes rather than process can be an effective approach to controlling energy usage. A process approach to energy usage might involve providing requests and guidelines to hotel guests regarding heat, cooling, and lighting levels. Some guests may not appreciate such requests and resist complying. Instead, it is possible to use an outcome-based approach to managing energy usage in a hotel or similar building, such as the control approach employed by WebGen Systems. WebGen is an energy management company that offers an Internet-based energy management system. The system tracks energy usage over time, considers weather, energy price, and current levels of energy consumption. Based on this information, specific adjustments are automatically made to the hotel's energy management system. For example, the system might adjust the temperature of water in a chiller or slightly raise the temperature level in a ballroom.

Discussion Questions

1. When do you think process control is the preferred control approach? Explain.

2. Is outcome-based control the best approach in a service setting? Why or why not?

3. What disadvantages might there be to outcome-based control? Do you think they outweigh the potential advantages?

Sources: B. Schmitt, "Water Treatment: Pouring on the Service," *Chemical Week* 164 (2001), pp. 20+; "Mission: Maintain Satisfaction: Smart Implementation plus the Right System Add Up to Happy Guests," *Hotel & Motel Management* 218 (2003), pp. M7+.

individual/
collaborative
learning
case 16.1

Profit vs. Equity: Beyond Short-Term Financial Performance

Making profits is a critical focus of business. Without sufficient profits, the business will fail. Maximizing profits is the goal of most business efforts. It is no surprise, then, that management commonly focuses attention and control efforts on profit levels. Take, for instance, a grocery store that is focused on profits and utilizes control mechanisms to maximize them. Part of a profit control system could involve measuring financial aspects of various areas of the business. Measurements could be broken down to the level of profitability per item. Consequently, a grocery store manager might decide to eliminate less profitable items, resulting in relatively immediate improvement in the profitability of the store.

As a contrasting approach, consider the same grocery store from the customer's perspective. Why does a customer continue to do business with a particular grocery store? There is a three-part answer that can be summed up with one concept: customer equity. Customer equity is the overall and long-term return that a customer receives from doing business with an organization. There are three components to customer equity: value equity, brand equity, and retention equity. Value equity has to do with the objective benefits and

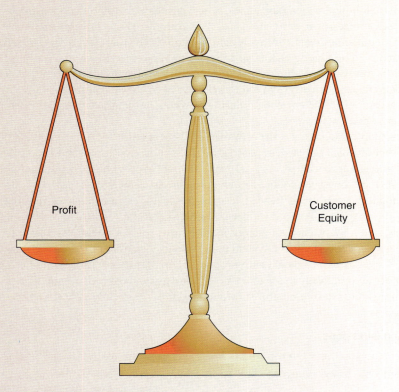

Profit or Customer Equity: Choice or Balance?

costs involved in dealing with the organization. For example, how convenient is the store's location and what are the prices and quality levels at the store? Brand equity is the more intangible and emotional aspects of the store. For example, does the store offer a sense of community or identification for the customer? Finally, retention equity is the benefits a customer receives from continuing to do business with an organization. So, why would a customer continue to do business with a grocery store? The answer would be because of positive levels of value, brand, and retention equities. Taking less profitable products off the shelves reduces convenience and may cause the customer to look elsewhere for the three forms of equity.

Critical Thinking Questions

1. Take the profit control approach. What other steps would you recommend in addition to retaining or deleting items based on profit levels?

2. Based on the customer equity approach, identify measures for each type of equity. How would you collect the data?

3. What actions could you take as a manager to maximize the levels of each of the three components of customer equity?

Collaborative Learning Exercises

1. Divide into opposing teams taking either the profit or customer equity approach as the focus for management control efforts. Profits are needed, but profits can't be made without customers. Is there a clear winner or other resolution to the debate?

2. Is there a way to combine or balance the profit and customer equity perspectives or are they opposed management control choices? With your team members, develop a control system that combines or balances the two perspectives. Share your system and ideas with the rest of the class.

Source: R. T. Rust, V. A. Zeithaml, and K. N. Lemon, *Driving Customer Equity* (New York: Free Press, 2000).

Balanced Scorecard: State of the Art

internet
exercise 16.1

The balanced scorecard has quickly become a popular management control technique. It is being used in a variety of settings, from manufacturing to services, and from nonprofit to profit organizations. Research the status of the balanced scorecard on the Internet. You will find numerous sites devoted to the topic.

1. Does the balanced scorecard appear to be maintaining its popularity?

2. As originally conceived, scorecards included four factors. Are additional factors being used? If so, what are they? Do you think they are useful?

3. What do you think accounts for the popularity of the balanced scorecard approach?

4. Can you find examples of balanced scorecards used by companies? If so, share them with the rest of the class.

video summary

Government vs. Google

Summary

Google, the nation's leading search engine, has maintained its independent streak as the company has grown from two guys in a garage to a multibillion dollar company. Now, that streak is showing up as the company is rebuffing the Bush administration's demand to review records of what millions of people have been googling, raising larger privacy concerns about online information. The Mountain View, California, company has refused to comply with a subpoena first issued last summer and revived this week when U.S. Attorney General Alberto Gonzales asked a federal judge in San Jose for an order to hand over the requested file.

Millions of people use Google every day to get information. The company fields some 3,000 searches per second. Some use the search engine to access sexual content, which is plentiful. For example, the search term "sex sites" turns up some 65 million hits in a matter of seconds. At issue is the 1998 Child Online Protection Act aimed at cracking down on "adult" sites. Courts have blocked enforcement of the law. The Department of Justice is now fighting to keep it and asking Google and others for more information, specifically, a list of all requests entered into Google's search engine during a random single week. That would total tens of millions of queries. In addition, it seeks 1 million randomly selected Web addresses from various Google databases. But Google executives said in a statement, "Their demand for information overreaches. We intend to resist their motion vigorously." Google expressed concern that they may not be able to protect the identities of individuals that could be extracted from the URLs that are disclosed.

This raises a really fundamental issue of privacy. It deals with the issue of to what extent the government has the right to access this information. Over the last 15 years, the amount of data that has been collected about all of us is enormous, and if the government has the ability to access that information, it opens a specter of a complete loss of privacy for everyone in America. The Constitution was written over 200 years ago in an era when the ability to be virtual didn't exist and couldn't have been conceived. The world is a different place. But are the issues at stake?

We should be able to have laws in place that protect our privacy and also respect law enforcement needs as we use the new technology. And we've managed to do this over the years with a whole range of new technologies, everything from the telephone to computer databases to junk faxes, even the telephone calls that we used to get, you know, in the evenings. This is as much a PR issue for Google as it is a legal issue because their concern is that being forced to comply with the subpoena is going to have a material adverse effect on people's willingness to use their service.

Discussion Questions

1. Consider the process of identifying gaps between actual and intended performance levels. How could the government use legislation to lower the threat of children being exposed to online pornography? What controls would they use to monitor the data? Would companies like Google have to play a role or could the government act independently?

2. Suppose the government enacted legislation that monitored people's use of search engines like Google by limiting the sites the search engine itself could report. Would this represent feedforward, concurrent, or feedback control? Why?

3. What is the content of the government's control efforts discussed in this video? Do you think this is what its focus should be? Explain your response.

chapter 17

Operations Management

Learning Objectives

1 Define operations management and its three stages: inputs, conversion, and disposition.

2 Describe materials requirements planning (MRP) and understand its use in operations management.

3 Be familiar with the conversion process tools of operations management, including Gantt charts, PERT networks, and statistical process control.

4 Explain the role quality management plays in the operations management process.

5 Understand and apply the principles of kaizen, just-in-time manufacturing, and kanban.

Taking a Page from Toyota's Playbook

Executives of Wipro Ltd. recently got a glimpse inside a Toyota assembly plant that produces Corollas near their headquarters in Bangalore, India.

Before the Toyota tour, Wipro had been struggling to get on track in back-office services. That might sound odd. With $1.7 billion in revenues, 42,000 employees, and a U.S.-traded stock that has advanced 230 percent in two years, Wipro is the embodiment of India's info-tech revolution. It's not only a leader in software development but also a pioneer in business-process outsourcing, where it does everything for clients from running accounting operations to processing mortgage applications. In that business, the company was respected for its low prices and dependability, but the work was too labor-intensive.

That's one reason Wipro decided to use Toyota as a model for overhauling operations. Its aim is to make business processes as simple, smooth, and replicable as the way Corollas slip off that Bangalore assembly line every 5.3 minutes. Wipro took on the tricky task of translating Toyota's vaunted principles for manufacturing into the realm of services. "What we do is apply people, technology, and processes to solve a business problem," says T. K. Kurien, the head of Wipro's 13,600-person business-process outsourcing unit.

Today, Wipro's paperwork processing operations in Bangalore, Pune, and Chennai bear an uncanny resemblance to a Toyota plant. Day and night, thousands of eager young men and women line up at long rows of tables modeled on an assembly line. Signs hanging over each aisle describe what process is being handled there—accounts receivable, travel and entertainment, and so on. Team leaders such as P. V. Priya, who oversees medical claims in Bangalore, set goals with their colleagues at the beginning of each shift. Just like in a Toyota factory, electronic displays mounted on the walls will shift from green to red if things bog down.

The goal for Wipro is to become the Toyota of business services. Toyota preaches continuous improvement, respect for employees, learning, and embracing change. "It's the soft stuff that makes a big impact on the hard numbers," says Kurien, a cheerful 45-year-old. There is plenty of hard-edged analysis, as well. Kurien last year assigned teams to examine business processes, break them into discrete components, and come up with streamlined services to sell to clients.

Almost immediately, Kurien spotted a surprising problem—cubicles. They're normal for programmers but interrupted the flow for business-process employees. So he came up with the idea of positioning people side by side at long tables and running processes up the line step by step. Wipro also adopted Toyota's kaizen system of soliciting employee suggestions for incremental improvements.

The initial response to all this "was a roaring disaster," admits Kurien. Some staffers felt like cogs in a machine, and they dragged their heels. After hearing from his middle managers, Kurien did a reboot. He set up classes to explain the concepts and show how the methods would make their lives easier.

The results are coming in. since the program started, the group has improved productivity by 43 percent and reduced the percentage of transactions that had to be redone from 18 percent to 2 percent. Customers are reaping rewards, too. Indeed, Wipro's paperwork-handling operations run with factorylike efficiency. When each shift starts, the teams, which are organized by process categories, gather with their team leaders for 10 minutes to discuss the day's goals and divide up tasks accordingly. Then they scatter to their desks. Wipro's employees seem sincerely excited about their jobs. Take 28-year-old Priya, who has worked for Wipro for nearly seven years. She has already submitted a handful of kaizen and is thrilled at how quickly her bosses respond. "Even though it's something small, it feels good. You're being considered," she says.

Kurien feels he has a long way to go. "On a scale of 1 to 10, we're still at 4," he says. But if Kurien succeeds, a few years from now management gurus may be trumpeting the Wipro Way.

Source: Adapted from Steve Hamm, "Taking a Page from Toyota's Playbook," *BusinessWeek Online*, www.businessweek.com, August 22, 2005.

CRITICAL THINKING QUESTIONS

1. *Do you think the kaizen process employed by Wipro could work without employees being empowered? Explain.*

2. *A common phrase is "If it ain't broke, don't fix it." However, quality approaches, and kaizen in particular, suggest that "the process can always be improved." In your opinion, which approach to managing the operations in an organization is better? Why?*

3. *Is there a downside to continuously making adjustments to improve a process?*

4. *What workforce skills are needed to make a quality improvement program, such as Wipro's, work effectively?*

We will revisit these questions at the end of the chapter in our Concluding Thoughts after you have read the following pages on operations management.

The heart and soul of many business operations is the production process. A new technique, such as kaizen, can greatly improve a firm's ability to deliver high quality products at a lower cost in a shorter amount of time. This chapter describes operations management methods for controlling production inputs and production processes.

What Is Operations Management?

Many organizations, both for-profit and not-for-profit, provide a product—whether a good, a service, or both. General Motors provides automobiles to its dealers, libraries provide books, and online databases provide information.

FIGURE 17.1

The Operations Management
Process

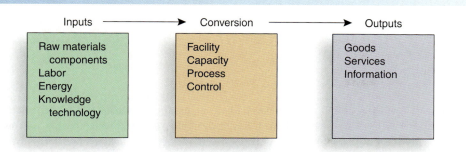

Operations management is the process an organization uses to obtain the materials or ideas, the process of transforming them into the product, and the process of providing the final product to a user. Operations management principles can be applied to a variety of departments within an organization. Typically, however, operations management refers to the firm's main product.

Operations management is closely tied to strategic management (Chapter 7), to planning (Chapter 5), and to information systems management (Chapter 18). Information systems today are closely linked to the firm's operations, as will be noted in Chapter 18.

operations management

The process an
organization uses to
obtain the materials or
ideas, the process of
transforming them into the
product, and the process
of providing the final
product to a user.

Three Stages of Operations

Operations management consists of three stages, as shown in Figure 17.1 above:

1. Acquiring inputs (the materials or ideas).
2. Controlling the conversion processes (transforming the materials or ideas into the organization's products).
3. Delivering the output (providing the organization's product to the user).

Although these stages are listed separately, they are highly interrelated. The inputs a firm acquires are influenced by the production process that is available as well as by refinements based on the customers' feedback. The production process is influenced by the type of inputs, such as skilled labor, that are available. Finally, the disposition of the product is influenced by the cost of production: What market can it be priced to? And how will the good or service be distributed and delivered to customers?

Planning

The foundation of operations management is **planning**. Planning typically begins with identifying the organization's customers and their needs. Market research helps company leaders target specific groups for its product. By determining the need for a product, managers can plan for the level of resources needed, the time involved, and the objectives that the operations management process must achieve. Managing the planning process was described in detail in Chapter 5.

planning

The management function
that assesses the
management environment
to set future objectives
and map out activities
necessary to achieve
those objectives.

Strategic Planning

Several types of strategic management decisions are part of operations management. After determining the need for the product and the market the firm wishes to target, organizational leaders must first determine if they want to make or buy their product. As discussed in Chapter 9, outsourcing allows a firm to concentrate on marketing and new product development.

Too Little of a Good Thing

THEME: CUSTOMER FOCUS

Immunex Corporation has a winner in its drug Enbrel, used to treat rheumatoid arthritis. The drug beat its optimistic 2000 sales projection by almost a third, and it became the fastest growing biological drug in history. Unfortunately, Enbrel became the largest supply shortage story in the history of prescription drugs.

Patients inject it to counteract the pain, swelling, and joint damage caused by the disease. The manufacturing process is complicated and time-consuming, however, using massive 10,000-liter tanks in sterile manufacturing plants. In spite of these quantities, the demand for Enbrel is so great that Immunex can't make enough of it. After a year on the market, it was obvious that demand would sooner or later outstrip supply. In March 2002, Immunex sent letters to doctors and to patients who were currently taking Enbrel that a shortage of two to three weeks might occur. Enbrel is a maintenance drug, not a cure. Thus, within about a month without the drug, arthritis symptoms typically return. In May 2002, the company again sent out letters informing doctors that the shortage might last longer than anticipated. In the meantime, there were approximately 20,000 people who were placed on a waiting list to receive the drug.

Enbrel's unexpected success created an overwhelming supply shortage in the drug industry. The drug was being rationed as patients across the United States were demanding it. When it wasn't available, doctors prescribed an alternative drug that required a doctor to administer it and a rigid medical regimen.

Immunex ended up being acquired by another company in July 2002. Two companies, Wyeth and Angen, now coproduce and market Enbrel. A production facility in Rhode Island and a state-of-the-art production facility in Ireland now provide the production capacity needed to capitalize on demand for the drug. Demand for the drug has increased even further since Enbrel received approval as a treatment for psoriasis. For the first nine months of 2005 Enbrel accounted for $2.6 billion in global sales. Enbrel is clearly a blockbuster now that production capacity problems appear to be resolved. Unfortunately, the supply constraints did not let Immunex enjoy the economic benefits of the drug they developed.

Sources: D. Shook, "Immunex' Supply-Side Cliffhanger," *BusinessWeek*, February 8, 2001; "Delays for Enbrel Continue," www.psoriasis.org/news/news/2002/20020524_enbrel.php, accessed May 20, 2003; "Alert! Enbrel Supply Shortage," http://arthritiscentral.com/enbrel/, accessed May 20, 2003; L. Loyd, "Wyeth Signs Three Biotech Product Deals—The Agreements Were an Indicator of the Direction that Major Pharmaceutical Companies Are Heading," *The Philadelphia Inquirer*, January 9, 2006, section C, p. 1.

---

make–buy analysis

An operations management tool used to help make the decision as to whether to produce an item or to purchase it.

A **make–buy analysis** is a tool operations managers use to help make this decision. The process begins with an assessment of whether the firm will lose or gain a competitive advantage by outsourcing the product or some aspects of the production process. Sara Lee found that outsourcing its manufacturing improved its competitive advantage. If outsourcing will hurt a firm's competitive advantage, the firm will continue making the product internally regardless of cost savings that may be obtained from outsourcing. Other factors in a make–buy analysis are the suitability of the product for outsourcing, the reasons for outsourcing, and the cost. The cost of buying the product may be less than the cost to the firm of equipment purchase and maintenance, labor and other inputs, inventory costs, administrative overhead, and so on.

capacity

The firm's ability to produce the product during a given period.

Once a decision has been made to make the product, the operations manager must consider capacity, facilities, process, and layout. **Capacity** is the firm's ability to produce the product during a given period. Creating capacity that exceeds the amount of products that can be sold is inefficient because unused capacity wastes the firm's resources. Not having enough capacity to meet demand also works against the firm, as described in Management Close-Up 17.1 above.

facilities

The design and location of an operation.

Operations management decisions also involve **facilities**, the design and location of an operation. Location decisions are based on factors such as the availability and cost of labor and energy as well as how close to suppliers or customers the facility needs to be.

Availability of labor and potential customers are important considerations in the facilities location for retail firms. By locating in areas with ample labor and a large customer population base, firms such as Ikea keep labor costs down and sales volume high.

Process decisions are also made regarding how a product or service will be produced. Operations managers evaluate the available production methods to see how efficiently they can achieve the operating objectives. Closely tied to process decisions are those regarding **facilities layout design:** What is the best physical arrangement for the facility that will allow for efficient production?

Once the strategic planning decisions have been made to lay the framework for producing the firm's goods or services, more focused planning must be completed for each stage of the operation.

Acquiring Inputs

An organization requires a sufficient supply of inputs to create various products. **Inputs** include materials, energy, information, management, technology, facilities, and labor. Individual organizations have different types of inputs. Sarnamotive Blue Water, Inc., supplies plastic products and components to the automotive industry. Sarnamotive's inputs include chemicals, natural resources, and technology. Inputs for General Motors include materials in the form of the finished products from its suppliers as well as energy, information, and so on. Dealers that sell General Motors cars have the finished automobiles as their most important input.

Managers oversee not only the selection of inputs and suppliers, but also the availability of the needed quantity of inputs, the quality of the inputs, the ability of suppliers to meet delivery dates, and the reliability of the suppliers. Obtaining supplies from foreign sources sometimes offers great dollar savings. Manager's Notebook 17.1 on page 650 suggests that there also can be substantial risk and difficulty in finding out if the supplies you are getting are really what you think they are. To manage inputs, operations managers continually monitor both performance and costs.

process

How a product or service will be produced.

facilities layout design

The physical arrangement for the facility that will allow for efficient production.

inputs

The supplies needed to create a product, which can include materials, energy, information, management, technology, facilities, and labor.

17.1

manager's notebook

Continued economic pressure has pushed manufacturers to search for ways to reduce operational costs. One way is to find a lower-cost supplier of materials. While many organizations looked to Mexico for lower-cost parts, China has the lowest labor costs in the world. It is expected that the number of components made in China for export will dramatically increase in the next five years. Unfortunately, organizational leaders eager to take advantage of the cost savings are finding that the materials they receive may not be what they think they are. Specifically, some may be generic knockoffs of parts that are made using lower quality standards. In short, these are counterfeit parts that may not work well.

In the electronics industry, parts that look like those made by reputable manufacturers can be made poorly by a Chinese manufacturer and then identified with the reputable manufacturer's label. These counterfeit parts are then sold to brokerage houses and distributed. Recently, an electronics customer in Florida ordered 400,000 capacitors only to discover that they were counterfeits made in China labeled with a reputable manufacturer's name. The Chinese government is finally taking increasing responsibility for limiting the occurrence of counterfeiting; however, the problem is not likely to disappear soon. Here are some steps you can take to lower the possibility that your supply of materials will be tainted by low-quality counterfeits.

- *Get an agent.* Find a person in the local area who can separate the good from the questionable suppliers.
- *Ask those who know.* If you are already doing business with a reliable Chinese supplier for one type of part, that organization may know of other reliable suppliers for other types of material you need.
- *Go through an independent distributor.* A distributor may be a third party between you and the source of manufactured material. This distributor can filter poor quality or counterfeit parts. If the distributor has been in the local area for long, the company probably has established relationships with reliable manufacturers.
- *Don't put all of your supply eggs in one basket.* As a measure of insurance, avoid obtaining all of your parts from one place. If it does turn out that there is a problem with the part, you won't be entirely dependent on that source.

Source: "How to Spot Counterfeit Parts: Caveat Emptor, or Buyer Beware, Is Appropriate Advice for Buyers Sourcing in China," *Purchasing* 131 (2002), pp. 31+.

Materials Requirements Planning

materials requirements planning (MRP)

The process of analyzing a design to determine the materials and parts that it requires in the production process.

A product's inputs are based on its design. **Materials requirements planning (MRP)** is the process of analyzing the design to determine the materials and parts that it requires in the production process. This information is then used for purchasing, inventorying, and planning. The MRP process increasingly is tied into the firm's information technology capabilities. MRP computer applications are discussed in Chapter 18.

While an MRP process may typically evoke images of a high technology environment and product, the process can be successfully used in low-tech situations. Consider, for example, the humble product of prepared horseradish. Silver Springs Gardens is one of the manufacturers involved in annually turning 24 million pounds of raw horseradish into 6 million gallons of prepared horseradish.[1] The company has multiple plants. Each plant traditionally had planners who determined production schedules. These planners considered account sales demand and stock on hand to manually create production orders.

Transfers of materials between plants were discussed via phone. Only after the orders were placed and negotiations were complete would the requirements for raw materials be known. Unfortunately, this process often took so long that the purchasing department did not have enough time to obtain needed materials. The manufacturer often faced having to inform customers that the company was temporarily out of stock. Silver Springs Gardens has resolved the problem and become more efficient by implementing MRP software. The software checks sales orders and stock levels automatically. It then generates production schedules and orders raw materials. The company has been able to reduce inventory levels as efficiency increased. Thus, even mundane processes can benefit from an MRP system.

LOC-In

Inventory

Most manufacturing operations require a stock of raw materials, inputs, and component parts on hand. Optimum **inventory** levels may be set when capacity decisions are made; the quantity of products to be created determines the amount of inventory the firm maintains. **Reordering systems** are used to help keep inventory levels more or less constant. In *fixed-point reordering systems*, the operations manager determines a minimum level of inventory; once this level is reached, inputs are reordered. In *fixed-interval reordering systems*, reordering is based on time—the operations manager determines that supplies need to be reordered every two months, for example. Just-in-time inventory levels are discussed later in this chapter.

2 **Learning Objective Check-In**

Scott Learning Company uses a computer system that analyzes the design of every product, which is also logged on the computers, and then determines the parts and materials that will be required for production. Once the appropriate materials are ordered, they are stored briefly in the back room until their use.

1. *The program that would be appropriate for Scott Learning Company to use in analyzing product design and determining resources needed is called _____.*
   a. *total quality management*
   b. *materials requirements planning*
   c. *system control*
   d. *bureaucratic control*
2. *What is the name given to the goods that are in the possession of Scott Learning Company, and that are being stored before they are used?*
   a. *Back orders*
   b. *Inventory*
   c. *Waste product*
   d. *Finished goods*

The Conversion Process

The second major stage of operations management is the **conversion process**—taking the product's inputs and converting them to the final product. The operations manager designs and controls the production system which should create high-quality, low-cost products that customers are willing to buy or use. An effective conversion process lowers the cost of creating the product or creates a better product for the same cost. Many software tools are available to help with the design and implementation of the conversion process; these are discussed in Chapter 18.

Designing the Process

The conversion process typically involves several steps that may occur either at the same time or in sequence. The process will be designed to accommodate these activities. For complex operations, the conversion process is designed in subparts. An aggregate plan shows the process for the entire operation, but each subpart requires individual analysis and design. Each subpart's schedule is taken into account in a master schedule.

inventory

The stock of raw materials, inputs, and component parts that the firm keeps on hand.

reordering systems

The process used to help keep inventory levels more or less constant.

conversion process

The operations management stage in which the product's inputs are converted to the final product.

table 17.1

Process Analysis Information

STEP	ORDER	RELATION TO OTHER STEPS	TIME
A. Get permit	1	None	4 weeks
B. Order equipment	1	None	1 week
C. Paint interior	2	None	2 weeks
D. Install electrical fixtures	3	Following C	1 week
E. Install floors	4	Following C	1 week
F. Install equipment	5	Following B, E	1 week
G. Test equipment	6	Following F	1 week

In designing the process, the operations manager should be careful to avoid overlooking less critical steps. Critical steps may depend on what are perceived as less important areas, but if they are not planned for, the entire process may be delayed.

Process design begins with an analysis of the general operation and identifying:

- Every major step.
- The order that the steps must take.
- The flow of the steps from start to finish, including their relationship to each other.
- The amount of time each individual step requires.

Table 17.1 above shows how this information is used to set up a new bakery's baking facility. If each step were done in order, the bakery would take 11 weeks to open. Because some of the steps can be done concurrently, however, the time can be shortened to 5 weeks.

Several tools are available to help analyze the steps needed to determine an efficient sequence and also to monitor the process. Three of the best known tools are a Gantt chart, a load chart, and a PERT network.

GANTT CHARTS   Developed by Henry Gantt in the early 1900s, **Gantt charts** provide a visual sequence of the process steps. A Gantt chart using the information in Table 17.1 appears in Figure 17.2 on page 653.

LOAD CHARTS   Another way to analyze the process is with a load chart. A **load chart** is a type of Gantt chart that is based on departments or specific resources, used in the process. Instead of the tasks listed in Figure 17.2, the load chart would list the people involved in each step and the time frame for their involvement, as seen in Figure 17.3 on page 653.

PERT NETWORKS   Another way to analyze the process, especially complex projects, is with a **program evaluation and review technique (PERT) network**. This technique was developed in the 1950s, when the work of thousands of contractors and government agencies needed to be coordinated for the Polaris submarine weapons system. A PERT network is illustrated in Figure 17.4 on page 653.

Gantt charts

A visual sequence of the process steps used in planning, scheduling, and monitoring production.

load chart

A type of Gantt chart that is based on departments or specific resources that are used in the process.

program evaluation and review technique (PERT) network

A tool for analyzing the conversion process.

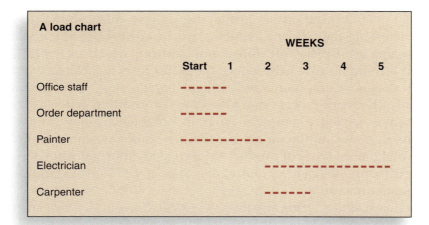

FIGURE 17.2

A Gantt Chart

Project Planning

FIGURE 17.3

A Load Chart

FIGURE 17.4

A PERT Network

FACILITIES LAYOUT   Once the major steps have been identified, the design of the actual work area is created. **Facilities layout**—the grouping and organization of equipment and employees—affects the efficiency of the production system. Workstations are arranged based on product layout, process layout, or fixed-position layout schemes.

facilities layout

The grouping and organization of equipment and employees.

Facilities layout is important in the operations management of retail outlets. At Sephora perfume stores, for instance, grand entrances are meant to suggest a "theater" of beauty. New and popular products and spotlighted near the door, and brands can pay a fee for featured retail space along the store's aisles, where the shelves at eye level produce the highest sales. To make room for niche brands of makeup that appeal to trendy customers, Sephora asks mainstream brands to reduce the size of their displays, thus increasing sales per square foot.

Facilities Layout

flexible manufacturing

Operations management techniques that help reduce the setup costs associated with the production system.

Functions in a *product layout* are organized so that each function is performed in a fixed sequence. Employees and equipment stay in one place, or workstation, as the product moves through the system. Mass production (assembly) lines are one type of product layout system. These systems have become efficient for relatively small levels of production, but traditionally they were used for large production runs.

In *process layout*, each workstation is relatively self-contained. The product moves to the workstation needed to perform the next operation, which may not be in sequence. Process layouts are often used to create custom-made products because they offer flexibility to make product changes. This layout does reduce efficiency, making it more expensive.

In a *fixed-position layout*, remote workstations assemble the product's components, which then are brought to the production area for final assembly. Fixed-position layouts are used for complex products that are difficult to assemble and for large products that are not easily moved, such as aircraft.

FLEXIBLE MANUFACTURING When changes are made to a product, time spent in setting up and reconfiguring the workstations is lost if the process must shut down during setup, increasing the cost and reducing efficiency. It is possible to design the process using principles of **flexible manufacturing**, which are operations management techniques that help reduce the setup costs associated with the production system. Computer-aided design, engineering, and manufacturing tools make the work process more flexible. For example, when a change in a component is needed, a computer program, not the machinery, might be modified, greatly reducing the time the machinery is not available for production and enabling more types of product to be created. Management Close-Up 17.2 on page 655 provides a closer look at one company's efforts to emphasize flexibility in manufacturing.

Flexible manufacturing also involves physical layout. A Y-shaped layout, for example, is often more amenable to flexible manufacturing than a straight-line layout. While one arm of the Y is being reconfigured, processes along the other two arms can continue. In a spiral layout, workers can easily physically turn to help with other steps to keep the work flow even.

Another consideration in flexible manufacturing is how employees work. Some firms use self-managed work teams to produce an entire product or component. Team members learn all the tasks in the production process, move from job to job, and fill in for each other, thereby creating a great deal of flexibility. Team members schedule work, order materials, and hire new staff for the team. Productivity and efficiency typically increase, and the supervisor position can often be eliminated, streamlining the hierarchy.

Monitoring the Process

Operations management is a continuous function. Once the process has been designed and implemented, the systems need to be monitored and improved. *Benchmarks* that set levels of production and costs are strategic management decisions. These benchmarks are used to evaluate the production process in a number of ways.

Getting Your Bearings

Since mid-2000, the United States has experienced a manufacturing recession resulting in the loss of nearly 3 million jobs. Some manufacturers coped with the difficult times by shifting operations to other countries with lower labor costs. At the same time, some U.S.-based manufacturers have not only survived but increased their competitiveness by emphasizing world-class quality and flexibility. Timken Company, a $3.9 billion maker of industrial bearings headquartered in Canton, Ohio, provides a prime example.

Timken made investments in building a sophisticated plant in the United States. This action came at a time when many of Timken's manufacturing competitors were shifting operations to lower-cost overseas facilities. The plant, located in Asheboro, North Carolina, is a model of flexibility in the production of small batches of goods without having to refit machine tools in between runs of different products. One of the keys to the flexibility of the production function is the library the company has developed featuring digital three-dimensional models of components. The models can be used as the design for a production run and can be tweaked for various custom features, when needed. The design is then sent out to networked machine tools. This process used to take half a day when refitting had to be done manually. Now, depending on the extent of modifications needed, the process takes 15 to 30 minutes. At the company's Asheboro plant, Timken can go from work order to finished part in four hours, a process that used to take six to eight weeks.

Timken Company increased flexibility at their Asheboro, North Carolina, plant by using a library of digital three-dimensional models of components.

Sources: A. Aston and M. Arndt, "The Flexible Factory: Leaning Heavily on Technology, Some U.S. Plants Stay Competitive with Offshore Rivals," *BusinessWeek*, May 5, 2003, pp. 90–91; L. Kren, "Decline of U.S. Manufacturing Threatens National Security," *Machine Design* 77 (2005): 173.

In **acceptance sampling**, a sample of materials or products is measured against the benchmark. Based on the results of this measurement, the entire run is either accepted or rejected.

Statistical process control uses quantitative methods and procedures to evaluate transformation operations and to detect and eliminate deviations. This type of control is in wide use today. Manager's Notebook 17.2 on page 656 lists several statistical process tools. By using statistical data about the process, operations managers can pinpoint problems and find solutions that address the problem. They can also see areas of improvement that will often circumvent a problem. By making the operations process more efficient, managers can also improve the firm's financial performance in most cases. Later in this chapter, systems for improving operations management quality are described in greater detail.

Another important goal of operations management is increasing the efficiency of the production process beyond the benchmarks. For example, if operations management can determine how to use fewer inputs or processes in the production system, the efficiency of the system will be improved and the operations will be more productive. Two methods are typically used to determine productivity: total factor productivity and partial factor productivity.

acceptance sampling

An operations management monitoring tool in which a sample of materials or products is measured against a benchmark.

statistical process control

An operations management monitoring tool that uses quantitative methods and procedures to evaluate transformation operations and to detect and eliminate deviations.

17.2

manager's notebook

Check Sheets Check sheets are quantity-based forms, where a check mark is made for a particular attribute. Check sheets can provide data when the attribute is tracked by time, location, or some other variable—to pinpoint workstations or processes that produce more or less than the average or that have fewer defects, for example.

Pareto Analysis The concept behind Pareto analysis is that 20 percent of an operation results in 80 percent of the gap between expected and actual performance. Pareto analysis involves specifying the causes of a problem and assigning a value (such as dollars or time) to each cause based on its contribution to the problem in order to determine the causes that have the most negative effects on the operation.

Process Flow Analysis Process flow analysis is a method of graphically representing the activities in a process, the exact tasks of these activities, and their organization or structure within the process. By diagramming the process, managers can identify variations and disruptions.

Cause-and-Effect Diagrams Also called *fishbone diagrams* and *Ishikawa charts*, cause-and-effect diagrams are a mechanism for identifying potential causes of problems and tracing back through interrelationships to identify the root causes. The main cause of a problem typically is a function of other causes, which can be identified by breaking the main cause down by area.

Process Capability Measures Certain specifications (S) can be defined as acceptable levels of variations, with a lower and upper limit set. By also setting acceptable variation in the process (P), we can evaluate the actual performance statistically as

$$C_p = \frac{\text{Specification width}}{\text{Process width}} = \frac{S}{P}$$

As the process variation narrows, the specification typically improves.

Control Charts Control charts plot data collected over time across a set of limits for the upper and lower boundaries of acceptable performance. Points outside the acceptable limits indicate a problem that needs to be solved to improve the operation.

Source: Adapted form S. Melnyk and D. Denzler, *Operations Management*. New York: McGraw-Hill/Irwin, 1996.

---

total factor productivity

The measurement of how well an organization utilizes all of its resources, such as capital, labor, materials, or energy, to produce its outputs.

Total factor productivity measures how well an organization utilizes all company resources, such as capital, labor, materials, or energy, to produce its outputs, according to the equation:

$$\frac{\text{Outputs}}{\text{All inputs}} = \text{Total factor productivity}$$

For total factor productivity to be valid, managers must convert all inputs to a common unit. Because inputs are typically initially measured in different units (labor may be measured in hours, materials in tons, energy in joules, for example), converting these units to their dollar cost allows them to be added.

partial productivity

The measurement of the contribution of a single input, such as labor or materials, to the final product.

Partial productivity measures the contribution of a single input, such as labor or materials, to the final product. The efficiency of materials would be expressed as:

$$\frac{\text{Outputs}}{\text{Materials}} = \text{Materials productivity}$$

The measurement of the partial productivity of labor is often used to compare the efficiency of firms within an industry.

SERVICE OPERATIONS MANAGEMENT

Form small groups of four or five students. Each group will choose a local service industry establishment, such as the public library, a video rental establishment, a dry cleaner, or a hand car wash. The establishment can be a for-profit or a not-for-profit firm. Before class, research the establishment—if possible, observe the organization in action.

1. Describe the service organization that you selected.
2. Define the target customers of that organization and what you think they value most.
3. List inputs that the service requires.

4. List the business processes that the organization uses to create its service.
5. Create a PERT network showing the business process from inputs through delivery of the service. Create a network for each process if the firm's activities require more than one process.

In class, meet with your group and share your results. Compare the PERT networks each member has created. Refine the network to show an efficient process for providing the service. Each group should then present its findings to the class.

Operations management is typically focused on the production process. The operations management approach can also be applied to other processes, such as monitoring and managing finances. Skills for Managing 17.1 above is an exercise for you in applying operations management to services.

Disposition of the Product

The end result of the firm's operations process is the product, whether it is a good or a service. Other areas of the firm, including marketing and sales, usually bear the responsibility for finding the user of the firm's product; actual delivery of the product may fall to customer service. Operations management, however, includes the customer-fulfillment process.

Customer fulfillment begins when an order is received, sometimes long before the firm's product will be delivered. An **order review/release (ORR) activity** is used to evaluate and track the order through the process, from creating order documentation, to material checking, capacity evaluation, and load leveling (releasing orders so that the workload is evenly distributed).

The final step of the customer-fulfillment process in operations management is the order disposition. The order must be checked to verify that it is complete. Records of labor hours, material amounts, and any problems in the production process are finalized so that the cost of producing the order can be arrived at and made available for pricing purposes.

order review/ release (ORR) activity

An operations management tool that is used to evaluate and track the order through the process, including creating order documentation, material checking, capacity evaluation, and load leveling (releasing orders so that the work load is evenly distributed).

LOC-In

3 Learning Objective Check-In

Crystal Shores is in the beginning stages of another conversion process for its products. This is an ongoing cycle that begins roughly every two to seven weeks, depending on the products. There are several steps that must occur at the same time in order to achieve production in the most efficient way possible.

1. *If Crystal Shores wants to use a visual tool to outline the sequence of machines and time per machine used, it could use an _____.*
   a. *MRP*
   b. *Gantt chart*
   c. *facilities layout*
   d. *total factor model*
2. *Sometimes the products undergo changes while they are already in the middle of production. If Crystal Shores wants to minimize its downtime and reduce setup costs associated with the production system itself, it should use a _____.*
   a. *flexible manufacturing system*
   b. *product layout*
   c. *PERT network*
   d. *load chart*

Managing Quality

During World War II, intense development in machinery and processes took place in U.S. factories to produce goods for the war effort and to use inputs more efficiently for manufacturing domestic goods. Innovations in the production process in the United States stagnated after the war, however. W. Edwards Deming, considered the father of quality management, taught Japanese firms how to use statistics to measure and improve quality—but U.S. firms had rejected his ideas. By the 1970s, firms in other countries had begun using computers to integrate manufacturing operations with strategic planning. The resulting products were better as they were being continually improved, and they became cheaper as the production process became more efficient. Their U.S. counterparts had been overtaken both in productivity and profitability.

The impact of quality improvement efforts in other countries on the U.S. economy was dramatic. Managers in the United States were forced to look hard at their operations. They began to take a second look at Deming's teachings and other means of improving quality. Quality management became an important issue to many firms by the middle of the 1980s. Company leaders began seeking a more efficient production process to lower production costs and ultimately increase profitability.

Top management must make improvement in productivity a strategic objective of the firm. Managers from different areas of the firm must work together to increase efficiency. Many of the steps to improve quality and efficiency cut across departmental boundaries.

Quality management techniques are not limited to operations management. Chapter 5 mentioned the role of the six-sigma objective in GE's planning process, and Chapter 14 emphasized the importance of quality in team performance. It is in the operations management area, however, that a quality philosophy is essential to the success of the firm. Identifying and implementing production improvements fall to operations management. Quality management, kaizen, just-in-time, and process reengineering are four methods of managing quality.

The Quality Management Approach

One of the main objectives of operations management should be to make the production sequence as effective as possible. Just what "effectiveness" means and how it can be achieved are critical issues. Traditionally, Western management approached production from the perspective of internal standards (often quantity produced), a focus on workers, and independent quality inspection. In contrast, the quality management philosophy approaches production from the perspective of external standards driven by customers, a focus on the system, and the belief that quality is integral to the work process.[2] Therefore, quality management becomes customer driven. It is the customer who is the source of standards for defining quality. The quality approach underscores the importance of the system in determining performance. Traditional Western management focuses on employee motivation and ability levels, whereas a quality approach emphasizes characteristics of the production system as the major influence on quality outcomes. Further, quality management emphasizes the empowerment of workers and their responsibility for the quality of the outcomes of work processes. Thus, workers in an organization, guided by a quality philosophy, are often responsible for inspecting the quality of their own work. In contrast, a traditional Western management approach typically keeps quality inspections separate, performed by separate personnel. According to Deming, inspection as a separate function puts fear into workers. He believed the work process was better if workers were responsible for their own work processes and the quality of outputs.

The quality management philosophy resulted in the development of a program called Total Quality Management. **Total quality management (TQM)** is based on the belief that all of an organization's activities should be focused on improving its product. TQM has been described as "a total commitment to quality and attitude expressed by everybody's involvement in the process of continuous improvement of products and services, through the use of innovative scientific methods."[3] One focus of TQM is on the use of SPC tools. Thus, a TQM program often emphasizes training workers in the use of SPC tools and then empowering workers to use the tools to measure the quality of work processes and the effectiveness of attempts to improve quality. While the TQM acronym virtually stands for every quality management perspective, Deming never espoused the use of the term. He believed that quality will be meaningfully improved by managers who understand the quality philosophy, not by applying a stand-alone, set program of steps. Recently TQM has become less visible, but not because quality is less important. To the contrary, quality continues to be critically important to the survival and competitiveness of organizations. Quality is now commonly viewed as simply part of the operation of an organization. That is, quality is often "baked in" to the management process, rather than treated as a separate element of the production recipe.

Four interrelated steps make up the quality approach according to Deming: plan, do, check, and act (also called the *PDCA cycle* or the *Deming wheel*). These processes are ongoing and will result in total quality management. At each step in the cycle, firms must focus on customer needs, emphasize participation and teamwork of all involved in the firm's activities (suppliers, employees, and customers), and establish an organizational climate of continuous improvement by all employees.

The quality management approach can be utilized by any manager. Management Is Everyone's Business 17.1 on page 660 offers suggestions for you to apply the quality management approach in your role as manager.

MANAGEMENT AND THE QUALITY PHILOSOPHY Deming's 14 points for management, as discussed in Chapters 1 and 14, provide the underlying management structure for the quality process. They define the tenets that make up the philosophy. Operations management also draws from Deming's theory of variance. Deming believed that variance causes unpredictability, which increases uncertainty and reduces control. Variations from standard work flows and activities can be seen as a major source of operations management problems. Correcting these variances by using quality principles to find and correct their source is one form of continuous improvement.

Common causes of ongoing variances that operations management should correct include weak designs, scheduling errors, chronic equipment problems, and inaccurate documentation. Individual employees can correct specific problems as part of their responsibilities, such as alerting their supervisor to late deliveries and suggesting ways to improve scheduling.

EMPLOYEES AND QUALITY Operations managers must be certain employees understand that the quality approach means each worker is responsible for improving quality. They must also be willing to act on any suggestions or problems that employees identify. **Quality circles**—groups of employees who meet regularly to discuss ways to increase quality—were a useful means

total quality management (TQM)

An organization-wide management approach that focuses on quality as an overarching goal. The basis of this approach is the understanding that all employees and organizational units should be working harmoniously to satisfy the customer.

quality circles

Groups of employees who meet regularly to discuss ways to increase quality.

of finding sources of and solutions to poor quality. As with TQM, there are now fewer references to quality circles since quality is integrated into the responsibilities of employees and teams of employees.

Goals should be set for each employee so that management can evaluate how well each has achieved these goals. When individual quality goals are met, employees should be recognized and rewarded.

CUSTOMERS AND TQM   Customers ultimately decide what constitutes quality through purchasing decisions. Other departments may identify what customers want as well as what the firm actually is providing to them. Operations management can focus on improving the **quality gap**—the difference between what customers want and what they actually get from the company. By consistently monitoring the production process, as discussed earlier in this chapter, managers can determine if improvements are taking place.

quality gap

The difference between what customers want and what they actually get from the company.

SUPPLIERS AND QUALITY   From a quality perspective, suppliers are regarded as partners with the firm. Poor quality in a product is often caused by poor quality in its inputs. The problem may be traced to the quality of the supplier's materials. On the other hand, it may be a function of the design and the materials the supplier was requested to provide. Involving suppliers during the design and production process takes advantage of their expertise in the materials that are available and any qualifications for using them.

Suppliers who are perceived (and perceive themselves) as partners with the firm will be proactive in solving problems. Operations managers should work to develop cooperative, long-term relationships with suppliers.

QUALITY AND PERFORMANCE IN SERVICE SETTINGS

The quality framework is often thought of in the context of producing goods. The approach applies equally well to organizations providing services. The following characteristics have been found to be most related to cost-effective performance in a large service organization.

- The extent to which the employee is satisfied with the internal processes of the organization.
- The extent to which the organization emphasizes doing things right the first time.
- The extent to which the structure of the organization makes it easy to focus on process improvement.
- A continuous learning culture.
- A multi-skill work environment providing clear knowledge of expectations.
- Task autonomy.
- Job satisfaction.
- Organizational commitment to the employee.
- Few restrictions to innovation.
- Rapid technology assimilation.

Source: C. Kontoghiorghes, "Examining the Association between Quality and Productivity Performance in a Service Organization," *The Quality Management Journal* 10 (2003): 32–42.

In addition to partnerships, many organizations are employing established standards and asking their suppliers to also adhere to those same standards. The International Organization for Standardization (ISO) is the world's largest developer of standards. It is a network of national standards institutes from 146 countries. ISO develops technical standards that guide, for example, production and distribution. The purpose of these standards is to make the development, manufacture, and supply of products and services safer, more efficient, and cleaner. In addition, the standardization is meant to make international trade easier and fairer. There are numerous ISO guidelines and standards. The ISO 9000 family of standards focuses on quality management in organizations. The ISO 1400 family of standards focuses on environmental management so that organizations minimize harmful impacts on the environment. While exploring the details of these standards is beyond the scope of this discussion, you can find more information about ISO standards at the ISO Web site (www.iso.ch/iso/en/ISOOnline.frontpage).

QUALITY AND THE PRODUCTION PROCESS Operations management uses quality techniques to focus on the production process. Products that can be manufactured with fewer components, for example, can be assembled more quickly and with fewer steps and typically have fewer defects. The quality of the product improves, the wasted labor spent in making and dealing with defective products decreases, and the firm's profitability is improved. While quality management is often associated with producing goods, the approach can also be applied to providing services. Manager's Notebook 17.3 above summarizes recent findings regarding quality indicators that were most important in service settings.

As discussed in Chapter 8, one way to combat defects is by adhering to the six-sigma philosophy. Sigma is a statistical measurement of defects in parts per million. Four sigma, where most firms operate, equals 6,210 defects per

Becca is a member of an employee group that meets every three weeks to discuss ways to increase quality in all aspects of production. Recently, the group identified some differences between what the customers say they want and what the company has actually been producing. Becca is assembling a report to give to her operations manager that should help them monitor the production process better in order to build quality into the products.

1. *What is the name given to the type of group Becca belongs to at work?*
   a. *Work group*
   b. *SDWT*
   c. *Quality circle*
   d. *Task force*
2. *The difference between what customers want and what they actually get from the company is called a(n) _____.*
   a. *avoidable cost*
   b. *kaizen*
   c. *production gap*
   d. *quality gap*

---

kaizen

The Japanese process of continuous improvement in the organization's production system from numerous small, incremental improvements in production processes.

LOC-In

Dance Strong Inc. manufactures all types of dance apparel, equipment, and training tools. The industry is very dynamic and while there are some traditional styles that remain largely unchanged, there are also many new and innovative styles that require products tailored to the trends. In order to remain as efficient as possible while still meeting customer demands, Dance Strong makes small, incremental improvements to its production lines. One advantage that Dance Strong has achieved is the fact that it uses the same types of fabrics and materials in the production of its most popular products as well as the custom products. This allows the company to forecast its own demand for resources and to minimize inventory. It also allows the company to create the product in the shortest possible amount of time.

1. *What principle is being applied by making incremental, continuous improvements to the production line's efficiency and design?*
   a. *Just-in-time*
   b. *Kanban*
   c. *Total quality management*
   d. *Kaizen*
2. *What principle is demonstrated by Dance Strong's making all of its products in the shortest amount of time possible?*
   a. *Kaizen*
   b. *Just-in-time*
   c. *Kanban*
   d. *Business process reengineering*

---

million. Five sigma equals 233 defects per million, which is considerably improved over four sigma. Six sigma, however, is the ultimate goal, where defects occur at the rate of 1 per 3.4 million—a product or process that is 99.999666 percent defect-free.

Kaizen (Continuous Improvement) and Efficiency

Kaizen is the Japanese term for the need for continuous improvement in the organization's production system from numerous small, incremental improvements in production processes. The principles of kaizen were introduced in 1985 by Masaaki Imai.[4] According to these principles, process should be dealt with in three steps: maintenance, kaizen, innovation.

The maintenance step is the status quo of the process—how it is done. Kaizen is the interim step of identifying small ways to improve maintenance. Innovation is the resulting changes to the process. After the process is modified, the innovated process then becomes the new status quo and the kaizen process begins again. Table 17.2 on page 663 lists suggestions from the Kaizen Institute for implementing kaizen in an organization. The kaizen principle of continuous improvement is now incorporated into the ISO 9000 standards and is a part of most quality improvement efforts. Thus, as with TQM, kaizen may not be readily visible in organizations, because it is integrated into organizational operations, rather than standing out as a separate program.

Kaizen is present and affects the lives of workers, particularly in terms of how they work as team members. Management Is Everyone's Business 17.2 on page 663 addresses some implications of continuous improvement for you as a team member.

One of the main principles of kaizen is reducing waste in materials, inventory, production steps, and activities that don't add value, such as moving parts from one machine to another. According to the Kaizen Institute, every second that is spent in adding value to a product is offset by 1,000 seconds of activities that add no value.[5] Sources of waste include inefficient facilities layouts. Implementing flexible manufacturing systems and facilities layouts is consistent with the kaizen approach. Another waste-reduction technique is using a limited number of suppliers, which enables the organization to control inputs. Just-in-time manufacturing, discussed next, is another method of operations management that firms use as part of their quality efforts.

Working as a Team A work environment based on quality principles and continuous improvement has important implications for what it takes to be an effective team member. The following are suggestions for you as a team member to be successful and a contributor in this type of work environment.

- The quality approach is based on efficiently and accurately satisfying customer needs. That means that teams need to know their customers and what they want. As a team member, you can help your team stay on track by keeping focused on the customer, internal or external, being served by your team.

- Your team needs to know what customers want. The need for this information means that you and your team may be doing things that aren't part of the traditional definition of work in which people perform tasks assigned by management. As a team member you may be involved in surveying, interviewing, and holding focus groups with customers.

- Measurement is critical to knowing the performance level of your team and the effects of any changes made by you or your team. Kaizen means taking steps to improve the work process, but you need to know if those steps really resulted in improvement and how much improvement. The work process and the steps taken to improve the process are owned by the team members. You need to know that the improvements actually produced the needed results.

table 17.2

Implementing Kaizen

MAINTENANCE

- Question current practices without making excuses or justifying them.
- Question everything five times to identify the root causes of waste and to come up with solutions.

KAIZEN

- Discard conventional ideas and methods in finding causes and devising solutions.
- Remember that kaizen ideas are limitless.
- Think positively of how to accomplish something, not negatively about why it can't be done.
- Focus wisdom on the kaizen process and solutions, not money.
- Understand that undergoing hardship increases wisdom.
- The wisdom of ten people is more valuable than the knowledge of one.

INNOVATION

- Begin implementing solutions right away—don't wait until the solutions have been perfected.
- Correct mistakes immediately, as they occur, before they can cause further problems.

Source: The Kaizen Institute, www.kaizen-institute.com.

Just-In-Time Systems

The concept of creating the firm's product in the least amount of time led to another operations management approach. The goal of a **just-in-time (JIT)** system is improving the firm's profitability. Managers develop a smooth, integrated production process in which steps are performed just as subsequent steps require them, from inputs and the conversion process through disposition of the product.

just-in-time (JIT)

The concept behind creating the firm's product in the least amount of time.

Computerized cash register transactions at Wal-Mart automatically trigger inventory restocking by the firm's suppliers. Wal-Mart's computer database is second only to the Pentagon's in capacity.

Like TQM and kaizen, JIT is implemented at the strategic level rather than the operations management level. Product design, employee compensation, accounting, and sales are all affected by JIT. Under JIT, product design can be as up to date as possible, because the production process won't begin until orders are received. Inventory levels can be more easily modified. On the other hand, product design must be finished when it is needed in the JIT production process or the cost of the product will increase.

In a JIT system, the firm's inventory of inputs—the raw materials, components, labor, and energy that the firm has available—are kept at the lowest level possible. Inputs arrive at the organization when, not before, they are needed. Close relationships with suppliers are critical to JIT inventory systems. Wal-Mart generates its inventory reorders with a computer network that receives data as each purchase is scanned at the checkout counter. When inventory levels for the product reach a predetermined level, information about the number of replacement items needed and where to send them is sent to the suppliers' computers. Suppliers agree to use this method of managing inventory and almost become Wal-Mart's warehouses, as the suppliers must maintain enough inventory to fill Wal-Mart's orders on demand.

JIT inventory systems are valuable in several ways. They save on warehouse space and labor, and financial resources are not tied up in inputs waiting to be used. They also play a major role in identifying production errors. Since inputs are received and put into the production process immediately, any defects in them quickly become apparent and replacements are sent by the firm's suppliers. Because orders are processed only after they are received, products are produced in small batches. Consequently, problems in the production process can be remedied before another batch goes through.

kanban

A form of JIT systems originated in Japan that uses cards to generate inventory; from the Japanese word for "card" or "sign."

KANBAN A form of JIT systems called kanban originated in Japan. **Kanban**, from the Japanese word for "card" or "sign," uses cards to generate inventory. Inputs are shipped to manufacturers in containers with a card in a side pocket. Upon receipt, the card is removed and returned to the supplier. The supplier then sends more inputs based on a predetermined schedule so that they will arrive just when the preceding shipment is used up.

The Kanban system is meant to change an organization's production system from one based on creating batches of a product to one driven by customer demand. In order to be driven by customer demand, the Kanban system uses the return of cards attached to containers to signal that more parts are needed. Conceptually, this is a simple and effective system, but the operational reality leaves room for improvement. For example, cards are sometimes not returned, with an estimate of 1 percent card loss per day among major auto suppliers.[6] Cards are sometimes misplaced, thrown in the garbage, or inadvertently placed in a pocket. While these errors may not occur frequently, when they do the non-returned cards can cause parts shortages, stop production, and cost a surprising amount of time lost in trying to diagnose the source of the problem. An e-kanban system promises to solve the problem of lost cards and to make the customer demand system even more efficient.

An electronic kanban system uses a scanner to read in a code on a container. Rather than having this information on a physical card, the information is sent electronically to the upstream supplier. The problem of lost cards is eliminated.

video: THE ENTREPRENEURIAL MANAGER

New Belgium
Brewery—
Operations
Management

Summary

Jeff Lebesch founded New Belgium Brewery (NBB) after a somewhat disastrous home experiment in 1980 in Golden, Colorado, where he tried to make beer himself. Then, he and Kim Jordan had been on a family vacation to Belgium and really liked the beer and decided they wanted to start beer operations on their own back in their home state of Colorado. They could not get loans from the banks and did not want to take on business partners, so they decided on a low capital investment of establishing the brewing facilities in their basement. Jeff and Kim's brewing creations were a hit within a couple months. Abby and Fat Tire, the first two beers, are still popular today. Fat Tire, the flagship brew, was named after Jeff's travels through Belgium on a fat-tire bicycle.

Jeff, an electrical engineer, and Kim, a social worker, were both very cognizant of the way they were impacting the environment and those around them. While they both love beer and enjoy brewing and creating new beers, they also find it very important to serve as good business role models. The company combines high-tech equipment with an environmentally conscious operations system. The technology they use, according to Kim, is not necessarily always technology that is totally proven. Sometimes, they are simply helping to "move the needle," so to speak.

Quality and productivity are essential elements of operations management for NBB's business. Operations management enables the firm to adhere to environmental friendliness and cost efficiency at the same time. It is in a company's interest to produce a high quality product at a reasonably low cost to yield moderately high profits. This is the reason quality and productivity are fundamental aspects of the company's business. Specifically, the brewery uses cost-efficient, energy-saving alternatives to operate a profitable business, while reducing its impact on the environment.

Discussion Questions

1. The video discusses NBB's conversion process, whereby inputs are converted to outputs. Identify those inputs and outputs, and name some of the ways that NBB achieves efficiencies through operations management.

2. Consider Deming's principles of total quality management (TQM) and the Japanese kaizen, the need for continuous organizational improvement. How does New Belgium Brewery apply these concepts in its manufacturing and other aspects of the business?

3. From a quality perspective, suppliers are regarded as partners with the firm. How does NBB use supply chain management to help control product quality? What other operations management concepts does NBB use that relate to the idea of maintaining quality throughout production?

Further, the demand information can be immediately sent to the suppliers. The electronic signal can be sent via the Internet and can, therefore, closely link the manufacturer and supplier even though they are geographically remote from each other. The electronic kanban system appears to deliver on its promise to solve problems and increase performance. Danaher Sensors and Control Group, for instance, conducted trial-runs with e-kanban to see if the system would reduce wasted time.[7] The organization found that it spent a lot of time expediting and chasing cards around with the traditional kanban system. The e-kanban system reduced this wasted time by about half, freeing up people to work on more value-added activities.

DRAWBACKS TO JIT   Some organizations utilize a modified JIT system because one major drawback of JIT is that having just enough inventory leaves the firm without a buffer. Thus, it becomes difficult to cover problems that sometimes arise, such as unexpected orders or labor disputes involving the firm's suppliers. Warehouse employees are forced to carefully monitor supplies to continue to be able to meet JIT deadlines with quality parts.

Another problem is keeping the labor supply stable. Unexpected demand means a firm must either increase its staff or pay overtime wage scales to meet order deadlines, since no inventory of products is available under a JIT system. The additional labor costs typically must be absorbed by the firm, cutting into profit margins.

A related problem is maintaining production equipment and other factors when demand is higher than expected. The firm's resources typically are focused on filling orders and not on maintenance of machines. Company employees may also not be able to take advantage of training opportunities to keep their skills up to date, another form of maintenance. Delaying maintenance for both equipment and skills puts the firm at a competitive disadvantage later.

Other Quality Management Systems

There are many exciting new ways to enhance quality in organizations. Whereas JIT systems are based on each area supplying materials or services to other areas for them to be built upon, and kaizen and TQM effect change in ongoing small increments over time, process reengineering is a new and different technique. Also, enterprise resource planning, or ERP, is an information technology form of quality management. Both process engineering and ERP are relatively new approaches for improving processes.

PROCESS REENGINEERING   A more dramatic approach to quality includes changing the entire production process rather than making incremental adjustments. In **process reengineering**, the firm is viewed as a complete process—a series of activities that produce the products and services necessary to fulfill the firm's mission. Therefore the objective is to change the entire process at one time. Process reengineering came on the scene in 1993.

Process reengineering focuses on processes rather than individual activities. Its goal, like that of the other quality management techniques, is to reduce waste and improve the firm's profitability. Process reengineering involves fundamentally rethinking and radically redesigning the entire process, including cutting out steps that aren't needed and reducing paperwork. The result should be improvements in cost, quality, timeliness, and service as a whole. Information technology, which has become an important part of process reengineering, is discussed in Chapter 18.

The management team at Ford reengineered the company procurement process when they discovered that their strategic business partner, Mazda, had five people in its accounts payable department while Ford had 500 people in its U.S. accounts payable department. As a result of the reengineering, a buyer in Ford's purchasing department now enters purchase orders into an online database and, at the same time, they are sent to the supplier. Upon receipt, the goods are verified against the online database. If they are acceptable, the database is updated and payment to the supplier is automatically authorized rather than the authorization being granted by the accounts payable department. If the goods are not acceptable against the online database, they are returned to the supplier.

As a result of this process reengineering, Ford greatly reduced the size of the company's accounts payable department. The unproductive activities of the accounting staff and the operations employees in maintaining records and verifying deliveries manually were also eliminated. This reengineering effort increased the efficiency of the entire organization.[8]

---

process reengineering

A method of changing the entire production process rather than making incremental changes.

Working as an Individual   The quality philosophy, tools such as MRP, kaizen, and kanban, and process reengineering, among other operations management applications, have a major impact on how work is done in organizations. These changes have important implications for each of us as workers who want to succeed in today's workplace. The following are some key suggestions for you as an individual employee.

- Empowerment is a routine approach in organizations. Solving your own problems and making decisions are now just part of the job. Empowerment means that increased responsibility is the nature of work in today's organizations. Looking for direction and waiting for others to solve problems is not the way to succeed in an empowered environment.

- Continuous improvement and process reengineering virtually guarantee that change is the only constant in organizations. As an individual worker, you need to adapt to the reality of change and accept it as part of the work process.

- Improvements and change may be inevitable, but they are not simply random events that happen to us. Get on board and be proactive in offering improvements. Further, make sure that you invest in improving and refining yourself as well. Broadening and improving your skills can make sure that you still have relevant skills and a place in the constantly changing workplace.

- Operational aspects may be in a state of flux, but we all need some constancy. Can you find a sense of stability in the core mission and values of your organization? It is much easier to deal with changes in work processes if you have clear understanding and fit with your organization's values.

- Empowerment means that you will likely have increasing levels of responsibility. You may be gathering data and making decisions in areas that used to be the domain of higher-level managers. This increased responsibility can be exciting, but you need to be prepared for these demands. Make sure you have the skills you need, such as skills in working with others and decision making, in order to make empowerment work for you.

From materials requirements planning to process reengineering, operations management is a vibrant and highly relevant area for any organization. The philosophies, principles, and tools of operations management impact the nature of work and have important implications for all of us. Management Is Everyone's Business 17.3 above highlights some key implications of the operations management area for you as an individual worker.

CONCLUDING THOUGHTS

After the introductory vignette that focused on Wipro Ltd., several critical thinking questions were posed. Now that you have read about the basics of operations management, it is time to revisit those issues. First, quality improvement efforts require the involvement and responsibility of those closest to the work—the workers! The workers can best understand and measure improvements in the work process. Without empowering the workers to make quality-related decisions, it is difficult to imagine how a quality program would get very far.

Second, continuous improvement might be considered the mantra of the quality approach. In today's competitive environment, taking the approach of "if it ain't broke, don't fix it" quickly results in the loss of competitive position. Other organizations will not be complacent and will continue to look for ways to do something faster, better, or more inexpensively. The fact that a process works is no reason for complacency. There is always room for improvement.

Third, remember that constantly adjusting a process can have a negative impact. If adjustments to a process become a preoccupation, they can distract attention from actually getting the work done and achieving key organizational outcomes. Further, constant adjustment, particularly when variance is within acceptable limits, can actually increase variance. As an example, consider resighting a gun every time you shoot it. The constant adjustment would likely decrease your accuracy and cause greater variance in your shots.

Finally, to be successful, quality improvement efforts require a variety of worker skills. Workers will need more than technical knowledge, such as information about statistical process control techniques. They must also be able to work effectively in teams and have good interpersonal skills so that problems can be identified and improvements can be evaluated.

Focusing on the Future: Using Management Theory in Daily Life

Operations Management

Mark Hasting, a Group Vice President for Target Corp., deals with operations issues on a daily basis, so he knows how critical acquiring inputs, controlling the conversion processes, and delivering the output are. Mark uses his knowledge of the operations process to make changes that improve Target's profitability and customer service.

Several years ago, Mark was tasked with the job of streamlining operations for Target. His first action was to convene a task force of experienced store managers. Without their input, he knew that he wouldn't be able to see the issues involved clearly or to create the ideas that were critical for reducing costs to an acceptable level. The task force agreed that the pricing process was an ideal target for streamlining, since it included both material and personnel costs.

Once the task force was assembled, they turned their attention to analyzing the conversion process—that is, looking at the major steps in the pricing process, the amount of time each takes, their order, and their flow. Each Target store uses a plan-o-gram prepared by Target's corporate offices to determine how and where products are displayed throughout the store. Since plan-o-grams change from week to week, pricing labels have to change as well. At Target, all pricing appears on the shelving holding the product, and all pricing is left justified to appear exactly under the first item on the shelf, reading from left to right. The task force knew that stores were responsible for using the plan-o-gram to print out a price label for each product. Price labels were printed on adhesive paper that cost approximately 25 cents for one 8.5 × 11 inch sheet. The adhesive labels were good because they were unlikely to fall off a shelf during the course of a week, but every time the plan-o-gram changed, Target store managers would have to print new labels and hire people to remove the label and the old adhesive and reapply new labels throughout the store. The process was time-consuming and costly.

The first idea for changing the process was proposed by a vendor who had met with one of the members of the task force. The vendor wanted to sell Target a new product—channel strips. These plastic strips can be put on the front of shelving, and they hold plain paper labels. The idea was a good one, and the group discussed how it would affect conversion processes—reducing both the cost of the paper used to create labels (plain paper was much less expensive than adhesive label paper) and the costs associated with employees who were hired to remove the adhesive left behind by old labels. Implementing the change is fairly straightforward and involves only purchasing the channel strips, setting them up, printing the new labels, and putting them in the strips.

As the group talked, however, it occurred to Mark that rather than putting one label up at a time, the process could be even more cost effective if the paper labels came in long strips, each strip the length of a four-foot shelving unit. Implementing this idea was complex, because it required finding a printer that could create four-foot labels at a reasonable price and convincing corporate management to make the change. Mark worked with numerous vendors, finally finding one who could supply the necessary hardware. Now, plan-o-gram packages are delivered from Target's corporate office complete with preprinted pricing strips, which are easily inserted into channel strips. The output of the process is that pricing is standardized, customers are satisfied because they know what different items cost, and Target saves money on both materials and personnel.

Another operations project for Mark involved reorganizing backroom operations. When Mark was a store manager, he realized that his employees were spending a considerable amount of time searching for items in the company back rooms. After talking with his employees and analyzing scanning data routinely provided by Target, he realized that employees had to scan location tags up to eight times to find an individual item. The reason for this was that items were stored in "sections"—lengths of four-foot shelving that were identified with scannable labels. The problem was that within each section, items were further organized into one-foot "waco" boxes, which were not labeled. Mark's solution to the problem was to put location scanning labels on each of the waco boxes, as well as on the shelving sections. Interestingly enough, this logical choice was difficult to implement. Operations at Target are highly centralized, and Mark's idea was not the commonly accepted practice at the time. In order to finally get the change put in place, Mark had to do his own research on the conversion process—measuring the number of scans it took to identify a given item in the back room. Fortunately, Mark was able to show that his new system reduced the average number of scans from over 8 to under 2, saving the organization time and money, while increasing customer satisfaction. As a result, Mark's idea was implemented companywide.

Mark describes another operations innovation that influences how Target handles inventory. Using the idea that the optimum inventory level is the amount of product that fits in the shelving space allocated to that product on the sales floor, Mark helped to create a program called "Make It Fit." This program encourages vendors to supply their product to Target in lots that exactly match the space available for the product on the sales floor. For example, if 12 bottles of shampoo fit into the shelving unit allocated to them, the vendors are asked to send cases that contain only 12 bottles of their product. Vendors that produce larger products, for example, liquid household cleansers, might be asked to ship cases of their product that contain only 6 bottles. This system works well, but not all vendors can comply with Target's request. To deal with the problem, Mark helped to create a system where excess items were reboxed once they got to the Target distribution center. This process change, combined with Target's sophisticated computerized reordering system, ensures that each store gets the exact amount of product they need from centralized distribution centers every day.

summary of learning objectives

Operations management is at the very heart of the competitiveness of an organization. This chapter has described the process of operations management and presented the major tools used in operations management. Effective operations management requires understanding of the stages of operation management and the tools used to manage these processes. The material presented in the chapter to meet each of the learning objectives set out of the start of the chapter is summarized below.

1 Define operations management and its three stages: inputs, conversion, and disposition.

- Operations management is the process of obtaining materials or ideas, transforming them into the product, and providing the final product to a user.
- Stages of operations management are acquiring inputs, controlling the conversion process, and delivering the output.

2 Describe **materials requirements planning (MRP)** and understand its use in operations management.

- **MRP** is an essential part of the input stage.
- It is the process of analyzing a design to determine the required materials and parts.

3 Be familiar with the conversion process tools of operations management, including Gantt charts, PERT networks, and statistical process control.

- Several tools can be used to determine an efficient sequence and to monitor the conversion process.
- **Gantt charts** provide a visual sequence of the process steps.
- **PERT networks** are a technique used to coordinate efforts on a project.
- **Statistical process control** is a group of quantitative techniques used to detect and eliminate deviations in the conversion process. Statistical process control techniques include: check sheets, Pareto analysis, process flow analysis, cause-and-effect diagrams, process capability measure, and control charts.

4 Explain the role quality management plays in the operations management process.

- Quality management approach focuses on the system; uses customer driven standards; approaches quality as integral to the work process; and empowers workers and uses *PDCA* cycle.

5 Understand and apply the principles of kaizen, just-in-time manufacturing, and kanban.

- **Kaizen** is the quality management technique of continuous improvement, identifying small improvement steps and focusing on waste reduction/efficiency.
- **In just-in-time manufacturing** steps are performed just as subsequent steps require them to keep inventory levels low. This requires close relationships with suppliers.
- **Kanban** uses cards to generate inventory.

discussion questions

1. Why do you think Deming's work was more widely accepted by Japanese firms than by U.S. firms?

2. Why is the supplier relationship so important in operations management? What problems do you think might occur for the firm if it used too many suppliers? Too few? Do you think being an exclusive supplier for a firm is advantageous for the supplier?

3. How do you think an Internet provider might structure its operations management for its product, which is a service rather than a good? Describe what you think would be the inputs, transformation process, and disposition of its service.

4. Why is the concept of reducing waste so important to quality management systems?

5. Why do you think statistical tools are important in a total quality management organization?

6. Can a service industry use just-in-time principles? Explain your answer.

7. In what circumstances do you think a firm would choose process reengineering to improve its operations management? When might it choose the kaizen process?

Quality Improvement for the Small Shop

management
minicase 17.1

World-class quality is usually associated with very large organizations, such as Toyota or Harley Davidson. Today, however, many smaller organizations are successfully applying the quality approach with limited budgets. Consider the example of Sunset Manufacturing, a family-owned, 35-person business in Tualatin, Oregon.

Sunset may be a small machine shop, but the owners have the objective of performing at a world class level. Sunset's customers were increasingly focused on cost reduction and quality. As a result, Sunset established teams of people focused on kaizen, being lean (doing more with less), and six sigma. They held a number of "events" in which there was a concentrated focus on an area of operation. One event examined ways to reduce setup times by standardizing components and reorganizing tool storage. As a result, average tool setup times went from 3.5 hours to 36 minutes, an impressive 83 percent improvement. This and other similar events resulted in a 75 percent reduction in scrap associated with setup procedures.

Discussion Questions

1. What obstacles does a smaller business face in trying to implement quality improvement efforts?

2. How could the obstacles identified in question 1 be reduced or eliminated?

3. What additional steps would you recommend to Sunset in their quest to perform at a world class level?

4. Do you think that "events" are the best approach to improving quality? Why or why not? What other approaches would you recommend?

Source: G. Connor, "Benefiting from Six Sigma," *Manufacturing Engineering* 130 (2003): 53–59.

management minicase 17.2

Visualize It!

Organizational processes can often be made more efficient and safer by using visual operations management (VOM). VOM is the use of visual aids to communicate messages in an organization. Symbols have the advantage of conveying a message quickly (consider how quickly you can respond to a stop sign) and they can also overcome language barriers.

VOM helps make the workplace understandable to new employees and visitors. The practice leads to improved safety as well as greater efficiency in operations. Recently, an organization instituted visual production control with a simple three-color board placed behind expensive stock. Because of the expense, the employer didn't want to carry too much of the material. On the other hand, the employer could not afford to run out of the material, which would shut down the production line. When the material was in the green level on the board, employees knew there was sufficient inventory. When the level went down to yellow, that signaled it was time to order more of the material. At the red level, the supplier of the material was to be contacted to expedite an order. Further, as the warehouse managers worked with suppliers to implement just-in-time practices, they lowered the heights of the colored boxes to correspond to lower levels of required inventory.

As another example of VOM, a four-page set of written instructions at an organization was reduced to an easy-to-follow, one-page diagram. The single sheet was laminated and posted in the relevant work area. This made instructions more accessible and easier to understand for everyone.

Discussion Questions

1. VOM can involve signs, markings on floors or walls, etc. Have you seen VOM at work in organizations? Describe.
2. What kind of visual communication could be used to increase productivity?
3. What kind of visual communication could be used to improve safety?
4. A visual guide may oversimplify and not convey all of the important nuances of a process. Do you think this is a reason for not using VOM? Why or why not?

Source: G. Stocker, "Use Symbols Instead of Words," *Quality Progress* 35 (2003): 68–72.

individual/ collaborative learning case 17.1

It's All about Variance

The quality approach is fundamentally about understanding and reducing the variance involved in a process. Limiting variation is the key to reducing the number of bad parts and having a more stable, predictable manufacturing output. In the service sector, lowering variance in processes can also reduce mistakes with customers and produce a smoother and more satisfying purchasing process. Limiting variance in a service setting can also be a difficult task.

Consider some of the variance that occurs in health care. People arriving at a hospital emergency room have no way of knowing how busy the hospital is or how long their visit may last. Some people may be lucky and arrive when other patients aren't there and be ready to leave, depending on treatment needed, in a matter of minutes. Others may wait for hours. The variance in this process is, in part, due to the variance in the arrival times of patients.

There are certainly many other sources of variance in health care. A community hospital in California experienced difficulty with variation in the surgery center. The hospital staff had developed a same-day surgery center that was quite successful, but scheduling soon became a serious problem. A process improvement committee was formed and discovered that part of the scheduling problem was due to surgeons who did not arrive on time for 7:30 A.M. surgeries. Further investigation revealed that patients sometimes did not arrive on time for their surgeries either, thereby compounding the problem. Also, some operating rooms were not set up and ready for early morning surgeries. In sum, scheduling variations in this case were found to involve the doctors, the patients, and other facility employees.

Critical Thinking Questions

1. Why is variance a concern in a health care or service setting?

2. Simulations and statistical models demonstrate that random variation in service delivery times can produce longer wait times than fixed wait times. That is, even if patients arrive at random times, the average duration of their stay will be less if the treatment times could be fixed. How could you make treatment times less variable?

3. Variance in arrival times is less under control of a hospital than variance in treatment times. Nonetheless, reducing this variance may be possible. How could you reduce variance in arrival times?

Collaborative Learning Exercise

Consider the example of the same-day surgery center. There are at least three sources of variance contributing to scheduling problems and delays. Understanding the sources of variance is only part of the management battle. What to do about the variance is the next critical issue. As a team, address each of the sources of variance. Identify ways to reduce, if not eliminate, the variance due to each source. What would be the benefits of reducing variance due to these sources? Share your suggestions and conclusions with the rest of the class.

Source: C. E. Noon, C. T. Hankins, and M. J. Cote, "Understanding the Impact of Variation in the Delivery of Healthcare Services," *Journal of Healthcare Management* 48 (2003): 82+.

Andersen Windows

internet
exercise 17.1

www.andersenwindows.com

Visit the Web site of Andersen Windows and read Andersen's timeline in the corporation history portion of the "About Andersen" section of the site. Then answer the following questions:

1. How did Andersen use effective operations management in its first 10 years?

2. Although Andersen may not have instituted a kaizen program, identify some examples of quality management techniques the company has used over the years.

3. What quality management principles can you see at work in the timeline?

video summary

Digital Domain

Summary

People come to companies like Digital Domain and say, "I want to see something no one has ever seen before. By the way, you've got 6 months and $5 million. Do it." Digital Domain is one of the largest digital production studios in the world. It provides a highly specialized service that helps movie directors create their vision. They never make the same thing twice. Even if they were presented with the same movie to make a second time, the approach would be radically different, because of the new tools and techniques that are available.

Their careful approach to operations management allows the company to plan for its future with regard to finances, materials, and personnel. Digital Domain is a manufacturer in that it creates state-of-the-art special effects, and it is a service provider in that it advises the filmmakers during each part of the process. Facility location, layout, and quality control affect the company's operations management. The company is in Los Angeles because that's where movies are made. In HR, they look in LA first, because that's where so many artists live and work. The artists they find internationally, however, are terrific additions to the domestic talent pool. The company's layout is much like an artist's loft. With regard to facility layout, there is a very clean and logical layout. The spaces are communal and are useful in a variety of ways. The conference center doubles as a late-night cafeteria, for example. With respect to quality control, the company prides itself on the reputation it has established in Hollywood. They strive for quality above all else.

Materials requirements planning is a computer-based operations management system that uses sales forecasts to make sure that needed parts and resources are available at the right time. Everything is managed on a just-in-time (JIT) basis, from materials to personnel. Because the projects vary in size and scope, the company has formed a long list of relationships that it can turn to in order to fill key personnel positions when a bigger project arises and they need to "scale up" production. A company becomes "lean" by increasing its ability to provide high quality goods while decreasing its need for resources. Digital Domain uses digitalization, but also is able to work with time using low-end computer graphics. They know how quickly the camera has to move, and so they try to do as much preproduction shooting as possible to contain costs when they are actually in production.

Mass customization has allowed the company to build on its own techniques. The technology does not stand still from project to project, but at least the firm is not starting from scratch. Each new project adds another tool at their disposal. Computer-aided design and manufacturing is a key component to Digital Domain's process. Since shooting film is expensive, using pen and paper or layers upon the pen and paper (ink or paint, for example) allows the company to control its costs even more. Since the company does so many projects simultaneously, it relies on computerized models like Gantt charts and PERT networks. This also helps the company know where they are at within the budget at a certain phase of any given project. If they are over budget, they realize it immediately and can make adjustments as necessary.

Discussion Questions

1. What is the role of quality in Digital Domain's operations management? Give examples from the video.

2. What methods does Digital Domain use in order to stay current in its industry, but also to be a lean manufacturer of its products?

3. How does Digital Domain use just-in-time techniques to run its operations and remain flexible?

chapter 18

Managing Information Systems

Learning Objectives

1. Specify the criteria that must be satisfied to make information useful for decisions.

2. Explain the difference between data and information and how to use each to achieve organizational goals.

3. Compare different types of networks, including local-area networks, intranets, extranets, and the Internet.

4. Understand the role of software and how it changes business operations.

5. Discuss the ethical issues in the use of computer technology.

6. Understand how productivity, efficiency, and responsiveness to customers can be improved with information technology.

FedEx Engineers Time

18

It's obvious that companies like FedEx could not exist without computer technology. As Rob Carter, the chief information officer at FedEx, is quick to assert, infotech is at the heart of everything the $29 billion package delivery service does for its customers.

The company's internal communications and technology systems keep its 90,000 vehicles and nearly 700 airplanes in touch with more than 200,000 employees and 39 airport hubs around the world; they make it possible for 6 million packages to reach their destinations in 220 countries flawlessly every single day. FedEx, the second most admired company in the United States (and fourth in the world, according to *Fortune* magazine), runs its information technology operations on a $1 billion annual budget that Carter strives to use effectively. "We focus a little more on revenue-generating, customer-satisfaction-generating, strategic-advantage technology," he says.

Some of those customer-oriented technology applications allow FedEx's biggest customers to integrate their own systems and databases with FedEx's data centers, connecting directly to the shipper's tracking systems and saving time and money for customers. "You don't want something someone has to key a bunch of stuff into," says Carter.

Even small customers can track their FedEx packages. Tracking "changed our business model," says John Dunavant, FedEx's manager of global operations control. To provide input for the company's tracking systems, packages shipped within the United States are scanned about 12 times between pickup and delivery; international packages are scanned 20 times as employees sort as many as 15 boxes per minute. FedEx has even figured out how to turn its tracking mechanism inside out to let customers track incoming packages, whether they're expecting any or not.

Other tech applications are powerful enough to allow FedEx customers to cut inventory and warehousing down to nothing, increasing their profitability. For its customer Motion Computing Inc., in Austin, Texas, FedEx picks up finished computers at a factory in Kunshan, China, and trucks them 50 miles to Shanghai, where they're loaded on planes for delivery directly to their final customers in as little as five days. "We have no inventory tied up in the process anywhere," says Motion's CEO. "Frankly, our business is enabled by FedEx."

Much of the 40 percent growth FedEx has experienced in the last few years comes from Asia, and particularly from China, where it not only holds enviable flying rights but also the truck fleet and 89 distribution hubs of its one-time Chinese delivery partner. The company is also building a brand-new super-hub in the heart of the fast-growing manufacturing city of Guangzhou, which FedEx will serve with giant new cargo planes.

FedEx supports its expansion with its continued investment in information technology. "From a technology standpoint," says Carter, "we're working with our [information technology] suppliers to get the best information on pricing, to make the most rational and aggressive decisions we can. We run this company on business intelligence and information."

"Technology is coming to us in much smaller bundles that cost a lot less," concludes Carter. "Our intent is to hold the line on IT spending and get more bang for the buck." Unexpected storms can still slow things up, though. Despite all its technology and its own meteorology team monitoring weather worldwide, FedEx has yet to figure out how to predict the weather.

Sources: Dean Foust, "FedEx: Taking Off like 'A Rocket Ship,' " *BusinessWeek Online*, www.businessweek.com, April 3, 2006; Geoffrey Colvin, "The FedEx Edge" (interview), *Fortune*, April 3, 2006, pp. 77–84; Ylan Q. Mui, "Shippers Feel the Rush," *Washington Post*, www.washingtonpost.com, December 17, 2005; Aaron Ricadela, "Logistics Companies Face Off with IT," *InformationWeek*, www.informationweek.com, September 19, 2005; Steve Lohr, "The Markets: A Technology Recovery in Post-Exuberant Times," *New York Times*, www.nytimes.com, October 26, 2004.

CRITICAL THINKING QUESTIONS

1. *How does FedEx apply its information technology software to lower costs and increase revenues for its customers?*

2. *How does the application of technology provide FedEx with ways to improve the performance of its own package-delivery performance?*

We will revisit these questions at the end of the chapter in our Concluding Thoughts. Information is like glue and it is like gasoline. It is like glue, because information systems hold together all company operations. It is like gasoline, because information fuels innovation and change. When IBM decided to change its management information systems to take advantage of new technology, the company's business processes were integrated with the information system. This chapter looks at information systems from two perspectives: how the firm's information systems and information technology are part of management and how management information systems are used by managers. Skills for Managing 18.1 on page 679 lists the skills managers use in managing information systems.

Managing Information

Information systems in some form existed long before today's technology was even dreamed of. The use of automated information processing became common at the end of the 19th century. In 1890, statistician Herman Hollerith designed the Punch Card Tabulating System to record that year's U.S. census. Census takers created the database with cards and punched holes in them that corresponded to answers to 240 questions. The collected data were then tabulated using electric current. The 1880 census, which had been performed by hand, took seven years to tabulate. Hollerith was able to complete the 1890 cen-

MANAGEMENT SKILLS FOR INFORMATION SYSTEMS MANAGEMENT

- *Analytical skills.* Managers need to be able to gather, synthesize, and compare data about their firms and about the options available to them.

- *Organization skills.* Data alone are rarely useful. Managers need to be able to make sense of information by organizing data to facilitate analysis and comparison. Organization skills are also essential in determining how to control data distribution.

- *Flexibility and innovation skills.* Managers must be able to be flexible in adapting standard business practices to new information technologies. Because information systems and technology are fast changing, looking for new ways of doing things is essential to being a proactive manager.

sus in only 12 weeks, saving $5 million for the U.S. Census Bureau.[1] Hollerith then began a data-tabulating firm, which merged with two other firms in 1911. The resulting firm was renamed International Business Machines in 1924, and Hollerith became known as the father of information processing.

By the 1960s, with the advent of affordable information technology, information systems experienced dramatic changes.[2] They have continued to evolve as technology developed. Management of information systems and technology has evolved as well. Today's systems allow greater use of information throughout the firm. They also generate new challenges in organizing, analyzing, and protecting information. The study of the design, implementation, management, and use of information technology applications in organizations is known as MIS, or management information systems.

Herman Hollerith's electric tabulating machine, first used in the 1890 U.S. census, reduced the time required to process census data from seven years to 12 weeks.

A management information system provides access to important information used in many of the management activities presented in previous chapters of this text. These include the planning process (Chapter 5), decision making (Chapter 6), human resource management (Chapter 10), communication (Chapter 15), control (Chapter 16), and operations management (Chapter 17). The planning process, for example, requires an economic forecast which depends on the availability of historical cost and revenue information. These items may be retrieved and manipulated using a management information system.

Data and Information

The term **data** refers to raw facts, such as the number of items sold or the number of hours worked in a department. By itself data can be useful at a rudimentary level. For instance, a retail clothing store can determine which style of jeans was

data

Raw facts, such as the number of items sold or the number of hours worked in a department.

the best seller based on data. By gathering and analyzing additional data about the jeans, however, the company can use the resulting information to determine past trends in sales, make forecasts about future sales, determine the profit margin, and make marketing decisions. The term **information** refers to data that have been gathered and converted into a meaningful context.

information

Data that have been gathered and converted into a meaningful context.

For information to be useful in decision making, it must be of high quality, timely, relevant, and comprehensive. The *quality* of information is determined by its accuracy and reliability. If the information that is provided to or by a firm is inaccurate or unreliable, it is likely to cause errors or to be ignored. *Timely* information is essential for decision making. Decisions about purchasing commodities, for example, that are based on market conditions may be costly if out-of-date information is used. *Relevant* information is also essential. A firm that markets products to foreign countries needs country-specific information that takes cultural differences into account; otherwise the information will be irrelevant. *Comprehensive* information contains the complete data set necessary to make a decision.

Information that is outdated or unclear can lead to poor decisions. When Firestone tires on Ford Explorers were linked to fatal accidents, Ford CEO Jacques Nasser defended his company's actions by claiming that Ford acted as quickly as possible to replace tires once its data supported a U.S. tire recall in August 2000. The firm had already recalled tires in other countries beginning a year earlier, based on Ford's analysis of property claims data from Bridgestone/Firestone. Had data been available to support an earlier U.S. recall, some lives might have been saved and Ford's reputation would not have been damaged.[3]

Ultimately in 2001 Ford decided to replace 13 million tires on Ford Explorers, costing the company $3 billion. Moreover, Ford CEO Jacques Nasser was fired in 2001 and replaced by Bill Ford, great-grandson of Henry Ford, the company's founder.[4]

LOC-In

1 **Learning Objective Check-In**

Christine analyzed all the data from 1940 through 1953. She ensured the accuracy and reliability of the data and also ensured the data set was comprehensive in nature. She intends to use the information she assembles from this data set to project sales for the next 10 years.

1. *The accuracy and reliability of a data set refer to its _____.*
   a. *timeliness*
   b. *relevance*
   c. *being comprehensive*
   d. *quality*
2. *Unfortunately, Christine's information will not be _____ and should not be used to make forecasting decisions.*
   a. *of high quality*
   b. *timely*
   c. *comprehensive*
   d. *accurate*

Databases and Data Warehousing

When Herman Hollerith tabulated the answers to 240 questions for the 1890 census, the result was a database, although the term *database* was unheard of at the time. **Databases** are programs that assign multiple characteristics to data and allow users to sort the data by characteristic. Databases are the heart of information systems.

databases

Computer programs that assign multiple characteristics to data and allow users to sort the data by characteristic.

Databases can be relatively small and specialized, such as those used for accounting systems and payroll records. These databases often are not designed for sharing among a firm's management. The database users typically create computer-generated *reports* for management purposes. These reports are customized to contain only the data that management needs for decision making. The advantage of these databases is that access to them is usually restricted, so that sensitive or confidential information is available to only a limited number of people.

Data warehouses are, in essence, massive databases containing almost all of the information about a firm's operations. In Chapter 17 we described how Wal-Mart manages its inventory using information about every item sold. Founder Sam Walton often said, "People think we got big by putting big stores in small towns. Really we got big by replacing inventory with information."[5] Wal-Mart's computer system receives over 8.4 million updates every minute from the checkout scanners. All of this information is stored in the firm's data warehouse, which can hold up to 12 terabytes of data (more than 12,000 gigabytes). Multiple users have controlled access to both retrieving and entering data in data warehouses. Wal-Mart's customers, for example, can access the firm's online shopping site to retrieve information on items in stock. In purchasing items using the site, customers are entering data into the data warehouse.

Many other large firms in other industries use data warehouses. Package delivery firms, such as FedEx and UPS, use data warehouses that contain data about millions of packages shipped daily. Customers can access these firms' online sites to track packages and to request services. Government agencies maintain data warehouses, as do large manufacturers such as automakers. As data warehouse technology becomes more common, smaller firms will also be able to use data warehousing.

The Internet is, in essence, a type of data warehouse. Information from millions of sources is available to Internet users. Information that is publicly available on Internet Web sites can be retrieved. At the same time, the ability to change a Web site's content is controlled and in most cases limited.

Data Mining

The amount of data contained in data warehouses is overwhelming. Finding useful data is the goal of data-mining software. **Data mining** is the process of determining the relevant factors in the accumulated data to extract the data that is important to the user. Automakers use data-mining software to find patterns among car buyers. They need to know which models buyers prefer in order to tailor marketing and production decisions accordingly.

Software applications use complex decision-making processes to find and analyze data, based on the user's input. A means of data mining for information on the Internet is the search engine, such as Yahoo! and Google. As with the data-mining software applications, the more refined the Internet search, the more likely it is that the user will receive relevant data.

The objective of data mining is to extract patterns, trends, and rules from data warehouses to evaluate (predict or score) proposed business strategies. This, in turn, improves competitiveness and profits and helps transform business processes. Data mining is used extensively in marketing to improve customer retention; cross-selling opportunities; market, channel and pricing analysis; and customer segmentation analysis.[6]

Applications of data mining are plentiful. Credit card issuers and insurers use data mining to identify subtle patterns within thousands of customer transactions to identify fraud, often as it happens.[7] Bell Canada uses data mining to identify patterns, group customers with similar characteristics, and create predictive target models to determine which customers should receive a particular offer for telephone service.[8] Some examples of how data mining reveals customer motives for purchasing products are provided in Management Close-Up 18.1 on page 682.

data warehouses

Massive databases that contain almost all of the information about a firm's operations.

data mining

The process of determining the relevant factors in the accumulated data to extract the data that are important to the user.

Data Mining Yields Valuable Customer Information

THEME: CUSTOMER FOCUS

Data mining is a new technology that yields valuable and surprising information about customer habits as well as the reasons why people use certain products. Data mining is the process of conducting computer-based searches through mountains of corporate transaction data. The goal is to develop useful information about both product purchases and consumer groups. A recent increase in data warehouses, a drop in secondary storage prices, and a plethora of consumer data from the Internet have come together in a way that makes data mining a value-adding activity.

SAS Institute is one of many organizations offering advanced tools to support data-mining efforts. SAS's Enterprise Miner provides an integrated suite of data-mining tools for businesses seeking to conduct comprehensive analyses of customer data. These tools can help uncover previously unknown patterns of data that reveal customers' buying habits and provide a greater understanding of underlying motivation.

Some basic rules are useful to make sense out of the data-mining analysis.

1. Keep data close to the customer. Data directly from the customer will be more recent and of higher quality.

2. Understand your customer. The more you know about your customers, the more likely you are to determine motives for their behavior.

3. Use past behavior to predict future actions. There are various statistical techniques that can be used to project expected actions.

4. Rely on your team. Turning information into business value takes teamwork and discipline.

New insights into marketing efforts can be obtained by using data-mining tools. For example, data mining showed that men who are sent out to buy diapers between 6 and 8 P.M. are also likely to pick up a six-pack of beer. Analysts have also discovered that although senior citizens buy hip hop music CDs by such artists as Snoop Doggy Dogg and Limp Bizkit, an effort to sell concert tickets at retirement homes would probably fail. Instead, a targeted marketing campaign emphasizing discounted music might sell more to senior citizens on fixed incomes buying presents for their grandchildren.

Data-mining analysts have reported results that have been used to lower automobile insurance rates for certain types of drivers. For example, sports car drivers have more accidents and therefore pay higher insurance premiums. However, people whose second car is a sports car are no more accident prone than other drivers so an insurance company lowered the premiums of these drivers and gained market share.

Source: Adapted from *The Economist Technology Quarterly*, "A Golden Vein," June 12, 2004, pp. 22–23; Ralph M. Stair and George W. Reynolds, *Fundamentals of Information Systems*. Boston: Thompson Learning, 2001, p. 122.

Information Technology

technology

The means of transforming inputs into products.

Technology is the means of transforming inputs into products. The roots of improvements in technology began when steam power and electricity became available. Railroads were created as a result of steam power. Herman Hollerith's census tabulation system revolutionized data processing because it used electricity. Today, the term *technology* is mostly associated with computer-driven equipment and processes.

Information technology includes six basic data-processing operations: capturing, transmitting, storing, retrieving, manipulating, and displaying data. These different functions of information technology can be seen in a grocery store's customer checkout system:[9]

1. It *captures* data using the bar code.

2. It *transmits* data to a computer that looks up the item's price and description.

3. It *stores* information about the item for calculating the bill.

4. It *retrieves* price and description information from the computer.

table 18.1

Six Functions of Information Technology

FUNCTION	DEFINITION	EXAMPLES OF DEVICES OR TECHNOLOGIES USED TO PERFORM THIS FUNCTION
Capture	Obtain a representation of information in a form permitting it to be transmitted or stored	Keyboard, bar code scanner, document scanner, sound recorder, video camera, voice recognition software
Transmit	Move information from one place to another	Broadcast radio, broadcast television, via regional transmitters, cable TV, satellite broadcasts, telephone networks, data transmission networks, for moving business data, fiber optic cable, fax machine, electronic mail, voice mail, Internet
Store	Move information to a specific place for later retrieval	Paper, computer tape, floppy disk, hard disk, optical disk, CD-ROM, flash memory
Retrieve	Find the specific information that is currently needed	Paper, computer tape, floppy disk, hard disk, optical disk, CD-ROM, flash memory
Manipulate	Create new information from existing information through summarizing, sorting, rearranging, reformatting, or other types of calculations	Computer (plus software)
Display	Show information to a person	Laser printer, computer screen

Source: Adapted from S. Alter, *Information Systems: Foundation of E-Business*, 4th ed. Upper Saddle River, NJ: Prentice Hall, 2002, p. 23.

5. It *manipulates* the information when it adds up the bill.

6. It *displays* information when it shows each price it calculates and prints the receipt.

Table 18.1 above defines the six functions of information technology and shows some technologies that focus on each of them.

The relationship between the technology and various processes has also changed. New processes are being developed because of available new technology, rather than the other way around, and change may be forced on a firm. IBM's decision to implement an Internet division ultimately changed the way it did business. As IBM CEO Gerstner explained,

> When you bring your company to the Web, when you truly integrate business processes to the Web, you expose—to yourself and ultimately your customers—all of the inefficiency that comes from silos or decentralized organizations. Banks are a great example: mortgage departments, credit-card departments, home-loan departments. Now, when a customer comes to you on the Web, they're expecting to be able to move across those departments. They're expecting to see a common look and feel. They don't want to see pricing presented in different ways. They don't want to be bounced from department to department.[10]

Technology has improved operations management, including productivity, efficiency, and customer responsiveness. A firm's information technology may incorporate its operations technology. Information technology includes equipment, networks, and software.

Managers of information systems and information technology need to establish policies for use of the firm's information technology. Misguided employee use can lead to hardware and software damage. Employee use of computers for unethical or illegal purposes puts the firm at risk, as can damaging e-mail. Manager's Notebook 18.1 on page 684 lists some general guidelines.

Since the Apple II ignited the personal computer revolution in the 1970s, computing power has doubled about every 18 months or less, and wireless technology has freed computer users from the need to physically connect to a network.

Equipment

Computer-based information technology began with the advent of mainframe computers in the 1950s. These machines allowed industry to automate information storage and retrieval for the first time. By 1964 individual workstations were linked to a firm's mainframe, allowing individuals to share information stored on the mainframe. The development of floppy disks in 1971 allowed users to share information easily with each other. In the early 1980s stand-alone personal computers were introduced to business. Soon these computers were being linked together within a firm as a *local-area network (LAN)* in which users could share information among themselves without using a mainframe. *Servers* were designed to store information for users linked to them, which allowed the development of data warehouses. The Internet provided a means for computers to connect outside a LAN using telephone lines. As information became more easily shared, the equipment became more powerful. Microprocessors, such as Intel's Pentium, are able to make complex calculations almost instantaneously. Internet connections moved beyond standard telephone lines to broadband and DSL, allowing data to be transmitted even more quickly.

Computers no longer have to have a physical connection to a network. Wireless networking allows users to access and provide information using the same technology as cellular and digital telephones. A signal is sent to a satellite or central location and then bounced to its destination. Wireless systems currently have some drawbacks, which no doubt will soon be resolved. Currently, if a wireless data transmission signal is lost even momentarily, the transmission ends and incomplete data may have been transmitted. Security and privacy of information transmitted using wireless technology may also be compromised.

Computer Networks

As noted earlier, a LAN is a type of computer network. Other types of networks employed by firms include the Internet, extranets, and intranets. Firms use networks in many ways, including for e-business. **E-business**, also called e-commerce, is the process of conducting business transactions using online resources.

Information posted on networks is a form of intellectual property and can be covered under copyright law. A link to the firm's copyright statement must be provided on every screen of the site. Individuals should be cautious about posting information from other sources covered by copyright. Making this type of information generally available without permission can leave a firm liable to lawsuits and damages.

LOC-In

2 **Learning Objective Check-In**

1. *Accuracy, Inc. (AI), has established a competitive advantage in its industry by virtually eliminating the need for any long-term inventory. In fact, the company uses a just-in-time system that surpasses all its competitors' systems. The firm is able to control costs because it is constantly updating its _____, which contains all of Accuracy, Inc.'s sales figures, inventory figures, and pending customer orders.*
   a. *database*
   b. *intranet*
   c. *data warehouse*
   d. *ERP system*
2. *After the raw facts about sales and orders have been gathered, they are analyzed to be meaningful _____ for various functional departments in AI.*
   a. *data*
   b. *information*
   c. *facts*
   d. *knowledge bases*

THE INTERNET   The Internet and the World Wide Web (one of the services on the Internet) revolutionized information sharing. For the first time, data could be shared in real time as text, voice, graphics, and video among anyone with access to the Internet. The **Internet** is a network of networks, connecting hundreds of thousands of corporate, educational, and research sites around the world. The Internet features several communication and information sharing capabilities:

- Electronic mail (e-mail) provides for communication of text messages and file attachments between computers.

- Telnet enables users to connect to other computers and interact with them as if the originating computers were directly connected to the remote computers.

- File-transfer protocol (FTP) sites are intermediate sites that are used to move files and data from one computer to another.

- The World Wide Web (the Web) employs the Internet's standards and protocols to allow users to get and contribute text, documents, images, and many other things.

EXTRANETS   When a company is able to link employees, suppliers, customers, and other key business partners in an electronic online environment for business communications, an **extranet**, or wide-area network, is created.[11] This network allows a firm's customers and suppliers to connect, through the Internet, to certain internal computer-based systems. Some extranets cannot be accessed by the general public. Access to these sites may be controlled by the firm by requiring registration or by issuing user names and passwords.

e-business

The process of conducting business transactions using online resources; also called *e-commerce*.

Internet

A computer network that is a network of networks, connecting hundreds of thousands of corporate, educational, and research computer networks around the world.

extranets

Also called *wide-area networks*, networks that link a company's employees, suppliers, customers, and other key business partners in an electronic online environment for business communications.

An example of an extranet.

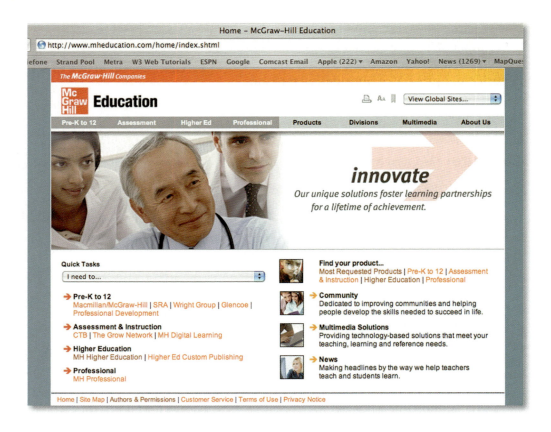

intranets

Private or semiprivate internal networks.

INTRANETS Private or semiprivate internal networks are called **intranets**. Unlike LANs, intranets use the infrastructure and standards of the Internet and the Web. An intranet site is typically a Web site with areas within it for employee use.

An intranet allows an organization's employees to communicate with each other and to access company information and databases using desktop or laptop computers. Access to intranets typically is limited to a firm's employees, and access to restricted data can further be limited to certain employees.[12] One of the advantages of an intranet is that employees can work at remote locations and still be connected to the firm.

Companies use intranets for many purposes. Managers must consider several factors before designing and implementing an intranet, as shown in Skills for Managing 18.2 on page 687.

When using intranets or extranets the computer department should be careful about allowing access to sensitive information. Network security is discussed later in this chapter. Information thieves can find other ways to access a firm's computer, as described in Management Close-Up 18.2 on page 688.

LOC-In

3 Learning Objective Check-In

Rick, who is in charge of parts and supplies for a boat dealer, uses his company's wide-area network to interface with suppliers and customers. The dealership controls access to the sites on the network by issuing user-specific names as well as passwords that change regularly.

1. *The network Rick uses to place orders for parts and other supplies is called a(n) _____.*
   a. *local area network*
   b. *extranet*
   c. *Internet*
   d. *intranet*
2. *This process of conducting business using online resources is called _____.*
   a. *interfacing*
   b. *e-business*
   c. *intranetting*
   d. *telnet*

BUILDING AN INTRANET

Form groups of four to five students. Each group will choose a medium-sized firm and design an intranet for the firm. Prepare a report for the firm's board of directors with a plan for the intranet, covering the following steps:

1. Define the firm's needs.
   a. How will you determine the users? What departments need access to the intranet? What individuals in those departments would need access?
   b. What content will be shared?
   c. How is the information going to be accessed and used?

2. Research some programs that firms use for Web development and recommend an intranet program.
   a. Do you need a flexible program?
   b. Is a standard program that has been in existence appropriate or should a new program be used?
   c. Can remote users easily access the program with standard computers?

3. Plan for testing the program and how you will measure the result.
   a. Who will be involved in the testing?
   b. What kind of feedback do you need from the testers?
   c. How will you incorporate the results into the program?

4. Prepare for the implementation.
   a. What information will you supply in advance of the implementation?
   b. How will you schedule the implementation?
   c. What kind of training will be necessary and who will provide it?

5. Follow up the ongoing use of the intranet.
   a. How will you measure the use of the system—who is using it and what information are they accessing?
   b. How will you provide information to different levels of user about the success of the intranet?
   c. How will you approach the need to update the intranet in terms of content and structure?

Each group will present its plan to the class, which will evaluate the plan.

Group Evaluation

1. Would access to the intranet allow information to fall into the hands of competitors? Can it be amended by users who might have information to contribute?

2. Does the group's intranet program allow for the site to be updated as technology changes?

3. Did the testing consider all potential users or just the users identified in step 1? Did the group get information about frequency of use, speed of access, appropriateness of content? Did the group plan to get all feedback before changing the program?

4. Did the group plan to send out regular reports about the intranet's implementation? How early would this information begin? Was an effort planned to get respected staff members to "buy into" the program? Did the group consider how to include updating information in the program's implementation?

5. Did the group monitor frequency of use? Did it plan to measure the type of information that is being accessed and how often? Did it plan for changing access based on its findings?

Source: *Intranet Design Magazine*, March 21, 2001, http://idm.internet.com.

Software

Software developments have profound implications for firms. Time and cost savings from implementing software that can drive processes have enabled employees to work more efficiently. Labor can sometimes be replaced by technology, freeing employees to focus on more challenging tasks. Information

Information Theft

THEME: ETHICS

The Internet has made information available to the public but it has also provided information thieves access to high-level material. When Qualcomm's founder and CEO Irwin Jacobs gave a talk on the wireless universe to journalists at a meeting in California, he illustrated his speech with a PowerPoint presentation from his laptop computer. Afterwards, he left the computer on the podium and moved several feet away to talk with a group of people. During that short discussion, his computer was taken.

Local police viewed the theft of the $4,000 computer as a commonplace occurrence, but the potential cost to the firm was much higher. The information stored on the computer had been saved at the firm's headquarters, but that fact brought little relief to the firm. The information on the hard drive could have been valuable to foreign governments, since Qualcomm was then negotiating to provide service to the People's Republic of China. Even more worrisome, however, was the possibility that other parties would be able to use information stored on the computer to figure out Jacobs's password, thus allowing access to the firm's main computers. Whether that happened may never be known.

It's bad enough, said Graham Titterington, senior analyst for technology consultants Ovum Ltd. in London, that senior executives carry sensitive information on a laptop, but if that laptop enables others to break into the firm's main computers, "that's the biggest possible security hole in the company's fence."

Sources: Peter Key, "Media Confab Includes Act of Brazen Thievery," *Philadelphia Business Journal*, September 29, 2000; Steve Barth, "Post-Industrial Espionage," *Knowledge Management Magazine*, March 2001, www.kmmag.com.

---

technology advances have also eliminated many positions and squeezed middle managers out of many organizations. Legal software, for example, is used to create standard contracts, wills, trusts, incorporations, and partnerships and perform other routine activities. Accounting and tax software is used for routine functions that had been performed by accountants. Medical software transforms information about symptoms and test results into a possible diagnosis for a doctor to consider. Computer-aided design (CAD) software can be used to graphically display and manipulate a product or component, making manual drafting virtually obsolete. New software affects almost every position within a firm.[13]

Operating system software tells the computer hardware how to run. *Applications* software is developed for a specific task. *Artificial intelligence (AI)* software can perform tasks such as searching through data and e-mail. Firms also use *speech recognition* software, which allows customers to speak numbers when placing orders over the telephone.

Almost every firm has software for accounting and word processing. The functions of each type, although specialized, are sometimes usable in other applications; a document created in an accounting program, for example, can often be inserted within a word processing document. Computer experts have also been able to integrate software systems so that data generated by one area of the firm can be linked to other areas, such as the operations management functions described in Chapter 17 and Wal-Mart's data warehouses.

Management Is Everyone's Business 18.1 on page 689 explains how the use of groupware software gives teams powerful new tools to collaborate even when they are physically separated from each other.

One form of integrated software has been implemented by many large firms. **Enterprise resource planning (ERP) software** combines all of a firm's computerized functions into a single, integrated software program that runs off a single database. This allows various departments to easily share information and

enterprise resource planning (ERP) software

A computer program that combines all of a firm's computerized functions into a single, integrated software program that runs off a single database, allowing various departments to easily share information and communicate with each other.

communicate with each other. ERP combined with the Internet is the basis of these firms' e-business. Large manufacturing firms were the original target market for ERP. Recently other types of organizations have implemented it as well.

Company leaders decide to implement ERP for three main reasons:

- To integrate financial data by providing one set of numbers for the company's finance department, sales department, and individual business units.

- To standardize manufacturing processes, especially so that a firm with multiple business units can save time, increase productivity, and reduce staff.

- To standardize human resources information with a unified, simple method for tracking employee time and communicating about benefits and services.

The main suppliers of ERP software and support are Baan, People-Soft, and SAP. The software differs, but the processes share basic characteristics. For example, the typical method for processing an order before a firm implements ERP involves several steps: (1) the customer sends in the order; (2) the customer service representative sends the order to the accounting department, which checks the customer's credit history and sends the order to the production floor; (3) the production floor sends the order to the inventory department, which supplies the inventory (and may need to order it) back to the production floor; (4) after production is complete, the order is sent to the shipping department, which schedules the shipment and sends the order to the customer and the paperwork to the accounting department for billing. If the customer has questions about the order at any time, he or she contacts the customer service representative, who may need to go through several layers to find out what happened to the order.

After implementing ERP, the company's order process is quite different, as the following typical path shows. The customer service representative may still take the order, or the order may be made online by the customer, who can then immediately see when the order will be filled and how much it will cost.

The customer service representative will immediately be able to see the customer's credit rating and order history, the company's inventory levels, and the shipping dock's trucking schedule. Once the order is put into the system, everyone else in the company can see the new order. When one department finishes with the order it is automatically routed via the ERP system to the next department. To find out where the order is at any point, the customer can log into the ERP system and track it down. The order process moves through the organization, resulting in orders being delivered faster and with fewer errors. Other major business processes, such as employee benefits or financial reporting, are also performed with ERP software, because the data that support them are now available (for example, the number of hours spent by an employee on a particular project is in the database, allowing payroll functions to be integrated).

Chapter 17 described how process reengineering and ERP are used for quality management. As with process reengineering, adopting ERP programs requires a major commitment by the firm, from the CEO down. All of the firm's processes are integrated at one time, which means changing how employees work. Planning and training can take one to three years before an ERP program is implemented. The cost of ERP is substantial—one survey showed the average total cost of implementing it at $15 million—and the cost and time savings it can provide may not be apparent immediately.

Some software analysts believe that niche vendors of Web applications will take over ERP's e-commerce functions, and that it will be possible to implement some of ERP's functions without needing to revamp the entire operation.

LOC-In

④ Learning Objective Check-In

1. Peter is the VP of Operations for a large manufacturing firm. He and other company leaders have been struggling to make more efficient, quicker decisions based on company data. The problem is that there are a number of "silos" or functional areas that need to share information, yet it can take up to a week or more to send the information back and forth between functions and then reach a decision. Peter would like to try _____, which could save the company time, improve productivity, and reduce labor hours spent simply communicating. This would combine all of the firm's data into one program running off a single database.
    a. customer relationship management software
    b. supply chain management
    c. enterprise resource planning software
    d. data warehousing

Information Ethics and Security

There are many types of temptation when computer networks are being utilized. Each computer system entails some management issues regarding ethics and security.

Computer Ethics

computer ethics

The analysis of the nature and social impact of computer technology and the development of policies for its appropriate use.

Management needs to be concerned about ethical uses of information. **Computer ethics** is the analysis of the nature and social impact of computer technology and the development of policies for its appropriate use.[14] Use of computers has created some unique problems that foster the need for development of ethics policies:

- Computer-generated errors are unlike human error.
- Computers are able to communicate over great distances at low cost.
- Computers can store, copy, erase, retrieve, transmit, and manipulate huge amounts of information quickly and cheaply.
- Computers can depersonalize originators, users, and subjects of programs and data.
- Computers can use data created for one purpose for another purpose for long periods of time.[15]

FIGURE 18.1

Ten Commandments for
Computer Ethics

Source: Copyright © 1991
Computer Ethics Institute. Author
Dr. Ramon C. Barquin. Reprinted
with permission.

Ten Commandments for Computer Ethics

1. Thou shalt not use a computer to harm other people.

2. Thou shalt not interfere with other people's computer work.

3. Thou shalt not snoop around in other people's files.

4. Thou shalt not use a computer to steal.

5. Thou shalt not use a computer to bear false witness.

6. Thou shalt not use or copy software for which you have not paid.

7. Thou shalt not use other people's computer resources without authorization.

8. Thou shalt not appropriate other people's intellectual output.

9. Thou shalt think about the social consequences of the program you write.

10. Thou shalt use a computer in ways that show consideration and respect.

An emerging ethical issue is employee use of computers for personal business or entertainment while on company time. Employees who browse the Internet and use it to play video games or engage in chat room activities with virtual friends are stealing work time from their employers. The computer should only be a tool for work activities. Further, employees who use company-owned computers (which are more likely to have broadband connections) to exchange personal music or video files with friends waste valuable storage space on music and video files that gobble up large chunks of computer memory. This slows the speed of the computer system to respond to the commands of users who are trying to serve customers. Thus, unrestricted employee use of a company's computer system could reduce the quality of services provided to customers, with negative implications to the bottom line.

While many company leaders take a flexible approach based on trust in regard to permitting employees to use the computer for nonwork interests, others are more restrictive. It is possible to monitor employee use of computers and sanction those who violate policies limiting the nonwork use of the computer. Companies that restrict the use of the computer to work activities should notify employees in advance. Workers should understand how the policy works and how it is enforced. Employers who monitor employee computer use without notifying employees in advance risk creating a less trusting work environment, which could in turn negatively affect morale.

Figure 18.1 above lists 10 commandments of computer ethics that provide guidance in ethical situations.

Security

Another primary consideration in managing information systems and information technology is information security. While the Internet makes information readily available, it may also allow unwanted parties a gateway to the firm. Companies can implement information security in several ways.

User names and passwords are one way to restrict access to information on a network. Sensitive or financial information transmitted using networks can be *encrypted*, using software that scrambles the data before it is sent and

Firewalls prevent unregistered users from accessing computer files. They may also advise when information being transmitted may be accessible by other parties.

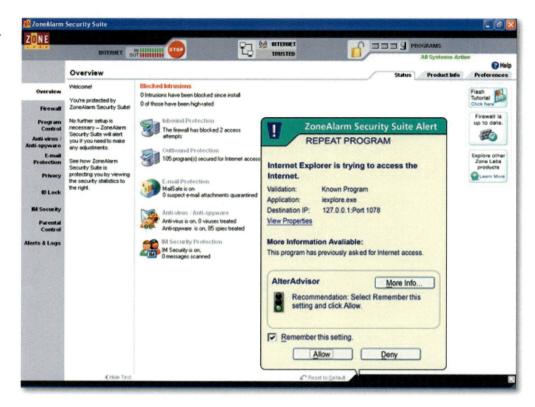

firewall

A combination of computer hardware and software that controls access to and transmission of data and information contained in a network.

then unscrambles it when it is received. Companies also use firewalls to protect sensitive or proprietary information available on a network. A **firewall** is a combination of computer hardware and software that controls access to and transmission of data contained in a network.[16]

Information systems are also at risk for computer viruses. The computer team should establish policies regarding downloading documents and other files from networks or e-mails. They should also provide tools for detecting and eliminating viruses.

Another threat to the security of an information system comes from spyware. *Spyware* is software that attaches itself to a personal computer without the user's knowledge, tracks the user's online activities, and occasionally sends pop-up advertisements across the screen. It may also monitor the use of the Internet and harvest personal information such as the user's e-mail address and location and even credit card detatils.[17]

Company leaders must be aware that almost any security system can be breached. New viruses are created and disseminated without warning. Security measures designed to prevent unauthorized access are not perfect. Even Microsoft periodically finds that hackers have broken into its systems.[18] Managers who are in charge of information systems that include sensitive data must be extremely vigilant in changing and updating security measures as often as is practical. A recent estimate of the damage caused by hackers to computer systems in the United States totals $17.5 billion per year. This damage estimate includes stolen money from accounts, swiping identities, and wrecking corporate computer systems.[19]

Sometimes it is employees, not hackers, who are at fault for compromising the security of sensitive information. For example, medical information covering a person's health history and use of pharmaceutical products is regulated by the Health Insurance Portability and Accountability Act (HIPPA), which requires that health care institutions, pharmaceuticals firms, and insurers use secure computer systems to protect the accessibility to health information. In a recent case, Eli Lilly,

Maintaining effective computer security includes quality technology and carefully crafted management policies. Here are some key elements to consider:

- **Secure the perimeter**. Build a secure perimeter around your company's computers by installing three components: a firewall, virtual private network (VPN) software for remote access, and virus detectors on your mail server. Mail should be the only non-VPN traffic that is allowed to cross the perimeter inbound (firewall settings allow you to do this).

- **Lock down computers**. Install antivirus and personal firewall software on all laptops, desktops, and servers. These are inexpensive and are available at most computer stores. Turn off unneeded functionality on all machines (a computer security service provider can do this).

- **Communicate and enforce policies**. Make sure that everyone in the company is aware that they should not run unapproved network applications: P2P file sharing (for example, many popular music-sharing services), instant messaging, and the like. Have the information technology (IT) staff monitor security bulletins from vendors for the products you are using. Finally, have a checklist ready so that when employees leave, the IT staff can immediately deactivate their passwords and VPN access.

Source: Adapted from R. D. Austin and C. A. Darby, "The Myth of Secure Computing," *Harvard Business Review*, June 2003, p. 124.

18.2 manager's notebook

---

a drug maker, was accused of violating customer privacy when employees accidentally revealed the e-mail addresses of 669 patients who were taking the antidepressant Prozac. The company settled out of court with the Federal Trade Commission and agreed to improve its security procedures.[20] In other cases, security systems are breached because passwords can be easily guessed or tricked out of employees. In 2002, an associate dean at Princeton University was removed from his post after admitting he used easily guessed passwords to access a student admissions site set up by Yale University. A survey of 500 corporations taken that year by the Computer Security Institute revealed that 80 percent of the companies reported that they had been broken into, resulting in combined losses of $455 million.[21] Manager's Notebook 18.2 above shows some points to consider in order to create a more secure computer system.

LOC-In

5 **Learning Objective Check-In**

Mark uses the company's computer network daily to track important financial information for the firm. He knows about other managers who have routed key information to external people who do not have their own valid access to it. While he would never do something like that himself, as it compromises the security of the firm's data and information, he is not sure whether he should turn the others in for doing it. He cannot pinpoint who is leaking the information, but he is aware of the valid user IDs, and has seen at least two IDs that are not valid consistently logged on to the network at one time or another.

1. *What type of issue is Mark struggling with?*
    a. *Firewall access*
    b. *Computer ethics*
    c. *Clan control*
    d. *Troubleshooting*
2. *What is one other way that Mark's company could ensure that sensitive information transmitted using its networks is hard for nonemployees to interpret?*
    a. *Encryption*
    b. *Password use*
    c. *Process control systems*
    d. *Transaction processing systems*

Information Systems

Information systems combine computers and other hardware, software such as data-mining tools, and human resources to manipulate data into usable information. Newer systems use computers with so-called business intelligence to analyze information.[22] Several types of information systems are used in firms.

Operations Information Systems

An operations information system maintains records and supports operations and decisions at a nonstrategic level. These systems may actually be part of a firm's management information system, or they may stand alone.

Process control systems are used to monitor and run machinery and other equipment. A process control system can warn an operator that a machine is overheating, for example, or can control the speed of a conveyor belt. **Office automation systems** are used to maintain and publish information for an organization. For example, e-mail and other electronic communication systems can disseminate information throughout the firm, to a company's customers, and to the public.

Transaction-processing systems are used to maintain data about transactions, such as inventory, sales, and purchase of supplies. Information from transaction-processing systems can be used for billing customers and managing a firm's payroll. Many supermarkets have transaction-processing systems connected to cash registers. These systems record data about items sold and payments received. Data from transaction-processing systems can be used in making management decisions.

Other Types of Information Systems

Besides operations information systems and management information systems, some advanced information systems are being developed. Expert systems are the most sophisticated information systems available. An **expert system** uses human knowledge captured in a computer to solve problems that normally require human expertise. Expert systems are a variant of artificial intelligence. They take specialized knowledge about a particular problem, apply qualitative reasoning, explain the solution, and learn from the experience.[23]

Neural network systems are another type of information system. This computer software imitates brain cells and the systems can distinguish patterns and trends by correlating hundreds of variables. They can perform many operations simultaneously, recognizing patterns, making associations, generalizing about problems they haven't seen before, and learning through experience.

Management Information Systems

Not all information systems are management information systems. A **management information system (MIS)** is an information system that provides information to managers to help make decisions. Although MIS programs traditionally have supported strategic management, all types of management use them today. An operations manager needs data about past operations to compare against present results to determine if business processes can be improved. Marketing managers need information to make decisions about pricing, distribution channels, and promotions.

Types of Management Information Systems

There are several types of MIS available in business today. *Information reporting systems* provide specific types of information for making structured decisions. *Decision support systems* give users decision models to manipulate data to project

---

process control systems

An operations information system that monitors and runs machinery and other equipment.

office automation systems

An operations information system used to maintain and publish information for an organization.

transaction-processing systems

An operations information system used to maintain data about transactions, such as inventory, sales, and purchase of supplies.

expert system

An advanced information system that uses human knowledge captured in a computer to solve problems that normally require human expertise.

management information system (MIS)

An information system (MIS) that provides information to managers to use in making decisions.

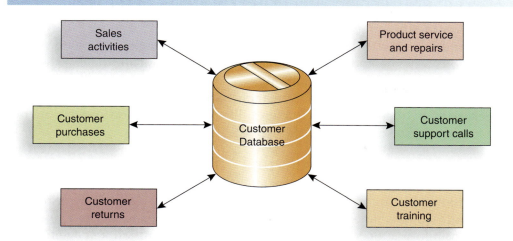

FIGURE 18.2

Example of Customer Relationship Management (CRM)
System

Source: Adapted from D. Kroenke,
Using MIS (Upper Saddle River,
NJ: Pearson, 2007), p. 32.
Adapted by permission.

possible alternative outcomes to decisions. *Group decision support systems* allow members of a group to interact with each other using computers to share information and solutions.

Executive information systems provide information to facilitate strategic decision making. These systems provide software that analyzes large amounts of data to clearly present timely information. They typically provide quick access to both internal and external sources of information.

A *human resource information system* (HRIS) is designed to collect, store, analyze, and retrieve data concerning an organization's human resources. Information that is collected and stored in the HRIS may include an employee's current rate of pay, pay history at the organization, the current status of the employee's benefits eligibility and usage, as well as a skills inventory that maintains records of the skills the employee has mastered. These can all be added to a performance management record that keeps a running account of the history of each employee's performance reviews while at the organization. It is important to protect the integrity and security of the HRIS, so that unauthorized users cannot gain access to sensitive employee data.

A *knowledge management system* (KMS) is an information system used for storing and retrieving organizational knowledge which can be in the form of data, documents, or employee know-how. The purpose of the KMS is to make the organization's knowledge available to employees, vendors, customers, investors, and other persons who need it.[24] Some of the key KMS applications consist of (1) the coding and sharing of best practices; (2) the creation of corporate knowledge directories; and (3) the creation of knowledge networks. For example, Siemens, a large German multinational telecommunications company, developed a KMS called ShareNet which was designed to be a global knowledge-sharing network for its 400,000 employees in 190 countries.[25]

A *customer relationship management* (CRM) system is an information system that maintains data about customers and all their interactions with an organization. CRM systems allow companies to respond efficiently, and sometimes instantly, to changing customer desires, which can increase sales revenues and customer retention while decreasing marketing costs.[26] A simple CRM system stores customer contacts and customer support calls. A more complex CRM system as shown in Figure 18.2 above provides data from all aspects of customer contact including sales activity, purchases, returns, training, support calls, and service and repair.

Effect of Management Information Systems on the Firm

Advances in MIS and technology continue to have profound effects on organizations and managers in organizations. Information technology is helping managers to coordinate and control the activities of their organizations, as well as helping them to make better decisions.

Modern computer-based information systems have become central components of many organizations' structures. Effective information systems are one source of a competitive advantage.

horizontal information flows

The flow of information from one department up through management layers and then back down to another department through other layers.

ORGANIZATIONAL STRUCTURE The development of computer-based information systems presents alternatives to the traditional vertical organizational hierarchy in existence since the 1850s.[27] By providing managers with high-quality, timely, relevant, and relatively complete information, management information systems have reduced the need for tall management hierarchies. **Horizontal information flows** are now viable, supplanting the flow of information from one department up through management layers and then back down to another department through other layers. The rapid development of mainframe–server–client computing configuration and organization-wide computer networks, including e-mail systems, file sharing, and intranets makes this possible. Management decisions can be reached with fewer layers of staff, as departments are now able to share information directly with each other.

Advanced information systems can also reduce the number of employees needed to perform many organizational activities. Managers can use this breakdown of barriers between departments to increase productivity and improve performance by employees. Management Is Everyone's Business 18.2 on page 697 explains that outsourcing arrangements, one approach that managers use to organize the structure of information systems, should be made only after carefully considering both the costs and the benefits of entering into these long-term relationships with a provider of outsourcing services.

COMPETITIVE ADVANTAGE The goal of increasing a competitive advantage has been behind the development and use of management information systems in many companies. With improved decision making based on the information available through a management information system, a manager can help the organization enhance its competitive position. The flattened organizational structure also increases an organization's efficiency and therefore its competitive advantage.

Computer networks also help marketing departments to become more responsive to customers. Managers are using management information systems to improve customer service by identifying areas where customer service can be personalized and where customer product support can be improved. Firms can also customize product offerings without incurring any extra costs.

Another competitive advantage area that MIS enhances is market entry. Using an MIS, a manager can identify markets that previously had been perceived as unapproachable. The firm's information technology also enables the firm to enter into joint ventures, partnerships, and strategic alliances; use new distribution channels; and sell goods globally.

e-commerce

Any business transaction executed electronically by companies or consumers.

E-COMMERCE One of the most significant sources of competitive advantage has been the addition of **e-commerce** to a company's operations. E-commerce combines the Internet with management information systems and transaction-

Working as a Manager   As a manager you may be tempted to hand the job of managing information technology (IT) over to another company that specializes in providing outsourcing services to clients. In fact, outsourcing the IT function to companies such as Accenture, IBM, or EDS is a growing business. Senior managers negotiate long-term contracts with IT service providers to run their entire IT functions. At a minimum, these providers are often able to provide IT capabilities for a lower cost and with fewer glitches than companies were able to provide for themselves.

In many cases, however, the outcomes of outsourcing relationships have produced dissatisfaction. This may occur especially when a company's business needs change. Service providers with standard packages of services may offer IT capabilities that are not flexible enough to meet changing requirements. They are often not responsive to problems as they arise. This may be due to the fact that the client organization did not negotiate a comprehensive contract in advance that anticipated and specified all the contingencies it would be likely to experience over the length of the outsourcing relationship. In addition, the relationship with the IT service provider often requires substantial investments of money and time, which entrenches the supplier, making it difficult to exit this relationship. The company needs to put in writing in the contract the "deal breaker" conditions that would void its relationship with the outsource provider to enable it to exit a relationship that is no longer beneficial. Without the provision of an "exit clause" in the contract a company is vulnerable if the service provider fails to meet its expected service obligations.

Managers should analyze very carefully both the pros and cons before agreeing to enter an IT outsourcing relationship. The key is to be aware of the trade-offs between owning the IT function or giving up control of it to an outside party.

Source: J. Ross and P. Weill, "Six Decisions Your IT People Shouldn't Make," *Harvard Business Review*, November 2002, p. 88.

Amazon.com offers much more than a bricks-and-mortar bookstore. (Copyright 2002 Amazon.com, Inc. All rights reserved.)

processing systems to create powerful new ways of doing business. The result is a new competitive advantage that emerges from generating value for the customer. E-commerce involves any business transaction executed electronically by parties such as companies (*business-to-business*) and companies and consumers

LOC-In

6 Learning Objective Check-In

1. *Charles Co. intends to publish information using e-mail and the Internet to disseminate press releases to its customers and to the public. It also wants to distribute internal announcements to everyone in the firm via e-mail. Because of the high frequency of these announcements, it does not want to send each announcement individually to its audiences. Which of the following would be appropriate for what Charles Company is trying to accomplish?*
   a. *Office automation system*
   b. *Process control system*
   c. *Transaction-processing system*
   d. *Expert system*
2. *Charles Co. also plans to use computer applications to improve its communication with customers. Specifically, it wants to implement a system that can maintain customer data, allow customers to update their data easily, and handle customer orders. Which of the following would be appropriate for this task?*
   a. *Process control system*
   b. *Knowledge management system*
   c. *Customer relationship management system*
   d. *Data mining*

(*business-to-consumer*).[28] Here are a few examples of how e-commerce has created a competitive advantage.

- Amazon.com, an electronic retailer of books, applied business-to-consumer e-commerce to sell books electronically over the Internet directly to customers. Amazon's Web site offers an electronic list of 3 million books, 20 times larger than that of the largest bricks-and-mortar retail store. The site features book reviews, customized book recommendations, and direct shipping of books to the customer's home. These value-enhanced customer services were not provided by the traditional book-retailing outlets.[29]

- Cisco Systems, the maker of Internet routers and other telecommunications equipment, saved $350 million in paperwork and transaction costs in the first year of its business-to-business e-commerce operation. Cisco Systems put its procurement operation online. This cut purchase order fulfillment times in half and produced dramatic savings in material and labor costs.[30]

- Retail stores have expanded the number of customers they serve by using business-to-consumer e-commerce strategies. For example, big box retailers such as Target (with "Partner's Online"), Lowe's (with "Lowe's Link"), and Wal-Mart (with "Retail Link") have created Internet stores which offer the same merchandise that a customer would find at the bricks-and-mortar store. These retailers have also discovered that customers who shop online provide useful market data that the companies can use for ordering merchandise in both their online and regular stores.[31]

Implementing Management Information Systems

Before implementing a management information system, managers need to consider the organization's principal goals and what types of information managers need to be able to measure how well they are moving toward achieving those goals. Managers also need to investigate what sources of information might be available to measure and improve the firm's efficiency, quality, innovation, and responsiveness to customers.

The firm's current MIS should be evaluated to determine the accuracy, reliability, timeliness, and relevance of the information provided. Also, the current system should be compared to the firm's competitors and others in the industry.

After determining that a change in the firm's MIS is warranted, managers need to convince employees to support the change by demonstrating how it will benefit them. Formal train-

Burpee.com, the Internet division of Burpee & Company, the seed company, sends new-product alerts to customers who maintain personalized Web pages on Yahoo, Google, and other popular Web sites. Ethan B. Holland, the company's director of e-commerce, says Burpee reaches about 10,000 people this way, and although the effect on sales is still small, "the investment has been almost nothing for us, so we're definitely getting money back."

Working as an Individual   Individual employees in companies use IT services daily to communicate with e-mail and to use business applications software such as word processing, graphics, and spreadsheet programs to perform their work assignments. They also browse the Internet to search for information and perform tasks such as purchasing an airline ticket or booking a hotel room for business travel. These business applications tools are in a continuous state of change as more functions are added in the software. For the individual, this requires a constant updating of personal computer skills to master the upgraded versions of the software and to learn new software applications that are adopted by the company. Here are some suggestions that individuals can use to cope with the changes in IT that occur on a regular basis.

- It is an excellent idea to take some time to cultivate a constructive work relationship with the IT person who serves as a liaison with your department or work area. For example, when IT people ask for feedback from users of their services from employees, they appreciate it when you take the time to be specific about how your needs are being met and what they could be doing to better support your technology needs. By showing an interest in helping IT staff by filling out their surveys or thoughtfully answering their questions when they solicit your participation, they are likely to reciprocate and be more responsive to your needs for support for IT services. For example, when you need to order a new software program they may know special ways to have it installed for you more quickly. The IT staff may also be willing to show you how to operate the software even though this may not be in their regular job duties.

- By taking the time to develop a vital relationship with an IT person, this individual will better understand your computing needs and work priorities. You are more likely to get better service than if you neglect forming a relationship with the IT person and simply expect service to be magically delivered to you instantly every time the computer system is malfunctioning.

- It is also a good idea to refresh your computing skills periodically by taking short training courses that cover software applications you are likely to use to do your work. Many companies provide these courses to employees who sign up for them on a voluntary basis in order to upgrade their computing skills during a half- or full-day workshop as well as to make them aware of new program features that have been added to upgraded versions of software.

ing programs and appropriate backup support must be incorporated in advance of the system's implementation. Employees at all levels should be involved in a continuing discussion of how best to exploit information technology to create a competitive advantage.

Technological Change

Managers also need to take other factors into account. Consistent technological standards should be used so that the system is accessible to various types of computer operating systems. Making the technology more user-friendly, especially to managers who have little or no prior computer experience, lessens resistance to the new MIS. Remember, some managers may perceive the new MIS as a threat to their authority and job security. The potential breakdown of department barriers by a new MIS may reduce managers' responsibility. Some may be tempted to thwart it by diverting resources from the project, working against the goals of the project, slowing its momentum, and neglecting it.

Finally, managers who use MIS should carefully consider the human element. Quantifiable information, as provided by an MIS, is not the only information involved in the firm's success. Electronic communication should supplement—not replace—face-to-face interactions. It is important to create policies and procedures that ensure continuing interaction among users of the firm's information systems. In Management Is Everyone's Business 18.3 above

table 18.2

Factors for Successful MIS Implementation

1. *User involvement*. Involve users in the design process. They can create an accurate picture of current work flows, costs, and time requirements for various functions as well as pinpointing potential problems. They will also understand why changes are being made and can prepare for them.
2. *Management support*. Strong visible support from higher management is essential.
3. *Time and cost evaluations*. Prepare realistic evaluations of the time and cost of implementing the system and weigh them against not implementing it.
4. *Phased implementation*. Introduce the system in gradual phases, which will allow problems that arise to be resolved before they affect later phases. Train employees in the new system before they begin using it. This training will ensure that they will have time to adjust to it and will reduce their resistance to the change.
5. *Thorough testing*. Test the hardware and software in terms of individual modules, sets of modules as the system is assembled, and the entire system before it becomes fully operational. Test for likely errors and try to anticipate unlikely errors. Involve users in the debugging process.
6. *Training and documentation*. Provide hands-on training and complete procedural documentation for the users so that they can understand the limitations and capabilities of the system.
7. *System backup*. Backup procedures and access to a backup computer system will enable employees to continue working while problems are evaluated and solved.

some suggestions are provided for individuals on how to cope with the constant changes that occur in IT as new and improved software and systems are implemented that have more powerful features.

Seven factors influence the successful implementation of information systems, as listed in Table 18.2 above.

CONCLUDING THOUGHTS

After the introductory vignette at the beginning of the chapter we presented some critical thinking questions related to understanding how FedEx uses information technology to improve its own business processes and those of its customers. Now that you have had the opportunity to learn about managing information systems in the chapter, let's think about these questions.

FedEx applies its information technology to build package-delivery systems that can reduce or even eliminate the customer's need for warehousing and inventory, saving its customers time and money by shipping products directly to final users. Its package tracking system improves customer satisfaction by letting customers integrate their ERP systems with FedEx's computers. Customer tracking capability also reduces the number of customer queries to FedEx's computers. Customer tracking capability also reduces the number of customer queries FedEx has to answer manually. Inbound tracking is another innovation that relies on FedEx's enormous database. FedEx also uses its massive buying power to negotiate lower prices and more powerful applications from its own technology suppliers, thus resulting in cost savings in its own operations.

Focusing on the Future: Using Management Theory in Daily Life

Managing Information Systems

Mark Hasting, the Target Corporation Group Vice President that you met in Chapter 17, didn't invent Workbench, Target's management information system, but he uses it every day. Workbench is an excellent example of how a large retail operation can use information and technology for planning, decision making, human resource management, communication, control, and operations management.

When Mark opens Workbench, the first thing he sees is the Target homepage. Here, he can peruse items of general interest—news about the retail industry, Target, and Target's vendors. There are even updates on Target's charitable contributions and racecar team. But Mark must quickly move on to his work for the day, and that is where the rest of the system comes into play.

In the Diagnostics Toolkit section of Workbench, Mark gets position-based information at any level he chooses—region, group, district or store. With a click, Mark can compare in-stock percents, team store leadership measures, guest experiences, food sales, team logistics, sales floor data and other detailed performance data. This information is invaluable for planning, decision-making, and controlling purposes. Each store receives a leadership score that quantifies its operational quality based on in-stock percents, team member claim frequencies (worker's comp claims), shortage percents, in-store detail visits, and customer survey results. These scores, like all of Target's other control data, are presented in a "stoplight" display format. If all targets are being exceeded, the figure is green; if targets are met or almost met, the figure is yellow; and if the target has been missed, the figure is red. This means that Mark can identify areas of strength and weakness within his group of stores at a glance and take immediate action based on the information.

The associates who report to Mark also use Workbench to assess their performance. Each team leader within a store can use Workbench to call up information on guest survey and district team leader visit results. In addition, team leaders utilize one of the most interesting features of the system to handle human resource issues—particularly coaching and counseling. Every time a cashier scans an item at checkout, his or her speed is automatically recorded by the cash register. At the end of the transaction, a red or green symbol pops up on the cashier's screen, indicating whether or not the transaction speed meets preestablished goals. Any time a cashier gets 10 green transactions in a row, a message is automatically sent to the team leader's pager, indicating that the cashier should be recognized for his or her work. If a cashier has more than 4 red transactions in a group of 10, the team leader gets a message that the cashier needs help with whatever kind of transaction is causing the delays—groceries, hard goods, soft goods, and so on.

Target's IT system has an "e-support system" which supplements formal training procedures and alerts corporate officers to problems in the field. This intranet feature allows Target employees to ask questions of other employees on the network and get an answer back within 24 hours. Information on what questions have been asked is consolidated by store, and if multiple stores have a similar problem, such as fitting an item onto existing display racks, teams are sent out into the field to assess the problem and develop a solution that can be implemented companywide.

When shopping at Target, you may hear an announcement over the loudspeaker asking team leaders to assemble for their "huddle." On every shift, team leaders meet to review key messages for the week, workload priorities, ways to improve guest experiences, product selling tips, and information about how Target is working to serve its four key constituencies—guests, team members, shareholders, and the community. This information is then passed on to associates, who use it to guide their work for the day. Workbench facilitates this communication process by providing talking points based on sales information, guest experience survey results, and logistics information.

The logistics information in Workbench ensures that Mark maintains control over all kinds of operational issues. By monitoring what items are in stock, price change processes, ordering processes, and things like food freshness, Mark can instantly identify areas that need his attention, as well as processes that may need reengineering. Key performance measurements (KPMs) allow Mark and other Target managers to control operations at storewide and higher levels. KPMs include information about sales (compared with comparable advertising period for the previous year), payroll performance, and margins.

summary of learning objectives

Information systems analyze data to create useful information. This chapter's discussion will help future managers, teams, and employees better understand the importance of managing information and information systems. The material in this chapter that meets each of the learning objectives set out at the start of the chapter is summarized below.

1 Specify the criteria that must be satisfied to make information useful for decisions.

- For information to be useful it must be of *high quality, timely, relevant*, and *comprehensive*.
- Information that does not meet these criteria is less useful at best and may lead to poor decisions.

2 Explain the difference between data and information and how to use each to achieve organizational goals.

- **Data** are raw facts that are useful on a rudimentary level.
- **Information** is created by gathering and analyzing different types of data to perceive patterns and relationships.
- Information systems help transform data into information for many purposes, including operations, communications, and management.

3 Compare different types of networks, including local-area networks, intranets, extranets, and the Internet.

- A *local-area network* is a cluster of computers that are linked together where users share information without the use of a mainframe computer.
- An **extranet,** is a network that allows a firm's employees, customers, and suppliers to communicate and share information with some control over access to the information with passwords and other security devices.
- An **intranet** is a Web site with areas within it for employee use. Access to intranets is usually limited to a firm's employees.
- The **Internet** is a network of networks that connects hundreds of thousands of computers of corporate, educational, and research sites around the world. It provides communication and information-sharing capabilities.

4 Understand the role of software and how it changes business operations.

- Operating system software tells the computer hardware how to run.
- Applications software is developed for a specific task.
- Artificial intelligence software can perform tasks such as searching through data and e-mail.
- Speech recognition software allows customers to speak numbers when placing orders over the phone.
- **Enterprise resource planning** software combines all of a firm's computerized functions into a single, integrated software program that runs off a single database.

5. Discuss the ethical issues in the use of computer technology.
- Managers must consider information *ethics* and *security* in their information systems.
- **Computer ethics** is the analysis of the impact of computer technology on society and developing policies for its appropriate use.
- Because a firm's information systems are vulnerable to unauthorized access, managers must also be vigilant in protecting the firm's sensitive information.

6. Understand how productivity, efficiency, and responsiveness to customers can be improved with information technology.
- Information systems combine computers and other hardware, software, and human resources to manipulate data. A firm may use *operations information systems*, **transaction-processing systems**, **expert systems**, and *neural network systems*. A **management information system (MIS)** is a specialized information system that provides information to managers to use in making decisions.
  - The development of management information systems has affected organizational hierarchies. The layers of middle management staff can be reduced, giving the firm a competitive advantage in becoming more efficient. The firm can also be more responsive to its customers by applying information from MIS.
  - Managers can also use MIS to identify and refine markets for the firm's product or service.

discussion questions

1. How do data affect information? What steps would you take to ensure that available data meet the major criteria for useful information (high quality, timeliness, relevance, and comprehensiveness)?

2. How do databases differ from data warehouses? Why would a firm choose to maintain databases instead of a data warehouse?

3. What factors do you think a firm would have considered in the early 1980s in deciding whether to provide mainframe computer terminals or to provide stand-alone personal computers for its employees to use?

4. What type of network would you recommend for a small manufacturing business with nationally based representatives and customers? What would you recommend for a retail operation with a single large store? Why?

5. Why is an enterprise resource planning system most appropriate for a manufacturing firm? Would you try to incorporate existing business processes into an ERP system, or would you suggest changing the processes? What benefits and disadvantages do you see in each alternative? Explain.

6. Do you think that computer ethics issues, such as protecting individuals' privacy, are important? Should computer network users expect that their information will be protected? Explain your answers.

7. How should a company balance the benefits of making its information accessible to customers and suppliers against the drawback of unauthorized users possibly gaining access to it? Do you think firms can be overly cautious about protecting information? Explain.

8. Why do strategic managers need different types of information systems than do other managers? Why would strategic managers need to meet with others, face to face, if they can get information electronically?

Online Knowledge Sharing at Xerox

In the early 1990s, Xerox Corporation had a nationwide database that contained information that could be used to fix its copiers, fax machines, and high-speed printers. However, the information was not readily available to the 25,000 service and field employees and engineers whose job it is to repair the machines at customer sites. Satisfaction with customer service was low.

The engineers at Xerox's Palo Alto Research Center (PARC) in California spent six months observing repair personnel, watching how they worked, noting what their frustrations were, and identifying what kind of information they needed. They determined that the repair personnel needed to share their knowledge with their peers. PARC engineers developed Eureka, an online knowledge-sharing system created to assist the service people with time-consuming and complicated repair problems.

Ray Everett, program manager for Eureka, describes the powerful impact the program has had on srevice: "You went from not knowing how to fix something to being able to get the answer instantly. Even better, you could share any solutions you found with your peers around the globe within a day, as opposed to the several weeks it used to take."

Since its inception in 1996, the Eureka knowledge-sharing system has been implemented in 71 countries. It has helped solve 350,000 problems and has saved $3 to $4 million in parts and labor every year. The system is available to all of Xerox's service engineers via notebook computers and is accessed through the Internet. Product fixes (50,000 of them), documentation updates, and product-update bulletins are delivered over the Web. Individual service employees and engineers can enter possible new solutions to problems into the system. The solution will appear in Eureka, giving credit to the author and noting the service employee's country of origin. An alert about a new solution is sent to validators who test the solution; if it works consistently, it is sent to all engineers via Eureka updates.

The 2004 version is designed to work over wireless Internet connections. Eureka is a constantly evolving and growing system that connects and shares the collective knowledge of Xerox's service force.

Discussion Questions

1. What knowledge is shared via Eureka? How is it shared? What type of management information system discussed in this chapter is most similar to Eureka?

2. How can Xerox influence its service and field employees to share information with the Eureka system? Could there be a reason why some employees decide to not share their "best practices" with Eureka? How could Xerox convince employees who hold back information from Eureka that it is better to share it?

Source: Adapted from E. Turban, D. King, D. Viehland, and J. Lee, *Electronic Commerce 2006* (Upper Saddle River, NJ: Pearson, 2006), p. 354.

Dun and Bradstreet Uses E-Commerce to Sell Financial Services

Dun and Bradstreet (D&B) collects and publishes corporate and financial data and data analysis about public and private companies. Customers use D&B's products to assess the creditworthiness of potential customers, to find and evaluate customer leads, to select potential suppliers, and to facilitate supplier negotiations. In business for over 160 years, D&B stores data from about 80 million businesses in over 200 countries worldwide. To provide the latest, most up-to-date information, D&B updates its databases more than 1 million times a day.

Throughout the years, D&B has used the latest technology to deliver its financial reports. In the beginning, reports were on paper and delivered via mail. Later, reports were faxed to customers, and still later they were delivered via private communications networks. With the advent of the Internet, however, D&B has an even more effective delivery medium: Web-based e-commerce.

At the D&B Web site (dnb.com) users can select from a menu of financial reports the kinds of information that suits their needs. The customer pays for the financial reports that are selected with the cost based on the number of companies and the type of reports that are ordered. The reports can be purchased online via the D&B commerce server.

Consider the advantages to D&B of delivering these reports via the Web. First, the site is up and running on a 24 hour/7 day per week basis, including holidays. Second, to purchase a report the user enters all customer data, saving D&B data entry and related administrative costs. Furthermore, by using Web-based e-commerce, D&B can change or extend its product offering simply by making a few changes to its commerce server database. There is no need to create, print, inventory, or mail a new catalog. Finally, the commerce server records customer puchase data that can be mined for information to guide future product offerings. Thus, by using e-commerce technology, D&B sells on a 24/7 basis, saves costs, distributes more current data, and gains marketing information.

Discussion Questions

1. By mining the data provided by the customers that use its financial services, D&B can gain useful marketing information for its ongoing products as well as ideas for new products. Explain how the market data gathered from the D&B e-commerce Web site can improve current products. How can this information be used to develop ideas for new products and to determine who the customer for the new product is likely to be?

2. Visit the D&B Web site at: www.dnb.com. Once at the Web site, click onto the link to "products and services." List five of the products or services that D&B offers to customers. Who are the core customers that use D&B services?

Source: Adapted from D. Kroenke, *Using MIS* (Upper Saddle River, NJ: Pearson, 2007), p. 240.

Hunting for Hackers to Help with Hacking

individual/ collaborative learning case 18.1

Breaking into networks has become a useful tool for illegally cutting corners. In October 2000, Microsoft discovered that someone had been breaking into the firm's network and looking at its source code of products under development. Other documents that may have been vulnerable included contracts, e-mail, and other components. Microsoft officials had little doubt that this break-in was an act of industrial espionage. Not surprisingly, Microsoft's security team is one of the best, with huge resources and incentives to maintain the integrity of the firm's information channels. If Microsoft can't keep its secrets secret, who can?

The United States is expected to need an additional 50,000 to 75,000 information-security professionals in the next few years. Computer-security professionals' salaries have leapt 50 percent in the past 12 months. Hetal Patel, an associate at PPS Information Systems Staffing in Baltimore, is a headhunter for information-security specialists. Even with the huge increase in salaries, there aren't enough people out there interested in this work, however, so companies are trying to improve their information-security defenses internally. These efforts create business for firewall engineers, intrusion-detection specialists, and programmers with expertise in cryptography algorithms. "It's very tough to find the engineers because there is so much competition," Patel says.

The small number of U.S. academic programs with an information-security emphasis graduate only 200 people annually, and only 14 universities are considered to provide information-security expertise by the National Security Agency. The International Information Systems Security Certifications Consortium, Inc., has issued only 3,000 certificates over the past four years. Most certification programs teach one particular type of equipment, while university programs teach the principles underlying everything. Understanding security principles has become more important for security experts, with complex technologies mixing multiple protocols and devices. Twenty-five years ago, firms had one operating system and one security product for it. New technologies and cross-platform operations create new headaches. And on-the-job training is essential.

Security experts feel that until the field gains academic status, as computer science did in the 1960s and 1970s, and receives money for academic programs, information security will continue to be threatened.

Critical Thinking Questions

1. Is it possible to create a security system to protect computer networks? Explain your answer.

2. How do you think hackers can gain access to systems as well protected as Microsoft's? Does it follow that companies with virtually all of their operations and information online would be expected to have the expertise to protect themselves?

3. How would you safeguard a firm's information from former employees—especially those who were responsible for its security?

Collaborative Learning Exercise

Your firm, DataStore, has recently found that its online databases have been broken into. Two members of your group have been assigned the responsibility for upgrading the firm's information security. They must outline the firm's security needs by detailing the firm's existing information technology, access to information, safeguards, and maintenance, and then provide the outline to two security firms, made up of the other members of the group. One firm can provide security based on an academic background, and the other must develop its security system from hands-on work only. Each security firm creates and presents a proposal that includes what it would do and why it should be chosen, and the DataStore staff must decide which to use.

Sources: Alex Salkever, "Security Net," *BusinessWeek*, November 28, 2000; Steve Barth, "Post-Industrial Espionage," *Knowledge Management Magazine*, March 2001.

internet exercise 18.1

Computer Privacy

Many firms that do business online have made privacy a key issue. Visit the Web sites of several firms, such as those listed and others of your choice, and answer the following questions:

1. Did the firm's Web site include information about maintaining visitors' privacy? Did it spell out how information about you would be used?

2. Now visit http://nclnet.org/technology/essentials/ and click the areas found there. Would you incorporate the safeguards from this consumer site into a privacy policy?

3. What kind of customer information do you feel firms have the right to know?

www.irs.gov
www.abercrombie.com
www.amazon.com

manager's checkup 18.1

The Ethics of Using the Corporate Computer

Suppose you work at a company that has the following computer use policy:

Computers, e-mail, and the Internet are to be used primarily for official company business. Small amounts of personal e-mail can be exchanged with friends and family, and occasional usage of the Internet is permitted, but such usage should be limited and never interfere with your work.

Which of the following activities on the corporate computer can you engage in according to the computer use policy? Mark the following activities as follows: **OK**, for activities that are permitted; **No**, for activities that are not permitted; and **?**, for questionnable activities:

_____ 1. Playing computer games during work hours.

_____ 2. Playing computer games on the company computer before and after work hours.

_____ 3. Responding to e-mails from an ill parent.

_____ 4. Watching DVDs during lunch and other breaks.

_____ 5. Sending e-mails to plan a party that involves mostly people from work.

_____ 6. Sending e-mails to plan a party that involves no one from work.

_____ 7. Searching the Web for a new car.

_____ 8. Reading the news on CNN.com.

_____ 9. Checking the stock market over the Internet.

_____ 10. Bidding on items for personal use on eBay.

_____ 11. Selling personal items on eBay.

_____ 12. Paying personal bills online.

_____ 13. Paying personal bills online when traveling on company business.

_____ 14. Buying an airplane ticket for an ill parent over the Internet.

_____ 15. Buying an airplane ticket for a personal vacation over the Internet.

Scoring: The permitted activities (marked "OK") should be: 3, 5, and 13.

The activities not permitted (marked "No") should be: 1, 6, 7, 11, and 12.

The questionable activities (marked "?") should be: 2, 4, 8, 9, 10, 14, and 15.

Give yourself 1 point for each correct answer. If your total points equal 12 or higher you have developed good ethical judgment regarding the use of a corporate computer.

Source: Adapted from D. Kroenke, _Using MIS_ (Upper Saddle River, NJ: Pearson, 2007), p. 309a. Adapted by permission.

Hillerich & Bradsby

video summary

Summary

The first name in bats is the Louisville Slugger. Hillerich & Bradsby, makers of the Louisville Slugger, started out in 1857 as J. F. Hillerich and Sons. In the beginning, they made butter churns, a popular item in that time. Their career in baseball began when John Hillerich's son, Bud, snuck out of school to catch a baseball game. He boldly promised star player Pete Browning that he could build him a better wooden bat that would not break. H&B ended up holding a majority of the bat market for years, until the acceptance of aluminum bats in the 1970s. In 1978, they expanded their capacity to manufacture aluminum bats. They also operate Power Bilt Golf (since 1916) and Louisville Hockey (since 1968). H&B has a family culture where employees look out for one another and care about each other. The management really tries to help employees understand where the company is going and how the individuals impact the company and its success.

The company promotes innovation by getting out to talk with users of its products, using sales reps and end-user talent as sources of information. Because of intensified competition, H&B took a long look at its internal systems as a way to streamline operations and give it a leg up on the competition. The executive management staff had a series of meetings looking at issues that needed to be addressed by H&B. These involved inventory, order entry, returns, and production problems. That led them to look at something that could address those issues all at the same time.

The company's old legacy system was not going to be supported anymore—it was expiring. This problem was common in the 1990s. The firm could either reconfigure the old system, which would be very expensive, or switch to a new enterprise resource planning system that could simplify all the processes of the firm by storing all the firm's information in one common database. ERP's benefits are bottom-line savings for the company and a boost to morale as redundancies fade away. Employees are forced to abandon their old methods for new ones. The cost of implementation, according to H&B, will be worthwhile financially down the road.

The various functional areas of the company did not have a viable means of communication before this system. To answer one question could take a week's time. The first step to implement the new system, the committee had to decide what their priorities were. They then chose SAP, a German company, to implement the program. There was an 18-month configuration period. Some long-time veterans struggled significantly with the new system. It raised everyone's stress level for a long period of time (about a year). The program took five years to start showing a payoff. The company considered pulling the plug during implementation. Now, the company ships 85 percent of its orders on time and complete, versus 40 percent before the implementation. Customer satisfaction among the firm's top customers is at 90–95 percent.

Discussion Questions

1. What were some of the reasons Hillerich & Bradsby implemented the new ERP system? Are these common reasons among businesses today?

2. What were some of the difficulties that H&B encountered when it changed systems?

3. What were the benefits of the ERP changeover? What benefits exist beyond the present investment in the system?

endnotes

Chapter 1

1. T. Zeller, "Microsoft Amends Its Policy for Shutting Down Blogs," *New York Times*, February 1, 2006; T. Zeller, "Internet Firms Face Questioning about Censoring Online Searches in China," *New York Times*, February 15, 2006, p. C-3; T. Zeller, "Web Firms Are Grilled on Dealings in China," *New York Times*, February 16, 2006, p. C-1; L. Grossman and H. Beech, "Google under the Gun," *Time*, February 13, 2006, pp. 53–54.; and B. Elgin, "Outrunning China's Web Cops," *BusinessWeek*, February 20, 2006, pp. 38–40
2. G. R. Jones, J. M. George, and C. W. Hill, *Contemporary Management*. New York: McGraw-Hill/Irwin, 2000, p. 42.
3. L. R. Gomez-Mejia, D. B. Balkin, and R. Cardy, *Managing Human Resources*. Englewood Cliffs, NJ: Prentice Hall, 2004.
4. Harris, 1915.
5. J. Heizer and B. Render, *Production and Operations Management*. Englewood Cliffs, NJ: Prentice Hall, 1996, p. 650.
6. Jones, George, and Hill, *Contemporary Management*, p. 54.
7. C. I. Barnard, *The Functions of the Executive*. Cambridge, MA: Harvard University Press, 1938, p. 65.
8. M. Mandel, S. Hamm, and C. Farrell, "Why the Economy Is a Lot Stronger Than You Think," *BusinessWeek*, February 13, 2006, pp. 20–32.
9. R.L. Daft, *Management*. Thompson: Southwestern Press, 2005, p. 62.

Chapter 2

1. G. de Jonquieres, "Foreign Direct Investment Worldwide Figures to Reach $430 Billion," *Financial Times*, November 11, 1998, p. 6; D. I. Oyama, "World Watch," *The Wall Street Journal*, June 1, 1999 p. A16.
2. C. W. Hill, *International Business*. New York: McGraw-Hill/Irwin, 2007.
3. World Trade Organization, *International Trade Trends and Statistics*. Geneva: WTO, 1998; see the special issue of *BusinessWeek* on globalization, February 3, 2003.
4. Hill, *International Business*.
5. "The Global 500," *Fortune*, August 7, 1995, pp. 130–131.
6. R. L. Hudson, "Europe's Great Expectations," *Wall Street Journal*, January 24, 2003, p. A-10.
7. E. Bellman and N. Koppel, "More U.S. Legal Work Moves to India's Low-Cost Lawyers," *The Wall Street Journal*, September 28, 2005, p. B-1.
8. F. Balfour and D. Roberts, "Stealing Managers from the Big Boys," *BusinessWeek*, September 26, 2005, p. 54.
9. M. Kripalani, (2005, Oct. 10). "A Quiet Shopping Spree Overseas," *BusinessWeek*, October 10, 2005, p. 54.
10. G. V. Naik, J. Karp, J. Millman, F. Fassiti, and J. Slater, "Global Baby Bust," *Wall Street Journal*, January 24, 2003, p. B-1.
11. T. Raithel, "Panel to Look at Changes Brought by Toyota," *Evansville Courier and Press*, July 2, 1999, pp. 3–4.
12. L. Gomez-Mejia, et al., *Managing Human Resources*. Upper Saddle River, NJ: Pearson Education, Inc., 2007.
13. Ibid.
14. G. T. Sims, "Corn Flakes Clash Shows the Glitches in European Union," *The Wall Street Journal*, November 1, 2005, p. A-1.
15. Hill, *International Business*.
16. Ibid., p. 6.
17. S. N. Mehta, "Enterprise: Small Companies Look to Cultivate Foreign Business," *The Wall Street Journal*, July 7, 1994, p. B-2.
18. Hill, *International Business*, p. 11.
19. J. H. Donnelly, J. Gibson, and J. M. Ivancevich, *Fundamentals of Management*. Burr Ridge, IL: Irwin, 1995, p. 67.
20. Y. El-Rashidi, "D'oh! Arabized Simpsons Aren't Getting Many Laughs." *The Wall Street Journal*, December 2, 2005, p. A-1.
21. C. Matlack and P. Burrows, "HP's French Twist." *BusinessWeek*, October 10, 2005, p. 53.
22. D. A. Ball, W. H. McCulloch, P. L. Frantz, J. M. Geringer, & M. S. Minor, *International business: The challenge of global competition*. New York: McGraw-Hill, 2002.
23. R. S. Greenberger and C. S. Smith, "CD Piracy Flourishes in China," *The Wall Street Journal*, April 28, 1997, p. A1.
24. C. Balfour and D. Roberts, "Stealing Managers from the Big Boys," *BusinessWeek*, September 26, 2005, p. 54.
25. J. Darling and D. Nauss, "Stall in the Fast Lane," *Los Angeles Times*, February 19, 1995, p. 1.
26. J. Graff, "Why France Is Burning," *Time*, November 14, 2005, p. 36.
27. G. Hofstede, *Culture's Consequences: International Differences in Work Related Values*, Beverly Hills, CA: Sage, 1984, p. 21.
28. Ibid.
29. C. Hymowitz, "More American Chiefs Are Taking Top Posts at Overseas Concerns," *The Wall Street Journal*, October 17, 2005, p. B-1.
30. P. Dvorak, "Stringer Faces First Big Test as Sony's Chief," *The Wall Street Journal*, September 19, 2005, p. B-1; P. Dvorak, "Culture Clash Crimps Sony CEO," *The Wall Street Journal*, September 24, 2005, p. A-6; and J. Wrighton & J. Sapsford, "For Nissan's Rescuer, Ghosn, New Road Rules Await at Renault," *The Wall Street Journal*, April 26, 2005, p. A-1.
31. J. Wild, K. C. Wild, and J. C. Han, *International Business*. Englewood Cliffs, NJ: Prentice Hall, 2002.
32. A. Taylor, "Got 300,000?" *Fortune*, January 20, 2003, pp. 118–125.
33. M. Fackler, "Wal-Mart Doubles Down on Its Investment in Japan," *The New York Times*, October 29, 2005, p. B-4.
34. Wild et al., *International Business*, p. 372.
35. Hill, *International Business*.
36. C. Chandler, "India's Bumpy Ride," *Fortune*, October 31, 2005, p. 134.
37. C. Rhoads, "Motorola's Modernizer," *The Wall Street Journal*, June 23, 2005, p. B-1.
38. M. Ihlwan, & D. Roberts, "Made in Korea, Assembled in China," *BusinessWeek*, August 1, 2005, p. 48.
39. R. Buckman, "Cellphone Game Rings in New Niche: Ultracheap," *The Wall Street Journal*, August 18, 2005, p. B-4.
40. Buckman, "Cellphone Game"; Ihlwan & Roberts, "Made in Korea."

41. B. Bremner, Z. Schiller, T. Smart, and W. Holstein, "Keiretsu Connections," *BusinessWeek*, July 22, 1996, p. 2.
42. Hill, *International Business*, p. 412.
43. R. Cohen, "For Coke, World Is Its Oyster," *The New York Times*, November 21, 1991, pp. DI, D5.
44. P. Oster, "Why Japan's Execs Travel Better," *BusinessWeek*, November 1993, p. 68.
45. L. Grant, "That Overseas Job Could Derail Your Career," *Fortune*, April 14, 1997, p. 166.
46. Ibid.
47. G. Koretz, "A Woman's Place Is ...," *BusinessWeek*, September 13, 1999, p. 28; H. Lancaster, "To Get Shipped Abroad, Women Must Overcome Prejudice at Home," *The Wall Street Journal*, July 29, 1989, p. B1; M. L. Wilson, "She Got the Last Laugh When Colleagues Bet She Would Fail in Japan," *The Wall Street Journal*, July 16, 1999, p. B1.
48. S. Shellenberger, "Separation Anxiety: Short Job Transfers Create Problems for Families Left Behind," *The Wall Street Journal*, October 27, 2005, p. D-1.
49. Cited in ibid.
50. G.W. Latta, "High Mobility International Employees," *WorldatWork*, 2005, p. 48; S. Trolman, "Rationalizing Global Incentive Pay Plans Look at the Big Picture," *Workspan*, August 5, 2005, p. 17; R. Rosenzwaig, "How Much Did We Spend This Year?" *Workspan*, July 5, 2005, p. 25; "Expatriate Programs," *Workspan*, July 5, 2005, p. 19; "Premiums and Allowances for Expatriates," *Workspan*, August 5, 2005, p. 13.
51. M. Gunther, "Can Factory Monitoring Ever Really Work?" *Fortune*, Fall 2005, p. 12.
52. M. Gunther, "Cops of the Global Village," *Fortune*, June 27, 2005, p. 158.

Chapter 3

1. M. Jackson, "50% of Workers Commit Unethical Acts, Survey Says," *Boulder Daily Camera*, May 12, 1997, p. 1B: "Business Ethics: Doing Well by Doing Good," *The Economist*, April 22, 2000, pp. 65–67.
2. F. D. Sturdivant and H. Vernon-Wortzel, *Business and Society*, 4th ed. Burr Ridge, IL: Irwin, 1990.
3. P. E. Murphy, "Creating Ethical Corporate Structures," *Sloan Management Review* 30 (Winter 1989), 81–89.
4. Eli Lilly & Company, Guidelines of Company Policy, 1990.
5. General Dynamics, Standards of Business Ethics and Conduct, 1988.
6. JD Edwards & Company, Corporate Ideals and Values, 1993.
7. M. Gundlach, S. Douglas, and M. Martinko, "The Decision to Blow the Whistle: A Social Information Processing Framework," *Academy of Management Review* 28 (2003), 107–123.

8. T. M. Dworkin and J. P. Near, "A Better Statutory Approach to Whistle Blowing," *Business Ethics Quarterly* 7, no. 1 (1997), 1–16.
9. M. Steinberg and S. Kaufman, "Minimizing Corporate Liability Exposure When the Whistle Blows in the Post–Sarbanes-Oxley Era," *Journal of Corporation Law*, August 2005, pp. 445–463.
10. Dworkin and Near, "A Better Statutory Approach to Whistle Blowing."
11. P. Dwyer and D. Carney, "Year of the Whistleblower," *BusinessWeek*, December 16, 2002, pp. 107–110.
12. W. Zellner, "The Whistleblower: A Hero—and a Smoking-Gun Letter," *BusinessWeek*, January 28, 2002, pp. 34–35.
13. M. Sashkin and K. J. Kiser, *Putting Total Quality Management to Work* (San Francisco: Berrett-Koehler, 1993).
14. I. Sager, "Tech's Kickback Culture," *BusinessWeek*, February 10, 2003, pp. 74–77.
15. A. Park, "Family Feuds Don't Get Nastier than This," *BusinessWeek*, February 10, 2003, pp. 62–63.
16. *Global Corruption Report 2003*, www.globalcorruptionreport.org.
17. "Pharmaceuticals: Pushing Pills," *The Economist*, February 15, 2003, p. 61.
18. D. B. Turban and D. W. Greening, "Corporate Social Performance and Organizational Attractiveness to Prospective Employees," *Academy of Management Journal* 40 (1997), 658–672; J. B. McGuire, A. Sundgren and T. Schneeweis, "Corporate Social Responsibility and Firm Financial Performance," *Academy of Management Journal* 27 (1988), 42–56; P. L. Cochran and R. A. Wood, "Corporate Social Responsibility and Financial Performance," *Academy of Management Journal* 31 (1984), 854–872.
19. S. V. Brull, "For All That Tobacco Money, Don't Stint on the Smoking War," *BusinessWeek*, May 10, 1999, p. 40; D. Noonan, "Lighting into Big Tobacco," *Newsweek*, July 24, 2000, pp. 30–31.
20. *The Economist*, "Big Trouble for Merck," November 6, 2004, pp. 61–62; A. Barrett, "Merck: How Much Misery After Vioxx?" *BusinessWeek*, November 22, 2004, pp. 48–50.
21. A. B. Carroll, *Business and Society*, 3rd ed. Cincinnati, OH: SouthWestern Publishing, 1996.
22. J. Greenwald, "Let's Make a Deal," *Time*, March 22, 1989, pp. 84–86.
23. B. McLean, "Why Enron Went Bust," *Fortune*, December 24, 2001, pp. 58–68; and W. Zellner and S. Forest, "The Fall of Enron," *BusinessWeek*, December 17, 2001, pp. 30–36.
24. N. Munk, "How Levi's Trashed a Great American Brand," *Fortune*, April 12, 1999, pp. 82–90.

25. B. Grow, "The Debate over Doing Good," *BusinessWeek*, August 15, 2005, pp. 76–78; L. Gard, "We're Good Guys, Buy from Us," *BusinessWeek*, November 22, 2004, pp. 72–74.
26. "Boeing v. Airbus," *Economist*, July 26, 1997, pp. 59–61.
27. A. B. Carroll, *Business and Society*, 3rd ed. Cincinnati, OH: SouthWestern Publishing, 1996.
28. M. Gunther, "A Pesky Environmental Group Called the Rainforest Action Network Is Getting under the Skin of Corporate America," *Fortune*, May 31, 2004, pp. 158–164.
29. J. H. Jackson, R. L. Miller, and S. G. Miller, *Business and Society Today*. St. Paul, MN: West Publishing, 1997.
30. N. C. Roberts and P. J. King, "The Stakeholder Audit Goes Public," *Organizational Dynamics*, Winter 1989, pp. 63–79.
31. R. Will, "Corporations with a Conscience," *Business and Society Review*, Spring 1995, pp. 17–20.

Chapter 4

1. J. C. Sarros, J. Gray, I. L. Demsten, and B. Cooper, "The Organizational Culture Profile Revisited and Revised: An Australian Perspective," *Australian Journal of Management* 30 (2005), 159–182.
2. L. Larson, "A New Attitude: Changing Organizational Culture," *Trustee* 55 (2002), 8–14.
3. J. P. Daly, R. W. Pouder, and B. Kabanoff, "The Effects of Initial Differences in Firms' Espoused Values on Their Postmerger Performance," *Journal of Applied Behavioral Science* 40 (2004), 323–343.
4. Ibid.
5. B. D. Gifford, R. F. Zammuto, E. A. Goodman, and K. Hill, "The Relationship between Hospital Unit Culture and Nurses' Quality of Work Life," *Journal of Healthcare Management* 47 (2002), 13–21.
6. J. Rossant, "Old World, New Mandate," *BusinessWeek*, January 31, 2000, p. 92.
7. R. L. Cardy, "HRM and the Virtual Workplace: Some Concluding Observations and Future Directions." In R. L. Heneman and D. B. Greenberger, eds., *Human Resource Management in Virtual Organizations* (Greenwich, CT: Information Age Publishing, 2002).
8. S. Robbins, *Organizational Behavior* (Englewood Cliffs, NJ: Prentice Hall, 2001), p. 693.
9. Jeffrey Pfeffer, quoted in J. Hamilton, "The Panic over Hiring," *BusinessWeek*, April 3, 2000, p. 131.
10. P. M. Wright and R. A. Noe, *Management of Organizations* (Burr Ridge, IL: Irwin, 1996), p. 185.
11. A. Nahavandi and A. R. Malekzadeh, *Organizational Behavior: The Person–Organization Fit* (Englewood Cliffs, NJ: Prentice Hall, 1999), p. 95.

12. R. Enderle, personal communication, November, 27, 2002.
13. D. Roznowski, "Johnson Control Employees Help to Reduce Cost, Waste, and Increase Safety Quality through Team Rally Event," *PR Newswire Association*, August 19, 1999.
14. E. Karachanns, J. R. Evaristo, and M. Srite, "Levels of Culture and Individual Behavior: An Integrated Perspective," *Journal of Global Information Management* 13 (2005), 1–20.
15. R. L. Heneman, M. M. Fisher, and K. E. Dixon, "Reward and Organizational Systems Alignment: An Expert System," *Compensation and Benefits Review* 33 (2001), 18–29.
16. C. Hymowitz, "Which Culture Fits You?" *The Wall Street Journal*, July 13, 1989, p. B1.
17. R. E. Quinn and J. Rohrbaugh, "A Spatial Model of Effectiveness Criteria: Toward a Competing Values Approach to Organizational Analysis," *Management Science* 23, (1983), 363–377.
18. Gifford et al. "The Relationship."
19. Cardy, "HRM."
20. P. Mornell, "Nothing Endures but Change," *Inc*, July 2000, pp. 131–132.
21. B. Trebilcock, "The Shadow Knows," *Logistics Management & Distribution Report* 41 (2002), 39.
22. E. E. Lawler, "Managing Change," *Executive Excellence* 19 (2002), 17–18.
23. K. Lewin, *Field Theory in Social Science: Selected Theoretical Papers* (New York: Harper & Brothers, 1951).
24. "Change Management: An Inside Job," *The Economist*, July 15, 2000, p. 61.

Chapter 5

1. D. Stipp, "Why Pfizer Is So Hot," *Fortune*, May 11, 1998, p. 88.
2. J. Muller, J. Green, and C. Tierney, "Chrysler's Rescue Team," *BusinessWeek,* January 15, 2001, pp. 48–50.
3. S. Holmes, "GE Little Engines That Could," *BusinessWeek*, January 20, 2003, pp. 62–64; www.ge.com.
4. L. Grant, "Why Kodak Still Isn't Fixed," *Fortune*, May 11, 1998, pp. 179–181.
5. W. M. Buckeley, "Kodak Swings to $1.03 Billion Loss," *The Wall Street Journal*, December 21, 2005, p. A-1.
6. Ibid.
7. www.gene.com, 2006.
8. www.ge.com, 2006.
9. S. A. Snell, "Control Theory in Strategic Human Resource Management: The Mediating Effect of Administrative Information," *Academy of Management Journal*, 35 (June 1992), 293.
10. C. O. O'Reilly "Corporations, Culture and Commitment: Motivation and Social Control in Organizations "*California Management Review*, Summer 1992.
11. *BusinessWeek*, September 17, 1985. Special feature issue on planning.

12. "The Year of the Dot.Bomb," *Business-Week*, January 15, 2001, p. 10; www.dotcomfailures.com, www.company.com.forrester research, *BusinessWeek*.
13. E. H. Burack, *Creative Human Resource Planning and Applications* (Englewood Cliffs, NJ: Prentice Hall, 1988).
14. D. Welch, "Detroit's Big Steeds Are Losing Traction," *Time*, 2001, pp. 37–40.
15. www.apple.com, 2006.
16. "FedEx, Post Office Combine Deliveries," *The Arizona Republic*, January 12, 2001, p. D1.
17. J. A. Byrne, "How Jack Welch Runs GE," *BusinessWeek*, June 8, 1998 p. 95.
18. A. Barrett, "DuPont Tries to Unclog a Pipeline, "*BusinessWeek*, 2003, January 27, pp. 103–104.
19. www.dupont.com, 2006.
20. "FedEx, Post Office Combine," p. D7; Altavista Co.
21. T. Satterfield, "From Performance Management to Performance Leadership," *Worldatwork* 2003, first quarter, *Journal*, pp. 15–20.
22. "Tenet's Bills to Calpers 50% More than Other Hospitals," *Sacramento BEE*, February 3, 2003.
23. D. W. Jarrell, *Human Resource Planning* (Englewood Cliffs, NJ: Prentice Hall, 1993), p. 73.
24. P. Tsao, "Reports of Cancer's Imminent Death Were an Exaggeration," *BusinessWeek*, June 8, 1998, p. 13.
25. J. Muller, "Thinking out of the Cereal Box," January 15, 2001, pp. 54–55.
26. M. L. Tushman and C. A. O'Reilly III, *Winning through Innovation* (Boston: Harvard Business School Press, 1997).
27. Ibid.
28. Ibid.
29. Ibid.
30. Ibid.

Chapter 6

1. C. M. Pearson and J. A. Clair, "Reframing Organizational Crisis," *Academy of Management Review* 23 (1998), 59–76.
2. E. Leonard, "The Only Lifeline Was the Wal-Mart," *Fortune*, October 3, 2005, pp. 74–80.
3. L. Gerstner, *Who Says Elephants Can't Dance? Leading a Great Enterprise through Dramatic Change* (New York: HarperBusiness, 2002).
4. N. R. Maier, *Psychology in Industrial Organizations*, 4th ed. (Boston: Houghton Mifflin, 1973).
5. A. A. Thompson and A. J. Strickland, (1998). *Strategic Management: Concepts and Cases*, 10th ed. New York: Irwin/McGraw-Hill.
6. S. P. Robbins and M. Coulter, *Management*, 5th ed. (Upper Saddle River, NJ: Prentice Hall, 1996), pp. 196–197.
7. M. Gladwell, *Blink: The Power of Thinking without Thinking*, (New York: Little, Brown and Company, 2005).

8. J. Hammond, R. Keeney, and H. Raiffa, "The Hidden Traps of Decision Making," *Harvard Business Review*, January, 2006, pp. 118–126
9. Ibid.
10. H. A. Simon, *Models of Man* (New York: Wiley, 1957).
11. M. Bazerman and D. Chugh, "Decisions without Blinders, *Harvard Business Review*, January 2006, pp. 88–97.
12. M. D. Cohen, J. G. March, and J. P. Olsen, "The Garbage Can Model of Organizational Choice," *Administrative Science Quarterly* 17 (1972), 1–25.
13. R. H. Hall, *Organizations* (Upper Saddle River, NJ: Prentice Hall, 1999).
14. A. Rowe and R. Mason, *Managing with Style: A Guide to Understanding, Assessing, and Improving Your Decision Making* (San Francisco: Jossey-Bass, 1987).
15. A. L. Delbecq, A. H. Van de Ven, and D.H. Gustafson, *Group Techniques for Program Planning* (Glenview, IL: Scott, Foresman, 1975).
16. M. Mankins, "Stop Wasting Valuable Time," *Harvard Business Review*, September 2004, pp. 58–65.
17. R. E. Quinn, S. R. Faerman, M. P. Thompson, and M. R. McGrath, *Becoming a Master Manager*, 3rd ed. (New York: John Wiley & Sons, 2003).

Chapter 7

1. J. McCraken, "Ford Focuses on Market-Share Slide," *The Wall Street Journal*, February 17, 2006, p. A-1; K. Lundegaard, "Ford, GM Make Big Push to Promote 'Flex-Fuel' Vehicles," *The Wall Street Journal*, January 10, 2006, p. B1; J. B. White and J. McCracken, "Troubled Legacy: Auto Industry, at a Crossroads, Finds Itself Stalled by History," *The Wall Street Journal*, January 7, 2006, p. B1; S. Silke, "Most Automakers See Their Sales Fall in December," *USA Today*, January 5, 2006, p. B1; M. Maynard, "Is There a Future in Ford's Future?" *New York Times*, January 8, 2006, p. 3; A. Taylor III, "Ford: The Hamlet of Dearborn," *Fortune*, October 17, 2005, p. 36; G. Chon, "GM and Ford Lose More Market Share," *The Wall Street Journal*, January 5, 2006, p. A13.
2. www.americanexpress.com.
3. G. Zuckerman, I. McDonald, and L. Hawkins, "If GM's Big Yield Vanishes, Investors May Do the Same, *The Wall Street Journal*, January 12, 2006, p. C1; M. Maynard, "Toyota Shows Big Three How It Is Done," *New York Times*, January 3, 2006, p. C1.
4. I. McDonald, and J. Adamy, "Whole Foods Fare's Pricey" *The Wall Street Journal*, January 3, 2006, p. C1.
5. *San Jose Mercury News*, "Gates Too Busy to Define Government." Story appearing in *Arizona Republic*, May 2, 1998, p. E1.
6. www.colgate.com, 2006.

7. R. L. Martin, "What Innovation Advantage?" *BusinessWeek*, January 16, 2006, p. 102.

8. A. Serwer, "Bruised in Bentonville," *Fortune*, April 18, 2005, p. 84; R. Berner, "Watch Out, Best Buy and Circuit City," *BusinessWeek*, November 21, 2005, p. 46; T. P. Coates, "Wal-Mart's Urban Room," *Time*, September 5, 2005, p. 44.

9. J. Useem, "One Nation under Wal-Mart," *Fortune*, March 3, 2003, p. 65.

10. S. Lohr, "Just Googling It Is Striking Fear into Companies," *New York Times*, November 6, 2005.

11. Wonacott, 2006.

12. Lundsford and Michaels, 2006).

13. Pasztor and Christie, 2006).

14. B. Einhorn, "Listen: The Sound of Hope," *BusinessWeek*, November 14, 2005, p. 68.

15. K. Durham, and R.A. Smith, "Behind Zooming Condo Prices," *The Wall Street Journal*, August 18, 2005, p. A-1.

16. M. Barboso, "State Mandate for Wal-Mart on Health Care." *New York Times*, January 13, 2006, p. A-1.

17. D. Carney, "Uncle Sam's Trustbusters: Outgunned and Outmoded." *BusinessWeek*, November 18, 2002, pp. 44–45.

18. B. Acohido, and E.C. Baig, "Gates Shares Spotlight with New Windows," *USA Today*, January 5, 2006, p. B-1.

19. Ibid.; R.A. Guth, "Microsoft, Palm Unite to Fight Blackberry," *The Wall Street Journal*, November 18, 2005, p. B1.; R.A. Guth, "Getting Xbox to Market," *The Wall Street Journal*, September 27, 2005, November 18, 2005 p. B1; D. Barboza and T. Zeller Jr., "Microsoft Shuts Blog's Site after Complaints by Beijing," *New York Times*, January 6, 2006, p. C3.

20. "The Big Picture," *BusinessWeek*, December 5, 2005, p. 16.

21. D. Grant, and A. Latour, "Changing Channels," *The Wall Street Journal*, November 21, 2005, p. A-1.

22. S. Hamm, J. Greene, and A. Reinhardt, "What Is a Rival to Do Now?" *BusinessWeek*, November 18, 2002, pp. 44–46.

23. R. Farzad, and B. Elgin, "Googling," *BusinessWeek*, December 5, 2005, p. 61.

24. P. Dvorak, and E. Ramstad, "TV Marriage: Behind Sony-Samsung Rivalry, an Unlikely Alliance Develops," *The Wall Street Journal*, January 3, 2006, p. A-1.

25. M. E. Porter, *Competitive Advantage* (New York: Free Press, 1990).

26. W. Echikson, "Designers Climb onto the Virtual Catwalk," *BusinessWeek*, October 11, 1999, pp. 164–166.

27. W. M. Bulkeley, "Kodak Swings to $1.03 Billion Loss," *The Wall Street Journal*, December 21, 2005, p. A1.; W.C. Symonds, and D. Burrows, "A Digital Warrior for Kodak," *BusinessWeek*, May 23, 2005, p. 42.

28. K. Barnes, "Alburn Sales Slump as Downloads Rise," *USA Today*, January 5, 2006, p. D-1.

29. M. Adams, "Independence CEO Says He Doesn't Regret Gamble," *USA Today*, January 5, 2006, p. B-5.

30. R. A. D'Aveni, "Coping with Hypercompetition: Utilizing the New 75's Framework," *Academy of Management Executive* 9, no. 3 (1995): 54.

31. M. S. Hunt, *Competition in the Major Home Appliance Industry* (Cambridge, MA: Harvard University Press, 1972).

32. M. A. Hitt, R. D. Ireland, and R. E. Hoskisson, *Strategic Management* (New York: Irwin/McGraw-Hill, 2001).

33. R. M. Grant, *Contemporary Strategy Analysis* (Malden, MA: Blackwell, 1998), p. 129.

34. U. Kher, "The Workhorse of Genomic Medicine," *Time*, January 15, 2001, p. 62.

35. www.canon.com, 2006.

36. J. White, and S. Power, "VW's Bernhard Says Labor Costs Dent Profit," *The Wall Street Journal*, January 9, 2006, p. A10.

37. Michael Hitt, R. Duane Ireland, and Robert E. Hoskisson, *Strategic Management: Competitiveness and Globalization* (Cincinnati, OH: South-Western Publishing, 1999), p. 26.

38. N. Stein, "America's Most Admired Companies," *Fortune*, March 3, 2003, pp. 81–98.

39. I. M. Kunii, "Making Canon Click" *BusinessWeek*, September 16, 2002, pp. 40–42.

40. R. M. Grant, *Contemporary Strategic Analysis* (Malden, MA: Blackwell, 2001).

41. M. Heinzl, "A New Crop of Gadgets Challenge the BlackBerry," *The Wall Street Journal*, November 2, 2005, p. D-1.

42. K. Hughes and C. Oughton, "Diversification, Multimarket Contact, and Profitability," *Economics* 60 (1993): 203–224; C. W. L. Hill, "Diversification and Economic Performance: Bringing Structure and Corporate Management Back into the Picture," in R. P. Rumelt et al. (Eds.), *Fundamental Issues in Strategy* (Boston: Harvard Business School Press, 1994), pp. 297–321.

43. "Upfront," *BusinessWeek*, August 6, 2001, p. 7.

44. S. Carey, "As Airlines Pull Out of Dive, Limited Charts Its Own Course," *The Wall Street Journal*, January 13, 2006, p. A-1.

45. K. Richardson, "Blockbuster's Backbreaker: No-Late-Fee Policy," *The Wall Street Journal*, January 5, 2006, p B1.

46. Hitt, Ireland, and Hoskisson, *Strategic Management: Competitiveness and Globalization*, p. 383.

47. D. Gullapalli, "Living with Sarbanes-Oxley," *The Wall Street Journal*, October 17, 2005, p. R1; A. Borrus, "Learning to Love Sarbanes-Oxley," *BusinessWeek*, November 21, 2005, p. 126; R. Sorkin, "To Battle, Armed with Shares, Big Holders Wield Their Shares to Push for Corporate Change," *New York Times*, January 6, 2006, p. C1; M. Jacoby, "The Global Agenda," *The Wall Street Journal*, October 17, 2005, p. R7; J. Burns, "Board Members Find Independence," *The Wall Street Journal*, January 12, 2006, p. C11; J. Weber, S. Holmes, and C. Palmeri, "Older Workers May Have a Hard Time Giving Up Private Offices," *BusinessWeek*, November 7, 2005, p. 100.

48. Hitt, Ireland, and Hoskisson, *Strategic Management*, p. 347.

49. Ibid., p. 28.

50. R. Berstein, R. "Men Chafe as Norway Ushers Women into Boardroom," *New York Times*, January 12, 2006, p. A-3.

Chapter 8

1. R. A. Cherwitz, and C. A. Sullivan, "Intellectual Entrepreneurship: A Vision for Graduate Education," *Change, 34* (2002): 23–28.

2. National Commission on Entrepreneurship, "Five Myths about Entrepreneurs: Understanding How Businesses Start and Grow," www.ncoe.org, accessed February 19, 2003.

3. Ibid.

4. http://www.census.gov/scd/sbol.

5. http://www.sba.gov/advo/stats/sbfag.html.

6. Ibid.

7. K.E. Klein, "Minority Startups: A Measure of Progress," *BusinessWeek Online*, August 25, 2005.

8. J. Hopkins, "Start-Up Succeeding Study Says," *The Arizona Republic*, February 24, 2003, p. D1.

9. C. Barrett, "Good Times and Bad: Innovation Is Key," *Information Week*, January 27, 2003, p. 20.

10. J. Eckberg, "Innovation Spells Success," *Cincinnati Enquirer*, October 14, 2002, p. B6.

11. B. Nadel, "Unraveling the Mysteries of Innovation," *Fortune, 152* (2000): 554–556.

12. D. Patnaik, "The True Measure of a Good Idea," *BusinessWeek Online*, December 21, 2005.

13. Ibid.

14. B. Nussbaum, R. Berner, and D. Brady, (2005). "Get Creative! How to Build Innovative Companies," *BusinessWeek Online*, August 1, 2005.

15. Ibid.

16. Ibid.

17. Ibid.

18. J. Pellet, "Leading Creative Charge" *Chief Executive, 1* (2002) 6–11.

19. D. Kirkpatrick, "Throw It at the Wall and See if It Sticks," *Fortune, 152* (2005): 142.

20. Pellet, "Leading Creative Charge."

21. J. Batelle, "The 70 Percent Solution," *Business* 2.0, *6* (2005): 134.

Chapter 9

1. D. Robey and C.A. Sayles, *Designing Organizations* (Burr Ridge, IL: Irwin, 1994).

2. Ibid.

3. Ibid.

4. R.C. Ford and W.A. Randolph, "Cross-Functional Structures: A Review and Integration of Matrix Organization and Project Management," *Journal of Management* 18 (1992): 267–294.

5. R.L. Daft, *Management,* 4th ed. (Fort Worth: Dryden Press, 1997).

6. K.A. Frank and K. Fahrback, "Organization Culture as a Complex System: Balance and Information Models of Influence and Selection," *Organization Science* 10 (1999): 253–277.

7. S. Brown and K. Blackmon, "Aligning Manufacturing Strategy and Business-Level Competitive Strategy in New Competitive Environments: The Case for Strategic Resonance," *Journal of Management Studies* 42 (2005): 793–815; J. Woodward, *Industrial Organizations: Theory and Practice* (London: Oxford University Press, 1965).

8. S. Das, "Designing Service Processes: A Design Factor Based Process Model," *International Journal of Services Technology and Management* 7(1) (2006): 85.

9. B. Evans, "Google Becomes an Irresistible Force," *InformationWeek,* December 19–26, 2005, p. 76; S. Smith, "A Date with Digital," *Mediaweek,* September 12, 2005, pp. 38–39.

10. M.S. Kraatz and E.J. Zaja, "How Organizational Resources Affect Strategic Change and Performance in Turbulent Environments: Theory and Evidence," *Organization Science* 12 (2001): 632–657.

11. G.R. Jones, *Organizational Theory,* 2nd ed. (Reading, MA: Addision-Wesley, 1998).

12. *The Economist,* "How to Manage a Dream Factory," January 18, 2003, pp. 73–75.

13. S. Lacy, "The Hardest Job in Silicon Valley," *BusinessWeek,* January 23, 2006, pp. 65–66.

Chapter 10

1. "USA Today Snapshots," *USA Today,* January 17, 2001, p. 1A.

2. D. Gonzalez, "World's Cultures Converge in State," *The Arizona Republic,* January 8, 2001, p. A1.

3. Rebecca Walker, *Black, White and Jewish: Autobiography of a Shifting Self* (New York: Riverhead Books, 2001).

4. T. Kenworthy, "Air Force Academy Hit by Drug Scandal," *USA Today,* January 16, 2001, p. 3A.

5. "Companies Try Creative Cutbacks: Managers Hope to Avoid Drastic Step of Layoffs." *USA Today,* January 8, 2001, p. D1.

6. www.latestandgreatest5@hrpomotions.com.

7. J.P. Wanous, *Organizational Entry,* 2nd ed. (Reading, MA: Addison-Wesley, 1992).

8. S. Armour. "Degrees in e-Commerce Seem Less Dazzling," *The Wall Street Journal,* January 16, 2001, p. B1.

9. F. Golden, "Probing the Chemistry of the Brain," *Time,* January 15, 2001, p. 55.

10. "The 100 Best Companies to Work For," *Fortune,* January 23, 2006, pp. 89–108.

11. L. M. Gomez-Mejia, D. B. Balkin, and R. Cardy, *Managing Human Resources* (Englewood Cliffs, NJ: Prentice Hall, 2007).

12. "Boeing Engineers to Get Bonuses," *USA Today,* January 8, 2001, p. A3.

13. G. L. White, "Ford Admits Last Year's Quality Snafus," *The Wall Street Journal,* January 12, 2001, p. A3.

14. T. Larimer, "Rebirth of the Z," *Time,* January 15, 2001, pp. 42–44.

Chapter 11

1. L. R. Gomez-Mejia, D. B. Balkin, and R. Cardy, *Managing Human Resources* (Englewood Cliffs, NJ: Prentice Hall, 2001).

2. C. Crossen, "How U.S. Immigration Evolved as the Nation Grew and Changed," *The Wall Street Journal,* January 9, 2006, p. B-3; S. Roberts, "Come October, Body Count Will Make 300 Million or So," *New York Times,* January 13, 2006, p. A.1.

3. M. L. Wheeler, "Capitalizing on Diversity," *BusinessWeek,* December 14, 1998, special advertising section.

4. Ibid.

5. G. Colvin, "50 Best Companies for Asians, Blacks, and Hispanics," *Fortune,* July 19, 1999, pp. 52–59.

6. R. O. Crockett, "African-Americans Get the Investing Bug," *BusinessWeek,* May 24, 1999, p. 39.

7. C. Prystay, and S. Ellison, "Time for Marketers to Grow Up?" *The Wall Street Journal,* February 27, 2003 p. B-1.

8. D. Jones, "U.S. Managers Earn Global Credentials," *USA Today,* February 26, 1997, p. A1.

9. M. L. Wheeler, "Diversity: Making the Business Case," *BusinessWeek,* December 9, 1996, special advertising section.

10. Ibid.

11. V. I. Sessa, S. E. Jackson, and D. T. Rapini, "Workforce Diversity: The Good, and Bad, and the Reality." In G. Ferris, S. D. Rosen, and D. T. Barnum (Eds.), *Handbook of Human Resource Management* (Cambridge, MA: Blackwell, 1995), pp. 263–282.

12. Wheeler, "Diversity."

13. T. H. Cox, and S. Blake, "Managing Cultural Diversity: Implications for Organizational Competitiveness," *Academy of Management Executive* 5, no. 3 (1991): 45–46.

14. M. C. Fine, P. L. Johnson, and S. M. Ryan, "Cultural Diversity in the Workplace," *Public Personnel Management* 19, no. 3 (1990): 305–319.

15. Wheeler, "Diversity."

16. G. S. Van Der Vegt, E. V. Ulert, and X. Huang, "Location Level Links between Diversity and Innovative Climate Depend on National Power Distance," *Academy of Management Journal,* 48(6), (2005): 1171–1182.

17. Fine, Johnson, and Ryan, "Cultural Diversity in the Workplace."

18. www.businessweek.com, 2006.

19. R. O. Crockett, "The Changing Landscape," *BusinessWeek,* January 27, 2003, p. 96.

20. H. Fineman, and T. Lipper, "Spinning Race," *Newsweek,* January 23, 2003, pp. 27–38.

21. C. Hastings, "Engaging in a Growing Workforce." *Workspan,* April 2003, pp. 35–39.

22. T. S. Bateman and S. A. Snell, *Management: Building Competitive Advantage,* 4th ed. (Burr Ridge, IL: Irwin, 1999), p. 320.

23. L. R. Gomez-Mejia, D. B. Balkin, and R. Cardy, *Managing Human Resources.* (Englewood Cliffs, NJ: Prentice Hall, 2004).

24. H. Green, "Chocolate Mess," *BusinessWeek,* January 16, 2006, p. 14; M. Jordan, "Blacks vs. Latinos at Work," *The Wall Street Journal,* January 24, 2006, p. B-1.

25. "Research National Phone Poll," *Chattanooga Times,* March 4, 1994, p. 1.

26. Jordan, "Blacks vs. Latinos."

27. "Research National Phone Poll"; Stephanie Mehta, "What Minority Employees Really Want," *Fortune,* July 10, 2000, p. 180.

28. J. Chu, and N. Mustafa, "Between Two Worlds," *Time,* January 16, 2006, p. 67.

29. Ibid.

30. Briefs, *Workforce Strategies,* 4(2) (February 22, 1993): WS-12.

31. Y. Armendariz, "Disabled Workers Can Telecommute," *Arizona Republic,* February 10, 2003, p. D-3.

32. S. Shellenbarger, "You Can Work from Home—Can You Coach Little League from the Office?" *The Wall Street Journal,* October 20, 2005, p. D-1.

33. R. Alonso-Zaldivar, "Immigrants at 7 million, Revised INS Report Says," *Arizona Republic,* February, 2003 p. A-5.

34. L. Koss-Feder, "Spurred by the Americans with Disabilities Act," p. 82.

35. J. Kanman, and H. Rozenberg, "Survey Looks at Residents with Recent Foreign Roots," *Arizona Republic,* February 7, 2002, p. A-8.

36. R. Doyle, "Assembling the future," *Scientific American,* February 2000, p. 30.

37. L. R. Gomez-Mejia, D. B. Balkin, and R. Cardy, *Managing Human Resources.* (New York: Prentice Hall, 2007); Crossen, "How U.S. Immigration Evolved."

38. Gomez-Mejia, Balkin, and Cardy, *Managing Human Resources.*

39. Overberg, El Nasser, 2005.

40. R. Mendosa, "The $152 Billion Engine," *Hispanic Business,* October 1996, pp. 28–29; R. Mendosa, "A Downward Count," *Hispanic Business,* October 1996, p. 18.

41. Gomez-Mejia, Balkin, and Cardy, *Managing Human Resources.*

42. E. Banach, "Today's Supply of Entry Level Workers Reflect Diversity," *Savings Institution,* September 1990, p. 74.

43. D. S. Fellows, "Striking Gold in a Silver Mine: Leveraging Senior Workers as Knowledge Champions," *Worldatwork Journal, 10*(4), (2001): 1–12.

44. C. J. Levy, "The New Corporate Outsourcing," *New York Times*, January 29, 2006, p. D-1; R. Bernstein, "The Undoing of a Done Deal," *BusinessWeek*, February 13, 2006, p. 54; K. Greene, "Bye-Bye Boomers?" *The Wall Street Journal*, September 20, 2005, p. B-1; M. W. Walsh, "When Your Pension Is Frozen," *New York Times*, January 22, 2006, p. A-1; J. Helyar, "50 and Fired," *Fortune*, May 10, 2006, p. 78–86; "Aging Workforce Presents New Opportunities, Challenges for Employers," *Workspan*, November 2, 2005, p. 16; P. Coy, "Surprise! The Graying of the Workforce Is Better News than You Think," *BusinessWeek*, June 27, 2005, p. 78; R. Pear, "Bush to Propose Vast Cost Savings in Medicare Plan," *New York Times*, February 4, 2006, p. B-1.

45. "Talking to Diversity Experts," 2003, www.fortune.com/sections.

46. Ameer, 2006.; Anna, 2006.

47. D. Bilefsky, "Denmark Is Unlikely Front in Islam-West Culture War," *New York Times*, January 8, 2006, p. 3; A. Cowell, "More European Papers Print Cartoons of Muhammad, Fueling Dispute among Muslims." *New York Times*, February 2, 2006, p. A-3; A. Cowell, "Cartoons Force Danish Muslims to Examine Loyalties," *New York Times*, February 4, 2006, p. B-1; M. Champion, "Muslim Outrage Mounts Over Cartoons in EU," *The Wall Street Journal*, February 3, 2006, p. B-2; A. Aji, "Syrians Burn Embassies over Cartoons," *Arizona Republic*, February 5, 2006, p. A-11; S. Nassauer, "France's New Race Relations," *The Wall Street Journal*, January 9, 2006, p. A-11.

48. P. Magnusson, "Wipsaved on the Border," *BusinessWeek*, October 10, 2005, pp. 64–66; B. Grow, "Tapping a Market That Is Hot, Hot, Hot," *BusinessWeek* January 17, 2005, p. 36; B. Grow, "Embracing Illegals," *BusinessWeek*, July 18, 2005, p. 55; J. Millman, "Changing Face of Immigrants," *The Wall Street Journal*, January 24, 2005, p. A-4; J. C. McKinley, "Mexican Pride and Death in U.S. Service," *New York Times*, March 22, 2005, p. A-6; J. C. McKinley, "At Mexican Border, Tunnels, Vile River, Rusty Fence," *New York Times*, March 23, 2005, p. A-8; C. Leduff and E. Flores, "The Everymigrant's Guide to Crossing the Border Illegally," *New York Times*, February 9, 2005, p. A-16; N. Thornburgh, "Inside the Lives of the Migrants Next Door," *BusinessWeek*, February 6, 2006, pp. 36–46; L. Valdez, "Migration a 2-Nation Concern," *Arizona Republic*, February 5, 2006, p. D-1.

49. D. A. Fahrenthold, "Cap on Migrant Workers Hurting Seafood Processors," *Arizona Republic*, January 16, 2005, p. A-16.

50. L. Greenhouse, "Broad Survey of Day Laborers Finds High Level of Injuries and Pay Violations," *New York Times*, January 22, 2006, p. A-17.

51. B. Kiviat, "Dessi Dollars. Inside Business Issue," *The Wall Street Journal*, August 2005, pp. A21–A23; R. L. Swarns, "Chamber and Two Unions Forge Alliance on Immigration Bill," *The Wall Street Journal*, January 19, 2006, p. A-15; Valdez, "Migration a 2-Nation Concern."

52. T. Egan, "Wanted: Border Hoppers," *Arizona Republic*, April 1, 2005, p. A-12.

53. J. Welch, and S. Welch, "What Is Holding Women Back," *BusinessWeek*, February 13, 2006, p. 100.

54. Wheeler, "Diversity."

55. Ibid.

56. Ibid.

57. Ibid.

58. Gomez-Mejia, Balkin, and Cardy, *Managing Human Resources.*

59. Wheeler, "Diversity."

60. A. Ashton, "Around-the-Clock Child Care," *Working Women*, February 2002, p. 14.

61. A. M. Newman, "Fair shares," *Working Women*, February 2002, pp. 64–71.

Chapter 12

1. D. S. Randolph, "Predicting the Effect of Extrinsic and Intrinsic Job Satisfaction Factors on Recruitment and Retention of Rehabilitation Professionals," *Journal of Healthcare Management, 50* (2005): 49.

2. A. H. Maslow, "A Theory of Human Motivation," *Psychological Review*, July 1943, pp. 370–396.

3. C. Alderfer, *Existence, Relatedness, and Growth: Human Needs in Organizational Settings* (Glencoe, IL: Free Press, 1972).

4. D. McClelland, *The Achieving Society* (New York: Van Nostrand Reinhold, 1961).

5. R. E. Boyatzis, "The Need for Close Relationships and the Manager's Job," in D. A. Kolls, I. M. Rubin, and J. M. McIntyre (eds.), *Organizational Psychology: Readings on Human Behavior in Organizations*, 4th ed. (Englewood Cliffs, NJ: Prentice Hall, 1984).

6. D. C. McClelland and R. Boyatzis, "Leadership Motive Pattern and Long-Term Success in Management," *Journal of Applied Psychology 67* (1982): 737–743.

7. N. Adler, *International Dimensions of Organizational Behavior*, 3rd ed. (Cincinnati, OH: South-Western Publishing, 1997); G. Hofstede, *Culture's Consequences: International Differences in Work Related Values* (Beverly Hills, CA: Sage, 1980).

8. F. Herzberg, "One More Time: How Do You Motivate Employees?" *Harvard Business Review, 81* (2003): 87–96.

9. P. C. Early, T. Connolly, and G. Ekegren, "Goals, Strategy Development, and Task Performance: Some Limits on the Efficacy of Goal Setting," *Journal of Applied Psychology 74* (1989): 24–33; C. E. Shalley, "Effects of Productivity Goals, Creativity Goals, and Personal Discretion on Individual Creativity," *Journal of Applied Psychology 76* (1991): 179–185. Most of these studies are based on the pioneering work of E. Locke, "Toward a Theory of Task Motivation and Incentives," *Organizational Behavior and Human Performance 3* (1968): 157–189. For practitioner perspective, see J. W. Marcum, "Out with Motivation, in with Engagement," *National Productivity Review 19*, no. 4 (Autumn 2000): 57–60.

10. J. S. Adams, "Inequity in Social Exchanges," in L. Berkowitz (ed.), *Advances in Experimental Social Psychology* (New York: Academic Press, 1965), pp. 267–300; S. Ronen, "Equity Perception in Multiple Comparisons: A Field Study," *Human Relations*, April, 1986, pp. 333–346; T. P. Summers and A. S. DeNisi, "In Search of Adam's Other: Reexamination of Referents Used in the Evaluation of Pay," *Human Relations*, June 1990, pp. 495–511.

11. P. M. Buhler, "Managing in the New Millennium." *SuperVision, 64* (2003): 20–22.

12. E. L. Thorndike, *The Fundamentals of Learning* (New York: AMS Press, 1971).

13. V. H. Vroom, *Work and Motivation* (New York: John Wiley & Sons, 1964); H. J. Arnold, "A Test of the Multiplicative Hypothesis of Expectancy-Valence Theories of Work Motivation," *Academy of Management Journal*, April 1981, pp. 128–141.

14. R. Grossman, "Putting in Rotation: Experts Say Job Rotation Programs Are Best Way to Gain a Broad View of the Business, Yet HR Often Leaves Itself Out of the Loop," *HRMagazine, 48* (2003): 501.

15. D. Abbott, "Stress and Strain," *The Safety & Health Practitioner, 21* (2003): 341.

16. T. Pollack, "Three Ways to Motivate People," *Automotive Design & Production, 114* (2002): 10.

17. J. R. Hackman, G. Oldham, R. Janson, and K. Purdy, "A New Strategy for Job Enrichment," *California Management Review 16* (1975): 57–71.

18. M. Memmotl, "Reich Knows High Cost of 'Success': He Paid It," *USA Today*, January 8, 2001, p. A1.

Chapter 13

1. J. R. Healey, "Chrysler Again Runs Low on Financial Fuel," *USA Today*, January 30, 2001, p. 1B; D. Goodman, "Can Chrysler Survive?" *Arizona Republic*, January 30, 2001, p. D1.

2. J. E. Garten, "The Mind of the CEO," *BusinessWeek*, February 5, 2001, p. 107.

3. S. P. Robbins, *Organizational Behavior*, 7th ed. (Englewood Cliffs, NJ: Prentice Hall, 1999), p. 413.

4. W. Adamchick, "Elliot Institute Must Distinguish Leadership from Management," *Nation's Restaurant News*, 37, (2003): p. 36

5. J. French and B. Raven, "The Bases of Social Power," in D. Cartwright (ed.), *Studies in Social Power* (Ann Arbor, MI: Institute for Social Research, 1959).

6. R. G. Lord, C. C. DeVader, and G. M. Alleger, "A Meta-analysis of the Relation between Personality Traits and Leadership Perceptions," *Journal of Applied Psychology* 71, no. 3 (1986): 402–410; D. A. Kenny and S. J. Zaccaro, "An Estimate of the Variance due to Traits in Leadership," *Journal of Applied Psychology* 68, no. 4 (1983): 678–685; D. A. Kenny and B. W. Hallmark, "Rotation Designs in Leadership Research," *Leadership Quarterly* 3, no. 1 (1992): 25–41; J. L. Denis, "Becoming a Leader in a Complex Organization," *Journal of Management Studies* 37, no. 8 (2000): 1063–1099; B. O'Reilly, "What It Takes to Start a Startup," *Fortune*, June 7, 1999, pp. 135–139; "The Top 25 Managers of the Year," *BusinessWeek*, January 8, 2001, pp. 60–79.

7. J. M. Kouzes, & B. Z. Posner, "The Credibility Factor: What Followers Expect from Their Readers," *Business Credit*, July–August, 1990, p. 92.

8. S. Kerr, C. A. Schriesheim, C. J. Murphy, and R. M. Stogdill, "Toward a Contingency Theory of Leadership Based upon the Consideration and Initiating Structure Literature," *Organizational Behavior and Human Performance*, August 1974, pp. 62–82; and R. Kahn and D. Katz, "Leadership Practices in Relation to Productivity and Morale," in D. Cartwright and A. Sander (eds.), *Group Dynamics: Research and Theory* (Elmsford, NY: Row, Peterson, 1960).

9. R. R. Blake and J. S. Mouton, *The Managerial Grid* (Houston: Gulf, 1964).

10. R. White and R. Lippit, *Autocracy and Democracy: An Experimental Inquiry* (New York: Harper & Brothers, 1960).

11. Robbins, *Organizational Behavior*, p. 419.

12. F. E. Fiedler, *A Theory of Leadership Effectiveness* (New York: McGraw-Hill, 1967): F. E. Fiedler, "Validation and Extension of the Contingency Model of Leadership Effectiveness," *Psychological Bulletin* 76 (1971): 128–148.

13. L. H. Peter, D. D. Hartke, and J. T. Pohlmann, "Fiedler's Contingency Theory of Leadership: An Application of the Meta-analysis Procedures of Schmidt and Hunter," *Psychological Bulletin*, March 1985, pp. 274–285; and C. A. Schriesheim, B. J. Tepper, and L. A. Tetrault, "Least Preferred Co-worker Score Situational Control, and Leadership Effectiveness: A Meta-analysis of Contingency Model Performance Predictions," *Journal of Applied Psychology*, August 1994, pp. 562–573.

14. R. J. House, "A Path Goal Theory of Leader Effectiveness," *Administrative Science Quarterly* 16 (1971): 321–338; R. J. House and T. R. Michell, "Path Goal Theory of Leadership," *Journal of Contemporary Business* 3 (1974): 81–97; R. House, "Weber and the Neo-charismatic Paradigm," *Leadership Quarterly* 10, no. 4 (2000): 15–26; R. House, P. J. Hanges, A. Quintanilla, P. W. Dorfman, M. W. Dickson, M. Javidan, et al., *Advances in Global Leadership* (Greenwich, CT: JAI Press, 1999), pp. 100–185.

15. "The Top 25 Managers," *BusinessWeek*, January 8, 2001, pp. 60–80.

16. "Pioneer Hewlett Dies at 87," *Arizona Republic*, January 13, 2001.

17. J. R. Meindl and S. B. Ehrlick, "The Romance of Leadership and the Evaluation of Organizational Performance," *Academy of Management Journal* 30 (1987): 91–109.

18. T. Bateman and S. Snell, *Management: Building Competitive Advantage*, 4th ed. (New York: Irwin/McGraw-Hill, 2000).

19. B. M. Bass and B. J. Avolio, "Developing Transformational Leadership: 1992 and Beyond," *Journal of European Industrial Training*, January 1990, p. 23; B. Bass, B. Avolio, and L. Goodheim, "Biography in the Assessment of Transformational Leadership at the World Class Level," *Journal of Management* 13 (1987): 7–20.

20. J. R. McColl-Kennedy and R. D. Anderson, "Impact of Leadership Style and Emotions on Subordinate Performance," *Leadership Quarterly* 13 (2002): 545–559.

21. F. Luthans and B. Avolio, "Authentic Leadership: A Positive Developmental Approach." In K. S. Cameron, J. E. Dutton, and R. E. Quinn (Eds.), *Positive Organizational Scholarship* (San Francisco: Berett-Koehler, 2003).

Chapter 14

1. R. L. Daft, *The Leadership Experience*, 2nd ed. (Cincinnati, OH: South-Western, 2002), p. 367.

2. W. E. Deming, *Out of the Crisis* (Cambridge, MA: MIT Press, 1986).

3. M. Sashkin and K. J. Kiser, *Putting Total Quality Management to Work* (San Francisco: Barrett-Koehler Publishers, 1993).

4. J. Bunderson and K. Sutcliffe, "Comparing Alternative Conceptualizations of Functional Diversity in Management Teams: Process and Performance Effects," *Academy of Management Journal* 45 (2002): 875–893, K. Bantel and S. Jackson, "Top Management and Innovations in Banking: Does the Demography of the Top Team Make a Difference?" *Strategic Management Journal* 10 (1989): 107–124.

5. G. Hertel, S. Geister, and U. Konradt, "Managing Virtual Teams: A Review of Current Empirical Research," *Human Resource Management Review* 15 (2005): 69–95.

6. C. J. Gersick, "Time and Transition in Work Teams: Toward a New Model of Group Development," *Academy of Management Journal* 31 (1988): 9–41.

7. A. Chang, P. Bordia, and J. Duck, "Punctuated Equilibrium and Linear Progression: Toward a New Understanding of Group Development," *Academy of Management Journal* 46 (2003): 106–117.

8. B. Nelson, *1001 Ways to Reward Employees* (New York: Workman Publishing, 1994).

9. W. H. Weiss. "Teams and Teamwork," *Supervision* 59, no. 7 (1999): 9–11.

10. J. R. Katzenbach and D. K. Smith, "The Discipline of Teams," *Harvard Business Review*, March–April 1993, pp. 111–120.

11. Daft, *The Leadership Experience*, p. 368.

12. L. Thompson, *Making the Team: A Guide for Managers*, 2nd ed. (Upper Saddle River, NJ: Pearson, 2004); E. Fan and D. Grueneld, "When Needs Outweight Desires: The Effects of Resource Interdependence and Reward Interdependence on Group Problem Solving," *Basic and Applied Social Psychology* 20 (1998): 45–56.

13. I. Berkow, "A Superstar, Iverson, Isn't a Role Model," *The New York Times*, February 2, 2001, p. C15; R. Zoglin, "Carsey and Werner, Last of the Mom-and-Pop Producers, Have a Hot Hand This Fall," *Time*, September 23, 1996.

14. T. Raz, "Taming the Savage Genius: The Delicate Art of Managing Employees Who Are Way, Way Smarter than You," *Inc.*, May 2003, pp. 33–35.

15. B. Fisher and A. Boynton, "Virtuoso Teams," *Harvard Business Review*, July–August 2005, pp. 117–123.

16. D. B. Balkin, S. Dolan, and K. Forgues, "Rewards for Team Contribution to Quality," *Journal of Compensation and Benefits* 13, no. 1 (1997): 41–46.

17. J. Varela, P. Fernandez, and M. Del Rio, "Cross-Functional Conflict, Conflict Handling Behaviors and new Product Performance in Spanish Firms," *Creativity and Innovation Management* 14 (December 2005): 355; Thompson, *Making the Team: A Guide for Managers*.

18. C. Osborne, *Dealing with Difficult People* (London: DK, 2001), p. 61.

19. J. Wecker, "Powers of Persuasion," *Fortune*, October 12, 1998, pp. 161–164; R. Lewicki and J. Litterer, *Negotiation* (Burr Ridge, IL: Irwin, 1985).

Chapter 15

1. D. Weeks, "Voice Mail: Blessing or Curse?" *World Traveler*, February 1995, pp. 51–54.
2. J. Fried, "Everything You Ever Wanted to Know about e-Mail," *Inc.*, October 2005, pp. 113–128.
3. M. Conlin, "Watch What You Put in That Office E-Mail," *BusinessWeek*, September 30, 2002, pp. 114–115.
4. A. Wellner, "Lost in Translation," *Inc.*, September 2005, pp. 37–38.
5. D. Brake, *Dealing with e-Mail* (London: DK, 2003).
6. A. Wellner, "Playing Well with Others: Office Cliques Sap Morale and Kill Productivity. Does Your Firm Have Them?" *Inc.*, January 2005, pp. 29–31.
7. C. Osborn, *Dealing with Difficult People* (London: DK, 2001).
8. C. Price, *Assertive Communication* (Boulder, CO: Career Track, 1994).
9. M. Munter, "Cross-Cultural Communication for Managers," *Business Horizons*, May–June 1993, pp. 69–78.

Chapter 16

1. B. J. Jaworski, V. Stathakopolous, and S. Krishnan, "Control Combinations in Marketing: Conceptual Framework and Empirical Evidence," *Journal of Marketing* 57 (1993): 57–69.
2. W. E. Deming, *Out of the Crisis* (Cambridge, MA: Center for Advanced Engineering Study, 1986).
3. D. A. Huffman, "Feedforward, Not Feedback," *Beverage World* 117 (1998): 170.
4. B. Pelletier and V. VanDoren, "Advanced Control Saves Energy," *Control Engineering* 50 (2003): 41–44.
5. "Better Safe than Sorry: The House That Numico Built," *Food Engineering & Ingredients* 28 (2003): 151.
6. R. Kaplan and D. Norton, "The Balanced Scorecard: Measures That Drive Performance," *Harvard Business Review*, January–February 1992, pp. 71–79.
7. G. H. Anthes, "Balanced Scorecard," *Computerworld* 37 (2003): 341.
8. D. Parmenter, "Balanced Scorecard," *Accountancy Ireland* 35 (2003): 14–17.
9. D. Williamson, "Managing the Key Cultural Dimensions of Control and Risk," *European Business Forum* 21 (2005): 41–45.
10. Deming, *Out of the Crisis*.
11. G. Godfrey, B. Dale, M. Marchington, and A. Wilkinson, "Control: A Contested Concept in TQM Research," *International Journal of Operations & Production Management* 17 (1997): 558–573.

Chapter 17

1. M. Gupta, A. Adams, and L. Raho, "Traditional Management, Quality Management, and Constraints Management: Perceptions of ASQ Members". *The Quality Management Journal* 10 (2003): 25–37.
2. A. Kumar, "Software Takes the Sting out of Horseradish Production: System Automatically Ages Ingredient and End-Item Lots Ensuring Stock Won't Be Wasted," *Food Engineering* 75 (2003): 781.
3. N. Logothetis, *Managing for Total Quality* (Hertfordshire, UK: Prentice Hall International, 1992), p. 5.
4. M. Imai, *Kaizen: The Key to Japan's Competitive Success* (New York: Random House, 1986).
5. R. Gourlay, "Back to Basics on the Factory Floor," *Financial Times*, January 4, 1994, p. 12.
6. D. Drickhamer, "The Kanban E-volution," *Material Handling Management* 60 (2005): 24–26.
7. Ibid.
8. M. Hammer and J. Champy, *Reengineering the Corporation* (New York: Harper Business, 1993), p. 35.

Chapter 18

1. Geoffrey Austrian, *Herman: Hollerith: Forgotten Giant of Information Processing* (New York: Columbia University Press, 1982).
2. Gareth R. Jones, Jennifer M. George, and Charles W. L. Hill, *Contemporary Management*, 2nd ed. (New York: McGraw-Hill/Irwin, 2000), pp. 624–625.
3. Jeffrey McCracken, "More Deaths Tied to Tires," *Detroit Free Press*, September 2, 2000.
4. H. Stoffer, "Explorer Ruling Helps Ford, but Legal Woes Remain," *Automotive News*, February 18, 2002; M. Miles, "Firestones, Ford Feud," *Tire Business*, December 17, 2001.
5. Wal-Mart, *Annual Report*, 1999.
6. R. M. Stair and G. W. Reynolds, *Fundamentals of Information Systems.* (Boston: Thompson Learning, 2001), p. 113.
7. "A Golden Vein," *The Economist Techonology Quarterly*, June 12, 2004, pp. 22–23.
8. Stair and Reynolds, *Fundamentals*, p. 113.
9. S. Alter, *Information Systems: Foundation of E-Business*, 4th ed. (Upper Saddle River, NJ: Prentice Hall, 2002), p. 22.
10. "O&A with Lou Gerstner," *BusinessWeek*, December 2, 1999.
11. R. H. Baker, *Extranets: The Complete Sourcebook* (New York: McGraw-Hill, 1997).
12. J. Stone Gonzalez, *The 21st Century Intranet* (Upper Saddle River, NJ: Prentice Hall, 1998).
13. P. E. Ross, "Software as Career Threat," *Forbes*, May 22, 1995, pp. 240–246.
14. J. Weckert and D. Adeney, *Computer and Information Ethics* (Westport, CT: Greenwood Press, 1997).
15. Don Hellriegel, Susan E. Jackson, and John W. Slocum, *Management*, 8th ed. (Cincinnati: South-Western Publishing, 1999).
16. P. Lashin, *Extranet Design and Implementation* (Alameda, CA: Sybex, 1997).
17. "Spyware: The Hidden Menace," *The Economist*, June 15, 2004, p. 61.
18. Steve Barth, "Post-Industrial Espionage," *Knowledge Management Magazine*, March 2001.
19. B. Grow, "Hacker Hunters," *BusinessWeek*, May 30, 2005, pp. 74–82.
20. "A Survey of Digital Security," *Economist*, October 26, 2002, p. 4.
21. F. Keenan, "You're Only as Good as Your Password," *BusinessWeek*, September 2, 2002, pp. 77–80.
22. IBM timetable, www.ibm.com.
23. E. Rich, *Artificial Intelligence* (New York: McGraw-Hill, 1983).
24. D. Kroenke, *Using MIS* (Upper Saddle River, NJ: Pearson, 2007).
25. S. Voelpel, M. Dous, and T. Davenport, "Five Steps to Creating a Global Knowledge-Sharing System: Siemens' ShareNet," *Academy of Management Executive*, May 2005, pp. 9–23.
26. D. Rigby and D. Ledingham, "CRM Done Right," *Harvard Business Review*, November 2004, pp. 118–129.
27. A. D. Chandler, *The Visible Hand* (Cambridge, MA: Harvard University Press, 1977).
28. Stair and Reynolds, *Fundamentals*, p. 11.
29. P. Evans, and T. S. Wurster, *Blown to Bits: How the New Economics of Information Transforms Strategy* (Boston: Harvard Business School Press, 2000) pp. 60–61.
30. Stair and Reynolds, *Fundamentals*, p. 174.
31. D. Rigby and V. Vishwanath, "Localization: The Revolution in Consumer Markets," *Harvard Business Review*, April 2006, pp. 82–92.

references

Chapter 1

Ante, S. E. (2006, February 13). Giving the boss the big picture. *BusinessWeek*, 48–50.

Barboza, D. (2006, February 25). Google cuts 2 features for China. *The New York Times*, C-1.

Barboza, D. (2006, February 9). Some assembly needed: China as Asia factory. *The New York Times*, C-1.

Barnard, C. I. (1938). *The functions of the executive.* Cambridge, MA: Harvard University Press.

Barnes, B. (2003, January 3). The new face of air rage. *The Wall Street Journal*, W-1.

Bartol, K. M., & Martin, D. C. (1998). *Management* (3rd ed.). New York: McGraw-Hill/Irwin.

Bateman, T. S., & Snell, S. A. (1999). *Management* (3rd ed.). New York: McGraw-Hill/Irwin.

Boulding, K. E. (1956). General systems theory: The skeleton of science. *Management Science, 2,* 197–208.

Burns, T., & Stalker, B. M. (1961). *The management of innovation.* London, UK: Tavistock Publications.

Chappell, L. (2006, February 7). Toyota to spurn Michigan (available at www.autoweek.com).

Cohen, W. M., & Levinthal, D. A. (1990). Absorptive capacity: A new perspective on learning and innovation. *Administrative Science Quarterly, 35,* 128–152.

Daft, R. L. (2000). *Management* (4th ed.). Fort Worth: Dryden Press.

Daft, R. L. (2005). *Management.* Thompson: Southwestern Press.

Dean, J. W., & Bowen, D. E. (1994). Management theory and total quality: Improving research and practice through theory development. *Academy of Management Review, 19,* 392–418.

Deming, W. E. (1986). *Out of the crisis.* Cambridge, MA: MIT Center for Advanced Engineering Study.

Donaldson, L. (1996). The normal science of structural contingency theory. In S. Clegg & C. Hardy (Eds.), *Handbook of organization studies* (pp. 57–76). Thousand Oaks, CA: Sage Publishing.

Duncan, W. J. (1989). *Great ideas in management.* San Francisco: Jossey-Bass.

Elgin, B. (2006, February 20). Outrunning China's web cops. *BusinessWeek*, 38–40.

Engardio, P. (2006, January 30). The future of outsourcing. *BusinessWeek*, 50–56.

Farnham, A. (1997, July 21). The man who changed work forever. *Fortune,* 114.

Fast, N. (1982). The Lincoln Electric Company. In F. K. Foulkes (Ed.), *Human resources management.* Englewood Cliffs, NJ: Prentice Hall.

Feder, B. J. (1995, September 5). Rethinking a model incentive plan. *The New York Times,* section 1, p. 33.

Foust, D. (2003, January 27). What worked at GE isn't working at Home Depot. *BusinessWeek,* 40.

Gomez-Mejia, L. R., Balkin, D. B., & Cardy, R. (2004). *Managing human resources.* Englewood Cliffs, NJ: Prentice Hall.

Gomez-Mejia, L. R., Balkin, D. B., & Cardy, R. L. (2001). *Managing human resources* (2nd ed.). Upper Saddle River, NJ: Prentice Hall.

Grossman, L., & Beech, H. (2006, February 13). Google under the gun. *Time*, 53–54.

Hamel, G., & Prahalad, C. K. (1994). *Competing for the future.* Boston: Harvard Business School Press.

Hammer, M., & Champy, J. (1993). *Reengineering the corporation.* New York: Harper Business.

Heizer, J., & Render, B. (1996). *Production and operations management.* Englewood Cliffs, NJ: Prentice Hall.

Huber, G. P. (1991). Organizational learning: The contributing processes and the literatures. *Organization Science, 2,* 88–115.

Hyde, P. (2003, January 22). Timesizing: Less work and more pay. What a crazy idea? www.timesizing.com.

Ignatius, A. (2006, February 20). In search of the real Google. *Time*, 36–50.

Jackson, J. H., Morgan, C. P., & Paolillo, J. G. (1986). *Organization theory* (3rd ed.). Englewood Cliffs, NJ: Prentice Hall.

Jay, A. (1970). *Management and Machiavelli.* New York: Harper & Row.

Jones, G. R., George, J. M., & Hill, C. W. (2000). *Contemporary management.* New York: McGraw-Hill/Irwin.

Jones, G. R., George, J. M., & Hill, C. W. (2001). *Contemporary management.* New York: McGraw-Hill/Irwin.

Kast, F. E., & Rosenweig, J. E. (1972). General systems theory: Applications for organization and management. *Academy of Management Journal, 15,* 447–465.

Krauthammer, C. (2006, February 13). Don't believe the hype. We are still no. 1. *Time*, 41.

Lawrence, P. R., & Lorsch, J. W. (1967). *Organization and environment.* Boston: Graduate School of Business Administration, Harvard University.

Lohr, S. (2006, February 16). Outsourcing is climbing skills ladder. *The New York Times*, C-1.

Maslow, A. H. (1954). *Motivation and personality.* New York: Harper & Row.

McCracken, J. (2006, March 1). Detroit's symbol of dysfunction: Paying employees not to work. *The Wall Street Journal*, A-1.

McGregor, D. (1960). *The human side of enterprise.* New York: McGraw-Hill.

Oh, H. (2006, February 6). Upfront. *BusinessWeek*, 14.

Peters, J. W. (2006, March 1). Both Ford and GM scale back. *The New York Times*, C-1.

Prasad, E. R., Prasad, V. S., & Satyanarayana, P. *Administrative thinkers.* New Delhi, India: Sterling Publishers.

Ripley, A., & Sieger, M. (2003, January 6). The special agent. *Time*, 34–40.

Roethlisberger, F., & Dickson, W. (1939). *Management and the worker: An account of a research program conducted by the Western Electric Company, Hawthorne Works, Chicago.* New York: John Wiley & Sons.

Schiller, Z. (1996, January 22). A model incentive plan gets caught in a vise. *BusinessWeek*, 89.

Schlosser, J. (2003, February 3) Uphill battle. *Fortune*, 64.

Sharplin, A., & Seeger, J. (1998). The Lincoln Electric Company, 1996. In A. A. Thompson, & A. J. Strickland (Eds.), *Strategic management* (10th ed.) New York: McGraw-Hill/Irwin.

Sheldrake, J. (1996). *Management theory*. London, UK: International Thompson Business Press.

Shellenbarger, S. (2006, February 16). Avoiding the next Enron: Today's crop of soon to be grads seeks job security. *The Wall Street Journal*, D-1.

Smith, A. (1937). *The wealth of nations*. New York: Modern Library.

Spencer, B. A. (1994). Models of organization and total quality management: A comparison and critical evaluation. *Academy of Management Review, 19*, 446–471.

Tzu, S. (1963). *The art of war*. Oxford, UK: Oxford University Press.

Vergano, D. (2006, February 9). U.S. could fall behind in global brain race. *USA Today*, D-1.

Weber, J. (2006, February 13). The new ethics enforcers. *BusinessWeek*, 75–77.

Womack, J. P. (2006, February 13). Why Toyota won. *The Wall Street Journal*, C-3.

Zeller, T. (2006, February 1). Microsoft amends its policy for shutting down blogs. *The New York Times*.

Zeller, T. (2006, February 15). Internet firms face questions about censoring online searches in China. *The New York Times*, C-3.

Zeller, T. (2006, February 16). Web firms are grilled on dealings in China. *The New York Times*, C-1.

Chapter 2

Balfour, F., & Roberts, D. (2005, September 26). Stealing managers from the big boys. *BusinessWeek*, p. 54.

Ball, D. A., McCullouch, W. H., Frantz, P. L., Geringer, J. M., & Minor, M. S. (2002). *International Business: The challenge of global competition*. New York: McGraw-Hill.

Bellman, E., & Koppel, N. (2005, September 28). More U.S. legal work moves to India's low-cost lawyers. *The Wall Street Journal*, p. B-1.

Bremner, B., Schiller, Z., Smart, T., & Holstein, W. (1996, July 22). Keiretsu connections. *BusinessWeek*, pp. 52–53.

Buckman, R. (2005, August 18). "Cellphone game rings in new niche: Ultracheap." *The Wall Street Journal*, p. B-4.

Chandler, C. (2005, October 31). "India's bumpy ride." *Fortune*, p. 134.

Cohen, R. (1991, November 21). For Coke, world is its oyster. *The New York Times*, pp. D1, D5.

Darling, J., & Nauss, D. (1995, February 19). Stall in the fast lane. *Los Angeles Times*, p. 1.

De Jonquieres, G. (1998, November 11). Foreign direct investment worldwide figures to reach $430 billion. *Financial Times*, p. 6.

Donnelly, J. H., Gibson, J., & Ivancevich, J. M. (1995). *Fundamentals of management*. Burr Ridge, IL: Irwin.

Dvorak, P. (2005, September 19), Stringer faces first big test as Sony's chief. *The Wall Street Journal*, p. B-1.

Dvorak, P. (2005, September 24). Culture clash crimps Sony CEO. *The Wall Street Journal*, p. A-6.

EI-Rashidi, Y. (2005). D'oh! Arabized Simpsons aren't getting many laughs. *The Wall Street Journal*.

Fackler, M. (2005, October 29). Wal-Mart doubles down on its investment in Japan. *The New York Times*, p. B-4.

Fortune. (1995, August 7). The global 500. pp. 130–131.

Graff, J. (2005, November 14). Why France is burning. *Time*, p. 36.

Grant, L. (1997, April 14). That overseas job could derail your career. *Fortune*, p. 166.

Greenberger, R. S., & Smith, C. S. (1997, April 28). CD piracy flourishes in China. *The Wall Street Journal*, p. A1.

Gunther, M. (2005, Fall). Can factory monitoring ever really work? *Fortune*, p. 12.

Gunther, M. (2005, June 27). Cops of the global village. *Fortune*, p. 158.

Hill, C. (2003). *International business*. New York: McGraw-Hill/Irwin.

Hill, C. W., & Jones, G. R. (1995). *Strategic management theory*. Boston: Houghton Mifflin.

Hofstede, G. (1984). *Culture consequences: International differences in work related values*. Beverly Hills, CA: Sage.

Hudson, R. L. (2003, January 24). Europe's great expectations. *The Wall Street Journal*, p. A-10.

Hymowitz, C. (2005, October 17). More American chiefs are taking top posts at overseas concerns. *The Wall Street Journal*, p. B-1.

Ihlwan, M., & Roberts, D. (2005, August 1). Made in Korea, assembled in China. *BusinessWeek*, p. 48.

Koretz, G. (1999, September 13). A woman's place is . . . *BusinessWeek*, p. 28.

Kripalani, M. (2005, October 10). A quiet shopping spree overseas. *BusinessWeek*, p. 54.

Latta, G.W. (2005). High mobility international employees. *WorldatWork Journal*, p. 48.

Matlack, C., & Burrows, P. (2005, October 10). HP's French twist. *BusinessWeek*, p. 53.

Mehta, S. N. (1994, July 7). Enterprise: Small companies look to cultivate foreign businesses. *The Wall Street Journal*, p. B2.

Naik, G. V., Karp, J., Millman, J., Fassiti, F., & Slater, J. (2003, January 24). Global baby bust, *The Wall Street Journal*, p. B-1.

Oster, P. (1993, November). Why Japan's execs travel better. *BusinessWeek*, p. 68.

Rhoads, C. (2005, June 23). Motorola's modernizer. *The Wall Street Journal*, p. B-1.

Rosenzwaig, R. (2005 July 5). How much did we spend this year? *Workspan*, p. 25.

Runnion, T. T. (2005 July 5). Expatriate programs. *Workspan*, p. 19.

Shellenbarger, S. (2005, October 27). Separation anxiety: Short job transfers create problems for families left behind. *The Wall Street Journal*, p. D-1.

Sims, G. T. (2005, November 1). Corn Flakes clash shows the glitches in European Union. *The Wall Street Journal*, p. A-1.

Taylor, A. (2003, January 20). Got 300,000? *Fortune*, pp. 118–125.

Trolman, S. (2005, August 5). Rationalizing global incentive pay plans look at the big picture. *Workspan*, p. 17.

Wild, J. J., Wild K. L., & Han, J. C. Y. (2000). *International Business*, Upper Saddle River, NJ: Prentice Hall.

Workspan. (2005, August 5). Premiums and allowances for expatriates, p. 13.

World Trade Organization (1998). *International Trade Trends and Statistics*. Geneva: WTO.

Wrighton, J., & Sapsford, J. (2005, April 26). For Nissan's rescuer, Ghosn new road rules await at Renault. *The Wall Street Journal*, p. A-1.

Chapter 3

Brull, S. V. (1999, May 10). For all that tobacco money, don't stint on the smoking war. *BusinessWeek*, p. 40.

Byrne, J. (1988, February 15). Businesses are signing up for ethics 101. *BusinessWeek*, pp. 56–57.

Carroll, A. B. (1996). *Business and society* (3rd ed.). Cincinnati: OH: South-Western Publishing.

Cochran, P. L., & Wood, R. A. (1984). Corporate social responsibility and financial performance. *Academy of Management Journal, 31*, 854–872.

Donaldson, T., & Preston, L. E. (1995). The stakeholder theory of the corporation: Concepts, evidence, and implications. *Academy of Management Review, 20*, 65–91.

Driscoll, D. (1998, March). Business ethics and compliance: What management is doing and why, *Business and Society Review, 99*, 33–51.

Dworkin, T. M., & Near, J. P. (1997). A better statutory approach to whistle blowing. *Business Ethics Quarterly, 7*(1), 1–16.

Dwyer, P., & Carney, D. (2002, December 16). Year of the whistleblower, *BusinessWeek*, pp. 107–110.

The Economist. (1997, July 26). Boeing v. Airbus, pp. 59–61.

The Economist. (2003, February 15). Pharmaceuticals: Pushing pills, p. 61.

The Economist. (2004, November 6). Big trouble for Merck, pp. 61–62; Barrett, A. (2004, November 22). Merck: How much misery after Vioxx? *BusinessWeek*, pp. 48–50.

Eli Lilly and Company, (1990). Guidelines of company policy.

Field, D. (1997, August 5). UPS strike stifles shippers. *USA Today*, p. 1A.

Freeman, R. E. (1984). *Strategic management: A stakeholder approach*. Boston: Pitman Publishing.

Frooman, J. (1999). Stakeholder influence strategies. *Academy of Management Review, 24*, 191–205.

Gard, L. (2004, November 22). We're good guys, buy from us. *BusinessWeek*, pp. 72–74.

Gelman, E. (1985, February 11). A giant under fire: General Dynamics faces numerous charges of fraud. *Newsweek*, pp. 24–25.

General Dynamics (1988). Standards of business ethics and conduct.

Global corruption report 2003. www.globalcorruptionreport.org.

Greenberg, J. (1990). Organizational justice: Yesterday, today and tomorrow. *Journal of Management, 16*, 399–432.

Greenwald, J. (1989, March 22). Let's make a deal. *Time*, pp. 84–86.

Grow, B. (2005, August 15). The debate over doing good. *BusinessWeek*, pp. 76–78.

Gundlach, M., Douglas, S., & Martinko, M. (2003). The decision to blow the whistle. A social information processing framework. *Academy of Management Review, 28*, 107–123.

Gunther, M. (2004, May 31). A pesky environmental group called the Rainforest Action Network is getting under the skin of corporate America. *Fortune*, pp. 158–164.

Hanson, A. (1990, July). What employees say about drug testing. *Personnel*, pp. 32–36.

Harrington, S. J. (1991). What corporate America is teaching about ethics. *Academy of Management Executive, 5*(1), 21–30.

Harrison, J. S., & St. John, C. H. (1996). Managing and partnering with external stakeholders. *Academy of Management Executive, 10*(2), 46–59.

Hemphill, T. A. (1994, Summer). Strange bedfellows cozy up for a clean environment. *Business and Society Review*, pp. 38–44.

Henderson, V. E. (1982). The ethical side of enterprise. *Sloan Management Review, 23*, 37–47.

Hoffman, W. M., & Moore, J. M (1990). *Business ethics* (2nd ed.) New York: McGraw-Hill.

Jackson, J. H., Miller, R. L., & Miller, S. G. (1997). *Business and society today*, St. Paul: West Publishing.

Jackson, M. (1997, May 12). 50% of workers commit unethical acts, survey says. *Boulder Daily Camera*, p. 1B.

JD Edwards & Company (1993). Corporate ideals and values.

McGuire, J. B., Sundgren, A., & Schneeweis, T. (1988). Corporate social responsibility and firm financial performance. *Academy of Management Journal, 27*, 42–56.

McLean, B. (2001, December 24). Why Enron went bust. *Fortune*, pp. 58–68.

Moore, T. (1982, November 29). The fight to save Tylenol. *Fortune*, pp. 48–49.

Munk, N. (1999, April 12). How Levi's trashed a great American brand. *Fortune*, pp. 82–90.

Murphy, P. E. (1989). Creating ethical corporate structures. *Sloan Management Review, 30*, 81–89.

Near, J. P., & Miceli, M. P. (1985). Organizational dissidence: The case of whistleblowing. *Journal of Business Ethics, 4*, 1–16.

Park, A. (2003, February 10). Family feuds don't get nastier than this. *BusinessWeek*, pp. 62–63.

Robbins, S. P., & Coulter, M. (1996). *Management* (5th ed.). Upper Saddle River, NJ: Prentice Hall.

Roberts, N. C., & King, P. J. (1989, Winter). The stakeholder audit goes public. *Organizational Dynamics*, pp. 63–79.

Sager, I. (2003, February 10). Tech's kickback culture, *BusinessWeek*, pp. 74–77.

Sashkin, M., & Kiser, K. J. (1993). *Putting total quality management to work*. San Francisco: Berrett-Koehler.

Savage, G. T., Nix, T. W., Whitehead, C. J., & Blair, J. D. (1991). Strategies for assessing and managing organizational stakeholders. *Academy of Management Executive, 5*(2), 61–75.

Sherman, S. (1997, May 12). Levi's: As ye sew, so shall ye reap, *Fortune*, pp. 104–116.

Steinberg, M., & Kaufman, S. (2005, August). Minimizing corporate liability exposure when the whistle blows in the post–Sarbanes-Oxley era. *Journal of Corporation Law*, pp. 445–463.

Sturdivant, F. D., & Vernon-Wortzel, H. (1990). *Business and society* (4th ed.). Homewood, IL: Irwin.

Trevino, L. K., & Nelson, K. A. (1995). *Managing business ethics*. New York: John Wiley & Sons.

Turban, D. B., & Greening, D. W. (1997). Corporate social performance and organizational attractiveness to prospective employees. *Academy of Management Journal, 40*, 658–672.

Weaver, G. R., Trevino, L. K., & Cochran, P. L. (1999). Corporate ethics programs as control systems: Influence of executive commitment and environmental factors. *Academy of Management Journal, 42*, 41–57.

Will, R. (1995, Spring). Corporations with a conscience. *Business and Society Review*, pp. 17–20.

Zellner, W. (2002, January 28). The whistleblower: A hero—and a smoking-gun letter. *BusinessWeek*, pp. 34–35.

Zellner, W., & Forest, S. (2001, December 17). The fall of Enron, *BusinessWeek*, pp. 30–36.

Chapter 4

Arndt, M., & Berstein, A. (2000, March 20). From milestone to millstone. *BusinessWeek*, pp. 120–122.

Baker, S. (2000, April 10). Telefonica: Takeover escape artist? *BusinessWeek*, pp. 58–60.

Barlow, W., Hatch, D., & Murphy, B. (1996, April). Employer denies jobs to smoker applicants. *Personnel Journal*, p. 142.

Bateman, T., & Snell, S. (1999). *Management: Building competitive advantage*. New York: McGraw-Hill/Irwin.

Bernstein, A. (1997, August 25). This package is a heavy one for the Teamsters. *BusinessWeek*, pp. 40–41.

BusinessWeek. (2000, May 15). The e.biz: Masters of the Web world, p. 25.

Conlin, M. (2000, June 12). Workers, surf at your own risk. *BusinessWeek*, pp. 105–106.

Crockett, R. O. (2000, April 17). A new company called Motorola. *BusinessWeek*, pp. 86–91.

Crockett, R., & Rosenbush, S. (2000, February 7). Doug Daft isn't sugarcoating things. *BusinessWeek*, pp. 36–38.

Currie, A. (2000, February). Merrill's internet conversion. *Euromoney*, p. 10.

Daft, R. L. (1997). *Management* (4th ed.). Fort Worth: Dryden Press.

Daft, R. L. (2000). *Management* (5th ed.). Fort Worth: Dryden Press.

Daly, J.P., Pouder, R. W., & Kabanoff, B. (2004). The effects of initial differences in firm's espoused values on their postmerger performance. *Journal of Applied Behavioral Science, 40*, 323–343.

Davidson, J. (2002). Overcoming resistance to change. *Public Management, 84*, 20–23.

Deal, T. E., & Kennedy, A. A. (1982). *Corporate cultures: The rites and rituals of corporate life*. Reading, MA: Addison-Wesley.

Deresky, H. L. (2000). *International management: Managing across borders and cultures*. Englewood Cliffs, NJ: Prentice Hall.

The Economist. (1999, October 23). Good scores or else, p. 28.

The Economist. (2000, July 15). Change management: An inside job, p. 61.

Gale, S. F. (2002). For ERP success, create a culture change. *Workforce*, September, pp. 88–94.

George, J., & Jones, G. (1999). *Understanding and managing organizational behavior*. Reading, MA: Addison-Wesley.

Gomez-Mejia, L. R., Balkin, D. B., & Cardy, R. (2001). *Managing human resources*. Englewood Cliffs, NJ: Prentice Hall.

Gomez-Mejia, L. R., & Welbourne, T. (1991). Compensation strategies in a global context. *Human Resource Planning, 14*(1), 38.

Greenwald, J. (2000, February 28). Lloyd's of London falling down. *Time*, pp. 54–58.

Griffin, R. W., & Pustay, M. W. (1998). *International business: A managerial perspective*. Reading, MA: Addison-Wesley.

Hamilton, J. (2000, April 3). The panic over hiring. *BusinessWeek*, pp. 130–131.

Hamm, S., & Kripalani, M. (2000, March 6). Software's tough guy. *BusinessWeek*, pp. 131–136.

Hof, R. D., Green, H., & Brady, D. (2000, February 21). An eagle eye on customers. *BusinessWeek*, pp. 67–81.

Hymowitz, C. (1989, July 13). Which culture fits you? *The Wall Street Journal*, p. B1.

Jones, G. R., George, J. M., & Hill, C. W. L. (2001). *Contemporary management* (2nd ed.). New York: McGraw-Hill/Irwin.

Karachanns, E., Evaristo, J.R., & Srite, M. (2005). Levels of culture and individual behavior: An integrated perspective. *Journal of Global Information Management, 13*, 1–20.

Kerwin, K. (2000, September 4). Fighting to stay on the road: Firestone's woes have dragged in Ford too. *BusinessWeek*, p. 44.

Kerwin, K., Burrows, P., & Foust, D. (2000, February 21). Workers of the world, logon. *BusinessWeek*, pp. 52–53.

Kiger, P. J. (2002). Axciom rebuilds from scratch. *Workforce, 81*, 52–55.

Kotter, J. P., & Heskett, J. L. (1992). *Corporate culture and performance*. New York: Free Press.

Kotter, J. P., & Schlesinger, L. A. (1979, March–April). Choosing strategies for change. *Harvard Business Review*, pp. 106–114.

Lewin, K. (1951). *Field theory in social science: Selected theoretical papers*. New York: Harper & Brothers.

Lewis, L. K., & Seibold, D. R. (1993). Innovation modification during intra-organizational adoption. *Academy of Management Review, 10*(2), 322–354.

Makri, M., Lane, P., & Gomez-Mejia, L. R. (2000). *Patent quality, firm performance, and CEO pay in high and low technology firms*. Unpublished manuscript, Management Department, Arizona State University.

Mandel, M. J. (2000, January 3). The new economy. It works in America. Will it go global? *BusinessWeek*, pp. 24–28.

Mandel, R. (2000, April 3). Up front. *BusinessWeek*, pp. 8–9.

Mitchell, M. A., & Yates, D. (2002). How to use your organizational culture as a competitive tool. *Nonprofit World, 20*, 33–34.

Moorhead, G., & Griffin, R. W. (2001). *Organizational behavior*. New York: Houghton Mifflin.

Mornell, P. (2000, July). Nothing endures but change. *Inc*, pp. 131–132.

Morris, B., & Sellers, P. (2000, January 10). What really happened at Coke. *Fortune*, pp. 114–117.

Nahavandi, A., & Malekzadeh, A. R. (1999). *Organizational behavior: The person–organization fit*. Englewood Cliffs, NJ: Prentice Hall.

O'Reilly, C. A., & Chatman, J. A. (1996). Culture as social control: Corporations, cults, and commitment. In B. Staw & L. L. Cummings (Eds.), *Research in Organizational Behavior, 18*, 157–200.

Peek, R. (2000, March). Jump-starting electronic books. *Information Today*, pp. 46–48.

Pettigrew, A. M. (1979). On studying organizational cultures. *Administrative Science Quarterly, 24*, 570–582.

Pfeffer, J., & Veiga, J. F. (1999). Putting people first for organizational success. *Academy of Management Executive, 13*(2), 38.

Quinn, R., Faerman, S., Thompson, M., & McGrath, M. (1996). *Becoming a master manager* (2nd ed.). New York: John Wiley & Sons.

Reingold, J., Stepanek, M., & Brady, D. (2000, February 14). The boom. *BusinessWeek*, pp. 100–118.

Reinhardt, A. (2000, January 31). I have left a few dead bodies. *BusinessWeek*, pp. 69–70.

Robbins, S. (2001). *Organizational behavior*. Englewood Cliffs, NJ: Prentice Hall.

Rossant, J. (2000, January 31). Old world, new mandate. *BusinessWeek*, pp. 92–93.

Sarros, J.C., Gray, J., Demsten, I.L., & Cooper, B. (2005). The organizational culture profile revisited and revised: An Australian perspective. *Australian Journal of Management, 30*, 159–182.

Schein, E. H. (1983). The role of the founder in creating organizational culture. *Organizational Dynamics, 12*, 13–28.

Speer, P. (2005). Managing change requires diligence, homework and a systematic approach to the CEO's office. *Insurance Networking News: Executive Strategies for Technology Management, 8*, 12.

Terpstra, V., & David, K. (1991). *The cultural environment of international business*. Cincinnati: South-Western Publishing.

Trice, H. M., & Beyer, J. M. (1993). *The cultures of work organizations*. Englewood Cliffs, NJ: Prentice Hall.

Van Maanen, J. V. (1975). Police socialization: A longitudinal examination of job attitudes in an urban police department. *Administrative Science Quarterly, 20*, 207–228.

The Wall Street Journal. (2000, May 26). General Motors Corp.: Saturn unit of General Motors is laying off about 490 workers, p. B10.

Watson, T. (2002). Goodnight, sweet prince. *Canadian Business, 75*, 77–78.

Welch, D. (2000, February 21). Running rings around Saturn. *BusinessWeek*, pp. 114–117.

Wilkins, A., & Ouchi, W. G. (1983, September). Efficient cultures: Exploring the relationship between cultures and organizational performance. *Administrative Science Quarterly*, pp. 468–481.

Wiscombe, J. (2002). CEO takes HR to prime time. *Workforce, 81*, 10.

Wright, P. M., & Noe, R. A. (1996). *Management of organizations*. Burr Ridge, IL: Irwin.

Chapter 5

Ahmed, N. V., Montagno, R. V., & Frienze, R. J. (1998). Organizational performance and environmental consciousness: An empirical study. *Management Decision, 36*(2), 57–63.

Ang, J. S., & Chua, J. H. (1979, April). Long range planning in large United States corporations: A survey. *Long Range Planning, 12*(2), 99–102.

Applebaum, S. H., & Hughes, B. (1998). Ingratiation as a political tactic. *Management Planning, 36*(2), 85–96.

Barkdoll, G., & Bosin M. R. (1997, August). Targeted planning: A paradigm for public service. *Management Planning*, pp. 529–540.

Barrett, A., Carey, J., & Brull, S. (1999, May 3). Bitter medicine ahead for drug companies. *BusinessWeek*, p. 50.

Barrett, P. (1998, June 8). Hot war over herbal remedies. *BusinessWeek*, p. 42.

Berner, R. (2005, October 31). At sears, a great communicator. *BusinessWeek*, p. 50.

Bonamici, K. (2005, June 27). Ford decides to let the pinto explode. *Fortune*, p. 77.

Brown, E. (1999, March 1). America's most admired companies. *Fortune*, pp. 68–76.

Brown, E. (1999, May 24). 9 ways to win on the web. *Fortune*, pp. 112–118.

Bulkeley, W.M. (2005, December 21). Kodak swings to $1.03 billion loss. *The Wall Street Journal*, p. A-1.

Burack, E. H. (1988). *Creative human resource planning and applications*. Englewood Cliffs, NJ: Prentice Hall.

Burack, E. H. Hochwarter, W., & Mathys, N.J. (1997). The new management development paradigm. *Human Resource Planning, 20*(1), 14–22.

Burrows, P. (1999, September 20). The big squeeze in the pc market. *BusinessWeek*, p. 40.

BusinessWeek. (2005, June 6). A multitude of medical miracles, p. 138.

BusinessWeek. (2005, August 1). The 100 top brands, pp. 90–92.

BusinessWeek. (1985, September 17). Special issue on planning.

Bylinsky, G. (1999, July 5). Hot new technologies, *Fortune*, pp. 168–176.

Byrne, J. A. (1998, June 8). How Jack Welch runs GE. *BusinessWeek*, pp. 90–110.

Byrne, J. A. (2003, February 17). Leaders are made, not born. *BusinessWeek*, p. 16.

Byrne, J. (1999, October 4). The search for the young and gifted. *BusinessWeek*, pp. 108–112.

Byrnes, N., & Judge, P. L. (1999, June 28). Internet anxiety. *BusinessWeek*, pp. 79–88.

Bymes, N. (2005, October 10). Cover story. *BusinessWeek*, p. 69.

Churchill, N. (1984, July–August). Budgeting choice: Planning vs. control. *Harvard Business Review*, pp. 150–164.

Chozick, A. (2005, September 19). Appearances are deceiving. *The Wall Street Journal*, R–7.

Cilmi, A.P. (2005, November). In a successful rewards and recognition program. *Workspan*, p. 19.

Cilmi, A.P. (2005, September 19).

Cohen, A.J., & Hall, M.E. (2005). Automating your performance and competency evaluation process. *WorldatWork Journal*, p. 64.

Colvin, G. (2005, October 3). "An executive risk handbook." *Fortune*, 69–70.

Cox, A., & Thompson, I. (1998). On the appropriateness of benchmarking. *Journal of General Management, 23*(3) 1–21.

Cravens, D. W., Greenley, G., Piercy, N. F., & Slater, S. (1997, August). Integrating contemporary strategic management perspectives. *Management Planning*, pp. 493–507.

Crockett, R. O. (1999, June 21). Motorola is ringing again. *BusinessWeek*, p. 40.

Crockett, R. O. (1999, August 30). Why Motorola should hang up on iridium. *BusinessWeek*, p. 46.

Donnelly, J. H., Gibson, J. L., & Ivancevich, J. M. (1998). *Fundamentals of management*. New York: McGraw-Hill/Irwin.

Einhorn, B. (1999, October 4). Big brother and the e-revolution. *BusinessWeek*, pp. 132–136.

Einhorn, B. (2005, November 14). Listen: The sound of hope. *BusinessWeek*, p. 68.

Ernst, R., & Ross, D. N. (1993). The Delta force approach to balancing long run performance. *Business Horizons*, pp. 4–9.

Faust, D., Smith, G., & Rocks, D. (1999, May 3). Man on the spot. *BusinessWeek*, pp. 142–147.

Fortune (2005, April 18). Jack Welch. "It's all in the sauce," p. 138.

Genentech Inc. Web site www.gene.com.

Giancola, F. (2005). A total rewards design tool that measures up. *WorldatWork Journal*, p. 6.

Gomez-Mejia, L. R., & Balkin, D. B. (1992). *Compensation, organizational strategy, and firm performance*. Cincinnati, OH: South-Western Publishing.

Gomez-Mejia, L.R., Balkin, D.B., & Cardy, R. (2005). *Managing human resources*. Englewood Cliffs, NJ: Prentice Hall.

Gorman, P., & Thomas, H. (1997, August). Strategy at the leading edge: The theory and practice of competence-based competition. *Management Planning*, pp. 615–628.

Grant, L. (1998, May 11). Why Kodak still isn't fixed. *Fortune*, pp. 179–181.

Green, G.T. (2005, November). Recognition and the generational divide. *Workspan*, p. 10.

Greising, D. (1998, April 13). I would like the world to buy a coke: The life and leadership of Robert Goizueta. *BusinessWeek*, pp. 70–76.

Grundy, T. (1997). Human resource management: A strategic approach. *Management Planning*, pp. 507–518.

Grundy, T. (1998). How are corporate strategy and human resources strategy linked? *Journal of General Management, 23*(3), 49–73.

Gurley, W. J. (1999, March 15). How the net is changing competition. *Fortune*, p. 168.

Hagan, J. (2005, November 8). Circulation continues to decline at most major newspapers. *The Wall Street Journal*, p. B–7.

Hanm, S. (1999, April 5). Netscapes storm the valley. *BusinessWeek*, p. 104.

Hax, A., & Majluf, N. S. (1996). *The strategy concept and process*. Upper Saddle River, NJ: Prentice Hall.

Hay, M., & Williamson, P. (1997, October). Good strategy: The view from below. *Management Planning*, pp. 661–665.

Hitt, M. A., Ireland, D. R., & Hoskisson, R. E. (1998). *Strategic management: Competitiveness and globalization*. St. Paul, MN: West Publishing.

Hof, R. D. (1999, October 4). A new era of bright hopes and terrible fears. *BusinessWeek*, pp. 84–98.

Hof, R.D. (2005, July 20). The power of us: Mass collaboration on the Internet is shaking up business. *BusinessWeek*, 78–81.

Holland, K.(1998, May 4). China slams a door in Amway's face *BusinessWeek*, 54.

Holmes, S. (2003, January 20). "GE little engines that could." *BusinessWeek*, 62–64, www.ge.com

Hoskisson, R. E., Hitt, M. A., Wan, W. P., & Yui, D. (1999). Theory and research in strategic management. *Journal of Management*, pp. 417–456.

Hymowitz, C. (2005, September 19). Middle managers are unsung heroes on corporate stage. *Wall Street Journal*, A–1.

Hymowitz, C. (2005, August 16). Balancing security and trust. *The Wall Street Journal*, B–1.

Jarrell, D. W. (1993). *Human resource planning*. Englewood Cliffs, NJ: Prentice Hall.

Kaplan, R. S., & Norton, D. P. (1993 September–October). Putting the balanced scorecard to work. *Harvard Business Review*, pp. 134–147.

Kluger, J. (2005, August 8). "Why NASA can't get it right." *Time*, p. 25.

Kochanski, J., & Sorensen, A. (2005, September). Managing performance. *Workspan*, p. 21.

Kovac, J. (2005, November). Smart goal setting. *Workspan*, p. 63.

Kress, N. (2005, May). Engaging your employees through the power of communication. *Workspan*, p. 27.

Kripalani, M., & Clifford, M. L. (2003, February 10). Finally, Coke gets it right. *BusinessWeek*, p. 47.

Kudia, R. J. (1979). The components of strategic planning. *Long Range Planning, 11*(6), 48–52.

Kumar, P. (1978). Long range planning practices by U.S. companies. *Managerial Planning, 26*(4), 31–33.

Kunii, I. M. Thorton, E., & Rae-Dupree, J. (1999, March 22). Sony's shake. *BusinessWeek*, p. 52.

Labich, K. (1999, March 1). Boeing finally hatches a plan. *Fortune*, pp. 101–106.

Landro, L. (2005, September 28). Compassion 101: Teaching M.D.s to be nicer. *The Wall Street Journal*, p. D–3.

Leonard, D. (2005, October 3). "The only lifeline was the Wal-Mart." *Fortune*, 74–80

Light, L. (1998, May 25). Litigation: The choice of a generation. *BusinessWeek*, p. 42.

Makridakis, S., Wheelwright, S., & McGee, V. (1982). *Forecasting methods and applications*. New York: John Wiley & Sons.

Mandel, M. J. (1999, October 4). The internet economy. *BusinessWeek*, pp.72–77.

Mandel, M.J. (2005, May 23). Sure, the trade deficit is scary – but we can handle it. *BusinessWeek*, p. 41.

McCracken, J. (2005, October 11). Delphi presses for cuts as Ford plans shake-up. *The Wall Street Journal*.

McCracken, J. (2005, October 28). Delphi seeks far-reaching givebacks. *The Wall Street Journal*.

McKay, B., & Vranica, S. (2003, January 9). Cracking the China market. *The Wall Street Journal*, pp. B1–B2.

Mullaney, T.J. (2005, September 5). Making it easy to size up a hospital. *BusinessWeek*, p. 102.

Munk, N. (1999, June 21). Title flight. *Fortune*, pp. 84–86.

Narisetti, R. (1998, March 12). How IBM turned around its ailing PC division. *The Wall Street Journal*, p. B1.

Nussbaum, B. (2005, August 1). How to build innovative companies. *BusinessWeek*, p. 61.

O'Connell, V. (2005, October 7). Rx from Marlboro man: Device that delivers drugs, not smoke. *The Wall Street Journal*, p. A–2.

O'Connor, R.V. (1986). *Corporate guides to long range planning* (Conference Board Report No. 687). New York: Conference Board.

Odiorne, G.S. (1987, July/August). Measuring the unmeasurable: Setting standards for management performance. *Business Horizons*, pp. 69–75.

Overholt, M.H. (1997). Flexible organizations: Using organizational design as a competitive advantage. *Human Resource Planning, 20*(1), 22–23.

Pearson, G. (1986). Business strategy should not be bureaucractic. *Accountancy, 97*(1112), 109–112.

Port, O. (1999, October 4). Customers move into the driver's seat. *BusinessWeek*. 103–110.

Preble, J.F. (1992). Environmental scanning for strategic control. *Journal of Managerial Issues, 4*, 254–268.

Prestowitz, C. (1998, May 11). Asia's flawed fundamentals. *Fortune*, p. 52.

Reingold, J., & Brody, D. (1999, September 20). Brain drain. *BusinessWeek*, pp. 113–122.

Revell, J. (2003, February 3). "Can Home Depot get its groove back?" *Fortune*, pp. 110–112.

Sager, I. (1999, June 21). Big Blue at your service, *BusinessWeek*, pp. 130–131.

Sager, I., Burrow, P., & Reinhardt, A. (1998, May 25). Back to the future at Apple. *Business Week*, pp. 56–58.

Sandberg, J. (2005, August 17). Sometimes colleagues are just too bad not to get promoted. *The Wall Street Journal*, p. B–1.

Sandersen, S. M. (1998). New approaches to strategy: New ways of thinking for the millennium. *Management Decision, 36*(1), 9–14.

Schlange, L. E., & Juttner, V. (1997, October). Helping managers to identify the key strategic issues. *Management Planning*, pp. 777–787.

Stepanek, M. (1999, June 7). Closed, gone to the net. *BusinessWeek*, pp. 113–116

Stipp, D. (1988, May 11). Why Pfizer is so hot. *Fortune*, p. 88.

Symonds, W.C. (2005, May 23). A digital warrior for Kodak. *BusinessWeek*, p. 42.

Taylor, A., III. (2005, October 17). Ford: the hamlet of Dearborn. *Fortune*, p. 36.

Tenet's bills to Calpers 50% more than other hospitals. (2003, February 3). *Sacramento BEE*.

Thurlby, B.(1998). Competitive forces are also subject to change. *Managerial Decisions, 36*(1), 19–25.

Tosi, H.L., Katz, J.P., & Gomez-Mejia, L.R. (1997). Disaggregating the agency contract: The effects of monitoring, incentive alignment, and term in office on agent decision making. *Academy of Management Journal, 40*, 584–602.

Tsao, P. (1998, June 8). Reports of cancer's imminent death were an exaggeration. *BusinessWeek*, p. 13.

Tushman, M.L., & O'Reily, C.A., III (1997). *Winning through innovation*. Boston: Harvard Business School Press.

USA Today. (2005, June 1). Godzilla rampage slows, p. D1.

Useem, J. (2005, June 27). Ford offers $5 a day. *Fortune*, p. 65.

Weir, D., & Smallman, C. (1998). *Management Decision, 36*(1), 43–50.

Wright, P. M., & Noe, R.A. (1998). *Management of organizations*. New York: McGraw-Hill/Irwin.

Xratz, E. F. (2005, October 3). For FedEx, it was time to deliver. *Fortune*, 83–84.

Chapter 6

Beteman, T. S., & Snell, S. A. (1996). *Management* (3rd ed.). Burr Ridge, IL: Irwin.

Bazerman, M., & Chugh, D. (2006, January). Decisions without blinders. *Harvard Business Review*, 88–97.

Benartzi, S., & Thaler, R. H. (1999). Risk aversion or myopia? Choices in repeated gambles and retirement investments. *Management Science, 45*, 364–381.

Bowen, J., & Qui, Q. (1992). Satisficing when buying information. *Organizational Behavior and Human Decision Process, 51*, 471–481.

Carter, B. (1997, December 26). Seinfeld says it's over, and it's no joke for NBC, *The New York Times*, pp. A1, A15.

Cohen, M. D., March, J. G., & Olsen, J. P. (1972). The garbage can model of organizational choice. *Administration Science Quarterly, 17*, 1–25.

Conlon, D. E., & Garland, H. (1993). The role of project completion information in resource allocation decisions. *Academy of Management Journal, 36*, 401–413.

Covey, S. R. (1989). *The 7 habits of highly effective people*. New York: Simon & Schuster.

Daft, R. L. (1997). *Management* (4th ed.). Fort Worth: Dryden Press.

Daft, R. L. (1999). *Leadership: Theory and practice*. Fort Worth: Dryden Press.

Dean, J. W., & Evans, J. R. (1994). *Total quality*. St. Paul, MN: West Publishing.

Delbecq, A. L., Van de Ven, A. H., & Gustafson, D. H. (1975). *Group techniques for program planning*. Glenview, IL: Scott, Foresman.

Eisenhardt, K. M. (1988). Agency and institutional theory explanations: The case of retail sales compensation. *Academy of Management Journal, 31*, 488–511.

Gerstner, L. (2002). *Who says elephants can't dance? Leading a great enterprise through dramatic change*. New York: HarperBusiness.

Gladwell, M. (2005). *Blink: The power of thinking without thinking*. New York: Little, Brown.

Grove, A. (1996). *Only the paranoid survive*. New York: Currency Doubleday.

Hall, R. H. (1999). *Organizations*. Upper Saddle River, NJ: Prentice Hall.

Hammond, et al. (2006, January). The hidden traps of decision making. *Harvard Business Review*, 118–126.

Hom, P. W., & Griffeth, R. W. (1995). *Employee turnover*. Cincinnati, OH: South-Western Publishing.

Howard, R. (1988). Decision analysis: Practice and promise. *Management Science, 34*, 679–695.

Huey, J. (1997, December 29). In search of Roberto's secret formula. *Fortune*, pp. 230–234.

Jackson, J. A., Kloeber, J. M., Ralson, B. E., & Deckro, R. F. (1999). Selecting a portfolio of technologies: An application of decision analysis. *Decision Sciences, 30*, 217–238.

Jones, G. R., George, J. M., & Hill, C. W. (1998). *Contemporary management*. New York: McGraw-Hill/Irwin.

Kiley, T. (1993, January). The idea makers. *Technology Review*, pp. 33–40.

Kreitner, R., & Kinicki, A. (1995). *Organizational behavior* (3rd ed.). Burr Ridge, IL: Irwin.

Leana, R. R. (1986). Predictors and consequences of delegation. *Academy of Management Journal, 29*, 754–774.

Leonard, E. (2005, October 3). The only lifeline was the Wal-Mart. *Fortune*, 74–80.

Mackenzie, R. A. (1972). *The time trap*. New York: McGraw-Hill.

McNamara, G., & Bromily, P. (1999). Risk and return in organizational decision making. *Academy of Management Journal, 42*, 330–339.

Maier, N. R. (1973). *Psychology in industrial organizations* (4th ed.). Boston: Houghton Mifflin.

Mankins, M. (2004, September). Stop wasting valuable time. *Harvard Business Review, 58–65*.

March, J. G., & Simon, H. A. (1958). *Organizations*. New York: John Wiley & Sons.

Mealiea, L. W., & Latham, G. P. (1996). *Skills for managerial success*. Burr Ridge, IL: Irwin.

Pearson, C. M., & Clair, J. A. (1998). Reframing organizational crisis. *Academy of Management Review, 23*, 59–76.

Quinn, R. E., Faerman, S. R., Thompson, M. P., & McGrath, M. R. (2003). *Becoming a master manager* (3rd ed.). New York: John Wiley & Sons.

Rimer, S. (1996, March 6). A hometown feels less like home. *The New York Times*, pp. A1, A8, A9.

Robbins, S. P., & Coulter, M. (1996). *Management* (5th ed.). Upper Saddle River, NJ: Prentice Hall.

Rowe, A., & Mason, R. (1987). *Managing with style: A guide to understanding, assessing, and improving your decision making*. San Francisco: Jossey-Bass.

Simon, H. A. (1957). *Models of man*. New York: Wiley.

Sitkin, S. B., & Pablo, A. L. (1992). Reconceptualizing the determinants of risk behavior. *Academy of Management Review, 17*, 9–38.

Sitkin, S. B., & Weingart, L. R. (1995). Determinants of risky decision making behavior: A test of the mediating role of risk perceptions and risk propensity. *Academy of Management Journal, 38*, 1573–1592.

Stoner, J. (1968). Risk and cautious shifts in group decisions. *Journal of Experimental and Social Psychology, 4*, 442–459.

Thompson, A. A., & Strickland, A. J. (1998). *Strategic management: Concepts and cases* (10th ed.). New York: McGraw-Hill/Irwin.

Thompson, R. (1993, July). An employee's view of empowerment. *HR Focus*, pp. 14–15.

Vroom, V. H., & Jago, A. G. (1988). *The new leadership: Managing participation in organizations*. Englewood Cliffs, NJ: Prentice Hall.

Waller, M. J. (1999). The timing of adaptive group responses to nonroutine events. *Academy of Management Journal, 42*, 127–137.

Whyte, G. (1989). Groupthink reconsidered. *Academy of Management Review, 14*, 40–56.

Wright, P. M., & Noe, R. A. (1996). *The management of organizations*. Burr Ridge, IL: Irwin.

Wu, G. (1999). Nonlinear decision weights in choice under uncertainty. *Management Science, 45*, 74–85.

Chapter 7

Acohido, B., & Baig, E.C. (2006, January 5). Gates shares spotlight with new windows. *USA Today*, p. B-1.

Adams, M. (2006, January 5). Independence CEO says he doesn't regret gamble. *USA Today*, p. B-5.

Afuah, A. (1998). *Innovation management*. New York: Oxford University Press.

Amato, I. (1999, June 7). Industrializing the search for new drugs. *Fortune*, pp. 110–118.

Armstrong, L. (1999, March 22). Amgen nurses itself back to health. *Fortune*, pp. 76–78.

Associated Press. (1996, February 7). Southwest Airlines earns triple crown award again. *Arizona Republic*, p. A15.

Barboso, M. (2006, January 13). State mandate for Wal-Mart on health care. *New York Times*, p. A-1.

Barboza, D., & Zeller, Jr., T. (2006, January 6). Microsoft shuts Blog's site after complaints by Beijing. *New York Times*, p. C-3.

Barnes, K. (2006, January 5). Alburn sales slump as downloads rise. *USA Today*, p. D-1.

Barney, J. B. (1995). Looking inside for competitive advantage. *Academy of Management Executive, 9*(4), 59–60.

Barney, J. B., & Hoskisson, R. (1990). Strategic groups: Untested assertions and research proposals. *Managerial and Decision Economics, 11*, 198–208.

Barret, P. (1999, May 3). Bitter medicine ahead for drug companies. *BusinessWeek*, p. 50.

Bergh, D. (1995). Size and relatedness of units sold: An agency theory and resource based perspective. *Strategic Management Journal, 16*, 221–229.

Berner, R. (2005, November 21). Watch out, Best Buy and Circuit City. *BusinessWeek*, p. 46.

Berstein, R. (2006, January 12). Men chafe as Norway ushers women into boardroom. *New York Times*, p. A-3.

Bettis, R., & Hitt, M. A. (1995, Summer). The new competitive landscape [Special Issue]. *Strategic Management Journal, 16*, 7–19.

Borrus, A. (2005, November 21). Learning to love Sarbanes-Oxley. *BusinessWeek*, p. 126.

Brody, D. (1999, April 2). Xerox. *BusinessWeek*, pp. 93–94.

Brown, E. (1999, March 1). America's most admired companies. *Fortune*, pp. 68–75.

Brown, E. (1999, May 24). 9 ways to win on the Web. *Fortune*, pp. 112–120.

Brush, T. A. (1996). Predicted change in operational synergy and post acquisition performance of acquired businesses. *Strategic Management Journal, 17*, 1–24.

Bulkeley, W. M. (2005, December 21). Kodak swings to $1.03 billion loss. *The Wall Street Journal*, p. A-1.

Burns, J. (2006, January 12). Board members find independence. *The Wall Street Journal*, p. C-11.

Burrows, P. (1999, September 20). The big squeeze in the PC market. *BusinessWeek*, pp. 40–41.

BusinessWeek. (1998, January 12), p. 32.

BusinessWeek. (1998, January 12). The 25 top managers of the year, pp. 54–60.

Bylinsky, G. (2000, June 26). Hot new technologies for American factories. *Fortune*, p. 288.

Byrnes, N. (1999, June 28). Internet anxiety. *BusinessWeek*, pp. 79–86.

Campbell, A., & Luchs, K. (1998). *Core competency-based strategy*. London, UK: International Thompson Business Press.

Campbell, A., Goold, M., & Alexander, M. (1995). Corporate strategy: The question for parenting advantage. *Harvard Business Review, 73*(2), 120–132.

Carey, S. (2006, January 13). As airlines pull out of dive, Limited charts its own course. *The Wall Street Journal*, p. A-1.

Charkham, J. (1994). *Keeping good company: A study of corporate governance in five countries*. New York: Oxford University Press.

Chon, G. (2006, January 5). GM and Ford lose more market share. *The Wall Street Journal*, p. A13.

Clarkson, M. B. E. (1995). A stakeholder framework for analyzing and evaluating corporate social performance. *Academy of Management Review, 20*, 92–117.

Coates, T. P. (2005, September 5). Wal-Mart's urban room. *Time*, p. 44.

Colvin, G. (1998, November 23). How Rubbermaid managed to fail. *Fortune*, pp. 32–36.

Crockett, R. O. (1999, August 30). Why Motorola should hang up on iridium. *BusinessWeek*, pp. 46–47.

Crockett, R. O. (1999, June 21). Motorola is ringing again. *BusinessWeek*, pp. 40–42.

D'Aveni, R. A. (1995). Coping with hypercompetition: Utilizing the new 75's framework. *Academy of Management Executive, 9*(3), 54.

Davis, J. B. (2003, February). Sorting out Sarbanes-Oxley. *ABA Journal*, pp. 44–50.

Desmond, E. W. (1998, February 2). Can Canon keep clicking? *Fortune*, pp. 98–107.

Dessler, G. (2000). *Human resource management*. Englewood Cliffs, NJ: Prentice Hall.

DeWit, R., & Meyer, R. (1998). *Strategy: Process, content, context*. London, UK: International Thompson Business Press.

Donaldson, T., & Preston, L. E. (1995). The stakeholder theory of the corporation: Concepts, evidence, and implications. *Academy of Management Review, 20*, 65–91.

Durham, K., & Smith, R. A. (2005, August 18). Behind zooming condo prices. *The Wall Street Journal*, p. A-1.

Dvorak, P., & Ramstad, E. (2006, January 3). TV marriage: Behind Sony-Samsung rivalry, an unlikely alliance develops. *The Wall Street Journal*, p. A-1.

Echikson, W. (1999, October 11). Designers climb onto the virtual catwalk. *BusinessWeek*, pp. 164–166.

Einhorn, B. (1999, February 15). Foreign rivals vs. the Chinese: If you can't beat them. *BusinessWeek*, p. 78.

Einhorn, B. (2005, November 14). Listen: The sound of hope. *BusinessWeek*, p. 68.

Eisenhardt, K., & Zbaracki, M. (1992, Winter). Strategic decision making [Special Issue]. *Strategic Management Journal, 13*, 17–37.

Fahey, L., & Narayanan, V. K. (1986). *Macroenvironmental analysis for strategic management*. St. Paul, MN: West Publishing Co.

Farzad, R., & Elgin, B. (2005, December 5). Googling. *BusinessWeek*, p. 61.

Fine, C. H. (1999, March 29). The ultimate core competency. *Fortune*, pp. 144–149.

Fineman, H., & Lipper, T. (2003, January 27). Spinning race. *BusinessWeek*, pp. 25–30.

Finkelstein, S., & Hambrick, D. C. (1996). *Strategic leadership: Top executives and their effects on organizations*. St. Paul, MN: West Publishing Co.

Fisher, A. B. (1996, March 6). Corporate reputations. *Fortune*, pp. 90–93.

Flynn, J., Carey, J., & Crockett, R. (1998, January 26). A fierce downdraft at Boeing. *BusinessWeek*, pp. 34–35.

Foust, D. (2002, September 9). The changing heartland. *BusinessWeek*, pp. 80–83.

Galbraith, J. R. (1995). *Designing organizations*. San Francisco: Jossey-Bass.

Genus, A. (1998). *Managing change: Perspective and practice*. London, UK: International Thompson Business Press.

Gibney, F. (1999, March 1). Nissan calls a low. *Time*, p. 48.

Godfrey, P. C., & Hill, C. W. L. (1995). The problem of unobservables in strategic management research. *Strategic Management Journal, 16*, 519–533.

Gomez, P. (1998). *Value management*. London, UK: International Thompson Business Press.

Gomez-Mejia, L. R., Balkin, D. B., & Cardy, R. (2001). *Managing human resources*. Englewood Cliffs, NJ: Prentice Hall.

Goold, M., & Luchs, K. (1993). Why diversify? Four decades of management thinking. *Academy of Management Executive, 7*(3), 7–25.

Grant, D., & Latour, A. (2005, November 21). Changing channels. *The Wall Street Journal*, p. A-1.

Greene, J. (2003, March 3). The Lenux uprising. *BusinessWeek*, pp. 78–86.

Grow, B. (2005, December 5). The great rebate runaround. *BusinessWeek*, p. 34.

Gullapalli, D. (2005, October 17). Living with Sarbanes-Oxley. *The Wall Street Journal*, R-1.

Guth, R.A. (2005, November 18). Microsoft, Palm unite to fight Blackberry. *The Wall Street Journal*, p. B-1.

Guth, R.A. (2005, September 27). Getting Xbox 360 to market. *The Wall Street Journal*, p. B-1.

Hall, R. H. (1996). *Organizations: Structures, processes, outcomes*. Englewood Cliffs, NJ: Prentice Hall.

Hamel, G., & Prahalad, C. K. (1993). Strategy as stretch and leverage. *Harvard Business Review, 71*(2), 75–84.

Hamel, G., & Prahalad, C. K. (1994). *Competing for the future*. Boston: Harvard Business School Press.

Hamm, S. (1999, April 5). Netscapees storm the valley. *BusinessWeek*, pp. 104–105.

Heinzl, M. (2005, November 2). A new crop of gadgets challenge the BlackBerry. *The Wall Street Journal*, p. D-1.

Hesseldahl, A. (2005, December 5). For every Xbox, a big fat loss. *BusinessWeek*, p. 13.

Hill, C. H. (2000). *International business*. New York: McGraw-Hill/Irwin.

Hill, C. W. L. (1994). Diversification and economic performance: Bringing structure and corporate management back into the picture. In R. P. Rumelt et al. (Eds.), *Fundamental issues in strategy* (pp. 297–321). Boston: Harvard Business School Press.

Hitt, M. A., Ireland, R. D., & Hoskisson, R. E. (2001). *Strategic management*. New York: McGraw-Hill/Irwin.

Hitt, M. A., Park, D., Hardee, C., & Tyler, B. B. (1995). Understanding strategic intent in the global market place. *Academy of Management Executive, 9*(2), 12–19.

Holstein, W. J. (2002, October 14). Canon takes aim at Xerox. *Fortune*, pp. 215–220.

Hoskisson, R. E., Hitt, M. A., Wan, W. P., & Yui, D. (1999). Theory and research in strategic management. *Journal of Management*, pp. 417–456.

Hughes, N., Ralf, M., & Michels, W. (1998). *Transform your supply chain*. London, UK: International Thompson Business Press.

Hughes, K., & Oughton, C. (1993). Diversification, multimarket contact, and profitability. *Economics, 60*, 203–224.

Hunt, M. S. (1972). *Competition in the major home appliance industry*. Cambridge, MA: Harvard University Press.

Ireland, D., & Hitt, M. A. (1999). Achieving and maintaining strategic competitiveness in the 21st century: The role of strategic leadership. *Academy of Management Executive, 13*(1), 43–58.

Jacoby, M. (2005, October 17). The global agenda. *The Wall Street Journal*, p. R7.

Jenison, D. B., & Sitkin, S. B. (1986). Corporate acquisitions: A process perspective. *Academy of Management Review, 11*, 145–163.

Jones, T. M. (1995). Instrumental stakeholder theory: A synthesis of ethics and economics. *Academy of Management Review, 20*, 404–437.

Kahn, J. (1999, June 7). Wal-Mart goes shopping in Europe. *Fortune*, pp. 105–110.

Kelm, K. M., Narayanan, V. K., & Pinches, G. E. (1995). Shareholder value creation during R&D innovation and commercialization stages. *Academy of Management Journal, 38*, 770–780.

Kerwin, K., & Ewing, J. (1999, September 27). Nasser: Ford be nimble. *BusinessWeek*, pp. 42–43.

Kosnik, R., & Chatterjee, S. (1997). *Corporate governance*. St. Paul, MN: West Publishing Co.

Kotha, S., & Nair, A. P. (1995). Strategy and environment as determinants of performance: Evidence from the Japanese machine tool industry. *Strategic Management Journal, 16*, 497–518.

Kumii, I. M. (1999, March 22). Sony's shake up. *BusinessWeek*, pp. 52–54.

Labich, K. (1999, March 1). Boeing finally hatches a plan. *Fortune*, pp. 101–106.

Lado, A. A., Boyd, N. G., & Wright, P. (1992). A competency based model of sustainable advantage: Toward a conceptual integration. *Journal of Management, 18*, 77–91.

Lohr, S. (2005, November 6). Just Googling it is striking fear into companies. *New York Times*.

Lundegaard, K. (2006, January 10). Ford, GM make big push to promote 'flex-fuel' vehicles. *The Wall Street Journal*, p. B1.

Martin, R. L. (2006, January 16). What innovation advantage? *BusinessWeek*, p. 102.

Maynard, M. (2006, January 3). Toyota shows big three how it is done. *New York Times*, p. C-1.

Maynard, M. (2006, January 8). Is there a future in Ford's future? *New York Times*, p. 3.

McCracken, J. (2006, February 17). Ford focuses on market-share slide. *The Wall Street Journal*, p. A-1.

McDonald, I., & Adamy, J. (2006, January 13). Whole Foods fare's pricey? *The Wall Street Journal*, p. C-1.

McGahan, A. M. (1994). Industry structure and competitive advantage. *Harvard Business Review, 72*(5), 115–124.

McGrath, R. G., MacMillan, I. C., & Venkataraman, S. (1995). Defining and developing competence: A strategic process paradigm. *Strategic Management Journal, 16,* 251–275.

Meznar, M. B., & Nigh, D. (1995). Buffer or bridge? Environmental and organizational determinants of public affairs activities in American firms. *Academy of Management Journal, 38,* 975–996.

Monks, R. A. G., & Minow, N. (1995). *Corporate governance.* Cambridge, MA: Blackwell Business.

Montgomery, C. A. (1994). Corporate diversification. *Journal of Economic Perspectives, 8,* 163–178.

Mullaney, T. J. (2005, September 5). Making it easy to size up a hospital. *BusinessWeek*, p. 102.

Munk, N. (1999, June 21). Title fight. *Fortune*, pp. 84–94.

Naughton, K. (1999, January 25). The global six. *BusinessWeek*, pp. 68–76.

Nerf, R. (1991, December 9). Guess who is selling Barbies in Japan now? *BusinessWeek*, pp. 72–76.

Peteraf, M. A. (1993). The cornerstone of competitive strategy: A resource based view. *Strategic Management Journal, 14,* 179–191.

Petrick, J. A., Scherer, R. F., Brodzinski, J. D., Quinn, J. F., & Ainina, M. F. (1999). Global leadership skills and reputational capital: Intangible resources for sustainable competitive advantage. *Academy of Management Executive, 13*(1), 58–70.

Pfeffer, J. (1994). *Competitive advantage through people: Unleashing the power of the workforce.* Boston: Harvard Business School Press.

Porter, M. E. (1990). *Competitive advantage.* New York: Free Press.

Porter, M. E. (1994). Toward a dynamic theory of strategy. In R. P. Rumelt, D. E. Schendel, & D. J. Teece (Eds.), *Fundamental issues in strategy.* Cambridge, MA: Harvard University Press.

Pound, J. (1995). The promise of the governed corporation. *Harvard Business Review, 73*(2), 90.

Prahalad, C. K., & Hamel, G. (1990). The core competence of the organization. *Harvard Business Review, 68*(3), 79–91.

Preble, J. F. (1992). Environmental scanning for strategic control. *Journal of Managerial Issues, 4,* 254–268.

Price, R. (1996). Technology and strategic advantage. *California Management Review, 38*(3), 38–56.

Reed, S. (1999, February 22). Busting up Sweden Inc. *BusinessWeek*, pp. 52–53.

Reger, R. K., & Huffs, A. S. (1993). Strategic groups: A cognitive perspective. *Strategic Management Journal, 14,* 103–123.

Richardson, K. (2006, January 5). Blockbuster's backbreaker: No-late-fee policy. *The Wall Street Journal*, p B1.

Rogers, B. (1998). *Seize the future for your business.* London, UK: International Thompson Business Press.

Rowley, I., Tashiro, H., & Lee, L. (2005, September 5). Canon: Combat-ready. *BusinessWeek*, p. 48.

Sager, I. (1999, June 21). Big Blue at your service. *BusinessWeek*, pp. 131–136.

San Jose Mercury News. (1998, May 2). Gates too busy to define government. [story appearing in *Arizona Republic*, E1].

Schendler, B. (1999, April 12). Sony's new game. *Fortune*, pp. 30–31.

Schrivastava, P. (1995). Ecocentric management for a risk society. *Academy of Management Review, 20,* 119.

Serwer, A. (2005, April 18). Bruised in Bentonville. *Fortune*, p. 84.

Sherman, S. (1995, November 13). Stretch goals: The dark side of asking for miracles. *Fortune*, pp. 231–232.

Siekman, P. (1999, April 26). Where build-to-order works best. *Fortune*, p. 160.

Silke, S. (2006, January 5). Most automakers see their sales fall in December. *USA Today*, p. B-1.

Sirois, C. (1995, August 25). Unifi, Inc. *Value Pine*, p. 1640.

Sorkin, R. (2006, January 6). To Battle, armed with shares: Big holders wield their stakes to push for corporate change. *New York Times*, p. C1.

Sparks, D. (1999, October 25). Partners. *BusinessWeek*, pp. 106–107.

Stiles, T. (1995). Collaboration for competitive advantage. *Long Range Planning, 28,* 109–112.

Symonds, W. C. (1999, April 5). Looking to lose just a few more pounds. *BusinessWeek*, pp. 64–70.

Symonds, W. C., & Burrows, D. (2005, May 23). A digital warrior for Kodak. *BusinessWeek*, p. 42.

Taylor A., III. (1999, January 11). The Germans take charge. *Fortune*, pp. 92–96.

Taylor, A., III. (1995, September 18). Ford's really B16 leap at the future: It's risky, it's worthy, and it may work. *Fortune*, pp. 134–144.

Taylor, A., III. (1999, April 26). Why DuPont is trading oil for corn. *Fortune*, pp. 154–160.

Taylor, A., III. (2005, October 17). Ford: the hamlet of Dearborn. *Fortune*, p. 36.

Time Magazine (2003, February 24). Milestones, p. 16.

UpFront. (2005, December 5). The big picture. *BusinessWeek*, p. 16.

Veale, J. (1999, August 30). How Daewoo ran itself off the road. *BusinessWeek*, pp. 48–49.

Vlasic, B., & Naughton, K. (1997, September 22). The small car wars are back. *BusinessWeek*, pp. 40–42.

Weber, J. (1999, June 14). As the world restructures. *BusinessWeek*, pp. 150–152.

Weber, J., Holmes, S. & Palmeri, C. (2005, November 7). Older workers may have a hard time giving up private offices. *BusinessWeek*, p. 100.

Weisul, K. (2005, December 5). A shine on their shoes. *BusinessWeek*, p. 84.

White, J., & Power, S. (2006, January 9). VW's Bernhard says labor costs dent profit. *The Wall Street Journal*, p. A10.

White, J. B., & McCracken, J. (2006, January 7). Troubled legacy: Auto industry, at a crossroads, finds itself stalled by history. *The Wall Street Journal*, p. B-1.

Wiles, R. (2003, February 18). Manage your money, control your future. *The Arizona Republic*, p. D-1.

Zellner, W. (1999, February 8). Southwest's new direction. *BusinessWeek*, pp. 58–59.

Zhang, H. (1995). Wealth effects of U.S. bank takeovers. *Applied Financial Economics, 5,* 329–336.

Zuckerman, G., McDonald, I., & Hawkins, L. (2006, January 12). If GM's big yield vanishes, investors may do the same. *The Wall Street Journal*, p. C-1.

Chapter 8

Armstrong, L. (1997, May 26). Powerwave technologies: Pump up the volume. *BusinessWeek*, p. 102.

Barker, E. (1999, June). Maker of rugged PCs crumbles in IPO bid. *Inc*, p. 25.

Baron, R. A. (1998). Cognitive mechanisms in entrepreneurship: Why and when entrepreneurs think differently than other people. *Journal of Business Venturing, 13,* 275–294.

Barrett, C. (2003, January 27). Good times and bad: Innovation is key. *Information Week*, p. 20.

Batelle, J. (2005). The 70 percent solution. *Business 2.0, 6,* 134.

Berringer, B. R., & Bluedorn, A. C. (1999). The relationship between corporate entrepreneurship and strategic management. *Strategic Management Journal, 20,* 421–444.

Bildner, J. (1995, July). Hitting the wall. *Inc,* pp. 21–22.

Borland, V.S. (2005). New directions for apparel and home fabrics. *Textile World, 155,* 53–55.

Brody, W.R. (2005). What happened to American innovation? *Chief Executive, 214,* 22–24.

Bruno, A. V., Leidecker, J. K., & Harder, J. W. (1987, March–April). Why firms fail. *Business Horizons,* pp. 50–58.

Bruno, A. V., & Tyebjee, T. (1985). The entrepreneur's search for capital. *Journal of Business Venturing, 1,* 61–74.

Burgelman, R. A. (1983). Corporate entrepreneurship and strategic management: Insights from a process study. *Management Science, 29,* 1349–1364.

Burgelman, R. A., Maidique, M. A., & Wheelwright, S. G. (1996). *Strategic management of technology and innovation* (2nd ed.). Burr Ridge, IL: Irwin.

Busenitz, L. A., & Barney, J. B. (1997). Differences between entrepreneurs and managers in large organizations: Biases and heuristics in strategic decision-making. *Journal of Business Venturing, 12,* 9–30.

Buttner, E. H., & Moore, D. P. (1997). Women's organizational exodus to entrepreneurship: Self-reported motivations and correlated with success. *Journal of Small Business Management, 34*(4), 1–13.

Byrt, F. (2005, Novermber 17). Clothes get wired at digital-edge design shops: Textronics foresees t-shirts that monitor heart rates, but market not yet certain. *The Wall Street Journal,* p. B4.

Callan, C., & Warshaw, M. (1995, September). The 25 best business schools for entrepreneurs. *Success,* pp. 37–54.

Carland, J., Hoy, F., Boulton, W., & Carland, J. (1984). Differentiating entrepreneurs from small business owners: A conceptualization. *Academy of Management Review, 9,* 354–359.

Cassidy, M. (2003, December 5). Creative marketing: The mouse tap. *Detroit Free Press,*www.freep.com/money/tech/mice5_20021205.htm, accessed February 19, 2003.

Cherwitz, R. A., & Sullivan, C. A. (2002). Intellectual entrepreneurship: A vision for graduate education. *Change, 34,* 23–28.

Covin, J. G., Slevin, D. P., & Covin, T. J. (1990). Content and performance of growth-seeking strategies: A comparison of small firms in high- and low-technology industries. *Journal of Business Venturing, 5,* 391–412.

DeCastro, J. D. (1997, March). When firms disappear have they really failed? *Colorado Business Review,* p. 3.

Dollinger, M. J. (1995). *Entrepreneurship.* New York: McGraw-Hill/Irwin.

Dubini, P., & Aldrich, H. (1991). Personal and extended networks are central to the entrepreneurial process. *Journal of Business Venturing, 6,* 305–313.

Eckberg, J. (2002, October 14). Innovation spells success. *Cincinnati Enquirer,* p. B6.

The Economist. (1993, July 10). Barefoot into PARC, p. 68.

The Economist (2005, December 10). Threads that think.

Engardio, P., Einhorn, B., Kripalini, M., Reinhardt, A., Nussbaum, B., & Burrows, P. (2005, March 21). Outsourcing innovation. *BusinessWeek Online.*

Fisher, R., & Ury, W. (1983). *Getting to yes.* New York: Penguin Books.

Gartner, W. B. (1985). A conceptual framework for describing the phenomena of new venture creation. *Academy of Management Review, 10,* 696–706.

Gartner, W. B. (1989). Who is an entrepreneur? Is the wrong question. *Entrepreneurship Theory and Practice, 13,* 47–64.

Gersick, C. J. (1994). Pacing strategic change: The case of a new venture. *Academy of Management Journal, 37,* 9–45.

Gomez-Mejia, L. R., Balkin, D. B., & Welbourne, T. (1990). Influence of venture capitalists on high tech management. *Journal of High Technology Management Research, 1,* 90–106.

Hambrick, D. C., & Crozier, L. M. (1985). Stumblers and stars in the management of rapid growth. *Journal of Business Venturing, 1,* 31–45.

Hamel, G., Doz, Y., & Prahalad, C. K. (1989, January–February). Collaborate with your competitors—and win. *Harvard Business Review,* pp. 133–139.

Heun, C. T. (2002, February 11). New "ink" veers display toward the good old look. *Informationweek,* p. 18.

Himelstein, L. (1998, September 7). Yahoo! The company, the strategy, the stock. *BusinessWeek,* pp. 66–76.

Hisrich, R. D., & Peters, M. P. (1998). *Entrepreneurship* (4th ed.). New York: McGraw-Hill/Irwin.

Hof, R. D. (1998, December 14). Amazon.com: The wild world of e-commerce. *BusinessWeek,* pp. 106–119.

Hofman, M. (1997, August). Desperation capital. *Inc,* pp. 54–57.

Hopkins, J. (2003, February 24). Start-up succeeding study says. *The Arizona Republic,* p. D1.

Jones, G. R., & Butler, J. E. (1992). Managing internal corporate entrepreneurship: An agency theory perspective. *Journal of Management, 18,* 733–749.

Kazanjian, R. K. (1988). Relation of dominant problems to stages of growth in technology-based new ventures. *Academy of Management Journal, 31,* 257–279.

Kirkpatrick, D. (2005). Throw it at the wall and see if it sticks. *Fortune, 152,* 142.

Klein, K.E. (2005, August 25). Minority startups: A measure of progress. *BusinessWeek Online.*

Kotter, J., & Sathe, V. (1978). Problems of human resource management in rapidly growing companies. *California Management Review, 21*(2), 29–36.

Kunze, R. J. (2001). The dark side of multilevel marketing: Appeals to the symbolically incomplete. Dissertation at Arizona State University.

Kuratko, D. F., & Hodgetts, R. M. (1992). *Entrepreneurship* (2nd ed.). Fort Worth: Dryden Press.

Larson, J. (2003). Musician beams with joy. *The Arizona Republic,* pp. D1, D2.

Lehn, D. I., Neely, C.W., Schoonover, K., Martin, T.L., Jones, M.T. (2004, January). E-TAGs: e-Textile attached gadgets. Paper presented at the Communication Networks and Distributed Systems Modeling and Simulation Conference.

Lesley, E., & Mallory, M. (1993, November 29). Inside the black business network. *BusinessWeek,* p. 70.

Lindsay, N., & Craig, J. (2002). A framework for understanding opportunity recognition: Entrepreneurs versus private equity financiers. *Journal of Private Equity, 6,* 13–24.

Lumpkin, G. T. (1996). Clarifying the entrepreneurial orientation construct and linking it to performance. *Academy of Management Review, 21,* 135–172.

Marsh, R. (2005, January/February). Ready, willing, & able. *BizAZ,* 37–43.

Martin, R.L. (2005, December 13). India and China: Not just cheap. *BusinessWeek Online.*

McNamee, M. (1997, September 1). Good news from small biz. *BusinessWeek,* p. 24.

Megginson, W. L., Boyd, M. J., Scott, C. R., & Megginson, L. C. (1997). *Small business management* (2nd ed.). Burr Ridge, IL: Irwin.

Meyer, G. D., & Dean, T. J. (1995, July). Why entrepreneurs fail. *Colorado Business Review,* pp. 3–4.

Mottram, B., Rigby, S., & Webster, A. (2003, January). The freedom to call your own shots. *Transmission & Distribution World, 55.*

Nadel, B. (2005). Unraveling the mysteries of innovation. *Fortune, 152,* 554–556.

National Commission on Entrepreneurship (2001). Five myths about entrepreneurs: Understanding how businesses start and grow. www.ncoe.org, accessed February 19, 2003.

Nussbaum, B., Berner, R., & Brady, D. (2005, August 1). Get creative! How to build innovative companies. *BusinessWeek Online.*

O'Reilly, B. (1999, June 7). What it takes to start a startup. *Fortune,* pp. 135–140.

Patnaik, D. (2005, December 21) The true measure of a good idea. *BusinessWeek Online.*

Pellet, J. (2002). Leading creative charge. *Chief Executive, 1,* 6–11.

Pinchot, G. (1985). *Intrapreneuring.* New York: Harper & Row.

Raz, T. (2003, January). The 10 secrets of a master networker, *Inc. Magazine,* pp. 90–99.

Riddle, D. (2000). Training staff to innovate. *International Trade Forum,* Issue 2, 28–30.

Russo, J. E., & Schoemaker, P. J. (1992). Managing overconfidence. *Sloan Management Review, 33*(2), 7–17.

Schlender, B. (1997, July 7). Cool companies. *Fortune,* pp. 84–110.

Schmitt, B. (2002, February). Growth signs for new "ink." *Chemical Week, 164,* 46.

Schubert, S. (2005). The ultimate silver lining: How Bill McNally turned his idea for an antibacterial fabric into $50 million sensation. *Business 20, 6,* 78.

Small Business Administration (2002). Small business by the numbers, www.sba.gov/advo/stats/, accessed April 6, 2003 (see "Small Business Frequently Asked Questions").

Statistical Abstracts of the United States. (1994). Washington, DC: U.S. Government Printing Office.

Stewart, W. H., Watson, W. E., Carland, J. C., & Carland, J. W. (1999). A proclivity for entrepreneurship: A comparison of entrepreneurs, small business owners, and corporate managers. *Journal of Business Venturing, 14,* 189–214.

The White House (2003). Taking action to strengthen small business, www.whitehouse.gov/infocus/smallbusiness/, accessed April 6, 2003.

Timmons, J. A. (1994). *New venture creation* (4th ed.). New York: McGraw-Hill/Irwin.

Usdansky, M. L. (1991, August 2). Asian businesses big winners in '80s. *USA Today,* p. 1A.

Useem, J. (1998, August). Partners on the edge. *Inc,* pp. 52–64.

Vincent, V. C. (1996). Decision-making policies among Mexican-American small business entrepreneurs. *Journal of Small Business Management, 34*(4), 1–13.

Williams, D. L. (1999). Why do entrepreneurs become franchisees? An empirical analysis of organizational choice. *Journal of Business Venturing, 14,* 103–124.

Chapter 9

Bartol, K. M., & Martin, D. C. (1998), *Management* (3rd ed.). New York: McGraw-Hill.

Brown, S., & Blackmon, K. (2005). *Journal of Management Studies, 42,* 793–815.

Budros, A. (1999). A conceptual framework for analyzing why organizations downsize. *Organization Science, 10,* 69–82.

Burns, T., & Stalker, G. (1961). *The management of innovation.* London, UK: Tavistock Institute.

Burrows, P. (1999, August 12). The boss: Carly Fiorina's challenge will be to propel staid Hewlett-Packard into the Internet age without sacrificing the very things that have made it great. *BusinessWeek,* pp. 76–84.

Byrne, J. A. (1998, June 8). Jack: A close-up look at how America's #1 manager views GE. *BusinessWeek,* pp. 40–51.

Caroll, P. (1993). *Big blues: The unmaking of IBM.* New York: Crown Publishers.

Clark, K., & Wheelwright, S. (1992). Organizing and leading "heavyweight" development teams. *California Management Review, 34*(2), 9–28.

Cobb, A. T. (1980). Informal influence in the formal organization: Perceived sources of power among work unit peers, *Academy of Management Journal, 23,* 55–61.

Crockett, R. O. (1998, May 4). How Motorola lost its way, *BusinessWeek,* pp. 140–148.

Crockett, R. O. (1999, June 21). Motorola is ringing again. *BusinessWeek,* p. 40.

Daft, R. L. (1983). *Organization theory and design,* St. Paul, MN: West Publishing Company.

Daft, R. L. (1997). *Management* (4th ed.). Fort Worth: Dryden Press.

Daft, R. L. (1999). *Leadership: Theory and practice.* Fort Worth: Dryden Press.

Das, S. (2006). Designing service processes: A design factor based process model. *International Journal of Services Technology and Management, 7* (1), p. 85.

Deal, T. E., & Kennedy, A. A. (1982). *Corporate cultures.* Reading, MA: Addison-Wesley.

Duncan, R. (1979, Winter). What is the right organization structure? Decision tree analysis provides the answer. *Organizational Dynamics,* pp. 59–80.

The Economist (1997, April 5). Conglomorates on trial, p. 59.

The Economist (1998, May 9). A new kind of car company, pp. 61–62.

The Economist (1999, January 9). How to merge: After the deal, pp. 21–23.

The Economist (2003, January 18). How to manage a dream factory, pp. 73–75.

Evans, B. (2005, December 19–26). Google becomes an irresistible force. *InformationWeek,* p. 76.

Fama, E. F. (1980). Agency problems and the theory of the firm. *Journal of Political Economy, 88,* 288–307.

Fama, E. F., & Jensen, M. L. (1983). Separation of ownership and control. *Journal of Law and Economics, 26,* 301–325.

Ford, R. C., & Randolph, W. A. (1992). Cross-functional structures: A review and integration of matrix organization and project management. *Journal of Management, 18,* 267–294.

Frank, K. A., & Fahrbach, K. (1999). Organization culture as a complex system: Balance and information models of influence and selection. *Organization Science, 10,* 253–277.

Freedman, A. M. (1988, October 20). Phillip Morris's bid for Kraft could limit product innovation. *The Wall Street Journal,* p. A1.

Garten, J. (1998, July 20). Daimler has to steer the Chrysler merger. *BusinessWeek,* p. 20.

Glasgall, W. (1998, April 20). Citigroup: Just the start? *BusinessWeek,* pp. 34–40.

Gomez-Mejia, L. R., Balkin, D. B., & Cardy, R. L. (1998). *Managing human resources* (2nd ed.). Upper Saddle River, NJ: Prentice Hall.

Gooding, R., & Wagner, J. (1985). A meta-analytic review of the relationship between size and performance: The productivity and efficiency of organizations and their subunits. *Administrative Science Quarterly, 30,* 462–481.

Hatch, M. J. (1997). *Organization theory.* Oxford, UK: Oxford University Press.

Hodge, B. J., & Anthony, W. P. (1979). *Organization theory.* Boston: Allyn and Bacon.

Hoskisson, R. E., & Hitt, M. A. (1994). *Downscoping: How to tame the diversified firm.* New York: Oxford University Press.

Jones, G. R. (1998). *Organizational theory* (2nd ed.). Reading, MA: Addison-Wesley.

Kirkpatrick, D. (1996, November 25). They're all copying Compaq. *Fortune,* pp. 28–32.

Kochan, T. A., & Osterman, P. (1994). *The mutual gains enterprise.* Boston: Harvard Business School Press.

Kraatz, M. S., & Zajac, E. J. (2001). How organizational resources affect strategic change and performance in turbulent environments: Theory and evidence. *Organization Science, 12,* 632–657.

Kruse, D. L. (1993). *Profit sharing.* Kalamazoo, MI: W. E. Upjohn Institute for Employment Research.

Lacy, S. (2006, January 23). The hardest job in Silicon Valley. *BusinessWeek,* pp. 65–66.

Larson, E. W., & Gobeli, D. H. (1987, Summer). Matrix management: Contradictions and insights. *California Management Review,* pp. 126–138.

Larsson, R., & Finkelstein, S. (1999). Integrating strategic, organizational, and human resource perspectives on mergers and acquisitions: A case survey of synergy realization. *Organization Science, 10,* 1–26.

Lawler, E. E. (1992). *The ultimate advantage.* San Francisco: Jossey-Bass.

McWilliams, G. (1998, February 9). Power play: How the Compaq-Digital deal will reshape the entire world of computers. *BusinessWeek,* pp. 90–97.

Meyer, M. (1998, July 6). The call of the wired. *Newsweek,* pp. 44–47.

Miller, A. (1998). *Strategic management* (3rd ed.). New York: McGraw-Hill/Irwin.

Miller, C., Glick, W., Wang, Y., & Huber, G. (1991). Understanding technology-structural relationships: Theory development and meta-analytic theory testing. *Academy of Management Journal, 34,* 370–399.

Mintzberg, H. (1979). *Structuring organizations.* Englewood Cliffs, NJ: Prentice Hall.

Montealegre, R., Nelson, J., Knoop, C., & Applegate, L. (1996). *BAE Automated Systems(A): Denver International Airport baggage-handling system.* Boston: Harvard Business School Publishing.

Moore, M. T. (1992, April 10). Hourly workers apply training in problem solving, *USA Today,* p. C1.

Murphy, K. R., & Cleveland, J. N. (1995), *Understanding performance appraisal.* Thousand Oaks, CA: Sage Publications.

Quinn, R. E., Faerman, S. R., Thompson, M. P., & McGrath, M. R. (1996). *Becoming a manager* (2nd ed.). New Yok: John Wiley & Sons.

Rebello, K. (1994, March 7). A juicy apple? *BusinessWeek,* pp 88–90.

Robbins, S. P., & Coulter, M. (1996.). *Management* (5th ed.). Upper Saddle River, NJ: Prentice Hall.

Robey, D., & Sayles, C. A. (1994). *Designing organizations.* Burr Ridge, IL: Irwin.

Silverman, G. (1999, August 16). Citigroup: So much for 50–50. *BusinessWeek,* p. 80.

Smart, T. (1996, October 28), Jack Welch's encore. *BusinessWeek,* pp. 155–160.

Smircich, L. (1983). Concepts of culture and organizational analysis. *Administrative Science Quartely, 28,* 339–358.

Smith, S. (2005, September 12). A date with digital. *Mediaweek,* pp. 38–39.

Van Fleet, D., & Bedeian, A. (1977). A history of the span of management. *Academy of Management Review, 2,* 356–372.

Whetton, D. A., & Cameron, K.S. (1995). *Developing management skills* (3rd ed.). New York: HarperCollins.

Woodward, J. (1965). *Industrial organizations: Theory and practice.* London: Oxford University Press.

Wright, P. M., & Noe, R. A. (1996). *Management of organizations.* Burr Ridge, IL: Irwin.

Chapter 10

Abelson, R. (2005, November 1). Dr. Saves-a-Lot. *New York Times,* pp. C-1, C-5.

Alpern, D. M. (1995, July). Why women are divided on affirmative action. *Working Woman,* p. 18.

Arizona Republic, (1997, January 25). Supermarket chain settles sex bias suit, p. E1.

Bernardin, H. J., & Cooke, D. K. (1993). Validity of an honesty test in predicting theft among convenience store employees. *Academy of Management Journal, 36,* 1097–1108.

Bloomberg News. (2006, January 13). Starbucks to add movie products. *New York Times,* p. C-5.

Blumenthal, R. (2006, January 13). In Houston, teachers get merit pay. *New York Times,* p. A-12.

BNA's Employee Relations Weekly. (1993, September 13). EEOC meets new, higher burden of proof in race bias case in California court, pp. 11, 991.

Branch, S. (1999, January 11). The 100 best companies to work for in America. *Fortune,* p. 118.

Burack, E. H. (1988). *Creative human resource planning and applications.* Englewood Cliffs, NJ: Prentice Hall.

Bureau of Labor Statistics. (1999). *Employment and earnings* (Tables 44 and 45). Washington, DC: Government Printing Office.

Carrell, M. R., & Heavrin, C. (1998). *Labor relations and collective bargaining.* Upper Saddle River, NJ: Prentice Hall.

Cowan, T. R. (1989). Drugs and the workplace. *Public Personnel Management, 16,* 313–322.

Damodt, M. G., Bryan, D. A., & Whitcomb, A. J. (1993). Predicting performance with letters of recommendation. *Public Personnel Management, 22,* 81–90.

Dessler, G. (2007). *Human resource management.* Upper Saddle River, NJ: Prentice Hall.

Eisenberg, D. (1999, August 16). We are for hire, just click. *Time,* pp. 46–50.

Filipzak, B. (1993, October). Training budgets boom. *Training,* pp. 37–44.

Fitzgerald, W. (1992). Training versus development. *Training and Development,* pp. 46–81.

Fortune. (2006, January 23). The 100 best companies to work for, pp. 89–108.

Foust, D., Grow, B., & Pascual, M. M. (2002, September 9). The changing heartland. *BusinessWeek,* pp. 80–82.

Goldstein, I. C. (1986). Training in organizations: Needs assessment, development, and evaluation (2nd ed.). Monterey, CA: Brooks/Cole.

Gomez-Mejia, L. R., & Blakin, D. B. (1992). *Compensation, organizational strategy, and firm performance.* Cincinnati, OH: South-Western Publishing.

Gomez-Mejia, L. R., Balkin, D. B., & Cardy, R. (2007). *Managing human resources.* Englewood Cliffs, NJ: Prentice Hall.

Gray, S. (2006, January 2). Fill'er up — with latte. *The Wall Street Journal,* p. A-1.

Griggs v. Duke Power Co., 401 U.S. 424 (1971).

Gunsch, D. (1993, September). Comprehensive college entry strengthens NCR's recruitment. *Personnel Journal,* pp. 58–62.

Henderson, R. I. (1997). *Compensation management* (7th ed.). Upper Saddle River, NJ: Prentice Hall.

Hill, C. W. C. (2007). *International business.* New York: McGraw-Hill/Irwin.

Hogan, R. (1991). Personality and personality measurement. In M. D. Dunnette, & L. M. Hough (Eds.), *Handbook of industrial and organization psychology* (2nd ed., vol. 1). Palo Alto, CA: Consulting Psychologists.

Holmes, S., Bennett, D., Carlisle, K., & Dawson, C. (2002, September 9). To keep up the growth, it must go global quickly. *BusinessWeek,* pp. 126–138.

HR News. (1994, February). No beard rule found to have disparate impact, p. 17.

Hunter, J. E. (1986). Cognitive ability, cognitive aptitudes, job knowledge, and job performance. *Journal of Vocational Behavior, 29,* 340–362.

Kasindorf, M. (1999, September 10). Hispanics and blacks find their futures entangled. *USA Today,* p. 21A.

Koretz, G. (1996, December 2). College majors that really pay. *BusinessWeek,* p. 34.

Levering, R., & Moskowitz, M. (2003, January 20). 100 best companies to work for. *Fortune,* pp. 127–150.

Longnecker, B. M., Petersen, B., & Hitt, R. (1999). Long-term incentives: How private companies can complete with public companies. *Compensation and Benefits Review, 31* (1), 44–53.

Lopez, J. A. (1993, October 6). Firms force job seekers to jump through hoops. *The Wall Street Journal,* pp. B1, B6.

Mandel, M. J. (1996, October 28). The high risk society: Coping with uncertainty. *BusinessWeek,* pp. 86–94.

McDonough, D. C. (1999, April 26). A fair workplace? Not everywhere. *BusinessWeek,* p. 6.

McEvoy, G. M., & Beatty, R. W. (1989). Assessment centers and subordinate appraisal of managers. *Personnel Psychology, 42,* 37–52.

Milkovich, G. T., & Newman, J. M. (2005). *Compensation* (8th ed.). New York: McGraw-Hill/Irwin.

Morris, B. (2006, January 23). No. 1 Genentech. *Fortune,* pp. 80–86.

Muchinsky, P. M. (1979). The use of reference reports in personnel selection. *Journal of Occupational Psychology, 52,* 287–297.

Murphy, K. R. (1993). *Honesty in the workplace.* Belmont, CA: Brooks/Cole.

Murphy, N. J. (1993). Performance measurement and appraisal. *Employment Relations Today,* pp. 47–62.

Newman, B. (2003, January 9). For ill immigrants, doctors' orders get lost in translation. *Wall Street Journal,* p. A-1.

Prasso, S. (2003, February 18). The UAW answers a cry for help. *BusinessWeek,* p. 8.

Ray, H. H., & Altmansberger, H. N. (1999). Introducing goal sharing in a public sector organization. *Compensation and Benefits Review, 31*(3), 40–45.

Reese, J. (1996, December 9). Starbucks: Inside the coffee cult. *Fortune,* pp. 191–200.

Reinhardt, A., & Holf, R. D. (1999, October 4). The search for the young and gifted. *BusinessWeek,* pp. 108–112.

Russell, C. J., Mattson, J., Devlin, S. E., & Atwater, D. (1990). Predictive validity of biodata items generated from retrospective life experience essays. *Journal of Applied Psychology, 75,* 569–580.

Rynes, S. L. (1991). Recruitment, job choice, and post hire consequences. *Handbook of industrial and organizational psychology* (2nd ed., Vol. 2, pp. 399–344).

Schwartz, N. D. (1999, May 24). Still perking after all these years. *Fortune,* pp. 203–210.

Shellenbarger, S. (2005, October 20). Work and family. *The Wall Street Journal,* p. D-1.

Stein, N. (2003, March 3). America's most admired companies. *Fortune,* pp. 81–94.

Symons, J. L. (1995, May–June). Is affirmative action in America's interest? *Executive Female,* p. 52.

Thottam, J. (2005, July 5). Reworking work. *Time,* pp. 50–55.

Time. (2003, March 10). Numbers, p. 17.

Useem, J. (1999, May 24). Read this before you put your résumé on line. *Fortune,* p. 290.

Useem, J. (1999, July 5). Getting job on line. *Fortune,* p. 69.

Walker, J. (1992). *Human resource management strategy.* New York: McGraw-Hill.

Wanous, J. P. (1992). *Organizational entry* (2nd ed.). Reading, MA: Addison-Wesley.

Wessel, D. (1989, September 7). Evidence is skimpy that drug testing works, but employers embrace the practice. *The Wall Street Journal,* p. B1.

White, E. (2005, November 28). How to reduce turnover. *The Wall Street Journal,* p. C-3.

Wright, P., Licthenfels, P., & Prusell, E. D. (1989). The structure interview: Additional studies and a meta-analysis. *Journal of Occupational Psychology, 6,* 191–199.

Chapter 11

Aji, A. (2006, February 5). Syrians burn embassies over cartoons. *Arizona Republic,* p. A-11.

Alonso-Zaldivar, R. (2003, February 1). Immigrants at 7 million, revised INS report says. *Arizona Republic,* p. A-5.

Alster, N. (2005, January 3). When grey heads roll. New York Times, p. B-3.

Anderson, J. (2006, January 10). Six women at Dresdner file bias suit. *New York Times,* p. C-1.

Armendariz, Y. (2003, February 10). Disabled workers can telecommute. *Arizona Republic,* p. D-3.

Ashton, A. (2002, February). Around-the-clock child care. *Working Women,* p. 14.

Banach, E. (1990, September). Today's supply of entry level workers reflect diversity. *Savings Institution,* pp. 74–75.

Bateman, T. S., & Snell, S. A. (1999). *Management: Building competitive advantage* (4th ed.). New York: McGraw-Hill/Irwin.

Berstein, R. (2006, February 13). The undoing of a done deal. *BusinessWeek,* p. 54.

Bilefsky, D. (2006, January 8). Denmark is unlikely front in Islam-West culture war. *New York Times,* p. 3.

Briefs. (2003, February 22). *Workforce strategies, 4*(2), WS-12.

Champion, M. (2006, February 3). Muslim outrage mounts over cartoons in EU. *The Wall Street Journal,* p. B-2.

Childs, T. (2005, Spring). Managing workforce diversity at IBM. Human Resources Management, 114(1), 73-77; www.ibm.com (2006).

Chu, J., & Mustafa, N. (2006, January 16). Between two worlds. *Time,* p. 67.

Colvin, G. (1999, July 19). 50 best companies for Asians, Blacks, and Hispanics. *Fortune,* pp. 52–59.

Cowell, A. (2006, February 2). More European papers print cartoons of Muhammad, fueling dispute among Muslims. *New York Times,* p. A-3.

Cowell, A. (2006, February 4). Cartoons force Danish Muslims to examine loyalties. *New York Times,* p. B-1.

Cox, T. H., & Blake, S. (1991). Managing cultural diversity: Implications for organizational competitiveness. *Academy of Management Executive, 5*(3), 45–46.

Coy, P. (2005, June 27). Surprise! The graying of the workforce is better news than you think. *BusinessWeek,* p. 78.

Crockett, R. O. (1999, May 24). African-Americans get the investing bug. *BusinessWeek,* p. 39.

Crossen, C. (2006, January 9). How U.S. immigration evolved as the nation grew and changed. *The Wall Street Journal,* p. B-3.

Doyle, R. (2002, February). Assembling the future. *Scientific American,* p. 30.

Egan, T. (2005, April 1). Wanted: Border hoppers. *Arizona Republic,* p. A-12.

Engardio, P., Matlack, C., Edmondson, G., Rowley, I., Barraclough, C., Smith, G. (2005, January 31). Global aging: Now, the geezer glut. *BusinessWeek,* pp. 44-47.

Fahrenthold, D. A. (2005, January 16). Cap on migrant workers hurting seafood processors. *Arizona Republic,* p. A-16.

Fellows, D. S. (2001). Striking gold in a silver mine: Leveraging senior workers as knowledge champions. *Worldatwork Journal, 10*(4), 1–12.

Fine, M. C., Johnson, P. L., & Ryan, S. M. (1990). Cultural diversity in the workplace. *Public Personnel Management, 19*(3), 305–319.

Fineman, H., & Lipper, T. (2003, January 23). Spinning race. *Newsweek,* pp. 27–38.

Fisher, A. (2005, March 31). How to battle the coming brain drain. *Fortune,* pp. 21–128.

Freudenheim, M. (2005, March 23). Help wanted: Older workers please apply. *New York Times,* p. A-1.

Gomez-Mejia, L. R., Balkin, D. B., & Cardy, R. (2007). *Managing human resources.* Englewood Cliffs, NJ: Prentice Hall.

Gomez-Mejia, L. R., Balkin, D. B., & Cardy, R. (2007). *Managing human resources.* New York: Prentice Hall.

Green, H. (2006, January 16). Chocolate mess. *BusinessWeek,* p. 14.

Greene, K. (2005, September 20). Bye-bye boomers? *The Wall Street Journal,* p. B-1.

Greenhouse, L. (2006, January 22). Broad survey of day laborers finds high level of injuries and pay violations. *New York Times,* p. A-17.

Grow, B. (2005, January 17). Tapping a market that is hot, hot, hot. *BusinessWeek,* p. 36.

Grow, B. (2005, July 18). Embracing illegals. *BusinessWeek,* p. 55.

Hastings, C. (2003, April). Engaging in a growing workforce. *Workspan,* pp. 35–39.

Helyar, J. (2006, May 10). 50 and fired. *Fortune*, pp. 78–86.

Jones, D. (1997, February 26). U.S. managers earn global credentials. *USA Today*, p. A1.

Jordan, M. (2006, January 24). Blacks vs. Latinos at work. *The Wall Street Journal*, p. B-1.

Kanmanm, J., & Rozenberg, H. (2002, February 7). Survey looks at residents with recent foreign roots. *Arizona Review*, p. A-8.

Kershaw, S. (2006, January 23). On Engine 22, it is women who answer the bell. *New York Times*, p. A-14.

Kiviat, B. (2005, August). Dessi dollars. Inside business issue, pp. A21–A23.

Koss-Feder, L. (1999, January 25). Spurred by the Americans with Disabilities Act, more firms take on those ready, willing and able to work. *Time*, p. 82.

Leduff, C., & Flores, E. (2005, February 9). The everymigrant's guide to crossing the border illegally. *New York Times*, p. A-16.

Levy, C. J. (2006, January 29). The new corporate outsourcing. *New York Times*, pp. D-1.

Magnusson, P. (2005, October 10). Wipsawed on the border. *BusinessWeek*, pp. 64–66.

McKinley, J. C. (2005, March 22). Mexican pride and death in U.S. service. *New York Times*, p. A-6.

McKinley, J. C. (2005, March 23). At Mexican border, tunnels, vile river, rusty fence. *New York Times*, p. A-8.

Mendosa, R. (1996, October). The $152 billion engine. *Hispanic Business*, pp. 28–29.

Millman, J. (2005, January 24). Changing face of immigrants. *The Wall Street Journal*, p. A-4.

Nassauer, S. (2006, January 9). France's new race relations. *The Wall Street Journal*, p. A11.

Newman, A. M. (2002, February). Fair shares. *Working Women*, pp. 64–71.

Pear, R. (2006, February 4). Bush to propose vast cost savings in Medicare plan. *New York Times*, p. B-1.

Prystay, C., & Ellison, S. (2003, February 27). Time for marketers to grow up? *The Wall Street Journal*, p. B-1.

Research National Phone Poll (1994, March 4). *Chattanooga Times*, p. 1.

Roberts, S. (2006, January 13). Come October, body count will make 300 million or so. *New York Times*, p. A-1.

Sessa, V. I., Jackson, S. E., & Rapini, D. T. (1995). Workforce diversity: The good, the bad, and the reality. In G. Ferris, S. D. Rosen, & D. T. Barnum (Eds.), H*andbook of human resource management* (pp. 263–282). Cambridge, MA: Blackwell Publishers.

Shellenbarger, S. (2005, October 20). You can work from home— Can you coach little league from the office? *The Wall Street Journal*, p. D-1.

Society for Human Resource Management. (2006). *HR resources.* http://www.shim.org/diversity.

Swarns, R. L. (2006, January 19). Chamber and two unions forge alliance on immigration bill. *The Wall Street Journal*, p. A-15.

Talking to diversity experts. (2003). http://www.fortune.com/sections.

Thornburgh, N. (2006, February 6). Inside the lives of the migrants next door. *BusinessWeek*, pp. 36–46.

Valdez, L. (2006, February 5). Migration a 2-nation concern. *Arizona Republic*, p. D-1.

Van Der Vegt, G. S., Ulert, E. V. & Huang, X. (2005). Location level links between diversity and innovative climate depend on national power distance. *Academy of Management Journal*, 48(6), 1171–1182.

Varadarajan, T. (2003, February 21). At least it is ok to back away with stereotypes. *The Wall Street Journal*, p. W-15.

Walsh, M. W. (2006, January 22). When your pension is frozen. *New York Times*, p. A-1.

Welch, J., & Welch, S. (2006, February 13). What is holding women back. *BusinessWeek*, p. 100.

Wheeler, M. L. (1996, December 9). Diversity: Making the business case. *BusinessWeek*, special advertising section.

Wheeler, M. L. (1996, December 14). Capitalizing on diversity. *BusinessWeek*, special advertising section.

Workspan. (2005, November 2). Aging workforce presents new opportunities, challenges for employers, p. 16.

Chapter 12

Adams, J. S. (1965). Inequity in social exchanges. In L. Berkowitz (Ed.), *Advances in experimental social psychology* (pp. 267–300). New York: Academic Press.

Adler, N. (1997). *International dimensions of organizational behavior* (3rd ed.). Cincinnati, OH: South-Western Publishing.

Alderfer, C. (1972). *Existence, relatedness, and growth: Human needs in organizational settings.* Glencoe, IL: Free Press.

Arnold, H. J. (1981, April) A test of the multiplicative hypothesis of expectancy-valence theories of work motivation. *Academy of Management Journal*, pp. 128–141.

Bass, B., Avolio, B., & Goodheim, L. (1987). Biography in the assessment of transformational leadership at the world class level. *Journal of Management*, 13, 7–20.

Bass, B. M. (1985). *Leadership and performance beyond expectations.* New York: Free Press.

Bass, B. M. (1990). *Bass and Stogdill's handbook of leadership: Theory, research and managerial application* (3rd ed.). New York: Free Press.

Bass, B. M., & Avolio, B. J. (1990, January). Developing transformational leadership: 1992 and beyond. *Journal of European Industrial Training*, p. 23.

Bennis, W., & Nanus, B. (1985). *Leaders: The strategies for taking charge.* New York: Harper & Row.

Blake, R. R., & Mouton, J. S. (1964). *The managerial grid.* Houston: Gulf.

Boyatzis, R. E. (1984). The need for close relationships and the manager's job. In D. A. Kolls, I. M. Rubin, & J. M. McIntyre (Eds.), *Organizational psychology: Readings on human behavior in organizations* (4th ed.). Englewood Cliffs, NJ: Prentice Hall.

Brooker, K. (1999, April 26). Can Procter and Gamble change its culture, protect its market share, and find the next Tide? *Fortune*, pp. 146–153.

Buhler, P. M. (2003). Managing in the new millennium. *SuperVision*, 64, 20–22.

Burns, J. M. (1978). *Leadership.* New York: Harper & Row.

BusinessWeek. (2001, January 8). The top 25 managers, pp. 60–81.

BusinessWeek. (2001, January 22). Can Texan Marjorie Scardino transform Britain's Pearson into a global media colossus? pp. 78–88.

Byrne, J. A. (1998, July 6). How Al Dunlap self-destructed. *BusinessWeek*, pp. 58–64.

Carvell, T. (1998, September 28). By the way … your staff. *Fortune*, pp. 200–206.

Chandler, S. (1999, October 17). Stumbling Sears seeks to launch 2nd revolution. *Arizona Republic*, p. D1.

Chang, J. (2003). Cracking the whip: In a perfect world, sales managers would use only positive incentives to get the best performance from their teams. But in less-than-ideal situations, is there a time and place for negative motivation? *Sales & Marketing Management*, 155, 241.

Charan, R., & Colvin, G. (1999, June 21). Why CEOs fail. *Fortune*, pp. 69–78.

Colvin, G. (1999, May 24). How to be a great CEO. *Fortune*, pp. 104–110.

Conger, J. A., & Kanungo, R. A. (1987). Toward a behavioral theory of charismatic leadership in organizational settings. *Academy of Management Review, 12*, 637–647.

Crockett, R. O. (2001, January 22). Motorola can't seem to get out of its own way. *BusinessWeek*, p. 72.

Darlington, H. (2002). People—your most important asset. *Supply House Times, 45*, 113–114.

Dickson, G. W., & DeSanctis, G. (Eds.) (2001). *Information technology and the future enterprise: New models for managers.* Upper Saddle River, NJ: Prentice Hall.

Early, P. C., Connolly, T., & Ekegren, G. (1989). Goals, strategy development, and task performance: Some limits on the efficacy of goal setting. *Journal of Applied Psychology, 74*, 24–33.

Fiedler, F. E. (1967). *A theory of leadership effectiveness.* New York: McGraw-Hill.

Fiedler, F. E. (1971). Validation and extension of the contingency model of leadership effectiveness. *Psychological Bulletin, 76*, 128–148.

Fisher, A. (1998, October 26). Success secret: A high emotional IQ. *Fortune*, pp. 295–298.

Foust, D., Smith, G., & Rocks, D. (1999, May 3). Man on the spot. *BusinessWeek*, pp. 142–152.

French, J., & Raven, B. (1959). The bases of social power. In D.Cartwright (Ed.), *Studies in social power.* Ann Arbor, MI: Institute for Social Research.

Garten, J. E. (2001). *The mind of the CEO.* New York: Basic Books/Perseus Publishing.

Gomez-Mejia, L. R., & Balkin, D. B. (1992). *Compensation, organizational strategy and firm performance.* Cincinnati, OH: South-Western Publishing.

Gomez-Mejia, L. R., Welbourne, T., & Wiseman, R. (2000). The role of risk sharing and risk taking under gainsharing. *Academy of Management Review, 25*(3), 492–509.

Grimaldi, L. (2005). Study proves recognition pays off. *Meetings & Conventions, 40*, 32.

Guyon, J. (1999, March 29). Getting the bugs out at VW. *Fortune*, pp. 96–99.

Hackman, J. R., Oldham, G., Janson, R., & Purdy, K. (1975). A new strategy for job enrichment. *California Management Review, 16*, 57–71.

Hamm, S., Sager, I., & Burrows, P. (1999, July 26). The lion in winter. *BusinessWeek*, pp. 108–120.

Hofstede, G. (1980). *Culture's consequences: International differences in work related values.* Beverly Hills, CA: Sage.

House, R. J. (1971). A path goal theory of leader effectiveness. *Administrative Science Quarterly, 16*, 321–338.

House, R. J., & Aditya, R. (1997). The social scientific study of leadership: Quo vadis? *Journal of Management, 23*(3), 409–475.

House, R. J., & Michell, T. R. (1974). Path goal theory of leadership. *Journal of Contemporary Business, 3*, 81–97.

House, R. J., Shane, S., & Herold, D. (1996). Rumors of the death of dispositional theory and research in organizational behavior are greatly exaggerated. *Academy of Management Review, 21*(1), 203–224.

Huey, J. (1994, February 21). The new post-heroic leadership. *Fortune*, pp. 42–50.

Hyer, N. L., & Wemmerlow, U. (2002). The office that lean built: Applying cellular thinking to administrative work. *IIE Solutions, 34*, 36–43.

Ivancevich, J. M., Lorenzi, P., Skinner, S. J., & Crosby, P. B. (1997). *Management: Quality and competitiveness.* Burr Ridge, IL: Irwin.

Jones, G. R., George, J. M., & Hill, C. W. (2001). *Contemporary management.* New York: McGraw-Hill/Irwin.

Kahn, R., & Katz, D. (1960). Leadership practices in relation to productivity and morale. In D.Cartwright & A.Sander (Eds.), *Group dynamics: Research and theory.* Elmsford, NY: Row, Peterson.

Kenny, D. A., & Hallmark, B. W. (1992). Rotation designs in leadership research. *Leadership Quarterly,, 3*(1), 25–41.

Kenny, D. A., & Zaccaro, S. J. (1983). An estimate of the variance due to traits in leadership. *Journal of Applied Psychology, 68*(4), 678–685.

Kerr, S., Schriesheim, C. A., Murphy, C. J., & Stogdill, R. M. (1974, August). Toward a contingency theory of leadership based upon the consideration and initiating structure literature. *Organizational Behavior and Human Performance*, pp. 62–82.

King, W. A., & Zeithaml, C. P. (2001). Competencies and firm performance. *Strategic Management Journal, 22*(1), 75–87.

Kirpatrick, D. (1999, May 24). Eckhard's fall, but the PC rocks on. *Fortune*, pp. 153–161.

Kulik, C. T., & Ambrose, M. L. (1992). Personal and situational determinants of referent choice. *Academy of Management Review, 17*, 212–237.

Kupfer, A. (1999, April 26). Mike Armstrong's AT&T. *Fortune*, pp. 82–86.

Le Pine, J. A., & Dyne, L. V. (2001). Peer responses to low performers: An attributional model of helping in the context of groups. *Academy of Management Review*, pp. 67–85.

Locke, E. (1968). Toward a theory of task motivation and incentives. *Organizational Behavior and Human Performance, 3*, 157–189.

Lord, R. G., DeVader, C. C., & Alleger, G. M. (1986). A meta-analysis of the relation between personality traits and leadership perceptions. *Journal of Applied Psychology, 71*(3), 402–410.

Manz, C., & Sims, H. P. (1990). *Superleadership.* New York: Berkeley.

Maslow, A. H. (1943, July). A theory of human motivation. *Psychological Review*, pp. 370–396.

McClelland, D. (1961). *The achieving society.* New York: Van Nostrand Reinhold.

McClelland, D. C., & Boyatzis, R. (1982). Leadership motive pattern and long-term success in management. *Journal of Applied Psychology, 67*, 737–743.

McClelland, D. C., & Winter, D. C. (1969). *Motivating economic achievement.* New York: Free Press.

McGregor, D. (1960). *The human side of enterprise.* New York: McGraw-Hill.

Mischel, W. (1973). Toward a cognitive social learning reconceptualization of personality. *Psychological Review, 80*, 252–283.

Muller, J. (2001, January 15). Thinking out of the cereal box. *BusinessWeek*, pp. 54–70.

Munk, N. (1999, April 12). How Levi's trashed a great American brand. *Fortune*, pp. 83–88.

O'Reilly, B. (1999, June 7). What it takes to start a startup. *Fortune*, pp. 135–139.

Osterloh, M., & Frey, B. S. (2000). Motivation, knowledge transfer, and organizational forms. *Organization Science, 11*(5), 538–551.

Palmer, B. (1999, June 21). Hasbro's new action figure. *Fortune*, pp. 189–192.

Randolph, D.S. (2005). Predicting the effect of extrinsic and intrinsic job satisfaction factors on recruitment and retention of rehabilitation professionals. *Journal of Healthcare Management, 50*, 49.

Reason, T. (2003). Incentive confrontation: A bitter dispute over bonuses highlights the hazards of incentive pay. *CEO: The Magazine for Senior Financial Executives, 19*, 46–51.

Robbins, S. P. (1999). *Organizational behavior* (7th ed.). Englewood Cliffs, NJ: Prentice Hall.

Ronen, S. (1986, April). Equity perception in multiple comparisons: A field study. *Human Relations*, pp. 333–346.

Rosenbush, S. (2001, February 5). Armstrong's last stand. *BusinessWeek*, pp. 88–91.

Sales & Marketing Management, 155 (2003). Little carrots, big results, p. 36.

Rynes, S. L., Gerhart, B., & Minette, K. A. (2004). The importance of pay in employee motivation: Discrepancies between what people say and what they do. *Human Resource Management, 43*, 381–394.

Saposnick, K. (2001). Achieving breakthrough business results through personal change: An interview with Rick Fox. Pegasus Communications, accessed February 26, 2003 at http://www.pegasuscom.com/levpoints/foxint.html.

Schlender, B. (1999, April 12). E-business according to Gates. *Fortune*, pp. 75–80.

Schurenberg, E. (1999, May 24). The fly boys. *Fortune*, pp. 236–240.

Schwab, D. P., & Cummings, L. L. (1970, October). Theories of performance and satisfaction: A review. *Industrial Relations*, pp. 403–430.

Shalley, C. E. (1991). Effects of productivity goals, creativity goals, and personal discretion on individual creativity. *Journal of Applied Psychology, 76*, 179–185.

Shellenbarger, S. (1997, March 19). Investors seem attracted to firms with happy employees. *The Wall Street Journal*, p. B1.

Shipper, F., & Manz, C. C. (1992, Winter). Employee self-management without formally designated teams: An alternative road to empowerment. *Organizational Dynamics*, pp. 48–61.

Simonton, D. K. (1987). Presidential inflexibility and veto behavior: Two individual situational interactions. *Journal of Personality, 55*(1), 1–18.

Spragins, E. (2002). Unmasking your motivations. *Fortune Small Business, 12*, 861.

Stogdill, R. M. (1948). Personal factors associated with leadership: A survey of the literature. *Journal of Psychology, 25*, 35–71.

Stogdill, R. M. (1974). *Handbook of leadership: A survey of theory and research*. New York: Free Press.

Stogdill, R. M., & Coons, A. E. (1957). *Leader behavior: Its description and measurement*. Columbus, OH: Ohio State University Press.

Summers, T. P., & DeNisi, A. S. (1990, June). In search of Adam's other: Reexamination of referents used in the evaluation of pay. *Human Relations*, pp. 495–511.

Symonds, W., Smith, G., & Judge, P. (1999, June 21). Fisher's photo finish. *BusinessWeek*, pp. 34–36.

Vroom, V. H. (1964). *Work and motivation*, New York: John Wiley & Sons.

Wahba, M., & Birdwell, L. (1975) Maslow reconsidered: A review of the need hierarchy theory. *Organizational Behavior and Human Performance, 15*(2), 212–240.

Weiss, H. (1977) Subordinate imitation of supervisor behavior: The role of modeling in organizational socialization. *Organizational Behavior and Human Performance, 19*, 89–105.

White, R., & Lippit, R. (1960). *Autocracy and democracy: An experimental inquiry*. New York: Harper & Brothers.

Zellner, W. (1999, August 16). Earth to herb: Pick a co-pilot. *BusinessWeek*, pp. 70–73.

Chapter 13

All a matter of priorities. (2003, February 10). *Editor and Publisher*.

Anders, G. (2003, January 13). Carly Fiorina, up close—How shrewd strategic moves in grueling proxy battle let H-P chief take control. *The Wall Street Journal*, Eastern Edition, p. B1.

Blank, D. (2003). A matter of ethics: In organizations where honesty and integrity rule, it is easy for employees to resist the many temptations today's business world offers. *Internal Auditor, 60*, 26, 31.

Biskupic, J. (2002), July 24). Why it's tough to indict CEOs. *USA Today*, pp. A1, A2.

Carpenter, L. (2002). Inspirational leadership. *Management Services, 46*, 34–36.

Foss, B. (2002, December 30). Corporate image: Greed, deceit, handcuffs, *The Arizona Republic*, p. D4.

Gale, S. F. (2002). Building leaders at all levels. *Workforce, 81*, 82–85.

Gitomer, J. (2005, April 18). Define leadership: Now redefine it in terms of you. *Business Record (Des Moines)*, pp. 23, 31.

Kaufman, B. (2003). Stories that sell, stories that tell: Effective storytelling can strengthen an organization's bonds with all of its stakeholders. *Journal of Business Strategy, 24*, 11.

Kraemer, H. M. J. (2003). Do the right thing: Practice values-based leadership. *Executive Excellence, 20*, 5–6.

Ronan, J. (2003). A boot to the system: How does a training company shake up its leadership style? It marches its managers off to boot camp. *T & D, 57*, 38.

Tyler, K. (2003). Sink-or-swim attitude strands new managers. *HRMagazine, 48*, 78–83.

Vasilash, G. S., Sawyer, C. A., & Kelly, K. M. (2005). Nissan: The extraordinary happens every day. *Automotive Design & Production, 117*, 48.

Chapter 14

Albanese, R. E., & Van Fleet, D. D. (1985). Rational behavior in groups: The free-riding tendency. *Academy of Management Review, 10*, 244–255.

Balkin, D. B., Dolan, S., & Forgues, K. (1997). Rewards for team contributions to quality. *Journal of Compensation and Benefits, 13*(1), 41–46.

Banker, R. A., Field, J. M., Schroeder, R. G., & Sinha, K. K. (1996). Impact of work teams on manufacturing performance: A longitudinal field study. *Academy of Management Journal, 42*, 58–74.

Bantel, K., and Jackson, S. (1989). Top management and innovations in banking: Does the demography of the top team make a difference?*Strategic Management Journal, 10*, 107–124.

Bunderson, J., & Sutcliffe, K. (2002). Comparing alternative conceptualizations of functional diversity in management teams: Process and performance effects. *Academy of Management Journal, 45*, 875–893.

Carbonara, P. (1997, March). Fire me. I dare you! *Inc.*, pp. 58–64.

Caudron, S. (1993, December). Are self-directed teams right for your company?*Personnel Journal*, pp. 76–84.

Chang, A., Bordia, P., & Dune, J. (2003). Punctuated equilibrium and linear progression: Toward a new understanding of group development. *Academy of Management Journal, 4*, 106–117.

Cohen, S. G., & Bailey, D. E. (1997). What makes teams work: Group effectiveness research from the shop floor to the executive suite. *Journal of Management, 23*, 239–290.

Daft, R. L. (2002). *The leadership experience* (2nd ed.). Cincinnati, OH: South-Western.

Daly, R. E., & Nicoll, D. (1997). Accelerating a team's developmental process. *OD Practitioner, 24*(1), 20–28.

Deming, W. E. (1986). *Out of the crisis*. Cambridge, MA: MIT Press.

Denton, D. K. (1992). Multi-skilled teams replace old work systems. *HR Magazine, 37*, 48–56.

Dumaine, B. (1990, May 7). Who needs a boss? *Fortune*, pp. 52–60.

Dumaine, B. (1994, September 5). The trouble with teams. *Fortune*, pp. 86–92.

Fan, E., & Grueneld, D. (1998). When needs outweigh desires: The effects of resource interdependence and reward interdependence on group problem solving. *Basic and Applied Social Psychology, 20*, 45–56.

Fisher, B., & Boynton, A. (2005, July–August). Virtuoso teams. *Harvard Business Review*, pp. 117–123.

Fisher, R., & Ury, W. (1981). *Getting to yes: Negotiating agreement without giving in*. New York: Penguin Books.

Geber, B. (1992, June). Saturn's grand experiment. *Training*, pp. 27–35.

Gersick, C. J. (1988). Time and transition in work teams: Toward a new model of group development. *Academy of Management Journal, 31*, 9–41.

Gross, S. E. (1995). *Compensation for teams*. New York: American Management Association.

Hammer, M., & Champy, J. (1993). *Reengineering the corporation.* New York: HarperCollins.

Hammer, M., & Champy, J. (1994, April). Avoiding the hottest new management cure. *Inc.,* pp. 25–26.

Hertel, G., Geister, S., & Kouradt, U. (2005). Managing virtual teams: A review of current empirical research. *Human Resource Management Review, 15,* 69–95.

Hosmer, L. T. (1995). Trust: The connecting link between organizational theory and philosophical ethics. *Academy of Management Review, 20,* 379–403.

Jones, G. R., & George, J. M. (1998). The experience and evolution of trust: Implications for cooperation and teamwork. *Academy of Management Review, 23,* 531–546.

Katzenbach, J. R., & Smith, D. K. (1993, March–April). The discipline of teams. *Harvard Business Review,* pp. 111–120.

Kets De Vries, M. F. (1999, Winter). High performance teams: Lessons from the pygmies. *Organizational Dynamics,* pp. 66–77.

Kidwell, R. E., & Bennett, N. (1993). Employee propensity to withhold effort: A conceptual model to intersect three avenues of research. *Academy of Management Review, 18,* 429–456.

Kirkman, B. L., & Rosen, B. (1999). Beyond self-management: Antecedents and consequences of team empowerment. *Academy of Management Journal, 42,* 58–74.

Kreitner, R., & Kinicki, A. (1995). *Organizational behavior* (3rd ed.). Burr Ridge, IL: Irwin.

Labich, K. (1996, February 16). Elite teams get the job done. *Fortune,* pp. 90–99.

Lawler, E. E. (1992). *The ultimate advantage.* San Francisco: Jossey-Bass.

Lewicki, R., & Litterer, J. (1985). *Negotiation.* Burr Ridge, IL: Irwin.

Maidique, M. A., & Hayes, R. H. (1984). The art of high-technology management. *Sloan Management Review, 25,* 18–31.

Mayer, R. C., Davis, J. H., & Schoorman, F. D. (1995). An integrative model of organizational trust. *Academy of Management Review, 20,* 709–734.

Montemayor, E. F. (1995, Summer). A model for aligning teamwork and pay. *ACA Journal,* pp. 18–25.

Nelson, B. (1994). *1001 ways to reward employees.* New York: Workman Publishing.

O'Lone, R. (1991, June 3). 777 revolutionizes Boeing aircraft development process. *Aviation Week and Space Technology,* pp. 34–36.

Osborne, C. (2001). *Dealing with difficult people.* London: DK.

Phillips, J. M. (1999). Antecedents of leader utilization of staff input in decision-making teams. *Organizational Behavior and Human Decision Processes, 77,* 215–242.

Rahim, M. A. (1983). A measure of styles of handling interpersonal conflict. *Academy of Management Journal, 26,* 368–376.

Raz, T. (2003, May). Taming the Savage Genius: The delicate art of managing employees who are way, way smarter than you. *Inc.,* pp. 33–35.

Sashkin, M., & Kiser, K. J. (1993). *Putting total quality management to work.* San Francisco: Barrett-Koehler.

Shaiken, H., Lopez, S., & Mankita, I. (1997). Two routes to team production: Saturn and Chrysler compared. *Industrial Relations, 36,* 17–45.

Shaw, M. (1981). *Group dynamics: The psychology of small group behavior.* New York: Harper.

Steers, R. M. (1984). *Introduction to organizational behavior.* Glenview, IL: Scott, Foresman.

Thompson, L. (2004). *Making the team: A guide For managers* (2nd ed.). Upper Saddle River, NJ: Pearson.

Tjosvold, D. (1993). *Learning to manage conflict: Getting people to work together cooperatively.* New York: Lexington Books.

Townsend, A. M., DeMarie, S. M., & Hendrickson, A. R. (1996, September). Are you ready for virtual teams? *HR Magazine,* pp. 123–126.

Varela, J., Fernandez, P., & Del Rio, M. (2005, December). Cross-functional conflict, conflict handling behaviors, and new product performance in Spanish firms. *Creativity and Innovation Management, 14,* 355.

Wageman, R. (1995). Interdependence and group effectiveness. *Administrative Science Quarterly, 40,* 145–180.

Wall, J. A. (1985). *Negotiation: Theory and practice.* Glenview, IL: Scott, Foresman.

Wecker, J. (1998, October 12). Powers of Persuasion. *Fortune,* pp. 161–164.

Weiss, W. H. (1999). Teams and teamwork. *Supervision, 59(7),* 9–11.

Whetton, D. A., & Cameron, K. S. (1995). *Developing management skills* (3rd ed.). New York: HarperCollins.

Zand, D. E. (1972). Trust and managerial problem solving. *Administrative Science Quarterly, 17,* 229–239.

Chapter 15

Brake, D. (2003). *Dealing with e-mail.* London: DK.

Conlin, M. (2002, September 30). Watch what you put in that office e-mail. *BusinessWeek,* pp. 114–115.

Creighton, J. L. (1998, January). The cybermeeting's about to begin. *Management Review,* pp. 29–31.

Daft, R. L. & Lengel, R. H. (1986). Organizational information requirements, media richness, and structural design. *Managerial science, 32,* 554–572.

Falcone, P. (1998, October). Communication breakdown. *HR Focus,* p. 8.

Fried, J. (2005, October). Everything you ever wanted to know about e-mail. *Inc.,* pp. 113–128.

Greengrad, S. (1998, September). 10 ways to protect intranet data. *Workforce,* pp. 78–81.

Knapp, M. (1980). *Essentials of nonverbal communication.* New York: Holt, Rinehart and Winston.

Labinch, K. (1999, March 1). Boeing finally hatches a plan. *Fortune,* pp. 100–106.

McCune, J. C. (1998, July/August). That elusive thing called trust. *Management Review,* pp. 10–16.

McDermott, M. (1996, September). Boeing's modern approach. *Profiles,* pp. 41–44.

Munter, M. (1993, May-June). Cross-cultural communication for managers. *Business Horizons,* pp. 69–78.

Osborn, C. (2001). *Dealing with Difficult People.* London: DK.

Pearl, J. (1993, July). The e-mail quandry. *Management Review,* p. 3.

Price, C. (1994). *Assertive Communication.* Boulder, CO: Career Track.

Rice, R. E. (1991). Task analyzability, use of new media, and effectiveness: A multi-site exploration of media richness. *Organization Science, 2,* 475–500.

Robbins, S. P., & Hunsaker, P. L. (1996). *Training in interpersonal skills* (2nd ed). Upper Saddle River, NJ: Prentice Hall.

Rogers, E., & Albritton, M. (1995, April). Interactive communications technologies in business organizations. *Journal of Business Communication, 32,* 177–195.

Sullivan, C. (1995, January). Preferences for electronic mail in organizational communication tasks. *Journal of Business Communication, 32,* 49–64.

Thumma, S. A. (1998, July). E-mail zaps the workplace. *HR Focus,* p. 9.

Townsend, A., DeMarie, S., & Hendrickson, A. (1996, September). Are you ready for virtual teams? *HR Magazine,* pp. 123–126.

Volkema, R., & Niederman, F. (1996, July). Planning and managing organizational meetings: An empirical analysis of written and oral communication. *Journal of Business Communication,* pp. 275–293.

Weeks, D. (1995, February). Voice mail: Blessing or curse? *World Traveler,* pp. 51–54.

Wellner, A. (2005, September). Lost in translation. *Inc.,* pp. 37–38.

Wellner, A. (2005, January). Playing well with others: Office cliques sap morale and kill productivity. Does your firm have them? *Inc.*, pp. 29–31.

Chapter 16

Blessings in disguise. (2003). *Snack, Food & Wholesale Bakery, 92*, 18.

Brandman, B. (2001). How $1.2 million of inventory vanished into thin air. *Transportation & Distribution, 42*, 31–38.

Cardy, R. L. (2004). *Performance management: Concepts, skills, and exercises*. Armonk, NY: M. E. Sharpe.

Deming, W. E. (1986). *Out of the crisis*. Cambridge, MA: MIT Center for Advanced Engineering Study.

Drickhammer, D. (2002). Goosing the bottom line. *Industry Week, 251*, 24–28.

Godfrey, G., Dale, B., Marchington, M., & Wilkinson, A. (1997). Control: A contested concept in TQM research. *International Journal of Operations & Production Management, 17*, 558–573.

Hartshorn, D. (2003). Solving accident investigation problems: Thorough accident investigations can be one of the most valuable exercises that companies undertake, yet too few have policies and programs in place to carry them out. *Occupational Hazards, 65*, 56–60.

Libby, T. (2003a). Budgeting—an unnecessary evil: A European idea to drop budgeting altogether is starting to find receptive ears in North America. *CMA Management, 77*, 30–33.

Libby, T., & Lindsay, M. (2003b). Budgeting—an unnecessary evil, part two: How the BPRT envisions a world without traditional budgeting. *CMA Management, 77*, 28–31.

Mann, J. (2003). Handwashing: Technology adds a measure of management. *Foodservice Equipment & Supplies, 56*, 39.

McClenahen, J. S. (2002). Mapping manufacturing: Remarkable results at Medtronic's medical-devices plant flow from value-stream mapping. *Industry Week, 251*, 62–64.

Mission: Maintain satisfaction: Smart implementation plus the right system add up to happy guests. (2003). *Hotel & Motel Management, 218*, p. M7.

Nozar, R. A. (2001). Guest's input helps develop standards. *Hotel and Motel Management, 216*, 36.

Rust, R. T., Zeithaml, V. A., & Lemon, K. N. (2000). *Driving customer equity*. New York: Free Press.

Schmitt, V. (2001). Water treatment: Pouring on the service. *Chemical Week, 164*, 20.

Williamson, D. (2005). Managing the key cultural dimensions of control and risk. *European Business Forum, 21*, 41–45.

Chapter 17

Aston, A., & Arndt, M. (2003, May 5). The flexible factory: Leaning heavily on technology, some U.S. plants stay competitive with offshore rivals. *BusinessWeek*, pp. 90–91.

Bickens, J., & Elliott, B. B. (1997). *Operations management: An active learning approach*. Cambridge, MA: Blackwell.

Braganza, A., & Myers, A. (1998). *Business process redesign: A view from the inside*. Boston: Thomson.

Bremner, B. (2000, May 23). Nissan's Ghosn: Can he bring back Japan's samurai spirit? *BusinessWeek*.

Connor, G. (2003). Benefiting from six sigma. *Manufacturing Engineering, 130*, 53–59.

D'Aveni, R. (1994). *Hypercompetition*. New York: Free Press.

Deming, W. E. (1986). *Out of the crisis*. Cambridge, MA: MIT Press.

Deming, W. E. (1981–1982, Winter). Improvement of quality and production through action by management. *National Productivity Review, 1*, 12–22.

Deming, W. E. (1986). Out of the crisis. Cambridge, MA: Center for Advanced Engineering Study.

Drickhamer, D. (2005). The kanban E-volution. *Material Handling Management, 60*, 24–26.

Faltin, D. M., & Faltin, F. W. (2003). Toe the line: No more Worldcoms. *Quality Progress, 36*, 29–35.

Gabor, A. (1990). *The man who discovered quality*. New York: Times Books.

Galuszka, P. (1999, November 8). Just-in-time manufacturing is working overtime. *BusinessWeek*.

Garvin, D. (1988). *Managing quality: The strategic and competitive edge*. New York: Free Press.

Garvin, D. (1984, Fall). What does product quality really mean? *Sloan Management Review, 26*, 24–25.

Gourlay, R. (1994, January 4). Back to basics on the factory floor. *Financial Times*, p. 12.

Hammer, M., & Champy, J. (1993). *Reengineering the corporation*. New York: Harper Business.

How to spot counterfeit parts: Caveat emptor, or buyer beware, is appropriate advice for buyers sourcing in China. (2002). *Purchasing, 131*, 31.

Imai, M. (1986). *Kaizen: The key to Japan's competitive success*. New York: Random House.

JIT just won't be the same: Security rules could affect cross border trade, (2003, May). *World Trade, 16*, 28.

Jones, G. R., George, J. M., & Hill, C. W. L. (2000). *Contemporary management*, 2nd ed. New York: McGraw-Hill/Irwin. The Kaizen Institute. www.kaizen-institute.com.

Kontoghiorghes, C. (2003). Examining the association between quality and productivity performance in a service organization. *The Quality Management Journal, 10*, 32–42.

Krajewski, L. L., & Ritzman, L. R. (2001). *Operations management: Strategy and analysis*, 6th ed. Upper Saddle River, NJ: Prentice Hall.

Kren, L. (2005). Decline of U.S. manufacturing threatens national security. *Machine Design, 77*, 173.

Logothetis, N. (1992). *Managing for total quality*. Hertfordshire, UK: Prentice Hall International.

Loyd, L. (January 9, 2006). Wyeth signs three biotech product deals—The agreements were an indicator of the direction that major pharmaceutical companies are heading. *The Philadelphia Inquirer*, section C, p. 01.

Markland, R. E., Vickery, S. K., & Davis, R. A. (1998). *Operations management: Concepts in manufacturing and service*, 2nd ed. Cincinnati: South-Western Publishing.

Melnyk, S., & Denzler, D. (1996). *Operations management*. New York: McGraw-Hill/Irwin.

Noon, C. E., Hankings, C. T., & Cote, M. J. (2003). Understanding the impact of variation in the delivery of healthcare services. *Journal of Healthcare Management, 48*, 82–98.

Porter, M. E. (1985). *Competitive advantage*. New York: Free Press.

Powell, T. C. (1995, January). Total quality management as competitive advantage: A review and empirical study. *Strategic Management Journal*, pp. 15–37.

Russell, R. S., & Taylor, B. W. (2000). *Operations management*. Upper Saddle River, NJ: Prentice Hall.

Skinner, W. (1969, May/June). Manufacturing—Missing link in corporate strategy. *Harvard Business Review*, pp. 136–145.

Slack, N. (1997). *The Blackwell encyclopedia of operations management*. Cambridge, MA: Blackwell.

Stevenson, W. (2001). *Operations management*, 7th ed. New York: McGraw-Hill.

Stocker, G. (2003). Use symbols instead of words. *Quality Progress, 35*, 68–72.

Taiichi, O. (1990). *Toyota production system.* Cambridge, MA: Productivity Press.

Young, S. M. (1992, October). A framework for successful adoption and performance of Japanese manufacturing practices in the United States. *Academy of Management Review, 17,* 677–701.

Chapter 18

Alter, S. (2002). *Information systems: Foundations of e-business* (4th ed.). Upper Saddle River, NJ: Prentice Hall.

Ante, S. E. (2000, June 19). The second coming of software. *Businessweek Online.*

Austrian, G. (1982). *Herman Hollerith: Forgotten giant of information processing.* New York: Columbia University Press.

Baker, R. H. (1997). *Extranets: The complete sourcebook.* New York: McGraw-Hill.

Black, J. (2001, April 26). Tracking customers while preserving their anonymity. *BusinessWeek.*

Buckhout, S., Frey, E., & Nemec, J. (1999, second quarter). Making ERP succeed: Turning fear into promise. *Strategy and Business.*

Cate, F. H. (1997). *Privacy in the information age.* Washington, DC: Brookings Institute.

Chandler, A. D. (1977). *The visible hand.* Cambridge, MA: Harvard University Press.

Cortada, W. J. (1997). *Best practices in information technology: How corporations get the most value from exploiting their digital investments.* Upper Saddle River, NJ: Prentice Hall.

Davis, G. B. (1997). *The Blackwell encyclopedic dictionary of management information systems.* Cambridge, MA: Blackwell.

The Economist. (2002, October 26). A survey of digital security, p. 4.

The Economist. (2004, June 15). Spyware: The hidden menace, p. 61.

The Economist Technology Quarterly. (2004, June 12). A golden vein, pp. 22–23.

Evans, P., & Wurster, T. S. (2000). *Blown to bits: How the new economics of information transforms strategy.* Boston: Harvard Business School Press.

Gilster, P. (1997). *Digital literacy.* New York: John Wiley & Sons.

Gonzalez, J. S. (1998). *The 21st century intranet.* Upper Saddle River, NJ: Prentice Hall.

Grow, B. (2005, May 30). Hacker hunters. *BusinessWeek,* pp. 74–82.

Hallows, J. E. (1997). *Information systems project management: How to deliver functions and value in information technology projects.* New York: AMACOM.

Hellriegel, D., Jackson, S. E., & Slocum, J. W. (1999). *Management,* 8th ed. Cincinnati, OH South-Western Publishing.

Jones, G. R., George, J. M. & Hill, C. W. L. (2000). *Contemporary management,* 2nd ed. New York: McGraw-Hill/Irwin.

Keenan, F. (2002, September 2). You're only as good as your password. *BusinessWeek,* pp. 77–80.

Kroenke, D. (2007). *Using MIS.* Upper Saddle River, NJ: Pearson.

Lashin, P., & Rich, E. (1983). *Artificial intelligence.* New York: McGraw-Hill.

Luconi, F. L., Malone, T. W., & Morton, M. S. S. (1996, Summer). Expert systems: The next challenge for managers. *Sloan Management Review.*

Miles, M. (2001, December 17). Firestone, Ford feud. *Tire Business.*

Pinsonneault, A., & Kraemer, K. L. (1993, September). The impact of information technology on middle managers. *MIS Quarterly,* pp. 271–292.

Rigby, D., & Ledingham, D. (2004, November). CRM done right. *Harvard Business Review,* pp. 118–129.

Rigby, D., & Vishwanath, V. (2006, April). Localization: The revolution in consumer markets. *Harvard Business Review,* pp. 82–92.

Ross, J. W., & Weill, P. (2002, November). Six decisions your IT people shouldn't make. *Harvard Business Review,* p. 88.

Ross, P. E. (1995, May 22). Software as career threat. *Forbes,* pp. 240–246.

Stair, R. M., & Reynolds, G. W. (2001). *Fundamentals of information systems.* Boston: Thompson Learning.

Stoffer, H. (2002, February 18). Explorer ruling helps Ford, but legal woes remain. *Automotive News.*

Teresko, J. (1999, February 19). Information rich, knowledge poor. *Industry Week.*

Voelpel, S., Dous, M., & Davenport, T. (2005, May). Five steps to creating a global knowledge-sharing system: Siemens' ShareNet. *Academy of Management Executive,* pp. 9–23.

Watson, H. J., Houdeshel, G., & Rainer, R. K. (1997). *Building executive information systems and other support applications.* New York: John Wiley & Sons.

Weckert, J., & Adeney, D. (1997). *Computer and information ethics.* Westport, CT: Greenwood.

glossary

a

absolute judgments   A performance appraisal approach in which the performance of employees is evaluated against performance standards, and not in comparison to each other.

academy culture   A type of organization culture that seeks to hire people with specialties and technical mastery who will be confined to a set of jobs within a particular function and will be rewarded by long-term association and a slow, steady climb up the organization ladder.

acceptance sampling   An operations management monitoring tool in which a sample of materials or products is measured against a benchmark.

accommodation strategy   A means of dealing with stakeholder groups when a firm decides to accept social responsibility for its business decisions after pressure has been exerted by stakeholder groups.

accountability   The expectation that the manager or other employee with authority and responsibility must be able to justify results to a manager at a higher level in the organizational hierarchy.

acquisition   The process of purchasing other firms.

actions   The specific steps the firm intends to take to achieve the desired objectives.

adjourning stage   A stage of team development in which teams complete their work and disband, if designed to do so.

administrative management   The management approach that examines an organization from the perspective of the managers and executives responsible for coordinating the activities of diverse groups and units across the entire organization.

adversarial relations   U.S. labor laws view management and labor as natural adversaries who want to have a larger share of the firm's profits and who must reach a compromise through collective bargaining.

adverse impact   A form of discrimination, also called *disparate impact*, that occurs when one standard that is applied to all applicants or employees negatively affects a protected class.

affirmative action   A federal government–mandated program that requires corporations to provide opportunities to women and members of minority groups who traditionally have been excluded from good jobs; it aims to accomplish the goal of fair employment by urging employers to make a conscious effort to hire members of protected classes.

aggressive communication   A forceful style of communication with others that expresses dominance and even anger. The needs and wants of others are ignored.

assessing   Evaluating the environmental data received to accurately specify the implications for the firm.

assessment phase   A career development step in which employees are helped to choose personally fitting career paths that are realistically attainable and to determine any obstacles they need to overcome to succeed.

attribution theory   The idea that the major function of the leader is to be blamed or given credit for a bad or a good situation, even if the leader has little or no control over the factors that led to the results.

authority   The formal right of a manager to make decisions, give orders, and expect the orders to be carried out.

avoiding style   Conflict resolution used when the individual decides it is better to avoid the conflict rather than to deal with it.

b

balanced scorecard   A technique designed to control and improve
(1) customer service,
(2) learning and growth,
(3) finance, and
(4) internal business processes

bankruptcy   A legal procedure that distributes company assets to creditors and protects the debtor from unfair demands of creditors when the debtor fails to make scheduled loan repayments.

base compensation   The fixed amount of money the employee expects to receive in a paycheck weekly or monthly or as an hourly wage.

baseball team culture   The fast-paced, competitive, high-risk form of corporate culture typically found in organizations in rapidly changing environments, with short product life cycles, with high-risk decision making, and dependent on continuous innovation for survival.

behavioral anchored rating scales   Performance appraisal tools that assess the effectiveness of the employee's performance using specific examples of good or bad behaviors at work.

behavioral appraisal instruments
Performance appraisal tools that assess certain employee behaviors, such as coming to work on time, completing assignments within stipulated guidelines, and getting along with co-workers.

behavioral perspective The management view that knowledge of the psychological and social processes of human behavior can result in improvements in productivity and work satisfaction.

benchmarking A strategic management approach that assesses capabilities by comparing the firm's activities or functions with those of other firms.

benefits A compensation component that accounts for almost 40 percent of the typical total compensation package and includes health insurance, pension plans, unemployment insurance, vacations, sick leave, and the like.

bona fide occupational qualification (BFOQ) A defense against discrimination in which a firm must show that a personal characteristic must be present to do the job.

bottom-up change Organizational change that originates with employees.

boundaryless organization design A management design that eliminates internal and external structural boundaries that inhibit employees from collaborating with each other or that inhibit firms from collaborating with customers, suppliers, or competitors.

brainstorming A technique to generate creative ideas for solving problems by reducing critical and judgmental reactions to ideas from group members.

brand managers A management role that coordinates the ongoing activities of marketing branded consumer products.

budgeting Controlling and allocating the firm's funds; *variable budgeting* allows for deviations between planned output and actual output by considering the fact that variable costs depend on the level of output, whereas fixed costs do not; *moving budgeting* creates a tentative budget for a fixed period of time and then revises and updates it on a periodic basis to take changes into account.

bureaucratic control A formal control approach involving a cycle of (1) establishing standards, (2) performance measurement, (3) identifying gaps, and (4) corrective action.

bureaucratic management The management approach that examines the entire organization as a rational entity, using impersonal rules and procedures for decision making.

business ethics *See* Ethics.

business network A firm's alliances formed with other businesses to achieve mutually beneficial goals.

business plan The business's blueprint that maps out its business strategy for entering markets and that explains the business to potential investors.

business process A value-adding, value-creating activity such as product development or order fulfillment.

business unionism Unions that focus on "bread and butter" issues such as wages, benefits, and job security.

C

capacity The firm's ability to produce the product during a given period.

career path The steps and a plausible time frame for accomplishing them for advancement to a career goal.

centralization The location of decision authority at the top of the organization hierarchy.

certainty The condition when all the information needed to make a decision is available.

chain of command The superior–subordinate authority relationship that starts at the top of the organization hierarchy and extends to the lowest levels.

change agents People who act as catalysts and assume responsibility for managing change.

charismatic leader A leader who can engender a strong emotional attachment from followers; charisma is associated with admiration, trust, and a willingness to believe what the leader says.

civil law The legal system that relies on a comprehensive set of rules that form part of a highly structured code; enforcement and interpretation of laws are made in reference to this code.

clan control Culture-based control.

classical perspective The management perspective formed during the 19th and early 20th centuries, with the evolution of the factory system and the formation of modern corporations, to meet the challenges of managing large, complex organizations.

club culture A form of organizational culture that seeks people who are loyal, committed to one organization, and need to fit into a group and rewards them with job security, promotion from within, and slow progress.

coaching Ongoing, mostly spontaneous, meetings between managers and their employees to discuss career goals, roadblocks, and available opportunities.

coalitions Political alliances between managers who agree on goals and priorities.

code of ethics A formal statement of the company's ethics and values that is designed to guide employee conduct in a variety of business situations.

coercive power Power based on the fear that the leader may cause people harm unless they support him or her.

cohesiveness The emotional closeness group members feel toward each other and how supportive they are of each other.

collective bargaining Negotiations between union and management with little, if any, government involvement.

common law The legal system in which precedents based on past court decisions play a key role in interpreting the meaning and intent of legal statutes.

communication The process of transmitting meaningful information from one party to another through the use of shared symbols.

communication channel Influences the quantity and quality of information that is conveyed to the receiver. Channels of communication include face-to-face conversations, group meetings, memos, policy manuals, e-mail, voice mail.

compensable factors A set of evaluation criteria used in job evaluation.

competitive behavior   Team behavior that views other people as rivals for a limited pool of resources and focuses on individual goals, noncollaboration, and the withholding of information.

compromising style   Conflict resolution used when the manager or team member makes some concessions to the other party and the other party is willing to reciprocate.

computer ethics   The analysis of the nature and social impact of computer technology and the development of policies for its appropriate use.

concentration strategy   A form of diversification strategy that focuses on a single business operating in a single industry segment.

concentric diversification strategy   A form of diversification strategy in which the firm expands by creating or acquiring new businesses related to the firm's core business.

conduct of training phase   A stage in the training process that ensures training will solve an organizational problem or need; this step is critical to ensuring that training will be beneficial to the organization.

confrontation strategy   One means a firm may use to deal with a stakeholder group whose goals are perceived to threaten company performance; the firm may use the courts, engage in public relations, or lobby against legislation.

conglomerate diversification   A form of diversification strategy that involves managing a portfolio of businesses that are unrelated to each other.

consideration   The behavioral dimension of leadership involving the concern that the leader has for the feelings, needs, personal interest, problems, and well-being of followers; also called *employee-oriented behaviors.*

content validity   The measurement that the selection process represents the actual activities or knowledge required to successfully perform the job.

contingency theory   The management theory that there is no "one best way" to manage and organize an organization because situational characteristics, called contingencies, differ; also, the view that no HR strategy is "good" or

"bad" in and of itself but rather depends on the situation or context in which it is used.

control   The process of comparing performance to standards and taking corrective action.

controlling   The management function that measures performance, compares it to objectives, implements necessary changes, and monitors progress.

conversion process   The operations management stage in which the product's inputs are converted to the final product.

cooperative behavior   Team behavior that is manifested in members' willingness to share information and help others.

cooperative strategies   Establishing partnerships or strategic alliances with other firms.

coordination   Linking activities so that diverse departments or divisions work in harmony and learn from each other.

core competencies   The unique skills and/or knowledge an organization possesses that give it an edge over competitors.

core values   A firm's principles that are widely shared, that operate unconsciously, and that are considered nonnegotiable.

corporate credo   A formal statement focusing on principles and beliefs, indicating the company's responsibility to its stakeholders.

corporate-level strategy   The corporation's overall plan concerning the number of businesses the corporation holds, the variety of markets or industries it serves, and the distribution of resources among those businesses.

corporate social responsibility   The belief that corporations have a responsibility to conduct their affairs ethically and to be judged by the same standards as people.

corporation   A form of business that is a legal entity separate from the individuals who own it.

cost leadership strategy   Providing products and services that are less expensive than those of competitors.

cultural symbols   The acts, events, or objects that communicate organizational values, used by management to convey and sustain shared meaning among employees.

culture shock   The reaction when exposed to other cultures (social

structure, religion, language, and historical background) with different norms, customs, and expectations.

d

damage control strategy   A means a firm may use to deal with a stakeholder group when it decides that it may have made mistakes and wants to improve its relationship with the stakeholders and to elevate its public image.

data   Raw facts, such as the number of items sold or the number of hours worked in a department.

databases   Computer programs that assign multiple characteristics to data and allow users to sort the data by characteristic.

data mining   The process of determining the relevant factors in the accumulated data to extract the data that are important to the user.

data warehouses   Massive databases that contain almost all of the information about a firm's operations.

debt financing   A means of obtaining financial resources that involves obtaining a commercial loan and setting up a plan to repay the principal and interest.

decentralization   The location of decision authority at lower levels in the organization.

decision acceptance   The aspect of decision making that is based on people's feelings; decision acceptance happens when people who are affected by a decision like it.

decision making   The process of identifying problems and opportunities and resolving them.

decision quality   The aspect of decision making that is based on such facts as costs, revenues, and product design specifications.

decision scope   The effect and time horizon of the decision.

decoding   Translating the symbolic verbal, written, or visual symbols into an undistorted, clear message.

delegation   The transfer of decision-making authority from a manager to a subordinate or a team at a lower level in the organization.

Delphi technique   A decision-making technique in which group members are presented with a problem and complete an anonymous questionnaire soliciting solutions; the results are tabulated, summarized, and returned to the group members, and each is asked again for solutions; the process continues until a consensus decision is reached.

departmentalization The horizontal basis for organizing jobs into units in an organization.

development and conduct of training phase A stage in the training process that ensures training will solve an organizational problem or need; this step is critical to ensuring that training will be beneficial to the organization.

development phase A career development step in which actions are designed to help the employee grow and learn the necessary skills to move along the desired career path.

devil's advocate The role of criticizing and challenging decision alternatives that are agreed on by other members of the group, to induce creative conflict and possibly alternative, better solutions.

differentiation strategy Delivering products and services that customers perceive as unique.

direction phase The step in career development that involves determining the steps employees must take to reach their career goals.

discrimination The unfair treatment of employees because of personal characteristics that are not job-related.

disparate treatment A form of discrimination that occurs when an employer treats an employee differently because of his or her protected class status.

diversification strategy A firm's strategic plan to create and manage a mix of businesses owned by the firm.

diversity The wide spectrum of individual and group differences.

divestiture The corporate process of selling a business in order to generate cash, which the corporation can better deploy elsewhere, or to refocus on its core related businesses, which are better understood by management.

divisional approach A departmentalization approach, sometimes called the product approach, that organizes employees into units based on common products, services, or markets.

division of labor The production process in which each worker repeats one step over and over, achieving greater efficiencies in the use of time and knowledge; also, the formal assignment of authority and responsibility to job holders.

dominating style Conflict resolution used when the manager or team member acts assertively and forcefully and persuades the other party to abandon his or her objectives.

downsizing A management strategy used to reduce the scale and scope of a business to improve its financial performance.

downward communication Sending a message from a high position in the organization to an individual or group lower in the hierarchy.

Drug-Free Workplace Act Federal legislation that requires employers to implement policies that restrict drug use.

dysfunctional conflict Conflict that has a negative effect on team and organizational performance.

e

e-business The process of conducting business transactions using online resources; also called *e-commerce*.

e-commerce Any business transaction executed electronically by companies or consumers.

e-mail Electronic mail.

empirical validity Statistical evidence that the selection method distinguishes between higher and lower performing employees.

employment at will A very old legal doctrine stating that unless there is an employment contract (such as a union contract or an implied contract), both employer and employee are free to end the employment relationship whenever and for whatever reasons they choose.

empowerment The process of transferring control of individual work behavior from the supervisor to the employee.

encounter stage The stage of socialization at which the individual begins to compare expectations about the firm's culture with reality.

enterprise resource planning (ERP) software A computer program that combines all of a firm's computerized functions into a single, integrated software program that runs off a single database, allowing various departments to easily share information and communicate with each other.

entrepreneur An individual who creates an enterprise that becomes a new entry to a market.

entrepreneurship The process of creating a business enterprise capable of entering new or established markets by deploying resources and people in a unique way to develop a new organization.

equity financing A means of obtaining financial resources that involves the sale of part of the ownership of the business to investors.

equity theory The view that people's perceptions about the fairness of the rewards they receive relative to their contributions affect their motivations.

ERG theory A theory of needs based on three core groups: existence, relationships, and growth (ERG).

escalation of commitment The refusal to abandon an earlier decision even when it is no longer appropriate, which happens because the decision maker is highly committed to a course of action and wants to stay the course.

espoused values The aspects of corporate culture that are not readily observed but instead can be perceived from the way managers and employees explain and justify their actions and decisions.

ethical policy statements A firm's formal guidelines that provide specific formulas for employees' ethical conduct.

ethical structure The procedures and the division or department within a company that promotes and advocates ethical behavior.

ethics Principles that explain what is good and right and what is bad and wrong and that prescribe a code of behavior based on these definitions. Business ethics provide standards or guidelines for the conduct and decision making of employees and managers.

ethics training A means of providing employees and managers practice in handling ethical dilemmas that they are likely to experience.

ethnocentric approach An approach to managing an international subsidiary that involves filling top management and other key positions with people from the home country (expatriates).

ethnocentrism A belief that may become prevalent among majority-group employees, meaning that they believe that their way of doing things, their values, and their norms are inherently superior to those of other groups and cultures.

evaluation The organization's reexamination of whether training is providing the expected benefits and meeting the identified needs.

expectancy theory The view that having the strength to act in a particular way depends on people's beliefs that their actions will produce outcomes they find valuable and attractive.

expert power Power deriving from the leader's unique knowledge or skills, which other people recognize as worthy of respect.

expert system An advanced information system that uses human knowledge captured in a computer to solve problems that normally require human expertise.

exporting A means of entering new markets by sending products to other countries and retaining production facilities within domestic borders.

external equity The perceived fairness of the compensation employees receive relative to what other companies pay for similar work.

external locus of control A strong belief that luck, fate, or other factors control one's progress, causing feelings of helplessness and decreasing intensity of goal-seeking efforts in the face of failure.

extinction Withholding of a positive consequence following desired behavior.

extranets Also called *wide-area networks*, networks that link a company's employees, suppliers, customers, and other key business partners in an electronic online environment for business communications.

extrinsic motivation Motivation that comes from the rewards that are linked to job performance, such as a paycheck.

f

facilities The design and location of an operation.

facilities layout The grouping and organization of equipment and employees.

facilities layout design The physical arrangement for the facility that will allow for efficient production.

facts Bits of information that can be objectively measured or described, such as the retail price of a new product, the cost of raw materials, the defect rate of a manufacturing process, or the number of employees who quit during a year.

Family and Medical Leave Act Federal legislation that requires employers to provide unpaid leave for childbirth, adoption, and illness.

feedback Information received back from the receiver, which allows the sender to clarify the message if its true meaning is not received.

feelings An individual's emotional responses to decisions made or actions taken by other people.

firewall A combination of computer hardware and software that controls access to and transmission of data and information contained in a network.

first-mover advantage The important advantage enjoyed by firms that recognize a market's potential before others do and thus typically outperform firms that are late entrants.

flexible manufacturing Operations management techniques that help reduce the setup costs associated with the production system.

force-field analysis A model of organizational change that states that two sets of opposing forces are at equilibrium before a change takes place and put at disequilibrium to make change come about: the driving forces, which are pushing for change, and the restraining forces, which are opposed to change.

forecasting Predicting what is likely to happen in the future, the intensity of the anticipated event, its importance to the firm, and the pace or time frame in which it may occur.

formalization The degree to which written documentation is used to direct and control employees.

formal planning A system designed to deliberately identify objectives and to structure the major tasks of the organization to accomplish them.

forming stage The first stage of team development, which brings the team members together for the first time so they can get acquainted and discuss their expectations.

fortress culture An organization culture with the primary goal of surviving and reversing business problems, including economic decline and hostile competitors.

franchising A means of entering new markets similar to licensing, mainly used by service companies, in which the franchisee pays a fee for using the brand name and agrees to strictly follow the standards and abide by the rules set by the franchise.

free riders Individuals who find it rational to withhold their effort and provide minimum input to the team in exchange for a full share of the rewards.

functional analysis A strategic management approach that establishes organizational capabilities for each of the major functional areas of the business.

functional conflict Conflict that stimulates team and organizational performance.

functional structure A departmentalization approach that clusters people with similar skills in a department.

g

Gantt charts A visual sequence of the process steps used in planning, scheduling, and monitoring production.

General Agreement on Tariffs and Trade (GATT) A treaty signed by 120 nations to lower trade barriers for manufactured goods and services. In 1993, the GATT negotiations in Uruguay, known as the Uruguay Round, created the World Trade Organization to ensure compliance by member nations.

geocentric approach An approach to managing an international subsidiary in which nationality is deliberately downplayed, and the firm actively searches on a worldwide or regional basis for the best people to fill key positions.

geographic-based divisions   A variation of the product-based departmentalization structure in which divisions are organized by geographic region.

glass ceiling   The intangible barrier that prevents women and minorities from rising to the upper levels in business.

global shift   A term used to characterize the effects of changes in the competitive landscape prompted by worldwide competition.

grapevine   Informal communication that takes place at the workplace.

groupthink   Team behavior that occurs when members prefer to avoid conflict rather than tolerate a healthy diversity of opinions; valuing social harmony over doing a thorough job.

h

Hawthorne effect   The finding that paying special attention to employees motivates them to put greater effort into their jobs (from the Hawthorne management studies, performed from 1924 through 1932 at Western Electric Company's plant near Chicago).

horizontal communication   Communication between a sender and a receiver at a similar level in the organization.

horizontal dimension   The organizational structure element that is the basis for dividing work into specific jobs and tasks and assigning jobs into units such as departments or teams.

horizontal information flows   The flow of information from one department up through management layers and then back down to another department through other layers.

HR tactics   The implementation of human resource programs to achieve the firm's vision.

human relations approach   A management approach that views the relationships between employees and supervisors as the most salient aspect of management.

i

illusion of control   The tendency for decision makers to be overconfident of their ability to control activities and events.

implementation guidelines   The planning step that shows how the intended actions will be carried out.

individualism   The degree to which a society values personal goals, autonomy, and privacy over group loyalty, commitment to group norms, involvement in collective activities, social cohesiveness, and intense socialization; ethical decisions based on individualism promote individual self-interest as long as it does not harm others.

information   Data that have been gathered and converted into a meaningful context.

information richness   The potential information-carrying capacity of data.

initiating structure   The behavioral dimension of leadership that refers to activities designed to accomplish group goals, including organizing tasks, assigning responsibilities, and establishing performance standards; also called *production-oriented behaviors*.

inputs   The supplies needed to create a product, which can include materials, energy, information, management, technology, facilities, and labor.

intangible resources   Resources that are difficult to quantify and include in a balance sheet, which often provide the firm with the strongest competitive advantage.

integrating manager   A management position designed to coordinate the work of several different departments; the integrating manager is not a member of any of the departments whose activities are being coordinated.

integrating style   Conflict resolution demonstrated by framing the issue as a problem and encouraging the interested parties to identify the problem, examine alternatives, and agree on a solution.

interdependence   The extent that team members depend on each other for resources, information, assistance, or mutual support to accomplish their tasks.

internal equity   The perceived fairness of the pay structure within a firm.

internal locus of control   A strong belief in one's own ability to succeed, so that one accepts responsibility for outcomes and tries harder after making mistakes.

Internet   A computer network with multimedia communication capabilities, allowing a combination of text, voice, graphics, and video to be sent to a receiver; a network of networks, connecting hundreds of thousands of corporate, educational, and research computer networks around the world.

intranets   Private or semiprivate internal networks.

intrapreneurship   A form of business organization in which new business units are developed within a larger corporate structure in order to deploy the firm's resources to market a new product or service; also called *corporate entrepreneurship.*

intrinsic motivation   Motivation that comes from the personal satisfaction of the work itself.

intrinsic reward design theory   The perspective that a potent motivator for work is the intangible reward people derive from performing well in a job they find interesting, challenging, and intriguing and that provides an opportunity for continued learning.

intuition   When a decision maker depends on gut feelings or innate beliefs as a basis for making a decision.

inventory   The stock of raw materials, inputs, and component parts that the firm keeps on hand.

j

job analysis   The systematic gathering and organizing of information about the tasks, duties, and responsibilities of various jobs.

job-based unionism   Unions that are organized by type of job.

job characteristics model   According to this model, the way jobs are designed produces critical psychological states which in turn affect key personal and work-related outcomes.

job description   A formal document that identifies, defines, and describes the duties, responsibilities, and working conditions.

job evaluation   A rational, orderly, and systematic judgment of how important each job is to the firm and how each job should be compensated.

job preview   Information about positive and negative aspects of the job that is provided to potential applicants.

job relatedness   A defense against discrimination claims in which the firm must show that the decision was made for job-related reasons.

job rotation   A formal program in which employees are assigned to different jobs to expand their skills base and to learn more about various parts of the organization.

job specification   The knowledge, skills, and abilities needed to successfully perform the job.

joint venture   A means of entering new markets where two or more independent firms agree to establish a separate firm; the firms normally own equivalent shares of the joint venture and contribute a corresponding proportion of the management team.

justice approach   An approach to decision making based on treating all people fairly and consistently when making business decisions.

just-in-time (JIT)   The concept behind creating the firm's product in the least amount of time.

k

kaizen   The Japanese process of continuous improvement in the organization's production system from numerous small, incremental improvements in production processes.

kanban   A form of JIT system originated in Japan that uses cards to generate inventory; from the Japanese word for "card" or "sign."

knowledge workers   Employees who manage information and make it available to decision makers in the organization.

l

labor contract   A written agreement negotiated between union and management.

labor demand   The forecast of how many and what type of workers the organization will need in the future.

labor supply   The availability of workers with the required skills to meet the firm's labor demand.

leadership substitute view   The leadership theory that contends that people overestimate the effect of leaders even when leader behaviors are irrelevant, so organizations need to develop mechanisms to replace or substitute the influence role assigned to leaders.

leading   The management function that energizes people to contribute their best individually and in cooperation with other people.

learning organization   The management approach based on an organization anticipating change faster than its counterparts to have an advantage in the market over its competitors.

legitimate power   The legal or formal authority to make decisions subject to certain constraints.

liaison role   A management role used to facilitate communications between two or more departments.

licensing   A means of entering new markets, primarily used by manufacturing firms, by transferring the rights to produce and sell products overseas to a foreign firm. In return, the licensing company receives a negotiated fee, normally in the form of a royalty.

line authority   The control by a manager of the work of subordinates by hiring, discharging, evaluating, and rewarding them.

line managers   The level of management positions that contribute directly to the strategic goals of the organization.

load chart   A type of Gantt chart that is based on departments or specific resources that are used in the process.

long-term/short-term orientation   The extent to which values are oriented toward the future (saving, persistence) as opposed to the past or present (respect for tradition, fulfilling social obligations).

m

make–buy analysis   An operations management tool used to help make the decision as to whether to produce an item or to purchase it.

management by objectives (MBO)   A performance appraisal strategy in which employees and supervisors agree on a set of goals to be accomplished for a particular period; performance is then assessed at the end of the period by comparing actual achievement against the agreed-on goals.

management by wandering around (MBWA)   Dropping in unannounced at a work site and engaging employees in spontaneous conversations.

management information system (MIS)   An information system that provides information to managers to use in making decisions.

managerial grid   A system of classifying managers based on leadership behaviors.

masculinity/femininity   The degree to which a society views assertive or "masculine" behavior as important to success and encourages rigidly stereotyped gender roles.

Maslow's hierarchy of needs   The theory that people tend to satisfy their needs in a specified order, from the most to the least basic.

materials requirements planning (MRP)   The process of analyzing a design to determine the materials and parts that it requires in the production process.

matrix approach   A departmentalization approach that superimposes a divisional structure over a functional structure in order to combine the efficiency of the functional approach with the flexibility and responsiveness to change of the divisional approach.

mechanistic organization design   A management design based on the classical perspective of management, emphasizing vertical control with rigid hierarchical relationships, top-down "command and control" communication channels, centralized decision authority, highly formalized work rules and policies, and specialized, narrowly defined jobs; sometimes called a *bureaucratic design*.

mentoring   Developmental activities carried out by more seasoned employees to help those who are learning the ropes.

merger   The process of integrating two firms.

metamorphosis stage   The stage of socialization at which the employee is induced to bring his or her values and ways of doing things closer to those of the organization.

monitoring   Observing environmental changes on a continuous basis to determine whether a clear trend is emerging.

monoculture The homogeneous organizational culture that results from turnover of dissimilar employees.

Muslim law The legal system based on religious Muslim beliefs that regulates behavior; strict interpretation and enforcement varies significantly from country to country.

n

NAFTA The major economic alliance in the Americas.

need for achievement A strong drive to accomplish things, in which the individual receives great satisfaction from personal attainment and goal completion.

need for affiliation A strong desire to be liked by others, to receive social approval, and to establish close interpersonal relationships.

need for power The desire to influence or control other people.

needs assessment A training tool that is used to determine whether training is needed.

negative reinforcement The removal of unpleasant consequences associated with a desired behavior, resulting in an increase in the frequency of that behavior.

noise Anything that can interfere with sending or receiving a message.

nominal group technique (NGT) A decision-making technique that helps a group generate and select solutions while letting group members think independently; group members are given the problem and each presents one solution without discussion; then all solutions are discussed, evaluated, and ranked to determine the best alternative.

nonconforming high performer A team member who is very individualistic and whose presence is disruptive to the team.

nonprogrammed decision The process of identifying and solving a problem when a situation is unique and there are no previously established routines or procedures that can be used as guides.

nonverbal communication The sending and decoding of messages with emotional content. Important dimensions include body movements and gestures, eye contact, touch, facial expressions, physical closeness, and tone of voice.

norming stage A stage in team development that is characterized by resolution of conflict and agreement over team goals and values.

o

objectives The goals or targets that the firm wishes to accomplish within a stated amount of time.

obliging style Conflict resolution demonstrated when the party managing the conflict is willing to neglect his or her own needs in order to accommodate the needs of the other party.

office automation systems An operations information system used to maintain and publish information for an organization.

off-the-job training Training that takes place away from the employment site.

one-way communications Communication channels that provide no opportunity for feedback.

on-the-job training (OJT) Training that takes place in the actual work setting under the guidance of an experienced worker, supervisor, or trainer.

operational action plan A management plan normally created by line managers and employees directly responsible for carrying out certain tasks or activities.

operational decisions Decisions with a short time perspective, generally less than a year, and that often are measured on a daily or weekly basis.

operational managers The firm's lower-level managers who supervise the operations of the organization.

operational perspective The management perspective formed during the 19th and early 20th centuries when the factory system and modern corporations evolved to meet the challenges of managing large, complex organizations.

operations management The process an organization uses to obtain the materials or ideas for the product it provides, the process of transforming them into the product, and the process of providing the final product to a user.

opportunistic planning A type of planning that involves programmatic actions triggered by unforeseen circumstances; it can coexist with formal planning and can help the formal plan function more smoothly.

optimizing Selecting the best alternative from among multiple criteria.

order review/release (ORR) activity An operations management tool that is used to evaluate and track the order through the process, including creating order documentation, material checking, capacity evaluation, and load leveling (releasing orders so that the work load is evenly distributed).

organic organization design A management design that is focused on change and flexibility, emphasizing horizontal relationships that involve teams, departments, or divisions, and provisions to coordinate these lateral units.

organizational culture A system of shared values, assumptions, beliefs, and norms that unite the members of an organization.

organization chart A graphic depiction that helps summarize the lines of authority in an organization.

organization design The selection of an organization structure that best fits the strategic goals of the business.

organization politics The exercise of power in an organization to control resources and influence policy.

organization structure The formal system of relationships that determines lines of authority (who reports to whom) and the tasks assigned to individuals and units (who does what task and with which department).

organizing The management function that determines how the firm's human, financial, physical, informational, and technical resources are arranged and coordinated to perform tasks to achieve desired goals; the deployment of resources to achieve strategic goals.

outcome appraisal instruments Performance appraisal tools that measure workers' results, such as sales volume, number of units produced, and deadlines met.

owners The parties that have invested a portion of their wealth in shares of company stock and have a financial stake in the enterprise.

p

parallel teams Sometimes called *problem-solving teams* or *special-purpose teams,* groups that focus on a problem or issue that requires only part-time commitment from team members.

partial productivity The measurement of the contribution of a single input, such as labor or materials, to the final product.

partnership A form of business that is an association of two or more persons acting as co-owners of a business.

passive-aggressive communication Style of communication whereby individual avoids giving direct responses to other's requests or feedback.

passive communication Style of communication whereby individual does not let others know directly what he or she wants or needs.

path–goal theory A contingency model of leadership that focuses on how leaders influence subordinates' perceptions of work goals and the path to achieve those goals.

pay incentives Compensation that rewards employees for good performance, including variable pay and merit pay.

performing stage A stage of team development that is characterized by a focus on the performance of the tasks delegated to the team.

personal network The relationships between an entrepreneur and other parties, including other entrepreneurs, suppliers, creditors, investors, friends, former colleagues, and others.

planning The management function that assesses the management environment to set future objectives and map out activities necessary to achieve those objectives.

policy A general guide for managers and employees to follow.

polycentric approach An approach to managing an international subsidiary in which subsidiaries are managed and staffed by personnel from the host country (local nationals).

pooled interdependence Team behavior where team members share common resources such as fax and copy machines, supplies, and secretarial support, but most of the work is performed independently.

portfolio analysis An approach to classify the processes of a diversified company within a single framework or taxonomy.

positive reinforcement A pleasurable stimulus or reward following a desired behavior that induces people to continue the behavior.

postheroic leadership perspective The view that most top executives, no matter how good they are, are limited in what they can do to solve problems, so that leadership responsibilities are spread throughout the firm.

power distance The extent to which individuals expect a hierarchical structure that emphasizes status differences between subordinates and superiors.

prearrival The first stage of socialization, encompassing the values, attitudes, biases, and expectations the employee brings to the organization when first hired.

prejudgment Type of perceptual barrier which involves making incorrect assumptions about a person due to membership in a group or about a thing based on earlier positive or negative experiences.

proactive management A management style in which problems are anticipated before they become pervasive and time is set aside on both a daily and weekly basis to plan goals and priorities.

proactive strategy A means of dealing with stakeholders when a firm determines that it wants to go beyond stakeholder expectations.

problem-solving team A group representing different departments that solves problems; sometimes called a *parallel team.*

process The way a product or service will be produced.

process control systems An operations information system that monitors and runs machinery and other equipment.

process reengineering A method of changing the entire production process rather than making incremental changes.

product managers A management role that coordinates the development of new products.

profit sharing Providing a share of a company's profits to the employees in the form of a bonus.

program evaluation and review technique (PERT) network A tool for analyzing the conversion process.

programmed decision Identifying a problem and matching the problem with established routines and procedures for resolving it.

project manager A management role that coordinates work on a scientific, aerospace, or construction project.

project team A group that works on a specific project that has a beginning and an end.

proprietorship A form of business that is owned by one person.

protected class The legal definition of specified groups of people who suffered widespread discrimination in the past and who are given special protection by the judicial system.

public offerings A means of raising capital by the sale of securities in public markets such as the New York Stock Exchange and NASDAQ.

punishment An aversive or unpleasant consequence following undesired behavior.

q

quality circles Groups of employees who meet regularly to discuss ways to increase quality.

quality gap The difference between what customers want and what they actually get from the company.

r

reactive management The management style of responding to the most urgent problem first when not enough time is available.

receiver Individual or party that receives message from sender.

reciprocal interdependence The greatest amount of interdependence that occurs when team members interact intensively back and forth with each other until their work is judged to meet performance standards.

recruitment The process of generating a pool of qualified candidates for a particular job.

referent power Power derived from the satisfaction people receive by identifying themselves with the leader.

relationship-building role The team-member role that focuses on sustaining harmony between team members.

relationship-oriented leadership A leadership style that focuses on maintaining good interpersonal relationships.

relative judgments A performance appraisal approach in which employees are compared to one another.

reliability The consistency of results from the selection method.

reordering systems The process used to help keep inventory levels more or less constant.

resource allocation The planning step that determines where the resources will come from (for instance, borrowing versus internally generated funds) and how the resources will be deployed to achieve the agreed-on objectives.

resource-based view A strategic management viewpoint that basing business strategy on what the firm is capable of doing provides a more sustainable competitive advantage than basing it on external opportunities.

responsibility The manager's duty to perform an assigned task.

reward power Power derived from the belief that the leader can provide something that other people value so that they trade their support for the rewards.

rights approach A means of making decisions based on the belief that each person has fundamental human rights that should be respected and protected.

risk The level of uncertainty as to the outcome of a management decision.

role modeling The leadership mechanism in which managers serve as examples of behaviors they would like employees to emulate.

roles Expectations regarding how team members should act in given situations.

rule written statement of the general permissible bounds for the application of particular policies.

S

satisficing Selecting the first alternative solution that meets a minimum criterion.

scanning The analysis of general environmental factors that may directly or indirectly be relevant to the firm's future.

scientific management A management method that applies the principles of the scientific method to the management process: determining the one best way to do a job and sharing the rewards with the workers.

segmented communication Flows of information within the firm that are far greater within groups than between groups.

selection The screening process used to decide which job applicant to hire.

selective perception Type of perception barrier whereby the receiver focuses on the parts of the message that are most salient to his or her interests and ignores other parts that are not relevant.

self-leadership Leadership that stresses the individual responsibility of employees to develop their own work priorities aligned with organizational goals; the manager is a facilitator who enhances the self-leadership capabilities of subordinates, encouraging them to develop self-control skills.

self-managed team (SMT) Sometimes called a *process team*, a group that is responsible for producing an entire product, component, or service.

sender Individual or party that initiates communication with another individual or party.

seniority A defense against discrimination in which companies with a well-established seniority system can give more senior workers priority, even if this has an adverse impact on protected class members.

sequential interdependence A series of hand-offs of work flow between team members in which output of

one team member becomes the input of the next team member, and so forth.

sexual harassment A form of discrimination that is broadly interpreted to include sexually suggestive remarks, unwanted touching, any physical or verbal act that indicates sexual advances or requests sexual favors, a promise of rewards or hidden threats by a supervisor to induce emotional attachment by a subordinate, and a "hostile environment" based on sex.

single-use plans Plans implemented for unusual or one-of-a-kind situations.

situational context The factors that are outside the control of the subordinate such as the tasks defining the job, the formal authority system of the organization, and the work group.

six sigma A quality standard that is equivalent to generating fewer than 3.4 defects per million manufacturing or service operations.

skills inventory A human resource inventory that keeps track of the firm's internal supply of talent by listing employees' education, training, experience, and language abilities; the firm can use this information to identify those eligible for promotion or transfer before trying to fill the position from the external market.

small business Any business that is independently owned and operated, that is small in size, and that is not dominant in its markets.

socialization The process of internalizing or taking organizational values as one's own.

social responsibility The belief that corporations have a responsibility to conduct their affairs ethically to benefit both employees and larger society.

span of control The feature of the vertical structure of an organization that outlines the number of subordinates who report to a manager, the number of managers, and the layers of management within the organization.

spin-off An independent entrepreneurship that produces a product or service that originated in a large company.

staff authority Management function of advising, recommending, and counseling line managers and others in the organization; it provides specialized expertise and is not directly related to achieving the strategic goals of the organization.

staff managers   The level of management that helps line managers achieve bottom-line results while only indirectly contributing to the outcome.

stakeholders   The groups or individuals who have an interest in the performance of the enterprise and how it uses its resources, including employees, customers, and shareholders.

standing plan   Plans created to help organizations deal with issues that come up on a regular basis.

statistical process control   An operations management monitoring tool that uses quantitative methods and procedures to evaluate transformation operations and to detect and eliminate deviations.

storming stage   A stage in team development in which team members voice their differences about team goals and procedures.

storyboarding   A variation of brainstorming in which group members jot down ideas on cards and then can shuffle, rewrite, or even eliminate cards to examine complex processes.

strategic action plans   Management plans based on macro approaches for analyzing organizational features, resources, and the environment and establishing long-term corporatewide action programs to accomplish the stated objectives in light of that analysis.

strategic alliances   Cooperative arrangements between competitors or potential competitors from different countries, possibly to establish a formal joint venture or collaboration between firms on specific projects.

strategic compensation   Compensation practices that best support the firm's business strategy.

strategic decisions   Decisions that have a long-term perspective of two to five years and affect the entire organization.

strategic HR planning (SHRP)   The development of a vision about where the company wants to be and how it can use human resources to get there.

strategic intent   The firm's internally focused definition of how the firm intends to use its resources, capabilities, and core competencies to win competitive battles.

strategic managers   The firm's senior executives who are responsible for overall management.

strategic meeting   Bringing people from different departments or divisions together to synchronize plans and objectives and to coordinate activities.

strategic mission   The firm's externally focused definition of what it plans to produce and market, utilizing its internally based core competence.

strategizing   The management skill of focusing on the firm's key objectives and on the internal and external environments and responding in an appropriate and timely fashion.

strategy formulation   The design of an approach to achieve the firm's mission.

subjective control   Informal approach based on global assessment of outcomes.

SWOT (strengths-weaknesses-opportunities-threats) analysis   A strategic management tool to evaluate the firm, which is accomplished by identifying its strengths and weaknesses, identifying its opportunities and threats, and cross-matching strengths with opportunities, weaknesses with threats, strengths with threats, and weaknesses with opportunities.

synergy   When individuals blend complementary skills and talents to produce a product that is more valuable than the sum of the individual contributions.

systems theory   A modern management theory that views the organization as a system of interrelated parts that function in a holistic way to achieve a common purpose.

t

tactical action plans   Management action plans at the division or department level that indicate what activities must be performed, when they must be completed, and what resources will be needed at the division or departmental level to complete the portions of the strategic action plan that fall under the purview of that particular organizational subunit.

tactical decisions   Decisions that have a short-term perspective of one year or less and focus on subunits of the organization, such as departments or project teams.

tactical managers   The firm's management staff who are responsible for translating the general goals and plan developed by strategic managers into specific objectives and activities.

tangible resources   Assets that can be quantified and observed, including financial resources, physical assets, and manpower.

task-facilitating role   The team-member role with the priority of helping the team accomplish its task goals.

task force   A temporary interdepartmental group formed to study an issue and make recommendations.

task-oriented leadership   A leadership style that emphasizes work accomplishments and performance results.

team   A small number of people with complementary skills who are committed to a common purpose, a set of performance goals, and an approach for which they hold themselves mutually accountable.

team cohesiveness   The extent to which team members feel a high degree of camaraderie, team spirit, and sense of unity.

team norms   Shared beliefs that regulate the behavior of team members.

technology   The means of transforming inputs into products.

Theory X   A negative perspective on human behavior.

Theory Y   A positive perspective on human behavior.

third-country nationals   Citizens of countries other than the host nation or the firm's home country.

360-degree feedback   Multirater feedback from peers, suppliers, other levels of management, and internal and external customers.

three-step model   A model of organizational change that features the three steps of unfreezing (melting the resistance to change), change (the departure from the status quo—also called movement or transformation), and refreezing (making new practices part of the employees' routine activities).

top-down change Organizational change that is initiated by managers.

total factor productivity The measurement of how well an organization utilizes all of its resources, such as capital, labor, materials, or energy, to produce its outputs.

total quality management (TQM) An organization wide management approach that focuses on quality as an overarching goal. The basis of this approach is the understanding that all employees and organizational units should be working harmoniously to satisfy the customer.

trait appraisal instruments Performance appraisal tools that evaluate employees based on worker characteristics that tend to be consistent and enduring, such as decisiveness, reliability, energy, and loyalty.

transactional leaders Leaders who use legitimate, coercive, or reward powers to elicit obedience and attempt to instill in followers the ability to question standard modes of operation.

transaction-processing systems An operations information system used to maintain data about transactions, such as inventory, sales, and purchase of supplies.

transformational leaders Leaders who revitalize organizations by instilling in followers the ability to question standard modes of operation.

transformational leadership A leadership style characterized by the ability to bring about significant change in an organization, such as a change in vision, strategy, or culture.

trust The willingness of one team member to increase his or her vulnerability to the actions of another person whose behavior he or she cannot control.

tuition assistance programs Support by the firm for employees' education and development by covering the cost of tuition and other fees for seminars, workshops, and continuing education programs.

turnkey projects A specialized type of exporting in which the firm handles the design, construction, start-up operations, and workforce training of a foreign plant, and a local client is handed the key to a plant that is fully operational.

two-way communications Communication channels that provide for feedback.

U

uncertainty The condition when incomplete information is available and must be used to make a management decision.

uncertainty avoidance The extent to which a society places a high value on reducing risk and instability.

unity of command The management concept that a subordinate should have only one direct supervisor, and a decision can be traced back through subordinates to the manager who originated it.

upward communication Sending a message from a position lower in the hierarchy to a receiver higher in the hierarchy.

utilitarianism A means of making decisions based on what is good for the greatest number of people.

V

validity The measurement of how well a technique used to assess candidates is related to performance in the job.

value-chain analysis Strategic management analysis that breaks the firm down into a sequential series of activities and attempts to identify the value-added of each activity.

venture capitalists Financial investors who specialize in making loans to entrepreneurships that have the potential for rapid growth but are in high-risk situations with few assets and would therefore not qualify for commercial bank loans.

vertical dimension The organization structure element that indicates who has the authority to make decisions and who is expected to supervise which subordinates.

vertical integration strategy A form of diversification strategy in which a firm integrates vertically by acquiring businesses that are supply channels or distributors to the primary business; producing its own inputs is backward integration, and distributing its own outputs is forward integration.

virtual teams Groups that use interactive computer technologies such as the Internet, groupware (software that permits people at different computer workstations to collaborate on a project simultaneously), and computer-based videoconferencing to work together regardless of distance.

visible culture The aspects of culture that an observer can hear, feel, or see.

voluntary contracts Because both parties enter the labor contract freely, one party can use the legal system to enforce the terms of the contract if the other party does not fulfill its responsibilities.

W

whistleblower policies A method by which employees who disclose their employer's illegal, immoral, or illegitimate practices can be protected; companies with whistleblower policies rely on whistleblowers to report unethical activities to the ethics officer or committee, which will then gather facts and investigate the situation in a fair and impartial way.

wholly owned subsidiaries A means of entering new markets in which a firm fully owns its subsidiary in foreign countries.

win–lose style Negotiating style used when there is a single issue that consists of a fixed amount of resources in which one party attempts to gain at the expense of the other.

win–win style Negotiating style requiring all interested parties to convert a potential conflict into a problem-solving process in which each party seeks to identify common, shared, or joint goals.

work group A group whose members are held accountable for individual work, but are not responsible for the output of the entire group.

World Trade Organization (WTO) *See* General Agreement on Tariffs and Trade (GATT).

photo credits

index

Page numbers followed by n indicate notes.

O